Heart of the Pines

Ghostly Voices of the Pine Barrens

John E. Pearce

ISBN 0-9679565-0-1

Library of Congress Card Number: 00-190338

This publication was assisted by a grant from the
New Jersey Historical Commission, a division of
Cultural Affairs in the Department of State.

Printed and bound by Quinn-Woodbine, Inc.,
Woodbine, New Jersey.

Published by the

Batsto Citizens Committee, Inc.

4110 Nesco Road
Hammonton, New Jersey 08037-3814

The photographs on the front and rear covers are views of the Mullica River at Green Bank
and are used with the permission of Mr. and Mrs. J. Hansell Lewis.

Heart of the Pines
Table of Contents

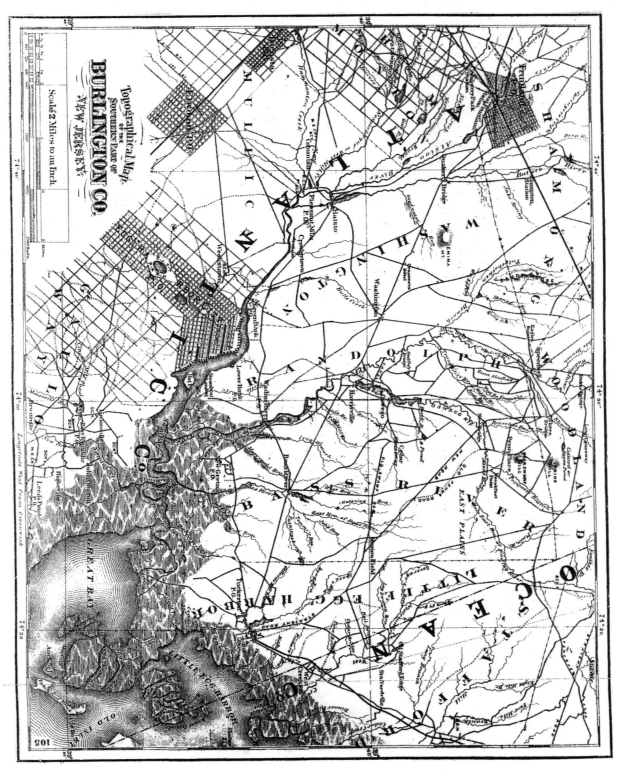

F.W. Beers, *State Atlas of New Jersey*, 1870, p. 105
Courtesy of Horace Somes

Medford Lakes

"Muskingum Bridge"

Indian
Mills

To Shamong
(1852)

Atsion

To Tabernacle
(1901)

To Woodland
(1866)

"Bridge at Head of
Union Forge Pond"

Keith Line

Mouth of Deep Run

To Shamong
(1852)

Speedwell

To Woodland
(1866)

"Lawrie's
Bridge"

Received from
Atlantic County
(1902)

Original Boundary of
Washington Township

Ocean County
formerly Monmouth County

Breakfast
Point

Present Boundary
of Washington
Township

Mouth of the
Batsto River
"The Forks"

Original
Boundary

Green
Bank

Bass River
(1864)

Original Boundary of
Egg Harbor Township,
Burlington County
(1740)
Incorporated as
Little Egg Harbor Township
(1798)

Lower
Bank

Mullica River

Atlantic County
formerly Gloucester County

Wading River

Mouth of the
Wading River

Present
Boundary

0   5
Miles

Old Washington Township

Information from Snyder's *The Story of New Jersey's Civil Boundaries 1606-1968*
Map is completely redrawn.

A Tribute to New Jersey

"On the shores of the Atlantic,
 Where the billowing waves do roll,
Is found the State, New Jersey,
 Of our hearts, and minds, the goal!"

The beautiful State; the historic State the State of our fore fathers; important since early times; one of the "Original Thirteen"; <u>That</u>, New Jersey, is you! <u>Why</u> do we say this? It is because long, long ago, you along with others, were discovered with other territory in the vicinity, and because of your insular position you were named after the "<u>Island</u> of <u>Jersey</u>" in the English Channel.

The beautiful State! Standing on your Coast, one may look out upon the cool waters of the Atlantic, which always send a fresh cool wind across the State, to cool it on the hottest days. Beautiful Woods are found from North to South, filled with many growing wild flowers, and a great variety of trees and shrubs.

"Home of our forefathers!" That is true. Washington crossed the Delaware that stormy night, and landed with his grave soldiers at Trenton, the State Capitol, and from there conducted campaigns which led him to all parts of the state.

Thomas Edison, one of the greatest inventors the world has known, lived here. The last years of his life were spent at East Orange, a small town in New Jersey. Then there is Charles Lindbergh, whose memorial non-stop flight across the Atlantic, will go down in the pages of history and remain there forever, - is a native of New Jersey, too. James Fennimore Cooper, whose stirring tales of Indians and fronteer - life, will forever be read by Americans both young and old, belongs to Jersey as well as Edison and Lindbergh.

Other names, such as Alexander Hamilton, Molly Pitcher, who so bravely took charge of the cannon when her husband had fallen - and Joyce Kilmer who wrote the poem "<u>Trees</u>" come to us as we name the sons and daughters of New Jersey. Then, too, there are such authors as Walt Whitman, Henry Van Dyke, - George Innes the Landscape Artist whose paintings "Autumn Oaks", "The Mill Pond", and "Early Morning" depict scenes similar to those found in New Jersey.

As to the beauty of forest, and "Wayside" and Stretch of Ocean Sands, we would say exaltingly, that mile after mile of white beaches lie bathed in the sun. Peach orchards bloom in April and May, and the inscense of scarlet leaves burns in Autumn. The friendly Pines spread their branches above the acres of flowers stretched in bright array. New Jersey, the "Garden State" - a Garden containing the "<u>blossoms</u> of <u>Culture</u>", and the "<u>flowers</u> of <u>Courage</u>," as well as the "Beauties of <u>Sight</u>, <u>Scent</u> and <u>Sound</u>. They are mingled in the hearts and minds of those who know and love her. The heavy Sweetness of the Magnolias and refreshing coolness of the Pine drift to meet the sharp salt tang of the Sea. The Country-side with its tall trees, its cozy cottages, its orchards, and furrows of tilled soil, and its sturdy people, recall the pictures of George Innes, and the poem written by Joyce Kilmer. And also we recall, that thro' these woods passed Walt Whitman, the "<u>father</u>" of "<u>free verse</u>", and Henry Van Dyke the poet-fisherman.

Rich in memories are the ivy-covered Walls of Princeton, over which ruled Woodrow Wilson before he became President of the United States. Rutgers, too, has contributed its share of the progress of Education. Nor, must one forget the excellence of the Smaller institutions - the Teachers Colleges, the Secondary and Elementary Schools.

Long, smooth highways, shining at night under the electric lights of Edison, who, lived and worked here, - stretch from the Atlantic to the Delaware from the Sands of Cape May to the Cliffs of the Palisades.

Once these highways were Indian Trails, tramped by Soldiers, wet with the blood of patriots and their oppressors. Echoes of Jersey's famous battles still ring thro' the Corridors of history - <u>Trenton</u>, where the Hessians feasted while Washington was crossing the Delaware; <u>Monmouth</u>, where brave Molly Pitcher fought in the place of her dead husband. The conditions that made the beautiful "Jerseys" the battle-ground of war, have made her the work shops of Peace. That Spirit which gave her leadership in a great patriotic Cause has given her even greater industrial initiative. Her farms are the gardens of half a continent and her sun-swept beaches are the reception centers of a Nation!

Leaders are not lacking. From her borders went Pike to conquer a mountain; Clara Barton to found the World-wide Red Cross; Marshall to discover Gold in California. Ideas and ideals pour fourth from a bountiful source.

Thus New Jersey, Whose soil has been so prolific of glorious growth, and upon whose scroll of history so <u>many</u>, <u>many</u> magnificent lines have been described to you, <u>New</u> <u>Jersey</u>, <u>Small</u>, but important, this solemn tribute is paid you

"Beautiful Jerseys of Historic fame!"

L.L.M. McConeghy
"West Wheat Road."
Vineland, New Jersey
March 1935

Laura Larrabee McConeghy lived in Green Bank from 1928—1933. During that time, she wrote volume after volume of volumptuous prose, extolling the virtues of her beloved little town in her work, "The Romance of Green Bank." After reluctantly moving to Vineland, she wrote the above paeon of praise to her state. I felt it was worth reprinting here that the people of New Jersey may know what it is to love their state.

Preface

The Mullica

This river forever
Homeward bound
Has my heart beneath its depths
Runs its course within my soul

With changeless beauty
It flows by swamps of
Cedar and sands of pine
With ebb and flow of tides
Its flowing knows no sense of time

With season's wind
Upon its face
Waters dance in
Sunlite trance or
Bound and race in
Turbulence under
Darkening sky

When air is still and windless
After nights repose
The river flows like silver glass
Mirrors cloud and shore alike
Within a looking glass
Renewing peace of mind
That it always was
Will always be
Now and ever there

For the river
Seeks the wave beyond
Salt marsh and meadows of
Golden grass
Mingling there with salt of seas
This timeless river
Forever homeward bound
Has found eternity

Jessie Lewis
Green Bank
2000

Most New Jersians know where Washington Township is located. It's in Glouocester County. Or perhaps they might think of the Warren County township of that name, or the Warren County borough of the same name. Perhaps they'd even think of the District of Columbia, the federal capitol named after the father of our country. But Washington Township, *Burlington* County? Nope. Never heard of it!

Yet those same New Jersians *have* heard about the pinelands, that vast stretch of pines and scrub oak that spreads throughout the south central part of the state. They know about its wonderful and precious ecosystem, of the vast underlying aquifer. They've heard tales of the backward "Pineys," half-witted, undernourished people who seem throwbacks to a more primitive time. They are familiar with the Jersey Devil, who haunts the dark swamps and forests of the pinelands. People from the more developed areas of the state think their extensive knowledge of the area entitles them to a certain status of superiority over the exploitative locals who would surely ruin this New Jersey treasure if given but a chance. In other words, they know absolutely nothing about the ancient Pine Barrens and its people. They just *think* they do. Well, guess what. Washington Township, Burlington County lies right in the heart of those very pinelands.

The "pinelands" is a political entity, not a natural one and certainly not a cultural one. The term was created by politicians to convince people from other areas of the state that this pristine wilderness was worth preserving. It *is* worth preserving, of course, but the name "pinelands" doesn't begin to encompass the variety of life and experience that can be found within this special place. Only the ancient name, "Pine Barrens," encompasses the vast historical, cultural, and natural history of this unique corner of the world.

I learned to love the Pine Barrens from my father. He was a state trooper back in the 1920's. His first duty station was in Chatsworth. He represented New Jersey's law and order to the people of the Barrens, riding horseback from village to village. I grew up in Pennsauken, a far more civilized place than Chatsworth, at least in the minds of its residents. My father, mother, sister, and I used to take rides through the Jersey Barrens to visit the people Pop had known when he was stationed there.

My father had a good friend, Henry Charlton Beck, who worked for the *Camden Courier Post*. Beck, too, fell in love with the Pine Barrens and its people. He traveled throughout the area, listening to people's stories and writing them down for newspaper articles. Later, he would collect those stories in a book, *Jersey Genesis*, which is still in print after over forty years. Henry Beck learned to love and respect the people of the Pine Barrens and wanted to show the outside world how very special they were. In the world of the cities and growing suburbs, the people of the Barrens were quaint oddities, harmless throwbacks to a way of life long lost to their more sophisticated neighbors. The press had created a negative view of these people. Beck was determined to set the record straight. In some ways, he did. In others, he, too, was lost in the pines.

Arthur Pierce was another good friend of my father's. His historian's approach to *Iron in the Pines* was completely different from Beck's folk history. He was a researcher, a real historian, who appreciated the industrial past of the Pine Barrens. I grew up with those strange names: Hog Wallow, Speedwell, Batsto, Atsion, Herman City, Sooy's Inn, Bridgeport, Green Bank, Lower Bank, and a host of others equally enticing.

Thus I fell in love with the Barrens at an early age under the capable tutelage of these three men: Henry Beck, Arthur Pierce, and my father. How could I have done otherwise? I became an archeologist by profession and worked for the State of New Jersey in my beloved Pine Barrens for several years. I've spent more than fifty years studying the details of the past in the Barrens. They still fascinate me.

The Pine Barrens are filled with stories. Over the past years, I've known a great many of the people of the Barrens and have counted them as friends. I knew Beck's guides, Leon Koster, and his sons, Rod and Hollis. Fred Brown of Hog Wallow, Percy Adams, Maurice Mick, Carrie Mick, and Jule Herman of Batsto, Clayton Ford of Tylertown, Bobby Wills of Bulltown, Sammy Simpkins, old Bill Wills, and Jess Nichols were all friends of my father and mine. I knew and respected them all. Each and every one loved this land and its little rivers. Each one had stories to tell, though sometimes they did like to stretch them a bit.

When I first came to Washington Township, it was heavily forested as it is today. I thought it had always been that way. Leon Koster told me that once he could walk out his lane in Herman City, look towards Batsto, and see the tower on the manion. That mansion is three miles from Herman City as the crow flies! There simply was no forest then. In fact, the first mile towards Batsto was agricultural land, including a cornfield.

Leon's grandfather had been a part owner of the Herman City glass factory. Leon himself had worked at Amatol, and later, he got a job in the paper mill at Pleasant Mills. The work was seasonal, and he was often roaming the woods and "doing" mossbunkers. I would later find that the seasonal employment life-style had been common during the iron and glass periods of Pine Barren's history as well.

Rod Koster knew the history of Washington Township better than anyone of his generation. He talked often about the woods. In some of his stories, his eyes would light up when he was stretching the truth just a bit. Rod was the storekeeper at Green Bank and later, he became a ranger for the State of New Jersey after a World War II stint in the army. I once asked Rod if there were hard times in the Pine Barrens during the Depression. His reply was, "No ….. it was always hard here." In a day when most people did not graduate from high school, seven of Leon's and Josie's eight children, including four girls, went to college, nursing school, or business school.

Hollis Koster, Rod's brother, was a botanist and a poet. He wrote about ferns, collected twenty-seven varieties of sphagnum moss and was published in "Poets of America." Hollis was smart, but not a storyteller like Rod.

Haze Wobbar told short stories usually about himself. Haze had a dump truck and was the head of the road gang for the township. Percy Adams, Clayton Ford and Sammy Simpkins worked for him. Each year he had to bid for his job, and the only other bidder was his next door neighbor, Arthur Holloway. Haze farmed about ten acres and also ran a store. "My potatoes," he used to say, "were as big as half dollars. Then there were the small ones."

Haze's father, Otto Wobbar, was the captain of a ship. Haze was the cook. His grandfather on his mother's side built outhouses at Batsto. Haze married Helena Davidson. Helena Wobbar and Josephine Koster were school teachers. Helena's storytelling was in the form of long poems she had memorized. Carrie Mick was the cleaning lady at the Batsto Visitors' Center. The state sent out a directive to lay off everyone over seventy years old. Carrie quipped, "I was over seventy when they hired me!" Jule Herman caught the Jersey Devil: an unshod feral mule.

Maurice Mick took care of the farm animals at Batsto. Through the middle of the day he would drive the stagecoach, to the delight of visiting children. In the late 1950's, the state took the stage coach driver to New York City. Maurice appeared on "What's My Line?" As a boy about 1910, Maurice carried a lunch pail to his father who was working at a steam sawmill just east of Batsto and north of the road to Crowleytown. The mill was cutting cedar from the swamp. That stream is now called Maple Branch. Maurice also trapped snapping turtles in the Mullica. I saw one snap off a broom handle. The turtle weighed fifty-eight pounds.

Russell Groff is the current local storyteller. He learned his "trade" from Jess Nichols, who had an automobile repair shop in his back yard in Green Bank. Now there is a new storyteller in Washington Township. He, like Russell, learned at Jesse Nichol's feet (or rather, stood peering under the hood at an engine). His story comes after years of work talking to everyone in the township. He has scanned hundreds of their photographs into his computer, in some cases taking out tears and scratches and bringing well-faded treasures back to life. His writing is accurate and witty, even if it is a tad verbose occasionally.

Heart of the Pines is the story of the people of Washington Township. It combines history, oral history, and genealogy into a story both comprehensible and informative … dare I say "entertaining." The book traces the early families in the township, incorporates its industrial past and includes the farmers of today – the cranberry growers. The familes weave the chapters together. The book can be read as town histories but should be read in its entirety to properly understand the people and places of Washington Township.

The heart of the pines has always been its people. There are families in Washington Township that have lived here since the township was formed three years after George Washington died. There are others whose lineage goes back much much farther. Still others, like myself, have only been here a short time. In my case, I married into an old family, and I've only been here fifty years.

Our identity in the Pine Barrens is found in the town, not the township. It is in the family and the fire company and the church. It is in Green Bank, Lower Bank, Wading River, and Hog Wallow. It has been in Batsto and Atsion, South Bend and Harrisville.

These intriguing Pine Barrens are not desolate stretches of sand and swamp. They are still alive with the love of a people who have made it their home for over three hundred years. Once there were iron furnaces and glass houses, paper mills and sawmills, taverns and ship yards.

The Pine Barrens gave it's first trees for lumber. It's second growth fed the iron furnaces. It's third growth fed the glass factories and the paper mills. Its fourth growth fed the early iron horses, provided lumber to build houses in New York and Philadelphia and firewood to heat them.

The last pristine cedar swamp was cut in the 1870's. The stumps are still there, some measuring over five feet in diameter. One tree was twenty-seven feet in circumference at chest height. Where now all is forest yet again, there were once farms that sustained generations of families. The Pine Barrens aren't primeval, but they are still loved by the people who have made them their home.

Heart of the Pines catches the heartbeat of a people whose progeny still linger beside the tannin-stained waters of the little rivers of the pines. This is their story, a tale of real people and their love for this land.

Budd Wilson
March 25, 2000

Old Mill House Forsaken

Bleak in autumn haze
The house forsaken
Endures unending time
Bereft in lonely years.

    (Driftwood dreams
    Wounding trench of tears
    Remembered hands
    Cupping childhood fears)

Shutters, broken,
Hammer on wood and wind,
Tattered garment
Swinging in sweeps of rain,
And windows
Dark of welcome
Forsake their watch.

    (No hailing light
    Or footsteps on the sill
    No more the hunter
    Home from the wooded kill)

Barren rooms in raveled light
Cast their shadows on
Vacant walls, silence
Echoes along hushful
Halls in chilling air.

    (Outcry of memory's
    Rustling skirt and
    Running step,
    Up an empty stair)

This oak-beamed shell
In loneness severed
From sullen hearth
In tireless sleep
Where loss impels despair
To coil against the
Kithless Keep.

    (And hollow cries a whippoorwill
    Within the ebb of time
    A house forsaken becomes
    An uncherished shrine.)

Jessie Lewis
Green Bank
2000

The Wind in the Pines

Nostalgia
Emma Van Sant Moore

Could I but live again those happy days of yore,
And roam once more through field and glen,
And play along the shore
Where the flowing river lapped my feet,
And rocked my boat so white—
Then I could tell you why the stars
Sing songs to me at night.

Could I but walk again those cool, dim forest aisles,
And wander 'neath the summer sun,
And practice childish wiles
To coax the birds, with whistle clear,
To come so close to me
That I could see the faintest mark
On wren or chick-a-dee—

Could I but take you with me the flower-strewn
    fields to roam,
And show you where the meadowlark
Had built her lowly home—
Oh, if you could but tread the paths
My youthful feet once trod—
I'm sure you'd know why I adore
All Nature and her God!

Emma Van Sant Moore extolled the homely charms of her Mullica valley birthplace in a small book of poems called *Mullica*, which was published by the Poets of America Publishing Company in 1960.

Two nineteenth century poems have charmed me from my youth. Both express beautiful sentiments, yet those thoughts are worlds apart. Perhaps it is the blend of Victorian romanticism and melancholy within my spirit which finds expression in their words. Many years ago, an English poet, Lord Byron, was overwhelmed by the magnificence of the Alps and penned:

There is a pleasure in the pathless woods,
There is a rapture on the lonely shore.
There is a society where none intrudes,
By the deep sea, and music in its roar:
I love not man the less, but nature more,
From these our interviews, in which I steal
From all I may be, or have been before,
To mingle with the universe, and feel
What I can ne'er express, yet cannot all conceal.

Childe Harold

When I was growing up, I spent many summers at Resica Falls in Pennsylvania's Pocono mountains. There I dreamt of untrod paths and exciting adventures. A warm, sunny afternoon, a gentle breeze, pink-blossomed mountain laurel luxuriant around me - how the spirit soars with the eagles! This was, indeed, a "pleasure in the pathless woods," a "rapture on the lonely shore." At Resica, with "true Scouting friends," firelight flickering over feathered "Indians" and legends of long ago, past and future joined as one, and we surely did find ourselves "closer drawn to God," as an old Scout song says. As we slept the sleep of the innocent, we truly were "at peace in a world of strife," or, as my second favorite poem states, "far from the madding crowd's ignoble strife."

Yet however beautiful the world of nature is, there is something in each of us that seeks our own kind. The woods around me were not "pathless." In the midst of the proverbial dark and stormy night, the ghosts of the past were present in the winds that moaned among the hemlocks. My spirit might soar with the eagles on uncharted ways, but I knew that others had walked that way before. I was not the first, nor would I be the last to sit beneath the roaring falls and feel one with nature's God. Stone "fences" wound their way through the woods, and occasionally the trails ran past cellar holes and small foundations which seemed out in the middle of nowhere. These were indications that life had been different on that land years ago. A millrace had been dug through the solid rock, and a tannery once stood below the falls. Others had exalted in life and loved beside those rushing waters. They knew a far different time from the one that was familiar to me, yet they, too, had shared in tears and laughter on the land they loved. Who were they, these children of the past? What useful toil occupied their hands? Did they feel like me? Love like me? Even die as I must die? Alas, I was never to know.

When South Jersey became my home, I longed for "real" trees, the tall and stately guardians of the forests I had loved, who braved the mountain winds, shaking their heads in defiance. Here the land was flat and sandy. The scrub oak and pine hardly seemed worthy to be called "trees," and the little brown-watered streams shared few of the charms of Pennsylvania's tumultuous flows. The beauty of the pine barrens is an acquired taste, as Hans Lewis of Green Bank once said about martinis. The outsider is confronted with intense heat, freezing cold, mosquitoes, pine flies, deer flies, and ticks. It's subtle beauty is almost missed by those outside the pines who are accustomed to more lush verdure.

Yet as I became more at one with the land, her ghosts reached out, caressing me and calling with their siren voices. The laughter of happy children canoeing down one of the "little rivers of New Jersey" mingled with the spirit-laughter of children long ago, who now rest from the trials of life in all-but-forgotten graves near lonely churches. These sounds were different from my Pennsylvania voices, yet somehow, they were strangely familiar. They were the voices of the past, echoing amongst the trees, sighing amongst these pines just as their kindred had breathed amongst the hemlocks of Resica.

Who were they, these people of the past, these children of the dawn, these men and women who lived their lives in the seemingly inhospitable pine barrens of New Jersey and were laid to rest amongst the pines they loved? I was kidding myself if I truly believed that I travelled in "the pathless woods" in a "society where none intrudes." These voices in the wind were those of others who had travelled the path of life long before me, or my parents, or even my grandparents. Some of these were the voices of those who luxuriated in unspoiled bounty before the coming of European settlers. Others were the voices of those who found the land and made it their own. Still others were the voices of those who defied the greatest power in the world to proclaim their rights as freeborn human beings to "life, liberty, and the pursuit of happiness." These were the voices of those who made life possible for me, and I knew next to nothing about them.

How could I ever know myself if I were ignorant of those who had gone this way before? I remember quite well the first time I walked towards the Green Bank Church in the dark of night. Even though I was with college friends, there was something forbidding about the darkness of the surrounding graveyard: spirits breathing, sighing, reaching out to touch us in the blackness of the enveloping night. I was a stranger in a strange land, yet I heard their voices. Who were these disembodied shades that seemed to make the night even darker and the air bite with a deeper chill?

The light of day revealed nothing more frightening than a lonely cemetery enfolding the little white church beside the ever-flowing river of life. It was another English poet, Thomas Grey, whose lines evoked the daylight truth. These half-legible, timeworn stones were all that remained of almost-forgotten fellow travellers who shouldered the burdens of life beside this river. Rich or poor, proud or humble, exuberant manhood or gentle maidens, they rest beside the river that brought them life and comforts them in death.

The breezy call of incense-breathing morn,
The swallow twitt'ring from the straw-built shed,
The cock's shrill clarion, or the echoing horn,
No more shall rouse them from their lowly bed.

For them no more the blazing hearth shall burn,
Or busy housewife ply her evening care;
No children run to lisp their sire's return,
Or climb his knees the envied kiss to share.

Oft did the harvest to their sickle yield,
Their furrow oft the stubborn glebe has broke;
How jocund did they drive their team afield!
How bowed the woods beneath their sturdy stroke!

Let not Ambition mock their useful toil,
Their homely joys, and destiny obscure;
Nor Grandeur hear with a disdainful smile
The short and simple annals of the poor.
Elegy Written in a Country Churchyard

The lands they once lovingly tended are grown up in trees again, as they had been before axe ever was set to clear the fields for harvest. Ancient homesteads carefully husbanded and passed from father to son for generations are now almost obscured beyond recognition and their families long absent from the land they loved. Once blasts from furnace and forge echoed prosperity and life. Now the lonely cry of the whippoorwill welcomes the night.

How dare the haughty extol the virtues of untrodden paths and mock the survival struggles of the past? They have paved and macadamized their past beneath them. Here, it still breathes amongst the pines. "I love not man the less, but nature more," Lord Byron said. Ah yes - to soar with the eagles. Yet I have learned to walk the paths long loved by those who have gone before and to appreciate the joys and sorrows which engulfed their lives.

This is the story of those who have gone before us in this land. I may walk this way but once, but I do not walk it alone. Those fellow travellers lead the way from darkness into light. This is their story, gleaned from fading gravestones, fragile records, and the living memories who will join their voices with those of the past in all too short a time. We can only know the way we are going when we know where we have been and comprehend those who have gone before us. It bothers me that the State of New Jersey has done so little to preserve the history its acquisitions have helped to erase, but that only means that we must work the harder to ensure that the light of the past is not completely extinguished.

What makes the story of the Mullica Valley so intriguing? Perhaps the answer lies in its representational aspects. This land and its people are exemplars of the settlement of Great Britain's Middle Colonies on the eastern seaboard of North America. Her heterogeneous mixture of men and women from many nationalities shadowed forth the union which emerged from the disjointed colonial ventures and the varigated peoples that formed and continue to form this unique American nation.

To the banks of this river of life came the Mullicas, a Swedish family of Finnish antecedents. Next, an unknown English family settled nearby. Perhaps this was Thomas Clark and his wife, who made their home across the river from Eric Mullica. Quakers, generally from lower New England, and perhaps from more western portions of West Jersey, built an established community of farms and mills nearer the bay. Scots fleeing from persecution in their homeland came to the head of navigation via Long Island. Next came a Frenchman, Peter Cavileer, from old New York. Then a Dutch family, headed by Yoos Sooy, also originally from New York, took up lands where the Mullicas had lived before them. The Leeks ventured from Long Island via Cumberland County a short generation after the Sooys.

As the eighteenth century blossomed, the seeds of revolution sprouted amongst common, ordinary people who accepted responsibility for their lives and those of their families and decided that they, and they alone, had the right to determine their futures. Entrepreneurs from the Burlington area and from the fast-growing city of Philadelphia saw opportunity in the pines and established infant industrial experiments. Those first iron manufactories of Atsion and Batsto were a signal to Mother England that her offspring were growing past the stage of parental regulation.

When war came to American soil, it was given birth and sustained, not by the rich and famous, but by the hearts and souls of common, ordinary people who were resolved to be free. After the most powerful nation on earth was confounded by these same "rude farmers" and seamen, they organized and controlled their own self-government as proudly as the Lords and Commons of Great Britain ruled in Westminster. Elijah Clark and Richard Wescoat turned their merchant interests into practical privateering ventures and rose to positions of respect amongst their compatriots for their abilities and intelligence. Batsto's iron production capacity spurred the interest of Philadelphia businessmen and members of the Quartermaster General's department in the Continental Army. Sea captains and ordinary seamen turned their peacetime skills into wartime virtues.

Plucky, self-made entrepreneurs like John Cavileer, Joseph Sooy, and John Leek, Sr., who had been brought to the Mullica Valley as young people or were born here, assembled landed plantations with the dream of providing moderate wealth for their children and grandchildren. Their sons and daughters continued their love of the land which extends in an unbroken chain to the present day.

When the conflict with Great Britain came to an end, these same strong families, along with others from more settled parts of the new state like the Richards family, plunged ahead to forge new wealth and new ventures in a land which they saw as productive and vital. Not until after the Civil War did the energy that had fed the Mullica valley begin to wane, and then its defeat came through no fault of those who had loved the land so much. When railroads replaced the sloops and schooners as primary means of transporting goods to market and the Panic of 1873 hit the country, the people of the pines had met their match.

In few other areas of New Jersey, or indeed, of the whole country, is America's past close enough to touch in the descendants of those early families, in the tiny houses built by their ancestors two centuries ago, in sand roads long rutted with the wheels of "sheet-topped" wagons carrying iron, lumber, charcoal, and glass which still run through pine woods and cedar swamp, in tiny, cedar-stained rivers and streams that once bore ore boats and sailing vessels alike.

The voices amongst the pines are those of men, women, and children who loved their land, who appreciated its vitality and its beauty, and who were laid to rest amongst their forebears next to the river which had given them life. The State of New Jersey owns eighty-two percent of Washington Township today, but it's people have not yet learned the true value of the treasure they possess. Though they may enjoy the recreational opportunities or appreciate the unique natural aspects of the Pine Barrens, they do not yet fully comprehend the invaluable clues to the wellspring of the American Dream that is represented here in such a complete microcosm. Destroy this human factor of the pines and only a pretty shell is left, empty of the very real people, our people, who struggled here to form a nation and weld it into a living, breathing organism.

Here in the pines, a technological generation can still find answers to the questions of life and hope for the future. On a star-spangled night deep in the pines, near a tannin-stained little river, the voices of the past still call to us. Those spirits breathing, sighing, reaching out to touch in the blackness of the enveloping night which I first encountered in the Green Bank churchyard were not threatening, but crying out for empathic consciousness. The faded names on crumbling stones are old, familiar friends now, and life's meaning has found increasing depth and breadth beside the brown waters of the Mullica. Blushing bride and hoary grandam, hearty youth and ancient sire, long in their graves and almost forgotten, come to life again. They speak to us of our roots, formed in the soil of this land though coming here from far-distant realms. Their spirits fashioned their dreams into realities, a process with which we still struggle in ongoing reincarnation.

This is their story. The people themselves are the real Heart of the Pines.

My River

Emma Van Sant Moore

When I reach the River Jordan
Will its banks seem quite as green,
Its smoothly flowing water
Be as crystal and serene
As the Mullica, my own?

Is it just a wide, straight river—
One last hazard to cross?
And will I miss, I'm wond'ring,
With o'erwhelming sense of loss,
The Mullica, my own?

And when I cross that river
Will I find an answered prayer,
"That my small bit of heaven"
Be not golden streets so fair,
But my Mullica shores?

If I no more may wander
That well-loved valley down,
Nor idle 'mong the ruins
Of a half-forgotten town
By the Mullica, my own;

Then let me find in heaven,
On the Jordan's farther side,
A Van Sant boat in the building
Beside a flowing tide
Like the Mullica, my own.

Should there be no more to meet me
Than Van Sants gone on before,
I'll hear the grandest singing
When I reach that far-off shore,
For they did their rehearsing
By the Mullica, of yore.

Flow on, my lovely Mullica,
Most wonderful of streams,
Thy bays, and coves and channels
Are part of all my dreams—
My Mullica, flow on!

from *Mullica,* 1960

Acknowledgements

Spring on the Mullica

Emma Van Sant Moore

O, to be beside the river,
And hear the fluttering of wings;
To stand enthralled at twilight,
While the robin sings

His last sweet notes of love and praise,
As he settles for the night;
Then to be awakened gently,
When he greets the morning light!

O, to watch once more, the sun come up
From far beyond the bay,
And hear that same glad robin
Herald in the day,

Would make my heart sing happily—
But in memory still I see:
How that lovely river looked in Spring—
O, what it meant to reel

Blue rifts in the cirrus clouds above—
White foam on the wind-lashed river—
Great flocks of duck flying north in the gale—
Nature's so benignant a giver!

A shimmer of green on the willow-trees,
They stand with feet in the stream,
While yellow as gold of a kingly crown,
Dandelion blossoms gleam!

A big, white goose gliding proudly by
With her downy, yellow brood—
Giving instructions—showing how to find
The most succulent bits of food!

O, dreamy days with beauty laden,
Down by the Mullica shore!
Each day I live in memory
Care-free days of yore.

from *Mullica*, 1960

As we all owe our lives to those who have gone before us, we also are indebted to those who take us by the hand and lead us through the intricacies of life. I've needed frequent guidance over the years, and I've certainly had a number of times, particularly during the last five years while working on this book, in which I needed to be led "through the dark valley."

My father, Walter Bowden Pearce, taught me the essentials of respect for others and an interest in the past. Muhlenberg College honed my skills in writing and perception, and all my Scouting friends gave me a deep appreciation for the land we can never truly own but only borrow in our life's journey. It was with them that I learned to soar with the eagles above crag and river, and with them that I learned to appreciate the love Native Americans have had for Our Mother the earth.

Mrs. Jesse Forman Lewis of Green Bank started me on this particular journey. She has a deep respect for the Mullica Valley that has come through generations of her Sooy family since old Yoos first set foot in Lower Bank in 1724. "If someone doesn't do something soon," she said, "there won't be anyone left who remembers. They're almost all gone now."

I am deeply indebted to the "Ancient Ones," who valued the Mullica Valley's past enough to research and write about it: Henry Charlton Beck, Arthur Pierce, and Charles Boyer. I salute those born on the land, whose abiding love focused in collecting photographs and writing short articles that illumined the dark recesses: Dorothia (McAnney) Somes, Augusta (Weeks) Cale, Theda Ashton, Alice (Adams) Weber, Martina (Adams) Eichinger, Rodney and Hollis Coster, and the other companions of Henry Beck's pilgrimages. Leah Blackman of Tuckerton, back in 1879, did so much to preserve the history and family ties of the area.

There were "outsiders," too, who loved the land so much that they gave years of their lives to see its past remembered: Laura Larrabee McConeghy, Edna and Charles I. "Cap" Wilson. Edna and "Cap," the first "Budd Wilson," spent their last years pouring over the Batsto collection in days when the State of New Jersey first took over the vast Wharton acres. "Cap," himself, took the Wharton ledgers to Trenton so they could be microfilmed and preserved. He and his wife made countless notes and lists of their contents that certainly have helped me sort through their material. "Cap" also was responsible for copying the entire list of marriages and births from a township records book that is now lost. Most of all, perhaps, they imbued their son, the second Budd Wilson, with their enthusiasm for the history of the Mullica Valley.

Then there are the older folks who still live on the land their great, great, great, great grandfather's tilled. I know perfectly well they won't like the characterization "old," for they are ever young in spirit if not in years, but I use it in the same sense as the Native Americans do when they honor their elders for the wisdom their years have given them. The "old" ones still breathe the spirit of their families and a deep love for the land that has nourished them in life and will enfold them in death: Stephen V. Lee, Jr., Bill Haines, Marjorie (Downs) Cavileer; Marjorie (Cavileer) Fox; David Cavileer; Lydie (Nichols) Guse; Marjorie (Ford) Ivins; Horace Cavileer; Arwilda (Ford) Walters and her husband, Bill; Howard Ware; Nelson and Evelyn Ware; Francis Mick; George and Nancy McCarten; Lillian (DeBow) Fritz; Walt and Virginia Priest; and many others who still live near their river of life. Jack Leek, Jr. is "retired," but like so many others in the pines, doesn't let that slow him down. Jack, Bill Haines, and Steve Lee, Jr. are the true inheritors of the spirit of the old entrepreneurs of Washington Township. They are knowledgable, strong, and decent men who have done well with their lives. My thanks to each of them for the time they spent with me.

There are the "Respected Elders" (not so old but older than I am): Budd Wilson, Jr. of Green Bank and Steve Eichinger of Wading River. Both have done much to bring the past alive. Budd has been a virtual encyclopedia of information from his wealth of knowledge and experience. Simply ask him a question no matter how obscure it might be, and he'll be off and researching until he's found an answer. He read this entire manuscript for both spelling and technical errors, though I've probably missed a couple of his corrections. I'll never forget his gentle suggestion after he read the section on Batsto that he thought I needed a little work on "processes." "Processes," I asked? "You know: iron manufacturing and glass making." "Oh." I thought I had that all figured out. Guess I didn't. He's a technician and very particular about the proper use of words.

When I first started this work, I told Budd I thought he ought to be writing it. After all, he knew so much and had a *multitude* of photographs and maps. He just smiled. I respect his quiet ways and his gentle guidance. He's always so precise: what he "knows," what he "thinks to be true," what he suspects is "possible," just as when he mentions the "digs" he has conducted, assisted in, or simply observed. I remember one time I said something with which he disagreed. Despite his far greater knowledge of the subject than my own, he quietly said, "I've always understood . . ." He didn't come right out and say I was wrong, mind you. He just politely suggested I needed a little more research in that area. He was right. And Steve Eichinger. Now there's another good man. He's lived all his life in Wading River and worked for the State of New Jersey at Bass River State Forest until his retirement last year. He knows every old road, stream, cellar hole, or depression on the land he has walked and ridden through his whole life. He's searched road returns and tax returns, poured over old maps, and has always been willing to jump in his truck to go exploring. I remember the time I mentioned to him that there were two bridges where the Tuckerton Road crossed the Wading River at Bodine's. He told me I was all wet. He had lived here all his life and *knew* there was only one bridge. I didn't even know where the cellar hole was for Bodine's Tavern. How could I know there were two bridges? Out in a rainstorm we went, bouncing up to Bodine's Field in his truck. Once there, he pointed out the cellar hole to me - and the location of the "one" bridge. "Now," says I, "come on downstream a little farther and look back up. What do you see?" The pilings of the second bridge, of course. We were both drenched, but we laughed happily together. We later discovered that these "two" bridges were really part of one long bridge called the "Great Bridge" in township minutes, so we both turned out right after all.

Other "Respected Elders" (again, mind you, not so much "elder") who have helped this traveller along the way are: Betty (Kathleen Crowley) Rubsom, Russ Montgomery, Don McCauly, and Bill Bell. I'm not quite certain where to put Murray and Jean Harris, but their genealogical work on the Cramers (or Cranmers or Crammers), as well as their support and friendship has meant so much to me. Mary Lewis Smith of Mount Holly helped me out on the Cramers, too, and Lorena Estlow Hyde in Ohio corresponded with me about her Sooy and Estlow families. June Methot and Dr. Peter Craig provided telephone help on sections of their books. The Rev. Robert Steelman sent me information on the Van Sant family that he and his brother, James, wrote for presentation to the Atlantic County Historical Society.

Next come the esteemed fellow travellers: Barry Cavileer, Horace Somes, Jr., and Pete Stemmer. Horace and his brother, Frank, absorbed a tremendous appreciation for the Wading River estuary from their parents, especially from their mother, Dorothia (McAnney) Somes. Dorothy was upset that Henry Charlton Beck had given the wrong impression of her beloved town and collected two milk crates full of photographs and notes on old Bridgeport. She always wanted to publish a little pamphlet on Wading River to set the record straight, but death robbed her of that pleasure. Out of her materials, however, I was able to glean almost a hundred pages on that tiny town in the pines. Her efforts were not for naught. Horace kept notebooks about the estuary when he was young. He tramped, slushed, and drove over every inch of the area. Into those notebooks he drew maps of every stream, rivulet, and ditch and carefully noted their names. He worked with Steve Eichinger across the river to insure their accuracy, and most of them have been listed in the section on Wading River.

I always knew Horace as the "Christmas Tree" man of Wading River. His family had turned his grandparents' farm into a Christmas tree farm, and I used to go over there every year for the one that would grace my living room. I actually stumbled across him when I started this history, however. Budd Wilson, Jr. had given me an old photograph of the Wading River School and told me it was on Turtle Creek Road. Over I went to find it, only nothing quite fit. I saw Horace on his way home and followed him into his driveway to air my predicament. He solved it for me immediately. What Budd had told me was Turtle Creek Road in the photograph was Cedar Lane. I had been driving up and down right past the old schoolhouse. That's when I found out how much information Horace had on Wading River. Horace has a deep love for the Wading River estuary and has tried to raise his sons to appreciate it as well. He and his wife, Barbara, are both members of the Lower Bank Fire Company and have risked their lives to save several people from burning buildings, rescued them in automobile accidents, and tearfully watched many an old house burn to the ground, unable to stop the destructive flames. Horace works for the State Forestry Service. Frank's wife, Mandy, is the Town Clerk for Washington, Woodland, and Bass River Townships.

Pete Stemmer lives over in Bass River Township in a house overlooking the Bass River itself. Pete started a project of his own to preserve his township's history. He began collecting old photographs of the New Gretna area. At first, he photocopied them into notebooks. Then he started scanning them for preservation in the computer at the New Gretna School. He heard that I knew something about scanning and contacted me for information. After that, it was like the dimly-sighted leading the blind. He's passed on to me a good many old photographs and tips through his contacts. Pete and I have kept the telephone lines busy with e-mail. I respect him very much and sincerely appreciate his friendship. We've both learned a lot from our endeavors.

To this list of "esteemed fellow travellers," I have to add Dudley Lewis of Green Bank. Dud was my roommate at college for two years, and he introduced me to Green Bank in the first place. We've travelled many a sandy mile first in his grandmother's 1941 Chrysler, then in his old Jeep, exploring the entire area of Washington Township. It's hard to tell a friend of over thirty years how much his friendship has meant. Maybe this little (hah!) history of his beloved township will say what I can't quite put into words.

I have yet to thank one of the younger generation. She's a madonna with three young children and a handsome husband who moved into an old house in Lower Bank not too long ago. How she found the time to spend with me, pouring over old photographs and telling me stories of the Cale and Cramer families, I'll never know, but I do appreciate it very much. Sarah (Cramer) Camillo is, after all, a scion of a couple of the "old" families, and she has a deep appreciation family and town history. Another of the "younger" generation I must thank is Holly Haines. She has inherited the Haines' business acumen . . . and the Haines' smile.

Then there is Beverly Weaver and Lisa Flick who were at Batsto. I sometimes get a little grumpy about the State of New Jersey and the dedication to historical preservation, and I deplore the ongoing disputes with the Batsto Citizens Committee, but I realize how difficult Ms. Weaver's job must have been to maintain so much on a shoestring budget. She found me four and a half hours in the Batsto research room, and that time was absolutely invaluable. Lisa was my "chaperone." How I wish it could have been hours and hours more. I hardly tapped the depths of what is stored in the Batsto vault. It's unfortunate that a lack of staff hampers research in such a treasure trove of information. The Batsto Citizens Committee has provided a great deal of help as well, though the members aren't aware of it. I read each and every past issue of the *Batsto Citizens Gazette* and combed their articles which contain so much valuable information on Batsto. Lois Ann Kirby of Medford, who, until her recent resignation was editor of the *Gazette*, has helped me out on several occasions. I was told she had information on Friendship, so I gave her a call one evening. She had never even heard of me, of course, but she was quite delightful. Unfortunately, she said she had no information on the Friendship Bogs whatsoever. Within the week, I received a call from her with strange news. Out of the blue, someone had sent her several pages on the history of the Friendship Bogs. Neither of us have an explanation for that coincidence. She has also helped me with information she received from the late Theda Ashton, whose family came from Batsto and Tylertown. Last but not least are two people who have given me advice and support in pursuing this endeavor. R. Marilyn Schmidt of Barnegat Light Press and Pine Barrens Press read most of my earlier manuscript work and gave me excellent counsel. Vince Laganella provided support through his unfailing friendship, by his enthusiasm for life and by his "can do" spirit.

There are many others who have given me of their time and knowledge either in person, over the telephone, or through the mail: John Milton Adams, Jr., who visited his grandfather's home near Calico back in 1939; Art Andrews, who used to live in the Captain Carlisle House in Lower Bank; Jack Cresson, an archaeologist who is currently a member of the Batsto Citizens Committee, Inc. and worked at Batsto; Harry Deverter, member of the Batsto Citizens Committee and one of my three Bass River compatriots; Bill Hawthorne, whose knowledge of Harrisville is extensive; Diane Kemble, scion of the Lower Bank Johnsons; Paul Lightman, formerly of the Old Mill at Pleasant Mills; Paul Ludwig, of Chip's Folly; Ruth MacDonald, who used to live with her husband at Bulltown; Herbert Schuck, whose wife was a descendant of Jesse Evans of Martha; Erva (Cramer) Enselin, who provided considerable information on the Van Sant family; Elaine Weber Mathis, who gave me photographs of the Fords and the Webers; and John Stanwood, whose wife, Constance is a Bodine descendant. Not mentioned here, but certainly cited within the book, are the numerous others who have given of their knowledge, their love of this "Heart of the Pines," and their friendship to an "outsider" who came to appreciate them for the wonderful people they are. My most sincere thanks to them all.

I was student-teaching in Maple Shade a few (no, more than a "few") years back and happened to mention to a senior with whom I was talking that I was heading down into the pines that night. That six-foot plus tall football player got a horrified look on his face and said, "Oh no! My God, be careful. Those pineys'l shoot you and bury you in some hole out in the woods!" He was serious. I tried not to guffaw. I could not believe that one end of Burlington County could know so little about the other. Actually, I can't believe the State of New Jersey knows so little about the area in which they have heavily invested over the years.

Quite frankly, I have found the residents of this "Heart of the Pines" to be some of the nicest people and the best friends I have ever met. I sincerely hope I have been a credit to them.

Back Home
Emma Van Sant Moore

I will go back a little while, and walk
In well-remembered paths of childhood days—
Back to the village store, and perchance talk
With natives of my birthplace, versed in ways
And customs of the valley.

I will go back in April, while sun, and sky,
And earth are shy of each other; while still
The silence of winter lies over the land. Then I
Will stand upon the river bank and fill
My soul with quiet beauty.

I will go back and see that lovely river—
So broad, and deep, and blue when at the crest.
The trees upon its banks will be a-quiver
With pride and joy of being newly dressed
In pale and tender green.

I will go back and see the white-sailed boats,
And hear the South Wind whistle through their shrouds.
I dare not hope that my small skiff still floats,
But gulls, white and gray as April clouds,
Will angle overhead,
And I'll be home again!

from *Mullica*, 1960

Getting Acquainted

Potbellied Stove

(From Memories of Green Bank)

Emma Van Sant Moore

Should a fairy appear tonight and say to me:
"You may have one wish fulfilled." I'd want it to be,

To see again from out the days of yore,
The pot-bellied stove in Uncle Billy's store.

To see the folk, who daily gathered there,
Seated 'round the stove on wooden box or chair.

To hear them, winter evenings, 'round that stove.
Making talk of river, of bay, and of cove;

Speaking of boats that had sailed—of boats being built,
Drawing near the stove and giving their chairs a tilt,

While they kept on talking—of sail-boats, gallant and fast—
Then talked of rudder, of rigging, of spar, and of mast.

Ah! this would be like music, sweet to my ear—
To daughter of shipbuilding men 'twould be good to hear.

But since I may have one granted wish—no more.
I'll look at the pot-bellied stove in Billy Sooy's store.

And perhaps see Uncle Billy as they tell of him—
Placing oysters to toast on that pot-bellied stove's broad rim.

He did this often, but one day—I've been told—
As some men sat close to the stove, away from the cold,

He carefully placed some oysters on the broad rim to steep,
And soon, soothed by the talk and heat, fell asleep.

The fire was hot. The oysters began to steam,
John Koster, sitting near—in his eye a mischievous gleam—

Took out his knife, opened and ate them all,
Letting the shells quietly into a bucket fall.

When Uncle Billy woke, he stoked the fire, looked around.
The men, wanting to laugh, talked on. Uncle Billy frowned

When he saw the oysters were gone from the stove's broad rim.
"What d'ye know! Hn, hn!" It puzzled him.

"I could swear I didn't eat those oysters, but the shells are cold.
Funny how forgetful a man gets when he grows old."

from *Mullica*, 1960

T his is the story of a people, the land they loved, and the river estuary that gave it life. We are about to take a journey through time and space along the Mullica estuary, from its confluence with Great Bay and the sea to the spot where the river's branches are just about wide enough to fit the slimness of a canoe and where tortuous meanderings and deadfalls choke the narrow proportions.

We will meet explorers and settlers, entrepreneurs and businessmen, judges and freeholders, immigrants and long-settled families, who, with hard work and perseverence brought prosperity and production to a "barren" land. These are a people who cherished the legacy of the land and heritage they inherited and loved the river which sustained them.

First, though, I want you to share my introduction to the Heart of the Pines, just as I did a few years back. I'll never forget the first visit I ever made there! It was 1968. Dudley Lewis and I were in college in Allentown, Pennsylvania, and he invited me to his home for the weekend. I grew up in a suburb of Philadelphia. I'd done a lot of camping with the Scouts and thought I was a country boy! Hah! Did I learn a thing or two on *this* trip! Ok ... Pemberton to Four Mile Circle, Route 72 to Route 563. And then ..... Chatsworth .... Jenkin's Neck .... Hog Wallow..... (they were *town* names?) *that* was bad enough, miles and miles of scrubby little pines and oaks and *nothing* else. As far as a Pennsylvanian was concerned, they weren't even *real* trees! And Dud didn't know the route numbers. It was the Chatsworth Road, the Hammonton Road, the New Gretna Road, the Egg Harbor Road.

When we hit a dirt road at the end of it all - I *knew* I was at the end of it all. Country boy, indeed! Green Bank ... River Road, ten houses, a graveyard and a minuscule church ... and beyond ... a sand road and swamp! My college roommate came from *here*? I envisioned mountain-hillbilly-hick, etc. etc. etc. He told stories as if he'd lived here all his life ... fascinating stories about fascinating people ... out of the near past, generation past, long past. I breathed a sigh of relief: *he* was born in Philadelphia and grew up in Baltimore and South Orange! Thank God! Civilization! He had only *summered* here in his mother's family home. Even *she* grew up in Atlantic City! I wasn't rooming with a back-country hick after all, thank God.

First thing he did when we got here was to take me to see Jess Nichols. He lived out on the Chatsworth Road and was an auto mechanic. Jess was skinny as the proverbial rail, shaved at least once a week, and kept a cinderblock garage out back of his home that was straight out of the '30s. Just about room in it to pull one car. The rest of it was piled high with parts from every car built in the United States since *at least* the Model T, maybe from even earlier than that! And he talked funny. He was "far" chief. Now just what was a "far" chief? I kind of smiled and said, "that's great" in a non-committal way. Conversation translated: "fire" chief. Oh.

Jess was born in a typical South Jersey saltbox, slightly extended (two *small* rooms and kitchen below, two *small* rooms above) in Bulltown (really out in the boonies). He was one of twelve children! Shades of 1930's Blue Ridge Mountains! Tell you something ... Jess was one of the nicest people I've ever met. Honest as the day is long, friendly, sincere, helpful ... and a damn good "far" chief - good mechanic, too, at least until the advent of the computer age. His wife, Margaret was a bit shorter and a lot broader than he was, but her smile was just as big. Here was a "salt of the earth" type: do anything for anybody, work long hours at the fire company annual clam bake, help her neighbors, enjoy her family and friends.

Courtesy of Patti Groff

Margaret and Jess Nichols
1991

Back to the Lewis family. The Lewises live in the biggest and oldest house in Green Bank. Samuel Driver built the original "South Jersey saltbox" about 1740. He was good friends with Eric Mullica (name sound familiar?) and the Sooy family (more about the Sooys later). Mrs. Jessie Lewis was a Sooy (The Washington Township branch pronounced it "Soo-ey" as in hog calling. Mrs. Lewis always pronounced it "Soy" and in "Soya Sauce".) Nicholas Sooy (one of them anyway) bought the house sometime after Sam's death in 1748. The deed, with his and his wife's signatures on it, still hung over the fireplace in the oldest section of the house. Josephus Sooy lost it in a bad debt, and it was brought back into the family a generation later. At least that's what she had understood.

About 1800, someone added a room, upper and lower, to the side of the old saltbox. Next generation added a bigger section: a double parlor and elegant hallway, with two large bedrooms above. Another somebody took out the walk-in fireplace in the kitchen when stoves became fashionable. Jess's father closed in a porch on the back that had become a laundry room and added screened porches at either end. Lewis's added a bathroom and later a closet off the 1800 section.

We took a ride around "town" in Dud's car — his grandmother's 1941 Chrysler: Green Bank, Bel Haven Lake, Hermann City, Crowleytown, Batsto, back road through Bulltown - we passed Jess Nichol's birthplace (it's since burned down) and my God, twelve kids in *that*? I gained a lot more respect for Jess.

Back in Green Bank, we stopped at the fire house. Dud proudly showed me the latest in fire fighting equipment: a 1951 International (keep in mind, this is 1968), a 1953 Chevrolet (formally seeing *mucho* service in the Philadelphia Fire Department), a 1950 dark green bomb Caddie ambulance, and outside, the best of all, a 1930 Reo. Did I mention I was from the Philadelphia suburbs? My father was a member of two fire companies: one with all new Hahns and one with all new Macks, both with the latest equipment. Ambler even had a heated paved apron in front of the firehouse so that the snow and ice would melt. To me, *THAT* was *fire*-fighting equipment. This was "far" out equipment. Oh, by the way: no coats, no Scott air packs, no nothing, except ancient fire trucks. At least they ran. Dud proved *that*. He started up all the engines in the cinderblock building without opening the building's doors. I edged toward the way we came in, thinking about being overcome by exhaust fumes - the irony of it all. Headlines in "The Ambler Gazette": *"Suburban Boy Found Dead From Fumes in Pine Barrens Fire House."*

I think Dud finally took pity on me: we walked outside. Dud went over and started the Reo. He had a pocket full of bulbs. Seems the Reo's electrical system was 6-volt and he had hooked up a 12-volt battery to it the last time he'd been home. Not healthy for 6-volt bulbs. So now you have it, two fire trucks inside, one fire truck outside, all sitting there going chug-achug-achug - and at that moment, a woman came running across the street yelling, "We've got a fire!"

Dud immediately ran to the "automatic" siren and, yes, squeezed the switch - the siren wound up as long as he held the switch and moaned down when he let go to open one of the doors. He ran in, scribbled something illegibly (I thought) on a blackboard by the door, ran back and squeezed the siren again, jumped into the International and took off down the road. The woman went home. ... OK ... Then someone else came speeding up in a car, jumped out of it and into the Chevy and took off. Yes ... yes ... That was two old trucks and two men. Did I hear the woman right: it was a *structure* fire? Oh yes, finally a pickup truck came along with a driver, a passenger, and four guys in the back. It skidded to a halt in front of the fire house. A man jumped out, checked the blackboard, and they all took off down the road.

At least half an hour went by. The sun was going down. It was getting cold. I was still standing in front of the fire house. The Reo was still going chug-achug-achug alongside of the fire house, so I figured that that was enough of that and shut off the key. It still went chug-achug-achug for a little while, then died in a wheeze. Some more time went by.

Suddenly a pickup truck came careening down the road, screeched to a stop, and Dud jumped out of the back. "We need the water in the Reo," he yelled. "I commandeered this pickup." He jumped into the Reo, started it up, slammed it into gear, took off, and *ran out of gas* directly in front of the fire house. Didn't seem to bother Dud any. Nothing *ever* seems to bother Dud any. Must be a pine barrens trait. He ran and got a five gallon can of gas out of his '41 Chrysler (doesn't everyone carry at least five gallons in the trunk?), pulled the seat out of the Reo (the gas tank was under the seat!) and filled up.

"Here, take this can and stop at Jess Nichols' and get more from the tank out back. Take my car," says he.

"Not on your life," says I. "I don't even remember which house is his house. I'm not going into someone's back yard and take gas from their gas tank, no way! Somebody's liable to shoot me." Headline in "The Ambler Gazette:" *Suburban Boy Shot Dead Stealing Gas in Pine Barrens.*

"I've got to have gas," Dud rejoined.

"Well, then, I'll follow you. Pull over in front of Jess's house and I'll know which one it is. At least that's safer."

"You got it," he replied. Mounting the gas tank (he did reinstall the seat), he shoved the Reo into gear, and away he went.

I ran to the '41 Chrysler (did I mention this was 1968?), prayed I could drive a standard shift, got it into gear, and took off after him. Yeah, you guessed it, he didn't pull over. OK ... so I followed him up the Chatsworth road. Thirty miles an hour. Yep. Top speed. It was getting dark: remember the blown lightbulbs? Headlights and four flashers. I provided the tail lights. Now *this* was going to a fire! Except that, now that I really looked, Dud wasn't in the driver's seat anymore, and the Reo was weaving back and forth across the road! All right. Sure. Now I'm in a 1941 Chrysler, following a 1930 Reo with no lights - and no driver, at the breakneck speed of thirty ... to a fire?

Then, finally, up ahead: the International, parked at a stream where it crossed the road. Dud reappeared in the driver's seat (thank God) and ditched the Reo (yes, 'ditched') in the sand shoulder of the road. Hopping out, he ran back to me, spouting the words, "Did you get the gas?"

"Hell, no I didn't get the gas! You didn't pull over."

"Well, I'm going to need it. Go back to the store and tell the woman there you need the gas for the fire company."

"Right." She's never seen me before in her life, and she's going to give me five gallons of gas for the "fire company." Right. He must have read my mind.

"She'll recognize the car."

Yep, she would *that*.

"Oh, by the way," he continued, don't go without giving the guys in the International the battery in the trunk. They came out to get water out of the river and stalled and their battery is dead."

"Right." Doesn't everyone carry a spare fire truck battery in the trunk of their car?

OK. Battery to the International ... '41 Chrysler back to the store ... get gas ... she did recognize the car (who wouldn't) but she kept eyeing *me* ... back to the bridge ... International still there. OK. I sauntered casually back to them after stopping.

"Where's Dud," I said, not wanting to suggest anything by the fact that they were still sitting where I'd left them.

Courtesy of Dudley Lewis

The 1930 Reo Decked Out for Christmas
(That's Santa, not Dudley, behind the wheel.)

5

"Back at the fire," was the reply.

"Well, he needs the gas I brought. He only has five gallons in the tank."

At that minute, there was Dud and the Reo "flashing" by down the road to Green Bank.

"Thanks a lot, guys," I shouted and took off for the Chrysler and the Reo. Figured I'd better follow that fire truck. *Somewhere* it was going to need the gas I was carrying.

All the way back to Green Bank ... thirty miles an hour. No lights. Dark. Will he run out of gas .... yes ... no. No... we made it.

So there we are, 1930 Reo - out of gas at the fire house once again. International still up beside the stream. Chevy, who knows? And Dud says, "we saved the gun club!" Now, *that* was a miracle! It was paneled in creosoted cut up telephone poles, too. It's a wonder they didn't lose the whole damn Wharton Tract!

"Why in the world did you keep ditching the Reo when you stopped," I asked. Naive me.

"Didn't have any brakes."

I should have guessed.

"And where did you disappear to on the trip there?"

"Oh, the Reo has a dual-speed rear axle, and I couldn't get it to go into high. There was a wrench on the floor, so I hooked my arm through the steering wheel and worked on the linkage with the wrench. Still couldn't get it to go into high, though."

Actually, this *is* the truth, the *whole* truth, and nothing *but* the truth so help me. I gained a very healthy respect for those firemen and their company. They *did* save half the building, and with not enough water to put out a campfire. Our wonderful suburban fire companies with all the latest equipment and an unlimited supply of hydrant water couldn't have done better. Eight men, three ancient antique trucks, and about a thousand gallons of water - half the building saved and no forest fire. They weren't such hicks after all, just local men with no cash and no way to get it, doing with what they had, and doing very well at that. Jess Nichols could go shaveless for a week and say "far" for fire all he wanted. He and the men of Green Bank Volunteer Fire Company were good men.

Howard ("Kingie") King, Jr.
During World War II

I later learned that Jess Nichols had rebuilt both trucks in his back yard from the frame up. The International had been an oil delivery truck that had to be completely rebuilt and the fire pump installed. Jess, you see, could make any engine run, even one that had been in the Mullica's brackish water for two full years. Jess always said that if it ran once, he could make it run again. Amazing man, Jess Nichols. Born and bred in Bulltown, Jess was definately a Piney, but he had commonsense intelligence and a native ability. He shared with his wife a community interest that organized and maintained both the fire company and the ambulance squad on practically no money.

The next day, we stopped at the Green Bank Store to get some 22 ammo for target practice: Walt Priest, prop. Walt was the epitome of the Piney: tall, gaunt, shaved once a week - gave us the ammunition, then showed us his "guns for sale - only to special people" division. Well, first impressions aren't everything, I was learning - the hard way. As I got to know Walt, I found out he, too, was really a great guy, but much to my surprise, he wasn't exactly born in the pines. He and his wife, Virginia, were born in Hammonton, but Virginia's family was from Green Bank. Virginia was the women that had eyed me up when I stopped for the gas for the fire company. Later, the couple built a house next to the store and 'retired.' Like so many of his generation in the pines, Walt was a little rough around the edges but a good man, nevertheless. Virginia was a dear!

Back to the Lewis's for evening dinner. Jessie Lewis, by the way, is a *fantastic* cook. Her father had rebuilt the old storehouse across the street by the river into a house when he and his wife decided to live there full time around 1947. The big house wasn't made habitable for the winter until the Lewises moved there the year their son started college (1965).

Jessie had a couple of good stories about herself when she was staying there alone from time to time while Hans was working. Seems like she was quite a quick draw. Her father had a local man, Howard King, Jr., a veteran of the Army Air Force in World War Two, who helped to keep an eye out on the property when they weren't there. One night, Jess was sleeping in her bedroom when a whole pile of cars pulled up out front. Jess jumped out of bed, got a shotgun, threw up the window and shouted "I've got a gun!" (And probably a bit more.) "Jesus-muh-God, Jess," Kingie shouted. "It's me! Watch that thing!" Apparently he was with a whole group of hunters and didn't realize Jess was staying in the old house. She pulled that gun on a State Trooper one night, too. If she was going to live in the pines, guess she figured she'd better be prepared. Jessie is some lady.

Then there was a "Jersey Devil" story. One night, horrible screams issued from the swamp across the river. All the men of Green Bank grabbed their guns and headed across the old drawbridge - in the morning, that is. Nothing turned up. Months later, a bear carcass was discovered. But the men would never talk about that night.

The following morning, we went to church. Remember, the Lewis's lived next to the graveyard next to the church, but we got there late anyway. We were walking up the road during the first hymn. I couldn't believe it. Wafting out of the open windows came - unmistakingly and at a *very slow* tempo - the melody to "How Dry I Am." *This* was a *Methodist* Church and *Methodists* were against drinking, at least they were supposed to be in 1968. There were ten people in church that morning: three Lewises, myself, the young minister who was still in seminary, four other people, and the organist, a *very* elderly lady, playing an ancient reed organ that you peddled, and it seemed that *every* tempo was s - l - o - w , so much so that you could memorize the tune during the first verse. Apparently the old bellows spring was getting a bit weak with age. If you tried to pump and play fast, the pedals went clear to the floor and you had no air. And yes, the tune of the first hymn really *was* "How Dry I Am."

So much has happened since those days in the late 1960's. The "far" company worked their butts off and bought two new trucks (The younger generation doesn't talk that way any more. Pity. I suspect that the accent, like those of Smith Island, Maryland, and the West Virginia mountains, dates back centuries.) Two years ago, they also built a new steel building next to their old house. The ambulance company has had several new ambulances and bought the old garage next to the fire house to house them. They still only have a handful of men - and women now - who serve their community unselfishly and bravely. The next generation has taken over the reigns. They're on the 911 system and are quite modern. Jess and Margaret Nichols are gone, sorely missed but fondly remembered. Walt and Virginia Priest still live next to their old store, but that's closed at the moment. The last owners lost it to the bank. Now there is no store in all of Washington Township. Hans Lewis spent a term as mayor of Washington Township. An enterprizing antiques enthusiast broke into the church and stole the one working potbelly stove and the communion table. I later learned the identity of the old organist of Green Bank: Gussy Weeks, as the Green Bankers called her, but more properly she was Augusta (Weeks) Cale. She played that old organ in the church until she died at ninety. A former mayor who lived in Lower Bank was murdered by a couple of local young men and his old house burned to the ground along with its priceless antiques. Yes, there is crime and tragedy, even in the pines.

When I first came to Green Bank, and for many years thereafter, the Washington Township building was a ramshackle old building on River Road. Today, it's all fixed up, clapboards painted a shining white, and a credit to the township. An excellent township committee serves the residents well in the last decade of the twentieth century. Bill Haines, Jr., of Haines and Haines (to call them 'cranberry farmers' just doesn't make it) succeeded Hans as mayor and went on to be elected to the Burlington County Board of Freeholders. Now, at least, Burlington County knows that Washington Township in the pines actually exists and really *is* a part of the county. My former roommate has been teaching at Mainland Regional High School for twenty years and still lives with his parents in the old house in Green Bank. His pride is a 32' 1937 Elco motor yacht which he carefully maintains. The '41 Chrysler, the '30 Reo, the '53 Chevy, the '51 International, and the 1950 dark green bomb of an ambulance are long gone.

Green Bank and Washington Township have made it through the twentieth century. At least the ambulance won't break down on the way to the hospital and the fire trucks won't run out of gas or battery power or the engines simply give up the ghost at a critical time. The times have changed, and the members worked hard to purchase new equipment. The men are younger and do shave more than once a week. Maybe I'm getting old, but somehow I miss the color and the spirit.

A Tribute

The River Mullica

Once more on Mullica's laurelled bluffs,
    The Summer flowers are budded.
Once more with Summer's golden ruff,
    The dales of the "Bank" are flooded.

Its Pines above, its waves below,
    The West-wind cross it, blowing,
Our river's praise on its rim bestow,
    As we behold it seaward, flowing.

Our River by its Valley born,
    Loves the beautiful and the lowly.
Blue skies smile, flowers wake with morn,
    But the River keeps on flowing.

Laura Larrabee McConeghy

A River Flows to the Sea

Ode to the Mullica River.

O, Beautiful Mullica River!
    With thy sparkling waves so free,
Winding thro' peaceful hamlets
    On thy journey to the Sea.

We love thee, Beautiful Mullica!
    With the ebb and flow of thy tide,
And thy ever changing beauty
    That forever shall abide.

Beautiful Mullica River!
    What tales thou could unfold
Of by gone days, when on they shores
    Dwelt many a warrior bold.

Flow on, O Beautiful Mullica!
    Cheering us on our Way,
With the glory of the SunSet
    Reflected at Close of day!

Mary Curry Birdsall
Green Bank
New Jersey

Mary Curry was born in Nova Scotia in 1867 and came to this country with her father, Captain Thomas Andrew Curry, a Master in the British Merchant Marine, and her half sister, Helena Davidson. Mary married Bill Birdsall of Green Bank and lived there for the rest of her life. Helena married Haze Wobbar and became principal of the consolidated Green Bank School. Mary Curry Birdsall died in 1953 and is buried in the Green Bank cemetery.

Heart of the Pines

TAKOKAN

There was a time when the brown waters of the river ran unseen to the Great Bay. Surrounding it were swamps filled with towering white cedars and sandy uplands crowded with huge and ancient oaks and pines. The leafy canopy would have been so dense that little sunlight filtered its way through to spackle the ground with light. Deer, bear, panther (catamount, mountain lion, or whatever you might choose to call the big cat), foxes, wolves, beaver, and raccoons populated the forest fastness, and the waters of river and bay teemed with fish and shellfish of every sort. This delightful valley was a paradise waiting to be discovered. And discovered it was.

The Lenape, or "True Men," "Grandfathers" the other Algonkian-speaking tribes of the Eastern Shore and New England called them, had made their permanent homes along the river which bore their name. In the summer, many of the bands moved eastward to the sea. The area through which they passed on their journey was initially uninhabited, and the seashore was a summer playground. There was no danger from attack from other tribes and the game was as plentiful as could possibly be imagined. In the autumn, they'd gather up their belongings and make the trek back to the River of the Lenape, some crossing to the western side, others remaining on the eastern.

"Takokan" they called what would one day be Lower Bank. "Takokan." We have no idea what the name meant in the Lenape language, but by the river's bank, they paused on their way eastward, and, in later years, even stayed for the summer. Eventually they set up a somewhat more permanent town up where the river forked. There they raised their children and grandchildren in a land of plenty.

The land had been formed countless centuries before at the end of the last ice age. The great glacier had pushed down into the more northern reaches, pulverizing rocks into sand under its huge weight. When the glacier melted, the resulting runoff carried the fine sand down the great rivers that formed in the valleys gouged by the once-mighty mountains of ice. As the rivers met the sea, they deposited their burden of sand to form the soil of a new plain. Gradually trees and plants took root, tapping the fresh water aquifers that underlay the porous soils. By the time the Lenape came into the picture, the land was filled with almost impassible forests, watered by numerous streams, and all led finally to the mighty sea that beckoned in the summer sun.

The Lenape's summer playground of plenty was theirs alone for hundreds of years, when suddenly a huge canoe floated into the Great Bay. The old men must have lost their stoicism at this startling revelation, but not one could imagine that their world would never be the same. In 1524, the ship of Verrazano, an Italian in French

Photograph by John Pearce

The River Approach to Lower Bank, *Takokan* - 1995

employ, dropped anchor in Great Bay. He was charmed with the sandy shoreline of what would become Nova Caesarea or New Jersey and, like so many after him, spent the summer playing on the beaches and bays of the coastline.

The Lenape would have discussed this awesome sight around their campfires of an evening, but as the years went by, the tales of the grandfathers simply became strange stories that seemed almost myths. For ninety years, the Great Bay did not know the splash of an anchor. Then in 1614, Captain Cornelius Mey, exploring for the Dutch, once more broke the peace of the bay. *Eyre Haven*, he named it. His crew, exploring the islands and creeks of the bay, found birds' eggs in such abundance that it was all they could talk about when they returned to their ship, the *Fortune*. *Eyre Haven*, Mey named it in Dutch, and *Egg Harbor* it has remained to this day. It would be a long time before the Lenape of Takokan would be again disturbed.

Not so their brothers and sisters in their ancient lands along the River of the Lenape. Mey had explored that river and had set up a fort. That was the beginning. The Dutch didn't make a go of it at first. They were more successful on Manhattan, which they purchased in a rather shady deal from relatives of the Lenape.

Sweden was more fortunate. The Swedish crown sent out colonists to the new world in the *Kalmar Nyckel* (*Key of Calmar*), which arrived on the shores of what would become known as the Delaware in 1638. They promptly set up a colony on Tinicum Island. The newly-appointed governor, John Printz, laid out what is today New Castle, Delaware, and called it "Stockholm." The Dutch didn't take kindly to the Swedes settling on *their* land, and when diplomatic protests failed, Governor Peter Stuyvesant sailed with six or seven hundred men in six ships from New Amsterdam on Manhattan Island to set things right. He demolished the Swedish forts and houses, but many of the Swedes remained on their lands along the river. [If the reader has an interest in the Swedish colony, Peter Craig's 1993 excellent work, *The 1693 Census of the Swedes on the Delaware*, is the best collection of material available on the subject.] Ten years after the Dutch Stuyvesant had dealt so forcibly with the Swedes, the English cannon gave the old man back in kind when they were pointed at Manhattan.

THE COLONY OF NEW JERSEY

Charles Stuart, the second of that name, reigned over England and Scotland as absolute king by divine right, or so he thought. So had his father before him, but he lost his head when his Parliament and their adherents disputed that right. His brother, reigning as James II, would lose his throne in the Glorious Revolution of 1688. For a few brief years in between, Charles II was happy claiming divine ownership over his dominions.

Charles II and his advisors had some appreciation for England's overseas colonies and realized that they could not be split by a Dutch wedge in the middle. Thus they instigated the relatively peaceful capture of New Netherlands and of all the Dutch-claimed lands east of the Delaware River.

To secure his new lands, Charles gave them to his brother, James, then Duke of York, as a proprietary colony. Maryland had already been founded after that fashion, having been granted to Lord Baltimore. Pennsylvania soon would be by virtue of a grant to William Penn. Proprietorship was a simple idea. It meant that the proprietor had the right to both own the land and to govern it as he saw fit, under the laws of the English realm.

James, Duke of York, soon granted his new lands east of the Delaware and west of the Hudson to two friends, Sir George Carteret and Lord John Berkeley, who proceeded to organize their territory as the Province of New Jersey. From 1664 to 1674, Carteret and Berkeley remained in ownership of the lands and set up a means to sell landholdings in their territories. In that latter year, however, Berkeley found himself in financial straits and sold his half share to Edward Byllinge, a Quaker.

Led by what he termed "The Inner Light," George Fox had started a religious movement in England whose members called themselves "Friends." They had a simple belief: God spoke directly to them without the intervention of churches or clergy. That all sounds innocent enough, but these early fanatics made themselves persona non grata by proclaiming the corruption of the Church of England, the Puritan churches, the Presbyterian churches, the Baptist congregations, and the Crown with every chance they encountered.

That did not endear them to their neighbors or to the government. When the government arrested them for disturbing the peace, most of their countrymen cheered. William Penn had become an adherent of the "friendly persuasion" and had long thought of a haven for the persecuted sect in the colonies. When Byllinge also found himself in financial difficulties, William Penn became one of the trustees administering his estate.

Penn convinced Carteret to divide the province in half along a line that stretched from just north of the Delaware Water Gap to the southern tip of Long Beach Island. William Penn and his shrewd Quaker associates got everything west of that line, while Carteret kept all the lands to the east. Carteret must have been delighted with the bargain. After all, he got all the lands near New York bordering on the Hudson, which included vast acres of fertile land. All the Quakers seemed to have received was sand and pine trees. To this day, the borders of Burlington County on the south and Monmouth/Ocean counties on the north, mark this division line between East and West Jersey with the single exception that Little Egg Harbor Township became part of Ocean County in 1891. Tuckerton became a separate municipality from Little Egg Harbor Township ten years later.

Penn was no slouch. He also had his eye on a greater prize: the vast lands to the west of the Delaware. In payment for a debt owed by the king to his father, Admiral Richard Penn, son William also received what would become the Colony of Pennsylvania, making him a proprietor in his own right. The Quakers were advancing!

Penn set out right away to create a "Peaceable Kingdom" in Pennsylvania. He set up a truly free form of government, subject, of course, to his rights as proprietor (he had the last say), and opened his colony to men and women of all religious groups. With his trusteeship of West Jersey he did the same thing.

In 1688, he set up a Council of Proprietors for West Jersey to oversee the sale and settlement of all lands within the colony that had not been sold previously. The proprietary estate was actually set up like a company with shares being sold to investors. These shareholders were given "warrant rights" in proportion to their shares. When someone wanted to buy a piece of land, he negotiated for "warrant rights" to it from a shareholder, then applied to the Council of Proprietors for a survey.

The Surveyor General of the colony would then have a survey made of the property which was put before the Council. If they approved, the survey was recorded. The purchaser of the land now held title to his property. Some of the surveyors arranged to purchase large tracts of land for resale. Other investors also bought a sizable number of acres for the same reason. Thus, if a person wanted to buy land still controlled by the Council, he applied directly to them. If he found a particular piece of land to his liking that someone else had already purchased, he bought it from them. This Council of West Jersey Proprietors still exists and operates as of this date.

LITTLE EGG HARBOR

All of this time, the waters of Mey's Little Egg Harbor River and its tributaries continued to flow undisturbed through a land whose primeval beauty was beckoning. Tribes of the True People still made extended stops at various spots along the river when on their way to their summer homes by the bay and seashore. The river teamed with fish, some of gigantic size by today's standards. Wildfowl filled the marshes. Huge virgin white cedars crowded the numerous swamps that bordered the river and its watershed. While the land may have been more sandy than that nearer the Delaware settlements, it still held valuable assets.

In 1690, the Little Egg Harbor watershed was poised on the edge of promise. Eric Pålsson Mullica, son of Pål Jönsson and his wife, Margaret, had sailed up the Delaware River with his parents and siblings aboard the *Eagle* in 1654 at the age of eighteen. By 1693, he had established himself on an estate near Tacony, had fathered several children, and had remarried after his first wife had passed away.

In 1693, he was one of the signers of a letter directed to the Swedish government requesting that they send out Lutheran clergy to minister to the spiritual needs of the Swedes who still had their homes along the Delaware. His name was also on the census list which was enclosed with the letter. By the time Pastor Rudman entered his duties at what would become Old Swedes (Gloria Dei) Church in Philadelphia and made a copy of the 1693 census over the winter of 1697-8, Eric, his second wife, and several of his children had left their comfortable home in the new colony of Pennsylvania and had removed to a place known in the Lenape vernacular as Takokan on the Little Egg Harbor River. Thus Eric, his sons, John, age twenty, Stephen, age thirteen, his daughter, Catherine, age fifteen, and their stepmother, Ingeborg Helm Mullica, became the first family to live in the wilderness in what is now called Lower Bank. When the Mullica family built their cabin in Takokan, there was not one other single settlement along the coast between the Shrewsbury River and the Great Egg Harbor River. They were truly alone in the wilderness.

In 1704, a Lutheran pastor named Sandel journeyed to "little Eggherbour" to preach to the "Widow Möllika" and her family, indicating that Eric had died prior to that year when he would have been sixty-eight years old and probably was buried near his cabin in Lower Bank. The following year, his son, Eric, Jr., who had remained behind on his father's old estate in Pennsylvania, along with his brother, John, who had accompanied their father, purchased land in West Jersey which would eventually bear their name: Mullica Hill.

Ingridh [*sic*] Mullica acted as godmother for her stepson's baby, another Eric, in 1714 in the Raccoon (Swedesboro) Lutheran Church, and it is presumed that she had moved to the Mullica Hill property from Takokan by that time. Her death is duly recorded in the church records of that place in 1719.

Records indicate that John Mullica sold the Takokan property to a Thomas Bishop on July 4, 1719 after the death of his mother, though his brother, Eric, Jr., sold fifty of that same one hundred acres to a Joseph Pearce three years later. No record of a deed to land in Takokan in the Mullica name has ever been discovered, though it was certainly under the jurisdiction of the West Jersey Proprietors. There doesn't seem to have been a challenge to its sale (either of them) by his sons, which seems to indicate he had some recognizable claim. Whatever the case, it is almost certain that Eric Mullica sleeps in the soil of his beloved Takokan somewhere in the present town of Lower Bank along the river which now bears his name.

CIVILIZATION ADVANCES

Meanwhile, the area of Little Egg Harbor was beginning to fill up. Henry Jacobs Falkinburg came from the Swedesboro area and bought land from the Lenape. He settled into his temporary, canvas-covered cave on one of the islands of Little Egg Harbor right after Mullica in 1698 or 1699. Edward Andrews joined him on a farm a bit inland from Falkinburg at Middle-of-the-Shore. By 1704, Andrews had helped to found a Quaker Meeting and gave land for the construction of a meeting house in 1708.

Around 1700, Thomas and Hannah Clark had settled on the Gloucester County side of the Little Egg Harbor River just down stream from the Mullica property. By 1718, their little village had grown to about forty homes, a store, a trading post, and a church.

Three years after Pastor Sandel preached to the "Widow Möllika" and her family, in Takokan, a group of Scots from the Long Island area sailed up the Little Egg Harbor River to its head of navigation, and unloaded their belongings on the western shore. Their passionate Presbyterianism induced them to build a small church at the same time as they were constructing shelter for themselves and their families. Tradition says that they copied the Scandinavian style of log construction for their church building and probably did so for their houses as well.

There is no indication that Thomas Bishop (or Joseph Pearce) ever actually resided on his land in Takokan though there is an indication from Pastor Sandel's diary that an Englishman did live near the Widow Mullica's at the time of his 1704 visit. In 1713, a John Pearce received a survey from the proprietors for land on which would be known in the future as "The Island." General Elias Wright, Wharton's manager, would try to find out the origin of the Pearce family almost two centuries later but failed. He found one mentioned in the East Jersey records but could never connect him to the West Jersey Pearce's. Still, he presumed that John and Joseph were either brothers or father and son.

In 1715, Richard Bull had a survey made for 151 acres upstream from the Mullica property, but there is no indication that he or his family lived on the land. He did lend his name to the Bull Creek, the Little Bull Creek, and Bulltown.

Eric Mullica and his family must receive credit for being the earliest family to make a permanent residence in coastal South Jersey above the Great Egg Harbor region and lends his name to the river which flowed past his cabin, but otherwise he had little influence on the area. The second man on the Lower Bank land is another matter.

PETER CAVILEER

Peter Cavileer is far more mysterious than is Eric Mullica. Soon after Mullica's sons sold the Takokan property of their father, one Peter Cavileer is on record as owning several hundred acres and a homestead in the vicinity of Lower Bank, Burlington County. The year is 1722; that much is known. Where did he come from, this Peter "Cavileer," and what was his real name?

Chevalier, Cavalier, Cavileer, was the French word for "knight," and it is believed that he was a French Huguenot, but little is actually known about his origins. The Huguenots were French Protestants, followers of John Calvin of Geneva, who were persecuted in their homeland areas of Brittany, Normandy, and the Channel Islands.

In France, the Huguenots had experienced persecution ever since Queen Catherine de'Medici engineered the St. Bartholomew's Day Massacre back in 1572. The crown finally forced either the conversion or expulsion of all Protestants from the realm of France with the revocation of the Edict of Nantes by Louis XIV in 1685, and many fled to other countries more hospitable to them, or to the new world. Holland shared their Calvinist theology and was most agreeable to their emigration.

"Cavaliers" are listed as residents of the colony of New Netherlands. Records exist of several "Peters" and "John's" (again spelled in the French fashion: Jean or Pierre, the Dutch fashion: Johannes or Pieter, or the English fashion as we know it). We have no idea whether they were related or not.

There are land grants in "Colonial Conveyances" in which a Peter Caveller [sic] deeded land along the Mullica River in Gloucester County (now Atlantic County) to John Smallwood in 1714, which seems to show that he owned property on the Gloucester County side of the river prior to the sale of the Mullica property. There is no indication that he actually lived on the property.

Was our Peter related to the other "Cavileers" in the Dutch colony of New Netherlands? Other "Peter Cavileers" apparently can be found in the early records of other colonies. It is entirely possible, however, that our Peter had come down from New Amsterdam (New York by this time) and that he recommended his new-found paradise to other friends of his back in the old colony.

Yoos Sooy

In 1724, two years after Peter Cavileer is recorded as having a homestead in the area, a middle-aged Dutchman and his family tired of their home at Cheesequake in northern New Jersey, and, like Eric had done years before, set out to find a new one. Yoos Sooy, his wife, and his two sons, Yoos II, and Nicholas, sailed into the Great Bay and up the river, dropping anchor off Mullica's old homestead. The Sooy family probably found Peter Cavileer waiting for them on the bank If our Lower Bank Peter was indeed from the New York "Cavaliers," he may very well have known Yoos Sooy and his wife. Surely the family had known her grandfather, sly old Dutch official that he was, and her famous father. Perhaps it was Peter Cavileer who persuaded Yoos and his wife to leave their home in northern New Jersey and venture into the wilderness near where he had made his homestead.

Being business-minded, Yoos spotted the obvious advantages of a good bank, high and dry, of surrounding high lands that could be cleared for farming, of cedar swamps with towering trees for ships' planking and lumber, of the possibilities for river trade, and figured he would just set down and stay a bit.

Yoos Sooy was born in Amsterdam, Holland, in 1685 and came to New Amsterdam (after it had forcibly had its name altered to "New York") in 1702 at the age of seventeen. He married Sarah Van Tienhoven, daughter of Dr. Lucas Van Tienhoven and granddaughter of Cornelius Van Tienhoven, the infamous secretary of the former Dutch colony, confidant of governors, and unscrupulous man of business. The young couple lived in New York until about 1720, giving them ample time to get to know any local "Cavaliers" in that little town. [Sarah's paternal great-grandmother was a Walloon by the name of "Cuvilier." The similarity of the names Cavileer and Cuvilier at least open the possibility that there was a relationship between the Cavileers and Adriana (Cuvilier) Vinge, the mother of Rachel (Vinge) Van Tienhoven, wife of Cornelius.

Though the reports from the records vary, it seems that Yoos and Sarah had a son, Yoos, Jr., born in 1709, but the baby didn't live. The following year, they had a second son, whom they again named "Yoos," after his father. In 1712, another son was born whom they called "Nicholas." (See Lower Bank for a complete discussion.) In the year 1720, the family removed to Middlesex County, New Jersey. Four years later, they came to Lower Bank.

Yoos Sooy died in 1737 and was buried on his property at Lower Bank at the age of fifty-two. Though Eric Mullica was no doubt buried in Lower Bank, the grave of Yoos Sooy is the oldest known grave anywhere in the vicinity. The spot where he is buried has remained private land and is surrounded by the decrepit remains of the old Pacemaker Yachts plant. The small plot contains at least three graves: Yoos Sooy's, John Cavileer's, and one that is unknown. In the midst of the rubble and debris of the Pacemaker plant lie the last remains of these two worthy men, the first, a pioneer of the area and forefather of the Sooy family, and the second, the son of a pioneer, ancestor of the Cavileer family and probably one of the first children to be born in Lower Bank.

Yoos and Sarah's two sons, Yoos II and Nicholas, amply carried out the dream of their enterprising father. Nicholas Sooy moved to Leed's Point and began a large family on the western side of the river that bears his family name. Yoos II (called "Joseph") remained on the eastern side of the river. Nicholas married Jean Ingersol of Great Egg Harbor and had six children. Yoos Sooy II married Elizabeth Smuts in the year of his father's death and had twelve children. Thus from those two sons of Yoos Sooy, there were eighteen children.

Peter Cavileer married Ann Tearney on the 11th of February, 1739, and had a son, John, who was born on the 20th of April, 1742. John had eight children, including another Peter and another John and died at the ripe old age of 71. Where father Peter was buried, we may never know, but son John lies head-to-toe with Yoos Sooy. Eric Mullica had come and gone, and, like the wind in the pines, left no trace of himself along the river that he loved. His children simply didn't care for a wilderness home, far from the settled areas along the Delaware. In Peter Cavileer and Yoos Sooy, however, the Mullica had found its champions.

Stephen and John Leek

In 1738, four years before John Cavileer was born, Stephen Leek and his son, John, came to the Wading River from Cumberland County, New Jersey. Stephen had been living on Long Island when the eighteenth century was born. Fifteen years later, he and his wife had a son, whom they named John, and, soon after his birth, the family set out to fulfill Stephen's dream of a landed estate. He bought land in Cumberland County and settled there first. John grew into a fine young man on his father's farm, but both father and son dreamed of bigger and better things. Hearing tales of the benefits of rivers, bays, and woodlands on the coast from his Long Island friends who had settled the Little Egg Harbor area, Stephen Leek, at the then-advanced age of fifty-eight, and his twenty-two year old son set out to make their dreams reality.

They bought land along the Wading River, inland from the estates of the Great John Mathis over on the Bass River, and started right in on their empire. By the time John died in 1777, the Leek estate included hundreds of acres, a shipyard, a huge wharf along the river, at least one coastal ship, and a thriving business in trade. Charles Loveland, the French family, and at least one branch of the Cranmer family took up land on the Bass River side of the Wading River at an early date. The Darnells seem to have settled on land on the Washington Township side, north of the present Route 542.

Samuel Driver

Samuel Driver came to Green Bank sometime in the early part of the eighteenth century. Tales have been told of how he was a friend of Eric Mullica's and of Yoos Sooy (who never met each other, the one being dead before the other arrived), of Driver being Sooy's surveyor (not established either), of Driver being a bachelor (though 'relatives' of his have shown up in Green Bank from time to time, and his *son* did sell the property to Joseph Sooy after his father's death). What we do know is that Samuel Driver came into the possession of the three hundred acres which a man by the name of Isaac Pearson had had surveyed in 1737 along the Mullica, built his house in what would become Green Bank, died in 1748, and was buried in the cleared land beside his little home. Nothing else has yet come to light. With a name like "Driver" though, it is more than likely that he was of English stock. John Driver, presumably Samuel's son, would sell his estate to Yoos Sooy's son, Joseph (Yoos II) in 1752.

On the Verge of Expansion

When the French and Indian War came to an end in 1763, you could have sailed on a fair sized vessel across Great Bay and up the Mullica with little difficulty. The lower part of the river was wide and deep. The surrounding marshes still provided nesting grounds for all sorts of birds, and the river hosted numerous varieties of fish and shellfish. Not until reaching the Bass River did the Little Egg Harbor start to narrow considerably.

Across the marshes from Great Bay, a couple of tiny dots would have appeared where Quaker families had built houses over in what is today Mystic Islands and Tuckerton. Up the Bass River at the head of navigation, John Mathis owned four farms. His children married into other Little Egg Harbor families, some moving towards the Andrews' mill to the east, some setting up homes on the southwest side of the big river.

If your ship didn't head up the Bass to John Mathis's house, you would find yourself sailing directly for a small settlement on the Gloucester County side of the Little Egg Harbor River at Chestnut Neck. Here, Micajah, John's eldest son, had bought property. Joseph Sooy's son, Joseph, also settled in the Chestnut Neck area, as did Micajah Smith.

Rounding the bend and passing Chestnut Neck, you would enter Swan Bay, an area where the river is surrounded by tidal marshland and which remains as wild today as it did in 1763. Another of the "little rivers" branches off to the north from Swan Bay which would have taken the adventurer to the Leek plantation, but your vessel would still have a distance to travel on the main river before it encountered the next cluster of houses at Clark's Landing. Visible in the distance were the houses of the Cavileers and perhaps those of a few others who had settled at Lower Bank. Yet another mile upriver stood the tiny house that Joseph Sooy had purchased from John and Mary Driver. Beyond "Green Bank" in 1763 were marshes and some high land until your vessel reached the head of navigation. Here, Elijah Clark, son of the Thomas who had settled Clark's Landing, had bought acreage six years before and had just built himself a fine mansion. Another enterprising young man, Richard Wescoat, had arrived in that vicinity three years before. These two men would find each other to be ideal business, social, and political companions and would help to forge the history of The Forks for the next thirty years.

If you were still adventurous, you'd have to hire a canoe and paddle hard against the strong current through the upper reaches of the five rivers and streams which joined at The Forks, but you would have found nothing for your efforts. Only if you managed to persevere though miles and miles of cedar swamps, marshes, and sandy upland would you chance to reach the Inskeep Sawmill at Goshen Neck on what would be later called the Atsion River.

The valley of the Little Egg Harbor presented no signs of great prosperity to the traveller of 1763, but it was on the verge of an economic explosion. The next hundred years would prove to be years of prosperity and excitement for the watershed.

AMERICAN FREEDOM

The inhabitants of the English colonies along the Atlantic seaboard in 1763 enjoyed more freedom than did any people in the world at that time or at any future time. They were part of the great British Empire, but Britain's control over her colonies had been somewhat indifferent. The king had appointed governors of the various colonies and, from time to time, Parliament had passed acts governing the shipping of local products, but every colony had its own legislature to set taxes and regulate parochial concerns.

Since the 1607 settlement of Jamestown, the American colonists had obtained more freedom in self-government than the people of England itself enjoyed. Although there was constant tension between royal governors, Parliament, and the colonial assemblies, by the end of the French and Indian War, the colonists had basically secured the exclusive right to tax themselves, to appoint most of the officials who administered colonial laws, raise troops, appoint military officers, build churches, schools, and set up whatever other institutions they wanted. Only in matters of foreign affairs did Britain exercise exclusive control, and even that control could be circumvented by smugglers.

The colonists had matured in self-government and expected to participate in decisions which effected their lives. Even the Navigation Laws which Parliament had passed from time to time were circumvented by lax enforcement and the actual lay of the land itself. The American coastline was cut by a host of rivers, bays and coves from the colony of Massachusetts Bay to Georgia, and those estuaries made it easy for the local inhabitants to circumvent any laws attempting to control shipping. Smuggling was a way of life for the citizens of every colony in America as it was for Englishmen themselves.

There are no records from those early days along the Little Egg Harbor, but it is almost certain that smuggling provided the financial underpinning for the estates and towns which grew along the river and it did for the inhabitants along the entire coastline. Successful merchants made their wealth through smuggling and were admired and respected by their fellow citizens as pillars of their communities.

There is little doubt that those early Presbyterian settlers at The Forks understood perfectly their favorable position at the head of navigation of the only river which pointed directly at Philadelphia across sparsely-settled terrain that was ideal for secretly transporting goods into that city. No doubt that's what Clark and Wescoat also understood quite well when they set up their enterprises at The Forks. Probably everyone along the river prospered from "illicit" trade.

Unfortunately, the 1763 end of the war with France overturned the balance of power upon which all depended. Britain was bankrupt. Her own taxes were exorbitant, and her rulers saw no reason why the colonies should not bear their share of the burden of empire. In addition to the taxes, Parliament and the royal ministers now saw a need to "protect" the colonies by stationing permanent forces there. Incidentally, of course, they would help "keep order" and back up the royal governors and the tax collectors in the performance of their duties.

The only enemy, from the colonists' point of view, had been soundly defeated and driven from the North American continent. From whom would they be defended? They knew exactly what the government in Britain had in mind. Permanent garrisons could only be used against the inhabitants themselves. If royal governors could call on royal troops to enforce their edicts and the laws of Parliament, the colonists would no longer enjoy the freedoms which they had grown to cherish over a hundred years! Trouble was brewing.

When the rupture with Great Britain finally came in the 1770's, almost all the inhabitants of the estuary were ardent supporters of the revolutionary elements. Some of the Quakers of Little Egg Harbor Meeting were neutral as their faith demanded, but the valley of the Little Egg Harbor River became a haven for privateers already experienced in annoying British patrol vessels. Even scions of Quaker families like that of the Great John Mathis found it profitable to support the war effort. For those of Presbyterian stock, like the Leeks, there was no question. Wescoat and Clark embraced the Revolution with spirit and dedication.

Parliament had tried to regulate the production of iron products in her American colonies since early in the eighteenth century, with little success. Governor Spotswood of Virginia built an iron furnace at the forks of the Rapidan and the Rappahannock and brought over German iron workers to run it at early as 1715. Three others, one owned by George Washington's father, Augustine, had been built by 1732. By the year 1750, the colonies of the Chesapeake estuary were sending over two thousand tons to England for sale (Morison, p. 143).

This was a disturbing development from the standpoint of iron manufacturers in England, with whom they were competing. Colonies were supposed to benefit the mother country, not compete with her, so they convinced Parliament to forbid slitting mills and forges in the colonies. Parliament was wasting its efforts, however. The resulting law did nothing to slow the development of the iron industry in the American colonies. According to Samuel Eliot Morison, Pennsylvania, New Jersey, and Massachusetts so completely disregarded this Act of Parliament that they granted bounties for the establishment of new iron enterprises. In 1775, he says, "there were actually more furnaces for producing pig iron, and forges for re-smelting the pigs into bar or wrought iron, in the thirteen colonies than in England and Wales."

Charles Read was the epitome of the adventurous entrepreneur. He was politically active in the colony of New Jersey and didn't hesitate to use his influence and contacts to advance his business interests. When he and a partner bought over a thousand acres on the upper reaches of the Little Egg Harbor River in 1755, he had grand dreams. He knew that the bogs of the area contained rich deposits of iron. He also knew that there was a tremendous demand for cheap iron produced right here in the colonies.

In the year 1765, he built a forge on his land near the Goshen Sawmill which he named Atsion. A year later, he completed his works a few miles below Atsion on a parallel branch of the main river which he called Batsto, which was the local name for the place. For more than sixty years, these furnaces and others like them would produce a flow of iron products which would enhance the local trade, support the shipping industry, undergird the colonial forces during the Revolution, and provide the basis for local prosperity. Unfortunately, Read wouldn't live to see the results of his dreams. He had to sell his furnaces almost as soon as he had them built and died a pauper.

The decade before the outbreak of hostilities with Britain brought fantastic prosperity to the valley of the Little Egg Harbor. Wescoat and Clark tapped into every aspect of the local economy so that all of the trade, legal and illegal, flowed through their enterprises at The Forks. John Van Sant settled in the area and built a very successful shipyard across the river from Wescoat's house and businesses. Joseph Sooy's son, Joseph, established himself in the little community at Chestnut Neck, and his brother, John, bought a plantation next to his father's acreage in 1771. John Cavileer became the respected father of a family rich in land and shipping. John Leek's plantation on the Wading included a farm, a shipyard, and a wharf.

By 1775, only twelve years after the end of the war with France, the Little Egg Harbor river was alive with ships and the industries which supported them. The Van Sant shipyard at The Forks sent ship after ship down the ways into the river. On both sides of the river near the shipyard were all the attendant industries that were so necessary to keep those ships sailing. The storehouses of Elijah Clark and Richard Wescoat were packed with trade goods. Batsto kept ships busy hauling its iron products. Batsto village grew with the influx of iron workers and their families. Chestnut Neck prospered as the lower landing for the larger vessels that couldn't navigate all the way to The Forks. Lower Bank supplied seamen and captains to man the vessels which sailed through Great Bay into the Atlantic.

Joe Sooy of Chestnut Neck got himself in a bit of hot water towards the beginning of the war. Joe was the son of Joseph and Elizabeth (Smith) Sooy of Green Bank and grandson of the famous Yoos. Born in 1738, he married Mary Leek of Wading River, the daughter of John Leek. He settled on a plantation in Chestnut Neck and was a sea captain by trade. He seems to have been a bit pompous and slow-witted, though I'm probably maligning him. Out in a boat near the inlet one day early in the war, he spotted a vessel standing just offshore that seemed to have no crew. Though he approached closer, he still couldn't discern anyone on board.

He tied up his boat and climbed up a conveniently-extended rope ladder to the deck where he confronted the first person he met there as if he had some local authority. Much to his chagrin, the vessel turned out to be one of His Majesty's transports loaded with foot soldiers. The tables had been turned on the good captain, and, instead of gaining an easy prize, he himself was the prize. Thus did Joseph Sooy become the unwilling pilot for one of His Majesty's ships. His story didn't end there, however. He was allowed to return to his home, but then he had to convince his fellow river folk that he wasn't a traitor who had willingly gone on board a British vessel to act as pilot.

Despite a deposition he made to that effect and the support of Wescoat and Clark, suspicion lingered around him for some time.

These were heady days for the river folk, and even the 1778 invasion by the British hardly registered a blip on the local prosperity. Merchants and seamen who had become skilled in prewar smuggling took to privateering with delight. Since even large merchant vessels were unarmed, a small cannon or two mounted on a rowed vessel would threaten a lone merchantman with destruction. A single hole through their bottom below the waterline would send her to the bottom. Thus, local people along the entire coast set out in vessels large and small to trip up the haughty British dowagers, made buxom with goods.

No wonder that the British schemed to put a halt to such depredations. These privateers were armed by the richer merchants of the area and sent out against the British shipping in such numbers and with such excellent results that the British sent an expedition to destroy this "nest of rebel pirates." Fortunately, they only managed to attack an earthwork that had no cannon, burn a couple of their own ships which the "pirates" had captured, and scare the begeebers out of the local militia before they found it prudent to retire to Great Bay in their ships.

They missed the main prize, however. Throughout the Revolutionary War, the furnace that Charles Read had built at Batsto in 1766 was a going concern, producing cannon and cannonballs for the Continental Army. This made it a prime target for a British raid. They would have liked to have gone all the way upriver and burned the Batsto Furnace as well as Chestnut Neck, but Pulaski's main army was on the way, and they didn't want to be trapped up the winding Mullica - up a creek without a paddle, so to speak - so they left. It was fortunate, some would say providential, they never did make it up to The Forks and Batsto, but in their reports, they made their foray into the Little Egg Harbor appear to be a great success nevertheless.

Before the British ships left Great Bay, however, they did accomplish another rather dastardly deed. A detachment of Pulaski's guard out in what is now Mystic Islands, which then was the main north-south route across Swimming-Over Point, was betrayed by a deserter, and troops from the transport fell on them by night slaughtered them. The mud-flats of the Mullica had a bit of revenge, though. The British flagship had to be burned because it went fast aground, a not uncommon occurrence in the area.

Joe Sooy's loss of his house and storehouse at Chestnut Neck went a long way towards reestablishing his local reputation. He built another house after the British attack, but most of the other inhabitants of Chestnut Neck moved inland a bit and over to the Nacote (pronounced "naked") Creek to reestablish their village. That creek was fairly narrow and would provide more protection from the marauding British. Thus was Wrangleboro (now Port Republic) founded. Joe died in 1801, "recommend[ing] my Soul into the hands of Almighty God, and my body to the earth to be buryed [sic] in decent Christian buryal [sic]" leaving his 'loving wif [sic]" his rebuilt house and field, "with the orchard and one half the barn... two cows and calves and one yoke of oxen ... also all my household goods and farming utensils with my swine and poultry ... also grass for paster [sic] and hay for her cattle, timber for firewood ... likewise all my provisions in the house and grane [sic] in the ground. His son, Augustus, would inherit the same lands and estate, subject to his mother's "dowry before sited."

Joseph Sooy's story ended happily. Another man's experience upriver at The Forks did not. A look at a map shows that the Mullica thrusts itself northwestward towards Philadelphia. If the seaward approach to that city on the Delaware was blocked, the closest link to the outside world would be at The Forks of the Mullica! That's exactly the situation that presented itself during the Revolution. The Delaware was closed to the colonists during the British occupation of the city and the blockade of the river which followed their evacuation. Benedict Arnold began his troubles while administering the city of Philadelphia after the British evacuated it. Goods were being shipped for the Province of Pennsylvania and the Continental Army via - guess where - The Forks of the Mullica. Arnold bought some of the goods himself, a common practice, but included their shipment along with that of the goods of Pennsylvania and the army in chartered wagons paid for by the army and the province. When Pennsylvania officials wanted to get back at him, they brought up this little point, and Washington had to reprimand his famous general. Miffed by this incident and married to the daughter of a notorious Tory, Arnold asked for and received appointment to the fortress of West Point. The rest is history. And it all began at The Forks.

THE RIVER OF LIFE

From the very beginning, the emphasis of the settlements on the Mullica was "trade." The land was full of trees that could be cut into lumber and shipped to the cities or charred to make charcoal and loaded onto transports for sale to the city folk to keep them warm in the winter. When the secret of the iron deposits in the riverbeds was discovered, iron could be cast or forged and likewise shipped via the Mullica to major ports along the Atlantic coast. The soil wasn't as productive as other inland areas, but it did just fine for subsistence farming. The main thrust was towards the sea, however, and all energies were channeled towards seafaring and related enterprises.

For almost two hundred years, the towns along the Mullica looked to the sea for their sustenance. Fish and shellfish were most abundant and there for the taking. If a man wasn't shipping out aboard a coastal schooner or larger trading vessel, he was usually engaged in one form of fishing or another. Later towns grew up around the iron forges and furnaces, starting with Atsion in 1765 and Batsto in 1766, and later, the glass manufacturing plants. Not until the advent of the railroads did the river lose its influence on the lives of the people of the Mullica valley.

For the First Families, intermarriage was a way of life. At first, there were no roads through the forests that surrounded the river, so the going was rough, except on the river itself. A young man who was looking for an eligible wife usually did not have to go far afield to find one. The large families of the early settlers provided ample opportunities for a prospective bride. Most of the families on the western side of the river married towards the south and those on the eastern side towards the north. There were no bridges across the Mullica lower than The Forks until that of Green Bank was built in 1855, so there was a practical side to the courtship pattern.

A FRESH COAT OF PAINT

Nicholas Sooy I, son of Yoos II, first established himself in the area of The Forks where he is reputed to have owned a tavern. Just prior to the Revolutionary War, he built a tavern on the Philadelphia/Little Egg Harbor Road which became known as Sooy's Inn and also called the Washington Tavern. His father, Joseph Sooy, owned the Driver Estate in Green Bank, his brother Joseph was Chestnut Neck's unwilling pilot, and his brother, John owned a plantation at Herman. His son, Nicholas Sooy II, was even more successful than his father. He bought his uncle John's plantation and used it as his own home. He also repurchased his grandfather's Green Bank estate from William Richards, the owner of Batsto, who had acquired the property after Joseph Sooy couldn't repay a bank loan. He spent his lifetime buying up the surrounding acreage, investing in local businesses and probably in trading vessels, and otherwise acting as a shrewd man of business.

Nicholas II had definately joined the ranks of the wealthy and influential in this area, which, in the early 1800's, included William Richards and his sons, Jesse of Batsto and Samuel of Atsion, Speedwell, and Martha, Jesse Evans of Martha, and several of the Cavileers of Lower Bank. Their rivals for influence in the township weighted the political influence in Washington Township towards the western side for half a century.

Photograph by John Pearce

The Mullica River Upstream from Green Bank - 1995

Families like the Taylors, the Maxwells, and the Leeks had moved into the area around the Wading River. John Leek, Sr. had contributed heavily to the War for Independence, and his son had gained the rank of captain in the local militia. Though John III sold his inheritance to Robert McKeen, his brothers and sisters continued to be an influence on both sides of the Wading River. Lower Bank was fast becoming a charming town of residences and farms for the captains who plied the coast and the men who sailed their ships.

The first half of the nineteenth century (1802) saw Washington Township formed from parts of Evesham, Northampton, and Little Egg Harbor townships. Batsto was booming. The area of The Forks was still prospering. Nicholas Sooy II would soon buy his brother John's estate at Green Bank (Herman) and his grandfather's old homestead just below it. Nicholas II would set up all sorts of business enterprises in the area, and they would focus considerable trade in the area of his estate. Martha Furnace was just beginning to produce. The Wading River Forge and Slitting Mill was active. Lower Bank was becoming a strong community of sea captains, laborers, ships' carpenters, farmers, and seamen. Atsion would have it's fluctuations, but it seemed to hold promise. Other furnaces and forges in the area of the new township had prospects.

Courtesy of Jesse Lewis

The State Access Area in Green Bank in the 1930s

Though some of the enterprises failed during those first heady years of the new century, by the 1830's others were being started: McCartyville with its paper plant was in operation below Martha. Crowleytown was a growing settlement that would see its glass house built in the 1850's. Nicholas II built a glass factory at Green Bank before McCarty had dug a single canal.

In fact, Washington Township was so prosperous that consideration was given to subdividing it. In 1852, part of its territory was taken to help make up Shamong Township. Bass River Township took another part in 1864. In 1866, part went to Woodland Township, and in 1870, Randolph Township (including Lower Bank) was set apart. The State of New Jersey must have felt that there was a sufficient population potential to form two townships where now there is one! They had a lot to go on.

By 1870, though, while everyone was looking so hopefully on the prospects of this area, dark clouds were gathering that should have dampened the excitement. Industry at Batsto was dead. The Forks was still prospering, though the half in Washington Township, Burlington County had declined in importance after the conclusion of the Revolutionary War, and no longer supported any industry between the Batsto and Atsion rivers. Crowleytown's glass works had gone bust, and Green Bank's trade gently faded away after Nicholas II died.

In what would become Randolph Township, Martha Furnace had closed twenty years before, and only holdouts remained in Calico. Lower Bank still saw prosperity and Harrisville near Bodine's Tavern was booming in the paper business. Bridgeport (Wading River) seemed to carry with it a real potential for growth. River commerce still continued but at a much slower pace.

Ships of some size came down the ways at local shipyards along the Mullica. The Van Sant family and others had shipyards, first at The Forks, then in Green Bank, and throughout coastal Atlantic County. The Van Sants were especially busy in both Burlington and Atlantic Counties. Sloops and brigs and other coastal vessels came down the ways at Green Bank, but the *Lillie Falkinburg* in 1873 would be one of the last. The Panic of that year would see to that.

The timber industry was still going strong, producing a huge amount of cut and trimmed lumber, clapboards, and shingles with which to build cities. Colliers continued their occupation of providing charcoal to Philadelphia and New York.

The iron industry, though, was gone. Even though there was still hope for the continued manufacturing of glass products, the boom times were over. The glass factory and town of Herman, built in 1869, would be a complete waste of money.

Coastal trade was still flourishing. A good many of the sons of the river towns shipped aboard the boats of their fathers or their uncles or their neighbors and explored the far ends of the earth in search of trade. In short, though the immediate future couldn't have looked brighter for the towns and settlements of the Mullica valley, reality was about to come down hard on the township.

THE COMING OF THE RAILROADS

What happened to the promise of this century? The answer: railroads. The nineteenth century was the century of the railroads, especially so after the Civil War. Railroads multiplied greatly during the second half of the century and could ship goods faster, more directly, and much more cheaply than could the companies involved in coastal shipping. The more rail laid, the less ships had to carry. The end of prosperity was near by 1870. Shipbuilding was declining. Tonnage was decreasing. Shipyards were closing. The Van Sant yard across from the cemetery in Green Bank produced three major ships in the 1870's: all three-masted schooners, but the panic of 1873 had hit them hard. Oh yes, the Van Sants continued to build vessels in Green Bank after that but the boats they built were mere shadows of past glory. Where once the ways had seen large ships and coastal schooners, now they held small fishing vessels. The iron furnaces folded in favor of those nearer the Pennsylvania ore fields. The glass factories never quite succeeded either. The new settlements of Hammonton and Egg Harbor - both on the railroad - flourished, while the towns on the Mullica died a slow death.

Washington Township almost made it. The Tuckerton Railroad proposed to build a line over through Bass River to Green Bank and then on to either Hammonton or Egg Harbor, whichever town would pay the most. Unfortunately, other railroads with more direct links to New York and Philadelphia got to those growing cities first. Both Egg Harbor City and Hammonton declined to pay anything for a Tuckerton Railroad connection that would only have benefited the clammers of that area anyway, and Washington Township lost its lease on the future.

Photograph by John Pearce

The State Access Area in Green Bank - 1995

The Paint Begins to Peel

By the time that the nineteenth century was fading, Green Bank, Lower Bank, and Wading River were like dowagers in their years of decline, slowly fading into obscurity, although they thought that there was still some life in them yet. Many of the residents were still deeply involved with the sea, but the commerce was heading elsewhere. Tourism was beginning to pick up, and day boats plied the Mullica. John Rapp and the Kosters ran the old Sooy homestead as a hotel during the Herman City days, and a steamboat actually made a scheduled run up the Mullica to their dock, but tourism never really took on. The tourists didn't care for the heat and mosquitoes, I guess. When the Herman City Glassworks flopped almost as soon as it was completed, the void left local trade and tourism as the only remaining businesses.

It seems that no one could forsee the deeping clouds on the horizen. In a passion of optimism, the State of New Jersey divided Washington Township in half, forming Randolph Township in 1870. Less than two decades later, the error was perceived.

Joseph Wharton was the next entrepreneur on the scene. He bought up thousands of acres of land with the idea that he could tap the underground aquifer for Philadelphia. With the idea of creating vast lakes throughout the pinelands, he seems to have closed down whatever was left at Batsto.

In the January 23, 1886 edition of the Mount Holly *Herald*, a correspondent noted that

> This [Batsto] *is indeed a deserted village and our township, Washington, is without her proper officers in consequence of renewals. Heretofore Batsto has ruled the roost and by force of numbers was enabled to fill nearly all the offices in the township with men from this vicinity. When Joseph Wharton suspended operations nearly all had to leave to find work elsewhere and now the township has no Assessor, Collector, Constable, Township Committee and other officials. The Pound Keeper and Road Overseer remain. It is suggested that Randolph and Washington townships be again united. According to the census of 1885 Randolph had 85 dwellings, 88 families and a total population of 355. Washington had 74 dwellings, 76 families and a total population of 333. Neither township has 100 voters in its limits. If the two were consolidated, it would make a township of respectable numbers and greatly lessen the township taxes. It seems a farce to have to keep up the expense of two township governments when one would be sufficient. Since the curtailing of operations by Mr. Wharton, Washington has further decreased in population and the consolidation is even more desirable.*

The New Jersey legislature, in a fit of pique, passed a law prohibiting the export of water. Basically, the legislators said *"No way, baby!"* to Wharton's water scheme, which put an end to that venture. Wharton then proceeded to develop parts of his holdings, including the old towns of Batsto, Atsion, and Washington, into experiments in farming and cattle breeding, but economic prosperity was still illusive for the area.

The possibility of running a railroad through the area was being discussed as late as 1897. A news item in the Mount Holly *Herald* dated March 22nd notes:

> *The much talked of railroad, from Hammonton to Tuckerton, is being agitated again with strong hopes of it being built. I understand that Mr. Jos. Wharton, of Camden, and a number of Philadelphia Capitalists, are moving in the matter and the proposed route is to be surveyed immediately. It would open up some of the best farming and fruit lands in the State, running through New Columbia, Pleasant Mills, Batsto, Herman City, Green Bank, Harrisville, Lower Bank, Bridgeport, Bass River, and on to Tuckerton and Long Beach. It would be one of the best freight paying roads of any that has recently been built in this State and will open up to pleasure seekers one of the finest beaches along the New Jersey Coast.*

Unfortunately, this dream never came to fruition. Without the industries at Atsion, Batsto, Martha, Green Bank, Crowleytown, Bulltown, and Herman, there were no major employers. Harrisville joined the list of failed enterprises in 1890. Without the coastal trade, there was no employment for the numerous captains, seamen, and those engaged in other maritime trades. The two townships were reunited in 1893, but nothing could restore the former prosperity of the area.

The existence of post cards of Green Bank from the early 1900's shows that someone still thought tourism a profitable business. Stephen Lee came to Speedwell to grow cranberries in 1868. Evans and Wills started the

Friendship Bogs soon after. The first of the Haines family came into Washington Township in the 1890's, and cranberries were coming into their own in cultivated bogs, but that was simply the promise of things to come when the century was young.

At the start of the twentieth century, Ephraim C. Sooy, Jr., a Kansas City businessman born in Green Bank, bought back thousands of acres of his family's former holdings from Mr. Wharton and set up all kinds of enterprises to provide work for the local people. Wharton's experiments continued even after his 1909 death. The twentieth century may have begun with faded glory, but at least there was some semblance of hope. The Great Depression destroyed even that.

Gone was the last of the river commerce. Gone were the tourists. Gone were the business ventures. Gone were the seafaring days. Gone were the trees which had fueled so many industries for two centuries. Gone were the landed estates of the old families. Those few scions that had braved out the close of the last century in the land of their forefathers were forced to leave in order to find work.

Some tried to stay. Watson Sooy was reduced to being the musically-gifted shopkeeper, the last remnant of the old Sooy trade empire. Ephraim Sooy, inheritor of the last of the large Sooy landholdings and of his grandfather's and great-grandfather's business acumen had gone west to make his fortune, returning only in old age to languish in the summer sun of the town of his youth. Ephraim died in 1927. When the Great Depression hit two years later, his Kansas City/Atlantic City family didn't have the money to pay the taxes on the Green Bank estate of Nicholas II. The property was sold to the State of New Jersey rather than have it confiscated for non-payment of taxes.

Proud descendants of powerful trading and manufacturing families were reduced to cutting the salt hay in the marshes and gathering pinecones in the woods and sphangum moss in the swamps. They were even betrayed by the scholars and writers who came into the area and manufactured the "Piney" myth. These people had been on the cutting edge of business, trade, and landed empires, and were now reduced to ignorant, unshaven, half-mad interbred morons from the backwoods. Nothing could have been farther from the truth.

The funny thing is, though, the people of Green Bank and Lower Bank who found their lives in the homes of their ancestors were pretty decent people. They were a hardworking, community-minded, proud people, of most respectable heritage, yet state historians ignored them and educated sociologists destroyed their image. If there is any paradigm for the area, it would be that of the popular television show, "The Waltons." During the Depression, people here were as varied and colorful as those found in any rural area of the period. Their children were educated through the eighth grade at a central school just as advanced as most others outside the major metropolitan areas and attended high school in Egg Harbor. Some found the means to go on to college. There were businessmen, landowners, sawmill operators, farmers, carpenters - the type of people you would have found anywhere. They were good people.

Like any community, Washington Township had its share of characters. One did not probe too deeply into some relationships. Generally speaking though, the residents of this heart of the pines were hard-working men and women who struggled, like everyone else, to make a living throughout the Great Depression and looked forward to a better day.

Then came the Second World War, and many of the young men left for good, either to die on the fields of Europe or in the Pacific, or to find their futures in more productive areas. Some of those who came home took jobs outside the area. Others tried to keep going right where they were, but they were confined to a subsistence life by the lack of any industry. The roads had begun to be paved in the forties and fifties, which made it easier to drive to work in Hammonton and Egg Harbor. The trains from those towns took people to Philadelphia and Atlantic City. Only the diehards preferred life in the pines with relative obscurity.

The State of New Jersey became more and more obtrusive in the area. They had already acquired the great Sooy Estate in the 1930's. In 1954, they took over the huge Wharton Tract. Influenced by the sociologists (who should have been politely invited to leave the second they poked their noses around town), the state found nothing worth preserving of the history and culture of Washington Township with the exception of Batsto Village and proceeded to allow ancient houses that came into their trust to decay or be deliberately burned. In the 1930's, the state had conscientiously tried to reforest a devastated land. By the nineteen eighties, they were concentrating on keeping up appearances in Batsto to justify the money spent and on returning the land to nature.

Environmentalists got the notion that the only good residents were those in the Green Bank and Lower Bank cemeteries, and the only good two hundred year-old house was the one that burned down. The state encouraged the recreational use of its vast lands, maintaining campgrounds with open-pit outhouses, but charged the local residents with polluting the groundwater with their septic systems. Where the thousands of campers in the Wharton State Forest defecated was never closely examined, and they far outnumbered the locals. Where Crowleytown had been, the state established a boat ramp for the launching of speedboats hauled in from outside the pines but made the residents tear out their docks or pay exorbitantly for "riparian rights" unless they could prove they already owned them. Two hundred years of ownership and use of property bordering the Mullica was not considered "proof." In the rush to accumulate land, it is rumored that overzealous bureaucrats even managed to "lose" pages from the deed books. Many an old house stood abandoned and burned during the night.

Wherein Lies the Future?

Are things any better as the twentieth century ends? The heart of the pines is no longer isolated. The roads that bring in the outsider and the tourist also make it easier for people to take jobs outside the immediate area. The State of New Jersey owns over eighty percent of the land in Washington Township, which helps insure a low tax base, a problem that has not been corrected even with recent legislation meant to assist the local taxpayer. Burlington County has hardly known that this end of its territory exists. The county and school taxes are some of the highest in the state, and the county provides little in the way of services.

The Pinelands Act and the resulting Commission have been a mixed blessing. *Everyone* who lives in this "core area" is interested in preservation of the pine barrens. They remain there because they love it, and they don't want to see it destroyed. On the other hand, some decisions of the Pinelands Commission have seemed ridiculous. Others seem outright discriminatory. The rumor circulates that you can do anything in the pinelands if you have enough money. True or not, when people come to believe that regulations are arbitrary, discriminatory, and designed to control or even steal their property for the benefit of others, they feel they are being deprived of their rights as Americans.

Recently, a proposition has been made to build a NASCAR auto race track at the edge of the pines in back of Tuckerton. Short of the jetport idea of the 1950's and 60's, nothing could be more destructive of the natural environment and the human habitat of the pine barrens than the volume of people, trash, and noise that such a track would bring to this sensitive area. It would ruin Bass River State Forest and alter the entire area for all time. Yet there are political connections. A few years back, a man living in a shed after his house burned down wanted to move an unwanted house one quarter mile down the road to his empty foundation and was denied permission by the Pinelands Commission. They preferred to see a two hundred year old house torn down than have it moved up the road. The man whose house had burned down continued to live in his shed. The old house is gone. Still, the Pinelands Commission is the last best hope of the pines.

The bad press dished out by the sociologists still plagues the residents of Washington Township and with absolutely no justification. Intelligent and educated people have asserted their interest in the politics of the town and have supported the local government with devotion. The township committee is a public-spirited group of citizens who are learning more and more about applying for grants and maneuvering with and around the county and state bureaucrats. The election of Bill Haines, Jr., to the Burlington County Board of Freeholders was a reassertion of Washington Township's position in the county and a demand for respect. Bill is young, intelligent, and certainly civic-minded. He is a former mayor of the township and a part of the largest cranberry-producing business in the area, Haines and Haines. Don McCauley, the immediate past mayor of the township, was another active and spirited individual who had a great deal of loyalty to this chosen land of his residence.

A River Flows to the Sea

What will the twenty-first century bring to these beloved towns on the Mullica? Sadly, I can't say. I'd like to see them stay exactly as they are now: quiet, peaceful, and well-loved. Yet the pressures remain. State and county officials are still trying to destroy the Pinelands Act which protects them. The Pinelands Commission often has given its enemies ammunition against them. Exploitation and destruction is still a possibility. With the election of a conservative congress in Washington, there is less pressure for natural preservation. Batsto officials have involved themselves in a meaningless quarrel with local supporters over emphasis. Old homes in the trust of the state are still allowed to deteriorate. Deep cuts in the budget of the DEP in New Jersey have left the department with insufficient staff and money for operating expenses as guardians of the history and natural resources of the area. The history of the Mullica valley is almost obliterated by time. Who will remember? Who will tell their children? Will the state continue to make life difficult for the residents of this pine barren's heart?

A masted ship has not been able to make its stately way up the Mullica since the construction of the Garden State Parkway in the early 1950's. The building of the Mullica River bridge with its 30-foot clearance was symbolic. It signalled the absolute ending of two and a half centuries of a way of life, and the State of New Jersey deliberately gave the coup d'grace. When bridgetender Tater Cramer left his "Old Iron Bridge" over the Mullica for the last time, he heralded an ending that has not yet become a beginning. So long as that Parkway bridge exists, not one single sailboat of any size will make it up to The Forks, nor dock at Green Bank or Lower Bank. Not one single sailboat will be built on the sites that saw the construction of hundreds of tons of ships. There will be no river commerce, no railroads, and little business development. In some ways, that's fortunate. Development, whether business or residential, would bring destruction with it. But where does that leave the residents of Washington Township? In 1998, there is not a single store in the entire township where you can buy a loaf of bread or a quart of milk. The little 'business' that is carried on in the old Pacemaker plant in Lower Bank, three canoe-rental places, the Mullica River Boat Basin, the Bel Haven Lake campground, and the two bars bring in precious few tax dollars. The only substantial income is provided by cranberry production.

On the other hand, the remnants of the old families, those newer residents who have deliberately chosen to forsake the rat race of more populated areas for the peace of the pines, the cranberry and blueberry producers, and those others who love the pines with all their hearts have some hope. Life has not changed all that much in the last half of the century. There is still hope that it won't change much in the next century as well.

There are threats. The state may blunder into destroying the very life of the pine barrens that they claim to want to preserve. Something has to be done to alleviate the local problems and give local people more of a say in their own governance. The river is being destroyed as well. The recreational draw of the upper Mullica has been growing over the years, but the wakes of powerboats and jet skis are destroying the sandy banks of the shoreline. Upstream from Lower Bank, the Mullica has shoaled and widened over the years as the banks crumble into it.

Not only will no sailing vessel ever get under the Garden State Parkway bridge, one could never navigate a channel that, always tortuous, has been filled in by the degeneration of the river banks caused by the wakes of speedboats. This 'wild and scenic river' is 'wild' only in the unregulated misuse by the numerous boat owners. What compromise can be made? Can local residents or even the river "win" by the halting of recreational usage? In 1995, the State put up signs forbidding water-skiing above Green Bank, which is, at least, a beginning. Now if it would only provide sufficient enforcement authority to ensure compliance with the laws and work to reduce the noise pollution from deep-throated boat engines.....

Even those interested in the pinelands for environmental reasons seem to conspire against acknowledging and preserving the historical remants that remain. They appear to be ecstatic about the unique and fragile bioculture of the area as if it were just as it was when the Native Americans made their moccasined journey to the seashore. They fail to acknowledge that this land had over two hundred years of use - and abuse - before they themselves were even born. Their beloved pinelands are fourth or fifth growth woodlands for the most part. They can dream all they want about untrodden ways as they paddle down one of the little rivers, but the fact is that there are a great many "ghosts" of the past that travel with them whether they acknowledge them or not.

The message to the residents and government of the State of New Jersey: a way needs to be devised to preserve and protect both the ecological *and* the cultural/historical riches of this very special area. It has valuable lessons to teach our children of life in New Jersey for over two hundred years before the automobile, suburban development, and shopping malls erased it from other areas of the state. Once an historical building is gone, it is irreplaceable, and a part of ourselves is destroyed as well. If the pine barrens are developed, we all will be the losers.

The message to the dwellers in the 'heart of the pines' can only be, "Hang On!" To all the residents of the State of New Jersey, the message is also clear: Treasure your land. Fight to preserve it. Learn your history and teach it to your children. Be proud of your past and confident of your future. Most of all, this land is *your* land and this heritage *your* heritage. Love it well. Treat it kindly. Protect it with your lives. It is a *very* special land with a *very* special heritage.

Atsion

Photograph believed to be by Bill Augustine
Courtesy of Budd Wilson

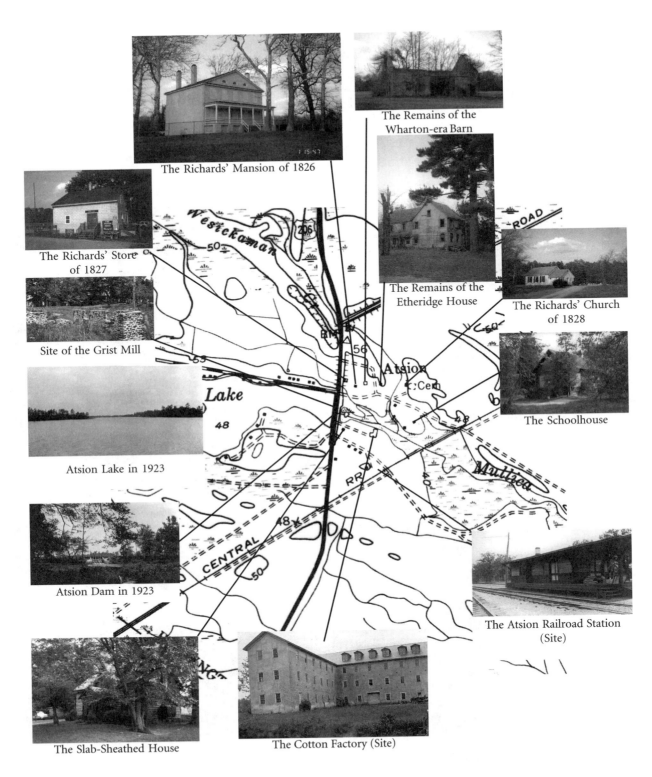

The Richards' Mansion of 1826

The Remains of the Wharton-era Barn

The Richards' Store of 1827

The Remains of the Etheridge House

The Richards' Church of 1828

Site of the Grist Mill

The Schoolhouse

Atsion Lake in 1923

Atsion Dam in 1923

The Atsion Railroad Station (Site)

The Slab-Sheathed House

The Cotton Factory (Site)

Atsion

ON THE CUTTING EDGE - 1765

Eighteenth century colonial America saw a huge explosion of settlement and expansion throughout the English colonies in the new world. By 1700, all of the original thirteen colonies were established and functioning, the native Americans had been pushed from the coastal areas by the sheer numbers of Europeans arriving and settling there, cities were growing into centers of trade and commerce, and coastal trade was blossoming.

Through 1763, however, a certain check on expansion existed in the control by the French and their Indian allies on the interior. While never numerous, the French had explored and claimed all the territory along the Saint Lawrence River northward to the Hudson Bay, westward around the Great Lakes, and down the watershed of the Ohio and its branches, the drainage basin of the Mississippi and Missouri Rivers, all the way to New Orleans. This extensive area of influence and the strong alliances and sympathy of the Native American nations throughout the area, with the sole exception of the Iroquois of upper New York, blocked the westward thrust of the English colonies. It also insured a dependence of those colonies on England herself, since the fledgling colonial powers did not have the inclination to unite amongst themselves nor the ability to confront the French over such an extensive area.

The English colonies were havens of opportunity for hard-pressed Europeans, and hundreds of thousands found the means to make passage across the Atlantic. New England still maintained a strong cohesiveness through its English heritage and its religious homogeneity. Here in these northeastern colonies, a fierce spirit of independence and a thirst for commercial trade cultivated a sense of identity and competence. New York, though since 1665 an English colony, was still controlled by the Dutch elite. Land along the Hudson was owned by several great families who leased landholdings rather than sold them. Emigrant people from Europe had been prevented from owning land to a great degree in their homelands and saw the restrictive nature of New York as a hindrance to the fulfillment of their dreams. Only New York City, based on strategic position and a fine harbor, grew and prospered.

Along the Delaware, the Swedes had settled early in the seventeenth century, only slightly inconvenienced by the Dutch claim to the lands. The Swedish farms were confirmed by the English when they took control and thus an agricultural base in the area was already established when William Penn formed the City of Philadelphia. People of Scots-Irish ancestry, fleeing from difficult circumstances in Ireland, settled the Pennsylvania frontier and provided a staunch and warlike fighting edge to settlement there. Between the frontier and Philadelphia, people from the German states created productive and peaceful farms.

The Philadelphia Quakers, talented and enthusiastic in business and trade, spread across the river into New Jersey. Upstate New Jersey had been settled by the Dutch prior to the English takeover, and was characteristically different from the lands along the Hudson. Here, small landowners had the opportunity to establish themselves in relative security. Southern New Jersey (originally the Province of West Jersey), which included the Mullica watershed, saw settlement from the Delaware side of the province, from the Philadelphia area, from East Jersey (now northern New Jersey), from Long Island, and from New England.

Business opportunity beckoned in New Jersey. Philadelphia entrepreneurs quickly spotted the commercial advantages of West Jersey: access to the Delaware, land that could be cleared and cultivated, a relatively small native population, sheltered from Indian depravations on the frontier by eastern Pennsylvania, and its position relative to both Philadelphia and New York. The Mullica was especially attractive to the enterprising businessman. It was fairly deep water from the ocean all the way to The Forks, cutting half the distance across the state toward Philadelphia. This meant that the entire area had access by water to both of those major colonial cities and by land the relatively short distance from The Forks to the Rancocas River at Vincentown or Lumberton, then down the Rancocas to the Delaware by water to Philadelphia. By 1765, much of the solid land along the tidal area of the Little Egg Harbor River had been cleared for farms, and settlements had been made on both banks.

Burlington and Mount Holly had seen the first real commercial development, and Mount Holly, the first local iron works. It didn't take a great deal of imagination to stand within the limits of Burlington City and look out over the relatively unpopulated land to the east, taking notice of streams to provide waterpower, bogs lined with iron ore, land for the cultivation of foodstuffs, trees for the charcoal necessary for smelting that ore, access to coastal trade already active on the rivers and bays, and settlements to provide anchors for new communities that could potentially be formed in that area.

When the French were defeated and the Treaty of Paris signed in 1763, a great weight was lifted from the shoulders of the colonies. Suddenly, energy and money that had been diverted to survival could be invested in commercial development. Energy would no longer have to be expended on defense nor taxes paid for the support of English troops. Manpower and ability could focus entirely on profitable enterprise. The colonies were on the verge of a major explosion in manufacturing and trade.

No one was more ambitious and foresighted than one particular Burlington City resident. The Honorable Charles Read of Burlington was an important man: Deputy Secretary of the Province of New Jersey, Member of the Assembly, Member of the Council of the Province, Judge of the Supreme Court, and finally, even Chief Justice of the Supreme Court of New Jersey. He was also an enterprising man, willing to accept the challenge of risking all in order to achieve great things.

For Read, the Jersey pine barrens were not desolate, unproductive lands, unwanted by any sane man. When he looked at the vast tracts of uninhabited lands along the upper branches of the Mullica river, he saw profits, large profits, pure and simple. He envisioned iron-producing plantations, glowing forges and furnaces, huge shipments of finished products, all of them moving along the Mullica valley through The Forks and on to New York, Philadelphia, and beyond.

Read wasn't the first to find advantage in the land that bordered the upper reaches of the Mullica River. On April 12, 1750, the Council of West Jersey Proprietors sold a fifty-acre survey on the Atsayunk, the Lenape name for the Atsion or upper Mullica river, to George Marple, an Englishman. Marple sold the land to James Inskeep on April Fool's Day in 1758. Inskeep intended to build a sawmill on the tract, which lay in Burlington County. This land was described as beginning "on the north side of Atsion Creek and thence crossing the branch of Sackemean [Wesickaman] thence crossing the creek below the mouth of afsd [sic] Sackemean Branch . . . thence crossing the afsd [sic] Atsion Creek to the corner first mentioned." Inskeep set up a sawmill called "Old Goshen."

Three years before Marple's sale to Inskeep, on March 31, 1755, Charles Read and Thomas Gardiner purchased 1,133 acres of land in the immediate area of Atsion. Read only kept title to five acres. Gardiner sold a half interest to Daniel Ellis, and, on September 10th, 1757, the two men gave a 999-year lease to Read.

On June 29, 1765, John Estell obtained rights to a vast tract of land which lay between the two branches of the Little Egg Harbor River. Estell was given the rights to dam the Atsion ostensibly to build a sawmill, but his actual purpose is a mystery. Estell did build a mill after damming the Sleepy Creek, a tributary of the Atsion, several miles below the future site of Atsion Forge, but he may also have been acting on behalf of Read, who soon took over Estell's rights to actually dam the Atsion proper.

Charles Read, shrewd businessman that he was, proceeded with caution. He contacted Inskeep and bought his land on July 19th, 1765. In this agreement, Read was to have all the "Iron in Goshen Neck within a mile and one half of the Mill" [the Old Goshen sawmill that Inskeep still operated]. Having thus assembled both a parcel of land, water rights to the Atsion River, and timber rights to a huge area, Read was ready to construct his forge, which he proceeded to do.

It soon became clear to him that he would need more capital for his investment than he had on hand. He was also planning to build a furnace at Batsto and had three other projects in the planning stage. Unfortunately he didn't have sufficient liquid funds for everything. In order to obtain working capital, he took in two partners, David Ogden, Jr. of Newark, also a member of the Governor's Council, and Lawrence Saltar of Nottingham, Burlington County, son of Judge Richard Saltar. Read was smart. He sold Ogden one quarter interest, but only sold Saltar 249/1000 interest, keeping controlling interest for himself. This January 9th, 1766 agreement mentions "a tract of land whereon the said Forge is erected," which means that Read had built the Atsion Forge between July 19, 1765 when he bought the property from Inskeep, and January 9, 1766 when he signed the agreement with Ogden and Saltar.

In these first iron-making days, Atsion Forge concentrated on converting pig iron into bar iron. The year after he built Atsion Forge, Read also constructed Batsto Furnace, eight miles downstream, and brought the pig iron produced there to Atsion to be worked by the forge. He analyzed the bog ore in the swamps that would form Atsion Lake and obtained rights to nearby ore, so he may have had building a furnace and producing his own iron in mind at that time, but he never accomplished this. That role was left for his successors. There is the possibility that the original Atsion Forge was actually a bloomery, capable of producing its own molten iron in small quantities, making it independent of surrounding furnaces for the most part.

As adventuresome as he was, however, his physical health didn't hold up under the strain. In October, 1770, when he was sixty years old and way overextended financially, he advertised his share of Atsion for sale in the *Pennsylvania Journal*, listing "four forge fires, two hammers and all necessary buildings with several servants and negroes who understood different branches of the business." There were no takers.

Being unable to sell his share in Atsion, his debts mounted steadily, and his health deteriorated further. Finally, on March 16th, 1773, he sold his share to Abel James and Henry Drinker, two business acquaintances. Unfortunately, it was too late for this enterprising man. He had risked all, and he lost all. Within three months of the sale, he turned over to trustees what was left of his assets and fled the colony. First, he went to Antigua to try to settle his deceased wife's estate there but was unsuccessful. He ended up in Martinsburg, North Carolina, where he set up a small shop and died destitute a year later. On December 27, 1774, Charles Read, Chief Justice of New Jersey, died alone in North Carolina. It was an ignominious end for such a great man.

Rebirth I - A New Furnace

The new owners were Philadelphia businessmen who were partners in a well-known shipping and importing firm in the City of Brotherly Love. They took over Read's Atsion Forge and also Inskeep's Old Goshen sawmill and over a thousand acres of woodland. On April 2, 1773, David Ogden sold his one-quarter share to Lawrence Saltar, who then owned 1/1000th less than fifty percent and continued to operate the business as manager. The three new "partners" (Saltar, James, and Drinker) fulfilled Read's plans for Atsion by building a new furnace that went into blast in April 1774. This permitted them to produce their own iron from ore rather than depending on Batsto to supply the forge. Batsto had been built and owned by Read, but now the two properties were in competition.

The partners knew that the Atsion Lake could be drained during the period when winter shut down the forge and furnace and that ore could be dug from the lakebed as Charles Read had planned. Much of the ore for the new furnace was dug out three or four miles upstream and floated downstream on barges.

Competition with Batsto spawned several lawsuits. Under the management of Lawrence Saltar and his brother Joseph, the workers dug a canal between Mechescatauxin Creek and the Atsion River to increase the flow of water over the Atsion dam and thus increase the water power to the forge and furnace. Unfortunately, this flooded areas downriver where the Batsto ore diggers were working, which cut down on the ore destined for that enterprise. The resulting lawsuit took seven years to settle. Another suit rose between the two iron plantations concerning timber rights and the use of the Atsion River.

Conflicting evidence is available concerning Atsion's participation in the War of American Independence. The Drinkers were Quakers and thus opposed to war as a matter of principle. Since Henry Drinker had control of the new furnace, he shut it down rather than be forced to support the war effort on either side. Drinker, in fact, was confined in Virginia by the Patriots. On the other hand, Saltar kept the forge working. Atsion produced evaporating pans for the Pennsylvania Salt Works at Toms River and supplied ships of the Pennsylvania Navy with iron, though it is not known whether that "iron" was in spikes, anchors, chains - or other more warlike material. Atsion did continue to make heating stoves throughout the period. The owners of Batsto had no such scruples and strongly aided the rebels. In fact, several shareholders of Batsto would be members of the Quartermaster General's department.

After the conclusion of the Revolution, iron-making continued to be profitable. A gristmill and three more sawmills were built, and two wharves in Lumberton on the Rancocas Creek were added to the estate. These Rancocas wharves made it easier to avoid Batsto by hauling the iron goods overland to the Rancocas for the short river trip to Philadelphia. Tons of pig and bar iron, kettles of all sizes, stoves, and plowshares continued to be shipped through The Forks to both Philadelphia and New York. The concern was taxed for three thousand acres of land, in addition to the business itself.

When Lawrence Saltar died in 1783, his heirs were left with slightly less than a half interest in Atsion. Abel James was declared bankrupt in 1784, and Henry Drinker bought his share. That left Drinker and the Saltar heirs in full possession of the furnace and forge town but also in the midst of disputes over the management.

Atsion did not escape the scourge of the pines: fire. In October 1794, the furnace burned to the ground and started a period of bad luck for the enterprise. Henry Drinker's wife, Elizabeth, noted in her journal that "H.D. thinks the loss, including repairs and loss of time will amount of one thousand pound and more money," a huge amount in those days.

Next, a scow with twenty-six tons of iron on it left the wharf at Lumberton bound for Philadelphia but disappeared. Apparently, John Saltar, a son of Lawrence, had hidden it on its way down river, but it had sunk in a storm, defeating both the Saltars and the Drinkers.

Washington Township had been formed in 1802, and part of Atsion was included. This gave Atsion a new focus for local politics. William Saltar would serve as a member of the Board of Chosen Freeholders in 1803-1804, but that would be the family's only participation in local political affairs. No one really knows how much of the original Atsion stood on the east bank of the river at that time, but apparently the homes of the owners did.

Drinker put the property up for sale in 1805 for 15,000 pounds and asked 12,000 for his share. Once again there were no takers, so he put it up for auction at the Merchant Coffee House. Jacob Downing, his son-in-law, bought the entire estate, including the shares of the Saltar heirs. Henry Drinker continued as half owner with his son-in-law.

A list of the assets of Atsion made for this 1805 "sale" show that the estate included 20,000 acres of land, 17,000 of which was pinelands, 2,500 acres in Goshen Neck, 100 acres of meadow lands, 100 acres of cedar swamp, a home built for the Talbert family, dwelling house, barn, stable, store house, out house, etc., nineteen houses for the workmen, the forge and coal house, the furnace and coal house, grist mill and smithy, two sawmills, dwelling houses, and fifteen acres of land to each.

Downing prospered for several years and continued manufacturing the Nine Plate stoves, firebacks, jamb stoves (five-plate stoves that stuck into another room from the back of a fireplace), anvils, forge hammers, and other castings at a nice profit. Within ten years, though, he was in trouble. In 1817, he mortgaged his interest in the "West Mill Tract," a part of the Atsion property, but defaulted two years later. The Bank of North America sold his half share to Samuel Richards on June 5, 1819.

REBIRTH II - AN EXPERIENCED IRONMASTER

Richards was the son of the Batsto entrepreneur, William Richards, and thus well-versed in the operation of the forge and furnace in the Jersey pines. Samuel was born on May 8, 1769 near Warwick Furnace in Pennsylvania where his father was working at the time. He was the third child and second son of William and Mary Patrick Richards.

Of all the Richards children, Samuel was the only one to surpass his father's business and commerical success. He learned the iron business from his father after William had acquired Batsto in 1784 when Samuel was fifteen. At twenty-one, he was managing the Philadelphia end of the business. In 1796, at the age of twenty-seven, he bought Pleasant Mills for his father from Joseph Ball. There were at least two sawmills on the Pleasant Mills property at the time of purchase. Samuel leased out the land to Benjamin Low, who built a mill that would reclaim wool, cotton, etc. from worn fabrics on the premises.

Samuel would marry twice: the first time to Mrs. Mary Smith Morgan on November 18, 1797. He relocated the family headquarters in Philadelphia to 111 North Water Street and made his home nearby. He and Mary had four children but lost all of them in a four year period from 1799 to 1803. They must have felt their old house was

The Atsion Mansion - 1923

Atsion Store - 1923
looking toward road (now route #206)

too filled with ghosts, for they changed their residence to 357 Mulberry Street (now Arch Street). Here they lived until Mary's death on May 3, 1820. Mary and Samuel would have another four children but would lose one of these in childhood, too.

Two years after Mary's death, Samuel married Anna Maria Martin Witherspoon, another widow. The groom was fifty-three and the bride thirty-nine, and the couple made their home at Ninth and Arch Streets. Both marriages seem to have been happy and successful ones. Though quite skilled and highly successful in business, Samuel was also a most congenial man. He was solidly built, good-looking, and had a dynamic personality.

Atsion was not in very good shape when Samuel Richards bought a half share in it. He put his cousin, John Richards, in charge, and the furnace was put in blast again on June 19, 1819 to fill an order for pipes placed by the city of Philadelphia. John sold his estate in Wading River and moved up to Atsion to do the work. By October 28th, the pipes were finished.

In January 1820, Richards advertised the property for sale. The following month, John Richards moved his family to Weymouth Furnace and the Account Book was closed. Carpenters, blacksmiths, forge workers, carters, hostlers, laborers, colliers, ore raisers - all were out of work and had to move elsewhere. The post office that the fledgling United States had established at Atsion in 1798 was moved down the Quaker Bridge Road to Nicholas Sooy's tavern at Washington in 1815. For a few years, the neglected works became picturesque ruins.

Of this early Atsion iron plantation nothing survives. Even the locations of the forge, furnace, houses, etc. are uncertain. J.F. Watson, passing through Atsion on his way to "Longbeach-Seashore" in 1823 wrote:

> Was much interested to see the formidable ruins of Atsion iron works. ... They looked as picturesque as the ruins of abbeys, etc., in pictures. There were dams, forges, furnaces, storehouses, a dozen houses and lots for the workmen, and the whole comprising a town; a place once overwhelming the ear with the din of unceasing, ponderous hammers, or alarming the sight with fire and smoke, and smutty and sweating Vulcans. Now all is hushed, no wheels turn, no fires blaze, the houses are unroofed, and the frames, etc., have fallen down and not a foot of the busy workmen is seen.

Anyone who expected Atsion to fade away, however, didn't count on Samuel Richards. He bought Henry Drinker's half share in 1824 and reestablished the Atsion Ironworks and village. He built a large and expensive mansion at Atsion in 1826, the company store in 1827, and in June of 1828, a church. He rebuilt the forge and furnace. The government even moved the post office back into town on the 13th of June, 1832. Business was brisk. The schooner *Atsion* made regular voyages from Batsto Landing on the north side of the Mullica at The Forks to New York and the Hudson Valley. Products shipped to Philadelphia went by way of the Lumberton wharves.

Thomas F. Gorden, in his *Gazetteer* of the State of New Jersey, in 1834 wrote,

> Besides the furnace there are here a forge, grist mill and three sawmills. The furnace makes from 800 to 900 tons of castings and the forge from 150 to 200 tons of bar-iron annually . . . There are about 100 men employed here between 6 and 700 persons depending for subsistence upon the works.

Samuel had learned the iron business from his father at Batsto and had long owned portions of Weymouth, Martha, and Speedwell furnaces. He was fifty-three when he purchased all of Atsion, and he built it into a prosperous and successful business. These years with Anna Maria were some of the happiest in his life. All of his business interests were making money, and he was known as having the "Midas touch." He and Anna Maria spent the summer months in residence at Atsion in their new mansion and travelled by coach to his other pinelands enterprises.

He entertained lavishly in his Atsion home and welcomed visitors to his furnace town. He and Maria had three children, but once again, Samuel experienced a parent's grief when they lost one in childhood. Thus, of his eleven children, five had died in childhood. A son from his first marriage, Thomas, followed in his father's footsteps and went into the iron business. Thomas' full sister, Sarah, married Stephen Colwell. Colwell was a Philadelphia lawyer when he met and wooed Sarah Richards, and Samuel was apparently delighted with his new son-in-law. He made him the manager of Weymouth Furnace and gradually turned more and more of his business affairs over to him.

It was during this period of prosperity that Samuel Richards also built two forges on the rivers to the east of Atsion. One of these was on the Atsion River about two and a half miles downstream. Here he actually built locks to raise the water level for the oreboats heading for Batsto. The other was called the Washington Forge and lay on the Batsto River about two miles above Quaker Bridge on the property of Hampton Furnace, which Samuel also purchased.

Things looked quite rosy for Atsion, but it all came to a shocking end with the death of Samuel Richards on the 4th of January, 1842. When Samuel died, he was a very wealthy man. He made provision for Anna Maria, divided Weymouth between his daughters from his first marriage, Sarah and Elizabeth Ann. His children by Anna Maria, William Henry and Maria Lawrence, each received exactly one half of the Atsion estate, which included over 128,000 acres by that time.

REBIRTH III - A SOUTHERN GENTLEMEN TRIES HIS HAND

The legacy at Atsion which Samuel Richards left his children seemed huge. Atsion was at the pinnacle of its prosperity, and there was no reason to suppose that it would not continue to be so for quite some time. Unfortunately, neither William Henry nor Maria Lawrence had any business sense. Like a spoiled child, William Henry had inherited enough money from his father to live as he chose, and he didn't choose to work in the iron business. Maria met William Walton Fleming of Charleston, South Carolina, at a party at her sister's mansion at Weymouth Furnace in the summer of 1848, and they were married a year later on June 14, 1849. Fleming took over several of the business interests of the Richards family.

In 1848, Fleming had started the W. W. Fleming Cobalt and Nickel Works on the Cooper River in Camden. He also was one of the organizers of the Camden and Atlantic Railroad and was a member of the Board of Directors for a number of years. When the first Camden and Atlantic train left Camden for the seashore resort on the first of July, 1854, it had an engine named *Atsion* on its head end.

Walton, as he was called, and Maria lived in the Atsion Mansion during the summer months but kept a winter residence in Philadelphia. Unfortunately, the bog ore industry chose this particular time to collapse. In 1852, Burlington County decided to create a new township, transferring Atsion from Washington Township to Shamong,

A Portion of the Cotton Factory Showing the Water Intake - 1923
The original part of the paper mill built by William Walton Fleming in 1852 or 1853 was a two-story structure.
Could this have been part of it?

severing long-held political ties with Batsto, Green Bank, Lower Bank, Wading River, and the other towns of the Mullica basin. Splitting the property between townships would have made things even more confusing if the business had been prospering. It wasn't.

Searching for a replacement for the iron forge and furnace, Fleming tried the next popular pineland's business: in 1852 or 3, he built a paper mill near the site of the ironworks. He took in two partners in the venture, Walter Dwight Bell, and Albert W. Markley. The mill was described in a legal summons issued in 1855:

> The said building is a stone mill erected for the manufacture of paper. The main building is two stories high about sixty feet long by fifty feet deep, and attached thereto and making a part thereof are a boiler and bleach house, forty-two feet by thirty-two, a machine house eighty feet by twenty-four; a water wheel and a wheel house, twenty-eight feet by twenty-four.

This venture hardly got off the ground, closing in about two years, or perhaps had never even operated.

In 1854, the financial situation in the northeast was unstable. Many businesses went bankrupt and their owners committed suicide. That fall, Fleming's house of cards collapsed as well.

By September of 1854, he was over a half a million dollars in debt, and, taking a note from the first owner of Atsion, he disappeared. His wife, Maria, must have thought things over quite a bit before love for her husband won the day. William Walton Fleming had lost a large portion of her inherited wealth and had left her to face the consequences. Love conquers all, they say, and Maria set out to find her vagrant husband. She finally located him in Brussels, Belgium, and the two were reconciled. Maria's mother joined them, and they continued to live in Belgium for the remainder of their lives.

In his will dated January 5, 1855, William Henry Richards directed that his share was to be sold and the proceeds invested. Eighteen years later, there were still no buyers. The Fleming assets were put up for sale by his creditors on April 7, 1859, and was advertised as "the largest public sale of Real Estate which has probably ever been made in this section of New Jersey." Walton and Maria's share of Atsion was sold on the 13th of April, 1861 to Jarvis Mason of Philadelphia for $66,000. That gentleman sold it a year later to Colonel William C. Patterson of Philadelphia for $82,500. Not a bad bargain for a worthless piece of property.

Patterson's dream was of a "planned community" based on farming. Calling his new project "The Fruitland Improvement Company," he envisioned a major development, with markets in Philadelphia and New York via the

new railroad which was pushing through the area. It was a good dream, but like so many other owners of this land, Patterson went bankrupt, and his estate was sold in 1871. From the height of 128,000 acres, the land had shrunk to 27,320. The property still included the mansion, "store, four barns, twelve tenant houses, 1 grist mill, 2 saw mills, and a paper mill; the latter without fixtures or machinery."

Patterson tried large-scale farming. He wanted to cultivate sugar beets and bought a steam cable rig in England to do the plowing. This expensive piece of machinery was supposed to be able to plow more land in one day than could twenty-five plow horse teams. Unfortunately, for him, the type of sugar beet he planted wouldn't grow in the Atsion soil. It remained for Joseph Wharton to try again in his era and succeed.

New prospects were just over the horizon, however. In 1854, William Torrey, John Torrey, and others launched the Raritan and Delaware Bay Railroad. In their vision, the rails would cut New Jersey in two, connecting with New York and Philadelphia via ferry service. In 1859, they had cut through the pines as far as Atsion, which became their temporary southern terminus. By 1862, they had built

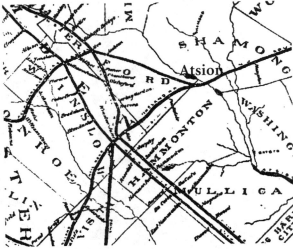

Map of the Railroads in the Vicinity of Atsion
This map shows the mainline through Atsion, built by the Raritan and Delaware Bay Railroad through Atsion to Vineland and Bridgeton, connecting with the Atlantic City/Philadelphia lines at Winslow Junction. The Camden and Atlantic Railroad built a freight branch connecting with the Raritan and Delaware Bay at Atsion. (taken from a map dated 1864-5)

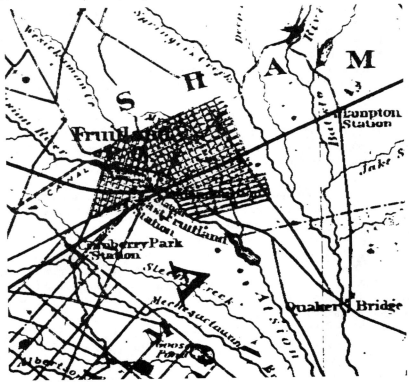

The Planned Community of Fruitland
as envisioned by Colonel Patterson 1862-1871 (F.W. Beers Map - 1870)

their line through the Atsion Estate and on to Winslow Junction, Vineland, and Bridgeton. When they started services between New York and Philadelphia, though, they ran afoul of one of the most powerful railroads in the area, the Camden and Amboy Railroad of Commodore Robert Stockton. Even though the United States declared the Raritan and Delaware Bay a military road in the midst of the Civil War, the courts still granted Stockton an injunction against them and ordered them to cease and desist. By 1867, the Torreys were bankrupt. The line was reorganized into the New Jersey Southern which later became part of the Central Railroad of New Jersey. It was during that year that the Camden and Atlantic Railroad built a 9.3 mile spur line to connect at Atsion with the New Jersey Southern. This branch apparently was for freight only, and there is no record of passenger service on it.

During the first half of the twentieth century, the Jersey Central's famous *Blue Comet* rushed through Atsion, carrying vacationers to the shore, for the line that had bankrupted the Torreys and threatened the Camden and Amboy became the Atlantic City line of the Central Railroad of New Jersey.

REBIRTH V - LET'S TRY COTTON THIS TIME

The next owner of Atsion, Maurice Raleigh, dreamed of an industrial community based on the railroad. He bought the property on May 10, 1871 for $48,200. It was Raleigh who enlarged the paper mill and turned it into a cotton factory. He built a carpenter's shop, a blacksmith's shop, a public school, rebuilt the Richards' church, and threw out that horrible name, "Fruitland" in favor of "Atsion" again. For ten more years, Atsion prospered. In 1880, Atsion boasted three hundred people and was a going concern.

Unfortunately, Raleigh's health weakened about that time, and he felt he would be unable to continue. A group that wanted to start an African American colony in the Atsion area approached him concerning a sale. They felt that the combination of a successful mill, a railroad access, and good farms would attract settlers to their community. For some reason, Raleigh way overestimated the value of his estate. He gave them a price of 1.3 million dollars! Needless to say, the deal collapsed.

Raleigh died on January 10, 1882, and his heirs planned to continue to develop his dream. They, however, wanted the name of the town changed to "Raleigh." The Raleigh Land and Improvement Company advertised lots at $25 an acre and emphasized its connections with New York, Philadelphia, and Atlantic City via the railroad.

Courtesy of Budd Wilson through the kindness of Charles Kier

The Paper Mill as rebuilt after 1871 into a
Cotton Factory - 1923
The building burned on March 27, 1977

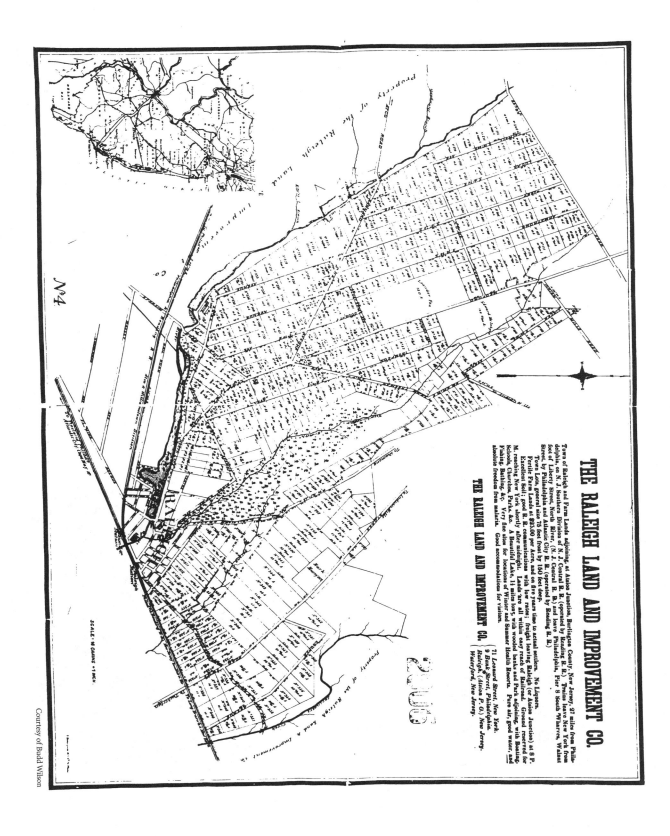

THE RALEIGH LAND AND IMPROVEMENT CO.

Town of Raleigh and Farm Lands adjoining, at Atsion Junction, Burlington County, New Jersey, 27 miles from Philadelphia, on N. J. Southern Division of N. J. Central R. R. (operated by Reading R. R.) Trains leave New York from foot of Liberty Street, North River, (N. J. Central R. R.) and leave Philadelphia, Pier 8 South Wharves, Walnut Street, by Philadelphia and Atlantic City R. R. (operated by Reading R. R.)

Town Lots, general size 75 feet front by 150 feet deep.

Fertile Farm Lands at $25.00 per Acre, and on five years time to actual settlers. No Liquors.

Excellent Soil; good R. R. communications with low rates; freight leaving Raleigh (or Atsion Junction) at 8 P. M. reaching New York shortly after midnight. Lands are all within easy reach of Railroad. Ground reserved for Schools, Churches, Parks, &c. A Beautiful Lake, 1½ miles long, with wooded banks and Park adjoining, with Boating, Fishing, Bathing, &c. Very fine sites for locations of Winter and Summer Health Resorts. Pure air, good water, and absolute freedom from malaria. Good accommodations for visitors.

THE RALEIGH LAND AND IMPROVEMENT CO.

71 Leonard Street, New York.
9 Bank Street, Philadelphia.
Raleigh, (Atsion P. O.) New Jersey.
Waterford, New Jersey.

SCALE: 10 CHAINS = 1 INCH.

N°4

Quaker Bridge Road became North Lake Avenue, and Atsion Lake was renamed Lake Roland. The map of the railroad lines shows two stations, one named "Atsion" on the main line to Winslow Junction, and one on the freight spur named "Raleigh." The Raleigh Land and Improvement Company failed. The mill was shut down within a year of Raleigh's death, and it would never reopen.

REBIRTH VI - THE INFAMOUS JOSEPH WHARTON

In 1892, Joseph Wharton bought the whole thing. Wharton wanted to utilize the pinelands streams and rivers as well as the underground aquifer to supply water to thirsty Philadelphia, but the New Jersey legislature refused to permit the export of water from the state. With characteristic enthusiasm, Wharton set about creating an agricultural empire in the pines. He wasn't in the habit of simply owning unproductive land. He created cultivated cranberry bogs where ore was once dug and turned the cotton factory into a cranberry house. East of the church, he even made a successful experiment in growing peanuts.

Also in 1892, Andrew Etheridge of Batsto was appointed caretaker of Atsion. Etheridge was efficient and well-liked and knew how to make Atsion turn a profit - which made Wharton like *him*. Wharton's death in 1909 didn't alter the pattern of life for the local people. His estate continued the overall management of the property, and Etheridge stayed at his post. His death in 1925 ended thirty-three years of faithful service. Leeson Small, Andrew Etheridge's son-in-law, succeeded him as superintendent, and Maymie, one of his daughters, continued to keep the books and run the store.

Burlington County Library Collection

The Old Mill
This photograph is from the Wharton Era when it was used
as a Cranberry Packing House

Requiem - The State of New Jersey

The State of New Jersey agreed to purchase the Atsion property in 1954 and actually acquired it a year later when they bought the second half of the Wharton Tract. The prospects were excellent for the preservation of this old pine barrens town that had gone through so many rebirths over three centuries. It inherited the Samuel Richards' Mansion, the store, the Etheridge House, the school, the Wharton barn, the cotton mill/cranberry house, and over a dozen of the houses from both the railroad era and later. The State rebuilt the exterior of the mansion and also restored the old store, removing later nineteenth century additions. This town seemed on its way to be a historical showcase of New Jersey history in the nineteenth and twentieth centuries, but it was not to be.

Instead of rebuilding and preserving, the State did nothing. The store became a Rangers' Station, the mansion was fenced and shuttered, and everything else was left to deteriorate. One entire street-full of houses was torn down. The cotton mill burned to the ground in 1977. What money was sent the way of Atsion was put into a recreational bathing facility on the lake. Play is what attracts people and justifies expenditures, not historic preservation.

As of 1998, the mansion remains off limits to visitors, deteriorating on the inside. The barn, the school, and one remaining house are in ruins. The Etheridge House burned to the ground in March of 1998, a victim of arson. One home belongs to Mrs. Lane, who moved there fifty years ago. The abandoned tracks of the Jersey Central still pass through the woods, but the stations of Atsion and Raleigh and the old hotel are gone.

Atsion today is a forlorn example of the past ignored and forgotten by the people of New Jersey as they splash and play in the lake that once provided power for mill, forge, furnace, and factory. Here are only weeds and ruins where so many people led productive lives for two and a half centuries.

The Slab-Sheathed House and the Old Mill - c. 1880

The Slab-Sheathed House and the Old Mill - c. 1960

The Old Mill and a Railroad-Era House - Wharton Era

The Old Mill - Possibly pre-1880

The Mansion of Samuel Richards

Samuel Richards' Mansion in 1995

Built by Samuel Richards in 1826, the old mansion of Atsion has seen many years pass by from its elevation beside the Quaker Bridge Road. When Richards constructed it, it faced the major highway of the day. It stood on the old Stage Road to the town of Washington and on through Bass River to Tuckerton. Now State Route 206 on its way south from Trenton to Hammonton bypasses the mansion on the west side. Once horses drew wagons loaded with iron products and cotton goods through the woods to market. Now the tractor-trailers, their modern counterparts, rumble past.

Samuel and Anna Maria Richards had been married for four years when he built this mansion overlooking his newly-acquired pinelands industrial town. They rode out to their property in a coach-and-four, which was the equivalent of the stretch limo of our time. Atsion was not as isolated as it may seem today. The sand road to Camden and Philadelphia saw a great deal of traffic, and many important couples from that city visited the Richards' mansion when they were in residence during the summer months.

Their carriages would pull up to the entrance on the north side of the house where they would alight and enter the long central hall of the mansion. When Samuel and Maria gave a party, the house was filled with the rich and famous from the Quaker City. The family quarters were elegant. The first floor boasts a huge double parlor and a central hall with a wide and elegant staircase to the second floor.

The columns which support the porch roof on the south side are made from pipe that was produced for the City of Philadelphia and are marked with a "P" for that city that may have come from the first production run which John Richards coaxed from the furnace immediately after the purchase of Atsion in 1819.

The east front featured a covered porch over the servants' entrance. Wagons bringing foodstuffs for the cellar kitchen could unload their wares protected from the elements. The servants entered into a narrow, transverse hall. They could climb narrow stairways to their quarters in the attic or go down an equally narrow staircase to the kitchen in the cellar.

Courtesy of Budd Wilson through the kindness of Charles Kier

The Atsion Mansion, North View - 1923

Unlike several of the smaller houses along the Mullica, the mansion had no "summer" kitchen outside of the main structure. Here, the kitchen was in the cellar and had a huge, eight-foot fireplace. Samuel Richards' is rumored to have enjoyed trying his hand at cooking now and then, quite the "modern" husband, except that the couple had servants to do the housework for them. Near the kitchen were the meat and milk rooms where the coolness of the ground and stone walls kept those items as fresh as the lack of refrigeration in those days would permit.

There was no central heating in the house. Each room had its fireplace, many with marble mantels.

This elegant Greek Revival mansion in the pines with its cool, stone walls would have made a lovely summer retreat from the heat of the city. It is no wonder that Samuel and Maria delighted in coming here each year.

There seems to be no record of whether Maria Lawrence Richards came here in the summers after her father's death in 1842, but she may well have continued to enjoy the respite from the city. Her half-sister was married to Stephen Colwell, her father's manager at Weymouth Furnace and now its owner, and Maria Lawrence enjoyed visiting their mansion when they were in residence. It was there at Weymouth, in fact, where she met her future husband. After her marriage to William Walton Flemming in 1849, the couple must have lived in the Atsion mansion while Flemming built and operated the paper mill on the site of the old forge and furnace.

Flemming lost everything in the business instability of 1854 and fled to Europe. After his wife found him and the two were reconciled, they remained in Belgium for the remainder of their lives. The Atsion mansion lay abandoned until the property was sold to William Patterson in 1862. Patterson and his successor at Atsion, Maurice Raleigh, seemed to have lived in the Atsion mansion at least part of the year, so the building was kept in repair if it no longer had the elegance of the Richards' period.

At one time, the mansion boasted a porch on both the south and west sides, the roof of which was supported by thirteen columns. Legend has it that Richards used these columns to symbolize the original thirteen states of the Union, but research indicated that the west front porch was a later addition. Some think that it was added during the tenure of Maurice Raleigh, but Brumbaugh, the former Archetect of Restorations at Batsto, believed that it was added in the Richards era soon after the mansion was constructed. The columns were iron pipes of the same diameter as those of the front porch but not as long. They had to be fitted with sleeves to give them the

The Atsion Mansion, Front View - 1923

proper length. Its seven supporting columns, combined with the original six, gave rise to the legend that Samuel Richards intended the thirteen columns to represent the original thirteen states.

When Joseph Wharton took over the Atsion property late in the nineteenth century, he had no use for the mansion. He completely rebuilt the one at Batsto for his own use but had no need for a second at Atsion. His manager on the spot, Andrew Etheridge, lived in a small house nearby, and the Richards' mansion was left vacant.

Human structures do not last very long without constant attention, and if they have no use, costly repairs are rarely made. The Atsion mansion decayed dramatically during the Wharton years. The 1923 photographs of the house show window panes missing, shutters falling apart, and the plaster cracked and falling off. There are people on the porches, but whether they were living there or simply posing for their photographs is not known.

The State of New Jersey restored the exterior of the mansion after they took over the property in 1955, but it remains tightly shuttered and fenced off from curious sightseers. Since the intent was to restore the mansion to the Richards' era, the west porch was removed. Unfortunately for this old queen of the pines, the interior was not restored and has deteriorated considerably.

It is a shame that, after spending so much to restore the exterior of this ancient house, the State of New Jersey has left it to silent ruin as the twentieth century draws to a close. If New Jersey historic preservationists want to find the most endangered architecture in the state, they should begin by looking in the pines and at the houses the state itself owns.

The Etheridge House

Andrew Etheridge was appointed caretaker of Atsion by Joseph Wharton in 1892 and managed the estate for thirty-three years. His family continued to live here until the State of New Jersey purchased the property in 1955, a period of sixty-three years.

Courtesy of Budd Wilson through the kindness of Charles Kier

The Etheridge House - 1928

Photograph by John Pearce

The Etheridge House - 1995
Destroyed by fire on March 1, 1998

After Andrew's death in 1925 and his burial at Batsto/Pleasant Mills, his son-in-law, Leeson Small, husband of daughter Bertha, became superintendent of the estate. Etheridge's daughter, Maymie, continued to keep the books as always, and his son John was station master at Atsion for forty-six years.

This house had been built for the manager of the Atsion property prior to the coming of Etheridge. A part of the structure was probably built in the early part of the nineteenth century. When he moved his family into the home, he added a kitchen onto the rear of the house. The kitchen had a wood stove for cooking and heating, and, like to many of the time, included a water tank on the side for hot water.

Andrew Etheridge's granddaughter, in Sarah Ewing's book, *Atsion: A Town of Four Faces*, published by the Batsto Citizens' Committee, relates that a little pantry off the kitchen held a big ice box, on top of which sat the cage of "Grandpop" Etheridge's pet parrot, who was named "Polly," of course. He also kept canaries in a cage in the dining room, which doubled as his sitting room.

Red and pink climbing roses covered the picket fences surrounding the home, which enclosed gardens blooming with a variety of colorful flowers throughout the summer season.

All lay abandoned by the State to the fate of time and weather. Cheerful welcome and cozy warmth are only memories. No longer was the home open to strangers, offering Atsion hospitality to the visitor. The old manager's house looked out forlornly on the meager remains of its once great empire in the pines until it was tragically destroyed by fire on March 1, 1998.

The Atsion Store

The Atsion Store in 1923

The Atsion Store was built by Samuel Richards the year after he built the Mansion on the rise immediately behind it. The year was 1827, and Atsion was seeing the first of many rebirths. It was to this building that the post office returned from the tavern in the town of Washington (Sooy's Inn) on the Stage Road, where it had been moved when Atsion had closed in 1815.

Hard cash was not very common in the early years of the nineteenth century. Local residents sold the produce from their gardens to the company store for credit, and ledgers were kept detailing their accounts. Part of the wages of those who worked in the iron furnace, forge, and attendant industries was paid in store credits. It was amazing the variety of goods that could be purchased from a little store like this. All necessities and frivolities of life that could not be home grown or manufactured were purchased through this store. Country stores like this were as much a thrill to the local people as are the large malls in our own time. Actually, they were the WalMarts of the day. Here women came to finger the cloth and dream of a new dress or skirt. Children, their eyes shining with anticipated delight, gazed longingly at the candies held by the glass jars on the counter.

At some time in the nineteenth century, a belfry was added to the store. The bell was used to signal the workers of the beginning and ending of the workday and also to warn of fires or other major events.

Maurice Raleigh was running the store in May of 1875 when it was robbed of over three hundred dollars worth of goods, quite a good sum in those days. The stock stolen included "boots, shoes, hats, shawls, jewelry, cutlery, and other [such] goods." A note of humor: the thieves carted the goods away on a railroad handcar! 'Course that was a quicker mode for making a getaway than a wagon on the sand roads through the pines.

During its last fifty years, Maymie Etheridge kept the store and its books, faithfully accounting for everything to the Wharton Estate. Maymie presided over a huge and varied stock which included bolts of cloth for dresses, pants, shirts, etc., hats for the men and bonnets for the women, flour, beans, crackers, pickles, etc., feed for the animals, oil and kerosene for lamps and stoves.

The store closed its doors for the last time in 1946. Most of the business in the area had disappeared through the long years of the Great Depression. World War II finished it off. The once-bustling Atsion was home only to the elderly, as the younger people looked elsewhere for work after the war's conclusion. The State restored it to its original appearance as Richards built it and now uses it as a rangers' station.

Photograph by John Pearce

The Atsion Store in 1995

The Atsion Railroad Station
of the Central Railroad of New Jersey
(No Longer in Existence)

Courtesy of Budd Wilson through the kindness of Charles Kier

During the 1930's, the famous *Blue Comet*, pride of the Jersey Central, that ran from Jersey City to Atlantic City, sped down from the terminal on the Hudson, through Winslow Junction, and on to Atlantic city. New York City folk crossed the Hudson on ferries to the Jersey Central Terminal (still there, by the way) and boarded the *Blue Comet* for a swift ride through the pines to the famous summer seaside resort. Tragedy and excitement enveloped this train when it was wrecked near Chatsworth in 1939.

The line was busy carrying freight as well as passengers. During cranberry season, five trains a day left Chatsworth hauling boxcars of cranberries to market, and many more boxcars were loaded at Atsion for the trip to either Philadelphia or New York. The last cranberry train left Chatsworth in 1949. Near to this station stood the Atsion Hotel which welcomed travellers to this center of industry in the Jersey pines.

A curiosity: the railroad map included in this chapter indicates that the rails heading towards the west were the Camden and Atlantic freight spur, on which the "Raleigh" station stood. It shows the rails to the southward as the Vineland Railroad and the "Atsion" station standing in the "Y" between the two. Maps of the town of Raleigh indicate that the Jersey Central line ran to the west and the Vineland Railroad to the south with the "Atsion" station sat in the "Y" and the "Raleigh" station northeastward of it. There is no doubt that the rails westward were the freight line and those to the south the main line of the Jersey Central. The station pictured above apparently was the "Atsion" station which stood between the tracks at the "Y.."

The only thing that remains are the tracks. The station is gone. The hotel is gone. The business is gone. The people are gone. Children splash in the Atsion Lake nearby, little knowing or caring that at one time, great trains rumbled past, filled with happy vacationers heading for the shore or carrying cranberries and other goods to market. Now only silence surround this site, and the wind howls softly in the pines.

The Samuel Richards' Church

Courtesy of Budd Wilson through the kindness of Charles Kier

The Richards' Church - 1923

Samuel Richards completed this church building in 1828. It stands off the Quaker Bridge Road, once the highway of choice, now almost forgotten as it loses itself in the pines. On June 13, 1828, Samuel Richards deeded the property on which he had already built the church to a board of trustees. The deed states that "Samuel Richards, with a view and desire to promote Christian Knowledge, has erected a house for religious worship at Atsion . . . and, in order that the said house may at all times hereafter be held for that purpose and the lot of ground on which the same is built and erected may forever be held as a site for a house of religious worship and for a burial place." The transfer by Samuel Richards to Jesse Richards, Thomas S. Richards, John Richards, Samuel B. Finch, Thomas Sorden, Samuel Bareford, and Henry Brown, trustees, was recorded on the 6th of August, 1828 (Book X 2 of deeds, page 276). It "conveys all that aforesaid house for religious worship and the lot or piece of ground thereunto belonging, situate at Atsion aforesaid & etc. " to have and to hold "as a site for a house of religious worship and burial place for the use of all religious denominations professing the Christian religion at or near Atsion" (Wharton ledger Vol. 25).

The adherents of many religious persuasions have used the old building over the years: Presbyterians, Methodists, Episcopalians, and, during Maurice Raleigh's proprietorship of Atsion, a "Free Union."

Next to the church is one of two burial grounds at Atsion. Many of the families who lived here during the successful and not so successful periods of Atsion's history left their beloved in this final resting place. Across the dam on the south side of the lake is Atsion's other cemetery. Very little remains today of what may have been the original cemetery in the Atsion vicinity. It has been traditionally known as the "Catholic" cemetery, because many of those buried here had Irish names. The first known consecrated Roman Catholic cemetery was Saint Mary's of the Assumption in Pleasant Mills which was established in 1827. It is known that many Scots-Irish men worked at Atsion, and that may account for the Irish names.

Archaeology research says that there were about sixty burials here over about one hundred square feet. For many years, the only visible stone was that of Eliza McNeal, who died in 1886 at the advanced age of 86. A partial stone nearby recorded the final resting place of Daniel McNeal, "A Native of Ireland." The earliest known grave is that of John Ross who died in 1804 at the age of twenty.

James Belangee, a well-known Quaker minister, visited Atsion in 1835 and recorded in his diary that "they seemed much prejudiced to us (Friends) as a society." He told the people here that he came "in love to have a meeting" and was finally permitted to preach at the "Presbyterian Meeting House."

The Presbyterians had been active in establishing missions wherever their staunch supporters settled. The Brainerds had preached in the Pleasant Mills area and had helped to gather a congregation there. Many Scottish "Covenanters" emigrated from their homeland early in the eighteenth century rather than be forced to join the Church of England. Both Pleasant Mills and Bass River originally had a contingent of Scottish families. Early in the nineteenth century, however, the Methodist fervor swept across South Jersey and the meetinghouses changed hands. Atsion was described in 1844 as having a furnace, 15 or 20 dwellings, and a Methodist Church.

By 1867, the meetinghouse had returned to the Presbyterian fold. This time the congregation was incorporated: "said congregation being assembled at their usual place of meeting for public worship . . .having duly advertised the assemblage as required . . . did assemble and elect Trustees: William C. Patterson, Philadelphia, J. Simpson, Africa, Thomas C. Parsons, Benjamin R. Nutt, and Rev. L. Roode, all of Fruitland, and so duly constituted a body corporate to be known as the Atsion Presbyterian Church of Fruitland."

It is said that the original building burned in 1869, and all the records were lost. Apparently, it was rebuilt by Raleigh after 1871 and was used as a Free Union church. By 1918, this church was Episcopalian. The Diocese of New Jersey of the Protestant Episcopal Church was active in missionwork early in the twentieth century. They established many "Missions in the Pines," including one here at Atsion and one in Jenkins. That missionwork petered out for lack of success and financing, and most of the nascent churches were sporadically supported by other denominations or by independent groups.

The oldest grave in the cemetery surrounding the church dates from 1837 for Sarah Ann Dunlop. Sarah Ann's parents were from Antrim, Ireland, and she was only four when she was buried here. Actually, people who were attached to the various furnaces and forges may not have been buried where they lived. When the areas were all under the Richards' family control, the workers and their families frequently moved from location to location as they were needed and were buried where they died. Batsto people, for instance, were buried at both Pleasant Mills and at Atsion. Weymouth folks were laid to rest in the Weymouth cemetery, but also at Pleasant Mills and Atsion.

Photograph by John Pearce

The Church in 1996

The Wharton-era Barn

Courtesy of Budd Wilson through the kindness of Charles Kier

Barns were always high-risk items. Farm animals and equipment were usually stored on the first floor, while grain for the animals and hay for their stalls found its place on the second floor. Bales could be hoisted up by means of a block and tackle. Then they were shovelled off onto the floor below. The combination of moist grain, manure, and flammable liquids in a wooden barn often proved tragic. Spontaneous combustion was always a possibility. A kerosene lantern accidently knocked over was not so easily extinguished. Such was the fate of the original wooden barn in this location.

Joseph Wharton was a practical man. When he built something, he built it to last. This barn was insured against fire: it was made from poured concrete. Wharton would never even have contemplated that abandonment and neglect would be the fate of his carefully maintained farm at Atsion.

This structure was built in the late nineteenth century and was intended to last a hundred years. By the looks of it, it may have just made it.

Photograph by John Pearce

The Wharton-era Barn - 1995

The Slab-Sheathed House

Photograph by John Pearce

This house stands just off Route 206 on the road to the ruins of the cotton factory. In the early days of Atsion, this land on the west side of the river lay in Gloucester County, now Atlantic, but became part of Burlington County in 1902. Behind it once stood a row of mid-nineteenth century houses where now there is only a road through high weeds. The State tore them all down some years back. Not far away is the last house of the railroad era: an abandoned ruin.

This house is thought to be one of the oldest structures in Atsion. It probably dates from the early iron era when forge and furnace glowed with fire, and the throb of the great forge hammer pounded nearby.

The house has a full-time resident, a dear lady of eighty-three, Mrs. Lane, who was originally from Camden. She and her now-deceased husband moved to this house over fifty years ago. She remembers Henry Charlton Beck making his rounds, collecting stories for his newspaper articles and books. Beck talked with her husband about the history of Atsion so many years ago.

Mrs. Lane remembers the January night in 1977 when the old mill went up in flames. How could she forget? She must have been afraid that the huge flaming structure which stood so nearby might reach out its burning embers and engulf her little house in flames as well. Fortunately, it didn't. Her house still stands to bear testimony to the past.

The Atsion Public School

Photograph by John Pearce

Although the American people differed dramatically in the value placed on an education, by the mid-1800's, it was generally agreed, in the northern states that is, that children should receive an education at the public expense, at least through the fifth grade.

Towns and villages built little schoolhouses like this one which were quite large enough to hold the ten to twenty children of various ages who lived in the area. They tried to employ someone, usually a young, unmarried woman or spinster, though sometimes a man, who could at least read and write. Not until later in the century could small, rural schools boast teachers who had any kind of advanced degree. Teachers received a pittance and boarded with parents when school was in session.

Home duties on the farms and jobs in the local industry (cranberry-picking when this particular building was in use) kept many young people from attending school on a regular basis, consequently, the ages of the pupils varied more than the grade level suggests. The first school at Atsion, Public School No. 94, was built by Maurice Raleigh in 1872. Sarah Ewing (*Atsion: A Town of Four Faces*) tells of an older lady, a Mrs. Gerber, whose mother boarded with the Etheridges while she taught in the old building around 1912.

This building replaced the old school. Built around 1916, it was an anachronism in an age when people were thinking of centralized schools. It was of a slightly larger design than those of the towns down the Mullica. Those were only little three-window buildings. This boasted four on each side! It didn't outlast them by much, though. In 1922, it was closed.

For a while, the building was used as a home, but it was abandoned to the weather when the State of New Jersey acquired the property in 1955.

The school building stands off the road, the last structure on the old Tuckerton Stage Road (the Quaker Bridge Road in these parts) before you cross the abandoned tracks of the Central Railroad of New Jersey. Brambles and underbrush clog the yard where once the happy voices of children were raised in delightful play.

The Grist Mill

Courtesy of Budd Wilson

Every community had to have at least two mills: a sawmill for preparing lumber for houses and business structures and a grist mill to grind the grain into usable flour and corn into meal. Atsion's grist mill stood east of Route 206 on the Mansion side of the river and was probably built during the Drinker years. The millrace ran from Atsion Lake, through the mill, and on to where it joined the river near the site of the forge and furnace where the cotton factory was built in later years. It was crossed by two bridges: a footbridge near the store and a wagon bridge near the cotton mill.

When Andrew Etheridge and his family moved to Atsion in 1892, the old mill was still standing, but at some time in the intervening years, it was struck by lightning and destroyed. Even the foundations are obscured. When the State of New Jersey built Route 206, the embankment for the road went over a portion of the site.

In the photograph above, if you look closely, you can see the Mansion and the store in the background behind the trees. The old photograph to the right, poor as it is, shows the location of the mill with regards to the dam.

Burlington County Library Collection

The Grist Mill - Date Unknown

The old Dam on the Atsion River (upper Mullica)

The Old Mill During the Wharton Era

Atsion - c. 1954

(1)   The Mansion (1996: Outside restored; inside a wreck)
(2)   The Store (1996: The Rangers' Station)
(3)   The Wharton Era Barn (1996: Ruins)
(4)   The Etheridge House (Burned 1998)
(5)   The Church (1996: private)
(6)   The School (1996: Ruins)
(7)   Site of the Railroad Station (1996: completely grown over)
(8)   Approximate vicinity of the hotel
(9)   The Cotton Factory/Paper Mill/Cranberry House (Burned 1977; 1996: Ruins)
(10)   The Slab-Sheathed House (1996: private)
(11)   Railroad Era Houses (Torn down by the State; 1996: completely grown over)
(12)   Railroad Era House (1996: Ruins)

The Remains of the Fleming Paper Mill, the Raleigh Cotton Factory,
and the Wharton Cranberry Packing House - 1996

Batsto and Pleasant Mills

Photograph by John Pearce

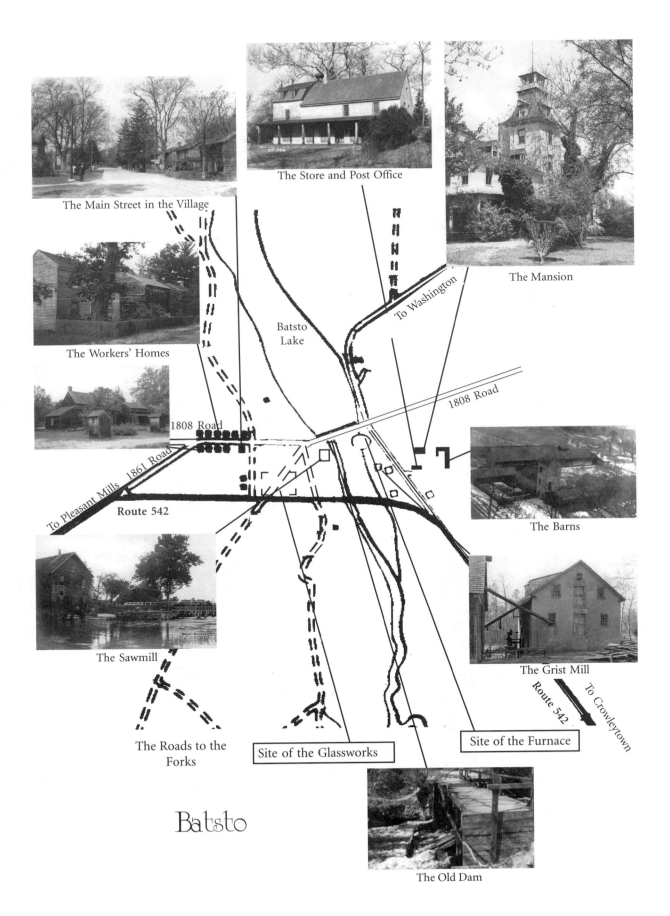

The Main Street in the Village

The Store and Post Office

The Mansion

The Workers' Homes

Batsto Lake

To Washington

1808 Road

1808 Road

The Barns

1861 Road

To Pleasant Mills

Route 542

The Grist Mill

Route 542

To Crowleytown

The Sawmill

The Roads to the Forks

Site of the Glassworks

Site of the Furnace

The Old Dam

Batsto

A Land of Dreams

A strange and enticing name has graced this area of the pinelands for well over two hundred years: Batsto! Out in the pines beyond Hammonton, above the navigable waters of the Mullica River at The Forks, a village of quaint little houses clusters about a large, imposing mansion, much as they have done for most of that two hundred-plus years.

In the last half of the twentieth century, this little village has slept peacefully in gentle repose beside the stream that also bears the same name. The main road, Route 542, from New Gretna to Hammonton, bypasses the town now, turning aside from its more direct route in front of the old store and post office, across the bridge at the dam for Batsto Lake, and on through the village.

The visitor to this state-owned and run town gets the distinct impression that this village has always slumbered through the years, bypassed by civilization, and that all its inhabitants have had to do was listen to the wind howling in the pines outside their little houses. Batsto seems the epitome of the forgotten pinelands town, sleeping in peaceful isolation from the rest of the world.

Not so! This deep-pines tourist attraction in the 1990s is but a shell of former glory, the victim of mistaken ideas of the pines isolation from the mainstream of life throughout the years.

Once upon a time, long ago, the thousands of acres around this town vibrated with life. Here, the entrepreneurs of colonial days challenged the authority of the British crown to regulate nascent industry in what they were fast considering to be "their" country. In the first heady days of independence, their successors built empires in the wilderness, as mighty for their times as any major industrial complex is today.

Here was a whole community of people, living decent lives, raising their children in the little houses, working in the various industries that grew around the paternal mansion, laughing and crying, shedding tears of joy and of sorrow, as generations worked in the pines and loved the land and the little rivers with all their hearts.

In the fifty years after independence was declared, hundreds of people lived in Batsto Village or nearby at The Forks or in Pleasant Mills. There was a hot, glowing furnace, a forge with its huge, throbbing hammer, plans for a glassworks, a sawmill to supply the growing demand for building materials in New York and Philadelphia, coastal schooners making their tortuous way up the Mullica as far as The Forks, where goods were unloaded and local products stowed away in their holds for shipment and sale. All along the Mullica, it is estimated that over a hundred ships might lay at anchor or tied to wharves on any one summer day, providing work for shipbuilders, cordwainers, coopers, blacksmiths, shipwrights, and a host of other attendant industries.

Lumbermen roamed the cedar swamps to find trees for ships' masts and planking. Colliers cut the pines and oaks for conversion to charcoal that fed not only the local furnaces and forges, but also the industries and homes of the great cities of New York and Pennsylvania. In the downstream villages of the Mullica valley lived the sea captains, their mates and crews, whose ships transported all these products. Where the two main branches of the Mullica meet in lonely silence today, two centuries ago, those streams that flow together to form the Mullica River joined their waters in the midst of vibrant life.

You can still hike the sand road through the pines from Batsto to The Forks today, but, standing there in the midst of the silence of the pines, gazing out on the brown waters of the little rivers where they meet, seeing nothing but herons and egrets and perhaps an eagle, there is little to suggest the vitality which once dominated this entire area.

When the successful conclusion of the French and Indian War in 1763 set the colonies free from their enemies on the western frontier of the seaboard states, the businessmen of the cities had great visions of enterprise. Even while the British manufacturing interests, fearing colonial competition, persuaded the parliament to forbid or highly tax colonial industries, old Britain seemed far away from the pinelands of New Jersey.

Land was available at reasonable rates. During this second half of the eighteenth century, much was still held by the Council of West Jersey Proprietors and all was potentially for sale. Speculators bought land from the Proprietors, expecting to resell it after a time at a good profit. By 1765, businessmen were eyeing this sparsely-populated area with scarce-repressed dreams of prosperity.

Batsto! What an intriguing name. Who in the world dreamed it up in the first place? Scholars, who always seem to have an erudite answer for everything, say it comes from the Swedish for "bathing place" and that the Native Americans took it into their own language.

Yes, I can just see it now: there is the Swede Eric Mullica making his way across the hot forests of pine and oak, skirting the cedar swamps, towards his destiny at Takokan, when he and his family meet the obstruction of a creek. Fording that, they almost immediately come upon a second! Grumbling a bit at first, the little family decides to make the best of it and take a dip. They're already half soaked from the waters of the first branch. They might as well have a little fun. "Badstu" - "Bathing place" in Swedish? It was called Swimming River as early as 1720 (Wharton ledgers).

Other scholars protest that it was the other way around: the Native Americans called it "Baastoo" or "Baatstoo," and the Europeans took it up. The Indians of the nearby village of Nescochague, lying as it did below the creek by that name beside the deeper waters at The Forks, hardly needed to cross two streams to get to the third to go "bathing." Anyway, Batsto it has been for over two hundred fifty years. Actually, there is a town in Norway, about an hour's drive from Oslo, Norway's capital, known by the name of "Batsto," and Norway was ruled by Sweden for many years. Perhaps, just perhaps. . .

First of all, let's get a picture of the area circa 1750. Most of southern portion of the Colony of New Jersey was covered by forests. As the townsfolk and farmers over in Burlington-Mount Holly and farther away in Philadelphia looked over towards the sea, they saw trees and rivers. Now, in 1750, the entire economy depended on two things: trees and rivers. So... here was opportunity in the making. The land was available at bargain-basement prices. All that was needed were men of vision and daring to exploit that opportunity. Such men were not wanting.

Research by John Hawes around 1900 indicated that Israel Pemberton, whose fame (and wealth) formed the basis of a fortune that enabled a descendant to lend the family name to that town up near Mount Holly, figured in this area, too. Pemberton bought a section of land somewhere in the vicinity of The Forks for a country estate, which he called "Whitcomb Manor" after the style of an English country gentlemen. Unfortunately, Hawes could not find an exact location for this supposed manor. K. Braddock-Rodgers repeated this information, but Woodward, who wrote on Charles Read and the Pembertons, father and son, doesn't mention it.

John Munrow, a resident of Mount Holly and a speculator in lands, bought three parcels of land in the area in 1758, one of which was described as being "between the Atsion River and Batstow Creek," also one on the west side of the Atsion and one on the east side of the Batsto. A year later, Vincent Leeds (remember "Vincentown" near where the Pemberton/Mount Holly roads cross Route 206?) bought a half interest in the Batsto lands. Munrow and Leeds only held it for two years when they found another dreamer to take it off their hands: one John Fort. John got a bargain. He got the land with little downpayment and monthly installments. He set up a sawmill and cut lumber but couldn't make a go of it. Foreclosure forced a sheriff's sale on May 9, 1764.

Now guess who was the Associate Justice who presided at the sale on the Court of Common Pleas? We've met him before. None other than the Honorable Charles Read: Assemblyman, Councilor to the Governor, Associate Justice of the Supreme Court, and would be iron speculator. All afternoon the court patiently waited for someone to come along with more money than brains (or should I say, some adventurous businessman), but only one appeared: a Richard Wescoat (also spelled "Wescott"). "Sold for three hundred pounds!" Judge Read cried and brought his gavel down.

It took a year, but on May 3, 1765, the honorable judge got what he wanted: an interest (half, that is) in thousands of acres of the Batsto tract. Wescoat made two hundred pounds on the sale, so he came off pretty well. Read also just happened to be the nephew by marriage of Israel Pemberton of Whitcomb Manor and certainly had the opportunity to acquire that property as well, if the manor ever really existed.

Read knew what he was getting into. He had made extensive surveys of the entire area, including that of Atsion to the north. He had assured himself that it was just as he suspected. These seemingly worthless pinelands were a gold mine. The streams contained plenty of water that could be dammed for power. The bogs boasted iron ore in abundance. Miles and miles of trees surrounded the area that could be cut for lumber and fuel. Local communities provided farm products, and the commercial river trade was poised for expansion.

Now all he had to do was use his influence on the assembly of the province to gain the right to dam those streams so that he could go ahead and construct his furnaces and forges. Not that there was any question about his getting it, considering his position in the government, that is.

And whereas the Honorable Charles Read, Esq., by his humble petition, set forth that he hath proved to demonstration good Merchantable Bar-Iron may be drawn from such Ore as may be found in plenty in the Bogs and . . . in such parts of this Province which are too poor for cultivation . . . and in order to erect the necessary Works, he had lately purchased a considerable Tract of Land lying on both sides of Batstow Creek near Little Egg Harbor in the County of Burlington; praying the aid of the Legislature to enable him to erect a Dam across the said Creek for the use of an Iron-Works; (N.J. Sessions Laws, 1766)

By the year's end, he had built the Batsto Iron Works though he didn't own it outright. He actually only held a part-interest in the project. Reuben Haines of Philadelphia, John Cooper and John Wilson of Burlington, and Walter Franklin of New York were induced to go in with him as partners in building the iron works, and Richard Wescoat still had his half interest in the land.

Within two years, Read dumped his half interest in the land by selling a half portion to Haines, a quarter to Cooper, and an eighth to Franklin and Wilson, his partners in the business.

The Honorable Charles Read was bankrupt and there was no recovery. Carrying all his titles and offices with him, he made a fast exit, first to try to recover a portion of his wife's estate in Antigua, then to a remote town in North Carolina. Here he died a year later, penniless and unmourned.

Reuben Haines was a brewer in Philadelphia, and, owning a full quarter interest in the land and who knows how much of the business, seems to have been the leader of the investors. Haines bought out Wilson in 1769, and, a day later, sold it to Joseph Burr, owner of a sawmill farther up the creek.

Batsto produced what was called "pig" iron: molten iron allowed to flow through channels into trenches made by scraping the heel of a worker's shoe in sand that made them seem like little piglets suckling their mother. These iron "pigs" were then hauled overland to Atsion Forge, that other abandoned Read project, to be made into bar iron, or shipped from The Forks directly to other forges nearer the cities.

A Spirit of Independence

Such was the situation in the pines when the 1770s began. When they closed, life would never be the same. In 1770, the distant speculators and the people on the land were loyal subjects of King George III, by the Grace of God, King of Great Britain and Ireland and His Majesty's Colonies in America. The colonies took advantage of the elimination of the threat of France in the new world by expanding their commercial speculation and trade at a frightening rate.

Parliament, determining that colonies were to be like children: seen but not heard, passed laws meant to protect British industries by restricting colonial ones. That did not sit well with anyone who had anything at all to do with manufacturing, neither owner nor laborer. The out-of-touch members of parliament also restricted trade so that the colonists would have to buy their products from Britain herself at the highest rates. That angered everyone as well. The rich saw their profits about to vanish. Those with less of the wealth saw poverty staring them in the face, and all to protect some fat, comfortable British merchants and manufacturers. As the decade aged, the tensions grew.

John Cox was a Philadelphia merchant, who, like many throughout the American colonies of Great Britain, gradually came to see British governance as a detriment rather than advantage to the colonial people. On November 16, 1760, Cox married Esther Bowes, the daughter of Francis Bowes. Bowes had owned a portion of the Black Creek (Bordentown) Forge. Perhaps that tweaked Cox's interest in the iron business, though it took ten years. He was an ardent supporter of the Patriot cause in that otherwise dull Quaker city, a member of the first Committee of Correspondence that those Massachusetts rebel cousins, Adams and Adams, had instigated, and also a member of the Council of Safety.

On October 12, 1770, John Cox and his partner, Charles Thompson, bought Reuben Haines' share of Batsto. That set them back a thousand pounds. On the very next day, they bought out Joseph Burr's one-eighth for 250 pounds. By the 24th, they had purchased John Cooper's one-fourth, and finally acquired Walter Franklin's one-eighth as well. Total cost: £2,350. That was a sizable amount in those days! Cox put up three-quarters of the money for the purchase and bought out Thompson's quarter-share three years later.

A Richards Comes To Batsto

William Richards was born in 1739 and was raised in iron furnace towns in Berks and Chester counties to the west and north of Philadelphia. He was the son of William Richards and had three cousins of the same name. William's childhood came to an abrupt halt with the death of his father at the age of 47. The boy, only thirteen at the time, had to grow up fast. His father had directed that all his property be sold and made small bequests to his other children. He gave his wife, Elizabeth, the income from his estate for the rest of her life and made his son, William, his residuary legatee. The boy was to live with his mother for another year and was then to be "put out to a trade which he likes."

Though he lacked a formal education and most of the advantages we would consider important today, William Richards made the best of what he did have. He had strength of character and a great deal of natural ability in business.

No question, his employers would be considered to be in violation of child labor laws today, but young William went to work with enthusiasm. He had little else. Apparently, he started at Warwick Furnace, and was the favorite of a John Patrick who worked there. In Arthur Pierce's excellent book, *Family Empire in Jersey Iron*, he quotes several entries in the Warwick books from 1765 through 1770 that mention the Patrick family. Among those entries is one concerning Michael Mick, who later worked in the South Jersey iron industry and whose son, Michael, Jr. became chief founder at Martha Furnace.

Richards worked at Warwick for eleven years and fell in love with John Patrick's daughter, Mary. Mary had only been eight years old when William came to Warwick, and he waited until she was nineteen to wed her in 1764. The couple had their first child, Abigail, a year later.

These were exciting years for a young colonial, for they were years of ferment and disagreement with Mother England. In the year 1765, the British Parliament passed the Stamp Tax which applied a tax to almost every official document in the colonies. Naturally, the colonies erupted in protest. Local men applied for the job of Stamp Distributor or were employed without their knowledge or consent by the crown upon recommendation. All were to feel the brunt of the anger of their fellow citizens. In Philadelphia, seven men paid a call upon the newly-designated stamp distributor, John Hughes, to "request" him to resign. Many of their names come down to us in history: Robert Morris (friend of Washington and financeer of the Revolution), James Tilghman, Archibald McCall, William Bradford, Charles Thompson (the "Sam Adams of Philadelphia" and future partner in the Batsto enterprise), John Cox (later member of the Quartermaster General's department of the army and owner of Batsto) and . . . William Richards.

In 1768, Richards left Pennsylvania and went to Batsto Furnace to seek a job. He left his family behind him and did not return until ice on the lake forced the halt in that year's blast. He seems to have worked here as a founder.

John Cox and Charles Thompson purchased Batsto Furnace in 1770 and almost immediately must have employed their friend, William Richards, as manager. This time, Richards moved his family from Warwick Furnace to Batsto, and with him came his young nephew, Joseph Ball.

During these first years of ownership, though, Cox was thinking profits, not cannonballs. No doubt, he, like most colonials, did not look forward to war with the mother country, though, also like most colonials, wasn't about to take sharp cuts in his financial welfare to maintain those ties to the homeland.

With war becoming ever more of a possibility between 1773 and 1776, the iron business grew in importance. Cox was chosen major of the Second Battalion of the Philadelphia Associators and later was elected its colonel. He also managed to buy another iron works at Mount Holly in 1776 from Thomas Mayberry. When those "damned Yankees" up in Boston shot up the British troops sent to capture the gunpowder stored at Concord, everyone knew that war couldn't be avoided.

It was apparently difficult to keep William Richards from his patriotic duty. He left Batsto and returned to Warwick Furnace in 1775 to be nearer the action in Philadelphia. On June 6, 1775, the Pennsylvania Assembly passed a resolution with regards to Richards which read: "reposing Special Trust and Confidence in your Patriotism, Valour, Conduct and Fidelity, Do by these Presents constitute and appoint you to be Standard Bearer to the Second Battalion of the Associators in the County of Chester for the Protection of this Province against all hostile enterprises and for the Defense of American Liberty."

Though later Richards was called "Colonel," Arthur Pierce could find no evidence that he ever actually bore that title in the ensuing conflict. The only mention of William Richards in the army records seems to be when he took the oath of allegiance to "The United States of America," renouncing loyalty to George III on May 30, 1778.

Colonel Cox hired Joseph Ball, William Richard's nephew, to be the manager of the Batsto Iron Works, when Richards left to join Pennsylvania's struggle for independence. Ball was very friendly with Cox, and his neighbors Richard Wescoat and Elijah Clark at Pleasant Mills. In fact, Joseph married Wescoat's stepdaughter, Sarah Lee.

The unofficial governing body sitting in Pennsylvania's State House in Philadelphia declared itself "official" and appointed George Washington of Virginia General of the "Continental Army." Cox became fully involved in the war effort.

Cox, ardent Patriot that he was, had no trouble getting a contract from the Pennsylvania Council of Safety (of which he was a member) for the production of cannonballs even before the Congress got its act in gear. Now lets remember: principles are one thing, but the wallet is always right there, too. Colonel Cox (he was using the title, now) was paid £2,481 and 55 shillings for those cannonballs. Colonial Patriots were sensible people. When the Congress called on the newly-organized "states" to provide manpower for the army, Cox was able to exempt his workers, except, of course, in case of invasion of the immediate area. Cannonballs and cannon were of such importance to fighting a war, that it was more important to produce them than to have the workers in the front lines of battle. After all, you couldn't just import them from, say, Britain, could you?

The Pennsylvania Journal in 1776 carried an advertisement for Batsto's products:

> MANUFACTURED ... AT BATSTO FURNACE: In West-New-Jersey and to be sold either at the works, or by the Subscriber, in Philadelphia. A great variety of iron pots, kettles, Dutch ovens, and oval fish kettles, either with or without covers, skillets of different sizes, being much lighter, neater and superior in quality to any imported from Great Britain - Pot ash and other large kettles, from 30 to 125 gallons; sugar millgudgeons, neatly rounded and polished at the ends; grating bars of different lengths, grist-mill rounds; weights of all sizes, from 7 lb. to 56 lb; Fullers plates; open and closed stoves of different sizes, rag-wheel irons for sawmills; pestles and morters; sash weights, and forge hammers of the best quality. Also Batsto Pig-Iron as usual, the quality of which is too well known to need any recommendation.

Two hundred years has made a great difference in our lives. I'm wondering, like the reader is, I'm sure, what is all this stuff?! At least we still know what "pots" and "kettles" are, and "morters and pestles," though they're not made of iron any more ... and "sash weights," though the younger generation won't know what they are, in all probability. Let's just say, they were making a great many implements that were commonly used in daily living, and not just cannonballs.

Joseph Ball was overseeing the production of cannon, however, and that at an early date. Remember, in 1775, British troops had fired on colonials at Lexington and Concord. The local militiamen swarmed to the environs of Boston, and the Battle of Bunker Hill (actually Breed's Hill) had been fought when the British took up the dare. That made things worse, of course. "Minutemen" from all over New England flocked to the hills surrounding Boston, which effectively kept the British penned in the city. The Congress at Philadelphia appointed Washington general of a nonexistent "Continental" army, sent him up to Boston to do what he could with the rambunctious New Englanders, and appointed a committee to try and help supply those amateur soldiers around the capitol of Massachusetts Bay. All of this took place in 1775, and it still took Congress another six months to actually have the guts to declare independence!

Ball enthusiastically applied himself to his job of producing iron for the war effort, but life was not always simple. Four months after the Congress finally got around to declaring the obvious, Colonel Cox wrote to his manager, Joseph Ball:

> Out of the 12 Howitzers in the first load 3 burst in proving and out of the last twelve 5 burst. The Captain who tried them and every one who saw them are clearly of the opinion they are by much too thin and that their bursting is owing to that and not the quality of the metal. They must therefore make new patterns much thicker ... I shall send some powder down by the next stage to try them there. .... It is no purpose to send them up not properly proved. I shall be down at Batsto next week."

There is, of course, an excuse for this. The making of cannon and cannonballs was a new enterprise for this homegrown iron industry. Men who knew how to produce kettles and pots could not automatically be expected to produce excellent cannon on the first try.

As the war took its toll on manpower, Ball also had problems getting enough workers to fill the positions he had available. He was in constant need for workers and advertised in the *Pennsylvania Evening Post* on the 26th of June, 1777:

> Wanted at Batsto and Mount Holly iron works a number of labourers, colliers, nailores, and two or three experienced forgemen to whom constant employ and best wages will be given - four shilling per cord will be paid for cutting pine and maple wood. For further information apply at Colonel Cox's counting house on Arch street, Philadelphia, to Mr. Joseph Ball, manager, at Batsto, or to the subscriber at Mount Holly.

Even during the Revolutionary War, there were ways to avoid military service, and that was an enticement for many.

SPIES, INTRIGUE, AND INVASION

John Adams of Massachusetts, ardent Patriot and member of the Continental Congress sitting at Philadelphia, estimated that only a third of the people in the colonies were in favor of complete independence. Another third were indifferent, or, like the Pennsylvania and New Jersey Quakers, outspoken against warfare of any kind. The last third were supporters of Crown, Parliament, Good Government, and Stability.

That left the door wide open for intrigue and betrayal. Tradition has it that one such loyalist kept a close eye on the Batsto Works from a house on the western shore of Batsto Lake. Though the house was not built until after the war, the legend probably has some truth in it. An intelligence report from Governor Tryon to the Earl of Dartmouth, February 11, 1776, records:

> *Shott supplied by John Cox from Batsto Furnace in New Jersey - sent in four waggons - first load - 650, 2nd - 400, 3rd - 1128, 4 - 445 / 2623; Weight - 1/2 of them 6 and the other 9 Pounders. Sent to Philadelphia for the ships of armed Privateers fitted out from that Port.*

Just down river was The Forks, the head of navigation on the Mullica. Here the products of Batsto were shipped to the cities of these new "states," and here also were gathered numerous privateers. The new country lacked a great number of things with which to fight the strongest country in the world, but their worst deficit was in the maritime department. Great Britain had the largest and most powerful naval fleet in the world, bar none. They had the ability to blockade the coastal ports rather effectively.

To counteract this, the various former colonies passed laws permitting private shipowners to commission their vessels as privateers. These papers were called "Letters of Marque" and were the only way a navy-less country could fight on the seas. This was guerrilla warfare on the high seas. Small, highly maneuverable vessels boasting a few cannon had a great advantage over an unescorted, huge, lumbering, unarmed merchant vessel, and these experienced captains and crews took every advantage. Like their counterparts up and down the coast, they were quite successful, so much so that British merchants were soon clamoring to the parliament, demanding that the navy and army which was costing so much would at least do something to swat the mosquitoes that were destroying their commerce.

The Mullica provided tremendous protection for these small privateer vessels. Local businessmen engaged in trade during the peaceful years found it risky business when British warships patrolled the coast. They could outfit their vessels with cannon, though, and use the war to turn a much greater profit. Experienced seamen could take their coastal schooners down the tortuous channel of the river into Great Bay and through the Old Inlet to the sea with little difficulty. Their relatively shallow draft enabled them to get over the offshore bar and capture British supply ships with impunity. Scurrying back into the safety of the river, they would take their prizes upstream to The Forks to be sold. All proceeds were divided amongst the owners, captains, and crews of such Letters of Marque vessels. Some modern-day apologists claim this was little short of piracy, but how else could a small, maritime country survive against the might of the British navy?

In addition, much of the cargo from these captured ships proved to be a tremendous help to the usually-strapped Continental Army. They were hauled overland in wagons to the Delaware, where Durham boats floated them across. Then more wagons were needed to transport them to Washington's army.

Richard Wescoat, at The Forks, was First Major in Colonel Richard Somers' Third Regiment of the Gloucester County Militia, and his home became the center of this important "trade." Batsto had become a source of precious cannon and cannonballs to the colonial army, and was thus also of first importance to the war effort.

The rebels knew this. So did the British. As early as September 1776, the local militia built a fort at Chestnut Neck, downriver on the Mullica, aptly called "Fort Fox Burrows," to provide protection against any British ships making it across the bar and into the river. The privateers were very successful, and all knew that it was simply a matter of time before they teased the British Lion a bit too much.

John Cox of Batsto and Elijah Clark of The Forks wrote to the Council of Safety:

Forks of Little Egg Harbor, June 12, 1777

Sir: - We this morning received information from CAPT. BRADLEY at the Foxborough, that on the 10th instant, about six o'clock in the evening, a brig appeared off Little Egg Harbor Inlet, and made a signal for a Pilot. JOSEPH SOWEY, with his brother and two boys, went off to conduct her into port, and were taken and carried off. Immediately on taking them on board the brig proceeded to the mouth of Great Egg Harbor Inlet, where she again threw out a signal for a pilot; on which Mr. Golder went off with his boat, and on approaching near enough finding she was a vessel of force, he immediately put about, and pushed for the shore, the enemy's boat pursuing, with ony two men showing themselves. On coming within 100 yards, a number of men showed themselves and fired on Golder and crew, who with some difficulty gained the shore, but were obliged to quit their boat, which fell into the hands of the enemy. As Sowey is one of our best pilots, we doubt not that he will be made use of by the enemy to bring in their tenders, and pilot them up the bay and river, which may be productive of most fatal consequences, the inhabitants being in a most helpless condition, and having a great number of cattle and other property that must immediately fall into the hands of the pirates, unless some spirited steps are immediately taken to prevent it. We have presumed to take from CAPT. SHALER, eight or ten pieces of cannon, belonging to a sloop of his lately cast away on the coast, which we have this day ordered to the Foxboroughs [sic], under his direction, with orders immediately to throw up a battery to defend the Inlet, and to annony [sic] the enemy as much as possible should they attempt an entrance. There are now at Foxboroughs [sic] a guard of about 20 men, and Col. Clark will immediately order down as many more, to assist in doing the necessary work. Powder and provisions will be immediately wanted. Shot can be procured here. We doubt not the Council will think it expedient to lose no time giving the necessary directions for effecting what they think ought to be done on this alarming occasion.

We are, with great respect, your most ob't and h'e ser'ts
(signed) John Cox
Elijah Clark

The Council of Safety didn't see fit to take up the matter until the 5th of July when their minutes record:

A memorial from Elijah Clark, Richard Wescott & John Cox was read, Setting forth that the Enemy's ships of War entered Little Egg Harbor Inlet and seized two brigs lying at the Fox Burrows, within the Inlet & carried them off, with a considerable quantity of Stock &c., and praying that Little Egg Harbor may be fortified &c. And that this Board issue the necessary orders for that purpose.

Agreed unanimously, That this Board is not competent to decide upon the subject matter of the said Memorial, and therefore, it be referred to the Legislature.

In other words, they passed the buck. These communications note the first time that the British attempted to stop the depredations from the Mullica "pirates."

The General Assembly, on September 20, 1777, took up the matter and

RESOLVED, That the Treasurer pay the Balance due to the said Elijah Clark and Richard Wescott, being Four Hundred and Thirty Pounts, One Shilling and Three Pence, and that their Receipt, or the Receipt of either of them, be a Discharge to the Treasurer for Payment thereof - that they be empowered and directed to sell such Stores as are not useful, and pay the Amount into the treasury, and to take Charge of the said Cannon and necessary Stores for the Use of the State.

Fort Fox Burrows (or Foxboroughs, as per the letter from Clark and Cox) was located on what was later known locally as "Fort Island," a portion of high ground surrounded by marsh.

During the winter of 1777 - 1778, Washington's troops languished at Valley Forge while the British reveled in Philadelphia. Captured supplies in great quantities were off-loaded at Chestnut Neck from the larger British vessels taken by the privateers, and carried upriver to The Forks in shallow draft boats, much like the ore boats from Batsto. Goods were offered at auction both at Chestnut Neck and at The Forks. Some was purchased for overland shipment to Washington's army, and this lifeline proved invaluable in continuing the struggle throughout that long, cold winter.

One of the leading privateers of Chestnut Neck was Captain Micajah Smith, who probably provided the proverbial straw that broke the camel's back. Along with Captain David Stevens and his schooner *Chance*, Smith's *Sly* managed to capture one of the most valuable prizes taken during the war. In August, 1778, Smith and Stevens brought in the *Venus*, of London, a large British merchant vessel. [Micajah Smith's son, Micajah, Jr., would later marry Jeana Sooy, the daughter of Noah Sooy, son of Yoos Sooy II and brother of Nicholas Sooy I. Her mother was Harriet Cavileer of Lower Bank. This *Chance* was likely one of the schooners in which Joseph Ball, John Cox, Charles Pettit, Richard Wescoat, and Timothy Shaler, were owners. All were associated with Batsto, and all profited handsomely from the sale of cargo from the *Venus*.] By the time of his triumphal return with the *Venus*, Captain Micajah Smith had already captured seven British vessels with his Sloop of War, *Sly* [some authorities list it as a schooner]. It is reported that his share of the sale of the *Venus* and her cargo amounted to over $30,000, a fantastic sum in those days. The wreck of the *Venus* still lies off Chestnut Neck at the bottom of the Mullica right where the British burned her.

In the autumn of 1778, New Jersey's rebel governor, Livingston, sent dispatch riders to Batsto and Chestnut Neck to warn the local people that the British navy had, at last, had enough. He warned that transports and troops were being sent out of New York to ravage the Mullica valley, destroy the Batsto Iron Works, and put an end, once and for all, to the privateers along the river. Chestnut Neck people were warned to save what they could. They sent most of the captured stores upriver, along with the vessels of light draft. Three ships made the open sea before the British navy put a stop to escape by blockading the coast, but ten vessels were caught still docked at Chestnut Neck.

Sir Henry Clinton, military governor of New York and commander-in-chief of His Majesty's forces in America, issued the command to "seize, pillage and destroy" this "nest of rebel pirates," and that was the intention of the British troops sent with the fleet. General Washington was also aware of the impending crisis and sent word to General Count Casmir Pulaski to take his legion to the area with the greatest haste. They arrived too late by a single day.

Sir Henry Clinton planned the expedition well. On September 30, 1778, Commander Henry Collins and his force of 1,690 men on nine British ships of war, two tenders, and two transports with three hundred Regulars and one hundred New Jersey Loyalists under Captain Patrick Ferguson on board, sailed from New York for the Mullica.

The British forces hove to off Old Inlet, the entrance to Great Bay and the Mullica, at noon on October 5, 1778. At daybreak on the 6th, the British troops began their invasion. At first, they were cautious. They took their lighter ships into the river and prepared to bombard the little fort. British troops drove away the militia that manned the fort, while others landed upstream to capture the town itself.

The militia seems to have included the sixty-man company of Captain Zephaniah Steelman, and also those of Captain Joseph Conover's company, both of Gloucester County. Numbering only in the area of a couple of hundred men and boys, the militia was outnumbered and outgunned. All they had to defend themselves were muskets which were no match for British cannon. They had no choice but to retreat towards Leed's Point. From their distant vantage point, they could see the smoke and flames from their homes, storehouses, and ships rising high above the marshes along their river.

Captain Ferguson supplied a description of the fort in his report:

> *The rebels had there erected a work with embrasures for six guns, on a level with the water, to*
> *rake the channel, and another upon a commanding eminence, with a platform for guns en barbette,*
> *in which, however, it was afterwards appeared that they had as yet placed no artillery.*

This does pose a question. What happened to the cannon from Captain Shaler's vessel that the legislature had paid Cox, Wescoat, and Clark to purchase the year before? Of that there is simply no record. Whether they would have made any difference in the outcome is debatable, but they weren't there, that's certain. Chestnut Neck is surrounded by marshland, and several cannon, placed to rake the hulls of the transports, may very well have made the British think twice about trying to take the fort. None of those who lost homes and property at Chestnut Neck, however, seemed to have complained about Cox, Clark, and Wescoat not delivering what was promised.

Perhaps, as has been suggested, they were needed elsewhere during the intervening year. Cox did manage to find a cannon or two to place on an island in the Mullica off Mordecai Landing just below The Forks.

The British high command had always intended that the troops proceed upriver and destroy the iron works at Batsto, as well as all the Mullica towns on the way, but they had gotten word of the approach of Pulaski's Legion. Navigating the lower Mullica had cautioned them against trying to sail even the smallest of their ships upriver where they could be prevented from getting back down again by the Legion. An overland march was also ruled out. After destroying all they could, they set sail for the open sea but ended up becalmed in Great Bay.

Now comes the story of betrayal. A man by the name of Juliat had deserted from the Hessian forces the year before and had joined Pulaski's Legion. On the pretext of a fishing trip, he and five others went out on the bay in a small boat and naturally were grabbed by the British. Juliat betrayed the location of the advance guard of the Legion to the British but also added, maliciously and untruthfully, that Pulaski had issued a "no quarter" order to his men. This infuriated the British troops, and plans were immediately made to turn the tables on this obstreperous general.

The advance guard of about fifty men was camped for the night out in what is now Mystic Islands, unaware of the impending doom approaching them from the bay. The surprise was complete. Every last one of the fifty was slaughtered as they slept.

The British were finally able to set sail for New York on the 22nd of October, leaving behind destruction and hatred, but failing completely at their purpose. They only hardened the attitudes of the local people against them and never made it to Batsto and the iron furnace there. [See Franklin Kemp's excellent book, *Nest of Rebel Pirates*, for a complete treatment of this subject.]

BATSTO OWNERSHIP CHANGES - MANAGEMENT DOESN'T

Under the able management of Joseph Ball, Batsto seems to have prospered throughout this period of the Revolutionary War. Now in 1778, there would be changes that provide a curious view into the internal affairs of the men who were in charge of supplying the army during the conflict.

By resolution of the Congress, John Cox became Assistant Quartermaster General of the Continental Army in March of 1778. Cox sold his interest in Batsto to Thomas Mayberry, an ironmaster who is supposed to have built a slitting mill at the Batsto works during his single year of ownership, but it may well be that the slitting mill was not built until 1783 by Joseph Ball. In 1779, Mayberry sold out to Joseph Ball at a great profit to himself.

Now comes the point of interest. Apparently another Assistant Quartermaster General, Charles Pettit, and the Quartermaster General, Nathaniel Greene, himself, acquired interests in the iron works. That meant that both were profiting from the production and sale of cannons and cannonballs to the army, of which they were the chief purchasing agents. Today, they would languish in federal prison. Back then, nobody seemed to think it strange. After the war, Charles Pettit would become the factor for Batsto in Philadelphia, selling its products in the markets of the city.

On April 20, 1779, Pettit wrote to General Greene:

> I have agreed for as many shares in Batsto as will now afford you, Col. Cox and myself one sixth each . . . the stock of coal being short, Mr. Ball blew the furnace out immediately on getting possession so that now she is idle, waiting for further stock. The only risk we run seems to be from the enemy and if they should learn we are casting cannon that may be something.

Though Pettit seems to have had a constant interest in the production and profits of Batsto, Joseph Ball, now as part owner, continued as manager. [Note: Samuel Pettit, a relative of Charles Pettit, married Hannah Sooy, daughter of Nicholas Sooy I and Sarah (Sears) Sooy of Green Bank on March 9, 1797.] It was during this period that Ball built a dam on the Mechescatauxin Creek, just northwest of Batsto Lake.

Batsto continued to prosper. In the summer of 1781, Joseph Ball built a forge on the Nescochague Creek. Up until this time, Batsto was confined to producing products that could be cast from molten iron. With Mayberry's slitting mill, things like nails could be produced. Iron pigs had to be shipped elsewhere for any other type of production. At around the same time, Ball also built something on the Mechescatauxin Creek that came to be called Ball's Folly. Some suggest that he may have tried an experiment in making gun powder. If he did, it wasn't a success. He may also have simply built a pond for ice skating, which would have been called a "folly" in the language of the time.

When the Quaker, Henry Drinker, shut down the Atsion Furnace, Lawrence Saltar kept the forge going, and some of Batsto's pig iron was shipped upriver to be forged at that location. When peace was declared in 1783, this little area of the pines had certainly done its share in seeing to the successful conclusion of this war for independence. Very few places in the colonies could lay claim to have produced as much war material than that manufactured at Batsto or that captured and brought to The Forks.

PEACE - AND AN OLD FRIEND RETURNS

On January 4, 1781, Charles Pettit, Assistant Quartermaster General, wrote William Richards a note addressed to him at Warwick Furnace:

> *From the favourable mention Colonel Cox has often made of you as a suitable person . . . I have for some time had it in contemplation to make some proposals to you respecting the management of Batsto Works, with which you are well acquainted. I have some time ago communicated this intention to Mr. Ball who has other matters in view for himself and therefore cannot long continue in charge of them.*

Within a short time, Richards was in charge of Batsto, though it seems he left his family behind at Warwick Furnace once again. Richards must have had a conflict with his nephew, Joseph Ball. Apparently Ball had not moved out of the mansion by the time his uncle arrived on the scene. In fact, Ball's residence on the hill may have been the reason Richards left his family back in Warwick.

Courtesy of Budd Wilson
Col. William Richards

With his management, Batsto began to prosper again. It was in 1781 that Ball started the building of a new forge on the Neschochague Creek which was intended to increase the profitability of the Batsto enterprise. Richards saw an excess of pig iron produced by the furnace and felt that it could not be sold at a profit if it had to "bear land carriage to market."

Ball was still around a year later. In fact, on April 26, 1782, Richards' diary notes that he "left the manamint [management] of Batsto Works to Mr. J. Ball." Richards didn't go very far though, for he was soon back at the helm.

The Battle of Yorktown and the subsequent surrender of General Lord Cornwallis seem to have caused an immediate slump in production. Munitions were not needed if there was no war.

By 1784, Batsto was for sale. An advertisement states:

> *A Furnace sufficiently large and commodious to produce upwards of 100 tons of pigs and castings per month. . .*
> *A Rolling and Slitting Mill, which, from the strength and construction of the works, and a large head of water, is capable of great execution.*
> *On the same dam are also a Saw-Mill and small Grist Mill.*
> *A Forge with four fires and two hammers, nearly new, well constructed and in good order, now at work, distant about half a mile from the Furnace, on another well adapted stream; on which is also an excellent, newly built Saw Mill; and near the Forge are some tenements for workmen and a large new Coal-House.*
> *Contiguous to the Furnace is a commodious Mansion-House, accommodated with a specious, well-cultivated garden. (Pennsylvania Packet, June 26, 1783)*

This advertisement brings up an interesting thought. The forge built by Ball that is listed as having "four fires and two hammers, may have been more than a simple forge or bloomery (a forge that also processed iron ore). It may have included all the processes of an advanced forge system (see "South Jersey Iron" in this section).

Richards, himself, bought Batsto. He didn't have much cash so he made the owners an offer to pay them in the iron he expected to produce. It doesn't seem like a very promising offer, but the owners had no other, and Richards was a known quantity. He formed a new company with Joseph Ball and Charles Pettit, each holding a one-third share. Richards was to be the manager of the works at an annual salary of 300 pounds. Pettit was to be the agent for the sale of Batsto goods in Philadelphia. Batsto continued to profit through several severe slumps in the market.

While there are no records to show it, Richards seems to have gained full control of the works by about 1790, and his son, Samuel, took over Pettit's job in Philadelphia.

Joseph Ball, Richards' nephew, continued his interest in the area even after the sale of Batsto. In 1787, he bought the house of his friend, Elijah Clark, that still stands by the lake formed from the damming of the Jackson (now Hammonton) Creek. On a more permanent basis, however, he lived in Philadelphia. Years of business success and association with the highest echelons of the military had given him respect beyond the confines of the pinelands towns. In 1791, he was elected a Director of the First Bank of the United States, and in the following year, along with Charles Pettit, helped established the Insurance Company of North America.

When Richards acquired Batsto, it included about 7,000 acres outright, plus the rights to mine the ore and cut the trees on thousands of acres more. Actually, Ball and Pettit weren't out of the Batsto picture completely. Each retained a one-third share. They agreed that Richards should manage the works, and Pettit would be the Philadelphia factor.

Richards' management continued to keep Batsto prosperous. In 1786, he rebuilt the furnace. It was not long before he was able to buy out Ball and Pettit and expand his estate. His management of the Batsto Works was more than simply that of a business enterprise. He saw himself as a paternal figure with all who worked for him. Everyone who needed anything applied to the "Big House," and Richards did his best to meet the need. He also insisted on one thing, however: His word was the law.

Colonel Richards did not plan on remaining at the helm all his life. His son, Samuel bought Atsion forge and furnace, and interests in Martha, Speedwell, and Weymouth furnaces. Another son, Jesse, was prepared for the Batsto management. In 1809, Colonel Richards, full of fame and wealth, retired to Mount Holly, where he lived another fourteen years.

JESSE RICHARDS MAKES HIS MARK

Courtesy of Budd Wilson

Jesse Richards

Son Jesse took over the reins of the Batsto management with his father's retirement and did so at a very promising time. Relations with both the French and the British were particularly strained, and war fever was again spreading amongst the people of the new United States.

The bog iron industry was approaching its highest point at this time, and the coming conflict with one or the other of those European nations promised a boom-time for the munitions of war.

Jesse lived in the mansion on the hill at Batsto, along with many members of his family. Life was not dull. His son, Thomas H., lived there with him. His brother, Samuel, who built the Atsion mansion in 1826, lived with his brother at Batsto off and on prior to that time. John Richards and his wife of Gloucester Furnace on the Atlantic County side of the Mullica were regular guests at the Batsto mansion.

When his father died in 1823, Batsto was auctioned off to settle his estate. It was purchased by Jesse's nephew, Thomas S. Richards, brother Samuel's son, who retained his uncle as manager. Six years later, Jesse managed to purchase a half interest in the Batsto establishment. Once again, he rebuilt the furnace which was producing about eight hundred tons each year.

Unfortunately, there were clouds on the horizon. The bog ore was near exhaustion. Competition from Pennsylvania furnaces was increasing just at the time when the bog ore was showing signs of giving out. Jesse Richards was not a man to be stopped by "little" problems. He was always searching for other ways to make the Batsto Works prosper.

During the 1830s, it is estimated that anywhere from two to three thousand shiploads of cargo were handled at The Forks. That makes an average of four to six shiploads per week heading up and down the Mullica just for Batsto alone. In 1837, Jesse Richards launched the schooner *Batsto*, and purchased another, the *Stranger*, for $3,000. The schooner *Frelinghuysen* was even built on the Batsto property in 1844.

There were at least two sawmills operating on the estate, producing lumber, shingles, lath, and other trimmed lumber for both local construction and for shipping elsewhere. Batsto was even making its own brick in the 1840s. By the 1850s, brick was being made by machine.

The Panic of 1837 that forced the collapse of William Walton Fleming at Atsion didn't seem to bother Batsto much. Diversification was the key. Jesse Richards kept so many modes of production going that he continued to make a profit, even if one was depressed.

On August 20, 1838, the furnace was stopped to put in a "hot blast," a new method of smelting iron ore. Jesse was keeping up with improvements. Unfortunately, the new method meant that the handwriting was on the wall for the charcoal-based furnaces of South Jersey. Not that anyone would notice, though. Business was still tremendous, but as the 1840s passed, each year showed a decrease in production. Jesse tried building a new form of furnace in 1841: the Cupola. He built another one in 1848. Then he had troubles with the cupola. In December of 1848 appears the notation: "Cupola idle for want of iron." In 1852, he built still another, but that was equally unsuccessful.

Jesse kept trying, though. In 1846, he built a glass factory, and the first glass was blown on the 6th of September of that year. A little over a year later on February 23, 1848, he built a second glass works. Three months after that, the first glass house burned to the ground. On the 29th of January, 1850, the second glass factory burned. Both were rebuilt.

There was one bright spot, though. On December 21st, 1846, a young man by the name of Robert Stewart came to work for Jesse Richards as his bookkeeper at a salary of $600 a year, plus house. He became a loyal employee and helped to carry the enterprise through its waning years.

THE GREAT HEART OF BATSTO CEASES TO BEAT

Batsto had yet to suffer its worst disaster. On June 17th, 1854, Jesse Richards died. He was buried in the Pleasant Mills churchyard, and the mourning of all of Washington Township was genuine. Jesse Richards had been an able manager of the Batsto estate, keeping watch over those who worked for him with paternalistic care and concern.

To his neighbors in Washington Township, he was always honest, open and sincere. He served as clerk of the township in 1809, 1811, 1840, and 1841, and as Judge of Elections in 1810, 1811, 1821, and 1831. From 1811 through 1814, 1820 through 1824, and 1826 through 1845, he served on the Burlington County Board of Chosen Freeholders, a total of twenty-six years in county office! His cousin Thomas K. Richards succeeded him on the Board of Freeholders, serving from 1848 through 1853. His son, Thomas H. Richards served on the township committee in 1838 and 1839, 1841 through 1843, and from 1846 until 1853. Only Jesse Evans of Martha exceeded Jesse in public service.

Richards was never a rich man, he simply managed well. He seemed to be everywhere in the huge operation, and no detail was too small to escape his notice. That Batsto prospered for so long while other enterprises in the pines and throughout the country collapsed is due solely to Jesse Richards' great business skill.

When Jesse died, the heart went out of Batsto. His energy and skill had carried it for so many years. Now that was gone. His sons, Thomas H., Jesse, Jr., and Samuel P. Inherited his estate, along with his three daughters, Elizabeth, Ann Maria, and Sarah. Thomas H. tried to carry on from the "big house" but lacked the skill. Facing poor economic conditions and cheated out of thousands by one of its agents, Batsto began to shrivel. In 1856 and 1857, the cupola failed to operate. On August 8, 1858, it was torn down. After ninety years of operation, the Batsto Iron Furnace was no more.

Nothing else seemed to work either. The glass factory was operating through the 1850s with the exception of 1857 when no glass was produced. One of the sawmills broke down and had to be repaired. Thomas Richards tried to encourage farming and planted cranberry bogs on the Batsto estate where once ore had been dug from the riverbeds. The railroads came close, but never close enough. Goods were carted to the banks of the Mullica over the road built in 1853 to the bridge above The Forks. Some were stored and then loaded on sloops, and much was carried across the river, continuing their wagon-ride to the railroad at Weymouth Station (Elwood).

Then came a true sign of the times: the workers went on strike "on account of not receiving cash." Throughout the previous century, most enterprises, especially rural ones, had operated on an almost cashless basis. Workers were paid in store credits, which at Batsto were most advantageous to them, though at other places, worked to the profit of the owner. They couldn't travel far from home, so they had to buy their goods at the "company store" anyway. By the time of the Civil War, however, all that was changing. Men who had "seen the world," or at least much of the United States, were demanding cash. Cash freed them to move elsewhere, or at least gave them the opportunity to find bargains outside of the company store.

Robert Stewart was, indeed, a tragic figure. In October, 1860, the Richards' heirs gave him the management of Batsto. Stewart kept his nose in the books and didn't presume to run for township or county office. He often didn't receive his own salary, and he loaned money to the estate, but his diligence availed him nothing. He finally even had to sue the Richards family for back wages. He put his whole heart into the town and did everything he could to keep Batsto running, but no amount of dedication and devotion could prevent the closing curtain from descending.

The Richards' estate once again suffered serious losses through its New York agent, and the heirs were forced to sell over thirty thousand acres to the Batsto Farm and Agricultural Company for real estate development. In 1867, the glass factories ceased their operations.

Then came the great fire. On the night of February 23, 1874, sparks from Robert Stewart's own chimney set the cedar shake roof of his house on fire. Like so many pinelands towns, Batsto lived in constant dread of that cry of "Fire!" in the night. It meant havoc, destruction, and loss. Bucket brigades were no match for tinder-dry houses. By sunrise, seventeen of Batsto's houses were gone, consumed by the raging flames. The survivors were the big house, the grist mill, the store, the glass factory buildings and one house out of eight that stood in a row facing the lake on the village side. Only the few houses which still remain were spared in the village itself. Over half the families who called Batsto home were destitute, without shelter or possessions.

WATER, LAND, AND GREED

Batsto was put up for sale. Joseph Wharton of Philadelphia knew a bargain when he saw one though most of his friends probably thought he was daft. He paid $14,000 for a moldering village in the pines. The iron furnace was but a memory in 1876. The glass factory buildings were abandoned and decaying. The charred ruins of the village had been cleared by this time, leaving only the few remaining houses which had been untouched by the great fire. To his Philadelphia business associates, Wharton had been gypped.

Wharton was not addled in the head at age fifty though. Born in Philadelphia on the 3rd of March 1826, he was the fifth child of William and Deborah (Fisher) Wharton, and the couple would have five more children before they were through. He was educated by tutors, and, at the age of sixteen, his parents sent him to work for three years on a Chester County farm owned by Joseph Dalton in order to improve his health.

Instead of attending one of the fine colleges in the city, he went to work as a clerk in a mercantile house in 1845. Two years later, he and his brother started a white lead manufacturing plant. He bought some stock in the Lehigh Zinc Company and, within six years, was running the business as general manager. In 1873, he established the first nickel and copper alloy plant in the nation across the river in Camden.

Wharton became a director on the board of Bethlehem Iron Company, which later became Bethlehem Steel and eventually gained controlling interest in the company. He built the first armor plate plant in the country and became sole owner of three blast furnaces in Wharton, New Jersey, and one in Phillipsburg.

Though he never attended college, he became one of the founders of Swarthmore College, endowed a chair in history and economics, and served as chairman of the Board of Trustees for twenty-five years. Besides Swarthmore, the University of Pennsylvania was the object of his benefaction. He gave $500,000 to establish the Wharton School of Finance at the university.

He was at the height of his powers when he bought Batsto, which was a minor part of his holdings. He had great ideas for the pine barrens land, however. Hiring General Elias Wright as his general manager, he worked with Wright to develop plans to ship water to thirsty Philadelphia by gathering it from the aquifer underlying the pines and by damming the rivers to form huge reservoirs.

Actually, it was a great idea, at least one hundred years before its time. Officials of the City of Philadelphia were somewhat interested in his potable water, but they wanted him to give them title to his lands. *That* he would not do. When the New Jersey legislature refused to allow him to export the water, he turned to agriculture.

He tried almost everything having to do with agriculture at one time or another. A year after his purchase, he had his workers growing sugar beets at Batsto. When this didn't seem to be working, he imported purebred cattle and fed the beets to them. He built a large range barn out in the fields at Washington and cleared a great deal of land in the area. Though there had been a road to Sooy's Inn (Washington) from Batsto, he constructed a completely new road that ended up at his barns rather than at the site of the old Sooy Tavern. He acquired Atsion and turned the abandoned cotton factory into a huge cranberry-packing house. He grew cranberries, farmed hay and wheat, even raised peanuts in Atsion. He spent over $40,000 just on rebuilding the mansion at Batsto, where he lived from time to time.

Joseph Wharton and His Plan to Supply Philadelphia With Water - 1891

Courtesy of Budd Wilson

Out from Batsto reached his long tentacles to entwine ever more land into his control. He was not well-liked by the residents of the Mullica valley and the pines - for good reason. Legal niceties were rarely observed in this area of casual relationships. Here, everyone knew everyone else. Most likely, the people down the street and the people up the road were relatives, no matter how many "times removed" they might be. Property transfers by will or sale went unrecorded in Mount Holly for years.

Wharton knew this, and he used this knowledge to benefit himself. He didn't care what people thought of him. All he cared about was making money. First he bought land outright. Then he turned surveyors' errors to his advantage. He'd take a small chunk of forgotten property into his control and suddenly end up with hundreds of surrounding acres - to the loss of the families that had owned them for a century.

John Cox had been respected and admired. Jesse Richards had been loved. Joseph Wharton was despised and cursed by many a pinelands family along the Mullica and inland. Everywhere a person turned, it seemed, he found the fingers of Joseph Wharton gripping at his land.

When Jesse Richards died in 1854, everyone on the east side of the Mullica mourned his passing. When Wharton died in 1909, everyone breathed a sigh of relief. His estate managers continued to carry on for another forty years, but they never went at it with the aggressiveness of Wharton himself. They concentrated on producing profits, not in grabbing everyone's land by legal but unscrupulous means.

On August 27, 1896, Joseph Wharton extended an option to purchase his entire estate to one Peter Garrahan. He listed his lands in aggregate as totaling more than one hundred thousand acres. Peter Garrahan had apparently offered one million, two hundred thousand dollars for Wharton's property, and Wharton decided to sell. The option was dated for November 1st of 1896, though the deal was not concluded. In 1897, Garrahan was still trying to buy the property through a Camden attorney, Mr. Woodall. Nothing seems to have come of this.

In 1912, just three years after Wharton died, the officials of the State of New Jersey proposed that the state purchase the land for one million dollars. These foresighted officials realized the immense value of the land which Wharton had accumulated and the water resources controlled by that land. The people of New Jersey did not. In 1912, it was considered utter foolishness to waste good money on a wilderness. Besides that, it was too far from North Jersey to do any good, so who wanted it. One hundred three thousand voters did. It wasn't enough. One hundred twenty-three thousand voted against it.

In 1917, twelve thousand acres of the Wharton lands were sold to Daniel Frozier. It was on this acreage that the Amatol munitions factory and storage area would be built during World War I.

Forty years later, the United States government gave a covetous eye to the pinelands for a jet airport supply depot, and the people of New Jersey finally got worried. The Air Force was frustrated by Pennsylvania farmers in placing their facility out in Lancaster and announced that the pinelands it would be. New Jersians have one virtue: they are covetous of what they have. If they wouldn't let Joseph Wharton and Philadelphia steal New Jersey water, they sure as hell weren't about to let the United States government have it.

Governor Alfred E. Driscoll fought the Air Force plan with vigor. The legislature joined in and voted to set aside two million dollars to purchase approximately 56,000 acres of the estate which surrounded Batsto and took an option on the rest. That would at least put a crimp in the Air Force plan. Driscoll quickly signed the bill. During Governor Robert Meyner's administration, another forty thousand acres were purchased for one million dollars.

New Jersey tackled Batsto with much enthusiasm. In 1958, the State put a huge restoration program into effect. Pains were taken to see that experts were employed and the work of repair, restoration, and excavation done correctly to preserve for all times the heritage of this vastly important area of the state. Among those employees of the 1960s was Budd Wilson, Jr. of Green Bank. Budd was responsible for excavating the glass house at Batsto and made a thorough report of the job.

A Batsto Citizens' Advisory Committee was organized by local residents and experts in the preservation and historical fields who lived elsewhere in the state but came to love old Batsto. Pine Barrens conservationists strongly supported the state's careful supervision of the old Wharton estate. Hopes were high. So was enthusiasm.

G. Edwin Brumbaugh developed an excellent plan for the development and exposition of the Batsto complex in 1960. In this plan, Brumbaugh structured his document on Dr. Edward Alexander's "The Interpretation Philosophy of Colonial Williamsburg," written in 1955. The plan would have developed Batsto into an historical site of the highest caliber, one of the best state historical sites in the nation. It correctly emphasized the three major periods in Batsto's life: the Colonial and Revolutionary period - 1765 to 1783, the Richards Family period - 1784 to 1876, and the Wharton period - 1876 to 1954. Unfortunately, the plan would have required both commitment from successive administrations in Trenton and money. The dreams were wonderful. The reality would not match them.

The Batsto administrators and the Citizens' Committee had tried hard in the fifties and sixties. They had supported the archeological examination of several buildings, the glass house site, and the furnace site.

In the late 1970's though, something serious happened. Tax revenues began to dry up. People were no longer willing to see their hard-earned money go down the drain to support vast state programs. The expenses never grew less, they only grew more. Coupled with that were the needs and demands of the cities. People in the highly populated areas of northern and western New Jersey had crucial needs. Parks and historical preservation were not high on the agenda.

While administration after administration concentrated on the problems of the cities, of the schools, of welfare, of state government bureaucracies, there seemed little justification for expenditures on a pinelands town which most of the people of the state never heard of anyway. From the beginning of the original Batsto Plan, the idea was to attract visitors by using the little houses for craftspeople who would perform their tasks on the weekends for visitors' delight, and this was accomplished.

Farm animals were kept in the old barns around the mansion, and a stage coach driver delighted children with rides through the old village. Then even that became too much for the state to support. By the late seventies and eighties, less and less was being done in the village. A beautiful and necessary visitors' center was constructed which provides a good museum for visitor orientation. and efforts were made to attract more people in on weekends for craft festivals, Civil War reenactments, and the like.

Yet in the 1990's, things only seemed to get worse. Charges were made that the farm animals were being neglected. They were. The two horses which had so faithfully pulled thousands of happy youngsters through the village on the old stage were found to be ill. No one even realized that one of the horses couldn't even eat because of a mouth problem. At least the animals were given away to good homes, and the state paid the vet bill for the horses after they were far away from their Batsto hell-hole. The administration counter-charged that the Batsto Citizens' Committee brought the animals to the town in the first place but didn't provide care for them though State employees had been caring for them since 1960.

In 1993, a new plan was developed that vilified the former plan of Mr. Brumbaugh and strongly supported the concept that the only period which ought to be emphasized at Batsto was that of Joseph Wharton between the years of 1880 and 1890. It appears as if the State of New Jersey found itself saddled with a trust and wanted to seem as if it was doing its utmost to support that trust but with as little financial input as possible. Since another site in the state would be used to exemplify the iron period, Batsto would not be needed for that purpose. Ignoring the glass period completely (acknowledging that would require financial input), the report concluded that the only viable period for support at Batsto was that of Wharton.

Dressing Batsto up like an aging Victorian dowager would require no new expenditure of funds, and the 1993 report blithely dismissed any other emphasis which *would* require money and effort. Of all the important periods in Batsto's history, the report picked the least important and most objectionable one - the Wharton era - on which to concentrate.

Giving credit where it's due, the state administrators were doing their best with limited means. The members of the Batsto Citizens Committee, experts in their various fields, had the interests of Batsto at heart. The shame was that everyone was shouting at each other instead of listening.

The *real* shame is that historical interpretation can be completely shallow and empty of historical significance. The builder of Batsto was a significant pre-Revolutionary New Jersey entrepreneur and politician worthy of being remembered. Batsto was instrumental in supplying Washington's struggling army and the new states of New Jersey and Pennsylvania with arms and ammunition during the war with Great Britain. The Richards family dominated the pines for well over seventy years and contributed heavily to the development of New Jersey as a viable state. Jesse Richards was especially active in the government of Washington Township during his administration at Batsto and worked cooperatively with all the local residents.

Wharton was surely a man of vision and a wealthy entrepreneur. There is no doubt that he was extremely notorious and influential in the area and there probably would not be a Batsto if he hadn't had the foresight to propose his water scheme. Yet his pinelands enterprise was a sideline for him. Even his biographers practically ignore his pinelands venture. His reputation suffered locally from his willingness to use every legal means to part old families from their properties, which was not likely to endear him to New Jerseyians. He seems to have had no particular interest in Washington Township and its people except as a distant enterprise designed to increase his already considerable wealth.

Almost no archeological work of any significance has taken place at Batsto in recent years, which is sad. The highly reputable and scholarly Batsto Citizens Committee was alienated. There was even a period in which their "Citizens Gazette" and their historical booklets were banned from the state-supported store at Batsto, despite the fact that they are the only inexpensive and best-researched materials available on the entire area. The Citizens

Committee had to go to court on the basis of freedom of speech to get the state to allow their materials back into the Batsto gift shop. Even at this date, publications of the Citizens Committee are not sold in the store unless the state purchases them from the committee. Local residents who are completely unconnected to the Citizens Committee have been aware of the "plight" of Batsto and are concerned for the future of this beloved little town. The controversy hasn't done anyone any good.

In this day of limited budgets, Batsto's state administrators chose to pick a quarrel with the one group they had which was providing both money and expertise in support of valid archaeological investigations and historical interpretation at the site. It was foolish and certainly a detriment to carrying out the responsibility of the State of New Jersey to care for this invaluable historical site.

Fortunately, things seemed to have changed for the better. Pat Martinelli was appointed to administer the Batsto Historic Site, and what a breath of fresh air she has been. She has expertise and knowledge in the field of historical preservation, and she is a most pleasant person. The atmosphere at Batsto has completely changed almost overnight. The rangers and guides are courteous, friendly, helpful, and interested for the first time in years. Tom Pogranicy, who is in charge of the whole Wharton State Forest, is also committed to making Batsto attractive to visitors. Farm animals are back in the pasture once more, tended by their owners in a special agreement Mr. Pogranicy worked out with a local 4-H club. This old town in the pines has become a wonderful, comfortable place once again. Long may it remain so!

Batsto is a gem. Set in the thousands of acres of pinelands, its center and preservation is unique in the state. Of all the state historical areas, money could be spent to rebuild the old furnace and/or the glass house. Children could really gain an appreciation for the past contributions of the State of New Jersey to the Revolution and to the birth of our country instead of seeing it as worth only a "So sorry. I'm only passing through," from Generals Washington and Clinton and everyone else since that time. Perhaps by such rebuilding, our children and their children can appreciate the huge part the state has played in the growth and development of our nation in its formative years. Perhaps that would lessen the jokes about only living in New Jersey because you can't live anywhere else, or you would. Of course, we don't want to forget Joseph Wharton either. His plans show great foresight, though he certainly didn't make any local friends by trying every trick of the legal trade to gain their property.

Here in the pines lie the state's one last hope. How we handle not just Batsto, but all of the pines, will determine our children's future. Development and exploitation threaten. The State of New Jersey fiddles while Rome burns.

Yes, this town of little houses, now so silent in the twilight, whispers to us in the pines. "Walk my streets and feel from whence you came. If I had not been, neither would you be. I am what made your day possible. Charles Read, William Richards, Joseph Ball, John Cox, William and Jesse Richards, and, yes, even that old fox, Wharton, are what made this country strong. Their efforts helped make this country free from the tyranny of the old world. Their struggle in the pines helped make it possible for Liberty Enlightening the World to lift her lamp to the 'tired and poor' of that same old world, beckoning them to a new life in a new world. It was to my streets that they came, those tired and poor of Europe. They lived in my houses. They worked my furnace. They tended the fires of my glass houses. They were my molders and blowers and shapers. I gave them their start. I gave them hope."

Walk through Batsto some quiet evening. Here the ghosts of the past speak to us of the present even more clearly than they do at Atsion. Here are real houses in which people lived and died. Here are what are left of their hopes and dreams. For a moment, it may even seem as if the past were alive once again, and the spirits of children long ago grown old laugh and play in the deepening shadows.

The Mansion on the Hill

Photograph by William F. Augustine, Courtesy of Budd Wilson

If only trees could talk! On the crest of Batsto's Mansion Hill stand several sycamores. They were planted long before the first stone was ever set in place for the present mansion, before the "main" road was ever laid out from east to west. These trees are ancient enough to have seen the furnace at their feet produce cannon and cannonballs for Washington's army. They were there before the first of the remaining houses was built in the village, before grist mill, sawmill, and barns.

If they could tell us of birth, life, and death in the Jersey pines, what would they say? Long ago, when they were planted, the only road into Batsto came down from the north. Traffic from Philadelphia bound for the iron town came eastward on the Road to Little Egg Harbor to Quaker Bridge, then turned southward towards Batsto. From the bay, it turned off the old road at Sooy's Inn (Washington) and travelled the pre-Wharton Batsto-Washington Road until it joined the Quaker Bridge Road near the middle of Batsto Lake. Together, it came in to Batsto at the base of the Mansion Hill. From here, the traveller could either continue down the eastern side of the Batsto River along Canal Street to the Mullica or turn into the village, presuming there *was* any village across the dam at that time.

On a commanding hill beside this ancient road through the forests once stood a large structure whose origin is lost in time. Back before 1960, J. Albert Sharkey conducted a good deal of archaeological work on the Mansion Hill, including exploratory trenches dug on the west lawn. These trenches crossed early foundation walls which he believed were the foundations of Israel Pemberton's Whitcomb Manor. If they were, the house was sizable. The width of the foundations equals that of the current mansion's west wing which may have been built over the eastern portion of those early foundations. Was this Whitcomb Manor? We actually have no idea where Pemberton's house was located or even if it actually existed. Charles Read owned Batsto for two years also. Did he build a "mansion" for the manager of the works? What house or building stood on the commanding hill above the furnace before the first stone was laid for the current structure? It may well have been the structure that housed the managers of Batsto during the busy years of the Revolution.

The giant sycamores still stand along the southern side of the present mansion, but on the west, they are far from the edifice as we know it. Instead, they follow the course of a road now long lost to memory and foundations that have been buried under the sandy soil for more than one hundred fifty years. Did these ancient trees once stand sentinel over the early Mansion of the Batsto Iron Works? The house, if house it was, was made of wood (the foundations are too light to bear the weight of stone) and had no cellar under it. We don't really know any more about the structure which once stood on these foundations.

When the business entrepreneurs moved into the Pine Barrens to build the bog ore industry of southern New Jersey, one of the first things to be constructed was a house from which they could supervise their extensive domains. Even if they only intended to live at their iron plantations for a part of the time, they wanted to preside over the works in comfort and comparative luxury. The Honorable Charles Read built the Batsto Furnace in 1766 and may well have intended to utilize a preexisting structure, possibly that of the illusive Whitcomb Manor of Israel Pemberton, as his mansion headquarters. Unfortunately, Read had almost immediate financial difficulties and sold his interest in the Batsto Works within two years. Batsto was producing iron by this time though, and there would have been need for some type of housing for whoever was the manager. William Richards was in the iron town by 1768 but does not seem to have been the manager until after John Cox and Charles Thompson purchased the works in 1770. Richards left Batsto in 1775, and his nephew, Joseph Ball took over management.

Courtesy of Budd Wilson

The South Front of the Jesse Richards Mansion
This photograph may actually date from the very early Wharton period prior to his addition of porch and tower.

Ball lived at the works in the "mansion," which also seems to have housed John Cox on his frequent visits, but where and what was this "mansion?" After the successful conclusion of the Revolutionary War, Richards returned to Batsto as manager in 1781, but Joseph Ball apparently did not move out of the "mansion." This failure to vacate the mansion, as well as management conflicts, almost made Richards return to Pennsylvania. An advertisement appeared in the "Pennsylvania Packet" during 1783 offering the Batsto Works for sale. Mentioned was a "commodious Mansion-House, accompanied with a spacious, well-cultivated garden." Was this "commodious Mansion-House" the tiny section #2 or the only slightly larger section #3 of the present mansion as shown below? Yet there are those elusive and intriguing western foundations. The archeologists who have worked on the mansion hill seem to think that #2 was built in the late eighteenth century, but #3 was constructed in the first quarter of the nineteenth.

William Richards purchased Batsto in 1784 and lived there until his retirement in 1809, at which time, son Jesse moved into the "mansion." William was said to have lived in "baronial splendor" in a "large and commodious" mansion on the premises, but once again this begs the question: just where and what was this "mansion?" A 1790 map of the area shows a house labelled "W. Richards" near where the main road would be constructed in 1808 rather than on the hill itself, but most of these maps were drawn from memory and are notoriously inaccurate.

Most of the mansion which has towered over Batsto Village for so long was constructed in the nineteenth century. Excavations have been performed at various times and studies have been made of construction methods and detailing, especially during the tenure of G. Edwin Brumbaugh as Architect of Restorations in the 1960's.

Budd Wilson, Jr. participated in and conducted digs at the furnace site and the glass house sites during the 1960's, explored under the cellars of the mansion's west wing, and observed the Sharkey trenches and the foundation walls they bisected. Jack Cresson did excavation work under the east wing between 1985 and 1988. All of these men came to conclusions based on their observations and the data they collected.

Batsto's mansion, as we know it, is most impressive. It's thick stone walls seem so much more permanent than the frame structures common throughout South Jersey, and perhaps even more so than the early structure they replaced. The Richards family thought in terms of permanence. Samuel Richards, son of William and brother of Jesse, built his mansion at Atsion out of the local sandstone in 1826, and evidence exists that his father started the stone mansion at Batsto even before that time.

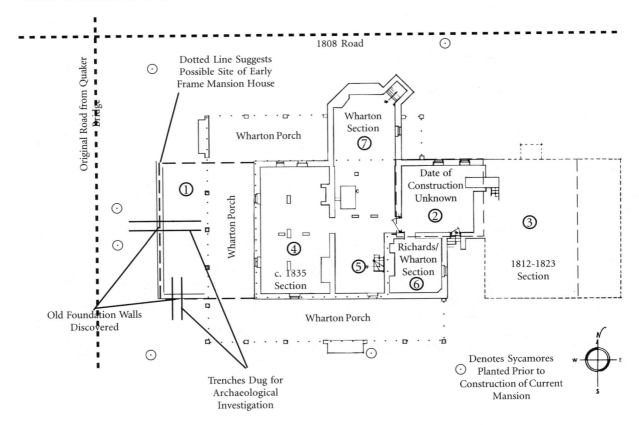

The North Side of the Jesse Richards Mansion
This view was taken during the era prior to
the Wharton reconstruction of 1878

As of the late-1980's, the following conclusions had been reached by those who had delved into the bowels of the Mansion on the Hill:

(1) At some early period, a large frame building occupied the western end of the mansion hill. Foundations exist underground outside of the western end of the current structure. It may have been the early mansion of revolutionary Batsto, but there is no historical indication as to when it was built or when it ceased to exist. There may be some evidence to suggest that it was destroyed by fire, which would had made subsequent builder(s) more inclined to work with stone. It may have faced west since the original road came in from the north and headed south to the river, and the early structure may have faced the road. The distance between the sycamores on the west end suggest that they may have framed the original steps to the frame mansion.

(2) The earliest existing part of the current structure is the section labelled #2 in the foundation plan. It has a parged (rough plastered) foundation like the Company Store, indicating that it may share the same construction date circa the late 1780's or perhaps even earlier. When this section was built, it stood either alone or was connected to a previously existing frame structure that occupied the space on the west end of the hill. It has a full basement, heavy stone foundation walls, and a drip course around the undisturbed sections of its walls. A drip course is a sloped extension of the foundation on the outside, built so that rainwater from the roof would hit the drip course and bounce off rather than run down the outside of the foundation wall and into the cellar. Gutters on the roof later obviated the necessity of this structural detail. This section also includes a walk-in fireplace that was later bricked up.

(3) Section #3 was added to Section #2 around 1812 - 1823, after William Richards had retired and Jesse had taken over the works. Jack Cresson of Moorestown did the archaeological work on the east end between 1985 and 1988 and determined that it was a later addition to section #2. It has a lighter brick foundation with no cellar. Underlying strata clearly show that the building was not standing when section #2 was built.

An agricultural zone existed prior to the construction of section #2. On top of that lies the debris that was dug out of the cellar hole when #2 was constructed. Above that is a layer of debris collected when section #2 was occupied prior to the construction of section #3. Finally, around the foundation walls of section #3 is a deposit formed when the foundations were dug for section #3. This order of strata clearly indicated that #3 was a later addition to section #2 and not the other way around. In 1988, Jack had to leave the mansion dig for work at the blacksmith's shop and the debris under the east end was never studied as completely as Jack would have wished. Though artifacts were found, there was insufficient time to examine them thoroughly. He has no doubt, though, of the dating of section #3.

(4) Jesse Richards built Section # 4 between 1832 and 1835, also adding Section #5 and possibly the first floor of Section #6. Budd Wilson's father, "Cap" Wilson, found evidence indicating that Jesse Richards made many purchases for furnishing his new section around the latter date.

(5) Joseph Wharton found the mansion in poor condition when he purchased Batsto in 1876. No one had lived here for ten years prior to his purchase, and there had been no money to keep it in repair. He added the tower of Section #6, and the dining room addition, Section #7. He also added a third story to Sections #2 and #3, built the massive staircase in Section #5, took off the Richards era porch and added another of his own, and completely rebuilt the interior of the house.

The immediate past administration at Batsto thought that Section #3 was the oldest section of the current mansion, despite the evidence of previous archaeological excavations under that section indicating otherwise and despite the construction techniques used on Section #2 that are older than those on Section #3. Whichever stone section was built first, neither seems sufficiently large enough to have been the home of William Richards and his nineteen children, even if they weren't all there at the same time. Was the one small section of the present house believed to have been built prior to 1800 the "large and commodious" mansion of William Richards? The original

Courtesy of Budd Wilson

Though the blotch on the photograph obscures it, this picture shows the mansion prior to the addition of the room at the top of the tower which was used as the first Batsto Fire Tower.

two-story section (#2) was not even large by the reduced expectations of those early times. Was it once but a stone addition to a large frame house, or was it built as a completely separate structure? Did the original structure succumb to fire or age before their first stone was ever set or did they both stand on the hill together at one time? Did Jesse Richards build Section #3 to replace the lost wooden structure?

The building which stood on the foundations found underground on the western part of the hill may indeed have been the mansion of the Revolutionary War period and may still have been standing as late as the William Richards era. That preexisting house may or may not have had a connection with the first section of the current structure to be built. The earliest section of the current mansion seems to have had no more than two rooms on each floor. It is built of stone, of which there are no other local examples with the exception of the old store, which is believed to be of an early date. The 1826 Atsion Mansion, the 1828 Grist Mill, and the other early stone outbuildings at Batsto, all date from the Jesse Richards era. The only other stone structure anywhere in the vicinity is an 1814 house at Leed's Point, which was originally the home of Daniel Leeds. In fact, this building may give us some indication of the dating of the Batsto Mansion. The original stone portion of this structure, without its frame addition, is about the same size as the east end of the Batsto Mansion, yet it is not large by today's standards.

Certainly even a four-room stone house is larger than the tiny wooden structures which must have composed the village in those early days, but there are Pennsylvania stone farm houses larger than either of these sections. The John Sooy House at Herman (the Old Homestead of the Sooy family) was not very large at the time period in question. Neither was the pre-1800 part of the old Driver/Sooy Farmhouse in Green Bank, but both had later additions made to them.

The Elijah Clark Mansion at Pleasant Mills/Sweetwater may afford a more likely idea of the type of home that may have existed at Batsto prior to the stone construction. This elegant colonial mansion is quite typical of a "large mansion" of the era and a fine example of the skills available to local builders before the Revolutionary War. If the small central, or perhaps the eastern, section of the present building was all that existed prior to Jesse Richards building of the western wing, what was the "large and commodious mansion" of William Richards?

Actually, this uncertainty is what makes archaeology and history fun. They present complicated puzzles, often with conflicting "solutions." Archaeologists and historians realize their limitations. We can only examine

The South Front of the Wharton Mansion

Courtesy of Budd Wilson

pieces of the puzzle and try to put them together. At any given time, even "experts" may well be completely wrong. The artifacts from the early digs were destroyed in the July 7, 1978 fire at Green Bank, which will necessitate archaeologists re-digging the area if any further light is to be shed on the early history of Batsto.

If the frame building which used to stand on the western portion of Mansion Hill was the original mansion, it would have made a suitable structure for the managers and owners of the Batsto Works. This structure would have occupied at least part of the physical space of the current west wing (#4) and extended almost to the sycamores on the west terrace, well beyond the current mansion, providing an ample house for the residence of John Cox and Joseph Ball. The foundation walls discovered on the west terrace of the present mansion, indications of preexisting foundations under the basement floor of the current west wing, the position of the sycamore trees relative to the present mansion and the location of the pre-revolutionary road from Quaker Bridge all seem to suggest that a frame edifice did occupy this commanding position on the hill overlooking the furnace.

A stone house (#2) may have joined the frame structure on the hill after the Revolutionary War, possibly after 1784 when William Richards returned to Batsto. Jack Cresson thinks that this central section was built prior to the time William Richards bought Batsto in 1784 and may have been standing during the Revolutionary War period. It is entirely possible that the first stone section was originally built as a completely separate house next to or behind the frame mansion of the colonial era. Either of these ideas would account for the small size of the first stone sections, which is to say that this section was never intended to *be* the actual mansion itself.

If it survived into the William Richards era, the wooden house may have been in deteriorating condition during the early Jesse Richards years, or perhaps Jesse simply wanted to make the entire structure fireproof. He may have built Section #3 as a replacement for the earlier structure.

At the commencement of the Wharton Era, General Elias Wright, employing the architectural firm of Sloan and Balderston of Philadelphia, had two additions made: the dining room extension towards what had been the front of the mansion facing the 1808 road (#7) and the tower in the rear "notch" (#6). He also added a story to the east end. The whole mansion was remodeled in the "Victorian" style, and the former front became the back. The workers rebuilt most of the rooms, added gables, casement windows, and an attic. Lighting, heating, and a water system were added to the building. The house was also made into two separate dwellings, the main house to the west and a caretaker's quarters in the east wing. A water tank was placed in the new tower and, in 1922, a fire observation room was built at the top.

Thus we now have some assurance that the major portions of the existing house were completed during the tenure of William and his son, Jesse Richards, as the period photographs indicate. We may also assume that a frame structure stood on the hill at the west end, though when it was actually removed is open to question. It is recorded that William Richards lived in "baronial splendor," and that would be difficult to say if his house included only the smallest surviving section. On the other hand, there is no proof that the frame structure was actually standing at the same time as any of the stone parts. It is an intriguing thought, however, and certainly helps to explain the lack of any seeming colonial antecedents in the present Mansion.

The Mansion, as it now stands, has thirty-six rooms, including a small room high above the third floor that had no access to it except by ladder until Joseph Wharton added a staircase. Legend has it that the room was used to hide escaped slaves during the period prior to the Civil War. There is no doubt that an Underground Railroad existed to assist runaways from the South in their perilous journey to freedom in the Northern states or Canada. The usual escape route was up through central Pennsylvania, however. Slaves making their way up the Delmarva Peninsula or through the main part of Maryland would have been able to go by land through Pennsylvania but would have had to find some way across the ever-dangerous Delaware Bay in order to get into New Jersey. They apparently did cross into Salem and Cumberland counties on their trip to New York City, but travelled through western Burlington County rather than through the pine barrens.

Unfortunately for the romantic legend, kind old Jesse Richards is reputed to have owned several slaves himself. New Jersey had abolished slavery in 1846, but the law had a loophole. It provided that slaves could stay with their former masters as "apprentices" and could not be "divorced" from such apprenticeships against their wishes. One of Jesse's daughters married a man who later became an officer in the Confederate army, and, as in much of South Jersey, there was a great deal of sympathy for the South at Batsto during the Richards era. There is no evidence that slaves were used to work the furnace, though they were used as house servants. Jesse Richards freed his slaves on his death in mid-1854, the year the Fugitive Slave Act was passed. The height of the Underground Railroad came after marshals fanned out through the North to capture escaped slaves as a result of this law. The

The North Side of the Wharton Mansion

legend may simply be a product of fertile imaginations and the intriguing nature of an almost inaccessible room, high in the Mansion. Unfortunately for the legend also, the room is a product of Wharton's remodelling and didn't exist prior to 1878.

The existing Mansion is the result of Wharton's remodelling and expanding work. Wharton was determined that his part-time home reflect his status and wealth, and this "Great House" certainly does that. From their mansion on the hill, successive generations of owners and managers could look out over their estate with a watchful eye. The Mansion dominates everything at Batsto. Every resident of the village would have to make their way up the hill to its door, hat in hand, to ask the master for help in any matter.

Mr. Brumbaugh, Architect of Restorations back in the 1960's, envisioned a return of the mansion to the Richards' period, though this may not be wise. So much of historical presentation today seems to prefer emphasizing only one particular period of a site's history, theoretically so as not to confuse the public. I doubt very much if the public would be confused by a mansion from the Wharton era overlooking a restored iron furnace and glass house from a different era.

Stripping away all later additions from a building often makes it less than it was. A better way would be to offer visual displays that elucidate the construction in each of its periods, leaving things as they are. Wharton's tower may not be as "authentic" as a house restored to the Richards' time, but it has raised its unique head into the pinelands' skies for nearly a century and a quarter, and we would all be the losers if the house were shorn of its crown.

The Southeast End of the Wharton Mansion
The buttonwoods still guard the mansion, as they have through the last two centuries.
The "dead soldier" in the foreground was an elm.

It is well worth the visitor's time to tour this old center of power on the hill to understand the pride of position each succeeding master of the estate must have felt as he gazed out over the extensive lands, industries, and people that were entrusted to his care. The Wharton additions have a charm and beauty of their own and provide a unique and attractive structure.

If one stands on the wide porch on a delightful Spring day, there is still something enticing and intoxicating about the view over the old town of Batsto. You can almost imagine it pulsing with life, as it did for so many years. For many, this little village was home for their whole lives, and their spirits still seem to breathe in the sighing of the wind.

The furnace ceased Vulcan's work almost a hundred and fifty years ago. The glass houses, too, are almost forgotten. Batsto has not had a resident manager/owner since Joseph Wharton died. Yet the ancient sycamores still stand their lonely sentinel over the Mansion on the Hill, just as they have for over two centuries.

The Barn Complex

1905

Courtesy of Budd Wilson

Of vast importance to every enterprise of this sort were the means of food production and transportation. There were no supermarkets in those days where people could buy any type of edible their heart desired. Everything had to be homegrown, and the barn complex was the heart of this operation.

The Pit Silo (1) and Range Barn (2) were built by Joseph Wharton as part of his experiment in cattle breeding. We are familiar with the silos that tower over the barns of today. The pit silo was their predecessor and was used for the same purpose. A pit was dug in the ground and covered over with a building. Inside was stored the grain which fed all the animals on the estate. Wharton also built a large barn complex at the town of Washington, a few miles from Batsto, where he kept approximately four hundred cattle. The Batsto complex held only about a hundred. At Washington, the pit silo separated the two sections of the barn.

The Pig Slaughter House (3) was used just for that. This was meat on the hoof, and a great deal of pork was consumed at Batsto during the nineteenth century. The animals' parts were boiled in a huge cauldron which is still inside this building and which was probably manufactured in the Batsto Furnace.

Records show that a water tower (4) was in use at Batsto before 1852, and the bricks in this water tower are the same as those used in the brick addition to the store in 1846. Inside this structure is a huge wooden cask which held the water. Water was pumped by a water ram to this tower for distribution to the various barns. The tower's height provided the pressure. Wharton built the tower on the Mansion to serve a similar purpose for the "Great House".

In the Carriage Barn (5) were kept all the conveyances necessary to the folk who lived in the Mansion. Whenever the master, mistress, or any of the guests needed transportation, a vehicle from this storage building was made ready for their use. The foundation for this building dates from the Richards period.

The Stable (6) housed the horses used by the ironmaster and his family. When someone ordered a carriage or a riding horse, the stableman would get one from this barn. Thus the finer horses were kept apart from those used in the business and on the farm.

The Threshing Barn (7) may have been built as late as the last half of the nineteenth century after Joseph Wharton had moved into the Mansion, but Brumbaugh dated it earlier than that. It was used for the threshing of wheat, a process of extracting the wheat germ from the husks so that it could be utilized. This building may have been moved to this site from another location.

A piggery (pig sty) (8) and sheep shed (9) complete the complex. A blacksmith/wheelwright's shop, a mule barn and a barn for the work horses also stand on the estate but are located a little distance away from the main complex above.

Note: According to the *Historical American Building Survey* made in 1971, for the National Register of Historic Places, the stone stable, cattle barn, threshing barn, mule barn, and wooded stable were built around 1830 during the tenure of Jesse Richards. The forage pits and sheep shed are circa 1865. The water tower is noted as being part of the Wharton complex of the 1870s. The piggery was supposedly a building that was moved to its present site.

The Pig Slaughter House, Water Tower, and Carriage Barn
1995

The Blacksmith Shop and Wheelwright's Shop

Courtesy of Budd Wilson

The Blacksmith Shop and Wheelwright's Shop - c. 1960

An integral part of every community into the twentieth century was the village blacksmith. Every metal part that was in need of repairs was taken to this Vulcan of the hearth. He made iron rims for wooden wagon wheels and iron rings for barrels, forged hand-wrought nails, and, in general, did any and everything that had to do with metal which the village people required in their daily lives. If there was no farrier in the community, he shod horses.

Having a furnace and forge handy made the South Jersey blacksmith's job a bit easier. Supplies didn't have to be brought by ocean voyage from somewhere far distant.

The blacksmith would be considered a common laborer today, but he was a respected member of the community in times gone by. It was an honorable job, requiring skill, strength, and endurance. Without his dedicated work, the life of the town would have broken down in short order. He had to be reliable and careful, for the lives of others depended on his work.

In this structure, the blacksmith's shop was in the section to the right, while a wheelwright's shop was to the left. Wheelwrights made the wooden wheels on which almost every moving vehicle ran. He also fixed the blacksmith's forged rim on the wooden wheels. John Wesley Miller was the blacksmith and wheelwright at Batsto during the last part of the nineteenth century. His son, Gus Miller took his father's place when his father was killed in an accident (see BULLTOWN AND TYLERTOWN).

This building was apparently built as two separate structures and moved to this location during the Wharton era. Budd Wilson, Jr. postulates that they originally stood near the river to the west of the furnace.

Interior of the Blacksmith's Shop

Interior of the Wheelwright's Shop

The Grist Mill

One of the main necessities of any estate like Batsto, or of any town anywhere, was a means of grinding the corn into meal and wheat into flour. This grist mill was built, at least as it now appears, by Thomas S. Richards in 1828, as an iron plate high in the wall attests, although a timber attributed to the mill bears the Roman numeral date of 1767. It is possible that Richards rebuilt a preexisting mill or used timbers from another structure in his 1828 project. This timber was found when the mill was rebuilt by the State of New Jersey. A 1783 advertisement for the sale of Batsto listed a grist mill on the property.

Just to the left of the mill is the corn crib. Huskers were able to stand in the upper level of the crib to remove the kernels from the husks and send them down the chute into the mill without having to load and unload them onto a wagon before they could be ground.

This mill, as originally built, was operated by a water wheel. The structure stands directly by the millrace and may have utilized an undershot wheel for power. With an undershot wheel, water rushed under a wheel with paddles which turned it. Far more efficient were overshot wheels where water was raised to a height above the wheel and dropped on to it. These wheels contained wooden "buckets" which caught the full amount of the falling water. Unfortunately, Southern New Jersey has very few places where water could be raised to sufficient height. Far more common were the breast wheels. These giant wheels could be as much as twelve to fifteen feet in width as well as in diameter. The water only had to be raised only six to eight feet high and contacted the wheel at midpoint. This provided less pressure than an overshot wheel, but was much more efficient than an undershot wheel.

Roland Robbins, principal archaeological investigator, determined in 1957 that it was turbine-driven at an early date in the nineteenth century. The late Mr. Dick Riker said, in an article on the Batsto Grist Mill which appeared in the Spring-Summer

Wooden pulleys and gears in the Grist Mill

1997 edition of the *Batsto Citizens Gazette*, that a Risdon water turbine made in Mount Holly was installed some time after 1832. "The water turbine was three times as efficient as the undershot wheel." A Pelton impulse turbine made by the D.A. Clay & Co. replaced the original turbine some time later.

The metal turbine sits in a lined pit and water is brought through a sluiceway and dropped into the pit, turning the turbine. The turbine was connected to a series of wooden gears and pulleys inside the structure which actually controlled the huge stones. The only known miller was Tom Baxter who worked by himself in the Batsto mill for twenty years between 1840 and 1860. Mr. Riker continues with figures for the 1850 production showing that the mill ground "10,000 bushels of grain, producing 250 tons of flour and feed a year."

The mill has two "runs" of stones but only one pair was used at a time. Riker says it is likely that one "run" was used "to mill small grains such as rye, buckwheat and barley, as well as wheat." Mr. Riker says that one of the "runs" were American-made granite stones which were made in one piece and brought by ship and cart to the mills where they would be used. The second "run" of stones in the Batsto mill are French Burr or Buhr stones. "Burr stones were imported as ballast stones in sailing vessels and then assembled, banded, and gaps filled with molten lead or Plaster of Paris."

Courtesy of the Batsto Citizens Gazette

Interior of the Grist Mill

I will let Mr. Riker continue:

> Grain on the top floor is fed down the chute (1), where the rate of flow can be controlled, into the hopper (2), where the flow can be slowed down if necessary, and on into the shoe (3). The shoe, agitated by the rotation of the damsel (4), assures an even and steady flow of grain to the eye (5) of the top stone. The damsel rides on the rynd, or stone cradle or bridge (6), which in turn is fastened to the upper or runner stone (7). The runner stone is driven by the mace (8), which is fixed on the end of a vertical shaft rising from a pulley and belt system that connects the ring and pinon gears in the basement of the mill. The mace locks into the runner or upper stone, and causes it to rotate when water is admitted to the turbine. The mace can also be raised or lowered by a lever under the stairs thereby varying the distance between the two stones. The pointed head on the mace is called the cockhead and the point itself is the cockeye.
>
> The grain is directed down the hole, or eye, in the center of the runner stone by a deflector called the shoe, into the gap between the runner stone and the bed stone (10), which is stationary. The miller adjusts the distance between the two stones to accommodate different grain sizes. He speeds or slows the runner stone by controlling the amount of water fed to the turbine. The speed with which the runner stone turns has to be closely controlled. Old sources indicate the proper speed for a five foot wheel is 97 rpm. A six foot stone would be spun at 81 rpm. [The Burr stones were more coarse and were rotated at a slower speed of 48 to 61 rpm.] The stones must never touch, and the miller 'keeps his nose to the grindstone' in order to smell for overheated stone or grain. The runner stone is dressed to be very slightly 'dished' and the miller adjusts the gap to approximately one sixteenth of an inch at the eye edge of the stone. At the outer edge, the stone just clears the bed stone. This provides for the 'flouring' of the meal as it moves from the inner edge to the outer edge of the paired stones. . . .

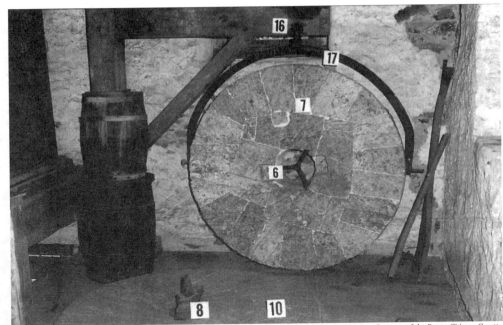

The Burr Stone

Centrifugal force carries the ground meal out along grooves cut in both sides of the casing or curb (11). The rotation of the runner stones moves the meal or flour to a chute that carries the meal to a basement bin called a cooling bin, where some of the heat generated by the grinding action can escape. There, a vertical endless belt with cups on it carries the meal or flour to the top floor again.

The force of gravity is again put to use, this time carrying the meal or flour down into the fifteen foot long bolter reel in the large bolter box on the back wall. The bolter separates the fines from the bran and husks as the meal or flour moves down the tipped tube of the bolter reel. It rotates at a speed of 36 to 40 rpm. Moving over a fine meshed fabric in the first half of the reel and a coarser mesh cloth in the second half, the flour would automatically separate into two grades. Material too coarse to pass through either mesh would exit the bolter reel at the far end and drop through a chute to the basement. The fine meal or flour would be bagged for human consumption while the coarser material, called middlings, would be bagged and sold separately for either human use or animal feed. The coarse material in the basement consisted of bran, husks and meal too coarse for the reel fabrics and would be sold for animal feed.

The heavy wooden framework near each run of stones is called a stone jack or crane (16) and is used by the miller to lift the runner stone and turn it on end so the miller can 'dress' his stones. The stone jack clamps (17) are placed on pins driven into holes drilled in the edge of the runner stone and the stone is lifted by turning the handle of the screw. Dressing the stone consists of recutting the grooves that carry the meal or flour to the edge of the stones when the mill is working. Eventually, the stones are worn from the act of grinding hard grain such as corn to a point where the grooves are no longer deep enough to move the meal outward. The miller very carefully pecks away with a 'mill pick' to deepen the grooves and sharpen the leading edge of each groove. Cutting the grooves requires considerable skill and is a slow and tedious job for the miller. When both stones are finished, the runner stone is lifted and put back in its place on the mace head. The grooves can be deepened many times before the stone is worn out. [reprinted with permission from the Spring-Summer 1997 issue of the *Batsto Citizens Gazette*]

While this old mill has remained still for some years, it is quite capable of grinding corn and grain with its great groved stone grinding wheels and its wooden pulleys and gears.

The General Store

Nathaniel R. Ewan, Photographer, Library of Congress
Courtesy of Budd Wilson

The store was another absolute essential for the people of the iron town. Transportation was poor in the pines and travel limited for the families of the workers who lived in the village. Within these walls, they had to find everything they needed for daily living.

For most of Batsto's first century and a half, hard cash was difficult to obtain. Paper money wasn't issued by the government until the Civil War, though banks and businesses did issue scrip. Unfortunately, script wasn't any good anywhere but at the bank or business which issued it. Much of the wages at Batsto were paid in store credits, by which the workers and their families could make purchases from this company store. At Batsto, they were always treated fairly, but many company stores liked to make a large profit for their owners at the expense of the workers. It wasn't until after the Civil War that workers began to protest. The Batsto workers went on strike in February of 1867 because they were not paid in cash.

It is estimated that an average of four to six ships a week made their way up the Mullica bound for The Forks in its heyday. On board were all the necessities of life for the villagers and the residents of the Great House. Jammed on the shelves of this store were bolts of cloth, articles of clothing, bonnets for the women, candy for the children, staples which were not produced at Batsto, halters and harnesses, patent medicines and elixirs - almost anything that the people of the town could want.

The eastern section of this building is thought by some to predate the Revolutionary War which would make it the oldest surviving structure in Batsto. Others think it dates from the early Richards period. Built of stone, which is unusual for South Jersey, the second floor had doors which opened at grade. The first floor doors on the opposite side opened at slightly above grade, necessitating a porch.

The original road from Quaker Bridge and Washington Tavern (or Sooy's Inn) came in from the north and divided as it came near the store. One branch went past the western side of the store, past the eastern side of the furnace and grist mill, and continued following the canal towards the distant Mullica. The lower section of this road was known as Canal Street and had several houses on it at one time, including two log cabins which were torn down in the nineteenth century. It was eventually extended to connect with the Batsto (or Stone) Landing on the Mullica and then ran on to Abe Nichols Landing and Crowleytown.

The eastern branch of the road ran between the mansion and the north face of the store building, though General Elias Wright made a beautiful Victorian lawn stretching around the front and side of the mansion which altered the road in that area.

The original company store was on the upper level of the building in a room which took up about three quarters of the building. G Edwin Brumbaugh, Architect of Restorations at Batsto in the 1960's, noted in a "Batsto Gazette" article that

> *it had a whitewashed, open joist ceiling; the walls were parged (rough plastered) and there was no baseboard at the floor. A vertical board partition (broken out around a steep stairs to the attic storage area) formed the west end of the room. Against this partition were two separate sections of shelving with counters in front.*
> *The balance of the room was a 'Sales Wareroom' with a steep, railed stairs to the floor below. The woodwork was painted black, and a stove, utilizing the chimney west of the board partition, completed the picture.*

Brumbaugh noted that the black woodwork was practical in a town made dirty by constant fires in the nearby furnace and was a custom followed in the workers' houses as well. He goes on to say that "the Batsto Account Book for 1810 to 1814 lists amazingly varied shipments to Batsto, from fabrics and clothing to implements and tools of all sorts, china, tableware, items of food, even furniture."

The Company Office lay behind the western partition with its own door to the outside. A stove stood in the center with its pipe running to the same chimney as the stove in the store. The room was completely plastered and had wooden baseboard.

The whole room below was used as a warehouse for storage and sale of the products of the nearby grist mill. Bins ran along the north wall for the various grains, and the rest of the floor space was used for sacks of flour and meal.

Courtesy of Budd Wilson

The North Side of the Company Store

The Southeast End of the Company Store

The western end was added in 1846-7, just after the coming of Robert Stewart as clerk. This brick addition was intended for the manager's office, which was moved out of the old section and into the new on June 12, 1847. Robert Stewart's office was on the upper floor with access from the north face of the building.

The Company Store was enlarged to include the area which had been office and the old office door became the new store door. The counters were turned to face the west. A large part of the room was retained for the storage of goods and larger items for sale. On the first floor, a storage room was added under the new office section, but the older grain room stayed the same.

The final change would come with the purchase of the Batsto Estate by Joseph Wharton in 1876. As has already been mentioned, General Elias Wright created a Victorian lawn for the mansion as was fashionable at that time and changed the location of the Company Store to the lower level. This took the traffic from in front of the mansion and moved it around to the other side of the building. The old road on the north side became part of the mansion's lawn.

A porch was added along the south and western sides. Since the north wall of the lower room had no windows because the building had been built into the hill on that side, four large windows were cut into the southern face to let in more air and light. A fireproof vault was added to the office.

Though Brumbaugh intended that both mansion and store would be restored to the Jesse Richards period, it is the Wharton period that has prevailed thus far.

High on top of the peak of this building resides a bell which was used to signal the laborers and workers within earshot. Its most frightening task must have come on that January night in 1874 when it rang out the warning of the fire which consumed much of the village.

The Sawmill

Courtesy of Budd Wilson

View from a postcard postmarked on Sept. 24, 1906

The first "manufacturing" business in the pinelands was that of producing cut lumber. Early pioneers used broadaxes to make hand-hewn timbers for their houses and barns but this was a laborious process. Quite early in the period of settlement, entrepreneurs set up sawmills, utilizing water power from the little rivers and streams of the area.

The first sawmill was built near Batsto by John Fort in 1761, though he was not able to make it a success. It was still standing when Charles Read built the first furnace in 1766, and a sawmill has continued in operation on the estate from that early date to the present. The early sawmills undoubtedly used a breast wheel for power. When the water was drained from this raceway during 1964 when the State of New Jersey was rebuilding the Wharton Saw Mill, Budd Wilson, who would become director of archaeology the following year, found evidence of an earlier mill structure which had been buried in the mill race.

The early saws were vertical blades which were moved up and down by a piston. They were really like a huge, two-man saw, held in the upright position by a frame. As the piston moved the blade up and down, the logs were fed into it by a carriage on which they rested. Power to move the carriage came from what was called a "tub" wheel. This was a small wheel set horizontally in a tub-like container, into which water was run via a trough. As the water poured through the "tub" it turned the wheel. This enabled the operators to have a separate source of power by which they could move the log carriage away from the saw blade, which was powered by the huge breast wheel.

By the time Joseph Wharton constructed this present mill, the turbine had come into being. Taking the idea of the tub wheel a step farther, someone invented a metal "wheel" or turbine which was larger and more powerful than the little tub wheel but operated on the same principle. This turbine soon replaced the huge wooden mill wheels of the past, though the old "water wheels" are far more picturesque.

Water from the lake is channelled into the turbine which is engaged from inside the mill by a single wheel. Power is transferred from the turbine to the machinery by a series of belts and pulleys. Safety is a major concern because, when the water is allowed to run through the turbine, every machine in the building is powered. An operator standing at the planer or jointer, for instance, cannot shut the power down on his machine if something goes wrong.

The wheel that regulates the water flow is near the great circular saw blades of the log cutter and the equivalent of the table saw, however. These huge blades, with their gigantic teeth, are the most dangerous machines at the mill. Both were totally unguarded. What the Office of Safety and Health Administration would have said if they saw men working under those conditions! Those blades could take off an arm or a leg in an instant or even cut a person in two if someone tripped into them.

The vertical saw and the circular saw each make quite identifiable cut patterns in the wood. The old pews of the Green Bank Church were said to be made with a vertical saw in the old Nicholas Sooy mill. Rough-cut circular sawn lumber has curved saw marks in it. If the lumber was planed after it was cut, though, it wouldn't show the marks.

All the lumber for every part of the houses in the village was cut at this sawmill. Logs were floated downstream to the mill where they were hauled inside to be cut. This mill has provisions for making square-cut lumber for framing, clapboards for siding, and shingles for the roofs.

It is a singular experience to be in the mill when all the machinery is operating. Though every machine is running at the same time and one certainly hears the sound of the belts and pulleys, it is strangely quiet compared to the mills of the twentieth century that were run by gasoline engines. There is no question that the coming of the internal combustion engine was an asset to the lumber industry everywhere. Once an engine was set in place and belts were connected to the power takeoff, the lumber mill became a movable operation. No longer tied to streams and rivers for power, small mills could be set up back in the woods. Here, the trees could be felled and cut into lumber, then loaded on wagons and hauled overland to a shipment point. When the timber ran out, the mill was simply packed up and moved.

Though noisier, the gasoline engine-powered mill was safer, too. If you had several machines in a mill, they weren't all running at the same time. You simply stopped the engine and changed belts to power another machine.

During the years in which the State of New Jersey has owned Batsto, several homes have been completely rebuilt using lumber cut at this mill. Though they have been thoroughly reconstructed, you can't tell it by their looks, except, perhaps if you examine them for saw marks, you'd see the circular pattern of the current mill, rather than the straight vertical line pattern of the old style saw blade.

The Sawmill after State Restoration

Front View of the Wharton-era Sawmill c. 1960 - Prior to Restoration

Rear View of the Wharton-era Sawmill c. 1960 - Prior to Restoration

South Jersey Iron

During the latter half of the eighteenth century, business entrepreneurs from the western towns of New Jersey like Burlington and Mount Holly, as well as from the Philadelphia area, found a veritable gold mine in the pine barrens.

The earliest settlers in the Mullica watershed had concentrated on building small farms and exploiting the timber of the area. This industry grew in proportion to the swelling population of New York and Philadelphia. As the cities grew, so did the necessity for building materials and firewood. When the first settlers sailed up the Mullica, they found stands of huge cedars, oaks, and pine spreading into the hinterland from the river and its tributaries. These first businessmen quickly built sawmills to process the timber into usable lumber. Others began converting it into charcoal and cord wood for consumption as fuel. All of these products were shipped from docks built by the early landholders like the Sooys at Green Bank and the Leeks at Wading River.

Perhaps it will never be known what amateur chemist first gazed into the dark cedar waters of the little rivers and wondered if they contained more than decayed vegetable matter, but certainly the Honorable Charles Read had experiments performed to determine if there was an iron content in the bogs along the rivers before he invested in the construction of Batsto and Atsion. When he found that they boasted a high iron content, he immediately began buying up land or the rights to mine ore on the land, and built furnaces.

After the tremendous profits made during the Revolutionary War by the owners of Batsto, there was no stopping increased investment in producing this native South Jersey product. Furnace after furnace was constructed, and all the streams and bogs of the area were exploited. The era of South Jersey iron ended as quickly as it had originated. By 1850, competition from Pennsylvania's natural ore fields and furnaces as well as a depletion of the ore beds and the forests which provided the fuel for the furnaces signaled the speedy demise of this once-profitable industry in the pines. While Batsto was, with diligent work and oversight, generally prosperous, as, it seems, was Martha, many of the other little furnaces were marginal at best.

Courtesy of Stephen V. Lee, Jr.

Speedwell Furnace
(1) the Water Wheel; (2) the Bellows Building; (3) the Furnace; (4) the Casting House

A furnace required beds of nearby ore, unlimited fuel, water power, oyster and clam shells for flux, and a means of moving its products to market. Batsto had these items in abundance. There was plenty of ore in the bogs of Washington Township. There was ample water power provided by the damming of the Batsto River. A huge supply of shells and means of transportation were available on the navigable Mullica to within a reasonable distance from the furnace site itself. Oyster and clam shells in quantity were as near as Great Bay. Finished products, whether cast iron items or pigs, could be floated downriver on barges to landings on deeper water where they were loaded into coastal vessels for transport to the cities, or they were loaded in carts and taken to Batsto Landing on the Mullica for loading on the ships.

By the mid-1800's, Batsto furnace was gone. We can gain insight into what it looked like though from the photograph of Speedwell Furnace. Its buildings lasted well into the period when photography came into popularity and thus are preserved for future generations. The photograph on the previous page is the only known photograph of one of the local South Jersey iron furnaces. Charles Boyer shows it as Hanover Furnace in his book, *Early Forges and Furnaces in New Jersey*, but this photograph came from Steven V. Lee, Jr. of Speedwell and is part of his collection of early Speedwell photographs, so we'll call it Speedwell Furnace. Several of the major buildings of the actual furnace are clearly visible, though they are much worse for wear in the passage of time. Not much happened at Speedwell after the collapse of the iron industry. The Lee family were interested in cranberry production, not in building new industrial complexes in the pines. They didn't need to tear down the furnace buildings to make way for something else. Perhaps that's why the buildings simply remained standing until they finally fell apart from age and the onslaught of the years.

The sands of the pinelands are filled with a chemical form of iron which leaches through them into the numerous streams and bogs into the dark cedar-waters. Here it combines with oxygen and decaying vegetable matter and precipitates back into the bogs. Over a period of years, the glop (what else does one call it?) at the bottom of the bogs becomes filled with iron content. Early entrepreneurs found that this material (that is a more genteel word) could be dug from the bogs with shovels. It could then be heated in furnaces by means of charcoal made from the local trees and mixed with flux composed of crushed oyster and clam shells, and the resulting molten iron poured off into pigs or cast into various necessary products. These products had a ready sale in the nearby cities, which were connected to the pines by the large number of coastal schooners plying the Mullica, Great Bay, and the Atlantic Ocean.

I always thought that the iron-colored rocks lying around the area were the ore dug from the streambeds. Not so. There certainly is iron in the hard sandbeds of the rivers, but it has too much sand mixed with it to be useful. The real "ore" that was mined from the bogs was the semisolid muck that was loaded with iron oxides called limonite. Only if left in contact with the open air for an extended period of time did it harden into the rocklike substance most of us would think of as "iron ore."

Given the presence of iron in the bogs, a furnace or "forge" would have to have power to run the bellows, without which there could be no "blast." A low-lying area would have to be dammed to form a lake, whose head would raise the level of the water high enough to power a water wheel. In the pines, the first wheels were probably breast wheels. In these, the water did not need to be raised to the entire height of a 15' wheel, but only to the halfway mark of about 8'. Given the fact that the pinelands terrain was low, this was a practical procedure. Breast wheels were almost fifteen feet wide, though, and we know that the Batsto wheel fit in a channel that was only five feet wide. Given the height of the lake above the bottom of the wheel, it is assumed that Batsto Furnace boasted an undershot wheel.

Site construction for a new furnace would have to begin by laying out a likely position for a dam that would back up the waters of a stream to provide power for the complex. Then a race would have to have been dug to bring that water to the furnace site. The lake could be deepened and the first ore obtained by the enterprise by digging it out of the area that would later be flooded by the rising waters backed up by the new dam. By the time the buildings were constructed, the lake would have been high enough to divert its waters through the head race and start the great wheel turning.

The main buildings of a furnace consisted of the water wheel, the bellows building, the main furnace itself, and the casting shed. In the photograph of Speedwell Furnace (or Hanover?), just a portion of the water wheel can be seen at (1) in the far left of the complex. Structure (2) housed the huge bellows which provided the draft for the fire in the furnace itself (3).

The furnace was made with an interior of brick, an exterior faced with stone, and looked like a truncated pyramid. Missing from the photograph is the wooden ramp that would have led from the hillside on the right to the top of the furnace structure. This ramp enabled the workmen to dump the charcoal, iron ore, and flux into the top.

The interior of the furnace widened from the top to a chamber about three quarter of the way down called the "bosh." The chamber then narrowed, and the molten ore ran into the crucible at the bottom of the furnace called the "hearth." After reaching the hearth, it was drained off into the casting house (4) and made into pigs or into various implements for the home and farm such as kettles, stoves, etc. Pigs had to be shipped to a forge or slitting mill for further work before it would become useful products.

In order to understand the process of producing iron in South Jersey, we must review the process itself which had been developed in Europe over centuries. Jack Chard, in an article in the Spring, 1971 issue of the "Northeast Historical Archaeology Journal," notes that "iron is never found in nature as the metal itself." "Iron ores, he says, are oxides, that is, iron combined with oxygen. "If charcoal is mixed with iron oxide ore and heated the carbon of the charcoal will combine with the oxygen in the iron ore to produce metallic iron and the gaseous oxides of carbon."

Even prior to the thirteenth century, primitive bloomeries were developed which were simple hearths "on which chunks of iron ore were heated with charcoal in a blast of air." At first, the wind supplied the air, but a bellows was soon devised from two boards and leather. The carbon in the charcoal

> reacted with the iron oxide ore, and metallic iron was produced as a spongy mass mixed up with partly fused slag and earthy matter. This pasty mass was dragged out from the hearth and hammered to consolidate it and squeeze out the foreign matter. . . . The bloomery was improved . . . as early as the 13th and 14th centuries by adding a low vertical shaft (perhaps six to ten feet high) to feed the charcoal and ore to the hearth, and get the benefit of some preheating of the charge. By around 1400 improved water-wheel driven bellows were developed and furnaces were built higher. This resulted in a striking change in the product of the furnace. The blast furnace was born. (Chard)

The spongy iron had to work its way down through the furnace and thus remained in contact with the hot charcoal for some time. Molten iron collected in the crucible at the bottom of the furnace. The earthy matter, or slag, remained at the top. This molten iron could then be drawn off at about half-day intervals and run into channels made in the sand of the casting floor. Unfortunately, this iron contained about 3 1/2% carbon, which made the resulting "pig" very brittle. The early bloomery had produced a mass of iron that could be forged. With the blast furnace, more carbon would have to be removed if wrought iron was to be made.

Chard goes on to say that a second process, called a finery, was needed to remelt the iron pig with a blast of air. The carbon in the iron reacted with the oxygen in the air, producing carbon monoxide and dioxide. What was left was pure iron. This finery process had a drop hammer and a water-powered bellows to supply the blast and produced pieces of iron called "anconies." These rough anconies were reheated and forged into finished wrought iron bars in a chafery. The combined process of furnace, finery, and chafery produced a much greater quantity of iron than did the old bloomery, and the total process was often referred to as a "forge," though the processes could take place in different structures built at different places along a stream or streams. Most local "forges" with multiple "fires" probably included all of these processes.

There was yet another process which was needed to make fine steel. Iron completely without a carbon content could not be hardened. About 1/2% - 1% carbon was put back in the iron by reheating bars of wrought iron sealed in boxes with a carbon-bearing material. What came out of the boxes could be hardened if it was heated to a red heat and quickly cooled in water or oil. Now, however, it was very brittle. In order to temper it, it was once again reheated, this time to between 350 to 750 degrees Fahrenheit.

These numerous processes do confuse the terminology of our South Jersey iron industry. A "forge" might be a simple bloomery, producing a small quantity of usable iron directly from ore, or it could be the whole series of processes which turned pigs produced by a nearby furnace into the finished product of wrought iron. A rolling mill might also be built to turn heated wrought iron into sheets, which could then be run through a slitting mill. Here, huge cutting disks sliced the sheets of metal into narrow strips for such things as nails. A label such as "forge" or "slitting mill" doesn't tell you how many of the different processes were contained in one structure.

Prior to the Revolutionary War, Great Britain wanted her colonies to produce only raw iron for export to British industries in the Mother County, and British laws prevented the manufacture of finished iron products. That didn't completely prevent the colonists from having illegal machinery to produced such products, but it did keep such production low. With the conclusion of the war, however, there were no restraints, and the iron business grew tremendously.

To get back to Batsto Furnace, as soon as the ice melted on the lake and race so that the huge water wheel could turn, the work of getting the furnace back in operation was begun. A cold furnace was first filled with charcoal and a fire lighted at the top. After the fire burned down to the hearth, another load of charcoal was dumped into the top of the furnace and lighted, only this time it burned from the bottom up.

When the charcoal, with air from the bellows, was white hot, the furnace was charged from the top. A layer of ore was spread over the charcoal, then a layer of flux (crushed oyster or clam shells, later crushed limestone), then another layer of crushed ore, etc. until the furnace was full. The furnace was said to be in "blast" when air was applied from the bellows. Once in "blast" it would be operating continuously for the next eight or so months.

In about twenty-four hours from the first charging, the molten iron worked its way down to the hearth, while the cinder, combined with the flux, floated on top of the molten iron. Tap holes in the sides of the furnace were used to draw off the cinder and flux twice a day and the resulting slag carted away and piled nearby. Sometimes this slag was also crushed and fed back into the furnace to gain every last bit of iron that remained. Eventually, though, the slag was completely discarded. These slag piles are often the only visible reminders of this once-prosperous industry in the pines.

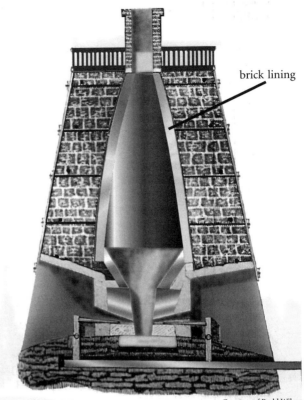

brick lining

Courtesy of Budd Wilson

A View Through the Tuyere Arches
into the Center of the Furnace
The mixture of crushed ore and flux was dumped into the top of the furnace onto the white-hot charcoal below. The molten iron was drawn off through the "tuyere" at the bottom. These two plates are from Overman's "The Manufacture of Iron," - 1850.

Courtesy of Budd Wilson

Side View of the Bellows
The bellows was powered by a water wheel and provided the air necessary for the fire to get to the white heat necessary to melt the iron ore.

Once the furnace was put into blast, it was worked twenty-four hours a day, every day, for the entire time the furnace was in blast. Usually, the men worked in two twelve-hour shifts, a grueling ordeal. No wonder the men frequented the nearby taverns to drown their exhaustion in hard drink.

Often, the owners of furnace or "forge" would build the accompanying processes to maximize their profits. Ball accomplished this at Batsto when he built the nearby "forge" on the Nescochague in 1781, and at Atsion, when Saltar, James, and Drinker built a furnace to join the pre-exiting forge in 1774. Nearby slitting mills, like the one built by Potts on the Oswego Branch of the Wading River would also complement the cycle.

One final note before we conclude this chapter on South Jersey iron. Most furnace complexes had a stamping mill of some kind to crush ore, slag, shells, and limestone so that they were ready to be mixed together and dumped into the top of the furnace itself, yet there seems to be no evidence that Batsto had such a "mill," at least not one powered by water. Other authors speak of great hammers shaking the earth with their pounding, but that was not apparently the case here.

Of course, while Batsto processed bog iron, there was no need for such hammers. The muck which was the bog iron was "roasted" to dry it out, at which point it was almost powdery. Shells and slag might still need crushing, but that was easily accomplished by a horse-driven stone wheel or fairly light hammers of 100 pounds or so. Only after "foreign" ore from northern New Jersey was brought in to supplement the dwindling bog ore about 1826 or 1827 was there a need for more crushing power, but there is still no evidence that a water-powered stamping mill was built at Batsto. Stamping and rolling mills were also used to crush the clay needed to make the pots at the Whister Glass Works, and Budd Wilson found one at the Batsto Glass Works, but again, it was a small affair, not a large, water-powered one.

No stamping mill is mentioned at Martha in the 1796 advertisement for sale by Isaac Potts. An 1805 advertisement does mention a stamping mill, but several 1809 entries in the Martha Diary seem to indicate that a water-powered mill was built at that time. Perhaps the earlier mill was a lighter-duty horse-powered mill, and the water-powered one was not built until the summer of 1809. Martha began using "mountain" ore (Martha's name for magnetite) at a much earlier date than did Batsto. The earliest reference in the Martha Diary seems to be for June 21, 1811, though it is certainly possible that it was used prior to that.

Courtesy of Budd Wilson

The Site of Batsto Furnace - Early 1960's

Jim Starkey, archaeologist for the State of New Jersey during the 1960's, supervised the "dig" at the furnace site. The furnace stood immediately below the southeast end of the dam on Batsto Lake where the pond is at the present time. This view is taken from the 1808 road as it approaches the dam crossing.

Conforming to the numbers on the photograph of Speedwell Furnace: (1) is the site of the water wheel; the bellows (2) would probably have been in close proximity to the wheel, while the furnace (3) came next (see photograph on the next page). The molding room (4) is off the picture to the left.

This photograph is taken towards the corner of the dam when the spillway would have allowed the lake's water into the race to drive the water wheel. The numbers correspond to those on the preceeding page. Once again, (4) is off the picture to the right. Budd Wilson, Jr. is center and Charles Hiller is in the foreground.

The location of the water wheel in the race.
The width of the trench suggests that a narrow undershot wheel was used to power the furnace bellows.
At the back of the site, Budd Wilson, Jr. is to the left and Charles Hiller to the right.

Budd Wilson, Jr. is in the middle of the photograph, James Albert Starkey, Jr. is in the back.

Batsto Glass

By 1840, Jesse Richards knew that iron production in South Jersey was on its way out. For almost eighty years, the bog iron deposits in the little rivers of New Jersey had provided a seemingly unending supply of iron ore for the little furnaces which hugged their banks. Thousands of acres of trees had fed the fires which roared in forges and furnaces until winter froze the great wheels which powered bellows.

Batsto had certainly done its part. Under his father, it had been the premiere producer of iron products in the area. Now, sadly, it was no longer competitive. Other great iron plantations had arisen after Batsto's founding and had floundered while Batsto was still producing, but Jesse could no longer ignore the inescapable fact that iron was dying in South Jersey.

Despite the inevitable, Jesse did not bear the Richards name for nothing. He became determined that his beloved town would live on, but it couldn't continue unless it provided work for those who lived in the village and nearby towns. Without work, the town would house but ghosts of the past in a very short time.

Jesse was willing to fight for what he believed in, and he believed in Batsto. In casting about for a replacement for the iron backbone, he didn't have far to look. All through southern New Jersey, glass manufacture was a growing business. South Jersey had excellent sands for the production of glass, an abundance of wood for fuel, and a ready supply of lime from a renewable resource: clam shells. Just down the road in Green Bank, Nicholas Sooy II had built a relatively successful glass factory that was producing both bottles and glass window panes using the German cylinder process pioneered in the American colonies by Wistar back in 1739.

Jesse decided to set up glass production near Batsto as early as 1845 when he went into partnership with James M. Brookfield at Nesco, up the road from Batsto, which was then called New Columbia. Brookfield was the "expert" at glassmaking and served as cutter on the new plant's first three firings. The partnership was shown on the Batsto ledgers as "Richards and Brookfield," while the glassworks was known as the New Columbia Glass Works. The Batsto plantation bore the expenses of this project, so it is obvious that Jesse intended it to be a replacement for the foundering iron business from the start. Jesse's brother was an experienced glass worker at Jackson, so he had excellent family advice available.

Only a year after he and Brookfield had started the New Columbia Glass Works, the partnership built the first glass house on the Batsto estate itself. That year was 1846, the year in which Jesse celebrated his sixty-sixth birthday, but he had no thought of retirement, as would later generations of Americans at that age.

Jesse kept up with the latest techniques in iron production, building a hot blast furnace in which to smelt iron in 1838. Though never as successful as his brother, Samuel, Jesse tried hard and bore the weight of hundreds of men, women, and children on his strong back for almost half a century. He had a great deal of determination, but, one thing he didn't have until his sixty-sixth year was Batsto itself.

Jesse had taken over the management of the Batsto plantation in 1809 when his father, William, retired. Unfortunately, when William Richards' will was probated in 1823, he left the estate in equal portions to all of his sons. That meant that the estate had to be sold in 1824. The place was bought by brother Samuel's son, Thomas S. Richards, Jesse's nephew. Not until 1829 was Jesse able to buy a half share in Batsto in his own right. For five years, he basically worked for his nephew, a rather humiliating circumstance for such a proud man.

The year 1846 was a triumph for sixty-six year old Jesse. At last he ascended to the seat of ownership and unchallenged power over the lands and people of Batsto. He knew that iron was on its way out, by that time. What he could not see, thankfully for this beloved man, was that Batsto itself was on its way out. In 1846, Jesse saw only hope and promise for his beloved enterprise in the pines, though he took a step in acquiring it that would eventually cause its demise many years later: he borrowed $13,425. That doesn't seem like much in today's world, but it was quite a sum a hundred and fifty years ago. It could never be repaid.

Brookfield built the first glass factory right in the Batsto village. Jesse decided that the ideal site for his new glass house was the field behind the sawmill, south of Bridge Street. The "Rent Roll" seems to indicate that the houses on Oak and Tuckahoe Streets, which ran on either side of the glass factory, were built after 1846 as well. When the complex was completed, it consisted of eight buildings: an oven, a pot house, two melting furnaces, a flattening house, a cutting house, a lime shed, and a wood shed, the whole spread over five acres. The only photograph of a section of the complex shows that the buildings were entirely of frame construction with the lumber cut in the Richards' sawmills close by. The Batsto clerk recorded under May 9th, 1846: "Raised new glass house." Four months later, on September 6th, he wrote: "blowed first glass at Batsto." The first recorded ship to sail down the Mullica carrying Batsto glass was the *John Wurts* which sailed for New York the following month.

That first blast, worked by blowers Charles Fisher, James Plunkett, Christopher Clark, George Heartman, Daniel Neippling, Lewis Hirsch, and John Barrett, ended on April 23rd, 1847.

During that first year of operation, the wooden glass house and pot room burned to the ground and had to be rebuilt. A second glass house was added to the complex in February of 1848. On January 29th, 1850, the new glass house burned to the ground. Though promptly rebuilt, it burned again in May of the following year and again in 1866.

Lest we think that this glass factory was a "small business," Sarah Ewing records the figures for 1850 in her excellent work, *Batsto Lights*, which show that this was quite a production.

Capital invested in the glass works	*$50,000.00*
Raw materials used, 8,000 cords of wood	*12,000.00*
5,600 lbs. Of lime	*1,568.00*
327 Hhd. of soda	*15,724.00*
Boxes	*2,500.00*
Pot makers	*600.00*

The investment produced 17,871 100-foot boxes of glass valued at $68,081.00, which was almost double the $36,000 worth of pipe produced by the iron cupola in 1850.

Except for one summer, that of 1866, the glass factory was never in operation during the months of June through August. A national recession halted production from June 1856 through September 1857. Otherwise, glass was being made continuously from 1846 through 1867.

After Jesse Richards died in 1854, only one factory remained in operation. His sons may have hired a man named J. Buckeleau to either manage the whole operation or at least to provide the workers. In 1859, it is recorded that "J. Buckeleau hands" began working at the furnace. In 1860, the notation changes to "Buckeleau and Holmes hands." The following year, the name of Buckeleau is no longer found.

Francis H. Holmes was a friend of Thomas Richards, Jesse's son, and his office in New York was consigned all of Batsto's glass in 1867. Holmes had taken over the production of glass at Batsto in May of that year, and, when the factory closed the next month, he received all the movable materials. The final date for its closing was June 15, 1867.

The Early Production of Window Lights

Glass was such a precious and valuable commodity in early America that many colonies laid a tax on homeowners based on the number of panes of glass in their house. Most of it had to be shipped directly from England, and housewives had to be content with animal hides or sheets of mica to keep out the cold and let in the light.

The earliest glass panes were the small diamond panes that appear so quaint today. These tiny bits of glass were all that could be safely transported across the ocean or in carts from town to town. Gradually, local industry began to produce crown glass, although there were only four or five glass factories of this type in the colonies. As Adeline Pepper records in her work on South Jersey glass,

> The blower would form a pear-shaped globule of glass which he then moved down to the "bottoming" hole, in from of which was a low wall to protect the man against the heat, where he twirled the parison which caused it to spread out. A helper then stepped up with a small gatherer of glass on a punty rod that he attached to the opposite side of the "blow." Then another workman touched a cold iron dipped in water to the blowpipe side, causing the pipe to separate. With one end of the parison now open, more twirling before the fire made the object basket-shaped.
>
> Suddenly, the blower would twirl the punty rod so fast that the basket, with a loud ruffling noise like the snap of a flag in the breeze, would flatten into a smooth round plate. … The disk, about 36 inches in diameter, was moved to a flat surface, separated from the rod, and placed in annealing ovens, warmed only to red heat. Sometimes the cooling process took two to three weeks.
>
> Small square or diamond panes were cut from the circle of glass, to be fitted into mullioned frames. The thick knot where the rod had been detached was excellent for panes around doors as the glass was translucent but not transparent.

This particular process was the English method, which produced small but fairly clear panes of glass. Another method, developed centuries before in Germany, started to gain popularity in the new United States. Pioneered by Wistar during the early 1700's, this cylinder method permitted large panes of glass to be manufactured but the resulting glass was not quite as clear as that in the English method and had ripples from the curvature of the cylinder. Those large panes of glass so beloved of Victorian architects were made possible through production techniques of the cylinder method.

GLASS PRODUCTION AT BATSTO

Glassmaking on the scale at which it was pursued at Batsto was a labor-intensive industry. It required wood-cutters to chop wood for the constant fires in the ovens and melting houses, scowmen to bring the wood downstream to Batsto village, carters to bring it to the glass house, haul in loads of sand and lime, and carry finished products to the docks or to the railroad for shipment elsewhere. Carts were pulled by horses, which meant that blacksmiths and wheelwrights had their place in the scheme of things as well. Carpenters were needed to make boxes for shipment of the finished product as well as to rebuild the glass houses. Sawmill workers had to keep a constant supply of lumber in stock for the rebuilding tasks and for construction of new houses for the workers. Experienced bricklayers built the various ovens and kilns necessary for production. All of these workers and their families had to be fed, which kept a host of farm workers busy as well. The most important men in the production of glass were the skilled craftsmen themselves who actually worked in the glass houses.

Glass production began with the raw materials: silica, soda, and lime. Sand (silica) was, of course, plentiful. Carters and scowmen, both on Batsto's payroll and acting as private contractors, were constantly bringing sand to the center of production. For five or six hours, it was burned in a calcining oven to rid it of moisture and any organic matter that had been mixed in with it. The heat also got rid of any carbonic acid in the sand. After it was cooled, it was sifted. Soda and lime were shipped in both by the Mullica and by the railroad to Weymouth Station (now Elwood) or from Atsion Station. Furnace ash, a form of soda ash, could also be used as part of the mixture or batch of raw materials.

Crushed shells were burned in a kiln and used for lime. Such a kiln once stood on the east side of Batsto Lake, about three hundred feet above the iron furnace site. The ledgers note that limestone was also shipped in for the same purpose. They note that the schooner *Mary* sailed from New York to Batsto carrying fifty tons of limestone, arriving at the village in June of 1854. The *Eureka*, a steamboat that long plied the Mullica, brought in limestone for Batsto's glass production.

Budd Wilson, Jr., who conducted the excavation of the glass factory site at Batsto, has provided original photographs taken from the *Annual Report of the Secretary of Internal Affairs of the Commonwealth of Pennsylvania* in 1900 that help to explain the process of glass production by the cylinder method. They were published again in a 1948 article that appeared in "The National Glass Budget" and are printed here to elucidate the method used to produce glass lights at Batsto.

Having assembled and prepared all the ingredients, vessels were needed in which they could be melted. Pot-making was an important skill. The pots had to be able to withstand the tremendous heat of the glass furnace without exploding, so it was important to see that they were properly made. Even at best, a pot would only last from three to six weeks.

The Pot House at Batsto measured thirty-four feet in width by sixty feet in length. Here, raw clay, burnt clay, called "German Clay" and pieces of broken pots to temper them were crushed and mixed together with in a large trough. The pots themselves were handmade inside cylindrical wooden stave molds which were bound together with iron hoops, much like barrels. We are familiar with a potter building up a pot on a wheel using long rolls of wet clay. The glass pots were built much the same way, though inside the mold. First, muslin was placed into the mold to cover the sides. Then the clay was built up around the edges and tapped in place with a mallet.

Finished pots stood about thirty inches high and tapered from around two inches thick at the bottom to about an inch at the top. After two days or so, the pots were deemed sufficiently dry and were removed from the molds. They then had to be smoothed every day until they were hard and dry. They then were cured for six to eight months.

Budd was unable to determine whether they were round or oval in cross section and notes that both types were used at the time.

A large supply of "green" pots was kept on hand, and, when needed, they would be moved to a "pot arch" where they were preheated to a red hot heat and kept that way for several hours to cure them. They were then taken to the melting furnace on a specially-designed pot carriage. The pots would have been carried into a room on the southwest corner where the temperature was kept at between eighty and one hundred degrees. They were then moved to the adjacent pot arch and heated to the temperature of the main furnace.

The building holding the melting furnace at Batsto was approximately sixty feet wide by eighty feet long. Along one side of each building ran a row of ovens that burned the soda ash and sand and also dried wood. Along the other side of each building were a storage room, a batch-preparing room, and the room in which the pots were cured. At each end was an ash pit. The glass furnaces themselves were trapezoidal in shape, measuring twenty feet

Courtesy of Budd Wilson, Jr.

Gathering the molten glass on the end of a blowpipe.

This series of photographs was taken from the *Annual Report of the Secretary of Internal Affairs of the Commonwealth of Pennsylvania* in 1900. While the photographs were not taken at Batsto, the glass production depicted is very similar to the methods used in the pines. One difference is that a separate oven was used to heat the batch. At Batsto, the batch was heated in the melting furnace.

six inches along one side and about seventeen feet on the other. The longer side was the glass blowers' side. The shorter side had a removable breast wall through which the pots with their batch were set.

Underlying the whole furnace was the firepit. Along the blowers' side were holes in the wall called ring holes, bye holes, and foot holes. The pots were placed on a siege in the front of a hole in the main furnace, and the end wall of the furnace was broken down so that the pot could be placed inside, after which it was sealed once again. The raw materials, called the batch, was prepared in a room along the west side of the building and put into the pots inside the furnace through a hole in the front of it. It took about twenty-four hours to turn the batch into molten glass or "metal." The foot holes were used to manipulate the pots onto the siege and were blocked with clay inserts when not being used. The blow pipes of the glass blowers were heated through the bye holes. After the pots had been placed on the siege and manipulated into place through the holes, the bye holes were blocked with clay "cookies," and the melting process began.

A master shearer was in charge of the melt. He saw that the furnace was properly stoked with wood by walking around and around the furnace,. At each end was a four-inch hole through which he shoved two to four foot long pieces of split wood called shiders to feed the fire. He kept this up for a period of six hours before he was relieved by another master shearer. When the furnace reached a white heat, the batch was shoveled into pots through the ring holes. As the heat increased and the batch melted, it was stirred either with a piece of wood or by a potato on an iron pole, and all impurities were skimmed from the surface. When the batch was fully melted and became clear, the furnace was opened up and allowed to cool for an hour, and the ash which had accumulated during the melt was removed.

All the holes were again plugged and the heat increased until the mixture was right for blowing. The master shearer's job lasted about two days and nights before he could turn everything over to the master blower. The window-light blowers were proud of their skill. The iron blowpipe weighed about thirty pounds and the molten glass gathered on the one end would weigh fifty to seventy pounds. Thus the blower had to lift over eighty pounds of pipe and hot molten glass and manipulate it without breaking it or burning himself or his helper. Two blowers usually worked a single pot, so, in a four-pot furnace, eight blowers worked along one side of the furnace, attended by eight helpers.

Forcing air through the blowpipe to form the hollow ball

A long narrow pit was built perpendicular to the furnace in front of each ring hole. This "swing" pit was the blower's position or berth. He would strip off his shirt and mount the foot board over the pit and walk up to the level of the furnace doors or ring hole. The pit and footboard were designed this way so that the blower could swing his blow pipe with its swelling bulb of molten glass on the end, the pit providing him clearance. On a string around his neck, the blower wore a wood mask called a cowl board which had eye slits filled with amber or blue glass. When he was ready to approach the tremendous heat of the furnace, he would clamp the mouthpiece of the cowl board between his teeth, protecting his face while leaving his hands free.

Each blower had a helper who was called a "tender" at the Batsto works though he was usually called a "gath-erer" elsewhere. The tender frequently started off the production by removing a plug called the "cookie" which stopped up the hole through which the batch had been placed into the pot, dipping the end of the blower's pipe into the pot of molten glass inside the furnace through the ring hole and gathering the molten glass on to the end of the blowpipe. The mass was then placed into a concave block of wood or iron either constantly doused with water or placed in a wooden tub of water and turned until a symmetrical shape was achieved. The process would be repeated a second, third, fourth, or even fifth or sixth time using progressively larger wooden blocks until the blower had enough material.

The blower then inflated the ball of molten glass by blowing through the opposite end of his pipe. He blew through a brass mouthpiece placed over the end of the pipe called a "bebee" and forced air through the pipe. This made a bubble inside the metal.

After moving to his bench over the swing pit, he swung the inflated ball over his pit, constantly turning it. He would carefully blow through the pipe until it lengthened into a cylinder. and create, basically, a huge, hollow glass bottle-like pendulum. Early in this century, in order to develop longer cylinders, the pipe would be hung from a swing-hole so that the cylinder would reach down into the pit. The weight of this swinging molten glass cylinder and the blow pipe were so great that the blower had to be chained in place. To many blowers, it was a matter of pride to scorn the chain, but accidents were plentiful, and many a blower was pulled off his high platform into the pit below by the weight of the swinging cylinder and pipe. As the pit was full of molten shards of glass, being pulled into it often meant death in a most horrible fashion. OSHA would have been appalled.

Courtesy of Budd Wilson, Jr.

The Swing Pit.
The worker on the left is swinging his blowpipe with the huge ball of glass attached so that it lengthens into a cylinder.

When the cylinder had reached the required length and the glass had cooled, the blower heaved it up to an iron crane and reheated it. He then held the huge glass bottle at the ring hole, blew into the opposite end of the pipe, and quickly sealed the end with his thumb. The expanding air blew a hole in the opposite end of the "bottle" which the blower quickly expanded to the side of the cylinder by turning it rapidly. It was now ready to be put in a cradle. Some blowers just couldn't resist swinging the huge cylinder overhead if he had an audience, and sometimes it broke apart and fragments of hot glass rained down on the workers below. Most of the time, though, the cylinder made it to the cradle without mishap, and the helper would touch the end near the blowpipe with a wet iron, breaking it from the pipe at that point leaving a piece called the "moille."

As it sat on its cradle, the cylinder was actually a five or six foot long bottle with a hole at both ends. After the glass had cooled somewhat, a thin strip or string of molten glass was wrapped around the cylinder and the ends were touched with a wet metal rod, breaking them off and leaving a perfect cylinder of glass.

A worker then threw sawdust into the cylinder and ran a hot iron rod back and forth along the bottom until it made a groove in the glass. The wet iron came into play again, and when the grove was touched, the cylinder split along whole length.

This split cylinder was carried into the flattening house, which, at Batsto, measured forty-six feet wide by eighty-six feet long and stood between the two melting furnaces. It included a flattening oven that was eighteen feet in diameter and had a center section with a five foot diameter. The curved sheet of glass was carried to the flattening oven where it was placed on a flattening table, turned to face the flattener, and reheated. When it became hot enough, it began to yield under its own weight. The flattener used a maple board to spread it flat and smoothed it with a wooden block on an iron rod by moving the wood from side to side. As soon as the glass would hold its shape, it was placed in an annealing oven for tempering. The sheet of glass measured approximately thirty-two by forty inches at this stage.

Cutting the ends off the cylinder.

After the glass had cooled, it was carried to the cutting house, a twenty-two by seventy-two foot structure. Here it was cut into window lights that varied in size from six by eight inches to twenty-six by thirty-six inches. Outranking in cast even the glassblowers were the cutters, who often came to work in a coat and tie. Their skill in knowing just how to cut the large and varied sheets of glass into its most efficient sizes without waste was much valued. They used a diamond-tipped cutting instrument and scored the glass along a straightedge. It was also their job to judge the quality of the glass and direct the packers to box them appropriately. The lights would then be packed into boxes for shipment.

The packing was also done in the cutting house, which measured twenty-two by seventy-two feet at Batsto. Wooden boxes made at the sawmill were used, and straw separated the layers of glass. Batsto graded the glass into several qualities. In the first years of production, the highest grade glass was called "Union Extra," the second grade "Union First," the third "Greenbush," and the fourth "Neponset." By 1851, the names used were "Star & Moon," "Jesse Richards," "Sterling," and "Washington."

Scoring and cutting the length of the cylinder

Storing the cylinders before moving them to the Flattening House

From 1846 to 1847, Batsto produced 6,511 boxes of window lights. By the 1850 - 1851 period, that quantity had risen to 19,550 boxes. The second factory, built in 1848, certainly helped to almost triple production. This quantity was the largest ever produced at Batsto when both factories were in operation through 1854. From 1854 through 1867, only one factory was operating, and of course the total number of boxes produced was considerably lower.

Between 1847 and 1854, most of the glass was carted to landings on the Mullica and shipped by coastal vessels to New York and Philadelphia. From 1854 through 1866, the boxes containing the window lights were loaded onto wagons and hauled overland to Weymouth Station (now Elwood) for shipment by rail. In 1866 until the factory ceased operations in 1867, the steamer *Eureka* carried the glass downriver to the cities.

Jesse Richards died in 1854, and, though the production of glass continued for another thirteen years, the light had gone out at Batsto with his passing. The fires were finally extinguished forever at the glass house on June 15th, 1867. For over twenty years, Batsto had produced window lights and trapezoidal lights for the streetlamps of Philadelphia and New York. Now all was gone. The skilled workers left to find employment elsewhere, and the debts crowded in on the Richards' heirs.

Courtesy of Budd Wilson

A Transport Sloop at the Atsion River Crossing of the Road to the Railroad
In the later 1800s, goods began to be shipped on the railroads. This dock and building stood on the Mullica near where the river comes the closest to the road in Sweetwater. It was in this location where the 1853 road out of Batsto crossed the Atsion (upper Mullica) River on a bridge which enabled wagonloads of glass to be carted to the railroad at Weymouth Station (now Elwood).

EXCAVATION OF THE GLASS FACTORY AT BATSTO

In 1960, James A. Starkey and Whitney Mullen conducted preliminary archeological excavation at the site of the Batsto Glass House in preparation for a thorough investigation and dig. The whole site was set with a ten-foot grid pattern, posthole corings were taken at the corners of the grid, and some exploratory trenches were dug between the corings.

The original intent was that at least part of the remains of the glass factory be reconstructed and part would be interpreted to the general public in situ. Budd Wilson, Jr. was the archeologist in charge of the excavation and worked with a former glassblower as a consultant and from two to eight laborers. He outlined the archeological work in an article entitled, "The Batsto Window Light Factory Excavation" in the Bulletin of the Archeological Society of New Jersey for December, 1971.

The next three years saw eight structures excavated: the flattening house, melting furnaces, the lime shed, the cutting house, an oven, the pot house, a wood storage area and a cellar hole that turned out to be unrelated to the glass factory itself. Among the artifacts were three types: building construction, industrial, and domestic. Stone, brick, refractory from the furnaces, nails, and some timbers made up the building construction material. Earthenware, stoneware, dark green glass bottles, clay tobacco pipe fragments, and a glass syringe were the domestic materials found. As could be expected at a site that operated for twenty years, the industrial artifacts were the most numerous. They included several thousand window glass fragments, cullet that would have been mixed with the batch, chunks of glass that had remained in the pots, pieces of discolored glass that were refuse, Moille, the part of the colored glass that had adhered to the blowpipes, glass threads and twists, and tubular pieces. Budd also found cast iron plates, grate bars for the ovens, sections of blowpipes, narrow gauge track, and gears.

The whole factory, including the wood storage area, covered over an acre of land. Budd noted that the buildings were of frame construction with siding of either clapboard or batten. The buildings which held the flattening furnace and the melting furnaces were gabled, with rather substantial foundations. The ovens were made of brick and other refractory material. He also says that both historical research and archeological excavation indicate that the melting furnaces had no large central chimney. An 1849 map of Batsto shows the location of the glass factory, and an 1875 drawing pinpoints all the buildings. An article published in the *New Republic* in 1875 indicates that the "roofs were caved in . . . and the walls were crumbling" at that time.

To help the reader understand the process of glassmaking and the excavation at Batsto, please refer to Budd's two drawings on the following page. Numbers indicate the buildings involved in the various processes and are indicated on the plan of the glass factory at Batsto on the top of the page. Letters designate the various areas within the Melting Furnace itself in the diagram at the bottom of the page.

Budd indicates that the process of producing glass actually began at the Pot House (#7), a thirty-four by sixty foot building the housed the facilities for making the German clay pots or crucibles that were used to melt the raw materials. These pots were made and stored in the Pot House until they were ready to be used.

There were two melting furnaces found at Batsto (sites #2 & #3). In describing Site #3, Budd notes that it was sixty by eighty feet and contained a large central room with two rows of smaller rooms to each side. We can refer to his diagram of the melting furnace on page 116. Pots were carried to the room at the southwest corner of the building (a) where the temperature was kept at between 80 and 100 degrees C. When needed, they were moved to the pot oven (b) and heated to the temperature of the main furnace.

They were then moved to the siege in front of the main furnace (c). The batch was taken from the Batch Room (d) and dumped into the pot through a hole in the furnace wall. The glassblower took his place at one of four benches on each side of the furnace in the swing pit (e), remove a clay plug in the furnace wall, and gather the metal on the end of his blowpipe. He then formed it on a hollowed-out wooden block until he had enough metal with which to make the cylinder. Forcing air through the blowpipe, he made a bubble inside the molten glass, gradually expanding this into a cylinder. He swung the cylinder back and forth in the pit below him until the glass was the proper thickness. The cylinder was broken from the blowpipe and the two ends cut off using strings of glass. The length of the cylinder was also cut.

Wooden racks held the cylinders until they were taken to the Flattening House (#1) where they were reheated and flattened by a worker smoothing the inside of the cylinder with a board. Finally, the resulting sheets of glass were taken to the Cutting House (#5) where they were cut into window lights of various sizes and packed for shipment.

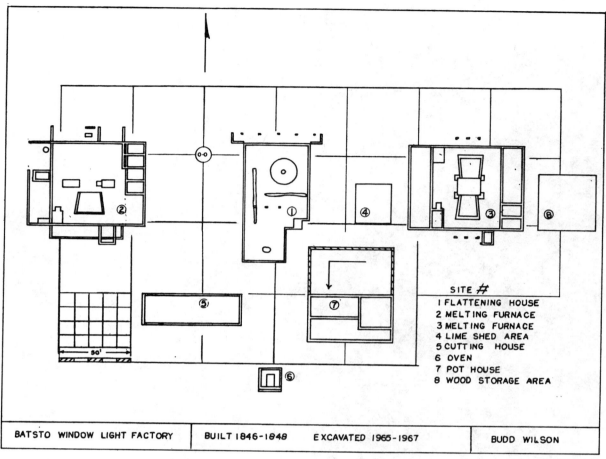

SITE #
1 FLATTENING HOUSE
2 MELTING FURNACE
3 MELTING FURNACE
4 LIME SHED AREA
5 CUTTING HOUSE
6 OVEN
7 POT HOUSE
8 WOOD STORAGE AREA

| BATSTO WINDOW LIGHT FACTORY | BUILT 1846-1848 | EXCAVATED 1965-1967 | BUDD WILSON |

Plan of the Glass Factory at Batsto

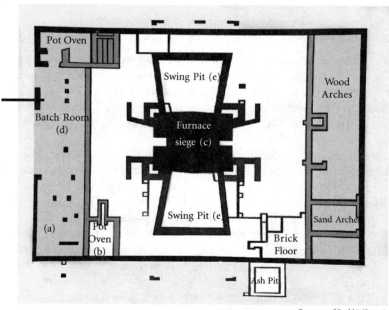

Illustration of the Batsto Glass House Interior
by Budd Wilson, Jr.

New Pond Dam

New Pond Dam

From the colonial days through the nineteenth century, water power was the most important requirement for the operation of an industry. In the pines, as elsewhere, water turned the wheels, and later the turbines, which powered the machinery of grist mills, sawmills, forge hammers, and furnace bellows. Without it, there was no means to power machinery until the steam engine became practical for general use. Every stream with a usable flow had several mills along its course, each with its mill dam and resulting lake to raise the water high enough to turn a wheel.

Every major stream which could be dammed for power was so. Atsion, Martha, Harrisville, and Hampton Furnace were all located on the little rivers of Washington Township. Even in areas where no town grew, grist mills and sawmills lined the streams. Obtaining permission to dam the river which ran through your land was the main task when acquiring ground for the construction of an industrial complex.

Batsto was blessed with two rivers and three tributary streams flowing together nearby which had the potential for supporting several local industries. John Fort dammed one of the rivers in the area for his sawmill in 1761, but the location of that mill and lake are unknown. Four years later, after acquiring Fort's property after the sawmill failed, Charles Read obtained permission from the Province to dam the Batsto River, and the resulting lake ran the furnace, grist mill and sawmill.

Elijah Clark, son of Thomas Clark, the founder of Clark's Landing on the Atlantic County side of the Mullica downstream from Lower Bank, bought three pieces of land at Sweetwater in 1757 and built a dam on what is now called the Hammonton Creek but has gone under several names including the Pleasant Mills Stream, Jackson Stream, and Clarks Mill Branch. He then built a sawmill on the resulting Clark's Pond.

A man by the name of Samuel Cripps had dammed the Nescochague Creek, which joins the Atsion River just behind the Batsto-Pleasant Mills Church, as early as 1740. In that year, he purchased land which was surveyed at 210 acres which was listed as "near Albertson's" on the "Pactcockeach branch." Here he built a sawmill below the new lake formed by the dam, and the pond was known as Samuel Cripps Mill Pond. The Nescochague was also known by the names Edgeackick, Edgeachaick, Checautoxin, Etomoquang, Nescochaque', and "West Mill" branch at various times. A Nathaniel Cripps is noted in the Wharton ledgers as owning the "Edgeackick Swamp" in 1728.

After the Revolutionary War, Joseph Ball, manager of the Batsto Works, decided to build a forge near the Batsto Furnace in order to take advantage of an excess production of iron pigs and the sale of a greater number of products than could be manufactured by the casting process alone. Samuel Cripps' mill was probably no longer in operation, and Ball built his new forge near that location. After the forge's construction, the pond was usually known as Forge Pond, though even as late as 1900, some maps still listed it as Samuel Cripps' Pond.

Joshua Lippincott

Ball also built the first dam on the Mechescatauxen, but its purpose is a mystery. Below the dam, Ball built something which has come down through history known only as "Ball's Folly." Unfortunately, there are no indications as to what Ball's Folly actually was. Ball was known to have experimented with the production of gunpowder, but his experiment seem to have failed (hopefully not in a big bang). Perhaps that was the reason for his new pond.

At any rate, when Joshua Lippencott and Augustus Richards bought the forge property on June 15, 1827, the deed granted the two men the right to dig a canal connecting the Nescochague with the Jackson (now Hammonton) Creek in order to increase the flow of water.

Late in the nineteenth century, more water was needed for the paper mill at Pleasant Mills. Consequently, a larger dam was constructed on the Atsion River just below its junction with the Mechescatauxen in 1895. The

New Pond Dam

119

resulting lake backed up the waters of both streams to form a sizable lake, and a new canal was dug to Forge Pond and Lake Nescochague. When it was completed, this canal cut across the Nescochague and traces of it are still evident. Large embankments were built on either side of New Pond dam with considerable underground cribbing. These embankments were extensive and are still quite obvious. Both dam and embankment were built to support local traffic.

All of the dams washed out in a 1939 storm. Only those at Lake Nescochague and Batsto were rebuilt.

Batsto Forge and the Nescochague

By the year 1780, the hostilities which had marked the war years since 1775 had calmed slightly, and the high-gear production of iron at Batsto had caused an overabundance of pig iron that had no immediate market. Joseph Ball, manager of the Batsto complex, surveyed the stacks of pig iron piling up near the furnace in front of his mansion with concern.

Batsto was set up to produce cast military products like cannon and cannonballs as well as domestic cast items, but it had no facility to forge the pigs into further products for sale. Until now, the pig iron had to be sold and transported to forges in the area, whose owners made the profit from their products. Ball decided to use the lull in the war to build a forge and slitting mill for the Batsto complex.

Having a forge of its own would enable Batsto to make wrought iron bars as well as bars for the slitting mill. A slitting mill was basically a giant, water-powered sheers that cut the thin bars that had been made from the pigs in the forge into nail rods which a smith then made into nails by hand.

By this time, William Richards had returned from his duties with the army, and Ball sent him to the Mount Holly Iron Works which had been burned by the British two years earlier. Here he was to get dimensions and pattern plates that could be used by the new Batsto Forge.

Ball, in the meantime, began the work to dam the Nescochague Creek near the Brainerd Church in Pleasant Mills. As has been previously mentioned, Samuel Cripps had dammed the creek as early as 1740, so Ball may have simply rebuilt the old dam rather than building a completely new one. He then had a forge building built, taking advantage of the water power provided by the lake.

The work was begun by digging a pit about eight feet deep, four feet wide, and twenty-five feet long, depending on the size of the hammer to be used. The bottom of this pit was paved with stone to a depth of four feet and the rest of the depth filled with sawn timbers cut 8" by 8" or 10" by 10" square. Long timbers were laid lengthwise in the pit side by side, while short timbers were laid crosswise. The whole structure was bolted together with through bolts.

This timber structure was not fastened to the stone foundation so that it could vibrate when struck by the giant hammer. This formed a shock absorber for the blows of the hammer, which could weigh as much as five hundred pounds.

An anvil block of solid wood was cut from a three-foot section of tree trunk, which was mortised and bolted in place. The entire structure was covered by sand to prevent the timbers from catching fire from the heated iron. On top of the anvil block was set the cast metal anvil itself. About ten feet away from the anvil, two

Typical Forge Layout
Drawn from a photograph of the forge at Saugus, Massachusetts by Kathie Howe

heavy timbers were set in place to support the anvil hammer. These timbers held the bearings in which rested the heavy pins which supported the cam shaft. This shaft was made of gum wood and was ten feet long by three feet in diameter.

The shaft had a large rim gear made of wood or iron set with wooden teeth which was driven by another wooden gear on the water wheel shaft. The cam shaft also had several knobs which came in contact with the striker plate on the hammer "handle" as the cam shaft turned. The knobs would catch the end of the handle, raising the hammer. Above the hammer was placed another timber which was flexible. The hammer would be raised by the cam shaft until it hit this "rebound" timber which acted like a spring. As the shaft kept turning, the knob catching the handle would come free, allowing the end of the hammer handle to go free, and the rebound timber gave it more spring, and therefore, more power in its downward movement than had it simply fallen by gravity. The great hammer would strike the anvil at the rate of about twenty-five times a minute.

The noise produced by the five hundred pound hammer striking the anvil at such a rate must have been simply incredible. A hammer lasted about a month and the anvil only a short time longer, so great was the velocity and pounding produced.

This forge must have been known as Friendship Forge at some period of time because this name is mentioned in the Wharton ledgers recording the bounds of the Meeting House Lot and Graveyard, "beginning at a small pine, on south side of Creek that runs from Friendship Forge to the forks of the Little Egg Harbor River marked with 4 blazes, 12 notches . . ."

The Mechescatauxen

Between the Nescochague and the Atsion lay the Mechescatauxen, Albertson's, or "Wild Cat" branch. In 1808, this branch was called the "Burnt Mill Seat," and the pond of water on it, the "Old Pond." This is where Ball built his "folly," whatever it was. The Wharton ledgers note that Jonathan Haines had erected a glass factory on this branch way up towards its source in Camden County. This rather well-known glass factory was called the Waterford Glass Works and was registered on April 8, 1828.

One of the ledgers records that "Swimming River runs out of a grate Pond above Haines Saw mill pond." This is mentioned in conjunction with a 1741 survey for Philo Leeds of 193 acres in the vicinity of the "Grate Pond." At a later unspecified date, John Burr transferred this same 193 acres to Joseph Burr with a "certain sawmill on a branch of the aforesaid Swimming river alias Badstoe Creek." It was the burning of this sawmill which must have given the name "Burnt Mill Branch" to the Mechescatauxen at a later date.

Mordecai Swamp and Mordecai Landing

Almost no information is available on the Mordecai of the swamp and landing near Batsto. Budd Wilson mentioned that he "understood" that the Mordecai in question was Mordecai Andrews of Little Egg Harbor Meeting (Tuckerton). As Leah Blackman and June Methot indicate, Mordecai Andrews, Sr., the son of Samuel and Mary (Wright) Andrews, was born on August 11, 1664 at Oyster Bay, Long Island. The family removed to the Burlington area, and finally settled near Mansfield. Though his parents were active Quakers, Mordecai was married in Freehold in a civil ceremony on July 14, 1691. His wife's name was Mary, but her family name was not recorded. The young couple removed to Little Egg Harbor about 1700 and became active in the Quaker Meeting.

His younger brother, Edward and his wife, Sarah (Ong) bought land south of the Tuckerton Creek, while Mordecai bought land where the town of Tuckerton was to develop at a later time. Mordecai and Mary had three daughters and a son: Alice, Edith, Mary, and Mordecai, Jr. On June 19, 1736, inventory was taken on his estate after his death, and it seems that he had owned about 1,330 acres. Probably Mordecai bought the swamp land near the head of navigation of the Little Egg Harbor River for the great cedars which stood there.

The land is believed to have been a part of the huge Richards holdings by 1800. Budd Wilson investigated the area of the landing some time ago and found evidence of ore, limestone, ballast rocks, and, of all things, coral. This would indicate that the landing was used during the iron period at Batsto and may have been replaced by Batsto or Stone Landing. The coral? It was probably used as flux. Just downriver, probing some years back indicated that there may be several wrecks lying under the river mud.

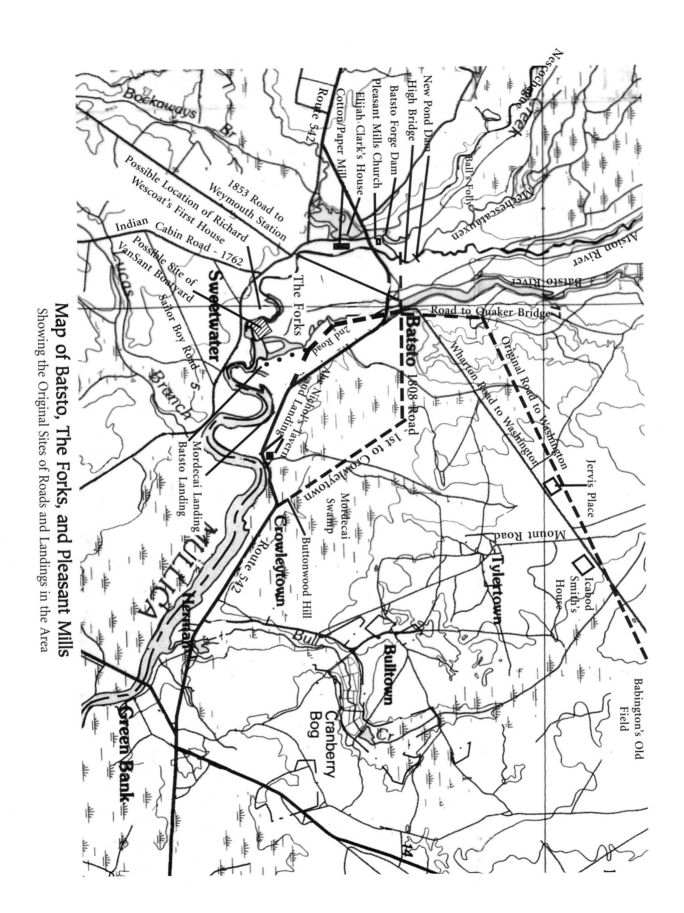

Map of Batsto, The Forks, and Pleasant Mills
Showing the Original Sites of Roads and Landings in the Area

122

The Village of Batsto

Nathaniel R. Ewan, Photographer, Library of Congress
Courtesy of Budd Wilson

There is something very special about walking down the main street of Batsto Village. These tiny weather-beaten houses of the past breathe with the centuries of life that has been lived here amongst the pines.

Built of Jersey White Cedar, their time-blackened exteriors have sheltered many families within their walls. Once there were many more of them in the village. A whole row used to stand on the western side of the lake. The road that runs perpendicular to Main Street was lined with houses on both sides as well. A total of six streets once comprised the town of furnace and glass house. It is estimated that, at the height of Batsto's prosperity, over five hundred people lived in the village or close by. That means that once there were a lot more houses here than remain today.

Batsto Village, like its people, is only a ghost of the past, a shadow of what once was, its reality obscured by the mists of time. Nothing at all remains from its glory days of producing cannon and munitions for Washington's struggling army. Newspaper articles from the period mentioning Batsto Iron Works indicate that there were both dwelling houses and "tenements" for the workers but their number and location is unknown. We are not even certain how many workers and their families lived at Batsto during that time when the fire of the furnace glowed in the night sky producing molten iron for the cannon molds in the casting house.

Tons of goods were shipped up the Mullica bound for Batsto. Tons more were shipped back down or carted overland to Philadelphia and directly to the Continental troops. Nearby, The Forks was also alive with activity. Ships and goods captured from the British were brought upriver and sold to the highest bidder. John Van Sant turned out coastal schooners and privateer vessels, captained and manned by local sailors.

Yet the Batsto of that era is a complete mystery, as is The Forks itself. No excavation has ever been done at that latter place, and Batsto's eighteenth century past has been obscured by its nineteenth century replacement. Dynamism and change are the signs of a growing and successful community, and those characteristics marked Batsto at the birth of the nation and of the new township in which it would play an important part. Batsto, today, is frozen in time, the shade of what once was but will never be again.

In the years immediately following the Revolutionary War, Batsto had two roads to Quaker Bridge on the Old Stage Road, one running on either side of the Batsto River. Another road ran to the Washington Tavern of the Sooy family further to the east on the Old Stage Road. Two roads also ran to the Mullica on either side of the Batsto River. The one on the western side of the river ran to a shipyard complex at The Forks. This was probably the yard of John Van Sant. Though Budd Wilson, in his article, "Batsto Village: Roads and Streets" in the Winter/

Spring issue of the *Batsto Citizens Gazette* for 1996, states that this shipyard was in existence since 1737, documents from theVan Sant family records indicate that John Van Sant bought thirty acres at The Forks from Richard Wescoat in 1760, on which it is assumed he built his shipyard. The eastern road out of Batsto towards the tidewater ended in a landing.

In 1781, the Batsto Forge was built on the Nescochague Creek. Passage between the furnace and forge would have warrented both a road and a bridge. There are indications that both existed prior to the construction of the forge. There had been a settlement at Pleasant Mills even prior to the construction of Batsto Furnace, so there would probably have been a road to get there.

In 1808, a new road was surveyed that would run between Bridgeport/Wading River and Batsto. The present Route 542 generally follows the course of this 1808 road from the Wading River to Crowleytown. From Crowleytown (or Crowleyville as it was sometimes called in the 19th century), the road ran inland over Buttonwood Hill. It then crossed a causeway through Maple Swamp which ended at a field east of the Mansion and village. It ran on across the dam and through the village to "High Bridge." At some time prior to 1840, this road was moved about five hundred feet towards the north on the eastern side of the village complex. Budd Wilson notes that both routes can be traced today by huge oak trees which once lined the edges of the roads.

In 1851, a new road was built from Buttonwood Hill to Batsto, bypassing the Maple Swamp causeway. This time, the road was built closer to the Mullica towards Mordecai Landing. This road began in the village about a hundred feet from the site of the furnace, right in front of the general store, then ran close by the mule barn and was called Canal Street in Batsto. The road continued on a straight line towards Batsto Landing, connecting with a road from Abe Nichols Landing.

During the 1850's, the Camden and Atlantic Railroad was building a line from the Delaware to the Atlantic Ocean at Absecon Island, and the Batsto manager wanted to build a connecting link to the rail line. Robert Stewart's books indicate that he paid to have a road built from Batsto to the new rail line at what is today known

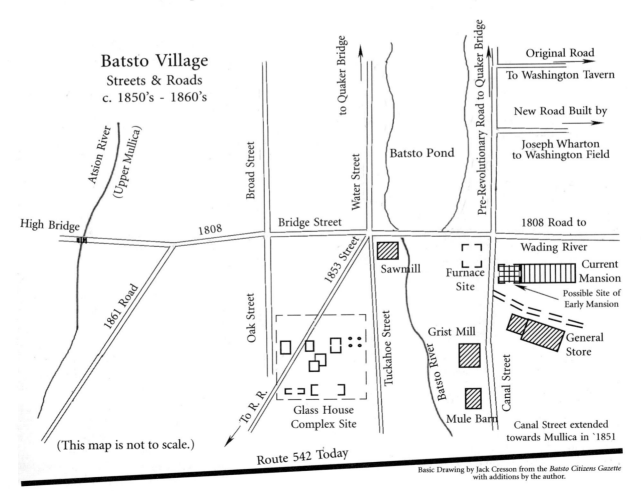

Batsto Village
Streets & Roads
c. 1850's - 1860's

Atsion River (Upper Mullica)

High Bridge

1808

1861 Road

(This map is not to scale.)

Broad Street

Oak Street

To R. R.

Glass House Complex Site

Route 542 Today

1853 Street

Bridge Street

Water Street

to Quaker Bridge

Tuckahoe Street

Sawmill

Batsto River

Grist Mill

Mule Barn

Batsto Pond

Pre-Revolutionary Road to Quaker Bridge

Furnace Site

Canal Street

Original Road

To Washington Tavern

New Road Built by

Joseph Wharton to Washington Field

1808 Road to

Wading River

Current Mansion

Possible Site of Early Mansion

General Store

Canal Street extended towards Mullica in `1851

Basic Drawing by Jack Cresson from the *Batsto Citizens Gazette* with additions by the author.

as Elwood but was then called Weymouth Station. This road began at the intersection of Water and Tuckahoe Streets next to the dam and sawmill and ran to the Mullica above The Forks. Here it crossed a bridge on the property of W.B. Miller and continued on to the railroad. Next to the spot where the road crossed the river stood a large warehouse. Though the railroad would eventually make river shipment unprofitable, Batsto's goods could be directed from this point either towards the railroad or loaded on schooners and sent downstream.

The western exit from the village wasn't laid out until just prior to the Civil War in 1859. Budd Wilson surmises that, since the cupola was torn down in that year, the remains of that old furnace were dumped as fill for the new road. This road poses a problem, however. A map of Sweetwater/Pleasant Mills indicates a road and bridge existed near the Batsto/Pleasant Mills church as early as 1854. However, Budd notes that Burlington County records indicate that the Freeholders met near the "new" bridge in 1861, apparently meaning the "new" bridge where the "new" road crossed the upper Mullica. Yet this road seems to have run from the village directly to the bridge near the church, just as it does today. Perhaps, as names are wont to go, the "old" bridge was "High Bridge" and the "new" bridge was that which had been indicated on the 1854 map. In other words, a "new" road does not indicate the absolute necessity of a "new" bridge being built at the same time if one already existed.

During the period of the glass manufacturing, the road to Quaker Bridge along the west side of the Batsto River ran to landings which were called 1-Mile, 2-Mile, and 3-Mile Landings and on the east side to a stone hill and sand pits.

Joseph Wharton tried his own hand at roadbuilding during his tenure. He laid out an entirely new road to Washington that ran directly to his cattle barns at that location rather than to the site of the old Washington Tavern. This section of Washington was called Washington Fields. He changed the western part of Canal Street, moving it eastwards towards the blacksmith shop. He also dumped ten feet of fill on the top of the site of the casting house which had been connected to the furnace. This is the beginning of the present road to Crowleytown.

Nathaniel R. Ewan, Photographer, Library of Congress

The "Spy" House

Legend relates that a British spy hid in this house during the American Revolution, but that is not the case. There was a spy at Batsto during those troubled years, but the first section of this house wasn't built until about 1820. The second half was constructed about 1870. When the house was rebuilt, workers found a "split-lath" technique not used on the other Batsto houses. In this method, lath was split rather than sliced into slats by a saw. It is one of the oldest houses at Batsto though it never housed a spy.

An Example of the Two Story Single House

Just to bring the road situation up to date before we begin talking about the village proper, in 1929, a road was built to take traffic out of the village entirely. This is the present course of Route 542. Prior to 1964, another road was built from the Washington road to Route 542, removing all traffic from that direction into the village. When the Batsto Visitors' Center was built, it was oriented on the old 1808 road into the village, a portion of which is the current entrance road for visitors to the Batsto Village complex. Parking was originally on the southwestern side of the old road but now lies to the northeastward of the Visitors' Center on the site of an old orchard.

Eighteenth century Batsto is almost a complete enigma. Almost nothing is known about the size of the village either in numbers of dwellings or in extent covered by them, although the number of cannon and shot produced during the Revolutionary War suggest that Batsto was not a small enterprize. Not one single structure remains of this famous iron town of the Revolution.

Nineteenth century Batsto, though well-documented, also presents many puzzles for the scholar. Information on the houses has to be pieced together from the various records. Historical accounts indicate that the Batsto work force grew from sixty to seventy workers in 1834 to over a hundred and a quarter ten years later. Though surely some of the men must have been bachelors, most had families with whom they lived in the village near

An Example of the Two Story Double House

the furnace and later, the glass houses.

Many of the official record books of the Batsto enterprise during the glasshouse period are extant. Two in particular provide information on the village itself. The "Rent Roll," dating from 1846 through 1871, indicates that there were at least seventy-seven houses on six streets which were occupied during this period, far more than the seventeen on two streets which remain. Thirty-two houses lined Bridge (Main) Street, twenty-four on Water Street which ran up along the lake, six on Oak Street, five on Tuckahoe Street, five on Broad Street, and eight on Canal. This latter street was the only street on the eastern side of the pond and ran along the canal, parallel to the river.

The "Rent Roll" also indicates that there were two log houses in the village as well as the more typical frame structures. Budd Wilson of Green Bank, former archeologist at Batsto, thinks that these were the remnants of the original houses built for the furnace workers and that they were a single story high, built with squared-off logs with chinking in the cracks between them. Nothing is known about the size nor the site of these early structures.

The "Rent Roll" and the "Day Books" record that twenty to twenty-nine new houses were built at the village in the first ten years of the glass house period from 1846 to 1856. Budd Wilson's article on the village, which appeared in the 1996 Spring/Summer edition of the *Batsto Citizens Gazette*, provides an intriguing insight into the mystery of historical study. Budd notes that the "Rent Roll" indicates general numbers of the houses constructed during a particular year as well as when and how many houses on each street began to be rented out to workers and their families. For instance, Budd notes that houses #14-26 on Bridge Street were first rented in 1848. He asks the rhetorical question: "If all the houses on Bridge Street between #14-26 existed before 1848, why [were] none of these two-story single framed houses rented?" The assumption is that they were all built and rented for the first time in 1848.

Courtesy of Budd Wilson

One of the Batsto Houses Under Reconstruction

Courtesy of Budd Wilson

There is also no indication that the houses on Tuckahoe Street or Oak Street were rented prior to 1846 either, Budd notes. Only the log house on Canal Street and the double house on Water Street lack a "rent commencing" date. What Budd postulates is that "all of the houses in the village, with the exception of the double house on Water Street, were built after 1846" for the workers of the glass house. The only remaining house from the period of the iron works is the so-called "Spy House," the two story double house on the pond. The houses on Canal Street were torn down in 1863.

On February 23rd, 1874, a spark from manager Robert Stewart's chimney at #4 Oak Street began a devastating conflagration that swept through the village, engulfing house after house. Houses on Oak, Broad, and Bridge Street were destroyed. Eighteen skeleton chimneys lifted their blackened bricks to the sky when the fire had done its worst. Elias Wright's 1876 map shows but thirty-six houses remaining in the village. Of these, only fourteen on Bridge (Main) Street, three on Oak, and one on Water Street still stand today. There are indications that a forest fire claimed more of the little houses of Batsto about 1900. The last house on Tuckahoe Street was torn down by the State of New Jersey after it took possession of the village.

Though the little houses line Main Street today seem so uniform in their appearance, there were actually several different types of houses built at Batsto in the years of the glass house enterprise. The most common type was the two story single frame house. Seventeen still remain of the thirty-four which are known to have been built. They are only 15'3" x 24'4" with a lean-to shed 10'8" x 12'3" on the rear.

The second most popular house-type constructed at Batsto during the mid-1800's was but a single story. Budd Wilson lists eleven of this type: eight on Water Street, two on Bridge Street, two on Canal, and one on Tuckahoe. Of frame construction, they may well have resembled that pictured in the material on Harrisville. Not one of these houses, absolutely tiny by modern standards, remains today.

Six double houses, two stories high, were built on Bridge and Water Street. The only remaining house on Water Street is of this type. These houses are 35'6" long by 15' wide and were constructed in the 1850's. #32 Bridge Street, the last house built towards the west, is dated as 1853 and varies slightly in measurement from the others, it being 33' long by 15'3" wide. All of these double houses had a 22' x 12' shed on the rear.

Two two-and-a-half-story houses were built at the west end of Bridge Street in the 1850's and have survived the ages. Two one-story double houses were also built at Batsto along the western side Water Street. None remains.

Courtesy of Budd Wilson

Its a shame that so many of the houses burned to the ground on that fateful night in 1874. It's difficult to get the feeling for the numbers of people who used to live in this little town from the few that remain. Some years ago, the State decided to bring in craftspeople to show weekend visitors the arts of yesteryear. Unfortunately, the little houses needed to be upgraded to make them safe for constant tourist traffic. The houses which had not already been rebuilt were torn apart and reconstructed, piece by piece, before the craftspeople moved in, with the single exception of the Weaver's House. To help protect them from that scourge of the Pine Barrens, fire, a complete hydrant system was installed. Where are the hydrants? Hiding in the outhouses and trash barrels, of course!

Batsto Village, throughout most of its history, was dynamic and alive, filled with vitality from the men, women, and children who called it "home." Now, come closing time, it sleeps in the shadows of the coming night, silent and empty like so much of the pinelands that once breathed life. The shell of what once was hardly hints at the noise, cinders, and activity that vibrated in the pines.

Wander through the village at twilight some evening and an eerie feeling may come over you. It is as if the laughter of children long grown old and departed from this world can be heard echoing down the street, mixing with the sounds of their parents' voices chatting on the quiet evening air. These are the ghosts of Batsto's past - New Jersey's past - our heritage. They still linger here in the silence of the coming night.

Photograph by John Pearce

Photographs taken in 1995 by John Pearce

The "Ghosts" of Batsto

All of the photographs on the next three pages are from the Wharton Era
in the first or second decade of the Twentieth Century
and are courtesy of Budd Wilson

The "Ghosts" of Batsto

Batsto Ball Team

Gus Miller (1872-1949)
The Blacksmith and Wheelwright
of Batsto - c. 1904

Circa 1910 - Photograph Taken in Front of the Grist Mill
Standing (L. to R.): Rev. Martha Jervis, Jules Gerber and his wife,
Amos "Boney" Ford, and Ada Coleman
Seated: Pauline Gerber and Mag Love.
Herbert Adams is holding his brother, Percy, and their mother, Mary, is next to them.
Percy was still living in Batsto as late as 1975.

The "Ghosts" of Batsto

MAIN STREET BATSTO, N.J. —

Jack E. Boucher, Photographer, Lynwood, NJ
Courtesy of Budd Wilson

Main Street

Courtesy of Budd Wilson

133

1995

134

Sweetwater/Pleasant Mills

Photograph by John Pearce

The Elijah Clark Mansion - 1996

A PRESBYTERIAN ENCLAVE

Pleasant Mills has been important enough over the years to demand a chapter of its own, but this is a history of Washington Township, and even by stretching its boundaries, we can't put Pleasant Mills in Washington Township. Its close relationship to The Forks, however, as well as the prominence of its two early families in the history of the township, warrants more than passing mention.

The story of Pleasant Mills begins far across the Atlantic Ocean in the country of the Scots. The people of Scotland had sided with Parliament in the mid-seventeenth century struggle with King Charles I known as the Puritan Revolution and thus were not loved by his sons, Charles II and James II when the Stuarts were restored to the throne of England. Both instigated severe acts against Scotland and its Kirk (church). By the 1680's, many had had enough of persecution by the crown and determined to settle outside of the British Isles. Led by George Scott, a party of Scots left Britain for the colonies in 1685 and settled on Long Island.

The remoteness of their new home may have given them more shelter from the vengeance of James II, but his governors, taking their cue from the king, despised the Scots. In 1688, Parliament invited William, the Prince of Orange (Holland) and his wife, Mary, the daughter of James II, to assume the crown of England and Scotland. William III was no more a friend of the Scots than the king he replaced. He organized the extermination of the MacDonalds of Glencoe and the MacGregors.

In 1707, several families from the party which had sailed with George Scott in 1685 made their homes at the head of navigation on the Mullica. Perhaps they wanted to get farther away from the royal authorities and saw the isolation of the Pine Barrens as a blessing. The Scots were known for their staunch and uncompromising faith, as solid and rugged as the mountains of the Scottish highlands, and that temerity in the face of oppression would stand them well in the struggle to found a new home in the wilds of New Jersey.

Tradition relates that the first structure they erected in the wilderness was a good, stout Scottish kirk of logs cut from the surrounding forest which they completed in the course of one day! That little church served to comfort and strengthen its people for half a century.

The Scottish settlers were attracted to the area by the presence of great cedar swamps that could be turned into lumber, the numerous streams which would provide water power for mills, and by the abundance of fur-bearing animals whose pelts could be sold for hard cash or traded for needed goods. Living closer to Philadelphia than the other settlers of the Mullica and Little Egg Harbor, the Scots managed to procure some of the necessities they could not make for themselves from that city, first by boat across the Delaware and up the Rancocas, then by pack-horse overland to the village by the forks of the Little Egg Harbor River.

They must also have been impressed by the opportunities that the Mullica estuary presented for smuggling. Smuggling was a way of life for the colonists and for the Scots in their homeland as a way of circumventing the hated English revenue officers, and the hazardous shoreline of New Jersey was not well-patrolled by the British navy. With Philadelphia nearby, goods could be brought upriver, loaded into carts, and carried overland to the city without paying import duties. This would play a very important roll as events led towards the middle of the century.

The Scots village at the forks of the Mullica had its first sawmill by the seventeen thirties. It was built by a Samuel Cripps on the Nescochague behind their kirk. Villages like that at The Forks, at Lower Bank, Clark's Landing, and Middle-of-the-Shore or Little Egg Harbor Meeting [Tuckerton], became more and more involved in trade, producing lumber products, shipbuilding, etc. There were always plenty of trees for lumber, charcoal, and pitch. Axes rang merrily in the woods, and sawmills were set up. Since grain was a necessity of life, a few grist mills were built for grinding the grain of local homesteaders, and the first harvesting of the salt hay that grew in the marshes was begun. What had been a wilderness when Eric Mullica came to the banks of the river not fifty years before was beginning to be transformed into an active, enterprising region of farmers, millers both of grain and wood, carpenters, woodsmen, shipbuilders, and blacksmiths. As coastal trade expanded, the Mullica was no longer isolated.

The Rev. John Brainerd, a Presbyterian missionary, visited the Mullica valley and the Little Egg Harbor region in general. Coming from Manahawkin through Bass River, he had to pass through Middle-of-the-Shore (Tuckerton). He found Little Egg Harbor Meeting an area of such staunch Quakers that he could make no head-way there. He did hold meetings in Bass River at Captain Charles Loveland's and at Captain John Leak's where at least there were some people who weren't Quakers. How he must have breathed a sigh of relief to get to The Forks and be amongst devoted advocates of the Kirk at last! David Brainerd, his brother, serving as a Presbyterian missionary to the Indians, converted most of the local natives who still inhabited the region to Christianity between 1742 and 1745. [See Brotherton]

Fortunes Made in Privateering

When Elijah Clark built his mansion above the confluence of the Batsto and Little Egg Harbor Rivers in 1762, he was a young man of great, but as yet unfulfilled, dreams. He was born in 1730 [Franklin Kemp says 1732 in *Nest of Rebel Pirates*] in the little town of Clark's Landing, down river from Lower Bank on the Gloucester (now Atlantic) County side when that town was in its infancy.

Elijah was the youngest of the four sons of Thomas and Hannah Clark, late of Saybrook, Connecticut. In 1700, according to Georgiana Blake in her 1934 article "Early Atlantic County," the pair had left their former home in New England for better prospects in New Jersey and had settled on the Old Gloucester County side of the river seven miles below the head of navigation and about the same distance from Great Bay. Arthur Pierce, in *Iron in the Pines*, notes that their little town had attracted other settlers and, by 1718, boasted forty houses, a store and trading house, and a church.

There by the Mullica, the couple had four sons: Thomas, Jr., David, Samuel, and Elijah. Thomas, Jr., the eldest, was only eighteen when his mother died, and Pierce relates an oft-told story about her replacement. Thomas, Sr. had a thriving business and four sons, three of whom were still in their youth. He knew they needed a mother and he a wife, and he dreamed of a woman by the name of Ruth whom he had known back in Saybrook. Unable to leave his business and his sons, he decided to send young Thomas, Jr. up to Connecticut with his proposal.

Thomas, Jr. was told to make his father's proposal to Ruth, but, if she refused, he was instructed to find someone in Saybrook who would be suitable as wife and mother. Just imagine sending your eighteen year old son to pick your wife and his mother! Young people grew up fast in the wilderness back then, and necessity required unique solutions. The journey had a doubly happy conclusion, for Ruth remembered Thomas, Sr. well and quickly gave her assent to his proposal. Thomas, Jr. also had the fortune to meet and fall in love with Sarah Parker in

Saybrook while he was courting Ruth for his father. He returned to Clark's Landing with his mother-to-be and immediately reversed direction and sailed back to Saybrook for his own bride, the "beautiful and brilliant" Sarah.

In 1757, at the age of twenty-seven [or 25 as per Kemp], Elijah Clark decided to settle down and bought the fifty acres above The Forks on the Gloucester County side of the river from his brothers, Thomas, Jr. and David, that would become his homestead plantation. He was too young to have known about the beautiful women of Saybrook and looked closer to home to find a mate. Though the actual date isn't known, it is assumed that about the time he bought his property, he also married Jane Lardner of Gloucester County. Jane was about ten years younger than her new husband, but the pair had seven children and a long, happy marriage.

Not long after he purchased the land from his brothers, he had two adjoining sections of land surveyed and conveyed to him by the Council of West Jersey Proprietors. The first deed was dated July 29, 1757 and the second, November 5, 1762. When he acquired his property, the descendants of the early Scottish settlers had lived in the Pleasant Mills area for over fifty years, but there was little else but their husbandry to break the silence of the forest.

Over the next thirty years, the activity at nearby Batsto insured growth and prosperity. The land at The Forks would see shipyards, docks, warehouses, and other industries related to shipping crowd the triangle of land between the two rivers. Smugglers, and later privateers (most of the time they were the same men) would make The Forks their strategic headquarters. Thousands of pounds of cannon and cannonballs would be shipped out of Batsto from various landings in the vicinity, and a vast wealth in captured British goods would be sold at auction just down river from Clark's new house, and Elijah Clark would be a part of all of it.

Elijah was an eighteenth century entrepreneur who was determined not to be satisfied with the limitations of his birthplace. Educated at Yale, Clark was a youth of great promise and ability. According to Pierce, he served as an officer in the colonial forces during the French and Indian War, but it must have been a militia position. That war didn't conclude until a year after he built his mansion, and he had spent time buying land and getting married. Clark built his mansion house in 1762, dammed the stream for a sawmill, and set about to make his fortune.

Smuggling had been a way of life for most of the colonials for as long as anyone could remember. Though the taxes levied by Mother England weren't onerous prior to 1763, the long seacoast, numerous bays and rivers, coves and harbors were impossible for the British to police, and businessmen were out to make money in any way they could. The Scots who had settled the Pleasant Mills area back in 1707 had had no love for the English anyway and knew their isolated community was ideal for circumventing mercantile law. The Little Egg Harbor River thrust its way inland towards Philadelphia for miles and their position at the end of navigable water, far away from revenue cutters and customs inspectors, was ideal. English butchery following the battle of Culloden and the outlawing of the tartan, the bagpipe, and the Gaelic language, must have made the Scots even more determined to defy British authority.

Clark must have had the same idea when he bought up his acreage. Oh, he dammed the stream next to his house and built a saw mill below the resulting pond, maybe even two, but if he was to be wealthy, it would not be for such a tame reason. His timing was perfect. Broke and desperate at the end of the exhausting conflict with the French and Spanish in 1763, the British crown and parliament decided that the colonies should help pay for their own defense, and passed a series of taxes to exact income from their western Atlantic possessions. Unfortunately, after a century and a half of freedom, self-rule, and hard-knocks education in their fundamental rights as Englishmen, the colonists knew all to well how to circumvent the government.

The area of The Forks was just perfect for clandestine practices. Ships could be brought across the treacherous bar at the inlet, then sailed through Great Bay and be brought up the tortuous channel to the head of navigation without any authorities in Philadelphia and New York being the wiser. There, untaxed goods from proscribed places could be unloaded and hauled overland to Philadelphia for sale, and taxes could be avoided. If the great Boston merchants like John Hancock were growing wealthy from smuggling, why not Elijah Clark? Why not, indeed!

Elijah Clark was an educated and cultured gentlemen. He was also a religious man. By the time Clark built his mansion, the Presbyterian log kirk was fifty-five years old, and the congregation had outgrown it. At the same time as the workmen were constructing his own house, Clark had them working on a new building to replace the old kirk. Indications are that both the original log building and Clark's new frame structure stood on the same ground as the present Batsto-Pleasant Mills church on the banks of the Nescochague Creek (which is not the stream that forms Lake Nescochague).

Clark was soon joined by another like-minded young man, Richard Wescoat, who bought property just down river from the Clark mansion in an area that would be known as "where the buttonwoods are" for well over a century after Wescoat had moved from the area. Between these two friends, The Forks would become the focus of revolutionary fervor.

The Clark/Wescoat Mansion on Lake Nescochaque

Wescoat and Clark bore remarkable similarities in their lives. Richard was only three years younger than Elijah Clark and was his equal in ambition. He was the namesake of his great great grandfather, Richard, who supposedly came to New England from Devonshire, England in 1620. The Wescoat line in England dates back to the twelfth century.

The first Richard died at Fairfield, Connecticut in 1651. His son, Daniel, married Abigail Gaylord, came to Fairfield, New Jersey in 1697, and died about five years later. *His* son, Daniel, Jr. married a woman by the name of Elizabeth, though her family name isn't known, and died in 1742. Yet a third Daniel (1707-1791) married Deborah Smith and fathered our Richard in 1733. Wescoat married a widow, Margaret Lee, on March 18, 1761. Both are listed as being from Burlington, New Jersey in the New Jersey Archives (Volume 22, Page 435) though Richard Wescoat had purchased his first property at Pleasant Mills by the time of his marriage. He and his wife eventually had six children. [Note: Wescoat's birth date is calculated from his gravestone in the Presbyterian cemetery at Mays Landing and agrees with Arthur Pierce's dating. Franklin Kemp has his birth in 1736].

The exact date for Wescoat's coming to the Mullica valley is not known, but the first survey recorded for him as listed in the Wharton ledgers is dated the 22nd of November, 1760 (recorded in Book K, Folio 237) for 40 acres. John Burr, Jr. is noted as the Deputy Surveyor and the description reads:

> *Situate on Little Egg Harbor River a little below Clark's Saw-Mill Creek. Beginning at a cedar corner to John Monrow's land by said river thence along Monrows line (1) S. 7º E. 7.50 chs. to a W. O. (2) by other lands. s.48º W. 14.50 chs. to a W. O. (3) 80º W. 13.50 chs. to a pine by the S.W. side of a cripple or swamp (4) N. 17ºW. 24.50 chs. to a pine by said river the several courses thereof to the beginning containing 46 acres and allowance for highways.* (Ledger Vol. 14, p. 338)

Page 129 of Volume 9 of the Wharton Ledgers also records another purchase Wescoat made two years later, in 1762, for 19 $^{19/100}$ acres (Recorded in Book L, Folio 46):

> Beginning at a pine on the bank of Little Egg Harbor River just above the Forks at a spring being corner of his former survey of 46 acres. Thence (1) S.52⁰ W. 15 chs. (2) S. 45⁰ E. 20 $^{1/2}$ chs. (3) ?N 58⁰ E. 4.50 chs. to the line of his former survey. (4) N. 17⁰ W. 22.4 chs. along his old line to the beginning containing 19 $^{19/100}$ acres and allowance.

Still another purchase the same year is dated October 25th, 1765 and is recorded in the Wharton Ledgers in Volume 14 and with the county in Book N. Folio 281. This time, Deputy Surveyor Peacock made the survey. The description given actually includes four other surveys, some of which he had already acquired, the whole totaling 285 acres.

Sparing the reader another incomprehensible description, just let me note for weird historians who like details that those surveys were recorded as follows:

Survey No. 151	46 acres	in Lib. K Folio 237
Survey No. 199	61 1/2 acres	in Book L Folio 203
Survey No. 169	19 19/100 acres	in Book K Folio 47
Survey No. 117	14 acres	in Book H Folio 363 (John Monroe's land)

All of this is mentioned simply to establish the approximate location of Wescoat's estate and residence. The above 46 acres is said to have been 50 chains above where he lived on the Mullica "where the buttonwoods are."

Another note in the ledgers accompanying the above description reads, "Wescoat lived at the Forks of the Mullica River where the big Buttonwoods now are." "Cap" Wilson added another note to this section of his summary of the ledgers that "the above was written about 1900 - the trees were still standing at the time."

While the buttonwoods may have been there as late as 1900, they are, unfortunately, no longer in existence. However, an old pamphlet history of Pleasant Mills by Charles F. Green says that the

> 'buttonwoods' were oft named in song and story. This famous group of trees stands or rather stood . . . near the confluence of the Batsto and Atsion creeks. . . . During the Revolution a watching station was fixed in the top of the tallest tree from which a view was obtained of all craft passing up and down the stream."

Green also says that one of Joe Mulliner's gang was an American deserter who, after capture, was "hanged on one of the buttonwoods which was long known as 'The Gallows Tree'.

Though there is a tradition that the auctions of privateer booty during the Revolution took place across from Elijah Clark's mansion (where, by the way, buttonwoods still flank the old mill), it seems that they actually happened downstream at Richard Wescoat's original homestead site off the end of the point at The Forks. Perhaps the fact that Wescoat later lived in Clark's house for a couple of years misled people into thinking that all the activity was up by the old mill. More than likely, though, Wescoat's property was somewhere in the vicinity where Indian Cabin Road leads off from the Pleasant Mills/Weekstown Road.

Arthur Pierce, for all his excellent work, could not determine the actual site of Wescoat's first home but assumed it was near the landing at The Forks, about a mile southeast of Elijah Clark's house. Wescoat kept a number of enterprises going and became, like Elijah Clark, a wealthy man.

The Rev. Carl Mangus Wrangel, dean of Swedish Lutheranism in America from 1758 - 1768, made a journey along the shore in this region in October of 1764. An entry in his journal notes

> October 11: After dinner I went in company with James Steelman and Mr. Price to a place called Little Egg Harbor, where a sermon was fixed for the following day. We arrived late in the evening at the home of an Irishman named Elisha [sic] Clark, by religion a Presbyterian. We were affectionately received and well treated in this house. He lived in the middle of the forest where, by the river called Little Egg Harbor, he had built a saw and flour mill. What especially delighted me here was to find that the man with his entire household feared God. He had built a small wooden church on his property, near the house, and two or three times a year there was preaching by Presbyterian or other ministers.

October 12: In the morning, after prayers and after we had eaten breakfast, we went out to see the place and the mills. About half a mile away we saw the loading site on the river, where more than twenty ships now lay to receive the products of the district. There was a tavern run by an Irishman by the name of Wescott [sic], who appeared to be making money to the harm of others and with little concern about God. (Shore Chronicles, Margaret Thomas Buchholz)

Considering the close friendship which Clark and Wescoat maintained over the years, one wonders if their personalities were really as different as Pastor Wrangel seems to imagine. Perhaps he was too harsh in his quick judgment of Wescoat.

During the years from Clark's settlement to the outbreak of hostilities with Britain, Clark and Wescoat worked hand in hand to increase their fortunes. Business after business would be built on the Burlington County side of the Little Egg Harbor River, while the Gloucester County side would be dominated by the enterprises owned by Clark and Wescoat.

In 1775, Clark was the Gloucester County representative to the New Jersey Provincial Assembly, and in the following year, he served as part of a special convention which met from June to August in Burlington, Trenton, and New Brunswick.

With the coming of the Revolutionary War, Clark and Wescoat would both be officers in the Gloucester County militia and would control the entire area by their influence. Clark served as Lieutenant Colonel of the Third battalion of Gloucester County militia, while Richard Wescoat was First Major. They both owned ships that were turned into privateers. They both participated in the auction of captured goods from warehouses right on their own property. And they both waxed rich - very rich.

Elijah Clark had served in a skirmish at Mount Holly in December 1776 and had made it up to Trenton in time to take part in that battle and in the one at Princeton. Clark was commissioned lieutenant colonel in the 2nd Regiment, Gloucester County Militia on September 20, 1777, his rank effective from 1775, but he resigned his commission after being elected to the New Jersey Assembly not two months later.

Wescoat volunteered for active duty very early in the war and was with Washington's army when they crossed the Delaware that snowy Christmas night in 1776. He was severely wounded in the subsequent Battle of Trenton and retired to his estate along the Little Egg Harbor River to recuperate. From that time on, his adventurous spirit being satisfied, he kept himself closer to home, though his revolutionary fervor continued unabated.

Though Wescoat later was called "colonel," Franklin Kemp, in *Nest of Rebel Pirates*, says that Wescoat never actually held that rank but was First Major until he resigned his commission on March 31, 1778. If this is correct, he was only a private citizen when the British attacked Chesnut Neck and threatened the Mullica valley.

During the war years, Wescoat was in charge of the government stores at The Forks, and both men joined in building Fort Foxboroughs at Chestnut Neck to protect the Little Egg Harbor River from British attack. The government had paid for several cannon for the fort, which Clark and Wescoat were supposed to have provided, but when the British did attack in 1778, there were no cannon there. They may well have been ordered elsewhere by the two men, perhaps even brought upriver to better protect their lucrative businesses in a place whose defense would be more under their immediate control.

No area was more involved in the Revolutionary War than was The Forks. Both Elijah Clark and Richard Wescoat were active in the anti-British activities which centered here. Both men directed the defenses of the Mullica valley and Wescoat succeeded Clark as head of the local militia. Both he and Clark were intimately involved with Joseph Ball and John Cox in the protecting the production of cannon and cannon balls at Batsto. Both were leaders in the promotion of privateering and profited from the sale of captured vessels and goods which were put up at auction right at The Forks.

Privateering was looked upon as a form of piracy by the British, who lost so much money to the "pirates." Britain had the greatest navy in the world in 1776, and the new government of the United States began without a single vessel. Washington, himself, commissioned the first official vessels, including General John Glover's *Hannah*, which was outfitted in Beverly, Massachusetts and crewed by Marbleheaders. Congress and the states issued "Letters of Marque" to wealthy ship owners who armed their vessels and signed up a captain and crew to sail them. Throughout the former colonies, owners saw the profits to be made from taking unarmed British merchantmen on the high seas and sailing them to some American port to be auctioned off. The owner of the vessel claimed the largest share, but captain and crew profited through shares as well. Privateering caught on very quickly, and it is estimated that the practice cost the British 60 - 70 billion dollars in terms of current values. If Britain's huge naval squadrons could not be attacked, she could be hit in the wallet where it hurt even more.

The inhabitants of the Mullica estuary were determined to have their share and outfitted a large number of vessels to engage in the lucrative practice. They had an ideal location. The inlet to Great Bay lay far down the coast from New York and considerably above Cape May on a shore that was extremely hazardous in a storm. This made patrolling the area a major difficulty. Also, large British ships of war couldn't get in through the inlet if they were chasing one of the shallow-draft privateers. The long, winding channel upriver made local knowledge imperative if a ship were to sail to The Forks. They were close enough to Philadelphia to haul the goods overland even if the British did control the Delaware with their navy. Finally, the river towns were filled with experienced seamen and captains. Thus The Forks would become a hive of privateering activity and would make fortunes for Elijah Clark and Richard Wescoat.

Properly speaking, The Forks was the triangle of land between the Batsto and Atsion Rivers, but in reality, the entire area bore that name and shared in the excitement that privateering generated. Captured ships that were too large to get so far up river were docked at Chestnut Neck, near where the Garden State Parkway crosses the Mullica river today. There, they were unloaded and stripped. Some of the captured goods were sold right at Chestnut Neck. What wasn't sold there was carried in shallow draft vessels upstream to Wescoat's for auction.

The two men made a fortune on the practice, but that was not considered a problem back then. No one thought ill of those who profited on the war effort. In point of fact, the United States couldn't have existed without the efforts of men like Clark, Wescoat, and those of the Mullica towns who captained and crewed their ships. When General Washington gave orders for a barracks to be built in the area of The Forks and stationed a company of Pennsylvania artillery there, he wasn't only thinking of protecting the Batsto Iron Works. He was also thinking quite seriously about today's equivalent of millions of dollars of captured British goods making their way up the Little Egg Harbor River and into the hands of patriots in New Jersey and Pennsylvania, as well as supplying his army.

All of this activity made The Forks a busy and exciting place during the war years. When the British blocked the Delaware entrance to Philadelphia, goods were brought up the Mullica, unloaded at The Forks, and shipped overland to that city. This area was as much a target for the British invasion force in the fall of 1778 as was Batsto. It must have disappointed them greatly to have achieved little more than the destruction of Chestnut Neck. Fort Foxboroughs did its work even if Clark and Cox's cannon weren't there, and the militia ran. The other half of the "nest of rebel pirates" at The Forks continued as before, as did the munitions production at Batsto. For all their burning and looting, the British forces achieved very little.

Washington had known of the planned British attack and sent Pulaski's Legion to prevent it. Unfortunately, Pulaski was a little late in arriving. Still, the Legion had a great deal to do with encouraging the quick exit of the British troops and ships from the area after their attack on the lower Mullica.

Count Casimer Pulaski was a Pole who had resisted a successful Russian invasion of his homeland. Having to leave his birthplace, he fled to America and joined the cause of the revolutionaries. The Battle of Brandywine made his reputation, and he received a commission as Brigadier General of Cavalry.

In 1778, he was commissioned by Congress to raise an independent corps of calvary and light infantry. Made up of men from seven nations, it was known as "The Legion." Its flag, woven of crimson silk by the Moravian sisterhood of Bethlehem, Pennsylvania, bore on one side a triangle enclosing an eye encircled by thirteen stars. On this side also was the Latin motto: "Non alino Regit" (No other governs). On the reverse, it simply had the letters "U.S." and another motto: "Unita Virtus Fortior" (Unity Makes Valor Stronger).

Pulaski was sent by Washington to defend the important Mullica valley from the British expedition. According to a pamphlet published around the turn of the century by Charles F. Green on Pleasant Mills, the British sent a force toward The Forks and Batsto after they completed the destruction of Chestnut Neck.

A youth named Blake, who had taken part in the battle and retreated with his comrades, was led by a spirit of adventure to return at nightfall and do a bit of scouting around the British camp. He saw the detachment leave Chestnut Neck, and followed it until camp was made for the night. The object of the movement was quite clear to him and making a detour through the woods he hurried to the Forks and communicated his tidings to the officer in command there. The commander acted promptly. Selecting several trusty messengers he sent them out to seek for volunteers. The response was quick and satisfactory and shortly after midnight ninety men, farmers, woodsmen and iron works, assembled at the post. ...

The improvised soldiery accompanied by fifty regulars from the post moved blithely on their way. A march of two hours brought them so near the British camp that the hail of the sentries could be plainly heard and here they halted. ... At daybreak, a blare of bugles announced that the British were on the move and soon their leading files appeared dim and ghostly in the light of early dawn. On they moved with rhythmic tread never dreaming of danger till they were in the very jaws of the ambuscade. The silence shattered by a sharp command, "Fire!" and then - in the words of one of the patriots, "we just cut loose and gave 'em hell." This demonstration by untrained woodsmen probably saved the Forks and Batsto iron works from destruction. ... The British fell back in confusion without an attempt to rally.

According to Green, Pulaski marched by way of The Forks, where he stopped for rest. At The Forks, he met the returning militia, who had made a successful ambush of the British near Chestnut Neck. Pulaski, himself, just missed the British at Chestnut Neck, arriving in time only to see the sterns of their vessels as they dropped downstream. There they stood in the midst of the smouldering ruins of Chestnut Neck's homes and storehouses, unable to vent their frustration at the audacious enemy. Some of the men must surely have dreamed about what they'd do if they ever got their hands on those *^&%$#@! Britishers! Unfortunately, the British *weren't* through with The Legion. Pulaski returned to The Forks and crossed the Atsion on October 8th, bound for the area of Little Egg Harbor now known as Tuckerton..

Unfortunately for this entire story, there seems no corroborating evidence for its veracity. Franklin Kemp, in his *Nest of Rebel Pirates*, doesn't entirely dismiss the possibility that militia skirmished with a small detachment of British troops, but simply says that there is no record of any major engagement. He makes no mention whatsoever of Pulaski's Legion heading anywhere except the Tuckerton area. Pauline Miller, of the Ocean County Cultural and Heritage Commission, is currently working on a booklet about the Affair at Little Egg Harbor, and I enquired of her the route Pulaski took to the Little Egg Harbor Meeting area.

She said his orders indicate that he was to head for Little Egg Harbor and not to Chestnut Neck. At that time, though, the Little Egg Harbor border was at the mouth of the Batsto River, and orders to proceed to "Little Egg Harbor" would not necessarily mean that area near the Meeting House. In any case, he arrived too late to do anything about the British at that location, because they had already boarded their vessels and dropped back down to Great Bay by that time. It would be a shame if Green's excellent story is a fabrication.

Ms. Miller says that he simply didn't have time to get all the way down to the battle site, return through Pleasant Mills, and then head for Little Egg Harbor Meeting. She also says that there is no record of the exact route he took on his journey. The only road in the vicinity from Cooper's Ferry (Camden) to Little Egg Harbor was what we know of now as the Stage Road. A main road led from Trenton, Pulaski's starting place, to the Medford area where it joined the Philadelphia/Little Egg Harbor Road. Also at Medford, that road split into three parts, the western/southernmost route passing through Atsion, crossing the Batsto River at Quaker Bridge. The only known road into Batsto at the time left the main road at the bridge and headed for the iron town, and beyond it, to Pleasant Mills. Indian Cabin Road, built in 1762, went from there to Chestnut Neck via a circuitous route around the intervening swamps. Ms. Miller may well be right in saying Pulaski just didn't have enough time to do all of that travelling.

Encamping in the area of what is now Mystic Islands, a detachment acting as his advance guard was surprised in the middle of the night and slaughtered by the British troops who had not entirely abandoned the area as had been thought. The outpost was encamped on fast land just inland from the "islands" which today make up Mystic Islands. The men were betrayed by a deserter who acted as guide to the British in navigating the tortuous channels towards Little Egg Harbor itself. Having been told by the deserter that Pulaski had issued a "no quarter" order, the British troops decided to give as they were supposed to get. Pulaski's outpost was completely surprised and most of the men died in the onslaught. Known as "The Affair at Little Egg Harbor," the bloody site is marked by a memorial stone set up by the Society of Cincinnati to honor the Americans who gave their lives that this nation might be free.

The British didn't stick around to confront Pulaski's entire Legion, and they had removed the planking from the bridge over the Big Creek to thwart the Legion's counterattack. At first light, Pulaski's men once again could only shake their fists in frustration at the British ships riding at anchor in the bay. Unfortunately for them, the British would live to fight another day. The valiant Count Casimer Pulaski was himself killed a year later in an abortive attack on Savannah, Georgia, after which, the Legion ceased to exist. The people of the Mullica valley had a great deal for which to be thankful, though. Had it not been for the timely arrival of Pulaski and his Legion, the British might very well have succeeded in their initial objective: burning Batsto Furnace and The Forks. Along the way, surely the homes of Joseph Sooy and his son John at what would become Green Bank, and the towns of Lower Bank and Clark's Landing would have been destroyed.

THE INFAMOUS GENERAL BENEDICT ARNOLD

The attack on Chestnut Neck and the potential for further alarms in the area did concern one gentleman. The wounded hero, Major General Benedict Arnold, had been placed in charge of the city of Philadelphia by General Washington when the British evacuated the town in the spring of 1778. Like so many other officers, he was not adverse to making a little money off the war effort.

Just prior to the British evacuation, Arnold, at Valley Forge, managed to acquire a half interest in the cargo of the *Charming Nancy*, which was still tied up at a Philadelphia wharf. Arnold sent a pass to the master of the *Charming Nancy* that would enable him to proceed down the Delaware unmolested should any American "officers and soldiers of the Continental Army" try to stop him.

Unfortunately, the schooner *was* stopped, not by a ship manned by "officers and soldiers of the Continental Army" but by a New Jersey privateer, the *Xantippe*. Her captain refused to honor Arnold's pass, seized the *Charming Nancy*, and sent her into Little Egg Harbor with a prize crew.

One can imagine how angry the wounded hero of Saratoga must have been. He was mollified, however, when an admiralty judge ruled against the *Xantippe* captain in his favor. When the news came that the British under Captain Henry Collins and Captain Patrick Furguson were heading with ships and troops to attack "that nest of rebel pirates," Arnold panicked.

Once again, the *Charming Nancy* and her cargo was in danger. He used his authority to commandeer twelve wagons, which were already hired out to Pennsylvania and some to the Continental Army, to save his property. The *Charming Nancy* had apparently been brought up river to The Forks for safety, and it was to The Forks that the twelve wagons headed as fast as Arnold's insistence could drive them.

Arnold did save his investment, but at a huge price to his reputation and his ego. A committee of the Pennsylvania legislature, made up of men who were definitely not Arnold fans, got wind of the arrangement and charged him with using government property for private profit. In commandeering the wagons, Arnold had used the legal loophole which allowed him to "remove property which was in imminent danger of falling into the hands of the enemy." When the Pennsylvania authorities found out that the property in question was *his* property, or at least half his, they knew they had him. Arnold was brought before a court martial and sentenced to be reprimanded by his Commander-in-Chief.

Arthur Pierce (*Iron in the Pines*) quotes Washington's rather mild rebuke:

> *The Commander-in-Chief would have been much happier in an occasion of bestowing commendations on an officer who has rendered such distinguished services to his country as Major General Arnold; but in the present case a sense of duty and a regard to candour oblige him to declare that he considers his conduct in the instance of the permit as peculiarly reprehensible, both in a civil and military view, and in the affair of the wagons as imprudent and improper.*

It's too bad that Washington was so gentle, but Arnold was, after all, the wounded hero of Saratoga. Arnold had been wrong on both counts; there is no question of that; but the man's ego was just beyond all bounds. Arnold felt unjustly betrayed by his commander-in-chief and, from that moment on, his harbored grudge festered.

He had channels of contact with the British through his new wife's Tory family, the Shippens, in Philadelphia, and he became ever more determined to use them to his advantage. He hadn't learned a thing about illicit passes and local state forces. It would be just such a "safe conduct" pass, given to Sir Henry Clinton's aide, Major John Andre, and intercepted by suspicious local militia, that would cause his ultimate downfall. He persuaded Washington to give him command of West Point, the fort which commanded the Hudson River and protected the entire New York valley, then proceeded with plans to betray it, and General Washington, to the British forces in New York City. All of this stemmed from his self-interested attempt to protect his investment in the cargo of the *Charming Nancy* from British attack at The Forks!

CLARK PASSES THE TORCH TO WESCOAT

The British foray up the Mullica must have given Clark much to think about. He had become a wealthy man in the sixteen years since he had built his mansion and did not want to risk it any further. Arthur Pierce records an advertisement which Clark placed in the *Pennsylvania Packet* on January 2, 1779:

His old friend, Richard Wescoat, wanted his mansion and property and made him an offer he couldn't refuse, so on April 2, 1779, he sold everything to his friend and comrade in arms for the large sum of 18,000 pounds. Wescoat gained twenty-three parcels of land both in the vicinity and at Mays Landing. He certainly must have grown *very* rich at the expense of the British.

Elijah and Jane Clark bought a farm in Haddonfield (Kemp, *Nest of Rebel Pirates*, says it was the Hinchman Farm near Woodbury) and moved there after the sale. He died at the age of sixty-five on the 9th of December, 1795. His wife lived another ten years, joining him in death on August 10th, 1804 at the age of sixty-six.

Wescoat didn't waste any time moving into the Clark mansion, but he, too, was thinking hard. There was little chance the British would repeat their incursion of the year before and threaten his tidy little business, but what would the end of the war mean for his future? His wealth had been dented by the payment to Clark, but the property was still salable. Casting his eye about for his next venture, he finally decided that, with the end of hostilities, he would move to the headwaters of the Great Egg Harbor River and see what profit that area held for him. Thus, on March 18, 1782, not quite three years after his purchase of Clark's plantation, Wescoat sold out to Edward Black and moved to Mays Landing. He died on March 9, 1825.

Though Wescoat didn't live in the Clark mansion very long, his daughter, Margaret, provided the model for the heroine of a romantic novel of the period, *Kate Aylesford*, and the Clark/Wescoat house is often known as the "Kate Aylesford Mansion."

Charles J. Peterson was a product of his time. Writing his novel, *Kate Aylesford*, in 1853, he exhibited all the characteristics of the era in his florid Victorian style and extravagant romanticism. Kate's beauty far exceeds that of other women. Her pure voice soars above all the other voices when she sings in church. She is the epitome of perfection, as Peterson's era thought heroines should be. As an only child, she is one of the most potentially wealthy young women in America. She is shipwrecked, trapped by a forest fire, kidnapped, hunted by blood-hounds, and rescued twice from death and an even worse fate by her hero, Major Gordon. When she finally marries her hero, it is George Washington who gives away the bride. One wonders how people could swallow so much melodrama within the covers of a single novel, but that was the characteristic of popular literature in that era.

Actually, Peterson, whose grandfather was one of the original trustees of the Pleasant Mills Church, did draw his inspiration from life, though he went a bit overboard in the details. Margaret Wescoat, Richard and Margaret Lee Wescoat's youngest daughter, was known to have been quite beautiful, high-spirited, and intelligent. Arthur Pierce records that she was educated at Burlington in a school for young ladies run by a cultured Englishwoman. While attending Mrs. Davenport's school, she and her classmates heard General Washington address the army in the Burlington public square and probably came into contact with him several times. She seems to have been married at a very young age to a man by the name of Leonard, who possibly died while serving in the militia. Pierce found the name of Azariah Leonard in the records of the Gloucester County militia, but notes that there is no way of telling whether this was the husband of our heroine. Nevertheless, she was a widow at eighteen.

Nathan Pennington was her real-life hero. He had volunteered for the army at the age of nineteen, had been captured by the British and sent to Quebec as a prisoner-of-war. He managed to escape and somehow ended up in

New Jersey where he was put in charge of captured property at Chestnut Neck. It was in that capacity that he sailed upriver one day on a prize ship bound for The Forks to consult with his major. This young war hero in his own right was welcomed into Major Wescoat's home by his youngest daughter, beautiful and vivacious Margaret, eighteen year old widow and heiress to her father's fortune. I wonder why Peterson bothered to exaggerate.

Pennington courted and married the lovely Margaret and followed her father to Mays Landing when Wescoat sold the Clark estate in 1782. He became a ship builder in what would become the Atlantic County seat and his place of business and site of his home was known as Pennington's Point for a good many years. He and Margaret had nine children, four sons and five daughters. Pennington must have come from a good family because his brother, William, served as governor of New Jersey from 1813 to 1815 and a town near Princeton is named after him.

Peterson drew most of his characters from real local people but scrambled the details with literary license. Though the creek behind the Pleasant Mills Church was called "Neskeetchey," "Echeocheague," "Edgeackik," "Edgeachaick," "Checautoxin," and even "Etomoquang" in early records, the actual word "Nescochague" applied to the lake stems from Peterson's novel, as does the name "Sweetwater." Though there may have been some tradition of the area being called by an Indian name meaning "Sweetwater," the name doesn't seem to appear in any records prior to the novel in 1853. All of the records refer to the area as "Clark's Mill Pond."

Edward Black was the new owner of Clark's Mills and the mansion. When Black looked at Pleasant Mills, he saw the advantages of a good head of water, Clark's sawmills, and the abundant timber available in the adjacent cedar swamps, but he didn't have enough funds to put everything together. It wasn't long before he had financial difficulties and sold out to Joseph Ball.

Ball was no stranger to the area. He was the nephew of William Richards, the new owner/manager of Batsto Furnace and had managed Batsto himself during the late war. Pleasant Mills was only a temporary halting place for Ball, though. He'd come out of the war a wealthy man through his efforts at the Batsto Iron Works, and he intended to be richer still. Joseph Ball bought the Clark/Wescoat property purely as a speculation, having no intention of settling down as a country squire. Philadelphia and its potential attracted him far more than being an adjunct to his uncle. He figured he could make a good deal on reselling, and indeed he did. When Ball died in 1821, he owned properties in Pennsylvania, Virginia, New Jersey, and the District of Columbia; he had been one of the original directors of the Insurance Company of North America, and had been on the boards of several other Philadelphia businesses and financial institutions.

Ball sold the Pleasant Mills estate to his cousin, Samuel Richards, and a partner, Clayton Earl, on August 24, 1796. When he did, though, he made an exception for the two acres surrounding Clark's Meeting House. Samuel Richards and Clayton Earl were rising stars as speculators and businessmen, too, and bought the property from cousin Joe with the same idea: making a profit on resale. And who was the potential buyer they had in mind? Why Daddy, of course! Who was "Daddy?" None other than William Richards, lord of the manor of Batsto. William had grown rich through his own keen business sense since the Revolution and had been buying up much of the surrounding area since he had purchased Batsto in 1784. His son and Earl weren't making too much of a gamble when they bought the Clark's Mills property.

It does not seem that Richards ever lived in the Clark/Wescoat mansion. Though he could have easily managed the Batsto works from the mansion in Pleasant Mills, he continued to live at Batso itself.

This poses a question. If, as many say, the only "mansion" at Batsto during the Richards' era was the tiny center section of the present structure, why did Richards and his large (nineteen children eventually) family continue to live there when he owned a commodious house just a short distance away? He could have made it from the Clark mansion to Batsto by horseback in ten minutes, why would he lived crammed into such a small house right next to the dirty, smelly, noisy iron works? For that matter, why would Mrs. Richards put up with it? Richards' ownership of Clark's mansion suggests that there was another mansion on the Batsto hill, a "large and commodious" one that would keep him there instead of losing him to Pleasant Mills.

For five years during the period of Richard's ownership, 1799 through 1804, the mills at Pleasant Mills were leased by Benjamin W. Low, and it was probably Low and his family who occupied the mansion house. Low was a man decidedly ahead of his time. He had invented a process for turning old woolen cloth into new wool. He even got a patent on his invention. Unfortunately, recycling was not profitable back then, and Low's business failed. Both his lease and his patent were sold at auction to pay his debts.

Richards also saw to it that the congregation of Clark's Meeting House, having outgrown their building which Elijah Clark had constructed back in 1762, was able to build a new one in 1808. Nephew Ball decided that this was a good time to turn the property over to the congregation itself and made provisions to that end. Arthur Pierce found the record of the deed which Ball made in 1808, giving the land to the trustees: William Richards and his son, Jesse, Simon Lucas (the lay preacher), George Peterson (grandfather of the future author of *Kate Alyesford*), Laurence Peterson, John Morgan, and Gibson Ashcroft.

The intent and purpose [is] that they hold the House now thereon erected and such other house as may hereafter be erected thereon as a House or place of public worship for the use and enjoyment of the ministers and preachers of any Christian denomination to preach and expound God's holy word, in particular for the use and enjoyment of Traveling and local ministers of the Methodist Episcopal Church. (quoted in *Iron in the Pines*)

Ball even envisioned the need for a schoolhouse and made provision for that, too, in his deed of gift, but when the local school was finally built, it was located elsewhere. Clark's had long been Presbyterian, but the Methodists were sweeping the country at the time, and Bishop Asbury dedicated the new building. In respect for the early Scottish covenanters who had pioneered the Christian faith in this area and to the Brainerd brothers who had given their lives in local missionary work, the new church was called the "Brainerd Church."

A COTTON FACTORY

Not much happened around the Clark mansion over the next few years, and there seems to be no indication as to its occupants, though the Richards' family continued to own it. The Wharton ledgers indicate that, on February 25, 1822, William Lippincott, Benjamin W. Richards, Edward York, Benjamin Say, and William York negotiated an agreement with Benjamin's father, William Richards, to lease the mill, mill stream, mill pond, water rights, and 200 acres of property for ten years at a fee of $250.00 per year. They also added a provision which would allow them to buy the property for $4,000 at any time within five years. Additionally, for another $4,000, they could buy the Batsto Forge stream (the Nescochague) and water rights. This would enable them to dig a canal to bring the waters of that stream into mill pond to increase the flow through their new mill. This large (for the times) cotton establishment would operate under the name of the William Lippincott Company. Actually, William Lippincott was Benjamin W. Richards' brother-in-law so things were still "in the family." Lippincott built a 3,000 spindle cotton mill at the confluence of the Hammonton Creek with the Atsion where Clark's Sawmill used to stand.

Unfortunately, William Richards died soon after on August 31, 1823. The executors, his sons Samuel, Jesse, Benjamin W., and Thomas, conveyed all the Batsto lands, including Pleasant Mills and Forge Pond to Thomas S. Richards, Samuel's son, on December 25, 1824. It was quite a Christmas purchase for twenty-one year old Thomas, as successful at business as was his father. His poor uncle Jesse, though, must have had a miserable holiday. Jesse had been struggling to make Batsto profit during the last years when his father had lived in retirement. It was he who had been living in the Batsto mansion and acting as paternal father of the community, but he had little money. It must have been galling to realize that, for all his work, his inheritance had ended up in the hands of his young nephew rather than in his own. Though he would remain manager and part owner of the works, he was now basically working for his nephew! Actually, though, as the Wharton Ledgers note, that it seems to have been understood that Jesse "should have an undivided half of all the land conveyed by deed (12) to Thomas S. Richards." Indeed, Thomas S. Richards and his wife conveyed as much to Uncle Jesse by deed dated March 25, 1829, though one might question why it took him five years to do it!

Seven days after Thomas S. Richards had been given title to the property, on January 1, 1826, Edward and William York sold their one-fifth shares in the cotton factory to William Lippincott and Benjamin W. Richards, giving each of them a two-fifths share, with Benjamin Say still holding a one-fifth share. Unfortunately, Benjamin Richards and the others took an action which would come back to haunt their heirs over twenty-eight years later: they took a mortgage on the property which they signed on May 8, 1826. Then, as has happened so very many times, Death's Dark Angel interrupted their plans. Lippincott died. His will left his son, Joshua, owner of his share in the property. His widow, Cristiana Lippincott, and Edward York, acting as his executors, signed over the two-fifths share to Joshua on October 9, 1826. William Lippincott left one poignant reminder of his tenure in the Clark/Wescoat mansion: on a downstairs window pane is scratched: "William Lippincott, September 8, 1823."

On January 1, 1827, three months after Joshua Lippincott received his father's two-fifths share, Benjamin Say got out of the business, selling his one-fifth to Benjamin Richards and Joshua Lippincott. All this seems simple so far, but it is about to become complex. The cotton mill had operated for about six years so far. Of the original investors, three had sold out (the Yorks and Say) and one had died (Lippincott), leaving only Benjamin Richards and Lippincott's son, Joshua, in possession and control. But, mind you, they were still renting the property from Thomas S. Richards.

Then, on the 17th of February, 1827, Benjamin Richards sold his half share of the lease on both tracts (Pleasant Mills and Batsto Forge) to Augustus H. Richards, his brother, for $1.00. On June 15th of the same year, Samuel Richards, Thomas Richards, and Benjamin W. Richards, as executors for their father, William, Thomas S. Richards

(Samuel's son) and Jesse Richards, as owners of the Batsto tract (and part owners of the forge tract) sold to Joshua Lippincott and Augustus Richards the Pleasant Mills Tract and the Batsto Forge Tract for $8,000 (and $1.00 to Thomas S. Richards) in accordance with the original 1822 agreement with William Richards. The conveyance specifically gave the new owners the right to dig a canal from the Batsto Forge Pond behind the Batsto-Pleasant Mills Church to the lake feeding the mill (Lake Nescochague) which was accomplished. Traces of this canal are still present today.

Courtesy of Horace Somes, Jr.

Joshua Lippincott and His Wife
from a tintype

Obviously, Augustus H. Richards was only acting in behalf of his brother, Benjamin, in the transaction, perhaps because Benjamin, acting as executor, would be selling the property to himself. Augustus returned title to the half share to Benjamin at the end of the summer on September 10th for the customary $1.00. The property is listed as 200 acres for the Pleasant Mills Tract and 100 acres for the Forge Tract.

The cotton factory continued to operate at a profit during the next twenty-seven years. It did have one close brush with a fiery death, however. In July, 1834 a serious fire threatened the entire structure. Several buildings were actually burned to the ground, but the whole complex was saved from a similar fate by the presence of a large crowd of people who were, as the *Camden Mail* of July 25th reported, "attracted thither to witness the performance of a traveling Circus company."

The action of William Lippincott and Company's mortgage venture came back to haunt Benjamin, though. Good old Augustus H. Richards, who had stood in for Benjamin in the 1827 transaction, had purchased the mortgage during the intervening years, and, in 1854, he foreclosed. On October 21, 1854, Benjamin's half share was sold to Augustus. Augustus promptly conveyed the deed to his nephew, Lewis H. Richards, son of George Washington Richards, on November 13th. This left Lewis holding a half share and Joshua Lippincott holding the other half. Lewis H. Richards took over the operation of the mill and estate.

Then Joshua died. His will, dated March 24, 1855, was proved in Philadelphia on August 16, 1856 and in New Jersey on February 16, 1857. Joshua's death was heralded by a spectacular fire, a conflagration that would make a Viking of old mad with envy. On November 27, 1855, the cotton mill was burned to the ground by a fire of "unknown origin."

The ruins remained black and gaunt through the next few years. Then, in the last year before the Civil War, Lewis H. Richards sold his share to John McNeil, Thomas Irving, Robert M. Pierce, and Benjamin F. Holbrook. The sale, dated February 8th, 1860, turned over the once-valuable property to the new owners for a mere $2,000. They borrowed $10,000 from George W. Richards to rebuild.

They weren't finished with problems, however. South Carolina's secession didn't halt Northern business matters. On December 10, 1860, Henry Allen sued Robert Pierce and Benjamin Holbrook, half owners of Pleasant Mills, for $702.71, and a Writ of Attachment allowed sheriff Ezra Cordery to seize the property ten days later. The partners: McNeil, Irving, Pierce, and Holbrook, secured still another mortgage for $9,000 on June 1st, 1861, but this time, they did not risk the Batsto Forge Tract. On July 12th, Pierce and Holbrook's half share was actually attached.

A New Business: Paper

During this eventful year of 1861, Irving and McNeil built a paper mill on the site of the burned cotton factory. The manufacture of paper was a growth industry in the first half of the nineteenth century. Paper available in the previous century was made by hand from cotton and linen fiber. By the early nineteenth century, a method was discovered to mass-produce paper and demand soared. The demand for paper was so great, as a matter of fact, that serious shortages of the raw materials developed, and manufacturers frantically tried a large variety of materials in their attempt to supply the needed quantities of paper. When we think of "King Cotton," we think of cloth, but a great deal of the crop went into paper production. That supply was interrupted by the secession of the southern states from the union and the commencement of the Civil War.

Paper manufacturers had already tried a variety of strange materials in their quest for cheap paper: hemp, bark, potatoes, cattails, wood chips, and, would you believe, even Egyptian mummies! Desperate times require desperate measures, and their linen and papyrus wrapping were seen as an inexpensive source of fiber. McCarty had already set up his paper mill on the Wading River some twenty-six years prior to that at Pleasant Mills, and he had had success using the salt hay which grew so plentifully on the meadows of the lower Mullica. The Harris brothers were now in full production in McCarty's old mill. It's too bad that Benjamin Low wasn't still around with his recycling idea. Perhaps he could have had success recycling cotton rather than wool.

Pierce and Holbrook's half share was finally sold to John W. Farrell on August 7, 1862. He also bought a one-quarter interest in the Batsto Forge Tract for $100. Thus, as of January 1, 1863, the Batsto Forge Tract was owned one-half by John W. Farrell and one-half by the children of Joshua Lippincott. The Pleasant Mills Tract was divided as follows: John McNeil, one-quarter share, Thomas Irving, one-quarter share, and John Farrell, one-half share. Irving, as managing partner, took up residence in the Clark/Wescoat mansion. Other partners lived in the house with the Irvings when they were visiting, and one, George W. Rich, actually lived there a number of years when he was acting as superintendent of the mill. Records indicate that, during the Civil War, Helen Mar Irving, Thomas' daughter, presented a flag to a company of Batsto Guards. She eventually celebrated her marriage in the mansion.

In 1864, McNeil and Irving took a ten-year lease on the Weymouth Mills which gave them an interest that would wean them from Pleasant Mills. What really did the trick was a sheriff's attachment against their interest in the company. McNeil and Irving continued operations. What had been Pierce and Holbrook's interest was conveyed to John W. Farrell. An operation that had existed on very shaky foundations quickly became more firmly based through Farrell's expertise and money. Once again, though, a mortgage comes into the picture. John Farrell borrowed $14,950 from George W. Wharton on his half shares of the Pleasant Mills Tract and the Forge Tract.

On February 9, 1865, John Farrell sold his share in the Pleasant Mills property to his son, William E. Farrell for $3,500. McNeil and Irving finally sold their share of Pleasant Mills to William Farrell on June 20, 1865 for $15,000. Farrell continued their Nescochague Manufacturing Company for another fourteen years. Apparently there was still some legal question concerning the original forced sale of Pierce and Holbrook's share back in 1862, so William Farrell bought them out completely on the 17th of January, 1870 for $50. The paper machine which Farrell installed in his mill was the second largest such machine in the world at the time.

When John W. Farrell and his son, William, took over the mill, they, too, moved into the mansion. William and his family were left in the house when his father later moved to Philadelphia.

In 1878, however, the "scourge of the pines" struck once again. For a second time, dawn's first light saw a smouldering ruin where a once-profitable business used to be. William E. Farrell reorganized the Nescochague Manufacturing Company (possibly declaring bankruptcy after the fire) as the Pleasant Mills Paper Company, to whom he sold his title on the 29th of May, 1880 for $1.00. Farrell was president and Herman Hoopes served as secretary. The new company proceeded to build a new paper factory on the ruins of the old. Hoopes must have had an investment in the property, but Farrell became sole owner once again in 1887.

Charles F. Green (*Pleasant Mills, New Jersey*) relates that Farrell was

> a shrewd man of business, thoroughly conversant with the papermakers' art, and the plant was his pride. Having set a high standard for its products, he maintained it, whether business was good or bad, and as J.H. Hall remarks in his history of Atlantic county, "Its market was the world."

Now remember "Death's Dark Angel?" Well, he came again, most inconveniently. William was not a particularly healthy man and his end-of-life romance with his nurse caused a scandal that had far-reaching consequences. Cecilia Hyslop of Troy, N.Y. was hired to look after the ailing William Farrell. Cecilia had found a woman's dream: a rich older man on his last legs. She took advantage of his last, brief period of health and married the old coot, who providently died soon after on March 9, 1893.

When the will was read, the family found out that the old guy had had the time to do more than get married. He left his entire estate to his new wife. His poor, old father, his brothers, and his sisters were left absolutely nothing at all. Naturally, they contested the will, and, as legal matters are wont to do, the case dragged on for five years. After Farrell's death, his manager, William Oliver, had moved into the mansion, but Oliver picked the wrong horse to back in the race. He testified on behalf of Farrell's father and family. The wife won, and Oliver

The Pleasant Mills Deveopment Company Summer Colony

was sent packing. To replace him, Mrs. Farrell hired Alexander J. McKeone to manage her mill. McKeone took up residence in the Clark/Wescoat mansion in 1899.

Mrs. Cecilia Hyslop Farrell did not remain single very long. She soon married L.M. Cresse of Ocean City. Cresse became president of the paper company, a position he maintained until his death in 1914.

By this time, the twice-widowed Mrs. Cresse had had enough of the paper business. In April, 1915, the mill was closed. Two years later, she sold the property to A.J. McKeone, the former manager of the plant, who wanted to reopen it. Unfortunately, the timing couldn't have been worse. World War One was raging in Europe and was about to drag the United States into its quagmire. The labor pool was minimal. Materials were very difficult to acquire. Shipping rates were exorbitant. In September, 1917, after two years of trying, McKeone sold out to the Norristown Magnesia and Asbestos Company in Pennsylvania. McKeone, however, retained possession of the Pleasant Mills mansion of Clark and Wescoat.

The new owners made alterations and put in new machinery, but the parent company folded in 1925, and the paper mill stopped production in April of that year.

McKeone eventually turned over the mansion property to his daughters, Elizabeth M. Rafferty and Katherine E. McKeone in 1925. When Mary and Raymond Baker bought it on November 17, 1954, "Sweetwater" was still "all in the family." Mrs. Baker was Alexander McKeone's granddaughter. During their tenure, the Bakers lovingly restored the old house to its former glory. The mill was not so fortunate.

FROM PAPER TO LEISURE TO BUST

In October of the same year, T.B. Bucholz of Philadelphia and Atlantic City was out looking for a site for the planned Atlantic City Motor Speedway. He happened to pass through Pleasant Mills and was very impressed with the beauty of the area. He saw the possibilities for developing Pleasant Mills into a Maine-style country club with bungalows for the moderately wealthy. The streams and lakes would provide an excellent setting for hunting and fishing, while rustic cabins would attract city folk looking for an escape.

In 1926, he made a deal with the Pleasant Mills Paper Company to buy the whole estate. He managed to convince others to invest in the Pleasant Mills Development Company, in which he kept a large interest and continued his general supervision of the planned construction. He saw to it that the remains of William E. Farrell, long buried in Pleasantville, were brought to Pleasant Mills and reinterred in the churchyard of the Batsto-Pleasant Mills Methodist Church. New ground was purchased for his interment, and his widow, now also the widow Cresse, donated the land to the church to enlarge the old cemetery. So many dreams and schemes have gone for bust in the pines, though, and this one proved no different. The stock market crash and the ensuing Depression effectively destroyed any hope of developing a Mecca for the moderately wealthy by throwing almost everyone to the bottom of the economic ladder for a decade.

Years of Neglect

The Great Depression forced almost everything in the country to decline. People barely scraped together enough to feed their families. Along the Mullica, things hadn't been prosperous since the dwindling natural resources and the railroads combined to move business elsewhere. By the time the Depression hit, people were used to getting by on what they could grow and hunt.

The old mill was another story, however. No one wanted the derelict, and it lay abandoned and decaying. People who had lost most, if not all, of their savings and their jobs had no interest in buying into a leisure community, and no one wanted to rehabilitate an outdated paper mill.

Water seeped under the shingles of some of the roofs, and rot finally caused them to collapse. Rotten floors followed the rotten roofs. Even the stone walls crumbled. Within twenty years of its closing, the mill looked like it had been standing vacant since the Civil War. The property was finally forfeited for unpaid taxes, and Mullica Township put the property up for tax sale.

Three hundred acres of land and the decrepit old mill were purchased by a man named Thomas McCorkle for $7,500. McCorkle formed the Pleasant Mills Company with the idea of continuing to promote real estate development and of forming a religious camp on the property. The end of World War Two and growing prosperity seemed to encourage confidence, but McCorkle found it more than he could handle.

Three years after his purchase, he sold everything to Ray and Mary Baker. Mary, as has been previously mentioned, was the granddaughter of Alexander McKeone, and her family still owned the Clark mansion. The Bakers were professional artists who fell in love with the picturesque old ruins and dreamed of using it as a center for the arts. McCorkle was encouraged by their dreams and sold them the property with the idea that the mill be used for the production and sale of art.

Artistic Dreams

Artists have wonderful dreams but are sometimes a little short on realities. The Bakers partially restored the mill and used it for the production of silk-screened materials, but the complex was far more demanding in time and money than the Bakers could supply of either.

Mary Baker had lived in Swarthmore, Pennsylvania, and, while there, had become acquainted with Ada Fenno. Mrs. Fenno's husband had been an Italian engineer, and she had inherited quite a bit of money when he died. She had a philanthropic nature and was involved with cultural projects of various sorts. Her love was the theatre. She took one look at the picturesque old ruins and saw possibilities. How delightful it would be to have a theatre in the pines! The Bakers were happy to sell the mill to her in 1952, and Ada proceeded to convert the old pulp room into a 250-seat theatre for the performing arts. She also bought an old house in Bulltown and fixed it up as a residence for her manager.

Her Pleasant Mills Playhouse threw open its doors to the public on July 3, 1953. During its brief day in the sun, the playhouse hosted real professional theatre. Actors Tony Perkins and Efrem Zimbalist, Jr. are among the alumni of Mrs. Fenno's dream. Unfortunately, even her wealth couldn't sustain its operation. The building was a constant drain on her finances. She hadn't counted on just how far out in the country Pleasant Mills was in the early '50's. The Actors Equity demanded full scale wages for their members who worked at the playhouse. A two hundred fifty-seat house was not large enough to support the productions. There wasn't sufficient land to provide parking for those who did come to see the performances in the pines. Finally, local residents weren't happy with all the people and traffic that brought the city's congestion to their quiet corner of the world.

After five years, Ada Fenno knew what she had to do: she closed her beloved playhouse. The year 1957 saw the end of her cultural dream for the pinelands.

Once again, the mill was abandoned to the elements. Mrs. Fenno lived in her apartments in Rome and in New York for another eighteen years, but she never forgot her playhouse in the pines. When she died in 1975, she left the property in trust to the town of Hammonton with the proviso that it be used for artistic and cultural purposes.

Paxamicus, a theatre group in New York, looked the place over with the idea of reopening the playhouse in the pines, but there was much local opposition. Arson finally prevented them from gaining an occupancy permit, and they abandoned the project.

In 1982, Paul Lightman formed the Pleasant Mills Foundation, a nonprofit organization, dedicated to promoting the arts. Paul actually lived in the old paper cutting room and offered programs in art, literature, and photography to the general public. Paul opened the buildings to meetings of the Daughters of the American Revolution and supported local garden clubs and historical associations. He became a speaker for the Pinelands Commission and has given talks all over New Jersey about his beloved pinelands. Like so many others, he has come to love this little corner of the world, its beauty; its serenity; its peace; but at eighty, he just doesn't have the ability to do everything that has to be done. The mill has become just too much for him.

Paul is passing on the torch to a new and younger set of visionaries who see potentiality for his beloved old mill in the pines. He doesn't do it without regrets, though. Stand amongst the buttonwoods which surround this old mill on a fine, sunlit day at almost any time of the year. You will see beauty and feel the whisper of peace as you have never known it before. Paul stands looking back on the crumbling old walls of his home, sheltered by the ancient sycamores that were young when privateers sold their prizes at The Forks. The crocuses thrust their way through the sandy soil, and a cheerful "hello" from another local resident echoes down from the road. Paul is moving to Atlantic City and knows that the beaches of the shore have their charm, but how can you trade Paradise, even for the whole world?

ADDITIONAL NOTE: According to tradition, a man by the name of Jack Mullin was the first to dam the stream on which Elijah Clark later built his mansion and sawmill. Mullin is supposed to have built a sawmill there by the 1750's, prior to Clark's purchase. Unfortunately, this legend cannot be substantiated. Arthur Pierce did an amazing amount of research for his *Iron in the Pines*, and even he gives Mullin's Mill a passing reference by stating that "Another mill, possibly legendary, was built by a Jack Mullin near the present pond at Pleasant Mills." I would take this to mean that Pierce had found no reference to Jack Mullin, despite his research.

In the records of Clark's property as recorded in the Batsto ledgers, no mention is made of a Jack Mullin or of a mill operating on Clark's property when he purchased the first acreage from his brothers. For that reason, I have not mentioned such a mill in the preceding text.

These photographs were originally one panoramic view of Sweetwater/
Pleasant Mills.
They were taken from the roof of the old paper mill.

All three photographs are courtesy of
Budd Wilson.

Romantic Ruins

The Main Complex Looking North

Three different mill complexes stood on these grounds in Pleasant Mills: a 3,000-spindle cotton factory (1821-1856), a paper mill (1861-1878), and a second paper factory (c.1880-1925). Each of the first two businesses were destroyed by fire, and it is not known whether portions of the walls were used in constructing the new buildings. Though all the paper machinery is gone, the remaining buildings portray a "modern" turn-of-the-century paper company somewhat different from that represented by Harrisville, a mid-nineteenth century complex.

Unlike Harrisville's brown paper, the Pleasant Mills companies produced much lighter material. At some time, the owners dug a leaching pond in the rear of the complex. The pulp was made in the building above on the right. Huge rollers used to span the walls of the center section. These rolled the pulp into paper. An adjoining boiler room produced heat which was used to dry the paper before it reached the cutting house at the far end.

The Rolling Room

The long sheets of paper were cut into standard sizes inside the cutting room, then taken to the warehouse in the rear for packaging and shipping.

During the early years of this century, this facility was considered one of the largest paper manufacturing complexes in the state of New Jersey. It's demise was due, not to its own lack of productivity, but to the bankruptcy of its parent company.

Photograph by John Pearce

The West Facade Looking South
The Cutting Room is on the left, Rolling Room in the center,
and the Pulp Room at the far end.

Photograph by John Pearce

A View from the Cutting Room, over the Rolling Room,
to the Pulp Room at the far end of the main complex.

The Pulp Room became the main theatre when Mrs. Fenno turned the buildings into a center for the performing arts. Paul Lightman has used the Cutting Room as living quarters during his stewardship.

154

The Warehouse
This building would have been filled with packages of paper waiting to be shipped to businesses across the country.
Despite the waiting Mullica, all of its products were hauled overland by trucks
and wagons to the railroads at Elwood.

The Old Mill has been loved by Paul Lightman for many years now, and it is with deep sadness that he is passing the torch to others. At eighty, his flesh is weakening, though his spirit burns as brightly as ever. These old walls have witnessed the entire century, and perhaps parts of them have seen almost another whole century before this one. They still bear mute testimony to the industry which once sustained the people of the pines.

The Batsto-Pleasant Mills Church

Photograph by John Pearce

The Batsto-Pleasant Mills Church - 1996
Built in 1808

Methodism in New Jersey was insignificant until after the Revolutionary War, though Methodist preachers had visited the colony prior to the outbreak of hostilities, but there is no record of the places in which they preached. The Rev. Benjamin Abbott made tours in the area during 1778 through at least 1792, but he did not record his every preaching point. He took advantage of every existing church building, regardless of denomination, and preached in open fields and in private homes. Robert Steelman, in *What God Has Wrought*, notes that he was an uneducated man, but he knew his Bible.

> *His diary is replete with such phrases as "the slain lay all around the house." These things may seem strange to modern ears, but all sorts of physical manifestations accompanied the preaching of Abbott. Sinners would scream for mercy. Men and women would fall prostrate as though dead. Others would run away in dread. The result was that the most wicked sinners were converted.*

Steelman is a little uncertain about the 1778 date but says if it is correct, Abbott was the first Methodist preacher to preach in the Atlantic and Ocean County areas.

Two circuits were established for New Jersey in 1781: the West Jersey Circuit and the East Jersey Circuit, though he notes that it is not certain whether they actually followed the old political division of the Jerseys exactly. Joseph Cromwell and Caleb B. Pedicord served the West Jersey Circuit. Pedicord earned a reputation as one of those who converted the infamous Joe Mulliner in a jail cell in Mount Holly before he was hung. Mulliner was the leader of the Refugees in the Batsto area, and his final act on the gallows was a magnificent performance. (See THE HEADLESS GHOST OF THE PINES)

In 1784, John Wesley, the founder of Methodism, ordained Thomas Coke to the office of Superintendent, and Coke made several visits to America. He first arrived in New York on November 3, 1784 and, at a Christmas conference in Baltimore, he and Francis Asbury were elected joint superintendents over the American church. Coke set apart Asbury as superintendent on December 27, 1784. The new church was named the Methodist Episcopal Church and *The Sunday Service of the Methodists in North America* was accepted.

In 1787, Ezekiel Cooper and Nathaniel B. Mills preached throughout the huge Trenton Circuit, which included Speedwell Furnace, Batsto, Bodine's, and Tuckerton, among numerous others. The circuit took six weeks to complete, so any individual location saw a preacher only once during that period.

The oldest circuit record in New Jersey, Steelman says, is that for the Salem Circuit, from May 1789 to March 1814. The circuit included all of South Jersey. Old Gloucester County was the northernmost area served. The area now Atlantic County was made part of a new circuit, the Bethel Circuit, in 1790.

The Rev. Richard Sneath preached the Bethel Circuit in 1798-1799 which included stops in Batsto. In the following year, he preached the Burlington Circuit and made stops at Lower Bank. Francis Asbury made a tour in 1791. On September 8th of that year, a Friday, he preached in Tuckerton. The next day, he began his trip to Batsto and "rode a dreary, mosquito path, in great weakness, to Batsto works." That Sunday, he preached there, either in Clark's Meeting House or in an open field, and "advised the people to build a house for the benefit of those men so busily employed day and night, Sabbaths not excepted, in the manufacture of iron - rude and rough, and strangely ignorant of God."

In 1809, Bishop Asbury and his associate, Henry Boehm, set out from Head of River, travelled through Mays Landing, English Creek, Absecon, and finally arrived in Pleasant Mills. They stayed at the Batsto Manor House, and, on Friday, April 21, 1809, Bishop Asbury dedicated the newly-constructed Batsto-Pleasant Mills Methodist Church, which had been built on the site of the old Clark's Meeting House the previous year. According to Charles Green, in his booklet on Pleasant Mills, the people of the area decided to name their new church after the Presbyterian ministers who had done such excellent work with the Native Americans in the area, and who had been so well-loved by the Pleasant Mills settlers. The first trustees of the new church were: William Richards, Simon Lucus, S. Gibson Ashcraft, George Peterson, Jesse Richards, Laurence Peterson, and John Morgan.

The strength of Methodism, in those early years, was not completely based on the dedication of their clergy, deep as it was. Methodist classes were organized everywhere, and lay people frequently conducted services and Bible studies during the lengthy weeks between visits of the circuit-riding clergy.

Simon Lucas, farmer and captain of the local militia, was a Methodist lay preacher at the Brainerd Church during the first part of the nineteenth century, and a colorful character he was! Often, the lay preachers equalled the ordained clergy in both passion and expertise and gained the respectful title of "reverend" from their grateful people, even though they were never actually ordained.

Passionate in his beliefs, Simon Lucus once embarrassed a young lady who came to church dressed in a bit more finery than Simon preferred. He strode over to her pew and commented that the broach at her throat reminded him of the devil's eye. She left the building, blushing and in great haste.

Lucas could be practical, though, as another story shows. When the herring were running in the river, great masses of them crowded their way upriver, and all the local men swarmed out to catch them.

Unfortunately, it was a Sunday, and, according to Charles Green, Jesse Richards and one of his daughters were walking to church, when they passed the men fishing in the creek. Jesse's daughter was scandalized. How, she asked her father, could Simon Lucas permit such a violation of the Sabbath? Her father scratched his chin and said he didn't know, but he'd ask him after church. On the way home, his daughter was once again affronted by the fishermen and demanded of her father whether he had asked preacher Simon about it. "Yes," her father replied. Simon said, "The time to catch herring is when the herring are here to catch." (Arthur Pierce, *Iron in the Pines*, and Father Beck, *Jersey Genesis*, quote the story also.) A gravestone in the Pleasant Mills cemetery shows that Simon Lucas and his wife shared a good many years on this earth. When he died at 87 and she at 83, they had both "known the Lord" for over sixty years.

Green notes that the period from 1826 through 1831 was the most noteworthy for the church in Pleasant Mills. Most of the conferences of the West Jersey District were held at the church during this period. Charles Pitman was the Presiding Elder of the district. People would travel to the church from miles around, setting up tents around the little building. After the business sessions were over, a camp meeting would start up that would last for days.

Robert Steelman, in his history of New Jersey Methodism, *What God Has Wrought*, quotes the Rev. James Newell on one camp meeting held on the Salem Circuit in 1809. One of the preachers was the Rev. Samuel Coates, and Rev. Newell says he would never forget it. I guess not!

[The sermon] *was on the resurrection and the judgment, the appearance of the white throne, etc. He sounded the trumpet and the trembling earth gave forth its unnumbered millions, while the ocean rolled its inmates to the shore, Death and Hell gave up their victims, all taking their course toward, and standing before the great white throne, all trembling to hear the fiat of God, the terrible Judge. The grandeur, the sublimity, the eloquence of this description of the scene at the last days can never be forgotten. All eyes were fastened upon him, streaming tears attested the depth of feeling, while he threw open the portals of the mansions of bliss, and crowned the happy righteous with glory - gave them palms of victory and harps of melody - then moving toward the front of the stand the preacher began to drop the wicked into hell; and at last with a mighty effort plunged the whole of the condemned into the abyss, the bottomless pit of eternal woe. Such an effect I never witnessed before or since. Such screams and cries for mercy; such praying and shouting all over the vast assemblage of the camp ground; from all classes - for all were affected. . . . The most respectable persons were down on the ground, rolling among the leaves, or prostrate among the seats; and a general surrender to the Lord seemed to prevail throughout the encampment.*

No less a person than Alexander Gilmore quoted this in his Centenary Memorial Sermon, "What Has God Wrought," delivered before the New Jersey Annual Conference in 1866. It was just such excitement that drew people from great distances in the days before television and movies provided a more sedentary thrill - and terror.

Most of the staunch supporters of this area rest in the surrounding cemetery, including Jesse Richards and his wife, and Nicholas Sooy I, the founder of the Washington Tavern on the Old Road to Little Egg Harbor, and his wife, Sarah, many of the Wescoat family, and old Simon Lucas himself.

At one time, the old high pulpit was removed from the building and a more "modern" speaking platform was installed, but it was wisely returned to its original style some years ago. It is easy to understand the pride of the people of Batsto-Pleasant Mills over the years in their little gem in the pines.

Enduring Beauty
Emma Van Sant Moore

There is no end to beauty in the pines;
Beyond the river shore—tall and far
They rise, like ocean billows bound with vines;
Yet reaching, ever reeaching for a star.
When tossed by wind, they have a muted roar,
That stirs the heart and gives the soul a lift
As when the green sea breaks along the shore,
Or thunderclouds collide like boats adrift.

from *Mullica*, 1960

The Interior of the Batsto-Pleasant Mills Methodist Church
The building was restored a few years ago to its original 1808 appearance with its raised pulpit.

Photograph by John Pearce

Saint Mary's of the Assumption

otherwise known as

St. Mary's Roman Catholic Church in the Pines

(No Longer in Existence)

Most of the early settlers of Pleasant Mills were either of the Presbyterian faith or of one of the other churches that were born of the Protestant Reformation. A great deal of distrust and hatred existed between the various Protestant denominations and the Roman Catholic Church, who viewed each other as heretics from the True Faith.

The religious wars of the sixteenth century in Europe left an exhausted populace no choice in religious matters. The religion of the prince would be the religion of the principality over which he ruled. No one believed that it was possible for people of different faiths to live in the same geographical area. Protestant countries persecuted Roman Catholics within their territories, and Roman Catholics persecuted Protestants within the boundaries of their countries, giving rise to martyred saints on both sides.

In England, adherence to the Roman Catholic faith meant treason against the crown, which, under Henry VIII, had declared itself supreme head of the Christian faith in England. Faithful Roman Catholics were beheaded and burned at the stake. When Henry VIII's young son, Edward, died, Mary Tudor succeeded her half brother on the throne and promptly had all Protestant leaders arrested and slain. When she, too, died childless, her half sister Elizabeth wanted nothing more than peace, stability, and prosperity, but the resulting national church did not include tolerance for Roman Catholics.

Scotland had known such fervor from the leadership of John Knox, a passionate follower of John Calvin in Geneva, that they had even driven their Roman Catholic Queen Mary Stuart to exile in England and her eventual death at her cousin Elizabeth's order.

Most of the French were equally passionate Roman Catholics, and major persecutions of Protestants erupted from time to time when thousands of Huguenots were killed. The German states, numerous as they were, constantly fought amongst themselves, ostensibly on the basis of religion.

Though politics had every bit as much to do with the antagonism between adherents of the different faiths as did religion, the hatreds and fears were very real. When settlers left their European homelands for the New World, they brought those prejudices with them. The Pilgrims and Puritans of the Plymouth and Massachusetts Bay colonies left their homes in England because of religious persecution, but they were equally intolerant of any who disagreed with their faith once they settled on this side of the ocean. They drove many dissenters to Rhode Island and were cruel in their banishment of adherents of the Quaker faith. Some were literally beaten out of the colony, and when they returned, they were hung from the gallows tree in Boston.

Maryland was founded by the Roman Catholic Calvert family, but they knew that Roman Catholic settlers would be far outnumbered by Protestants and tried to ensure religious harmony in the colony. It didn't work. When Protestant colonists outnumbered Roman Catholics, they withdrew religious toleration for their enemies.

Rhode Island became one of the earliest hosts of toleration and religious freedom, but the colony was considered a maverick by the rest of New England. The Quakers, however, after their initial fervor in New England which drove them to denounce the Puritan faith even during Sunday services, became firm advocates of a live-and-let-live policy. Consequently, Pennsylvania and West Jersey inherited from them a sense of security in living with religious toleration.

The French and Indian War jarred everyone in the English colonies into a passionate fear and hatred of Roman Catholicism. The Roman Catholic French in Canada used Native American Indians, converted by Franciscan and Jesuit priests, to slaughter their "heretic" New England neighbors. This did not help them to "win friends and influence people," except in the negative, of course.

Until the successful conclusion of the Revolutionary War, Roman Catholics were few and far between in the colonies which would become the United States. Yet with the beginning of the nineteenth century, as a product of the Revolution in acknowledging that "all men . . . are endowed with certain unalienable rights," the idea of tolerance between faiths was catching on.

With the onset of the industrial age, people from Roman Catholic countries in Europe began to immigrate to the United States to find new homes and jobs to keep their families from starving and to give themselves and their children a chance which they would not have if they were to remain in the old country. Roman Catholic German and Irish families were especially eager to find new lives, but they were equally passionate in their faith. In the cities, they could at least find some security and support by living close to others of the same faith and extraction.

Country areas were more difficult. If there were churches in the towns and villages, they were undoubtedly of some Protestant faith, and poor Roman Catholic working families didn't have enough money to buy land and build a church of their own faith. That's why Saint Mary's of the Assumption was such a miracle. Buried deep in the pines, in the midst of an area that was being swept by Methodist revivalism, a small chapel of the Roman Catholic faith was built with the cooperation and good will of the Protestant families who lived in the area.

Irish and German Catholic families had been attracted to the Batsto/Pleasant Mills area by the jobs offered in the Richards enterprises, but the fervency of their faith had no release. Priests from Philadelphia visited the area and said Mass for gatherings of Catholics in their tiny homes, but the families yearned for a real church in which to worship.

In 1826, kindhearted Jesse Richards offered to give his Catholic families a piece of land on which they could build their church and made generous contributions towards its construction costs as well. Work was soon begun, and by the following year, a small church proudly held high the cross on its steeple in the pines. This little church was the first of the Roman Catholic faith to be built south of Trenton and possibly the third in all of New Jersey.

Father Edward R. Mayne, a convert from one of the Protestant faiths, served as the first pastor of the mission, but he only was able to journey down from Saint Augustine's in Philadelphia once a month. Unfortunately, though Father Mayne began services in Saint Mary's, it couldn't be dedicated because Philadelphia had no bishop that year. The former bishop, Bishop Conwell, had gone to Rome, and the Right Reverend Patrick Kendrick wasn't appointed Bishop of Philadelphia until 1830. On August 15th of that year, though, Bishop Kendrick made the journey into the pines to dedicate Saint Mary's of the Assumption.

In about the year the church was dedicated, the people built a house nearby. They thought that they could rent it to a family who would care for the priest when he was in the area, but the priest stayed at the Batsto Mansion with Episcopalian Jesse Richards and his family. Jesse's daughter even took care of the altar. The house was rented to Jerry Fitzgerald. It was later sold to Dr. Charles D. Smith, who provided local medical services. When Dr. Smith moved to Elwood, the building was sold to Dr. James Stille of Atlantic City.

Unfortunately, Father Mayne caught tuberculosis and went to Florida for his health. The climate seemed to help him, and he became the pastor of a church in Saint Augustine. Sadly, though, there were no miracles for him, and he died when he was in his early thirties.

Research by Mrs. L. Dow Balliett and Laura Lavinia Willis of the Atlantic County Historical Society in 1915 established the following list of priests who served Saint Mary's:

> 1833 - The Rev. James Cummisky from Phildelphia
> 1834 - The Rev. William Whelan from Philadelphia, occasionally
> 1835 - The Rev. Patrick Reilly from Philadelphia, occasionally
> 1836 - The Rev. Edward McCarthy, S.J., from St. Joseph's Church, Philadelphia, monthly
> 1837 - The Rev. Richard Waters, S.J., from St. Joseph's Church, Philadelphia, monthly
> 1838 - The Rev. Edward Sourin, from St. Charles Seminary
> 1839 - The Rev. James Miller, C.M. from Philadelphia
> 1840- 1843 - The Rev. William Loughran, from St. Michaels Church, Philadelphia
> 1844 - The Rev. B. Rolando, C.M., from St. Charles Seminary
> 1845-1848 - The Rev. Hugh Lane, from St. Phillip's Church, Philadelphia
>   Three Redemptorists from St. Peter's, Philadelphia made occasional visits
> 1848 - St. Mary's became a mission of Gloucester under Father Waldron, and Fathers
>   Finnegan and Hannegan attended occasionally through 1859
> 1849 - The Rev. Hugh Kenny, St. Michael's Church, Philadelphia
>   Redemptorist Fathers Bayer, Cowdenhave, and Hotzer from Philadelphia
>   occasionally
> 1850 - The Rev. J. Finnegan, from Gloucester, N.J.
> 1857 - St. Mary's became a mission of St. Mary's in Camden

Father McCarthy's Latin baptismal record shows only eleven baptisms, but among them are names which are still recognized in Washington Township:

August 9, 1835: Nicholas, born December 26, 1834, of Samuel Crowley and Parnelia Saney [Sooy]
October 11, 1835: Samuel, born March 28, from Abraham Nichols and Mary Ann Crowley
September 11, 1836: James, born February 5, 1836 from James McCambridge and Anna Miller
October 9, 1836: Charles, born May 13, 1836, from Samuel Crowley and Parnelia Saney [Sooy]

Nicholas and Rebecca Crowley would later live in Herman and be the parents of James Morell Crowley of Green Bank (See Herman and Green Bank). Abraham Nichols kept a tavern in Crowleytown and is the ancestor of most of the Nichols who live in the township today (See Bulltown). James McCambridge kept the Eagle Tavern near Speedwell. His sister married the first Stephen Lee (See Speedwell).

The year 1860 seems to have been the watershed for Saint Mary's. The visit of a priest was on December 11th of that year. For the next four years, the chapel had no priestly visitations at all. Then in 1865, a young woman from the Dillet (or Dellet) family spoke to a priest in Philadelphia and told him the situation at Saint Mary's. He directed her to speak to a priest in Camden, presumably because the church had been under the administration of the Camden parish as a mission. She spoke to a Father Byrne in Camden who actually had the initiative to come down to see the little church for himself. He found it in good shape, but it seems that many of the Catholic families had lost interest in it and had strayed from their faith during the years they had been ignored. Of course, most of the families had moved away when iron production had stopped at Batsto, and glass manufacturing had almost ceased as well. While Father Byrne was in Pleasant Mills, he boarded with a Protestant, Mr. Patterson, and said Mass in a private home.

The following year, it became one of the missions of the church in Egg Harbor, and Father Turnes tended to the few families in the area until 1877. His successor, Father Esser, continued the ministry in the pines through 1885. When the Hammonton parish was formed, the mission was transferred to that church, but there were few Catholics in the area any more. Alexander McKeon, manager of the mill, and his family, attended Mass in Hammonton. The Hammonton priest took the pews and a painting of the Crucifixion and used them in his church, and the little chapel lay vacant. Then in April, 1900, a forest fire swept through the area, and Saint Mary's of the Assumption was no more than a memory.

The cemetery that adjoined the church remained well-tended into this present century, though, it, too, fell on hard times as the century wore on and its faithful caregivers passed away. Many of its stones were victims of vandalism. The oldest remaining stone is that of Mary McCambridge, who passed away in 1835. The last known grave is that of George McCambridge in 1906. Beneath the trees of Pleasant Mills like the last remains of the Froelingers. He may have spelled it differently, but those whose mouths water at the taste of salt water taffy should recognize the inventor's name. These are George Fralinger's parents, immigrants from Germany. Franz Froehlinger is given credit for fathering sixteen children. He died at the age of sixty-six on February 15, 1857, and was buried here by Saint Mary's of the Assumption.

The Valley for Me

Emma Van Sant Moore

"For me the mountains, " some folk say,
    "And the clean, rarefied air!"
But I'll take the winding valley way
    Beside a river fair.

Some folk say, they like not the mists
    That rise in the valley land—
I wonder if the clouds that touch the hills
    Differ much from the mists where I stand.

Folk seem so alone on the mountain-top—
    So many fall by the way—
I'll keep the friendship of the humble folk
    And in my valley stay!

I do not like my head in the clouds—
    High places are not my goal;
I'd rather dwell in the valley below
    And feed my thirsting soul

On the beauty of river flowing free—
    White sails in a freshening gale!
Let those who will, climb the mountain peak—
    I'll stay in the sheltering vale!

from *Mullica*, 1960

Bulltown and Tylertown

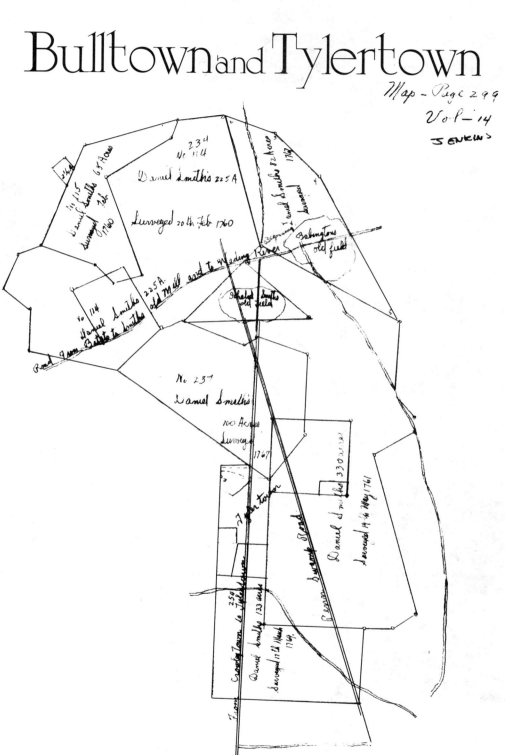

A map from the Wharton Ledgers, Volume 14, page 229 of Daniel Smith's acreage in the area of Tylertown. Across the top runs the original road from Batsto to Sooy's Inn (Washington) and from thence to Smith's Old Mill (see TRULY FORGOTTEN TOWNS), the road to Penn Swamp, and the road from Crowleytown to Tulpehocken. See the map at the end of the BATSTO section for the location of Smith's Old Field and Babington's Old Field.

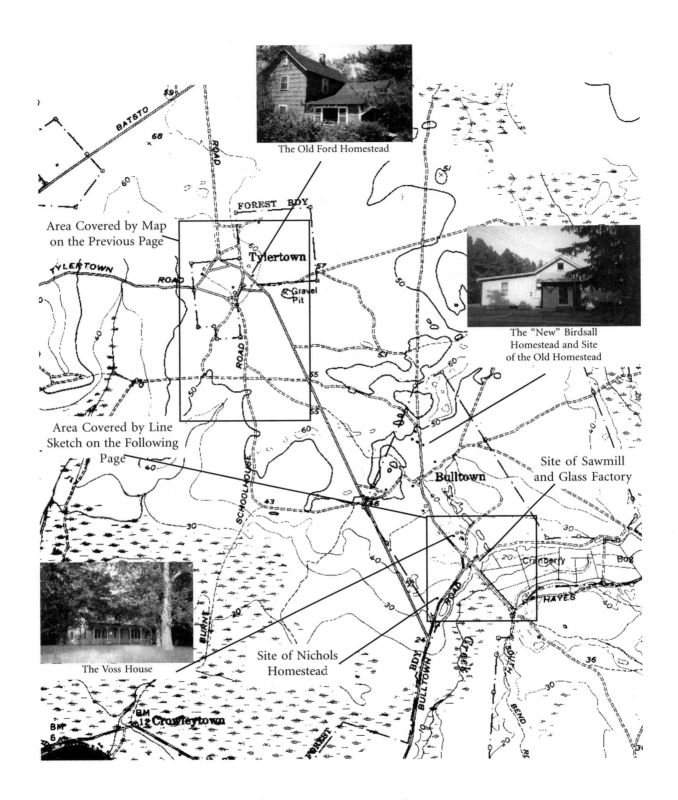

The Old Ford Homestead

Area Covered by Map on the Previous Page

The "New" Birdsall Homestead and Site of the Old Homestead

Area Covered by Line Sketch on the Following Page

Site of Sawmill and Glass Factory

The Voss House

Site of Nichols Homestead

Bulltown and Tylertown

Bulltown and Tylertown

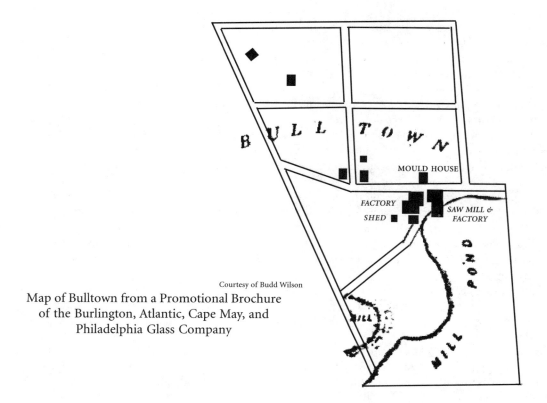

Courtesy of Budd Wilson

Map of Bulltown from a Promotional Brochure
of the Burlington, Atlantic, Cape May, and
Philadelphia Glass Company

The name "Bulltown" evokes rich images of raging bulls, red capes, and elegantly-dressed Spaniards. Unfortunately, they have nothing whatever to do with this little town in the pines. The origin of the name is much more mundane than that. Richard Bull, colonial surveyor, lent his name to several local entities: the Bull Survey, Bull Creek, Little Bull Creek, and to Bulltown itself, through which the Bull Creek runs. The origin of the name Tylertown is not so easy. It must have come from a family by that name who either lived in the vicinity or held the original survey, but the actual source isn't known.

Though the old township records list it as both Tylertown and Tyler Town, no family by the name of Tyler is known to have lived there at an early date. There was a Samuel Tyler, twenty-five years of age, living in the township when the 1850 census was taken, along with his wife, Sarah (23), and his two daughters, Emily (3) and Alwilda (1), but there is no way to prove just where he lived, and the name certainly predates him. Budd Wilson, Jr. of Green Bank says that the name did supposedly come from a Samuel Tyler, but if so, it must have been this Samuel's father.

The township birth records for 1848 - 1877 list the first birth for Tylertown as that of Lavinia Ford, daughter of Charles and Elizabeth Ford, on June 10, 1848, followed on September 9th of the same year by the birth of Hannah Ford, daughter of Reuben and Birtha [sic]. The first birth of record for Bulltown was that of Sarah Elizabeth Reed, daughter of Henry and Elizabeth Reed on May 27, 1853.

The earliest surveys in the area were made for Daniel Smith during the 1760's. Smith owned over eleven hundred acres in the vicinity of Tylertown and had a sawmill on the West Branch of the Wading River above the current Evans Bridge. When did the actual towns originate? No one knows. The probability is that they were settled soon after the township was formed, but they were close enough to Batsto to have supported settlements even earlier than that. Of all the families along the Mullica estuary, those from these two communities exhibited characteristics of what one might call "piney." Many retained a particular way of speaking whose pronunciations echoed the tones of English as it had been known several centuries earlier. The families were hardscrabble farmers, working together, dawn to dusk, to keep body and soul together. They ate what they could raise, consequently their diet wasn't as varied as that of the people along the river where foods and goods were brought in from other areas.

The Mullica gave breadth and depth to those who lived beside her waters. So many of the men in the river towns had the opportunity to see other places by serving as captains or crew aboard the numerous vessels that set sail for the sunrise or were involved in the shipping of goods in those vessels, and they developed an expanded perspective in their lives. Those who lived away from the river rarely saw much more in their lifetimes than their immediate surroundings, and thus their visions of life were more parochial. The families of the back country tended to marry each other, just as the river people sought mates from families of similar means. Thus did Fords marry Fords and Pattens, and Millers, and Nichols. Their horizons may have been limited by scrub pines and oaks, but they were certainly *not* inbred idiots! Theirs was a struggle for survival as epic as those families who went west and pioneered new settlements on the Great Plains or in some remote mountain fastness. They may have been a tad less sophisticated than their brothers and sisters along the river, but they still should be respected for their efforts to survive. Several branches of these families did, indeed, seek contacts - and spouses - along the river and fit smoothly into the life they found there, and their descendants are no different from anyone else, except, perhaps, for their deep appreciation for the land and for living in the present.

Bulltown and Tylertown once had the potential to be thriving communities back in the woods above Green Bank. Haze Birdsall had first lived with the Wilson family in nearby Green Bank, then built his homestead on the Bulltown Road after he married a Tylertown girl, Sarah Ann Miller. Those names are prominent in the area a century and a half ago: Reed, Miller, Birdsall, Ford, Patten, *especially* Ford. The name Ford appears in the township records for the period covered more than that of any other, though there seems to have been several distinct Ford families at a very early period.

The height of prosperity came just before the outbreak of the Civil War. During the 1850's, Sam Crowley III of Crowleytown teamed up with Haze Birdsall and dammed the Bull Creek for waterpower. They built a sawmill, which Haze ran, and a glass factory. Then at the same time, they built a number of houses for the workers and a big house for Crowley.

Sam was the owner of a large number of cedar swamps as well as solid timberland and a great deal of lumbering and coaling was done in the area. Crowley took in partners both here and at Crowleytown and called the resulting glass producing operation the Burlington, Atlantic, Cape May, and Philadelphia Glass Manufacturing Company. The plant at Crowleytown was built in 1850, and that of Bulltown in 1858.

The children of Bulltown went to school at Crowleytown, which, at that time, was connected to Bulltown by a direct road through the woods that is almost gone today. The original schoolhouse at Crowleytown stood on what is called "Burnt Schoolhouse Road," which is all but impassable. One need not ask what happened to this early school. The name of the road says it all.

A couple of houses still huddle along this old Bulltown Road, but that is all. The lake is gone. It has been a cranberry bog for several generations now. The many houses that Haze built are gone; the glass plant is gone; the sawmill is gone. In making the transit from Batsto to Green Bank, a distance through the woods of about seven miles, if you happen to pass more than one car on the road, it is a heavy traffic day.

The Bulltown Glassworks

Photograph by John Pearce

Samuel Crowley III, the famed husband of four wives and father of twenty-one children, got around. He was a sea captain/entrepreneur, who, like so many others in the pines, began his life on the sea and shifted to land-based operations as he got older. Either he or his father, Samuel, Jr., is mentioned in the Batsto Store Books as owning and/or serving as master of the schooners *Belvidier* in 1832-1834, *Anna Maria* in 1837, *Stranger* in 1846, *July R. Clark* in 1854, and the sloop *Rebecca* in 1857.

Samuel III built a glasshouse at Crowleytown in 1850 (See CROWLEYTOWN) but had to sell it soon afterwards for lack of ready cash. He then hired Hazelton Birdsall to build him another up the road in Bulltown.

In those days, Crowleytown and Bulltown were a lot closer together than they are today. Now, come on. Did the towns move farther apart? Of course not, but in the pines a single road makes all the difference. Years ago, this whole area was crisscrossed by roads that connected every town and hamlet in the entire core of the pinelands. Now only Routes 70 and 72 to the north, Route 563 to the east, Route 542 to the south, and Route 206 to the west are paved: with one exception, the Bulltown Road. This is actually a combination of sections of other roads that starts at Green Bank and ends up at Batsto.

It was not so a century ago. A direct road ran from Bulltown to Crowleytown, and the children of Bulltown attended school in Crowleytown, not in Green Bank, as one would assume from the location of the only paved road today. You could go to Green Bank, and South Bend, and Tylertown, and the town of Washington, and even way up to Speedwell, and do it all from roads which radiated out from Bulltown. Even on the topographic maps of the 1950s, though, the "Burnt Schoolhouse Road" to Crowleytown is only marked as a faint trail through the swamps. In our "modern" era, you simply have to drive around the whole core of the pinelands unless you have a four-wheel-drive vehicle, and even then, you'd better do your driving by daylight with plenty of gas in the tank.

In 1858, Haze Birdsall, at Crowley's direction, dammed the Bull Creek, built a sawmill, a 5-pot glass factory, and numerous houses, including a "mansion" for the master, Samuel Crowley III. Crowley's second glassworks made bottles, and rumor has it that some Mason jars were blown here after Crowley left Crowley-town.

About 1870, Crowley's company with the big name died along with the glass plants he created, and Bull-town slipped into obscurity. By the early twentieth century, the houses which Haze Birdsall had built in the town had fallen apart from neglect. The glass factory was gone. The sawmill was gone.

In the 1890s, a man by the name of Gustav Voss bought the old Bulltown Glassworks property and turned the abandoned lake into a cranberry bog. Ruth (Cramer) MacDonald, the wife of Bill MacDonald, who later lived in the Voss house, says that the real boss was Mrs. Voss. Gustav and his wife were only in residence during the summer months, and Mr. Voss spent most of his time in Philadelphia even when his wife was in Bulltown.

The big question is, did he remodel the "mansion" of Samuel Crowley III, or did he build an entirely different house for himself? There is little doubt that this house has all the trim details of later construction. That may mean little, however, and many houses were modernized so completely as to look like much newer houses than they actually are.

Laura Larrabee McConeghy, in a work on the genealogy of the families of Green Bank in 1935, says that Delwyne P. Crowley, son of Samuel III's third marriage, was born in the old Nicholas Sooy II homestead on the river in 1860. She notes that "Capt. Delwyne's parents resided in this "Old Homestead" a short time while they were rebuilding the "Bulltown house." Is this the house which the Crowleys were rebuilding?

Ruth (Cramer) MacDonald remembers being told that the house originally had much longer front windows that were replaced with the present double windows. This may be a hint that the house is older than it appears. Until further archetectural research is done, we will not know.

Courtesy of Jeanette (Ford) Ford

Earle Hill - c. 1955

Courtesy of Jeanette (Ford) Ford

Bill Patten - c. 1955

If Voss built this house himself, what happened to the "big" house of Samuel Crowley III? According to the map on the first page of this chapter, it must have stood very much where this house now stands. One would think that, of all the old buildings of the glass factory, the mansion would have been the one most useful to the property's future owner. Perhaps it was.

Early in this century, Charlie Delong owned the property at Bulltown for about twenty to thirty years.

During the middle part of the century, Earle Hill of Lower Bank and Bill MacDonald went into partnership to raise cranberries and blueberries. Bill lived in the Voss house while Earle continued to live in Lower Bank.

Jeanette (Ford) Ford tells of her first experience at cranberry picking at about the age of twenty. A friend got her to work with her picking cranberries by hand, but the work was exhausting. After just half a day, Jeanette's hands were sore and bleeding, and she couldn't continue to pick. Later, she tried scooping. While equally tiring, she was determined not to quit and managed to put in a full day's work. That was just the beginning of several years of working the bogs for her.

When these photographs were taken, much of the picking was done by machine. The bogs were drained and this machine run over the plants, knocking the berries into the louvers which transferred them into a bin. Even this method is no longer practiced in this area.

Earle and Bill finally split up the partnership, Earle continuing to raise the cranberries and Bill concentrating on the blueberries. Earle's son, Ronnie Hill continues to cultivate the bogs of Bulltown in 1997.

Bill finally sold the house to Mrs. Fenno. She also bought the abandoned mill at Pleasant Mills which she turned into a theatre, and she used this house as a residence for her manager. Mrs. Fenno had great dreams of a playhouse in the woods which would bring people to Pleasant Mills from all the surrounding communities. Her cultural dreams were greater than her practicality. People didn't come.

When Mrs. Fenno died, the State of New Jersey acquired the property at Bulltown. For many years, Youth With A Mission leased the old house to a Christian drug-rehabilitation program called "Covenant House." They ran a most successful program for young

Courtesy of Jeanette (Ford) Ford

Earle Hill and Bill MacDonald
inspecting the cranberry picking machine
c. 1955

The dry-picking machine that Earle Hill was using to harvest the cranberries at this time was a "Western," a new item on the market when this photograph was taken. It was invented by an Oregon grower, Joseph Stankiewicz and was first offered for sale in 1947. Its third edition is still in use.

Almost all of the local growers wet-harvest today, but the Cloverdale Farm outside of Barnegat, New Jersey still does dry-picking. Katherine E. Collins, who owns Cloverdale, provided the information on the Western dry-picking machine. Ronnie Hill confirmed that they used Westerns in the 1950's harvesting.

Wet-harvested cranberries are sent to Ocean Spray for processing. Only dry-harvested berries can be sold as whole berries.

Courtesy of Jeanette (Ford) Ford

Bill Patten
Bill lived in Jenkins and married
Ida Nichols of Bulltown
c. 1955

people and brought a good many back from catastrophe to be responsible citizens. Then the State of New Jersey, in its wisdom, thought a vacant house was more likely to fall apart than an inhabited one, so they terminated the lease.

Now the old mansion stands empty. The complex was fully equipped with a swimming pool and a commercial kitchen. It should have been to be put to good use, but it wasn't. In the summer of 1996, the State of New Jersey bulldozed the pool, the attached sheds, and the barn. Budd Wilson, former archaeologist at Batsto has always wondered if the barn was actually the old Bulltown Glass House that had been moved from its site by the dam to this location on the hill overlooking the former lake. Unfortunately, the bulldozer eliminated any chance anyone will ever have to find out if he is correct.

The house continues to stand vacant, waiting for the malicious torchbearers. There is a rumor that the state intends to bulldoze the house, too, in the near future, which is a shame. It's too bad that some use could not be found for it.

Courtesy of Jeanette (Ford) Ford
Like other growers in the area, Earle Hill and Bill MacDonald hired men from Puerto Rico to work for them. Many of the Puerto Rican families settled in the Jenkins area and remain there to this day, adding to the variety of life in the pinelands.

Courtesy of Jeanette (Ford) Ford
These two men are unidentified but worked at the side of other local people in the harvesting of cranberries and picking of blueberries. Both photographs are of the 1955 vintage.

The Birdsall Family

The Birdsall family of Bulltown may have been descended from Amos and Martha (Headly) Birdsall of Waretown. During the War of 1812, Captain Amos Birdsall (b. 1777) commanded the schooner *President* which was captured by the British ship *Ramillies* off Barnegat Inlet. Amos and his wife were Quakers, though apparently not all of their family remained so.

The story generally given is that Amos and Martha Birsall had a son, Aaron, who married Esther Arnold. Aaron and Esther had three sons, one of whom they named Hazelton. Unfortunately, June Methot, in *Blackman Revisited,* lists Amos and Martha's children and does *not* include an Aaron. The late Theda Ashton, a descendant of Hazelton's wife's brother, gives Haze's father's name as Amos. If she is correct, then it must be Amos Birdsall, Jr. who is meant, and Amos, Jr. is on June Methot's list. In any case, Hazelton was born in Barnegat on October 31, 1820. It is said that Haze lost his parents at an early age, and in 1831, when Hazelton was eleven, he attended First Day Meeting at Little Egg Harbor Meeting in Tuckerton with his aunt and never went back to Barnegat. A Quaker family from Green Bank, Curtis and Sarah Wilson, took him home with them and raised him along with their own three children. Later he married Sarah Ann Miller, eldest daughter of Joseph and Rebecca (Cobb) Miller.

Courtesy of Budd Wilson

The Old Birdsall Homestead
September 1905

Haze built his house in Bulltown, which received its name from the original survey of this area known as "The Richard Bull Survey." Haze was a carpenter and shipwright, a trade he had started to learn from his father before his untimely death and Haze's exodus to Washington Township. He built a lot of houses on the Bulltown tract when Bulltown boasted a glass factory, sawmill, grist mill, and the like. Haze ran the sawmill and served as the local blacksmith and wheelwright in the Bulltown area, so he was quite a busy man.

Haze also acted as the local undertaker. He built coffins for all the local people, and the old hearse in his barn was frequently put to use in all of Washington Township.

Haze and Sarah Ann (Miller) Birdsall had twelve children: Esther Arnold (b. November 30, 1846; d. January 2, 1928), James (b. October 14, 1848; d. September 2, 1926), Joseph M. (b. August 5, 1850; d. April 28, 1936), Rebecca Jane (b. 1852; d. October 8,

Courtesy of Budd Wilson

On the porch of the Old Birdsall Homestead
Summer of 1924

1854), Aaron (b. September 1854; d. January 25, 1855), Abigail Ann (b. December 25, 1855; d. June 20, 1948), Robert Crowley (b. November 19, 1857; d. March 16, 1893), Hannah Matilda (b. October 14, 1859; d. October 1, 1936), Alfred Hance (b. September 24, 1861; d. August 30, 1939) William Hazelton (b. 1864; d. 1942), Abraham (b. 1866; d. September 10, 1908), and John (b. May 20, 1871; d. November 21, 1879). Much of this information was provided by Lois Ann Kirby from the genealogical work of the late Theda Ashton.

Esther Birdsall would become the second wife of Otto Wobbar and live in South Bend, just above Green Bank. James was a glassblower and shipwright and married Anna Adaline Gaunt Cobb, the daugher of Reuben and Jane (Weatherby) Gaunt and widow of Henry Cobb. Joe remained on the farm at Bulltown and married Lucinda Johnson, who died young. Rebecca died within two years of her birth. Her brother, Aaron, died within five months of his birth. Abigail married Jarvis C. Jones of Tuckerton, and (2) William Nichols, son of Samuel Sr. and Nancy Nichols of Tylertown. She served as a practical nurse. Robert Crowley married Sarah Emma Sooy, daughter of Nicholas (son of Noah Sooy) and Sarah (Messarole) Sooy. Matilda married Alfred Holloway, and later, John F. Walford. She was a practical nurse like her sister, Abigail. Hance married Mary Jane Reed, the daughter of Henry and Elizabeth (Cobb) Reed of Green Bank and was a carpenter. William married Nevada Hall, the daughter of John and Amanda (Sooy) Hall of Lower Bank and was a carpenter also. Nevada died in 1914, and, in 1917, he married Mary Curry, half-sister to Helena Wobbar, his nephew Haze Wobbar's wife. "Aunt May" died in 1953. (See GREEN BANK) Abraham married Anna Marie Southard, the daughter of Amos and Ellen Southard of Nesco. John died at the age of eight and a half.

Haze Birdsall lived in his house in Bulltown until his death on April 23, 1907. Sarah Ann (Miller) Birdsall died on March 1, 1910. Hazelton and his wife were life-long members of the Methodist Church in Green Bank, but they were buried in Pleasant Mills with their children who had gone before them: John, Aaron, Rebecca Jane, and

Robert. Sarah's family, the Millers, are buried nearby. So are Curtis Wilson and his wife, who had raised the boy, Hazelton Birdsall, as their son so many years before. So, too, is their son, Alfred Hance, and his family: his wife, Mary Jane (Reed), and their daughter, Dollie (Dorothy). The Reed family is there, too.

Haze and his wife had raised eight children and lost four. They saw the rise and fall of Bulltown as a real community. Haze had built the glass factory and the sawmill with his own hands as well as all the houses for the workers. By the time he and Sarah Ann died, everything was gone forever.

Fortunately, neither Haze nor Sarah lived to see the destruction of their beloved home, for, in January of

Courtesy of Budd Wilson

The "New" Birdsall Homestead - 1935

1928, the Old Birdsall Homestead burned to the ground. Joseph Birdsall was living there at the time of the fire, and he built a new home on the site of the old Birdsall house in Bulltown, where he lived with his sister, Abbie Jones, until his death in 1936.

Their sister, Esther, was the second wife of Otto Wobbar of South Bend and mother of Haze Wobbar and Augusta (Wobbar) Crowley of Green Bank, and Lottie (Wobbar) Weeks of Weekstown. Their brother, William, built a little house at 1014 River Road in Green Bank, which he later enlarged with a series of additions. (See GREEN BANK)

They're all gone now: Haze and Sarah, Bill and May, Joe, Abbie, and Esther. Gone are the little houses of Jersey cedar that Haze and Bill and Joe built throughout the township. Gone are the families that lived and died in them, and gone are the memories of what once was.

The "New" Birdsall Homestead was purchased by the members of the Tri-County Gun Club who enlarged it extensively and use it as a hunting facility.

While Ronnie Hill still works the Bulltown bogs and lives there with a couple other families, the old Voss house alone speaks of what once was a comfortable little town.

The Birdsall Family
"Taken at Uncle Joe's at Bulltown"
September 18, 1932
Front Row: Augusta Weeks, Augusta (Wobbar) Crowley
Middle Row: Abbie Birdsall, Esther (Birdsall) Wobbar, Joe Birdsall
Back Row: May Birdsall, Will Birdsall

Alfred Hance Birdsall
Son of Hazelton and Sarah Ann (Miller) Birdsall
of Bulltown - c. 1900
("Hansel" Birdsall is written on the back of the
photograph.)

His youngest child, Dorothy.
1889 - 1972
He also had an older daughter, Rebecca,
and a son, John.

175

A view looking north on the Bulltown Road.
The 1928 house is on the right. It still stands as the central portion of the Tri-County Gun Club.

Tri-County Gun Club - 1995

176

The Miller, Cobb and Wilson Families

Very little is known about these families today, for they've long since rested in the Batsto/Pleasant Mills Cemetery. The story that has been passed down is that Curtis Wilson and his wife, Sarah, met the boy, Hazelton Birdsall of Barnegat, at the Tuckerton Friends Meeting one day and brought him home with them to raise as a son. He married Sarah Ann Miller, whose parents, Joseph and Rebecca Miller, lived nearby. In some versions of the story, it is Joseph Wilson who raised the boy, Hazelton, not Curtis.

A Curtis Wilson is listed as being eighty-one years old in the 1850 census. His wife, Sarah, is recorded as being seventy-seven at the time. The year Hazelton Birdsall went to live with the Wilsons is given as 1831, which would have made this Curtis Wilson sixty-two at the time, and his wife, Sarah, fifty-eight. In the same census, Joseph is listed as being forty-four, but there is no one else mentioned in the household, suggesting the probability that Joseph Wilson was not married at that time. Joel Wilson (49) and his wife, Mary (46) are listed, along with their children: Ruth (9), Susanna (8), and Henry (7 mos.). Haze Birdsall (spelled Hays Birchall) and his family are there as well with Haze's age showing as twenty-nine. This would have made him ten years old in 1831, giving credence to the story that Curtis and his wife, Sarah, raised the boy, not Joseph and his wife. No other "Curtis Wilson" appears on the list.

Stones in the Batsto/Pleasant Mills cemetery read:

Curtis Wilson, Private Co. F, 2nd Regt. Cav. N.J. d. 1879 age 49 yrs.
Lucinda, wife of Curtis Wilson, Sr. January 12, 1834 - November 3, 1902.
Curtis Wilson, Jr. d. March 10, 1899, age 35 yrs. 6 mos. 9 days.
Sarah Wilson d. May 23, 1822 age 75 years.

Now this is a puzzlement. Curtis Wilson, Sr. has to be the son of the Curtis Wilson listed in the 1850 census, thus making him actually Curtis Wilson, Jr. This in itself is not surprising, for the custom of the time was for the junior to take the senior after his father's death, moving everyone up a notch. However, since there is no other Curtis Wilson listed in the census except the one who is eighty-one in 1850, the real Curtis, Jr. had to have been out of the township at that time. He was the one married to Lucinda and died in 1879. It must have been their son, really Curtis, III, who died in 1899. No stones mark the graves of Curtis and Sarah Wilson, if indeed they are buried in the same plot, which is probable.

Another curiosity is the identity of the other "Sarah Wilson," who died in 1822 at the age of seventy-five. This has to be either the mother or the grandmother of the first Curtis Wilson.

Consequently, the story that has been passed down is probably correct: that it really was an elderly Curtis and Sarah Wilson who took in the young boy, Hazelton Birdsall, and raised him until he married, Sarah Ann Miller, daughter of Joseph and Rebecca (Cobb) Miller. The story also mentions that Curtis and Sarah had three children of their own. Joel, forty-nine in 1850 and Joseph, forty-four in that year, are two prime candidates. But who was the third? The Curtis, Sr. whose stone shows him to have died in 1879 at forty-nine would have been but one year old in 1831. Sarah, at fifty-seven, using the census figure, would have been too old to have had a one-year old child. Could this Curtis, Sr. have been the son of Joel and not the son of Curtis? Once again, I heave a big sigh . . .

I had originally thought that the Wilson family lived near Bulltown, which is why this information is included in this section, but recent information seems to indicate that their home was in Green Bank. If this is the case, the orphaned boy they raised was certainly connected with Bulltown, and his wife's family, the Millers, lived between what we know as Bulltown and Tylertown.

Joseph Miller's family is found among those old records, too. He was forty-five in 1850, and his wife, Rebecca, was forty-one. Sarah Jane was twenty-two and had already married the twenty-seven year old Haze Birdsall. The Millers still had several other children at home with them: Ruth Ann (17), Alfred Hance (15), Thomas Stewart (12), Edward James (10), John Wesley (9), Jonathan Sprague (7), Jesse Lemuel (4), Mary (2), and Caleb (1).

The late Theda Ashton, a twenty-five year member of the Batsto Citizens Committee, was a descendant of Joseph and Rebecca (Cobb) Miller. The Spring/Summer edition of the Batsto Citizens Gazette for 1997 includes an article taken from an oral history taped in her home in Paulsboro, N.J. in 1994 and relates that Joseph Miller (1804-1891), her great-great-grandfather, was born in Monmouth County and originally came from Lakewood to Gloucester Furnace, across the Mullica from Lower Bank in Gloucester (now Atlantic) County.

Joseph married Rebecca Cobb (1809-1883) of Tylertown in 1826 when he was twenty-two and she was seventeen. Rebecca's father was Constant Cobb and her mother, Deborah (Ford) Cobb. Constant's parents are reputed to have been Thomas and Lucy Cobb of West Creek. Rebecca was their second child. Their first, Nancy Ann, was born in 1807. Rebecca's birth year is usually given as 1813, but this would have made her only thirteen when she was married. While not impossible, it always seemed to pose a question for Theda. In searching family records, she discovered the possibility that Rebecca was born in 1809, not 1813, and left a note to that effect in her papers when she died. Lois Ann Kirby, in her Batsto Gazatte article, followed Theda's notation rather than the traditional birthdate. Constant, Jr. followed Rebecca in 1814, Elizabeth in 1820, and Thomas in 1822. They also had a sister, Deborah, but no birthdate is given for her. Of the marriages that are known, Thomas Cobb married Ann Sprague, and Constant, Jr. married Susanna Crowley. After the death of Constant, Sr., his widow married James Patten. Now comes the unique twist. When her mother died, daughter Elizabeth married her step-father.

We'd better get back to Joseph and Rebecca (Cobb) Miller. The couple bought land in Tylertown and built their home there. They had a total of eleven children, seven boys and four girls. According to Theda, all of their sons fought in the Union Army during the Civil War and came home safely with the exception of the eldest, Edward James, who died of typhoid fever in Winchester, Virginia, where he is buried. The census of 1850 shows Thomas Stewart being two years older than Edward James, so perhaps Theda's memory was a little shaky on that

John Wesley Miller
(1840-1899)

point. Theda was descended from John Wesley Miller, whose Civil War discharge, dated June 27, 1863, lists him as being five foot nine inches tall, of dark complexion, with black eyes and black hair. John Wesley Miller married Ellen Downs Ford of Tylertown on April 4, 1861 in Lower Bank with the Rev. Nicholas Van Sant officiating. Ellen was the daughter of Charles and Elizabeth Ford. He is listed in the township records as being twenty-one, and she is sixteen.

The couple had a total of ten children, but five of them died young. Those who survived to adulthood were

Elmer (b. 1864), Maggie (b. 1867), Augustus ("Gus") (b. 1872), Cora (b. 1876), and Ella (b. 1883). By the time Gus Miller was born, the family had moved from Tylertown to Batsto. John Wesley and Ellen Downs (Ford) Miller lived in house #21 at Batsto, and Theda had a copy of a lease for that house, dated 1878, showing that they paid $2.00 a month rent. John Wesley Miller was the blacksmith and wheelwright at Batsto and apparently had another shop in nearby Elwood. He died in 1899 at the age of fifty-eight in a buggy accident coming home from Elwood.

Gus Miller lived in Batsto his entire life and was a fixture there until his death in 1949. His photograph at the age of thirty-two is included in the section on "The Ghosts of Batsto."

No one seems to remember where the Cobbs lived, but the site of Joseph Miller's homestead lies off a sand road above Bulltown. Where the paved road bends to the west above the site of the old glass factory, the Millers would have continued on northward, but the road is impassible today.

Ellen Downs (Ford) Miller
(1842-1932)

Back in the 1930's, a Green Bank resident, Laura Larrabee McConaghy, wrote an extensive and flowery paean of praise to beloved town by the Mullica and included a passage on the site of the Miller homestead. Even in her time, the site had been swallowed up by the surrounding forest, yet a solitary dogwood still bloomed in the spring, the single reminder of the family who once made this spot their home. She recalls the memories of Augusta Crowley, who played there as a child, remembering

> *the walkway leading from the gate to the porch* [of the house] *with lilac and rose bushes growing and blossoming on either side. Also apple, peach, pear, quinces and Walnut trees in the Orchard, with grape-vines and honeysuckle. These grandchildren liked to play in the shade of two large Buttonwood trees in the front yard. Last, but not least - the "Dogwood tree," which has stood thro' all the storms and watched the old home tumble down. ... The Miller family have all passed to their reward, but every spring, the "Dogwood Tree" is arrayed in all her beauty, reminding one of the 'Resurrection' Morn - when this old family will again be united!* - Laura Larrabee McConaghy

"The Woodland Orchard!"

These apple-trees were lost for good
When the little house which stood
Near by to keep them safe and sound
Sank moldering into the ground,
And the children went away.
The Waiting forest Won the day,
And came and took the orphaned trees
Upon its dark, and kindly knees.

The sun comes down more golden here
Than it comes ever in the clear;
The grass is greener for the Wall
Of forest all around it.
There are no feet to trample it down,
Except the little ones in brown,
Beneath a deer that comes to stand
And wonder at this lost, sweet land.

You might say this was a spot
Where tame and Wild for once forgot
Their old fear; the partridge feeds
On fruit Sprung of men's tended seeds
And pecks the apples touched by frost.
But these are trees that have been lost;
Here one draws a careful breath,
This loveliness is so like death!

"This Old Miller Plantation in the Forest!"
- from "Genealogy of Families of Green Bank Country," Laura Larrabee McConaghy
c. 1935

The Dogwood Tree in the Wildwood

In the quiet of the Wildwood,
   Where a Homestead used to be,
In all its wondrous beauty
   Stands a stately Dogwood Tree.

Its blossom laden branches
   Seem pointing to the Sky,
As tho' in benediction,
   To those no longer nigh.

Its all so still and lonely;
   No more the open door.
For the *dear loved ones who dwelt there,*
   Have *passed* to the *other Shore.*

But the lovely *Dogwood* liveth,
   As a Sentinel, guarding the Way
To that dearly loved old Homestead
   Forsaken for many a day!

So, I bow my head in tribute,
   'Neath that wealth of blossoms rare,
For to me, all *God's lovely trees,*
   The *Dogwood* is *most fair!*

Written by Mary Curry Birdsall
June 1933, Green Bank, New Jersey
"Born in the Land of Evangeline,'
'The Grand-Pre Land,' Nova Scotia

The Nichols Family

Lydie Guse is the last of the Nichols generation able to remember growing up in the old homestead in Bulltown. At eighty-three, she is still pretty sharp, despite several minnie-strokes. Deafness has softened the outside world and raised the decibels of her own voice as a result, but age and infirmity hasn't dulled the spirit that has made her vibrant and alive throughout her life.

Lydie's parents, Franklin C. W. and Belle Nichols, raised their twelve children in the old house on the Bulltown road with love, joy, and hard work. Lydie can't remember her grandparents at all, though it's likely they had lived nearby. What she does remember is all the work. Every member of the family had to help with the daily chores. They kept a farm and did everything themselves. They slaughtered the hogs, did the canning and pickling, made the bread, fixed the roof when it leaked, tended the cows. They couldn't get into trouble, because there just wasn't time to fool around.

Lydie remembers that, each day, her older siblings walked all the way down Burnt Schoolhouse Road to Crowleytown to attend school. She was too young to go there herself. By the time she was ready for the three R's, the new consolidated school was open in Green Bank, and Bert Crowley used to pick everyone up in his schoolbus. She, like all the older generation, remembers Bert. His friendliness and cheerfulness enlivened many a long bus ride to and from school. Bert also was a deliveryman. If any of the families on his route needed anything, Bert would bring it. Often, he would drop off food supplies while on his rounds with the school children. Coal he had to deliver later. It wouldn't fit on the bus.

Will and Alonzo Nichols were Lydie's uncles. They lived up in Tylertown and had a cranberry bog all the way over in Weekstown on the Elwood road. Their thin, craggy features were caught by Bill Augustine in a photograph back in the very early 1940's.

Jessie Lewis remembers how much Lydie liked to dance. They were of an age, Jessie and Lydie, and Jess liked to party, too, back when she was twenty and very much alive with youthful vigor. Age has tamed their bodies, but not their spirits! There's still a gleam in Jessie's eyes when she remembers Lydie and the "Rump-Bump." I'll let that dance go without an explanation. You figure it out.

Jess Nichols, Lydie's younger brother, had the same spirit and zest for life as his sister. Jesse married Margaret Groff, and that pair were truly the salt of the earth. Jess and Margaret lived in Green Bank in a rancher just down from the intersection of Routes 563 and 542. Jess ran a garage, the old-style type with parts piled on the floor five feet deep, old oil soaking into the concrete floor, and cinder block walls covered with belts, gaskets, and parts for every conceivable automobile since the Model T Ford.

Jess was a true mechanic. He could make anything run. He once even rebuilt an engine that had been under salt water for a lengthy period of time. He had patience, too. Little Dudley Lewis spent his summers pestering Jess with his curiosity, and Jess would calmly explain everything to the boy.

Jess was also responsible for starting the Green Bank Volunteer Fire Company and kept its early equipment running almost singlehandedly. A great many tinderbox houses that went up in flames were saved because of Jess Nichols, and those like him, who "answered the call" at any hour.

Margaret Groff Nichols worked just as hard as Jess. She was a great cook and a wonderful friend. Fire company clam bakes were the staple of Fathers' Day in Green Bank for years. Margaret would always be working with the other "Fire Ladies" for days ahead of time, getting all the food prepared for the big celebration. Her stuffed clams were out of this world. Outside, Jess would help tend the charcoal pits, where roasting goodies sent enticing aromas all over Green Bank. This was a rather poor area, and hard work kept things going.

The stones labeled "Franklin C. Nichols" and "Belle Nichols" in the Green Bank cemetery tell almost nothing about their lives. Franklin C. W. Nichols was born on the 29th of December, in 1858 and died just shy of his eighty-first birthday on December 12, 1939. Belle was born in 1882 and died in 1954 at the age of 72. Their life of toil on a hardscrabble farm had not been easy. Nor had it been simple to bring up ten girls and two boys in a tiny house back in the woods, but they had fought the good fight.

The story of the Nichols family actually begins over a century before Jess and Lydie were born with Jacob and Sarah Nichols who had two sons, Israel (b. about 1780) and Samuel. Samuel lived across the river in Weekstown (then Weeksville), and his issue would just confuse things that are quite difficult enough. Interestingly enough, he is referred to as "Over-the-River-Sam." Israel married a woman by the name of Catherine (b. about 1785).

The 1830 census of Washington Township lists only one Nichols family: a household of eight under the name of Israel Nichols, and the couple had five sons and two daughters. The 1850 census also lists a Jane (12), who apparently died in her teens. Hollis Koster sent notes to Edna Wilson half a century ago that indicate December 4, 1857 as the date of Israel Nichols's death and say that he died a widower at the age of eighty-five, but he would have been only seventy-seven according to the 1850 census data. Though the rest of the family would be buried in Green Bank, no stone appears in that cemetery for either Israel or Catherine.

Abram (or Abraham) was probably the eldest son, born about 1807. By 1836, Abram was on his way to making a comfortable life for his family, for in that year, he purchased property at Crowleyville from Samuel Crowley, Jr. and built himself both a tavern and a landing on the Mullica. The tavern stood on the inside of the bend where Route 542 turns towards Batsto just beyond Crowleytown. (See CROWLEYTOWN)

Abram Nichols married a woman by the name of Mary Ann, and by the 1850 census, the couple is listed as having eight children: Catherine (18), Sarah A. (17), Samuel (16), Israel (14), John (12), Alonzo (7), Melissa (4), and Charles (8/12). His father, Israel, is still on the list as being seventy, his wife, Catherine, as sixty-five, with daughters Jane (12) and Mary Ann (22) and son Samuel (21).

Mary Ann Nichols, Abram's wife, died on the 11th of April, 1857 at the age of forty-four years and two months. Her daughter, Mary Ann, died just about five weeks later at the age of ten years. On the ninth of March, 1859, the widower Abraham Nichols married Elizabeth Wintlin (or Wintley as per Hollis Koster's notes) of Lower Bank at Sooy's Inn, Washington. William Sooy, J.P. conducted the ceremony.

The 1860 Census also shows Abram Nichols still keeping his Crowleyville tavern, married to Elizabeth, and having six children living with him: Israel (22), John (19), Alonzo (16), Charles (10), Mary (7), and Jane (7). Another Nichols appears in the township in 1860: one Samuel C. Nichols (24), a glassblower, his wife, Cordelia, and a son, Horris (1). Samuel seems to have been the eldest son of Abraham and Mary Ann Nichols. The 1880 census lists Charles C. Nichols (33), who had become a doctor, and his wife, Elsie (26) and son, Hall (5). By 1880, Abraham, at the age of seventy-three, had apparently given up his tavern and become a farmer. His wife was sixty-two. Abram and his second wife, Elizabeth (Wintlin), have no stone in the Green Bank cemetery, but his first wife, Mary Ann, is there.

Joel appears to be Israel and Catherine's second son, though no birthdate is available. Joel and his wife have but one child, a girl under five, in the 1840 census. His name doesn't appear in the 1850 census, so he may have moved outside the township. When Sarah Jane Nichols, daughter of Joel and Sophia, married Charles Parker of Green Bank on August 31, 1856, however, she is listed as living in Green Bank.

Sedmon was born about 1818 and died on December 3, 1841 at the age of twenty-three years and nine months. Hollis Koster's notes show Sedmon having a wife, Hannah, and a daughter, Tobitha, who was born about 1839 and died on April 2, 1844 at the age of five. The township records show an Abram Nichols (21), son of Sydmon [sic] and *Elizabeth* Nichols, married Mary Ford (16), the daughter of Charles and Elizabeth Ford, on April 21, 1861. I can't explain the difference in Sedmon's wife's name, but the dating would have made Abram about a year old when his father died. The 1840 census shows only three persons in Sedmon's family at the time the census was taken: Sedmon, his wife, and his daughter, but that is the year in which Abram would have been born. The 1860 census doesn't show a twenty-year-old Abram. Confusing. The 1870 census lists a seventy-two year old Hannah Nichols keeping house for Jesse Parker (40), a stage driver, but thirty years earlier, she would have been twice the age of Sedmon. I'd bet that the township records are correct: Sedmon's wife's name was Elizabeth. So who was Hannah?

No birth date is available for Susan Nichols, but Hollis Koster's notes indicate that she was the first wife of David ("Fiddler") Ford and was obviously deceased in 1862 when he married a second time. Her name does not appear on the 1850 census under Nichols, but there is a Susan Ford married to David whose age is given as thirty-seven, which must be Susan (Nichols) Ford, making her birth year about 1823.

Jacob, born about 1826, was twenty-three, when he married Martha Ford who was nineteen in a ceremony performed by The Rev. Nicholas Van Sant on March 4, 1849. Jacob's residence is given as Green Bank. Martha was the daughter of John and Mary Ford of Lower Bank. In the 1850 census, Jacob is listed as being twenty-seven, married to a Martha Ann (22) and had a daughter, Charlotte (b. 5/12/1850). Martha (Ford) Nichols must have died by 1856, for in that year, Jacob married Eliza Parmer of Green Bank on July 14th in a ceremony performed by William Woolston, J.P. The 1860 Census shows him as thirty-nine, married to Eliza, also thirty-nine, and having two children: a son, John (9) and a daughter, Susanna (3). He's listed as a laborer.

Samuel, according to his gravestone, was born about 1828, and married Ann (Nancy) Ford. The couple is listed in 1880 as having seven children: George (28), John W. (26), Frank (21), Alonzo (19), Isaac Ellsworth (14), Georgianna (11), and William (6). They also had a daughter, Mary A., who was apparently married by this time. The 1870 census adds Laurence (8) and Ella (6) to the list, but they must have died as children because they aren't on the 1880 census. The couple also had a son, Israel, born on August 31, 1871, but his name doesn't appear on the 1880 census either.

Mary Ann (b. 1836 according to her cemetery stone) never married and died at the age of twenty-six in 1862.

Lydie (Nichols) Guse, who still lives on Route 542, and her brother, Jess, Green Bank mechanic and "far" chief, were the children of Franklin, grandchildren of Samuel and Nancy, and great-grandchildren of Israel and Catherine, so we'll follow the children of Samuel and Nancy.

George Nichols, a sailor of twenty-eight in 1880, died at the age of seventy-six on March 13, 1928.

John W. Nichols, another sailor of twenty-six in 1880, lasted seventy-one years before he joined his family by the little Green Bank church on June 1, 1927.

Franklin Nichols (b. 12/29/58), husband of Belle (b. 1882) and father of the ten girls and two boys from Bulltown, was listed as a laborer in 1880 and died December 12, 1939 at the age of eighty-one. Belle died in 1954.

Alonzo Nichols, a laborer of nineteen in 1880 according to the census of that year, and his brother, Will, just a boy of six, were photographed by Bill Augustine late in their lives. Alonzo died in 1948 at eighty-six. It seems that Alonzo was actually a year older than his stone indicates. The township records of his birth show March 4, 1862 as his birth date, not 1863.

Hollis Koster's notes say that "Ellsworth" Nichols was born in 1866 and never married. His gravestone says that he was fifty-five when he died in 1925, which would make his birthdate 1870. Unfortunately, the censuses don't list an "Ellsworth," only an "Isaac E." Since "Isaac E." doesn't fit in anywhere else, the "E" must have stood for "Ellsworth," and this is our elusive Ellsworth Nichols. The 1880 census gives his age as fourteen, indicating 1866 as his birth year. He isn't even on the 1870 census unless the "Ella" is actually "Ellsworth."

Georgianna was born on March 8,1869 and married William Patten of Tylertown.

William"s gravestone states that he was born in 1870 and died a year after his brother, Alonzo, at the age of seventy-nine, but the 1880 census indicated him as a child of six in that year, making his birthdate about 1874.

William F. Augustine Collection
Special Collections and University Archives
Rutgers University Libraries

Will and 'Lonzo Nichols - c. 1940

Samuel and Nancy Nichols lived in Green Bank with their family when their daughter, Mary Ann, was born in 1856. In 1862, at the birth of son, Howard Alonzo, and in 1868 when daughter, Georgiana came into the world, they were still living in Green Bank. By the time son, Israel, was born in 1871, they had moved to Tylertown.

Samuel is listed as a laborer on the census lists prior to 1870 and on the township records of births for that period. By 1880, he is listed as a farmer. Samuel died on the 9th of October, 1885 at the age of fifty-seven, while Nancy lived until the 7th of July, 1908.

His grandson, Jesse, and his wife, Margaret, are gone now, too. Jess died in 1990, Margaret followed soon behind. Jess and Margaret were never rich in this world's goods. They came from old but poor families and weren't much of a success the way the world measures success. They came into the world with nothing and left it with nothing, but in between, they enriched every life they touched with their spirit of love, enthusiasm, and generosity.

Clam bakes have become a thing of the past as well. Insurance problems and rowdy types from a distance insured that they would have to go. The fire company has new trucks and younger people to handle the hoses, but no suburban chief with million-dollar engines could be more proud of his company than Jess Nichols had been, despite the ancient, decrepit and secondhand engines that made up his "far" company.

Even the old house at Bulltown is gone now. It burned to the ground years back before the men of Jess's company could get all the way up there to put it out. It had stood the test of time, though. It was old: pegged together rather than nailed, as Lydie remembers. Now it's just a junk-strewn clearing on the way to Bulltown. There are few left to remember the hard life Frank and Belle lived here with their twelve children, but they gave them strength, joy, and enthusiasm for life that made their lives a blessing to others.

The Fords of Tylertown and Green Bank

Photograph by John Pearce

The Ford House at Tylertown - 1996
Demolished in 1997

The old Ford house in Tylertown is gone. An abandoned ruin for many years, Ray Ford, who lives next door, finally tore it down in 1997. There are more listing for "Fords" in the Washington Township records for the mid-nineteenth century than there are for any other name. Unfortunately, there are no records to indicate the relationships among the many families. The older Fords have always claimed that there were at least three different and distinct families by that name that resided in the township throughout the last century. Whether or not some or all of them stemmed from the same family at some very early time is beyond the scope of this book.

Ray Ford may seem like the epitome of the "piney," but his heritage in this area can be traced back to a Stephen Ford, born about 1770. Stephen and his wife, whose name isn't known, were the parents of Jeremiah Ford (b. 1794). Jeremiah married Sarah Jane Cramer, whose father, Sylvanus Cramer (b. c. 1770), married her mother, Sarah Jane Gifford (b. c. 1775) about 1793. The location of their home is unknown.

Jeremiah and Sarah Jane's son, Reuben, married Tabitha Cobb, the daughter of Constant Cobb, Jr. and Susanna Crowley, and the couple had three children: Hannah (b. 7/14/1848, m. Jacob Hyson and d. 7/4/1895); Josiah (b. c. 1849, m. 1) Liz Mick and 2) Virginia Brewer; and Sarah (b. 1851 m. 1) Asa Ford and 2) Charles Ford.

Reuben apparently died, and Tabitha (Cobb) Ford married his brother, Josiah. Ford records show the children of this second marriage as: Robert Stewart Ford (b. 5/3/1854 m. Anna Matilda Ford d. 3/5/1927); Mary Elizabeth (b. 7/6/1855, m. James Birdsall, son of Haze and Sarah Ann (Miller) Birdsall, and died in childbirth); Kate Ann (b. 1856, d.c. 1870); Phoebe N. (b. 1858, m. George Ford); George W. Ford (b. 3/18/1868 d. 1/28/1909); William Watson (b. 10/10/1865, did not marry but lived with Minnie Rossell, no death date on stone); Jonathan C. (b. 1/20/1868 d. 8/29/1934); Samuel Tyler (b. 1875 d. 1945) and Susanna (b. 10/26/1873 d. 5/5/1964 m. Arthur (Jerry) Miller. This information was received from Elaine Weber Mathis through her mother, Elsie (Ford) Weber, and though Susanna (Ford) Miller.

The township records give slightly different dates for the births of some of these children. They show that Josiah and Tabitha (or Tobitha) Ford gave birth to a son, Robert, on August 26, 1854 in Tylertown. The couple had a second child, Mary Tabitha (or Tobitha) on July 6th, 1855, again in Tylertown. Ten years later, William Watson was born in Bulltown on October 10th, 1865 and died in 1951. The records note that a "Joseph" and "Tobitha" had a son, Jonathan C. on January 26th, 1868 in Tylertown. ("Joseph" in the records, should read "Josiah.")

Josiah is listed as a laborer on each record and probably worked at Batsto, Bulltown, and possibly Crowleytown while living in Tylertown. The family may have actually moved to Bulltown for a while, since Watson was born there.

A stone for Josiah Ford bears his date of death: 3 December 1902. That of his wife, Tabitha, reads that she was born on the 6th of May, 1831 and died on December 2nd, 1901. There are no other entries for Mary Tabitha Ford except that for her birth. Watson Ford is buried at Green Bank, and, though his stone has no date of death, he died in 1951. It adjoins another similar stone bearing the name of Minnie Ford, born in 1879. Minnie died in 1965. A stone for Jonathan C. bears the dates 1868 and 1934.

Robert Stewart Ford, listed as a laborer like his father, Josiah, in the records, married Anna Matilda (called "Emma" in the township records) Ford (b. 10/4/1860), daughter of George Washington Ford, and his wife, Phoebe (Gaunt). One of the last entries in the township records is that of the birth of a *son*, George Washington Ford to Robert and "Emma" in Bulltown in September of 1876. There are no other births listed for this couple in the records, but they eventually had several other children, including Howard Augustus, Alburtis (1884-1963), Horace, Phillip, Calvin (b. 1891), Emma Rose (1889-1967 m. Harry Ford), Jesse A., Hattie (Matilida?) (b. 10/1897 d. 5/30/1969), Josiah (b. 2/1886), and Robert S., Jr. (b. 9/ 1892 m. Anna Vacella). The family lived in the house that is now the Green Bank Liquor Store on the corner of Rts. 542 and 563, at least after the birth of their son, George Washington.

Anna Matilda Ford died on April 25, 1908 and was buried in Green Bank. Robert Stewart then married Mary Mateland, a Scot (b. 1865). When Robert Stewart Ford died on March 5th, 1927, he was buried beside his first wife. Hattie Ford married George Carney and was the mother of George, Bill, and Armand Carney (*See* GREEN BANK).

As an indication of how confusing family trees can be, there were at least three George Washington Fords. One was the *father* of Anna Matilda Ford. One was the *brother* of Robert Stewart Ford, and one was the *son* of Robert Stewart and Anna Matilda (Ford) Ford.

In any case, George Washington Ford, the son, married *another* Ford, Julia Belle, who does not seem to be any relation to his Ford family, and they raised their children in a house on Lance Run Road, immediately behind that of Chink Simpkins. The couple had eight children: Gertrude Leona, married James Patten; George Clayton, married Sadie Patten; Henry Nickleye, married Demmie Friel; Bertha Clarence Ford, married James Simmerman first, then John Rodenbough; Margaret Emaline, married Clarance Lloyd

Courtesy of Elaine Weber Mathis

George Washington Ford (husband of Julia Belle Ford) and Samuel Truex, his brother-in-law. Samuel Truex married Emma Jane Ford (the sister of Julia Belle) and lived just up the road from Chink Simpkins. George W. & Julia Belle Ford lived in a house behind Chink's.

Mathis; Blanche Arwilda, married William Walters; Lavinia (or Lavenia) Bernice apparently remained unmarried, and Elsie Leola, married Charles William Weber, Jr., one of Salt-hayer Charlie Weber's sons. Julia Belle Ford was the half-sister of John Wesley Ford of Herman. George Washington Ford died in 1954, and his wife, Julia, in 1971.

George Clayton, born in 1903, raised his family in the Ford house in Tylertown. His son, Ray Ford, still lives next door to the old homesite. Ray's two sisters, Hilda and Flora, married the Hefley brothers. One still lives behind the site of her grandparents' house on Lance Run Road. Arwilda (Ford) Walters and her husband, Bill, live on Route 563 across from the ambulance building in Green Bank, and their children live close by. Arwilda served as the Green Bank bridge tender for many years. Elaine Weber Mathis, daughter of Charles Weber, Jr. and Elsie Leola (Ford) lives in New Gretna.

Crowleytown

Photograph by Bill Augustine
Courtesy of Budd Wilson

This photograph looks across a bend in the Mullica towards the location of Crowleytown.
It was taken from Abe Nichols Landing. His tavern stood to the left across Route 542.

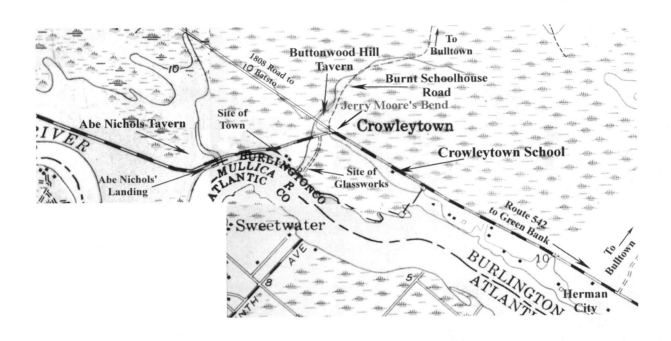

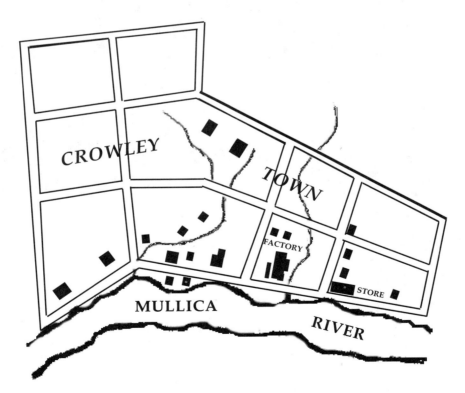

Courtesy of Budd Wilson

186

Crowleytown was once a thriving town which included a glass works, a school, and many houses. Its bustling streets were filled with the laughter of children as they ran and played. Housewives tidied their little homes, and fathers labored long hours at the nearby glass factory. Captain Samuel Crowley III married Parnell Sooy, daughter of Noah Sooy and Sarah Weeks in 1834 and started a town. After several years, four wives, and twenty-one children, he was entitled to have it named after him! According to the records of Washington Township during the mid-1800s, this village was known as Crowleyville.

Crowleyville's story actually begins early in the 1800's when the virile Sam III was only a little tyke. His father, Samuel Crowley, Jr. and his mother, Tabitha, owned land in this vicinity at that time and probably lived here as well. Little is known about the senior Samuel. Samuel III is credited for the first cultivated cranberry bog in the area c. 1830, but it is his father, Samuel, Jr. who should receive the recognition. Samuel III was only eleven years old in 1830. We know that in 1836, Abraham Nichols bought land from Samuel, Jr. that was on the river part way between Crowleyville and Mordecai Landing. Here he built a tavern and a landing. This property was right where the present Route 542, coming from Batsto, makes a sharp left hand turn.

Story has it that some years ago, a State Trooper tried to see how fast his patrol car would go on that straightaway out of Batsto. He didn't make the turn. He got out of the car all right, but he had to stand there dripping wet, looking at his patrol car, submerged up to its bubble gum machine in the Mullica, wondering how he could explain *that* to everyone back at the barracks.

Abraham Nichols' tavern stood just across the road from the bend, and the Township Committee met there in 1854, 1855, 1857, and 1864. The 1870 census still lists Abraham Nichols as a hotel keeper, but in 1880, he is recorded as a farmer. The years 1865 through 1870 are missing from the township records, but when they resume, the Annual Meeting is held in Herman from then until it moves to Green Bank. Abraham Nichols Tavern is never mentioned again. Thus, it seems that the Nichols "hotel" ceased operations between 1870 and 1880.

Crowleytown itself is just up the road toward Green Bank, at the next bend. The original road to Batsto from Green Bank went straight at this bend across a slight rise called Buttonwood Hill. If you take the sand road across from the entrance to Crowley's Landing today, Buttonwood Hill is about fifty feet from Route 542.

Here once stood the tavern of the Wills family. Robbie Wills was born in that tavern, and some of the older Washington Township folks still remember him trudging up Burnt Schoolhouse Road to Bulltown to work in Earle Hill's bogs in the 1940's.

Courtesy of Budd Wilson

Robbie Wills - c. 1955

The Buttonwood Hill Tavern of the Wills family was in operation at least by 1850, for on the census of that year, George Wills (41) and his wife, Mary (41), are listed as maintaining a hotel, along with their children: William Hy (16), Aaron (16), George (14), James (12), Moses (10), Mary Ann (8), Amos (6), Martha Jane (4), and John (2). They do not appear on the 1860, 1870, or 1880 censuses, though local memories recall Robbie Wills (b. 1891) living in the old tavern building. The Buttonwood Hill tavern could not have been in operation as a tavern after 1860, at least not one operated by the Wills family. It may well have been in operation at an earlier date.

Crowleyville's days of glass began with the lusty Samuel III, but the data is very confusing, to say the least. In 1851 at the age of forty, Samuel Crowley III actually built an entire town on this bend in the river, including a glass factory, houses for the workers, a hotel, and stores. He tried to raise money for the enterprise but failed to gain the needed investments. Consequently, he sold the glassworks to a group of New York investors, who named it the "Atlantic Glass Works." Meanwhile, Crowley started over up Burnt Schoolhouse Road at Bulltown, building a small glass house there in 1858 which ran until 1870.

After several disastrous fires at the Crowleytown works, the investors abandoned it in 1866. Crowley and other investors founded the Burlington, Atlantic, Cape May, and Philadelphia Glass Company which included both the Crowleytown and the Bulltown glass works.

There is a notation in the Wharton Ledgers that Isaiah Weeks and Samuel Crowley III leased two lots and fourteen houses at $400 an acre on April 1, 1862. There is another listing that shows that Isaiah Weeks leased the property to the Burlington, Atlantic, Cape May, and Philadelphia Glass Company for $10,000, though someone wrote in the ledger that this "looks like a swindle," which means that probably Wharton's General Wright thought the venture was all hype and no substance. It may well have been just that, because there's no evidence that it ever produced very much. In November of 1869, the president of the company, John Dougherty, leased the entire works to one of the directors, George Langdon, for $16,500 in stock. Samuel Crowley III seems to have remained on the Board of Directors. Despite all the changes in ownership, the effort to manufacture glass at Crowleytown failed, and the glass house blew down in 1874.

One rather famous event did take place on this lovely bend in the Mullica. The usual story is that, in 1850, John Mason, one of the first investors in the construction of the original glass house, designed a canning jar that was to become famous. Partner and entrepreneur Samuel Crowley III blew the first jars of this design. Mason was a tinsmith from Vineland whose design for a metal cap and rubber seal revolutionized the canning practice. Mason made the moulds for this new type of jar, and they were eventually made in several different factories.

As usual, though, there are other versions. According to Adeline Pepper in *The Glass Gaffers of New Jersey*, the first glass manufacturing company built here was the Atlantic Glass Company in 1851. "The blower of the experimental [Mason] jar at Crowleytown's Atlantic Glass Works was Clayton Parker, an expert glass man from Bridgeton. Mason's first patent was March 7, 1856." Ms. Pepper goes on the explain that the date -Nov. 30th, 1858- was molded into thousands of jars up until about 1902 and has no significance to the manufacturing date or the origin of any particular jar. Samuel Crowley III isn't even mentioned.

She does say that a Mason jar was found at this location some years ago. It had almost square angles at the base like the patent drawing and unlike later models. In addition, though inscribed with the usual MASON'S/ PATENT/NOV. 30TH/1858, it has two dots under the "TH."

She goes on to say that an advertisement appeared in "Philadelphia As It Is" by R.A. Smith a year after the glassworks was built. It reads:

Atlantic and Milford Glass Works
Crowleytown and Milford, Burlington Co., N.J.
Manufacturers and Dealers in Every Description
of Druggist Glassware
J. Huffsey & Co.
Office, No. 50 N. Fourth St., above Arch, Phila.

Ms. Pepper does say that the Atlantic Glass Works had an 8-pot furnace which was worked by a dozen blowers. John Huffsey, brother of Samuel Huffsey, owner of the Milford Glass Works in the 1850's, was the agent and later the manager of the Crowleytown glass works. She continues that Burling Brothers took over the opera-

Photograph by John Pearce

Crowleytown - 1995

tion of the glassworks in 1858, and it closed down in 1866. Not once does she mention Samuel Crowley III.

Immediately following the article on Crowleytown, is one on Bulltown which begins:

"Samuel Crowley III, also built the 5-pot Bulltown furnace, 2 1/2 miles east of Crowley's Landing" and includes a plan of the two glassworks labeled "Plan of the Property belonging to the Burlington, Atlantic, Cape May and Philadelphia Glass Manufac. Co. Situated in Washington Townp Burlington, Co. N.J." Is she implying that the "Atlantic Glass Works" and the "Burlington, Atlantic, Cape May, and Philadelphia Glass Manufac. Co." are one and the same? (They weren't.)

Did Clayton Parker blow the first jar with Crowley looking over his shoulder, or did Crowley blow it himself? More than likely, entrepreneur Crowley knew how to run a business. He hired experts to blow the glass. In fact, that's exactly what an article by J. G. Wilson in the Summer and Fall issue of the Batsto Citizens Gazette for 1986 says. John Mason contracted with Samuel Crowley to make the jars. "The best glassblower of the works, Clayton Parker of Bridgeton, was delegated to carry out the project."

Though the glassworks ended with the Civil War, Crowleytown remained a viable village. It finally petered out during the depression. Buttonwood Hill Tavern is gone. So, too, is Abraham Nichols Tavern. Samuel Crowley III died on the 22nd of January 1887 just a month shy of his seventy-seventh birthday and was buried in Green Bank. Robbie Wills of the Buttonwood Hill Tavern lies there, too. He died in 1967.

The State of New Jersey acquired the property and created a picnic area with boat-launching facilities there (also for washing State Police cars). By that time, little was left of the glass village of Samuel Crowley III. One large house kept lonely vigil there for several years, but an arsonist burned it down thirty years ago. Only the Crowleytown school remains, and it stands just down the road from the site of the village proper. The first schoolhouse in the area stood a little way up the road known as "Burnt Schoolhouse Road," which leads off the the right at Buttonwood Hill. Other than the last Crowleytown school building, there is no trace of the little glass works community by the Mullica, home of the first Mason jar.

Information on the Crowleys just recently received from John Milton Adams, Jr., a descendant, makes it clear that the person many writers have called Samuel Crowley, Jr. was really Samuel Crowley III. The line began with Samuel, Sr. (1745-1810) who married Mary Woos and is buried in the Pestleton Cemetery, near Ancora. Samuel, Sr. had two sons, Samuel, Jr. (1788-1864) who married Tabetha Ford (1789-1867) and Sebastian (1790-1881) who married Martha Ford. Their daughter, Susan, married Samuel Ford, from whom John Milton Adams, Jr. is descended. Samuel, Jr. had a son, Samuel III (1811-1887), who married 1) Parmelia Sooy, 2) Abby Ann Wilson, 3) Hannah Weeks, and 4) Catherine Taylor and sired twenty-one children. For the record, their names are: of Parmelia (Sooy) Crowley: Nicholas, Charles, William H. and Elizabeth; of Abby Ann (Wilson) Crowley: Phebe, Joseph, Permelia, Mary Etta, Serena, John, and Theodore; of Hannah M. (Weeks) Crowley: Abbie, Margaret, Adelia, Delwyne P. and Isaiah; and of Catherine Taylor: Kate, Minnie, Warren M. Samuel Ellis, and Nathaniel B. Samuel, Jr.'s brother, Sebastian, also a sea captain, had a son of the same name.

I received this information as *Heart of the Pines* was going to press but tried to incorporate this information into the text. Unfortunately, I may have missed in a few places. It does show that the man everyone has always called Samuel Crowley, Jr. is really Samuel Crowley III. Mr. Adams does note that he can't verify the accuracy of the information because he did not actually collect it himself, but it does appear to be correct. Samuel Crowley III is buried in Green Bank, along with his wives. His name appears as "Samuel Crowley, Jr." on his stone.

Samuel Crowley

This photo is labelled "Samuel Crowley," with no designation as to which Samuel it is. Judging from the clothes, it is probably Samuel Crowley III, husband of four wives and father of twenty-one children, sea captain, and builder of two glass factories. John Milton Adams, Jr., who has preserved the photograph, says he isn't sure which Crowley it was, but notes that the photograph was given to him by Helen Leek Mack.

Courtesy of John Milton Adams, Jr.

The Children of Crowleytown

This picture, like the others of the last little one-room schoolhouses in Washington Township, was taken in about 1890.
This was near the end of an era, both for the little school, and for Crowleytown itself,
though perhaps no one realized it at the time.
The children are, from left to right:
Front Row: Herb Tull, Horace Patten, James Patten, Estella Wills, William Simpkins, Mary Emma Simpkins, Eugene Ford
Second Row: Emma Nichols, Lizzie Gerber, Florence Wills, Leon Koster, Julius Gerber
Third Row: Kathie Gerber, Lin Ford, Susie Wills, Pauline Gerber
Teacher: Hattie (Koster) Ford
During the 1930's, "Aunt Hattie" Ford ran the Green Bank Store.

The Crowleytown School
in 1997

(Sorry about the prominance of
the trash cans, folks.)

190

Green Bank

This view of Green Bank was taken prior to the bridge's replacement in 1926.
It probably dates from the first decade of the twentieth century.

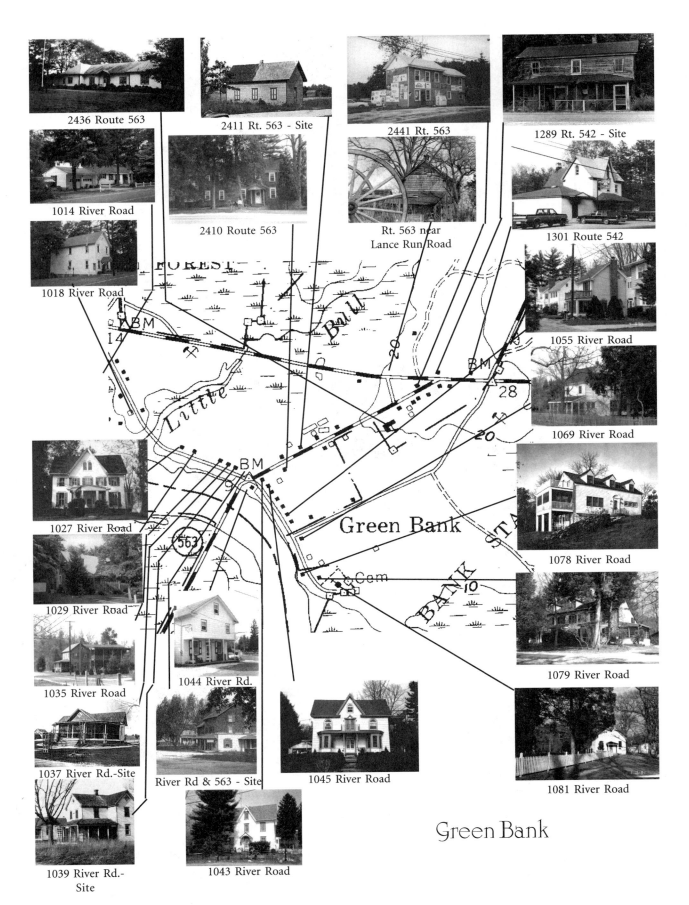

2436 Route 563

2411 Rt. 563 - Site

2441 Rt. 563

1289 Rt. 542 - Site

1014 River Road

2410 Route 563

Rt. 563 near
Lance Run Road

1301 Route 542

1018 River Road

1055 River Road

1069 River Road

1027 River Road

1078 River Road

1029 River Road

1079 River Road

1035 River Road

1044 River Rd.

1037 River Rd.-Site

River Rd & 563 - Site

1045 River Road

1081 River Road

1039 River Rd.-
Site

1043 River Road

Green Bank

192

Beauty, they say, is in the eye of the beholder, but the eye cannot but behold a special glory that shines at a summer's sunrise on the upper Mullica. Stand along the river in Green Bank at sunrise some morning and experience the radiance of a new day as the mists rise from the dark, cedar water that flows silently under the old drawbridge, and you will have an experience of special peace.

Green Bank, where the river narrows and the eastern bank rises to its greatest height, is a town that evokes images of the Eastern Shore. Quietly residential today, the town was not always so. At the lower end near the quaint Methodist church, Nicholas Sooy II built his storehouse and extensive docks twenty years after Washington Township was formed. An active glass factory once filled the center portion of the town during the middle part of the nineteenth century. The Van Sant family worked two shipyards in Green Bank during that century. Joel, Sr. had one by the store of William H. Sooy and, later, his sons ran one across from the cemetery.

Green Bank today is a sleepy little town by the Mullica, except in summer, when Air Force training jets explode low overhead, deepthroated speedboats and poorly muffled jet skis jar the nerves, and loud radios from the state park scare away the wildfowl. Stately older homes mixed with newer ones line the River Road facing the ever-flowing Mullica.

The old church with its ancient cemetery still stands guard over the road's southern end. In that cemetery, the town of the past sleeps in eternal rest. Jessie Lewis, scion of the great Sooy family, presides over her home next door, a portion of which is the oldest house in Green Bank and perhaps in the entire area. Farther down the River Road, modern descendants of old families live side by side with relative newcomers to the town. All love the tranquility and beauty of this little town by the river.

Susan Dunphey lives in the old Sooy Storehouse. Don McCauley, the retired mayor of the township, lived in one of the original "Glass House Lot" houses until he moved to Florida in 1998. The Montgomery brothers, Russ and Jim lived side by side, Jim in one of the older "Glass House Lot" houses, until he died that same year. Russ lives in a new modular that replaced his father's old house that had been too termite-ridden to be restored. The Jaeckles, Schoenwetter, and Braun families come next, fairly new arrivals to the area. Bridge-tender Betty (Crowley) Rubsam lives in the old home of her parents on the corner. Betty is the former actress Kathleen Crowley. Her son, Matt, lives across the street in the old store, built by Nicholas Sooy II, and later run by Aunt Hattie Ford and later by Rod Koster.

The Walters family, children of Bill and Arwilda (Ford) Walters, own several homes at and near the juncture of River Road with Route 563. Bill came to the area in the very early 1930's, while Arwilda's family dates back to the times of the iron furnaces. Budd Wilson, former archaeologist for the State of New Jersey, lives in the Sooy/Wobbar home.

Green Bank is small-town America, much the way things used to be. Everyone knows everyone else. People smile at each other, wave to each other, speak to each other (most of the time). When the old store/post office closed its doors years ago, the people lost a vital part of their community. The center for gathering, conversation, gossip, and socialization was gone. Matt Rubsam intends to set things right sometime very soon. The pot belly stove may not be back, but Matt intends his store to be a community center once again.

Green Bank is a special town, a special place. Legend has that the town began with Samuel Driver. Sam is said to have lived at Red Bank in Gloucester County, and, in 1737, had Isaac Pearson do a survey for him of three hundred acres. Sam dreamed of having his own homestead by the river, and his new-found land stretched from beyond the present church to Little Bull Creek, near Budd Wilson's house today. Sam built a little house at the down-river end of his property in 1742, and there he remained for the next six years until his death. Even then, he didn't travel very far. He was laid to rest about a hundred yards from his house, his grave forming the nucleus of Green Bank's loved ones for the next two hundred years.

This has, at least, been the understanding for generations. However, the Wharton Ledger No. 2 Volume 12 suggests a different possibility. Apparently, General Elias Wright, in searching out property deeds for Joseph Wharton, found that Isaac Pearson bought 300 acres "situate at a place called Red Bank on the Easterly side of Mullicas River" which was inspected and approved on August 9, 1737. The Deputy Surveyor, John Burr, made the resulting survey on October 31, 1737, which was known as Survey No. 17. An accompanying map indicates that Driver purchased 106 adjacent acres known as Survey No. 43 but built his house near the corner of Survey No. 17. There seemed to be no actual record of transfer of Survey No. 17 from Pearson to Driver, although there is a record in Grantor Deeds 4671 dated March 10, 1752 stating that John and Mary Driver made a deed to Joseph (Yoos II) Sooy for "a place called Red Bank, Burlington County in consideration of the sum of 170 pounds." This transaction was recorded on the 23rd of March (Book A.I. of Deeds, p. 369) in the office of the Secretary of State. The property thus sold is described as "Isaac Pearson's 300 acres." John was Samuel Driver's son.

John Driver made one exception: "Before executing, the burial place where my honored father deceased lies buried on the premises of four rod square of ground is always and only excepted for our family." Notes on the ledger indicate that Driver and Sooy lived on the property but question how John Driver got the property. It is suggested that perhaps his wife, Mary, was Isaac Pearson's daughter. John Driver was Samuel's son. Sam died in 1748. In all probability, Samuel Driver received the property from Isaac Pearson prior to the 1742 construction date of his house. Son John and his wife then sold the property to Joseph Sooy in 1752, four years after his father's death. Samuel Driver also obtained another 222 acres locally in two different surveys: #21 for 200 acres and #22 for 22 acres in August 1738. He obtained another 106 acres in survey #43 on August 8, 1747, the year before his death. There is a note in the Wharton ledgers that says that when Driver made his surveys, he owned Pearson's 300 acres. Certainly he built his house on that land in 1742.

This record is doubly interesting however. Yoos II's *son*, Nicholas Sooy I, has always been thought to have been the purchaser of the Driver Estate, but Elias Wright's title search indicates Nicholas I, who owned the

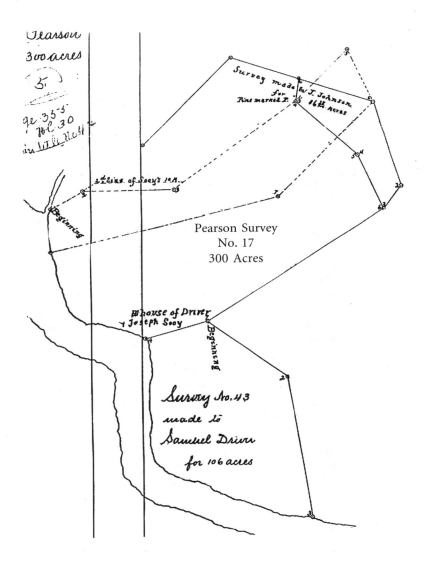

Copy of a Map from the Wharton Ledgers c. 1895
Showing the Pearson and Driver Surveys

Washington Tavern on the Road to Little Egg Harbor, may have lived in the Driver house at 1079 River Road as a child but did not own it as an adult. Secondly, note what the plantation is called: *Red* Bank! Samuel Driver's original home was supposed to have been in Red Bank, Gloucester County, and he may well have named his new plantation after his old home. Yet the name "Red Bank" is attached to the Pearson Survey, prior to Driver's acquiring it. When did *Red* become *Green*? Very early, no doubt. Bisbee quotes another Surveyor General's Office record from 1747 which mentions "Samuel Driver's Plantation at Red Bank," but the name is definitely *Green* Bank in the days of the Sooys.

Bisbee also notes that the name was "Upper Bank" on an 1849 map of Burlington County, but the records of Washington Township for the middle of that century call it nothing but Green Bank. Apparently, *Green* Bank it was after the time Joseph (Yoos II) Sooy bought it in 1752, and *Green* Bank it has remained ever since.

On February 13, 1787, a Jacob Ridgeway entered a judgement against Joseph Sooy in the courts. The execution of the judgement was made on the 15th of May, 1787 for a debt of 126 pounds, two shillings, and no pence with costs listed as two pounds, six shillings, six pence. Joseph Sooy's 300 acres of the Pearson Survey were sold at a sheriff's sale to William Richards of Batsto on June 26, 1790. This transaction was acknowledged on June 3, 1790. This deed conveyed "300 acres of land at a place called Green Bank on the east side of Mullicus river in the Western Division of New Jersey Particularly described as in Isaac Pearsons 300 acres."

William Richards owned the entire three hundred acres for over thirty years, selling it to Joseph Sooy's grandson, Nicholas Sooy II on the 14th of March, 1823 for $3,500, a

Bisbee does provide further confusion about the name. He also says that the place name was first mentioned in a 1710 survey done for John Osborn, Jr. "for 10 acres on south side of Little Egg Harbor River against a little Isle called Red Bank" (SGO Basse book p 5, 1710). Now, Green Bank was never an "Isle," even back in 1710 and isn't on the *south* side of the Mullica at all.

Another note mentions a survey for John Leek in 1761 "at Red Bank near Wading River." Bisbee begins his section of *Red* Bank (Washington Township) with the words: "*Located between Wading River and Lower Bank on the Mullica River.*" *Green* Bank is not between Lower Bank and Wading River. Confusing, to say the least.

Of course, Bisbee's conclusion about Green Bank being called "Sooy's Inn" is totally wrong. Sooy's Inn was Nicholas Sooy I's Washington Tavern on the Stage Road, not Green Bank.

transaction which was acknowledged the same month and recorded at Mt. Holly in Book O 2 of Deeds page 438. This transfer specifically states that Richards was selling Nicholas Sooy II

1st a tract containing 300 acres particularly described the same as Survey No. 17 made to Isaac Pearson for 300 acres; [This tract contains all of Green Bank from the church to Little Bull Creek]

2nd tract containing 10 62/100 acres and was surveyed to Joseph Sooy in L101;

3rd tract containing 50 acres and was conveyed out of a tract called the Bull Tract to Joseph Burr and by him to Joseph Sooy and by Sooy mortgaged to the Loan office and by the Commissioners of said office conveyed to William Richards;

4th tract is a survey made to Samuel Driver and by Driver conveyed to the said Joseph Sooy and by said Sooy mortgaged to the Loan office and by the commissioners of Said office conveyed to said William Richards;

5th Also 2 acres which the said Richards purchased of Michael Garout (this is part of Survey No. 22 made to Samuel Driver for 22 acres.)

Nicholas Sooy II and David Mapps recorded a joint Quit Claim for disputed cedar swamp land between the old Pearce Survey in Lower Bank which Mapps owned and the Driver Survey No. 43 (see map). This took place on January 26, 1824.

Over the fireplace in the old Driver Homestead on 1079 River Road hangs a faded deed dated 1811, transferring what is supposed to have been the land of the Driver Survey from Nicholas Sooy I to Nicholas Sooy II. Unfortumately, it is almost illegible. The recorded transfers as outline above seem to indicate that Nicholas Sooy I *never owned* any portion of the Driver Survey. So what *did* Nicholas I sell to Nicholas II in 1811 that has always been considered the deed to the Driver Survey?

In any case, Nicholas Sooy II built most of the older extant homes to house his children and their families during the last century. Not until his death in mid-century was the old estate divided up. In his will, dated 1850, he left about 175 acres lying on the south side of Pearson Survey to his son, William H. Sooy; another 105 acres to his grandchildren Ephraim C. Sooy, Jr. and Lydia, his sister, children of his deceased son, Ephraim; and additional acreage on the northern border of the Pearson Survey to his son, Josephus. The so-called "Glass House Lot", which lay on both sides of the present Route 563 where it crosses the Mullica, was divided equally between his sons. Both Josephus and William H. lost their lands in bad debts.

A large portion of Sooy lands were reassembled by Ephraim Sooy, Jr. early in the late nineteenth century, then lost again, this time to the state, during the misery of the Great Depression.

When Henry Charlton Beck haunted the Mullica Valley, Green Bank was home to some colorful characters. Leon Koster and his sons, Rodney and Hollis, lived in the "old homestead" of Nicholas Sooy II which stood on the outskirts of Green Bank at a place called "Herman" or "Herman City" after the building of the glass factory there in 1870. Rodney was a World War II veteran, and Hollis, a well-known naturalist. "Snapper" Cobb lived in a nearby house on Route 542 which is still standing. "Chink" Simkins lived on Lance Run Road. Haze Wobbar lived where Budd Wilson lives today and tipped many a glass with Jessie Lewis's father, Zeke Forman.

During the fifties and sixties, Walt and Virginia Priest ran first the old store on the corner by the bridge, then built a new one out on Route 542. Jess Nichols ran an auto repair shop behind his home on Route 563 and served as fire chief for a number of years. His wife, Margaret, worked hard for many a fire company clam bake. Arwilda (Ford) Walters was bridge tender, though her husband, Bill, often responded to the boat horns from the river. More precisely, Bill's dog responded. Bill was and is quite deaf, and it was their dog who heard the horns and alerted Bill to head for the bridge.

Every generation has its "characters." Most of the old "characters" are gone today, replaced by new ones, unique and spirited people who give color and life to this old town on the Mullica.

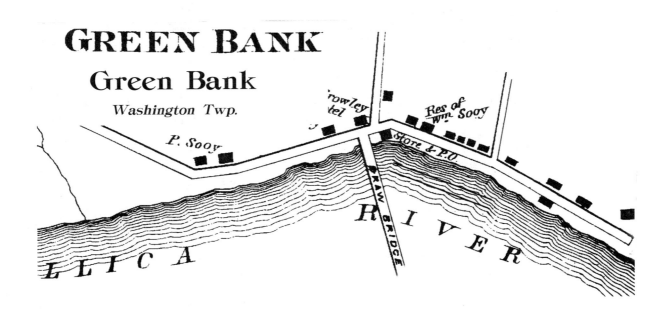

Map of Green Bank - 1876
Taken from J.D. Scott's *Atlas of Burlington County*

The Old Farmhouse of Samuel Driver
1079 River Road

Photograph by John Pearce

Green Bank began when Isaac Pearson purchased 300 acres which was inspected and approved on August 9th, 1737. John Burr, Deputy Surveyor, did the survey on October 31st, 1737. This 300 acres was "situate at a place called *Red Bank* on the Easterly side of Mullicas River."

By 1742, Sam Driver had acquired the Pearson Survey and, in that year, built the original section of this house for himself on the Pearson Survey: a typical South Jersey saltbox structure with one room below, a bedroom above, and a sleeping loft under the eves, with a kitchen in the back section. Though there have been some changes, the original section of 1079 River Road, the oldest house in Green Bank and, perhaps, the oldest in the township, remains much the same today as it was when Driver built it. Wharton Ledger No. 2, Volume 12 records that Samuel Driver owned an additional 106 acres down river from the Pearson Survey and later purchased other, smaller parcels of land in the vicinity.

When you pass through the front entrance, you enter a room of about fifteen feet square with a fireplace on the south wall. Directly ahead lies the door to the kitchen. Next to the fireplace, in the east wall, a door opens on a very narrow and winding staircase to the second floor. Originally, the bedroom upstairs had no wall on the staircase side, but did have a hole in the ceiling for access to the loft above. Mother and father slept in the bedroom, the children in the loft. There was no insulation of any sort in the walls of this house, which must have made for mighty cold winters. It was especially so in the loft. Our modern children who expect bedrooms of their own and central heating are mighty soft compared to those children of yesteryear.

The door to the kitchen retains hand-blown glass panels, and the height is low enough to make anyone over 5'7" stoop as they pass through. Keeps you humble!

Photograph by John Pearce

The oldest grave in the Green Bank Cemetery is that of Samuel Driver - 1748

1935

The original kitchen had a huge, walk-in fireplace on the east wall, but that was removed years ago when cooking stoves became popular.

That was all of the little house that Samuel Driver built in the wilderness of the New Jersey pines in the first half of the eighteenth century. The exterior was covered with hand-hewn clapboards, the wider style common in South Jersey rather than the narrower ones of New England, and the roof was shingled in hand-riven cedar shakes. Actually, the entire structure of the house was made from the tall cedar trees that loomed toward the sky in the dense swamps that surrounded Green Bank in those days.

Samuel Driver died in 1748 and was laid to rest in his side yard. His stone would be the first of many in what would become the Green Bank Cemetery. It has always been presumed by the family that, in the latter half of the century, Nicholas Sooy I purchased the entire Driver Survey: three hundred acres bordering the Mullica, including this house, and that in 1811, Nicholas sold the house to his son, Nicholas II. Josephus Sooy, son of Nicholas II, is supposed to have inherited the property when his father died. He then lost it in a bad debt.

According to title searches done by General Elias Wright for Joseph Wharton, who owned this property at the turn of the century, Joseph Sooy, son of Yoos of Lower Bank, bought this three hundred acres from John Driver in 1752 and lived here with his family until he lost it in 1787. Jacob Ridgeway sued him on February 13, 1787, and the sheriff was directed to sell the property on the 15th of May of that year. The amount of the judgement: 126 pounds, two shillings.

John Hollinshead, "late" Sheriff, sold the whole three hundred acres and farmhouse to William Richards of Batsto on June 26, 1790, and it remained his property until 1823, the year of his death, when Nicholas Sooy II, Joseph's grandson, bought it back into the family. On his death in 1851, Nicholas II left the house and its surrounding acreage to his son, William H. Sooy, not to William's brother, Josephus.

Somewhere around the turn of the century (eighteenth to nineteenth that is), an addition was made to the little house of Samuel Driver and Joseph Sooy though it is uncertain whether this was done prior to Joseph's losing the place or after William Richards bought it. To the north side was added a room that in all probability was used as a parlor or main room. This, too, had a fireplace, and probably also had a door to the outside in the west wall. This room stretched along almost the whole side of the old Driver house from the front to the end where the great fireplace glowed day in and day out with the promise of good food. On the second floor was a bedroom, or perhaps two, though at this point, the only access to the new section on the second floor was a very low corridor under the eves, connecting with the little, old winding staircase in the original section. A door may have given access between the original bedroom and the new one, which would have made life a bit easier for anyone over four and a half feet in height. There seems to be no indication from the construction as to the actual date this section was built.

John Richards, William's grandnephew, is supposed to have lived in Green Bank from 1810 to 1813. Here he kept a store and served as Justice of the Peace. On May 30, 1811, he married Rebecca Ludwig of Reading, Pennsylvania, and the couple rode to Green Bank on horseback after the wedding. Two years later, John bought land in Wading River and moved there. Did John build this first addition to this house? When William Richards bought the property, it was still one plantation. Most of the early houses were built by Joseph's grandson, Nicholas II, for his children, workers at his glass factory, and others. The property was not subdivided until his death in 1851. If John Richards did live in Green Bank, it is likely that he lived here, in the only house that we know existed at the time, although he may well have lived in some other dwelling built on the plantation.

Not long after 1800, the house experienced another building boom. Once again on the north end, a central staircase and a double parlor were added. This section had two formal bedrooms on the second floor and a small nursery room at the head of the stairs and completed the major work on the house as we know it. The usual time estimate for this construction is around 1830, which would be consistant with the repurchase of his grandfather's property by Nicholas Sooy II in 1823. Nicholas himself did not live here. He had also bought the "Old Homestead" of his uncle John on the Burr Survey nearby and was living there. It seems that his son, William H. Sooy, lived in this house with his wife, Mary, at least that's what Nicholas II's 1850 will implies.

William H. Sooy mortgaged the 175 acre farm to the Union National Bank at Mount Holly for $5000 on September 20, 1875 (BuCo Book S2). The debt being unpaid, Sheriff George P. Conover, sold the property to the Union National Bank on February 24th, 1879, for $1,000. At the end of the same year, on November 10th, the bank sold the 175 acres to Edwin B. Giles for $4,000 (BuCo B10 of Deeds). Two months later, Giles sold the farm to Joseph Wharton.

Recent information has come to light about the tenants of the property during the late eighteen hundreds. According to materials assembled by the Van Sant family, whose ancestors were famous for shipbuilding, Joel Van Sant started the first shipyard in Green Bank down by the Sooy Store sometime in the nineteenth century. Lillie, oldest daughter of Joel Van Sant II, in a letter to Emma Van Sant Moore, seems to indicate that there was a second yard by the river across from the cemetery. "Uncle Doughty lived in half of the house that we lived in, it was next to the church yard." She seems to indicate that this was "in the lower part of the Bank" [ie. Green Bank].

Photograph by Augusta Weeks

Views of the south-east end Driver Homestead during the 1930s
after the death of Ephraim C. Sooy, Jr.

Joel Nicholas Van Sant IV, writer of a manuscript on the Van Sant shipyards, presumes that the shipyard was started prior to 1875, based on the birth dates of Lillie and her siblings, and continued in operation until at least 1884. Of interest is that Lillie Van Sant seems to indicate that the Van Sant family lived in the house "next to the church yard," which could only be 1079 River Road. The years 1875 through 1884 span the ownerships of William H. Sooy, Edwin B. Giles, and Joseph Wharton.

John Van Sant had started the shipyard at The Forks which figured prominently in the American Revolution. Family members also had shipyards at Barnegat, Tuckerton, Somers Point, Atlantic City, New Gretna, and Ocean City. Another Joel Van Sant, Higbee Van Sant, Sr. and Higbee, Jr. apparently built ships in Cincinatti, Ohio during the early part of the nineteenth century. The Rev. Nicholas Van Sant, Jr. of Lower Bank visited these relatives in 1854-56, and said that they were descendants of Nicholas Van Sant, Sr. [see Lower Bank]

William H. Sooy's nephew, Ephraim C. Sooy, Jr., would figure prominently in bringing the Driver/Sooy Homestead back into the Sooy family. Ephraim, Jr. or Eph as he was called, bought the house and much of what is now Green Bank State Forest from the Wharton Estate early in the twentieth century. He installed the William Woolston family as caretakers of his estate, and they apparently lived in the old house for a time.

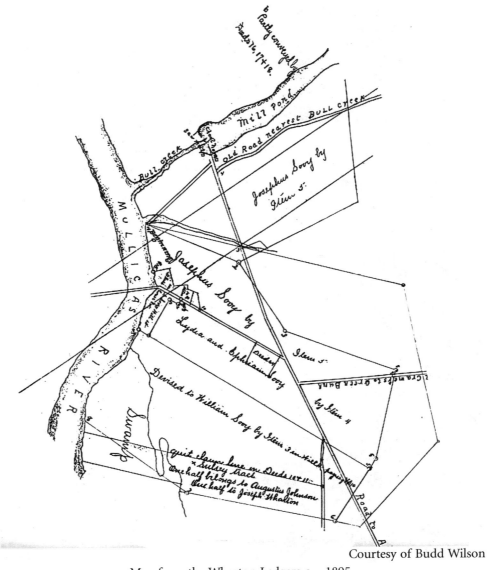

Courtesy of Budd Wilson

Map from the Wharton Ledgers c. - 1895
Showing Distribution of the Sooy Properties
Joseph Wharton owned the Driver Homestead at 1079 River Road at that time.

Eph's father and mother were Ephraim C. and Lucy Ann Haywood. Lucy Ann was the daughter of the Methodist Episcopal minister in West Creek, New Jersey, and Ephraim C. was the son of Nicholas Sooy II. When tragedy struck the young family (a full discussion appears under the material for 2410 Route 563: the Sooy/Woolston/Wessler House), Eph was first taken in by his maternal grandfather, then by his uncle, William H. Sooy and his aunt by marriage and his mother's aunt as well, Mary (Haywood) Sooy, and raised in their home at 1045 River Road.

When he was twenty in 1868, Eph had a hankering for adventure and went to sea as mate aboard a steamer, but soon gave up the idea of following the sea. A year later in 1869, he headed west and established himself on a large ranch in Kansas. He told an interesting story about the hardships of life on the plains, especially about the blizzard in the winter of 1872. He almost froze to death trying to round up a thousand head of cattle that had stampeded along the valley of the Beaver Creek. In her manuscript "The Romance of Green Bank," which she wrote in the mid-1930's, Mrs. McConeghy records that Ephraim, Jr. had told her a story about riding amongst a herd of buffalo: "They were on all sides of us as far as the eye could see. I must have seen a million that day. It was a wonderful, wonderful sight." Later, he worked as a carpenter in

Courtesy of Jessie (Forman) Lewis

Ephraim C. Sooy, Jr.

Great Bend, Kansas, and still later, set up a milling business in Walnut Creek. Finally, he moved to Kansas City, Mo. and was connected for years with various mills and manufacturing businesses. He even had interests in silver mining in Mexico. He met and married Jessie Hargrave, and the couple settled down and had four children before her untimely death at the age of fifty in 1901.

The Rev. Charles Nesbet, Pastor of the Central Presbyterian Church in Kansas City, Mo., said at his funeral service: "Mr. Sooy was thirty-one years a member of this church and twenty years a Ruling Elder. He gave of his prayers, his money, his love. There are four things that have made him a princely man - the spirit of gentleness, kindliness, optimism, and loyalty. He always looked on the bright side and was loyal in every relationship."

He invested his own money in the propagation of the Gospel through missionary work. Three missionaries served under the gifts of Eph for a total of twenty-seven years and three months. An accounting was given of the results of their labors at the time of his death:

Courtesy of Jessie (Forman) Lewis

Jessie (Hargrave) Sooy
1850 - 1901

A FEW RESULTS OF THIS INVESTMENT

Pastoral Visits made to Homes	*20,816*
Miles Traveled	*5,090*
Bibles and Testaments Distributed	*180,768*
Churches Developed from this Work	*34*
Sermons and Addresses given	*5,861*
Hopeful Conversions Reported	*6,564*
Lives helpfully touched, fully	*115,000*

Laura McConeghy comments:

"Are these only bare figures? No, for back of each figure there is a human soul. Thousands of eager, smiling, children and young people have been gathered from pitiful mountain homes, mining towns full of temptation, lumber camps far back in the forest or from the open country, to be taught the Bible and their feet turned toward God. This work is so vital, constructive, far-reaching. The investment has paid great spiritual returns. God has been honored and His Kingdom built up through the life and gift of Ephraim Cline Sooy."

Ephraim Cline Sooy, Jr., had four children: Lucy, Bertram, Elizabeth, and Norman, but Bert died at the young age of twenty-one. Lucy and Norman were mid-Westerners and had little interest in the pinelands property of their Sooy ancestors. Elizabeth was another matter altogether. She had married Ezekiel Forman, whose family had a long history on Maryland's Eastern Shore. She and Zeke moved from Kansas City, where their daughter, Jessie was born, to Atlantic City, but, when Zeke developed ulcers on his eyes, his doctors told him to take it easy. Father Eph fixed up the old home of his birth at 2410 Route 563 for the little family, and they lived there for several years.

When Ephraim died in 1927, his estate passed to his children. Lucy and Norman continued their residence and interests in Kansas City. Elizabeth adored Green Bank. Zeke, Elizabeth, and

Jessie (Sooy) Forman as a child in the 1920s, visiting the home of her grandfather, Ephraim C. Sooy, Jr.

The Lewis Clan in 1944 on the porch of the Old Store.
L to R: Hans Lewis, Jessie (Forman) Lewis, Phyllis Lewis, Bob Lewis,
Dudley Weimer, and Herb Lewis.
(Hans, Bob, and Herb are brothers.)

The Old Farmhouse under the Forman care during the 1940s.
Note that the south porch has not yet been added.

Jessie did finally move back to their house in Margate, but they lost it during the depression in 1939. They finally decided they'd fix up the old Storehouse as a home and move in, and that's what they did in the mid 1940s.

Zeke Forman and his wife Elizabeth (Sooy) Forman added a porch on the west end off the parlor, porches at the two front doors, and enclosed a back porch to make a room off the kitchen. Zeke also added a porch off the eastern end of the original house. Eph had been a practical man and managed to squeeze in a bathroom on the second floor rear. Thankfully, that ended the trips to the outhouse, but the lack of plumbing had made this new "johnny" a bit difficult to flush. Jessie says that a huge barrel of water used to stand on the back steps and that it was her cousins' job to fill it each morning. No one remembers how they filled the clawfooted tub. That water was what they used to flush the toilet. Hans Lewis later added a dormer and a new bathtub to Eph's little "convenience" room.

Their daughter, Jessie, had grown into a fine young woman by the 1940's and married James Hansell Lewis (or Hans as he is called) of Mount Airy in Philadelphia in 1943. During World War II, Jessie travelled to be near her husband. After the war, they had a son, whom they named Dudley for a family friend, Dudley Weimer, who had been Hans's Best Man. The family moved to Dickeyville in Baltimore, Maryland, and later, they lived in South Orange, New Jersey.

Each summer, though, they made the pilgrimage to Green Bank. Jess dearly loved the old Driver homestead. Of all the places they had been, this was home to her, and her husband and son came to love the place as well. Their son basically grew up here. This summer home was more home to him than where they lived in the winter. He was raised on the tales of the local men of their experiences in times long past and absorbed a deep appreciation for Green Bank and the pinelands.

When Jessie and Hans decided to move to Green Bank permanently, they had the old house completely restored. New electrical wiring was placed in the walls, which now were insulated against the winter's cold. Wallboard covered the old, cracked plaster that was falling off the walls, and new random-width pine floors were laid on the first floor. The parlor was sinking at both ends, built as it was on a single course of sandstone for a foundation, so that was shored up. Rather than tear the structure apart to install a heating system, they chose electric heat and modernized the kitchen. Over the years, the Lewis family has added a full bath off the dining room and a large coat closet as well. When Hans retired, he decided to start painting the house. At the end of the second year, he had just made it around once and it needed painting again! That was when the vinyl-siding people were called in. All in all though, the structure is both the oldest and most original structure in Green Bank and retains its flavor of the past.

After college at Muhlenberg in Allentown, Pennsylvania, Dud returned to Green Bank, teaching the eighth grade in the school for a couple of years. Then he accepted a teaching position in Cooperstown, New York, and remained there for three years. Winters were too much for him, though, and he received a teaching position at Mainland Regional, where he has been ever since. Green Bank once again became home.

As of 1998, Jessie Sooy Forman Lewis still reigns a queen in the house of her ancestors. She has headed up the local food distribution program for many years, been active on the county level with the senior citizens, and even testified before the State Senate when the Pinelands Bill was under discussion. Her decisiveness, strength of character, and determination definitely reflect the Sooy personality of her mother, her grandfather Ephraim C., her great-great grandfather Nicholas II, and her great-great-great-grandfather, Nicholas I. Hans is no slouch either, having been active in the township's Republican politics and having served a term as mayor. During the 1970s, Hans, Jess, and Dud were instrumental in building up the Green Bank Ambulance Squad and have always been ready to help their fellow citizens. Dud served as captain of the squad for several years and was in the fire company as well.

The old house vibrates with memories of past lives that have lived within its walls. Sometimes in the quiet of the nights, the house creaks and groans, speaking with voices of its own of the things that it's seen: of the vast woodlands and swamps that were exploited for their timber, of the busy river commerce that made the Mullica a highway, of the Sooys who lived and died here in the little town of Green Bank.

Over the mantel in the parlor still hangs the portrait of Lucy Ann Haywood Sooy, that young wife who lost her infant son and husband within a month, and died herself at twenty-six, leaving Lydia and Eph to be raised by her father and aunt/sister-in-law. On the wall in the same room is the portrait of The Rev. Joel Haywood, her father, of West Creek.

The old house has been an integral part of the Sooy family since the second Yoos (Joseph) bought it in 1752 from Sam Driver's son, John. The house breathes memories.

Courtesy of Jessie Lewis

The north and newest section of the Old Farmhouse.
This picture is also from the 1940s, when the house was loved by
Ezekiel and Elizabeth (Sooy) Forman.

Photograph by John Pearce

Jessie (Forman) Lewis, Hans Lewis, Dudley
Lewis

204

The Shipyards of Green Bank

During the nineteenth century, busy Green Bank had no less than two ship yards operating along the river. Both were run by the Van Sant family though that family's records are fuzzy about the actual dates of operation.

Lillie Van Sant, great granddaughter of the Rev. Nicholas Van Sant of Lower Bank, in a letter to her sister, Emma, indicated that her grandfather, Joel Van Sant, son of the Rev. Nicholas and grandson of John, who ran the ship yard at The Forks, built a ship yard in Green Bank early in the century. Indications are that this yard was next to the Green Bank store. Since all the land in Green Bank belonged to Nicholas Sooy II or, after his death in 1851, to his sons, Joel Van Sant probably rented the property from the Sooys.

A bit later in the century, he and his son, Joel II, built another yard downriver across from the cemetery. Joel Van Sant was born on November 22, 1811 and died November 5, 1895. The Van Sant family history notes that Joel and his sons built many vessels in several local towns, among which were Manahawkin, Mays Landing, Green Bank, New Gretna, Tuckerton, and on the Alloways Creek. His grandson, Captain Joel Frank Van Sant III (1885-1967), indicated in his journal that his grandfather had at least one ship named after himself that was celebrated in a song which began: "It was on the schooner *Joel Van Sant*/commanded by Captain Oliphant," and each verse ended with the line, "So we headed her in for Hawkin (Manahawkin)." His grandson had been told that the *Joel Van Sant* was a charcoal schooner which hauled local charcoal to New York and Philadelphia.

Joel Van Sant II was born on March 19, 1841 and helped to construct gun boats for the United States Navy in Tuckerton during the Civil War. He was "held in arms" at the commencement of the battle at Gettysburg, but he and his fellow "soldiers" never made it past Philadelphia. By the time they reached that city, they received word that General Lee had been defeated, and, no longer being needed, they were sent back home to New Jersey.

The Van Sants apparently moved from town to town, setting up shipyards as they went. Perhaps they simply found the best timber available, set up a yard nearby, built a few ships, and moved on. At Green Bank, they built at least three large ships during the 1870's: the *L.A. Seiver*, the *Lillie Falkinburg*, and the *Harvey W. Anderson*, all three-masted schooners over a hundred feet long. Captain Joel F. Van Sant III indicates that

> The *Lillie Falkinburg was named for my mother's twin sister, who was married to Captain William Henry Falkinburg, who perhaps had a master's share in the schooner, possibly a 16th or a 32nd. It was customary in those days to sell shares in a schooner before she was built. They all made money in those days and lived well, but the crash while Grant was president ruined a great number of people. I do not think my father ever recovered enough to keep even with an increasing family. With less earning power and the long period of low wages and business stagnation, his spirit must have been broken.* (Van Sant Family papers)

According to other records, the *Lillie Falkinburg* was built in Green Bank in 1873. It had a gross tonnage of 216.58, a net tonnage of 205.75, a length of 115.8 feet, and a beam of 30.8 feet. It ran a ground at Lewes, Delaware while carrying a cargo of lumber from the James River to New York. It was owned, at least in part, by Marshall Loveland. If this building date is correct, it must have been the last large vessel built in Green Bank prior to the Panic of 1873.

The families of both Joel Van Sant II and Doughty Van Sant, his brother, lived in the old Driver/Sooy Homestead at 1079 River Road, which they must have rented from William H. Sooy, but Joel II may have lived elsewhere in Green Bank before moving there. His daughter, Lillie's letter to her sister is quite confusing since it was written when she was very old. "We moved to Green Bank (from Tuckerton). Then they started the yard down the lower part of the Bank and we moved up there. Uncle Doughty lived in half of the house that we lived in. It was next to the church yard." There is no indication when Joel I first moved to Green Bank nor when the yard by the church yard was dismantled, but on March 15, 1877, Samuel Van Sant (b. 1844), Joel II and Doughty's younger brother, bought Josephus Sooy's 2/5th share of the house at 1047 River Road, next to the location of his father's ship yard. The following May 7th, he bought the other 3/5th share of that property from William H. Sooy, Josephus's brother..

Joel II seems to have moved to Hammonton about 1884-5. On June 14th, 1890, Samuel Van Sant and his wife, Phoebe, conveyed Lot H back to William H. Sooy for $500. Thus 1885-90 seems to have been the outside limit for the operation of the Van Sant ship yards in Green Bank.

The Last Days of the *Lillie Falkinburg*

The *Lillie Falkinburg* was a three-masted schooner, built at Green Bank in 1873 by the Van Sants. She had a gross tonnage of 216.58, a net tonnage of 205.75, stretched 115.8 feet from the tip of her bowsprit to her stern, and had a beam of 30.8 feet. Owned by Marshall Loveland and sailing out of Tuckerton, the ship ran aground at Lewes, Delaware while carrying a cargo of lumber from the James River to New York. The actual date of her demise is not known.

It doesn't seem possible that a ship this big was ever built in little Green Bank, let alone sailed down the Mullica to the sea.

The Old Storehouse
1078 River Road

Prior to World War II

Courtesy of Jessie Lewis

For a great many years, this old building has stood beside the Mullica, a part of all the activities of life on the river though its construction date is unknown.

Traditionally, it has been thought that this structure was built by Nicholas Sooy II after acquiring the Samuel Driver property from William Richards in 1823, but it may have been constructed at an earlier date. It's frame is pegged together, and hand-forged nails were also found in the building. The rafters were sawn with either a vertical saw or a pit saw, and the general construction resembles that used in the original section of the Driver house across the road (1079 River Road). Thus it may well be that it was built prior to Nicholas Sooy II's time, and there is the chance

Photograph by Augusta Weeks

1935

that Joseph Sooy built it when he lived here in the eighteenth century. Samuel Driver himself may have erected it at the same time as he built his home by the river in 1742.

Nicholas Sooy II was active in commercial pursuits and had an excellent eye for business. River commerce would have been one of his prime interests, and this is the first known storehouse built in Green Bank for the storage and transfer of goods being shipped to and from the Green Bank area.

For well over a hundred years, this old storehouse saw constant activity, with cargo-carrying ships

Courtesy of Jessie Lewis

Elizabeth Sooy Forman
This photograph was taken during World War Two

sailing and warping their way upriver and sliding down with the tide and current. Products produced locally like lumber, charcoal, iron products, glass products, and the like, were stored here prior to shipment to the cities. Goods for sale to the people and businesses of the area were unloaded from the coastal schooners, which were then reloaded with the locally-produced items in return. Commercial trading was lucrative, and this old building saw it all. At one time, a large dock stretched out from the base of this building, thrusting itself into the river, where coastal schooners and sloops tied up.

Courtesy of Jessie Lewis
Late 1940s

The nineteenth century did not end very well for the Old Storehouse, though. Nicholas II, prior to his death in 1851, moved the business down the road to the corner, intending to keep the old Storehouse for precisely that: storage. Gradually, though, the river trade shifted to the Upper Dock and the new store.

For almost forty years, the ancient building stood, gazing forlornly out on the river at its feet, perhaps envying the attention paid to the "new" store upstream, but helpless to alter its fate. During these years, Ephraim C. Sooy, Jr., came often to his beloved Green Bank. He stayed in Atlantic City but would make the journey out to Green Bank frequently.

Ephraim, Jr. spent his life in Kansas City with his family. True, his heart was in Green Bank, but he always had to go home in the autumn to the city of his adoption. Besides that, his second wife was a city-person and couldn't quite adjust to rural Green Bank. She stayed in Atlantic City while E.C. made his pilgrimage to his birthplace.

Ephraim, Jr.'s daughter, Elizabeth, had married Zeke Forman of the Eastern Shore of Maryland. They lived first in Kansas City, then moved to Atlantic City. When Zeke's eyes had trouble with ulcers and the doctors warned him into a less strenuous life-style, Elizabeth, Zeke, and their little daughter, Jessie, moved into the old house on the Chatsworth-New Gretna Road that her father fixed up for them. When Ephraim, Jr. died in 1927, all his property passed to his children.

Courtesy of Jessie Lewis
Ezekiel and Elizabeth (Sooy) Forman
in their newly-created home.

208

Then came the crash of 1929. That wreaked havoc in the lives of everyone, rich or poor, and the Sooy family was not spared. They lost almost all of the Nicholas Sooy II estate left to them with the sole exception of the five acres that included the Samuel Driver homestead and this old Storehouse by the river, which they clung to with tenacity. The Forman family had moved back to their home in Margate during the early 1930s, but they lost their house in 1939. For a while they lived in various apartments, but their thoughts were in Green Bank.

The Old Storehouse as rebuilt by the Formans in 1946-7.

After World War II, Zeke and Elizabeth decided to fix up the old storehouse for their retirement house, and they did a wonderful job of it. That empty old building became a darling showplace and comfortable dwelling for their remaining years. How proud they were of their snug little cottage by the Mullica and what wonderful views they had from the double porches they built on the river end of their new house. The old Storehouse had a new lease and once again vibrated with life.

Daughter Jessie had grown up by now and had married James Hansell ("Hans") Lewis, from Mount Airy, in Philadelphia. It was wartime. Hans was in the military, and Jess was living as near to his station of duty as possible, so Elizabeth and Zeke had all the space they needed.

Dudley Lewis, early 1950s

That little boy is growing up!

The big house remained unwinterized, used only in the summer, but both the old home of Samuel Driver, and the re-modeled new home of the Formans, were well-loved and much appreciated. Green Bank was home to them, proving the truth of the words of that old song, that no matter how far you wandered, there's no place like home.

After the war was over, Jess and Hans settled down into building a family of their own. Jessie, child of Green Bank, still had to return home once in a while. Oh yes, it was to visit her dear parents, but it was also to feel in touch with her past. Each summer, she and her new little addition, whom they named Dudley, would come "home" for a long visit. Although they lived in Baltimore, then in South Orange, Green Bank was always *home*. When her parents passed away, Jess, Hans, and Dud came only in the summers. Thus they transferred their lives to the old homestead of Samuel Driver. To help pay the inevitable taxes, they rented out the Old Storehouse.

Finally, when Dudley was ready for college in 1965, Jess and Hans decided that they were ready for Green Bank full time. After winterizing the big house, they moved in. The Old Storehouse continued to be a rental property.

Things remained thus for many years until 1994, when they decided to sell the little house to their then tenant, Susan Dunphey, who, like Jess's father, was into real estate. Susan adores the little house with its spectacular views of the river and continues the long line of life within those four walls.

Courtesy of Susan Dunphey

Susan Dunphey- 1995

Photograph by John Pearce

Nicholas Sooy's Old Storehouse - 1995

The Superintendent's House
1061 River Road

Photograph by Augusta Weeks

1935

    This house has been owned by the State of New Jersey for many years. It was no doubt built in the mid-nineteenth century and follows the style of that period. It served as the home of the caretaker of the Sooy Estate before it served the same purpose under the State of New Jersey. This property was not part of the Glass House Lot of Nicholas Sooy II but stood on property inherited by his son, William H. Sooy, as was the Driver/Sooy House at 1079 River Road.

    Jessie Lewis remembers this house being called the "Jenny Broom House" when she was a child. Jenny Broom married William Woolston who served as caretaker for the Sooy Estate for many years. An interview with Woolston by Henry Charlton Beck suggests that the "Jenny Broom" house stood on the property at 1014 River Road. Beck records Woolston as saying that it was here that his wife, Jenny, was born. This house was later torn down by Bill Birdsall when he built his little cottage. In any case, the William Woolstons lived in many locations around Green Bank over the years, including the Old Driver Farmhouse and may well have lived in this particular house for a number of years as well. This house did belong to the Sooy Estate, and Woolston did serve as caretaker for many years.

    During the 1930s, this house was the home of Mr. and Mrs. Clifford Terry. Mr. Terry was the Keeper of the State Forestry Department and ran the reforestation nursery in the Green Bank State Forest.

    Ephraim C. Sooy, Jr., had owned all the land that now comprises the Green Bank State Forest, including the Old Driver Farmhouse, the Old Storehouse, and a great many acres of land in the early part of this century.

    Ephraim died in 1927, and his children inherited the vast estate, both here and in Kansas City. Unfortunately, the Great Despression struck with a vengeance soon after, and, like so many others across the nation, the heirs found themselves paupers where once they had seemed so well off. Ephraim C. had owned all the property in Green Bank that remained in the Sooy family of the great Nicholas Sooy II estate. He had even repurchased the Old Driver Farmhouse (1079 River Road) that his uncle, William H. Sooy, lost to the bank. Now his heirs had to struggle. There was no money with which to pay the taxes, so the whole property was put up for auction. The State of New Jersey was the only bidder and acquired everything in 1931, including this house which had been the home of the supervisor of the Sooy Estate, with the single exception of the Driver Homestead and five surrounding acres.. This was called, "How to Get a State Forest - In One Easy Step"!

Into this house, the state moved Mr. Clifford Terry to manage their considerable acreage. Most of the land around Green Bank had been stripped of trees in the nineteenth century to stoke the many glassworks and iron furnaces . Wood not needed for them was made into charcoal and shipped as fuel to Philadelphia and New York. Timber was cut and dressed for shipment to the cities as well. The first part of the twentieth century saw tremendous emptiness where there once stood great trees. The State of New Jersey made a concerted effort at rebuilding what commerce had destroyed. Their employees planted experimental "farms" of white pine in many areas and watched over the newly acquired state lands.

The Terrys were originally from Plainfield, New Jersey, but they were such congenial people, however, that they weren't resented. They made their home a center for social and cultural activities especially for the young people. They kept a library, which, for Green Bank in the 1930s, was extensive. Mrs. Terry was appointed "Librarian" of the community by the County Librarian, Miss Clark, and the appointment was approved by the State Librarian, Miss Askew, at Trenton. The community library was a great help to the residents of the little town of Green Bank. The Terrys were active in the affairs of the Green Bank school and the Parent-Teachers Association. The Terrys were succeeded by Art Conrad and his family. Art was also an employee of the State of New Jersey at the Green Bank State Forest. He and his family lived in this house for a period of about thirty-five years.

Though the state had used this house for employees of the Wharton State Forest (under which the Green Bank State Forest fell

Courtesy of Jessie (Forman) Lewis

Howard King, Jr. and Florence Terry
During World War II

for administration) since the Great Depression, it found that it no longer had a need for such housing. Rather than rent out the property, they abandoned it to deterioration like most of the other houses in their possession. The State of New Jersey seems to have no appreciation whatsoever for historic preservation, except where Batsto is concerned. During 1995, Mayor Don McCauley negotiated with the state to acquire the house on a long-term lease for the use of the people of Washington Township. The township was finally successful in their quest and is now seeking funds for restoration.

Photograph by John Pearce

1995

The Green Bank Glass House

In 1837, perhaps as early as 1834, Nicholas Sooy II decided to get into the glass business. Glass looked good at the time. It was the up and coming business of South Jersey, and Nicholas II wanted to get in on the ground floor. He laid out a sizable lot for the glass house and for workers' houses along the river in the middle of the original Pearson/Driver Survey.

In those days, the Bridgeport (Wading River) to Batsto Road ran approximately where Route 542 does today, at least in this area, but Route 563 wasn't even considered. The short section of Route 563 from Route 542 to the bridge may well have been there, though the bridge itself was not. It wouldn't be built for another eighteen years or there about. This section of road probably joined with that running downriver to the Driver house at 1027 River Road where his son, William H. Sooy, lived with his family.

Nicholas Sooy II and his brother-in-law, Arthur Thompson (his sister Elizabeth's husband), formed a partnership in about 1837 to get into the glass business. Nicholas laid out the glass house lot so that the main pad of the business lay to the northwest of what is now Route 563. The remainder of that lot stretched along River Road downriver from the corner. At some time during this period, several houses were built along the river south of the glass house itself that were meant to house those who worked in the business. These probably include 1055 River Road, 1053, 1051 (no longer in existence) and 1047 (no longer in existence). It seems that three other houses were built upriver from the glass house for the same purpose. Three were listed in Nicholas II's will as part of his son, Josephus's inheritance, but two were long gone before present memory. The third is possibly the one at 1032 River Road.

The two men seem to have set up a bottle works on the property, but Nicholas was not in the habit of running a business himself. Like all good entrepreneurs, he wanted to control businesses and make money. He did not want to risk much to do so. Consequently, by the beginning of the 1840's, he was looking for an expert to run the place for him. He found his expert in the person of Green Bank native William Coffin, Sr. Coffin had become the founder and co-owner of a successful glassworks in Hammonton and also in Winslow. He seems to have been getting on in years by the start of the decade, and Nicholas Sooy II persuaded him to return to the town of his birth and operate a window-light and hollow ware furnace. Boarden Westcott built a flattening house at Green Bank in 1842, and Nicholas leased the glassworks to Coffin.

In addition to bottles, Green Bank's glass house also produced window glass in the cylindrical method that was common in this area. William died only two years later, but the work was continued by his son, Bodine Coffin, though the business does not seem to have been very profitable. By the end of the decade, the glassworks was already laying off workers. Arthur Thompson, Sooy's partner, died in 1849. The glass factory closed by 1850.

Nicholas Sooy II then leased the glass factory to the E. L. Wells and Company of Philadelphia from March 1, 1850 to March 1, 1852. Before the lease expired, Nicholas Sooy II died (June 29, 1851), and the glass industry was left to his sons. Apparently E.L. Wells and Company didn't make enough of a profit either and did not renew the lease. From May 1, 1852 to August 1, 1853, D. O. Ketchum and Company leased the works. Both of these companies seem to have made only bottles. The flattening oven, so necessary for producing window lights, had not been used since Bodine Coffin failed, so it was sold.

Just after Nicholas' death, several things happened to change Green Bank dramatically. On January 11, 1853, Samuel and Catherine Sooy transferred their one-fifth share in the lot "called glass house works, dwelling houses, wharf, store houses and all buildings thereon situate" (Vol. 12, Wharton ledger) to Samuel's brother, William. A month later, on February 5th, Nicholas Sooy III and his wife Hannah transferred their one-fifth share in the glass house lot to his brother, Josephus. That left William owning two-fifths, Josephus owning two-fifths, and their nephew, Ephraim, Jr., then only a child, owning one-fifth.

When the D.O. Ketchum Company left Green Bank, the bottle furnace remained idle for about four years. At that time, the South Jersey glassmakers went on strike. Some Glassboro blowers apparently approached the Sooy family and arranged a lease/partnership agreement with him. One of the Sooys would act as the clerk of this labor-owned company, and they would produce glass on a cooperative basis. This arrangement didn't last very long either, and with its collapse, glass production in Green Bank ended.

In 1855, the iron and wood swing bridge was built which connected the town to Atlantic County. In 1857, the glass house ceased its operations. In 1858, Nicholas II's son, William H. Sooy, built a new home for himself at 1045 River Road. At some time during this period also, one of the Van Sants ran a boatyard immediately next to the store in what became William's front yard. Perhaps it was after William H. built his new house in 1858 that the shipyard was moved down river near the Old Storehouse. It is also probable that the Green Bank Hotel was not built by Sebastian Crowley until after the glass house ceased operations.

In 1971, Bill Carney would be digging in the riverbank in his front yard and find a large, stone structure. Carney was born in an old house which used to stand at 1047 River Road but which he later tore down and built a new one. Carney's find was identified by Budd Wilson as a lime kiln that had been part of the glass house complex.

The maps on this and the next page are from a Wharton ledger that was compiled about 1895. The first map shows the actual glass house lot as Nicholas Sooy II had it laid out. The second map shows the riverfront of that large lot split up into smaller lots for houses. River Road doesn't show.

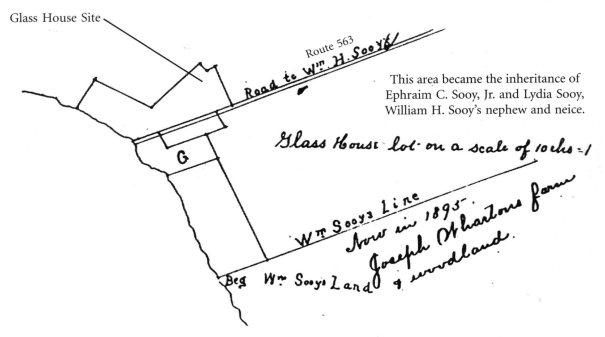

Courtesy of Budd Wilson

The Glass House Lot

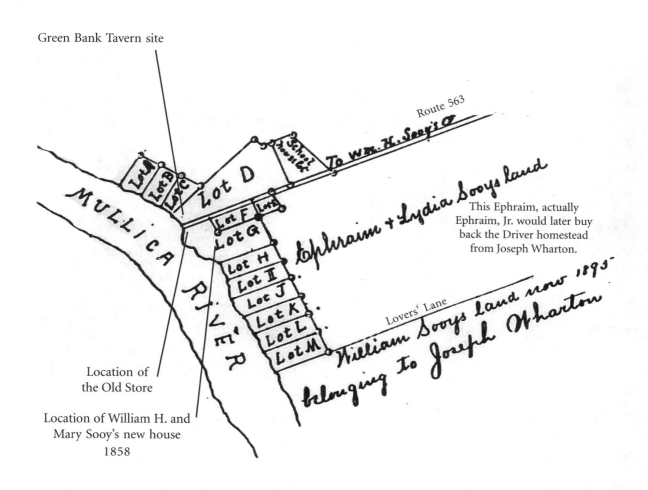

Green Bank Tavern site

Route 563

To Wm. H. Sooy's

Lot A

Lot B

Lot C

Lot D

School House

Lot E

Lot F

Lot G

Lot H

Lot I

Lot J

Lot K

Lot L

Lot M

MULLICA RIVER

Ephraim + Lydia Sooys land

This Ephraim, actually Ephraim, Jr. would later buy back the Driver homestead from Joseph Wharton.

Lovers' Lane

William Sooys land now 1895 belonging to Joseph Wharton

Location of the Old Store

Location of William H. and Mary Sooy's new house 1858

The Glass House Lot
Apparently after the glass house closed, the property was actually divided into separate lots and sold.
Houses already stood on some of them at the time.

The Weaver/Shafer/McCauley House
1055 River Road

Photograph by Augusta Weeks

1935

This house, along with its neighbors, was probably constructed in the first half of the nineteenth century to house the craftsmen of the glassworks and their families. Nicholas Sooy II owned the property on which the glasshouse was erected and leased it to an operator. The glasshouse lot included property on both sides of what is now Route 563.

In his will of 1850, Nicholas II gave this entire property to his sons, Samuel Sooy, William Sooy, Josephus Sooy, Nicholas Sooy, Jr. (III) and to his grandson Ephraim C. Sooy, Jr. Each inherited a 1/5th share, but Samuel quickly sold his share to his brother, William H. for $520 in a deed dated January 11. 1853, acknowledged the same day, and recorded on April 19th. Not to be outdone by his brother, Josephus persuaded his brother, Nicholas W. Sooy (III) to sell him his one-fifth share a month later, on the fifth of February for the same amount, $520. E.C. Sooy, Jr. held on to his share until 1875. By that time, he got $1,300 out of his Uncle William in a deed dated the first of February.

Josephus mortgaged his entire estate, including his shares of the Glass House Lot to the First National Bank of Vincentown on the 17th of December, 1872 for $14,000. Still another mortgage is recorded in the Burlington County books. This time, Josephus remortgaged all of the same property to his brother, William H. Sooy, to secure $11,466.10. The date was the 17th of February, 1874. Josephus defaulted. The "Master" appointed by the court to handle the property was John C. Ten Eyck, who proceeded to have the lands of Josephus Sooy surveyed. He divided the Glass House Lot into twelve parcels for sale.

On the 25th of July, 1876, a 2/5th share of Lot L, which contained this house, was sold to the First National Bank of Vincentown for $200 to satisfy the debts of Josephus Sooy. William H. Sooy bought this 2/5ths share from the bank in 1877. William H. Sooy sold his whole share in this lot to John S. Frick, James Durand, and William A. Ripley on January 12th, 1880. Durand sold his share to Frick and Ripley on June 28th, 1882. They sold out to Elizabeth Adams on March 24th, 1891.

This house was the home of Mr. and Mrs. Harry Weaver during the 1930s. Harry Weaver, a Philadelphian, was a veteran of the Spanish-American War. He married Annie Ford, daughter of Maurice and Hester (Sooy) Ford, who owned and operated the Green Bank hotel. In her last years, Hester Ann (Sooy) Ford lived in this house with her daughter. Hester Anne actually outlasted Harry Weaver by a year, since he passed away in 1933. Harry tried to run a chicken farm on the property but had to give it up when his health failed. Harry had taken great pride in his home and had always tried to be a good neighbor. Annie (Ford) Weaver was active in the Ladies Aid of the Green Bank church and in the Parent-Teachers' Association of the Green Bank school. She had been one of Watson Sooy's voice pupils and was active in the choir at the church. After the double blow of losing her husband and her mother in one year, she rented out the home and took up residence in Atlantic City.

In the 1950s, Annie Weaver rented her house to the Shafers for the summer and moved into a shed in the rear of her property. When Annie died, the Shafers bought the home. Don McCauley visited the Shafers, his aunt and uncle, frequently during the period of their ownership of 1055 River Road. Finally he purchased this house from them and moved to Green Bank permanently. Don had lived in Audubon, New Jersey and worked for the Bell Telephone Company prior to moving to Green Bank. He was elected mayor of the township but, in 1998, after heart by-pass surgery, he resigned and moved to the warmer clime of Florida.

Photograph by John Pearce

His Honor the Mayor
Don McCauley

1995

Photograph by John Pearce

217

The Frances Montgomery House
1053 River Road

Photograph by John Pearce

1996

When the Glass House Lot was split up by the mortgage sale, this house stood on Lot K. Josephus' two-fifths share was sold to James E. Allen on July 25th, 1876. William's three-fifths share of this lot was sold to Frick, Durand, and Ripley on January 12, 1880, along with Lots J & L. Durand sold his share to Frick and Ripley in 1882. There are indications that this property was then sold to Louis V. McCarthy in 1893.

Frances (Montgomery) Carlson, called "Fanny" and "Monty," bought this house on River Road with her husband, Howard "Whitey" Carlson in about 1939. At the time of the purchase, the house was meant to be a residence for her mother. Frances was the daughter of Burke and Ella (Cramer) Montgomery. Her mother was the youngest daughter of Richard and Mary Ann (Van Sant) Cramer of Lower Bank (see LOWER BANK: THE CRAMER HOUSE ON "THE ISLAND") and the sister of Nicholas Van Sant Cramer.

Born in Lower Bank herself, Elvira Augusta Cramer had fallen in love with and married a young man from the Eastern Shore of Maryland, Burke Montgomery. Their children, Russell and Frances, thus had ties to the township that proved enduring.

Frances spent several years as the schoolmarm in the little old one-room schoolhouse which preceded the present Green Bank School prior to 1920. "Fanny," as they called her, was no typical schoolteacher, though. She apparently was a very attractive woman, a "classy-looking lady," Hans Lewis recalls.

In 1930, she married "Whitey" Carlson, a trooper in the second class of the New Jersey State Police, and the two lived in Green Bank, though no one seems to know in exactly which house. It is possible that they either rented this house or lived next door in the house her brother, Russell, eventually purchased. Jessie Lewis remembers well the perfect manners with which "Monty" graced Green Bank for many years. After her death in 1985, her nephew, James Burke Montgomery, acquired the house and lived there until he passed away in 1998.

The Judge Russell Montgomery House
1051 River Road
(No Longer in Existence)

Courtesy of Russell Montgomery, Jr.

Date Unknown

This house stood on Lot J of the Glass House Lot and followed the same fate as Lots K & L when Josephus' property was sold to satisfy a mortgage. John C. Ten Eyck, Master, sold Josephus' 2/5ths share to the First National Bank of Vincentown for $300, and the lot included a house at the time. Frick, Durand, and Ripley bought a 3/5ths share in this house and lot along with its neighbors on Lots K & L in 1880, which subsequently devolved on Frick and Ripley in 1882.

During the first half of this century, it was the home of the Corbin family. Billy and Jenny (Broom) Woolston, who seemed to have lived in half the houses of Green Bank, lived here for a while, too.

About 1940, Russell Montgomery and his wife, Margaret (Higgins) moved his family into this house from Red Lion. Russ wasn't really an outside transplant to the area when he acquired this house from the New Gretna Building and Loan. His sister, Frances, had lived in Green Bank for years, and had purchased the house next door to this one the year before, and their mother, Ella, was the youngest daughter of Richard and Mary Ann (Van Sant) Cramer of Lower Bank. Russell thus had ties to Washington Township through his mother's family, and, when he moved to Green Bank, he was, in a sense, "coming home."

Russell worked for his cousin, Charlie Leek, down at Lower Bank during World War II, and he appears in the photograph of the crew at C.P. Leek and Sons in the chapter on Lower Bank. He also served as the local Justice of the Peace. The "Judge" once let Jessie (Forman) Lewis off with a warning for pulling a shotgun on a state trooper. One wonders if the state trooper was his brother-in-law! Judge Montgomery must have gotten quite a laugh out of the incident regardless. Late one night, the trooper had pulled up out in front of Jessie's house at a time when her husband was away, and she was by herself. She didn't know it was a trooper, so she did the safest thing. She pointed a shotgun at the stranger and ordered him off her property.

Russell and Margaret Montgomery had three children: Russell, Jr., Shirley Janet, and James Burke. Russ, Jr. remembers visiting his Lower Bank relatives when he was little, even before his parents purchased this house in Green Bank and moved into the township. Russell's aunt, Mary Ida (Cale) Cramer, "Granny Cramer" or "Aunt Mel," as she was known in her hometown, still lived in the old Cramer homestead on "The Island" in Lower Bank, as did his cousin, Roy.

"Judge" Russell Montgomery died in 1960; his wife followed him twenty-four years later in 1984. Russ Montgomery, Jr. and his wife wanted to restore the old house, but when they took it apart, they found it so ridden with termites that they had no choice but to tear it down and start over. Their charming modular stands in this location today. Their children: Russell III, Linda, and Janet, live outside of the township.

Russ, Jr. expresses a great deal of thankfulness that State regulations have kept his beloved home free from the development that has overwhelmed so many other areas along the New York/Washington metropolitan corridor. He and his wife have a deep appreciation for the serenity that still flows with the river past their front door.

The Carney House
1047 River Road
(No Longer in Existence)

William F. Augustine Collection
Special Collections and University Archives
Rutgers University Libraries

Bill Carney and His Son, Billy, at the Limekiln Discovered in 1971

A very old house dating from early in the nineteenth century used to stand on this property. It was Lot H when the Glass House Lot was split up. The First National Bank of Vincentown sold Josephus Sooy's 2/5th share in this house and lot to Samuel Van Sant for $320 on March 15th, 1877. On the 7th of May in the same year, Samuel Van Sant bought William H. Sooy's 3/5ths share for $480. He then mortgaged the entire lot and house back to William's wife, Mary, on the 24th of May to secure $800. On June 14th, 1890, he conveyed the lot back to William H. Sooy for $500.

In this century, it was owned by George Carney who worked for Haze Wobbar on the Roads Department. George and his wife, Hattie (Ford) had three sons: George, Bill and Armand. George, Jr. drowned in the Mullica at the age of eight in 1926. Bill and Armand lived in the area until their retirement a few years ago. Before their mother's

Courtesy of Budd Wilson

The Glassworks' Kiln

Billy, Armand, and George Carney - 1937

death in 1969, Bill and Armand tore down the old house and built a new one. Bill later lived in it with his wife, Jacqueline, daughters Loreen and Karen, and his son, William, Jr. Armand and his wife, Pat, lived outside of New Gretna.

In 1971, while digging in the riverbank in front of his house, Bill and his son discovered a limekiln that had been part of the Glasshouse property in the mid-eighteen hundreds. The discovery made the Sunday edition of the *Phildelphia Inquirer* on June 27, 1971. The reporter quoted Carney as saying, "Passing boats, over the years, eroded the banks on the river. I was trying to move dirt from the higher parts of our property to lower land around the bank [when the shovel hit what seemed to him like a big boulder]."

Budd Wilson, who was the archeologist for Batsto at that time, came down and checked out the structure. He determined that the stone used to build the circular pit was not local rock and that there was fired red clay instead of mortar holding the rocks together. He identified the unearthed structure as a kiln from the Green Bank Glass Works. Green Bank's glasshouse was in operation for about twenty years from around 1837 to 1857 and utilized kilns for the extraction of calcium oxide from limestone.

Ships brought the limestone down from Staten Island and unloaded it near this kiln, where it was heated.

Several years ago, Bill retired and moved to Florida, selling the house to the Schoenwetter's. His brother, Armand, who worked for Pacemaker Yachts as their demo captain, has also retired and lives in Virginia. Bill, Jr. lives with his family in Linwood.

Armand Carney c. 1940

The Sooy/Ford/Houser/Braun House
1045 River Road

This was the home of William H. Sooy, the second son of Nicholas Sooy II and Rebecca Weeks. He was born on February 4, 1816 (his stone says "May 20") in the "Old Homestead," and married Mary Ann Haywood, sister of Joel Haywood of West Creek and aunt of Lucy Ann Haywood, Joel's daughter, who married his younger brother, Ephraim. The couple built this house in 1858, when William H. was forty-two.

William H. Sooy was a member of the Democratic Party in his younger years but later became an ardent Republican. During the Civil War and in the years following, he was Internal Revenue Assessor, in addition to serving as Justice of the Peace, Town Clerk and Freeholder of Burlington County for many years. He kept the general store (now 1078 River Road) and dealt in lumber products. He ran his business out of the Green Bank Store across the street from his home.

William and Mary had four children: Joel H. (who moved to Bristol and was in the oyster business), Anna M. (married Edward Johnson and lived in Atlantic City), Watson T., and Franklin W. (an artist who lived in Asbury Park). It was William H. and his wife who took on the responsibility of raising the young children of William's deceased brother, Ephraim, and Mary Ann's neice, Lucy Ann, when they were orphaned. Both he and his wife were active members of the Green Bank Church. In fact, as per his father, Nicholas Sooy II's will, he and his brothers *inherited* the Green

Photograph by Augusta Weeks

The William H. and Watson Sooy Home
in 1935, the residence of Hattie Koster Ford

Bank Church. Their father placed it in their charge to be maintained as a Methodist Episcopal Church and maintain it they did. William H. undertook the rebuilding of the church in 1871, when it took on the form it would know for the next century and a quarter.

Having four children of their own and two of their deceased brother and niece/sister-in-law, this house was always filled with young people. William H. and Mary Haywood welcomed the younger generation and set an example for them in appreciating music and culture. Many a good time was had in this old home and people from the village gathered here for parties, musical rehearsals and recitals, and general good fun.

The lot on which this house and the Old Store across the street were built was Lot G of the Glass House Lot. William only owned a 2/5th share in the property when he built his house, his brother, Josephus, owning another 2/5ths and his nephew and ward, Ephraim C., Jr. 1/5.

Josephus, of course, mortgaged his share to the First National Bank of Vincentown in 1872. Ephraim sold his

Courtesy of Budd Wilson

The two people in the middle are
Hattie and Watson Sooy

223

uncle his 1/5th share in the entire Glass House Lot on February 1st, 1875 for $1,300, and William sold his own house and lot to Ephraim's sister, Lydia on the 1st of September of the same year for $2,300, perhaps to protect it from creditors. This was Lot G, but also included probably a 3/5ths share in lots E & F. When Josephus' property was sold by the bank, a 2/5ths share in E & F was sold to Joel H. Sooy, William's son. Lot F must have had a house on it at the time, because it is listed as worth $161, while Lots E & I were worth $20 each, and Lot M $37.50. Josephus' 2/5ths share in William's own house and lot was sold to the First National Bank of Vincentown for $2,050. Niece Lydia sold her ownership of Lots E, F, and G back to her aunt, Mary Ann Sooy, William's wife, on October 2nd, 1876. In 1877, the First National Bank of Vincentown sold Josephus' 2/5th share to Mary A. Sooy for $850 and for the first time, William and Mary Sooy owned their entire house and lot, they managed to hang on to it for the next nineteen years until William's death on October 2, 1896. Mary Ann Haywood Sooy died on April 1, 1905 at the age of ninety. I only record all of this to indicate that life was not necessarily less complicated or more secure a century ago than it is today.

Frank and Watson Sooy, sons of
William H. Sooy

Joel Sooy, son of William H. Sooy
and brother of Frank
and Watson Sooy

When William H. Sooy was running the Old Store, his son, Joel, was apparently the postmaster. When Joel resigned the office, his father was appointed in his place. The official notice of William H. Sooy's appointment as postmaster is the document on the right.

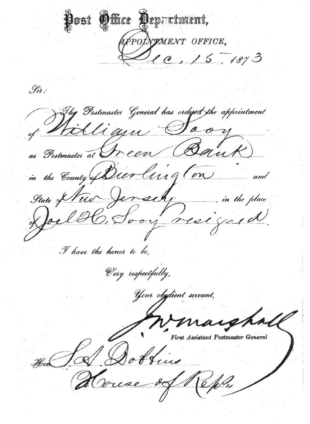

When Mary Sooy passed away in 1905, her sons, Joel, Frank, and Watson Sooy inherited the house and business, and Watson moved into the house. Watson, born February 14, 1848 in Green Bank, was educated at Providence Conference Seminary, later known as the Greenwich Academy, in Rhode Island. He taught school for a while, then returned to the relative security of his native town. Back in Green Bank, he married Harriet Lane, daughter of Peter and Rebecca (Van Sant) Lane of Lower Bank who was also a teacher. It is said that he "engaged in the fisheries," which probably meant that he either owned a fishing vessel or two or that he bought fish from the local fishermen and sold them to wholesalers in New York and Philadelphia. He also continued his father's trading business at the crossroads store near his home. Watson and Harriet Lane also continued the tradition of good times in their home that Watson's parents had established. Watson had been trained musically and gave music and voice lessons to the young people in the community.

Watson died in 1926, and Hattie followed him the following year. The home was eventually bought by Hattie (Koster) Ford. Hattie's husband, who had died in 1934, prior to her purchase of the house, was Jesse Ford. Jesse and Watson Sooy had been third cousins. Jesse Ford was the son of Maurice Ford, Sr. and Esther Anna Sooy. Esther Sooy was the daughter of Nicholas Sooy and Sarah Messarole. This Nicholas Sooy was the son of Noah Sooy and Sarah Weeks, the brother of Nicholas II and son of Nicholas I and Sarah Sears. Hattie (Koster) Ford was the sister of Leon Koster who owned the "Old Homestead" of the Sooy family.

"Aunt" Hattie Ford outlived her husband and was well known as the "storekeeper" of Green Bank in the "new" now the "old" Green Bank store close by the bridge. She also served as postmistress for many years.

In the 1950s, George Houser purchased the home and operated a garage on the property to the rear of the house.

The home was recently purchased by Charles R. Braun III, family and totally modernized. Charlie Braun was raised over in Egg Harbor and worked for Arena Olds/Pontiac in Hammonton prior to going into business for himself. In 1996, he completed work on restoring the bulkheading on his property where one of the Van Sant shipyards stood in the nineteenth century.

1995

Photograph by John Pearce

The Sooy/Crowley/Rubsam House
1043 River Road

1935

Photograph by Augusta Weeks

William H. Sooy and Mary Haywood built this house for their son, Watston T. Sooy, in the last part of the nineteenth century. It stands on ground which was part of Lot G of the Glass House Lot which William H. Sooy had inherited from his father, Nicholas II and on which he had also built his own house next door to this one.

Watson was a talented young man. Gifted musically, his parents saw that he received a good education, though the details are a bit uncertain at this date. The Sooy geneology says that he was educated at the Providence Conference Seminary, now the Greenwich Academy in Rhode Island, but Laura Larrabee McConaghy notes in her 1930s manuscript, "The Romance of Green Bank," that he was trained at the Boston Conservatory of Music. Both may be true.

What we do know is that Watson T. Sooy and his wife Harriet Lane were music lovers and, in the days before television and radio, trained young people to sing and play instruments for their entertainment. They actively supported the Green Bank Church, and Watson directed the choir for many years.

Watson and Harriet's home was the center of social activities in Green Bank, and they worked together to make the old church come alive with music and song for Sunday services. Harriet Sooy donated simple furnishings for the pulpit of the little church, including several walnut cane-seated chairs, an altar table, and candlestick holders, which graced that humble place until some enterprising antiques enthusiast stole the altar table and candlestick holders in the late 1960s. Not even a church is sacred any more! The Watson Sooys were always ready to contribute to the financial welfare of the little church and left what was then the princely sum of $1,000 to the church from their estate.

Laura Larrabee McConeghy waxes eloquent:

> "Oh, how deeply you are missed from your place in the daily life that goes on in the little village. The life in which you were the 'Lode Stars'! Your passing left a vacancy that will never be filled, and how greatly you are lamented! You left behind an influence for good that will never

1995

fade, and like the ocean, go on and on, to come back in the heart of some one who loved you and your excellent work. Thus do your 'works follow you!' Whenever your name is spoken, it is in loving 'Remembrance' of your beautiful Christian Character, and influence that remain and will linger as long as Green Bank endures!"

After the death of his parents, Watson and his wife moved into their house next door. According to Laura Larrabee McConeghy, Captain James Morrell Crowley and his wife, Augusta (Wobbar) Crowley bought this house and gave it to their son, Birdsall, and his new wife, Miss Alyce Michels, as a wedding present. Betty (Crowley) Rubsam, who still lives in the house, says that her mother would have been furious at the suggestion that Captain Crowley *gave* them the house. Bert and Alyce struggled for years to pay off the mortgage, so it certainly *wasn't* a gift. Betty even remembers her mother saying that she provided food and drinks for the workers who constructed the "new" Green Bank bridge back in the 1920's to help make the mortgage payments.

Bert and Alyce were popular young people in the Green Bank community of the 1930s, interested in community affairs, and strong in support of church and school. Alyce, though born and raised in Blue Bell, Pennsylvania near the borough of Norristown, seemed to fit in with everyone very well. She and Bert were the leaders of the "younger set."

Courtesy of Jessie Lewis

Watson and Hattie Sooy

227

Four Generations
Billy Crowley, Bert Crowley, Augusta (Wobbar) Crowley, and Grandma Wobbar, Augusta's mother

Birdsall and his mother, Augusta (Wobbar) Crowley

Mrs. Crowley was active in the school and served for four years as the president of the Parent-Teacher Association. She helped to support the building of a lunchroom at the school and maintaining a "matron".

Birdsall drove a schoolbus. He also delivered the mail and brought ice, milk, coal, and sundries to the people of the township.

The Birdsall Crowleys had two children: Billy and Betty Jane. Betty Jane was the "darling" of Green Bank as a child and grew to be a most beautiful young woman. She entered the competition for Miss New Jersey in 1949 and won! Though she, and all of Washington Township with her, was disappointed at the loss of the Miss America pageant that year, Betty Jane Crowley went on to become an actress of some renown.

During the 1950s, under the name Kathleen Crowley, she acted in films and on the nacent television, taking parts in *Bonanza* with Lorne Greene, Dan Blocker, and "Little Joe" Michael Landon, as well as in *The Virginian, Thriller, 77 Sunset Strip, Westward Ho the Wagons*, and many other shows. She was also chosen to be the first to open the gates of Disneyland in California. Her father, Birdsall, died at the height of her career in 1955. Mother Alyce passed away in 1972.

Betty married John Rubsam and, in the late 1960's, wanted to have a child but didn't want him raised as one of the spoiled Hollywood jet set. She and her husband returned to her birthplace to raise Matthew with the support of friends and neighbors, and a love of the pinelands and the Mullica. Her husband, John, left for California years ago, and Betty managed to scrape together the money to see that her son got a fine education, first at the Perkiomen School in Pennsburg and then at Ursinus College in Collegeville, Pennsylvania.

Courtesy of Budd Wilson

Rebecca Crowley

For several years, Betty has been seen heading for the old bridge when a boat gives its one long blast, one short blast, for the bridge to open. Betty has carefully and conscientiously tended that bridge, day in and day out. Matt learned to love the freedom of the pinelands and the river and decided to stay in his family's town. He now lives in the "Old Store" across the street from his mother's home, runs a pizza take-out restaurant, and is planning to reopen the store eventually.

Courtesy of Jessie Lewis

Matthew Rubsam - Age 9

Courtesy of Budd Wilson

Billy Crowley

Betty Rubsam tending the bridge at Green Bank
1995

Betty (Crowley) Rubsam
1995

9-585

"The beginning of it all
at the 'Miss America Pagent.

Love always,
Betty Jane"

The 1949 Miss America Pagent

In 1949, the contestants for the pagent didn't starve themselves or work out in a gym to look their best. They didn't even wear much makeup. In a recent newspaper interview, Betty noted that the first set of false eyelashes she ever saw was on "Miss New York City" that year. The contestants also did their own hair. Many even made their own gowns. Betty recalls that she paid around $19 for the material of her gown which her mother made at home. The contest winner that year, Miss Arizona, paid $3,000 for her gown, and that may have given her the edge. Betty was 5' 2 1/2" tall and weighed 110 lbs. at the time of the pagent.

The photograph above was taken at the talent competition, for which Betty sang "Mighty Like a Rose". She accompanied the song with a monologue she had written herself.

The strikingly beautiful actress, Kathleen Crowley, of Green Bank in the early 1950's.

Kathleen Crowley was a finalist in the Miss America contest and used the prize money to study at the American Academy of Dramatic Arts and did her first year of stock at Kennebunkport, Maine. She was chosen by Robert Montgomery to play the lead in his production of *A Star is Born* and later was also the lead in *Jane Eyre* on television. She was on the cover of *Cue* magazine and the subject of a spread in *Life*. In May, 1952, she went under contract at 20th Century Fox. When she became a free agent two years later, she starred in *Target Earth* (1954). Her credits go on to include *The Flame Barrier (1958), Female Jungle, Curse of the Undead,* Disney's *Westward Ho the Wagons (1956) and Downhill Racer (1969)*. In television, she starred in The Lux Playhouse production of *Coney Island Winter (1958)* and in *On Trial: the Case of the Gril on the Elsewhere*. In *Batman*, she acted with the late Burgess Meredith. *The Lawyer* (1970) was her last film before moving home to Green Bank.

The Old Store
1044 River Road

1935

The Old Store was long the center of the social and political life of Green Bank and of Washington Township as a whole. William H. Sooy, son of Nicholas Sooy II, kept a storehouse and community store at the "Old Store-house" on the river at the lower dock (1078 River Road). The old store was fine for the storage of goods loaded and unloaded from the river traffic, but it was somewhat out of the way for a community store. Besides that, it was never fitted out as a proper store for the retail trade.

Though William H. Sooy is thought to have built this store at the same time as he constructed his new house at 1045 River Road, there is evidence that it was already built by 1850.

A bequest to his sons in Nicholas Sooy II's will shows that it was already standing by the time he wrote it in 1850. The will gives the glasshouse lot to his sons and to his grandson by his deceased son, Ephraim, in equal shares. It reads:

> I give and bequeath to my sons, Samuel Sooy, William Sooy, Josephus Sooy, and NIcholas Sooy, Jr., and also my grandson Ephraim Sooy - "The Glass-Works" and lot of ground there on said "Works" stand.
>
> Beginning at a "Poplar tree" one chain and fifty links to the west of the "Store House" - standing near the edge of the River. Running (1) North (43 degrees) East, Seven chains and fifty-five links. (2) South (55 degrees) East, two chains and twenty-eight links. (4) South (47 degrees) East four chains to the Road to the "Green Bank Store". Along said Road South (65 degrees) West four chains, (5) South (33 degrees) East one chain and fifty links. (6) South (63 degrees) West one chain and sixty-four links. (7) South (29 degrees) East ten chains and fifty links to William Sooy line. South (66 1/2 degrees) three chains and twenty-five links to the River. Thence up the River the several courses to the place of beginning.

In describing the Glass House Lot, Nicholas II says that the "poplar tree" that forms the corner of the "Glass House Lot" stands one chain and fifty links from the "storehouse." In the middle of the Glass House property, he also mentions that the line follows the road which leads to the "Green Bank Store." This can only be the present Route 563. Since the Green Bank bridge did not exist when Nicholas II wrote his will, the road could only have led to the riverbank location of the Green Bank Store.

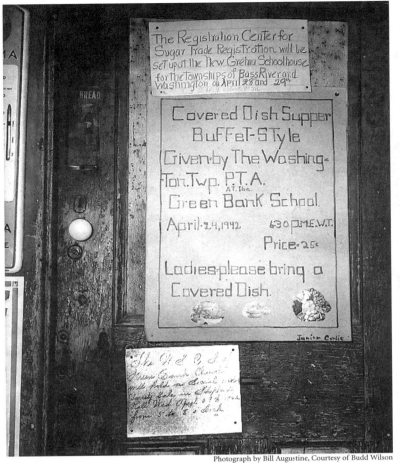

The Door of the Old Store - 1942

Photograph by Bill Augustine, Courtesy of Budd Wilson

Courtesy of Budd Wilson

Shirley (Koster) Bratton

Though it was long thought that William H. Sooy moved the Sooy retail goods into this building at the "Upper Dock" after his father's death, the shift from the Old Storehouse may well have happened before his father's 1851 death.

From this point on, the Sooy business centered on this location. The Old Storehouse and "Lower Dock" was gradually abandoned. Ocean-going vessels tied up at the dock behind the store, and "day" boats for tourists plied the river from their docks by the new bridge behind the store.

When William H.'s son, Watson, inherited the business on his father's death in 1896, the river traffic that had made the Mullica a prosperous highway had all but ceased, and Watson was reduced to being a shopkeeper.

In the upstairs room, the local lodge of "Odd Fellows" met until 1930, when the members moved it to Egg Harbor City. The place was the scene of constant activity, with ships tying up at the old wharf out back on the river, unloading their goods for sale and loading the products of the area's natural resources.

When Watson died in 1926, his third cousin, Jesse Ford, and his wife Hattie (Koster), ran the store. After Jesse's death in 1934, his widow, "Aunt Hattie," continued to operate the store and also bought the Sooy house. This was an old-fashioned store of the type that graced every hamlet in America. It had its wooden floor, shelving lining the walls, serving counter, cracker barrel and pickle barrel, housed the local "post office" - a few postal boxes in one corner - and a woodstove. It was around this latter fixture that, on any given day, could be found gathered the older men of the community, leaning back on their wooden chairs, passing on the local news, discussing the fishing, the weather, politics, and all other items of interest. For almost a hundred years, this store was the daily resort of the people of Green Bank. It was the center of their social life and of their entertainment world.

The door to the store was always filled with public notices for all to see. Rodney Koster, son of Leon and Josie Koster, who lived in the "Old Homestead" of the Sooy family, inherited the store from Hattie (Koster) Ford on her death in 1944. Rodney continued to run the store for a while, then turned it over to his sister, Shirley (Koster) Bratton. Shirley's first marriage ended in divorce, and she married again to George Clayton Ford, Jr.

The Green Bank Store
c. 1940
Aunt Hattie Ford was
running the store at this
time.

The interior of the old store
remains much the same as
it was back when this photograph was taken. The
current owner, Matt
Rubsom, plans to reopen it
sometime soon. The only
thing missing, besides the
people that is, is the pot bel-
lied stove (and perhaps
F.D.R.'s photograph!).

The Old Store - 1995

Photograph by John Pearce

When Shirley's health started to fail, it was leased to Virginia and Walt Priest, who ran it until they built their own building out on Route 542.

How sad the day when this old store closed its doors for the last time as a community store, replaced by the more modern one out on the Hammonton-New Gretna Road that Walt and Virginia Priest built for the convenience of the automobile trade. Green Bank lost its post office and became a rural delivery route out of Egg Harbor. The name "Green Bank" would not be seen as part of mailing addresses again until 1995, when, due to the changes necessary for the 911 emergency number, all rural route designations were changed to actual addresses to make it easier for emergency vehicles to find a particular residence. Thus once again, "Green Bank" became an address recognized by the U.S. Postal Service, although the Zip code remains that of Egg Harbor City, from whence the mail comes.

A couple of years ago, Matt Rubsom, Betty (Kathleen Crowley) Rubson's son, started a pizza take-out business in the lower part of the old store that once housed trade goods brought upriver by coastal schooners. Matt lives on the second floor in an apartment created from storage space over the old store. The store itself is now the storage area. Matt is currently (1995) serving on the Washington Township Committee.

For some odd reason, Matt had a difficult time convincing the Pinelands Commission that this store, a place of business for almost a hundred years, had housed a business at all! Amazing!

Photograph by John Pearce

Matt Rubsom - 1995

236

"Cousin Eph and the Boy"

Ephraim C. Sooy, Jr., on one of his many summer visits to Green Bank from Kansas City, on the porch of the "Old Store". The "boy" may be his son Bert, who died at the age of twenty-one on August 21, 1903. The Old Store was the backdrop for many a photograph.

The Upper Dock Behind the Old Store - 1909

The Area of what was the Upper Dock - 1995

The Old Green Bank Hotel
Corner of River Road and Route 563
(No Longer in Existence)
and the
Hester Anne Ford Cottage
1039 River Road
(No Longer in Existence)

Courtesy of Budd Wilson

The Old Tavern that faced the bridge at Green Bank - Circa 1909

The Last Days of the Hotel Sebastian Crowley

In the earliest days of the colonies, roads of any sort were few and far between. They began as Indian trails through the woods and passage was only for those riding horseback.

In the pinelands of New Jersey, extensive roads were not laid out until just before the Revolutionary War. In the early part of the eighteenth century, the stage route to Middle-of-the-Shore (Tuckerton) led down from Mount Holly through Oriental, which is near Tabernacle (a paved portion of this original road is still called the "Tuckerton Road") and Hampton Gate, down through the tiny hamlet of Washington where Nicholas Sooy I owned a tavern, through to Bodine's Tavern (at Bodine's Field) where it crossed the Wading River, then to Bass River Tavern, and finally to Little Egg Harbor Meeting (at Tuckerton). The Quakers from Burlington used to attend Yearly Meeting in Little Egg Harbor via a trail that led down from what would later be known as Atsion, across Quaker Bridge (built in 1774), and on to the town of Washington where it joined the old stage road for the trip to Little Egg Harbor.

Across the tidal part of the Mullica, there were no bridges. Anyone going south from Cooper's Ferry (Camden) and Philadelphia would have to head in that direction prior to reaching the Mullica. The most convenient travel was by boat, down the rivers, out into the ocean, and then on to wherever. Travel by "road" was most inconvenient: filthy, hot (or cold), and very, very time-consuming.

Every little town, therefore, boasted a "tavern." It was usually the largest building for miles around (although it could still be quite small by modern standards), usually providing some standard (or sub-standard as was frequently the case) fare, with a few beds (in which people slept three and four together - and not just family members either), and some locally-produced alcoholic beverage (usually drunk straight from the jug, giving them the nickname "Jug Taverns"). The Tavern was the gathering place for the men of the towns. Here they escaped from their wives for a little while and could discuss business and politics over a cup of hard cider, rum, or some other potent beverage. Most of the political discussions leading to the Revolution happened in taverns across the emerging nation.

During the nineteenth century as roads improved, so did the taverns. Stage routes were set up and actual schedules published. In the early part of the century, the old Nicholas Sooy I Tavern in Washington, the famed Sooy's Inn, was a popular spot. By the second quarter, Sooy's son, Paul Sears Sooy, had taken over the management. By the third quarter, it was gone, and the tavern business moved with the stage route to Lower Bank, Green Bank, and Crowleytown. The stage used the "mail stage" road to Wading River early in the nineteenth century. Later it was routed through Bass River (New Gretna) where a drawbridge had been built in 1824, Wading River (across a drawbridge built in 1814), Green Bank, and on to Batsto/Pleasant Mills. By 1855, when the first bridge spanned the Mullica at Green Bank, one could even take the stage south.

Sebastian Crowley apparently built this hotel/tavern in Green Bank sometime around 1860 after the Glass Works was no longer operating and the bridge had been built. It was certainly in business during 1862 when the annual Town Meeting was held here. Who was Sebastian Crowley? Some sources say he was one of the twenty-one children of Samuel Crowley III (There are sources who say Sam had 32 children.) of Crowleytown and Bulltown, but his name is not listed among them. As it turns out, there were two Sebastians. One was the brother of Samuel Crowley, Jr. and the uncle of Samuel III. The other was his son, Sebastian, Jr.

Sebastian Crowley, Sr., like his brother and his nephew, began with the sea. He is listed in the Batsto Store Books in connection with the schooner *Anna D. Coffee* in 1841, and the schooner *Patriot* in 1843 and 1847. It is also possible that he owned or was master of the schooner *Anna Maria* in 1837 rather than Samuel, Jr. or III, because the Store Books only list "S" Crowley as that vessel's owner or master.

Given the time frame for the hotel in the last half of the nineteenth century, it was probably Sebastian Crowley, Jr. who ran the hotel. Under his proprietorship, it no doubt prospered. The stage route was active during this period, and the hotel was one of the stops for refreshment of passengers and horses.

During the last half of the century, road travel became much more practical, if not much more convenient than a century earlier. With the advent of the automobile, the tavern was becoming a thing of the past. More people were travelling, of course, but they could also go a lot farther between stops. Granted the roads hadn't actually improved very much, but automobiles, slow as they were, did cover a greater distance than a horse and did it faster.

Now there was simply no need for a tavern in every town. A growing support for temperance didn't do the tavern business any good either. Oh, the men may have wanted to continue their discussions over a mug of grog, but their women preferred them snoozing in the local store.

In the 1876 sheriff's sale of Josephus Sooy's property, the sale was advertised to take place at the "Hotel Sebastian Crowley." A 2/5th share for Lot D, containing the hotel, was sold to the First National Bank of Vincentown for $335.00. Apparently Crowley only rented the land, and perhaps the building as well, from the Sooys. On the 29th of September, in the same year (1876), William H. Sooy mortgaged his 3/5ths share in lots A, B, C, and D to John M. Hall. This mortgage is marked as cancelled. On the 14th of March, 1877, the same lots were mortgaged to the First National Bank of Vincentown (who, by now, must seem to own most of Green Bank). On August 28, 1885, the bank sold Lots C & D to John Lingerfield for $600.

By the early 1900's, the Green Bank Tavern was maintained by Maurice (pronounced "Morris") Ford and his wife Hester (or Esther) Anne Sooy. They would take in and feed the local traveller, but the tavern business was almost a memory. The couple had three sons and

Photograph by Augusta Weeks

1935

two daughters (Jesse, Nicholas, Anna, Harry, and Elizabeth) that must have filled the old tavern even when they were the only ones there. Maurice and Hester raised their children in the old tavern, but when the kids moved out, it was a bit big for their needs. Up went the "For Sale" sign, and they moved to the little house next door.

Maurice and Hester found comfort in the "little house." The "For Sale" sign stayed up. Maurice Ford died in 1926, and Hester continued to live in the little cottage for a while, then moved in with her daughter, Mrs. Harry Weaver. The "For Sale" sign stayed up. Laura McConeghy commented in *The Romance of Green Bank* that Hester was "beautiful in figure and face, that was crowned with a wealth of beautiful white silvery hair which was always adorable. Her fine face had escaped the ravages of 'Time' in wrinkles and 'old-age' features, and her bright, shining blue eyes were ever soft in kindly expression."

Her son, Jesse, and his wife, Hattie (Koster) Ford had been living in the old hotel while his parents lived next door. When his mother moved in with his sister down the road, Jesse and Hattie moved into her cottage. It was here that Jesse died in 1934, though he was actually buried from the old hotel. Hattie then bought the Watson Sooy house at 1045 River Road and moved there.

Mother Hester also passed away in 1934. She died at the age of eighty-four and was buried in the graveyard by the Green Bank Church, along with her beloved Maurice. The "For Sale" sign on the old tavern stayed up.

The tavern is gone. The little house next door is gone. Maurice and Hesther are hardly remembered by the current generation that lives on the property where their little house stood. The tavern lot is vacant. Only one who pauses to read the gravestones by the old church might wonder who Maurice Ford, b. 1844, d. 1926, and Hester Anne Ford, b. 1850, d. 1934, were or where they lived. What joys did they know? What anguish? Now they rest from their labors along with all those they knew and loved.

Daniel Walters bought the property some years back and tore down both the cottage and the old hotel. By this time, the hotel had been abandoned so long that there were actually trees growing up through the middle of it. On the cottage property (1039 River Road), he built a modern duplex, and on the opposite end of the hotel lot, he built his own home (2407 Route 563). Dan Walters is the son of Bill Walters, who resides at 2419 Route 563. Bill's wife, Arwilda (Ford) Walters, was long the bridge-tender of the Green Bank drawbridge.

Courtesy of Budd Wilson

The Hester Anne (Sooy) Ford Cottage
Circa 1909

The Clark/Updike Home
1037 River Road
(No Longer in Existence)

Photograph by Augusta Weeks

1935

Courtesy of Budd Wilson

The Rev. and Mrs. Joseph C. Clark
1935

During the 1930s, this quaint little home stood on the property that is now 1037 River Road and was occupied by Mr. and Mrs. Joseph Clark. The cottage was designed and built by the Clarks as their retirement retreat.

Mr. Clark was actually the Reverend Mr. Clark and had served many congregations prior to his retirement in Green Bank. He continued to serve in the Green Bank church for a couple of years as the pastor before finally retiring completely.

The Rev. Mr. Clark had been a merchant in Pleasant Mills for many years before receiving the call to the Methodist ministry. Upon his ordination, he worked especially in the Evangelistic Mission Service of the Methodist Episcopal Church, serving in forty-four different congregations in South Jersey over the years, most without any compensation. Laura Larrabee McConaghy says of the Rev. Mr. Clark: "A gentleman to the pulpit born, and an advocate of the type of religion which Francis Asbury and John Wesley expounded, and the colonial churches of South Jersey were adherents of. A firm believer in the maintenance of the Sunday School as being the upbuilder of the church. He has been a faithful instructor in the Adult Bible Class . . . and always faithful at the church service."

Mrs. Clark, according to Mrs. McConaghy, was the daughter of Sebastian Crowley, son of Samuel Crowley III, the father of James

242

Morrell Crowley, but none of his twenty-one children was named "Sebastian," and James's father was Nicholas Crowley, Samuel Crowley III's son. Sebastian Crowley, Sr. was actually the *brother* of Samuel, Jr. and the *uncle* of Samuel III (father of Nicholas, grandfather of James Morrell). Mrs. Clark was probably the daughter of Sebastian Crowley, Jr. who kept the nearby hotel. She was born in Tuckerton, but her family moved to Green Bank when she was just a child, her father taking over the proprietorship of the Green Bank hotel that stood just a short distance from her retirement home. At some time, also, the family lived in Crowleytown. Watson Sooy held choir rehearsals in the Clark home when Ella Crowley was the organist of the church, and Eva Crowley and the Van Sants were members of the choir. The Van Sants were prominent in the little church and helped with the music, along with Watson, Joel, and Annie Sooy.

The Rev. and Mrs. Clark's son, Atwood, died in Florida around 1935. The parents found out about it through a broadcast over the radio station, an announcement of a search for the young man's parents. How much grief they must have suffered.

Mrs. Clark died on the 14th of February, 1936. Laura McConaghy says in tribute to her: "Mrs. Clark was highly esteemed, and a valued friend, and townswoman, a woman of high integrity and zeal and earnest religious purposes. In community life, she was a zealot for uprightness and righteousness. A kind, considerate neighbor and sympathetic in sorrow and grief. Much will she be missed by the 'Dwellers of the Bank.'" She was buried at the side of her brother, Jesse Crowley in the Green Bank churchyard. The memory of the Clarks died with their generation. Only her gravestone bears mute testimony to this lovely old couple, devoted to each other and to God, who made Green Bank their last home. There is no stone for the Rev. Mr. Clark.

After the death of Mrs. Clark, Jack Updike and his wife moved into this little house. Jack held an engineer's certificate, enabling him to operate "anything pushed around by gas to Diesels and fuel oil." Jack was the son of John Updike of Wading River and was born in their house on Turtle Creek Road. In his earlier years, he had shipped aboard food-fish boat out of Anglesea and menhaden fishing boats as well as acting as master aboard several large yachts that were owned by the wealthy at the turn of the century. In his later years, he tried his hand at carpentry and painting. He knew every twist and turn, every nook and cranny of the Mullica and its tributaries.

Jack's main love, though, was ducks. Jack Updike, you see, was a decoy carver, a very *good* decoy carver! By the time Henry Beck interviewed him, he'd admit to have carved a thousand. His wife immediately protested that this was a *most* conservative figure. Jack studied ducks, studied them most carefully. He studied how they looked, how they sat in the water, how they flew. He knew ducks. "Got to know ducks, really *know* 'em" before you could carve a reasonable decoy.

Jack knew all the swamps 'round about Green Bank, swamp white cedar being the best wood for decoys in his estimation. Beck, in *Jersey Genesis*, includes an extensive and interesting interview with this well-known carver that is worth reading in its entirety. Every decoy-carver had his own particular design that was as identifiable as a signature. Jack's skill was right up there with Harry Shourds of Tuckerton, Joel Salmons of Parkertown, and John McAnney of New Gretna. The works of all these masters are highly prized today.

Decoys were meant to sit on the water just like the original birds. Jack believed that the best design for all weather was the hollow top/solid bottom design. That kept them light enough to carry and heavy enough that they didn't bob all over the place in rough weather. "All I know is, you got to be plenty smart to fool a duck," he commented to Henry Beck.

After being vacant for many years, the little cottage of the Clarks was purchased by Bill Walters and his sons. The house had so deteriorated that they tore it down and built a new one in its place. That new house on the property is currently (1995) occupied by Mr. Alan Gregory.

Jack Updike at Work in his Decoy Shop - c. 1950

243

The Sooy/Hollaway/Murray House
1032 River Road

1935

Photo by Augusta Weeks

This home is typical of the smaller houses built in the area during the nineteenth century. It appears to have been built on Lot A of the Glass House Lot and may have been the home of Dr. Charles Nichols, who bought the lots on March 26th, 1880 from the Vincentown bank for $750. Lot A was listed as having a house on it as early as the first evaluation by "Special Master" Ten Eyck for the forced sale of Josephus Sooy's property in 1876.

It became the home of Thomas Kimble Sooy who was active in community affairs at the turn of the century. Thomas K. Sooy was the son of Benjamin and Eunice B. (Kimble) Sooy. Benjamin Sooy was a farmer and was born September 17, 1819, the first son of William H. and Rebecca (Weeks) Sooy. This William H. was the son of Nicholas Sooy I and Sarah Sears, the brother of the Nicholas Sooy II., and the uncle of the William H. Sooy who built 1045 River Road. Thomas had a brother, William H. Sooy, Jr., who became the Green Bank blacksmith.

Thomas' mother, Eunice Bevis Kimble, was born on January 6, 1824, the daughter of Samuel and Hannah Kimble of Pleasant Mills. Samuel Kimble was a sea captain who made many trips to China and other foreign ports in search of trade goods. As the Sooy genealogy notes, he was an expert navigator, which was probably the reason why he's buried at Pleasant Mills rather than in the deep. Benjamin Sooy died in 1872, and both he and his wife, Eunice lie in the Green Bank cemetery.

Thomas Kimble Sooy was born on the 16th of September, 1858 in the Wading River homestead of his parents, the ninth child of Benjamin and Eunice, when his father was forty and his mother thirty-five. He married Martha Crowley (b. 1864, d. 1935), and they had five children, three of whom died in infancy. Their first child, Kathryn, died at the age of twenty-nine. Their only son and surviving child, Lewis Sooy, moved to Newark and was in the insurance business. Thomas K. represented Washington Township as a member of the Board of Chosen Freeholders of Burlington County for several terms and served on the Township Committee. He was the postmaster for Green Bank for twenty years and conducted a general store (though the location is unknown today). He died at the age of seventy-eight on the 21st of October, 1937 in Egg Harbor City, where he had moved after his wife died in 1935. His service was held in the Green Bank church, and he rests in the old cemetery nearby with his father and mother, and his whole family.

When Thomas K. Sooy's wife, Martha, died in 1935, he sold this house to Mr. and Mrs. Arthur Hollaway. They originally came to Green Bank from Pleasant Mills, where they continued their church ties, even though they were living in Green Bank.

Arthur Hollaway served as the Highway Commissioner of Washington Township for a number of years. Their son, Ralph, married Winona Ford, and, in 1935, the couple had one son. The Hollaways supported the school activities and always donated to the support of the Green Bank church, even though they retained their membership in the Pleasant Mills church. Mrs. Hollaway had an interest in gardening and kept the grounds around the house in beautiful condition.

This home, extensively remodelled and enlarged, is now owned by Mr. Joseph Peter Murray, Esq. and his family.

Photograph by John Pearce

1995

The Wobbar Store
1029 River Road

Courtesy of Budd Wilson

May 31, 1930

The Wobbar Store was built and operated by Haze Wobbar, who lived in the old Josephus Sooy house at 1027 River Road. It was built on the river side of the road, and during the 1920s through the 1940s, it was in competition with the corner store at the bridge, operated by the Fords.

The building was moved across River Road in the mid-1950s and made into a home. Haze and Helena Wobbar lived here while their daughter, Ruth, and her second husband lived next door. When that marriage failed, the Wobbars moved back into their old home and sold this house to Jim Montgomery. It was later sold to Earl and Shirley Ford, then to the Mathews. Joan Mathews Ross lives there in 1997. Her first husband was Daniel Leeds Mathews, a descendant of both the Leeds and Mathis families. It is interesting that "Mathis" is supposed to have been a corruption of "Mathews" in the first place. When she and her husband moved to Green Bank, they were, in a sense, returning home.

Courtesy of Budd Wilson

1928

Photograph by Augusta Weeks

1935

246

Actual Date Uncertain

Actual Date Uncertain

1950s

1995

The Sooy/Crowley/Wobbar/Wilson House
1027 River Road

1935

The original Pearson/Driver Survey included three hundred acres from the southeast side of the Green Bank cemetery to Little Bull Creek or Driver's Run which runs near the northwest side of this house. When Joseph Sooy (Yoos II) bought the acreage from John Driver in 1752, the only known house on the entire survey was that of Samuel Driver (1079 River Road), into which Joseph moved with his family. Joseph had married Elizabeth Smuts in 1737, the year of his father's death in Lower Bank. In all probability, he continued to live on the old homestead there until he moved upriver fifteen years later. It is more than likely that the first six of the couple's twelve children, Joseph, Sarah, John, Mary, Nicholas, and Noah were born there. The seventh, Luke, born in the year the Driver estate was purchased, may well have been born in Green Bank, as, in all likelihood, were the remaining five children the couple would have.

Joseph lost the Green Bank lands in 1787. Where he and his family lived after that is a mystery. The Driver estate did not return to the Sooy family until his grandson, Nicholas II, bought it back from William Richards in 1823.

This house stands on a portion of ground that marked the northern boundary of the old Driver property purchased by Nicholas Sooy II. Budd Wilson, archaeologist and current owner of this house, says that there are indications that Paul Sears Sooy, the son of Nicholas I and brother of Nicholas II, built this house in the 1820's. If so, he built it on land owned by his brother. Also, when his father, Nicholas I, died in 1822, Paul Sears Sooy took over the operation of the Washington Tavern on the Tuckerton Road. Paul Sears Sooy was the youngest child of Nicholas Sooy I and Sarah (Sears) Sooy and was twenty-two when his father died in 1822. His brother, Nicholas II, was eighteen years his senior. The problem is that Nicholas didn't acquire this property from Richards until 1823. Paul Sears Sooy was born in February of 1800 and married Elizabeth (called Betsy) Cavileer, the daughter of Peter and Eleanor (called "Eva" in the Sooy genealogy, "Eleanor" in that of the Cavileers) Cavileer, at Harrisville (no date given). He may have lived here rather than at the Washington Tavern itself. Paul Sears Sooy died June 25, 1868, and Elizabeth died on October 14th, 1872.

248

Brother Nicholas lived on his uncle John's plantation a half mile up river, not in the old Sooy/Driver house. His son, Samuel, was the only one of his sons old enough in the 1820's to be needing a house. He married Catherine Leek on May 3, 1827. Perhaps it was Samuel rather than his uncle, Paul Sears, who originally constructed this house, yet an 1849 map of the township lists it as the home of P.S. Sooy.

In any case, the house was built in a Federal style, much as the newer part of the Old Driver Homestead at 1079 River Road. What we can know with some certainty is that Nicholas II's son, Josephus, lived here with his wife and children and inherited it from his father in 1851.

Josephus Sooy married Louisa Reeves on the eleventh of September, 1845. The couple had three children: Mark R., J. Leander, and Lucy A.

Leander grew up to become a noted Methodist minister in Trenton and Camden and wrote a "History of the Methodist Episcopal Church of Trenton, N.J." which is on file in the Pennsylvania Historical Society.

Mark R. Sooy entered the University of Lewisberg in Pennsylvania in 1864 and graduated from Princeton. He taught Latin and Greek in Wyoming Seminary at Kinston, Pa. in 1870-71 and was later head of the Mount Holly Institute. He became a prominent lawyer and founder of the New Jersey Bar Association.

Mark's son, William Frank Sooy was educated at the Peddie School of Hightstown, New Jersey, and studied law under his father. He later held the position of Vice-Chancellor of New Jersey and served as the captain of Battery B., New Jersey Field Artillery, in World War One. His brother, Mark Reeves Sooy, Jr., graduated from Lafayette College in Easton, Pennsylvania, and the University of California but died at the young age of forty-four.

An interesting note in the Sooy genealogy says that Mark R. Sooy moved to a farm near Mount Holly in 1855. Since he would only have been nine years old in 1855, it is presumed that his family moved from Green Bank at this time. While no birthdate for William Frank Sooy is given in the Sooy genealogy, it is noted that he was born in Mount Holly.

Josephus inherited about 105 acres which included a portion of the original Pearson/Driver Survey from the present Route 563 to Little Bull Creek. He also inherited an even larger piece of land from Little Bull Creek to Bull Creek that stretched up the South Bend Road which then had no name. He also inherited a 1/5th share of the Glass House Lot along with his brothers and nephew.

He sold a small lot on the north side of the Batsto/Wading River Road to Reuben L. Gauntt on November 29th, 1855 for $200 and another lot at the point between the present routes 542 and 563 to George Ford for $200 a month later. On the 17th of September, 1857, he sold another small lot to George Ford which adjoined the first parcel. This is the property where the liquor store now stands.

Josephus managed to get himself into financial problems by mortgaging all of his Washington Township properties to the First National Bank of Vincentown on the 17th of December, 1872 to secure a loan of $14,000. Two years later, he gave a second mortgage on the same lands to his brother, William H. Sooy, for $11,466.10. He apparently defaulted on both and a Bill to Foreclose was entered with the Chancery Court at Trenton on the 30th of September 1875. On March 7th, 1876, the

Courtesy of Budd Wilson

D.P. Crowley, step-brother of Nicholas Crowley, the father of Captain James Morell Crowley aboard the *Nemo* on the Mullica near Hog Island off Lower Bank in August 1934

court ordered that the properties of Josephus Sooy "be sold in parcels and in order and manner aforesaid [in the Master's Report]." Some of his lands were sold to Joseph Wharton, but this property where Josephus had lived with his family prior to 1855 was sold to Samual Taylor by the First National Bank of Vincentown on the 24th of February, 1877 for $1,900.

Captain Samuel Taylor married Parmelia Crowley, a daughter of Captain Samuel Crowley III and may have been the brother of Captain Crowley's fourth wife, Catherine Taylor. It was probably during their ownership that the house was "modernized": the roof was raised and made more peaked, the front dormer was added, and a wing was built in the rear to bring it more up to date with the homes of the period as exemplified by the home of Josephus' brother, William H. Sooy, at 1045 River Road. The Taylors mortgaged the property to Drissilla M. Cox on the first of July, 1883 to secure $1,500. Cox assigned the mortgage to the Burlington Savings Institution on November 11, 1890.

Apparently the mortgage was never satisfied, for, on January 20, 1898, the Burlington Savings Institution sold the property to thirty-six year old Captain James Morrell Crowley, step-nephew of Captain Taylor, for $1,000. Captain Crowley was born in Port Republic on August 23, 1862, the son of Nicholas Crowley of Crowleytown and Rebecca Johnson of Port Republic who were married in that town in June of 1858. James Morell Crowley had already purchased lots A & B of the Glass House Lot from the Vincentown bank on July 9th, 1891.

James Morrell Crowley was the son of Sam Crowley III's first wife's son, Nicholas, and thus was related to Nicholas Sooy I. 'Rell, as he was called, married Sarah Augusta Wobbar, daughter of Otto and Esther Wobbar of South Bend. Captain James commanded coastal trading ships and made his home port in Green Bank. He continued to follow the sea for forty-three years until ill-health forced him to abandon his lifelong love. 'Rell was a born seafarer: his father and his grandfather having followed the call of the sea. His sister, Annabelle, married Captain George Leek, who also commanded vessels. Seven of his uncles had been seafarers. His uncle, Delwyne P. Crowley sailed the seas for fifty-two years before retiring and moving to Tuckerton. Delwyne (D.P.) Crowley then maintained a winter harborage called Crowley's Basin in Tuckerton. Delwyne was born in the old Nicholas Sooy II homestead on the river, where his parents lived for a short time while they rebuilt their home in Bulltown.

'Rell and Augusta had only one child, Birdsall (b. 1894), named after his grandmother's family. Birdsall Wobbar Crowley served in the Coast Guard Patrol during World War I. When he married Alyce, they bought the house on the corner of River Road across from the bridge and the store.

James Morrell Crowley died on December 17, 1922. On May 24, 1923, Birdsall and his mother, Augusta, sold this house to J. Hazelton Wobbar, son of Otto and Esther Wobbar of South Bend, Augusta's brother and Birdsall's uncle.

Haze Wobbar had sailed as a mate and cook on board Captain James Morrell Crowley's ship. He met and married a

Courtesy of Budd Wilson

Helena Wobbar,
Will and May Birdsall,
Ruth Wobbar, and
Grandma Esther Wobbar

schoolteacher, Helena Gould Davidson (1878-1968), late of Nova Scotia, when she was teaching at the school in Weekstown and may have first lived in an old house that stood at 1014 River Road prior to its razing by William Birdsall.

Haze had a garage near the Green Bank School and also opened a store on the riverbank across from his home. Captain Crowley Loveland (obviously a relative somewhere along the line) used to winter his yawl *Vagabond* at the dock in front of this house and beside the Wobbar store.

During the 1930s, Hazelton Wobbar was the Highway Commissioner of Washington Township and was also in charge of the school bus route. Haze was known to be "a man of few words, decided in thought and action, a kindly neighbor and friend, willing to aid those who are not as well-to-do in life as he." He was a good friend of Zeke Forman, who lived in the Old Driver Homestead at 1079 River Road.

Helena Davidson Wobbar continued her educational career, serving as teacher and principal of the Green Bank School for many decades. As the teacher of the sixth, seventh, and eighth grades and the principal, Helena Wobbar had tremendous influence on every child that lived in Washington Township for over thirty years as her pictures proudly attest.

Helena and Hazelton had one child, Ruth, born in 1918. Ruth married Harrison Browne of the United States Marine Corps, who was stationed at Quantico, Virginia, on February 21, 1935. They had a daughter, Marilyn, who later became the wife of Budd Wilson, the current (1995) owner and resident of this old house. Budd, the archaeologist for Batsto for a number of years, is a an expert in many areas of archaeology and a fine architectural historian as well. He excavated the glass factory at Batsto. Budd preserved many of the pictures used in this book, and we owe a great debt to him for his interest, generosity, and cooperation.

Budd was born in Pennsauken, New Jersey, on March 25,

Courtesy of Budd Wilson

Hazelton and Helena Wobbar with their daughter, Ruth

Courtesy of Budd Wilson

Ruth Wobbar is the little girl in the sleigh.
The gentleman's identity is not known.

251

1934. His parents were Charles I. Wilson, Sr. (also called Budd), and Edna May Wilson. Budd, Sr. was the Chief of Police of the Benjamin Franklin Bridge for many years but fell in love with the Mullica area. His love was confirmed when he met and became friends with both Arthur Pierce and Henry Charlton Beck. In 1953, he contacted Jewel and John Herman at Batsto in order to rent one of the Batsto houses for the summers, and they let him know that the Rebecca Crowley House (1154 Route 542) was available. Budd, Sr. and Edna jumped at the chance to rent this old, riverfront house, and the family came here in the summers from then on. He and

Courtesy of Budd Wilson

Budd as a budding archeologist fresh from college, holding a cannonball mold from Batsto on the river near the Old Sooy Homestead of the Kosters - early 1960s.

his wife, Edna, were very active at Batsto during the 1950's and took copious notes of both local records and the Batsto ledgers themselves. It was "Cap" Wilson who took the ledgers to Trenton to have them microfilmed. Though technically amateurs, "Cap" and Edna were vital in preserving a great deal of information on Batsto and Washington Township.

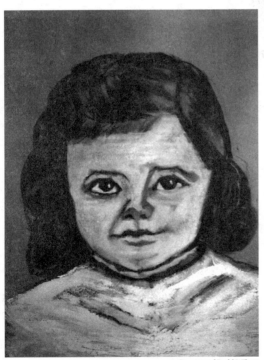

Courtesy of Budd Wilson

Marilyn, daughter of Ruth (Wobbar) Browne, granddaughter of Haze and Helena (Davidson) Wobbar, taken from a drawing she did of herself when she was a child.

Young Budd was here off and on during his college years but moved here permanently in 1961 after he had graduated. He first met his future wife, Marilyn Browne while they were canoeing. Marilyn was the daughter of Ruth (Wobbar) Browne, granddaughter of Haze and Helena Wobbar, and lived in this house at 1027 River Road. After not seeing her for some time, he happened to pass by her house and found her picking pansies along the front walk. His first words differ depending on whether you asked him or asked Marilyn. He says he said: "Hello, how are you? May I see your house?" She said he said: "Hello, may I see your house?" Not a very romantic beginning for a deep love, but not bad for an archaeologist. In any case, Marilyn and Budd were married in 1974. Their marriage was shattered on October 31, 1989, with Marilyn's death as the result of an automobile accident in Egg Harbor City.

Budd is deeply interested in the history of the area and has enthusiastically provided many hours of fascinating discussion on the subject. His reference library is comprehensive and amazingly large, covering just about every subject relating to the pinelands. Budd is a true scholar with a most inquisitive mind, who simply enjoys learning about any and everything. He seems to know every cellar-hole, house-site, and vanished town anywhere in the vicinity. When Budd talks, his extensive knowledge fascinates the listener for hours.

Budd's father, Charles I. Wilson, Sr., was an amateur archaeologist himself, and Budd gained his enthusiasm for the task from his father's interest. Archaeology and history, related disciplines, are as fascinating as criminal investigations, and just as complex. The careful digs and voluminous research that must be done provide constant leads, dead ends, and complexities. Only when all the data is collected can the historian or archaeologist draw final conclusions.

The archaeologist and historian are dealing with real life people in the past: their way of life, their history and interests, the events they shaped and which shaped them, the buildings they built, the tools they used, the common household articles that they accepted as part of their daily lives.

It seems we know so little about the lives of those who came before us even in the recent past. As each year passes, it becomes more difficult to find the clues which shed light on their lives. Budd is, in the end, a "Light-shedder" for those who were born, lived, loved, worked, celebrated triumphs and suffered losses in this land of the Mullia valley. Viva, Budd!

Courtesy of Budd Wilson

Charles I. (Budd) Wilson, Jr. and his wife,
Marilyn (Browne) Wilson - circa 1985

Photograph by John Pearce

The home of Budd Wilson - 1995

Shepherd's Hall
The Washington Township Town Hall
1018 River Road

South Side of Shepherd's Hall - 1995

According to Laura Larrabee McConaghy, Shepherd's Hall was built in 1903 for the local lodge (Washington Camp #176) of the Patriotic Order Sons of America. This Order was founded in 1847 as a "civilian patriotic fraternal order of American-born men 'who place fealty to country above every other consideration.'" During the early part of this century, several prominent townspeople were members of this lodge. William Asa Johnson, grandson of Nicholas Sooy II and owner/operator of the sawmill and grist mill on the Bull Creek, was known to be active in its affairs.

The order is still in existence today and has its headquarters in Valley Forge, Pennsylvania. According to the *Encyclopedia of Associations*, the order "seeks to : enhance appreciation of our heritage of freedom; establish a feeling of devotion to country, its institutions, the Constitution, and respect for the flag; support and defend the public schools; oppose foreign interference in state and national affairs and all "subversive movements' against our constitutional government and the powers of law and order; work for 'adequate restriction' of immigration and advocate a firm program and legislation for the national defense and the nation's security."

The years between 1830 and 1850 were turbulent years for the nascent democracy which was the United States. The slavery issue was not completely buried by the Missouri Compromise of 1820 and continually threatened to overwhelm the unity and patriotism which had bound the country together. It was a time of tremendous expansion, in population, in western settlement, and in business. Political and social issues were the constant topic of all citizens. It was also a period which saw the formation of a great many organizations and lodges for patriotic and social purposes, among which was the United Sons of America, whose main thrust at the time was the promotion of public education throughout the country. During the 1840s, members of the United Sons of America felt that something should be done to increase patriotic ardor and knowledge amongst the young men of the country, and Dr. Reynell Coates of Philadelphia issued the call for the first meeting of the "Junior Sons of America," held on December 10, 1847 in the City of Brotherly Love. Coates was the organizer, chief promoter, writer of the constitution and bylaws of the organization, as well as of the ritual. All "camps" chartered were given the name of "Washington Camp" with a specific number. The organization rapidly expanded into the adjacent mid-Atlantic states, New England, the mid-west, and even into the South.

At the beginning of the Civil War, most of the membership entered either the Union or Confederate armies. Only seven disabled men from Reading, Pennsylvania, kept the organization afloat. All the other lodges were disbanded. These few members continued their interest and, in 1864, issued a call for renewal of the order. The new state camp of Pennsylvania was formed in August, 1866, and other lodges were subsequently chartered. By the turn of the century, the Patriotic Order Sons of America, as it had been styled, counted thousands of members.

The order has continued to hold rallies, sponsor events, and donate towards historic preservation and educational goals. In the early part of this century, it purchased the house that was the headquarters of General Washington at Valley Forge and carefully maintained it until it was taken over by the Commonwealth of Pennsylvania as part of the Valley Forge State Park. It has placed monuments to various patriots, including Betsy Ross and Francis Scott Key, author of the "Star-spangled Banner." It made the original donation of land to the Commonwealth of Pennsylvania for the Washington's Crossing State Park and has contributed to the memorial building and grounds there.

Its "Goals for the 90's" are substantially unchanged from those which inspired the young men of the pre-Civil War era or those of Washington Township at the turn of the century:

> *To increase the integrity of all American citizens.*
> *To sustain the power of all American citizens - by voting and using the power of the ballot, with respect for each other and in impeachment when necessary.*
> *That those who come among us shall have the fullest respect for real Americans, in heart and in name, and strive to become real Americans. Appreciate our Heritage of Freedom under God and become vigilant citizens.*
> *Support constitutional government. Have devotion to Country and its symbol, the Flag of the United States. Object to any desecration of Constitution or Flag with patriotic zeal. Provide a respectful method for the disposal of flags when there is the need.*
> *We will make all effort to instruct each other so as to act as American citizens - to establish justice, domestic tranquility, the common defense. To promote the general welfare. To secure the blessing of liberty for ourselves and for our descendants.*

Photograph by John Pearce

North side of Shepherd's Hall - 1995

Under our Platform of Principles to provide a thrust toward good legislation, Local, State and National, that will give the opportunity for the right to know, to think, to believe, and to utter freely, according to conscience, above all other liberties.

To observe and support the laws of the land and the regulations of this Fraternity, as becomes sons of freemen. Willing to submit to the restraints of social order; but acknowledging no other bonds but those of duty to God, our Country, and Ourselves.

Support and defend the American system of public schools favoring compulsory school attendance age 8 through 14 years. To help support/decide/resolve major school problems by public vote. Responsible control to be held by officers elected by the people.

Dedicated to the aid of our older Brothers, the maturing of ourselves, the encouragement of each other - taking upon ourselves those opportunities which are part of our republic's life. (from the informational booklet of the Patriotic Order Sons of America - 1995)

Many of the records of the national order for Pennsylvania and New Jersey were lost in a fire in 1978 and in a flood in 1980, but the charter for Washington Camp #106 recently came to light hiding in Green Bank itself. The New Jersey State Camp issued the original warrent for the Washington Camp under the date of September 27, 1912, and the charter itself is dated July 10, 1913. It lists the following men as charter members: Fremont Bozarth, Atwood Clark, Charles Clevinger, James W. Crowley, Geroge W. Ford, Harry Ford, Harvey Ford, Jesse A. Ford, John W. Ford, J.W. Ford, Nicholas Ford, Geroge Gerber, Phillip Gerber, , Barris Jerue, Earl Jerue, Walter Jerue, John R. Koster, Harold G. Maxwell, Phillip Maxwell, Charles Ryan, A. Lyall Salmons, Lewis Sooy, T. K. Sooy, Edmund Weeks, Morris V. Weeks, Robert Wills, and Leslie Wills.

In a deed transferring the surrounding property from William and Rebecca Johnson to Haze Wobbar in 1917, this lot is excepted. The deed gives the name of the lodge as "The Star of Hope Lodge, Order of Shepherds of Bethlehem." This does not seem to be the same lodge as that of the Patriotic Order Sons of America. It is possible that the building was actually built for the Star of Hope Lodge. Perhaps a chapter of the P.O.S.O.A. was started by several of the original lodge members as successor to the Star of Hope Lodge. Certainly William A. Johnson was an integral part of both lodges and simply may not have changed the name on the deed.

The first record of this building's use as a site for the town meeting is in notes taken by Charles I. ("Cap" or "Budd") Wilson, Sr. They indicate that the Township of Washington paid a rental fee of $5.00 for use of "Shepherd's Hall" in 1906. In 1919, the rent had doubled to $10.00. This would have been quite a hefty fee in those years if it was only used for one meeting a year.

The Town Committee negotiated the purchase of the hall under then mayor Earle Hill, and the building has been used as a regular Town Hall ever since.

The upstairs room of this building is used only for storage today, but remains unchanged from its days as a lodge hall. Members would enter the building for a meeting through a southeast side door, then climb a narrow stairway to the second floor. The doorway at the top of the stairs leads to a small antechamber. Though rather small, this hallway, actually divided in half, was used as a preparatory room. Here members donned their sashes, and visitors were probably examined for the "signs" of membership prior to entering the main lodge hall. The sashes remain hanging on pegs in the anteroom at the rear, just as the members of the lodge left them for the last time many years ago. Members then entered the lodge hall. It has a vaulted ceiling and a raised platform at both ends. The walls are panelled in tongue-and-grove wainscoting, and, though it was electrified at some time, the hanging bracket for four kerosene lamps is still there. One interesting item: there are at least three different types of balloting boxes of the past stored in the room.

The first floor has been modernized for the use of township meetings. The pent over the front door is also a modern addition but was tastefully constructed in the style of the building.

The Birdsall/Porter/Reismiller/Braddock Residence
1014 River Road

William Birdsall, brother of Joseph and Abbie Birdsall and son of Hazelton and Sarah Ann (Miller) Birdsall, was born in the Old Birdsall Homestead in Bulltown. His first wife was Nevada Hall (b. 1864, d. 1914), the daughter of John and Amanda (Sooy) Hall. Amanda was the daughter of Samuel Sooy, son of Nicholas II. When Nevada died, he married Mary Curry, who was the daughter of Captain Thomas Andrew Curry of Nova Scotia, a Master in the British Merchant Marine service and the half-sister of Helena Wobbar.

The original house which stood on this property is believed to have been the inheritance of Hester (Sooy) Johnson from her father, Nicholas Sooy II and later the home of Jenny Broom, wife of William Woolston. Haze Wobbar bought the property from William and Rebecca Johnson on August 20, 1917 for $900 and may have lived in the old house when he was first married. He sold it to his uncle about 1923 when he bought 1027 River Road. Bill tore this old three or five-bay house down in order to build the original part of his new house.

Bill was a carpenter and shipwright in his younger years, a trade he learned from his father, Haze. In his later years when age made travelling around the country building houses a bit too strenuous, Bill went into the poultry business and had rental boats on the river during the fishing season. He was also the Warden and Keeper of the drawbridge. He was known to be "fearless in the cause of right" and "would not cater to deception or unfair dealing. "He was a "genial, happy, and hale fellow with all who come his way. Hospitable and generous to a fault!"

Courtesy of Budd Wilson

Will and May Birdsall with Ruth Wobbar
Photographed before their original home
which stood at 1014 River Road

Courtesy of Budd Wilson

Will and May Birdsall in front of their new home
at the same location

May Birdsall was a member of the Ladies' Aid of the Green Bank Church, a teacher in the Junior Bible Class in Sunday School, and a member of the choir. She was also active in the Parent-Teacher Association at the Green Bank School.

Elliot Porter, a well-known photographer, lived in the Birdsall house during the 1960s and was responsible for most of the final form this house has taken. He eventually built a new home on the other side of River Road and sold this house to the Reismillers. Mr. Reismiller now lives on Lovers' Lane in Green Bank.

The Birdsall House is currently owned by the Lee Braddock family. This is one house that certainly grew with time.

Courtesy of Budd Wilson

William and May Birdsall
The identity of the elderly woman is not known.

Courtesy of Budd Wilson

The date of this picture is not known, but it is obviously earlier than the one to the right: no porch to the left.

Photograph by Augusta Weeks

Circa 1935

The date of this picture is unknown but obviously sometime later than the 1935 picture on the previous page.

Elliot Porter

1995

The Sooy/Forman/Wessler House
2410 Route 563
Chatsworth-Egg Harbor Road

Courtesy of Jessie Lewis

The house as it appeared prior to the remodelling of E.C. Sooy in the 1920s.

This early home, purported to be the second oldest house in Green Bank, was a residence of the Sooy family and part of Nicholas Sooy II's estate. His son, Ephraim, lived here with his young wife, Lucy Ann Haywood, and their story is touching.

On March 8, 1819, Nicholas Sooy II and his wife, Sarah Sears, were blessed with the birth of twin boys whom they named Ephraim and Josephus. As young men, Ephraim and his older brother, William, courted the Haywoods from West Creek. William married Mary A. Haywood, sister of Joel Haywood, and Ephraim married his daughter, Lucy Ann (born June 30, 1822) on the 28th day of August, 1842, when Ephraim was twenty-three and Lucy Ann twenty.

The young people were deeply in love and established themselves in this home on the road perpendicular to the river near the crossroads with River Road, and, no doubt they had sincere hopes and dreams for the future, but their dreams were not to be realized. Things began well though. Ephraim and Lucy Ann had two children less than two years apart: Lydia, born November 20, 1843 and Franklin, born October 22, 1845.

The first tragedy to strike the little family was the death of little Franklin on August 19th, 1847, two months shy of his second birthday. Ephraim and Lucy Ann were devastated but still filled with hope. Lucy was pregnant at the time of Franklin's death, and they looked forward to the birth of another child the following January.

Photograph of her portrait by Dudley Lewis

Lucy Ann (Haywood) Sooy

260

Unfortunately, tragedy struck again. Ephraim took sick and died one month after his son on the 16th of September, 1847 at the age of twenty-eight, leaving Lucy Ann (Haywood) Sooy, at twenty-five, a widow with a four-year old girl and pregnant with another child. Ephraim C., named after his deceased father, was born on the 8th of January in 1848, four months after his father had been laid to rest in the cemetery, close by the Green Bank Church. Lucy Ann Haywood Sooy never fully recovered from the loss of both son and husband within one month, and she died on March 23rd, 1849, at the age of twenty-six, leaving a little daughter of five and a son of fourteen months.

Sister Lydia was taken into the home of her Uncle William and his wife in Green Bank. Ephraim C., Jr., was taken in by the Reverend Joel Haywood, Lucy Ann's father, the Methodist Episcopal minister in West Creek, New Jersey. Later, Eph also came to live with his sister in the William Sooy family.

Grandfather Joel Haywood was not some backwood's clergyman. According to Polly Miller of the Ocean County Cultural and Heritage Commission, Haywood was responsible for the setting apart of Ocean County. Her 1997 pamphlet about the minister is entitled, *Joel Haywood: The Founding Father of Ocean County.*

Haywood was a dedicated member of the Whig party and was disturbed when the Democrats, in 1844, maneuvered to create two new townships in northern Monmouth County that would send Democratic members to the Board of Freeholders, tipping the balance of power in the county.

Photograph of his portrait by Dudley Lewis

The Rev. Joel Haywood
West Creek Methodist Episcopal Church

In 1849, in the midst of heightened tensions, Haywood wrote to the State Legislature and requested that Stafford and Dover Townships be set apart as a new county to be called Ocean. Though the resulting bill passed the Assembly with no difficulty, the situation was different in the State Senate. The senators divided along strict party lines, and the bill carried by only one vote! Haywood continued to shepherd the fledgling county, defending it against an attempt by the Democrats in Monmouth to re-annex part of its territory.

Joel Haywood, the son of Thomas Haywood, was born on December 9, 1798, in West Creek. His great-grandfather, James, had worked for the Proprietors of East Jersey as a sales agent and had bought land in the area which became Stafford Township in 1743. Joel's father, Thomas, built a house in West Creek which his son, Joel, enlarged during his lifetime.

Joel was self-educated, learned the blacksmith trade from his father, and was a devout Methodist. He was a member of the Board of Trustees of the West Creek Methodist Episcopal Church and served as its minister for over forty years.

His nephew, James Edwards, who lived with the Haywoods for a few years while teaching school in West Creek, wrote in his little book on the Edwards family that "He [Joel Haywood] was a master of wit and humor, although usually maintaining the gravest countenance. Looking at the stern visage peering out from his portrait above, one can surely perceive the "gravest countenance" part, if not the wit and humor.

Courtesy of Jessie Lewis

Ephraim C. Sooy, Sr.

Haywood served as the first representative of the new Ocean County to the State legislature and, in 1853, ran unsuccessfully for the governorship of New Jersey. He was a founding member of the Republican Party and attended their first convention held in Philadelphia. That 1856 convention nominated John C. Fremont for president, but did not succeed at the subsequent election. Instead, the Democratic Pennsylvanian, James Buchanan, received sufficient votes to become President.

Somehow, Haywood found time to assist in rescuing several people from shipwrecks along the immediate coast and pushed for the establishment of a governmental service to help save lives in such disasters. He encouraged Congressman William A Newell to support legislation establishing the Life Saving Service, which, at a later date was merged into the United States Coast Guard. Newell later became the Governor of New Jersey and was known as the "Father of the Life Saving Service," but Newell himself gave that title to Joel Haywood for his tireless efforts in behalf of shipwrecked victims of the sea.

Joel had married Lydia Pharo in 1821 and the couple had eight children before her death in 1842. He then married Lydia's neice, Mary Ann Pharo and fathered four more children. His eldest daughter, Lucy Ann, married Ephraim Sooy of Green Bank while his sister, Mary Ann, married Ephraim's brother, William.

Ephraim C. Sooy, Jr.

This young man was left without a father before he was even born and without his mother a year later. Despite this early tragedy, he was determined to make something of his life, and indeed he did. He died a wealthy man in 1927 at the age of 79. This photograph was probably taken before 1868 when he left Green Bank to make his way in the world.

Lydia Sooy

Lydia was four years old when her father died and six when her mother passed away. She went to live with her aunt and uncle, William H. and Mary Sooy while their grandfather, The Rev. Joel Haywood of West Creek, took baby Ephraim, Jr. The boy later joined his sister and cousins in Green Bank, probably after the death of his grandfather in 1865.

After the tragic death of his daughter and son-in-law, Joel Haywood took the baby boy, Ephraim, Jr. into his home and raised him as a son. His granddaughter, Lydia, apparently spent the majority of her time with her uncle and great-aunt, William and Mary Ann (Haywood) Sooy in Green Bank but also made extended visits to her grandfather's house.

Ephraim C. Sooy, Jr. lived with his grandfather for several years but joined his sister and his cousins in the Green Bank home of William H. and Mary Ann (Haywood) Sooy probably after his grandfather's death in 1865, a month after Lincoln's assasination, when he was seventeen.

Ephraim was always fond of the sea, and being surrounded by seamen, had his young life filled with the romantic tales of the ocean waves. When he was twenty, he served as mate on a steamship, but that apparently disillusioned him as to a career on the sea. It didn't stifle his ambition.

At twenty-one he went West and lived on a ranch in western Kansas. Eph started several businesses in the Kansas City, Missouri area, including the Hay Press, a casting business, which his descendants have maintained to this day (1995). Thus he established a branch of the Sooy family in the mid-west. He married Jessie J. Hargrave, having four children by her: Lucy, Bertram (who died at the age of twenty-one), Elizabeth, and Norman. Jessie (Hargrave) Sooy died on the 26th of March, 1901, and Ephraim married again the following year, this time to Evelyn Hammel, who survived him.

Eph was to return to this town of his birth in his old age, summering in Green Bank for many years in the old Driver homestead at 1079 River Road. The portrait of his mother, Lucy Ann, still hangs over the mantle in the parlor of the Old Driver Homestead, now occupied by his granddaughter and her family.

Eph and Jessie Hargrave's daughter Elizabeth married Ezekial Forman, whose family dated back past the Revolution on Maryland's Eastern Shore. They had one daughter, Jessie, in Kansas City, but soon moved to Atlantic City, where Zeke was in real estate. When Zeke's eyes were giving him problems, Eph fixed up this house of his birth on the Chatsworth Road for his daughter, her husband, and their little girl, adding an addition to the northern end. Zeke managed Eph's Green Bank estate and and raised chickens.

After Ephraim C.'s death in 1927, Zeke and Elizabeth Forman took up summer residence in the old Driver homestead and sold this house to Daniel and Laura McConeghy. The McConeghys came from northern Pennsylvania but fell in love with Green Bank. Laura McConeghy wrote an extensive

Courtesy of Jessie Lewis

Jessie Forman about 1922

Courtesy of Jessie Lewis

Jessie Forman and her father, Zeke on the "chicken farm" about 1924.

manuscript on "The Green Bank Country" called *The Romance of Green Bank* from which the 1935 pictures in this book and many of the family notes were taken. Without her efforts in chronicling the details of local families and houses, very little would be known of Green Bank's history indeed. In Laura Larrabee McConeghy, Green Bank found an outsider who became its champion and retained her love for the Mullica valley until she died.

The McConeghys lived in this house for six years, from 1928 to 1933, Mr. McConeghy continuing to run the chicken farm. The property also boasted a fine orchard, whose trees bore peaches, pears, and cherries. After the McConeghys moved, the house was purchased by Mr. William Woolston, a close friend of Ephraim C. Sooy's. Indeed, the Woolston family lived for a time in the old Driver homestead on River Road before Eph returned to Green Bank and fixed it up for his summer home.

William Woolston was the son of Jane and Peter Woolston, who lived in Green Bank at 1156 Route 542 (later the home of Alanson and Sylvia Cobb, today the home of Ken Cramer, Jr., 1156 Route 542).

According to Henry Beck, based on an interview with Woolston himself, William was born in Green Bank in 1859 (his gravestone says 1860), the son of Peter and Jane Messick Woolston of Green Bank, in one of the houses along the river. His father was a sea captain engaged in the lumber trade and dealt especially with ship timbers.

On one of his stops in Chincoteague, Virginia, he met and fell in love with his future wife. Their son grew up with the smell of the salt air and the call of high adventure in his blood and went to sea as a cook at the age of seventeen on the *Hazel Dell,* captained by Watson Cale of Crowleytown. The boy helped his father in the lumber trade and later commanded vessels himself.

In the eighteenth, nineteenth, and early twentieth centuries, the Mullica was heavily trafficked by ocean-going vessels, many of which were ships of some size. Quite a number of the residents of Green Bank and Lower

Photo by Augusta Weeks

This photograph was taken by Augusta Weeks for Laura Larrabee McConeghy's "Romance of Green Bank." Mrs. McConeghy and her husband lived here for about seven years. Note the addition made by E.C. Sooy, Jr., for his daughter and her family.

Bank were captains of these vessels. Others shipped aboard as mates or crew members. Its no wonder that so many of the young men of the period dreamed of adventure on the high seas.

According the Laura Larrabee McConeghy, in her *Romance of Green Bank*, written when William Woolston was still alive, Jane and Peter Woolston lived in the Cobb House at 1156 Route 542 (this could be said to be "along the river" for the back part of the property does stretch to the river, but it could not be referred to be a part of "Sailorman's Row, the houses facing the river above and below the bridge." Beck does say that "The Woolstons were away for a time at Herman" which may mean that William and Jenny lived in the Cobb House "for a time," which threw off Mrs. McConeghy. She does say, however, that William was born in Toms River and moved here with his parents when still an infant. This is in direct conflict with Beck's statement that his father was from Green Bank and is probably wrong. The Woolstons had been in Washington Township at least two generations prior to this William.

William met and married Jenny Broom, the daughter of William and Catherine Broom, whose house stood at 1014 River Road and was torn down by Bill Birdsall in 1886. The Sooy Genealogy says that William married Amanda Rebecca Sooy, the daughter of Mark C. Sooy (brother of Laura (Sooy) Maxwell (see 1289 and 1301 Route 542). (Amanda was Ephraim C. Sooy, Jr.'s third cousin once removed.) This has to be another William Woolston, however. Ah, the confusion of past relationships!

William and Jenny moved from Herman to Mount Holly for a time, returning to Green Bank with two sons. At this point, William was employed by Will Johnson, the owner of the grist mill and sawmill on the Bull Creek. Later, he apparently worked for both William H. and Watson Sooy and served as caretaker for the Sooy-Forman estate, caring for the old Driver homestead for his friend, Ephraim C. Sooy, Jr. and, after his death, for his daughter, Elizabeth, and her husband.

As an old man in the 1930s, William Woolston was employed by the State Forestry Department as the first warden of the Green Bank State Forest, which the State had taken over from the Sooy family. Jessie Lewis remembers that the Superintendent's House on River Road was called the "Jenny Broom" house when she was a child in the 1930s. William and Jenny might have indeed lived there while he was working for the State. They seemed to have lived in a good many of the houses of Green Bank over the years.

Beck speaks of the tale of Woolston's conversion at the age of nineteen by the preaching of the Rev. J. Swain Garrison. "Uncle Billy," as he was called in his later years, and his wife, Jenny, were active members of the Green Bank Church and served as custodians, lovingly cleaning the little church each week in preparation for the Sunday service. He seems also to have served as a lay preacher and treasurer of the church. Billy died in 1939 at the age of eighty, and Jenny died in 1957 at eighty-nine.

The house has survived at least one major fire, and, in 1996, is the property of the Wesslers.

Photograph by John Pearce

The Sooy/Forman/ Wessler House - 1995

The Collins/Ford/Cavileer/Capaccio House
2441 Route 563

1935

Photograph by Augusta Weeks

When Nicholas Sooy II died in 1851, he left about seventy acres, bounded by Little Bull Creek, Route 563, and stretching across Route 542, with the exception of the Glass House lot, to his son, Josephus as his inheritance. On the 29th of November 1855, Josephus Sooy sold two small portions of the land, the purchase price for each being $200, the first of about three acres on the north side of "the road leading from Joseph Allen's to Sooy's Mills" (Route 542) to Reuben L. Gauntt, and the second of two acres to George W. Ford. This latter was the point of land between the present Routes 542 and 563. Through a second deed, dated September 17th, 1857, and again for an acknowledged $200, the conveyance was made again of the same piece of land from Josephus Sooy to George W. Ford. Apparently, there were some errors in the original deed that were corrected by the second, although this second deed covers a slightly larger piece of property than the first.

Ten years later, on the 18th of November, 1865 George W. Ford sold the property to William F. Cramer for a consideration of $210. It would appear that there was no house on this property as of yet. Not quite four months later, on March 21, 1866, Cramer sold it to Joseph Allen for $500. On the 10th of August of the same year, Allen sold it to Elizabeth Collins for $500. It seems that Mr. Cramer bought the property with the intention of constructing a house for resale, which was accomplished first to Joseph Allen, then to Elizabeth Collins, which would give a date to this house of 1866. Since structures were rarely mentioned in property deeds and $200 was a considerable sum for such a small piece of vacant land, it may me that one part of this house predates the 1855 sale of the land from Josephus Sooy to George W. Ford and the second part was added to the first in 1866.

In any case, Elizabeth and Richard Collins made this their home in the late nineteenth century. Richard was the son of an eminent surveyor, Matthew Collins. It seems that Elizabeth survived her husband, though there is no known date for his death, nor is there a stone inscribed for him in the Green Bank cemetery. Elizabeth dated her will the 7th of June, 1879, and it was proved on September 8, 1879. Nathaniel D. Van Sant of Lower Bank was her executor. She left land in both Washington and Mullica Townships to her son, James S. Collins, her daughter, Ursula Sooy, her grandson, Richard C. Mathis, and her granddaughter, Julia Ralor, in equal shares. She died on the 14th of August, 1879 in the eighty-second year of her life.

Lydia Ursula (b. March 23, 1832) had married William H. Sooy, Jr. (b. August 7, 1831), the blacksmith of Green Bank, and lived in the house which used to stand on the property at 1289 Route 542. She apparently inherited this house as her share of her mother's property. The couple had several children: Rebecca Elizabeth, Henry, Mark C., Laura A., Wina, Harry, and Mary. The Sooy genealogy notes that these latter three came from gravestone inscriptions, but, if so, they don't seem to be in the Green Bank cemetery. "Harry N." certainly does appear as the son of Willima H. and Ursula Sooy. He died at the age of twenty years, nine months, and twenty-one days, a sad tragedy for his parents. There are four stones for "Mary" Sooy, but none of them seems to have been for a daughter of William H. and Ursula Sooy. Perhaps the genealogist confused "Henry" for "Harry," which seems likely, and somehow got the others mixed up.

Laura (Sooy) Maxwell, wife of Captain Joseph Maxwell, inherited the house upon the death of her mother. She lived with her husband in what is now the Green Bank Inn. Her brother, Mark C. Sooy, inherited the house at 1289 Route 542 and seems to have continued the blacksmith operation of his father.

This house was later purchased by Robert Ford of the Tylertown Fords. Robert Ford reared a large family in this house that included Green Bank residents Mrs. Rose Ford, Mrs. Hattie Carney, and Mrs. Jessie Corliss. In the 1930s, Rose Ford and Hattie Carney were on the Board of Education. Mrs. Carney studied voice under Watson Sooy and was a soprano soloist. She used her gifted voice in the Green Bank Church for many years.

Jesse Cavileer of Lower Bank was the next purchaser. Then came Mike Capaccio. He purchased all three of these Collins/Sooy houses in the late 1930's after the death of Laura (Sooy) Maxwell. Mike's son, Ralph, lived in the Sooy house for a while, but it was later abandoned. Mike turned the Maxwell house into a bar, and made this house his liquor store. After his death, his widow sold the property, and it continues to be used as the local liquor store.

1995

Photograph by John Pearce

The Captain Maxwell House
1301 Route 542

Photograph by Augusta Weeks

1935

This house was either built by William Henry Sooy, Jr. (1831-1878) for his daughter, Laura, when she married Captain Joseph Maxwell or was constructed by the Maxwells themselves soon after their marriage. William Henry was the son of William H. Sooy, Sr., son of Nicholas Sooy I and Sarah Sears. He married Lydia Ursula Collins (b. March 23, 1832), daughter of Richard Collins and granddaughter of Matthew Collins.

William Henry and Lydia had seven children: Rebecca Elizabeth (who married William Miller), Henry (died unmarried), Mark C. (married Estella Hall), Laura A. (married Joseph Maxwell), Wina (died at age 33), Harry, and Mary A. This house, like that of her grandparents, Elizabeth and Richard Collins, (the Liquor Store in 1995) and that of Mark C. Sooy next door, reverted to Laura Sooy Maxwell.

William Henry Sooy's brother, Thomas K. Sooy, also lived in Green Bank at 1032 River Road. Thomas Sooy served as a member of the Washington Township Committee, Township Treasurer, and County Freeholder.

Captain Joseph Bush Maxwell was the son of Captain William Maxwell and Rachel Ann Hatfield who lived in Wading River. Joseph probably went to sea with his father as an apprentice and rose to chief officer. He followed the sea for over fifty years as captain of a number

Photo by Elliot Porter

Early 1950s
(Mike Capaccio is the man in the lower corner.)

of vessels. During World War I, the government of the United States issued a call for all trained sailors, and Captain Maxwell offered his services. He successfully sailed transports to and from France for the duration of the war.

Captain Maxwell was known to have been "a man of high purpose, strictly honorable in business and community life, and highly esteemed by all his townsmen." Joseph and Laura Maxwell were staunch Methodists and supporters of the Green Bank Church. Mrs. Maxwell served as a director on the Board of Education in Green Bank. They had four children: Mary Sooy, Elizabeth U., William H. and Mark Sooy. Captain Maxwell died in 1936 and was buried in his beloved Green Bank. His wife, Laura, died two years later and lies next to him in the cemetery.

Soon after the death of Laura (Sooy) Maxwell, Mike Capaccio bought this house and opened the Green Bank Inn. He also purchased the Collins house (now the Pine Barrens Liquor Store) and the Mark C. Sooy house (which stood on the property at 1289 Route 542). All three of these homes belonged to Laura Sooy Maxwell at one time.

Mike Capaccio c. 1944

The Green Bank Inn has passed through a succession of owners and today seems to have a special popularity with bikers on summer weekends. The bar is very rustic but would never be recognized by Captain Maxwell should he walk through the door some dark night. It was a Capaccio addition to the house.

The old captain may have found his eternal peace, however. If he had any interest whatsoever in returning to his final home on earth, his strict Methodist beliefs would have had him haunting this tavern in the pines long before now.

1995

The William H. and Mark C. Sooy House
1289 Route 542
(No longer in existence)

The date of this photograph is unknown, but it could be as late as the 1960's.

As has been previously noted, all the land between the Little Bull Creek and the present Route 563, with the exception of the Glass House lot, as well as land across Route 542, was the inheritance of Josephus Sooy from his father, Nicholas Sooy II in 1851. Josephus sold a three-acre portion of his land to Reuben L. Gauntt on November 29, 1855. Ten years later, on the 17th of October, 1865 Gauntt sold it to Elizabeth Collins for $300. Elizabeth would buy the property and house just across the street on Route 563 a year later. Once again, no mention is made of a structure on this property at the time of its purchase by Mrs. Collins. You will also recall that Elizabeth and Richard Collins's daughter, Ursula, married Green Bank's blacksmith, William H. Sooy, Jr., and the couple lived here while her mother lived across the street.

There were three William H. Sooys living in Green Bank during the last half of the nineteenth century. Nicholas Sooy II's son of that name, built his home on the corner lot where Route 563 crosses River Road. Nicholas Sooy II also had a brother, William H., who married Rebecca Weeks of Weekstown. Their children were Benjamin, Samuel, William Henry, Edwin Clark, Arthur, Elizabeth, Maria, Frances Anne, and Sophia. The William H. Sooy who lived here was the *son* of William H., Sr., the brother of Thomas K., and *cousin* of William H. down the road.

William H. Sooy, Sr. would buy a homestead farm in Wading River off of Turtle Creek Road (see WADING RIVER), on which his son Benjamin and his family would live. Arthur lived on a farm near the site of the old Washington Tavern on the Old Stage Road.

Since William H. Sooy, Jr. was born in 1831 and, therefore, was thirty-four when his mother-in-law bought the property and his wife, thirty-three, we must assume that he began his blacksmithing practice here soon after moving in. Jessie Lewis remembers the blacksmith shop next to this house when she was a girl, but it wasn't being used at that time. Archaeologist Budd Wilson of Green Bank surveyed the property for the second Mrs. Capaccio when she built her new house on the lot and found considerable evidence of the blacksmithing trade at the side of the old house, confirming Jessie Lewis's memory.

William H., Jr. and Lydia Ursula Collins Sooy were succeeded in the house by their son, Mark C. Sooy, who seems to have continued his father's blacksmithing practice. Mark married Estella Hall, and the couple had two children: Amanda Rebecca Sooy (b. September 6, 1883) and John Milton Sooy (b. September 6, 1886). John married Lillian Mae Green and their son, Bruce, was born in this house. His grandfather, Mark C., raised the boy after the death of his parents at an early age. Bruce later became a career officer in the military and lives in California (1995). On a recent visit to Green Bank, Mark Sooy recalled that his grandfather also had a modest auto repair business in his blacksmith shop. He had a pit, over which he could pull a Model T Ford schoolbus to work on it.

William H. and Lydia Ursala (Collins) Sooy's daughter, Laura, married sea captain Joseph Maxwell and lived next door in what is today the Green Bank Inn.

William H. Sooy, Jr., the blacksmith, died in 1878 and was buried in Green Bank, the town in which he had spent his entire life.

Apparently, Laura Sooy Maxwell bought this house from her nephew and niece on the death of her brother, Mark C. and still owned it when she died in 1938. It was purchased from the estate by Mike Capaccio after her death, along with the Maxwell and the Collins houses. While Mike turned the Maxwell house into a tavern and the Collins house into a liquor store, he found no use for this property except as storage. His son, Ralph, lived here for a while, then Mike abandoned it.

Gradually, time decayed the roof, windows were smashed, rain poured in, and nature's elements worked their inevitable destruction.

Courtesy of Budd Wilson

Bruce Sooy and
Ruth (Wobbar) Browne
mid-1940s

After Mike's death, his second wife, Helen wanted to build a new house for herself on the property, but the Pinelands Commission would only permit one house on the property, so this old place had to go.

The Chink Simpkins House
Route 542 near Lance Run Road
(No Longer in Existence)

The home of "Chink" Simpkins in the early 1940s

Henry Charlton Beck, in his book *Jersey Genesis*, paints a colorful and entertaining picture of the old gentleman who lived here in the 1930s. "Chink" Simpkins lived in Washington Township for the better part of a century, as colorful and humorous a character as you'd ever want to meet. ("I sort of got chucked up and stuck here like driftwood on the bank.") In his later years, he had cut wood for fifty cents a cord, worked the cranberry bogs, gathered huckleberries, fished for herring, and had done just about anything to keep going. "Chink" was notorious for hard work and hard drinking, and he'd been good at both. Beck quotes him using one of the old Mullica remarks when downing a drink of Jersey Lightning (Apple Jack) here along the river: "Godalmighty, him's hard but him's good."

"Chink" was born William H. Simpkins in 1858, the eldest child of Samuel and Elizabeth Simpkins' brood of nine. He was listed as being twenty-one on the 1880 census, and his siblings were Jesse A. (19), John (17), Mary J. (14), George (12), Sarah E. (10), Walter (8), Lewis (5), and Lizzie (3). Samuel was listed as a waterman in 1860, but by 1870, he seems to have given up the sea temporarily and is listed as a laborer.

"Chink" shipped aboard the vessels of Captain Watson Cale, Captain Hen Taylor, Captain Bill Leek, and Captain Otto Wobbar, mostly in the coastal trade of timber and charcoal to New York and is listed on the 1880 census as a sailor. He married Sarah Hester Ford, daughter of Samuel Pitman Ford and Margaret Emeline (Ford) Ford and sister of Julia Belle (Ford) Ford, wife of George Washington Ford. "Chink" and Sarah lived in several places within the township, notably on the Watson Cale place in Lower Bank. When that was sold, he and his wife bought this little house and farm on the Batsto-Wading River Road in Green Bank. His brother, John, lived across Route 542 in the house currently belonging to "Dutch" Jones.

Courtesy of Virginia Priest

William Henry "Chink" Simpkins

William Henry and Sarah (Ford) Simpkins had four children: Mary Emma, Ada, William, and Andrew. Mary Emma (b. 4/5/84, d. 1930) married Andrew Vassella of Hammonton. Virginia (Vassella) Priest is their daughter.

Once, he even came back from the dead, or at least that's the tale he related to Henry Beck. At the age of eighty, he came down with pneumonia, and there was no hope he'd survive. The doctor assured his family and friends that he'd done everything he could, but there was no chance old "Chink" would survive 'til morning. The doctor didn't count on Mullica stubbornness. No sooner was he out the door, than the old man managed to sit up in bed, struggling for air. "To hell with the doctor," he gasped, and from that moment on, he never stopped talking. Every time those around him tried to quiet him down, he flung profanities at them and kept right on talking. When the sun came up the next morning, old "Chink" was still talking. Guess all that chatter and cussing was too much for either God or Satan. Both decided they didn't want him yet! "Eighty years alive and two dead," he told Beck. "Sort of uneven. Ain't sure which is best yet, bein' dead or alive. You ought to try being dead some time."

Sarah died at the beginning of World War II in 1941 at the age of seventy-six, but "Chink" lived on. He continued to live here with his son, Andrew, until the draft board came a calling one day. Andrew was sent oveseas and gave his life for his country during the Normandy Invasion on

Courtesy of Virginia Priest

Mary Emma Simpkins, her mother, Sarah (Ford) Simpkins, and her brother, William

Courtesy of Virginia Priest

"Chink" Simpkins and his wife, Sarah

June 21, 1944. The Simkins family placed a marker on their Green Bank plot that proudly states his rank: Private First Class in the Twenty-second Infantry.

After "Chink" died for the second time in 1959 at the age of 101, the old house stood empty and forlorn. It slowly deteriorated through the 1960s, becoming ever more decrepit with years, until the trees and underbrush finally reclaimed its own.

"Chink" Simpkins, hard worker, hard drinker, and river humorist has returned to the dust of the earth, along with his old home - a memory almost forgotten.

Right: Virginia and Walt Priest
October 1997
Virginia is the granddaughter of "Chink" Simpkins and still has the photograph of his old house hanging on her dining room wall. I especially like the plaque next to it: "The best antiques are old friends."

May old friends always gladden your hearts, Walt and Virginia!

Photograph by John Pearce

Photograph by John Pearce

Above: Nelson and Evelyn (Simpkins) Ware - 1998
Evelyn is John's granddaughter. Evelyn Simpkins Ware and Virginia Priest are second cousins.

Nelson is holding the hundred year-old gun of his uncle, John Updike, and displaying the last of Uncle Jack's famous decoys.

Photograph by John Pearce
The Home of John and Georgianna Simpkins

Courtesy of Nelson and Evelyn (Simpkins) Ware

John and Georgianna (Ford) Simpkins
John W. Simpkins, "Chink's" brother, was born February 13, 1863 and married Georgianna Ford (b. October 18, 1868) c. 1884. He and his wife had at least six children: John, Jr., Samuel Lewis, Eva M., Viola, Merrle, and Frank. They lived in the house now owned by "Dutch" Jones, across Rt. 542 from "Chink's" house. Georgianna died on June 18, 1944, and John followed her a year later on September 8, 1945.

The Miners/Albor House
Route 542

1997

Dolly Albor taught in the Green Bank consolidated school for many years. From the time that the new school was opened in 1920, she served under the direction of principal Helena Wobbar. After Mrs. Wobbar retired, Dolly succeeded to the position. Thus, a great many adults from Washington Township received their early instructions from Miss Albor. This faithful teacher never married but lived with her brother, Joe, in this house near the nebulous border between Green Bank and Lower Bank.

The story actually begins with Fred and Minnie Miners, Dolly's grandparents, in the second half of the nineteenth century. Fred kept a blacksmith shop across Route 542 from this house. Fred and Minnie also owned several pieces of property in Bass River Township. The 1910 tax book indicates that they owned the 25-acre Gregory Bog, believed to be along Route 679, and 78 acres of the Levi French Tract. They also paid taxes on the land where the Merrygold Estates is today and on the old Adams Hotel property in New Gretna, as well as an additional house and lot adjoining that property. The taxes continued to be paid in their names at least through 1919, though Fred died in 1914.

Fred Miners (b. 6/2/1842, d. 7/9/1914) and his wife, Minnie (b. 7/18/1842, d. 5/3/1926) had two children, Fred, Jr. (b. 1/12/1872, d. 3/13/1941) and Matilda (b. 3/16/1866, d. 2/1/1883). The story is that Matilda "married" a Joe Albor, a union which was adamantly opposed by her parents. Joe and Minnie (Miners) Albor had two children, Joe, Jr. and Mary (called Dolly), after which, Matilda brought the two children back to her parents' house. If this is the case, then it all happened before Matilda was seventeen, for Maltilda died a month and a half prior to her seventeenth birthday. My "source" indicated that there was something more than this, so it is entirely possible that Matilda and Joe Albor weren't married at all.

So who was this Joe Albor, Sr.? The township records for 1848-1877 record that Joseph *Alber* and his wife, Ellen, had a son, William M. on September 20, 1854. Those same records indicate that Joseph and Helene *Albert*, had a son, Charles, on May 23, 1856, and a daughter, Elizabeth on March 9, 1858. Joseph and Helen *Albur* had a son, Richard, on May 19, 1861. In all cases, Joseph is listed as a laborer at McCartyville/Harrisville which indicates that whether the spelling was Alber, Albert, or Albur, it was probably the same couple. Did this Joseph Albor (of whatever spelling) take up with a young girl from Green Bank after his wife's death? If so, he would have been her father's age. No wonder the Miners detested the relationship.

Fred, Sr. and Minnie Miners are buried in the Green Bank cemetery along with their son, Fred, Jr. and their daughter, Matilda. No one seems to know what happened to Dolly and Joe Albor. They seem to have just faded away. It is believed that both are buried in Green Bank or Lower Bank, yet neither has a stone bearing their name.

South Bend
The Wobbar Homestead
(No Longer in Existence)

1935

Photo by Augusta Weeks

Otto H. Wobbar was born in Bremenhaven, Germany, on July 8, 1836, the son of Nicholas and Margaret Wobbar. It is said that as a young boy he often watched the ships entering and leaving the harbor and longed for adventure. Rather than have him serve the compulsory seven years of military service, his parents decided to send him to the United States. He arrived in New York City at the age of fifteen after a voyage of six weeks. His cousin, John Rapp, took him into his home until he was twenty-one, when he shipped out as a sailor.

While working as a sailor, he met Watson Cale, the captain of a vessel that transported charcoal from Bass River (now New Gretna) to New York. Cale must have taken a liking to the twenty-two year old German, for in 1858, Captain Cale invited him to take a trip up the Mullica on his ship. Apparently he found Lower Bank most attractive in more ways than one (he met and married Hannah Gauntt in 1859 at the age of twenty-three). Hannah and Otto had three children: John, Lizzie, and Mary.

Tragically, Hannah died at an early age, leaving Otto, a man of the sea away for months at a time, with three children to care for. The decision wasn't easy to make, but there was no alternative: the three children were given away at graveside. John was given to the family of Billy Maxwell of Wading River. The boy took the name of Maxwell and started a whole Maxwell family who aren't really Maxwells but Wobbars. He later built a home on the corner of Turtle Creek Road and Route 542 (See WADING RIVER/BRIDGEPORT).

On December 30, 1870, Otto Wobbar married again, this time to Esther Arnold Birdsall. Esther was the daughter of Hazelton and Sarah Ann (Miller) Birdsall of Bulltown and was born in Crowleytown on November 30, 1846. Otto built a little house for Esther just above Green Bank which was called South Bend. The name doesn't seem to appear in the local records at an earlier date and may have been what he called his homestead outside of Green Bank.

He and Esther had three children: Sarah Augusta, Charlotte, and Joseph Hazelton. Augusta later married Captain James Morrell Crowley. Lottie married Jonathan Weeks of Weekstown, across the river, and Hazelton

276

Wobbar married a Nova Scotian girl, Helena Davidson, and lived in the Josephus Sooy house at 1027 River Road in Green Bank. Hazelton later ran the little store on the river across from his house, and, for several decades, Helena was principal of the Green Bank School and taught the sixth through eighth grades. Their granddaughter, Marilyn, became the wife of Budd Wilson, who (in 1995) resides in the old home looking out on the river.

Otto followed the sea for thirty years before finally retiring to his home in South Bend with his wife, Esther. He had become the captain of at least one ship before he left the sea. Henry Charlton Beck, in a 1933 "Courier-Post" article, says that Wobbar's *Argo* joined the *Frances* and an unnamed vessel as sunken hulks in the Mulllica off the old Herman City Hotel of the Kosters.

> When she lay idle off-shore this gentleman, Otto Wobban [sic] ordered his crew to stop bailing to check a leak, he had seen the hand-writing on the wall, apparently, insofar as Hermann City was concerned. "Cut in for Gus Koster's ice house," he ordered, and the ship stuck in the mud, exactly where she is today.

Otto and Esther shared another thirty-four years together before death separated them. Otto died in this home on June 24, 1921, and his dear wife followed him on January 2, 1928. They rest from their labors in the cemetery by the river in Green Bank.

About two years later, a young man by the name of Bill Walters came from Brooklyn, New York. Bill had heard that there was opportunity for an enterprising man in the pines of New Jersey in the middle of the Great Depression and had the idea of starting a chicken farm. He married Arwilda Ford, moved into this house, and raised three youngsters here. In 1946, Bill and Arwilda moved into the Kirby house at 2419 Route 563 in Green Bank proper.

The house at South Bend is no more. The fire company finally burned it down as part of a training exercise. The South Bend road leaves Route 542 from the south side of Bel Haven Lake in Green Bank and eventually joined the Bulltown Road although you can't get through with a car in 1995.

Copied from a shipping ledger currently in the possession of Sarah (Cramer) Camillo, this short note shows Otto Wobbar signing on to a vessel under the command of Captain Watson Cale in 1865.

Esther (Birdsall) Wobbar, Otto Wobbar,
Jonathan Weeks, Lottie (Wobbar) Weeks

White Town

White Town is one of the forgotten towns of the pines and probably should have been included in that section of this work, but it lies so close to Green Bank as to have been considered part of it. White Town is mentioned in only two years in the Washington Township "Record of Births 1848-1877." In the year 1854, on June 25th, a little boy, Walter, was born to Nicholas and Sarah Sooy in White Town. In July of the same year, on the sixteenth, Samuel and Ann Nichols became the proud parents of their son, Samuel W. Once again, in August of 1854, a daughter, Rebecca, was born to Ampley and Elizabeth Heyson on the eleventh of the month. The following year, David and Susannah Ford had a son, David H., born on April 14, 1855.

The occupations of all the fathers, with the exception of Nicholas Sooy, was that of "laborer." This Nicholas was neither the famous tavern owner at Washington, who died in 1822, nor his wealthy son, who died in 1851, but the Nicholas Sooy, son of Noah and Sarah (Weeks) Sooy who married Sarah Messarole.

Where was this "White Town" that was so thoroughly forgotten that even the illustrious Henry Beck never even tried to find it when he was interviewing the local people for his newspaper articles. He did talk to "Snapper" Cobb, and the subject of this little town came up in the conversation. "Snapper," whose real name was Alanson, said he was born near there but that he had gone to school in Crowleytown, not in Green Bank, which indicates that his parents moved from the immediate area after his birth.

The Whites, for whom White Town was named, were a wealthy family from Burlington City, whose descendants spread out all over New Jersey. One of them must have settled near Green Bank at least by the beginning of the nineteenth century, and other families built houses nearby. No more than half a dozen houses ever stood in the hamlet, and all were abandoned by the end of the century.

At least three White families are listed in the 1850 census: David (50) and his wife, Hannah (37), and their daughter, Rebecca Jane (18); Alanson (44) and his wife, Amy (44), and their children, Benjamin (23), Lucy Ann (17), Cordelia (14), Lemuel B. (12), Emeline (8), Alanson (6), Catherine (4), Alfred (1/12); and finally Mary (50), Benjamin (30), Reuben (22), and Sarah (19). Another White, Cordelia (15), lived with D.M. McCollam and his wife, Louisa.

Alanson "Snapper" Cobb, the son of William and Emmaline Cobb, was seventeen in the 1880 census and eight in the 1870 census. His father is listed as a laborer. His siblings, listed in 1880, were Edward (15) and Mary Jane (12). In all probability, Emmaline's maiden name was White, probably the Emmaline listed in the 1860 census as the eighteen year old daughter of Alanson and Amy White. She also had a brother named Alanson who was a year younger than she was.

In 1860, there were only two White families in the township: Alanson, Amy, and their children, and David (59) and Hannah (47). Mary White is listed as living with the Thomas family. Mary doesn't appear in the earlier censuses, so she probably came from elsewhere. In 1870, only the family of Alanson White is listed. Three White girls: Annie (12), Mary A. (15), and Sarah E. (18), live with Catherine and Samuel Turner, a glassworker, and must also have come from outside of the township since their names do not appear on the 1860 census. The only Whites left in 1880 were Alanson (74), listed as a stone mason. The curiosity is that he is listed as "head of household" with Rachel (41) as his wife and his children: Alanson (36), Ada (12), Lenora (8), and Howard (4). Either he had lost his first wife, Amy, and had remarried a women only four years older than his son and started a whole new family, or the census is wrong and the son, Alanson, is married to Rachel and his father is living with them. The latter is more likely.

In the 1860 census, Alanson White is listed as a blacksmith. In 1870, he appears as a carpenter, and in 1880, he is a stone mason. William Cobb, "Snapper's" father, is listed as a waterman in 1860 and as a laborer in 1870 and 1880.

Whether any of the Whites remained in White Town by 1890 is open to question. The only White in the Green Bank cemetery is that of Mary Ann, the year and a half old daughter of Benjamin and Catherine White, who died on September 24, 1855. Two Benjamins appear on the 1850 census: the son of Alanson and Amy White, who was twenty-three, and another Benjamin who was thirty, and the brother of Reuben (22) and Sarah (19). A Mary (50) is living with them also, perhaps their mother. No Benjamin appears on the 1860 census.

So . . . where was White Town? Just above the intersection of Routes 542 and 563 next to the Green Bank Inn, a sand road leads off into the woods on the northeast side of Route 563. The area was logged several years back and is so overgrown the road is impassible. Back in the late 1960's however, it led back to the abandoned ruins of the old Civilian Conservation Corps camp. The site of White Town today lies off the beaten track, but in former times, it stood on the main road from Washington to Lower Bank. At Washington, is was known as the Green Bank road. The old road cut across what is now Route 563, went through White Town, then met what is now Route 542 near the Miners/Albor House.

During the 1930's, Green Bank played host to one of those government camps for young men that were a result of President Franklin Roosevelt's Depression-breaking legislation. The C.C.C. gave young men an opportunity to both work and gain knowledge of forestry, construction, and the like in a period of time when there was simply no work to be found. Some, like Horace Somes, Sr. of Wading River, met local girls and never returned to the place of their birth. Others moved on to new places of employment. Many lost their lives during World War II. Long after the C.C.C. buildings were abandoned, the archeologists at Batsto used one of the buildings for storage of historic items from their digs, as well as old papers and maps. It was the only place that the State of New Jersey would give to the men who were doing the important research for the storage of their artifacts. An arsonist proved to the state authorities the hard way that an isolated building out in the woods is no place for valuable objects, even if they were only valuable to historians.

This, in any case, was the location of White Town. For many years, a single old chimney played sentry for the entrance road to the C.C.C. camp. In all probability, that lone chimney was all that remained of the little village now lost in the pines.

The Spell
Emma Van Sant Moore

I have an understanding with the pines,
Magnolia, laurel and green-briar vines.
They weave about me such a spell
Of quiet peace, that I know full well—
Although my feet have wandered far,
It is for me a sure lodestar
That draws me back and e'er inclines
'Mid Jersey pines.

Another of native poet Emma Van Sant Moore's charming poems of the pine barrens and the Mullica valley.

Views of Green Bank circa 1909

The Old Store
Corner of River Road and
Route 563

Courtesy of Jessie Lewis

View of River Road
Looking Downstream
from the Crossroads
with Route 563

Green Bank, N.J.

Courtesy of Jessie Lewis

Green Bank, N.J.

View of River Road
Looking Downstream
from the Crossroads
with Route 563

Courtesy of Jessie Lewis

Views of Green Bank circa 1909

View of the Old Store and Tavern
Corner of River Road and Route 563
"I thought you would like to have a picture of George in his auto.
The other one is Tom Sooy and his son Lu. October 8, 1913."

The Corner of River Road and Route 563
The bridge is just to the right of the picture.

Views of Green Bank circa 1909

River Road Looking Upriver from the Intersection of River Road and Route 563

The Batsto-Wading River Road (Route 542) Bridge over Bull Creek
This bridge may have been slightly closer to the old mill pond dam than the present bridge at this location.
The Sooy/Johnson Sawmill stood just across the bridge to the right. The grist mill site is to the immediate right where Bill Bell has his canoe rental business today.

Views of Green Bank circa 1909

The Upper Dock Behind the Old Store
The schooner has to be over a hundred feet long!

The Old Iron Swing Bridge of 1855
This bridge was replaced with a drawbridge in 1926

The People of Green Bank
1910 - 1940

Courtesy of Budd Wilson

L to R: Shirley Koster, Alyce
Crowley, Ruth Wobbar

Courtesy of Budd Wilson

The Birdsall Sisters: Esther Wobbar,
Abbie Jones, and Tillie Salford

Courtesy of Budd Wilson

The woman's identity is not
known

Courtesy of Budd Wilson

Delbert Weeks & Alva Cobb

Courtesy of Budd Wilson

The gentleman's identity is
unknown.

Courtesy of Budd Wilson

Ruth Wobbar is sitting in the rear seat with her mother,
Helena next to her. The others are not identified.

The People of Green Bank
1910 - 1940

On the Front Porch of the Wobbar House
1027 River Road
Jonathan Weeks, Sarah A Crowley, Alva Cobb, Augusta Weeks, Mathew Maxwell, Delbert Weeks, Birdsall Crowley

In Front of the Old Store
The men are not known,
nor is the year, but the car
is turn-of-the-century.

Jesse   A.   Sooy

Jesse Alfred Sooy was the son of Nicholas Sooy, grandson of Noah Sooy and Sarah (Weeks) Sooy, the brother of Nicholas Sooy II and son of Nicholas Sooy I.

Jesse was born in 1843, and died in the Civil War in 1864. He was only twenty-one when he was killed. This family lived in Green Bank for several generations, and, in all probability, the above photograph is of this Jesse A. Sooy.

There were others from Green Bank who served in the Union army. Maurice Ford, who married Hester Sooy and later lived in the old Green Bank tavern, served in Company E, Third New Jersey Volunteer Cavalry during the war. Maurice was born a year after Jesse Alfred Sooy in 1844. Theodore Sooy, born in 1837 to Samuel and Catherine (Leek) Sooy, grandson of Nicholas II, also served during the Civil War. William Mathias Johnson, son of William Johnson and Esther (Sooy) Johnson and grandson of Nicholas Sooy II, served with Company C, 9th New Jersey Infantry Volunteers. He was the brother of Edwin B. Johnson and uncle of William Asa Johnson (see "Herman" for the Johnson family).

The Sooy genealogy does list another "Jesse A. Sooy" though. *This* Jesse A. was born on July 20, 1873 and married Irene Wilson of Lambertville, N.J. He was the son of Ezekiel Sooy and Keturah (Prickitt) Sooy, the son of *another* Ezekiel Sooy and Sarah (Crowley) Sooy. Now things become confusing. Ezekiel (the one that married Sarah Crowley) was supposedly the son of Noah Sooy (the same Noah who married Sarah Weeks, his first wife, brother of Nicholas Sooy II, by his *second* wife, Mary (no surname given). This family of Sooys, though, did not seem to live any where near Green Bank. *This* Jesse A. Sooy lived in Trenton, N.J. and had no particular connection with Green Bank. Given the Green Bank source of the photograph, it is highly unlikely that the photograph is of this Jesse A. Sooy.

The Green Bank Church
1081 River Road

Courtesy of Jessie Lewis

The Green Bank Church
c. 1910

The origins of this little meeting house are, like so many other things in the Jersey pines, shrouded by the mists of time. The people of Green Bank have long celebrated the date of 1748 as the building date of the first log structure on this site, but this date is based only on oral tradition. The absence of a written record of the building of the Green Bank church does not of itself mean that there was *not* a church building in this vicinity at a very early period. In order to delve into the mystery, we must reexamine the ownership of the Green Bank plantation during its early years.

Green Bank was a private estate until the death of Nicholas Sooy II in 1851, and no part of the original 300 acres was sold to others until that time. It passed from Samuel Driver to Joseph Sooy to William Richards to Nicholas Sooy II intact, so there were not really many people who lived in the area except for these families and those who worked for them until after 1851.

We know that Samuel Driver was in possession of the Isaac Pearson survey of 300 acres at the time of his death in 1748. He was laid to rest next to his house in a grave that would form the nucleus of the Green Bank cemetery.

When John Driver, presumably Samuel's son, sold the plantation to Joseph Sooy, son of Yoos, in 1752, he excepted a four rod plot where his father had been buried. On the 19th of July, 1771, Andrew Anderson sold 151 acres of the Richard Bull Survey to John Sooy, Joseph's son, giving father and son adjoining plantations. Another of Joseph's sons, Nicholas I, built a tavern on the Road to Little Egg Harbor at about the same time.

On July 27, 1782, Joseph's twenty-one year old daughter, Jemima, died, and she was buried in her father's side yard next to the grave of Samuel Driver.

Joseph Sooy lost his plantation when Jacob Ridgeway sued him on February 13, 1787, and the sheriff was directed to sell the property on the 15th of May of that year. Sheriff John Hollinshead sold the whole three hundred acres and farmhouse to William Richards of Batsto on June 26, 1790, and it remained his property until just prior to his 1823 death, when Nicholas Sooy II, Joseph's grandson, bought it back into the family. Joseph Sooy and his family appear to have been the only inhabitants on the land during his tenure. His sons built homes elsewhere in the vicinity. John Richards lived in Green Bank during the William Richards' period of ownership, and David Mapes is supposed to have lived there prior to buying his farm in Lower Bank, but other than that, it seems that there were few families who called it their home. Thus it is unlikely that one or two families would need a church in the vicinity. Not so with the next owner.

Nicholas Sooy II was a very successful businessman who owned vast tracts of land along the Mullica from Wading River to Crowleytown. He had at least one fish factory out in Great Bay, negotiated the sale of lumber and charcoal through his storehouse and dock, loaded those products aboard his own coastal schooners, and resold them in New York, Philadelphia, and in cities all along the American coast. Nicholas built several houses for the members of his large family on his Green Bank estate, though he himself lived in his uncle's house in what is now Herman.

The first mention of the church building itself is in his will, written in 1850 and probated on his death in 1851:

> *"Twentieth : - I give and bequeath to my four sons, Samuel Sooy, William Sooy, Josephus Sooy, and Nicholas Sooy, Jr., the "Meeting House" and one acre of ground for the use of a grave-yard. The "Meeting House" to be for the use of the Methodist Episcopal Church, to them and their heirs, and assignees for ever, and for no other purpose."*

Local tradition indicates that his son, William H. Sooy, who inherited the surrounding property on his father's death, rebuilt the structure in 1871. Stanger, in *The Methodist Trail in New Jersey*, records the rebuilding date as 1861 rather than 1871. Whichever date is correct, the little church would hardly have needed the extensive rebuilding William performed if it had been built within ten or twenty years. William H. Sooy did such a thorough job that it would be doubtful if an expert could find a means of dating it beyond his reconstruction.

Many of the people who settled the wilderness of the American colonies were a very religious people. They fled the intolerance and oppression of their homelands in Europe for the freedom of the American wilderness.

Courtesy of Jessie Lewis

The Green Bank Church
Probably 1940s or possibly early 1950s

Some came especially for religious freedom. Others came for economic opportunity and the possibility of owning land. Very early on, they and their neighbors constructed places of worship, usually a log cabin, in which they could gather for Sunday services. Most of the denominations based in Europe did not send out a great quantity of ordained clergy, so lay people led these weekly worship services.

Whenever a minister happened in the area, he was invited to stay in a someone's home and asked to preach in the local church building or even in an open field. It didn't matter what denomination he represented. People were too hungry for the Word of God to care which brand they happened to get at the moment.

The Quakers at Little Egg Harbor built their Meeting House in 1709, within ten years of the arrival of the first Quaker settler in the area. The Presbyterians near The Forks, built their church immediately upon *their* arrival in 1707. Presbyterian missionaries passed through this area in the mid-seventeen hundreds and preached in local homes of families who welcomed them. The Loveland and Leek families in Bass River and the people of The Forks were especially happy to see them. The Rev. David Brainerd converted most of the local Indians to Christianity during his stay at the Forks between 1742 and 1745. The Rev. John Brainerd made a journey down from Manahawkin to Bass River, and probably on to the area of The Forks in the first half of the century as well. Generally, these itinerant preachers conducted worship in local homes or barns. The log church that those early Presbyterians built was, no doubt, a special treat for these devoted servants of the Lord.

Methodist societies were organized throughout southern New Jersey after the conclusion of the Revolutionary War. Robert Steelman, in his history of the Southern New Jersey Conference of the United Methodist Church, *What God Has Wrought*, notes that though Methodist preachers had been active prior to the war, most of those who had been born in England were loyalists and returned to the Mother Country during the fighting. John Wesley wrote a pastoral letter to the Methodists in 1773 entitled, "A Calm Address to Our American Colonies" in which he contended that the "liberty" held dear by so many of those in the colonies was contrary to the fundamental laws of their country, Great Britain, and disobedience to the commands of their rightful sovereign, King George.

Needless to say, this did not endear his followers in the colonies to those who supported the revolutionary cause. During the war years, only Francis Asbury, of those born in England, remained in the colonies, and American-born preachers were beaten and abused by mobs and even imprisoned for their "treason." From 1778 to 1780, Asbury remained secluded in Delaware and did not preach.

The year 1780 seemed to have been the turning point for Methodism. In that year, there were only one hundred ninety-six Methodists in all of New Jersey. From that time on, though, Methodism grew exponentially.

Photograph by John Pearce

The Green Bank Church - 1995

Photograph c. 1970 by Budd Wilson

Three years later, there were over a thousand Methodists in the state, according to Steelman. Until the end of the war, however, the American Methodist preachers were unordained lay preachers. Wesley finally decided that God had showed his will in the American victory and that there should, therefore, be an American church.

In Great Britain, the Methodists were still part of the Church of England, but no Anglican bishop would ordain Methodist clergy for the new American states. Wesley ended up ordaining two men first as deacons, then as elders, and a third to the office of Superintendent. Though Superintendent Coke would later call himself bishop, as would Francis Asbury, Wesley never quite approved of the designation.

What the newly organized Methodist Church did have was zeal for the Lord, and her clergy and lay preachers served their Lord with unflagging enthusiasm. The Methodist missionaries swept all before them. Areas that had been predominantly Quaker or Presbyterian or adherents of any other denomination quickly succumbed to the dynamic preaching of the horsebacked advocates of Methodism. They were circuit-riders, but not like any with which we are familiar today. Dedicated men spent their lives in the saddle, travelling from one village to another, preaching the Gospel of Christ in homes, tiny churches, barns, or in open fields, until they had converted entire populations. Where there hadn't been church buildings before, they were built now. Where a building had been used by the preacher of any denomination venturing into the area, they now became exclusively Methodist.

Steelman says that, in 1785, Francis Asbury left New York on September 7th of that year and travelled down through New Jersey to the "Morris River," preaching at various locales along the way. After he preached at Monmouth, there are no entries in his journal for a week, and Steelman postulates that he must have travelled down "through Batsto and Atlantic County for his next appointment on the 17th" at Port Elizabeth, Cumberland County. He and his party had to stop at various private homes along the way for the night and may well have stayed at John Sooy's in Green Bank (Herman), or perhaps with Joseph Sooy in Green Bank proper. The problem is that, in 1785, there was no bridge at Wading River and no direct road from town to town. The easiest road "through Batsto" would have been the Road to Little Egg Harbor through Bodine's and Sooy's Inn.

Once again, Steelman notes that Methodist preachers Ezekiel Cooper and Nathaniel B. Mills travelled through Mercer, Burlington, Ocean, and Monmouth counties in 1787 and preached at Speedwell Furnace, Batsto, Bodine's Tavern, Bass River, Tuckerton, and Manahawkin. No mention is made of a stop in Lower Bank or Green Bank, and it would seem that their route followed the Philadelphia/Little Egg Harbor Road.

Steelman records that The Rev. Richard Sneath rode the Bethel Circuit, going "down the Tuckahoe Road to Doughty's Tavern, over to Mays Landing, down to English Creek, Bargaintown and Absecon to Port Republic, then up to Batsto, through Egg Harbor and up the present Route 30 to Tansboro, Williamstown, and Bethel" in 1796. Once again, the northeast side of the Mullica seems to have been neglected.

Asbury, himself, made a trip along the coast of New Jersey in 1791, stopping at Potter's Church in Lanoka Harbor and in Tuckerton two days later. He left there on a Saturday and, as mentioned in the Batsto chapter,

"rode a dreary, mosquito path, in great weakness, to Batsto works," preached there on Sunday, *"and advised the people to build a house for the benefit of those men so busily employed day and night, Sabbaths not excepted, in the manufacture of iron - rude and rough, and strangely ignorant of God."*
(Steelman, p. 34)

Is it possible he stopped briefly to give a sermon along the way? If he did, he didn't mention it in his journal, and his most likely path was still the Road to Little Egg Harbor through Bass River, Bodine's, and Sooy's Inn.

In 1799, the Reverend Richard Sneath traveled the Burlington Circuit, and this time, his route included Lower Bank. According to Steelman, his path took him from Moorestown, to Burlington, Lumberton, Mount Holly, Buddtown, Browns Mills, Pemberton, Bodine's, Lower Bank, New Gretna, Tuckerton, Manahawkin, Waretown, Good Luck, and Toms River. At least one of the Methodist preachers made it to Lower Bank this time.

Several of the early preachers did not keep very good notes as to where they preached. Often, they would simply note the route they had taken and the names of the people with whom they had stayed and at whose home they preached. It is very likely that one or several of these clergymen made stops at private homes in the vicinity and preached in the open air or in barns to the people along the Mullica.

Oral tradition also has it that "camp meetings" were held in the field next to the old home of Nicholas Sooy II in Herman. The Methodists were quite fond of camp meetings. Preachers would come from a distance, be

Photograph c. 1970 by Budd Wilson

housed by local families, and spend a week or even two weeks conducting emotional preaching and testimony sessions, but once again, local traditions of such meetings may stem from the first half of the nineteenth century rather than from an earlier period.

Francis Asbury was once again in the Batsto area when he preached at the dedication of the new Pleasant Mills Church in 1809. On his trip there, it is said, he stopped at the home of Nicholas Sooy I in Green Bank (Herman), and preached in an open field either next to the Sooy house or in a field that would later become the Glass House site in Green Bank.

Unfortunately, Nicholas Sooy I did not own the Herman property in 1809. It was his son, Nicholas Sooy II, who bought the Herman property from his cousins, the heirs of his uncle, John Sooy, in 1815. John Sooy had died back in 1792, and it is presumed that his widow and her children continued to live in their house until it was sold.

Whoever owned the house, Francis Asbury did dedicate the Batsto/Pleasant Mills Church in 1809, staying at the Batsto Manor House with the Richards family. According to Steelman, he preached at Batsto on Friday, April 21st. On Saturday, "they rode along the Mullica River to Tuckerton where Asbury preached Sunday morning and afternoon." Once again, no mention is made of any stops along the way for preaching services, and the distance would have taken the better part of a day to cover, but it is still entirely possible that he did stop in the vicinity of Green Bank or Lower Bank. At least the new road connecting the towns had been built in the previous year.

After the 1799 mention of Lower Bank as part of the Burlington Circuit, the next specific mention of either the Lower Bank or Green Bank church is on an 1836 list of churches of the New Brunswick District as given by Steelman. Here, Lower Bank and Green Bank take their places along with Barnegat, Bass River (New Gretna), Brookville, Forked River, Manahawkin, Tuckerton, West Creek, and points north. The Port Republic church is listed in the Camden District, and Batsto/Pleasant Mills is listed as part of the Trenton District.

Frank Stanger, in *The Methodist Trail in New Jersey*, says that Nicholas Sooy II built the Green Bank church prior to 1850 "although we have no record of the exact date."

Since many Methodist churches met in private homes, the mere presence of a name on the list does not mean that there was a church building in that location. We know, for instance, that the property for the Lower Bank Church was not purchased until 1842, yet Lower Bank's name appears on the list in 1836.

Again local tradition also tells us that the lumber used in the construction of the church building and the interior furnishings came from the sawmill of Nicholas I, which stood next to the Bull Creek, at the location of the later William Johnson sawmill, at the dam which is now the outlet for Bel Haven Lake.

It is entirely possible that either Nicholas I or Nicholas II operated the mills at some time after brother or uncle John's death in 1792, and there are indications that the mills stood on Bull Creek about 1803, but a date after Nicholas II's 1815 acquisition is more likely.

One further curiosity: the building does not appear on an 1849 map of Burlington County. Information for such maps had to be gathered prior to the actual date of publication, but it is strange that the church does not appear if it existed for too many years before that date.

So where are we with this precious little church in the pines? More than likely, the existing structure was built by Nicholas Sooy II with lumber sawn in his sawmill on Bull Creek at some time after his acquisition of the property from William Richards in 1823.

Photograph c. 1970 by Budd Wilson

If a member of the Richards family built it with Nicholas Sooy II's help, a date between 1815 and 1823 is possible. If a Richards built it without Sooy participation, the date could be pushed back to 1794. An earlier date is very doubtful.

In any case, it is most likely that both Lower Bank and Green Bank hosted both circuit-riding preachers of the Methodist faith and camp meetings from the period of 1799 on, though those visits may have been painfully far apart. There seems to be no record of a Methodist society in either town until that of 1836, and no mention of a Methodist house of worship in either until the construction of the old Lower Bank Meeting House in 1842.

The Green Bank church has been lovingly maintained by its local people for almost two centuries, though it has never had a large membership. Its devoted few have had a deep love for their little church and its ancient burial ground by the Mullica where so many of the people of the past have labored and loved and been laid to rest.

Photograph by Budd Wilson, Jr.

The Green Bank Cemetery

Christmas Card of Watson Sooy
showing the Green Bank Church

The Pulpit
Photograph taken before the
Altar Table was stolen.

The Green Bank Church - 187th Anniversary - July 7, 1935

Courtesy of Budd Wilson

Jonathan and Lottie Weeks

Courtesy of Budd Wilson

Augusta Crowley and Helena Wobbar

The Green Bank Church
188th Anniversary
July 12, 1936

Courtesy of Budd Wilson

Courtesy of Budd Wilson

Courtesy of Budd Wilson

Two Hundredth Anniversary Picture
July 11, 1948

The Choir in 1949
L to R: Marilyn Browne, Betsey, Shirley Simpkins, Doris, Betty,
Agnes Walters, HazelBrowne, Lillian Walters, Barbara Wills

Green Bank Methodist Church

The following is a list of names of the preachers as far back as we have been able to learn who preached in this church:

Robert Given	1844	Joseph Clark	1918-1919
Edwin Waters	1850	Alfred Burr	1919-1920
Ferrot		Charles Ebell	1921-1925
Charles M Griffin		C. Mott Cramer	Part of 1926 (sick)
Shellhorn	1862	Jesse Richards Parl	1926-1927
		Peter Sampson	1928-1929
Lucius Manchester	1863	Norman Pangburn	1929-1931
Peter Burd	1867	Albert Bitters	1931-1932
Lewis Atkinson	1872	Russell Nixon	1932-1934
James E. Lake	1873	Charles Rhubart	1934-1935
Wm A Lilly	1877	Nathan Trainer	1935-1936
Alfred Wagg	1879	U. G. Hagaman	1936-1938
S. P. Cossoboon	1879	Donald Weist	1939-1941
John W. Magee	1881	Edward Jelley	1941-1942
Lively		R. Blaine Detrick	1942-1945
Eugene F. Sherman	1883	Wm. F. Parker	1945-1946
George W. Pine	1884	Champin Goldy	1946-1949
George E. Reybold		*Lower Bank Circuit - merged with New Gretna*	
Wm. Goodenham	1888	*1946*	
Verona A Lonier	1889	Howard Shoemaker	1950-1952
Noble	1892	and Wm. Bowen	
S.K. Moore	1892-1893	*We are back in Lower Bank Circuit - 1952*	
Fergus Slater	1894-1895	Donald Phillips, Jr.	1952-1953
Joel Rose	1895-1896	Earl C. Horick	1953-1954
J. S. Garrison	1896-1897	Franklin H. Bird Jr.	1954-1957
Joseph Johnson	1898-1899	Bernard Shropshire	1957-1958
J.W. Veal	1900-1902	Gerald Huntsinger	1958-1959
J.W. Wainwright	1902-1903	Daniel Stone	1959-1961
J. Tower	1903-1903	George Groom	1961-1963
Frank Vanhise	1905	L. David York	1963-1965
James Ryan	1906-1907	Clyde A. Phillips	1965-1967
Bruerre	1907-1908	Donald H. MacLaren	1967-1969
Wm Wagson	1908-1909	Carl Farrell	1969-
J. Horner	1909	Walter Jeinkoskie	1969-
J.L. Lowden	1909-1912	Fred Sciscoe	1980-1990
Geo. W. Southard	1912-1916	Jana Purkis-Brash	1990-1991
James Budd	1916-1917	Bud Erbb	1992-
Franklin Bowen	1917-1918		

In This Sacred Chapel

by

Jessie F. Lewis
September 29, 1991

Under dawn soft mist
Of turning day,
This tranquil church,
Stands apart
From strands of pine.
Marble markers define
Release in peace
Silently line by line,
Embracing earth,
Marking end of life's
Unyielding time.

Within walls of charity,
Holding past and present
In their holy spell,
Love's indwelling spirit
Lends rest and sanctuary
From cradle to wedded grave,
A seminary of hearts
To conceive an inner citadel.

Empty rows of ancient seats
Bear witness to toll of time,
Bittersweet the memory,
Mindful of unseen presence,
Their example enscrolls the heart
Becoming our paradigm.

The enduring word of God
Upon the lasting altar
Attend all passions
Of human hearts,
From love and charity
To greed and hate,

Mirror of crowning glory
Or abysmal despair,
When lamps of oil
Replenish life's luckless flame too late.

Joy and sorrow mingle
With all sacraments
Of the Church,
To baptize, to marry,
To share the host
To bless and to bury.

The hush of stillness
Bids all bonded souls
To face their dawning, no need to fear
What penance hold,
Love carries the imperfect
Beyond their darker threshold.

Blest are they
Who come here seeking
And feel love
Enfold their pleading,
For there will be
No more despairing,
Their yearning, no more the needing.

Here is God
With answering love
To share our joy
To bury our sorrow,
To fortress our strength
And embrace our hearts
As we brave our own --

tomorrow.

Early Schools of Washington Township

The State of New Jersey was tardy in promoting free pubic elementary education within its borders. Though schools for the poor and academies for the rich were in operation by 1830, completely free public elementary schools were nonexistent at that time. Though the legislature did not provide for free public elementary education in the state until 1871, Washington Township records indicate the existence of schools that were at least partially funded with public money as early as 1831. Those who could afford to pay to support the teachers and the schools had to do so. Only the poorest families received public support. The first Superintendent of Education, appointed in 1848, wrote that "a merciful man ... would not winter his horse" in the existing district schoolhouses (see *A New Jersey Anthology*, edited by Maxine N. Lurie, N.J. Historical Society, 1994, p. 14).

The first school committee mentioned in the township records consisted of William H. Sooy and Nicholas Sooy of Green Bank, elected at the township meeting held at Town House, Quaker Bridge, on March 8, 1831, and one hundred dollars was to be raised by taxation for the use of the school in that year. The men mentioned were probably Nicholas Sooy II (b. 1782 d. 1851) and his brother, William H. Sooy (b. 1798 d. 1861). Nicholas II was a highly successful business entrepreneur who lived in the "Old Homestead" in Herman/Green Bank. William H. (one of three) was a lawyer who lived about a quarter mile up the Atsion Road from the Washington Tavern.

The following year, 1832, Jesse Evans of Martha joined the Sooy brothers as a member of the School Committee. Town Meeting voted to raise only fifty dollars for the use of the school in that year. (At the same meeting, it was voted to raise $400 for the use of the township for roads, etc.) The year 1832 saw a controversy of some sort within the government of the township and the major families of Green Bank and Lower Bank withdrew from the local government. The names of Sooy, Weeks, and Cavileer disappear from the annual records for several years.

At the second township meeting in 1832, held a month later than the

Courtesy of Budd Wilson, Jr.

The Green Bank School - October 1916

This little schoolhouse stood on the property at 2411 Route 563. The building was turned into a house when it was no longer needed for its original purpose. Susanna (b. 1873) and Arthur W. (b. 1860) Miller lived here until their deaths: his in 1931; hers is not recorded. Later, the old school was torn down and a new house built on this lot.

first one, the actions of the previous meeting were declared null and void. Samuel B. Finch was elected as the sole member of the School Committee, replacing the Sooys and Jesse Evans. Finch was also one of the Chosen Freeholders from 1831-1833. Later that same day, yet another town meeting convened and declared the previous one invalid. This time, Jesse Richards and Samuel Goforth were elected to the School Committee. Jesse Richards was, of course, the patriarch of Batsto. Mr. Goforth's identity is unknown. Resolution #6 of this meeting still stipulated that only $50 was to be raised for the "use of the Schools in Township to Educate the poor Children for the year 1832."

The year 1833 saw a huge increase in the funding for the schools. While township taxes remained at the $400 level, the school tax rose to $200! Joseph Townsend replaced Goforth on the committee with Jesse Richards. An additional building or buildings must have been constructed that year, for in 1834, the school tax returned to the customary $50. Goforth returned to the committee with Jesse Richards and was joined by Samuel L. Richards and James Maxwell of Wading River.

In 1835, the committee again expanded and the Richards family claimed a majority. Jesse and Samuel L. were joined by Thomas H. Richards, Ephraim Cline, and James McCambridge of Speedwell. Once again, the annual receipts for educating the poor was set at only $50. In 1836, only Jesse Richards and Ephraim Cline remained on the school committee, joined by Samuel Weeks, the tavern keeper from Lower Bank.

The composition of the school committee continued to change through the years, but not until 1839 was the tax level raised. In that year, Town Meeting voted $250 for the use of the School Fund. Once again, the size of this figure must indicate the construction of another school, for in 1840, the figure went back to $50. That seems to have been a sufficient amount to support education for those unable to pay for many years. In 1843, there isn't even any mention of funds for the schools. Then in 1844, the sum is once again raised to $150. The notes for 1845 clearly state, however, "no Money be raised for the use of Public Schools." Jesse and Thomas H. Richards are the only members of the school committee for that year. No funding figure is listed for 1846, though in 1847 and 1848, it is $50 again.

In 1847, there were seven schools: Batsto #2, Speedwell #3, Harrisville #4, Bridgeport #5 (Wading River), Mullicus #6 (apparently Lower Bank), Green Bank #7, and Crowleytown #C. In 1848, the amount raised was still $50, but in 1849 and 1850, it rose to $75. In 1851 and 1852, it stood at $200. In 1852, Speedwell was made part of Shamong Township and removed from Washington Township's list of schools. The resulting reorganization left six schools. In 1853 through 1855, $300 per year was raised. In 1856, it jumped to $600 but was lowered to $400 the following year.

The year 1855 was the first in which the township tax and the school tax were balanced. Apparently, the Town Meeting tried to minimize the burden on the local taxpayers caused by the rise in school taxes by lowering the funds available for the management of the township. School taxes just kept their upward spiral. In 1856, only $300 was raised for the township but $600 for the schools. In 1857 and 1858, it was $400 and $400. In 1859: $400 and $600. In 1860, the last year of peace prior to the commencement of the Civil War, the township taxes jumped a whopping 375% to $1,500 and the school taxes by 33% to $800. That meant that in one year, the overall taxes for the township went from $1,000 to $2,300 at a time when the local glass industry was floundering and the railroads were decimating the river trade. Worse was yet to come.

In 1861, not quite three months after the secession of South Carolina and her sister states of the lower South, the township meeting held at Sam Weeks' tavern in Lower Bank on the 12th of March voted $2,000 for the township and $1,000 for the schools! That must have proved a bit much for the residents to swallow. Only one of the four members of the Township Committee retained their positions in 1862, and the tax was dropped to $1,000 for the township and $500 for the schools. No figures are given for 1863, but in 1864, at the height of the national conflict, only $800 was raised for the township and $500 for the schools, though there is a note that $6,497.00 was received in cash for volunteers and $10,584.29 was raised for that purpose (local municipalities helped to provide bonuses for men who would sign up in the state units that were sent into the war).

The township records do not resume again until the year 1872 when only $250 was raised for the township. A figure for the schools is not mentioned nor are the members of a school committee. An act of the legislature in 1871 had made the school committee independent of the township government and gave it the power to raise their own funds.

During the late nineteenth century after Harrisville became part of Bass River Township, there were six schools within Washington Township (including Randolph): Batsto, Crowleytown, Green Bank, Lower Bank, Washington, and Wading River. They were typical one-room schoolhouses with a single teacher instructing all the elementary grades.

The following quotation about the schools of Washington Township is taken from the "History of Schools in Burlington County," written by the County Superintendent, Edgar Hass, in 1876.

Washington Township

Formerly, this township included Randolph, part of Shamong, and part of Woodland.

Batsto, Dist. No. 97. Although this place was settled in the year 1766, yet there have been but few or no educational facilities afforded to the children. In 1827, there was a log-house 10x12 feet, used in common by a small school and the church, but, in a short time, this not meeting the demands of the neighborhood, the children attended school at Pleasant Mills, Atlantic County, until about 1844, when the present schoolhouse, a one-story frame, 28x32 feet, was erected by the inhabitants of the town. It was occupied by a pay-school, until the time of the establishment of the public schools, when it took the name of "Batsto School," Dist. No. 1, now, No. 97. The tuition of each pupil in attendance, was $1.00 per month, a tax that many poor people could not afford to pay. About the time the present school law was enacted, the school numbered about sixty pupils, but owing to the failure of the manufacturing interests in the community, the number of children has been greatly reduced. Though laboring under many difficulties, yet the Trustees have managed to keep the school open eight months in the year. The school is well supplied with books, maps, charts, etc. It is now in the charge of Emma J. McIlvain. Trustees: Joseph McIlvaine, J.W. Shields. Joseph M. McIlvaine, Dist. Clerk.

Crowleytown, Dist. No. 98. The first school-house in this place of which we have any mention, was built in the year 1857. It was a one-story frame, 14x18 feet, worth about $100, and used until 1867, when it took fire and burned down. A new one, 26x38 feet, was erected the following year, at a cost of $770. The glass works having ceased operation in 1865, the number of pupils has since been somewhat diminished. Present teacher is Miss Mary F. Cale. Trustees: E.A. Koster, Watson Cale, Dist. Clerk.

Green Bank, Dist. No. 99. The first school-house in this District was erected in the year 1835. It was a one-story frame, 16x18 feet, and worth about $150. It was used until 1868 when the present one, 20x30 feet, was erected at a cost of $425. It is surrounded by one half of an acre of ground, and now occupied by the school in charge of James E. Allen. Trustees: Asa Weeks, Towers Sooy, William H. Sooy, Dist. Clerk

302

At that period of time, public education in the rural areas (including the areas close to the city that we'd call "suburban" today) did not provide for schooling beyond the sixth or possibly the eighth grade. Parents could pay to send their children on to private schools in preparation for college if they chose, but the vast majority of people made due with the basic reading, writing, and arithmetic taught in these little school buildings by underpaid women and men whose dedication and sacrifice has never been fully appreciated.

Teens were expected to be a part of the life around them and not continue as adolescents. Boys found employment. Girls married at an early age. Not until the second half of the twentieth century was there sufficient wherewithal and time for young people to continue their education beyond the rudimentary levels.

Both men and women acted as school teachers in the one-rooms schools of Washington Township. Generally, the women were single and boarded with someone from the town where the school was located. The reports of the State Superintendent of Schools for the last half of the nineteenth century show that the Washington/Randolph Township schools were only open about seven months a year. The reason given is that there were not enough children to warrant employing a teacher.

The condition of education in the rural districts of New Jersey at that time may be surmised from the 1861 report of Theos. T. Price, Town Superintendent for Tuckerton, which is at left.

The building of the "new" Green Bank School in 1919 changed everything dramatically. Things got 'modern'. No longer did the children walk to a school in their own town. Now they had to ride a school bus. These rural children experienced the niceties of busing before city and suburban children did. For the first time, all the children in the township went to one school for the first eight grades. When they were ready for high school, they were bussed to Egg Harbor High School.

In 1998, the Green Bank School still contains the first to the eighth grades with kindergarten added. The school now boasts six new classrooms which were added a few years ago in a separate building. Egg Harbor High School is no longer. High School students are bussed to Absegami Regional High School.

Mrs. Helena Wobbar, originally from Nova Scotia, the wife of Haze Wobbar, was the principal and teacher of the sixth through eighth grade classes for many decades. For much of that time she was assisted by Miss Barnes, and by Dolly Albor.

For over thirty years, these women taught the children of Washington Township with diligence and love and influenced the people of the township immeasurably. Somewhere on that school property should be a monument to Helena Wobbar and the other early teachers for their lifelong commitment to the youth of Washington Township.

Helena Wobbar never complained that she was wasting her life in some backwater hamlet, receiving little remuneration and having no future. She was proud of her students and proud of her work, and justly so.

A surprising number of the little schools of Washington Township survive. Wading River's is part of a house on the Turtle Creek Road. Lower Bank's was sold to Fred Noyes, Jr. and moved to Smithville as part of the Noyes' complex of stores. Jenkins school is now the Jenkins Chapel, though two predecessors at Washington burned in the 1880's. Crowleytown school is a private home on Route 542 just downriver from Crowley's Landing. The schools which stood in Batsto, Green Bank, Speedwell, and Harrisville are gone. Speedwell's fell to the widening of Route 563. Friendship's is in Tabernacle. Green Bank's was abandoned and finally torn down. Batsto's seems to have just faded away. It stood on the river side of the present Route 542 where it crosses the site of the old sand road to Weymouth Junction. Harrisville's last school building perished in the fire of 1914. The original school burned in the 1880's. Both were rented facilities.

The 'New' Green Bank School

(All Photographs are courtesy of Budd Wilson, Jr. unless otherwise noted.)

Courtesy of Nelson Ware

November 1921

Augusta Koster
6-8th Grade 1927-8

Richard Cavileer
6-8th Grade 1927-8

304

The Lower Grades of the Green Bank School - 1920

Front Row: Morris Mick, Leslie Leek, Samuel Fox, Victor Sooy, Clyde Adams, Ralph Holloway, Warren Coffee
Second Row: Charles Nichols, Isaac Maxwell, Eddie Weber, Thomas Maxwell, Robert Lippincott, Merle Wills, Charles Weber, Maurice Ford **Third Row:** Marie Weber, Janice Koster, Lavinia Bryant, Anna Leek, Dorothea McAnney, Bernice Maxwell, Alice Cramer, Hilda Ford, Eliz. McCormick, Edith Sooy, Ella Patten **Back Row:** Mrs Rita Wooston (teacher) Albert Sooy, Marian Adams, Lorena Ford, Iona Woolston, Lucinda Weber

The Upper Grades of the Green Bank School - 1920

Front Row: Norman Sooy, John Burr, Earl Maxwell, Unknown, Unknown, Cullis Weeks, Samuel Simpkins
Middle Row: Hollis Koster, Glendon Koster, Howard Ford (?), Susy Maxwell, Alice McAnney, Marie Weber **Top Row:** Gilbert Cramer, Lem Maxuel, Jr., Verna Cavileer, Miss Hewett, E. Jensen, Emily Weber, Unknown, Mary McAnney

8th Grade Class - 1927
Martina Adams, Lucinda Weber, Helena Wobbar, Margie Cavileer, Clara
Cramer, Edward McCullough, Hilda Weber, Hilda Ford
(Rodney Koster absent)

Girl Reserves Picnic
June 1932
Along the Mullica River
at Green Bank

Girl Reserves
1932 - 1933
Mary DeCamp, Mildred Patten, Sadie Mick, Ruth Cavileer,
Virginia Leek, Lola Nichols, Marjorie Ford, Ida Ford,
Mrs. Wobbar, Edith Parks, Evelyn Ford, Bertha Ford, Marion
Corliss, Dorothy Nichols, Eleanor Ford

8th Grade Class - 1928
Florence Weber, Edna Stewart, Sara Thomas,
Augusta Koster, Mrs. Wobbar, Ada Jones

8th Grade Class - 1930
Thelma Gaskill, Ruth Wobbar, Julia Smith, Harold Cavileer
Eva J. Barnes, Acting Principal
Helena Wobbar, Principal

The Teachers
May 1934

Mrs. Wobbar
(Principal and
Teacher)
Hilda Hewitt
(Helping
Teacher)
Miss Barnes
(Teacher)

306

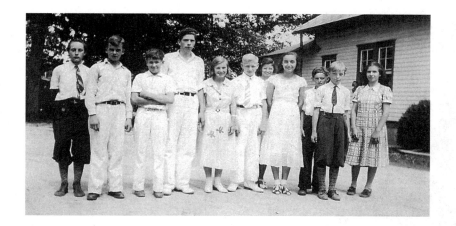

Safety Patrol 1938 - 1939

Cale Cavileer, Edward Patten, George Mick, George Ellice, Anna Patten, William Carney, Edith Taylor, Norma Ford, Calvin Downe, Donald Cavileer, Laura Ford

Henry Mick
6-8th Grade
1927-8

Randel Leek
6-8th Grade
1927-8

Ruth Crammer
6-8th Grade
1927-8

8th Grade Class - 1940
Evelyn Simpkins, Ida Nichols, Margurite Updike, Lillian DeBow, Laura Ford, Gladys Cramer, Mrs. Wobbar, boys: Calvin Downs, James Smith, Caleb Cavileer

Those Participating in the Play, 'Old Fashioned Girl' given by the Eighth Grade Class of 1935:

H.D. Wobbar, Mary DeCamp, Lucy Patten, Sadie Mick, David Cavileer, Darthy Thomas, Betty Leek, Irene Bell, Chas. Rhiebart, Miriam Leek, Elsie Ford, Violet Patten, Burrell Ford

4-H Jr. Forestry Group 1935 - 1936
Mrs. Wobbar, Harold Maxwell, Harold Downs, Francis
Mick, Billy Crowley, Howard Ware, Weldon Bell, Bobby
Bell, Walter McAnney, George Ellice, William Patten, James
Patten, Emil Brown

The School Buses

8th Grade Class - 1938
Edith Taylor, Phylis Ford, Norma Ford, Nelson Ware,
George Mick, Bill Carney, Edward Patten.
Mrs. Wobbar is on the right.

Menu Club 1941 - 1942
Miss E.M. Smythe, Ida Ford, Margaret Core,
June Ayles, Doris Cavileer, Mrs. Helena Wobbar
Kneeling: Helen Smith, Eleanor Downs,
Betty Crowley

8th Grade Class of 1941 - 1942

Upper Row: Doris Cavileer, Laura Brown, Betty Crowley, Helen Smith, Margaret Core, Rose Downs, Mrs. Wobbar
Lower Row: George Raynor, Thomas Cramer, Howard Patten, Richard Leek, Wesley Core

Florence Weber   Jesse Cavileer
6-8th Grade 1927-8

8th Grade Class of 1942 - 1943

Ida Ford, Jane Ayres, Ernest DeStefano, Donald Groff, George Mathis, Clarence Patten, William Simpkins, Clayton Ford.

Lydia Ford   Edna Stuart
6-8th Grade 1927-8

Class Date Unknown

Thelma Gaskill   Pearl Ford
6-8th Grade 1927-8

The Teachers
Date Unknown

Marion Maxwell
6-8th Grade 1927-8

Edwin Downs
6-8th Grade 1927-8

8th Grade Class - 1944

Boys: Norman Ford, Donald Cavileer, Arthur Sooy, Harry Ayres,
Girls: Hattie Ford, Marjorie Downs, Helen Groff, Mrs. Wobbar

John Quigley
6-8th Grade 1927-8

Probably 1937

Jim Patten, Bing Yates, Mary Mick, Harold Maxwell, Ida Ford, The
Bell Twins: Robert and Weldon, Peggy Corlis, Billy Crowley (Sr.)

Winnona Ford
6-8th Grade
1927-8

Ada Jones
6-8th Grade
1927-8

Sara Thomas
6-8th Grade
1927-8

310

Class Date Unknown

First Row: 1. Margarie Ford 2. Adelia Maxwell 3. Unknown
Second Row: 1. Eleanor Ford 2. Bertha Ford 3. Unknown 4. Violet Maxwell 5. Virginia Leek
Third Row: 1. Courtland Koster 2. Jim Patten 3. Ralph Ford 4. Edith Parks 5. Ruth Cavileer
Fourth Row: 1. Unknown 2. Jess Nichols 3. Bobby Mick 4. Bruce Sooy 5. ? Mick 6. Paul Brown 7. Unknown

Field Day Exercises
Green Bank, N.J.
May 25, 1922
Dance: "A Hunting We Will Go"

Class Date Unknown

Edna Crammer

Elsie Weber

Esther Ford

Ruth Wobbar

Arwilda Ford

6th - 8th Grade Class
1927 - 1928

Sadie Nichols

Lyda Nichols

Mrs. Helena Wobbar
Teacher

Randall Leek   Harold Cavileer

Arwilda Ford

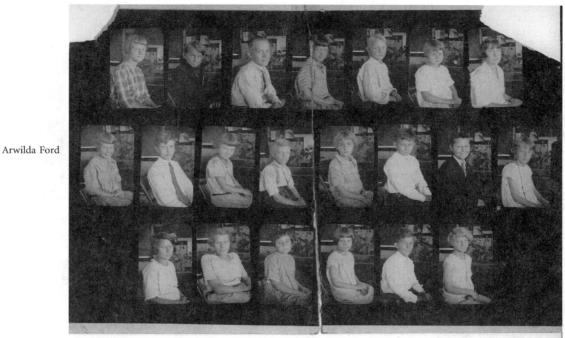

Class Date Unknown

Courtesy of David Cavileer

1935 or 1936 Graduating Class
Front Row: Mary Dekamp, Sadie Mick, Miriam Leek, Darthy Thomas, Lucy Patten, Violet Patten
Second Row: Charles Hawkins, Charles Rhubart, David Cavileer, Burrell Ford

Ann Inman

Eighth Grade

Class of 1951

Elaine Adams

Anna Priest

Tommy Ade

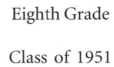

Alex DeStefano

Charles Sampayo

Marilyn Browne

Alexander McIntosh

Charles Nichols

314

1948
Elaine Adams, Virginia "Jeanie"
Priest, Hazel Browne

1950

Barbara Woolston is on the left.

"Aggie" Walters

1948
Shirley Siefert & Agnes Walters

1953
Center:Agnes Walters; R: Marilyn Browne

Elaine Adams
June 6, 1951
Green Bank School

1953
Agnes and Dean

315

Hilda Ford
Age 10
May - 1946
July 25th

Flora Ford
Age 12
May 1946
May 25th

Elaine Adams, Ann Inman, Marilyn Browne

Hazel Browne

Bobby Breitzman

Bobby Breitzman

"To Mrs. Wobbar from Vinnie
June 7, 1953"
George McCarten and Dolly Albor

Harrisville

Courtesy of Budd Wilson

The Howard Feyl Collection

    Howard Feyl was a young man who attended the Y.M.C.A. camp held at Harrisville at the beginning of the second decade of this century. He took several photographs at that time, both before and after the fire that destroyed the paper village. Bill Hawthorne became friends with him late in life, and Mr. Feyl gave his collection of photographs to Bill. Bill permitted Budd Wilson, Jr. to copy the photographs for the Batsto research library, to keep a copy himself and give one to Steve Eichinger of Wading River. My copies of these photos are taken from the ones in Budd Wilson's collection.

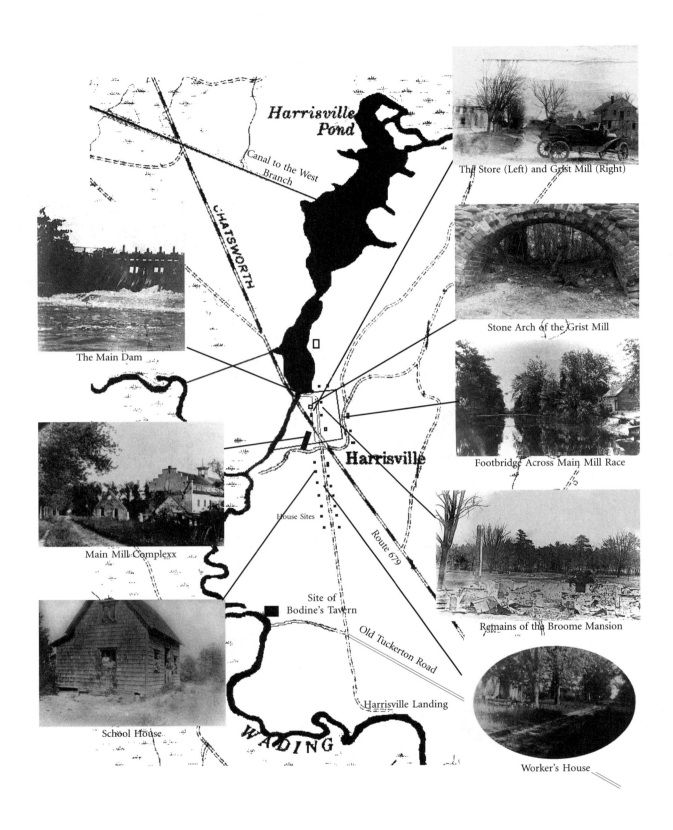

Harrisville Pond

Canal to the West Branch

CHATSWORTH

The Store (Left) and Grist Mill (Right)

The Main Dam

Stone Arch of the Grist Mill

Footbridge Across Main Mill Race

Main Mill Complexx

Harrisville

House Sites

Route 679

Remains of the Broome Mansion

Site of Bodine's Tavern

Old Tuckerton Road

Harrisville Landing

School House

WADING

Worker's House

Harrisville

Gone With the Wind

Some stories should naturally just begin, "Once upon a time, a long, long time ago." Those stories are usually romantic tales of knights and ladies and of a way of life, as Margaret Mead put it, "gone with the wind."

The reader is inspired to dream by the ruins of once-great abbeys where cowled monks chanted vespers in high-vaulted chambers, or of castle ruins brooding over a mist-shrouded coastline, where lords and their ladies-fair danced to many an ancient tune. Perhaps the remains of a Southern mansion, burned during the War Between the States, evoke fantasies of a more genteel way of life.

The pinelands seem so empty of such inspirations of fancy. Here were no lords and ladies, no great castles and churches, no plantations with hundreds of slaves toiling in the fields. Here were only adventurous men who dared to dream of wealth in the pines. Here the common man labored in forge and furnace, glass house and paper mill, tilled his fields and cared for his cows, trying to make a life for his wife and children.

What is left of the sweat of their brow, their heartaches and their triumphs? Very little, indeed. Time, neglect, and raging fire have effectively wiped their memory from the land that gave them life. Trees have reclaimed their farmlands, forest fires have destroyed the last traces of their little homes, and their families have moved elsewhere, perhaps not even remembering their roots in the pines.

One forgotten town, though, defies the ages. Just off the Chatsworth-New Gretna road stand the last remnants of McCartyville, or Harrisville as it has been called since 1851. Lost in the dense growth just off the highway rise stone walls that still tower over the landscape. In 1999, they are almost invisible, covered as they are by summer growth and fenced off from the curious who would hasten their destruction.

For over a hundred years, this spot was home to hundreds of men and women who raised their families in the tiny houses and strolled along neat, gas-lighted streets in early evening. Here the clanking and pounding of great machinery echoed through the pines, producing paper for the Philadelphia and New York markets.

Now only the last remnants of the mill's sandstone walls recall the throbbing life that once thrived deep in the pines.

Once Upon A Time

The second half of the eighteenth century was an age of adventure. Colonists in the English province of New Jersey had their minds set on dreams of a better life for their families, of homesteads and businesses across every portion of the land, of eventual wealth and prosperity. The little rivers of South Jersey beckoned them with the promise of unlimited water power, a wonderful prospect in the pre-gasoline engine and preelectric motor days. Rivers provided the power for the production of all kinds of useful goods and carried those goods to market on their bosoms. Rivers were the lifelines that bound early society together.

Evi Belangee, Jr. came early to the pines of New Jersey. In about 1750, fifteen years before Charles Read started Atsion and Batsto, Belangee built himself a "Skit" mill on the West Branch of the Wading River, northwest of the later location of Harrisville. The generally accepted thought is that a skit mill was a combination sawmill and grist mill that probably used the same waterwheel to run both mills within the same building.

Everyone had to farm to some extent in order to survive in such a wilderness area. There were no stores in which to buy food, so vegetables had to be grown in home gardens. Every settler raised cows, pigs, and the like for their meat, and the animals had to be fed by grain produced right there on a person's farm. Grain had to be ground into flour in order to make bread, and that was the purpose of a grist mill. In 1701, the first grist mill anywhere in the area was established in Little Egg Harbor on what would become the Tuckerton Creek.

Belangee thought the West Branch of the Wading a likely spot for another such business venture, but he was smart. The second major local industry was timber. Of that, there was plenty. The vast forests of trees could be chopped and brought to his mill, cut into boards, shingles, and lumber, then floated down the river to the Mullica and shipped via that great highway of commerce to Philedelphia and New York.

Every settlement needed both a grist mill and a sawmill in order to grow and prosper. Batsto, Atsion, Green Bank, Lower Bank, and Wading River - all boasted such mills at an early date.

Where did his business come from, though? Prior to the Revolutionary War, this area did not boast any significant population, so Belangee probably processed his own timber for shipment and sale elsewhere and ground his own grain, that of those who worked for him, and that of local farmers. With the growth of settlement and commercial ventures that accompanied the conclusion of hostilities with Great Britain, Belangee's foresight was rewarded.

According to K. Braddock-Rogers of the University of Pennsylvania, in a paper he wrote for the "Journal of Chemical Education" in 1931, Belangee also dammed the East Branch of the Wading River in about 1760 and built a sawmill on the site. Arthur Pierce, in *Iron in the Pines*, cites Braddock-Rogers' work and comes to the same conclusion. Remains of this dam were visible when the State of New Jersey rebuilt the main dam nearby several years ago. The site of Belangee's dam is couple hundred yards upstream to the north from the main dam at Harrisville lake and lay across the old channel of the East Branch. Belangee's dam only raised a head of water of about five or six feet, but that was sufficient to power a water wheel. His mill must have prospered for it remained in operation for over sixty years.

Many historians have made the mistake of locating the skit mill on the East Branch of the Wading River rather than on the West Branch, but this does not appear to be the case. On the 1836 map of McCartyville, Belangee's original 109 acres is listed under the name of Thomas Ballinger with the date of 1743. This parcel cut across the East Branch above where the two branches join. It's southwestern border was upstream from Bodine's Tavern on the Road to Little Egg Harbor.

Potts Didn't Make Pots

Anyone familiar with Revolutionary War history ought to recognize the name of Isaac Potts. Prior to the beginning of the war, Potts owned a forge outside of Philadelphia but leased its actual operation to another. By the time Washington's weary army limped into its winter encampment at the Valley Forge, Potts' forge had been burned by the British. He did still own a house in the vicinity, though, which became the winter home of the General-in-Chief and his wife, Martha, for the winter of 1777-1778.

After the war, this same Isaac Potts ventured into the South Jersey pines and built a furnace on the East Branch of the Wading River which he named for *his* wife, Martha. In 1795, he also built a forge and slitting mill a bit south of his furnace at Martha. The property for the forge and slitting mill was purchased from John and Francis Bodine of Bodine's Tavern on the old Road to Little Egg Harbor. Potts enlarged Belangee's dam to gain a little more height to the lake.

Furnace, forge, and slitting mill were all necessary parts of early iron production, as previously mentioned. A furnace produced pig iron and other miscellaneous cast items: kettles, pots, stove plates, cannonballs, and the like, that are made from molten iron poured into molds. A forge then reheated the iron pigs, formed them into bars, and made them into other useful implements such as those produced by a blacksmith. A "four fire" forge, as mentioned in Potts' newspaper advertisement when he sold the business two years later, may have been a bloomery, producing a modest quantity of iron directly from ore and having the finery and chafery processes to refine it. A slitting mill had a huge set of rotary sheers that cut sheet iron into nail rod, wagon-tires, etc. According to Pierce, Ezekiel Reed invented a nail-cutting machine in 1786 which made nails from nail rod as part of the function of a slitting mill.

The complex on the East Branch of the Wading was meant to be complementary to the forges and furnaces in the area. The Wading River Forge and Slitting Mill bought iron pigs from Martha, forged it into iron bars, then pressed those bars into sheets and sliced them with the huge sheers.

Potts, like other early investors, probably did not plan to stay in the business long. He invested money to build an industry, then sold it at a considerable profit to himself with little risk. Two years after he had built the forge and mill, Isaac sold it to George and William Ashbridge of Philadelphia, and to a local resident, Joseph Walker. The actual date was April 24th, 1797, and Potts got $20,000 for the 350-acre parcel from the brothers and Walker.

On the Main Road

This section of the pinelands was not as isolated as it seems when Walker and the Ashbridges purchased their mill and acreage. Just downriver was Bodine's Tavern. This popular public house stood on the banks of the Wading River where the main, and only road, from Tuckerton to Cooper's Ferry (Camden) crossed the river. Until the Wading River Bridge on what is today Route 542 was built in 1814, this was the only crossing for through traffic. Coastal schooners could make it up to the town of Wading River south of Bodine's, and the Martha workers were always making the trip downstream for good times at the tavern.

During the next nine years, the Ashbridges and Walker bought Belangee's saw mill, but the Philadelphia brothers were anxious to get their money out of the place. They finally sold their interest to their partner, Joseph Walker, in 1806. Walker seems to have had a new partner waiting in the wings, so to speak, and sold a half interest to John Youle, who made "patented" cambosses (ships' stoves). He and Youle continued to operate the complex until 1815, building new forge fires and a second grist mill.

August 14th, 1823, was not a good day for the Wading River Forge and Slitting Mill. It had gone through several owners and partnerships since 1815, but on that day in 1823, everything was consumed by that pinelands terror: fire. One of the owners at the time, John Hallock, built a castor-oil mill on the property after the fire, but it was not successful.

Finally, at a public sale in September, 1828, Samuel Richards, brother of Batsto's Jesse Richards, owner of Atsion, and part-owner of Martha and Speedwell furnaces, bought the property for $1,895. He apparently got a bargain. The acreage of the slitting mill property had increased by this time to three thousand acres. Whether Richards ever did much with the old mill site is doubtful. Four years after his purchase, he sold it to William McCarty, Thomas Davis, and Isaac Ashmead for $7,000, making a neat profit of $5,105, or 365% for a four-year investment. (Bill Hawthorne says it went back to Read first, then to McCarty, et al. See NOTE on this page.) Pierce indicates that there is no evidence showing that the Wading River Forge and Slitting Mill was still in operation when the "estate" was sold to McCarty.

PAPER IN THE PINES

McCarty, Davis, and Ashmead had no interest in continuing the iron production of the past. That industry was falling apart because of competition from Pennsylvania iron furnaces. Unlike other areas that were trying glass-manufacturing, the new investors thought they'd try making paper. Once again, waterpower was of vital importance to the new industry. The partners incorporated their concern as the "Wading River Manufacturing and Canal Company" and named the new town after the dominant member of the concern: McCartyville.

McCarty was apparently enthralled by canal-building and went to work right away at the Wading River site. He built a new dam below that which had powered Belangee's mill, by which he raised the head of water a few feet higher than previously. He then dug two canals from the lake to the location of his new paper mill. The smaller of the two canals was to power his grist mill, then flow into the larger one just after it left the paper mill.

McCarty and his partners were not exactly original thinkers. By 1834, others had thought of paper, too, and at least twenty-nine were already operating in the state. McCarty built an entire town in the pines, including a new saw mill, grist mill, company store, a boarding house, numerous dwellings, including one for whomever was running the place, and the huge mill itself. It was McCarty who planned the town layout as it would remain for its entire existence.

The main canal ran a total of 1,585 feet from the lake to the mill building and was dug completely by hand (not a great feat in South Jersey sand though certainly one worth noting). According to author Bill Hawthorne, the canal was lined with stone and had a depth of approximately fourteen feet when it entered the main building. The grist mill canal was also lined with sandstone and got its water from the main mill race just after it exited the lake. It ran for about 220 feet into a small pond in front of the grist mill, then on into the mill and out the back. The outflow ran next to the sawmill to give it power and finally into the tailrace of the main mill about 420 feet further along. Both then ran into the Wading River.

The village of McCartyville covered about 2,360 feet from north to south and was bordered on the south by the Old Stage Road. The road to Speedwell Furnace cut across the center of the village, and the road to Martha Furnace ran up the side of the main mill race towards the north.

NOTE: According to a list of owners included in an article by Bill Hawthorne in the "South Jersey Magazine" of Winter 1976, Walker must have sold his share to John Youle at some time during this period, for Hawthorne records that Youle sold a half interest to Bartholomew Ward and another half interest to Justin Layman (no dates given). Ward then sold his half interest to the New York Machine Fac. Co. and Layman his half share back to John Youle, Sr. John, Sr. conveyed his half to his son, John, Jr. The New York Machine Fac. Co. sold their half to William P. Rathbone, who then sold it to Philo Andrews. John Youle, Jr. sold his half to John Hallock. After the fire of August 14, 1823, Hallack sold a quarter interest to Samuel J. Read and another quarter interest to Timothy Pharo. Pharo then sold his quarter to Samuel J. Read. That should leave Samuel Read owning half and Philo Andrews the other half. Apparently, Read and Andrews went bankrupt and the 3,000 acres of the Wading River Forge and Slitting Mill property was sold at a public sale in September, 1828 to Samuel Richards for $1,895.00.

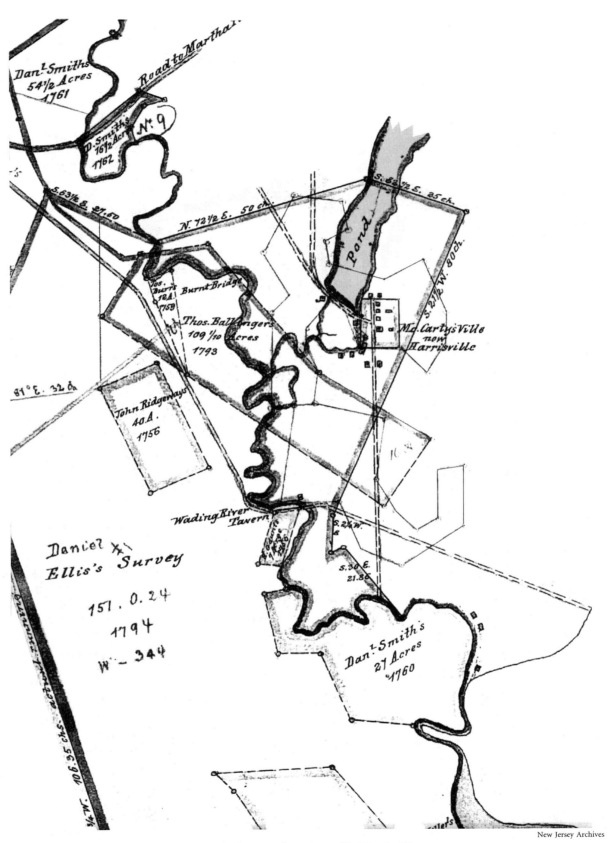

Detail of Map of McCartyville/Harrisville

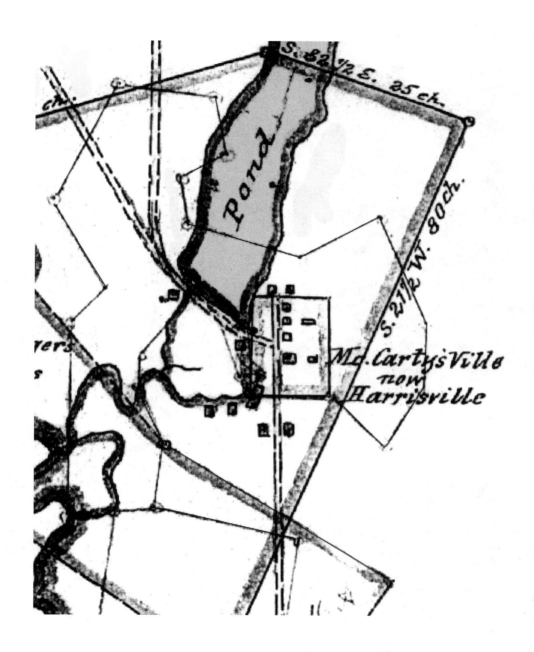

Copied March 14th 1861.
By Saml S. Downs, Deputy Surveyor, Tuckerton N.J.

MAP OF LANDS
Belonging to the
WADING RIVER MANUFACTURING & CANAL CO.
at
Mc. Cartysville, N. J.
By
ENOCH HAMMEL Dep. Surveyor.
1836.

Detail of Map of McCartyville/Harrisville

The Paper Mill after its abandonment at the turn of the century.
This building was built by McCarty in 1834 and was substantially unchanged
during the ownership of the Harris brothers.

McCarty had really built himself a valuable asset in the pines. In its first three years, its capital assets had gone from $65,000 to $200,000!

McCarty sold his controlling interest to the main company, still called the Wading River Manufacturing and Canal Company, in February of 1836, but he remained as a director of the company, with Thomas Davis, Henry Carey, Isaac Lea, and Laurence Johnson. Actually, this was a smart move on McCarty's part. He received $55,750 for the sale of his assets but retained his management and his stock interests in the company. Thus he insulated himself from financial disaster just a year before the panic of 1837.

The assets of the company, as defined in the sale, included a 550-acre farm and a schooner. In its incorporation papers, the company obtained the rights to dig a canal from McCartyville to tidal water on the lower Wading River and to charge a usage toll of eight cents per ton per mile, but there is no evidence they ever used this option. They did offer $25,000 in stock in 1837 to finance additional construction. A canal would have brought shallow-draft vessels up a couple of miles closer to the two major industries.

As Arthur Pierce correctly noted, a deed from this period (BC Book X 11, p. 516) indicates that McCarty dug a canal from the lake at Harrisville to the West Branch of the Wading River in order to raise the water level in the lake. This canal was approximately one and three tenths of a mile long. The deed conveys "all right, title and interest . . . in and to the water-power, Tumbling Dam on Speedwell Creek (the West Branch of the Wading River) above the Mill, and the Canal to convey it into Wading River." A tumbling dam, by the way, is a dam that always has water going over it, as opposed to one like the main dam at Harrisville that could be completely shut off and the water diverted through the mill race, if necessary.

The Wading River Manufacturing and Canal Company also ventured into the area of a new fad: the production of silk. Silk from the orient was a precious commodity to the early United States, and people dreamed of riches gleaned from locally-produced silk. Mulberry trees were planted in great numbers throughout the town, and silk worms imported. Unfortunately, the experiment was a failure.

Paper *was* making money, and the company prospered. Once again, though, fire reared its ugly head. In November, 1846, the huge paper mill was heavily damaged. The Wading River Manufacturing and Canal Company borrowed money from the Burlington County Bank at Medford, Mahlon Hutchinson of Philadelphia, and Thomas A.

Haven of Burlington to rebuild the mill in 1847, but that was the beginning of the end for this formerly successful company. By 1851, the Burlington County Bank would control McCartyville.

THE HARRIS BROTHERS

Richard Harris, thirty-two years old in 1851, had learned the paper manufacturing business under William McCarty along with his younger brother, Benjamin and was now returning as an owner. He and his brother William, twenty-eight that year, had signed an agreement to purchase the three hundred acres that comprised the center of the enterprise, including all its improvements. They borrowed the $6,000 required by the contract in order to purchase the property but had to make payments over the next three years. Not until 1856 would the property become legally theirs.

Those three years did not go smoothly, though. Thomas Haven died suddenly after signing the agreement, and the Burlington County Bank cancelled the agreement. The brothers finally petitioned the court in 1854 to have the original agreement honored. Not until April 17th, 1855, did the Orphans' Court of Burlington County issue a decree order that Virginia Haven, administrator of Thomas Haven's estate, issue a deed to the Harris brothers for the property. They now owned Haven's one-fourth part of the property for the sum of $875 paid to the estate. The other three-fourths had been sold to John H. Simon of Philadelphia by the Burlington County Bank on the first of June, 1854.

Courtesy of Budd Wilson
Ruins of the Main Building
Date Unknown

Simon delayed until 1856, but he finally sold his interest in the property to the Harris brothers for $8,000. He made the offer, quickly accepted, to finance the Harris loan if the brothers would put up their quarter interest as collateral, which they did. Finally, on the 2nd of November, 1856, the Harris brothers owned McCartyville and all its buildings. Their brother, Benjamin, and their father, John, joined with them to see that the terms of the agreement with Simon were met by June 1, 1860. Seven months later, brother William sold his interest to the firm for $2,000. Another seven months went by and brother Benjamin sold his part to the firm as well. This made John Harris, the father, and his son, Richard, the sole owners.

In 1858, they mortgaged the property to A. Eugene Smith from Philadelphia for $12,000 to gain money for improvements. The Civil War brought a heightened demand for paper, and Harrisville profited greatly. The Harris brothers were beginning at a most favorable time, indeed!

Another asset to the production at Harrisville was access to the railroad for shipment of its products. The Raritan and Delaware Bay Railroad pushed its way through the northern section of the pinelands through Chatsworth and Atsion, though it missed the heart of the pines completely. A scheduled stop, Harris Station actually was eleven miles north of Harrisville itself, but its existence did help in the shipment of paper products to both New York and Philadelphia.

It was also at this time that the whole subject of a realignment of townships was being discussed by the State of New Jersey and Burlington County. In 1864, Bass River Township was created from Little Egg Harbor Township, and a portion of Washington Township, including much of the land around Harrisville, was given to the new township. No doubt, officials felt that they were giving Bass River a real asset in taxable property that would go a long way in helping the new township survive. Though deprived of the paper town, Washington Township continued to be closely related to it. Many residents of the township were employed in Harrisville in later years, and it remained influential in the lives of those who lived in the area.

Richard Harris, the manager in residence, enlarged the main canal and modernized the papermaking process. He needed to raise the level of the lake, so he improved the canal from the West Branch of the Wading River to the lake which McCarty had dug previously. This has often led historians to think that Harris was the first to dig the feeder canal. This author canoed the West Branch many times, always confronting an underwater obstacle below Godfrey's Bridge which impeded the canoes without ever realizing that this obstruction is all that remains of the McCarty dam rebuilt by Richard Harris in 1865 to divert more water into his improved feeder canal.

The canal is clearly visible, but let me give you a hint about walking through, no, even *near* any grasses, *especially* in shorts. While searching for this canal some years back, I got the worst (and so far, the only) case of chiggers! I knew better than to brush up against anything, but I failed to shower thoroughly when I got home. Chiggers, for the uninitiated, drive you absolutely crazy with their itch in most uncomfortable places for one solid month. *Nothing* stops the itch. The only solution, I'm told, is to cover them with clear nail poilish. Where I was concerned, I would have had to take a *bath* in nail polish. Be warned! Now, as to the ticks and the hazards of Lime's disease. . . Ah, this really is a nice place, you just have to be careful!

In that same year, 1865, Richard Harris incorporated the business and renamed it the Harrisville Manufacturing Company with a capital stock of half a million dollars. Its directors were Richard Harris himself, C. Heineman, W. Woodfall, Joseph S. Fisher, Howard Harris, and A. Eugene Smith. Smith, it will be recalled, was the mortgage-holder on the property. Fisher was Richard Harris's brother-in-law, being married to Ann Eliza Harris. At thirty, Howard Harris was the youngest of the Harris brothers, and was a successful real estate broker.

He also dug the famous artesian well, out of which still runs the iron-laden water of the pines. Of this well, he wrote, "*In 1866, I had an artesian well sunk at Harrisville, to obtain a supply of pure water, free from iron, from which ingredient we had a great deal of trouble, causing our wrought-iron boiler to rust out rapidly.*" The driller did strike iron-free water at first but determined to dig deeper for a greater flow. Big mistake! Harris notes that "*the result was, no water of any volume; and that which overflowed was impregnated with iron very strongly, which was the very thing I wished to avoid. At this I concluded to abandon the project and declined to bore any further.*" The hole was dug with an eight-inch drill using horsepower. Iron pipe casings were driven into the well and joined together with a heated iron collar which shrank as it cooled.

John Harris, father of the brothers, retired from the firm in 1866, but brother William came back on board during the same year. A financier by the name of Joseph Newhall wanted to invest in the company, and the Board of Directors offered him a one-third share in the property. Brother William was also given a one-third share. Together, the two men paid $27,000 for their interest and assumed the two previous mortgages of John Simon and A. Eugene Smith.

Richard and Howard Harris were the only two of the brothers who would actually live at Harrisville. Richard Harris lived in his mansion which was located within the arms of the main mill race near his mill, sawmill, grist mill, and company store, which he operated profitably. The other brothers continued to live in Philadelphia and manage their other businesses.

IMPENDING DISASTER

Harrisville was active and prosperous throughout the 1860's. At the turn of the decade, no one could foresee the tragedy that would engulf this little town in the pines during the following ten years.

Richard Harris was fifty-one in 1870 and had been managing the business well over the preceding decade. On May 2nd of that year, however, John W. Harris, Sr., died. His death only began the list of tragedies that would hit the family over the next eight years. Between 1870 and 1878, John, Jr., Benjamin, and William died, along with three of their sisters. This left all the family business in Philadelphia and New York in the hands of Richard and Howard. Richard continued to operate Harrisville, but Howard had to spend all of his time travelling between the two major cities to keep an eye on the Harris businesses there.

The period after the Civil War was also a period of unbridled industrial expansion and speculation. New manufacturing plants were being built all across the country, including those to make paper. Harrisville was basically over fifty years old at this point and was only capable of producing a rough, brown paper much like today's butchers' paper. Despite their best efforts, the two remaining Harris brothers couldn't reverse the tide that was sweeping over them.

When their mother, Sarah, died in 1881, Howard and Richard sold the family mansion on Locust Street in Philadelphia, and invested the funds in their business enterprises. In 1887, they went looking for another mortgage to help them continue their operations. They obtained a mortgage of $20,000 from a casual friend of the family, Maria C. Robbins, and Howard's son, John, also got one from a John H. Pratt, Jr. for $2,000. John Pratt was a nephew of the Harris brothers, his mother being Howard's twin sister, Virginia. John Pratt took as security the plot of land on which had stood Martha Furnace. This infusion of money enabled them to reorganize the company, and on October 1, 1888, Howard Harris and his two sons obtained full control of the Harris Paper Company.

Howard's son, John W. Harris III, lived in the mansion at Harrisville, but conveyed his interest to the company soon after its reorganization. Real estate was always an interest to the entire Harris family, and John III continued that interest.

John directed his interest towards the newly-formed Bass River Township and the town of New Gretna. He, his wife, Phoebe, and their four children attended the Presbyterian Church of New Gretna every Sunday, was elected a Justice of the Peace, founded the Building and Loan Society of New Gretna, and was a part of the formation of the New Gretna Town Hall Company. His mother, Rebecca, was a Cramer, the daughter of Joseph and Sarah (Thompson) Cramer. Joseph, the son of Caleb S. Cramer, was born May 15, 1804 in Bass River, and died on July 20, 1852. It is said that when his grandfather, Joseph Cramer, died, he left land for the church and that John III was on the building committee. Though a deed to the Presbyterian Church in New Gretna in 1896 lists Joseph's surviving heirs, the church was built earlier than this. Perhaps Joseph's grandson, John W. Harris III, was on the building committee for the addition to the church.

Unfortunately, John III's success and community respect did not stave off the final collapse of Harrisville.

FOR WHOM THE BELL TOLLS

For over one hundred years, a town had survived along the East Branch of the Wading. In 1890, it would receive its death knell. The Harris family defaulted on its mortgage to Maria Robbins, and she started procedures to foreclose on their property. The Court of Chancery in Trenton, on July 9, 1890, issued a writ of execution to sheriff George F. Harbert to sell all the land in both Bass River and Randolph Townships. The sale was to include absolutely everything: sixteen and a half acres in Randolph Township, 352 acres in Bass River Township, the paper mill, saw mill, grist mill, mansions, workers' houses, storehouses, and all tools, machinery, etc. belonging to the Harris Paper Company. The Harris family was finished in the Jersey pines.

Sheriff Harbert published notices of the impending sale in two Burlington County newspapers, but Maria Robbins herself was the only bidder on February 28th, 1891. She obtained the property for $10,000 to satisfy her $20,000 mortgage. Within four days, she sold title to the property to Alexander W. Harrington for a mortgage of $20,000. He sold a half interest to Emanuel Ettenheimer and Joseph Schneider for $9,736, who organized the New Jersey Manufacturing and Improvement Company. Harrington, however, went bankrupt within two years. Maria certainly made poor choices for her mortgages. In March, 1893, the property was attached to protect Harrington's creditors.

Three years later, good, old Joseph Wharton bought the property on July 17, 1896. Sometime in between, the great machinery at Harrisville had fallen silent, and the workmen had taken their families and moved to other locations in order to find work. John Harris III continued to live in the Harris Mansion with his family, but this scion of a great family presided over crumbling buildings and weed-choked streets. Where once the gas lights revealed only neatness and quiet prosperity, now there was the darkness of decay. Richard Harris had insisted on clean, smooth roads, and neat lawns. Now the undergrowth was reclaiming its own.

Human vultures swooped in on the defenseless town and stole every movable thing in sight. The gas lamps were the first to go. Machinery soon followed. Sandstone was torn from the mill and its outbuildings. Wharton hired guards, but even that didn't seem to keep away the scavengers. Harrisville was dying.

ONE LAST SWAN SONG

Dying in 1909, Joseph Wharton did not live to see either the last great triumph of Harrisville, nor of its Viking funeral. The commencement of the twentieth century held great promise for the youth of America. There was a new spirit in the air. Various organizations were springing up all over the country for the training and benefit of young men and women. Dan Beard and Ernest Thompson Seton organized groups of boys on a wilderness and frontier theme. Lord Baden-Powell of England returned with fame from the Boer War in South Africa and organized the Boy Scouts. His wife countered with the Girl Scouts. Both organizations were readily transplanted to the United States. The Y.M.C.A. also began to promote summer camps as an ideal way to help the young people of the cities to regain an appreciation for their roots and to escape from the confines of the cities for the summer.

An Atlantic City physician, Dr. M.S. Lyon, president of the local Y.M.C.A., had pestered Wharton several times for permission to start a boys' camp at Harrisville. Wharton always feared the danger of fire in his woodlands, however, and refused his permission. After his death, though, Lyon tried again, this time using his friend Charles Widden, an Atlantic City attorney and friend of General Elias Wright, the manager of the Wharton Estate, to prevail on that gentlemen to allow a Y.M.C.A. camp in the pines.

Wright consented, and by the summer of 1910, Camp Lyon was open for business. Lyon and his committee hired as Camp Director George O. Draper, twenty-one year old graduate of Springfield College in Massachusetts and director of the Atlantic City Y.M.C.A. Chapter's Physical Department. Some of Draper's boys requested permission to form a Scout troop for any of those boys who wanted to become a Boy Scout. The Atlantic City Y.M.C.A. would become the sponsor of a Scout Troop. This insured that Camp Lyon would be both a Y.M.C.A. camp and the first organized Scout Camp in the area. The young boy responsible for this early Scout troop was Howard Feyl, fourteen years old at the time. He would later become the Scout Executive for the local council and remain as such until he retired in 1959. Bill Hawthorne, who knew Mr. Feyl personally, says that Mr. Feyl maintained that this first Scout troop at Harrisville was not officially part of the Boy Scouts of America but was a troop formed by the Y.M.C.A. on the scout model.

The happy campers were brought by boat from Atlantic City, up the Mullica to Wading River. There they were met by a wagon that carted the campers up the sandy road to the town. While the camp officials used some of the buildings, the campers were housed in tents. For a $6.00 fee, the campers were fed, housed, and welcomed to participate in all the camp's activities. The actual row of sixteen tents stood on the east side of Harrisville Lake in one long row.

Howard Feyl Collection

Howard Feyl Collection

The Scout Troop at Camp Lyon
"To the Colors"

In the Camp Lodge
This is the only known interior of a Harrisville structure. The building was located on the
north side of the dam upstream from the location of the old slitting mill site.

Swimming in the Harrisville Lake

Mahlon Broome and his wife, Sarah Holloway Broome
Mahlon was the last manager of Harrisville

Shelter from the Noonday Sun

In the cupola of the main mill building, George Draper posed with some of the boys attending Camp Lyon.

Among the boys perched high above the old paper mill can be identified Warren Somers, Jr., later an owner of the Somers Lumber Company in Atlantic City, and Earl Hann, later a respected Methodist clergyman from that ocean resort.

Campers actually elected their own governing council of eight boys, who chaired departments of sanitation, improvements, social activities, guard duty, woodcraft, nature study, athletics, and religious work. The days began at 6:30 A.M. and were filled with activities until 9:00 P.M.

Draper lived with his wife in one of the old houses of Harrisville, and, in the fourth season, another old house was turned into a camp lodge. This housed rainy-day activities as well as a darkroom and a classroom. In 1912, the old general store was reopened as a camp store to provide the youngsters with sundries and supplies. Check-in was done at the Broom Mansion and the old schoolhouse/church was the camp headquarters.

For four years, there was hope for this village in the pines. It was not to be. At 6:00 P.M. on Sunday, April 19, 1914, a fire raged through the entire area. When the flames died down, one hundred years of history was gone forever.

The Main Mill After the Fire

Howard Feyl Collection

The Thursday edition for April 23, 1914 of *The Evening Union* (Atlantic City) carried a short news item on Page 6:

Mysterious Blaze Wipes Out Village
Harrisville on Border of Atlantic County is Destroyed

Mount Holly, N.J. April 22 - All that was left of Harrisville, which at one time was a thriving and active community with a paper manufacturing plant as the industry around which the village was built, was destroyed by a fire of unknown origin on Sunday night, word to that effect having reached here today. Harrisville is not far from Batsto and near the line between Burlington and Atlantic Counties.

The fire consumed the mill property, the general store building, two large houses, and numerous small buildings surrounding them. All were unoccupied, uninsured and belong to the Joseph Wharton Tract.

(Quoted in an article by Bill Hawthorne in the *South Jersey Magazine* for Spring, 1976)

Headlines in the *Atlantic City Review* for Saturday, April 25, 1914 noted: "'Camp Lyon Burned Out' All Tents Owned by Y.M.C.A. Swept Away By Flames At Harrisville. Started In Old Mill." Camp Lyon was to

Main Street Looking Towards the Mill after the fire.
The fire of 1914 brought to a close one hundred years of history.
It is fortunate that the fire swept through prior to the opening of the Y.M.C.A. camp that season, or there
may have been tragedy. As it was, the damage to the town was complete.
Nothing remains but the remnants of walls and foundations.

open on June 25th and run through July 16th. The article noted that at least seventy-five boys had set their hearts on going to camp that year, and everything was in blackened ruins. The Y.M.C.A. wasn't deterred yet, though. They were putting out a plea for donations. They said that each tent cost $25.00 and that the tents would bear the donors' names.

The *Evening Union* for June 20th stated that

> the advanced guard . . . left this morning to establish the summer camp of the Association (the Y.M.C.A.) at Lake Harris, Wading River, N.J. The "Huskies" of the association, who were detailed to pitch the camp, embarked on the power cruisers "Mame," "Captain McDevitt," and the "Wilhelmina." About two tons of canvas and other camp material with provisions were taken along. Dr. Lyon was in charge of the advance guard with aides in Scout Master McKnight and Physical Director Draper. (Quoted in Bill Hawthorne's article)

It is interesting to note that no recent account suggests that the 1914 camp season was ever held at the burned-out ruins of Harrisville. The advance group must have found tragic devastation when they arrived at Harrisville Landing and trudged up through the woods to the site of their beloved Camp Lyon. If all the buildings and trees in the area had been consumed by the fire, it would have been impossible to camp within the perimeter of the burned area.

Bill Hawthorne suggests that not all the buildings were destroyed in the fire. He says he knows that at least three houses survived and that one was moved to a new location near Batsto.

There is a sadness in this account. Most of the forgotten towns of the pines simply faded away with time and forest fires. It seems that Harrisville's destruction was the product of arson, and that crime destroyed the last remains of almost a century's dreams. Boys had climbed to the cupola in the old paper mill and surveyed the territory for miles around from their high perch. Perhaps they had dreamed of soaring with the hawks, rising higher and higher on the thermal currents of the pines. Maybe they just enjoyed the exhilaration of height and the excitement of the challenge. They had slept beside the lake and learned the lessons of cooperative living. Some had raised their hands in the Scout sign and pledged, "On my honor, I will do my best . . ." Duty to God, to country, to others, to self: they were young men growing up free. Now their dreams for that summer of 1914 were gone.

All too soon, those very young men would be old enough in 1917 to give "their last full measure of devotion" for their country on the battlefields of Europe, and they had lost one last summer of their youth to the unthinking selfishness of a arsonist. Whoever started that fire on the fateful day of April, 1914 accomplished more than the destruction of a few old buildings. They had destroyed a dream. Camp Lyon was no more. In a way, I hope that the reporters for the *Evening Union* and the *Atlantic City Review* were wrong and that it was a forest fire that took away their dreams. At least that would have been a bit more impersonal.

On a summer's evening beside the lake, you might still hear the laughter of young people echoing through the trees where they're camping at Bodine's Field campground, but no longer does the bugle sound the haunting "Taps." The State of New Jersey has surrounded what's left of the ruins of the main paper plant with a high fence, and they are so overgrown you could drive by on the main road and never know they were there. Not a single sign reminds the casual visitor of the history that was Harrisville, of gas lights, neat streets, and tidy houses. The last remaining vestiges of Harrisville are slowly crumbling into dust. If you're by that lake some dark night, don't be too startled if you feel a tap on the shoulder. It may just be that Old Broome, the last manager of Harrisville, is welcoming you to his beloved town. Mr. Broome used to meet "the boys" at Wading River/Bridgeport with his horse and wagon to carry the happy campers to and from their summer in the pines. The solitary resident of an almost forgotten town, he haunted one of the abandoned Harris mansions for many years until the fire deprived him of his home. Broome, too, has become a ghost of the pines.

Courtesy of Marian Broome, Mahlon's grandaughter, via Benjamin
Broome and Elizabeth Souder Broome
Mahlon Broome
1826-1919
The last manager of Harrisville
who was called "Old Broome" by the boys
of the Y.M.C.A. camp

Courtesy of Marian Broome, Sarah's grandaughter, via Benjamin
Broome and Elizabeth Souder Broome
Sarah Holloway Broome
Wife of Mahlon Broome

Two Views of the Main Paper Mill Building
Built by McCarty in 1834
The entire structure stretched for 313 feet and was sixty-five feet wide at its broadest point. The above photograph is from the early Wharton Era. When General Wright came to Harrisville in behalf of Joseph Wharton, the east paper machine room, originally built in 1832 by McCarty, had been destroyed by fire, but the main mill was untouched. In the picture below can be seen the large door through which the raw materials were first brought to the cleaning and cutting room.

The School/Church by the Lake on the Martha Road

The Main Harrisville Road towards Bodine's Tavern
One of the worker's houses can be seen on the left.

336

The Footbridge Across the Main Mill Race.
This bridge connected the buildings on the east side of the race with the Harris and Broome Mansions,
the store, the grist mill, and the sawmill on the western side.

The Old Dam at Harrisville
Probably built by the Harris Brothers when they needed a higher head on the lake, this dam washed out in 1939.
A new wooden dam was built and lasted until it was replaced in 1974 by the State of New Jersey.

Two views before and after the fire of 1914

This photograph shows the company store on the left and the grist mill on the right. Both buildings sat in the middle of the area formed by the races of the main canal and that of the grist mill canal. Next to the company store was the Broome Mansion and beyond that, the Harris Mansion. The main paper mill does not show but would be far in the back right side of the photograph. The view is after the buildings were abandoned, but prior to the fire which destroyed them.

The photographs on this page were from the Howard Feyl Collection

The fire of April 1914 has raged through the area, destroying everything in its path. Only the walls of the store and grist mill remain.

George Draper is standing in the middle of the Turbine Room after the 1914 fire.

The Ruins of the Broome Mansion
Mahlon Broome and his wife, Sarah, lived in the house that had
stood in this location until the 1914 fire destroyed it.

Photographs courtesy of Nelson Ware

340

Harrisville

This view of the north end of the main plant shows one of the Harris mansions in the background. Steve Eichinger believes the man on the right to be Levi Austin Downs, but he was born in 1857, making him too young to appear in a tintype as an older man. It is more likely that the tintype dates from the late 1850's or early 1860's and that the gentleman in the wagon is his father, Benjamin Franklin Downs. A suggestion for the other man is Samuel McKeen. The Wading River/Bridgeport pair has just finished delivering a cartload of salt hay that will be made into paper at the mill.

The Mill Complex

The buildings in this picture all look in excellent shape and may indicate that this photograph was taken prior to the time in which the mill ceased operations.

Courtesy of Horace Somes

342

The Production of Paper at Harrisville

from "Fragments of Early Industries in South Jersey"
by K. Braddock-Rogers
University of Pennsylvania
Reprinted from the "Journal of Chemical Education"
Vol. 8, No. 10 and 11
October and November, 1931

The raw material for the paper was marsh grass from the marshes of the Mullica River. It was bought for three dollars a ton and was brought to the mill landing on twenty-ton barges, from the landing to the mill by mule team.

From the barges, the marsh grass went to the cookers. These were in a shed whose floor level was several feet below the surface of the ground and it held five vats, ten feet in diameter. Live steam was forced into these vats, which leached out the salts and soluble material. The condensing steam and wash liquors were run off through a tunnel to the sluice. The grass went to the large stone vats fifteen feet in diameter and there it was chopped up by vertically-revolving knives into pulp. From the macerators, the pulp was pumped to a storage tank where it was very slowly agitated to keep it from packing. This storage tank was a deep well, lined with [sandstone] and built above the ground about ten feet. It was twenty-two feet square. The pulp was then ready to be made into paper. In later years, a building in which were two drums with knives was built. The drums slowly revolved to cut the grass which was then allowed to drop into another tank. From the construction of the building, it is easy to see that it is of very much later date. The walls have stones of mica schist and calcite while the brickwork is far superior to that in the original arches. . . .

The paper is said to have had great tensile strength and to have been of a peculiar brown color. This color was due to the iron in the water which was used, for it must be remembered that the Wading River flows through and helped to lay down the enormous limonite deposits. Many attempts were made at the plant to make a white paper, but all failed. The finish was put on the paper by passing it very slowly over a roller where it was buffed by another roller going in the opposite direction and at a considerable speed.

The finished paper was loaded on barges at the landing and floated down the river to the ships for transportation to New York and Philadelphia. In later years, the paper was hauled by mule and ox term through the woods to Harris Station on the railroad (which is now the Central Railroad of New Jersey) from where it went directly to New York.

Courtesy of Nelson Ware

Joe and Sadie (Downs) Ware at the Ruins of Harrisville
Early 1920's

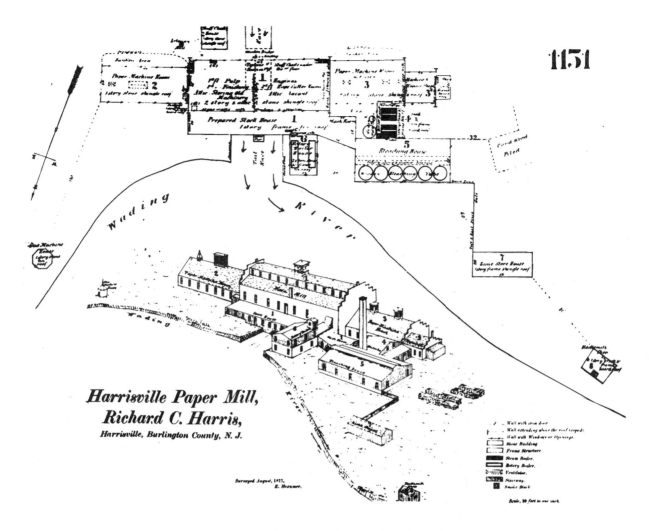

Harrisville Paper Mill,
Richard C. Harris,
Harrisville, Burlington County, N. J.

Surveyed August, 1877,
E. Hexamer.

Harrisville Paper Mill
Richard C. Harris
Harrisville, Burlington County, N.J.
Surveyed August 1877
by E. Hexamer

Owner: Richard C. Harris

Superintended: - by the owner.

Name: - Harrisville Paper Mill

Location: - situated at Harrisville, Burlington County, N.J.

Construction: - Good.

Communication: - Buildings adjoining communicate by openings, wooden and iron doors, as shown on plans. The window in stone wall between boiler and bleach house will be bricked up. There will be an iron door between the Boiler and Paper Machine Houses.

Age: - Buildings erected 30 years ago.

Power: - Machinery propelled by waterpower, ample supply of water throughout the year.

Height: - Main Mill, 15' 15' 18' 25'. Paper Machine Rooms, 12-30'. Boiler House, 12' - and 18'. Rotary House, 10' and 9'.

Length: - See plan.

Walls: - Of stone, from 20" to 30" thick.

Cornice: - of Main Mill of brick. Other bldgs, no cornice.

Gutters: - None.

Columns: - Of iron.

Roof: - As per plan.

Scuttle: - In roof of Main Mill, and ladder to it.

Floors: - Stone floor in Lime House, brick floor in Builder House, other floors of 1 " pine flooring boards, not arranged for flooding.

Ceilings: - Of part of Attic of Main Mill, lathed and plastered. Paper Machine Rooms, boarded ceilings. Others not finished.

Ladders: - None permanent. Several wooden movable ladders on hand, reaching to the roof of the Main Mill.

Lightening Rod: - With numerous points on roof of Main Mill. None on Stack.

Elevator: - Small elevator in Main Mill, from 1st to 2nd story only.

Hoisting: - Outside of Main Mill at (b), see plan.

Porch: - None

Tower: - Wooden cupola on roof of Main Mill, as shown on view.

Boilers: - 4 Exter Boilers, located as per plan, enclosed by brickwork, in proper distance of woodwork.

Smoke Stack: - Of brick, rising 5 or 6 feet above the peak of the roof of the Main Mill.

Steam Engine: - None.\

Turbines: - On 1st floor of Main Mill, about 125 Horsepower.

Heating: - Rooms warmed by 5" cast-iron steampipes, resting on iron, and by a stove.

Stove: - 1 Cast-iron stove in Paper Machine Room, east of Main Mill, well protected; no stovepipe.

Lighting: - Rooms lighted by gas manufactured in a stone building 125 feet from Mill, of gasoline (Springfield Gas Machine), about 4 barrels of gasoline kept in an Iron tank in Gas Machine House. Rope Cutter Room lighted by an enclosed gas lantern.

Watchman: - None; proprietor and hands employed live on adjoining premises.

Hours of Work: - Day and Night.

Machine Shop: - Adjoining, west of Paper Machine Room; very little repairing done; no new machinery made.

Forge: - Brick forge in Blacksmith Shop, on ground floor, side wall of shop near forge covered by brick on inside.

Wood Shavings: - Made in case of repairs only and cleaned out as soon as made. Carpenter's bench in Machine Shop. One carpenter employed. One circular saw in Paper Machine Room, west of Main Mill.

Stock: Old rope, bagging, and salt hay stored in piles in the open air in safe distance of Mill.

Rope Cutters: - 2 Rope cutters and one duster (no devil) in second floor of Main Mill, on wood floor and ceiling (two words here are undecipherablec[sic]). Cutters allowed to run on a loose pulley, man having charge. Cut rope wet down immediately after being made and taken to rotary boilers.

Sorting: - Rope and bagging sorted in cutter Room in quantities sufficient for one day's running.

Bleaching: - Done in two rotary boilers and six stationary wooden bleaching tubs. Unslacked lime kept in a separate building.

Sizing: - Operations done by steam.

Oils: - Natural oils used on machinery, not stored on the premises, taken into the Mill in small quantities in tin cans. Occupancy: - as per plan.

Provisions against fire: - Two pumps, marked (c, 0) on plan, driven by belt. One 2 " hose connection on the east pump in the Main Mill, and one 2" connection on the other pump used to fill tanks; one small steam force pump (piston) in the Boiler Room, no hose connection.

Hose: - About 30 feet of 2" rubber hose near pump   in prepared Stock House.

Water Tanks: - One wooden water tank on roof of Main Mill, about 2500 Gals. Two in yard, about 2000 gals.

Casks: - Several wooden water casks on every floor of Main Mill, always full, with buckets near by.

Fire Extinguishers: - Two; one in Main Mill and one in Boiler House.

Fire Engine: - None.

Care in Management: - Good.

General condition of the property: - Good.

External Exposures: - None.

Machinery: - 2 Rope Cutters, 1 Duster, 2 Rotary Boilers, 6 Stationary bleaching tubs, 5 Pulp Engines, 1 Paper Machine with Calendar, 1 Patent Washing Machine, 2 power and 1 lever press, 1 patent glazing calendar, 1 paper cutter, 4 steam boilers, 3 pumps, (1 steam and two belt) and 7 turbines.

The above is courtesy of Steve Eichinger

EPILOGUE

The State of New Jersey acquired Harrisville along with the other properties of the vast Wharton Estate in the early 1950s. Nothing has been done to preserve the area other than fencing off the ruins of the main paper mill building. The site is completely overgrown, though the canals are still clearly visible. The ruins of the houses, grist mill, and store are gone. Only shallow cellarholes remain. The main mill walls have been slowly crumbling over the years, as well. Someday in the not too distant future, these ruins of the pines will simply be a pile of sandstone obscured by undergrowth. Not even a single sign indicates to the casual visitor the one hundred fifty years of history that transpired in this lonely pinelands spot. Harrisville is almost forgotten.

Courtesy of Budd Wilson

The Ruins of the Paper Mill During the 1970s

THE MISSING MILL

The Wading River Forge and Slitting Mill has provided a mystery for every writer on the subject of Harrisville. No one could find any reference to it during the Harrisville period, nor could they pinpoint a location for it from archeological remains. In the 1960's, Bill Hawthorne was sent to Harrisville to determine the density of pine to oak in the vicinity as a college project and fell in love with the old ruins. He spent many years trudging around the half-obscured roads, measuring cellar holes, plotting road locations, and thoroughly investigating the site. He even tracked down Howard C. Feyl, who, as a camper with the Atlantic City Y.M.C.A. at the end of the first decade of the twentieth century, took the series of photos that appear in this chapter.

In 1976, while searching through a photo album in the Atlantic County Historical Society, he came across two photographs that had been identified as "Weymouth" Furnace and realized right away that the site was not Weymouth but Harrisville. He had an argument with the Atlantic County Historical Society which insisted that the site in question was Weymouth. Bill went to Harrisville and found the unique forked tree that appears by the lake on the right hand side. This was Harrisville! There was no way the terrain at Weymouth matched that in this picture. Bill was excited. He thought he had found photographs of McCarty's first paper mill.

Then in the Feyl Collection of Harrisville, he found a photograph of the *exact same buildings*, taken *after* the disastrous fire that destroyed most the Harrisville buildings in 1914. To check out the Weymouth identification, he even asked Howard Feyl if he had ever taken any photographs at Weymouth and received an answer in the negative. This *was* indeed Harrisville. Bill went back to Harrisville and searched the site. There he found the site strewn with old, rusting cut nails of the type made by a slitting mill. He also saw evidence of at least two mill races and felt that this must be the site of that enigmatic mill, the Wading River Forge and Slitting Mill, as well as McCarty's mill. Yet something kept nagging him about the pictures. In the winter of 1976, he wrote an article for the *South Jersey Magazine* in which he said that the buildings were the original McCarty paper mill and published the photographs for the first time.

Twenty years after they had been written, Steve Eichinger of Wading River brought Bill Hawthorne's articles to my attention. An immediate problem was discovered. These buildings stood beside the lake to the *north* of the dam. McCarty's mill itself stood *south* of the dam and had been rebuilt by the Harris brothers after the McCarty-era fire. If these buildings were not the McCarty mill, and they could not have been, what were they? Steve and I walked the site once again and saw the definite evidence of several mill races in the vicinity. There was little

Looking North from the Dam at Harrisville - Date Unknown

question that something had stood here that was not related to the McCarty plant or to the later business of the Harris brothers.

In the company of Dudley Lewis of Green Bank the next day, I walked the area once again. Dudley looked at the photos and, like Bill Hawthorne, something bothered him, too. What *was* wrong with the photographs? They *were* photographs of Harrisville, but something was definitely wrong. Dud pulled out the topographic map and studied it carefully. It was March of 1997 in the late afternoon, and the sun was in the southwest. That was it! In order the have the lake of the left side, as in the photographs from the historical society that Bill Hawthorne had published, the sun would have been in the *north*, a physical impossibility. These photographs had been printed in reverse! As they are printed on this and the preceding page, they have been reversed from the originals so that the sun appears on *south* side where it should be, and lo and behold, it works!

So what were the buildings? Steve Eichinger had a sketched map of the area which showed Belangee's Mill and the Wading River Forge and Slitting Mill located right here along the lake. Was it possible that these were the ruins of that long-lost slitting mill complex? As on the map, the spillway for Belangee's Mill (1760) appears just beyond the race in the photograph below. These ruins had to have lasted into the twentieth century for Howard Feyl to have photographed them after the 1914 fire. All this time, the mystery forge/slitting mill had been right under the noses of everyone.

I then made contact with Bill Hawthorne, whom I did not know at the time, and went over the whole subject with him. Bill had identified the structures as McCarty's original paper mill and the site of the slitting mill. He thought that the view was towards the dam, as it would have to be if the actual photographs were not reversed. But they *were* reversed. The sun can't be in the north. *That* was what was bothering him about those pictures! Bill had been wondering about them for the last twenty years. Now it was perfectly clear.

The road heads *away* from the dam, not *towards* it. The building could not be McCarty's mill because it stands on the *northwest* side of the dam, and McCarty is credited with digging the canals on the *southeast* side to what is known as the main mill building during the Harris administration. McCarty's mill was supposed to have been rebuilt by Harris into the main mill. The building in these photographs could not have stood on the southeast side of the dam and river. He concurred with the present author that they could only be the ruins of the long lost slitting mill and forge.

The Same View of the Ruins of the Wading River Forge and Slitting Mill - 1914

The Southwest Corner of the Wading River Forge and Slitting Mill
Note the Harrisville Lake in the distance on the right.

In all probability, the Wading River Forge and Slitting Mill had ceased operations after the 1823 fire and before McCarty built his paper mill and village complex on the other side of the river in the 1830's, although McCarty's new dam would not have deprived the forge/slitting mill of its water power, as the existing upper sluiceway shows.

There is evidence that John Hallock used the building as part of his castor oil/linseed oil production after the fire. Hallock came to the Tuckerton area from New York around 1812, purchasing the former plantation of Mordecai Andrews. In 1818, he obtained a patent on a screw press and on a process using it to extract castor oil from caster beans. Four years later, he received a second patent on a new machine that would manufacture both castor oil and linseed oil. After the 1823 fire at the Wading River Forge and Slitting Mill, in which he owned a one-quarter interest, Hallock built one of his newly patented machines in the location and sold his half interest in his Tuckerton plantation. While the Tuckerton machine was apparently powered by a horse, the Wading River machine may have utilized the power of the river through the sluice of the former forge and slitting mill. Hallock was financially over-extended and his holdings on the Wading River and at Tuckerton were sold in 1825.

During the McCarty and ensuing Harris era, the old mill probably fell into ruins and remained picturesque reminders of the past until the 1914 fire reduced the whole town to rubble. Construction of Route 679 and the picnic area in this century destroyed every trace of the "missing" mill.

There is one further piece of corroborating evidence. Bill Hawthorne recalled Howard Feyl mentioning that the Y.M.C.A.'s Camp Lodge had stood on the road which ran up the west side of the lake towards Jenkins, quite a distance from the dam. In the original photograph, one can just spot the roof of that lodge where the road curves to the left in the distance. The mill building actually appears on the 1836 map of McCartyville found on p. 322.

When the state rebuilt the dam a few years ago the water level in the lake was down to the original streambed, and Bill Hawthorne, ever interested, took his camera and photographed the area in front of the upper overflow. Here, in the lake bed, were the remains of pilings and timber that appeared to be sluice gates which had been covered by the lake since McCarty dammed it for his paper mill. These remains were slightly northward of the site of the above buildings, right where Belange's mill was supposed to have been built.

Thus, at long last, the puzzling mystery of the missing forge and slitting mill and the site of Belangee's Mill has been solved.

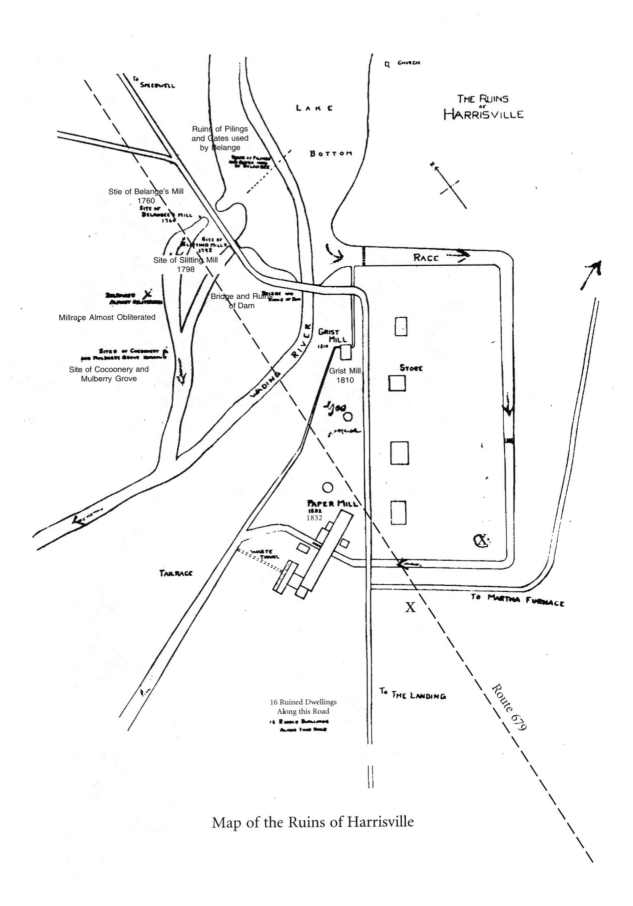

Map of the Ruins of Harrisville

The Ruins of the Main Plant at Harrisville
The couple in the photograph are Joe and Sadie (Updike) Ware and was taken before 1928.

Map of the Ruins at Harrisville
(Preceding Page)
Taken from the one appearing in K. Braddock-Rogers' article:
"Fragments of Early Industries in South Jersey"

This map of Harrisville was provided to the author by Steve Eichinger of Wading River from an 8" x 10" photograph of the original. Steve did not know the original source of the photograph or of the map.

There are inaccuracies: The Gas Plant is not in the correct location, nor are some of the buildings within the main mill race. However, the map does note the location of both Belangee's Mill and the Wading River Forge and Slitting Mill. The position of the latter corresponds with the photographs on the previous page. The construction of Route 679 may have destroyed these early sites but the mill races are still visible. The date given at the main mill, 1832, corresponds to the McCarty paper mill. The gas plant was located where I've placed a "O" directly above the words "Paper Mill." The depression is still visible at the site.

I have set new printing to the text that was legible in the original with a magnifying glass but illegible in the reproduction. I have marked with "X's" the sites which Steve's mother and aunt (Martina Adams Eichinger and Alice Adams Weber) used to point out as the location of two "mansions." Though there is a large cellar hole at the southernmost location, all writers so far have indicated that the "mansions" were only within the main mill race. No "mansion" is mentioned at the northernmost site. Since the Harris family had many members, it is not inconceivable that each had a large house in which they stayed while visiting Harrisville, but the actual mansions usually mentioned were those of Richard Harris (the on-site manager) and that called the "Broome" Mansion.

State Route 679 is my addition as well in order to give orientation. The sawmill was immediately southeast of the grist mill, though it isn't shown on this map.

351

The Ruins of the Grist Mill - Circa 1974

Herman City

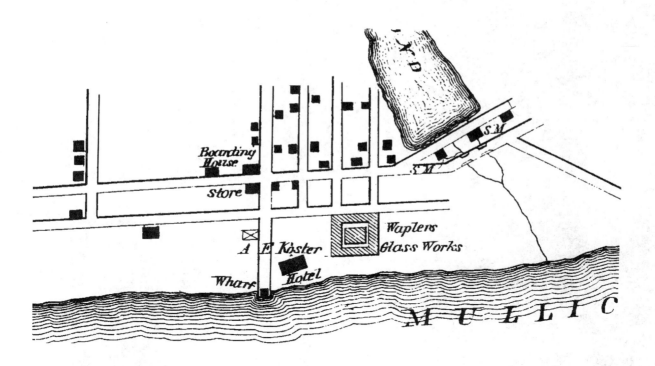

Map of Herman City - 1876
Taken from J.D. Scott's *Atlas of Burlington County*

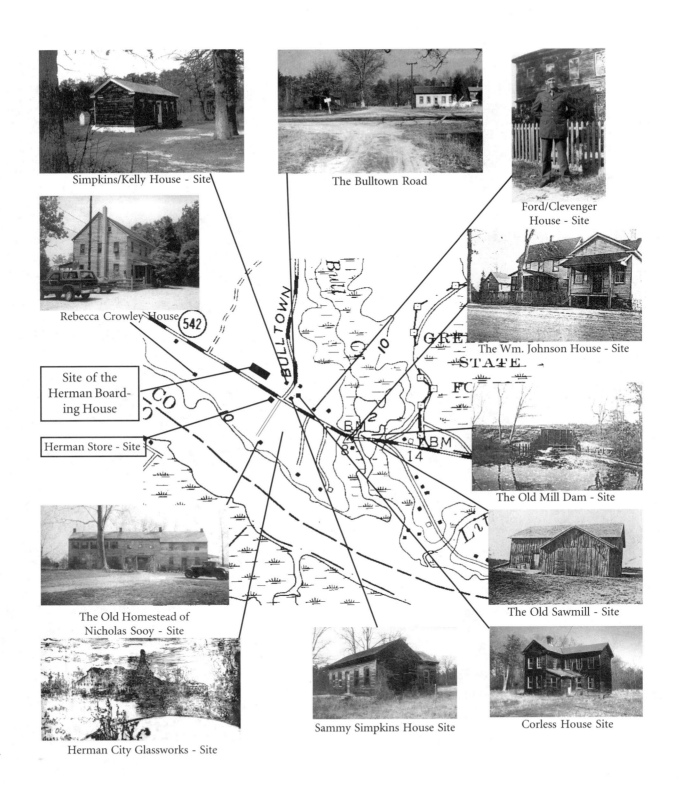

Simpkins/Kelly House - Site

The Bulltown Road

Ford/Clevenger
House - Site

Rebecca Crowley House

The Wm. Johnson House - Site

Site of the
Herman Board-
ing House

Herman Store - Site

The Old Mill Dam - Site

The Old Homestead of
Nicholas Sooy - Site

The Old Sawmill - Site

Herman City Glassworks - Site

Sammy Simpkins House Site

Corless House Site

Herman City

Herman City Glass Works and Village
(No Longer in Existence)

Directly connected with the nineteenth century history of Green Bank is the construction of Herman City. Nicholas Sooy II had owned many thousands of acres along the Mullica, including the old Driver Survey. Driver had purchased all the land which comprises Green Bank proper from the church to Little Bull Creek, which runs near the Sooy/Crowley/Wobbar/Wilson House (1027 River Road). John Sooy built the first section of what he surely intended to become a baronial house upriver from the Driver property across the Bull Creek. His nephew, Nicholas Sooy II, added the second section, and perhaps even the third, to the house.

When Nicholas Sooy III sold his patrimonial land, it was divided into several portions. The Old Homestead was apparently owned by John H. Rapp outright, but the land immediately downriver was held by several businessmen, including Rapp and Francis Wing. Taking notice of the business methods of Nicholas Sooy II, Rapp and Wing decided to lease this land for development.

During the 1869, Rapp and Wing contracted with Joseph Wapler to build and operate a glass factory on property next to the old Sooy homestead. Wapler not only built a huge glass factory, but also a number of houses for the workers and managers in the plant. The new village was named after a man named Charles Herman who apparently had a sizable investment in the new glassworks and was president of the Gloucester Land and Town Association.

The glass factory was larger than the other local glass houses in the vicinity, and, unlike them, was designed to burn coal. Though covered with earth, underground draft tunnels still remain where the factory once stood. The main products of the factory were bottles and flasks, but it also made chimneys for kerosene and gas lamps, Christmas tree ornaments, and buttons.

The Herman Glass Works was in operation for only six months in the year 1870. Why these gentlemen thought they could succeed after the failure of the Green Bank Glass Works and the Batsto Glass Works is not

Courtesy of Budd Wilson

The Bulltown Road and Route 542 at Herman
This view is taken from the entrance to the Old Homestead of Nicholas Sooy, looking across Route 542 up the Bulltown Road. None of the houses in the picture survive. To the right of the photograph is Bel Haven Lake.

known, but they may have counted on the promised railroad through the area which never materialized. The workers in the new village of Herman moved away to find work, and most of the homes were abandoned. Francis Wing later sold his portion of the property to Joseph Wharton.

Like the builders of many other towns whose aspirations and expectations exceed their rationality, the creators of Herman had dreamed great dreams. In typical pretentiousness, the village of Herman (or Hermann, as some spell it) appended "City" to the name, predicting future glory. The glass works went up and ended production in the same year. So quickly are dreams destroyed.

Rapp's Herman City was a planned community that was laid out in a systematic gridiron pattern with over twenty streets and four large squares. It was designed to stretch from Bull Creek to Crowleytown and was laid out on the northeast side of the Batsto-Green Bank road. The only part of the town that was ever built included somewhere between fifty and sixty houses across the Batsto-Green Bank road from the Herman City Hotel and the glass works. The houses planned were of two types: a one-story L-shaped house and a two story L-shaped house. This larger house had a central staircase that rose to the second floor. They were designed without much trim or ornamentation and were meant to be strictly utilitarian.

The houses pictured on this page and the one following stood in the area where the Bulltown Road connects with Route 542, the Hammonton/New Gretna Road, on the northwest side of the present Bel Haven Lake. They were the last remnants of the fifty-odd houses that formed the village of Herman. Only six houses remained into the 1950's, and all were torn down after the State of New Jersey acquired the property.

"History" may be the record of great events and the people who shaped them, but the real "American heroes" were and are the ordinary people who live their lives as best they can, struggling to make a living and raise their children for a future they themselves will never see. Every time another old house is lost, gone also are the memories of those ordinary and extraordinary folk who made them their home. The hopes and dreams, the joys and sorrows of the men, women, and children who lived in them are lost to those who come after them.

In the 1930's, this was the home of Merrle and Helen Simpkins. Merrle was the son of John W. Simpkins and the brother of Sammy Simpkins, who lived across the Bulltown Road. A family by the name of Kelly lived here later.

Courtesy of Charles F. Kier

The One-Story Houses of Herman City

This appears to be the house on the corner of Bulltown Road and Route 542 where Sammy Simpkins lived. Sammy was the son of John W. Simpkins, the brother of "Chink" Simpkins. He was born January 29, 1906 and married Myrtle Winton. He died on December 31, 1969.

Courtesy of Charles F. Kier

Courtesy of Budd Wilson

Early Sketch of the Herman Glass Works from an 1896 Newspaper

William F. Augustine Collection
Special Collections and University Archives
Rutgers University Libraries

All that remains of the Herman City Glass Works are now-buried ruins.
This photograph was taken about 1940. That part of the foundation which still remains above ground was
recently (1996) used in the filming of a movie.

357

The John Wesley Ford House
(No Longer in Existance)

While touring the Batsto-Pleasant Mills Methodist Church with a church group from Barnegat Light in 1996, we were hosted by a delightful lady of seventy-seven who was acting as docent for her daughter, Merle. Not until we were about to leave did she mention that she had attended the Green Bank School in her youth. She was a Ford, she said, but not from the same Ford family as the other Fords in Green Bank. Turns out, she was mistaken about not being related.

There were a lot of Fords in Washington Township in the 19th century, that's for sure! There were more people with the last name of Ford than of any other surname, as a matter of fact. Our Batsto-Pleasant Mills docent was born in Green Bank in 1919 and given the name, Anna Marjorie Ford. She was the youngest of three daughters born to Daniel Leonard (b. 1893) and Florence (Clevenger) Ford (b. 1896), her sisters being Lydie Ethel, (b. 1915), and Bertha Augustus (b. 1917).

Her grandparents on the Ford side were John Wesley Ford, Jr. and Sarah Elizabeth (Nichols) who lived in this house in Herman. John Wesley and Sarah Elizabeth (Nichols) Ford had five children: Mary Emma (1885-1980), Samuel F. (1885-1953), Arthur (c. 1894-?), John Wesley III (1882-1952), and Daniel Leonard (1893-?). Mary Emma, called just plain Emma, married Charles G. Clevenger. Interestingly enough, her brother, John, married Charles' sister, Ada, and her brother, Daniel Leonard, married another sister, Florence.

Though Margie was born in Green Bank, her parents moved to Batsto soon after her birth. Her father worked in Amatol, then at the paper mill in Pleasant Mills. After that closed, he worked for the Wharton Estate. Margie's sister, Lydie later married Charles Holden of West Virginia, while her sister, Bertha, married Maurice Ford II.

Rod Koster - c. 1944

Rod is standing in front of the home of John Wesley Ford, and later of Bertha Ford and Emily Clevenger, in Herman. It stood facing Route 542 across from the lane to his own home on the river. Rod is standing on the edge of the road.

Margie remembers walking the four miles from Batsto to Herman many times to visit her grandparents. The distance didn't seem so great in her days of youth. In later years, her sister, Bertha Ford and her aunt, Emma Clevenger, lived out their days in this old house. It was finally torn down when the State of New Jersey acquired the property.

John Wesley, called "Jackie," claimed he was born in an old, weather-beaten house in Lower Bank that had the tradition of being one of the oldest post offices in the United States, but no one today remembers exactly where it stood. He said he remembered carrying bricks for the construction of the great chimney of the Herman Glass Factory, but he was only eight when it was built.

He was typical of the Mullica residents of that period who found work wherever he could. John Wesley Ford, pictured opposite page 223 of Henry Charlton Beck's *Jersey Genesis*, gave Beck a lengthy interview. Beck reported that Jackie did "'spells of coalin' and woodchoppin'" in Bulltown, Tylertown, and Herman City" before he got a job at the fish factory run by Captain Cyrus Smith over in Mystic Islands near where the Tuckerton Wireless was built. Smith's factory, and another out on Crab Island owned by a Sooy (probably Ephraim C. Sooy, Jr.), made oil, glue, and fertilizer from menhaden, or mossbunkers as the local people called them.

They had other names too: greentails, Sam Days, mossybunkers, bony-fish, mud-shad, "minnies to you, maybe," he told Beck. He and his fellow crewmen worked the fishing steamers that worked the local waters and brought fish to the factories for "whatever factory men would pay." John Wesley also remembered that Leon Koster, Rod's father, also worked at the fish factories for a while. A lookout could spot the school of fish off the shore by their oil slick, and, when one was spotted, the men set out in dories with their nets to bring them in.

John Wesley Ford was also responsible for preserving the memory of a special New Jersey heritage: the early covered wagons, predecessors of the Conestogas that bore thousands westward across the mountains.

Soon the sheet-topped wagons to the swamps will go,
Loads of merry pickers, seated all in a row;
They jumped into the thickets and whistled merrily
While scooping in the treasures of the huckleberry tree. (Jersey Genesis)

John Wesley Ford, Jr. was the son of Margaret Emeline Ford (b. 4/9/1842). Margaret married John Wesley Ford, Sr. in 1858 at the age of sixteen and had a son, John Wesley, Jr. in either 1860 or 1862 (His gravestone says 1862). The information from one part of the Ford family is that J.W. Sr. was killed in the Civil War. Other information is that he died in 1902. Regardless of how or when he died, Margaret Emeline Ford married for a second time in 1863 at the age of twenty-one. This time, she married Samuel Pitman Ford (b. 3/4/1842), the son of Joseph (b. 1812) and Sarah Anne (Pharo) Ford (b. 1818). Joseph was listed as a laborer in the 1850 census. Son Samuel would later be listed as a soldier. Robert and Susannah Ford, the parents of Margaret Emeline Ford, wife of John Wesley, had only two children that are known, Margaret and her brother, Robert.

We have no idea whatsoever who the senior John Wesley's parents were.

So Margie (Ford) Ivins is wrong about her relatives. Samuel Pitman and Margaret Emeline Ford were the parents of Julia Belle Ford who married one of the numerous George Washington Fords (see The Fords of Tylertown and Greenbank in BULLTOWN AND TYLERTOWN.) Thus it seems that John Wesley Ford, Jr., her grandfather, was the half-brother of Julia Belle Ford, who married George Washington Ford and became the parents of Gertrude Leona, George Clayton, Henry Nickleye, Bertha Clarence, Margaret Emaline, Blanche Arwilda, Lavenia Bernice, and Elsie Leola Ford: the *other* Green Bank Fords.

Courtesy of Charles F. Kier

The Two-Story Houses of Herman
This house is typical of the two-story houses of Herman. It faced Belhaven Lake and, during the 1930's, was home to the Corless family. John Wesley, Jr. and Sarah Elizabeth (Nichols) Ford's house was identical to this one, but it faced Route 542. The Corless house was behind it, slightly closer to the Bulltown Road.

The William Johnson Residence
(No Longer in Existence)

Photograph by Augusta Weeks

The William A. Johnson House and Store - 1935

Esther Sooy (born December 24, 1813), daughter of Nicholas Sooy II, married William Johnson (born April 22, 1814) in 1835 or 1836 and lived in a house which once stood at 1014 River Road. (Bill Birdsall later came into possession of this property and tore the house down in order to build his little cottage.) Esther and William Johnson had two sons, Edwin B. and William Mathias, and one daughter, Sarah Elizabeth.

William Johnson was accidently killed on the 17th of November, 1840, at the age of twenty-six. Five years later, Esther married David Lowery, who was twenty-one years older than she was. She had two more children by David, Mary and Ephraim.

In his 1851 will, her father, Nicholas Sooy II, gave the property (1014 River Road) to his grandsons, Edwin and William Johnson when they became of age, through his daughter Esther. He also left them the mill property near the dam on the Bull Creek. Sooy had constructed both a sawmill and a grist mill at this spot perhaps as early as 1803. The grist mill lasted until 1903, the sawmill, as rebuilt, until 1939.

Edwin B. Johnson was born on March 3, 1837 and died November 18, 1885. He lived in Green Bank and married Amanda Cramer, daughter of Asa Cramer. Some time after the death of his grandfather, Edwin and Amanda (Cramer) Johnson came into the possession of the mill property, and they lived in this house close by. The couple had one son, William Asa Johnson, and were staunch supporters of the Green Bank Church.

Edwin's *brother*, William, was born on March 22, 1841 and died on January 27, 1918. On February 2, 1863, he married Anna Elizabeth Corson. William Mathias Johnson served with Company C, 9th New Jersey Infantry during the Civil War and received pension #1050718. His widow died on April 17, 1939. They had three daughters and one son: Esther, Amanda, Anna Vesta, and William Corson. All moved away from Green Bank.

The Bull Creek property reverted to Edwin and Amanda's son, William Asa Johnson, on the untimely death of his father at the age of forty-eight. William Asa Johnson married Rebecca Birdsall on February 10, 1904. Rebecca was the daughter of Alfred Hance Birdsall, son of Haze Birdsall (of Bulltown) and the brother of Bill (of Green Bank), Joe and Abbie (of Bulltown) and of Esther (Birdsall) Wobbar. Their daughter, Mary Amanda, was born on December 31, 1904.

William A. Johnson continued the operation of the grist mill and sawmill on the Bull Creek that his great-grandfather, Nicholas Sooy II had built. The gristmill burned to the ground in 1901, and William converted at least part of the lake into a cranberry bog. The sawmill stood just below the original dam and was washed out two years after the burning of the grist mill in 1903. William Asa Johnson rebuilt the sawmill on the same location and continued its operation. This second sawmill washed out in 1939 and was not rebuilt.

William and Rebecca Johnson's daughter, Mary, had talent both for music and for business, serving as her father's bookkeeper and typist. She also ran a gift shop on her own. William Johnson was a major grower of cranberries, producer of milled lumber through his sawmill, and ran a community store next to his home. Miss Mary also kept a boathouse on the Bull Creek and rented out rowboats and motor boats to summer visitors.

William served as treasurer of the Green Bank Church for a good many years and was generous in his support. Mrs. Johnson served as the president of the Ladies' Aid. Mr. and Mrs. Johnson also served as officials of the "Shepherd's Lodge" of Green Bank, whose building on River Road is now (1995) the Town Hall of Washington Township. Will Johnson served Washington Township faithfully for fifty years as the township clerk and tax collector. From 1914 through 1916, he was on the Burlington County Board of Chosen Freeholders.

The store that Miss Mary supervised so well is long gone. The grist mill and saw mill on the Bull Creek are even beyond memory. The house, like so many others have done over the years, stood abandoned. Even its gaunt wreckage is now gone, felled by a bulldozer in 1995, and the memory of the family that lived there for four generations has no trace in the present. How sad!

The old cranberry bog was converted into a lake by the Bell brothers, who rented out trailer and tent spots there for some years before they sold it. Bill Bell now concentrates on his canoe rental business and runs a boat yard where Miss Mary's rowboats and motorboats swung lazily on their moorings on the old Bull Creek.

Photograph by John Pearce

The Johnson House in 1995 - Demolished September 1995

361

Photograph by Augusta Weeks

The Sawmill in 1935
When the Nicholas Sooy II sawmill washed out in 1903,
William Johnson built this mill as a replacement.

Courtesy of Budd Wilson

Helena Wobbar, Ruth Wobbar, and Mabel Yates
by the Sawmill
Sunday, September 11, 1920

1935
The Mill Dam
William Johnson converted the mill lake into a cranberry bog, rebuilding the dam and relocating the roadway (now Route 542) after the gristmill burned in 1901.
The sawmill stood immediately to the left.

The Johnson Sawmill met the fate of its predecessor
in 1939 and was not rebuilt.
A huge storm in August of that year washed out every dam in the area and many of the bridges as well.

The Old Sooy Homestead
The Site is off Route 542
(No Longer in Existence)

Photo by Augusta Weeks

The Old Homestead as it appeared in 1935.
The Mullica River is behind the house.

Sooy. That name had been synonymous for stability, strength, and dedication to family in the Mullica Valley since old Yoos came down from Cheesequake and New York back in 1724. Yoos' son, Yoos, Jr., or "Joseph" as he had anglicized his name, bought the old Driver place at Red Bank in 1752 and moved in with his half dozen kids. It was probably Joseph and his family that was responsible for changing "Red" to "Green." Before he and Elizabeth were through, they had six more, and those twelve children had started somewhat of a local dynasty by the end of the century. Joseph lost his house in a bad debt in 1787, but there seems to be no records of where he went after that. Perhaps he and his family just continued to live in the old house, renting it from its new owner, William Richards of Batsto.

His son, Nicholas Sooy I, named after Joseph's brother who had moved south of the river to Leeds' Point, became a tavern owner, possibly first in Pleasant Mills, then, just prior to the Revolutionary War, at a new tavern out on the old Road to Little Egg Harbor where all the roads from just about everywhere came together. Sooy's Inn it was called, though he later named it for the famous general he so highly respected: the Washington Tavern.

Another son, John, bought this particular piece of property just above the old Sooy Homestead on the Driver Survey, and started a new traditional family locus.

The property had a bit of a history before John Sooy came along. The land was originally part of the Richard Bull Survey for 151 acres made on the 9th of February, 1715. Bull was a surveyor for the proprietors, but it seems that this particular land he intended to keep for himself. He lent his name to Bull Creek (called Wackerra Sprout in 1744 as per the Wharton Ledgers #9, p. 39) and Little Bull Creek, and later to Bulltown and its glassworks. Richard must not have had any children, for his nephew, Thomas, became his heir-in-law when he died. Thomas sold this particular 151 acres to Philip Wallace on the 4th of January, 1731 for 40 pounds. Philip's will, written on August 25th, 1753 (the year after Joseph Sooy bought the Driver Survey), was proved on March 24th, 1755. His estate descended upon his sons, John and Thomas. John took little time in getting out from under what he must have considered to be a worthless hunk of real estate, for he made a Quit Claim deed to his brother on March 1st, 1756 for the immense sum of five shillings.

Thomas Wallace didn't last much longer than his father. His will was written on November 20th, 1758 and was proved on December 18th of the same year. He directed that his property was to be sold by his executors: his

The Old Homestead from the river end - circa 1960

son, John Wallace, his brother-in-law, Joshua Lippincott, and his wife, Hope. These sold it to Joseph Burr six years later on September 20th, 1764. There had to have been some particular reason for this sale, perhaps to satisfy Wallace's requirement that his property be sold, because five days after he bought the acreage, Burr sold it to Henry Jones for 60 pounds. Henry Jones, you see, had married the widow Wallace during the intervening years, and they wanted to hang on to the property.

Apparently Henry and Hope (Wallace) Jones weren't able to fulfill their dreams by the Mullica, though. On the 9th of February, 1767, they sold it at a loss to Andrew Anderson for 20 pounds. Andrew didn't get to do anything with it either, and this is where the Sooy family comes in to the picture.

On the 19th of July, 1771, Andrew Anderson sold this 151 acres of the Richard Bull Survey to John Sooy, son of Joseph Sooy, then the owner of the Pearson/Driver Survey just across Little Bull Creek. John Sooy was born in 1742 and was twenty-nine when he paid $80 for this land. It was John and his wife, Abigail (Osborn), who must have built the first section of this house overlooking the Little Egg Harbor River sometime after this purchase.

Mr. Brumbaugh, the Architect of Restorations at Batsto during the 1960's, thought that the original section of the house was the two-story end closest to the river, but on examination of internal evidence, Budd Wilson and Hollis Koster, who used to live here, found that there were strong indications pointing to the original section of the house being the first story of the center section.

If Mr. Wilson and Mr. Koster are correct, John Sooy built the first story of the center section as his home on the river and moved his family into it before the outbreak of the Revolutionary War. While John Sooy owned the property, it seems evident that their house became the "homestead" to the Sooy clan. Nicholas Sooy II, the son of tavern-keeper Nicholas I, is listed as being born in this house on the 20th of February, 1782. Nicholas and Sarah (Sears) must have ventured down the Green Bank road from time to time and stayed with his older brother, John, and his family, especially in times like childbirth. Perhaps father Joseph even breathed his last within these walls. It was probably not long after the first section was built that John added the second, then built another story over the original section. The growing extended family would have definitely needed the space. By the time he died, at least the full center section and the river end looked out over the Mullica. Mr. Wilson took extensive measurements on the old house and notes that they seemed all wrong at first glance. Apparently, it was built using the German foot rather than the English, which would reflect the Sooy Dutch heritage.

When John Sooy wrote his Last Will and Testament on the 16th of May, 1792, he was only fifty years old, yet the will is marked "proved" on the 17th of October in the same year. "I do give and bequeath" he wrote, "unto my sons, John and Osborne, the home plantation I live on, to be equally divided between them (N.J. Arch. 1st Series, Vol. 8, p. 335)." Abigail was pregnant when her husband died, and the resulting son, Thomas, would be entitled to a one-third share along with his brothers. Two other sons, Richard and Charles, inherited John's upper plantation, whose location is not known. Apparently, John Sooy owned half of his brother Joseph's plantation as well. This share of brother Joseph's land as well as forty-three acres on the other side of the river, known as Mud Point, were to be sold to pay his debts. He also had three daughters: Sarah, Phoebe, and Eliza. Phoebe married Godfrey Estlow who had bought fifty acres on the west branch of the Wading River in 1791 and built himself a sawmill. Abigail herself received two feather beds, three cows, one yoke of oxen and was entitled to possession of the homestead until the youngest son (Thomas) was of age. Lewis Darnell of Wading River and Noah Sooy took inventory of the estate on June 8th, 1792 and valued it at 81.18 pouinds. John Sooy's widow married Samuel Odell, who, with her sons, was an executor for her first husband, and, on December 23, 1815, she and her sons sold their plantation property to Nicholas Sooy II for $1,400.

Nicholas Sooy II, fifth child and third son of the owner of Sooy's Inn, Nicholas I, had been born in the "Old Homestead" in what was then considered part of Green Bank on February 20, 1782. At twenty-one, he married Esther Weeks (b. December 30th, 1783) on August 13th, 1803. Esther was the daughter of Ezekiel Weeks of Weekstown (then Weeksville) across the river from Green Bank, and the older sister of Job and Samuel Weeks who later had so much to do with the history of Lower Bank. Nicholas II accumulated a great deal of land along the Mullica during his lifetime, including this, his uncle John's plantation, the 300 acres of his grandfather's plantation (the Pearson/Driver Survey) and several other large parcels along the 1808 road all the way to Wading River. The most prominent citizen of Green Bank for half a century, he built several houses in the vicinity for his children, was instrumental in either the building or the rebuilding of the Green Bank Church, and owned the property on which the Green Bank glassworks was built.

Nicholas Sooy II and Esther Weeks had ten children: Elizabeth, Samuel, Mary, Sophia, Esther, William, Ephraim and Josephus (who were twins), Sarah, and Nicholas III. The final two-story section on the southern end of the house was probably added by Nicholas Sooy II in the first half of the 19th century, although John Rapp may have added the third section when he bought the property later in the century and turned it into a hotel. The house was quite lengthy, but only eighteen feet in width! Seen from the river, it had the appearance of a rather small, nondescript house. From the main drive, however, it took on the imposing appearance seen in the picture above. A traveler on the Mullica would have seen the same imposing view of the rear of the house when approaching from downriver.

To Nicholas II, this house must have symbolized his enduring legacy to his family. His grandfather had lost the Old Driver Homestead to a bad debt in 1787. His father, respected as he was, was simply a tavern keeper on the Old Tuckerton Road. Nicholas II had created what he hoped would be the nucleus of a landed aristocracy. His children had married well. He owned thousands of acres of land, a prosperous shipping business, several ships, and even a glass factory. In 1823, he bought back the homestead that his grandfather had lost. He provided each of his children with a house and land. To the doorstep of his homestead came rich and poor alike. He was respected and admired. Jesse Richards of Batsto had died, loved, respected, but broke. Jesse Evans had seen his beloved Martha Furnace shut down forever before he went to his final rest.

Nicholas Sooy II was at the height of success when he met his Maker. When he breathed his last within these walls, he closed his eyes in peace, knowing that he had provided his family with ample tools to continue his success in life. When Nicholas Sooy II wrote his will in 1850, it was with fondness that he gave his "Old Homestead" to his namesake, Nicholas III.

To his "dear and beloved wife," he bequeathed one-third of all his extensive real estate, "together with all my household and kitchen furniture, one horse and harness, and two horse buggy - or rather wagon - and one Deerbons wagon - and five cows - all my farming utensils in full right of her dowery, so long as she shall remain my widow." Esther (Weeks) Sooy lived for another thirteen years.

When he died on the 29th of June, 1851, the "Old Homestead" became the patrimony of his fifth son and youngest child, Nicholas III (listed in the will as "Jr."). Nicholas III held on to the beloved homestead for eighteen years, but on the 24th of May, 1869, he sold this symbol of the stability and endurance of his family to John H. Rapp and Luman Wing for $4,500. Rapp and Wing had big ideas for the Richard Bull Survey and the Old Homestead of the Sooys. They envisioned a new planned community, surrounding a huge glass factory. The homestead would be the centerpiece hotel, standing at the head of a fine steamship dock on the river.

Though Rapp and Wing are poised on the banks of the Mullica, getting ready for big things, we have to go back a few years and trace the immigrant path of a young German who would figure prominently in the next era of the Old Homestead. Augustus Koster was born in Hanover, Germany in 1840 and had at least three brothers, two of whom were missionaries in China. The third brother, Charles Koster, came to the United States prior to Augustus' arrival. That came in 1854 when he was fourteen years old. Augustus settled in Brooklyn, home of many German and Scandinavian immigrants. That's where he eventually met Augusta Rapp, daughter of John H. Rapp, who would later have plans to build a new city in the Jersey pines. He and Augusta were married on July 30, 1868 and apparently moved to the new Herman City soon afterwards.

The ancient homestead of the Sooy family figured in Rapp's plans for his new town, and the young couple became the host and hostess of the Herman City Hotel. Despite John Rapp's death and the failure of the glass factory, the Kosters continued their operation of the hotel. During the latter part of the nineteenth century, steamboats from New York used to make their way up the Mullica and docked at the wharf at the Herman City Hotel, giving it the name "Steamboat Wharf." Augustus served as tax collector and assessor of Washington Township for several years. He also was president of the District Board of Education. Augustus died in 1925 at the age of eighty-five.

Augusta and Augustus's son, Leon, had the place into the 20th century, but it was only a shadow of its former self. Leon Koster married Josephine Garton, a teacher from Hammonton. Josie's father had been a soldier in the British army for ten years prior to his coming to the

Courtesy of Budd Wilson

Leon Koster

United States. Josie and Leon filled the old homestead with nine children: Hollis, Rodney, Courtland, Shirley, Janice, Augusta, Helene, Kathleen, and Glendin. There was no need for a hotel way out in the woods by this time, though there are indications that the Kosters rented out rooms in the old Sooy homestead.

One of their children became a nurse, another, Glendin, completed his studies at Drexell University. In fact, all of the Koster children had a college-level education with the single exception of Rodney. Mrs. Koster served as secretary for the Parent-Teacher Association at the Green Bank School, and as a substitute teacher and Leon was employed by the State of New Jersey in the Forestry Department. Their many children moved to other areas though, leaving their brothers, Rodney and Hollis, as caretakers of the family estate after Leon and Josie passed away. Both Rodney and Hollis acted as guides to Henry Charlton Beck during the thirties when that newspaperman collected stories about the Mullica area. Hollis was an expert on the flora of the Pine Barrens.

Rodney served in the army during the Second World War. When he returned to Green Bank at the war's conclusion, he lived with his father and brother in the Old Homestead until Leon Koster's death in 1960. It was during this period that he ran the Old Store (1044 River Road), and was succeeded by his sister, Shirley.

When Rodney died in 1984, Glendin continued to pay the taxes. The family negotiated with the State of New Jersey for purchase of the property. A price was finally agreed upon,

Courtesy of Elaine Weber Mathis

Glendin Koster and George W. Ford

and the state came into possession of the ancient seat of the Sooy family.

The Old Homestead burned to the ground in a spectacular fire in the summer of 1987. Like so many other abandoned buildings in the Pine Barrens, it was believed to have been the work of an arsonist. The Old Homestead of the Sooys had stood overlooking the Mullica for over two centuries. Now it was gone forever. Glendin Koster lived to know of the loss of his family's home for three generations, outliving his brothers and sisters. He finally passed away in February of 1995.

The lane that used to lead to this old house begins at the base of the Bulltown Road where it exits on the Batsto/Wading River Road (Route 542). At the entrance to the site of the Old Homestead, stand two huge oak trees that must have been planted when John Sooy built the first section of the home that would become the ancestral "mansion" of his family and that of his eminently successful nephew. They tower high into the air and are mute testimony to the size of the trees of the ancient forest that once covered this entire area. Leon Koster used to tell the story of how he purchased the two old trees from the state for fifty cents apiece. There used to be several of the huge

Courtesy of Budd Wilson

Rodney Koster - 1940's

Courtesy of Budd Wilson

Rodney & Shirley Koster - 1940's

Courtesy of Budd Wilson

Courtland Koster - 1940's

oaks lining Route 542, and the state decided to cut them down. Leon loved the old trees and bargained with the state for their preservation. To all our modern-day specialists, who maintain the pinelands soil cannot support anything but scrub oak and pine, these trees shout to the world that once, when Indians roamed the banks of the Mullica, there were indeed "real" trees spreading their dense foliage high above the sandy soil of the pinelands.

They are all that are left of over two hundred years of history, but in 1996, they are marked. This time, when the New Jersey Department of Transportation or the Wharton State Forest comes along, there will be no Leon Koster to ransom these grandfathers of the primeval forest. With their demise, there will be nothing to teach our children that once this land supported something besides scrub oak and spindly pines. We will have erased the natural history of the Mullica valley just as the myth of the piney has effectively obliterated the human drama which has played itself out beside the brown waters of this river of life.

The Mullica still flows to the sea, but it passes empty clearings where ancient homesteads used to stand, and the woods are silent.

Courtesy of Budd Wilson

Shirley Koster - 1940's

Leon Koster
1956

Courtesy of Budd Wilson

Courtesy of Elaine Weber Mathis

The Herman City Hotel

Courtesy of Budd Wilson

Rodney Koster - 1956

369

The Woolston/Cobb/Cramer House
1156 Route 542

During the mid-eighteen hundreds, Jane and Peter Woolston lived in this house on the road near the river. Peter and Jane's son, William, later became the guardian of the Sooy estate, and, when the state took over most of that property, he became the first Forest Warden for the State of New Jersey.

Back in the 1930s, Henry Charlton Beck interviewed a colorful old character of Green Bank, 'Lance' Cobb, who lived in this house with his wife. 'Alanson' was his given name, but everyone called him 'Lance'.

Lance, at seventy-six, was typical of many of the older folk of the

Photograph by John Pearce

area: spare in frame and speech. These were the days before Social Security, and older Americans continued to work unless they were totally unable to do so. "Snapper" Cobb was no different.

"Snapper" got his nickname from his seasonal occupation, "fyking" snapping turtles. As anyone with a taste palet knows, snapper makes great soup. Devotees of fine restaurants may not know what they're eating when they order snapper soup laced with sherry, but those delectable morsels of meat floating in broth are pieces of snapping turtles.

Snappers, we are told, are everywhere. It is said that every still body of fresh water contains at least one snapping turtle (more than likely, several). Snappers have a huge head, compared with other turtles, and their jaws are quite powerful. Even small ones can chomp through a frozen fish with a single bite. Imagine what they can do to a human foot or hand! Think about that the next time you take a dip in a beautiful lake. Thankfully, they rarely bother with humans when they're in the water. They usually head in the other direction when a human sloshes by, which is most beneficial to the unsuspecting human. On land its another matter altogether. If you ever spot a big turtle with a huge, triangular head and a jagged-edge shell, don't mess with it! You'll come out the looser.

"Snapper" Cobb, in his "retirement" years, did anything he could to make a little money in the midst of the depression. Like everyone else, he lived off the land. He did some subsistence farming to provide vegetables and the like for himself and his wife, but his main occupation was "fyking" snapping turtles. "Fykes" were large, hooped nets that were baited with mossbunkers and set out in the swamps and riverbanks . Biggest snapper "Snapper" Cobb had ever caught, he admitted to Beck one day, was twenty-seven pounds. That's one big snapper. He'd been told that a Lower Banker had caught one that weighed forty-six pounds! Just remember, water-skiers and jet skiers: those turtles with the big strong jaws still lurk in the muddy depths of the Mullica.

Lance Cobb used to fish for herring every spring when they were running. Herring was a marketable commodity, too, and plentiful in the late spring along the Mullica. Herring runs used to start in late March, but you didn't put out the half-pound gill nets until April when the bigger ones were running. "Herring was once so thick in this here river that you could almost walk across on 'em," Cobb told Henry Beck. "They used to go up as far as they could get beyond Batsto, almost to Atsion in the old days."

There's a story told about a local hell-fire-and-damnation preacher who was confronted one Sunday by a parishioner who delighted in pointing out that some of his "sinful" neighbors had skipped church that morning to go fishing for herring. The preacher thought for a minute and then commented that the time to fish for herring was when the herring were there. Somehow, God would understand! Not the answer the busybody expected at all.

The family of Ken Cramer, Jr., lives in this house today.

"Snapper" Cobb with his nets
c. 1940

The Sophia (Sooy) Sawyer/Rebecca Crowley House
1168 Route 542

Courtesy of Budd Wilson

Sophia, the forth child and third daughter of Nicholas Sooy II and Esther (Weeks) Sooy, was born on the Fourth of July 1811. She married David Sawyer, the son of Dr. Ephraim Sawyer of Tuckerton and moved into this house which her father built for her upriver from the "Old Homestead" which her father had purchased from his cousins. David and Sophia had six children: Ephraim, Erastus, Sabra, Thomas, Sophia, and Esther.

Thirteenth: - I give and bequeath to my daughter Sophia Sawyer, a certain lot of land where she now resides, Beginning at William Woolston's Corner at the side of the main road leading to a line between myself and hers, which line was affixed by myself and her husband, David Sawyer: then along said division line on a straight course to the River: then up the River the serveral courses thereof to Curtis Wilson's line, then along said line to William Woolston's line, then along said line to the place of beginning. I also give her eight hundred dollars for which amount I have already given her in cash.

Courtesy of Budd Wilson

Rebecca Crowley

The actual construction date of this house is not known, but it was definately prior to the death of Nicholas Sooy II in 1851. As originally built, the house was only a story and a half, very much like the little houses at Batsto and was L-shaped. At some time, the roof was raised to make a full height second floor and the L-section filled in so that the house became rectangular. It retained the original fireplace and narrow, winding staircase until the state "restoration" for offices under the Bureau of Parks.

During the second half of the nineteenth century, the house came into the Crowley family. Nicholas Crowley was the son of Samuel Crowley III (of the twenty-one-children-and-four-wives fame) and his first wife, Parnell Sooy. He married Rebecca Johnson of Port Republic in that town in June of 1858, and the couple made Port Republic their home.

Four years later, on August 23, 1862, Rebecca gave birth to a boy whom they named "James Morrell". James, or rather "'Rell" as they called him, became enamored of the sea and captained his own vessels. In the latter part of the century, he acquired the house at 1027 River Road in Green Bank and lived there with his wife, Augusta Wobbar. His mother lived in this house on the Hammonton/New Gretna Road during the last years of her life.

In the 1930s and 1940s, the Mathis family lived here. Charles Wilson, Sr. (called "Budd" or locally, "Cap"), Chief of Police of the Benjamin Franklin Bridge for many years, fell in love with the Mullica valley when he was still a young man in the New Jersey State Police. After he met Henry Beck and read his books, the area became his passion. While searching for a home to rent in the area, he was directed to this house by friends who lived at Batsto.

Charles and his wife Edna moved here while their son, Charles, Jr., (also called "Budd") was in college. Budd Sr. and Edna found the house in need of having its rear porch replaced and undertook the reconstruction themselves. Through the 1950s, the house also had a "summer kitchen" to the rear, clearly visible in several of the photographs on the next pages.

Budd Wilson, (Charles, Jr.), often visited them during his college years, and he, too, fell in love with Washington Township. Although he was forced to find employment elsewhere for some years, his heart was always by the Mullica. He moved here permanently in 1961, and, in 1974, married Marilyn Browne, daughter of Ruth (Wobbar) Browne, granddaughter of Haze and Helena Wobbar.

His father was interested in archeology and was fascinated by the various "digs" in the area. Budd took up archeology in college and later served as archeologist for the State of New Jersey in the excavation of the glassworks site at Batsto. In 1995, the house contains the regional offices of the Department of Environmental Protection, State Park Service - Region I.

An interesting note: across the Batsto-Green Bank road from this house once stood about five houses which were known as "Skin" Row though the reason for this strange cognomen is beyond memory.

The Sawyer/Crowley House - Circa 1900

The Sawyer/Crowley House
Circa 1900

The Rear Porch of the Crowley House
As Reconstructed by the Wilsons
Circa 1954 - 1956
Edna Wilson is standing on the porch.

East View of the House
Between 1953 and 1956
The summer kitchen can still be seen to the left of the house.

Edna Wilson
Circa 1954 - 1956

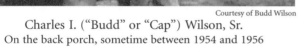
Courtesy of Budd Wilson

Charles I. ("Budd" or "Cap") Wilson, Sr.
On the back porch, sometime between 1954 and 1956

Courtesy of Budd Wilson

Edna Wilson
On the back porch, sometime between 1954 and 1956

The Rear of the House
Circa 1953 - 1954
The doors nailed to the porch posts are from the old Crowleytown School

The Rear Porch Under Reconstruction
Circa 1954

The Sawyer/Crowley House
1995
Currently housing the regional offices of the
Department of Environmental Protection,
State Park Service - Region I

Photographs by John Pearce

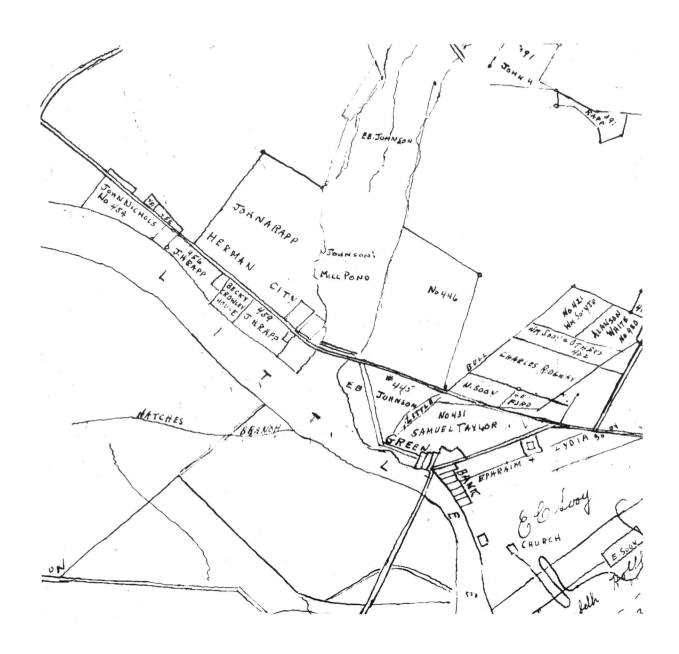

Map of Herman

This map of Herman is taken from the Wharton Ledgers and was drawn about 1890.

Hog Wallow

and

Pineworth

The old Haines Cranberry Packing House at Hog Wallow
This building, used for cleaning and packing cranberries, burned to the ground in a spectacular fire in July of 1974.

Hog Wallow and Pineworth

TRANQUILITY, HOSPITALITY, AND FRUGALITY IN THE PINES

The Pine Barrens are a wonderful anachronism. Despite the ever-present peripheral pressures for all-consuming development, the core area of the pines still reflects a life long past, when a person could walk for miles through forests without seeing a single building, unthreatened by traffic and smog and congestion. They are different than they once were, of course. Much of the land was exploited in the infant days of our country. Giant cedars were toppled for their timber. The swamps and freshwater marshes were mined of their natural iron deposits. Vast areas were stripped for farming. Yet the fragile land somehow remained resilient.

Deep within the pinelands flows a tributary of *Little Hauken Run* called *Hospitality Brook*. *Little Hauken Run* is itself a tributary of the West Branch of the *Wading River*, and both streams drain the Haines's cranberry bogs at Hog Wallow. According to Henry Bisbee in *Signposts: Place Names in History of Burlington County, N.J.*, an 1873 map of the area calls this stream *Tranquility Branch*. He says that it was named *Tranquility* as early as 1740, though in 1759 it was labelled *Frugality*, "a *Branch of Tranquility*." In 1760, it had gained the name of *Indian Run*. The name *Hospitality* first appears on an 1895 map and is repeated on the 1956 U.S. Geological Survey topographical map of the Jenkins Quadrangle. Whichever name one chooses: *Tranquility, Frugality*, or *Hospitality*, it would seem appropriate for a stream which drains the bogs of this prosperous family enterprise in the pines. Here there is a harmony of man and the land, of a family where mutual respect and love still are the rule rather than the exception.

Bill Haines loves his family and the land which sustains it. There's a depth to him that speaks of a virtue anchored in the land that gives life. He is very much a product of the pinelands but certainly not a "Piney," that inbred, half-imbecilic caricature created by the intellectual elite for the public's titillation and their own profit. His weathered face and gentle demeanor speak of a strength and confidence born of the land. His is a family of three daughters and a son and their families who still live with mutual respect and love, sustained by the strength of the land which has nurtured them. Educated at Rutgers as well as by the surrounding forests and streams of the pines, Bill is a wise, shrewd, generous, and successful man.

William S. Haines, Sr. stems from a family that can trace its roots back to the seventeenth century in New Jersey. He knows a date, 1677, and a place, Burlington. There's even a story about the first Haines in New Jersey living in a cave in Hainesport. New arrivals had to do that sometimes. They had little but the clothes they wore way back then, so their first "home" in the new world was often a hole in the ground which was covered by a roof made from the surrounding forests. Bill thinks that first Haines in the new world was of Welsh origin, and, if so, he passed the strength of his homeland's hills to his posterity in the pines.

MARTIN LUTHER HAINES

The Haines family story in the pines begins at the end of the last century about 1890. His grandfather, Martin Luther Haines, lived on a farm in Vincentown, New Jersey. He was no simple farmer, however. During the Civil War, Martin Luther served as a captain in the Union Army, and, after returning home, both practiced law and taught in the public school in Vincentown. While in the army, he had seen examples of the infant cranberry-growing business and developed an interest in it. When he came home from the war, he was unwilling to settle for the bounds of a simple farm and soon purchased bogs in Southampton and Tabernacle Townships.

"Martin Luther" wasn't his given name, though. His parents had named him after the great Democrat Andrew Jackson's protege and

Courtesy of William S. Haines, Sr.

Martin Luther Haines

381

handpicked successor, Martin Van Buren, but, having had a fight with the Democratic Party, Martin Haines opted for the famous church reformer over the political hack and changed his name.

Martin Van Buren Haines, or as he came to call himself, Martin Luther Haines, was an enterprising man. Besides his legal career, his teaching career, his farm and his bogs, he also owned a store in Vincentown, outside of which some long-forgotten photographer caught him in a moment of relaxation sometime at the end of the century in the photograph on the previous page.

With ever an eye to profit, he decided to add lands nearer the core of the pinelands to his extensive bogs at the Birches, Two Bridges, Burr's Mills, and Peach Farm closer to Vincentown. It was about the year 1890 in which Martin Luther and a partner, George McCambridge bought some bogs and upland in upper Washington Township, Burlington County in an area known as "Hog Wallow." Outside of the Haines's main buildings is still a shallow depression which fills up with water in a good rain. Perhaps it was just this spot which was the original swimming pool for the local hogs gone wild after their owners moved away following the collapse of the iron industry in the area.

Bisbee implies that the name "Hog Wallow" is of more recent origin than that of "Haines Bog," but Bill Haines doesn't believe it. Others may have referred to the area as "Haines Bog" after the coming of Martin Luther to the area, but the Haines Family has always been proud of the colorful old name of "Hog Wallow."

The Haines/McCambridge partnership didn't last very long however. Two strong men rarely see eye-to-eye for a long period of time, and certainly these two were no different. The property was split between them with George McCambridge taking the cultivated bogs in what would later be known as Pineworth and Martin Haines taking the wild bogs around Hog Wallow.

The Second Generation - Ethelbert, Ernest, and Ralph

For the Haines family, 1890 was a memorable year in more ways than one. In that year when Martin bought the bogs at Hog Wallow, he and his wife, Ella Joyce, also had a son, whom they named Ralph. Already blessed with Ethelbert, Ernest, and Edith, the couple were delighted with their third boy, and Martin Luther probably planned his enterprises well to provide a lasting heritage for his sons.

Martin Luther Haines spent the remaining fifteen years of his life happily building bogs around Hog Wallow. Though still not an old man, he died in 1905, weakened perhaps by the privations of the Civil War years and by his unsparing zeal for his various enterprises.

In the mean time, George McCambridge sold his interest in the lower bogs to a partnership consisting of Jake and George Worth, Blanchard White, and Earl Lippincott, Sr. (not one of the Wading River Lippincotts). According to Stephen V. Lee, Jr. of Speedwell, George Worth was not part of the partnership with his brother but bought bogs in the area on his own. Mr. Lee says that the brothers weren't even on speaking terms. It may well have been at this time when the area was christened with the name "Pineworth" after the Worth brothers.

George Worth soon sold out his interest to James Aquila Jones. Blanchard White just seems to disappear. Jake Worth and Earl Lippincott, Sr., continued to operate their share of the Pineworth bogs which passed to their sons, Jake, Jr. and Earl, Jr. Bill Haines eventually brought them back into the Haines sphere in 1972, almost a century after his grandfather had given up his partnership in them.

Martin Luther's sons, Ethelbert and Ernest took over the operation of the Hog Wallow bogs after their father's 1905 death. They saw to it that their little brother, Ralph, only fifteen at the time of his father's passing, got the best of educations. Ralph actually graduated from the University of Pennsylvania and hung out his shingle as a practicing attorney, as his father had been, in the county seat, Mount Holly.

The lure of the pines was too much for him, however. In 1920, at the age of thirty, he went into partnership with brother Ethelbert in the Hog Wallow bogs. Brother Ernest took over the complete operation of the older Haines bogs in Tabernacle and Shamong Townships: the Birches, Burr's Mill, and Two Bridges, as well as the Peach Farm. Ethelbert eventually bought out John Aquila Jones and his Pineworth bogs, turning over a half share in the lands to his wife, Bertha. Bertha was from Ore Hill, South Carolina, and returned home after her husband's death. Her heirs sold that share to Bill Haines, Sr., so that section remained in the Haines family as well.

Ethelbert and his brother Ralph constructed several buildings on the Hog Wallow property, some of which remain standing in 1995. Built by Ethelbert Haines sometime between 1900 and 1910, the oldest structure in the complex is now the home of Bill Haines, Sr. The huge old Packing House in the photograph on the first page of

Courtesy of William S. Haines, Sr.

Ethelbert Haines overlooking Oswego Lake

this section was also constructed in the very early part of the twentieth century, a little later than the house. It succumbed to a spectacular fire in the midsummer of 1974.   Everyone was thankful that it was surrounded by bogs rather than trees or the burning embers might have started a truly memorable conflagration.

It was under Ethelbert and Ralph's administration that the farm became a part of the Ocean Spray Cooperative in 1948.

Courtesy of William S. Haines, Sr.

Ralph Haines

Ralph had married Cordelia Abrams Reynolds (b. 1893, d. 1990), three years younger than himself. The couple lived on Mill Street in Vincentown and had two sons, Martin Luther II and William S.

Bill Haines was born in 1921, though not on the Hog Wallow farm nor at Vincentown. In the 1920's, people were beginning to think that babies should actually be born in hospitals, not in the home, and Cordelia always felt that the Philadelphia hospitals were better than the local ones, so she insisted that her husband take her to Pennsylvania for the birth of their son.

The Third Generation - William S. Haines

Bill was born with pinelands blood coursing through his arteries just as surely as anyone could be, even though he didn't actually grow up there. During the summers, he would live out at Hog Wallow and work with his uncle, Ethelbert while he was on vacation from school and gained a deep love for the land.

His parents sent him to Rutgers University, but Bill just couldn't keep away from the pinelands. The lure of megabucks in industry wasn't strong enough to bar him from the pines. He left Rutgers after only a year and came home to work on the farm, commuting back and forth from Vincentown every day.

When Bill started working with his uncle full time, the farm consisted of about five hundred acres of bogs and uplands. As far as local farms went, that was a sizable amount of land, but Bill was determined to see things got even bigger.

In 1946, Bill married Sarah Jennings and moved permanently to Hog Wallow. Sarah was the widow of Paul Norcross and had two very young daughters, Karen and Betty Ann, who were three and six years old when their mother remarried.

Karen married Bob Breitzman of Egg Harbor, and the couple have four children: Sharon, Rob, Jennifer, and Donald. Betty Ann married Aldo McCoy of Vedalia, Georgia, and they have just one child, a son, William Scott Doerr. These two families still live close on the Hog Wallow property.

Bill and Sarah did what they could to populate their corner of Washington Township and had the joy of having two children as well: Bill, Jr. and Holly.

Bill, Jr. married Crystal Smith and had three children: Stefanie, Rebecca, and William S. Haines III, whom they call "Tug".

Bill, Jr. married twice, the second time to Nadine Costa, daughter of Catherine and Joseph Costa. Catherine is a former New Jersey State Senator. Nadine and Bill, Jr. share three lovely children themselves: John Michael, Sarah, and Victoria.

Courtesy of William S. Haines, Sr.

William S. Haines - circa 1927

Bill and Nadine live in a Victorian-style home they built on Hambone Ridge in Pineworth. Holly lives in the old Captain Somers house in Lower Bank.

When Bill's father, Ralph, died in 1965, Bill became the owner of the enterprise in the pines. Almost every building on the property: employee homes, machinery shop, storage sheds, outbuildings, and the newer packing house were built after Bill took over the operations.

New Jersey's Largest Cranberry Farm

Bill Haines, Sr. and his family have not only loved and protected their land in the Pinelands, they've made it productive and profitable as well. Growing cranberries is a water-intensive process. Each acre of bog needs ten acres of protected upland to support it. That relationship of cultivated land to pristine forest means that the vast majority of acreage must be carefully preserved in order for the bogs to produce. Development and overuse are anathama.

When Bill, Sr. took over the operation of Haines and Haines from his father, there were about five hundred acres in the farm. In 1995, there are over eleven thousand acres, almost nine hundred of which are devoted to growing cranberries. An elaborate system of irrigation channels connect the bogs in order for them to be alternately flooded and drained. In spring and summer, the bogs are dry, giving the plants time to grow and produce. When the harvest is near, they are flooded. During the winter, the bogs remain flooded to protect the plants from

Planting the Bog - circa 1950
L. to R.: Ethelbert Haines, Gene Rosar, John Melton, Walter Ball

freezing. Dikes, ditches, and wooden dams channel the water over the landscape to ensure sufficient water to each and every bog over the vast farm.

Raising cranberries has changed considerably over the years. In the early days, harvesting cranberries required a great deal of labor. The ripe berries were handpicked in dry bogs, and many local folk would travel from farm to farm during the season to help in the harvesting. They would crawl through the bogs, raking their fingers through the vines to dislodge the berries, then pick them up and place them in a box.

Two different types of scoops were invented to make the job easier, both of which are museum pieces today. The Makepiece scoop was designed on Cape Cod, Massachusetts, while the Applegate scoop was invented by a David Applegate who lived in Chatsworth. Using a scoop saved the pickers hands, but both methods were backbreaking work.

Pickers would spend hours a day bent over in the dry bogs, using the scoops like combs to gather the berries. They would dump them in one-peck wooden boxes. When filled, these boxes would be emptied into a one-bushel packing box. These packing boxes would be trucked to the packing house where the berries would be separated from the leaves and pieces of twigs which had been collected with them. Good cranberries bounce, so, after cleaning, they would be put into a machine that would bounce them down seven stages. Those which failed to bounce at all were discarded. During the 1940's, a man by the name of Darlington invented a machine for dry-picking the berries. This device had a row of cones that would rake the vines, lift the culled berries up in a series of rotating cylinders, and dump them in a bag at the top. Another locally-used picker, the Western, was invented by Joseph Stankiewicz of Oregon (see BULLTOWN for a photograph).

Bill Haines was the pioneer of harvesting techniques in the area. In the 1950's, Bill developed the first method to harvest the cranberries from a flooded bog. The bogs would first be dry-harvested. Then the bogs would be flooded, and , using an airboat, the flooded bogs would be agitated to loosen the berries that had been trapped under the vines. They were corralled from the surface using a huge, U-shaped wooden gathering "boom." This would increase the yield of the dry-harvested bogs. Bill went into partnership with John Lee, Stephen V. Lee, Jr.'s brother, and they went from farm to farm with their airboats.

Picking the Cranberries - Early 1950's
On the Worth Tract west of Hog Wallow and north of Pineworth
L. to R.: Ethelbert Haines, Margaret Grant, Betty Grant, Elizabeth ("Beana") Coia

In the early 1960's, Bill pioneered the wet-pick method used today by designing a harvesting machine used in a flooded bog. In this method, the bogs are flooded to about two inches over the vines, and Bill's special machines are used to agitate the vines and persuade them to let go of their berries (See WADING RIVER for photographs). Many of these machines are small enough for men to walk behind them through the bogs. Others are actually ridden by their operators. Several operators move in succession around the bogs, knocking loose the berries, which then float to the top of the water. A large boom, much like those used to surround oil spills on rivers, lakes, and the ocean is placed around the bogs, and the berries are worked to one end. A conveyor belt lifts the berries into a dump truck, which then transports them to the packing house.

Local farms like Bill's don't need to completely clean and test bounce the berries today. The local packing house workers simply clean them of the leaves and larger twigs and send them off to the Ocean Spray Receiving Station in Chatsworth for processing.

Both harvesting and packing cranberries required a large amount of seasonal labor just a few years ago. An individual laborer could only pick between two to four bushels over a four to six hour period. Then the packing houses demanded another large group of workers to watch the machines which cleaned and separated the berries. Local workers provided the first seasonal labor in the cranberry bogs of Washington Township, and many of the older residents still remember working in them when they were young. As the farms expanded, additional labor was needed. Labor suppliers like Nick Coia of Hammonton arranged to bring in seasonal help, first Italian immigrants, then people from Puerto Rico. Some of the latter liked the pinelands so much that they sent for their families and remain there today.

Courtesy of William S. Haines, Sr.

Nick Coia and Ethelbert Haines - Late 1940's or early 1950's
Timmy Coia runs a trucking company for Ocean Spray as well as the Haines's packing house.

Bill Haines, Sr. did a great deal of experimenting with cranberry production techniques and helped improve the quality of the crop and the efficiency of production. He was instrumental in the establishment of the Cranberry and Blueberry Research Center on the road to Oswego Lake.

Bill Haines, Jr. graduated from Cook College in 1975 and returned to the family enterprise in the pines. Named the New Jersey State Board of Agriculture's Outstanding Young Farmer in 1987, he formed the Pine Island Cranberry Company the following year. This is the actual management company which oversees the daily operations of the farm. Father and son installed New Jersey's first solid-set irrigation and frost protection system for cranberries and have applied integrated pest management practices. They have also been actively involved in testing USDA experimental plant varieties.

Their farm was also one of the first in the country to use a water sanding system which promotes growth and helps keep diseases from taking hold in the plants. Invented by neighboring farmer, Abbott Lee, sanding is a process of spreading a fine layer of sand on the flooded bogs both in the fall after harvest time and also in the spring.

Harvesting time is hectic, to say the least. Every last hand is needed to gather the berries from the far-flung bogs, clean them in the packing house, and send them on to Ocean Spray. The remainder of the year is occupied with planting, fertilizing, pollinating, sanding, pruning, and otherwise cultivating the cranberry bogs. There are flood gates and dams to be repaired and replaced, roads to be maintained, and dikes to be rebuilt. On top of that, Haines and Haines is always building new bogs.

As if all this activity with luscious cranberries weren't enough, Haines and Haines also maintains many acres of that other pinelands crop, blueberries. Developed from the wild blueberry, the cultivated blueberry is a delicious treat that thrives in Washington Township. In recent years, though, blueberry fields have been forced to yield to cranberries. Unlike the latter, blueberries still have to be handpicked and that's an expensive process. The relationship of profit to production costs are much better for cranberries than for blueberries.

No one understands the value of the land more than the Haines family. Since cranberry growing requires millions of gallons of clean, pure water, they have a tremendous stake in preserving the land for both present and future. Dealing with Department of Environmental Protection regulations, though, is both expensive and time-consuming. The Pinelands Commission hovers over all as well. So do intellectuals and ivory-towered educators who think that the only thing uneducated local-yokels want is the total exploitation of their precious pristine pinelands. Nothing could be farther from the truth, of course.

Over the years since he attended Rutgers, Bill, Sr. has been involved in numerous community and agricultural activities. He has served as president and member of the Board of Directors of the Tru-Blu Cooperative and a member of the board of Ocean Spray Cranberries. He has been a supervisor of the Burlington County Soil Conservation district, is a past president of the Burlington County Board of Agriculture and is a past president of the Cook College Board of Managers. He's serves on the Research Committee of the Rutgers University Research Council and has been chairman of the Washington Township Planning Board.

Bill, Jr. served as mayor of Washington Township and was also a member of the township Planning Board. He is a past president of the county Board of Agriculture and Young Farmers and Ranchers as well as past vice president of the New Jersey Farm Bureau. He is now a member of the Board of Chosen Freeholders of Burlington County.

The Haines family exemplifies the best of pinelands traditions in a harmonious blend of unspoiled wilderness and productive usage. The land could not have more devoted trustees.

Courtesy of William S. Haines, Sr.

The Old Cookhouse at Hog Wallow
In the days of itinerant labor, meals were provided on the property,
and cookhouses like this one were a necessity.

Holly Haines and her father, Bill, Sr. - 1996

Picking Cranberries - Late 1940's
Hog Wallow

Jenkins Neck

and

Maxwell

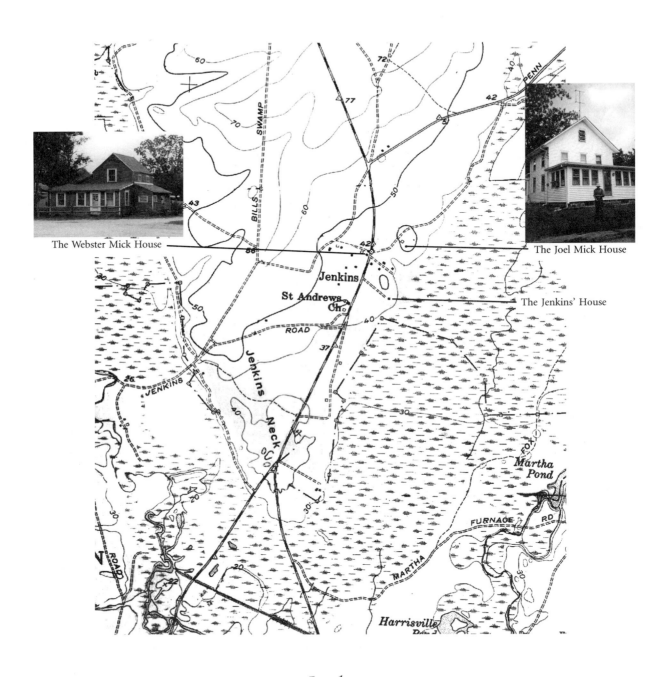

The Webster Mick House

The Joel Mick House

The Jenkins' House

Jenkins

What in the world was so special about old Jenkins' neck that a town was named after it? Was it particularly long and skinny? Did he break it somewhere out in the woods a long time ago? There was a War of Jenkins *Ear* which began in 1739 between Britain and Spain, but there was no skirmish out in these parts that had anything to do with a *neck*. Was this place out here in the pines the place where a man named Jenkins necked with his girlfriend at some long distance past?

Well, we can laugh all we want, but a "neck" is, after all, a piece of fast land between two bodies of water. In this case, it is solid land between the east and west branches of the Wading River, or, as some would have it, between the Wading River proper and the Oswego River. You wouldn't realize that, of course, if you drove up Route 563 through Jenkins today. You can't see either river from the main road. Much of the surrounding land is swamp long before it reaches flowing water.

Francis Mick of Jenkins claims that Jenkins and Jenkins Neck are two different places. Francis is seventy-six years old and was born in the same house in which he still lives. His father, Joel Mick, bought the house before 1920, so Francis doesn't remember quite that far back. Jenkins Neck, he says is down the road towards Green Bank a bit. Jenkins proper is right there where he lives. There aren't many references to the area in the old township records of births, but each is listed as "Jenkins Neck," which seems to have been the original designation for the entire area. The Bowhers, Barzella and Martha, of McCartyville, had a son on February 2, 1848 in "Jenkins Neck" whom they named William Israel. On September 21, 1861, Charles and Elizabeth Hollaway had a daughter, Margaret Aron [sic], in Jenkin's Neck. The family is listed as living there as well.

The year 1866 saw a population explosion in Jenkins Neck. On May 1, William and Roxanna Hollaway welcomed a son, William J., into the world. Two months later, on the 27th of July, the Battersons, Jane and John, had a daughter, Sarah. September saw two births: on the second, Sarah E., daughter of Joseph and "M" McNinney (probably a McAnney), and on the ninth, Uriah, son of Josiah and Phoebe Adams. In the entire period that the records cover, from 1848 through 1876, they are the only recorded births in Jenkins Neck. If there is a difference between Jenkins and Jenkins Neck, it is probably the Mick family that was responsible for the distinction.

So who was Mr. Jenkins? Bisbee (*Martha: The Complete Furnace Diary and Journal 1808-1815*) says that one Zachariah Jenkins served in the American Revolution. He also notes that he is not on the militia list in 1793, which probably indicates that he was exempt from serving due to his prior record of service. Bisbee assumes that, if he were of age to serve in the Revolutionary War, he had to have been around sixty years old in 1808. In 1797, he is listed as living in Northampton Township, a portion of which became Washington Township in 1802. An 1806 record notes that he paid a tax on horses and property. Despite his research, he couldn't find any reference to Mr. Jenkins' death. A "Granny Jenkins" is mentioned in the Martha Diary under the date of April 11, 1811, though there is no indication whether she had any relation to our Zachariah. Henry Charlton Beck says in *Jersey Genesis* that the town was named for Isaac Jenkins who began the operation of the Tuckerton stage in 1816. He notes, though, that a stage was running on a regular schedule between Philadelphia and "Middle-of-the-Shore" (Tuckerton) prior to that date, so if the 1816 date is correct, Isaac Jenkins couldn't have been the *first* to establish such service.

The township records of births and marriages for 1848 to 1877 do not mention a single "Jenkins," nor is his name found in the Census of 1830, the earliest one available for New Jersey. If Zachariah Jenkins had any children, they must have all moved out of the township at a very early date.

There was a house in Jenkins that was connected with the Jenkins family. Budd Wilson, Jr. of Green Bank had the opportunity to examine it prior to its being destroyed in a fire in 1981. Apparently, the first house built on the site was a log cabin, constructed by, yes, Zachariah Jenkins, soldier of the Revolution, prior to 1790. That which was the "middle" section of the house when Budd examined it was built between 1790 and 1810, probably as an addition to the log cabin. By this time, it was the home of Zephaniah Jenkins. Jenkins and Martha are actually rather close together, and it is known that people lived in Jenkins and worked in Martha. It is likely, then, that the "Granny Jenkins" mentioned by the 1811 entry in the Martha diary was indeed the wife of Zachariah Jenkins and mother of Zephaniah.

Budd's notes say that Zephaniah Jenkins had a stage to Tuckerton that was later taken over by an Adams. Leah Blackman gives the name of the Jenkins that ran the stage as Isaac and says he began the route in 1816 but then questions the date since she knew that the stage ran at an earlier one. The relationship of Zephaniah and Isaac has not yet been determined, but everything would be quite simple if they were brothers. Budd's research shows that this house passed to the Adams family from Zephaniah Jenkins and apparently the stage business did also.

Adams sold it to a Holloway, but there were four Holloway families in the township in 1860, and there's no way of telling which one lived here unless further information comes to light. The possibilities are: Joseph (a laborer) and Lettice Holloway (both 49 in 1860), and their sons, Godfrey, Peter, and Henry; Charles (a teamster) and Elizabeth Holloway (48 & 38 respectively), and their children, Anna, Sarah, Alice, John, Charles, Samuel, Emma, Alfred, and Mary E.; Joseph (a team driver) and Martha Holloway (29 & 25 respectively), and their children, Thomas and Sarah; and Elizabeth Holloway (59) and her children, Alfred, Mary and Thomas.

As has been previously mentioned, the township records from mid-century take note of the birth of Margaret Aron [sic], daughter of Charles and Elizabeth Hollaway [sic] in Jenkin's Neck on January 1, 1854. This seems to be the Charles and Elizabeth listed in the census of 1860, but there is no daughter, Margaret Aron. Perhaps she died as a child. Also, Chalres is listed as a laborer in the township birth records and as a teamster in the census. This isn't really a problem, because people often switched jobs. The closest place Charles Holloway could have worked at either job would have been Harrisville. It is possible that he worked at the sawmill in Martha during the early 1850's, then switched to Harrisville when it closed down. In any case, his family seems to have the greatest potential for living in this house during that period.

Budd notes that the two story section was built in 1850-1851 by a man from Lower Bank. This is just a guess, but with the years involved, I would assume that this section was built while the Holloway family lived there. The main house included a 6-foot fireplace on the south end, and a set of stairs was built in next to the fireplace.

After the Holloways moved out, several Micks lived there. It would be interesting to know just which Micks lived here. An addition was added to the north side about 1870. The property then went to a Thomas, then a Singer. On October 13, 1981, the two-story section burned completely. Thus is the history of the Jenkins House in Jenkins, sketchy but enticing. There were others who left their name in this area besides the Jenkins families.

Godfrey Estlow ran a sawmill on the west branch of the Wading River near Jenkins in the first part of the nineteenth century. He had married Phoebe Sooy, the daughter of John Sooy of the Burr Survey in Green Bank/ Herman, and their son, Christopher, was a sawyer at Martha Furnace in 1848. He and his wife, Ann, had a son, Hezekiah Estlow, on Christmas Eve that year. His mother, Phoebe (Sooy) Estlow, died at Martha in June of 1849. Christopher and his family were still in Martha eight years later. A letter in the possession of Lorena Estlow Hyde of Ohio is dated July 16, 1857 and is directed to Christopher Estlow, Martha. Mrs. Hyde has helped this author many times in reference to Godfrey and Christopher Esltow and to John Sooy. Over the years, she has done a great deal of research on her family and the properties owned by the Estlow family.

In April of 1859, Christopher bought property in Red Oak Grove, Ocean County and moved there. He later purchased Wells Mills, where he died. Christopher and his wife, as well as their son, Jesse A. and his wife, were buried just outside of Warren Grove in the Reevestown Cemetery.

Godfrey Estlow's name is remembered in that of the state camping ground and the bridge across the West Branch of the Wading River in Jenkins: Godfrey's Bridge (see THE TRULY FORGOTTEN TOWNS OF THE PINES). There are still Estlow descendants throughout the general area of Southern Ocean County.

Left: Charles Holloway

Right: Elizabeth Holloway

Charles and Elizabeth Holloway of Jenkins Neck were the parents of Sarah Holloway, who married Mahlon Broome, the last manager of Harrisville.

Photographs courtesy of Marian Broome, great-granddaughter of Charles and Elizabeth Holloway.

The Mick Family

The family that has been identified with Jenkins for many years is that of an Irishman, who seems to have started his journey towards Washington Township with William Richards over in Pennsylvania. Perhaps you will remember that William Richards of Batsto was associated with Warwick Furnace in the other Quaker state. As a youth in 1754, he was apprenticed to John Patrick, an important person at Warwick Furnace. Ten years later, he married his master's daughter, Mary. He remained on a very amicable basis with her brother, Samuel, for the rest of his life. There seems no question that the Patricks, betrayed by their name, came from the Emerald Isle, nor is there much of a question about the original origins of the next name to surface at Warwick Furnace. In the Warwick store books, under the date of September 16, 1765, appears the name of Michael Mick, who purchased molasses on that day.

It seems a most mundane record for the first mention of a man who would found the Mick clan in Washington Township, but it does kind of stick to you after a while. The next time the name "Mick" surfaces Michael's 1783 marriage to Mary Moore on December 4th of that year. He must have had his son, Michael, Jr., soon after, for Michael, Jr. married Delia Diviney on the 26th of March, 1802. If junior was born nine months after his parents' marriage (no guarantee of that, of course) he would have been only eighteen or possibly nineteen in 1802.

The name Michael Mick stands out in a listing in the militia records submitted by the Subscriber Deputy Commissioner of the Township of New Hanover, returned to the County of Burlington on April 12, 1793. There, as part of the Company of Hanover Furnace, Township of New Hanover, the report notes that Michael Mick was elected a captain. If Michael Mick was twenty when he purchased molasses at Warwick Furnace on that day so long ago, he would have been forty-eight when he was elected captain at Hanover Furnace. Michael Mick turns up in references at Batsto during the tenure of William Richards, so he may have gravitated here where his old companion and contemporary reigned.

The Martha diary mentions Mick several times, but by the early part of the nineteenth century, the prominent figure locally seems to have been his son, Michael, Jr. Michael, Sr. is listed in 1808 in the Washington Township Tax List, but not as a householder, though his son does have that designation. In the same year, his name and that of his son, Michael, Jr., is among those who were woodchoppers at Martha Furnace. The following year, Michael Mick, Sr. and Jr. appear on the tax list as part of the Martha company once again, and, on the actual Martha list, his name appears under "Workmen." Jr.'s name seems missing from the list of workers. Both appear as "Workmen" in 1810 but neither is listed in 1811. By 1812, both find their way back on the list of workmen, though only Michael, Jr., is on the tax list for that year. Michael, Jr. and "Israel" Mick are listed as workmen in 1813, and junior's name appears again as an oreraiser. The senior Mick's name is absent on the list. He is back on in 1814, though junior and Israel are missing. Actually, Michael, Sr. was a very intelligent and trustworthy man whose talents were employed at Weymouth and Speedwell, as well as at Martha, and it seems he was at Weymouth in 1813. From 1808 until 1813, Michael, Jr. served as Chief Founder at Martha Furnace, second only to manager, Jesse Evans. The services of both Michael Mick, Sr. and Junior were needed at the other local furnaces when rebuilding was necessary. Israel Mick must have been a second son of Michael, Sr. as he is listed on the 1830 census as being between thirty and forty that year.

The Martha Diary records that Delia Mick "gained one" on October 29, 1808. A son, Joseph, was born September 23, 1810. Winter was the time when work was slow, after all. Michael and Delia Mick's house at Martha burned down on April 10, 1810.

The Weymouth diary notes that Michael Mick "began to take out the hearth" at Weymouth on the twenty-second of February, 1814. Mary Mick's death at Weymouth was duly recorded in the Weymouth diary under March, 1814: On the first of the month "Mrs. Michael Mick departed this life about 4 P.M. Extremely cold." On the third, "Buried M. Mick's wife at Batsto. Raised Moulding Room." Life went on, even when funerals were in progress. This has to be Michael Mick, Sr.'s wife. Her stone at Batsto/Pleasant Mills reads: Mary Mick, d. March 1, 1814. Her age is not legible, but she married Michael Mick, Sr. in 1783, thirty-one years before her death. A curiosity: next to Mary Mick's headstone is one for Borick Mick, d. 1794. Who was he? Perhaps a son of Mary and Michael, Sr.?

Bisbee lists, under "Marriages at Martha," that Deliah [sic] Mick had a son on December 7, 1814. There are suggestions that there had to be other Micks than the ones mentioned so far. On April 4, 1814, Bisbee's *Martha: The Complete Furnace Diary and Journal 1808-1815* notes the marriage of "Mick-Mick - Israel and Elizabeth."

Where did Elizabeth come from? Who were her parents? Needless to say, there is much fertile ground for genealogical detective work here.

The 1830 census lists three Mick families in Washington Township. Israel Mick is listed as having nine in his family: males - two under five years of age, three of five but under ten, and one of 30 but under forty; females - one of ten but under fifteen, one of fifteen but under twenty, one of thirty but under forty. Michael Mick is listed as having seven in his family: males - one of five but under ten, one of ten but under fifteen, and one of fifteen but under twenty; females - one of five but under ten, one of forty but under fifty. This may indicate that Michael Mick is either no longer living or is not in the township at the time. Michael Mick "Two" is listed as having three in his family: males - one under five and one of twenty but under thirty; females - one of twenty but under thirty. Since Michael Mick, Jr. would be considerably older than "twenty but under thirty," the first "Michael" listed must be his family. Thus it would seem that Michael Mick, Sr. is no longer living in 1830. Perhaps even Michael, Jr. has passed away. "Michael Mick Two" would have to be actually Michael Mick III.

By 1840, only one Mick is listed, a Robert Mick, whose family totals three: males - one of five but under ten, and one of thirty but under forty; females - one of thirty but under forty. Is this a brother of Michael III? If it is, where have Israel and Michael III gone?

What is curious about these listings is that Martha Furnace had ceased operations around the time that Jesse Evans sold it to Francis French and William Allen in 1847, although a sawmill may have continued to operate there. Likewise, Speedwell Furnace was not operating at the time and had been sold to James McCambridge, the owner of the Eagle Tavern on June 30, 1850. A sawmill may have continued to operate there, too, which would have provided work for Joseph Mick. Another curiosity is that part of Speedwell had been ceded to Shamong Township prior to 1862, when William Mick was born at that place and was recorded in the Washington Township records. The Mick family may have lived in Speedwell proper on land that still remained a part of the old Township. Speedwell itself was ceeded to Woodland Township in 1866.

The Census of 1850 indicates that Joseph Mick, age 27, lived in the township with his wife, Sarah, also 27, and their five children: Charlotte, age 9; Elizabeth, age 7; Israel, age 5; Peter, age 3; and Joseph, age one. No other Micks appear. Joseph would have been born in 1823 or thereabouts. Thus it is possible that he was the son of either Israel Mick or Michael Mick, Jr., both of which had sons of the right age in 1830. The township records for 1848 - 1877 list John and Phoebe Mick having a son, Charles, on the 3rd of April, 1853. John is listed as a laborer at Martha Furnace and the birth happened at Martha.

The 1860 census lists four Mick families in Washington Township. George Mick (53), is listed as a wood chopper. Robert Mick (54), a sawyer, and his wife, Ann (41), appear together. Joseph Mick (38), a laborer, and his wife, Sarah, also thirty-eight, are listed with their children: Charlotte (19), Elizabeth (15), Israel (14), Peter (12), Joseph (9), John (7), Charles (4), and Alice (3). Finally, there is John Mick (54), also a laborer, and his wife, Phoebe (52), and their children: Elizabeth (16), John, Jr. (15), Michael (13), Eliza (9), and Charles (6). This last is the "Charles," son of John and Phoebe, whose birth was listed in the township records. Did this family still live in Martha in 1860? As the township records show, on September 15, 1862, Joseph and Sarah Mick had a son, William, at Speedwell. Joseph is listed as a laborer at that place. There are no other listings of any sort for the Mick family in the township records.

By 1870, Only a Michael Mick remains on the list with his family. Michael was twenty-three that year, and his wife, Mary J. Mick was twenty-two. Three boys are listed with them: Reuben (6), Robert (4), and John (2). This must be the Michael Mick, son of John and Phoebe Mick, who was thirteen at the time of the 1860 census.

There are no Micks on the 1880 census save one: Charles, who was twenty-six at the time, lived with Jane Gaunt (62) and her children, Briney (22) and William (19). A granddaughter, Emma J. Gaskill (2), also lived in the household.

It is not known just when the Mick family came to Jenkins, but it seems probable that they did not move there until the first decade of this century. As has been noted above, in 1853, when their son, Charles, was born, John and Phoebe's family lived in Martha. Joseph and Sarah Mick lived at Speedwell when their son, William was born in 1862. Since only Michael's young family remained in the township in 1870, it is possible that Joseph and Sarah Mick were still in Speedwell and were counted in Shamong or Woodland Township.

It is this Joseph who seems to have been the progenitor to whom Francis and George Mick of Jenkins (1997) can be traced. Both Israel and the elder Michael (probably Michael, Jr.), listed in the 1830 census for Washington Township, had sons who would have been around seven in that year and thus be candidates for the father of Joseph, listed in the 1850 census as being twenty-seven years of age, married to Sarah, and having three sons:

Israel (5), Peter (3), and Joseph (1) and two daughters: Charlotte (9) and Elizabeth (7). Their son, William, whose birth is mentioned above as being at Speedwell in 1862, is listed on the Randolph Township census for 1880, along with his mother, Sarah (58) and his sister, Sarah (14). Joseph must have died by this time.

Joseph and Sarah Mick's son, Israel (b. c. 1845), appears on the Washington Township census for 1860, along with his brothers and sisters: Charlotte (19), Elizabeth (15), Peter (12), Joseph (9), John (7), Charles (4) and Alice (3). Thus it would seem that the family moved from Speedwell to Randolph Township prior to 1880.

Only one Mick appears in the Washington Township census in 1880: the Charles who had been born in 1853, and he was boarding with another family. This Charles may be Israel's brother, who is listed on the 1860 census as being four years old at that time. Michael's family must have moved from the township by that time. Charles's mother, brother William, and sister, Sarah, are on the Randolph Township census for that year and may have lived in Jenkins or even just outside of Speedwell. The location of the rest of their family is uncertain. They appear on neither the Washington, Randolph, or Shamong Township censuses from 1860 through 1900.

Israel appears again on the 1910 census for Washington Township (Randolph is no longer a separate township) as living in Jenkins Village. He is listed as having been married to his wife, Mary, for twenty-three years. It was his second marriage and her first. Thier children: Thomas R. (21), Joel H. (18), Webster (13), and Richard A. (11). Francis Mick, at seventy-six the oldest surviving member of the Mick family of Jenkins, recently confirmed that his father, Joel, bought the house in which he still lives around 1910, though he wasn't certain of the exact date.

In the 1920 census, Webster (21) and his brother, Richard (21), are listed as boarders with the Joel Mick family in Jenkins Neck. This Joel is their brother, who is twenty-eight at the time, and married to Melissa (30) and having Henry (5), Haines (3) and Sady (11/12). Their mother, Mary (61), a widow, lives with them. Israel must have died at some time during the preceding decade. When this was mentioned to Francis, he said, yes, he remembered his uncles living with his family when he was very young. He also remembered that his mother was a Patten and that his Uncle Webster married her sister, Nancy. Webster bought the little house on the west side of Route 563 and raised his family there. George Mick, the son of Webster and Nancy (Patten) Mick, lives in a new house which he built just below the old Joel Mick house of his cousin, Francis. George's son, George, Jr. has his home right next door to that of his father. Until recently, George ran Mick's Canoe Rentals and a store near his parental house on the other side of the main road, but he tired of the hazards of dealing with drunken and belligerent canoeists who interpret "recreation" as license.

Just to recapitulate: George's father, Webster, and Francis's father, Joel, were

Photograph by John Pearce

The Joel Mick House
This house had four rooms when Joel bought it back about 1910: two rooms down and two up. Joel closed in the front porch and made additions to the rear.

Photograph by John Pearce

The Webster Mick House
Joel Mick's brother, Webster, boarded with Joel's family until he purchased this little house nearby, probably about 1920.

the sons of Israel and Mary Mick. Israel was the son of Joseph and Sarah Mick of Speedwell, who, in all probability, was himself the son of either Israel or of Michael Mick, Jr., sons of Michael Mick, Sr.

Another Mick family also lived in Jenkins in 1920. It was headed by William Mick, age fifty-seven, married to Laura. Their children were: William, Jr. (21), Joseph (16), Bessie (14), and Emma (11). This family also appears on the 1920 census of Washington Township as follows: William (49), Laura (44) [a first marriage for both of them; married for twenty-two years in 1910.] and their children: Elise (21), Laura (14), William B. (11), Joseph (6), Bessie (4), and Emma (4/12). This family also appears on the Washington Township census for 1900. This may well be the William Mick, son of Joseph and brother of Israel, who was living with their mother, Sarah, in 1880. It would seem that he was the only William Mick of anywhere near the right age to have been fifty-seven (or thereabouts) in 1920.

Other Mick families also appear in the Washington Township censuses over the years, but their connection to the present-day family is uncertain. In 1840, only Robert Mick and his family appear in the census at all. In 1850, there is a John (40) and Phoebe (39) Mick and their children: James (20), George (15), Elizabeth (8), John (6), Michael (4), and Eliza (1).

In 1860, the same family appears again, along with our Joseph and Sarah whom we traced above. There is also a George Mick (53) that *may* be a son of either Israel or Michael Mick of the 1830 census. There is also one Robert Mick (54) and his wife, Ann (41). Robert is listed as having been born in Virginia. They have no children and do not appear in the 1870 census.

A George Mick family which seems to appear out of nowhere on the Randolph Township census for 1870. It includes: George (31), his wife, Lucy (28), and their children, William (10), Eliza (8), John B. (6), George (4) and Rusling (2). This family does not appear in either Randolph's 1880 census or in Washington Township's census thereafter, but it is likely that this George is the son of John and Phoebe Mick who is listed as being fifteen in 1850. His brother, Michael, listed as thirteen in 1860, is probably the Michael (23) married to Mary J. (22) in

1870. Their sons are Reuben (6), Robert (4), and John (2). Reuben crops up once again in 1900 as being born in 1869, thirty years of age, and married for fourteen years to Mary Anna Mick, also born in 1869. Yes, the ages are slightly off, but he's the only Reuben Mick that appears in any of the censuses. The same Reuben appears on the 1910 census as being forty-six years old, married twenty-five years to Mary J., who is listed as being forty. Their sons are William E. (14), Howard S. (10), and Paritis (3). This family doesn't seem to be around by 1920.

All this adds up to two conclusions. Though it wouldn't satisfy the Daughters or the Sons of the American Revolution, George and Francis Mick and their families are probably direct descendants of the Michael Mick of Warwick Furnace who was a captain in the militia in 1793 at Hanover Furnace and later was in Martha Furnace, where he presumably died. George's great-grandfather, Joseph, was the youngest son of either Michael Mick, Jr. or of Israel, his brother. It is possible that he was the eldest son of Michael Mick, III, (all listed in the 1830 census but without the names of their children) thereby adding another generation.

The second conclusion should be obvious. Though we seem to get the idea that country life was static in past, it was far from that. Even single families appear and disappear in particular locations. Only one or two branches of a large family may have continued to reside in the land of their ancestors. All the others went elsewhere to find work, just as most people continue to do today.

For all of you who have plowed through these arcane ruminations, I feel your pain. All of us who have an interest in someone else's genealogy just have to be a bit squirrely. To the Micks of hot, buggy Jenkins: I salute you and your heritage. It's one of which you can be proud.

Photograph by John Pearce

Francis Mick
Francis, son of Joel, is the oldest surviving member of the Mick family.

The Jenkins' Chapel

This tiny little chapel in the pines began life somewhere about the middle of the last century as one of the early schoolhouses in Washington Township. For thirty years, the Jenkins' children learned their Three-R's here, close to their homes, before the local school board decided to consolidate their educational system into a "regional" elementary school at Green Bank. Prior to 1920, Jenkins children had probably never been as far from home as that town on the Mullica, and it must have been a great adventure when their school bus headed for Green Bank on that first day of school at the new location.

The little schools at Batsto and Green Bank would crumble away. The Crowleytown and Wading River schools still exist as houses. Lower Bank's would end up at Smithville. The abandoned building at Jenkins was to hold a higher place in the scheme of things.

The Episcopal Church had caught the missionary fervor in the years from the Great War to the Second World War. In all the solitudes along the eastern seaboard, chapels were set up and missionaries provided to bring God into the lives of the isolated country people. Jessie (Forman) Lewis of Green Bank still remembers her summer as a missionary's assistant in the hamlets and glens of Virginia's Blue Ridge. The rural and isolated pinelands of New Jersey were not neglected.

The Right Reverend Paul Matthews, Bishop of the Diocese of New Jersey, decided to plant missions throughout the pinelands. His plan for "Children's Missionaries in the Pines" included using the old Richards' church at Atsion, as well as establishing a chapel in the heart of the pines. There were Methodist churches in the river communities, but who would bring Christ to the pineys of the woods?

In 1917, Bishop Matthews sent the Rev. Cornelius W. Twing into the benighted depths of the pines *on horseback*, no less. Rev. Twing was a circuit rider, much like the Methodist preachers of old had been, and he held services in various spots. One of them was the school house at Jenkins.

When the building was abandoned, the diocese negotiated with the Washington Township School Board for it. In 1925, they finally settled on $100 for the structure and a sign went up out in front: "St. Andrew's Chapel." Bill Haines of Hog Wallow remembers that back when he was a child attending an Episcopal church near his home in Vincentown, the children were given little cardboard churches as penny banks so that they could contribute to the "Children's Missionaries in the Pines."

The Reverend Mr. Twing died in 1926, only a year after the purchase of the old school building, but he had spent thirteen faithful years riding horseback through the pines to Woodmansie, New Freedom, Bozarthville, and Chairville, as well as Atsion and Jenkins. The Rev. Howard S. Frazer succeeded the Rev. Twing and continued the ministry through the nineteen thirties, though the horse was traded for an automobile by then. Still, life was never easy, nor were the missions particularly productive. The poverty of the Great Depression ensured that the Episcopal Church had nothing left to spare for isolated missions when millions were starving across the country. Though many survived both depression and war, prosperity and suburban growth sounded their death knell. By the late 1950's, almost all were no longer staffed.

According to Robert Hagaman of Weekstown, the Rev. Carl Farrell is given credit for negotiating with the Diocese of New Jersey for the use of the building when he was minister of the Lower Bank Circuit of the Methodist Church in 1969, though it seems that the Rev. Clyde Phillips, his predecessor, had held services there during his tenure at the Lower Bank Circuit in 1965 through 1967. Robert Hagaman started as a lay minister at Jenkins in 1970. Eight years later, he and his sister, Harriet, incorporated the nondenominational chapel and paid the Episcopal Diocese ten times what they had originally paid the school board for the building. Of course, over sixty years had passed since then and inflation had upped the ante. Actually, the diocese had lost money on their enterprise in the pines, but they certainly had provided a much-needed ministry to many isolated communities.

Robert Hagaman still makes the journey from Weekstown through Green Bank and up to Jenkins every Sunday. It only takes twenty-eight people to fill the chapel to the splitting point, but sometimes there is no one there at all except the faithful minister. In the quiet of the pines, one often gets the flavor of days gone by. No minister of the Gospel has ever been successful in the pines if he insisted on tallying up the numbers.

A final note before we leave this old schoolhouse-turned-chapel in the pines: this particular school was actually the *third* to serve the children of the Jenkins area. When I was talking with Francis Mick, he mentioned that the original schoolhouse for the area had stood on the Jenkins-Washington Road beyond Godfrey's Bridge campground and that it had burned down. I don't know how he knew this. Perhaps his father told him about it, or maybe he found evidence of burned timbers in the area. He did say he was too young to have attended school there. I figured it was just a tale. Not so.

In checking the reports of the Burlington County Superintendent of Schools, which are part of the state records in the State Library at Trenton, I came upon the following note in the report for 1884-5. "The small schoolhouse in District No. 103 was destroyed by fire, and a new one costing some $300 has been put in its place." District No. 103, by the way, was Washington, in Washington Township, Burlington County. Later annual reports show that this second building also succumbed to fire only three years after it was built! It was then decided to place the third building nearer the center of population which had shifted from Washington to Jenkins. Thus this little schoolhouse in Jenkins was built in about 1889 and was open for the first time in 1889-90 school year. Hat's off to you, Mr. Mick! You've preserved a memory of something that happened thirty years before you were born, and you were quite right!

Maxwell

The 1956 topographic map of the Jenkins quadrangle indicates the location of the town of Maxwell, a cluster of houses spanning Iron Pipe Road on the southwest side of Route 563, about two miles below the junction with the Chatsworth/New Gretna Road. The Maxwell name is well-known in the area, and no doubt this town was settled by a family of that name either late in the nineteenth century or early in the twentieth, as it is not listed on the 1870 map.

Iron Pipe Road is the section of the Old Philadelphia Road from Sooy's Inn in Washington to Bodine's Tavern. It crosses Route 563 at Maxwell, and heads for the Wading River below Harrisville. Through the last two miles before it comes in proximity to the river, it passes through extensive swamps, but as it nears the river, it hits solid ground directly across from the site of Bodine's Tavern.

According to Bisbee in his *Sign Posts: Place Names in History of Burlington County, N.J.*, one "James Maxwell farmed a one hundred acre plot here around 1890." According to the township records, a James and Sarah Maxwell lived at McCartyville and gave birth in Bridgeport to a son, John Robert in 1852. In 1855, with McCartyville now called Harrisville, the couple had another son, William Franklin. By the birth of son, Edwin, in 1858, they were at Martha. John and Leah Maxwell of Bridgeport had a daughter, Martha, in the 1852, and two years later, had a son, John. The same couple had a son, James, at Turtle Creek (Bridgeport) in 1857. William B. and Rachel Maxwell of Bridgeport had a daughter Mary in 1854 and a daughter Rachel in 1862. Perhaps it was James, son of John and Leah Maxwell of Bridgeport who was farming in Maxwell in 1890. This John was Billy Maxwell's brother (see WADING RIVER/BRIDGEPORT). Others of the family remained in Bridgeport.

Courtesy of Budd Wilson, Jr.

The Maxwell House

My Childhood in Green Bank

(from Memories of Green Bank)
Emma Van Sant Moore

No tales of wizardry dimmed the bright joys of childhood;
No horrifying tales of witches and ghosts could blight
The childish mind with awe, and dread, and fear!
But only words of God that told of His love and might.

The forest was a place of dear enchantment,
Where happy hours were spent in grapevine swings,
And watching birds, whose songs made glad the heart,
While searching for the flowers that grew in fairy rings.

The memory of those childhood days lives on—
Like perfect fruit—no bitterness at the core,
Because the hand of affection each day turned
A page—sparkling with bright gems of Nature's lore.

So proud I was when sister on occasion
Took me to visit Eddie Allen's school,
And still I can remember the boy who stood
In a corner, wearing a dunce cap labelled "fool!"

I remember watching older boys and girls—
Brothers, sisters, and cousins—oh, so many—
Coast down the river bank on winter days:
I, too small to take a part, nor wanted any.

Enough for me to sit beside the window—
The window of the house where I was born,
And watch the sleds glide far across the river—
The Mullica—for love of which my heart is often torn

With longing—oh, so poignant and so deep!
And as the years go by, I yearn still more
To relive those days fond memory brings to mind,
And play on sun-bright summer days along the shore.

The shipyard of my grandfather was to me
A place of deep contentment and of joy,
Where I could find sweet-scented blocks of wood
That were dearer far to me than any costly toy.

How I loved to watch those long, thin chips of white,
That deftly handled adz stripped from the bole
Of spruce-tree, straight and tall, which once had stood
Erect in northern forest, with green boughs scented—whole!

I liked to see them marked with chalk and line,
Then squared with adz, so patiently applied:
And soon sharp edges all were rounded—gone,
The while I waited breathlessly by father's side!

Soon, round and smooth, and polished—tapering tall—
Those masts—such things of beauty then to me—
Were raised and stepped in ships that proudly bore
Them down the river—over many a far-flung sea!

And the little white church in the oaks, at the village end—
Whenever I enter it—seems still the same
As when I worshipped there in childhood days,
It stands—a silent benediction in His name!

from *Mullica,* 1960

Lower Bank

This view across the Lower Bank Bridge towards Lower Bank was taken in the first decade of the twentieth century.

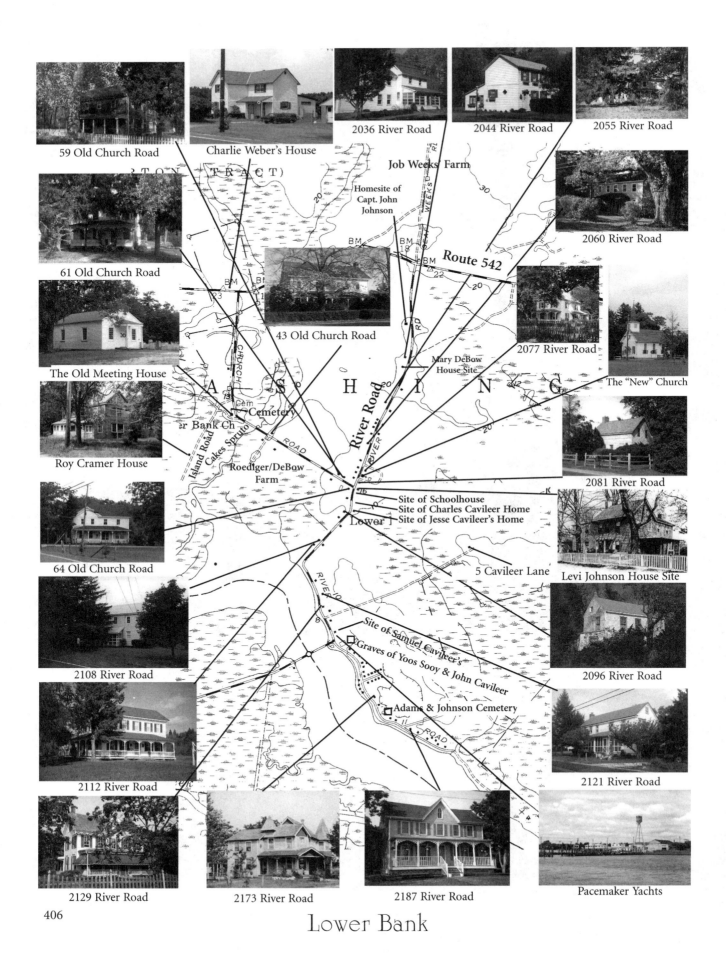

59 Old Church Road

Charlie Weber's House

2036 River Road

2044 River Road

2055 River Road

61 Old Church Road

Job Weeks Farm

Homesite of Capt. John Johnson

2060 River Road

The Old Meeting House

43 Old Church Road

Route 542

2077 River Road

The "New" Church

Roy Cramer House

Mary DeBow House Site

2081 River Road

64 Old Church Road

Roediger/DeBow Farm

Site of Schoolhouse
Site of Charles Cavileer Home
Site of Jesse Cavileer's Home

Levi Johnson House Site

5 Cavileer Lane

2108 River Road

2096 River Road

2112 River Road

Site of Samuel Cavileer's
Graves of Yoos Sooy & John Cavileer

Adams & Johnson Cemetery

2121 River Road

2129 River Road

2173 River Road

2187 River Road

Pacemaker Yachts

406

Lower Bank

Eric Mullica

There was a time, barely over three hundred years ago, when the dark waters of The River only knew the touch of human hands through the occasional dip of a Lenape paddle as wandering tribes of Native Americans made their way from their winter homes along the Delaware to the seashore for the summer. Whatever prompted Eric Pålsson Mullica to leave his settlement near the new city of Philadelphia and head off into the wilderness of southern New Jersey with his new wife and his youngest children? No one will ever know, but that's just what he did.

Eric's story is believed to have begun in the settlement of Mullica, in the village of Fågelsjö, an enclave to Mora Parish in the province of Dalarna, on the borderland of Hälsingland, Sweden* in the month of April, 1636. He was one of the older children of at least six in the family of Pål Jönsson, also known as Pål Malich, and his wife, Margaret. According to the most recent and accurate research by Peter Stebbins Craig in his 1993 book entitled, *The 1693 Census of the Swedes on the Delaware*, Pål Jönsson, Margaret, and their children, John, Eric, Anders, Annakin, Christian, and Hendrick arrived in the colony of New Sweden in 1654 aboard the *Eagle*.

Pål Jönsson was called "The Finn" in the early records, indicating that he was probably of Finnish extraction, spoke Finnish as his primary language, and had married a Swedish woman. Finland was a part of the Kingdom of Sweden during the 17th century, and people from Finland were considered Swedes. A title like "The Finn" indicated that he spoke Finnish rather than Swedish as his first language. According to Dr. Craig, though, "all the 'Finns' who came to the Delaware came from provinces in present Sweden . . . and bore Swedish names. Conversely, those settlers coming from Finland proper were Swedish-speaking and were *not* called Finns."

Some Finns recently visiting Budd Wilson of Green Bank claimed that they were relatives of Eric Mullica and that the name was originally Moelke. Therefore, Eric was not Swedish at all but Finnish, even if he was born in Sweden. As Dr. Craig's research indicates, his father was indeed Finnish, though his mother was probably Swedish, and the family lived in Sweden proper before they emigrated to New Sweden.

Pål and his wife, with their younger children, left the area of New Sweden for Maryland, where he was granted citizenship on the twenty-ninth of July, 1661 and apparently died within three years. On April 14, 1664, Pastor Lars Lock drew up a deed dividing his property amongst his wife and the children who had accompanied him to Maryland.

Eric Pålsson and John Pålsson remained along the Delaware. By the way, Swedish names of this period can be confusing. The general practice was not to use the family surname as we are accustomed to do, but to add "son" or "dotter" to the father's name. Thus Eric, who was the son of Pål, would have been called "Eric Pålsson" more frequently than "Eric Mullica."

Eric married Ingeri, the daughter of Olof Philipsson, who had arrived from Letstigen, Värmland in 1656, two years after Eric and his family had landed in the colony. Their first child, Anna, was born in 1668. Two years later, their first son, Anders, was born. Then came Olof (1673), then Eric, Jr. (1675).

*This was indicated to Dr. Peter Craig through research in Sweden and communicated to me by phone. He wanted me to know that the entry in his book was in error when it stated that Eric was born in Mora, Delsbo parish, Hälsingland.

Part of the waterfront
property that
belonged to
Eric Mullica as it
appears today.

The John Cavileer III
House is on the right
and the Coulter House
is in the center.

Photograph by John Pearce

As Dr. Craig goes on to note, the same year his son, Eric, Jr. was born, Eric, Sr. and two other men had a 950-acre tract surveyed for them near the present Frankford Creek on October 20th, which was called "Tacony," and the Mullica family must have settled there soon after that date.

Charles Werner of New Gretna did extensive research on Eric Mullica which he published privately in 1930. He also found that Eric Mullica received a patent for land on the Delaware River at the mouth of the Sissowokinnk (now Wissonoming) Creek, a part of Philadelphia today, which was called "Towocawonink" in the Lenape (Delaware) language, Tacony today. The date of the patent, issued by Governor Edmund Andros of New York, is July 18, 1676. Werner also found that Mullica and other area residents appealed to the Court at Upland (now Chester, Pa.) for the setting out of a new settlement on the river in 1677.

Several more children were born to the couple in the succeeding years: John (1677), Helena or Ella (1680), Catharine (1682), and finally Stephen (April 30, 1684) for a total of eight. In 1687, Eric and other Swedes conveyed land in the "Liberties of the City of Philadelphia" to the Society of Traders in Pennsylvania. His name also appears on a petition for relief from a tax in 1692.

The focus of Dr. Craig's 1993 book, *1693 Census of the Swedes on the Delaware,* is the census of the Swedes living along the Delaware in that year that was made to induce the Swedish authorities to send out Lutheran pastors to minister to the religious needs of the Swedish settlers. The original of this list has lain in the Swedish National Archives since it was received three hundred years ago, and Dr. Craig had the benefit of using this original for his work.

Historians have known about the existence of this census for many years through a copy made by Pastor Andreas Rudman in the first record book of Gloria Dei Church in Philadelphia. Pastor Rudman was one of three clergymen sent out in response to the 1693 request, and he made his copy in 1697 after arriving in the New World. Unfortunately, his copy contains errors. The original census was discovered in time to be photographed and made part of the Finnish exhibit on New Sweden at the University of Delaware in 1988 called "Delaware 350." On that list, the name "Erick Mollika" appears as #43 with a family of eight.

Dr. Craig agrees with other historians that the list was compiled by Charles Springer, who was uniquely educated in both Swedish and English. It was apparently sent along with a letter, dated the 31st of May, 1693 and signed by over thirty Swedish settlers, which detailed the situation on the Delaware and requested assistance from the crown. The letter was addressed to Johann Thelin, the postmaster of Gothenburg. Eric Mullica's name appears among the signatories.

At some time before he and part of his family left Tacony for the wilds of New Jersey, his wife, Ingeri, died, and his daughter, Anna, married an Englishman, John Reynolds. It was apparently after the letter and census were sent that Mullica married Ingeborg Helm, the daughter of Israel Helm and set out for his new home "Takokan."

Israel Åkesson Helm sailed from Sweden with his father, Åke Israelsson in 1641 on the *Charitas.* Åke was a musketeer but died a month before the ship arrived in the colony of New Sweden on October 7 of that year. The boy lived with Governor Printz's family from 1643 to 1648. After he turned eighteen on the first of March 1648, Printz hired him as a soldier. He went back to Sweden in 1653 and returned on the *Mercurius* two years later. In 1662-3, he returned to Sweden once again and helped Governor d'Hinojossa sign up new settlers for the Swedish colony on the Delaware.

When d'Hinojossa arrived in New Sweden aboard *de Purmelander Kerck* on December 3, 1663, Israel Åkesson was with him. The grateful governor appointed him justice of the Upland court, a position which he retained until 1681. By 1668, he had acquired the surname "Helm." Governor d'Hinojossa had also given him exclusive rights to the Indian fur trade amongst the up-river Swedes, and Helm acquired rights to 600 acres in the Province of West Jersey across the Delaware from what would become Pennsbury Manor. Apparently, the West Jersey authorities reduced this claim to around 100 acres by the time Helm sold his Upland estate on March 9, 1679/80. Helm finally received a deed to his West Jersey property on May 3, 1686 and built a house for himself there. His will was proved on March 2, 1701/02.

No record of a survey or grant has ever been found in Mullica's name for land along the river which would bear his name, though the proprietors of West Jersey were issuing them at this time. However, it is quite certain from Pastor Rudman's notes that Mullica, his second wife, and his younger children were living there in Takokan by the time the clergyman arrived in 1697. Mr. Werner notes that Pastor Rudman's list, dated April, 1698, gives two references to the family of Mullica:

> *Takokan, near Little Egg Harbor — Eric Molicka, born in Helsingeland and Mora Parish, 62 years of age in April 1698. His wife Ingabor, sister of Peter Cox's wife. Their children: John 20 years; Stephen 13 years the 30th April; Catherine 15 years.*

*Tahokaning, [Pennsylvania] Olave Mollicka 24 years; Eric Mullica 22; Anna Mollica, Helena, sisters;
Anna Runnels, Engl., professing our religion. Her daughter Elsa, son Olave.*

At some time between 1693 when he signed the letter to the crown and 1698 when Pastor Rudman composed his list, Eric Mullica, his wife, and three of his children by his first wife had taken up residence on land along the river that would bear their name at a place called Takokan, in what is today Lower Bank, New Jersey.

That makes the town of Lower Bank the oldest permanent settlement north of the Great Egg Harbor region and south of the Shrewsbury, quite an honor for the quiet little pinelands hamlet of today. [The Quaker settlement at Little Egg Harbor (Tuckerton) was made in 1699.]   Unfortunately, we don't know the exact spot on which he built his wilderness house. Back in the early part of this century, a location on the property of Mr. Lewis A. Adams of Lower Bank which lay about two hunderd feet from Mr. Adam's house was pointed out as the site of the Mullica cabin. Next to that spot stood the remains of two ancient walnut trees which were rumored to have been planted by Mullica himself. One blew down in 1885 and the other in 1890. In 1930, the two stumps still remained close by the riverbank.

Thanks to Dr. Craig's research, we now know that Eric died prior to 1704 while he and his family were still living at Takokan. Pastor Andreas Sandel kept a diary in which he recorded a visit to Takokan from Philadelphia which he made in the year 1704. Dr. Craig is currently editing the Sandel journal, and the translation which he provided me is by Dr. Richard H. Hulan. Under the date of September 27th, he notes, "I set out for the ocean, to a place that is called Eggherbour, because some Swedes lived there, to preach for them."

On the 28th he wrote that his guides knew he wanted to see all the Swedes "who lived thereabouts, and they did not know the way to little Eggherbour." The previous evening (the 27th) they sent "across the River to Mollickas people, who we heard also wished to go that way and show us the route." When they set out on the 28th, "Olof Mollicka," Eric's son*, was among his party. The travelers "arrived at little Egg Harbor in the evening just at sunset."

The following day, September 29th, he notes: "In the morning I gave a little sermon for those who lived there, namely Möllika's mother [actually his step-mother], a widow; her daughters and two unmarried sons; and one son who was married, Anders Möllika, who lived nearby." Thus it would certainly seem that Eric Mullica had died in Lower Bank prior to Pastor Sandel's 1704 visit to the "Widow Möllika" and her family.

Eric's son, John, sold the 100-acre "plantation" where his father had built a home to one Thomas Bishop on July 4, 1719. At that time, Lower Bank was in North Hampton Township, Burlington County. It is interesting to note that on August 8, 1722, his brother, Eric, Jr. also conveyed one-half of the same tract, amounting to fifty acres, to

---

*Olof Mullica, the second son of Eric Mullica, did not move to Little Egg Harbor with his father and step-mother but remained in the area of Philadelphia. According to a footnote on p. 10 of Dr. Hulan's work, by 1704, Olof had married and had settled on a branch of the Raccoon Creek at the present Mullica Hill.

Photograph by John Pearce

View of the Mullica downriver from Lower Bank 1995

Joseph Pearce (or Pierce). If the whole one hundred acres had been sold by John in 1719, how did "Eric, Jr." sell half of it three years later? Ah, the intricacies of land transactions in the pines!

On March 2, 1704, Eric, Jr. and John jointly purchased a two hundred seventy-three acre tract near their brother Olof's home in the area of what would become known as Mullica Hill. In 1705, Richard Bull, Deputy Surveyor for the Province of West Jersey, surveyed the 242 1/2 acre parcel for Eric, Jr., and baptismal records exist for Eric, Jr.'s children at the Raccoon Church, Swedesboro, N.J., in the years before 1719, indicating that his family lived in the vicinity at that time..

According to the records of the church, "Ingridh M_____" stood as godmother for Stephen Mulicka's [sic] son, Eric, when he was baptized on January 24th, 1714. Charles Werner assumed that this was the baby's grandmother (actually his step-grandmother) and that she had either journeyed to visit her children for the baptism, or she had moved to that location prior to 1714. The death of Ingrid Mulicka [sic] is duly recorded in the church records on August 10, 1719. Eric, Jr.'s wife, Marget, died on the 5th of February 1742, and "Eric" Mullika's [sic] demise is listed in the year 1765 of "a decay in his 36 year of age." This has to be Eric, III, the baby baptized in 1714. The death of John Mullica, Eric's son, is noted under 1766 as follows: "Sept. 10 John Mullicka [sic] died the 15th. 97 years of age." Actually, John Mullica would only have been eighty-nine years old in 1766.

Eric, Jr. had remained behind in Pennsylvania when Eric, Sr. took off for the woods in the first place. John had accompanied his parents on their venture to the pines. John's share of the Mullica Hill property was only fifteen and a half acres out of the 242 1/2, but the property was not sub-divided until June 21, 1740. On December 7th of that year, John and Eric, Jr. sold their property to Daniel Sutton.

Leah Blackman wrote her "History of Little Egg Harbor Township" which was, as the 1963 issue by The Great John Mathis Foundation notes, "all but buried at the back of a report of the 1880 West Jersey Surveyors' Association." As knowledgeable as Mrs. Blackman was, she seems confused about Mullica. In this section, she doesn't even seem to know of Eric Mullica:

> In ancient writings this river is called *Mullicas, Mulican* and *Mullica.* It is impossible to say which of these designations is the original, or from whence the name originated. It may have been the Indian name for the river. I adhere to the name of *Mullica,* because I deem it the prettiest of the above designations.

Later in her work, she does mention "the Mullica Indians, whose name was derived from Eric Mullica, a Swede, who settled very early on the east bank of Little Egg Harbor river, near Batsto, . . ."

Mrs. Blackman took her cue from eighteenth century writers who chose to spell with remarkable inconsistancy: "Mollicas" in a survey of 1726, "Mullicus" in the writings of John Barber and Henry Howe, and "Mulicus" in 1778.

Eric Mullica ought to be given a lot of credit for his temerity. After all, he, his second wife, and his younger children left their relatively secure land on the Delaware and, with courage, set out into the uncharted wilderness to the land which was to become his last resting place. One hopes that Eric, at the end of his life, found his peace in this land by the river which bears his name.

Where was the famous Mullica homestead? No one has known. During the 1920's, Mr. Lewis Adams firmly believed that a cellarhole on his property was the site of Mullica's cabin. Others have suggested that the Mullica property was that actually occupied by the Pacemaker Plant itself, on which Yoos Sooy and John Cavileer were buried. Until now, there was no proof for either theory. Mullica's cabin was long gone before anyone ever considered its site important.

Roy Cramer, the tax collector for Washington Township in the 1940's, always claimed to C. P. Leek that Charlie's boatyard stood on the original Mullica homestead. He claimed he had a tax map to prove it, but Charlie never saw that map and neither did anyone else.

However, information has recently surfaced which sheds light on the Mullica homestead situation. Budd Wilson found a copy of a map, the original of which is currently in the Batsto collection, in which General Elias Wright employed Sam S. Downs to survey the properties of the William Richards estate for Joseph Wharton. The map apparently belonged to Ezekiel Forman of Green Bank but came into the State's possession and was never returned to him as had been requested in writing on the map.

Sam Downs' survey commenced on the 21st of May, 1880. When he drew up his own survey map thirty-two years later, Sam had in front of him the survey which Daniel Wills had made in 1848. The 1880 survey clearly shows the fifty-acre portion of land which Eric Mullica, Jr. sold to Joseph Pearce in 1722. A second fifty-acre parcel next to it, shown as transferred to Charles Reed [sic], August 10, 1764, may have been the other fifty acres of the 100-acre homestead of the old Swede. Probably this "Charles Reed" is none other than the original founder of Batsto!

At least as far as we can assume from this well-researched map and survey for the grasping Mr. Wharton, the Mullica estate included most of the riverfront property in modern-day Lower Bank. The fifty acres sold by Eric, Jr. to Joseph Pearce stretched approximately from the current Coulter house at 2121 River Road through the old Pacemaker property. The second fifty acres went from there down to the Adams homestead, on which 2173 River Road was built. Perhaps Lewis Adams guessed right in the location of Eric's cabin after all.

A notation on the map seems to indicate that the boundry-point on the river was the corner of Augustus S. Johnson land and that belonging to Lorainy Adams. Lorinah Brush Adams was the wife of Stephen Adams and the grandmother of Lewis Adams (See THE ADAMS HOUSE in this chapter). We know Augustus Johnson owned approximately 207 acres in the vicinity which had originally belonged to John Cavileer. John was buried on his own property next to the grave of Yoos Sooy which is in the old C.P. Leek/Pacemaker property (see THE CAVILEER/JOHNSON/HENDRICKSON/COULTER HOUSE in this chapter). Apparently, this cemetery is in the center of what was the Mullica homestead in Takokan.

There is an additional assumption, as yet unproved but a reasonable one nevertheless: Yoos Sooy's homestead (see article following on YOOS SOOY) must have been on the same land. That's why he was buried there. At least half of the same property must have been sold or otherwise transferred to Charles Read in 1764. Yoos Sooy II (called "Joseph") had, by this time, purchased the Samuel Driver Homestead in Green Bank (1752) and his brother, Nicholas, had moved to Leed's Point.

The "Legend of Eric Mullica" has fascinated lovers of the Mullica Valley for over a hundred and fifty years, the details of his story have been the subject of much invention. Stories are told that he was friends with Peter Cavileer and Yoos Sooy of Lower Bank, and with Samuel Driver of Green Bank, but he was long buried in Lower Bank's soil by the time they came along.

The Sooy Family Genealogy, like all other writings on the Mullica Valley, says that Eric was born in 1623 and came to America in 1637 or 1638 on the *Key of Calmar* or on the *Griffin*, the first ships to bring Swedish settlers to these new lands, and that he settled in Lower Bank in 1645. Only Charles Werner of New Gretna and of course, Dr. Craig, did the necessary research to establish the details of Eric Mullica's life and the probable time period in which he came to the banks of the river which would bear his name.

I've always wondered where these oft repeated details came from, and, exploring the Wharton Ledgers at Batsto, I came across the following item written by General Elias Wright, Joseph Wharton's manager. Wright begins by saying that he got the story from a letter written by Thomas H. Richards, son of Jesse Richards, in 1864, but only quotes the beginning of it: "Eric Mullica, a Swede, settled on a high bluff on the East side of the river (Little Egg Harbor River) before 1680. His plantation was a favorite resort for the Indians. They adopted his name & etc." Wright notes that Richards had died prior to the time at which he was entering it in the Wharton Ledgers, Volume 28, on page 7, in the late 1800's.

He quotes more extensively from a letter the surveyor, George Sykes, wrote to Samuel P. Richards, another son of Jesse Richards, which was dated "Sykesville, March 21st, 1866."

> Eric Mullica, the original settler, appears to have been a man of position and means. He was born in Sweden, emigrated from there, when very young. Was living in 1693, being the head of a family of eight persons, and died about the year 1723, at the advanced age of one hundred years. The year he came to this country cannot now be ascertained. If he came in the "Key of Calamar" or the "Griffin," the two first Swedish emigrant vessels, on their first voyage, which was made in 1637 or 1638, he could have been only about fifteen years old; Nor is it known at what period he settled with his friends and retainers at the "Lower Bank." He may have settled under a grant from the Crown of Sweden; though so far as his title under the proprietors of the English Government was concerned, he appears to have been only a squatter. The records in the Surveyor General's office at Burlington of the earliest Surveys made in that neighborhood, after the transfer from the Duke of York in 1664, frequently refer to "Mullica's Plantations, Mullicas River," "Mullicas Road," & etc. showing that he must have been settled there before any of the English settlers. Some years previous to his death, he removed from Egg Harbor to Greenwhich Township, Gloucester County, and settled at "Mullicas Hill," where he died.

> About a year before his death, he conveyed a part of his property at or near the Lower Bank to Jesse Pearce, son of Joseph Pearce, by deed dated August 8th, 1722. It is probable that John Pearce, to whom this survey was made in 1713, was also the son of Joseph Pearce.

Unfortunately for historical accuracy, Thomas Richards, George Sykes, and Elias Wright inadvertently created a legend that would echo on for well over a hundred years. The earliest historians in the twentieth century no doubt obtained their information on Eric Mullica from the Wharton Ledgers account and have repeated the details until they seem to be "fact." Of course, Thomas H. Richards, in 1865, and George Sykes, a year later, are almost a hundred and fifty years after Mullica, and there is no reason to suppose that their "facts" are anything other than supposition. Wright seems to have been the first in a lengthy series of people who have repeated this tale until another hundred years has enshrined them as sacred truth. Dr. Craig's excellent research has given us an accurate picture of the First Pioneer of the Mullica valley.

It is still entirely possible, though not terribly likely, that he owned (or squatted on) land at Takokan prior to having moved there, but if there's no written record . . . I've also wondered if the acreage actually belonged to his father-in-law, Israel Helm. Helm's own plantation was across the Delaware from Penn's mansion at Pennsbury, according to Dr. Craig, not in Takokan, but he may have owned the hundred acres Mullica and his daughter settled on along the Little Egg Harbor River. As to Mullica and his wife, though, that 1693-1697 period is about as close as we can get to dating his permanent arrival by the river which would bear his name.

Before departing from the Mullica story, though, I think a little credit should be given to Charles Werner of New Gretna, who, almost seventy years ago, did exhaustive research into Eric Mullica that should have gone a long way towards setting the record straight. He must have spent quite a bit of his own money to have his little book published in 1930 in the midst of the Great Depression, but it seems to have had no influence whatsoever on more modern historians who have dutifully parroted the Wharton Ledgers Bible.

Werner made mistakes, as Dr. Craig pointed out. He was using a faulty copy of the Census of 1693 which he thought Pastor Rudman had compiled himself in 1697-8. He thought the Mullica children were a product of the second, rather than the first marriage. He knew there was no record of Eric Mullica, Sr.'s demise and burial in Mullica Hill, but he couldn't resist the temptation of "The Legend" and thought Mullica died there rather than in Takokan. Yet he didn't know of Pastor Sandel's journal, and those entries make all the difference in the world. Peter Craig's definitive work should certainly set the record straight on Eric Mullica for the first time in over three hundred fifty years.

There is one more intriguing note to be made from Pastor Sandel's diary before we leave Eric Mullica. After his entry about preaching to the Widow Mullica and her family, he goes on to say, "There were no more Swedes, but it was said that one English family lived alongside there." Who was this mysterious "English family?" Could Peter Cavileer have possibly been in Lower Bank as early as 1704? It may well have been Thomas Clark who had settled across the river at Clark's Landing by this time. Perhaps it may have been some other family whose name has been lost to history. The brown waters of the Mullica continue to flow past shores now inhabited by people of names other than Mullica, and the River keeps her secrets.

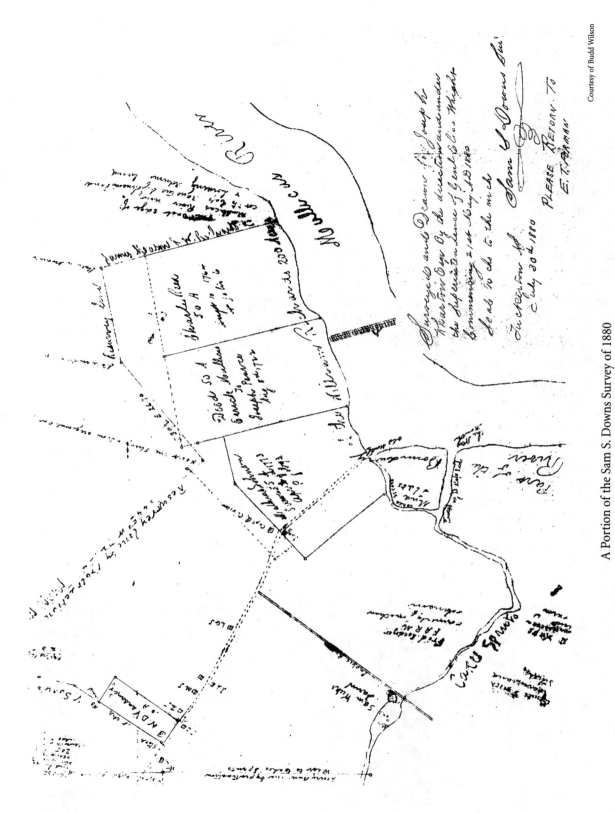

A Portion of the Sam S. Downs Survey of 1880

This survey was commissioned by General Elias Wright, General Manager for Joseph Wharton, of the William Richards Estate.

413

Peter Cavileer

At some time after Eric Mullica had died and his family had removed from Lower Bank, another family came to the banks of the Mullica. In 1722, there is record that Peter Cavileer owned several hundred acres and a homestead in the vicinity of Lower Bank, Burlington County.

Chevalier, Cavalier, Cavileer, however it was decided to spell it when it was written, was the French word for "knight," and it is believed that the family were French Huguenots, originating from Brittany, Normandy, and the Channel Islands. The Huguenots were French Protestants, followers of John Calvin of Geneva, who were terribly persecuted in their homeland.

In France, there were constant difficulties between the Catholics and the Protestants. Queen Catherine de' Medici had no love for heretics. In 1572, she engineered the Saint Bartholomew's Day massacre on August 24th, during which thousands of Huguenots were killed. Involved in the plot were the the duke of Anjou, later King Henry III, and Henri, duc de Guise. It all began at the wedding of Henry of Navarre, a leading Protestant, and King Charles IX was forced to go along. There was some peace when Henry of Navarre, deciding that Paris was "worth a mass," as he himself said, converted and succeeded to the throne as Henry IV, but things got worse again after his murder. The crown finally forced either the conversion or expulsion of all Protestants from the realm of France when Louis XIV revoked the Edict of Nantes in 1685, and many fled to other countries more hospitable to them, or to the new world. Holland shared their Calvinist theology and was most agreeable to their emigration.

It is no surprise, then, to find "Cavaliers" in the colony of New Netherlands during its heyday. Records exist of several "Peters" and "John"s (again spelled in the French fashion: Jean or Pierre, the Dutch fashion: Johannes or Pieter, or the English fashion as we know it. Whether they were related or not, we do not know.

Baird, in *Huguenot Emigration to America* (p. 80) says that all the families of this name were probably from St. Lo, Normandy. Stapleton, in *Memorials of the Huguenots in America*, lists a Pierre Chevallier at Charleston, South Carolina, a Jean Le Chevalier in New York, and a Phillip Chevalier in Delaware, all as early as 1677. There is also a record of a French refugee, Peter Cavalier and his wife and a child, landing in Virginia on September 20, 1700.

There are land grants in "Colonial Conveyances" in which a Peter Caveller [*sic*] deeded land along the Mullica River in Gloucester County (now Atlantic County) to John Smallwood in 1714, indicating possession *prior* to that date. This need not indicate that Peter, whoever he was, lived on the spot, simply that he owned property here as early as 1714.

What we do know is that there is a record of a "Peter Cavileer" owning several hundred acres and a homestead in the vicinity of Lower Bank in 1722. Cavileer married Ann Tearney, also a resident of Burlington County, and the couple had a son, John, who was born in 1742. Whether he was connected to the family in New York (the former New Amsterdam) is not clear. However, it is intriguing that the next known family to move to the Mullica had also lived in New York for many years.

John Cavileer,
son of Peter Cavileer,
was buried in the Cavileer/
Sooy Burial Ground when
he died in 1813.

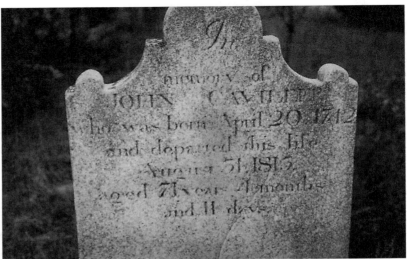

Photograph by John Pearce

414

Yoos Sooy

When Yoos Sooy came from North Jersey in the early seventeen-hundreds, he sailed along a dangerous and deserted coast. Inlet after inlet beckoned him, enticing him with rich lands beyond, prime for settlement, but Yoos sailed on. What made him swing the helm over when he reached this breach in the barrier islands? Did he know Peter Cavileer? Had Peter induced him to leave his Cheesequake home for the Mullica valley? No one will ever know, but he sailed into a world of sunlight and water and sand that is substantially unchanged to the present day.

Yoos was born in Amsterdam, Holland, in April of 1685 with wanderlust infusing him. New York was no longer a Dutch colony, but young Yoos emigrated there, wooing the granddaughter of the most important official next to the governor in the old Dutch administration. Yoos married Sarah, granddaughter of the wealthy and prominent Cornelius Van Tienhoven and daughter of Dr. Lucas Van Tienhoven, his son and heir and a renowned physician, in tiny New York City in the year 1707 on the 19th of August when he was twenty-two years old. Not bad for a young man on the make. Sarah was the fifth child of the good doctor and his wife, Tryntje (Broding) and had been baptized on the 12th of January 1681. She was a young widow by the time Yoos found her, her husband, Jan Balch, having died not long after their marriage.

Holland had become a world trading power of note since she broke away from the dominance of Spain. The commercial trading interests of the Dutch West India Company founded colony after colony for the simple purpose of making fat Dutch burghers fatter (at least in their bank accounts and probably in their waistlines as well). There are indications that young Yoos was employed as a captain by The Company and, in that way, found himself in the former New Netherlands. It is noted in the Sooy Family records that Yoos thrust himself on New York in 1702, at the ripe old age of seventeen.

He couldn't have been a sea captain for many years at the age of seventeen. Some young men in their late teens were sea-captains though, even at this tender age. They were the sons of wealthy Dutchmen who purchased ships and sailed them under their own house flag to all parts of the world. Their sons would take a berth aboard their father's ship at a very early age, and by seventeen or eighteen, would have learned enough to command, so it is a possibility that Yoos Sooy *was* a sea-captain of sorts. Perhaps he sailed for The Company after he had arrived in the colony.

Holland had claimed the North River (as the Hudson was then called) and its surrounding territories for herself, based on the explorations of Henry Hudson in 1609. [Remember Rip Van Winkle and the tale of thunder in the Catskills being the crew of the famed Hudson playing at ninepins high in the mysterious mountains?] For the equivalent of $24.00, The Company via Peter Minuit bought Manhattan, took over both banks of the Hudson River north to what would become Albany, and settled it with a landed gentry.

The company administration left something to be desired, however. Founded on avarice, the sole motive of officials and authorities was to make money, and the sole loyalty of The Company's employees was to their own self-interest. Only three governors presided over the nascent colony before the English found it in their interest to take over in 1664, *their* claim based on the threat of blasting the Dutch off Manhattan with the power of the English naval cannons. Patriotism might have made Governor Peter Stuyvesant fight to the finish, but self-interest is sometimes the wiser course. The sturdy Dutch burghers would have none of the former and certainly had plenty of the latter. Stuyvesant was a wise man to capitulate.

Cornelius Van Tienhoven was an "experienced" man. He had held the second most important post in the colony under each of the three governors and knew how to insinuate himself into every profitable circumstance. He was born in Breukelen, a province of Utrecht, and came to New Amsterdam in 1633. In a short time he went from "book-keeper" for The Company to "Colonial Secretary." He also served as mayor of New Amsterdam and as treasurer of the colony. In 1647, he received a patent for land on which he developed a plantation which he named "Breuckelen" after the area of his birth.

A royal commission sent to explore why the colony was falling apart at the seams about 1650 reported of Cornelius Van Tienhoven:

> *A great deal might be said of this man, more even than we are able to set forth. For brevity sake, however, we shall select here and there a few traits. He is crafty, intelligent, subtle, and sharp-witted - good gifts when properly applied. He is one of those who has been longest in this country; is thoroughly acquainted with every circumstance relating both to the Christians and to the Indians.*

With the Indians even he has run about like an Indian, with little covering and a patch [sic] before him through lust for the prostitutes to whom he has ever been excessively addicted, and with whom he has had so much intercourse that no punishment nor menaces of the Director can drive him from them. He is a great adept at dissimulation, and even when laughing, intends to bite, and professes the warmest friendship where he hates the deepest. To everyone who has business with him, and there is scarcely one who has not, he gives a favorable reply, promises assistance, yet, assists scarcely anyone but heads them off continually on some course or other - except the minister's friends.

In his words and acts he is loose, false and deceitful, given to lying, prodigal of promises, and when it comes to performance, nobody is home. With the exception of the Director and his party, the whole country cries out against him, as a villain - a murderer, and a traitor, and that he must quit this country or there will not be any peace with the Indians.

[From notes made by Elizabeth (Sooy) Forman]

Nice guy! Cornelius's mother-in-law is rumored to have incited her son-in-law to massacre the Indians "for it is recorded that she danced through the Town Kicking before her the severed head of a murdered Red Skin." I hope that Sarah was a beautiful and well-tempered woman, for Yoos's sake. He certainly was marrying into quite a family! Old Cornelius was removed from office in 1656 and fled to the West Indies. He was never heard from again.

Cornelius was long gone when Yoos got to New York and married his granddaughter in 1707. Come to think of it though, the girl's father was a successful surgeon, which, in those days, was equivalent to being a bit of a butcher! Hack saw, please? The couple lived in the city until about 1720, when they bought a "plantation" in Middlesex County, New Jersey, on the Cheesequake Creek. For some reason, this spot didn't please them, and they removed to Little Egg Harbor, Burlington County, four years later.

The river mouth and Great Bay merge somewhere amidst salt-marsh banks when the flowing waters narrow to about a mile. In Yoos's time, a small ship could make its way across the bay, disturbing huge flocks of geese, ducks, brant, and other water fowl that would darken the sky as they flew off. The sun-bleached sail of his ship would have been no match for the whiteness of the egrets that stalked through the marshes searching for their dinner. Even the proud Great Blue Herons were no strangers to the Little Egg Harbor River, as the Mullica was then called. The bay was paved with oysters and clams, and fish of all sorts inhabited the waters of both bay and river. Nature was prolific in this isolated place. The glory of Great Bay as gateway to the Mullica would appeal to both the esthetic nature and the cold, calculating lust for a good Dutch profit.

If the tide was running out, Yoos and his crew would have had to throw over the anchor and wait for a more favorable time to ascend the river. No power of wind and sail can fight an ebbing tide combined with a strong natural current. Only when the tide flows in can a boat sail up the Mullica and navigate its tortuous curves through mile after mile of marshland.

Azure blue painting the dome of the sky, brilliant sun warming the skin, fresh salt breeze off the ocean propelling the sailing ship up river towards his destiny, Yoos Sooy stared watchfully for a place to begin his empire. Yet for miles, there was not one foot of solid land! Oh, a couple little spots - one foot is an exaggeration - but not much to speak of, and certainly not much on which to build an empire of trade. Over the bay, up the river, mile on tortuous mile, nothing but water and marsh, birds and shellfish and fish - but no solid earth.

Then, as they rounded a bend in the river, there were houses on the left bank! Houses, of all things, in Yoos Sooy's magical river paradise! The town was Clark's Landing and, by 1718, boasted forty houses, a church, and a storehouse. Tied up to real wharves were several small boats.

That must have made the "bank" to starboard, just upriver, look all the more attractive. Solid land that could be cleared for farming! A goodly river! Access to the sea! Yoos's Dutch trader's eyes must have glowed at the unlimited prospects for himself and his family. He was almost forty years old in the Year of Our Lord 1724 - too old for starting over in the wilderness, but for those hardy and independent Dutch tradesmen, no age was too old for making money. Perhaps his old friend from New York, Peter Cavileer, was even standing on the bank waving a welcome.

Yoos looked at that good, solid, dry land and imagined a large "plantation" home, storehouses, warehouses, wagons, and, of course, ocean-going ships anchored at wharves: his wharves! Even the proximity of Clark's Landing could be turned to his advantage. There he could find companionship for himself and his wife and extra hands for employment on his plantation. If he wanted to build a boat, there were skilled workers just downriver.

416

Yoos Sooy died in Lower Bank in 1737 at the age of fifty-two and was buried on the banks of his beloved river. His grave was made on private ground which is now surrounded by the old Pacemaker Plant. His stone remains, almost illegible, a mute testimony to the dreams of this adventurous man. His wife, Sarah, presumably moved to Leed's Point with her son, Nicholas, for when she died in 1744, she was listed as a resident of Great Egg Harbor. in a legal document, signed by her sons, Joseph and Nicholas, giving up their right to administer their father's estate.

As in most old families, the lineage is difficult to figure out due to repeated names in the various branches and has certainly confused genealogists and historians. Yoos II (called "Joseph") married Elizabeth Smuts (or "Smith") in Cape May (See NOTE on the following page) on the 3rd of December in the year of his father's death, and they had twelve children: Joseph (1738); Sarah (1740); John (1742); Mary (1744); Nicholas (1747); Noah (1750); Luke (1752); Elizabeth (1754); Rebeca (1757); Phebe (1759); Jemima (1761); and Hannah (1763).

Poor Elizabeth! That's almost one child every two years for twenty-five years! There's no record of where *she's* buried. I think of that line from the burial service: *"...and now rest from their labors."* Elizabeth was one woman who surely deserved her "rest!"

Brother Nicholas was a laggard in terms of numbers, though he wasn't much easier on his wife. He married Jean Ingersol of Great Egg Harbor in 1743, and they had only six children: Joseph (1744); Jane (1745); Samuel (1747); Susanah (1748); Nicholas, Jr. (1749) and Richard (1751). Except for Jane and Samuel, all were born *one* year apart!

Here we have two families living in close proximity, in which there are three "Josephs" (including Yoos II who was called by his anglicized name "Joseph"), and three "Nicholases."

Nicholas, son of Yoos II, had *thirteen* children, including another Nicholas, another Elizabeth, another Jemima, another Sarah, and a Josephus (instead of Joseph). Nicholas, Jr., son of Nicholas, son of Yoos, had *ten* children, including *another* Elizabeth, *another* Samuel *another* Mary, *another* Josephus, *another* Sarah, and *another* Nicholas.

THAT means that within three generations of one family, all of that family living within the same general area, and following only one son from each of the original sons of Yoos Sooy, there are: three "Josephs," four "Nicholases," three "Elizabeths," three Sarahs," two "Samuels," two Marys," two "Josephuses," two "Jemimas," and I may have gotten lost in the figuring process! Try and straighten out who owns what parcel of land with all of that in one place!

Thank God for little favors! Yoos's son, Nicholas, moved to Leed's Point, south of the Mullica, after his marriage to a girl from that area and here raised his family of six. Yoos II (Joseph) remained on the northeast side of the river with his brood of twelve. This seemingly inconsequential move is about the only thing that helps us know who's who in this large and prolific family.

Why am I even taking time to mention this mess? The Sooy family in the pines, along with the Cavileers, the Leeks, and several other major families, represent the "first families" of the pinelands. Those families reach over three centuries into our own time and included in their occupational ventures most if not all of the "pinelands" industries, huge land-holdings, intermarriages between the these families and the major families of the surrounding areas, and were the stable core of the entire vast area of the central pines. Though many have moved great distances away from their roots, especially in this day of mobility, others still are anchored in this land of their parents, and grandparents, and great-grandparents and great-great-grandparents, with a heritage and a pedigree as decent as any produced in New England or in the South.

They were and are a hardworking and decent people, not backward, uneducated, mentally-weak, interbred "Pineys" of fable and sociological fiction. These people provided for themselves and their children a stable community, a strong sense of religion, as decent an educational opportunity for their children as most rural areas did, a sense of pride in family and place, and a love of the pinelands and of the river which flowed ever at their doors.

Photograph by John Pearce

"Here Lyes Interrd The Body of yoos Sooy who Departed this Life the 28th september Anno D° 1737 - 52 years"

417

Photograph by John Pearce

The Grave of Yoos Sooy - 1995

NOTE: A genealogical chart in the possession of Sooy scion, Jessie (Forman) Lewis that was written by her mother, Elizabeth (Sooy) Forman from original sources, place the birthdates of Yoos and Sarah's sons as follows: Yoos, Jr.: July 3, 1709; Yoos II (presumably Yoos, Jr. had died in infancy) October 25, 1710; and Nicholas ("Luykas") August 3, 1712. June Methot (*Blackman Revisited*) also follows this dating and order of birth.

According to the genealogy of the Sooy Family Association however, Nicholas was born July 3, 1709, Joost (Yoos) on October 25, 1710, and Luykas (who seems to have died as a baby) on August 3, 1712. Both versions claim to be from the same church baptismal records. If we follow the dating of Methot and Jessie Forman Lewis, Yoos II would have been twenty-seven when he was married and Nicholas thirty-one at his wedding. If it is as in the Sooy Family Genealogy, Nicholas would have been thirty-four and Yoos II thirty-one.

There is also a variation in the name and place of origin of Yoos II's (Joseph, Sr.) wife, Elizabeth. The Sooy Family Genealogy gives her as Elizabeth Smith, daughter of John and Mary Smith of Leed's Point, an English Quaker girl. Other sources give the name as "Smuts," and say that the wedding was in Cape May. This latter spelling conforms more with a Dutch origin for the wife of this Dutch scion. I can't vouch for the veracity of either of these variations, so I am presenting both here in hopes that someone will eventually prove the birth order of Yoos and Sarah's sons and the national origin of Elizabeth Sooy.

As to the spelling of Yoos's name, most of the early records seem to spell it "Joost." The "J" would have sounded like a "Y" and the final "T" might have been easily dropped, leaving the actual pronunciation as "Yoos." Given the penchant for inconsistencies in phonetical spelling, there are many variants of the name. "Yoos" is on his gravestone, and I have used this spelling throughout this work. As to his son, Yoos II, at a very early date he anglicized his name to "Joseph," as evidenced by a legal paper he signed in 1744 on the death of his mother.

A word before we conclude: most of those who have so painstakingly researched and written material on this family have made errors, sometimes major ones, and I don't pretend to be above reproach either. I've simply tried to keep track of the Sooys of Washington Township as best as possible.

The above signatures are from a 1744 legal document signed by Nicholas and Joseph (Yoos II) Sooy, the sons of Yoos Sooy, in which they gave up their right to administer their father's estate. The originals are on microfilm in the New Jersey State Archives.

418

Here Lyes Interrd
The Body of yoos
Sooy who Departed
this Life the 28 th sep
tember Anno Do

William F. Augustine Collection
Special Collections and University Archives
Rutgers University Libraries

The Late Fred Noyes, unofficial mayor of Lower Bank, at the stone of patriarch Yoos Sooy prior to the construction of the Pacemaker Plant.
This photograph was included in Henry Charlton Beck's *Jersey Genesis.*

A Schooner Heads for the Sea

A large, two-masted schooner is going through the old swing bridge at Lower Bank on its way to Great Bay and the Sea. Photograph was probably made during the first decade of the twentieth century.

Courtesy of Budd Wilson, Jr.

Courtesy of Budd Wilson, Jr.

Lower Bank at the Turn of the Century

A peaceful, pastoral setting of farms; that would aptly describe Lower Bank in the nineteenth and early twentieth centuries.

The view is northwest upriver towards Green Bank. In this old photograph, River Road stretches from the direction of the Batsto/Bridgeport Road (Route 542) on the far right towards the Mullica River off the picture to the left.

Only the Lower Bank Methodist Church and two of the houses visible in this photograph remain standing in 1995. The Daniel Cale II House (1) at 2090 River Road is still standing as a private home. The Lower Bank school building (2) is in Smithville as part of the "Historic Smithville" complex of shops. The house which was part of the Johnson family homestead (3) was destroyed by arson a few years ago. The Captain Jacob Johnson Store (4) still stands between the church (5) and the Johnson homestead site but is not visible in this picture. The roof of Marge (Cavileer) Fox's house (1995) (6) is just visible in front of the Victorian house roof in the center of the photograph. The Victorian house in the foreground (7) belonged to Captain Jesse Reuben Cavileer. Captain Jesse (b. 1840; d. 1927) first lived in (8). Late in the century, he built himself a fine Victorian home and turned the old house into a barn. This beautiful home was struck by lightning and burned to the ground early in this century. Charlie and Nettie Cavileer bought the house/barn (8) and turned it back into a home. This home also burned. (9) This house may have been built by a man named Bartlett and was owned by George Maxwell. It was torn down in recent years and a new home was built back behind where the barns are located in this photograph.

Lower Bank in the Nineteenth Century

River Road at the Turn of the Century
Looking towards the Mullica

Lower Bank, like its sister towns of Green Bank and Bridgeport, was a town of farms, shipping, and trade during the nineteenth century. The majority of residents stemmed from the few families which had settled here in the eighteenth century whose sons and daughters had intermarried with the families in the surrounding Mullica towns. The Cavileer family shared prominence with the Weekses, the Allens, the Johnsons, the Van Sants, the Adamses, the Cramers, and the Cales.

As in the other towns of the estuary, Lower Bank was involved in the usual trades. Loggers worked on the Great Swamp from the Lower Bank side towards Bridgeport. Shingles, timber, charcoal, and cordwood was exported to New York and Philadelphia in ships built by Lower Bankers, captained by Lower Bankers, and crewed by Lower Bankers exactly as was so in the other Mullica towns. Boats, large and small, were built in a ship yard which once stood where River Road turns to follow the Mullica.

Extensive docks stretched into the Mullica that saw a multitude of boats tied to them from small fishing craft to large, three-masted schooners. Fish, oysters, and clams were taken from the river. Wild fowl were hunted during the autumn migrations. Sphagnum moss was harvested from the cedar swamps. Salt hay was gathered from the meadows. Carpenters built houses when they weren't working on boats. Blacksmiths shoed horses, forged iron rims for wagon wheels, and made all types of ironware for homesteads and ships alike. No doubt there were coopers [barrel makers], cordwainers [leather workers], rope makers, men expert in tarring rigging lines. Millers ground the local grain, and sawmill operators processed the timber. In all probability, Lower Bank was a more self-sustaining town than was either Green Bank or Wading River, but that tied all three towns together.

From the junction of River Road with the Green Bank/Wading River Road, houses stretched down both sides of the lane to the river. After the road made the bend at the Mullica, it hugged the river for another mile or so until it ended at the ferry landing. Most families, whether sea captains or laborers, lived in what would today be considered small homes whose cedar clapboards remained generally unpainted. They had no electricity, no indoor plumbing, no insulation in the walls, no screens on the windows. Men and women worked from dawn to dusk. Their recreation was an occasional picnic or sail, if the man of the house owned a boat. Church socials broke the monotony of the routine.

Photograph by John Pearce

River Road - 1995

A woman's work around the house was as wearing as that of the men at their trades. It was an endless round of washing, ironing, cooking, cleaning, and caring for their generally large families. Illness or injury was a serious matter in the absence of medicines and doctors. It was a strong and self-sustaining community that prospered during the nineteenth century, but their prosperity was dependent on the river. When the railroads bypassed the area and scuttled the shipping industry, the handwriting was on the wall for this town in the pines.

A profitable business in Lower Bank seems to have been the sale of spirits. Legend has it that there were seven taverns in the town and that they were all put out of business by the indomitable Methodist minister, the Reverend Nicholas Van Sant, who thundered from the pulpit of the Old Meeting House for a good many years. At least two of them flanked the Old Meeting House: Sam Week's tavern, just across a stream called by the singular name of Cakes Spruto, and Josie Allen's out where the present Old Church Road meets the Green Bank/Wading River road. It must have irked the Rev. Van Sant to have old Sam's tavern so conveniently on the road between the bulk of the town and his little church to tempt the men to sin on the Sabbath, but how the men must have missed their jug which went far in relieving their tired, aching bones when the Rev. Van Sant had his way.

For many years, the only way to cross the Mullica was a small ferry which shuttled passengers back and forth to the Atlantic County side of the river. From old maps, it appears that the steamboat landing was approximately where River Road currently ends. The ferry landing seems to have been on the other side of the small creek which enters the Mullica at this point. The ferry apparently sailed from here to the old road from Egg Harbor City which passed through Gloucester Furnace and Gloucester Landing to the Mullica across from Lower Bank on the Atlantic (Old Gloucester) County side. When it was first established, it may have run downriver to Clark's Landing, since that was the nearest town in the eighteenth century. By the nineteenth, Clark's Landing was no longer a viable town. Gloucester Furnace, and later, Egg Harbor City, were the important areas of that century, and the ferry probably took the more direct route across the river. The dates of operation of this ferry are not known, but it ceased plying the waters with the construction of the Lower Bank bridge in 1863.

The bridge was authorized to be constructed where River Road bends to the south to follow the river bank, but it was never built there. The state legislature passed the authorizing legislation on February 25, 1863. One month later, it passed another bill which allowed the bridge to be constructed further downstream near the residence of Samuel Cavileer where it was subsequently built. The original road on the Atlantic County side of the

Mullica did not run along the line it does today. Instead, it ran downriver on a causeway through the marshes, turned abruptly inland at Landing Creek, crossed that stream at Gloucester Landing, and continued on through Gloucester Furnace.

Near the Old Meeting House runs the one creek in Lower Bank which was suitable for a mill. In fact, there may have been two: a saw mill and a grist mill. The creek bears a strange name: *Cakes Spruto*. Jonathan Johnson dammed the stream and built a grist mill after his 1809 land purchase from David Mapps. Later, Samuel Weeks, who ran the tavern nearby, maintained a sawmill on the pond formed by Cakes Spruto, which may have replaced the earlier Johnson grist mill. When Randolph Township was formed in 1870, the stream became the border between that township and the remnant that remained Washington Township.

Bisbee (*Signposts*) records that a 1713 survey lists this stream as *Cakes Sprater*. Another survey forty-six years later was still calling it *Cakes Sprater*. Still another record from 1759, talks about the mill pond at the head of *Cakesproots*. The 1808 road returns called it *Caky Sprater*.

Bisbee notes that Leah Blackman, in *The History of Little Egg Harbor*, mentions that one Joseph Cake, Jr. married Helena Cramer of Little Egg Harbor around 1758. Prior to the formation of Washington Township in 1802, this whole area was still part of Little Egg Harbor Township. Bisbee says that there is a Swedish word *Spruts*, meaning "to sprout out water," making *Cakes Spruto* mean literally, Cakes Spring. There is evidence to support this theory in the Wharton ledgers where one of the names of Bull Creek in Green Bank is Wackerra Sprout.

At one time, Old Church Road, or Old Meeting House Road, as it was originally called, was a part of the road that ran from Lower Bank to Washington via Green Bank and White Town. When it was first used, it ran behind the cemetery rather than in front of it. Traces can still be found where it headed for Green Bank through the woods. It met the present Green Bank/Wading River Road near where Lovers' Lane meets Routes 542 and 563. Another nearby road began nearby and ran past White Town and then on to Washington and the Road to Little Egg Harbor.

One branch of the Johnson family had its homestead farm on the River Road about halfway between the present Route 542 and the river. Captains Levi, Mahlon, John, and Jacob Johnson, sons of Mathias IV, lived here

Photograph by John Pearce

The Johnson Store - 1995
2081 River Road - The Paul Seybold Home

during the mid-nineteenth century. The Johnsons were connected with the sea though Levi and John occupied themselves with farming when age made the sea a bit much for them.

Their brother, Captain Jacob, operated the store on the old homestead property during the last half of the nineteenth century after he had retired from his waterborne life. The Johnson store was filled with all the items necessary to the local populace which they could not produce for themselves. Its shelves were no doubt stocked from wares brought upriver by Johnson ships captained by Johnsons and landed on the dock which stood where the River Road turns at the Mullica.

Lower Bank was not a static town but dynamic and alive. Shipping filled the river with boats of all sorts. Those who would have been listed as laborers worked at whatever task needed broad shoulders and strong arms. Generally, even the common laborers were skilled at a number of trades which they could use as the need arose.

Lower Bank, like her sister towns hugging the banks of the Mullica, is a relaxed, sleepy little town, a "bedroom" community. Her residents are either retired or work elsewhere. No one succeeded Harold Maxwell when he closed his store back in the late 1950's. Where Pacemaker Yachts once employed hundreds of men, now a few individual businesses attract commuting workers from elsewhere. The church is almost empty on a Sunday morning.

Lower Bank, like Green Bank and Wading River, and in fact, like many small towns on the Eastern Seaboard, is slumbering compared to years ago. It is a delightfully serene community filled with friendly, casual people, but as a community, as a cohesive, vibrant fellowship, it is fading away. Only the fire company provides a means to join people together for the common good. Fund-raising dinners and activities are still a way for the residents to see each other and socialize. How different this town is as we enter the twenty-first century from what it was a century and a half ago.

Only when a town has a reason for existence can it maintain a sense of community. We are all too used to living out our own lives independently of each other, most unlike those who came before us. The Lower Bankers of the nineteenth century knew they needed each other to survive. We, too, need to learn that lesson.

If in the following pages, I seem to dwell overmuch on family relationships which may bore the reader to tears, there's method in my madness. It is precisely these interrelationships which brought strength and cohesion to our communities of long ago. It is what gave Lower Bank life. Only as we realize our own similar interdependency, can we make our communities something besides a place to sleep.

Lower Bank, like Green Bank and Wading River, is very special, filled with people who have much to give to each other. May she always stay just that way!

The Van Sant Family

One of the most influential families to move into the Lower Bank area during the nineteenth century was that of the Reverend Nicholas Van Sant. The Rev. Mr. Van Sant presided over the religious life of Washington Township for over thirty-eight years, performed most of the marriages throughout the widespread rural township during that period, and preached the Word of God to the people of Lower Bank and Wading River from the pulpit of the Old Meeting House.

The brothers James F. and the Rev. Robert B. Steelman prepared a working paper for the Van Sant Genealogical Workshop of the Atlantic County Historical Society for presentation in 1999 that outlines the Van Sant genealogy. They note that *The Van Sant Family of New Utrecht and Bucks County, Pennsylvania* by Barbara A. Barth in the New York State Genealogical and Biographical Record, Vol. 127, Numbers 3 and 4 records that Nicholas's father, Captain John Van Sant was a descendant of Stoffel/Christoffel Harmenszen, who arrived about 1651 in New Amsterdam. A Stoffel/Christopher Vansant (possibly a grandson) was baptized on Staten Island on October 22, 1701. At some period during his youth, Stoffel and his parents moved to Bucks County, Pennsylvania. He later moved to Hartford, Connecticut, where he married Hannah Risley, daughter of John and Mary (Arnold) Risley of that city. *The Risley Family*, in The American Genealogist, Vol. 25, p. 236 confirms the marriage, though Hannah's name is wrongly entered in the church records as "Mary." Their first child, John, was baptized on January 7, 1727/8. He married a woman named Martha and the baptisms of their children were recorded at Portland Church: Rachel (3/8/1752), John (4/7/1754), and Jonathan (3/22/1756 - 5/13/1757).

That this is the same John who came to Burlington County is confirmed by a deed between John Vansant and his wife, Martha, and John Loveland of Middletown Township, Hartford County, Connecticut on October 15, 1760, which lists John as a resident of "Egg Harbour in the County of Burlington in the Western Division of the Province of New Jersey."

It would seem that John and Martha Vansant, with their two surviving children, John and Rachel, came to the area of "The Forks" between 1757 and 1760 (the date of Jonathan's death in Connecticut and the date of the deed giving this as their residence).

Other writers on the Van Sant family have listed another son, Christopher, who was born on December 10, 1769, the son of John Van Sant and a Sarah Dole. The date that John's first wife, Martha, died is unknown, but she was still alive in 1774, which would make Christopher her son, if indeed, Christopher is John's son in the first place. The Steelmans note that Ella Montgomery of Green Bank, a descendant of John's youngest son, told them that her grandfather, Nicholas, had a half brother by the name of Christopher, who lived in Bargaintown. Letters from ex-Governor Samuel R. Van Sant of Minnesota, dated August 29, 1932, confirm this.

After his wife, Martha, died, John is supposed to have married a Polly Bowen in 1775, but this is undocumented. John and Polly (Bowen) Vansant were supposed to have had a son, Joel, who was born the year after his parents' marriage. The Steelmans note that there are also several other Van Sants, "both male and female, that generally cannot be accounted for except as children of Captain John and ... would all appear to have been children of Polly Bowen."

According to Samuel R. Van Sant in a letter dated August 29, 1932, John married yet a third time to a Rebecca (Simkins?), a widow, in 1787. They had a son, Nicholas, who was born on November 9, 1788. That Nicholas was John's son is confirmed by both his Bible, now in the possession of The Rev. Robert Steelman, and in a deed dated May 1, 1869, wherein Nicholas, sold the land at "The Forks" to Samuel P. Richards for one dollar. In the deed, Nicholas is called "his only child and heir at law..." Obviously, Nicholas was not John's only child.

Thus, prior to the commencement of hostilities that culminated in war with England, John moved his family to the vicinity of "The Forks" on the Old Gloucester County side of the Mullica. Here he took up an occupation which would characterize his family for at least four generations: shipbuilding. In 1760, he purchased approximately ninety acres from Richard Wescoat on the Washington Township side of the Mullica, which became the site of his shipyard.

When the Revolution broke out, Captain John Van Sant either converted one of his vessels for use as a privateer or built an entirely new one for that purpose. Though he seems to have engaged in active service, his shipyard continued to build privateering vessels for other owners during the war as well. A record of the fitting out of the privateer galley *Alligator*, owned by Joseph Ball of Batsto, is in the possession of the Historical Society of Pennsylvania.

The Van Sant family recalled that Captain John, later in life, continued to bemoan the fact that he was paid for his efforts in "Continentals," paper money issued by the Continental Congress that was worthless by the end of the war. So devastated were many financial backers of the Revolution that "Not worth a Continental" remained a common phrase throughout the nineteenth century. Captain John's ship was burned at the battle of Chestnut Neck when the British determined to wipe out that "nest of rebel pirates" that so plagued their shipping from the Mullica estuary.

At some time after Nicholas's birth in 1788, John moved to Bass River and set up another shipyard.

On December 23, 1808, Simon Lukas joined Nicholas Van Sant and Mercy Davis in marriage. Mercy was born on the 13th of March, 1789. Fred Cramer ("Family Bible of Nicholas and Mercy Van Sant") states that Mercy had "sought the Lord" at the age of eighteen in 1807 and united with the Methodist church at Pleasant Mills under the care of the Rev. Joseph Totten. Nicholas Van Sant was converted "about the same time."

Mercy's mother had been married twice, first to a man by the name of Davis, who was probably Mercy's father, then to a gentleman by the name of Moore. Mercy seems to have used both her birth father's name and her stepfather's as well. Her mother was supposedly the daughter of Richard Wescoat of Pleasant Mills. The newlyweds set up housekeeping in Bass River, where Nicholas worked in his father's shipyard.

Courtesy of Sarah (Cramer) Camillo

The Rev. Nicholas Van Sant, Sr.
Ordained Minister of the Gospel

During the War of 1812 with Great Britain, Nicholas Van Sant enlisted and served at Cape May Point, though it seems that he really wasn't in any real action. He was listed as a pensioner of that war, however.

In the Atlantic County Historical Society Year Book Volume I, Number 2, for October 1977, Sarah Ewing says that Nicholas worked at his father's Bass River yard until 1815 when he and Mercy moved to Port Republic. After the birth of their fourth son, James, in 1816, she says he moved his family to Absecon, where he had found work in a shipyard. He and his family remained in Absecon for about ten years, after which they returned to Port Republic, and Nicholas built his own boat yard there.

The couple had eleven children, eight of them sons: John Wesley, Joel, Samuel, James, Rebecca, Samuel II, Nicholas, Nathaniel Doughty, Mary Ann, Isaac Newton, and Phebe Moore. According to a family Bible, all the children from Rebecca to Phebe were born in Gloucester (now Atlantic) County. The first Samuel, the couple's third child, born on July 17th, 1814, died at the age of five and a half years old on January 27, 1820. Phebe Moore, their eleventh child, died at two years of age on October 1, 1835.

This sizable family became noted for their two family devotions. The sons were all skilled in ship building, and they were all *very* devout Methodists.

John Wesley Van Sant was born in Bass River, Burlington County, on January 9, 1810. At the age of twenty-nine, he "went West," living both in Rock Island, Illinois, and later in Leclaire, Iowa. John Wesley served as a licensed preacher for several years and lived to the age of 94 on February 24, 1904. It was his son, Samuel R. Van Sant, who became the governor of Minnesota in later years. This Samuel tried to get into the Union Army at an early age (he says at 16, though he wasn't mustered in until September 1, 1861, which, given his birth date of 1843 would have made him eighteen when he actually succeeded in getting in.)

The second son of the Reverend Nicholas and Mercy (Davis) Van Sant, Joel, was born on November 22nd, as per a typed copy of the family record found in the Van Sant Bible, and printed in an article by Fred Cramer entitled, "Family Bible of Nicholas and Mercy Van Sant" in the Atlantic County Historical Society Quarterly Newsletter for August 1996 and confirmed by the Rev. Mr. Steelman) and married Catherine Wilson on the 23rd of January 1832.

Joel and his wife lived in Lower Bank for many years, although they apparently lived in Atlantic County for a while as well. Fred Cramer notes that family records indicate Joel ran a shipyard at Green Bank and was a devout member of the Methodist church. Joel died on November 5th, 1895, just shy of his eighty-fourth birthday and was buried at Lower Bank. His son, Joel, Jr. is listed as a ship carpenter in Green Bank at the time of *his* son, Oscar's birth in 1874.

After leaving Green Bank in the early 1880's, Edward and Joel Jr. built a shipyard in Atlantic City near Wabash and Maryland Avenues. Their brother, Doughty, joined them when they moved their business to the newly-dredged Gardener's Basin ten years later.

James was born on November 9, 1816. He became a Methodist minister like his father, married four times, and died at the age of eighty-one and is buried in Petersburg, N.J.

Daughter Rebecca was born on May 25, 1819, married Peter Lane in 1836. The couple took over the operation of the Port Republic boatyard and later lived in Lower Bank. She died on February 18, 1899.

Samuel II, born September 23, 1821, had the shortest life of all his brothers and sisters with the exception of the two who died as children, living only to the age of sixty. He married Susanna Hays and, like his father and older brother, served as a Methodist minister. One of his sons, S. Monroe, likewise bore the title "Reverend." Samuel II died at the age of eighty in Island Heights, N.J. on April 24, 1881 and was buried in Toms River.

Courtesy of Sarah (Cramer) Camillo

Mercy (Davis) Van Sant
"Devout Mother in Israel"

Nicholas, Jr. was born on December 7, 1823 at Absecon. He enlisted in the Union army at the age of seventeen and served throughout the war. After the conflict, he became a Methodist preacher. Nicholas, Jr. married (1) Amelia Pauline Moses on December 9, 1844 and (2) Josephine L. Tunis on December 30, 1885. After a long and full life, died at Madison, N.J. on May 3, 1902 or 3 and was buried in Paterson, N.J.

Nathaniel Doughty Van Sant was born on the 1st of May, 1826 in Wrangleboro, N.J. and died when he was more than eighty on February 12, 1906. Like his grandfather, he was a skilled ships' carpenter. Called "Uncle Thannie" in his later years, he was very influential in the Lower Bank church where he served as a deacon. On July 28, 1848, Nathaniel married Sarah Carter. He lies buried in the old churchyard in Lower Bank.

Mary Ann was born on the 17th of April, 1828 in Wrangleboro and married Captain Richard Cramer on December 21, 1845. She and the good captain had seven daughters and two sons.

Reverend Nicholas and Mercy (Davis) Van Sant's youngest son, Isaac Newton, was born on May 31st, 1830 in Wrangleboro and married Margaret Bush Adams on September 21, 1847. Guess what he did for a living? In the township records, he is listed as a "carpenter," which probably meant he worked on both ships and houses, but the other family occupation beckoned. Like his father and three of his brothers, he finally became an ordained Methodist minister. James, Samuel, Nicholas and Isaac all served as "Itinerant Ministers," the fancy name for circuit-riders. Nicholas and Isaac were members of the former Newark Conference while James and Samuel served in the former New Jersey Conference of the Methodist Episcopal Church. In a letter to this author, the Rev. Mr. Steelman notes that there is a family story, "attributed to my boat-building grandfather, John Van Sant, that Van Sant boys were usually either Methodist preachers or boat builders, and the lazy ones were preachers."

Phebe Moore was born on June 17, 1833 at Wrangleboro, N.J. She died there on October 1, 1835 and is buried in Blackman's Cemetery.

Nicholas was ordained as a Methodist clergyman on April 17, 1831 and thereby started the second occupation which would characterize this active family. Reverend Nicholas was the preacher at Smith's Meeting House in Wrangleboro (now Port Republic), Old Gloucester County, during the first years of the nineteenth century and also ran a shipyard there. Smith's Meeting House stood across the street from the present church, and the shipyard was next to it.

John Van Sant finally gave up his yard on the Bass River and, with his wife, Rebecca, moved to the Port Republic home of his son. The old privateer captain died there in 1820 at the age of ninety-four. His wife, Rebecca, lived another eleven years and was eighty when she died. Mrs. Ewing confirms that Nicholas's shipyard on the Nacote (pronounced "naked") Creek stood "in a cove at the end of a lane leading to the creek, opposite St. Paul's United Methodist Church." She also notes that the Van Sant home stood across the road from the shipyard, and still stands today.

In 1841, ten years after his mother's death, Nicholas Van Sant and his wife moved to Lower Bank to organize a congregation of the Methodist Episcopal Church in that place. Their son, James, continued working at the shipyard in Port Republic until he, too, received the call to the ministry ten years later. When James left, his sister, Rebecca, and her husband, Peter Lane, took over the business. They, too, moved to Lower Bank at a later date.

Shipyards in Green Bank, Lower Bank, Bass River, and Tuckerton were operated by the Van Sant family during the eighteen hundreds, as well as several yards in Atlantic County. Their reputation for sound vessels and religious zeal made them famous throughout the entire region. During the years for which we have records from the township of Washington, 1848 through 1877, Reverend Van Sant performed the vast majority of the marriages recorded in the township, travelling by horseback to every town for the ceremonies though the bulk were performed in Lower Bank itself.

The Reverend Nicholas Van Sant of Lower Bank died full of years and honor at his Lower Bank home on the sixth of March, 1879, four months after his ninetieth birthday. He was laid to rest beside the church he served so faithfully amongst the beloved members of his flock. His stone in the Lower Bank cemetery reads,

> *He was a member of the Methodist Episcopal Church for 73 years, and a local preacher almost 60 years, was ordained April 17, 1831, lived with the wife of his youth 70 years. Honest in his dealings, uncompromising with sin, firm and fearless in the advocacy of Temperence [sic], earned and unswerving as a Christian skilled in the Word of God, he was instructive as a preacher, and always preaching by his holy life. Exemplifying the Christian graces and virtues, his long life was remarkable in Goodness and Usefulness, Honoring his parents, his days were long in the land and his numerous posterity rise up to call him Blessed.*

> *Servant of God well done!*
> *Thy glorious warfare's past.*
> *The battle fought, the race is run*
> *And thou art crowned at last.*

His wife, Mercy, passed away on the eighth of the following January in the ninety-first year of her life and was buried beside him. Her stone in the old burial yard speaks as eloquently as his:

> *Converted in youth, she continued a faithful member of the ME Church. Living the church, she was punctual in attendance in the means of grace even in old age. Possesing [sic] a rich experience. In prayer she devoutly and eloquently talk'd with God; and in the class her experience was given with a positiveness and joyous glow which frequently culminated in shouting the praise of God. Exemplary in her home, she live'd to see her children converted and four of her sons ministers of the Gospel, and most of her children's children brought to Christ. Her death was peaceful and triumphant.*

> *O may I triumph so,*
> *When my warfare's past,*
> *And find in death, my latest foe*
> *Beneath my feet at last.*

The Cavileer Family

The first Peter seems to have been in Lower Bank by 1722, not long after Eric Mullica's demise. There is no record of his whereabouts prior to that time, but it is assumed he was of French Huguenot extraction. He didn't marry for about eight years after he came to the area, but when he did, he married a Burlington County girl, Ann Tearney. A son, John, was born to the couple on April 20, 1742, almost twelve years after their marriage. No other children are listed in the genealogy of the Cavileer family, though it seems strange that it took the couple so long to have children.

John Cavileer, on the other hand, left a record. His gravestone stands near that of Yoos Sooy in the area of the old Pacemaker Yachts plant near the Lower Bank bridge. John married another Ann, whose surname is unknown, and the couple had nine children, four sons and five daughters: Peter, Charles W., Elizabeth, Sarah, Mary, Hester, Ann, John, and David.

Like all the other old families on the Mullica, most of the family looked for spouses in nearby locales. On September 11, 1797, John and Ann's eldest son, Peter, married Eleanor Sooy, the daughter of Joseph and Mary (Leek) Sooy. The family genealogy indicates that they were married at Harrisville, but Harrisville as such, even as McCartyville, wouldn't be thought about for another thirty years. Only Bodine's Tavern and the Wading River Forge and Slitting Mill were up in that direction at that early date.

Charles married Elizabeth Weatherby of Bridgeport. Elizabeth married David Lewis. Sarah seems to have fallen for an Irishman, Benjamin O'Mear. Mary married Solomon Leeds, a member of the famous Leed's Point family in Old Gloucester County south of the Mullica. Hester married Jacob Gale, another Bridgeporter. Ann married Thomas Dixon. John married into the Weeks family, his wife being Elizabeth Weeks. Finally, David married a Cramer, Mary, the daughter of Caleb Cramer, Sr.

Peter and Eleanor became the proud parents of twelve children: Peter, Jr., Mary S., Samuel S., Elizabeth, John Dennis, Amelia, David, Sarah Louisa, Elvira, Joseph G., Millicent, and Charles Wesley.

The third generation of the Cavileers did as much intermarrying with the other families on the Mullica as the second. Peter married Ann Mulford, but apparently died young. No birth date is given, but as his parents were married in 1797 and he died in 1825, its fairly safe to conclude that he wasn't more than twenty-eight when he died.

Mary S. married William Loveland Leek, the son of William and Catherine (Loveland) Leek of Bridgeport. The couple had five children, three girls and two boys. Once again, their choice of spouses was made locally. Catherine married William M. Cale. Mary Elizabeth married James Johnson. Jane Ann married Edwin Clark Sooy and ran the store in Bridgeport. Joseph Henry married Phoebe Lovenia Sears. William Towers married Charlotte Johnson. Edwin Clark and Jane Ann (Cavileer) Sooy's oldest son, William Augustus Sooy's first wife was Mary A. Cramer. Their daughter, Etta, married William Augustus Maxwell, a sea captain and store operator in Bridgeport. Their second son, Edwin Clark Sooy, Jr. married Abby Ann Turner and took over the operation of his parents' store in Bridgeport. All of these people are discussed in more detail in the section on Wading River/Bridgeport.

Samuel S. married Martha Ann Allen of the Bass River Allens. The couple's first son was Samuel Henry Cavileer, born in 1839 and lost at sea on September 16, 1876. Their second son, Gilbert Hatfield Cavileer, was born in 1843 and died in 1928. They apparently lived in Port Republic most of their lives and are buried there.

Elizabeth married Paul Sears Sooy, the son of Nicholas Sooy I, of Green Bank. Paul Sears Sooy took over the operation of Sooy's Inn (the Washington Tavern) on the old stage road when his father died.

When John Dennis married Mary E. Leach, he joined his brother Peter in marrying outside the township.

Amelia married William DeBow on August 24, 1828, and became the second wife of Samuel Weeks prior to September 10, 1860 when they sold land in Mullica Township, Atlantic County.

David married Phoebe Ann Cale, another local girl.

Sarah Louisa married Maja Leek whose boyhood home was the old Wading River Tavern (see Bridgeport/Wading River).

Elvira married a Charles Schell, origin unknown. The Schell name does not appear on the township records during the third quarter of the century.

Joseph's wife's name was Honoria, but her surname is not given.

Only Millicent's name appears in the genealogy.

Charles Wesley married his cousin, Elizabeth L. Cavileer, the daughter of John and Elizabeth (Weeks) Cavileer.

When you read over the genealogies of the local families you quickly realize how intertwined the families really were. The families of the river towns: Green Bank, Lower Bank, and Wading River/Bridgeport were completely interrelated in almost every generation throughout the nineteenth and early twentieth centuries. It is very safe to say that *everyone* related to *one* old local family is also related to *every other* old local family all along the river.

That does not mean that they were inbred. They certainly were not. Though the families were related, those relationships spanned generations, and therefore were not particularly close. There were a few instances of marriage between first cousins, but that was not forbidden years ago.

While families could be said to have had their origins in a particular town, their progeny spread throughout the locality from Crowleyville to New Gretna and beyond to Tuckerton and south through Leed's Point. Though Peter Cavileer and Yoos Sooy made their homes in Lower Bank for instance, their children and grandchildren lived all along both sides of the Mullica and Wading rivers and beyond. Thus the cemeteries in Green Bank, Lower Bank, Wading River/Bridgeport, New Gretna, Leed's Point, Tuckerton, and even as far away as that in Atsion contain the graves of one, huge, extended family.

Many of the residents of Lower Bank today share in the heritage of the past two centuries. Barry and Caleb Cavileer, for instance, are the sons of Caleb and Mina (Schwenger) Cavileer. Caleb was the son of Benjamin Franklin and Marjorie Nevada (Mathis) Cavileer. Benjamin's parents were Caleb Napoleon and Laura Jane (Headley) Cavileer. Caleb Napoleon's parents were Lorenzo Dow and Hannah Elizabeth (Weatherby) Cavileer. Lorenzo's first wife had been Elizabeth Sooy, daughter of Noah and Sarah (Weeks) Sooy. Lorenzo Dow's parents were Charles W. and Elizabeth (Weatherby) Cavileer. Charles W.'s father was John Cavileer, son of the pioneer, Peter, who is buried in the old Pacemaker plant in Lower Bank. Margery (Cavileer) Fox, Barry's aunt, was the sister of Caleb Franklin Cavileer. Doris Rebecca (Cavileer) Ryder, is Margery's younger sister.

Horace Cavileer's home and clam shack are on the turn of River Road at the river itself. Horace is an old and experienced waterman, who knows the tides, weather, and seasons of the Mullica and its Great Bay. Horace was born on the 27th of October, 1918, the son of Reuben Cavileer, Jr. and Laura E. (Broom) Cavileer. Reuben's father was Reuben, Sr., of course and his mother was Joanna (Loveland-Rose) Cavileer. Reuben, Sr. was the son of Samuel and Mary Ann (Cavileer) Cavileer. Samuel was the son of Charles W. and Elizabeth (Weatherby) Cavileer.

That makes Horace the third cousin of Margery (Cavileer) Fox and her sister, Doris (Cavileer) Ryder and the third cousin once removed of Barry Cavileer.

Walter Knickerbocker Cavileer, Jr., who married Marjorie Downs (see WADING RIVER/BRIDGEPORT) was the son of Walter K., Sr. He was the son of John and Armenia (Johnson) Cavileer. John was the son of John and Elizabeth (Weeks) Cavileer. John was the son of John and Ann Cavileer, the son of Peter. That means that Walter Knickerbocker Cavileer, Jr. and Horace were third cousins once removed and Barry Cavileer is W. K. Jr.'s third cousin twice removed.

David Cavileer is the son of Jesse Reuban and Daisy (Brooks) Cavileer. Jesse's parents were James Veldren and Rachel Matilda (Maxwell) Cavileer. James's parents were Reuben and Elizabeth (Lewis) Cavileer. Reuben's parents were John and Elizabeth (Weeks) Cavileer. That makes Barry David's fourth cousin once removed and Horace's fourth cousin.

There are still twenty "Cavileers" listed in the local phone book who live in Lower Bank, Port Republic, Hammonton, Egg Harbor, Absecon, Pleasantville and even in Atlantic City, all of whom are directly related to this extensive family. Barry, Caleb, David, Horace and their families still live in the town of their forefathers, as do Margery (Cavileer) Fox and Doris (Cavileer) Rider. Many others are also related through the female side.

Peter Cavileer, the eldest son of John Cavileer, served on the township committee in 1806 and 1808. His brother, John Cavileer, Jr. held the same responsibility from 1816 through 1822, and from 1826 through 1831. He also served as one of the Commissioners of Appeal in 1805, 1808, 1817, 1820-1824, 1826, 1830-1831, constable in 1820, Commissioner of Highways and Pound Keeper in 1827. David Cavileer served a year as constable in 1813 and Overseer of Highways in 1814. Charles Cavileer was a Commissioner of Appeal in 1822 through 1831, Pound Keeper in 1826, 1829-1831, and Surveyor of Highways 1829-1831.

In the fateful year of 1832, something happened which shattered the calm of Washington Township. Three "Annual Meetings" were held, each declaring the actions of the previous meeting null and void. Nicholas Sooy II and the Sooy family, Job Weeks and the Weeks family, and John and Charles Cavileer and the Cavileer family withdrew from public service. It was years before members of these families served again in public capacity and even then, it was the next generation who took up the reins. It is too bad that the cause of the unrest was not noted in the records and is lost to history.

Lorenzo was Surveyor of Roads in 1850. Lorenzo D. was constable in 1851 and Judge of Elections in 1862. Charles W. was on the Township Committee in 1864. Rainer Cavileer was a Commissioner of Appeals in 1896 through 1899 after Randolph Township was merged with Washington. Whether or not they held positions in this short-lived municipality is not known. No records exist.

The Cavileers are one of the few "first families" that still flourishes as the twentieth century draws to a close. Their fortunes have varied as the generations succeeded one another, but they have been an anchor to the past for this tiny, pinelands town by the Mullica.

Gathered near the Leek Boatyard are the brothers George, Charlie, Raymond, and Sam Cavileer.
Henry Charlton Beck got the brothers together for a reunion when he was writing his book, *Jersey Genesis*, around 1940.

The Weeks Family

According to Elmer G. Van Name who wrote *The Weeks Family of Southern New Jersey*, the name Weeks (or Wyke, Wike, Wicks, Wykes, Wycks, Wyckes, Weax, and Weekes) is "derived from an ancient Saxon word, Wyke, meaning a village, or from a baptismal source, meaning 'son of William.'" This latter interpretation may be the more reasonable one, since the practice of calling someone "son of..." was common in Northern Europe and Saxon England for centuries [see ERIC MULLICA]. There is no guarantee that everyone bearing the name "Weeks" in the United States even derive their heritage from the same European country.

The oldest provable member of the Weeks family in the Mullica valley was Ezekiel Weeks who was born about December 17, 1750. Van Name indicates that Ezekiel may have come from England to New Jersey via Connecticut and does not seem directly related to any of the other Weeks families in this country, but Van Name also says that it is obvious he is not the originator of his branch of the family. Though he interviewed many people in attempting to coordinate a genealogy, he admits that his work is only tentative. The Weeks genealogy remains a bit more sketchy than those of several of the other old families of the area.

Van Name notes that there were many bearing the Weeks name who lived in the colony of New York as early as the seventeenth century. One James Weeks is listed on February 19, 1690 as an Ensign of Foot at Oyster Bay, Queens County, New York, and others bearing the names of Ezekiel, Henry, James, Richard and Job are listed as members of the militia of Queens County in 1715. The 1790 census continues to show that members of these early families remained in New York. Unfortunately, there is no proof of a connection between the Mullica Weeks family and those in New York, even though they share common Christian names. He does note that Jacob, Henry, and Caleb Weeks of Long Island, apparently owned land in Burlington County in 1724, though there is no proof that they lived on those lands. Nor could he find any proof that the Weeks families who settled in Salem or Cape May counties had any relationship to those who settled in old Gloucester County (now Atlantic County) in the Mullica valley.

The Mullica Weeks family thought that their ancestor in America was one of four brothers who came to America from Devonshire, England, in 1635. Brother George settled in first in Salem, then in Dorchester, Massachusetts Bay, brother Thomas in Huntington, Long Island, brother Francis in Oyster Bay. The fourth brother, Joseph, drowned in an accident during the landing on these shores. The family thought that Francis (actually Francis Robert) had a grandson by the name of Robert, and a great-grandson, Robert, Jr. who was the father of Ezekiel of the Mullica. Not so, says Mr. Van Name.

The genealogist will only admit that Ezekiel was probably the fifth generation in America and moved to old Gloucester County from Connecticut. He was born December 17, 1750 and is recorded as a householder in old Galloway Township in February, 1780. That Ezekiel was not the only Weeks in the area at the time is indicated by the fact that on April 17, 1762, Job Weex [*sic*] of Great Egg Harbor transferred to Ezekiel Weex and James Weex, of the same place, low land and cedar swamp on the south side of the new road from Egg Harbour to Gloucester, containing 36 acres. The sale was not recorded until sixty-nine years later on July 25, 1831 (G1D C3:524). This land was not in what would become Weekstown but on the same side of the Mullica, south of Lower Bank, near Gloucester Landing (off Clark's Landing Road). Ezekiel would only have been twelve years old when this transfer was actually made.

Who was this Job Weeks? Who was James Weeks? Was Job Ezekiel's father? Was James his brother? Quite possibly. We do know that Ezekiel named two of his sons Job and James. On March 23, 1798, Ezekiel was appointed administrator of the estate of one James Weeks of Gloucester County. When his fourth son was born on May 8,1798, he was named James.

Ezekiel may have had other brothers as well. A John Weeks served as a private during the Revolutionary War (SJR 815) and was taxed in Egg Harbor Township in January 1781 on five cattle. He was taxed in Little Egg Harbor Township (which included what is now Bass River Township and the Mullica River portion of Washington Township) in July, 1784 as a householder. A Job Weeks (born May 8, 1755, in Gloucester County, served in the Revolutionary War and applied for a pension (File S30777). He served under Colonel Richard Westcott (or "Wescoat"; see BATSTO) in the company of Captain Arthur Westcott (or "Wescoat") for six tours of duty of six weeks each. He also served aboard the privateer sloop *Chance* and the schoooner *Rattlesnake*. At some time after the war, he moved to Salem County, N.J., then to Ohio County, Virginia, then to Warren County, Ohio, then to Indiana, and finally to Kentucky.

At some time prior to the birth of his first child in 1782, Ezekiel married Elizabeth Johnson, the daughter of Mathias, Sr. and Elizabeth (Brookfield) Johnson (1762-1841) of the Lower Bank Johnsons. On June 3, 1784,

The Old Weeks Homestead in Weekstown - 1935
This house was destroyed by fire a good many years ago.

Ezekiel Weeks and his brother-in-law, Joseph Johnson, obtained a survey for fifty acres on the north side of Pine Creek or Newton Creek in Galloway Township "formerly surveyed to Richard Westcott and 'now in the possession of said Ezekiel Weeks and Joseph Johnson.'" The following year, on February 26, 1785, Elizabeth's brother, Joseph, sold thirty-six acres of land in old Gloucester County, originally surveyed to Richard Wescott (or "Wescoat") and sold to Joseph's father in 1778. These land transactions are the first *recorded* purchases of land by Ezekiel and Elizabeth (Johnson) Weeks in what would become Weeksville (now Weekstown), Galloway Township (now Mullica Township), Gloucester County (now Atlantic County). We must not forget that he was listed as a householder in the township as early as 1780, meaning that these are *additional* purchases, *not* the initial one. Ezekiel died in 1817 at the age of sixty-seven and was buried in Lower Bank.

Ezekiel and Elizabeth (Johnson) Weeks had at least eleven children whose names are known, the first of whom was Daniel, born on January 20, 1782. Like the other families who called the Mullica valley their home, many of the Weeks children would choose the sons and daughters of other local families as their spouses and thus cement ties with those families throughout the area.

Son Daniel would marry Anne Weatherby. Her father, William Weatherby, is listed as being from Pennsylvania but her mother was Elizabeth Mathis of Little Egg Harbor Township. The Weatherby family lived off Turtle Creek Road in Bridgeport/Wading River, and William served as Clerk of Washington Township in 1803, as one of the Commissioners of Appeal in 1804 as well as Surveyor of Highways that year, and as Clerk in 1806 through 1808. In 1810 and 1811, he was a Commissioner of Appeals and served as Assessor in 1814, after which his name does not appear on the lists. Anne Weatherby's sister, Elizabeth, married Charles Cavileer, son of John Cavileer. Daniel died in 1845 in Atlantic County.

Daughter Esther was born on December 3rd, 1783 and would marry Nicholas Sooy II, the owner of Green Bank (see Green Bank).

Sarah, born on March 12, 1785 married Nicholas's brother, Noah. Their daughter, Parmelia, would marry Samuel Crowley, III. Another daughter, Hannah, would marry William Leek. A third daughter, Betsy, married Lorenzo Dow Cavileer. Now Lorenzo's father, Charles W. Cavileer was married to Elizabeth Weatherby. That means that Lorenzo's mother and his wife's aunt by marriage were sisters.

William, born September 2nd, 1788 married Margaret Bevis.

Elizabeth, born February 10, 1791, married John Cavileer, Jr. of Lower Bank (see THE CAVILEER FAMILY). John Cavileer, Jr. was Charles W. Cavileer's brother.

Job, born October 10, 1793 married Sarah Pettit. Sarah was the daughter of Samuel Pettit and Hannah Sooy, the eldest daughter of Nicholas Sooy I and sister of Nicholas II. Samuel Pettit was from the same Pettit family as Charles, the Secretary of New Jersey from 1772 to 1778 and part owner of the *Chance* with Joseph Ball, Richard Wescoat, and John Cox of Batsto and The Forks (see BATSTO). This couple would move to Lower Bank and become the progenitors of the Lower Bank clan of the Weeks family in later years.

Photograph by Augusta Weeks

Jonathan and Charlotte (Wobbar) Weeks' Store - 1935
Weekstown

Rebecca, born January 17, 1796 married William Sooy, another son of Nicholas Sooy I and brother of Nicholas Sooy II (see WADING RIVER/BRIDGEPORT).

James, born May 8, 1798, married Phebe Wilson, the daughter of Curtis Wilson and Sarah Sooy.

Photograph by Augusta Weeks

Jonathan and
Charlotte (Wobbar) Weeks
about 1935

Samuel, born March 17, 1804, married Mary Cranmer, daughter of John Cranmer and Hannah Johnson. Samuel and his wife lived in Lower Bank, had seven children. It was Samuel who was supposed to have had the dispute over an unpaid bill with the Methodist Episcopal Society trustees, including his brother, Job.

Hannah, born December 8, 1801, married a man named Thompson, and Isaiah, born July 29, 1806, married Hannah Cramer. There may well have been more children than this.

I hope I'm only occasionally carried away on these genealogical interweavings. Actually, I'm just having fun! The interrelationships among the families of the Mullica valley are far more complex than they seem and span both sides of the river.

The Jonathan Weeks who married Charlotte Wobbar, daughter of Otto and Esther (Birdsall) Wobbar of South Bend and who was active in the Green Bank Methodist Church during the first part of the twentieth century (see GREEN BANK and SOUTH BEND) was born on May 15, 1858. Jonathan and Charlotte's daughter, Augusta, was responsible for the 1935 photographs of Green Bank in that section as well as those of the Weeks houses on this and the previous page. Jonathan and his wife ran a store from their home which still stands on the corner in Weekstown though it is no longer maintained as a store. Jonathan died on November 15, 1935 and was remembered as a fine, old gentleman. His father was Joseph Weeks and his mother, Hannah Sooy, daughter of Josephus and Sarah (Thomas) Sooy and granddaughter of Nicholas I. His paternal grandparents were William and Margaret (Bevis) Weeks. William, was of course, the son of Ezekiel.

Charlie Weber
The Last of the Salt-Hayers

Photograph by John Pearce

Charlie Weber's House - 1995
1427 Route 542

Charlie Weber's farm isn't a farm any more. Charlie himself has been gone for over fifty years, but there are still older people around who remember the man who worked well into his seventies as the last of the South Jersey Salt-Hayers. "There was a worker!" say men and women with a smile and a shake of the head, men and women who, like Charlie, have worked hard all their lives and are approaching eighty themselves. Charlie was one of them, though born over in Weekstown in Atlantic County.

Charlie's parents were Germans, lured to the pines by entrepreneurs who had dreams of developing Egg Harbor City as a great port and farming community in the mid-eighteen hundreds. Gloucester Furnace had been established in 1813, and, as an iron furnace, had all the advantages: plentiful ore, river transportation, clam shell lime, abundant fuel, and ready markets in Philadelphia and New York.

The furnace itself was built on a tributary stream of the Mullica called Landing Creek about two miles from the river itself. Unfortunately, the best place for the furnace was *not* on tidal water. A landing had to be built further down the stream about half way to the Mullica. Finished products were hauled overland by horse and wagon to the landing, where they were loaded on barges or shallow-draft sloops for a still further trip to deeper water. In fact, the road from Gloucester Furnace to Gloucester Landing crossed Landing Creek on a bridge and continued along an embankment built through the marshes to the Mullica itself immediately opposite the present end of River Road in Lower Bank. Perhaps there were docks on the Mullica as well as at Gloucester Landing. Evidence still remains of the latter at low tide. At its height, Gloucester Furnace produced as much as twenty-five tons of iron a week in custom castings, stoves, and pipe. By mid-century, however, Gloucester Furnace, like the other South Jersey iron furnaces, was out of business.

There were others who had plans for the Atlantic County side of the Mullica though. The pre-Civil War era was rife with antagonism towards "foreigners," and the Know Nothing Party made political hay out of hatred. The German states, as yet divided into numerous principalities, had an overabundance of people and a distinct lack of land. Young men faced an uncertain future since they were often restricted from following any occupation other than that of their fathers. Laws prevented marriage, because there was no land to support more families in the German states. Youths were conscripted into the armies of the various rulers, which were, in turn, rented out to other nations as mercenaries. Incessant wars in Europe impoverished everyone, and left farmers and townspeople alike without hope. The failure of the revolutions of 1848 seemed to make it certain that they would never find fulfillment in their homelands.

It is little wonder, then, that German men and women turned their dreams towards the new lands across the ocean where hard work was rewarded with freedom and with land. The Camden and Atlantic Railroad ran its first train to Atlantic City in 1854 with the engine "Atsion" pulling the coaches. That meant that the lands near its path could be developed into farms with a ready access to large markets.

Several men of German extraction, including P.M. Wolsiffer and the physicians William and Henry Schmoele, saw a haven for Germans in the pines of Atlantic County and founded the Gloucester Land and Town Association. Within the next two years, the Association had purchased forty-one thousand acres of land from the west bank of the Mullica to the railroad line, eight thousand from William Ford and thirty-three thousand from Stephen Colwell, the owner/manager of Weymouth who was married to the half-sister of Maria (Richards) Fleming and William Henry Richards of Atsion.

The Gloucester Land and Town Association had great plans for their new paradise in the pines. They envisioned a rather large city that was anchored both on the railroad and on the Mullica. Egg Harbor City they called their development, which included a sizable central town surrounded by farms. Their promotional ability must have been rather good, for new German settlers flooded into the area from their restrictive homelands overseas. Unfortunately, early success does not always presage sustained growth, and Egg Harbor City never fulfilled its early

Charles W. Weber, Sr.

promise. Though the town grew near the railroad, it could never be called a "city," and the Mullica end remains much as it has been for the last two hundred years. In fact, it was more of a harbor when Gloucester Furnace was operating that it ever was at a later date.

It was in part of this migration, in 1864, that Charlie Weber's parents and his older sister and brother left Prussia, the land of their birth, for the Jersey pines. Though the elder Weber fell in love with what would one day become his son's farm in Washington Township, he couldn't afford to purchase it and had to settle for land near Weekstown. Charlie's older brother, Otto, and his sister, Marie, had been born in Prussia, but Emilie, Lucinda, Charlie (b. July 29, 1869), Edward, and Harry were born here. It was with pride that Charlie Weber told Henry Beck a half century ago that he had finally managed to acquire his father's dream farm in Lower Bank. To land-less Europeans with no prospects, land meant both status and wealth. With land, you would never starve. When you walked about your farm, you could do so with pride. It was *your* farm, and if you worked hard, no one could take it away from you.

Charlie's brother, Otto, got in trouble with the law because he held that strong opinion. He had been buying a farm over in Weekstown but ended up with insufficient funds with which to make one of the payments. On the day before he would have been in arrears, the man from whom he had been buying the farm showed up with his wife and the materials with which to spray "his" apple trees. That one day cost him his life. Otto Weber lost his temper, shouted at the man that it was still his farm until midnight. A heated altercation followed, after which the man sprayed Otto in the face with the chemical he was carrying. Otto really blew then. He dashed into his house, got his gun, and shot the man, right in front of his wife. Otto got ten years behind bars, and, it is assumed, lost his farm, too.

Otto wasn't the only family member who had a hot temper. Charlie had that problem also. George McCarten of Wading River remembers Charlie getting into a fight with his father, Stan McCarten. Charlie was of normal stature and George's father was a strong man. Charlie wouldn't

Pauline Marie (Sascher) Weber
Charlie's Wife

437

give up, though, until George's father had him in a head lock with his face pressed into the ground. Another story has Charlie confronting Chink Simkins on the old causeway from Green Bank to Weekstown. For many years, that road was only wide enough for one cart at a time. but neither Charlie nor Chink would yield. With their horses head to head, the two men started fighting. Eventually, Charlie is supposed to have grabbed a wrench and hit Chink in the eye with it. That summarily ended the fight. With Chink incapacitated, Charlie went on his way.

Charlie never stopped working. Like many other residents of the pines who had emigrated into the area over the last century and a half, Charlie Weber set himself to do whatever would make money. He always had his homestead farm to sustain him, but he would fish or harvest salt hay to supplement his income.

Along the Mullica, salt haying had been going on since the late 1600's. The roots of the salt hay held together a rich accumulation of humus which had to be protected. The meadows were carefully tended by their owners or renters with a series of dikes to regulate the water flow and prevent them from being washed over in a storm and thus losing them back to the river. There were almost three hundred thousand potential salt hay acres in southern New Jersey, and much of it still remains.

Charlie rented salt hay meadows on the lower Wading River and cared for a fine yearly crop of the valuable commodity. Salt hay was used on farms to protect young plants, because it didn't carry weed seeds that had the potential for choking out new growth. It was also a packing material of choice for Batsto, Green Bank, Egg Harbor City, and Hammonton glassware and was used in road construction as well. In the heyday of the furnaces, it was used in the pit-casting process for making iron pipe. Some paper manufacturers, including those at Harrisville, even experimented with making their product from the versatile material. During the Great War, it was a commodity that was much in demand. Huge bales of salt hay were shipped all over the East Coast to manufacturers, farmers, and nurserymen.

Edward and Charles W. Weber, Jr.
at the age of ten years old

The Mullica must have been a wonderful sight about the middle of the last century, covered with schooners and barges hauling glass products, lumber, firewood, and charcoal down river and returning with manufactured goods for sale in the Mullica towns. Even in his last years, Charlie could remember the numerous sailing barges, piled high with salt hay from the downriver meadows, turning the Mullica white in the evening with their return upriver.

Charlie himself used a barge that depended on oar-power, or rather, tide power. He went up or down the river, depending on the direction of the tidal flow, and steered with his oars. His two horses were housed at one end in covered stalls. A small cabin, with two bunks, a stove, a makeshift table, and provisions stood at the other. Salt-hayers from Wading River and Lower Bank would tie up their barges in Scow Ditch or Turtle Creek Cove if they needed to remain overnight near the marshes. Wagons and mowers would be taken down early in the year and left in the marshes for the season.

The horses had to be specially dressed for their work on the marshes, for marshes, are, after all, simply mud. They had snowshoe-like contraptions tied to their feet to prevent them sinking into the soft ground, and they were covered with hoods and blankets of coarse burlap and even "decorated" with aprons of the same material. All of this would help to keep them from sinking into the muck and also protect them from the voracious mosquitoes and greenheads.

Charlie's last barge was forty feet long, and had been built in Port Republic. Kate and Prince were his faithful team, and hitched to mower, rake, or wagon, Charlie and his team would walk over twenty miles a day harvesting the salt hay. After mowing, then raking it, the salt hay was loaded onto wagons and carted to the waiting barges. The barges were then sailed, or, after motors came into prominence, pushed upstream to dry land for hauling, baling, and shipment.

Charlie Weber usually tied his barge near the location of the old shipyard at the bend where River Road meets the Mullica. That was the nearest point to his farm which was high ground, and it made the trips back and forth convenient. Often, however, he tied his barge up near the Adams cemetery below the bridge. He found it easier to get the horses on and off the barge at that point, and the bridge-tender didn't have to open the swing span, or as it was in Charlie's later years, the draw.

Charlie died on Armistice Day, November 11, 1947. There was real sadness when Charlie Weber was laid to rest over in Egg Harbor. Charlie Weber had been a colorful part of the life of Lower Bank for so many years, and now he was gone.

His death signaled the end of an era that had lasted almost two centuries. Salt-hayers had lived with the river and the land, and, like the cranberry growers of today, lived in harmony with land and water. They made the marshes productive without destroying them, and helped to support a huge population of wildfowl, river mammals, and fish. They grew their product without chemical fertilizers that pollute and harvested without gasoline or diesel-powered machines. They helped to make the Mullica valley verdant.

Now they are gone, and the State insures that they will never be again. Jet skis spewing oil and causing wakes that wash the fragile banks into the water are acceptable. Productive growth is not. Instead of biodegradable natural packing materials, we use "peanuts" made of almost indestructible foam that are discarded in landfills and don't decay for hundreds of years. Progress!

Charlie Weber worked right up until the end, the last of the salt-hayers. His twin sons, Charles William, Jr. and Edward, helped him, but they became watermen rather than salt hayers. Not for Charlie was a comfortable retirement in front of the television. He, like so many others along the Mullica, accepted the challenge of life and lived it to the fullest. His endurance is a legacy to us all.

The family of Robert J. Cook lives in Charlie's old house today. One of his fields was subdivided, and the Frank Mandrona family lives in a new house that was built just a few years ago.

Some evening at sunset, stand below the bridge and let your gaze linger on the Mullica downstream. Maybe, just maybe, you will see the strangest sight you ever did see: an old wooden barge with cabins at either end, piled high with fine, curved salt hay, making its way through the twilight on the river. Old Charlie Weber is coming home.

Charlie Weber, his horses, Kate and Prince, wagon, hay barge, unloading salt hay in Lower Bank.
The structure meant to house the horses is clearly visible on the near end of the hay barge.

Charlie Weber with
Prince and Kate out
in the salt hay
meadows.

David Mapps and "The Island"

As you leave Charlie Weber's house on the Green Bank/Wading River Road and head down Old Church Road into Lower Bank proper, the paved road makes a turn past the Lower Bank cemetery and the Old Meeting House itself. Right at the bend, a dirt road continues straight ahead past the side of the cemetery and on into the woods. Though the modern traveller is prevented from following its course all the way to the Mullica by a gate, the road does run down to the river. Here we find a point of land overlooking a bend in the river, and the view is spectacular. All of Lower Bank stretches out in front of you, and, at certain times of the year when the sun rises out of the Mullica's dark waters, the sight must be overwhelming.

This land, bounded on one side by the Mullica, on another by a brook called Cakes Spruto, and on the third by cedar swamp, was first surveyed to John Pearce in 1713. Elias Wright, Wharton's manager, searched extensively for information on the Pearce family but came up with very little. In the Wharton ledgers, he wrote:

I find no Will of John Pearce, but find the following -

Perth Amboy June 17th 1736
Their Letters of Administration now granted by the Honorable John Hamilton, Esq. president of his Majesty's Council and Commander in Chief of the province of New Jersey, To Mary Pearce appointing her administratrix of all and singular the goods and rights and credits of John Pearce late of Perth Amboy aforesaid deceased, being sworn according to law before John Hamilton.

Wright goes on to indicate:

I find conveyances from John Pearce, Sr. and John Pearce, Jr. for land in Cape May County of Record in Trenton but no conveyances relating to Gloucester county.

Edwin Saltar, in his 1890 *History of Monmouth and Ocean County* (p. xliv), notes that a John Pearce of Middletown, sold land to Thomas Whitlock in September of 1693 and his cattle mark was recorded four years later. A Jeremiah, Joseph and Thomas Pearce were listed as taxpayers in Old Shrewsbury township in 1764.

Saltar goes on to say that the Pearce family settled at Woodbridge, N.J. and Joshua Pearce married his wife, Dorothy, there on January 14, 1674. "John was a noted Quaker of that place 1687 and thereabouts. John Pearce, father of the first of the name in Monmouth, it is said, was from Wales and a Baptist; he was persecuted on account of his faith and came to this country."

While there is no proof that this Pearce family in Monmouth County is the family from which Lower Bank's John Pearce

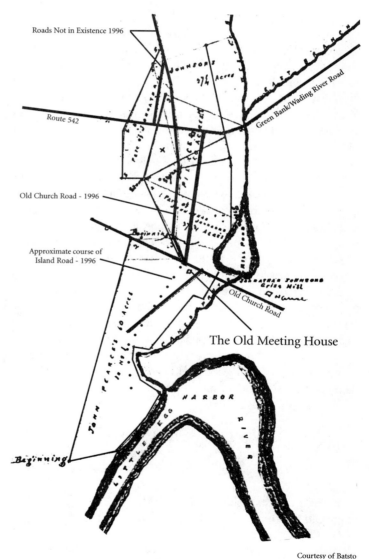

Copy of a Map from the Wharton Ledgers
Showing the Location of the Pearce Surveys

originates, it is entirely possible that this is the case. If so, the indications are that they were speculating in land and did not develop their Lower Bank holdings.

Daniel Mathis and John Foreman sold the two tracks surveyed to John Pearce, one of sixty acres and one of forty acres, to one David Mapps on March 13th, 1790 for a consideration of sixty pounds. The sale was acknowledged on the 23rd of October, 1790 and recorded at Mount Holly in about 1797. The deed thus executed recites no antecedent title, according to Elias Wright, meaning that there is no indication how Mathis and Foreman came into the possession of the property in question.

Mapps is reputed to have been the son of a white mother and an African American father, who, though not a slave, was bound out for a period of years when he was a youngster. This was not an uncommon practice, as even William Richards of Batsto fame had been bound or "apprenticed" when he was a teenager. Men and women who wanted to come to the "New World" but didn't have the passage money, often bound themselves for a set term of years in exchange for their passage. At the end of their servitude, they were sometimes given property on which to settle, and certainly no stigma was attached to them for being former bound servants. This is not to suggest that all had an easy time of it. They didn't. They were literally "owned" by their masters during their period of service, and their lives were completely dependent on their masters. Mapps is also thought to have been born in old Monmouth (now Ocean) County and to have been raised by a man named Ward or Wardel.

Nothing more is known about the early life of David Mapps, but his later one in Washington Township was exemplary. It is thought that he originally resided in Green Bank and was employed as a carter for Batsto. One of the stories told about him is that he carried ore for Joseph Ball. During the Revolutionary War, Ball offered him a contract to carry cannonballs to Philadelphia, but Mapps, true to his Quaker principles, refused. While this story may have some truth in it, Mapps did not officially join the local Friends Meeting until the end of the century.

David and his wife, Grace, bought the John Pearce Survey in March of 1790, and the couple apparently moved from Green Bank to their new farm at that time. It must also have been in this decade that Mapps acquired a 60-ton schooner and left land transport for water transport. He and his wife were accepted into the Little Egg Harbor Meeting of the Society of Friends in July of 1799. By this time, Mapps had developed a reputation for honest dealing and was well-respected by his neighbors.

The Pumpkin Story has been handed down for generations in the Lower Bank area and concerns Mapps. Apparently a local captain was in the habit of acquiring provisions for his vessel by stealing them from his neighbors. One dark night, he anchored off the point where David Mapps' farm was located and stole some pumpkins. Unfortunately, the river is rather shallow as it rounds the point, and the thieving captain's vessel got stuck in the mud. At first light, Mapps noticed both his missing pumpkins and the grounded ship, quickly putting two and two together. He rowed out to the schooner, confronted the captain, and quietly suggested that every pumpkin be placed back next to the stem from which it was taken. If the captain chose that course of action, nothing further would come from his thievery. The captain did choose to comply.

David is also known for his building of a school and meeting house for the use of his neighbors and for travelling Friends. The earliest date confirming both the building and location that this author could find is found in a deed made by David Mapps to Jonathan Johnson in 1809. On the 18th of January of that year, Mapps sold a piece of property along Cakes Spruto to Johnson for a consideration of $45. It was acknowledged on the 26th of the month and recorded in Mount Holly on October 19th, 1813. Johnson would later flood this property when he dammed Cakes Spruto for his grist mill.

This deed reads in part:

> Conveys all my right, title, and interest in land Beginning at a pine by the West side of Cakes Spruto about one chain above where the road crosses said Run that leads from Johnathan [sic] Johnsons to the meeting house. . .

This deed establishes that Mapp's Meeting House was built prior to 1809 and was also located in the same spot as the Old Meeting House today. It also proves that his meeting house preceded the construction of Johnson's mill on the Cakes Spruto.

Historian Charles Green, in *Pleasant Mills, New Jersey, Lake Nescochague, a Place of Olden Days: An Historical Sketch*, relates another story of this well-known African American Quaker of Lower Bank that supposedly took place during the War of 1812:

The Colonel [William Richards of Batsto] *had finished an order for 50 tons of cannon shot which were to be delivered to New York. The only vessel in the river available for this service was a 60-ton schooner, owned and managed by a colored man, named David Mapps, who with a crew of his own race, traded regularly between New York and Little Egg Harbor. David was a Quaker and stuck to the tenets of his faith like brick dust to a bar of soap. Proceeding to the wharf where the schooner lay, Colonel Richards called the dusky skipper on deck.*

"David," said he, "I have a freight for you, one that will pay you well."

"And what may it be?" queried David.

"I want you to take a load of cannon balls to New York as soon as the wind and tide will get you there," said the Colonel.

"Did thee say cannon balls?" asked friend Mapps.

"Yes," replied the Colonel, "they are for the defense of the country and the government needs them."

"I'd like to oblige thee," was David's mild yet firm rejoinder, "but I cannot carry thy devil's pills that were made to kill people."

No argument could change his decision and Colonel Richards was obliged to find other means of transportation for his devil's pills.

Joseph Hoag, a Friend, recorded in his diary towards the end of 1817 that "We had a satisfactory meeting at The Bank, where we staid [sic] the night with David Mapes [sic], a coloured man who is a respectable Friend." (*Journal of the Life of Joseph Hoag*, London, 1862, p. 224f)

In the following year, William Williams of Tennessee recorded in his journal (*Journal of William Williams*, Cincinnati, 1828, p. 226) another visit to the Mapps' home.

Had a meeting at Lower Great Egg Harbor; and after meeting rode twenty-seven miles to David Maps' [sic]. He and his wife are both colored people and are possessed of good talents, and he is a man of considerable property, and much business. They are both members of our Society [the Society of Friends], and are useful in their places; and my mind felt as much comforted under their roof, as in any house, since I had left home; so that while I was with them, I was brought to think of the power of truth. It not only changes and alters a person's conduct, but as it were, in appearance, is able to change the Ethiopian's skin, so that black and white, as to the thoughts of colour, appear as one in the truth. Here we met our friends, Mary Witchel and Mary James, from Pennsylvania, who had appointed a meeting near here, in a house which our friend David Maps [sic] had built for the use of his neighbours, as a school house and meeting house.

A Mildred Ratcliffe also found that "God is no respecter of persons," when she stayed in the home of Grace and David Mapps on March 20, 1820 (*Memoir of Mildred Ratcliffe*, Philadelphia, 1890, p. 133).

The famous antislavery editor, Charles Osborn, visited the Mapps' home on May 8th of the same year and wrote (*Journal of Charles Osborn*, Cincinnati, 1854, p. 177):

We rode twenty-seven miles [from Galloway] *to the house of David Mapp* [sic], *a man of color. He and his wife are respectable members of our society. They are well settled, and are in the way of entertaining Friends travelling in truth's service. They have no children of their own, yet have several in family, children and laborers, all people of color, and who appeared to be well ordered. Marks of industry and neatness appear in their affairs, which, with their kind attention to their friends, render their abode a comfortable stage for Friends to put up at, as they are passing through the parts.*

Maria Child, the biographer of the Quaker Isaac T. Hopper of Philadelphia (*Isaac T. Hopper: A True Life*, Boston, 1853, p. 210) relates the following:

On the occasion of the annual gathering in Philadelphia, they [David and Grace Mapps] *came with other members of the Society to share the hospitality of his* [Hopper's] *house. A question arose in the family whether Friends of white complexion would object to eating with them. "Leave that to me," said the master of the household. Accordingly when the time arrived, he announced it thus: "Friends, dinner is now ready. David Maps [sic] and his wife will come with me; and as I like to have all accommodated, those who object to dining with them can wait till they have done." The guests smiled, and all seated themselves at the table.*

The actual date is not known, but at some time, Mapps moved from Lower Bank to Tuckerton. His wife, Grace, died at the age of sixty-nine on December 16, 1833. Following her death, Mapps married Anna Douglas of Philadelphia. The couple apparently took vows in front of a magistrate in that city, which caused a tumult in the Little Egg Harbor Meeting. Anna Douglas must have been a Quaker, for the Meeting decided that David Mapps be "retained in the society's membership" despite his aberration. They would surely have excluded him if the woman wasn't even a Quaker. It is a matter of record in the Mount Holly Book E of Wills that David Mapps wrote a new will on the 3rd of June, 1835. This will appointed Timothy Pharo, William Lippincott, and Elihu Mathis as Executors of his estate and Ann Mapps as Executrix. This indicates that he had to have married Ann prior to June 3, 1835.

The couple had two children despite David's advanced age at the time of his second marriage. The girl was named after David's first wife, Grace, and the boy, David, after himself. His daughter became the first African American to graduate from a recognized college, for Grace A. Mapps gained her degree from McGrawville College in New York in 1852. She became a teacher, which is also what her mother is supposed to have been. The year after her graduation, she was the principal of the Girls' Department of the Friends' high school at the Institute for Coloured Youth, a position she held for eleven years. She wrote an article for the "Anglo-African Magazine" in 1859 and is said to have been able to understand and teach the Greek language.

She resigned from her position as principal in 1864 to care for her ill mother, who, by that time, lived in Burlington, New Jersey. Her father, David, must have died in 1838, for his will is listed as "proved" on February 27th of that year. He left an estate of $5,276.69, quite a considerable sum for anyone at that time. He made bequests of property in Monmouth (now Ocean) County to his nephews Charles, Anthony, and Joseph Still, and also a portion of his Lower Bank property to Joseph and Joel Sulsey. The Sulseys were among many others who benefited from Mapps' generosity, and their relationship to him is not known. Perhaps they were some of the young people which he and Grace had taken in to their Lower Bank home and raised as their own.

There may be an unfortunate coda to the story of this beloved African American sea captain from Lower Bank. No record exists of the location of Mapps' grave in the Friends' cemetery in Tuckerton. While investigating the grave of Lucy Evans, close by the site of the old Meeting House in Bridgeport/Wading River, a meeting house which David Mapps may have helped to construct, Steve Eichinger told this author a story about a nearby depression. He said that the story had come down to him that this was once the grave of an African American who was buried here. Local white folks didn't like the idea of an African American man being buried amongst the whites so they dug up the body during the night and moved it to another location.

There is no provable connection between this unknown African American whose eternal rest was so tragically disturbed by such prejudice, but this depression in the ground may have been what was intended to be the final resting place for Captain David Mapps of Lower Bank. Lucy Evans, after all, died in 1834 and was the last Quaker in attendance at the Bridgeport Friends Meeting. In 1835, Mapps remarried and was living in Tuckerton, though he had certainly helped build the Bridgeport Friends Meeting. As there is no record of his burial at the Little Egg Harbor Meeting, perhaps he was laid to rest not fifteen feet from his fellow Friend, Lucy Evans, near the walls of the Bridgeport Friends Meeting. If so, those "local men" did the residents of the area a disservice when they allegedly dug up his body with the night's darkness hiding their perfidy.

That was not the only sign of bigotry to haunt the memory of this man who had done so much for the people of his chosen home. For over a hundred and fifty years, the road leading through his property to his home by the Mullica was known as "Nigger Island Road." Not until recently were the residents of the township embarrassed by this continual reminder of generations of prejudice. The road through the Pearce Survey, long the home of David and Grace Mapps, Quaker Friend and friend to all, is now simply known as "Island Road." The name of Mapps is almost forgotten.

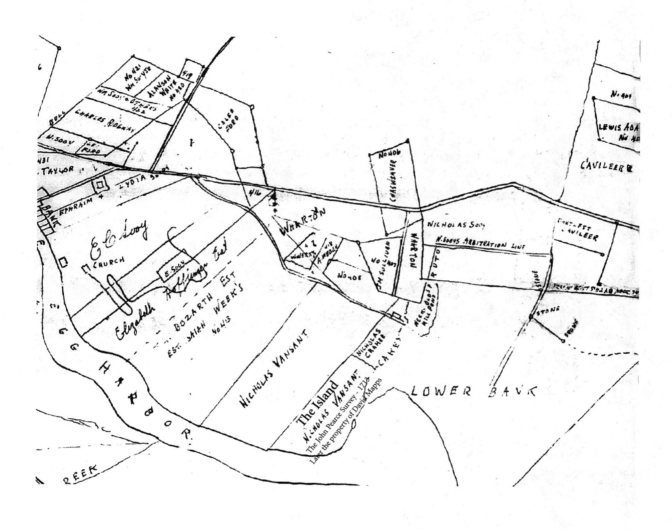

Map Showing "The Island" Portion of Lower Bank

This turn of the century map shows "The Island" section of Lower Bank which lies across the Cakes Spruto brook. This section was not included in the short-lived Randolph Township but was left in what remained of Washington. According to this map, Nicholas Vansant [sic] owned the entire property with the exception of that belonging to Nicholas Cramer. Nicholas, Sr. died in 1879. This may have belonged to Nicholas, Jr., but more than likely, was still part of the estate inherited by his children. Nicholas, Jr. was a Methodist minister and it is not known that he resided in Lower Bank. Nathaniel Van Sant, Nicholas, Jr.'s brother, is credited by Beck with building the Cramer House on "The Island" and selling it to Nicholas Cramer.

The Cramer House on "The Island"

The Cramer House - 1996

At one time, an old house stood at the very end of Island Road on a beautiful spot overlooking the Mullica. Whether this house had been the farmhouse of David and Grace Mapps, we don't know. What we do know is that Nicholas Van Sant, the minister, owned the property during the third quarter of the nineteenth century, apparently buying it from Joel Sulsey, one of the beneficiaries of the Mapps' will, and that Van Sant's granddaughter, Julia Lane, lived there.

Beck records that the Rev. Louis Atkinson laid the cornerstone of the "new" church when it was built in 1875 and also married Julia Lane from "The Island." Once again, though, details get mixed up. The Rev. Atkinson is listed as having served the circuit in 1872, just prior to the construction of the new church, though it may well have taken the parishioners a couple of years to build. It is very likely that he was retired from the active ministry by 1875 but still living in the old house on the island and participated in the laying of the cornerstone.

Julia was the daughter of Rebecca (Van Sant) and Peter Lane. Her mother was the daughter of the Rev. Nicholas and Mercy (Davis) Van Sant and the sister of John Wesley, Joel, James, Samuel, Nicholas, Jr., Nathaniel D., Mary Ann, and Isaac. Peter and Rebecca's other children were Nicholas V., Josiah, Mary E., Arabella, Cathern, Harriet, and Peter, Jr. Harriet would later marry Watson Sooy, son of William H. and Mary (Haywood) Sooy.

Later in life, having become a widow, Mrs. Julia (Lane) Atkinson married another preacher of the circuit, the Rev. J. Swayne Garrison, who served the circuit in 1896 and 1897. The Rev. Garrison was apparently an old hellfire and brimstone preacher who is given credit for converting William Woolston of Green Bank, well known in the early nineteen hundreds as the caretaker of the Sooy estate.

The map on the previous page shows The Island belonging to Nicholas Vansant [sic]. While no date appears on the map, other indications are that it was entered into the Batsto Ledgers at the end of the nineteenth century. Since The Rev. Nicholas died in 1879, it is possible that the property was still in his estate at the time the map was drawn. Beck records that it was another son, Nathaniel, who built the Cramer house, an indicator that he either shared administrative powers over his father's estate or that he had received a portion of it after the estate was dissolved . It is possible that the Lanes, and later the Garrisons, rented from the Van Sants. While we know that

446

David Mapps had his house near this location, we don't know whether the actual structure that was the Lane/Garrison house was where Captain David and Grace Mapps lived when they owned their farm in Lower Bank.

Unfortunately, the Lane/Garrison house burned to the ground prior to 1925, and, despite the beautiful location on the river, no one has built another in its place. A new gate prevents the casual explorer from heading down Island Road to its site. Ruth (Cramer) MacDonald, who lived in the Lane/Garrison House with her aunt and uncle for a time, remembers her aunt, Julia (Lane) Garrison, saying that they had taken off a part of the original house which they didn't want and had moved it to the Cramer House where it was used as a kitchen. Perhaps a portion of the old house on the river still survives!

Inland from the Lane/Garrison house stands the Cramer house which is now vacant. In Father Beck's time, it was the home of "Granny" Cramer. Beck admits an utter failure at straightening out the Cramers, or Crammers, or Cranmers. This widespread and numerous family has a variety of preferred spellings. At least as far back as Leah Blackman in the 1880's, the legend was common that the Cramers (of whatever spelling) all descended from Thomas Cranmer, Henry VIII's Archbishop of Canterbury.

Father Bill Paul, modern successor to Father Beck in serving Saint Peter's-at-the-Light in Barnegat Light, quipped recently that two women once came to a celebration of the Eucharist and proudly informed him that they were descendants of Archbishop Cranmer. With a straight face, Canon Paul said, "I never knew he was married." His joke wasn't appreciated.

Actually, Henry VIII didn't allow a married clergy. He may have displaced the pope as head of the English Church, but he wasn't about to give up his cherished beliefs. He, himself, might have as many wives as he wanted and eliminate them as he chose, but his clergy had to be celibate. There are indications that Thomas Cranmer married a Lutheran woman from the continent but kept the marriage strictly secret, for reasons that should be completely obvious, considering his boss's penchant for summary executions. Whether any of the local Cranmers, Crammers, or Cramers were actually related to the famed archbishop is up for grabs.

Beck follows Blackman in tracing the local family from four different men who moved their families down from the New York area in the late 1600's, but Murray and Jean Harris of New Gretna have published an extensive genealogical treatment of the Cramers (of whatever spelling) through the Gloucester County Historical Society, and their work is now the authoritative work on the Cranmer/Cramer family.

Beck tells of "Granny" Cramer who was born Mary Cale, daughter of Captain Watson Cale and Anna Maria Cavileer (see 2060 River Road). Local folks called her "Aunt Mel." Her siblings were Daniel, John, Sarah, William, Reuben, Franklin, two Rebeccas, and Carrie. She told Father Beck that three of her brothers had been drowned many years before. One had lost his life on Great Bay. Two others were lost at sea when their father's ship, a three-masted schooner, the *Walter Palmer*, went down. She was a carrier of phosphate rock, railroad ties, and other similar cargo and sunk with all hands.

At any rate, this house was supposed to have been built by no other than dear, old "Uncle Thannie" Van Sant, though for once he isn't given credit for having lived in it. Instead, it was Nicholas and Mary (Cale) Cramer who moved into Uncle Thannie's house on "The Island."

Actually, it was all in the family. Nicholas's middle name was "Van Sant" after his mother's family, for Mary Ann Cramer (April 23, 1828 - December 28, 1913) was the sister of Nathaniel Van Sant and the daughter of the Rev. Nicholas. She married Richard Cramer (September 1816 - November 18, 1896) on the 12th of January 1845.

Courtesy of Sarah (Cramer) Camillo

Richard Cramer
1816 - 1896

According to material provided by Murray and Jean Harris of New Gretna, Richard Cramer's parents were Jacob and Elizabeth Cramer. Jacob was born between 1770 and 1780 and died between 1840 and 1850. Jacob and Elizabeth lived in Washington Township. Jacob himself was the son of John Cramer, Jr. and Margaret (Smith) Cramer. John, Jr. served in the Continental line and is listed in the DAR Patriot Index.

To go back even further, John, Jr.'s father was, of course, John, Sr. John, Sr.'s parents were William, Jr. and Rachel Cranmer. William was the son of the first William and Elizabeth (Carwithy) Cramer of Elizabethtown, from which all local Cramers (or Cranmers, or Crammers) are descended. (See WADING RIVER: CRANMER/CRAMER FAMILY OF WADING RIVER)

William Cranmer, Jr. bought land in West Creek with his brother, John, on May 9, 1702 and by 1707, they were both members of the Little Egg Harbor Meeting. William, Jr.'s son, John Cranmer, is supposed to have built the first building of the Little Egg Harbor Meeting. His wedding to Mary Andrews, daughter of Mordecai and Mary Andrews of Little Egg Harbor in the building he had built with his own hands, was reported to the Monthly Meeting on April 4, 1721. Unfortunately, the couple had no children. After his wife's death, he married

Courtesy of Sarah (Cramer) Camillo

Mary Ann (Van Sant) Cramer
1828 - 1913

Rebecca Stout, daughter of Richard, Jr. and Penelope Stout. It is this marriage from which all his descendants issue.

Before we digressed, we were talking about Richard Cramer of Lower Bank. Richard first married Fanny Weeks, the daughter of Daniel and Ann (Weatherby) Weeks, who was born about 1810. They had one son, William O. who married Amanda Palmer.

On December 21, 1845, Mary Ann Van Sant became his second wife in Green Bank. Richard and Mary Ann (Van Sant) Cramer had nine children, most of whom married into local families. Francis E. [Fannie] married Stephen H. Adams, whose homestead was in Lower Bank on the Mullica. James married Arabella Johnson, and later Susie (Reed) Bell. Nicholas Van Sant Cramer married Mary Ida Cale, the daughter of Captain Watson Cale. Rebecca L. Cramer married William Spafford Leek, the son of Captain John and Martha (Rose) Leek. Among their children was their eldest son, Charles Platt Leek (II), Jack Leek's (Pacemaker/Ocean Yachts) grandfather. Mary married (1) Frank Broome and (2) Captain Pitney Blackman. Elvira Augusta married Burke Montgomery. Florence Cramer, born in 1862, died in 1877 at the age of fifteen of scarlet fever. Myra B. married Gilbert Irons. They would return to Lower Bank, living in retirement in the Old Weeks' Tavern at 43 Old Church Road. Richard Cramer died at Lower Bank on November 18, 1896, and his wife, Mary Ann (Van Sant) on December 28, 1913, also in Lower Bank.

To get back to our story after all that genealogical digression, Nicholas Van Sant Cramer and his wife, Mary Ida, lived in this house built by his uncle Nathaniel Van Sant. Nicholas was confined to a wheelchair most of his life, and Mary Ida did almost any household job to bring in money for her family.

Nicholas passed away in 1928 at the age of eighty-two. His wife would last another twenty-two years. The older Lower Bankers still refer to "Granny" Cramer as "Aunt Mel." Mary Ida (Cale) Cramer, daughter of Captain Watson and Anna Maria (Cavileer) Cale and the last of ten brothers and sisters, died in 1950 at the age of ninety-two.

Nicholas and Mary had four children: Nicholas Ambrose, Florence, Harvey, and Clinton Roy. The eldest son, Nicholas Ambrose (he went by "Ambrose"), was born on January 31st, 1893, and, on the 10th of December, 1916 he married Nora Mae Dampley (November 10, 1896 - October 30, 1970) of Atlantic City. The couple lived in Atlantic City, and Ambrose worked in the post office there. Ambrose and Nora Mae had five children. Their youngest, a son, Wilbert Stanton Cramer (b. July 8, 1930), married Gloria Marie Wolff (b. November 27, 1932) and lives in Lower Bank. Their daughter, Sarah (b. July 17, 19962) married James Camillo on the 7th of May, 1983 and has three children. She is the source of many of the photographs in this section and in those on the Cale residences. Sarah's sister is Debra (Cramer) Bucher. Grandfather Ambrose died in 1965 and Grandmother Nora Mae in 1970.

Florence A. Cramer, born at Lower Bank on December 21, 1888, married Arthur Skelton, who had been born about 1882 in Maine. Arthur worked as a hotel painter, and the couple had three children: Evelyn, Doris, and Arthur.

Harvey Cramer, born on September 4, 1881in Green Bank, married Florence Wells in Camden on July 5, 1903. He and his wife had nine children: Mary Ida, Gilbert, Alice, Claire, Edna Lavinia, Gladys, Thomas, Calla, and Kenneth. Kenneth married Betty (Koster) Wilson and lives on Old Church Road very near his cousin, Wilbert Stanton. Ken and Betty Jane (Wilson) have two children: Kenneth, Jr., who lives with his family in Green Bank in the Snapper Cobb House, and a daughter, Sharon, who married John Core of Lower Bank.

Courtesy of Lilian (DeBow) Fritz
Roy Cramer - c. 1944

Nicholas and Mary (Cale) Cramer's son, Roy (1884-1972), was one of Beck's guides in Lower Bank. Roy Cramer lived on in the old house after his parents joined their families and friends around the Old Meeting House. He was married twice: first to Ella Garrison, the daughter of Jonathan and Sarah (Johnson) Garrison and the sister of the Rev. J. Swayne Garrison and Lizzie (Garrison) Allen, by whom he had a daughter, Ruth, who later married Bill MacDonald. After his divorce from Ella, he married Gertrude Bardsley.

Roy was "self-employed," which, in the Mullica valley, meant he'd do almost anything to make a buck. He worked as a carpenter, and, in fact, he built the house across the street from the "new" church for Alfred Allen. He also turned the Crowleytown school into a house after the schools were consolidated at Green Bank. After talking to his grandniece, I'm not sure I'd want to buy one of those houses.

Sarah, Roy's grandniece, tells a story about the time Roy laid a new floor in an upstairs room in this old house. He had done all the work with the door to room closed. When he got to it, he found that he couldn't open it. The door had been cut to the proper height for the old flooring, and the new flooring came above the bottom of the door. After venting his frustration with several loud shouts, which brought the family running upstairs to see what was the matter, he finally figured out that he'd have to remove the pins from the hinges and take down the door in order to get out.

Roy may not be remembered for his carpentry. He is remembered, however, as an excellent woodsman and did a great deal of trapping. He served Washington Township as tax collector, assessor, and fire warden as well.

Roy Cramer always claimed that he had proof that Eric Mullica's cabin stood right about where old Charlie Leek's boatshop was, immediately next to the burial place of Yoos Sooy and John Cavileer. C.P. Leek used to say that Roy bragged that he had tax maps that showed the location, but there weren't any tax maps prior to 1937 in Washington Township. Though records exist back to the turn of the century, they only list acreage and improvements but do not locate taxed parcels.

However, as mentioned in the beginning of this chapter, there is a map that belonged to Ezekiel Forman of Green Bank and now in the possession of the State of New Jersey at Batsto which indicates that Charlie Leek's boatyard was indeed on part of the original Mullica homestead. Perhaps old Roy had seen that map!

Roy Cramer
1884-1972

The Old Meeting House

The Old Lower Bank Meeting House - 1995

A great deal of confusion and rumor surrounds the building of Lower Bank's Old Meeting House. Henry Charlton Beck, in *Jersey Genesis*, quoted Ella (Johnson) Underhill as saying that "the old church that wasn't a church at all at the beginning. It was a school . . . moved to its present location in 1810." Another source says that it was built by a noted Black sea captain, David Mapps, as a school and meeting house. Still another author says that John Cavileer, Samuel Weeks, Job Weeks, and Isaac Cramer were responsible for moving this building to its present location and turning it into a church around 1810. An entry in *The Weeks' Family of Southern New Jersey* notes that there is a deed recorded in the Burlington Country records citing the following:

> *On May 9, 1842, Ann Mapps, et al, Executors of the estate of David Mapps, sold to Job, James, and Samuel Weeks, and others, as trustees, 1 rood of land in Washington Twp. upon which to build a Methodist Episcopal Church (BuD G4:498).*

There is an intriguing story concerning the construction of the "new" Lower Bank Methodist Church in 1875. It is said that Samuel Weeks, one of the founders of the Old Meeting House, was owed money by the congregation, and the people failed to pay him. In particular vindictiveness, he took the large pulpit Bible from the church building, locking the door behind him. The congregation would simply not have the use of their Meeting House until the bill was paid.

The Lower Bank congregation, however, left him holding the bag (or Bible rather). They were reported to be so incensed at his temerity that they immediately made plans to build another church building. Rebecca Leek and Levi Johnson are reported to have given the ground for the new church edifice, and the Methodist Episcopal Conference helped them raise the money for its construction. If old Sam Weeks wanted to deprive them of their church, let him have it! Actually, the congregation is said to have paid Samuel Weeks his due, but it was too late. They continued to hold services in the old church until the new one was built but then left it vacant, a mute testament to Sam Week's folly in threatening his fellow Lower Bankers.

This is an interesting and colorful story, but Lower Bankers say it isn't true. Though there are difficulties with dates and people, it still might have some basis in fact, however.

Current research indicates the following: David Mapps, a respected African American sea captain, purchased one hundred acres of land between Lower Bank and Green Bank which had been originally surveyed to John Pearce as early as 1713. At some time and by an unknown means, the property came into the possession of Daniel Mathis and John Foreman, who sold it to David Mapps in a deed dated March 13th, 1790 for a consideration of sixty pounds. This deed was acknowledged on October 23rd, 1790 and recorded in Mount Holly about 1797. This deed conveyed to Mapps "1st John Pearce survey of 60 acres" and "2nd John Pearce survey of 40 acres." General Elias Wright, who located this deed in the Burlington County books, noted that "no antecedent title is recited." In other words, there is no record as to how Mathis and Foreman obtained the Pearce survey. The Old Meeting House stands on land once part of the Pearce survey.

David Mapps and his wife, Grace, were admitted to the Little Egg Harbor Meeting in 1799, and David served as an overseer and was on the school committee.

On the 18th of January 1809, David Mapps sold a parcel of land to Jonathan Johnson. General Elias Wright in the Wharton ledgers recorded that the deed "conveys all my right, title, and interest in land Beginning at a pine by the West side of Cakes Pruto [sic] about one chain above where the road crosses said Run that leads from Johnathan [sic] Johnson's to the meeting house . . ." It was on this property that Johnathan Johnson erected his grist mill

An article in volume 21 of the 1936 issue of the *Journal of Negro History* by Henry Joel Cadberry entitled "Negro Membership in the Society of Friends" quotes one William Williams, who, in 1818, made a journey in the area of Lower Bank and related that "Here we met our friends, Mary Witchel and Mary James, from Pennsylvania, who had appointed a meeting near here, in a house which our friend David Maps [sic] had built for the use of his neighbours, as a school house and meeting house."

The same article goes on to quote from *The Journal of Charles Osborn* (Cincinnati, 1854, p. 177) that, on May 8th, 1820, Osborn's diary says, " Third-day, 9th - We had a meeting in a school and meeting house, near David Mapps."

Still another traveller, Thomas Shilltoe, late in 1827 wrote: "Third-day, we proceeded to the township of Washington, near the Mullicus river and took up our abode with David Mapps and his kind wife, both coloured people, and members of our religious Society: we attended an indulged meeting in a new meeting house, about three miles from our quarters at a place called Bridge Port." (*Journal of the Life, Labours, and Travels of Thomas Shillitoe*, London, 1839, ii, 274f.)

Of these three references, the third obviously states that the "new" meeting house was the one at Bridgeport. The second could be at either Bridgeport or Lower Bank, but seems to refer to Lower Bank. The first, however, seems definitely to refer to this Old Meeting House in Lower Bank.

All of this seems to suggest the following scenario: The Old Meeting House dates to at least 1809 in its present location. A great probability exists that David Mapps constructed it on his own property some time after he purchased the land from Foreman and Mathis in 1790 with the idea that it would be used by himself, his neighbors, and travelling Friends as both a school and a "Meeting House."

Mapps made his will in 1835 when he remarried and moved to Tuckerton. When he died in 1838, he left his property to his widow and their children, as well as to several other beneficiaries. The meeting house he had constructed on his property is not mentioned specifically. Ann Mapps, his second wife, sold the meeting house property to the trustees of the newly-formed Methodist Church, Job, James, and Samuel Weeks to use as a Methodist Church. Sam Weeks was a carpenter who had bought land from David Mapps and built himself a tavern just down the road from the Old Meeting House on the other side of Cakes Spruto. The trustees may well have asked him to make the necessary repairs to the building for the congregation's use. When the repairs were completed, the trustees may not have had the money to pay Weeks for his work, so Weeks took the Bible and locked the door until he got his due.

Lower Bankers say that this story is apocryphal, of course, but there is another indication that it may have some truth behind it.

The Weeks Family of Southern New Jersey also records that:

> On Jan. 26, 1850, Levi G. Johnson and wife, sold to Job Weeks, Samuel Weeks, Jr., Nicholas Vansant [sic] and four others, as trustees, 35 feet square on the northeast side of Main Road nearly opposite Hall's store, at Lower Bank, Washington Twp., for a school house with the privilege of

holding meetings of the Methodist Episcopal Society, also temperance meetings, Sabath Schools, political meetings of both parties, Democrats and Whigs. Job Weeks, Jr. was a witness (BuD Y4:97).

Levi Johnson's homestead was on River Road, and the house stood immediately opposite the end of Old Church Road. The old Lower Bank School building was just down the road from this house towards the river. This description obviously applies to the land on which the schoolhouse was eventually built and not to the land on which the "new" Lower Bank church now stands, which was also originally part of the Levi Johnson homestead on River Road.

If the Methodist trustees had acquired the meeting house and property in 1842 when they bought the Mapps' property, why were the same trustees *and the minister* (Reverend Nicholas Van Sant), acting as trustees for the construction of a *public school*, insisting that permission be gained via the transfer of the deed for the schoolhouse land to hold meetings of a Methodist Episcopal society on the newly-acquired property, unless, of course, Sam Weeks had locked them out of their new Meeting House.

The dispute may have been settled amicably after all. We do know that the trustees eventually acquired more land from the Johnsons and built the "new" Lower Bank Methodist Church in 1875. In all probability, the congregation of the eighteen seventies simply wanted more room in a modern structure, and a more central location in the town. The "new" church is far more imposing than the Old Meeting House. More than likely, the trustees and congregation quietly settled the dispute with Samuel Weeks around 1850 and continued holding their service in the original old Meeting House that David Mapps had built. In any case, the original place of worship for the people of Lower Bank has seen only a yearly anniversary celebration for over a hundred years.

If the Methodist Society existed much earlier than 1842, Samuel and his brother Job were probably not founders. Samuel, son of Ezekiel and Elizabeth Weeks, was born on March 17, 1804, making him just six in 1810. Job Weeks, his brother, was seventeen, having been born on October 10, 1793. On the other hand, an 1842 date would be far more reasonable, the two men being thirty-eight and forty-nine respectively. Job Weeks's son, Samuel B., would have been twenty-six in 1842. No date is given for the birth of Samuel, Jr., though it would appear that he was born after his brother, William Henry, whose birth date was April 13, 1835.

The Samuel Weeks, Jr. mentioned in the purchase of the schoolhouse property in 1850 was probably not the actual Samuel Weeks, Jr. (Samuel's son) but Samuel B. Weeks, Job's son. Job Weeks's son would have been about thirty-four by this time, while the *real* Samuel Weeks, Jr. would probably have been less than fifteen. Still further? John Cavileer, Sr. died in 1813, making an 1810 date possible but not one in 1842. His son, John, Jr. (who married Elizabeth Weeks, Job, Sr.'s sister) would have been just the right age to have been a church trustee in 1842.

A further curiosity: Lillian (DeBow) Fritz and Marjorie (Cavileer) Fox both mentioned that there was a fire in the Old Meeting House around 1880 and that the windows were replaced at that time. Budd Wilson, archaeological historian of Green Bank has always wondered why the roof of the Old Meeting House has such a low pitch to it. They simply didn't build them that way at an early date. Perhaps the roof was replaced after the fire. Yet the ceiling is curved like that of the 1808 Batsto-Pleasant Mills Church. Would they have bothered to rebuild such a ceiling if they had to replace the roof? These are questions that may never find a satisfactory answer.

A minute-book of the trustees of the Old Church in the possession of Budd Wilson has a notation in it which may throw doubt on the age of the building. The first page with writing on it (page 2) has a brief summary of the history of the Old Meeting House as it was known in 1909. The first entries are in the hand of George S. Maxwell of Wading River, and the "Early History" may have been written by him also although it is very difficult to make a comparison of the handwriting. It reads:

Early history of the M. E. Church at the Grave Yard at Lower Bank

May 9th, 1842 is the date of deed of the site the church now stands on. The Description of this deed reads: Beginning at a point S.E. Cor of the Lower Bank Meeting house at a tall oak, Showing there was a place of worship there before the present one was built in 1842.

The present site was bought from the Mapps Estate through the executors Wm. S. Lippincott, Anne Mapps, [and] Timothy Pharo. The consideration was Ten Dollars for one rood of land. The Trustees were Wm. H. Sooy, Job Weeks, Samuel Weeks, Reuben Cavileer, James Weeks, Joseph Allen, [and] Asa S. Cramer. [All punctuation has been added for clarity.]

Later, in the lists of donors to the refurbishing of the Old Church, it is mentioned that there was a woman who had been there in 1842 and was still alive in 1909. She should have known whether they had built a new building or simply remodeled the old one. The mention of the Meeting House in the original deed does indicate that "there was a place of worship there" when the Methodists acquired the land, but it does not prove that they tore the old one down before they constructed their new one, as the 1909 author supposes. Obviously, whoever wrote this brief summary of the history of the Old Church believed that it *was* an entirely new building in 1842, not a reconstructed one. While this is possible, and the surviving structure may only date to 1842, it is equally possible that the Methodists incorporated the earlier Meeting House of David Mapps into their new Methodist structure. Probably the only way to find out, though, would be to completely dismantle the Old Meeting House. If we count the 1842 work as a renovation rather than a construction, it was extensively rebuilt in 1842, 1888, 1909, and 1937.

George S. Maxwell notes that a meeting was held in the Old Church on September 18th, 1909

> *for the purpose of electing a board of trustees for Said Church there being present Walter Downs, Lemuel H. Maxwell, Geo. S. Maxwell, Rev. Joseph E. Horner, and Thornton B. Southwick. Meeting was called to order and prayer was offered by Rev. Joseph E. Horner After which Mr. Horner was elected Chairman. When the following person [sic] were duly elected Trustees of the Old Church at Lower Bank at the Grave Yard*
>
> *Geo. S. Maxwell & Levi Downs of Wading River. Ethan Hall & Joseph E. Johnson of Lower Bank, and Mahlon Broms of Jenkins.* [The names of Ethan Hall and Mahlon Broms are crossed out in pencil and the word "deceased" written next to them in what possibly may be a different hand.]

It continues:

> *In organizing Geo. S. Maxwell was elected President of the Board and J.E. Johnson was elected Secretary & Treasurer. Gilbert Irons takes the place of Ethan Hall deceased and George Thomas takes the place of Mahlen Brooms deceased.*

The following page reads:

> *1st Reopening of the Old Church*
> *1st Service November 4th, 1909*
> *History of the condition and repairs of the old Church at the Grave Yard*
> *at Lower Bank NJ.*
> *It was in sad condition. The roof was partly off causing the walls to fall so the floor was covered with lime. 68 window glass were broken & putty out of all the others, so they were ready to fall. The portico was nearly down. Such was the condition; the friends got together & resolved to put the dear Church in good repair.*
> *The work was done as follows. By putting on a new Shingle roof. New portico putting in window glass & puttying all the old ones. plastering all the broken walls. painting all the woodwork and graining the same in oak. painting the wall & ceiling with "Alabastine" in a pretty Soft Shade. that with - new carpet Made the Church very attractive.*
> *The first service for the reopening was in the evening of Thursday Nov 4th 09. Preaching by the Rev. S.G. Patt of the Central ME Church of Atlantic City had a fine Audience & powerful Sermon Hebrews 12 Chap 1 & 2 Verses. The thought of the sermon was we were encompassed about with many witnesses referring to the many Sainted on who had worshiped there & had preached from that Sacred disk [sic] & thought that they might be present with us in Spirit in this Service.*
> [All punctuation and spelling are as per original.]

George S. Maxwell carefully noted every contribution made to the restoration fund of the old church and who collected it. The list reads like a Who's Who of Wading River and Lower Bank. In a running list, he also recorded the expenses of the work. Joseph E. Johnson made the largest contribution: $25.00. Others came in as little amount as $.50. Most were in the $1.00 to $2.00 range. Lest one get the idea that these were piddling amounts, the expenses proclaim otherwise. Apparently some of the merchants made contributions by reducing their bills:

H. Bozarth	7,500 shingles	37.50	Pd	32.50
Jn Cale	for labor on roof & porch	25.00	Pd	22.50
H. Kayser	paint - stove	32.23	Pd	31.00
	Cleaning Church	5.65	Pd	4.65
Steve Adams	painting Walls	4.00	Pd	3.00
	Plastering Walls	9.00	Pd	9.00
JE Johnson	2 old post from portico	1.00	Pd	1.00

The expenses and donations continued with many of the local people contributing their time as well as funds. Some income was derived from selling unused items:

Sold one package Alabastine	25
The old stove in the church 50 ys	25
5 qts Linseed oil	82
1 bl of (? - something beginning with an "S")	20

These are cents, for the total of the above items is given as $1.52. On the same page, one of the contributors is noted as

> Mrs Elizabeth Deacon who was one of the contributors when the church was built in 1842.
> She is now 85 yrs old gives 2.00

The names of the contributors in the list are ones with which we will become familiar in Lower Bank and Wading River. They include Jesse R. Cavileer, James V. Cavileer, Olive Adams, Jesse Ford, Lemuel Maxwell, Charles Cavileer, Gilbert Irons, George S. Maxwell, Jr., Charles Leek, Stanley Vansant, Hattie Sooy, G. W. Woolston, Howard McAnney, Sadie Updike, Lettie Cale, John Cale, W.T. Sooy, J. S. Garrison, Mahlon Brooms, Wm. Guss Maxwell, Walter K. Cavileer, J.E. Johnson, and many others, all of whom are gone now, and almost forgotten with the passage of time. Most lie buried next to the Old Church they loved so well.

The reckoning as of November 7, 1910 was:

Rec^d in subscription through J.E. Johnson	107.75
Special Collection including basket call	59.74
Donated by Labor as per report on other page	84.41
Amt collected by Geo. S. Maxwell	30.98
	282.88
Bills pd by Geo. S. Maxwell	18.17
bill pd by J.E. Johnson	162.73
Amt Donated in labor	84.41
	$265.31
Bal on hand Nov 7. 1909	17.57

Joseph E. Johnson continued the account after the meeting, noting additional income of $122.11 making a total receipts in cash of $301.33; additional bills brought the total spent on the rehabilitation of the Old Meeting House in 1909 - 1910 to $423.29.

Each year thereafter, during the month of October, a week was set apart to hold preachings in the Old Church each day. J.E. Johnson continued to take the minutes of the meetings until 1920. The minute-book concludes with an accounting which lists a balance on hand of $28.31.

Another book, also in the possession of Budd Wilson of Green Bank, begins on August 19, 1937. C. Roy Cramer signed the first page as secretary and noted that those elected to the Board of Trustees were Chas. Thomas, Howard McAnney, James Updike, B.F. Cavileer, and C. Roy Cramer. The latter was elected president and secretary of the board with B.F. Cavileer as treasurer. August 26, 1937 was set as a cleanup day for the cemetery, and letters were sent out requesting donations for the same. On the scheduled date of the cleanup, Roy Cramer reported that $22.50 in donations had been received. Unfortunately, the cleanup expenses were $30.01. The week-long meetings that had been customary in the 'teens had been reduced to day-long services by the late '30's. Meeting days were held in 1938 and 1939, though a page is blank where the 1940 one would have been listed. Roy Cramer noted under October 12th, 1941 that three clergymen preached during the three services held that day for the celebration of the 161st Anniversary of the Old Church. This is the first recorded reference to 1780 as the building date of the church. From that day through the last entry in the book, that of October 18, 1953, Roy Cramer duly notes the anniversary date acknowledging a 1780 building date. The trustees of the Old Church have continued to hold a service in the building each year to date, and the adjoining cemetery is well-maintained.

Elizabeth Perinchief, in her *History of Cemeteries in Burlington County 1687-1975* records that a mill stood *on the property* prior to the construction of a church building there. This can only be accurate if she noted the 1759 mention of a mill pond on the Cakes Spruto or if she was considering the 1842 date of construction for the Meeting House.

The 1809 deed of Mapps to Jonathan Johnson does mention the Meeting House but does not mention a mill nor a cemetery. Elias Wright later noted on the map of the property in question that "Jonathan Johnson's Mill pond subsequently Weeks Mill pond" took up most of this property. Thus it would seem that the Meeting House preceded the mill, or at least, the only mill we actually know of at this time.

Another Wright map notes the location of Johnson's Grist Mill on the east side of Cakes Spruto at the foot of the millpond. Ronnie Hill used to say that there was a sawmill on that creek, too, but he indicated the "sawmill" was located where the map shows the grist mill. A late nineteenth century map of Lower Bank does indeed locate a sawmill where the grist mill had been located. Samuel Weeks may have replaced the Johnson grist mill with his sawmill rather than simply adding another race to the dam. Then again, the same map of the Green Bank area shows two sawmills on Bull Creek where we know there was both a grist mill and a sawmill.

The oldest dated graves in the cemetery are those of Mary Bodine (1815), Anna Maria Cavileer (1817), and Ezekiel Weeks (1817). Thus it seems that the cemetery was started soon after the mill was built when Mapp's Meeting House was standing and before the Methodist Meeting House of 1842 was constructed.

This is the largest of Lower Bank's cemeteries, and here the honored and beloved dead of this town and of Wading River lie in the soil of their cherished land close beside the Old Meeting House. Many of the stones are worn by the years, and some are missing entirely, but they are the last tribute to the folk who laughed and cried, suffered and died in the Lower Bank of old.

The Weeks Tavern
43 Old Church Road

1995

Photograph by John Pearce

Sam Weeks of the purloined Bible and locked church door fame is listed as a carpenter in the old township records, but Mrs. Ella (Johnson) Underhill, Beck's spring of local knowledge, mentioned him as the owner/operator of an inn. Mae Hill, current owner of this old house, close by the Old Church Road, heard the same story and has no doubt of its veracity. In fact, Samuel Weeks is listed as a hotel keeper in the 1860 census.

Mae and her husband, Earle, moved to Lower Bank in the year they were married: 1937. Earle was originally from Swartswood, N.J. while Mae hailed from New York City (hasn't lost her accent yet, she proudly maintains). For the first few years, they rented the Old Parsonage at 61 Old Church Road and kept a blueberry field out on Route 542. Sometime between 1940 and 1942, she doesn't remember the exact year, they bought this property consisting of 63 acres and moved into Sam Weeks' old inn.

Earle dug cranberry bogs on the property and eventually went into partnership with Bill MacDonald in both cranberry bogs and blueberry fields up in Bulltown. When they later came to a parting of ways, Earle kept the bogs, while Bill continued with the blueberries.

Earle served on the township committee for over thirty-one years, much of the time as mayor and was well-known for his strong, pinelands advocacy. He probably would have been considered a piney par excellence for his "down-home" appearance and brusque ways, but he was far from typical and not a native of the area at all. When Earle died in 1988, Washington Township lost a truly dedicated advocate.

Earle and Mae had two children, Ronnie and Tanya. Ronnie, the current (1998) mayor of the township, farms the cranberry bogs which had belonged to his father in Bulltown while Tanya married Joey Bishop's son.

Mae still greets the visitor with a cheerful smile though she definitely does not like to have her picture taken. Mae now regrets something she did many years ago when they moved into this old house. She and Earle found boxes which contained a great many letters from Samuel Weeks' wife, though she doesn't remember whether it was his first wife, Mary (Cramer), or his second wife, Amelia, that had been stashed in the attic for a good many years. Mae sat down and read them all, but they proved to be a great embarrassment. Apparently, Sam

Weeks' wife had some of Sam's irascible personality, for the letters were full of rather nasty gossip about everyone hereabouts. Much of it was scandalous. Perhaps it could even have been considered libelous. In any case, kind-hearted Mae thought that a good many people could be hurt if they got out, so she destroyed them. Now she realizes just how valuable they would have been to the history of Lower Bank.

That's not all Mae threw out fifty-odd years ago. A doctor had lived in this house sometime after Sam Weeks and his bitter-penned wife passed on. Mae found several ledgers containing lists of his patients. Not thinking, these, too, were destroyed. In acts of such seeming innocence, the past is left in a dim mist.

Mae does remember a story about the good doctor, however. Seems this doctor was an alcoholic and didn't hesitate to prescribe while he was inebriated. He had vials full of pills of all colors: red, blue, green, pink, etc. and, when consulted by a patient, would hand out packets of the particular color which supposedly matched the symptoms. Unfortunately, much of the time he was handing out pills, he was drunk. He'd awake from his stupor the following morning and suddenly wonder just what he had prescribed to whom. He'd written down the names of his patients but not the color of the pills given them. In a panic, he'd hitch up his buggy and go from patient to patient, asking them the color of the pills he'd given them. No doubt, he had to change the pills once in a while this second time around and hope that what he had first given his patients wouldn't hurt them. Returning home in the afternoon, he'd take up both his new patients and a new bottle and begin the whole charade over again.

Sam Weeks was born on March 17, 1804, the ninth child of Ezekiel and Elizabeth (Johnson) Weeks, the founder of Weekstown. He married Mary Cramer, daughter of John and Hannah (Johnson) Cramer, though the date isn't known, and they had seven children. His older brother, Job, had already moved to the vicinity of Lower Bank and bought a homestead on what is today called Seaf Weeks Road but was, for more than a century, known as Job Weeks Road that is the continuation of River Road towards Harrisville. It was also part of the original road from Wading River to Lower Bank prior to the construction of the 1808 road (Route 542).

Gilbert "Gibe" and Myra (Cramer) Irons
The couple are standing on the front steps of their house at 43 Old Church Road, Sam Weeks' Tavern.

Sam was induced to serve as Overseer of Highways with Charles Cavileer in 1831 at the age of twenty-seven. Then came the fateful year 1832, and his name does not again appear in any office until 1836, when he served as a Surveyor of Highways. He took the same position in 1837 through1839, and in 1840 was elected as a member of the Board of Chosen Freeholders of Burlington County for a one-year term. In 1843, he served as a Commissioner of Appeal. In 1851, he was elected as Justice of the Peace and served as a Chosen Freeholder again in 1852, after which his name no longer appears on the list of officeholders.

On January 29, 1835, David Mapps [sometimes spelled "Mapes"] and his wife sold property to Samuel Weeks of Washington Township, Burlington County, land that had been part of the homestead farm of Hugh Johnson, and, on March 17, a year later, Levi G. Johnson sold Sam land that had been part of the Johnson estate as well. It was from David Mapps' estate, it will be remembered that the land for the Old Meeting House just down the road was obtained by Sam and his brother, Job. It may well be that these two transactions of Mapps' property was the land in the vicinity of this house. In all probability, this building was constructed soon after Sam and his wife obtained the property.

Sam was not content in being a carpenter, innkeeper, and thorn-in-the-flesh for his brother and the other devoted Methodists. He seems to have also engaged in many land transactions during his lifetime, as did most of the other successful residents of the township. Sam and Mary's son, William Henry, served in Company G, 4th New Jersey Volunteers during the Civil War.

The Weeks Family of Southern New Jersey gives no date for the death of his wife, Mary, nor the surname of his second wife, Amelia, but Amelia was the daughter of Peter and Eleanor (Sooy) Cavileer, great granddaughter of the first Peter. Mary Weeks' stone in the Lower Bank cemetery reveals she died on April 2, 1858 at the age of fifty-four. The Weeks genealogy does note that, on September 5, 1867, Sam Weeks made his will, naming his wife, Amelia, his five surviving children, and his granddaughter, Ema Louisa, the bulk of his estate, which spanned both Burlington and Atlantic Counties. He died on November 11, 1875 at the age of seventy-one.

Prior to Earle and Mae Hill's purchase of the property, Gilbert Irons (b. 1861) and his wife, Myra (b. 1864) lived in the house. Mae thinks he just rented rather than owned it, but Marjorie (Downs) Cavileer remembers that Gibe Irons was the nemesis of her husband, Walter Knickerbocker Cavileer, Jr. Irons, it seems, was a dyed-in-the-wool Republican while Walter K. was an equally staunch Democrat. Walt served as mayor of the township for some years, while Gibe was the unofficial one. It must have been fun to watch these two go at it fast and furiously, constantly finding fault with each other's ideas. Myra was the daughter of Richard and Mary Ann (Van Sant) Cramer and the sister of Nicholas Van Sant Cramer, Ella (Elvira) (Cramer) Montgomery, and Rebecca (Cramer) Leek. Myra (Cramer) Irons died in 1930, and her husband, Gibe, in 1932.

This house has fostered at least two tough and tenacious Republicans, though Mae maintains she never voted straight anything. Wonder what old Sam was?

The Roediger/DeBow Farm
(No Longer in Existence)

Directly across Old Church Road from the Weeks Tavern, now the home of Mae Hill, is DeBow Lane. This was once a lane which led from the road to the Roediger/DeBow House at its end. Frederick and Ann Roediger came from Germany some time prior to 1850 and purchased approximately 77 acres of land from a man who lived on Island Road.

Frederick was a cabinetmaker by trade, skilled in all forms of woodcarving, a master of the fine and elaborate details of which the nineteenth century Europeans were so fond. Unfortunately, rural America wasn't able to support such an artist in wood, and Frederick turned to gardening. That's actually how he's listed on the township records at the birth of his daughter Emma in 1856 and how his great granddaughter, Lillian (DeBow) Fritz describes him. Family legend has it that he did try an experiment with planting mulberry trees and raising silk worms, but the silk worms ate more than he planted, and the experiment failed.

The township records for Emma's birth also have another intriguing element. Under "Residence of Parents" is listed both "Germany" and "Mount," though his great granddaughter had never heard the name "Mount" before. Mount was on the Old Stage Road, halfway between Washington and Quaker Bridge, where, in mid-century, Jonathan Cramer kept the Mount Tavern. Another curiosity, Emma is listed as being born in Atlantic County.

Frederick and Ann had four children: Frederick (b. 1853, d. 1919), Emma (b. 1856), Mary Louise (b. 1862), and Lena (birthdate unknown). Mrs. Fritz does not know the date on which the Lower Bank farm was acquired, so it is possible the Roedigers came into the township through Mount.

Lena married Gerald Moore, and they lived in Crowleytown. They had one son, Byrd. Frederick married a girl by the name of Mary (b. 1868, d. 1945). The couple had one son, John, and lived in Philadelphia, though both are buried in Lower Bank.

Emma married Albert Samuel Sooy, son of Towers and Sabrina (Weeks) Sooy. Sabrina was Job Weeks's daughter. Towers Sooy was the son of Samuel and Catherine (Leek) Sooy and grandson of Nicholas II and Esther (Weeks) Sooy.

Courtesy of Lillian (DeBow) Fritz

Charles DeBow - 1899
at the age of six

Mary Roediger married John DeBow, and the couple had three children: Charles Walter (b. 1893, d. 1964), Viola, and Maude. Not long after the marriage of their daughter, the Roedigers had a rude shock. They had been buying their farm with monthly payments to the former owner. They made their last payment and rejoiced that the land was finally theirs. Unfortunately, the holder of their note died suddenly before he had time to give them a receipt for the last payment and title to the land was never registered in their name. Their grandson, Charles, had to go to court years later to gain final title to the farm.

Charles DeBow married a girl from Cuba, New York, Helen Joyce Sibert. Lillian (DeBow) Fritz remembers her mother saying that, when she applied for Social Security, she received an inquiry from the government of the United States asking whether or not she was a naturalized citizen. They thought she had been born in Cuba, the island that is, even though she had very clearly written Cuba, NEW YORK. Helen provides another humorous note. She always hated the name "Helen," so she went by the name of Cora, that being more pleasing to her ear.

Daughter Viola married Weldon ("Spider") Bell, and the couple became the proud parents of William, Weldon, Jr., Robert, and Irene.

Daughter Maude married Horace Patten, and they had Austin, Violet, Maude, and Ella. They also raised their granddaughter, Ramona as a daughter. She must have loved her very much, for at Maude's funeral, Ramona was listed as one of her daughters, not as her granddaughter.

As to Mary Louise (Roediger) and John DeBow, both family and neighbors remember that, in later years, John DeBow lived in Philadelphia while his wife, Mary, worked the farm.

This was no easy task for poor Mary as she got up in years. She had a dislocated hip and walked with two canes, but she still managed to work an 11 acre farm and sell her produce in Atlantic City.

Every few days, she would hitch her horse to the farm wagon, load it up with vegetables, and drive all the way to that resort town so that she could get her produce to market. While in Atlantic City, she would stay with the Van Sant family, which was related to the Van Sants who lived in Lower Bank. Doughty Van Sant built a shipyard at Gardiner's Basin after that area was dredged in 1892. He and his son, Stanley, continued to operate the shipyard there until 1970. It must have been the Doughty Van Sant family who "put up" Mary DeBow while she was selling her produce.

It is most difficult to imagine how an older woman with a dislocated hip could find the stamina to do all that, but she did. She was certainly "physically challenged," but she met that challenge head on.

Mary Louise (Roediger) DeBow finally passed away in April of 1947. Surely, she fought the good fight and deserved her rest. She lies with her fellow Lower Bankers in the cemetery next to the old church.

The Pattens and the Bells remained residents of Washington Township, but Lillian, though reaching adulthood here, married a Philadelphia man, Charles Fritz, and lived in that city for much of her adult life. She and her husband finally returned to the land which gave her birth and built a new home on a parcel of the old Roediger/DeBow Farm.

The old farmhouse which Frederick and Ann Roediger built and Mary (Roediger) DeBow defended with

Courtesy of Lillian (DeBow) Fritz

Mary DeBow on her 80th Birthday - 1942
She is standing in front of the Roediger/DeBow House
which is no longer in existence.

such perseverance and strength is gone. The farm has been split up into homesites. Even the Roediger and DeBow names are gone from Washington Township, preserved only by the name of a lane down which Mary DeBow drove her horse and wagon to Atlantic City each week.

Charles DeBow, John Roediger,
and Byrd Moore
at the funeral of their mother and aunt,
Mary DeBow, in April 1947

Lillian (DeBow) Fritz - 1996

The Captain John Carlisle House
59 Old Church Road

1917

Courtesy of Arthur Andrews

Art Andrews, who bought this property in 1961, investigated its history and discovered that Captain John Carlisle had purchased fifteen acres from Robert Horner, who had originally acquired it from the Sooys. Captain Carlisle immediately started the construction of this house using ships' carpenters. Apparently, Art found no record of the exact year of its completion, but in 1821, Carlisle bought fourteen more acres of land from Isaiah Johnson. When the good captain died in 1828, the property devolved to his children, Richard Risley Carlisle, an actor, and Elizabeth (Carlisle) Egbert. It seems that Captain Carlisle's wife, Achsah (Allen) Carlisle was still living at the time, and daughter Elizabeth transferred her half share to her mother. Achsah (Allen) Carlisle was the daughter of Joseph and Mary (Leek) Allen. Her mother, Mary, was the sister of Captain John Leek, Jr. of Wading River.

Captain Carlisle's memory lives on because he kept an account book, beginning in 1813 until his death in 1828. These old account books give an interesting glimpse into the life of a day long gone. Henry Beck, in *Jersey Genesis*, quotes several entries, including one where Carlisle bought a new pair of oyster tongs to replace "those borrowed but never returned"- the price was $1.50. There was another in which credit was allowed for "38 pound of early corn meal at 3 cents a pound." There were still others showing Captain Carlisle spent a quarter for help in bringing up "goods" from his ship, paid John Townsend $3 for "1 ½ days plowing with two horses, and purchased five tons of salt hay from Joseph Allen, Jr. for $18.31.

In 1834, Richard Carlisle sold his half share to Captain Benjamin Edwards and his wife, Lucy Ann (Weeks). His mother, Achsah (Allen) Carlisle, sold Edwards her half share as well. Benjamin Edwards was a sea captain whose name is associated with the *Mark*, under the date of 1847 in the Batsto Store Books and with the *Chesepeke* [sic] in 1849. Both ships were schooners of undetermined size. His wife, Lucy Ann Weeks, was born c. 1811, the daughter of Daniel Weeks and granddaughter of Ezekiel and Elizabeth (Johnson) Weeks. (See Note 1 on the next page)

Benjamin Edwards was born in Delaware c. 1797, it seems he and his wife lived in that state after their marriage. Their first four children, Daniel (b. 1828), John (b. 1830), Sarah (b. 1835), and Charles (b. 1837) were all born in Delaware. Though he owned the house in 1834, he did not move here until some time after 1837. The Edwards' fifth child, Lucy Ann, named after her mother, was born in New Jersey in 1847. They were also purported to have had two other children, Irene and Elizabeth.

Captain Benjamin and Lucy Ann (Weeks) Edwards sold the house to Samuel Sooy in 1848. Samuel, in turn, sold it to Captain Jesse Allen in 1852. Captain Jesse Bodine Allen (b. November 29, 1818; d. March 12, 1873) and his wife, Hannah (Weeks) Allen (b. 1818; d. 1892) lived here during their married life. Jesse was the nephew of Achsah (Allen) Carlisle, the wife of the house's builder, and his wife was Job Weeks' daughter. Captain Jesse is connected with at least two schooners in the Batsto Store Books: the *John Little*, under the date of 1852, and the *John Fritts*, in 1853.

Captain Jesse's father, Joseph Allen, Jr., and his mother, Sarah (Bodine) Allen, kept an inn that used to stand on the corner of Old Church Road and Route 542 immediately across from Charlie Weber's house on what is today called "Korny Korners." This inn, according to Beck's research, was a stop on the stage route which led through Wading River and Green Bank early in the nineteenth century. Perhaps it is also one of those famous seven put out of business by the zeal of Lower Bank's famous Methodist preacher, Nicholas Van Sant. Sarah's family ran the Bodine Tavern on the Old Stage Road where it crossed the Wading River, a couple of miles up the road past Job Weeks' place.

Captain Jesse and Hannah (Weeks) Allen continued the operation of his parents' tavern on the Green Bank/Wading River Road while living here on Old Church Road. They had two children, Sarah Elizabeth and Charles Taylor. Captain Jesse Bodine Allen died in 1873 and the house devised to his wife, Hannah (Weeks) Allen. (See Note 2) The couple's daughter, Sarah Elizabeth, married James W. Cavileer, son of David and Phoebe Ann (Cale) Cavileer, son of Peter, son of John. Their son, Charles Taylor Allen married Achsah Amanda Cramer, daughter of Charles Burris and Ellen (Adams) Cramer, granddaughter of Charles and Mary (Gaskill) Cramer of Wading River, on January 28th, 1876, and they succeeded his parents in making this house their home. Charles was born on February 1, 1851, the year before his parents bought this house from Samuel Sooy, at Turtle Creek (Wading River), where they were living at the time. Achsah (Cramer) Allen was born on March 20, 1858 and died September 6, 1911. The couple had two children, Ellen A. Cramer Allen (b. 1876), who married Asbury Kier Scott, and Esther Matilda Allen, who married Aaron R. Willitts. Charles' mother, Hannah, transferred the house by deed to her daughter-in-law, Achsah (Cramer) Allen on September 14, 1892. In 1902, Achsah bought additional land from Captain Robert and Margaret Somers.

In 1907, Achsah gave half of the property to her daughter, Ellen (Allen) Scott, and half to daughter Esther Mathilda (Allen) Willitts. When Achsah (Cramer) Allen died in 1911, her husband, Charles, married Lizzie Garrison, the daughter of the Rev. J. Swayne Garrison and his wife, Julia (Lane). Charles died in Lower Bank on October 6, 1922.

Henry Beck met Ellen (Allen) Scott at the time he was writing his material for *Jersey Genesis*. She was born in the year of the Centennial, 1876. Ellen Scott was fascinated by history, but she couldn't tell Beck much about Captain Carlisle. She did, however, have Carlisle's ledger, inscribed with his name across the top. She also had a diary that had been written by her great-grandfather, Charles Cramer, which kept a record of purchases and noted daily events, including deaths, drownings, and notable happenings such as: "July 14, 1832: My wife tuck a rattle-snake that was measured and was six feet long." Ellen Scott had traced the Scott line back to a Thomas Wright, Lexham, Norfolk, England, who was born in 1422 and died in 1529. She eventually sold Charles I. Wilson, Sr. the Charles Cramer diary, and he placed it in the Batsto collection. Sadly, no one knows what happened to Captain John's ledger, for Ellen met a tragic end.

Joe and Sadie (Updike) Ware had lived next door in the Parsonage for a couple of years. After Nelson Ware's birth in 1924, Ellen Scott moved into the smaller section of the Carlisle House and the Wares moved into the larger section. They were only here for a year, however, before they moved to the Island. Ellen Scott had Roy Cramer tear down the smaller part of the house at some time in the 1930's or 1940's, prior to Henry Beck and Bill Augustine's visit.

NOTE 1: Daniel Weeks was the brother of Job and Samuel Weeks who also lived in Lower Bank, of Esther, who was married to Nicholas Sooy I, of Sarah, wife of Noah Sooy, Nicholas' brother, of Rebecca, wife of William Sooy, also Nicholas I's brother, and of Elizabeth, wife of John Cavileer. When she and her husband, Captain Benjamin, moved into this house, they were certainly surrounded by family! Mr. Andrews says that Achsah Allen was Lucy Ann Weeks' grandmother, but this is incorrect. Her grandmother on the Weeks' side was Elizabeth (Johnson) and her maternal grandmother was Elizabeth (Mathis) Weatherby. Actually, Captain Jesse Allen, husband of Hannah (Weeks) Allen, was Achsah (Allen) Carlisle's nephew. Achsah's *brother* was Joseph Allen, Jr., the father of Captain Jesse.

NOTE 2: Lillian (DeBow) Fritz says that one of the Allens used this house as a tavern for a while. Since Josie and Jesse both kept the inn out on the Green Bank/Wading River Road *and* owned this house, she may be mistaken.

Meanwhile, back to the tragedy. Ellen Scott raised her grandson, Allen Bodine Scott, in this house while the boy's mother, Melva, lived in Philadelphia. Local rumor has it that Allen Scott had adjustment problems. During World War II, he used to taunt the Coast Guardsmen who were guarding the bridge and boatyard with saying he'd be governor when the Nazis took over. This earned him at least one severe beating. Over a period of time, he charmed his grandmother into thinking that he really enjoyed her company and coaxed her out to a remote place for picnics. Then, on July 18, 1954, he took a rifle with him on their journey and reputedly shot her to death.

The manhunt was on, and local people reported spotting him all over the place: Atlantic City, Pleasantville, Absecon. Actually, he had fled all the way out to the State of Washington. The long arm of the law finally caught up with him, though. He was tried, convicted, and sentenced to life imprisonment.

Father Beck must have been saddened by this tragic end to the life of his Lower Bank informant. Ellen's half share in the house passed to her daughter, Melva Scott Dougherty. On September 23, 1955, Melva also received the other half, by deed, from her aunt, Esther Mathilda (Allen) (Willitts) Curtis. Melva sold the house to Arthur and Dorothy Andrews, who lived here for several years and rebuilt it completely. Dorothy had been the founder of the first parents' association for retarded children chartered in Pennsylvania, now known as the Pennsylvania Association for Retarded Citizens. After Dorothy's death, Art sold the house in 1986.

The Stuart Kerzners owned this very early nineteenth century home until they sold it recently.

1995

Photograph by John Pearce

William F. Augustine Collection
Special Collections and University Archives
Rutgers University Libraries

A photograph of the Carlisle House, as it appeared in Henry Beck's time, superimposed over the Carlisle ledger. The ledger is currently in the Batsto library.

The Parsonage
61 Old Church Road

Photograph by John Pearce

1995

This house has been known as "The Parsonage" for some years, having been given to the Lower Bank Circuit of the Methodist Episcopal Church by Alicia (Somers) Smith over half a century ago. Alicia (Somers) Smith was the daughter of Captain Robert and Margaret Somers, whose home still stands at 2187 River Road overlooking the Mullica. It was rented to various families, including those of the local ministers, even while Captain Somers still owned the house, a practice which continued when the circuit had no need for it.

A map from the last quarter of the nineteenth century lists it as the home of Mrs. James Cavileer. Captain James W. Cavileer (b. 4/6/1841, d. 8/5/1902) was the son of David and Phoebe Ann (Cale) Cavileer. On January 20, 1870, he married Sarah Elizabeth Allen (b. 9/6/1848, d. 12/18/1926), daughter of Jesse Bodine and Hannah (Weeks) Allen who lived next door at 59 Old Church Road. Apparently the couple lived in this house for several years. James was a sea captain, and it is strange that the map maker's information lists the house as Mrs. James Cavileer's house, not simply "J. Cavileer" as are the other homes of sea captains. Maybe Captain Jim was away at sea when the information was gathered for the map, or perhaps Mrs. Captain Cavileer actually owned the house through her father and mother next door.

No one seems to know exactly when Captain Somers bought the house, but it was probably prior to the time Sarah Elizabeth (Allen) Cavileer died in 1926. Mrs. James Cavileer moved to Hammonton after her brother's death, selling this house to Captain Robert Somers in time to rent it to its next occupants, Sadie and Joe Ware.

Sadie was an Updike from Wading River, and the young couple lived in the home of Joe's parents at Batsto when they were first married. Here they had their first child, Anna, in 1918. They moved in with John and Anna Updike at the Benjamin Downs farm on Turtle Creek Road in Wading River soon after. The elder Updikes died the year before Sadie and Joe's first son, Howard, was born on the 23rd of May, 1921. It wasn't long after his birth that his parents moved to the Old Parsonage. Joe bought some used sawmill machinery and set up a mill in Lower Bank downriver from the bridge. When sawmill machinery was freed from water power, the mills were set up wherever there was timber to be cut. The machinery purchased by Joe Ware began life in a mill at Sandy Ridge, a spot to the west of the Friendship bogs. When timber there was exhausted, it was moved to New Gretna where it was in the MacDonald mill. Ware brought it to Lower Bank. The mill was powered by a 20 horsepower Fairbanks-Morse engine that ran on kerosene and included a log carriage, a rip saw, and a shingle machine, amongst other machinery.

Howard remembers that the Old Parsonage belonged to the Methodist churches even then, but he also recalls that Captain Somers used to come and mow the grass, which probably means that he may have still owned it at that time. Joe and Sadie's third child and second son, Nelson, was born in November of 1924 in this house.

During the year following Nelson's birth, Sarah Elizabeth (Allen) Cavileer died, and the Ware family moved next door to the Carlisle/Scott house. The following year, the Wares moved again, this time to a house at "The Island" near the Cramers, but tragedy was soon to strike. The young mother had tuberculosis, and she passed away in 1928, leaving her husband with two little sons and a six year old daughter.

Despite tragedy at home, Joe continued to operate his sawmill and even set up another across the river in Atlantic County near the site of Gloucester Furnace. For years, he shifted the equipment back and forth between the two mills. Needing a wife and a mother for his children, Joe remarried, this time to Emilie Weber, daughter of Charlie Weber of Lower Bank. In 1932 or 1933, the family moved to a house in Green Bank that still stands on Route 563, but Joe continued to run his Lower Bank and Gloucester Furnace mills. When Henry Charlton Beck and Bill Augustine came nosing around, they found Joe hard at work in his Lower Bank mill.

Finally, in the late 1940's, Joe and his wife decided to build a mill next to their Green Bank house. The Wares built their new mill and moved the log carriage to the site. A "log carriage," for those of you not familiar with sawmill terminology, is the mechanism that actually holds the logs and moves them towards the sawblade. They were just finishing up their last order of blueberry crates when the Lower Bank mill caught fire and much of the remaining equipment was damaged. Howard Ware was a little vague about the year of the conflagration which destroyed his father's Lower Bank mill. He couldn't remember whether it was 1946 or 1947, but he did remember that the fire was not a complete disaster. Raymond Bozarth was actually able to rebuild the Fairbanks-Morse engine which was the heart of the enterprise.

When Joe Ware died in 1948, his sons were still in their twenties and his widow proved herself to be a worthy daughter of hard-working Charlie Weber. Emilie Weber Ware (everyone always called her by all three names) was a no-nonsense woman, determined to carry on the Green Bank sawmill. Her strength and determination supported her through the rest of her life.

Howard Ware, at 76, lives on North Maple Avenue in New Gretna in a house which he built himself. His brother, Nelson, lives in Lower Bank. Both are friendly and hard-working, and, like most of the scions of the old Washington Township families, unwilling to let age get them down.

To get back to the Old Parsonage, in the late 1930's, the house was again rented out to another couple who would add much to Lower Bank and Washington Township, for it became the first local home of Earle and Mae Hill before they bought old Sam Weeks' Tavern after Gilbert and Myra (Cramer) Irons died.

As the 20th century was drawing to a close, the Lower Bank circuit was faced with dwindling membership. For years, they had had new ministers every two or three years, and many times, they were ministers-in-training rather than fully ordained clergy. Then a controversy arose in the Weekstown church, which threatened Green Bank and Lower Bank with closure. The Weekstown congregation disagreed with the policies of the United Methodist Church and withdrew to form their own independent church. Though the Methodist Conference tried to keep the Weekstown church open, they had to admit their failure and sold the building to its former congregation. This left only the two Washington Township churches to support the minister.

Unable to afford repairs on the house, the two churches sold the property a few years back and invested the proceeds to their mutual interest. The Old Parsonage is now a private house which is currently owned by Thomas Haes.

Courtesy of Nelson Ware

Nelson, Sadie (Updike), and
Howard Ware - c. 1926

Anna, Nelson, and Howard Ware

Howard, Joe, and Nelson Ware

Joe Ware and his shingle machine - c. 1940

468

The Ware
Sawmill in
Lower Bank

Photographs courtesy of Nelson Ware

The Ware Sawmill in
Green Bank (Right and
Below)

The little building to
the right is the first
automobile shop of
Jesse Nichols.
This view is looking
towards Rt. 563 from
the rear of the sawmill.

469

The Job Weeks Farm
(No Longer in Existence)

Job Weeks, born on October 10, 1793, was the third son and sixth child of Ezekiel and Elizabeth (Johnson) Weeks. On July 10, 1815, he married Sarah Pettit, daughter of Samuel Pettit and Hannah Sooy (Nicholas Sooy II's sister). His wife's uncle sold him one hundred acres in Washington Township which he had acquired from his father, Nicholas Sooy I, in 1811. This may well have been the point at which Job and Sarah (Pettit) Weeks moved to the Lower Bank area. The couple purchased another one hundred acres from Archibold Sooy eight years later, and one hundred ninety acres from the estates of John Cramer and Nicholas Sooy I. In 1836, he purchased still another 1,897 acres, along with Nicholas II and William H. Sooy (presumably Nicholas II's brother of that name). Other acreage is recorded as being purchased by Job Weeks, either outright or with partners.

Old letters indicate that his homestead stood on what is today known as Seaf Weeks Road which appears to be an extension of River Road on the north side of the Batsto/Wading River Road (Route 542). On old maps, this is called Mullicus Road and formed part of the original (pre-1808) road from Wading River to Lower Bank, or Mullica's Plantation. After Job built his farm, it became known as Job Week's Road. The modern "Seaf" apparently comes from Job's ninth child, Josephus S.

Job and Sarah's first son, Samuel was born on July 5, 1816 and was a mariner. He died at the age of forty-eight of typhoid fever. A Samuel Weeks is connected with at least one ship in the Batsto books, the schooner *Winslow*, as either owner or as master in the year 1837. Job's son, Samuel, was only twenty-one in 1837, and it is entirely possible that he was a captain at this age. It is also possible that it was his uncle Samuel, carpenter and tavern owner, who was master and/or owner of the *Winslow*. Samuel was only thirty-three in 1837. Job Weeks was also connected with a ship in the Batsto Store Books in the year 1847, the schooner *Esther and Sarah*. By this year, the *Winslow* is listed under the names of Sam Kemble (1846) and Benjamin Sooy (1847).

Daughter Mary's husband is not known. Son Job, Jr. married Hannah Adams, and daughter Sabrina (or perhaps Sabine) married Towers Sooy of the Wading River Sooys.

Hannah married Captain Jesse Allen, the son of Joseph Allen, Jr. and Sarah (Bodine) Allen. As has been mentioned in connection with the Allen house at 59 Old Church Road, the Bodines ran the tavern at the point which the old Stage Road crossed the Wading River, and the Allens ran another on the corner of Old Church Road and the Green Bank/Wading River Road.

Nicholas S. Weeks was a ship carpenter and died in Camden. Sarah Elizabeth was born in 1830 but died three years later. Ezekiel died in infancy in 1839. His birth date is unknown. The birthdate of Josephus S. is not known, but he married first, Sallie McCollum, and after her death in 1876, Mary Cale of the Lower Bank Cales.

Job Weeks was induced to serve Washington Township as constable in 1829 through 1831 and, in addition to his position as constable, he was an Overseer of the Poor in 1830. At the first annual meeting of 1832 held on March 13 at Town House in Quaker Bridge, Job was elected as an Overseer of the Poor and as a Commissioner of Appeal with John Cavileer and Wiliam H. Sooy. Samuel Weeks replaced him as constable. Nicholas Sooy II was on the township committee and the school committee. William H. Sooy, his son, also was to serve on the school committee as both men had done in 1831, the first year in which there *was* a school committee. Paul Sears Sooy was to be Pound Keeper.

However, something happened in 1832 that shook up the township. A second "annual meeting" was held on April 3rd where in the former meeting was declared illegal and a new slate elected. This time, the names of Sooy, Cavileer, and Weeks are missing from the list. Yet another "annual meeting" was held on the same day at the Washington Tavern, now operated by Paul Sears Sooy, at which the former two meetings were declared void. Once again, the names of Sooy, Cavileer, and Weeks do not appear on the new list of officeholders. At all of these meetings, Jesse Richards of Batsto remained president and Isaiah Hall clerk of the township. The second and third lists (of the two meetings held on April 3rd) remained substantially the same, which means that the entire assemblage must have journeyed from Quaker Bridge to the Washington Tavern, several miles down the old Stage Road on the same day. William H. Sooy would serve the township again in 1833 and for many years thereafter, but Nicholas Sooy II's name would never appear on the township office list again. Not until 1837 would Sam Weeks serve as Surveyor of Highways and on the school committee. His brother, Job, would serve again for one year as Overseer of Highways in 1844.

Job Weeks, Sr., son of Ezekiel, died on December 29, 1864. His wife, Sarah, died on September 15, 1880.

In 1995, there is nothing at all where the ancient homestead of Job and Sarah Weeks raised their children nor has there been in recent memory. The pastures have grown up in trees, and the house long since returned to dust.

Lower Bank

Randolph Twp.

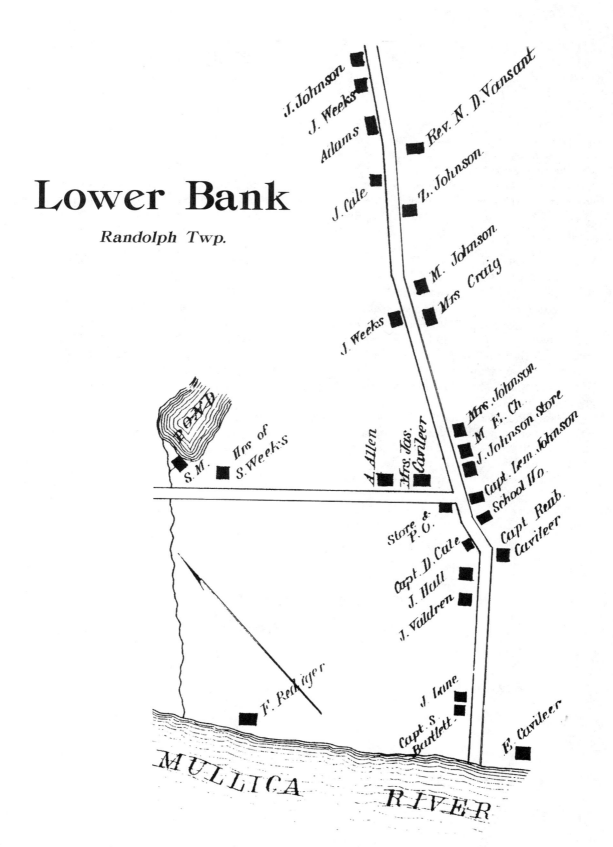

J. Johnson
J. Weeks
Adams
J. Cale
Rev. N. D. Vansant
Z. Johnson
M. Johnson
Mrs. Craig
J. Weeks

POND
S. M.
Hrs of S. Weeks

A. Allen
Mrs. Jas. Cavileer

Mrs. Johnson
M. E. Ch.
J. Johnson Store
Capt. Lem. Johnson
School Ho.
Capt. Reub. Cavileer

Store & P. O.
Capt. D. Cale
J. Hull
J. Valdren

F. Reatiger

J. Lane
Capt. S. Bartlett

E. Cavileer

MULLICA   RIVER

Map of the Inland Section of River Road, Lower Bank - 1876
Taken from J.D. Scott's *Atlas of Burlington County*

The Home of Captain John Johnson
(No Longer in Existence)

We entered Lower Bank from Charlie Weber's out on the Green Bank/Wading River Road (Route 542). Now we must retrace our steps and come in again from that artery, this time heading for the Mullica on River Road.

The majority of houses along this first stretch of Lower Bank's main road were small, one-and-a-half or two-story houses owned by laborers and sea captains alike.

The first house from the corner on the right hand side was the home of Captain John Johnson. John Johnson was born in 1811, the sixth child of Mathias Johnson IV and Ann (Homan). He was the brother of Captain Levi Johnson, who lived in the old homestead on River Road at the head of Old Church Road (2085 River Road), and of Mahlon Johnson (2055 River Road) and of Jacob Johnson who ran the store next to the "new" church

He married Margaret (Cramer), the daughter of Isaiah and Rachel (Randolph) Cramer, in Washington Township on December 31, 1835 and the couple had ten children: Elmer (b. 1836), Anna (b. 1838, d. 6/9/1865), Isaiah C., Mary A. (b.c. 1843, d. 9/9/1873), Sarah L. (1845-1930), George Henry (b.c. 1848), Rachel (b. 1852), William (b. 2/6/1853, d. 4/14/1923), Martha Adella (1855-1927), Rebandia (b. 1858).

Though he went to sea and became the captain of a ship like his brothers, he had retired by 1860 and is listed as a farmer in the census for that year. Captain John may have been the captain of the first vessel to sail down the Mullica with Batsto glass in its hold. The ship credited with that honor is the *John Wurts* in October of 1846. Her captain was "J" Johnson. This had to be either John or his brother Jacob, both of Lower Bank.

The Johnson house stood on a fifty-three acre parcel that was still listed as the John Johnson Estate in 1942. Captain Johnson died on the 9th of January 1891, at the age of 78 years, and his wife died eight years later, on the 6th of February 1899.

Harold Atherholt's aunt bought the property from the estate sometime between 1942 and 1947, because Harold and his aunt were living there when he acquired, then sold, the house at 2044 River Road to Irvin Homiller. Harold was born in 1905 and died in 1959. His wife, Dorothy, was born in 1913 and lived until 1972. Both are buried in the Lower Bank cemetery.

The house burned to the ground in the 1970's.

The Johnson Family

The Johnson family was one of the most important families in Lower Bank during the nineteenth century and can be traced to Mathias and Elizabeth (Brookfield) Johnson who are reported to have lived in Connecticut prior to puchasing land in Little Egg Harbor Township at Lower Bank in 1740, though the original deed of that date has not been found. The earliest located to date is a sale of 51 1/2 acres by Richard Risley to Mathias Johnson for forty-eight pounds in 1769. This particular piece of property was surveyed by the Council of Proprietors on December 5, 1757 as part of a 9,782 acre parcel to the West Jersey Society. One thousand of those acres were surveyed by the West Jersey Society to George May on January 5, 1760, five hundred acres of which May sold to Richard Somers on April 1st of the same year. This is presumed to be the same Richard Somers who had his home in Somers Point and was a colonel in the Gloucester County militia during the Revolutionary War. His son, John, surveyed one hundred acres of that land to Richard Risley on January 28-29, 1765, 51 1/2 acres of which Risley sold to Mathias Johnson on November 24, 1769. This latter indenture was witnessed by John Leek and Joseph Burr. It was acknowledged on April 7, 1819 before Caleb Cramer, Commissioner, and was recorded on April 9, 1819 in Mount Holly, N.J.

The exact location this first Mathias chose for his homestead site is not known, but it is presumed to have been on a portion of the property in Lower Bank which later came into the possession of his heirs. Mathias and Elizabeth (Brookfield) Johnson had seven sons and two daughters: William (1747-1818), Jacob, Jonathan (d. 3/18/ 1822), Mathias, Jr., Joseph, Uriah, Asiah, Elizabeth (b. c. 5/8 (or 22) /1761, d. 4/6/1841), and Hannah (b. 9/16/ 1765, d. 10/16/1827).

William was supposed to have married a Phoebe Sooy, but this relationship does not appear in the Sooy genealogy. In the information provided by the Johnson family, the name Poole is in parentheses after Sooy, and this may be Phoebe's correct name. Augustus (Captain Gus) Johnson, who lived on the corner of Old Church Road and River Road in Lower Bank was their son. Augustus was forty-four in 1850, married to Sarah (54), and had three daughters: Margaret (20), Parmela (17), and Phoebe (15). Daughter Armenia is listed as twenty-four in 1860, though she's not on the 1850 census. She later married John Cavileer III and lived in the Victorian house on the river.

Jonathan Johnson was the one who bought land from Captain David Mapps to form a millpond for his grist mill on the Cakes Spruto in 1809. The site of his homestead isn't known either. He married a woman by the name of Mary who died on October 19, 1826 at the age of seventy-three years, nine months, and nineteen days. Jonathan and Maria had at least two children, sons by the name of Hugh and Malcolm. Malcolm's stone in the Lower Bank cemetery bears no dates. According to a note in *Jersey Genesis* from the Carlisle ledger, "Hugh Johnson was drowned and found opposite Clark's Landing. And was buried the 26." The date given is July 23, 1833. Hugh's name doesn't appear on a stone, but those of his wife and two sons do. Hugh married a woman named Maria who died on February 16, 1829 at the age of thirty-four. Hugh and Maria also lost a son, Bornt, who died when he was five months old. Hugh, Jr. died at the early age of twenty-six on June 12, 1855.

Mathias, Sr. and Elizabeth's daughter Elizabeth married Ezekial Weeks and began the Weeks line in the Mullica valley, and *their* daughter, Esther, married Nicholas Sooy I. Nicholas and Esther ran Sooy's Inn (Washington Tavern) on the road from Cooper's Ferry to Tuckerton.

Daughter Hannah married John Cramer III, son of John, Jr., son of John, son of William, Jr., son of the first William. John Cramer III's sisters married into the local families as well. Ann Cramer married Charles Allen; Sarah Cramer married James Gale, Sr.; and Phebe Cramer married Francis French Sr.

The son from whom the four captains (John, Jacob, Mahlon, and Levi) were descended was Jacob. The name of Jacob's wife has been forgotten, but they had at least two sons: Mathias III (his uncle was Mathias, Jr.) and John. Jacob divided his share of his father's property between his sons, but Mathias III bought his brother, John's share. Mathias III had seven children: Mathias IV, John, Isabel, Sarah, Blenna, Elizabeth, and Mary.

Mathias Johnson IV was born on December 9, 1778 and married Ann Homan (b. 2/25/1780) on May 10, 1801. Ann (Homan) Johnson died on August 20, 1844. He died on August 26, 1849. The couple had eleven children: Achsah (b. 6/3/1803), Mahlon (b. 4/24/1805, d. 8/2/1872), Rachel (b. 2/6/1807), Levi (b. 1/4/1808, d. 1889), Daniel (b. 10/25/1809), John (b. 10/22/1811, d. 1/9/1891), Samuel (b. 10/25/1813), Jacob (b. 11/20/1814), Mary (b.11/30/1816), Reeve (b. 6/27/1819), and Sarah Ann (b. 11/6/1821). Mathias IV and Ann (She signed a deed in 1822 as "Nancy") lived in a little cabin that used to stand a distance behind what is known today as the Johnson Cottage at 2077 River Road, and it was here that their first five children were born. In 1810, Mathias IV and Ann (Nancy) built themselves a new home, the Johnson Cottage, where their remaining six children were born.

Mahlon married Hannah Jervis and lived at 2055 River Road.

Daniel married a Sarah Ann (b. 1817) who died at the age of thirty-two. Their daughter, Anna Emaline, died in 1847 at the age of two. Grandfather Mathias is buried in the same plot as Sarah Ann and Anna Emaline.

Jacob Johnson married Jane Leeds, according to the Johnson family material, but the 1860 census lists "Margaret" as his wife. On the census, the couple is listed as having six children: Alice, Brainard, Lewis S., Rachel, Stephen, and Jacob E.

John married Martha Cramer and lived at the first house on the west side of River Road in from Route 542. They are listed on the 1860 census as having nine children: Elmer, Isaiah, Mary, Sarah, Rachel, George, William, Adella, and Rebandi. Though he, too, was a sea captain, he had turned farmer by the time he was forty-nine in 1860.

Levi married Hannah Wilson, daughter of Joseph and Sarah (Howell) Wilson, on the 6th of February, 1831 at Pleasant Mills, and the couple had nine children: Walter, Lemuel (1833-1909), Anna, Emma, Sarah Jane, Joseph Edmund, Arthur Mathias, Henry, and Mary Ella. Levi and Hannah (Wilson) Johnson built what became known as the Johnson Homestead at 2085 River Road.

Lemuel Howell Johnson had two daughers and a son, but his wife's name is not known. When he died in 1903, he was buried with his father and mother at Lower Bank. Anna and Emma died young. Arthur Mathias Johnson (1843-1913) married Louisa Glover and had three boys and a girl. Henry Howell Johnson (1846-1899) married Maria Oliver, and they had one son. Mary Ella (1848-1933) married Charles Platt Leek (1843-1918) in 1888. This C.P. Leek was the uncle of the Lower Bank C.P. Leek II who had C.P. Leek and Sons boatyard. Mary Ella (Johnson) Leek operated The Mullica Hotel in Atlantic City at least from 1930-1931, possibly for a longer period of time.

Joseph Edmund Johnson (b. October 12, 1840) married Henrietta Allaire Spain on December 13, 1866, and the couple had five children: Florence Allaire (m. Frank Van Sant in 1889), Ella Howell (m. Charles R. Underhill in 1898), Ada Hope (m. William F. Kemble in 1904), Josie Edna, and Walter Simmons (m. Ruby Miller).

Ella (Johnson) Underhill would later live in the Johnson Cottage and give Henry Charlton Beck quite a bit of information on Lower Bank, the Johnsons, and the Jersey Devil. Her sister, Ada Hope (Johnson) Kemble was the mother of Edmund and Karel Kemble and lived in the Levi Johnson Homestead with her husband, William Fritz Kemble.

The Weeks/Lewis House
2036 River Road

1995

Photograph by John Pearce

This early nineteenth century house was the home of Job Weeks, Jr. His father, Job Weeks, Sr., had his farm on the north side of Route 542 and his uncle was the tavern keeper, Sam Weeks. Job and Sam were trustees of the Methodist Church when they obtained the property in 1842 and Job, Jr. joined his father and the minister, Nicholas Van Zant, as trustees of the original school in Lower Bank at the end of that decade.

Job, Jr. was born in May of 1821, the third of nine children, no doubt on his father's farm on Job (now Seaf) Weeks Road. According to Van Name (*The Weeks Family*) he married Hannah S. Adams (b. April 12, 1821), the daughter of Reuben Adams and Emma (alias Amy Riley). Van Name also records that on December 13, 1842, Samuel and Mary Weeks sold 7.25 acres in Washington Township to his nephew, Job Weeks, Jr. On the 1942 tax maps, this particular parcel is only listed as 6.25 acres, but who's to say whether it was the same acreage.

Job, Jr. and Hannah appear five times in the extant Washington Township birth records for 1848 through 1877 where Job is listed as a "carpenter" four times, in 1848 when son Reuben was born, 1853 when son Charles D. was born, in 1855 on the birth of Charles S., and in 1863 when son Job H. was born. He is listed as a "laborer" in 1865 when daughter Amy was born.

Job, Jr. and Hannah had a total of eleven children, four of whom died young. At least five of his children married spouses from Philadelphia and lived in that area. Jesse A. (b. 1844) married Anna Allen; Josephine A. married William A. Miller of Philadelphia; Reuben A. married Emma Cohill in Philadelphia; Anna married James Edward Allen; Charles Stokes; Albert (M.D.) married Mary E. Umstead of Phoenixville, Penna.; Job Harry (M.D.) married Georgianna Baymore Weeks, the widow of his brother, Charles Stokes Weeks (both were reported as living in Philadelphia as late as 1943); Ephraim (b. 1846), Charles D. (b. 1853), Harry E. (b. 1861) and Amy (b. 1865) all died in their first year of life.

475

Hannah S. (Adams) Weeks died on June 29, 1899. Job Weeks, Jr. died on July 19, 1908. Both were buried in the Lower Bank cemetery.

Early in the twentieth century, this house was the home of the Fox family. Bill Fox, Margie (Cavileer) Fox's husband, (see 2096 River Road), grew up here. Next came a family by the name of Peiffer.

The 1937 tax records indicate that a William Stark, soldier, owned the property. Stark was a veteran of the Spanish American War and was a distant relation of the current owners, the Lewises. J. Herman Lewis (1913 - 1988) and his wife, Irma, often brought their sons, Bill and John, from Philadelphia to Lower Bank for vacations. Bill Stark was actually a cousin of Mr. Lewis's aunt and always said that he wanted the Lewis family to have the house after he was gone, but he died intestate, and Herman had to buy it at a tax sale. Mrs. Lewis herself just recently passed away.

The Mary DeBow House
(No Longer in Existence)

In the 1942 tax records, Mary DeBow owned the house which used to stand third from the corner of Route 542 and River Road. This puzzles her granddaughter, Lillian (DeBow) Fritz, because the house was in her husband's family, and he was still living at the time. He did, however, live in Philadelphia while she lived in Lower Bank on the DeBow farm, so perhaps Mary paid the taxes on the property.

Beck says that the house burned to the ground in the summer of 1940, and granddaughter Lillian (DeBow) Fritz agrees with him, but the tax map and accompanying book indicate "improvements" on the DeBow property as late as 1942.

Jersey Genesis says that this no longer existing house was owned by a succession of Leeks and Cales, and was the home of Isaac Van Sant. He goes on to say (his source is Ella Johnson Underhill) that Nathaniel ("Uncle Thanie") Van Sant, who lived in a house across River Road (which is no longer there) moved into Isaac's house when Isaac left to become a clergyman. Now Isaac was the ninth child and seventh son of the Rev. Nicholas Van Sant. Nathaniel was the seventh child and sixth son of the good Reverend and married to Sarah Cramer.

While Nathaniel never entered the Methodist ministry, he did have quite a lot to say about Methodism in Lower Bank for a good many years. Uncle Thannie ascribed to the old New England notion that musical instruments were implements of the devil and should not be heard in church. The unadorned human voice was the only instrument that truly pleased God. By the late nineteenth century when Uncle Thannie presided over the ecclesiastical morals of Lower Bank, even the New Englanders had permitted organs and melodeons in their meeting houses. Not Uncle Thannie!

Beck quotes Ella (Johnson) Underhill as saying that he "sold the place to the Cales later on and moved into a house that most of us remember better as the real Uncle Thannie's." Tantalizing. In 1996, no one remembers which house *was* the *real* "Uncle Thannie's." Also intriguing is that Marjorie (Downs) Cavileer says that Uncle Thannie's house is part of Horace Cavileer's house at 2108 River Road. Horace says he never heard of Uncle Thannie.

On the 1876 map, this house is listed as belonging to an Adams.

The Captain John Cale House
2044 River Road

Courtesy of Sarah (Cramer) Camillo

The Home of Captain John C. Cale and His Wife, Lettice

Though some captains' homes are large and imposing, many lived with their families in modest homes just like this one. In fact, this was the home of a sea captain, Captain John Cale and his loving wife, Lettice.

Ship captain's houses along the seacoast were often ornamented with Captains' Walks or Widows' Walks. Placed on the ridge of the house, they provided places for retired captains to watch for their ship to enter the harbor, or, if the captain was still at the helm, for his wife to gaze anxiously at the horizon for his return. Many a legend exists of women haunting their "walks" years after their captain-husbands were lost at sea.

Lower Bank has not a single example of a captains' or widows' walk, but it does have a story of a ship lost at sea and of the woman who waited a lifetime for the return of her one true love.

John and Lettice's story is a sad tale of unfulfilled love, for Captain John sailed off in his ship one day and never returned to his loving wife. John Cale was born in 1843 and married Lettice Winterbottom in Green Bank on the 17th of May, 1867 when he was twenty-four and she was twenty. John's father was Captain Watson Cale. The bride's parents were Thomas and Sarah Winterbottom.

This house was their "love nest," and the couple were infatuated with each other. A year after their marriage, on November 11, 1868, the couple was blessed with the birth of a daughter, Olive W. Two years later, William was born. Four years after William, Walter came along. Things seemed perfect for the young family. Unfortunately, life would not allow them continued happiness.

Eleven years after they were married, Captain Watson Cale had a bad case of the gout and couldn't get out of bed. Instead, he sent his son, Captain John, as captain of the *Walter Palmer* for this one trip. It was a fateful decision. Some time later, Captain Watson woke up in the middle of the night in great anguish. Startling his wife, Anna Maria, who was sleeping beside him, he got out of bed and went to the window. His wife was shocked, for Watson hadn't been able to get up since his son had left on the *Walter Palmer*.

478

With tears streaming down his rugged, windblown face, he cried to his wife that he could see his ship going down in the ocean. It was quite a while before she could get her husband calmed sufficiently to return to his bed. The incident had been so shocking to her that Anna Maria made it a point to write down the exact time at which her sea captain husband had left his sickbed for the window.

There is an emptiness in waiting, in not knowing the fate of a loved one. The finality of the grave is that you can know without doubt the final disposition of someone you love, but a "missing in action" or a "lost at sea" tells the heart absolutely nothing. It clings to hope and dreams that which will never be fulfilled.

One year later, a seaman appeared on Captain Watson's doorstep with quite a tale. He had been on a vessel which had almost floundered in a storm the year before. In the storm-tossed darkness, they could just make out the outline of the *Walter Palmer*, which they had last seen clearly in the light of day. The seamen and his crew watched helplessly as the *Walter Palmer* began to break up. At dawn the next morning, the storm had subsided, and the remaining ship searched hours for survivors but found none. The *Walter Palmer* had gone down with all hands. [Ella Johnson Underhill told Henry Beck that it was cut in two by a steamer.] With a trembling voice, Mrs. Cale inquired of the date and exact time that the man had seen the *Walter Palmer* sink beneath the waves, then climbed the stairs to her bedroom. From the dresser drawer, she took that small piece of paper on which she had written down the hour and minute at which Captain Watson had gotten up from his pain-wracked sickbed and stood sobbing at the window. Though her hand trembled and her eyes filled with tears, she could read that same fateful date in 1878 and the exact minute the seaman had reported that the *Walter Palmer* had gone down with all hands.

Lettice never accepted that she would not see her beloved John again, and, for the rest of her life, rarely left her little home on River Road. Each evening, she continued to set a place for her Captain John, always hoping beyond hope that he would return to share their modest fare once again. As the sun fell below the western horizon, she would light candles in the windows to guide his way up the River Road. Every night, she must have tucked her young children into bed and whispered that their daddy would soon be home. They would grow in years, marry, and have children of their own, but the void in their lives would never be filled.

Courtesy of Sarah (Cramer) Camillo

Lettice and her Captain John

The following poem was written by Lettice Winterbottom in the back of a ledger at some time prior to her marriage to Captain John Cale. It would prove prophetic.

To Lettie

How long wilt thou forget me Lord.
Must I for ever mourn'd
How long wilt thou with draw for and
O' new to return!

Oh! hear and to my longing eyes
Restore thy wonted light;
Draw on my spirit lest I sleep
In death's most gloomy night,

Since I have always placed my trust
Beneath thy mercy's wing,
Thy saving health shall come; and then
My heart with joy shall spring.

Written by

Mils. Lettie M. Winterbottom

Lettice (Winterbottom) Cale was faithful to her John for another forty-nine years. Just imagine, forty-nine years of never leaving the house for fear her captain would return while she was gone; forty-nine years of setting a table-place that would never be used; forty-nine years of lighting candles in the window each and every night. Lettice was thirty-one the year Captain John walked down River Road to his ship for the last time with their ten year old daughter laughing and skipping beside her beloved father. Lettice Cale died in 1927 at the age of eighty, faithful to the end, but she had continued heartbreak. Her son, Walter, had died in 1890, just a couple of weeks shy of his twenty-first birthday, and her daughter, Olive, died three years before her mother. Olive's husband, Lewis Adams, hung himself in his barn just prior to Lettice's death.

Her love accompanied her to her final resting place in the Lower Bank cemetery. Next to her stone stands another, dedicated to her beloved husband, which doesn't begin to reveal the anguish she must have borne for so many years. It says simply, "Captain John Cale: Lost at Sea."

In the 1942 tax records, this house stands on a lot with 2060 River Road and is listed as still belonging to a Cale, another John, husband of Augusta (Weeks) Cale.

Harold Atherholt lived with his aunt in the old Captain Johnson house, the first from the corner of Route 542. Sometime after 1942, he gained ownership of this property. In the early 1940's, either when John Cale still owned it or after Mr. Atherholt succeeded to the ownership, one of Charlie Weber's twin sons and his wife rented it. In 1947, Atherholt sold it to Irvin Homiller and William Rathfon, father and uncle of the current owner and occupant, Warren Homiller. The Homillers have expanded the original structure somewhat over the years.

To Lettice

How long wilt thou forget me Lord.
  Must I forever mourn.
How long wilt thou with draw for and
  O, never to return!

Oh! hear and to my longing eyes
  Restore thy wanted Light;
Dawn on my spirit lest I sleep
  In death's most gloomy night.

Since I have always placed my trust
  Beneath thy mercy's wing,
Thy saving health will come; and then
  My heart with joy shall spring.

Written by Miss Lettice W. Winterbottom

This is another poem that was written in the back of the old ledger in the handwriting of Lettice Winterbottom. It eerily foreshadows the painful years she would have to endure alone.

The ledger in which these poems were written
is in the possession of Sarah (Cramer) Camillo.

Κεερ Ιt!

Yes for I love thee - I will keep it well -
This little lock of auburn hair! - and now
Methinks I saw it waving round thy brow,
And curling o'er thy forehead's gentle swell.
As when I kissed that forhead in thy youth.
And thou wirt pleased thro' blushed that suffered
Thy cheek, to such susceptions all unused.
Years have rolled on: yet do I not in truth
Forget that happy moment: and I feel
Such joys as only virtue can reveal,
When memory lifts the veil of by-gone year.
And spreads her long-loved pictures to her view!
I gazed on her enchantments, and the tears
That dim my sight, from my emotions true!

481

Courtesy of Sarah (Cramer) Camillo

The Home of Captain John C. Cale and His Wife, Lettice

Photograph by John Pearce

1995

The Johnson/Coup/Ayres/Bragg House
2047 River Road

1996

This tiny house was, at one time, the second house from the corner on the left side of River Road. Another old house, about which little is known, stood next to the new home of Barry Cavileer, 2039 River Road. By 1995, it had deteriorated so much that it was a hazard and the township insisted that the remains be removed. It was listed in 1942 as owned by Thomas Crane. This was the house in which Nathaniel (Uncle Thannie) Van Sant lived before moving across the street to the De Bow House when his brother, Isaac vacated it.

The history of this little house in the photograph above seems to have begun with Zachariah Johnson, at least a map of Lower Bank from the last quarter of the nineteenth century so labels it. Zachariah was the son of Mahlon and Hannah Johnson, who lived at 2055 River Road, where Zachariah was born. He is listed in the 1860 census as being thirteen years old and living with his parents. In 1870, he was twenty-three and still with his parents. In 1880, he is thirty-three (a marvelous consistency in his age, given the census penchant for being inaccurate as to ages) and married. His wife, Mary E. is twenty-nine, and the couple have two children: Carrie C. (7) and William (6). Neither Zachariah nor Mary have stones in the Lower Bank cemetery, so they may have moved away before their deaths.

During the 1940's, Albert Ayres and his family lived in this house. Ayres was related to the DeBow family, he being the half brother of Helen (Sibert) DeBow, the wife of Charles DeBow.

In the 1942 tax records, the name Richard Coup is attached with this property, much to the consternation of Lillian (DeBow) Fritz. She maintains that the Ayres family lived there at that time, as the dates attached to the photographs attest, and that they owned the house. Actually, Margie (Cavileer) Fox says that her husband, William, bought the property for Albert Ayres, who, in turn, paid him back over time.

According to Margie, the one she remembers living there before the Ayres moved in was a mean old German whom everyone locally called "Old Johann." All the kids in town avoided him like the plague. So who was Richard Coup? Lillian (DeBow) Fritz reveals: Richard Coup *was* "Old Johann."

Albert Ayres died in 1974 and was buried in Lower Bank. His wife, Mary, has her name on the same stone, but there is no death date. After the Ayres, several families rented the property. The Bradshaws lived here at some time since then, but Margie Fox doesn't remember exactly when.

The house is currently the home of the George Bragg family.

Courtesy of Lillian (DeBow) Fritz

Albert Ayres - 1944

Courtesy of Lillian (DeBow) Fritz

Mary Ayres - 1944

June Ayres, Lillian DeBow, and Aunt Mary Ayres
in front of the Ayres House

The Captain W. Watson Cale House
2060 River Road

1995

Photograph by John Pearce

The Cale family was one of the old families of Washington Township in the nineteenth century. Though the name has entirely disappeared from Lower Bank, there are still Cale descendants within the other river families. This house was purchased by Captain William Watson Cale, perhaps as his retirement home, in the 1870's, but the good captain never actually lived here. It is known that Captain Watson lived in Green Bank in his early days and in Crowleytown when he was older. It does seem, though, that he never did move into this house, despite the fact that the bulk of his family lived in Lower Bank.

William Watson Cale, son of Daniel and Rebecca Cale, was born on January 4, 1816. Watson followed the life of the sea, serving as captain on several local vessels.

He married Anna Maria Cavileer, daughter of John and Elizabeth (Weeks) Cavileer, and the couple had ten children. Their eldest, Daniel E. Cale married Mary Fredericka Adams (See 2090 RIVER ROAD).

Watson and Anna Maria Cale's second son was John C., born in 1843, who married Lettice Winterbottom and was lost at sea in 1878 (See 2044 RIVER ROAD).

Daughter Sarah Virginia (b. June 29, 1845) married John Little (no known relation to Robin Hood's sidekick). William G. was born in 1847 and died on February 26, 1865 at the age of eighteen. Reuben is simply listed in the Cavileer genealogy as "died and was buried at Green Bank," but he was born on February 11, 1849 and died on July 20, 1863. Frankin Pierce Cale was born

Courtesy of Sarah (Cramer) Camillo

Captain Daniel Cale
from a tintype

on October 26, 1852 and eventually married Matilda Jaunkie. Next came a little girl, born on September 26, 1853, but she died shortly after birth.

Rebecca Elizabeth was born on August 1, 1857 and married John Bevis Weeks. Many people remember her being called the "Second Rebecca," knowing that she bore the name of the baby that died. The curiosity is that the baby's gravestone in Green Bank bears the name "Mary," not "Rebecca."

Mary Ida was born on October 12, 1858. She married Nicholas V. Cramer (b. 1846; d. 1928) and died in 1950. The couple lived out on "The Island" in Lower Bank. Mary Ida was known by the Lower Bankers as "Aunt Mel" and by Father Beck as "Grannie Cale" (See THE CRAMER HOUSE ON 'THE ISLAND'). She outlived all her brothers and sisters.

On the 10th of November 1864, Carrie May became the last child born to Watson and Anna Maria. She married Alexander Gravatt, but her marriage wasn't a happy one. Her husband is said to have been an alcoholic who, one cold night in 1905, locked Carrie May out of the house. By the time she found shelter, she was so weakened physically that she came down with pneumonia and died soon after. Her wonderful husband didn't want his children any more than he wanted his wife, and he gave them away at graveside when Carrie May was buried in Green Bank. One son, Frank, rose above the meager circumstances of his childhood to eventually own the Steel Pier and quite a large part of the town of Atlantic City as well.

Watson Cale was a well-known and re-

Courtesy of Sarah (Cramer) Camillo

This is believed to be a portrait of
Captain William Watson Cale

spected sea captain who sailed his vessels many a long mile over the ocean waves. A list of his vessels would include the *Mary Clinton*, the *John West*, the ill-fated *Walter Palmer*, and the *Hazel Del*.

It was Watson Cale who was responsible for introducing Otto Wobbar to the Mullica valley and Green Bank for the first time. Otto had signed on to Captain Cale's ship and was with her when it put into New Gretna in 1858. Cale persuaded the young man to come home with him to Green Bank where Otto met his future first wife, Hannah Gauntt. Otto continued to sign aboard vessels captained by Watson Cale for many years.

Watson Cale served as Tax Collector in 1858 through 1861. All of these meetings were held in Lower Bank at the Samuel Weeks' Tavern just up Old Church Road. When the meeting shifted to Sebastian Crowley's Tavern at Green Bank in 1863, Watson Cale's name doesn't appear. At the 1876 meeting held at the Herman Boarding House (the Herman City Hotel of Rapp and Koster), he was elected to the Township Committee. The records for 1877 through 1886 are missing, but a short note in the March 10, 1881 a Mount Holly newspaper mentions that he was elected to the Board of Chosen Freeholders from Washington Township.

Three things indicate that Watson never actually moved into this house as he intended. First, he could not have been elected to the Washington Township Committee in 1876 if he lived here because Lower Bank was part of Randolph Township from 1870-1893. A second indicator is his 1881 election to the Chosen Freeholders from Washington Township. Still a third is that he is listed as a resident of Washington Township in the 1860 through 1880 censuses. Though the rest of the Cale family is associated with Lower Bank, it seems that the town cannot lay claim to the patriarch. Captain Watson never actually lived in Lower Bank himself but remained in Crowleytown, when he relocated from Green Bank.

Watson and Anna Maria suffered great tragedy in their lives. In 1853, they lost their infant daughter. Their second son, John, was lost at sea in 1878 at the age of thirty-five, leaving a grieving wife and three young children. Their third son, William, was apparently drowned in Great Bay at the age of eighteen. In "Granny" Cramer's interview with Father Beck, she says that *two* of her brothers were lost at sea when their father's ship went down. There seems to be few references to Franklin Pierce Cale, and it may be that he accompanied his brother, John, on that fateful voyage that claimed both their father's ship and their lives.   Unfortunately for Aunt Mel's story, another source says that Franklin Pierce did indeed die on a ship, but that vessel was in New York harbor, and the young man died of appendicitis. If so, there were two grieving widows in the Cale family.

Captain Watson Cale died on April 23, 1884. Anna Maria followed her husband eight years later on March 4, 1892. Both are buried in Green Bank. As to this house at 2060 River Road, memories recall it as being "John Cale (II)'s House" in the 1940's, but no one remembers *him* actually *living* here either. As far back as living memory goes, the house was rented to a number of tenants, but the 1942 tax map shows this house as "John Cale's" and the lot includes his Uncle John's house at 2044.

Art Conrad, who succeeded Clifford Terry as the Superintendent of the Green Bank State Forest, bought the house in the 1940's. Conrad actually lived in the Superintendent's House on River Road in Green Bank and rented this house to a series of tenants. Thus, through much of its history, this old house, intended as the retirement home of one of the area's most well-known sea captains, has been rented out to tenants. In 1996, the Frank Cerreto family lives here.

The Captain Mahlon Johnson House
2055 River Road

Photograph by John Pearce

1995

Captain Mahlon Johnson, the brother of Captain Levi Johnson, built this home on a portion of the Johnson family property in the first half of the nineteenth century. Mahlon and Levi were anomg the first captains to command ships which sailed with Batsto glass in their hold. Both married women named Hannah. Ella Johnson, Captain Levi and Hannah's granddaughter, noted that the husbands' names were always joined with their names to distinguish the two women: Hannah Levi and Hannah Mahlon.

Mahlon Johnson was born in 1804 and died on August 2, 1872. Hannah (Jervis) was born in 1811 and died sixteen years after her husband on the 28th of February, 1888. Both rest in the Lower Bank cemetery.

The house was later purchased by Harold Augustus Maxwell, the son of Captain William Augustus and Angeline Adelia (Jones) Maxwell of Wading River, and his wife, yet a third "Hannah," Hannah Elizabeth Matilda (Cavileer), daughter of Caleb Napoleon and Laura Jane (Headley) Cavileer. Harold was born in Wading River in 1893. His wife, Benjamin Cavileer's sister and aunt of Marge (Cavileer) Fox and Doris (Cavileer) Rider, was born three years later in 1896. Her birthplace was at 5 Cavileer Lane and his was at his father's house on Turtle Creek Road.

The couple had four children, Violet Elizabeth, Laura Adelia, Harold Augustus, Jr., and Estelle Vivian.

There is a charming love story that was recorded about this pair. Hannah Cavileer of Lower Bank fell in love with William and Angie's son, Harold, and found a rather unique way of telling him so. She carved his initials on the back of a box turtle and started it off in his direction.

Unfortunately, the turtle had something else in mind and went off in another direction. Hannah had to communicate with Harold Maxwell in more conventional ways. The happy pair was married on the fifteenth of June, 1917. Turtles are slow, we know, but this one was ridiculous. Forty years later, that same turtle ended up at the home of Harold and Hannah Maxwell in Lower Bank, and Harold finally got the message so lovingly carved those many years ago! Harold hugged his wife with love and sent the turtle on its way. Ten years later, the old turtle showed up at the Maxwell residence once again, much to the enjoyment of everyone in Lower Bank.

Harold served as postmaster of Lower Bank from 1940 to 1955 when the post office was closed, and the town of Lower Bank became part of a rural delivery route out of Egg Harbor City. Harold and Hannah also kept a little store on the first floor of their home which provided the local children with a source of candy and their parents with emergency staples.

A longtime member of the Lower Bank Fire Company, Harold was still serving as secretary at the age of eighty!

The Lower Bank Fire Company gave him a testimonial on his 76th birthday on May 30, 1969, at which he read the following poem:

> *You tell me I am getting old, I tell you that is not so.*
> *The house I live in is worn out, and that of course I know.*
> *It has been in use for a long, long while, it has weathered many a gale.*
> *I'm not surprised that you think it is getting somewhat frail.*
> *The color is changing on the roof, the windows getting dim,*
> *The walls a bit transparent and looking rather thin.*
> *The foundation is not as steady, as once it used to be.*
> *My house is getting shaky, but my house is not me.*
> *My few short years can't make me old, I feel I'm in my youth.*
> *Eternity lies just ahead, a place of joy and truth.*
> *I expect to live forever there, life will go on, its grand.*
> *You tell me I'm getting old, you just don't understand.*
> *The dweller in my little house is young, happy and gay,*
> *Just starting on a life to last throughout eternal day.*
> *You only see the outside, which is all that most folks see.*
> *You tell me I'm getting old. You have mixed my house with me!*
>
> (Author Unknown)

Hannah (Cavileer) Maxwell's eternal day began in 1983. Harold followed two years later in 1985. Both Harold's ninety-two year old "house" and Hannah's eighty-seven year old one found their final rest in Lower Bank's cemetery. We rejoice that they were "just starting on a life to last throughout eternal day."

This house now belongs to the Francis Ford, Jr. family.

The Johnson Cottage
2077 River Road

Photograph by John Pearce

1995

The Johnson Cottage stands on a portion of the old Johnson homestead next to the "new" Lower Bank church. It is one of the older houses in Lower Bank but its true age is obscured by late nineteenth century details. Mathias Johnson IV (b. 1778) and his wife, Ann (Homan), lived in a little cabin quite a way back in the woods behind this house. They had eleven children, and, after the birth of their fifth child, Daniel, in 1809, they decided to build a bigger house for their family. Consequently, they built this house the following year.

Their son, Levi Johnson, "modernized" this delightful little house, and his sister, Achsah (Johnson) Gale/ Pharo, apparently lived here for some years. She was succeeded by her son, Henry, and his wife, Maria (Oliver).

After they moved elsewhere, the house was rented out, sometimes to the Methodist preachers who were serving the Lower Bank Circuit, and once to William Spafford Leek and his wife, Rebecca (Cramer). The Leeks lived here when their son, Charlie (C.P. Leek of boatyard fame), was a baby. Since Charles Platt Leek II was born in 1877, they would have lived in this house at the beginning of the last quarter of the nineteenth century. Levi and Hannah Johnson's daughter, Mary Ella, was married to William Spafford Leek's brother, Charles P. Leek, so it was still "all in the family."

When Levi and Hannah's granddaughter, Ada, and her husband, Will Kemble, needed a home, they were given this house in which to raise their sons, Karel and Edmund. After the death of her parents, the Kembles moved into the old homestead which stood just down the River Road.

During the late 1930's and early '40's, Charles Reginald Underhill lived in this house with his wife, Ada (Johnson) Kemble's sister, Ella. Charlie Underhill and "Uncle" Will Kemble shared more than wives who were sisters, granddaughters of Captain Levi Johnson. Charlie and Will also shared a love of technological invention.

Charlie Underhill was born in Chappaqua, New York, and was mostly self-educated. He had been born deaf, so he couldn't go to college. Instead he took correspondence courses in mathematics, engineering, and physics.

From 1892 to the end of the century, he worked at Western Electric. He then took on a job as chief electrical engineer with the Varley Duplex Magnet Company of Jersey City and Providence, Rhode Island. Westinghouse later employed him as a consulting engineer, as did several other large companies. He lectured in several of the top universities in the county and even invented telegraphic signalling devices.

Mr. Underhill and Mr. Kemble were, technologically speaking, two peas in a pod, but they parted company in the area of philosophy. Mrs. Ella (Johnson) Underhill provided Father Beck with many details concerning early life in Lower Bank. It was she who came up with the 1810 date for the old church (which was wrong), and the story about it being a school before being made into a church. She also came up with the story about Sam Weeks, the church Bible, and the locked door.

She remembered that Job Weeks lived up the road that heads northward off of Route 542 at the end of Church Road. She even retained the details that his children were Job, Sam, Hannah, and Josephus. Originally bearing the name of Job Weeks himself, that sand trail through the woods now goes by the name of his son, Josephus, or "Seaf" Weeks, who stayed with his father at the old homestead and lived there with his daughters, Louie and Flora. Job Weeks (now Seaf Weeks) Road originally was a direct route to Harrisville.

Mrs. Underhill was a wealth of information about Lower Bank to Henry Beck, but that wasn't her only notoriety. She was also rather famous for having spotted the Jersey Devil on one of his noted visits to Lower Bank. In fact, she even claimed Lower Bank, not Leed's Point, was his birthplace!

Ada (Johnson) Kemble, "Mother Kemble", as she was called by the locals, moved back into this little cottage and gave up the old homestead for her son, Karel's, family after the death of her husband, Will.

Jessie (Forman) Lewis of Green Bank remembers visiting "Mother Kemble" in this house. Ada (Johnson) Kemble was a tiny, little lady and her house was perfect for her. "Even the furniture was tiny," Jessie says, "but everything was perfectly exquisite! It was just like a doll house!"

The home belongs to Michael Achey in 1996.

The Lower Bank Methodist Church

The "New" Lower Bank Church
The date of this photograph is unknown but it is probably from the very early part of the twentieth century.

Despite the story that the Methodist parishioners built this building when Sam Weeks purloined the Bible and locked the doors of the old one on Old Church Road, the years just don't add up. If there was a quarrel over money, it must have taken place at the end of the 1840's, and the fact is that this building wasn't constructed until twenty-five years later.

Frank Stanger, in *The Methodist Trail in New Jersey*, relates that the Board of Trustees of the Lower Bank church met on October 9, 1874 for the express purpose of discussing the construction of a new building for the congregation. The church had grown over the years, and the old Meeting House was no longer adequate for their Sunday services. Stanger gives the names of the members of the board as follows: John Cavileer, president; Joshiah Laur, treasurer; N. D. Van Sant, secretary; Levi Johnson, Augustus Johnson, Joseph Weeks, and J. Alfred Allen.

John Cavileer was probably John III, husband of Armenia (Johnson) Cavileer, who would eventually build the large Victorian home on the river. John was forty-three that year. Joshiah [sic] Laur is a puzzle. There is no one by that name on either the 1870 or the 1880 census. The closest would be Josiah Lane, the son of Peter and Rebecca Lane, who would have been thirty-three in 1874. N.D. Van Sant is probably Nathaniel D. Van Sant, son of the Rev. Nicholas and Mercy (Davis) Van Sant, the retired minister of the church, forty-eight in 1874. Levi Johnson lived in the Johnson homestead, a portion of which would be sold to the congregation for the new building. Levi was sixty-six. Augustus Johnson lived on the corner of River Road and Old Church Road across the street from Levi and was seventy-one. Joseph Weeks was probably Josephus Weeks, son of Job Weeks. J. Alfred Allen was the son of Jesse and Hannah (Weeks) Allen and was forty-eight.

The "New" Lower Bank Church

This photograph was obviously taken at a very early date. Though it is winter, the trees appear about the same size as those in the photograph on the preceeding page, which may indicate that it was taken about the same time.

Stanger also gives the name of the minister at that time: L. M. Atkinson. The Rev. Louis Atkinson was the husband of Julia Lane, daughter of Rebecca (Van Sant) and Peter Lane and granddaughter of the Rev. Nicholas and Mercy (Davis) Van Sant. The list of clergy serving the circuit (See GREEN BANK) shows a James E. Lake serving there at the time, but it may be wrong. More likely though, The Rev. Atkinson had retired but still lived in Lower Bank, as did The Rev. Van Sant, and The Rev. Lake was actually serving the circuit.

Stanger says that the lot for the new church was purchased from Levi and Hannah Johnson for $75.00. Local tradition says he *gave* the lot to his congregation, but there was certainly a fee exchanged. Perhaps the Johnsons put the money in the following Sunday's offering. The total cost for the construction of the church was $1,925.23. Stanger also records that the Ladies' Aid helped to finance the building. They certainly must have sold a lot of cakes to make that kind of money out of Lower Bank, but times were still prosperous for the river traffic, even though the unseen sword was hanging over their heads at that very time.

The cornerstone gives the date of construction: 1875. The Reverend Louis Atkinson, who probably still lived in his house on "The Island" at the time, laid that cornerstone. If he was well enough, the elderly Reverend Nicholas Van Sant himself was no doubt present for the festivities as well.

The Reverend Van Sant, founder of the congregation, died in 1879 and was buried from this new church, rather than from his little old building beside the cemetery. His wife, Mercy, must have participated in the decision, but one must contemplate whether the faithful old man would not rather have been laid to rest from the structure he had helped to construct and in which he had preached so many times over the years. It probably just wasn't large enough to hold the crowds that had come to celebrate his entrance into glory on that day so many years ago.

Photograph by John Pearce

The "New" Lower Bank Methodist Church - 1995

The Captain Jacob Johnson House and Store
2081 River Road

Courtesy of Budd Wilson, Jr.

The Jacob Johnson Store - circa 1910
The horse-drawn vehicle was either a water or a kerosene wagon.
The unpaved roads became so dusty in the summer that water from tank vehicles like these was sprayed on them to keep air breathable. A very similar type of tank vehicle was used to deliver kerosene.
Budd Wilson, Jr. says, that from his knowledge, it was probably a kerosene wagon.

Jacob Johnson, son of Mathias Johnson IV and Ann (Homan) Johnson was born in what is now called the Johnson Cottage at 2077 River Road on November 20, 1814. He married Margaret Jane Leeds (b. 3/14/1819). The 1860 census lists the couple as having six children: Alice (19), Brainard (17), Lewis S. (11), Rachel (9), Stephen (8) and Jacob E. (3). He was forty-six and she forty-one in that last year of peace before the outbreak of the Civil War.

Jacob became a sea captain like his brothers, John, Mahlon, and Levi, and may have been the first captain to carry glass from Batsto. He built this home and store on a portion of the old Johnson homestead property. When he retired from the sea, he set up a store next to his home. This he must have done prior to the 1860 census, for he is listed as a merchant in those records. Edmund Kemble, son of Ada (Johnson) and "Fritz" Kemble, said that, during the Johnson era, the little building to the left of the store was used for travelling salesmen who came to ply their wares in the area, but the building *was* the store at a later date and may have been so under Captain Johnson. Margaret Jane (Leeds) Johnson died in Lower Bank on May 6, 1869, but no record could be found of Jacob Johnson's death. He is still listed as a retail grocer in the 1880 census.

It seems as if someone continued to run the store and post office after Jacob's death, but I have been unable to find out just who this was. In about 1926, Lizzie (Garrison) Allen served as postmistress and kept the store here. Lizzie was the daughter of the Rev. J. Swayne and Julia (Lane) Garrison. She was the second wife of Charles Taylor Allen, who died in 1922.

Lizzie's store was in the smaller building, and she lived in the larger one with her sister, Ella (Garrison) Cramer and her neice, Ruth, who later married Bill Montgomery. Lizzie (Garrison) Allen had been the postmistress at Cape May and held the same position in Lower Bank until her retirement about 1940, when Harold Maxwell took over as postmaster. He continued the post office here for a few months until he was able to convert the porch on his home at 2055 River Road into the new post office and store. This is the home of the Paul Seybold family as of this writing.

The Captain Levi Johnson House
(No Longer in Existence)
2085 River Road

Courtesy of Diane Kemble

This house stood on River Road, across from Church Road for a hundred and sixty years before it was deliberately set on fire as part of a robbery and murder just a few years ago. It was built on a portion of what had been the original homestead of Mathias Johnson, the first Johnson in Lower Bank. Landowners, entrepreneurs, and sea captains, the Johnson family was one of the most influential families in the Mullica valley, yet their memory is almost gone from the land they had made their own for almost two centuries.

To trace the property back to the first Johnson in Lower Bank: Mathias Johnson, Sr. bought this property for his homestead farm probably in 1769, though possibly as early as 1740, and his son, Jacob, acquired it on the death of his father. Jacob's will was written on August 13, 1778 and probated on November 24th of the same year gave the land to his sons, Mathias IV and John. Captain Levi G. Johnson purchased this property from his father, Mathias IV with five acres of ground for $110 and built this house in 1832. He extended it by additions in 1860.

Levi was a sea captain and carried iron products in his vessels from Batsto to New York City. He was supposed to have been the captain to load aboard his ship the first glass produced at Batsto, but there is a slight uncertainty in this. The first recorded vessel to sail with Batsto glass in her hold was the *John Wurts* in 1846. Budd Wilson, Jr.'s list of vessels mentioned in the Batsto Store Books lists the *John Wurts* as under the command of or owned by "J" Johnson in 1847. It is entirely possible that either John or Jacob Johnson had bought their brother's vessel by 1847, and that it really had been Captain Levi who was at the helm when the first Batsto glass came down the Mullica in the year before.

In any case, Levi Johnson is mentioned three times in the Batsto Store Books as owner/master of vessels during the mid-nineteenth century: the schooner *Confidense* [sic] is the first, in the year 1830. Then comes the schooner *Henry Clay* in 1832 and again in 1839.

It was Levi who provided land near the homestead for both the school in 1850 and for the new church in 1874. He was born in 1808 and married Hannah Wilson, daughter of Joseph and Sarah (Howell) Wilson, on the February

6, 1831 at Pleasant Mills. They had nine children: Walter, Lemuel (1833-1909), Anna, Emma, Sarah Jane, Joseph Edmund, Arthur Mathias, Henry, and Mary Ella.

Henry Charlton Beck says that Levi had his first boat built in the yard which used to stand hard by the river where River Road turns to follow the Mullica. Naming the vessel after his sons, the *Walter Lemuel*, Captain Levi planned to carry glass from Batsto to New York for Jesse Richards. The only way this can be accurate is if Levi were serving as master aboard the *Confidense* [sic], the *Henry Clay*, and perhaps the *John Wurts* and did not own them himself, which is a good possibility, of course. There is another problem with Beck's tale as well.

According to Beck, the launching ran into a hitch. The year was 1856, and Captain Johnson's wife had made a special chicken potpie for all those involved in the launching, but John Hall, who had helped build the boat, took a note from Samuel Weeks and held up the ceremonies for an unpaid bill of five hundred dollars. Jesse Richards was in such need for another vessel to haul his products that he hurried down to Lower Bank with the cash as soon as he was notified of the problem, and the launching finally got underway. The potpie, however, was cold by that time. It makes a nice story, but Jesse Richards died in 1854. He would have had a difficult time hurrying from Batsto to Lower Bank with the necessary money two years after he

Anna Johnson

died. Another interesting point is that the *Walter Lemuel* is not mentioned in the Batsto Store Books. In 1856, the cupola at Batsto ceased operating, and the glass factory produced nothing in 1857. If Levi built the *Walter Lemuel* in 1856, he was not depending on Batsto to provide shipping goods.

Captain Levi traded up, some years later, by selling the *Walter Lemuel* and buying the *Walter Palmer*. With this vessel, he engaged in the coastal trade as far away as Boston and Charleston. After Captain Levi retired from the sea, Captain Watson Cale served as her captain. The *Walter Palmer* had a rather inglorious end, however. While under the command of Captain John Cale, a steamer apparently hit the vessel and cut her in two, or at least that's the version of the story told by Levi's granddaughter, Ella.

River Road looking north at the intersection with Old Church Road
The Levi Johnson Homestead is on the right.

Beck records that Captain Levi experimented with raising potatoes during the Civil War, much to the disdain of his neighbors. His first harvest was over a thousand bushels, for which he received a dollar each, having the last laugh on his fellow Lower Bankers. He also bought bogs from William Sooy and began cultivating cranberries.

Ada (Johnson) Kemble remembered visiting her mother's sister, Aunt Becky, and her Grandmother Spain, when she was a child. She told of a time when her grandmother told her Uncle Levi she would like to go to church. He hitched up the wagon, put a rocking chair in the back of it, and placed Ada's grandmother in the chair. They set out for the church, but, unbeknown to Levi, the rocking chair walked itself to the rear of the wagon bed and slipped off into the road, grandmother and all! Levi didn't hear the chair hit the ground, so the wagon kept going down the road. When he finally looked around to check on the old lady, he found the wagon empty. He stopped the horses, jumped off the driver's seat, saw the rocking chair down the road a considerable distance, and ran back as fast as he could to see if Grandmother Spain had been hurt. When they got to her, they found her, not at all disturbed by the mishap, rocking away in her chair in the middle of the road, with her hands folded on her lap, cheerfully singing the hymn: "The Lord Will Take Care of Me."

Captain Levi's last years were not the happy ones he deserved. His granddaughter, Ella (Johnson) Underhill remembered that he went blind some time before he died. He had bought two mules when Ella was two years old. Every time her father, Joseph Edmund Johnson, wanted to figure out how old the mules were, he always started counting from his daughter's age. In later years, Ella summered in Lower Bank before moving here again on a permanent basis, and when the local young people threw a birthday party for her, they always said they were celebrating the mules' birthday.

Ella remembered her grandfather, Capt. Levi, going into the stalls and feeling around with his cane. She marvelled that the mules seemed to sense that he was blind and never kicked if he hit one of them accidentally. Hannah Johnson died in 1888. Her husband, the renowned Captain Levi, died a year later. Both were buried in Lower Bank.

Levi and Hannah's son, Joseph Edmund Johnson and his wife, Henrietta Allaire (Spain), succeeded his parents in this house. They had five children: Florence, Ella, Ada, Josie, and Walter. Ella married Charles Underhill

Courtesy of Diane Kemble

The Levi Johnson Homestead

and lived in the Johnson Cottage. Ada married William F. (Fritz) Kemble. Walter married Ruby Miller.

Joseph E. Johnson was a sea captain like his father, and he joined his old companion of the sea, Captain Dan Cale for a photograph which is included in this chapter on Lower Bank (see 2090 River Road). Captain Joseph died in 1921 at the age of eighty-one. Henrietta, his wife, had died in 1903.

Captain Levi had left his property to his children on an equal basis by his will, probated on January 9, 1890. Although, Ada's father, Joseph E. Johnson, had lived here with his family, the property still belonged to the estate of his father. When Captain Joe died, the surviving siblings signed over their shares to their sister, Mary Ella (Johnson) Leek. Ada (Johnson) Kemble acquired this property from her aunt, Mary Ella, not from her father.

Levi and Hannah's granddaughter, whose family would later make their house their home, was swept off her feet by one of the most unique men ever to have found his way to the Mullica valley. As Henry Beck tells it in *Jersey Genesis*, William Fritz Kemble was a graduate of Drew Seminary when, in 1898, he climbed a Pocono mountain near the Delaware Water Gap and confronted his God. From that time on, metaphysics rather than religion governed his thinking. His father was the Reverend Samuel T. Kemble, a Philadelphia preacher, who could paint glowing images of the Arch Fiend to terrorize his flock. Kemble came down from the mountain convinced that his father's message was all hogwash.

Courtesy of Jessie Lewis

Ada Johnson Kemble

He met and married Levi Johnson's granddaughter, Ada Hope. Going into business as a real estate promoter with her father in 1904, the two men bought land in North Yonkers and Hastings-on-Hudson, then resold it for a huge profit. Lower Bankers heard rumors he and Ada lived in a big mansion overlooking the Hudson River. He was riding high when a panic in 1907 made the bottom drop out of real estate, and he ended up broke. It was during this first decade of the twentieth century that Ada and Will had two sons, Karel and Edmund.

It was also about this time that he started to develop his ideas on employee testing. Professors of psychology at Penn and Columbia, however, looked down their educated noses at him and sniffed. The Baltimore and Ohio Railroad and the Underwood Typewriter Company didn't feel the same way, though, and Kemble was soon using his testing methods on their employees. Will Kemble sought the advice of no less a personage than Thomas Eva Edison. Edison was delighted with the idea of some standardized means of psychological testing that could help businessmen with employee selection. During 1915, he worked on plans for prefabricated houses but discarded

them because the resulting houses were not beautiful. In 1917, he finished a book on psychological testing and published *Choosing Employes By Test*, to the acclaim of the international press. His ideas were hailed by all the leading business magazines, but, as luck would have it, World War One intervened.

Turned down by the army because of his age, Kemble went prospecting for oil in Louisiana. Dropping his oil leases, he then turned to journalism, working for McClure's as a columnist. He submitted plans to Washington for armored trucks that were acknowledged by the government, then ignored. He decided to become a landscape architect, setting up the Beaux Arts Nurseries on his father-in-law's Lower Bank prop-

Courtesy of Jessie Lewis

From a Christmas Card - c. mid-1950's

erty. He, Ada, Karel, and Edmund moved into the Johnson Cottage which still stands next to the "new" Lower Bank church. When her father died, the Kembles moved into the old homestead.

He got the contract for the Marvin Gardens development in Atlantic City, expanded his Lower Bank nursery, and bought a new one in Long Branch. Once again, the bottom dropped out of the economy, and no one was buying ornamental shrubs. He lost the Long Branch nursery but managed to salvage the Johnson homestead.

Eleven years after he had published his first book, Kemble tried for success again with a manuscript entitled *Taxless Government*, but this time, he couldn't find anyone who wanted to print it. The world of the Twenties was just not ready for a government run without taxes.

His greatest creation philosophically was "The Circular Equation." This appears to have been an esoteric analysis of the existence of humankind that was quite abstruse. As the Great Depression gripped the country in ever tighter coils, Kemble decided that all ideas of social structure had to be misguided. Somehow there had to be an alternative to making money, saving money, and losing money. Consequently, Lower Bank became the site of an experiment in American collectivism. His "Kolektovist Kolony," called "Fellowship Colony," worked the land as a farm, trading for needed supplies which they couldn't produce. The government even loaned them six cows and a bull. Kemble called himself the "Kolektovist Keeper of Heaven, New Jersey."

Unfortunately, government involvement was its downfall. Roosevelt came up with the Works Progress Administration and the Civilian Conservation Corps which provided real wages and meals for out-of-work men and set up camps within walking distance of the Kolektovist Kolony. That put an end to Will Kemble's experiment.

Lower Bankers were a tolerant sort, and they simply looked the other way when Kemble's ideas seemed radical and perhaps even rather dangerous. Other small towns would have ridden the wierdo out of town on a rail, but Lower Bankers actually liked Will Kemble. Besides, he had married one of their own, and they figured "live and let live." In *Taxless Government*, Kemble had postulated that "Government indulges in material theft when it lays upon us needless taxes to support a great body of leisurely working people when we have to work so earnestly ourselves." Lower Bankers kept on working - and paying their taxes.

Perhaps one of the reasons Will Kemble was respected in this little town, despite his aberrations, was for his role as the town Santa Claus. Evelyn Cavileer Bash, a cousin of David Cavileer, published an article some time back on her childhood memories of Lower Bank's Santa Claus, and her words still bring a tear to the eye.

She writes that her first "encounter with the Country Santa Claus" was when she was about five or six years old and her family was visiting her paternal grandparents, Captain James Veldrin and his wife, Rachel Matilda (Maxwell) Cavileer in their home at 2112 River Road. She narrates that she was in the midst of hanging her stocking on the mantle when she heard the sound of sleigh bells. Even at her tender age, she was surprised because there was no snow on the ground and no one around town owned a sleigh.

Little Evelyn immediately thought it was Santa Claus, of course, and ran to the window, when what to her wondering eyes should appear, no, not a sleigh and eight tiny reindeer, but a Model-T Ford. As she tells the story,

> As I stared out the window, a man's face suddenly appeared on the other side of the glass. I hadn't seen him approach. I was staring into a lean face and close-cropped beard. On the other side of the window, he was staring back at me. I screamed in terror and ran to hide behind the sofa. . . .
>
> Dad headed for the front door. Before he reached it, I heard the door knocker. I watched from my hiding place as Dad threw open the door. On the threshold stood a very tall, thin man in a long fur goat, galoshes and a small-brimmed wool hat pulled down over his grey eyes.
>
> 'Is there a little girl here named Evelyn?' the man asked. . . .
>
> 'Can't stay,' the man answered. 'I've got to be on my way. There are a lot of presents for me to deliver to boys and girls of Lower Bank tonight. . . .
>
> 'Evelyn!' my father called again. 'Don't keep Santa Claus waiting. Hurry! Come now!'
>
> Reluctantly, I rose from my hiding place and walked slowly toward the tall man whose head almost touched the chandelier. I walked as if mesmerized, my eyes staring into his.
>
> He held out a package. 'Now you be a good little girl and I'll see you next year,' he said. . .
>
> I heard the car engine start and watched as the Ford crunched down the gravel road. . .
>
> 'It's a pretty little baby doll. Look! I held the doll for the grown-ups to see. 'But he wasn't really Santa Claus, was he, Dad?'
>
> 'He wasn't the Santa Claus you're used to seeing in the picture books,' Dad answered. 'But believe me, little girl, he's as real a Santa Claus as you'll ever find anywhere. He's the Country Santa Claus - the Santa Claus of Lower Bank.' (Courtesy of David Cavileer)

When Evelyn Cavileer grew up enough to understand, she learned all about Will Kemble's eccentricities, but, as she concludes her tale: "Every Christmas, no matter where I am, the vision of Will Kemble as the Country Santa Claus lives on in my memory."

I long for those days when things seemed so simple, when children were children and didn't have to worry about being sexually abused or kidnapped, a time when a tall, thin man with a scruffy beard and a wool hat brought her a little doll at Christmas, and taught her a lesson about the season of love that she would never, ever forget. Will Kemble died a good many years ago, and so have most of the children to whom he brought gifts that he couldn't afford in the midst of the Depression, but there is still a Santa Claus in Lower Bank. If Evelyn (Cavileer) Bash could be a little girl for one more Christmas Eve, she could still stand at her grandfather's door (though now the house belongs to Chick Croce) and see a strange man through the window. There wouldn't be a Model-T parked outside now, and perhaps Lower Bank's Santa Claus would seem familiar somehow, for today, Lower Bank's Santa is her cousin, David Cavileer.

When Will died, mother Ada moved back into the Johnson Cottage, and her son, Karel, lived with his wife and three children in the old homestead. Tragedy was to strike the family later in life, though. Karel served a term as mayor of Washington Township and was one of the founding members of the Lower Bank Volunteer Fire Company. He had inherited some of his father's unique mode of reasoning, however. Hans Lewis of Green Bank remembers trying to get Karel to give a donation to the ambulance squad one day, a donation which Karel refused. It seems he felt that there was absolutely no need for an ambulance. As long as you had a car, you could drive to the hospital yourself, if you had to go. An ambulance? Hrumph! Waste of good money!

Marie Kemble passed away before the final scenes of tragedy were performed. In the early hours of New Year's Day in 1994, some local young men broke into the old homestead with robbery on their mind. They murdered Karel in his bed and set a blaze which burned the house down around him. One young man turned himself in to the police on the urging of his father and was convicted, but he never would reveal his accomplices. When Karel was murdered, over two centuries of Johnsons in Lower Bank came to an end.

Karel and Marie's son, Doug, the little boy in the photograph both above and below, was killed in an automobile accident in the spring of 1995. Karel's daughter, Diane, lives with her family in New Hampshire, and Hope is in California. Edmund, 89 years old in 1996, is living out his last years in Asbury Park. A single sign near the site of the old Johnson homestead announces forlornly, "Beaux Arts Nurseries." It's a sad parting we take of the Johnsons of Lower Bank.

Memories of Christmas Past
The Kemble Children: Diane, Douglas, and Hope

The Lower Bank School

The Weeks Family of Southern New Jersey records that:

On Jan. 26, 1850, Levi G. Johnson and wife, sold to Job Weeks, Samuel Weeks, Jr., Nicholas Vansant [sic] and four others, as trustees 35 feet square on the northeast side of Main Road nearly opposite Hall's store, at Lower Bank, Washington Twp., for a school house with the privilege of holding meetings of the Methodist Episcopal Society, also temperance meetings, Sabath Schools, political meetings of both parties, Democrats and Whigs. Job Weeks, Jr. was a witness (BuDY4:97).

For almost seventy years, the children of Lower Bank attended school in this small building on River Road. To find the original site, stand in front of 2090 River Road, facing southeast. The school stood on the other side of the road a little to the left. Johnson family records indicate that Levi Johnson donated the land and six other families contributed $25.00 each out of their own pockets to build the school.

During those years, all the children walked to school and had classes in the same small room. Harriet Lane taught in this little building before she married Watson Sooy of Green Bank. She was the daughter of Rebecca and Peter Lane and the sister of Julia Lane, who lived on "The Island." The last schoolmaster was Lewis Adams, grandson of Stephen Adams, who lived on River Road below the bridge.

After the consolidated Green Bank School was opened in 1920, the Lower Bank Methodist Church bought the old school and used it as a community hall. The church sponsored Ice Cream Socials and other town activities for young and old alike, but maintaining the building became expensive for the small congregation.

When Fred (Fritz) Noyes, Jr. offered to take it off their hands, they jumped at the chance. Fred, Jr. and his wife, Ethel, were developing the Historic Towne of Smithville over in Atlantic County. They were interested in acquiring old, historic structures as part of their "village," and the church people were glad to get themselves out from under the responsibility of maintaining it. Fred moved the old school building to his "Historic Smithville" where it remains today as part of the complex.

Courtesy of Thomas Cramer

The Old Lower Bank School
in its original location on River Road

Courtesy of Lillian (DeBow) Fritz

The Children of Lower Bank and their Schoolmaster - c. 1900

Front Row (L. to R.): Schoolteacher Lewis Adams, Hannah Cavileer, Myrtle Cavileer, Viola DeBow, Virginia Adams, Eddie Johnson, Lewis Bozarth, Douglas Cavileer, Rutherford Barnett, Curtis Cavileer, Milton Ford.

Second Row: Beatrice Adams, Margaret Cavileer, Vivian O'Dell, Esther Bozarth, Adina Barnett, Paul Bozarth, Charlie DeBow.

Third Row: Jesse Cavileer, Alzena Barnett, John Cavileer, Eugene Barnett.

504

The Captain "Gus" Johnson Home
64 Old Church Road

1995

Photograph by John Pearce

This nineteenth century house was the home of Captain Augustus "Gus" Johnson, the son of William Johnson (1747-1818) and grandson of Mathias I (d. 1778). Augustus S. Johnson was born on August 29, 1803, married Sarah Ann Bush (b. May 31, 1794), and made this house and homestead his home. Captain Johnson made a couple of very judicious purchases of land until he owned several hundred acres along the river and many additional acres more inland.

Augustus Johnson's name first appears on the list of township officeholders at the second disputed meeting in 1832 as a member of the Township Committee. At the third meeting, his name is still on the list. The following year, though, his name isn't on the list and doesn't appear again until 1846 when he was Judge of Elections. In 1847, he is again judge, as he was in 1848 and 1849. In 1850, he was Township Assessor. In 1854, he was Judge of Elections again but then didn't serve until 1859, when he was judge for yet another year. In 1860, Jesse E. Broom was elected judge but apparently couldn't or wouldn't serve, for the notation appears after his name: "A.S. Johnson appointed." The year 1861 saw him reelected as judge. He didn't serve in 1862 but became Overseer of the Poor in 1863. That is the last year his name appears on the lists. Sarah Bush Johnson died on the fifteenth of May, 1879. Augustus passed away on September 7, 1896, having celebrated his ninety-third birthday!

Augustus and Sarah's older daughter, Armenia, was born on March 3, 1834, married John Cavileer III and was given almost the entire riverfront from the present Coulter house at 2121 River Road to the original Leek Boatworks beyond the bridge. Their younger daughter, Phebe M. is listed in 1860 as being twenty-three.

No further record could be found of Phebe M. Johnson, but the next owner was a Margaret Allen. The 1860 census lists a Margaret Allen (29) with a daughter, Gertrude (3), but her husband's name does not appear. In 1870, she's added a Margaret (13) and an Edward (4) to her family, but still no husband is listed. In 1880, her son, Montgomery (b. 1866), appears as being fourteen years old, yet his name isn't on the 1870 census. For the first time, Margaret Allen is listed as a "retail grocer," which indicates that she opened a store in her house between 1870 and 1880. After his mother's death, "Monty" ran a store and kept the Lower Bank Post Office here. He died in 1938 and was buried in the same plot as his mother and an Edmund Allen (12/7/1825 - 1/14/1866) who must have been his father. Ruth (Cramer) MacDonald told me that she had always heard that "Monty" Allen was born after his father died, this would confirm what she had been told.

The next known owners were Jonas and Edna (Heineman) Corson who lived here during the nineteen forties. The Heineman family were relatives of Captain Robert Somers. This house was listed as the property of a Mrs. Willitts in the tax records of the late 1930's. This may be Mathilda (Allen) Willitts, Ellen Scott's sister. Local people remember that the property was used as a chicken farm at one time. In 1996, it was the home of Mrs. Edith Clarke, but she recently remarried and has sold the house.

The Hall/Captain Daniel Cale House
2090 River Road

Courtesy of Sarah (Cramer) Camillo

The Dan Cale Family and Their Newly-Remodelled Home - c.1915
L to R: Warren Cale, Mary Frederika (Adams) Cale, Captain Daniel E. Cale, Julia Cale

    If you were looking for "old" houses, you'd be fooled by the 1920's look of this one. It was known as "The Isaiah Hall Storehouse" throughout the nineteenth century, even after it was converted into a home. Though there is no provable construction date, a recent title search went back to October 27, 1821 when Isaiah Hall sold it to John Carlisle. The Halls actually lived next door at 2096 River Road and used this for storage and as a store. A note in *The Weeks Family of Southern New Jersey* mentions that the school lot was "nearly opposite Hall's store." John Carlisle was the sea captain who lived across Old Church Road from this structure, so he probably continued to use it for storage (see THE CAPTAIN JOHN CARLISLE HOUSE). Richard Carlisle sold it to Benjamin Edwards, another Lower Banker, on April 17, 1824. Edwards kept it for twelve years and sold it back to Isaiah Hall on September 5, 1836. This time, the Hall family kept it for several years, not selling it again unil January 18, 1865, when it was purchased by Joseph Adams.
    The next transfer date discovered was not until February 15, 1901, but there is some discrepency here. The deed says that the "F.B. Cale" estate transferred it to Mary F. Cale on that date, nor is there any indication as to how or when it went from Joseph Adams to "F.B. Cale." Unfortunately as well, there simply is no "F.B. Cale" in the Cale family. Mary Fredericka Cale, the wife of Captain Dan Cale, was Joseph Adams's daughter. If that's confusing, so is the next transfer. On July 1, 1920, the estate of W. Watson Cale transferred the property to John C. Cale II, his grandson. If Mary F. Cale, John's mother, owned the property and lived in it, how did Captain Watson, her father--in-law, get it from her? Watson had died in 1884, that questionable blank period in the transfer history. Perhaps Joseph Adams had sold the house to him in the first place, and there was some question about the irregularity of the 1901 transfer to Mary Fredericka Cale, so her son, John, resecured the title in 1920.

The Hall/Cale House Prior to Remodeling - c. 1910

Not until 1976 did the house change hands again. After the deaths of John C. and Augusta (Weeks) Cale, Josephine M. Gager acquired it. Her estate sold it to James and Sarah (Cramer) Camillo, who live there now. Sarah, through her father, is a direct descendant of Captain Watson Cale through his daughter, Mary Ida.

That's the title history of the house, but the human history is far more fascinating. Though Captain William Watson Cale lived in Crowleytown, his son, Captain Daniel, decided he preferred Lower Bank and lived in several houses in the immediate area. The family story is that Watson signed the mortgage for this property so that his son's family would have a permanent place to live.

Captain Daniel E. Cale had married Mary Fredericka Adams, daughter of Joseph Perkins and Julia (Hall) Adams. Remember, this is the Hall storehouse and the Hall family lived next door. Dan and Mary had six children: The eldest is believed to have been Watson Andrew, though no dates are known for him. Julia (b. 1864; d. 1957) came next, then Iola (b. 1873; d. 1957), Warren M. (b. 1876; d. 1951), and John C. (b. 1882; d. February 25, 1974). A sixth child, a boy they named Everett, was born on July 2, 1887, but he died on the 8th of May in the following year. Iola became the second wife of Harry Daniel Adams. Julia married John F. McKeen (1862-1907) of the Wading River McKeens. Warren married Mrs. Edna Irene (Capp) Heitshu on June 4, 1900, and John finally married Augusta Weeks.

Though no actual date for the remodelling of the house is known, it is thought to have been accomplished during the first decade of the twentieth century, as the photograph on the previous page seems to indicate by the ages of the family standing proudly before their "new" home.

Mary Fredericka Cale's death in 1918 spared her one more tragedy in the family. In 1922, Julia P. (Cale) McKeen's daughter, Elva M. had an accident in the river near the bridge. Whether she was swimming or whether she fell in, no one knows, but she was caught in a current and couldn't get out. By the time she was hauled to shore, she was covered with mud and her lungs were filled with the Mullica's dark

Captain Daniel E. Cale - c. 1865

507

waters. Her rescuers carried her to this home of her grandfather, but all their efforts were in vain. At the age of twenty-six, Elva McKeen died right in the foyer. Captain Daniel died not four years later in 1926.

John, who was still single when his father died, had bought a house in Pleasantville and was living there. John was a carpenter by trade, and, in the rear addition to this house stands a built-in cupboard whose drawers are signed by their builder: John Cale.

Actually, John had more than his own life for which to thank old Captain Watson. When John finally did seek wedded bliss, he married the granddaughter of the man his grandfather had introduced to the Mullica valley in the first place, Otto Wobbar (see GREEN BANK: SOUTH BEND).

John had had a lengthy romance with the daughter of Jonathan and Lottie (Wobbar) Weeks over in Weekstown. John had been born in 1882 and "Gussy" in 1899, making him seventeen years older than she was. Gussy was a vivacious and cute young girl, so it's no wonder that she captured the heart of middle-aged John. The age difference didn't mean as much back then as it seems to do today. Gussy's own mother was eighteen years younger than her father.

Though they went together for many years, they didn't get married. The story is that the marriage was opposed by John's father, Captain Dan, so John didn't marry until after his father's death. Though this "end of life" love story is romantic, it must be somewhat inaccurate. John took his good old time getting around to it even after his father was no longer there to obstruct his wishes. He waited *twenty-three years* after his father's death in 1926 to marry his sweetheart. The couple may well have been "ships passing in the night" for a good many years, but there must be more to it than his father's opposition.

Courtesy of Sarah (Cramer) Camillo

Cullis Weeks, Augusta Weeks,
and John C. Cale II c. 1920

She had to wait thirty years for the fulfillment of her romantic dreams. In the meantime, she built a respected life of her own, though perhaps it was a bit lonely for her. Her parents were active in the Green Bank church, and Gussy played the old pump organ for many years. Her father died on November 13, 1935, while her mother lived until 1964.

Gussy assisted Laura Larrabee McConeghy in her *Romance of Green Bank* project by taking photographs in 1935 of many of the old Green Bank homes that are included in that section of this book.

When John and Gussy were finally married, it was the first time for both of them. John Cale married Augusta Weeks on October 4, 1949 when he was sixty-seven years old and she was fifty. Her marriage didn't keep her from her organ-playing. Every Sunday, she was at her place at the old pump organ with the Methodist Hymnal open before her. John, lover and husband, waited for her outside under the trees.

Both organ and organist were getting a bit worn with the years, though. The metal springs on the foot pedels were weakening, so she had to play slowly in order to maintain air pressure. This author remembers very well his first visit to the Green Bank church in 1967, during his college days, when the very s - l - o - w notes to the tune of "How Dry I Am," (believe it or not, a tune used in the old Methodist Hymnal) came floating out of the open windows as he walked to the church that fine morning. Gussy died in the late 1980's and was buried in Lower Bank beside her beloved John. She must have had the date of his death, February 25, 1974, carved on their stone, but when she died, there was no one left to see to it that her date of decease was carved into their joint stone. The spot remains blank to this day, and no one seems to remember even the exact year the organist of Green Bank left the little church in the pines for a more heavenly realm. For the record, it was March 10, 1989.

Josephene and Ralph F. Gager bought the house from the estate of John Cale on December 29, 1976. They lived in it until their own deaths some years later. James and Sarah (Cramer) Camillo purchased it from their estate on October 2, 1995 and live there today with their children: Aaron Paul (b. January 17, 1988), Bethany Marie (b. May 16, 1990), and Abigail Sarah (b. January 18, 1995).

The house is filled with memories of the Cale family. Best of all though, the new owners of the house "inherited" photographs galore from the Cale family. The Gagers had found them in the house when they moved in, and their estate passed them on to the new owners, knowing that Sarah was related to the Cales. While she knows the identities of many of those photographed so many years ago, the vast majority have no identifying markings on them. Along with the house, also, came two ledgers. On the back pages of one, Miss Lettice Winterbottom, the future wife of Captain John C. Cale, had written three poems before she was married. Another lists accounts from several ships known to have been captained by Watson Cale.

The past still lives in Lower Bank.

Courtesy of Sarah (Cramer) Camillo

John C. Cale II

The Dan Cale Family c. 1910
Standing L to R: Watson Andrew Cale (this could be
Julia's husband, John F. McKeen), Mary Frederika
(Adams) Cale, Captain Daniel E. Cale, Warren M. Cale,
Seated L to R: Iola, Julia, granddaughter Elva,
and John C. Cale II

Mary Fredericka (Adams) Cale
and Captain Daniel E. Cale c. 1915

Captain Daniel Cale and his son, John C. Cale II c. 1920

John C. Cale II c. 1920

John C. Cale II is on the right.
The identity of the others is not known.

Captain Daniel E. Cale c.1920

Only in their Dreams Does the Wind Howl in the Rigging and the Salt
Spray Wash Across the Quarterdeck.

Captain Daniel E. Cale and Captain Joseph E. Johnson

c.1920

The Hall/Cavileer/Fox House
2096 River Road

1995

Photograph by John Pearce

Marjorie (Cavileer) Fox has lived in this house for seventy-five years. Margie's father moved her family here in 1921, and she's been here ever since.

Margie was born in the old house at the very end of Cavileer Lane (5 Cavileer Lane), the eldest daughter of Benjamin Franklin and Marjorie Nevada (Mathis) Cavileer on November 8, 1915. Benjamin had been born in that house back in 1894, for it had been the home of his father, Margie's grandfather, Caleb Napoleon Cavileer. Marjorie lived there with her parents and younger brother, Harold Everett (b. October 16, 1917) until 1921 when her parents rented this house out on River Road. It was here that Caleb Franklin, Donald Joshua, Doris Rebecca, and Benjamin Earle were born and raised. Her parents built a newer house in town which eventually became Caleb Franklin and Mina's house.

Margie's father bought the house from John Hall in 1934, the year before her planned marriage. Marjorie married William Howard Fox (b. April 12, 1914) on April 12, 1935, and the couple made this house their home, buying it from her father over a period of time.

Bill worked as a laborer for the State of New Jersey, also worked for C.P. Leek and Sons, had vegetable gardens and grew blueberries. The couple had two children, Eileen, who married Warren Homiller, and William Howard, Jr. who married Anna Ramp in 1965. Eileen later received a divorce from Warren and remarried a man by the name of Stephanos and lives in Barnegat. William, Jr. and his family live in Weekstown.

Marjorie is still active in community affairs. She spent thirteen years serving as the Washington Township Clerk from 1977 through 1990. Each Sunday, you may see her travelling back and forth to Jenkins, because she continues to play the piano for the services held in the Jenkins' Chapel each Lord's Day.

Marge is a wonderfully warm and friendly person who is a wealth of information on Lower Bank and Washington Township. She says that this house was built about 1840 or 1842 but has had several additions made to it over the years. As far as she can tell, the house was always in the Hall family from its construction until her father bought it from John Hall. Actually, it was probably built prior to 1821 when Isaiah Hall sold his old house next door to Captain John Carlisle.

There are Hall names: Isaiah, Ethan, John - she can't remember who was father or who was grandfather, but John had moved from Lower Bank to Bridgeton, New Jersey, and had lived there for many years before selling the family home in Lower Bank to the Foxes. Isaiah, she says, built new windows for the Old Church after the fire. What fire? She says in the 1880's. She also says that the congregation considered moving the old building to a portion of the Hall property but finally decided not to. Perhaps they debated moving it to River Road and rebuilding it but finally decided to build a whole new church. Local people simply rebuilt the old structure rather than see it fall apart.

Isaiah Hall served as Township Clerk from 1828 to 1836. In the disputed elections of 1832, Isaiah's name appears as clerk at all three meetings. At the second, the word "unanimous" stands after his name, the only person who received that endorsement. He also served as Judge of Election in 1836 through 1838. In 1838 and 1839, he was on the Township Committee. John Hall's name appears as Judge of Election in 1844. John Hall served as Assessor from 1851 to 1852. In 1858, John was Township

Margie (Cavileer) Fox
1996

Clerk. After that, the Hall name disappears from the records.

Isaiah is the only Hall name to appear on a gravestone in the Lower Bank cemetery. His stone says he was born on April 15, 1787 and died on the 24th of January 1840. Since John served as Township Clerk as late as 1858, he would have had to have been Isaiah's son.

The 1850 census lists three men by the name of "John Hall," and at least one was the son of the other. In 1850, the elder John was forty-three, married to Anna (35) with four children at home: Lydia (19), John Mott (17), Ephraim C. (13), and Julia A. (6). The other John M. Hall was twenty-one, married to Amanda (22). Apparently, his mother, Julia, was sixty. By 1860, there is only one Hall family, that of John, now fifty-two, and his wife Annamarie (46), John M. (28), Ethan C. (24), and Julia A. (17). John, Sr. is listed as a ships' carpenter, while John M. and Ethan are listed as mariners. In 1870, the list has been reduced to John (63) and Ann M. (56), Ethan C. (33), and Julia A. (26). Ten years later, It's down to John (73) and Julia A. (36), who is still keeping house for her father.

The "John Hall" who sold this house to the Foxes had to be John Hall, Jr., brother of Ethan, or perhaps even a third John. John, Sr., son of Isaiah, who was seventy-three in 1880, was long gone before the Foxes bought the house. Julia Hall eventually married Joseph Perkins Adams and gave birth to a daughter, Mary Fredericka, who married Captain Daniel E. Cale and lived in her mother's family house next door.

The puzzle presented by the census of 1850 is that there are three "John Halls." Obviously, John Hall (43) who is married to Anna (35) is the father of John Mott (17), but who is the other "John M. (21)," married to Amanda (22), who has his mother, Julia (60), living with him? Is this a cousin of the same name? If so, then Julia Hall, mother of Mary Frederica (Adams) Cale, was named perhaps for her great aunt.

Another Victorian used to stand next to Marge Fox's house towards the river. This house she thinks was built by a man named Bartlett and was owned by George Maxwell, Fritz Noyes, Lydia Lyons, and Ed McGlinn. In recent years, this house was found in such wretched condition that the present owners of the property, the Bretnalls, had to tear it down and build a new one.

To get back to Margie's brother, Cale, who was born in this house: Caleb Franklin Cavileer was born on July 7, 1926. He married Wilhelmina Schwenger (called "Mina" b. July 7, 1926). The couple had three children, Barry, Caleb Paul, and Nevada (Jacobs). Two of Caleb's brothers live locally, Donald in Mays Landing and Benjamin E., Sr. in Egg Harbor. A third brother lives in Long Creek, North Carolina.

Caleb was a graduate of the Command and General Staff College in Leavenworth, Kansas and retired from the Army Reserve as a Lieutenant Colonel. He served as coordinator and administrative supply technician at the Storck

Army Reserve Center and was Past Commander of the Third Battalion, 309th Regiment. He was also a Past Commander of the Storck Army Reserve Center in Northfield.

He was a charter member of the Lower Bank Fire Company and a trustee. He served as the company's treasurer for twenty years and was the Fire Chief for ten years. He also served a year as lieutenant, seven years as First Lieutenant, four years as Captain, and a year as vice-president.

He was a member of Hiram Dewey Lodge, Free and Accepted Masons, in Egg Harbor City and the Good Fellowship Club; American Legion Post of Egg Harbor City, and past president National Cranberry Growers Association.

Caleb died at the age of fifty-eight on the twentieth of November, 1984 and was buried in the Lower Bank cemetery. Well did he deserve the tribute of his fellow firemen:

Our Chief

He'll always be the Chief, a name he earned with pride.
Even when his term was over and he had to step aside.
He rose through the ranks, to the pinnacle of success.
Took years of special training - a dedication few possess.
His lungs have tasted toxic fumes, his skin has felt the
*   flame.*
Aches and bruises went hand in hand, like thunder in the
*   rain.*
As a soldier of the Florian, our patron saint of old.
He fought his share of battles, too numerous to unfold.
Destiny makes us brothers, he'll never be alone.
What he sent into lives of others, has come back to his
*   own.*
From those who worked beside him, it's said in fond be-
*   lief.*
May God be always with him. He'll always be Our Chief.

Caleb Cavileer led a distinguished life of public service, and his family has a right to be proud of him. He was no inbred "Piney," isolated in the backwater of a little town. He was a man of character and strength, scion of an old and respected family, who served his country and the town of his ancestors well.

Courtesy of Horace Somes

Caleb Cavileer

Courtesy of Lillian (DeBow) Fritz

Cale Cavileer and Nelson Ware - c. 1944
in front of the Ayres House, 2047 River Road

The Captain Jesse Reuben Cavileer House
(No Longer in Existence)

The First Jesse Reuben Cavileer House
This photograph is labelled "Captain Jesse Cavileer,"
so it must be the captain himself in the carriage.

    Across the street from Margie (Cavileer) Fox's house used to stand the magnificent Victorian of Jesse Reuben Cavileer. Jesse and his wife originally lived in the house in the photograph above which stood next to their new "modern" one, but the couple turned their old house into a barn after moving into their new mansion.

    Captain Jesse Reuben and Mary Elizabeth (Adams) Cavileer modelled their new house after the one which his Uncle John and Aunt Armenia (Johnson) Cavileer had built on the river, though he added a round turret to the front of his.

    Charles Cavileer and his wife, Elizabeth ("Nettie") L. (Cavileer) bought the house-turned-barn from Jesse and made it back into a house. Charles was the son of Peter and Eleanor (Sooy) Cavileer. His grandparents on the Cavileer side were John and Ann (Tearney) Cavileer. Elizabeth was Jesse's sister. Thus Charles Wesley Cavileer was both Jesse Reuben's first cousin once removed and his uncle by marriage. Actually, Elizabeth and her husband, Charles, shared grandparents so they were first cousins. Elizabeth's sister, Anna Marie, was the wife of Captain William Watson Cale. Another sister, Mary Ann, married Samuel Cavileer, whose house stood where the present Pacemaker Plant is located today. Her brother, John Cavileer III, married Armenia Johnson.

Born in 1840, Jesse was the son of Reuben and Elizabeth (Lewis) Cavileer. He first married Sarah Guibel. Later, he wed Mary Elizabeth Adams (b. 1870, d. 1918). The couple's first child, a son whom they named Lincoln, died at the age of four and a half months. Though eventually married, their second child, Jesse, had no children. Their third child, Douglas married Etta Kesler and they had two sons, Ralph and Lewis. Jesse Reuben's brother was James Veldrin Cavileer, who lived on River Road where it meets the Mullica.

An interesting note appears in the September 30, 1876 edition of the Mount Holly Herald:

> *The reported loss of the three mased schooner,* T. Harris Kirk, *commanded by Captain Jesse Cavilerer of Lower Bank, Randolph township, with the loss of all on board, proves to be a canard, as the vessel only left the Delaware breakwater on Monday, 26th instant. for New York.*

The photograph of River Road early in this century which appears in this chapter was taken from the windmill at the rear of the Cavileer house. Lightning bolts from heaven are terribly capricious, though, and it was a lightning bolt which struck Jesse and Mary Elizabeth's beautiful house some time before 1921 when six year old Margie moved to the Hall house with her parents. Marjorie (Downs) Cavileer called this Victorian "Douglas Cavileer's house," but Margie Fox says she thinks it burned while Jesse was still living there. Mary died in 1918 at the age of forty-eight, so she may have been spared the tragedy of losing her beautiful home. Jesse, having met with the double tragedy of losing his wife and his home, died in 1927 at the age of eighty-seven.

Elizabeth Cavileer's husband, Charles, just seems to disappear. There is no stone for him next to his wife's in the cemetery, so he either was not buried in Lower Bank, or his stone is missing. The Cavileer genealogy gives two different suggestions for the date of his death, either December 5, 1886 or in 1888. We do know that he lost both his brother, David, and his nephew, W. Nelson Cavileer, to the sea in 1876. The Mount Holly Herald for September 30th of that year records the sad news:

> *The schooner* Robert F. Stockton, *Captain W. Nelson Cavileer of Bridgeport, Randolph township, was lost off Hogg and Smith's Islands, Capes of Virginia, in the storm of Sunday week. The body of Captain Cavileer was picked up on Wednesday last by Captain Almy of the steamer Resolute near Black River lighthouse.*

The fortunes of the house-turned-barn-turned-house of Charles and Elizabeth declined after Elizabeth died on July 4, 1903. Like so many other old houses in the pines, it burned to the ground in the 1970's. An old man had moved into it and had piled up all kinds of junk inside. The first time it caught on fire, the Lower Bank Fire Company was able to put it out. Unfortunately, the old drifter moved right back in after the fire and continued to live in the same squallor without repairing the fire damage. There was no running water in the house, and the only bathroom facility was an outhouse.

The old man had a sad end. It was winter, and someone passing by on the street saw the front door standing open. They thought that was strange and called the police. The police called the Green Bank Ambulance Squad. When the squad arrived, they found the old man, sitting in a chair in the yard. They thought he had gone out to sit in the yard the previous afternoon. He apparently fell asleep and never awakened.

When the old house caught fire a second time not long after the man's death, the fire company could do nothing but keep the fire from spreading to the surrounding houses and woods. The first home of Captain Jesse Reuben Cavileer, erstwhile barn, and home of his cousin/uncle Charles was no more.

The Horace Cavileer House
2108 River Road

1995

Horace Cavileer is seventy-eight years old this year and still a waterman. His entire life has been spent on the waters of the Mullica and Great Bay, harvesting oysters and clams. His clam shack at the corner where River Road turns and follows the Mullica has been well-known for a long time now. Though he only "lives" in this house occasionally, it still retains fond memories of his childhood.

Horace's father, Reuben Cavileer, Jr., bought the house from a man by the name of Cy Lane for $500 back around the turn of the century. Horace doesn't remember the exact year, but it was before he was born in 1918 anyway. Cy Lane had brought two houses to this location that used to stand farther up the road and joined them together making a double house, which it remains today. Reuben, Jr. owned 6.46 acres surrounding this house and 52.96 acres immediately across from it on the other side of the road, stretching all the way up the river to the Coulter property, which then was part of the John Cavileer, III land.

Marjorie (Downs) Cavileer remembers that at least part of this house was originally the home of Nathaniel ("Thanie") Van Sant, son of the famous minister, Nicholas Van Sant, perhaps when it still stood in its original location inland on River Road.

Reuben Cavileer, Jr. was the son of Reuben, Sr., and Joanna (Loveland) Rose, widow of James A. Rose, Reuben, Sr.'s second wife. Reuben, Sr.'s first wife, Sarah Ellen, was the daughter of Benjamin Franklin and Ellen (Chew) Downs of Wading River, Marjorie (Downs) Cavileer's grandfather. His great grandparents were Samuel and Mary Ann (Cavileer) Cavileer. Samuel Cavileer was born in 1853 and died in 1932. His house used to stand on a portion of the Pacemaker property. Horace quips that his great grandmother was the bridge-tender at one time, for which she received $5 a month and a rupture. That was back in the days when the bridge-tender had to open the bridge by using a giant key and a great deal of effort.

Reuben, Jr. married Laura E. Broom, whose mother came from England in 1865 and settled in Harrisville. Horace says that Laura's father lived in Bridgeton and hitched his horse up every morning at three A.M. to ride to work in the paper town. Talk about a commute! (Talk about pulling my leg! Bridgeport I'd believe. Bridge*ton*: impossible!) His job was to take care of the horses for the paperworks, but he must have found the time to fall in love with an Englishwoman.

Horace and his older brother, Richard, were born in one of the upstairs bedrooms "along with the sweet potatoes" he is fond of remembering. His father stored sweet potatoes in an upstairs bedroom to keep them from freezing in the winter. Born on October 27, 1918, he arrived just after the harvest.

Horace at 78 is still the same hard worker he has been all his life and still loves his wife of forty-five years. He served in World War II, but he remembers that women of marriageable age were hard to find when he came home.

> *I got engaged before I went into the army, but I thought I might get killed and I wanted the money to go to my parents. ... When I came home, they were all taken. I used to like to roller skate and I went over to Mays Landing to roller skate and that's where I met Del* [his wife, Adele Brant]. *I figured I'd like to go out with her again. I went there for a month and every night they had skaten', and she never comed. And only once she did come, and I found out where she lived then. I went with her three years without gettin' married.*

Horace and Del live in a rancher beside the river, but he still keeps up the old house across the road. Del vividly remembers the flood waters of 1962 and points out a spot on the wall of their house about three feet above the ground as the eventual height they reached. Del won't give up the security of the old house as their place of refuge should the Mullica rise once again.

Del said she had a good story that happened a long time ago. Seems as if one of the local men took his horse and wagon into the Great Swamp for logging. He cut cedar after cedar and kept piling the logs on the wagon until they reached a great height. Unfortunately, the horse and wagon sank down into the mud so far that the horse couldn't pull either himself or that wagon out of there.

> *He had to go every day to see how the horse was. He couldn't get him out of the swamp with all the cedar on the back of the wagon, and he finally had to take a gun and shoot the poor horse! Right in the swamp! Up to his kneebones in the mud. The horse! Now picture somethin' like that! They sware up and down its the truth! I thought, geez, couldn't he have kind of estimated it before he went into the swamp? When he loaded that wagon down and then he couldn't pull it out of there. He was a real nice horse!*

Photograph by John Pearce

Horace Cavileer - 1996
1918-1999

The summer sun has disappeared far upriver and the mosquitoes are out in force. Horace, like so many others along the river, would continue to talk of friends and family long gone to their rest, but the day will begin early, and Horace will be back at work in his clam shack. He's even willing to allow that, though born beside the Mullica, the darn mosquitoes bother him, too!

The Captain James Veldrin Cavileer House
2112 River Road

Courtesy of David Cavileer

c. 1926

Charlie Croce is a retired State Police lieutenant and has seen just about everything. He served in the Air Force during World War II and was as a ball-turret gunner on B-17 bombers. During his Air Force service, he was awarded the Distinguished Flying Cross and the Air Medal with four oakleaf clusters.

As a State Trooper, Charlie had been in cities and suburbs and knows just about every locality, yet he chose the New Jersey pinelands in which to retire. Some friends must have thought he was crazy when he bought thirty-seven overgrown acres in Lower Bank that came complete with a house which had never known the likes of plumbing and whose electrical system was a nightmare.

In 1988, when Charlie bought this house, it was surrounded by brambles as high and as thick as those which surrounded Sleeping Beauty's castle! The roof was in tolerable shape, but some of the windows were gone, and the interior had been stripped.

With characteristic vigor, Charlie set about making this old home a showplace on the Mullica. He cleaned out the entire property, made the house secure against the weather, redecked the porch and replaced the Jersey White Cedar siding with new boards cut from logs taken from

Photograph by John Pearce

1995

Courtesy of David Cavileer

The Rev. Jesse Cavileer and his wife, the former Daisy Brooke of Chicago

his new property and cut into lumber at a local sawmill. He was able to save the upstairs floors and polished them to a fine shine with polyurethane, but the downstairs wide-plank floors were beyond simple refinishing. Those he had to cover with linoleum. Upstairs he made four small bedrooms into two of reasonable size, and, of course, plumbed and wired the whole house. The original structure had a summer kitchen in the rear, but it was so far gone that Charlie had to tear it down. Summer kitchens were used throughout the hotter areas of the country but are usually found in the South. Old Southern New Jersey houses frequently included them, though you rarely see them farther north.

Charlie didn't have to look very far for his home's former occupant. David Cavileer, who lives just across River Road, was raised in this house. James Veldrin Cavileer, son of Reuben and Elizabeth (Lewis) Cavileer, was a sea captain, and knew a shrewd bargain when he saw one. Story goes, he bought this house at a tax sale for $500. Dave doesn't have a date for his "deal of a lifetime," but Charlie Croce says it was around 1884, when the sea captain, looking for a fitting domicile, settled on this bargain in his home town. He also has a name associated with the house prior to Captain James, one Thomas Bartlett, but he doesn't know if Bartlett was the actual builder. *Jersey Genesis* gives the builder's name as Captain Jim Bartlett.

Courtesy of David Cavileer

Daisy (Brooke) Cavileer

There are no Bartletts listed in the Washington Township census for 1850 at all. In 1860, there are two families living here. The first is William (30), a laborer, and his wife, Harriet (24), and their children: John E. (3) and Deborah (1). The second family with the Bartlett name is that of Simeon Bartlett (34), listed as a sea captain in 1860, with his wife, Elvirah [sic] (29), and their children: Emalay (9) and Samuel (7). By 1870, the William Bartlett family is gone and only that of Simeon remains. In 1880, there are no Bartletts in either Washington or Randolph Townships.

A map of circa 1870 labels this house as that of Captain S. Bartlett. Thus, in all probability, there was neither a Jim Bartlett nor a Thomas Bartlett who was the original builder but Captain Simeon Bartlett. Captain Simeon seems to have moved into the area after 1850 and moved away by 1880. These, then, become the outside dates in which the house could have been constructed.

Courtesy of David Cavileer

The Rev. Jesse Reuben Cavileer

Captain James Veldrin Cavileer married Rachel Matilda Maxwell, and the young couple had six children: James Veldrin, Jr., Evelyn French, Jesse Reuben, John William, Curtis Monroe, and Alvan Maxwell. The latter only lived four days, but the other children were all eventually married.

Their third son, Jesse Reuben, was named for his uncle, Captain Jesse Reuben Cavileer, who built himself a fine Victorian across from the Hall/Fox house and lived to see it destroyed by lightning [see THE CAPTAIN JESSE REUBEN CAVILEER HOUSE]. He became an ordained Methodist minister and married Daisy Brooke of Chicago. During their first years together, their marriage was blessed with children: first a son, Jesse Reuben, Jr., then a daughter, Ruth, and finally, on April 6, 1922, a second son, David.

When David was born, the Rev. Jesse Cavileer was serving at a church in Maryland where he lived with his growing family. Fortune did not continue to shine on this clergyman's family. Six days after the birth of little David, mother Daisy died. A grief-stricken Jesse tried to carry on, but the church and three children were just too much for him.

Courtesy of David Cavileer

David Franklin Cavileer - c. 1944

In 1925, when little David was three, Jesse packed up his family and moved them back to the town of his birth, Lower Bank, to the home of his parents on the Mullica. Captain James passed away only two years later, but Jesse and his family continued to live with his mother, Rachel Matilda (Maxwell). Jesse later remarried. His daughter, Ruth, married a physician, Dr. Thomas Cochran, and David married Calla Cramer.

Courtesy of David Cavileer

Lower Bank's Santa Claus

David grew into a fine young man. He served as an MP during World War II. At war's end, he returned to Lower Bank and his grandmother's house by the river. Grandmother Rachel died in 1946, outliving her sea captain husband by nineteen years. The Rev. Jesse passed away only six years later, and was laid to rest in the old cemetery in Lower Bank where his family had been buried for many generations.

Son David continued to live in the now-venerable house on the Mullica for another eight years after his father's death. He finally built himself a rancher just across River Road in 1961. David's new house had all the modern conveniences, including indoor plumbing and electricity.

From 1961 until rescued by Charlie Croce in 1988, the old captain's house lay derelict and abandoned. Mike Capaccio, owner of the Green Bank Tavern, bought the property but did nothing to halt its decay. Time and the elements almost triumphed again, as it has so many times in the pines, but fortunately, Charlie Croce came along and had imagination. He also wasn't afraid of hard work.

Today, he can be justly proud of his fine home and thirty-seven acres of lawns, marsh, and cedar swamp sweeping down to the Mullica. When he stands on the end of his ninety-foot dock and contemplates the majestic sweep of the Mullica as it flows towards the sea, he can imagine it crowded with coastal schooners

Courtesy of Lilian (DeBow) Fritz

David Cavileer - c. 1944

Photograph by John Pearce

David Cavileer - 1996

Photograph by John Pearce

Charles (Chick) Croce - 1996

bringing timber, charcoal, iron products, and glassware downstream, destined for New York, Philadelphia, and other East Coast ports.

As he turns towards his shining white house, gleaming golden in the light of the setting sun, he can imagine Captain James Veldrin Cavileer gazing down from an upstairs window at the ever-flowing Mullica and dreaming of the sea which once brought him such adventure.

David Cavileer, genial teller of jokes and tales, still lives in his house across the street. Fit and hearty at seventy-four, David must have inherited some of his father's piety. While not an ordained minister, he still acts as Lay Preacher for the Green Bank and Lower Bank churches. His face may be a little more lined than it was when he was twenty in the midst of the Second World War, but his body is still strong and his eyes shine with youthful vigor. Dedicated Methodist as he is, he still quietly boasts that not a drop of liquor has ever passed his lips. Perhaps that does partially account for his physical well-being. No doubt another factor is his indomitable spirit and sense of humor. He is still playing the local Santa Claus each and every Christmas, the most recent "Santa" in a long-standing tradition of this old town on the Mullica.

c. 1940

c. 1960

David Franklin Cavileer - 1996

The Cavileer/Johnson/Hendrickson/Coulter House
2121 River Road

1995

Photograph by John Pearce

This old house hugs the river road between the bend where it turns inland and the bridge which crosses the Mullica. Now owned by George and Mary Coulter, the property has had several families associated with it over the years. When the Coulters purchased the property in 1994, they did a title search which turned up a number of previous owners but gave no indication as to the actual date of the construction of their house.

At some time prior to 1783, one Henry Burr lawfully seized 507 acres of meadowland in the vicinity, including the acreage on which this house now stands. In 1783, John, Thomas, and Henry Burr inherited it from their father. Ten years later, John Burr became the sole owner of 407 acres, transferred to him by his brothers. Two years later, John Burr sold James Gale 207 acres, including that portion along the river where this house now stands.

Having possessed the property for six years, in 1801, Gale sold "all that tract of meadow" to John Cavileer for $149.62. John Cavileer was the son of the first of his line to come to the Mullica valley, Peter. John was born on April 20, 1742. When he died on August 31, 1813, he was laid to rest in the family plot of Yoos Sooy which is now part of the old Pacemaker Yachts plant just down the street from this house.

John and Ann Cavileer sold the property to their eldest son, Charles W. and his wife, the former Elizabeth Weatherby of the Wading River Weatherbys for $212 in the year of our second war with England, 1812. Charles and Elizabeth held on to it until 1836, when they sold it to John Lewis. Eight years later, Lewis sold it to John H. Black. Possibly John Black went bankrupt, because two years later, in 1846, the sheriff, Charles Collins, sold the title to Augustus Johnson. Augustus Johnson held on to it for forty years, finally transferring it to his daughter, Armenia Cavileer, in 1886. Armenia was married to John Cavileer, the grandson of the John and Ann Cavileer who had previously owned the property. In 1924, Armenia died and left it to her daughters, Augusta Matthews, Martha ("Mattie") Cavileer, and Elizabeth Rose, and to her son, Walter Knickerbocker. Since two of the sisters had died before their mother, the entire property went to Mattie and Walter. In 1948, Walter K. Cavileer sold it to Charles Platt Leek II and his wife, Edith, who had been renting it at the time. He also sold Leek the land at the Lower Bank end of the bridge for his first boatyard.

PRICE LIST

EUGENE HENDRICKSON
Northfield, N. J.

WHOLESALE

Black Ducks	$17.00	doz.
Blue Bills	17.00	"
Cub Heads	17.00	"
Diving Fowl	17.00	"
Old Grandy	17.00	"
Yellow Legs	5.00	"
Brant	24.00	"
Geese	5.00	ea.

RETAIL

Black Ducks	$20.00	doz.
Blue Bills	20.00	"
Cub Heads	20.00	"
Diving Fowl	20.00	"
Old Grandy	20.00	"
Yellow Legs	6.00	"
Brant	30.00	"
Geese	6.00	ea.

Courtesy of George and Mary Coulter

A Price List of Hendrickson's Work

Courtesy of George and Mary Coulter

Gene Hendrickson at Work in his Shop

The Coulters couldn't find just when the Leeks sold it to decoy-carver Gene Hendrickson of Northfield, but Gene definitely lived here during the 1950's and was justly famous for his excellent decoys which still grace many a mantelpiece and display shelf along the eastern seaboard. His daughter, Nancy, is recorded as owning it in 1972, the year in which she sold the property to Franklin and Elaine A. Ecker. The Eckers moved into the house on the first of December, 1972, and sold it to Joseph S. and Anne M. Benny exactly three years later on December 1, 1975.

The Bennys had a longer term of residence than most, living here until the thirty-first of May, 1994, when George and Mary Coulter bought the property.

Unfortunately, there is no record of the building date of the earliest part of the structure, though details may indicate that either John Cavileer or his son, Charles, built the upriver section in the early part of the nineteenth century. The house is actually composed of two houses that have been joined together by some enterprising individual.

The story the Coulters heard was that the southeast half of the house first stood in Nesco and was floated downriver to Lower Bank where it was joined to the preexisting structure. Interior details do indicate that the house is certainly made up of two structures which were once separate. Perhaps it was during the ownership of Augustus Johnson, whose family included many sea captains, that the feat took place. It may have been accomplished prior to the construction of the first bridge at Green Bank in 1855, which would have restricted the channel.

Photograph by John Pearce

Mary and George Coulter - 1995

The Captain John Cavileer III House
2129 River Road

Photograph by John Pearce

1995

John Cavileer, the third of that name in his direct line, was born on October 22, 1831. Before his death on September 12, 1900, he had gained a great reputation as a successful sea captain, ship owner, and merchant in the Mullica Valley.

John married Armenia Johnson, the daughter of Augustus S. and Sarah Ann (Bush) Johnson (b. March 3, 1834; d. February 29, 1924), and the couple had seven children: Sarah Augusta, Elizabeth, Martha, Walter Knickerbocker, Avalinda, Harry, and Albert. Despite his success in business, tragedy stalked the family. The couple's last three children lived but one day. Sarah Augusta married a man by the name of Matthews but died at the age of forty-one without having a child. Martha lived to be sixty-eight but never married. Elizabeth married James Rose, but there is no indication of children. Walter Knickerbocker Cavileer married Elizabeth Lenore Burwell and had three children: Gladys, Florence Genevieve, and Walter Knickerbocker, Jr.

John Cavileer III built a sizable fortune from his early days as a sea captain and, in his later years, was a successful shipping magnate. He acquired most of the land along the river, land which had been owned by his grandfather, the first John Cavileer, through his marriage to Armenia Johnson. Her father transferred ownership of the acreage to John and Armenia in 1886. This property included the Coulter House at 2121 River Road, in which Captain John's brother, Ezekiel, would live for some time. At one point, this merchant-sea captain owned most of the land bordering on the now Route 542, all the way from Lower Bank to Wading River.

This particular piece of property apparently included the land which was originally the homesteads of Eric Mullica and Yoos Sooy. The map at the beginning of this chapter clearly shows a fifty-acre parcel transferred by Eric Mullica, Jr. to Joseph Pearce in 1722 as including this area from the Coulter House to what became the Leek boatyard.

Captain John had been dreaming of a mansion to suit his status as captain and ship owner for some time, and the acquisition of the property overlooking the Mullica was prime land. Legend has it that he brought timbers down from Maine in one of his own ships with which to construct this house, though why he would go to all this trouble and expense in the midst of a land that was still producing construction timber itself is not known.

John and Armenia only enjoyed the house for a little over ten years prior to John's death at the age of sixty-nine. Armenia lived on for another twenty-four years before passing away three days before her ninetieth birthday. When she died in 1924, she left the property to her children, Martha and Walter Knickerbocker. Sarah Augusta and Elizabeth had predeceased their mother.

It was Walter Knickerbocker Cavileer, who, without telling his sister, sold the original boatyard and site of the burial place of Yoos Sooy and John Cavileer, to Charles P. Leek II. When Martha found out about it, she was furious with her brother. Unfortunately, the deed was signed, sealed, and delivered, so to speak.

Walter K. Cavileer also sold his father's house to Leon Herron for $7,000. Herron later sold it to Bernard Champon, who, in turn, sold it to the current owner, Albert Hughes, no doubt for considerably more than $7,000!

Walter K. Cavileer, Jr. married Marjorie Downs, daughter of Hannah and Edward Downs of Turtle Creek Road, Wading River. Walter K., Jr. and Marge had two children, Nancy and Colleen. Marjorie (Downs) Cavileer still lives in the little house immediately next to this house which her husband's grandparents had built a century ago. Marge is a delightful person who enjoys sitting under the trees in front of her home, surrounded by ducks and geese, enjoying the beauty of the Mullica flowing before her.

Photograph by John Pearce

Marjorie (Downs) Cavilieer - 1996

For many years, Marge responded to every horn on the river, for she served as tender of the Lower Bank bridge. Sitting in front of her riverfront house on a summer's afternoon, she still feels a response deep inside of her whenever some present-day boater sounds his horn for the bridge.

Courtesy of Sarah (Cramer) Camillo

The Cavileer House - c. 1915

The Caleb Napoleon and Benjamin Cavileer House
5 Cavileer Lane

Photograph by Dudley Lewis

1996

Behind the Pacemaker Plant, on a long sand lane leading off of River Road and named for the Cavileer family, lies one of the reputed haunts of the Jersey Devil, at least according to Mrs. Ella (Johnson) Underhill.

This very old house is guarded by two large dogs to keep away prowlers who would venture that far back. Betty Braddock lives there now. Before her, Gene Hendrickson, the decoy carver, lived there for a while. The center portion of the house dates to the very early nineteenth century.

Horace Cavileer says that his grandfather, Reuben Cavileer, Sr., used to live back at this house, but he exchanged land with Samuel Cavileer and moved out to the riverfront. Samuel was Reuben's father and lived in a house fronting the river which stood near Cavileer Lane on what is now Pacemaker property. Reuban Cavileer, Sr. (b. 1853) and Caleb Napoleon Cavileer were first cousins.

Thus it was probably Samuel, or perhaps his estate, which sold the property to his nephew, Caleb Napoleon. The property-switching gets to be as complex as the family tree.

In any case, Caleb Napoleon Cavileer was the son of Lorenzo Dow (Samuel's brother) and Hannah Elizabeth (Weatherby) Cavileer. Caleb Napoleon was born on December 30, 1857 and married Laura Jane Headley, daughter of Benjamin Franklin Headley in Tuckerton. Caleb Napoleon and Laura Jane parented nine children, four boys and five girls.

Their third son and fifth child, Benjamin Franklin Cavileer apparently came into the possession of this house. Benjamin was born on the 15th of September, 1894. He married Marjorie Nevada Mathis on April 25th, 1915, and they had six children. The couple had their first two children on this farm, Marjorie Naomi and Harold Everett. They then moved to a rented house at 2096 River Road, where they had their remaining children: Caleb Franklin, Donald Joshua, Doris Rebecca, and Benjamin Earle.

Marjorie married William Howard Fox and still lives in the house on River Road. Doris Rebecca married George Rider and lives across the street from Marjorie Fox. Caleb Franklin married Mina Schwenger and were the parents of Barry Franklin, Caleb Paul, and Nevada Cavileer.

Cale Cavileer was fire chief of the Lower Bank Fire Company and died 1984. His widow, Mina, just passed away in 1996.

This old farm of Caleb Napoleon and Benjamin Cavileer consists of 120.2 acres, bordering on Johnson land which became the Beaux Arts Nurseries early in this century.

Mrs. Underhill said that, at one time, there was a lane, known by the name of Leeds, which entered this property from the upper section of River Road and ran through the Johnson property. When her grandfather built a cow barn behind the "new" church, this road was cut off.

This house is supposed to have predated the Cavileer ownership by some years. Moses Leeds is said to have lived there, giving his name to the lane leading off the upper part of River Road through the Johnson property. Moses was born the year in which the Declaration of Independence was signed in Philadelphia, his wife, Rachel, the year after. The couple had a son, Levi, born in 1809, and a daughter, Lydia, born in 1827. Before their own deaths, Moses and Rachel would bury both son and daughter in the Lower Bank cemetery, Levi at the age of twenty-eight in 1837 and Lydia at the age of seventeen in 1844. When Rachel went to her rest in 1850 and Moses followed three years later, there would be no heirs. It is probably about that time that the property came into the Cavileer family.

Now just where does the Jersey Devil fit in? Another name for the famous devil is the Leeds Devil. "Mother" Leeds was one of its reputed "mothers," but whether the legend came from Leeds Point in Atlantic (Old Gloucester) County or from Lower Bank, no one knows. Perhaps it was Moses' own mother who uttered the fateful curse on her thirteenth child. Ella (Johnson) Underhill did report several sightings of the famed devil near her home which was close to Leeds Lane. Maybe the curse was playing itself out in the next generation when Moses and Rachel were forced to bury both their children at early ages. If this was the birthplace of the Devil, the Cavileers dispelled the curse for all time.

C. P. Leek and Sons
The Famous Name of "Pacemaker"

c. 1970

Charles Platt Leek, II was a well-known and colorful figure in the Lower Bank of the early twentieth century. Charlie, the son of William Spafford and Rebecca (Cramer) Leek, was born May 14, 1877. He married Edith Young (b. 1879; d. 1959), daughter of Edgar and Phoebe Ann (Headley) Young on Christmas Day in 1898. Charlie and Edith had three children, Cecil Gilbert (b. June 12, 1899; d. October 9, 1982), Olga Winona (b. March 1902), and John Everett (b. May 1904; d. 1957).

Charlie Leek and his brother, Walter, ran a yacht yard in Atlantic City in the second decade of the twentieth century, but about 1918, Charlie got tired of the rum running that was going on in that area and moved to Lower Bank with his sons. Charlie didn't drink and was proud of it (grandson Jack says he makes up for it), so he didn't have any sympathy for the illegal trade that dominated the resort town.

The Second Boatyard Building of C.P. Leek and Sons

The Crew of C.P. Leek and Sons - 1942
81-foot Custom Boat CG 81002

CG 81002 was built as a yacht for one of the hotel owners in Atlantic City but was seized for government use by the U.S. Coast Guard at the beginning of World War II. It was used by the government throughout the war and ended up in California where it was sold and turned back into the yacht it was intended to be.

The crew assembled in front of her includes many who were prominent in both C.P. Leek and Sons and in the local towns.

(1)   Sal Zitto
(3)   William Fox of Lower Bank
(5)   Weldon Bell of Lower Bank
(6)   Jack Updike of Green Bank
(7)   Byrd Moore of Crowleytown
in front (left to right):
Harold Maxwell of Lower Bank
Monty Somers of Lower Bank
Russell Montgomery of Green Bank
C.P. Leek is the man with the eye patch
Fred Noyes, Sr., the "Mayor" is on C.P.'s left
Ted Haggis, boat designer, is on C.P.'s right

Charlie bought the Coulter House on River Road from Walter Knickerbocker Cavileer, heir of Captain John Cavileer, III and also purchased the site at the end of the bridge which he and his family would develop the property as one of the most well-known yacht yards of this century. The boatyard site included the graves of Yoos Sooy and John Cavileer (Peter's son) and may have been the land on which Eric Mullica set up his homestead.

Charlie and his family organized the C.P. Leek Company Boat Works, constructed a building in the corner formed by the bridge and River Road and began to build boats. As the business expanded, he built a second wooden building on the opposite side of the road. This building is still standing, though the original building is now flanked by block extensions to either side.

When Cecil and John became old enough to shoulder part of the business burdens, C.P. Leek became C.P. Leek and Sons. Charlie's specialty was in constructing one-off designs for wealthy businessmen. He built a good, solid boat, of which he could be proud. Cecil had married Lillian Warner in 1920, and John Everett wed Rachel (Cope) Schindler. Thus the sons were ready to start a family. John and Rachel had Marie D. (b. 1927), John Everett, Jr. (b. 1930), and Donald (b. 1933). Both Donald and John, Jr. followed their father and grandfather in the family business.

The commencement of World War II changed things considerably. Charlie was almost finished the construction of a yacht for one of the Atlantic City hotel owners, when the United States Coast Guard seized it for the government. His son, John, left the company and went to work at the Philadelphia Naval Yard. Later, he became the Naval Inspector for South Jersey and returned to Lower Bank to inspect his father's boats, which Charlie was now building for the government. "Grandpop didn't like that at all!" recalls Jack Leek.

John had plenty to inspect at C.P. Leek and Sons, who built buoy tenders for the government during the war. They also constructed two 72' sub-chasers on the English design.

In 1945-1946, Charlie's yard returned to custom boats as the war was drawing to a close. He built a couple of yachts for Frank Wheaton, of Wheaton Glass during those years.

In 1946, son John left his navy job and became part of Egg Harbor Boats. Two years later, when his son, Jack graduated from high school, he went back to Lower Bank and helped to start Pacemaker Yachts.

The first of the famous Pacemakers went down the ways in the spring of 1949. Jack remembers that it didn't have a name and the christening was approaching. The family couldn't figure out what to call it. They were just about to put the mahogany over the plywood transom when Uncle Cecil walked up to it, took a paintbrush, and wrote *Pacemaker* on the unfinished transom. It was a good name for an excellent boat, a name that would become famous all over the country. Actually, though, while they called their boats Pacemakers, the company continued with the name C.P. Leek and Sons until after old Charlie's death. Cecil was the engine and electrical man for the company, while John, Sr. was designer, woodworker, and business manager.

Custom Yacht c. 1938

The *Alice T* - c. 1940
Custom yacht built for a Norristown, Pennsylvania Dodge dealer

The Leek family realized that they would need a much larger physical plant if they wanted to achieve their dreams. During the early years, they continued to buy surrounding parcels of land on which to expand their business, one of which was Samuel Cavileer's house and land. This house was torn down when the newer buildings were built.

John, Jr. (Jack) married Beatrice Yanko and the couple had two sons: John Everett III (b. December 23, 1951) and Ralph Nicholas (b. June 14, 1960). His brother Donald married Jean Corbett, and they have two sons and two daughters: Donald, Jr. (b. March 7, 1956), Kim Michele (b. June 24, 1957), David Charles (b. December 11, 1958), and Aimee Jean (b. September 11, 1962). He has since remarried to Jane Hofheimer.

Charlie Leek died on March 22, 1959. His wife, Edith, died nine years later. Both were buried in the Lower Bank cemetery. John, Sr. and Cecil gradually turned the operation of the business over to John, Sr.'s sons, Jack and Donald. In 1963 or '64, the brothers organized the company with a new name: *Pacemaker Yachts*, and they continued to produce some of the finest yachts in the world. In their best year, they employed over 800 people and built 2,000 boats!

In those mid-1960's, Pacemaker Yachts was still committed to building wooden boats. In 1960, the company's general manager told a *New York Times* reporter that "People are more comfortable in wooden boats. Wood gets away from the hospital-like appearance of fiber glass." Customizing was also another consideration. Wood was a far easier material to work with when it came to changing things to suit particular owners.

Though Pacemaker took pains to build a boat exactly the way the new owner wanted it, the company was geared to mass-production. Each model, from 26 feet through 53 feet, had its own assembly line. The 39-footer's line always included seven boats in various stages of construction. An interesting note, hulls were always inverted to make planking easier.

By 1965, the production yachts of many other companies were being built from fiberglass, but Pacemaker Yachts seemed committed to continuing the time-honored tradition of solid wooden boats. ["If God wanted boats

C.P. Leek and Sons

The center building burned and the oldest boatyard buiding next to the water was torn down.

The interior view
in one of the Pace-
maker Yachts build-
ings at the height of
production.

Courtesy of
John Leek, Jr.

made out of fiberglass, He would have made fiberglass trees!"] The company would eventually start a plant in Egg Harbor City to produce a fiberglass version of Pacemaker designs rather than make Pacemakers themselves from that material. Unfortunately, the age of the wooden boat was past, and by the end of the decade, even Pacemaker would succumb. The busy yachting crowd found that fiberglass boats required far less maintenance than wooden vessels and much less tender loving care. Nostalgia was not for the many. Wooden boats would remain the realm of the purist, not the weekend sailor.

In 1968, Jack sold the business to Fuqua Industries but continued working for them at Pacemaker Yachts for another nine years. In about 1976 or '77, Fuqua sold it to Mission Marine, a California-based company that built Islander Yachts. Unfortunately, Mission Marine seemed bent on getting as much out of the company as they could in as short a time as possible. They "bought with mirrors," as Jack says. They didn't have any money for production, so they got the suppliers to give them 120 days grace period. According to Jack, it took them just two years to run one of the most successful yacht businesses in the world into the hole.

Jack left Pacemaker soon after the sale. He was supposed to continue to work for Mission Marine, but he soon learned exactly what they had in mind for his former company and just how much they needed him in the downward spiral. He quit, wanting nothing to do with the shady business.

Brother Donald retired from the business, but Jack wasn't ready for that. Jack organized a new company on the Atlantic County side of the Mullica the year he left Mission Marine, and the first Ocean Yachts boats was finished on January 1, 1978. About the same time, he built a fine, new home, also on the Atlantic County side of the Mullica between Green Bank and Lower Bank.

Jack has turned the day-to-day operations of Ocean Yachts over to his sons, John III and Ralph. John III is the yacht builder and president of the company. Ralph is vice-president and head of sales. John III's son, John IV has also entered the business, much to the satisfaction of his grandfather.

Jack, Jr. is now "retired," as if an active and dynamic man like Jack, born to business and the Mullica, could ever sit back and do nothing. Actually, he can dump the daily responsibilities and go have a good time if he wants to. He's been successful and has made enough to be comfortable in his retirement. More power to him!

Courtesy of John Leek, Jr.

The Leeks
Ralph, John, Jr., and John III

A Pacemaker Yacht on a Demo Run
Armand Carney of Green Bank is at the helm.
Armand was Pacemaker's demo captain.

Miss Heritage - The Last Wooden Boat Built on the Mullica

Christened on July 6, 1996, *Miss Heritage* is a c. 1919 flat-bottomed runabout design of C. P. Leek. thus the "C.P. 19". John Leek, Jr. is at the helm headed upriver across from The Old Storehouse in Green Bank.

Lining Up for Demos at Ocean Yachts - 1996

Photographs by John Pearce

John (Jack) Leek, Jr. calculates that his family is responsible for building upwards of 22,000 boats since his grandfather started the ball rolling so many years ago. That's quite an accomplishment, and a great example of an American family's success story in achieving the American Dream. Jack is justly proud of his family, past and present. No wonder he's always interested in the future, not the past.

For years, Jack and his family have provided Fourth of July fireworks for the people of the Mullica valley that would rival those of any town in New Jersey. He and his sons started out setting them off on a barge anchored in the river off Green Bank but moved them down to his home some years back. At first, Jack, John, III, and Ralph set them off themselves but were concerned that it was risky business. It was too easy to shoot yourself.

Jack did the only thing a man could do under the circumstances: he found an explosives manufacturer from Vineland who would do the annual display for him. Jack's fireworks are the highlight of the Mullica towns on the Saturday nearest the Fourth. Everyone who either has a boat, or has a friend with a boat, manages to anchor off Jack's house for the show. Jack throws a party for two hundred fifty guests at his house. At dusk, the show begins, and what a show it is! When it concludes, it does so to the cacophony of boat horns honking in appreciation. Jack's graciousness has been a highlight of these little towns along the Mullica. The whole experience is so moving, a spirit from the past when everyone knew everyone else, when family meant something, and when townspeople could gather to celebrate Independence Day with heartfelt joy.

Jack is still a lover of wooden boats, and he has a new toy in 1996. *Miss Heritage* is the last wooden boat to be built on the Mullica (even if it was constructed on the Atlantic County side). She is a step hydroplane built on a 1919 C.P. Leek design with a huge, eight-cylinder engine in her. She was christened on fireworks day, July 6, 1996, which was also Jack's wife's birthday. Jack loves running her up and down the Mullica. He says she doesn't really pick up and move properly until you reach 30 miles per hour!

Photograph by John Pearce

John Leek IV and John Leek III
aboard a new Ocean Yachts
August 15, 1996

Tommy Hamilton, former head of Collective Bank in Egg Harbor, and Lloyd Wimberg of the Wimberg Funeral Home in the same town own new runabouts of vintage design, and the three like to race each other. Jack modestly says, however, that the race is actually between Wimberg and Hamilton. *Miss Heritage* is at least ten knots faster than either of the other boats.

Charles Platt Leek II
c. 1940
C.P. is examining plans for his latest vessel on his dock at Lower Bank.

The Adams House
2173 River Road

The Home of Lewis and Olive Adams - c. 1910

It is a shame to begin with tragedy, but this interesting old house saw the untimely demise of its owner back in the 1920's. Lewis Adams was the son, perhaps the illegitimate son, of Sarah Lorinah Adams, born on the third of May, 1864. He married Olive Virginia Cale (b. 1867), the daughter of Captain John and Lettice Cale, on October 17th, 1893, and the couple had a son, Gerald, who died in infancy, and two daughters, Beatrice Winterbottom Adams (b. September 30, 1897; d. October 7, 1982) and Ethel Virginia Adams (b. June 17, 1900; d. December 5, 1982).

In all probability, given the approximate era in which this house was constructed, Lewis Adams built himself a fine home on Adams family property in the 1890's after his marriage to Olive Cale. Here the family lived for twenty-five years. Despite his perhaps questionable origins, Lewis Adams gained the respect of his neighbors. For many years, he was the schoolmaster at the Lower Bank school and is shown with his charges in a photograph towards the beginning of this chapter.

He was also instrumental in fighting the removal of the Lower Bank bridge in the 1920's. The old wooden swing bridge, at that time over fifty years old, had fallen into considerable disrepair. Burlington and Atlantic Counties wanted to remove the bridge entirely, forcing Lower Bankers to travel upriver to cross the Green Bank bridge on their way to Egg Harbor, lengthening their trip to that town by over five miles. Adams organized the Lower Bankers in opposition to that plan and led his friends and neighbors to victory. The counties agreed to replace the old structure with a new drawbridge rather than simply removing it.

At the height of his personal triumph, Lewis Adams hung himself in the barn behind his home on the twenty-first of February, 1927. One of his daughters found him, which must have been quite a shock for her. Which of the two actually saw her father in that state is not remembered by the locals, but Beatrice would have been twenty-nine at the time and Ethel Virginia only twenty-six.

Why did he do it? No one will ever know. He had lost his wife, Olive Virginia, on September 13, 1924, less than three years before his demise. His daughter, Ethel, would marry William Henry Fetter on March 25th, slightly less than two months after her father's suicide. Daughter Beatrice would never marry. Perhaps he never got over his wife's death. Maybe it was the threat of losing one of his daughters in marriage. Perhaps it was the combination of losing his wife and daughter in such close proximity. No one locally seems to remember any scandal that would have caused his untimely demise. The reason has been buried in time.

Lewis Adams was buried in the family plot not a hundred yards from his home along the Mullica. Stephen H. Adams and Lorinah Brush Adams, Lewis's grandparents, lie here along with their grandson.

The Adams line can be traced back at least two generations beyond Stephen. Leah Blackman, in her *History of Little Egg Harbor*, gives a thorough account of the Adams family. Hezekiah Adams moved into the Bass River area sometime in the mid-1700's about the same time that John Leek, Sr. and Charles Loveland settled on their homesteads. Though Mrs. Blackman doesn't give Hezekiah's wife's name, she does list his children: Joseph, Hezekiah, Jr., Jeremiah, Charles, David, Dorcas, and Mary. His children married into local families. There is no listing for Joseph, but Hezekiah, Jr. married Margaret Humphrey; Jeremiah married Elizabeth Jenkins; Charles married Hannah Jenkins; David married Elizabeth Robbins; while Dorcas and Mary married brothers: Isaac Cramer and Caleb Cramer, Jr. respectively.

David and Elizabeth (Robbins) Adams had eleven children, in keeping with the large-family ideal on farms and homesteads of the time: Stacy, Moses, Charles, Isaiah, Mary Ann, Stephen, John, Washington, Sarah, Eliza, and Joseph Perkins.

Stephen Adams was born on February 20, 1808 and is listed on the 1850 census as a hotel keeper. His tavern may have been the core of this house, which his grandson, Lewis, later expanded. Stephen and Lorinah's children were: Benjamin, Chalkley C., Sarah A., Stephen H., Joseph M., Analiza, Rebecca, Sarah J., Emma J., and Lovinah. Stephen died on the 19th of July, 1851, but his wife continued to keep the tavern. Lorinah (Brush) Adams died on August 22nd, 1888 in the eighty-eighth year of her life. Sarah Lorinah Adams was the mother of the ill-fated Lewis.

Isaiah Adams, Stephen's brother, became one of the leading men of Little Egg Harbor Township. It was Isaiah who kept the famous Bass River Tavern, the first stop out of Tuckerton on the old Stage Road. He was rather unique

Photograph by John Pearce

1996

amongst tavern-keepers due to the fact that he was for total abstinence. Anyone wanting a drink of hard liquor would have had to make the journey to Bodine's Tavern up the road. They couldn't be served at Bass River.

Isaiah was not satisfied with simply being a tavern-keeper. Like Nicholas Sooy I at Green Bank, Isaiah was an entrepreneur. He cleared a large farm in the vicinity of his tavern and built a house suitable for his status. He was involved in the lumber business, ship building, and other similar enterprises. On his farm, he planted orchards of apples, peaches, cherries, and other fruits and was one of the most enterprising and skillful agriculturists in the township. He served as a State Legislator and held offices within his township.

Mrs. Blackman records that he was very well-liked by his neighbors. He had an obliging disposition, was always ready to help a friend or a complete stranger, contributed to all the local churches without discrimination, put up travelling clergy in his home, and tried to help the suffering and destitute. He saw to it that his children had an excellent education.

Isaiah Adams died at, as Mrs. Blackman so quaintly puts it, "the commencement of the late rebellion" [the Civil War]. He was succeeded in the Bass River Tavern by his nephew, Franklin, son of his brother, Moses. Because of the declining traffic on the old road, Franklin Adams closed the hoary tavern and built a new one in New Gretna proper.

One hundred and thirty-five years had obliterated everything that Isaiah accomplished. The Bass River Tavern is gone. Located on the western branch of the Bass River at the "Upper Bridge," even its exact site is almost forgotten. Pilgrim Lake Campground occupies land in the vicinity. Of Isaiah's extensive and famous farm, nothing at all remains. Most of the surrounding land is owned by the State of New Jersey and has returned to second growth woodland. Much of the area was flooded during the depression when the C.C.C. created the lake at Bass River State Park.

As to the Adams house, a man by the name of Frank Henderson succeeded to the ownership, purchasing it from Lewis Adams's daughters after his untimely demise. Henderson built an ice house by the river. He would cut ice from the river in winter and store it in his ice house. In season, the local fishermen would bring their stripers to Henderson's ice house to be boxed and iced for shipment to the Philadelphia and New York markets.

Lewis Adams' daughter, Beatrice, built a little house right on the river on a portion of the former homestead property and lived there the rest of her life. She died in 1982, the same year in which her sister, Ethel (Adams) Fetter passed away.

One final note. Lewis Adams delighted in telling everyone that the Adams property was the site of Eric Mullica's homestead. He would even point out two old trees which have long since disappeared, that he claimed once flanked the Mullica cabin. We now know that his claim may have had some merit.

The Captain Robert Somers House
2187 River Road

1995

Photograph by John Pearce

Built during the waning years of the nineteenth century, this beautiful home overlooking the Mullica River has had but three owners in its entire history. Captain Robert Somers was the original builder of this late 1800's house below the bridge in Lower Bank.

He and his wife, Margaret, had two children, Monty and Alicia. Alicia Somers was born in 1890, and her brother, E. Montgomery, in 1892. Alicia married Clarence Smith (b. 1889; d. 1956) and was a college instructor. She inherited the house upon the death of her father and lived here for the last years of her life. She died in 1978 at the age of 88 and was buried in the family cemetery along the river. Monty served in World War One and died in 1966.

The Haines family of Hog Wallow bought the house near the time of Alicia's death. Under the capable direction of Holly Haines, who now makes it her home, the entire structure was restored to its original splendor.

Bridge at Lower Bank, N.J.

View of the Lower Bank Bridge
Looking Towards Atlantic County
c. 1910

The Great Flood of 1950

C. P. Leek's original boatyard building is on the left. The Lower Bank bridge is almost completely under water.

The Great Flood of 1950

This photograph was taken at the base of the Lower Bank bridge looking upstream. The house on the right was the home of Samuel Cavileer which was later torn down as part of the expansion for Pacemaker.

Boys Will Be Boys
c. 1935
The house in the background belonged to Samuel Cavileer, Horace Cavileer's great-grandfather.
It was torn down when the Pacemaker Yachts Plant was expanded to its present form.

Dave Cavileer

Lillian DeBow and Dave Cavileer
c. 1944

The Newest Version of the
Lower Bank Bridge
1995

Looking Towards Lower Bank from the John Lewis House on the
Atlantic County side of the Mullica.
The Pacemaker Plant is in the background and the bridge to the left.

Lower Bank

Photograph by John Pearce

552

Martha Furnace

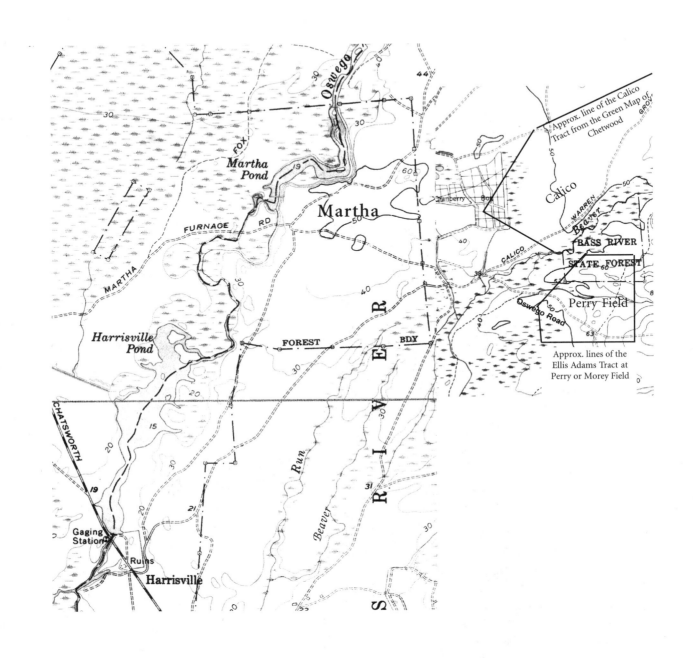

Martha Furnace

554

THE ROAD TO MARTHA

The road to Martha begins at Harrisville and runs up the east bank of the Harrisville Lake, then follows the East Branch of the Wading River (called the Oswego River) until it reaches a bridge to the west side. Nearby is the site of Martha Furnace, a going concern at the beginning of the nineteenth century, but today its location is all but lost in the pines. The road to Martha in 1995 is fit only for four-wheel drive vehicles, especially where it curves through the site of Martha itself. It used to cross the bridge and continue on until it reemerged on the Harrisville/Chatsworth road, but huge, water-filled holes have made that journey impossible, even for Jeep-type vehicles. A fenced mound of brick and earth is all that's left of this profitable furnace, and nearby, the site of the mansion can be found only by noticing the various non-indigenous trees which were planted almost two hundred years ago.

At some time prior to 1758, an unknown entrepreneur dammed the Oswego Branch of the Wading River and built a saw mill which he called "Swago," about two miles above the location of Evi Belangee, Jr.'s mill. The location wasn't completely lost in the pines prior to the Revolutionary War as it seems today. The Stage Road from Burlington and Mount Holly passed about a mile to the south of Belangee's mill, which meant that the sawmill was only about three miles from this main thoroughfare. Just below the point at which the Stage Road crossed the Wading River at Bodine's Tavern was also the highest point of navigation, which meant that goods from the Oswego Sawmill could be shipped at that point after only a three-mile trip through the woods. Sometime before the end of the century, William Newbold and Samuel Hough owned and operated this mill.

Isaac Potts, a Philadelphia businessman we've heard of before, bought the mill from Samuel Hough and the executors of Newbold's estate on the first of October, 1793. The following year, he also bought land from John Bodine, the owner and proprietor of Bodine's Tavern. Potts was an entrepreneur, investing in land, building businesses, then selling them off at a profit. He had to have already owned the land near the Oswego ("Swago") Saw Mill, because it is noted in the Martha Diary that the furnace went into blast on September 29th, 1793 and made its first casting at three in the morning of the 30th of that month, prior to his purchase of the saw mill on the following day.

Potts & Co. was involved with iron production in Pennsylvania. It ran the Great Valley Works and owned the land on which the forge at Valley Forge was constructed. Isaac Potts must have noticed the tremendous potential for the bog iron industry at that time and decided to take advantage of the growing interest in the area. Potts, his new furnace named "Martha" for his wife, had it in blast by the end of 1793, and offered it for sale three years later, on February 11, 1796. By this time, the furnace lands totalled about 20,000 acres of pinelands and additional acres of cedar swamps. Arthur Pierce in *Iron in the Pines* quotes this figure from an advertisement placed in the February 11, 1796 *American Weekly Advertiser*. The advertisement indicates that the furnace property also included a "grist mill, saw mill, and some preparation for erecting a forge." Curiously, Henry Bisbee in *Martha: The Complete Furnace Diary and Journal* (1976) came up with a Little Egg Harbor tax duplicate, dating from 1795

Courtesy of Budd Wilson, Jr.

A Portion of the Martha Furnace

Budd Wilson, Jr. as archaeologist for the State of New Jersey, excavated Martha Furnace in 1968. This photograph and the others in this section are from his collection of slides.

through 1797, that indicates Potts was only assessed for a furnace, thirty acres of improved land, and 2,000 acres of unimproved land.

A sizable village had grown up near the furnace, and Potts seems also to have built a grist mill, in addition to the saw mill purchased from Hough and Newbold. At the time of the sale, the village included a large frame house, a log barn, a coal house, bellows house, bridge house, moulding rooms, and quite a number of small houses for the workers. Potts had built the Wading River Forge and Slitting Mill on the Oswego Branch of the Wading River south of Martha in 1795, so as of that date, he had constructed a complete iron-producing facility on the river.

As has been noted before, a furnace such as Martha produced cast iron in the form of "pigs." It

Courtesy of Budd Wilson, Jr.
Site of the Furnace - 1968

also made cast-iron products directly from the molten ore. A forge further refined the ore into hammered products. A slitting mill turned the iron into bars which could be cut by huge rotary shears into various products like nails. When he offered the whole complex for sale, he certainly could be proud of his achievement. Unfortunately, others didn't share his enthusiasm for iron in the pines. While he managed to sell the Wading River Forge, it took him five years to unload Martha Furnace.

WADING RIVER FORGE AND SLITTING MILL

Isaac Potts sold the Wading River Forge and Slitting Mill to William Ashbridge, his brother, George Garret Ashbridge, and Joseph Walker on the 24th of April, 1797. William Ashbridge sold his share in the forge to Joseph Walker on April 4, 1802, giving him a two-thirds interest. Walker sold out to John Youle in 1809, but the forge burned in 1810. When George Ashbridge died (no date given in the Wharton ledgers), his one-third share of the land was inherited by his daughter, Mary, the wife of a Newark physician, John S. Condit. Dr. John and Mary Condit sold their share to Samuel Richards on May 7, 1829. Samuel apparently sold his share to Jesse Evans when the latter purchased Martha Furnace from him in 1841.

Courtesy of Budd Wilson, Jr.

ANOTHER "GREAT" MAN COMES TO WASHINGTON TOWNSHIP

John Paul, Charles Shoemaker, Morris Robeson, and George Ashbridge finally bought Martha from Potts in November, 1800. The George Garret Ashbridge who had been one of the purchasers of the Wading River Forge and Slitting Mill was the cousin of this George Ashbridge, so the entire complex was still related. These businessmen formed the Martha Furnace Company and hired a manager to live on the site and oversee the production.

Apparently the business didn't fulfill expectations. The company was put up for sale four years later in 1805.

As advertised in the Trenton *Federalist*, the estate had been reduced in size from 20,000 acres to 15,000 acres, but still included the blast furnace, gristmill, stamping mill, the entire town, and ore rights. It also noted that the West Creek Forge (also called the "Westecunk Forge" after the creek which runs through the nearby town, and the "Stafford Forge") provided another market for the pig iron produced at the furnace.

Once again, there were no buyers. According to Pierce, the company decided to hire another manager, and engaged Jesse Evans in 1805. This may be incorrect. Jesse Evans had to have been in Washington Township, perhaps even at Martha, prior to 1803, for in that year and until 1807, he served as one of the township's representatives to the Board of Chosen Freeholders. That honor would not have been given if he had recently moved into the area,

Courtesy of Budd Wilson, Jr.

Budd Wilson, Jr. in the excavated remains of Martha Furnace - 1968

or unless, of course, he was heading one of the important local industries. He may in fact have been the original manager hired by Messrs. Paul, Shoemaker, Robeson, and Ashbridge in 1800 after they bought the business from Isaac Potts.

Jesse was born in Old Evesham Township in the Lumberton area in 1770, and, when he was twenty-five years old, married Lucy Ann Kellum of Beverly, Massachusetts, who was a year older than he was. Bisbee notes that the first mention of his name is in an advertisement in the *New Jersey Mirror* of 1799 concerning a new iron plow developed by Charles Newbold. He and Lucy Ann moved to Little Egg Harbor Township between 1800 and 1802, but the area would not remain a part of that township for very long. On November 19th, 1802, the new Washington Township was formed, and Jesse jumped into local politics with enthusiasm. At the first meeting of the township, held at Bodine's Tavern below Martha in March of the following year, he was elected both a Chosen Freeholder and a member of the township committee.

Jesse proved not only a good manager for Martha, he also was a godsend for the township. Along with Jesse Richards of Batsto, Evans became one of the most active and prominent citizens of the new township, serving in several capacities over the years: Justice of the Peace, Assessor, Judge of Elections, and even as Chosen Freeholder. Year after year in the early township records, the name of Jesse Evans appears, along with those of Jesse Richards and Nicholas Sooy I and II.

Jesse Evans served as president of town meeting in 1804, 1806, and 1822, and clerk in 1807 and 1810. He also spent a total of thirty-seven years on the township committee: 1803 - 1807, 1809 - 1814, 1819 - 1828, 1830 - 1832, 1834 - 1843, and 1845 - 1847. No one else came close to beating his record, not even Jesse Richards.

MARTHA FURNACE UNDER JESSE EVANS

When Martha was finally sold on April 6, 1808, it passed into the hands of Samuel Richards and Joseph Ball. Richards, the brother of Jesse Richards of Batsto and owner of Atsion Furnace, had interests in Hampton Furnace and Weymouth Furnace as well. Ball, the nephew of William Richards and cousin of Jesse and Samuel, had operated Batsto during the Revolutionary War for Cox and his partners. He also held an interest in Weymouth Furnace and was a speculator in lands over an extensive area. Of all the previous owners, only George Ashbridge did not sell his one-quarter interest in Martha. Thus he became a partner with Ball and Richards in the iron town. Jesse Evans was retained as manager by the new owners.

The Furnace Site During the 1968 Excavation

In 1834, during the successful management of Martha by Jesse Evans, the village contained a school, a grist mill, as many as forty to fifty houses for the workers, a "mansion" for Mr. Evans and his wife, the furnace, a stamping mill, and a sawmill. It boasted upwards of four hundred residents. The furnace was located on the river at the base of Calico Ridge. Jesse Evans' house stood to the south of the furnace complex.

Martha Furnace used a tub-type bellows to produce the forced air necessary to sustain the great heat needed to melt the iron ore. Martha made the usual Jersey-furnace products like Batsto and Atsion: firebacks, stoves, kettles, sash weights, cambooses (ships' stoves), and cast-iron cooking pots. Although there seems to have been plans from time to time to build a forge nearing the Martha property, none was ever built. In the early years, it must have shipped much of its production to the Wading River Forge and Slitting Mill, two miles down the river, to be made into wagon tires, nails, etc.

Jesse proved to be an adept manager, making Martha profitable for almost half a century. Jesse also travelled around the country quite a bit. He and his wife went to Tucker's Beach, south of Long Beach Island, attended township and county meetings, made court appearances (court was held at the various taverns along the Stage Road), took his mother to Pottsgove, Pennsylvania, and went on surveying trips. He helped build a school house at Martha and is even recorded as building a desk for the school.

Jesse was successful for most of his life, a well-respected and loved gentleman.

THE MARTHA DIARY

Martha is special among the old furnaces of New Jersey in that someone kept a diary from March of 1808 until May of 1815. Arthur Pierce states that diary was found in a safe in the semi-abandoned main building of the paper mill at Harrisville about 1910. Henry Bisbee says it belonged to John Harris, Esq. of Mount Holly in 1917. Both may be true.

Pierce noted that the location of the original diary was unknown when he published in 1957, but Bisbee, after extensive sleuthing, found that a New York dealer had sold it to The Eleutherian Mills Historical Library at Greenville, Delaware. The book had originally been purchased from an antiques dealer, Albert Collier, in Bordentown.

Pierce says that two copies were made from the original prior to its disappearance. One was owned by historian Charles Boyer. South Jersey historian Nathaniel R. Ewan made his copy from Boyer's. Another copy was made by Captain Charles I. ("Cap" or "Budd") Wilson of Herman City, the father of Budd Wilson of Green Bank. Bisbee adds that the copy owned by Boyer was originally made by D. G. Baird of Beverly, and this copy became the property of the Camden County Historical Society. Another copy is in the Rutgers University library. In 1976, Bisbee published the entire diary from the original, not from one of the copies.

It is not known who wrote the entries in the diary in the first place. Pierce assumes Caleb Earl, the clerk at Martha, kept the journal, but Bisbee disproves this. He notes that, from the handwriting, there seems to be two distinct authors. Caleb Earl, (Sr.) Esq. was a merchant in Juliustown, Springfield Township, and he died before the diary ends. His son, Caleb Earl, Jr. did become clerk in 1814, and we know from an entry made in April of 1814 that "Caleb Earl, Jurn., wt 129 lbs." He was nineteen that year. In August, "JEN" noted that Caleb Earl, Jr. had gained nine pounds. Who was "JEN"? No one at Martha had these initials. Caleb Earl, Jr. was the clerk at Martha by the time the diary concluded, but he is noted as absent from Martha and the diary continues uninterrupted. Harvey Moore's booklet on Martha states that a "Caleb West, a self-effacing humorist" wrote the diary, but there was no one at Martha by that name.

Bisbee apparently submitted handwriting samples of the diary and of both Caleb Earls to the F.B.I for analysis. Their conclusion was that it was written by three, possibly more, writers. The signatures of the Caleb Earls were not sufficient to determine whether or not either of them had made entries. Bisbee concludes that "one writer, with some exceptions, made entries in the diary from 1808 through 1811. Thereafter, three and perhaps more persons made entries."

The Martha Diary presents a vivid picture of life in a South Jersey iron community during the first part of the nineteenth century. The residential village contained about four hundred people at the height of Martha's prosperity. Travel between towns was minimal, and men worked long, hard hours. For the workers there were no eight-hour days and paid vacations. The only time off they got was in midwinter when the furnace went out of blast, the water wheel frozen solid from the cold. Three miles downstream was Bodine's Tavern on the Stage Road. To the east was the Bass River Hotel, and up the road to the northwest was Sooy's Inn at the town of Washington. On holidays such as voting day and "training" day, the men delighted in travelling to Bodine's or Sooy's by the wagon-load. It was good they went by wagon, because most were too drunk to ride the long way home at night. Bodine's was only about three miles from Martha, a bit too close to suit manager Jesse Evans. The Bass River Hotel never posed a threat to Bodine's or Sooy's: the proprietor was an advocate of abstinence. The entry for January 7th, 1809 notes that the furnace was put out of blast that day and that "all hands [were] drunk."

Most of the hiring and firing was done by the chief founder, Michael Mick, Jr., who also seems to have run the day-to-day operations of the furnace while Jesse Evans maintained overall supervision. His father, the first Michael Mick, who was also at Martha during the period of the diary, is probably the progenitor of the Mick family of Jenkins. These little iron furnaces in the pines were self-sustaining units, and Mick was often forced to rehire the very persons he had previously fired. Experienced hands were far better than inexperienced ones, even if the possessor was drunk occasionally. Some of the more skilled workers moved between the various furnaces owned by Samuel Richards.

The history of the pinelands towns is punctuated by that word "fire." Little wonder. Most of the buildings were constructed of wood which dried out in the hot sun. The surrounding forests of pine and oak became tinder-dry in the summer. The iron and glass industries themselves were based on fire. Bellows-induced white-hot fire was needed to melt the iron at every stage. It's no wonder that fire was so dreaded. Martha's day came on the second of June, 1813. The furnace was entirely destroyed, but the surrounding woods and town escaped. Samuel Richards and Joseph Ball arrived from Atsion two days later and decided to rebuild. They arranged to have bricks brought down from Speedwell Furnace, and other equipment, including a bellows, were borrowed from those other Richards' establishments, Atsion and Hampton Forge. By the eleventh of August, Martha was back in business.

The Martha diary ends in May 1815, but that date doesn't end the Martha story. Richards bought Joseph Ball's share from his heirs in 1822, and the iron business seems to have continued to make a profit. Competition from Pennsylvania was closing in, though.

THE STAMPING MILL QUESTION

While researching the Batsto complex, the presence of a stamping mill at that location was questioned. A stamping mill was used to crush magnetite ore (called "mountain" ore at Martha and "foreign" ore at Batsto), brought in from northern New Jersey to supplement the bog iron, which was "roasted" and needed no crushing. A light-duty mill was used to crush the seashells for lime and the slag for reuse.

No evidence exists that Batsto ever had a water-powered heavy-duty mill, only a horse-powered one, even after "foreign" ore was imported around 1826 or 1827. At Martha there is ample indication of a water-powered mill. When Martha Furnace was offered for sale by Potts in 1796, no mention is made of a stamping mill in the complex. An 1805 advertisement for sale does list one, so it is presumed that some type of stamping mill existed at that time, but there would have been no need for a water-powered one until they started to import magnetite.

In 1809 and 1810, the following entries are found in the Diary:

January 1809	*Farrell commenced in stamping mill*
July 1809	*Stamping mill in full blast*
June 1810	*Mr. Evans and Luker went for stamping mill shaft*
July 1810	*Sawing shaft for stamping mill*
July 15, 1810	*Maurice Simons came today to begin stamping mill.*
July 23, 1810	*Moses Gaskill began to work at the Stamping Mill. Digging out flume for stamping mill*

Courtesy of Budd Wilson, Jr.

Archaeologist Budd Wilson, Jr. at the Furnace Site - 1968

July 28, 1810	*Trunk for stamping mill*
July 31, 1810	*Ventling making castings for stamping mill*
August 2, 1810	*Wheeling cinder to stamping mill flume*
August 11. 1810	*Moses Gasgill cut off his finger working at the Stamping Mill*
August 13, 1810	*P. Cunning working about the Stamping Mill*
August 15, 1810	*Maurice Simons finished the Stamping Mill*
August 16, 1810	*Patrick Cunning started the Stamping Mill*

(Entries are taken from both Arthur Pierce's and Bisbee's version of "The Martha Diary.")

In a way, these entries are a puzzle in themselves. They are taken from two different versions of the diary, but they do seem to make sense. Apparently, there was a light-duty horse-powered stamping mill at Martha prior to 1810. Thus the entry about "Farrell commenced in stamping mill" must refer to the earlier horse-powered mill.

The July 1809 entry is a puzzlement. A *furnace* is said to be "in blast" when the bellows are powered. Since a stamping mill had neither fire nor bellows, perhaps "in blast" was their slang for "working on a full schedule" or "working at capacity." We still use the term "going full blast" today.

By 1810, Jesse Evans must have decided to make preparations for the use of "mountain" ore from northern New Jersey which required a water-powered stamping mill. Consequently, he got construction going on a new mill. He accompanied a man by the name of Luker to look for a likely tree to use for the stamping mill shaft. Having found one, it was cut in July. Maurice Simons began the

Courtesy of Budd Wilson, Jr.

Edna Wilson of Herman, Budd Wilson, Jr.'s mother, is on the left.
Alice Adams Weber of Wading River is on the right.

construction of the new stamping mill on July 15th, and, on the 23rd of that month, the water flume to the new mill was dug. Five days later, the flume was enclosed in a wooden trunk. On the 31st, they made the necessary castings at the furnace.

The last entry referring to the stamping mill is really strange. Why would they haul cinders to the flume? Would they wash them and then reuse them? More than likely, there had been a cave-in at the flume for the stamping mill and the men were hauling cinders to be used in the repair job.

The first *recorded* date for the use of "mountain ore" at Martha is June 21, 1811.

JESSE EVANS

Jesse's first wife, Lucy Ann (Kellum), was a devout Quaker, but little is known concerning Jesse's relationship to the Friends. If he was a Quaker, business matters or indifference seemed to have kept him from regular attendance at Meeting. There have been some who would question whether Jesse Evans was a member of a Quaker Meeting at all, because he attended the Little Egg Harbor Meeting in Tuckerton with his wife so infrequently.

In the first part of the nineteenth century, the Quakers were ruptured by disagreements that resulted in a division of the "Friends." Those of the Little Egg Harbor Meeting who adhered to the teachings of the Hicksites built a Meeting House at Bridgeport/Wading River in 1825, and Lucy Evans travelled down the road from Martha to Bridgeport each First Day for meeting. The Methodists were sweeping the area during these years, and many joined the churches built for that denomination, but Lucy remained faithful. Lucy Evans remained so faithful that the time came when she was the sole minister and member of the congregation at the Bridgeport Meeting, sitting in solitary and silent meditation each First Day until her death in 1834 at the age of sixty-six. She was buried in the old Quaker graveyard at Bridgeport/Wading River.

No mention is made in any record extant that Jesse and Lucy Ann had any children. Bisbee notes that *The Camden Mail* printed a death notice for a Jesse Evans, Jr. on October 7, 1835, at Joseph Burr's Ferry, aged twenty-five years. At the end of the month, another notice simply states that he died in Philadelphia. If the age given is correct, Jesse Evans, Jr. was born in 1810, about ten years after Jesse and Lucy Ann moved to Martha.

When his friend, John King, died on March 25, 1813, he left eight children under the age of fourteen and three older ones. Jesse and Lucy Ann (Kellum) took the four youngest children into their home: Mary age 5, Margaret age 4, Lucy age 2, and John less than a year old. It is possible that this last child, named John, took Jesse's name and was known as "Jesse, Jr.". Thus it may be he who died at Burr's Ferry in 1835. He would have been twenty-three years old. It wouldn't have been the first time that a newspaper got the details wrong. (Note: Bisbee, *Martha: The Complete Furnace Diary and Journal 1808-1815,* has in his list of births at Martha: "Evans, Lucy Ann *nee* Kellum, a son, Jesse, Jr. Probably 1809." He doesn't say where he got this information. He may have calculated it from the death notice rather than found it in any record.)

Jesse Evans waited almost two years after his wife's death before remarrying. At the age of sixty-six, he married Lucy Ann King, his former ward, age twenty-five, at Martha in December of 1836. Over the next few years, he fathered five children: Elizabeth (1837), Lucy Ann (1839), Jesse (1841), Rebecca (1842), and David (1845*). When David was born, Jesse Evans would have been seventy-five years old!

Mr. Herbert Schuck of Bordentown recently gave me a copy of notes his wife's grandmother, Irene Cornelia FitzRandolph Evans Harbut, made in 1943. Irene Cornelia was the daughter of Jesse's son, David. Among her genealogy work was the following about old Jesse:

> He must have been a "dandy" of his day. He wore velvet knee britches (black), and white lace ruffled front, and his knee buckles and slipper buckles were blue and white sapphires. I have always worn one as a broach. He also wore a bracelet, his chain [and?] his watch. Jess had the topaz stone in a ring, the chain is solid gold. Jesse Evans came from Wales, that is all I know of his whereabouts.

On August 26, 1841, Samuel Richards, always a sharp businessman, sold out to Martha's longtime manager, Jesse Evans, who was left to bear the brunt of decay and death. Jesse paid $10,000 for his home of over forty years, but his purchase of love was to no avail. The ensuing decade would see the great hammer of Martha cease its ore-pounding, and Jesse Evans was destined to watch as the fire was extinguished in the furnace for the final time. Charcoal production continued until the end of the decade, but the majority of workers and their families were forced to leave the area in order to find work. Jesse and the second Lucy Ann finally gave up in 1847 and moved back to the area of his birth, now a part of Medford Township.

Washington Township lost a great man who had given his life in the service of the people of the township from its founding until that fateful year, a period of forty-five years. The furnace was no more. When Jesse and the second Lucy Ann moved from Martha, a way of life with iron in the pines had come to an end forever. He died at the age of seventy-nine on March 29, 1849 at Medford, but his grave has never been located. His granddaughter's notes continue:

> Grandfather Jesse Evans lived on the main street in Medford, N.J. I have seen the red brick three-storied house which was known as the Evan's homestead. . . . He was considered a rich man in his time. Grandmother, Lucy King Evans, went south with Aunt Bess and Uncle Rice Gualle in 1876, the year I was borned. Grandmother Lucy King Evans died and was buried in Florida.

*These dates were taken from Bisbee. David Evans's gravestone in Bordentown states that he died in 1900 at the age of 51. This would mean that he was born in 1849, the year of his father's death. Jesse would have been seventy-eight when David was conceived. David died after a fall from a bicycle.

Jesse Evans, no doubt with tears streaming from his eyes for his beloved home, sold out to Francis French and William B. Allen in 1848. They continued to operate the sawmill for a few years, but in 1858, they resold the 23,000 acre tract to Francis B. Chetwood, president of the Raritan and Delaware Bay Railroad. The company had planned to build the rail line through Martha Furnace, Harrisville, Green Bank, Egg Harbor and on to Mays Landing, but by the time Chetwood bought the Martha Tract, the surveyors had found that route impractical. When the Raritan and Delaware Bay Railroad laid its rails, it was through Shamong (Chatsworth) and Atsion, not through Martha. In that simple act, Martha and Harrisville were doomed to obscurity, and Green Bank would become a sleepy little town on the Mullica, stirred only by memories of past glory.

On February 11th, 1858, a boy named Edwin was born in Martha to James and Sarah Maxwell, but this may well have been the Maxwell family that had the farm in what is known today as Maxwell. It was close enough to Martha that it could easily have been considered a part of that town. A month and a half later, Samuel and Caroline Albertson had a little girl on March 28th. James Maxwell is listed as a carpenter, and Samuel Albertson, a sawyer. On August 29th, 1861, Hannah Angeline was born to John B. & Jane Ann [no surname given - possibly "Batterson"] at "Chitwood." These were the last births recorded for the town of Martha in the Washington Township records, but the site of Martha became part of Bass River Township in 1864. The last marriages recorded were of John Borough Batterson and Mary Jane French on the 3rd of November, 1849, and Henry Hollaway and the daughter of George & Sarah Rhyal [no name given] on October 10th, 1860. The Batterson/French wedding was conducted at Toms River, while the Hollaway/Rhyal wedding was conducted at Lower Bank.

When Chetwood purchased the tract, he reserved 300 acres for himself and changed the name to the Oswego Tract. The remainder he resold to Amory Edwards between 1860 and 1863. Edwards was a speculator and a director of the same railroad of which Chetwood was president. Though the name "Oswego" appears on the 1870 map of lower Burlington County, the township records continue to call it Martha until the 1861 birth mentioned above. After 1861, it is called "Chitwood." Bisbee notes that "Chitwood" was listed in the "Industries of New Jersey" of 1882 as a "hamlet two miles above Harrisville." It is probable that "Chitwood" was simply the local pronunciation of "Chetwood."

The "Lost" Site of Calico

Some of Martha's workers and their families were supposed to have lived in a little town called Calico, though that name does not appear in the Martha Diary or in the Washington Township records.

When Bisbee (*Signposts*) and Beck (*Forgotten Towns*) were doing their research in the early and middle part of the twentieth century, they recorded the location of this forgotten town at between two and five miles from the site of Martha itself, a healthy hike for the workers. Budd Wilson of Green Bank and Steve Eichinger of Wading River both have said that there

Courtesy of John Milton Adams, Jr

John Milton Adams, Jr. with his father, John Milton Adams, Sr. at Perry Field near Calico in 1939.

were houses on the road to the east of Martha Furnace itself, but apparently they were considered a part of Martha. Beck actually visited the site with two men who had intimate connections with Calico. Hugh O'Neill of Camden had been born there, and Kirk Cramer of Berlin's grandfather had called Calico his home. Kirk did locate his grandfather's house, or at least, the remains of its chimney, still marking the place where so much of his family's life had happened.

John Milton Adams, Jr.. visited the site of his grandfather's (Ellis Adams) house in Perry Field (or Morey Field) near Calico with his father in 1939. He says that Calico was on the Calico-Warren Grove Road, after the Oswego Road branches off and after crossing Beaver Branch. This would be a little over a mile or a mile and a half from Martha. Perry Field was on the Oswego Road, not far from Calico.

THE BRIDGE TO NOWHERE

The site of Martha, like so much other land in the pinelands, was sucked up by Joseph Wharton in 1896 along with Harrisville, but even by this time, nothing remained of the Martha Furnace. The little wooden houses of the workers, Jesse Evans' "mansion," and all the furnace works had succumbed to time and the elements. Wharton apparently had no particular use for the area in the long run, and Martha returned to a state of obscurity.

On July 1, 1968, Budd Wilson of Green Bank, in his capacity as archeologist for the State of New Jersey, began excavations at Martha Furnace. He found that the brick and stonework that was uncovered crumbled very easily and that it was difficult to determine just what was structure and what was rubble. After investigation, he found that the furnace measured 22'6" square and had but one bellows hole and that the hearth, originally square, had been blown out of shape by the blast. He could locate neither the gutter into which the molten iron flowed, nor any evidence of the sow and pig beds. He did find that the furnace was built on 8" thick wood cribbing that was sawn on only two sides. Also uncovered was a 2' thick wall which extended eastward from the furnace for a distance of 39 feet. This wall is believed to have acted as a retaining wall against the north hill and probably held the north wall of the casting house. A few fragments of stoneware were also found which bore various designs including a wreath, garland, and ship, a Grecian figure with a dog, a cathedral, a sunburst and floral designs. Little else remained of this pinelands enterprise, the nearby village, or the mansion. When the excavations were completed, everything was covered up once again.

Of Jesse Evans, strong in character, public spirited, and lusty in his old age, nothing remains where he made his home for almost fifty years. Wind breathes in the leaves of ancient trees planted by the residents in their little village by the river. A bridge still crosses the Oswego Branch at Martha, but the road beyond is impassable. It is truly a bridge to nowhere.

The Ore Beach at Martha

564

LINES WRITTEN ON THE LIFE OF

LUCY ANN EVANS

THE WIFE OF JESSE EVANS, OF MARTHA FURNACE, BURLINGTON COUNTY, N.J.

Since the death of dear Lucy, some years have expired,
In which we've accomplished one thing we desired,
To gather up the fragments, that nothing be lost,
Of all that is good, without trouble or cost.
That portion implanted in every ones breast,
If duly considered, will lead us to rest;
The truth of this doctrine will fully appear,
If we follow the example of Lucy our dear.
Surrender up all to our Lord and Master,
Be willing to become as sheep of his pasture,
No wolf can devour, or serpent betray,
If we in his power do trust night and day.
All habits of evil he'll help us remove
And place our desires on him and his love.
There was one she indulged in, so under disguise
The effect it produced, occasioned surprise,
That tobacco or snuff, should an evil possess,
That went to destroy rather than bless:
Being fully convinced of the truth of the fact,
There seemed a reluctance in nature to act.
One night in a dream, as in the garden she stray'd
To view the fine flowers and plants there display'd,
She saw a tobacco stalk and rejoiced at the sight,
As the things which she loved she could view with delight.
So examining it closely in every part,
She there found a serpent wound up in its heart.
Then staring astonished, she shortly awoke
And gave to tobacco its finishing stroke.
The next great sacrifice that she had to make,
Was her habits and dress must go to the stake,
Became willing to do, or suffer for his cause
Whose power induced her to submit to his laws.
No mortal to counsel her, no will to obey
But his who commanded, and pointed the way,
She yielded submission, and saw with delight
His yoke was made easy, and burden made light.
In all things of importance, took him for her guide
Who never deceived her, but did often provide
Such things as she needed, to heal or to cure
The poor, sick or afflicted that came to her door.
The lame and the sick to her would apply,
On whose counsel for truth they could always rely.
She was not quick to speak, but retiring to feel
What the Master would teach in order to heal.
The sick and afflicted in her had a friend
Who often assisted their sufferings to mend.
One case I refer to, we'll freely record,
Where her feelings were moved to send a regard;
A poor man in sickness, and want in extreme
Was told her laid suffering, no one to redeem;
She was then in the stage, going down to the city,
Yet still she was moved with compasion and pity -
Took the money she intended to lay out for a dress,
And sent it to relieve a poor man in distress.
Another adventure of a similar kind
Has just presented itself to my mind:
Early one morning, on a very cold day,

She felt an impression, to go without delay
Some miles in the woods, where two old people dwelt,
And act in accordance with what she had felt.
She went to the storehouse, and there did proceed
To provide such things, as she thought they had need,
And then told her husband that he must go with her,
As he well knew it was very cold weather,
And take a supply both to warm and to feed,
Nor ever deny what they really did need;
So on they proceeded through cold, ice and snow,
Through branches and thickets as far as they could go,
Some obstruction prevented the carriage going through,
They lift up their eyes, and the house was in view,
Then taking their present, proceeded on foot,
and with some trouble arrived at the spot.
No dwelling was near them, entirely alone,
No ear that could hear them, their sigh of their moan,
Both stricken with age, he, confined to his bed,
And without some relief, would soon have been dead.
J. Evans turned out and gathered some wod,
While she spray'd about and got them some food.
Thus fed and comforted, the sick and the poor
They went home rejoicing, for who could do more.
When going on journeys she has seen on the road
Poor emigrant strangers, without bed or board,
Then stop'd at a tavern, and paid for a meal,
For the heart of a stranger, they knew she could feel.
Even while she was moving in the gay walks of life,
She fulfilled the station of Matron and Wife;
Her virtues were known for many miles round,
And a better example was not to be found.
Great burns, wounds and sores, she was called on to dress,
Where Doctors relinquished for want of success;
She had no books or receipts on which to rely,
But trusted her master the want would supply;
When impressions were clear, she straight to work went,
Not doubting at all concerning the event.
And yet there were cases, and those not a few,
She plainly would tell them she nothing could do.
When waiting to feel, and there would nothing present,
The power to heal was not to her sent.
Her fame was so great, and doctrine so sound,
The country did shake for many miles round.
Her pious neighbors, who the Truth did admire,
Would often go see her, and sometimes enquire
Her humble example, in thought, word and deed,
Would generally furnish the things they had need:
Encouraged by her precepts, to seek a connection
With those of good habits and greater perfection,
And in process of time, of the lover of piety,
There were no less than five who joined the Society.
These things we've recorded, are chiefly designed
To bring to remembrance, or store in the mind
The principles of Virtue, as here brought to view,
Which will ever remain, both ancient and new.

AURORA

8th month 25th, 1848

The Site of the Jesse Evans Mansion

The East or Oswego Branch of the Wading River at Martha

Speedwell

Speedwell Furnace at the Turn of the Century

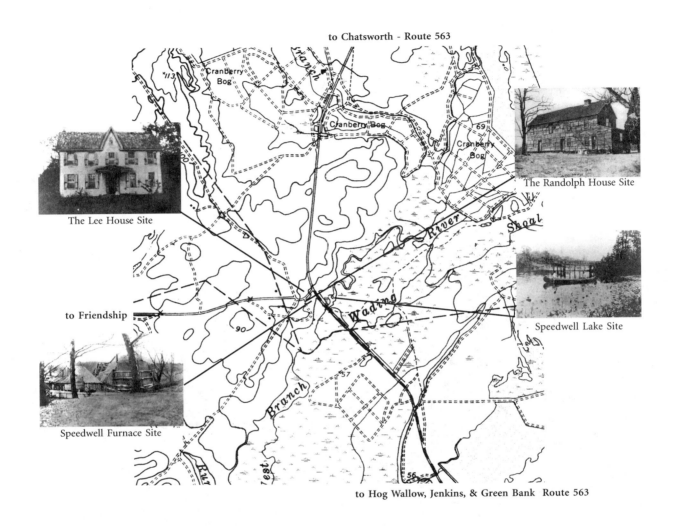

to Chatsworth - Route 563

Cranberry Bog

Cranberry Bog

Cranberry Bog

The Randolph House Site

The Lee House Site

Speedwell Lake Site

to Friendship

Speedwell Furnace Site

to Hog Wallow, Jenkins, & Green Bank Route 563

Speedwell

Speedwell

The Benjamin Randolph House at Speedwell

The Sign of the Golden Eagle

Lying north by east of Harrisville and north by west of Washington where Route 563 (the Chatsworth Road) crosses the West Branch of the Wading River, Speedwell, like so many other places in the pines, is intriguing. As to the origin of the name, Bisbee opts for the common wildflower, Speedwell, a name used in colonial days for the culver-root (*Veronica Virginica*) rather than the place name in England or the Mayflower's consort.

Speedwell is hardly noticed by the motorist of 1996, speeding southward from Chatsworth towards Green Bank. Route 563 heads down a slight rise and crosses two little bridges that span streams which join nearby to form the West Branch of the Wading River. This is Speedwell. Route 563, at this point, formerly a part of the back road to Chatsworth rather than the main one, cuts between the site of the furnace and the furnace pond.

Speedwell was part of the original Washington Township as constituted in 1802 but was given to Shamong Township when it was formed in 1852. Woodland Township took the section in 1866, as well as another portion of Shamong that had once been Washington Township. It originally boasted one of the little one-room school-houses of the Washington Township school district, as the 1847 listing indicates. Only one birth is recorded for Speedwell in the township records from 1848 through 1877: that of William Mick, son of Sarah and Joseph Mick, laborer, on September 16, 1862. Like so many other places in the pines, though, the story of Speedwell begins somewhere else.

Benjamin Randolph was a Philadelphia cabinet maker of great skill. Prior to the hostilities which resulted in the Revolutionary War, Randolph had an establishment near Third and Chestnut Streets in the City of Brotherly

Love and was renown for the beauty of his craftsmanship. He built tall case clocks, mirror frames, picture frames for artists, including his neighbor, Charles Willson Peale, caskets, and furniture. His most famous workmanship was lavished on beautiful Chippendale furniture, especially chairs, much of which has survived to our time. Several of his pieces are part of the collections of the Pennsylvania Museum of Fine Arts and the Boston Museum of Fine Arts.

Benjamin's great grandfather was the first Fitz Randolph, as the family name was in his time, to emigrate from Robin Hood's famous shire in old England to the new world. Edward Fitz Randolph settled in Scituate, Massachusetts about 1630, and, seven years later, married Elizabeth Blossom on May 10, 1637. There the couple had ten children and lived in Scituate for thirty-two years. About 1669, the Fitz Randolphs and six of their children moved to Piscataway, New Jersey, hoping to further their fortunes. The second and third generations moved from Piscataway to the area of what would become Princeton, and a grandson, Nathaniel Fitz Randolph II gave four and a half acres of property, right in the middle of the town, for the establishment of the College of New Jersey, later to be known as Princeton University. On the Fitz Randolph land would be built Nassau Hall. Despite the gift of the land, the Fitz Randolph family continued to use a small, family burial ground on the premises. Over the years, the site was forgotten, but, in 1909 when the foundations of Holden Hall and its famous tower were being dug, the bones of Nathaniel Fitz Randolph and his family were found and reinterred in the walls of the tower.

The first Benjamin Fitz Randolph was the tenth and last child of Edward and Elizabeth Fitz Randolph. Our Benjamin's father, Isaac, was born on April 10, 1701 and married Rebecca Seabrook of November 28, 1728. Isaac was a cousin of Princeton's Nathaniel, but he was neither prosperous nor of high station. At one point, he drove the Philadelphia/New York stage. He and Rebecca had eight children, and our Benjamin was the sixth. When Rebecca died, Isaac remarried and three more children were the result. Isaac, for some long-forgotten reason, dropped the "Fitz" from the family name.

Benjamin Randolph was born in South River on January 30, 1738. Two of his brothers died before maturity. Only his older brothers, James and Daniel, would, with Benjamin, live to add lustre to the Randolph name. Benjamin, while in his early twenties, was in the lumbering business in South Jersey. It was about 1760 that he, with two partners, William Hendrickson, and T. Laurie, acquired the Speedwell property. On the west branch of the Wading River, he, and perhaps his brother, Daniel, built a sawmill. Daniel Randolph ran the sawmill until the Revolutionary War gave him other things to do.

Benjamin moved to Philadelphia and became a "joiner," which was a carpenter skilled in interior woodwork. On the side, the practiced his furniture-making ability until he earned a reputation for his excellent work in that field. In 1763, he married Anna Bromwich, the daughter of William Bromwich, a staymaker. Randolph was a member of St. Paul's Church, on Third Street below Walnut, and the young couple were married there with the rites of the Church of England on February 18, 1762.

Benjamin's father-in-law died about two years after this, and the income from his estate enabled him to expand his business. He bought a new shop which he called the "Sign of the Golden Eagle" on Chestnut Street in 1767. Though Anna had given birth to two little girls by this time, their new home and shop was apparently a bit larger than the family needed, so they decided to take in lodgers. One of their first was John Gualdo and his little daughter, Frances.

John was a musical genius who could play almost any instrument. He started a music store on Front Street, not far from the Randolph shop, and employed men skilled in the repair of musical instruments. Unfortunately, in the midst of a highly successful series of concerts, his mind went, and he spent the rest of his short life chained in a cell in the Pennsylvania Hospital. The Randolphs took on the responsibility of raising his daughter, Frances, as their ward after John died in 1772.

These were exciting years to be in Philadelphia. Though the Quakers still had a great influence on Penn's City, the city's central position in British America made it subject to the revolutionary excitement which was spreading amongst those colonies. Two years after John Gualdo's death, representatives from the colonies met at Carpenter's Hall to remonstrate to the British crown for the harsh measures which the British parliament had burdened their American subjects.

Randolph's spirits were ardently patriotic. He was a member of the First Mounted City Troop, gaining him the title of "Colonel." Thus it was that, in 1774, when a certain Virginia planter, the former Colonel Washington, arrived in the city for the First Continental Congress to which he was a delegate, he was directed to the Sign of the Golden Eagle on Chestnut Street to find lodgings. When he returned the following year, he went back to room with the Randolphs.

When the Second Continental Congress met in 1776, another Virginia planter roomed with the Randolphs. He liked the craftsman's work so much that he commissioned Benjamin to build him a portable writing desk. That desk was destined to have one of the most famous documents in the world written on it, for the Virginia planter was none other than Thomas Jefferson.

In later years, Jefferson would give the desk to Joseph Coolidge, Jr., the husband of Jefferson's favorite grand-daughter, Ellen. The original desk survives and is on display in Washington, D.C.

The famous desk bears this note:

> *Thomas Jefferson gives this writing desk to Joseph Coolidge, Jr., as a memorial of his affection.*
> *It was made from the drawing of his own, by Benjamin Randolph, cabinet maker at Philadelphia,*
> *with whom he first lodged on his arrival in that city, in May 1776, and is the identical one on which*
> *he wrote the Declaration of Independence.*

Benjamin Randolph took part in the battle of Princeton as a member of the Philadelphia Light Horse. Tra-dition says that he was a guide to Washington's army in their night crossing of the Delaware and their march on Trenton. He had grown up in the Princeton area and knew all the back roads, so he may well have led the Conti-nental Army through the snow for their dawn attack on the sleeping German soldiers.

In March of 1777, he wrote to General Anthony Wayne that he had captured two deserters from Wayne's corps "at a place called Speedwell Mill, of mine." There are indications that he may even have acted as an agent for Washington while the army was encamped for the winter in Morristown. When the British were threatening his home and shop on Chestnut Street towards the end of that year, Benjamin took his family to Speedwell. "Lost in the pines" was just what Benjamin Randolph, ardent patriot, hoped his family would be.

For himself, Randolph had no such plans. In November, he was in the town of Burlington. During the battle of Fort Mifflin, Randolph carried a flag of truce to General Howe which was refused.

When the British moved out of Philadelphia, Randolph moved back in along with his family. They found the city much abused and their old home a shambles. The loyalists of the city had seen to it that the soldiers

The East End of the Randolph House

plundered the effects of this well-known advocate of the revolutionary cause. Benjamin totalled up the costs and arrived at a huge figure for his losses: 2,811 pounds, ten shillings. To make matters worse, his wife, Anna, died. She was buried in St. Paul's churchyard, her grave marked with a carved mahogany "stone."

Randolph had lost almost everything except the Speedwell property. Now he had three young girls to care for. He immediately put up for sale the remaining pieces of his cabinet making business. No one was buying new furniture at that particular instant, so he felt he could recover a little from the sale. He used the Sign of the Golden Eagle to set up a merchandizing business, and, in fact, sold some linens to William Richards of Batsto in 1781, duly noted in Richards' diary. He tried his hand at privateering, investing some of his ready cash in a couple of such commercial enterprises.

He also tried to sell the Speedwell tract. His brother, Daniel, had been running the saw mill at Speedwell but had moved to Freehold at the beginning of the war. He joined Captain Joshua Huddy in defending the Toms River blockhouse and was imprisoned with him at the Suger House prison. He was more fortunate than Huddy. Tory Governor William Franklin and his loyalists hung the ill-fated captain, but Daniel Randolph was exchanged. Brother James built the Revolutionary Salt Works in Monmouth County and served in the militia there.

Benjamin advertised the Speedwell site as having a "good new two-story house, framed and covered with cedar, good cellars walled up with stone, good brick hearths and oven . . . good log house for the sawyer, a large commodious barn and stabling for sixteen or eighteen horses." He noted that the mill went with "two saws, newly repaired." Included in the sale were four horses, thirty head of cattle, a peach orchard, an apple orchard, and two hundred acres of iron ore and rights to seven hundred additional acres.

Benjamin succeeded in selling the Speedwell tract on April 24, 1780. Unfortunately, the buyer defaulted. In February, 1781, he managed to sell it a second time only to have to foreclose on those buyers. On December 4, 1783, he ended up with the property once again.

Early in 1784, he found out that his family wasn't entirely "safe" during their sojourn at Speedwell. John Jacob Sluyter, the man Randolph had made the manager of his sawmill there in 1779, apparently had charmed his daughter Mary, and, on May 11, 1784, the couple were married at St. Paul's and moved to the Randolph house in the pines.

The Last Days of the Randolph House
This view of the house is from the site of the furnace.

A Cabinetmaker Builds a Furnace

Randolph himself moved to the town of Burlington, New Jersey on September 1, 1784. He also started the construction of an iron furnace on his Speedwell property. As part of the complex, he managed to build all the necessary buildings and a new house for himself by the beginning of winter. Property borders in the pines have always been rather uncertain and confusing, and Benjamin had a new survey made at the same time he was building his furnace. On November 3, 1784, he bought another 522 acres, bringing his total acreage to 1,717. On the corner of his property near the site of his house and furnace, he placed a stone, into which is still carved "B.R./ 1785."

Speedwell furnace was never the success its neighbors Batsto and Martha became. It was too far from navigable water to make transportation of the pig iron very profitable. Some was sold to nearby Union Forge (near the present Chatsworth), the Wading River Forge and Slitting Mill, and Stafford Forge, but everything had to be carted overland. He might have floated some of his product downriver to a point near the Wading River Forge, but the sand roads probably saw a good many cartloads hauled to the other area forges.

Three years after he placed his marker stone, Benjamin Randolph, now fifty years old, remarried. He chose a widow with five children, Mary Wilkinson Fenimore. Mary had been a Quaker, but she was disowned by the Burlington Friends Meeting on September 1. 1788 for marrying an Episcopalian. There were other complications. Benjamin still had his daughter, Anna, and his ward, Frances, in his household. Both he and Mary were responsible to their children for the estates of their former spouses. The couple agreed to have no claim on each other's estate. After the marriage, Benjamin and his two girls moved in with Mary's family in the Fenimore house in Burlington.

Something didn't work out, though. One year later, Benjamin signed over the title to Speedwell to his daughter, Anna. Within two years of his wedding, he was giving Speedwell as his address and apparently living there full time - without his wife and her family.

Courtesy of Budd Wilson
From the collection of Stephen V. Lee, Jr.

The Really Last Days of the Randolph House
Looking south from the Speedwell/Friendship Road. The furnace ruins were behind the house.

The Abandoned Spillway

Randolph died on the 21st of December, 1791. He left two-thirds of his estate to his daughter, Anna, one-third to his ward, Frances, and to his widow, Mary, "twenty pounds and no more." His other daughter, Mary, was probably given a portion of his estate when she married John Sluyter as was often the custom. His wife wasn't even listed as one of the executors. She, of course, challenged the will. She lost, despite the fact that there had been no written agreement between herself and her husband denying her right to at least part of his estate.

Anna Randolph continued to live at Speedwell, and, in fact, bought another 1,273 acres for 300 pounds. She leased the furnace to John Sluyter, but he failed on January 14, 1797. The Sluyters moved to Georgia, but Anna would own the Speedwell property for another forty-four years. She moved to Morristown soon after the estate was settled to live with Frances.

In 1798, she leased Speedwell to Joseph Walker and John Youle. These two partners bought the Wading River Forge and Slitting Mill in 1802 and the Stafford Forge in 1808. When Walker died, Youle took another seven-year lease. Most of the Speedwell pigs were shipped to Stafford Forge after the burning of the Wading River Forge in 1810.

After Youle's lease expired, Anna Randolph found a new lessor in the person of Mark Richards (no relation to the Richards family famous in Washington Township). Richards ceased production in 1829.

On December 23, 1833, Anna decided to sell Speedwell. The new owner was Samuel Richards.

Anna died just a little over a year later on February 28, 1835.

The Randolph name did not immediately pass from the scene. Though the site of Speedwell Furnace became part of Shamong Township when that municipality was formed in 1852, a new township created from old Washington Township in 1870 bore the name of the illustrious patriot, expert cabinetmaker, and ironmaster. Unfortunately, Randolph Township only lasted for twenty-three years.

Courtesy of Budd Wilson
From the collection of Stephen V. Lee, Jr.

Speedwell Lake
Stephen Lee, Sr. on the lake with his children, Stephen, Jr. and Jean

SPEEDWELL DIES WITH A WHIMPER

Samuel Richards, son of William Richards and brother of Batsto's Jesse, was a highly successful ironmaster. He owned Atsion Furnace, Martha Furnace, and Weymouth Furnace, all highly successful enterprises. Even he couldn't make a go of it at Speedwell.

He tried, though. He rebuilt the furnace buildings and got things working again, but activity was sporadic. Something was always happening to cause a halt in production. Samuel Richards had given up on it before he died seven years later.

It took Stephen Colwell, Samuel's executor, eight years to sell this abandoned iron works. When he did so on June 30, 1850, he got only $1,750 for it from James McCambridge. McCambridge had been running the Eagle Tavern which stood to the northwest of Speedwell Furnace on one of the three "stage roads" between Philadelphia and Tuckerton. The tavern could not have been profitable after the demise of Speedwell Furnace. The Speedwell workers had provided most of the business of the tavern. Of the three stage routes, this was the least used, so there wasn't much business coming that way. The McCambridge family continued to live there, though, until the house burned down early in this century.

NOTE: Much of the research on Benjamin Randolph was done by Budd Wilson, Jr. of Green Bank for an article published in the Batsto Citizens Gazette Volume XVI Number 2 in 1982. He also provided me with additional information on the subject over our many hours of consultation for this book.

THE LEE FAMILY OF SPEEDWELL

Stephen Lee, the first "Stephen Lee of Speedwell," was born in Ireland in the early part of the nineteenth century, but, like many of his fellow islanders, he turned his hopes and dreams towards the new world.

After the Civil War, American energies, which had been spent on self-slaughter for four long years, were turned to business, and the climate was ripe for expansion. Stephen Lee took advantage of the situation by marrying James McCambridge's sister and, on August 28, 1868, by purchasing 2,007 acres from his new brother-in-law for $8,000. Lee's purchase included the site of the old Speedwell Furnace.

He saw his future in the bright red berries which the early Plymouth colonists had called "crane-berries." The Wampanoags of Massachusetts Bay, an Algonkian-speaking tribe of the eastern seaboard, had called them *ibimi* or "bitter berries," but they had also found them quite tasty and useful. The Native Americans used them for clothing dye and as a delicacy. They also made them into a poultice that could be used on wounds.

Local cranberry production had been pioneered by Samuel Crowley, Jr. down near the Mullica in the first part of the century, and Stephen Lee was enthusiastic about their cultivation in upland bogs. At Speedwell, Lee built a large house near the remains of the abandoned iron furnace. This magnificent house stood across the country road from the home built by Benjamin Randolph, cabinetmaker and furnace entrepreneur, which, by this time, was in ruins.

Speedwell was a decaying relic by the time Stephen Lee came to the pines, though it may still have boasted an active sawmill. The furnace had long since ceased producing its famous South Jersey iron, though its former pond attracted migratory birds and the woods were filled with deer and other forest animals.

Speedwell must have been quite picturesque when the first Stephen made it his home. The ruins of the old furnace still hugged the hillside behind the decaying mansion of Benjamin Randolph. The former furnace pond backed up behind its dam and played host to geese, ducks, egrets, and other wild birds. Deer, raccoons, possum, skunks, and fox graced the enfolding forests. Around the Lee house, the remaining houses of the furnace village

Courtesy of Budd Wilson
From the collection of Stephen V. Lee, Jr.

The Lee House at Speedwell - Prior to 1930

huddled in the pines. Even the little log school, formerly of Washington Township, still stood as a reminder of the area's prosperous past.

As the 1870's progressed, Stephen Lee and his son, James, dug a series of bogs in which they determined to grow cranberries. The Panic of 1873 must have given them a setback, but the family continued to pursue their dream of a cranberry empire in the pines. Farming, even cranberry farming, did not produce a great deal of wealth in those early days, but with farmland and woods, there was always food.

Stephen Vincent Lee, the second "Stephen" and grandson of the first Stephen, the first to add the "Vincent" to his name, raised a family of six children at Speedwell.

His son, Stephen V. Lee, Jr. (the third "Stephen") was born in 1910 and was nineteen when the New York Stock Exchange laid over and died. The resulting catastrophe for the country destroyed the value of the cranberry crop - and everything else for that matter. His family shut down the operation and moved to a nearby town to find work, but their hearts were in their "home" at Speedwell.

Courtesy of Budd Wilson
From the collection of Stephen V. Lee, Jr.
Side View of the Lee House

Courtesy of Budd Wilson
From the collection of Stephen V. Lee, Jr.)

The Lee Family
Mary, Anna (mother), Sarita, Jean, Stephen, Jr., John (held by Stephen Jr.), Ann, and father, Stephen Vincent Lee, Sr.

577

The Lee Family
Mary, Stephen, Jr., Anna (mother), Jean, Ann,
Stephen, Sr. (father), John, and Sarita

Then came another disaster. In 1930, while young Stephen's uncle was in residence in the Speedwell house, the roof was set on fire by a spark from the chimney. There were no fire companies in the pines in those days, and, like so many other old houses, the Lee house burned to the ground.

The Great Depression left most of the people in the United States in comparative poverty. People fled from the country to the towns, from the towns to the cities, and, in the cities, to bread lines stretching for blocks. Out in the mid-west, fertile lands turned to dust as drought sucked the last drop of water from the ground. As the dust swirled around them, family after family loaded their possessions on wagons, pickups, and cars, trudging westward in search of work and food.

New Jersey's pinelands continued much as they had always been. Here people could farm produce to feed themselves and their neighbors. They could raise their chickens and cows and hunt in the woods for meat. The Speedwell Lake provided prime fishing territory. In short, families could at least struggle along with food on the table, even if the clothes on their backs were becoming a bit threadbare. Let the unemployed

A Barn at Speedwell - 1919

"scholars" from Philadelphia, New York, and Boston under the Works Progress Administration sneer at backwoods "Pineys" and invent tall tales about inbreeding and imbeciles, these people of the pines had the last laugh. They, at least, knew exactly where their next meal was coming from, which is more than could be said for the effete bespectacled snobs from the cities whose trade in words was now almost valueless.

Like so many of his generation, Stephen V. Lee, Jr. had to leave the pines to fight for his country during the greatest war the world had ever seen. He managed to survive both the Normandy Invasion and the great battles of the Pacific, and finally returned home to his beloved Speedwell.

Though World War II had forced young Americans to grow up fast, it also ended the tragedy of the Depression. Young men, returning from Europe and the Pacific, were filled with determination and purpose. Like his young countrymen, Stephen Lee had a dream: to reclaim the land of his ancestors and rebuild their dream of cranberry production in the pines.

Courtesy of Budd Wilson
From the collection of Stephen V. Lee, Jr.
Ann Lee and her brother Stephen V. Lee, Jr.
About 1915

Borrowing $4,000 from the Ocean Spray Cooperative, that's exactly what he started to do. It takes about seven years to build a bog, so the task was not quickly accomplished. Stephen used many of the original bogs dug

Courtesy of Budd Wilson
From the collection of Stephen V. Lee, Jr.
Mae Keating, a Lee cousin,
and Ann Lee
They are standing beside the old log schoolhouse which was torn down when Route 563 was paved.

Courtesy of Budd Wilson
From the collection of Stephen V. Lee, Jr.
Stephen Vincent Lee, Sr.,
Grandson of the first Stephen Lee

Jean Lee, Stephen, Jr., Ann Lee, and Mae Keating
Early 1920's

Stephen Lee, Jr.
Early 1920's

by the first Stephen and even was able to save some of the original stock.

There was one thing he wasn't afraid of: hard work, and that's exactly how he reclaimed the land and returned it to production. Over the years, he dug bog after bog, until today, his farm includes one hundred twenty-five acres of cranberry-producing bogs and over a thousand acres of upland.

While only one ninth the size of the Haines farm down the road, the Lees are prosperous and proud of their achievements. Not rivals at all, Stephen Lee and Bill Haines are the closest of friends and have shared technology and ideas over the years.

Stephen's son, yet another Stephen Vincent Lee (this one the third) went into the Air Force, serving as a flight instructor at the U.S. Air Force Academy at Colorado Springs for several years. He didn't return to the pines until after the death of his mother, Marjorie, in 1973. Marjorie Lee had run the business end of the cranberry operation, and her death left a vacuum in the family business that needed to be filled. Stephen, III must have given the whole idea some very serious thought before he gave up his Air Force career for the Jersey Pines but return home he did.

His younger brother, Abbott, studied agriculture at college and seemed always dedicated to succeeding his father in the production end of the farm. At present, both brothers and their families live near their father in the "town" of Speedwell. By the way, there is a fifth "Stephen." The fourth Stephen Vincent Lee is pursuing a career far from the Jersey Pines.

Stephen Vincent Lee, Sr., John Lee,
and Stephen V. Lee, Jr.

Courtesy of the Batsto Citizens Gazette

The Speedwell School

The old Speedwell School was built around 1775 and stood in what is today the right-of-way for Route 563. When the road was widened in this century, it was torn down. The gentleman in the photograph is the brother of Anna Lee and the uncle of Stephen V. Lee, Jr. The building was used both as a school building and a house.

Courtesy of Budd Wilson
From the collection of Stephen V. Lee, Jr.

Today, the old furnace buildings are gone. The Randolph House is gone. The Lee House is gone. The old school is gone. The lake across the Chatsworth road has drained to a swamp, but Speedwell still has a delightful country flavor.

Sheltered by the pines and supported by its history, Speedwell is an oasis in the midst of thousands of acres of bogs which grow blood-red at the autumn harvest.

Cranberry production in 1996 is *the* industry of northern Washington Township. It is exciting, demanding, and profitable. Unlike the old iron industries, it does not destroy but enhances the land that sustains it.

Around forty-five pinelands families are directly engaged in the production of cranberries in 3,500 acres of bogs. In 1940, there were 11,400 acres of bogs, but False-blossom disease almost destroyed the industry. By 1960, the acreage under cultivation was reduced to 2,700. In the mid-1960's though, Ocean Spray mixed cranberry juice with apple juice and a whole new product revived the industry.

In much of the country, farming and ranching have become big business with family farms loosing out. The pinelands, however, are still the stronghold of the family farm that provided the backbone of America.

The vision of the first Stephen Lee and of Martin Luther Haines was right on the mark. Ocean Spray's sales over the last ten years have exceeded a billion dollars annually! The last berry boxcar on the Central of New Jersey was loaded in Chatsworth in 1949. Now almost 95% of the crop is processed into sauce and juice.

The Lee family and the Haines family have found perhaps the best way to both preserve the pinelands and make them productive. Here, nature balances with industry in one harmonious melody of the pines.

A "Pig" of
Speedwell Iron
This "pig" is still cherished
by the Lee Family of
Speedwell.

Courtesy of Budd Wilson
From the collection of Stephen V. Lee, Jr.

A Hunting Party

Early in the twentieth century, hunting was a popular pastime at Speedwell as it is in the century's last decade. Hunting parties were brought out from the cities for weekends of roughing it in the pines.

Courtesy of Budd Wilson
From the collection of Stephen V. Lee, Jr.

L. to R. An unknown reporter; Gifford Pinchot of Pennsylvania, a famous environmentalist; General Hugh Scott; Stephen Lee, Sr.; Stephen V. Lee, Jr.; a *Philadelphia Inquirer* reporter; a man by the name of Rendell who owned a newstand in Mt. Holly; and Charles Morton, the Game Warden - circa 1918. Gifford Pinchot (1865-1946) was appointed by President Theodore Roosevelt to head the Division of Forestry which became the U.S. Forest Service in 1905. Pinchot became chairman of the National Conservation Committee in 1908 and left the Forest Service in 1910. He served as governor of Pennsylvania from 1923-1927 and from 1931 to 1935. Hugh Scott (1853-1934) served as Chief of Staff of the U.S. Army from 1914-1917.

Camp Speedwell
In the 1920's, cousin John Lee ran a camp for both girls and boys in Speedwell.

Stephen Vincent Lee, Jr. - Early 1920's

Stephen Vincent Lee, Jr. with his sons, Abbott and Stephen V. Lee, III
June 1996

The Site of the Speedwell Furnace - 1996
Vince Laganella, formerly of Manahawkin and now of Charleston, S.C., accompanied the
author on a photographing trip to Speedwell and Friendship in March, 1996. He is standing
on the site of the furnace. Behind him is Route 563. To the right is the spillway, and beyond
Route 563 to the right is swamp, all that's left of the Speedwell Lake.

Wading River
(Bridgeport)

"To be ignorant of what occurred before you were born is to remain always a child. For what is the worth of human life, unless it is woven into the life of our ancestors." - Cicero

Most of the material and photographs in this section were lovingly assembled over a period of many years by Dorothea (McAnney) Somes, who maintained a life-long interest in preserving the history of the community of her birth. Others from the Wading River area made contributions of photos and notes to her project, including Mildred Honaker, Steven Eichinger, and Stephen Potter. Dorothea did not live to see her project completed, but, through the courtesy of her son, Horace Somes, Jr., all her efforts have finally been brought to fruitition. A considerable amount of help has also been given by Steve Eichinger, a life-long resident of Wading River and a member of the Old Bridgeport Society, founded by his aunt, Alice Adams Weber. Whenever possible, I have noted the original sources of the photographs. The quotation above is one which Mrs. Somes collected to be included in her booklet on her beloved town.

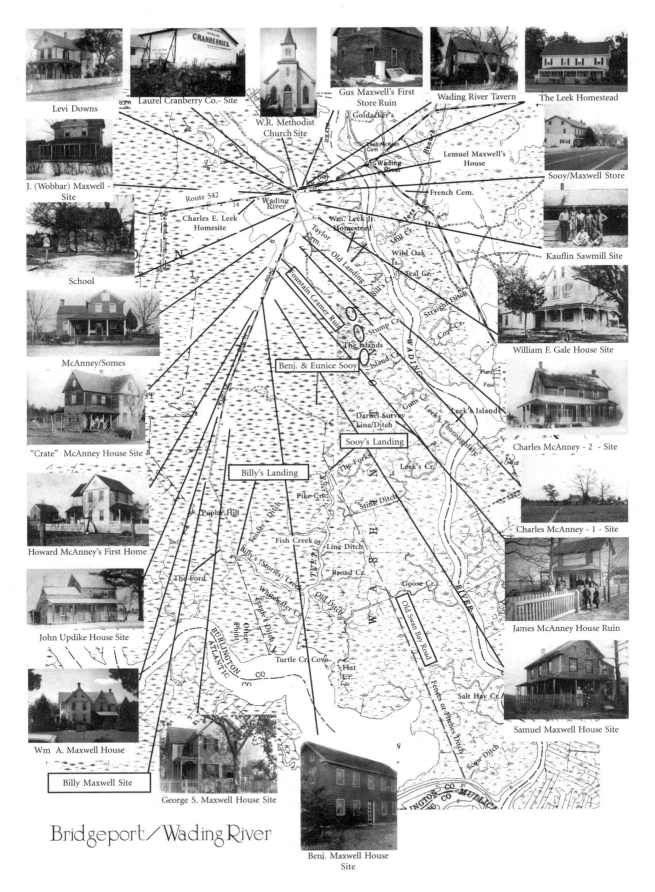

Levi Downs

Laurel Cranberry Co.- Site

W.R. Methodist Church Site

Gus Maxwell's First Store Ruin

Wading River Tavern

The Leek Homestead

J. (Wobbar) Maxwell - Site

Sooy/Maxwell Store

School

Kauflin Sawmill Site

McAnney/Somes

William F. Gale House Site

"Crate" McAnney House Site

Charles McAnney - 2 - Site

Howard McAnney's First Home

Charles McAnney - 1 - Site

John Updike House Site

James McAnney House Ruin

Wm A. Maxwell House

Samuel Maxwell House Site

Billy Maxwell Site

George S. Maxwell House Site

Benj. Maxwell House Site

Bridgeport/Wading River

Dreams of Empire

Stephen Leek, age fifty-eight, and John Leek, age twenty-two, trudged along the Indian trail that followed the Little Egg Harbor River from Biddle's Island on the Bass River. All the land through which they were passing belonged to John Mathis, who, even at this early date, was starting to be called "great" by his neighbors. Everything John Mathis did seemed to work out to his advantage.

He had purchased much of the land bordered by the Bass River, the Mullica River, and the Wading River. He had already built himself a house on his island and had started to clear the land on both sides of the Bass River for farms. Yes, he envisioned more than one, and a man of his determination would find a way to carve himself an estate from this wilderness. John Mathis intended to be a wealthy old man with a large family, and John Mathis was a man who would accomplish his dreams.

Stephen Leek had come down from Long Island and settled in Cumberland County, New Jersey, soon after the birth of his son in 1715, and he, too, had dreams. Like Mathis, he dreamed of a landed estate and family to carry on the Leek name, and he projected all his dreams on to his little son. Cumberland County seemed so far away from everything. Many of his former friends from East Hampton, Long Island, had settled farther north along the seacoast, and he heard the tales of beautiful rivers, great stands of white cedar, oak, and pine.

The Great Bay teemed with fish and shellfish, and the air was darkened by wildfowl when the huge flocks took flight. That area of Little Egg Harbor was growing fast and was an opportunity that just couldn't be passed up. For twenty years he had heard the stories of his former neighbors as they filtered down to Cumberland County. Finally, he decided to act.

John and his father first did something else that was most important in their lives. They got married, John for the first time and Stephen for his third. Stephen Leek had no dreams of more children, but he did want the company of a good woman, and Sarah was that. He was content to let John and Phoebe supply their new home with children to carry on the Leek name. John didn't disappoint him. Through his son, John, Jr. and his grandchildren, Stephen Leek would end up being related to almost everyone along the Mullica River. Stephen and Sarah's daughter, Sarah, would be a happy afterthought.

Stephen and his son headed northward for Little Egg Harbor. "See the 'Great' John Mathis," they were told. "There is plenty of land for hard-working folks." And see John Mathis they had.

The "Great" John was very pleased with the pair. Both appeared to be hard-working, intelligent, and eager to build an empire in the pines, so he steered them to some fine land on the border of his own acres over by the Wading River. John and his father were delighted with their prospects. The Mullica and Wading Rivers were both navigable, beautiful streams that would bring trade right to their doorstep. John had already had a taste of the sea and dreamed of having his own ship one day. How proud he'd be to sail up those rivers from the Great Bay and dock at a wharf in front of his own house!

That year, 1738, would be the year of beginning for the Leeks. The few miles inland from John Mathis's island were quickly passed, and when they finally reached the edge of the Wading River as Mathis had directed them, they knew they were home. I wonder if young John plunged into the river, whooping and shouting with glee as his proud father looked on from the bank. This was the answer to their dreams! This would be their land and the birthright of John's children and grandchildren and great grandchildren! Here the river would give them life, and the land would nurture them.

The pair lost no time in applying for grants. Through John Mathis, they arranged for proprietary surveys to be conducted on eighty-one and a half acres hard by the Wading and Mullica Rivers on the eastern side, stretching inland towards the Mathis property. Eighty-one and a half acres! It didn't seem like much, compared to what John Mathis owned, but it was all theirs, and it was only a start, after all!

Stephen and his son must have begun right away to build themselves a home on their new land. They may have started small, but they knew: In a few years, they'd have themselves a larger house to rival even that of the "Great" John Mathis!

As time went on, John purchased more land, both upland for farming, swamp land for timber, and marshes for salt hay and hunting. Opportunity was endless. He managed to acquire a ship of his own, not a very large one at first, but it could carry their meats and furs and timber to market, and it made John Leek a sea captain!

When father Stephen died in 1753 at the ripe old (then, at least) age of seventy-three, he had held his grandson and granddaughters in his arms, shared the love of three women, established an ever-growing homestead that would give his family permanent roots, and had seen his son grow into a man of substance, respected and admired by all his neighbors.

John, Phoebe, and Sarah, Stephen's third wife, laid the old man to rest in the ground out behind their home on a hillside overlooking the river he had come to love so well. "SL" they carved on his gravestone. Not much for a man who had worked hard for many years, but in the wilderness, even those two letters graven in stone were more than most had to mark their final resting spot.

Much happened over the next twenty or so years. John operated his homestead and his ship quite successfully and was pleased with what he accomplished. His son, John, Jr. grew into a fine young man. He was also the proud father of four daughters.

John, Jr. married the beautiful Martha Rose and set about having a family at the homestead beside the Wading River. His sister, Phoebe, married into the family of the "Great" John Mathis. Job and Phoebe (Leek) Mathis's son married the daughter of the famous privateer captain, Macijah Smith. His other sister, Mary, married Captain Joseph Sooy, Jr., son of Joseph Sooy of Green Bank. Other young Leeks married into the Maxwell, Gale, and Downs families. Life was great.

Unfortunately, the growing cloud cast by the Mother Country over the expanding wealth of her colonies threatened to overwhelm the hard-working farmers, tradesmen, ship owners, and entrepreneurs who were carving an empire from the wilderness.

When the open break finally came in 1775, John Leek knew exactly where he would stand. The little realm along the Wading River would mean nothing if England were allowed to strangle trade, restrict exports, and limit manufacturing. Taxes would crush the colonists. England, he was sure, was killing the goose that laid the golden egg, and he'd have none of it.

He was sixty years old in 1775, an old man. He couldn't go roaming about the countryside fighting battles. His roving days were over. The privations would have to be suffered by his son, just as his son would reap the glory, but John Leek would do his part. He scraped together every piece of hard cash he could get his hands on for the support of the patriot cause. He was rich in lands, and those lands would always produce. He had ships, and they could be outfitted for privateering. The fish, clams, oysters, birds, deer, muskrat, and beaver were always there to recreate his wealth, so he could afford the hard cash.

John, Jr. had never loved the sea as had his father, but when he joined the patriot forces, he gained the title of "captain" in his own right. Now there were two "Captain John Leeks" along the Wading. When John Leek, Sr. died suddenly in 1777, his family was deeply saddened. They had lost the pioneer of their homestead, the strength and mainstay of their lives and their far-flung enterprises.

He was laid to rest beside his father on the hillside behind the house he had built with his own hands, where he could look out over the marshland and river that had comprised his empire and which had given him life. In his last will and testament, he left the portion of his land on which had been constructed a Presbyterian Meeting House and which included a small cemetery for the local residents of Wading River. John Leek, Jr. also left the homestead to his grandson, John Leek III rather than to his son, perhaps to protect it if the war did not have an outcome favorable to the patriots.

A REVOLUTIONARY AGE

When Captain John Leek, Jr. came home after the war with Great Britain, he faced a new world. His father was no longer there to be the backbone of the Leek empire. John, Jr. had to stand on his own two feet and defy the world, but the opportunities were fantastic! A new country. A new world order. New challenges to be met.

In those last years of the eighteenth century, John Leek, Jr. had every right to be a proud man. He was the third generation on the land. His family was related to every one of the old families of lower Little Egg Harbor. He had achieved the renown due to a

Photograph by John Pearce

Gravestone of Captain John Leek, Jr. Even though the stone reads "Senʳ", this is actually the stone of Revolutionary War Captain John Leek, Jr. Evidentially they were calling him "Sr." and his son "Jr." by the time of his death in 1790. It does make for confusion.

great patriot in the late war. Captain John Leek, Jr. didn't see the new century. He died on the thirteenth of May in 1790 and was laid to rest beside his parents on the hill behind the homestead. The Leeks had built a sizable empire in the pines through that last half of the eighteenth century, so when they carried John, Jr. to that now-growing resting place behind the ancestral house in 1790, his children could be proud.

An infant national government had heralded a new age which the Revolution had only begun. Proud and cocky, the United States of America thrust herself into conquering the newer lands to the west. Dreams were there for the making.

The grave of Martha Leek
Wife of John Leek, Jr.

The old Road to Little Egg Harbor had always bypassed the Leek estate to the north. They had enough traffic with the growing trade on the rivers. Travellers stayed at the Bass River Tavern, then headed on up the road to Bodine's and on to Sooy's, but towns on the west side of the Wading were growing. Lower Bank was becoming a nice little community. In 1808, the commissioners of the surrounding townships laid out the new road from the Wading River to Batsto that would eventually replace the old Tuckerton Road. John Richards, who had lived in Green Bank, knew the advantages that area had in the way of trade and shipping, so when he moved to Wading River in 1813, he knew that the area would grow.

When the legislature passed a bill in 1814 to permit the construction of a bridge across the Wading River near the Leek family wharf, the Leeks were probably delighted. Finally, they'd be able to visit their friends across the river without having to row across! The stage and cart traffic from Tuckerton inland would pass right in front of their house, and they wouldn't be isolated quite as much as they had been.

Burlington County soon took advantage of the state's grant of permission, and authorized the building of a wooden swing bridge hard by the Leek Homestead and wharf. Instead of bypassing Lower Bank, Batsto, and Pleasant Mills on their way to and from Philadelphia, the new bridge and road would enable travellers to go right through these towns and also make connections with the ships on the Mullica. It also connected the tidal area of Bass River with the other growing towns in the newly-formed Washington Township and enabled the development of the Harmony area of Bass River Township, later to be called New Gretna.

John Richards, nephew of William Richards of Batsto and Jesse's cousin, and also the cousin of Samuel Richards of Atsion and Martha, was born in Pennsylvania in 1784. At the age of twenty-three, he became fascinated with the iron industry in Southern New Jersey when he visited his Uncle William at Batsto. In 1810, he actually moved to the Green Bank plantation, then owned by William Richards, and married in 1811.

In 1813, at the age of twenty-nine, he moved from Green Bank and bought a piece of fast land and a cedar swamp in Wading River on the Washington Township side, built a new house and store on his property, and moved his young wife into his new homestead.

According to his grandson, Louis Richards, he also built a bridge across the river which was probably the original swing bridge authorized by the State of New Jersey in 1814. No other bridge is known to have existed below Bodine's.

John and Rebecca Richards did not remain in Wading River for very long. In 1816, Jesse and Samuel Richards his first cousins, hired him to superintend Washington Furnace in Monmouth County. In 1819, Samual, needed him to oversee a run of pipe at his newly-purchased ironworks at Atsion. Then in 1820, he headed for another Richards' ironworks, Weymouth, as resident manager. Richards sold his property in Wading River and never came back. He would later purchase Gloucester Furnace on the Atlantic County side of the Mullica across from Lower Bank with his first cousin once removed, Thomas S. Richards, son of Samuel, and move there. When Gloucester Furnace finished its last blast in 1848, John moved to Mauch Chunk, Pennsylvania (now Jim Thorpe), where he bought the Carbon Furnace, which he ran for six years.

Where was this plantation of John Richards? No one seems to know. In his 1825 will, Thomas Taylor, another landowner on the west side of the river, mentions his "Ridge Survey" as being "above John Richards plantation." Trouble is, we don't know where this "Ridge Survey" was either. Perhaps it lay along what is today known as "Ridge Road" on the north side of the Batsto-New Gretna Road (Route 542). The lower portion of this road in Wading River

The Bridge at Billy's Landing - circa 1941
Orville McAnney, Howard W. McAnney, Ruthren Gale, Louise Gale,
Howard McAnney (Orville's son) and Alice McAnney.

was known as the "Road to Harrisville" a century ago. The Richards Plantation may have been part of property later owned by Maja Leek or by the Laurel Cranberry Company in the nineteenth century.

Other homesteads had been established on the west bank, including those of Thomas Taylor, James Maxwell, and two men by the name of Moore and Haines. That meant more neighbors, more trade, and more money. When did they start to call this place Bridgeport? It had been a "port" of sorts for years, with the Leek ships coming and going, but it wasn't a "bridge-port" until there was a bridge.

On February 12, 1817, John Leek III sold the homestead to Robert McKeen, Esq. McKeen planned to rebuild the wharf that had fallen on hard times during Jefferson's embargo, and planned on the trans-shipment of goods from the upstream enterprises. John III and his wife disappear from the Wading River scene at this time, but brother William's family continued to be prominent in the affairs of the area.

Sea captains, baymen, sailors, sawyers, iron masters and workers, lumbermen, tradesmen,

Billy's Landing on Billy's (or Storey's) Creek

Batsto-Bridgeport Road Intersection
Turtle Creek Road to the left and Ridge Road to the right

business entrepreneurs, colliers, laborers, all felt a kinship along these rivers. Hundreds of vessels plied the Little Egg Harbor River each year, and many made their way up the Wading as well. Products were shipped to New York and Philadelphia through "Bridgeport." The east-siders didn't mind that the west-siders called their area "Bridge-port," too. They were all proud to be "Bridgeporters." That made them different from the Lower Bankers and the Green Bankers, the Crowleyville people and the Batsto people. When McCarty started that paper mill upstream, they knew that every load of paper destined for the city would have to be transshipped at Bridgeport, for sailing vessels of any length and draft could not make it up to the Landing above Leek's wharf.

THE GOLDEN YEARS

Amongst the towns along the Mullica, Bridgeport was different. Bridgeport had a whole river just to itself. A man could walk out his back door and see great flocks of ducks rise up from the marshes. He could take his gun and bring home dinner without making much of an effort.

The Wading River area is a blend of the land and sea, an area which is neither totally pinelands nor totally coastal, and that physical blend was reflected in the lives of the people who lived there. Most of the people who settled in the area worked in several occupations, many of them seasonal. Some served aboard coastal schooners that carried goods to Philadelphia and New York markets and beyond. These seamen knew that they had a productive homestead to which they could return after a long voyage, and, when they tired of the sea, they could make a living from the land. Others remained with the land all their lives. Both shifted emphasis depending on the season. Homesteads were made up of a variety of types of land, much of which was not contiguous. Upland fields were used to grow all types of crops during the summer. Cows were pastured, pigs and chickens were raised. Salt hay meadows provided a salable crop as well as food for the animals. Forests provided lumber, firewood, and charcoal. Swamps could be worked for their valuable white cedar. In the fall and winter the farmers joined with those who worked at the iron furnaces and glass plants to use the Mullica and Wading River estuaries for their rich resources. The numerous streams yielded muskrats and fish, the salt marshes waterfowl, and every man knew that he and his family would not starve in this rich land, no matter what the business climate happened to be.

591

Two old roads stretched off into the marshes from the uplands. Turtle Creek Road itself heads off into the swamps and marshes beyond the homestead of Billy Maxwell. In 1995, the potholed road ends abruptly at Billy's (or Storey's) Creek. Once there were extensive docks for small boats and hay barges at this landing, and their remnants could be seen as late as the 1960s. For almost two centuries, the road crossed a wooden bridge at Billy's Landing and continued on out to the Mullica itself. The road ended at Zeagles Ditch on the Mullica, upstream from the mouth of Turtle Creek. At this point were kept drying racks for the nets that were used in fishing as well as houseboats, in which the men could spend their nights when the fishing was good. Striped bass, perch, and catfish were caught in the waters of the two rivers in great abundance. Eels were speared where they wintered in Turtle Creek Cove.

Part of the way down the Turtle Creek Road from its intersection with the Batsto-Bridgeport Road (Route 542), a road went out towards the Wading River to the farm of Benjamin and Eunice Sooy. Just below their farm, the road crossed a bridge near the forks at the head of the Turtle Creek. The road continued on in almost a perfectly straight line out through the marshes midway between the Wading and Mullica Rivers. For much of the distance, it paralleled Fences or Fitches Ditch and intersected with a short, hand-dug canal on the Mullica. This canal was aptly named "Scow Ditch" and was made to shelter the flat-bottomed hay barges ("scows"). Both roads provided access to the extensive salt hay meadows. According to Horace Somes, Jr., salt haying continued into the 1940s when aerial photographs indicated that the meadows were still being burned off in the winter to induce a better crop of salt hay during the next season.

During the nineteenth century, the "town" of Bridgeport/Wading River had several identifiable parts. On what became the Bass River Township side, the community stretched from Charcoal Landing above the Tub Mill Branch (below the McCartyville, Harrisville, Martha Landing at what is now Beaver Branch) downriver around a curve known as the Devil's Elbow and into the Broad Place above the bridge opposite Chip's Folly. It continued on down the eastern side of the Wading River past the high bank at Goldacker's, through the area where the Leek Homestead stood, past French's Cemetery, past the sawmill and its millpond where Route 542 crosses the Ives Branch down to the Merrygold Branch, half way to New Gretna. Most of the shoreline downriver from the bridge was marshland while that upriver has a distinct pinelands character although there were extensive flats of wild rice from the Broad Place to the bridge. Tub Mill Branch was the original boundary of Washington Township when it was separated from Little Egg Harbor in 1802.

An old road left the main road between the bridge and the Leek Homestead, travelling upriver to a place known as Goldacker's in the twentieth century. At this spot, a high bluff overlooks the river. On the crest of the bank, Horace Somes, Jr. found an aboriginal stone pestle, indicating that Native Americans may have used the area. Actually, arrowheads and flaked scrapers have been found at several points in the Wading River area. On the road to Leektown and the Old Stage Road, another road led off to the river.

In 1995, Chip's Folly Campground overlooks "Broad Place" on the Wading from this point. Chip's Folly became the first campground in the area when the Ludwig family bought the land after World War II. Prior to that, the land had been owned by an oil man from Philadelphia whose name was Zurn. He ran a retreat for his wealthy friends, complete with two-story, screened barge on the river. It was near this property that the original Road to Little Egg Harbor passed on its way from the Bass River Tavern to Bodine's Tavern and on the Philadelphia.

Speaking of Bodine's Tavern, it was at this spot on the river, now part of Bodine's Field campground, where the river got its name. It is not known when the first bridge was thrown across the Wading River at Bodine's, but prior to that time, travellers on the old road had to "wade" across the river at this point on their journey from Little Egg Harbor to Philadelphia and Burlington. It is thought that this road existed as an early Indian trail through the area before it was settled by those of European extraction.

Between Bodine's and Wading River were several landings, three of which have names that are remembered: the Landing (for McCartyville/Harrisville, Wading River Forge, and Martha Furnace), Charcoal Landing, and Anderson's Landing.

On the eastern side of the 1814 Wading River Bridge, the main road ran south parallel to the meadow line to New Gretna. It passed the cemetery of the French family on the north side of the road before it crossed the Ives Branch. This creek was called "Mill Creek" from the main road to the river after the mills that were built on it. The millpond lay to the north of the road with a sawmill next to the road and a gristmill to the south of the road.

The road along Ives Branch to Leektown passed some extensive cranberry bogs above the millpond. An interesting note: near the site of the millpond, there was an old house that belonged to Steven Silkotch in the 1960s. In April of 1966, his "poultry farm" had thirty-one ducks, three geese, four cats, and two dogs! This old house was reputed to be the spot last visited by the Jersey Devil by McCloy and Miller in their 1976 book, *The Jersey Devil*. The house burned to the ground in the 1980s. The Merrygold Branch was probably the easternmost point which could be considered the boundary of Bass River's Bridgeport/Wading River.

Upriver on the Washington Township side, Maja Leek had blueberry fields and cranberry bogs to the east of Ridge Road which followed the only high ground in the immediate area. South nearer the river towards the Batsto-Bridgeport Road (Route 542) were the extensive cranberry bogs of the Wading River Cranberry Company. Just north of the bridge was a place on the river called "Wild Oat" Cove where that plant grew in abundance along with a considerable amount of wild rice.

Then came the intersection of the Batsto-Bridgeport Road with Turtle Creek Road and Ridge Road where the imposing Wading River Tavern, the home of Maja and Sarah Leek, stood sentry over the bridge. Here clustered the general stores, homes, and, after 1890, the Wading River Methodist Episcopal Church. Before Turtle Creek Road was created, the original road used to follow the edge of the uplands down the western side of the river to a spot where the road terminated at the river. There may have been a landing in this location. Numerous ships seem to have dumped their ballast here, for even today, the bottom of the river at this point is covered with ballast stones on both banks.

Far more numerous than the houses on the main road were the farms that stretched down Turtle Creek Road on the "neck" of high ground between the swamps of the Wading River and the Great Swamp. This latter feature clearly delineated the western boundary of the town and kept Bridgeport forever separate from Lower Bank. The Great Swamp was filled with huge white cedar trees all the way from the Mullica marshes above Log Bay to the main road. Stumps indicate that the oldest trees were from four to five feet in diameter.

The local inhabitants had names for every brook and land feature in the watershed. Each feature was an old, familiar friend to those who spent their lives in Bridgeport/Wading River. On the west side of the Wading River were The Islands, Bill's Creek (different from Billy's Creek), Stump Creek, Island Creek, Gum Creek, Leek's Creek, Goose Creek, and Salt Hay Creek.

On the east side were Mill Creek, Wild Oak Island, Teal Creek, Straight Ditch, Cove Creek, and Crooked Reach. On the Turtle Creek, starting at the point below the Forks and the Sooy Place where the Old Swan Bay Road crossed it, there were Stink Ditch, Fish Creek, Line Ditch, Broad Creek, Billy's (or Storey's) Creek, Old Ditch, and Whitewater Creek. Flat Creek enters the Mullica between the mouth of Turtle Creek and Swan Bay.

In Bridgeport/Wading River, a man knew his neighbors. As time went on, all the families were related by marriage. When they gathered for Sabbath worship, first in the Presbyterian Church on the east side of the river, later in the Methodist Church on the west side, or for socials or games of one sort or another, they always had a wonderful time. The women could walk across the bridge for tea or to attend a quilting or a church meeting, and, as the century went on, these Bridgeporters became ever closer.

By century's end, this tight-knit group of interrelated families shared a joyous and supportive fellowship. Divided by government, separated by a river, Bridgeport was still one, joined by a bridge. Of course, when the United States Government got involved, there was a slight problem.

In 1858, there were enough people in Bridgeport to warrant a post office of their own, but when the government set one up, it was confused. There was another Bridgeport in New Jersey. In the days before zip codes, that was one sure-fired way to get the mail mixed up. So . . . "Wading River" the post office was named. Actually, the area on both sides of the river *had* been called "Wading River" in colonial days, though it had gained the name "Bridgeport" after it had a bridge. By the time the government got out of the post office business in Bridgeport, excuse me, Wading River, the new name had replaced the old. For years, the locals had called their split town, "Bridgeport." To outsiders, they called it "Wading River." Which was it? At one point, the Washington Township records even referred to it as "Turtle Creek" after the road where most of the houses were being built.

In 1900, you could walk from the Sooy store and Gus Maxwell's little shop next to the imposing Leek mansion, all the way down Turtle Creek Road and pass two score farms with fine houses surrounded by white, picket fences. The Methodist Church proudly raised her steeple near the intersection of the main road and the road to Billy's Landing.

This was a land of happy families, proud of their new church - and their baseball team, especially when it squared off against those of Lower Bank or Green Bank or Batsto.

The ball games were played in the field that was then ours (back of where Lemuel Maxwell built his home and back of Uncle Gus' little house - next to grandma's). Later they moved it up

across from Uncle John Maxwell's place which was an empty lot then. (Mildred Honaker, March, 1980) [This second field sat back from the northwest corner of Route 542 and Ridge Road.]
I know they had a baseball team for they had picnics to make money to get their suits. I went around and asked for cakes for them to sell. [Rachel Maxwell Adams, March 1, 1977]

The Wading River Cornet Band, composed of a baker's dozen of the local men, entertained the town at picnics and concerts with their music. They were even good enough to play at the 1876 Centennial Celebration in Philadelphia, which certainly must have been a source of great pride to them and their families. Over a century later, their faces still gaze proudly and hauntingly out of the photograph taken for this wonderful occasion. Maja Leek, Charles McAnney, Edward Sooy, George Washington Leek, Levi Downs, Captain Jesse Williams, Frank Downs, William Gale, Captain George Valiant, James Gale, John Maxwell, Austin Downs, Sr., and Samuel Maxwell: all had homes and families in Wading River in the late nineteenth century.

Several of the townsmen owned vessels of various sizes which engaged in the fishing or coastal trade. Known owners and their vessels include:

Adjutant	Maja Leek
Atsion	Oliver Loveland
Albert	James Maxwell
Vulcan	William Gale
Samuel & Franklin	Robert McKeen
Huntress	Robert McKeen
Packet	McKeen & Taggert

RELAPSE

What happened to the town in the early twentieth century? Gradual decline. Railroads stole the river trade. The timber uplands and cedar swamps were stripped bare. The farms never could compete with Midwestern ones with deep, rich, and fertile topsoil. A scheme to sell lots in a real estate venture, the "Gateway to Atlantic City," failed miserably, despite the best efforts of some of the local people. There just was no way to make money here anymore. Even the waterfowl were destroyed by over-hunting before hunting regulations took effect. Moss-gathering, pinecone collecting, and berry-picking replaced farming and shipping and logging. The Depression delivered the final blow. Sure, people could still hunt, and fish, and grow truck gardens, but that didn't make much money. The old families that had tended the land so faithfully for over two centuries were dying off or moving away. Many of the old houses caught fire and burned to the ground or were abandoned.

By 1950, the church was a ruin, the Leek Mansion had been sold and resold and was now turning rather seedy. The stores of Sooy and Maxwell were closed. The post office was gone. The dreams of the "Gateway to Atlantic City" had faced harsh reality, and the young people moved away.

Even the character of the estuary has changed. Years ago, the sea level was lower than it is today, and the saltwater did not intrude as far up the rivers as it does now. The United States Geological Survey has been studying the changes to the ecological system in the present century, and it's evidence suggests that both the river flow has decreased and the salt water has intruded into areas where it was previously absent. As Horace Somes, Jr. of Wading River notes in an unpublished manuscript (1995):

The impacts upon plant life have been striking, particularly in the marshes and adjacent forests. As saltier water pushed inland, the banded zones of different types of marsh plants that are respectively adapted to salt-brackish-fresh tidewater have shifted inland. On the Wading River, expansive wild rice beds have disappeared from below the bridge. As late as the 1960s, the mudflats - or 'middle ground' - on both sides of the channel were covered with this plant. It was never as tall as the rice you can find in the Delaware Valley, where truly-fresh tidewater allows it to grow to twelve feet in height. In our area, where there has always been some hint of salt in the tidewater, it grew only several feet above the water surface. This was fine for those who poled boats through the rice to hunt [railbirds]. . . . But the days of bagging twenty-five birds on a flood tide are gone. The rice remains upriver at the Broad Place, but the cover there was never as good for the birds. . . .

Along with the reduction of wild rice, the saltier water also pushed other valuable wildlife plants out of our marshes - arrowheads, wild oats, cattail, and three-square. Also, an alarming amount of the brackish marshland along the Wading and Mullica is being taken over by foxtail reedgrass, or Phragmites - the common invader of spoiled areas along the shore, which was introduced here from Europe - along with the starling! This choking growth is of minimal value, even to muskrats - who prefer cattails and three-square. Also, the impenetrable reed jungle - up to ten feet in height - makes access to the marsh very difficult. The only consolation is that the reed also is not salt tolerant and eventually will be replaced by the cordgrasses of the true saltmarshes.

Subtle changes in the floristic composition of the marsh may be lost on the average person. More evident, however, is the retreat of the forest or swamp edge as the water level rises and the tide marsh advances. This is particularly apparent where the loss involves white cedar - which probably has been the most important wood product of the South Jersey forests. Because of the natural longevity of the wood - which also made a superior boat lumber - the skeletons of the cedar trees remain long after the swamp has been killed either by too much water or salinity. These dead snags may be seen protruding from the new marsh vegetation for decades, such as at the bridge approaches at Wading River, Lower Bank, and Green Bank.

The land has changed. The river and marshes have changed. Those who live by the river have changed. The residents of Wading River in 1995 are still good people. They are still friendly. They still know each other well. Remnants of the old families who remain in the area or who live in nearby towns still fondly remember "Old Bridgeport." But things are just not the same. They live in the country, which is far better than in the crowded cities or suburbs, but there's not the same closeness as there used to be. There are no white picket fences. No church socials and picnics and annual "strawberry festivals" - no church. No baseball games - no baseball field anymore.

Young people no longer feel the land and marshes. The pulse of the river no longer flows in their veins. The speed of life and technology has replaced the breathing of the land and waters. Life no longer moves with the rhythm of the tides.

Like the residents of the other surviving towns of the Mullica Valley, the people of Wading River live surrounded by state-owned lands. Most of what was can never be rebuilt because of pinelands regulations. Wading River, like Lower Bank and Green Bank, is frozen in time. Wading River itself is classified as a "Preservation Zone," and the Pinelands Commission has steadfastly refused to recognize it as a Pinelands Village, claiming it has too few houses and is split between two municipalities. Apparently state plans for land acquisition count far more than history and reality.

Horace Somes, Jr. makes an observant statement in his manuscript:

Today, we look at the extensive marshlands and forests - some of which are overgrown fields and forgotten towns - as open space for recreational and aesthetic enjoyment. Few people really live on and use the land today; and we have become a culture of servers, not producers -- possibly our epitaph.

Our world moves at too fast a pace. Speedboats and jet-skis haul recreation-seekers at a dizzying pace down the Mullica and the Wading. Few would slow down long enough to explore the numerous creeks and ditches that meant so much to the people of the past. A little creek has a name? Who cares! Life is passing by so fast, it doesn't even know there's a creek there in the first place. It is an irony that the very recreational uses which stimulate the pockets of the state legislature to appropriate funds for natural preservation are gradually destroying the estuaries and marshes. A land that was loved and treasured by those who lived close to its bosom in the past is now forgotten except for the momentary thrill. We really lose something precious to human life when we lose touch with the land and the rivers that feed it. The times change.

This is still a town with two names though, a town replete with memories. Residents of the town may say "Wading River" rather boldly when asked where they live, but deep inside, the remnants of the older families still fondly whisper, "Bridgeport." If you listen closely on a stormy night, perhaps you can hear the music of the Wading River Cornet Band playing jaunty Civil War era marches echoing through the trees where homes and fields once stood.

The Washington Township side of Bridgeport/Wading River

(Route 542 is in the upper right hand corner with the Wading River Bridge just off the picture to the right.)
This photograph and the other aerial photos included in this book were made in the late 1930s and rephotographed about 1978 by Horace Somes, Jr. Much of the darker-colored cedar swampland areas along the river have been taken over by marshes since that time. Also, much of the cultivated land has returned to woods.

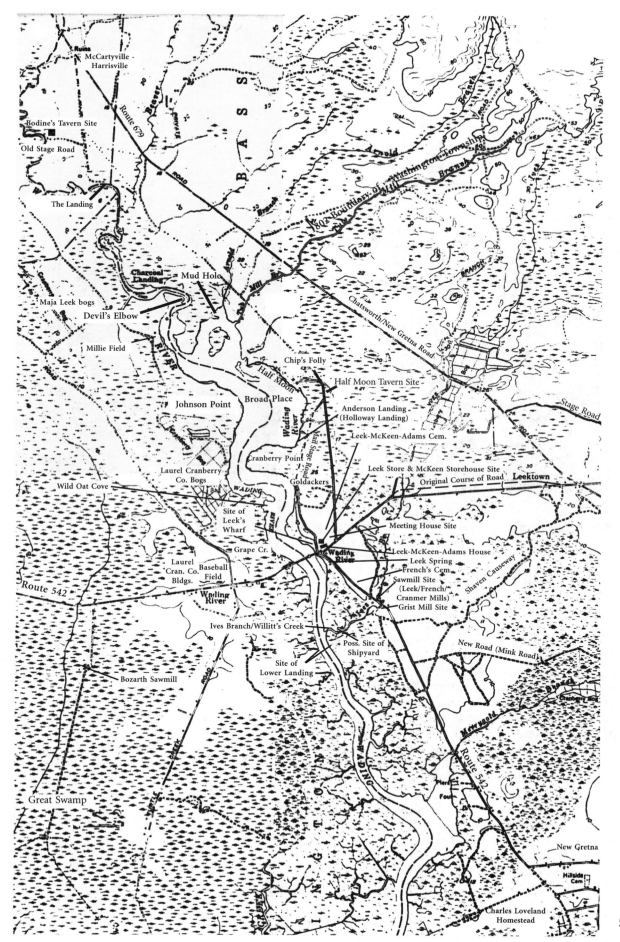

Ruins
McCartyville -
Harrisville

Route 679

Bodine's Tavern Site

Old Stage Road

The Landing

B A S S

1802 Boundary of Washington Township

Mill Br.

Arnold Branch

Branch

Charcoal Landing
Mud Hole

Maja Leek bogs

Devil's Elbow

Millie Field

Chatsworth/New Gretna Road

Half Moon

Chip's Folly

Half Moon Tavern Site

Johnson Point

Broad Place

Anderson Landing
(Holloway Landing)

Wading River

Leek-McKeen-Adams Cem.

Cranberry Point

Laurel Cranberry
Co. Bogs

Goldackers

Leek Store & McKeen Storehouse Site
Original Course of Road   Leektown

Wild Oat Cove

WADING

Mud Stage Road

Site of
Leek's Wharf

Meeting House Site

Grape Cr.

Wading River

Leek-McKeen-Adams House
Leek Spring
French's Cem.

Laurel
Cran. Co.
Bldgs.

Baseball
Field

Sawmill Site
(Leek/French/
Cranmer Mills)

Shaven Causeway

Wading
River

Grist Mill Site

Ives Branch/Willitt's Creek

New Road (Mink Road)

Poss. Site of
Shipyard

Route 542

Site of
Lower Landing

Bozarth Sawmill

Route 542

Great Swamp

WADING

New Gretna

Hillside
Cem

Charles Loveland
Homestead

The Leek/McKeen/Adams House

The Leek/McKeen/Adams House
This view is prior to the rebuilding of the Wading River Bridge in the 1920's. That project placed a considerable amount of fill in the area and brought the ground level almost up to the edge of the porch.

The story of Bridgeport/Wading River actually begins with a man who settled on an island in the Bass River very early in the eighteenth century. According to Leah Blackman in her *History of Little Egg Harbor*, John Mathis was born in Wales about 1690 and emigrated to the American colonies with his brother, Charles, when he was still a young man. The brothers settled on Long Island at Oyster Bay, but Charles soon took his family to Shrewsbury in Monmouth County, New Jersey. In 1713, John Mathis joined with William Birdsall and Moses Forman in purchasing from Daniel Leeds what was then known as Biddle's Island in the Bass River. The next year, both Forman and Birdsall sold their shares of the island to Mathis and moved to other locations. In any case, Mathis was living on his island when he bought out his partners.

Leah Blackman said that the Biddle's Island purchase included approximately two hundred fifty acres of land, but current research could only locate a single fifty acre purchase from Leeds to Mathis. Over the next decades, John Mathis continued to purchase property in the Bass River/Little Egg Harbor River area until he became the largest landholder in the vicinity. At one time, he ran four farms along both sides of the Bass River and his children married into other families in the Bridgeport/Wading River area.

Those years also saw others settle in the area who had family names still recognized today: John Cranmer married Mary Andrews, the daughter of Tuckerton's first family and settled in Bass River somewhere near the Wading River. Robert Allen of Shrewsbury, New Jersey married Edith Andrews, the sister of John Mathis's wife, Alice, and settled an area that would later be known as Allentown, outside of the present-day New Gretna on North Maple Avenue (Route 679). Stephen Cranmer also settled in the Bass River area.

Not long after these well-known men came to Little Egg Harbor, they were joined by John Leak [Blackman's spelling] and Charles Loveland. Unlike their neighbors in Little Egg Harbor, many of the residents between the Bass and Wading Rivers were Presbyterians, including Loveland and Leak. According to Leah Blackman, Captain Charles Loveland was engaged in the slave trade between New Guinea and the American colonies. His family intermarried with those of Washington Township. John Leak was also a sea captain, but there is no evidence that he was involved in the slave trade.

The Leak family (spelled variously: Leake, Leek, or Leeke) has been traced back to England to a Phillip Leeke [*sic*] who was born in that country about 1611 (In 1661, he declared that he was fifty years of age.). He took the oath of allegiance to the Colony of Connecticut on the first of July, 1644. The year before he had been fined a shilling for showing up late for "training" day, the day the militia of the colony turned out for military training (read: getting drunk and having a good time).

In 1645, he was elected to the Great and General Court (the Connecticut legislature) for that year, and in 1646, he was chosen as examiner of measures. In January 1646/7, he was elected as one of the collectors of funds to support the college of Harvard. Somewhere about that time, Phillip married Joanna Ackeley (There is some uncertainty about his wife's maiden name.), and the couple had six children: Phillip, Ebenezer, Mary, John, Joanna, and Thomas.

In 1658, he purchased fifty-nine acres of land and a house from Ralph Dayton in New Haven. Ralph Dayton moved his family from New Haven to East Hampton, Long Island. Phillip Leeke's two sons, Phillip and Ebenezer, followed him there some years later, and Phillip, Jr. married Dayton's daughter, Elizabeth.

Ebenezer married Hannah Baker, daughter of Thomas and Alice (Dayton) Baker, who was also of East Hampton, formerly of New Haven. He was a weaver and cooper (barrel-maker) by trade and was appointed constable of East Hampton in 1699. He died there on June 10, 1726.

His son, Stephen, was born on Long Island about 1680 and was married three times. He was documented as a "husbandman" in East Hampton in 1706. Stephen and his first wife, whose name is not known, had a child who died a baby on August 2, 1705 while he was still living in East Hampton. A little girl born to the couple on October 4, 1709 fared no better, dying on November 9, 1710. His wife died on October 12, 1713, leaving him an eligible bachelor of thirty-three. He then married Mary Shaw. Their son, John, was baptized at East Hampton, New York on September 25, 1715 and must have been born shortly before. At some time during the first year of his son's life, Stephen and Mary moved to Cumberland County, New Jersey, where he was recorded as living by December, 1716. The dates are not clear for the next events in his life, but at some time, his second wife, Mary, died, and he was married for a third time to a woman named Sarah.

June Methot (*Blackman Revisited*) records another child of Stephen and Mary, a girl named Hannah, who later married a man by the name of Garrison. Ms. Methot could not determine whether John's sister Rachel was the daughter of the second wife, Mary, or the third wife, Sarah. She does note that Rachel probably married Thomas Ford on July 2, 1747.

As per Methot, Stephen and Sarah had a daughter, Sarah, who possibly married Thomas Choate on January 2, 1754.

Helen Leek Mack (*The Leek Family of Southern New Jersey*) made it clear that she didn't know which of the girls were born to Mary and which to Sarah.

John Leeke became a sea captain and married Phoebe Devinney on January 12, 1735. It was John who apparently dropped the "E" at the end of his surname.

The exact date on which Stephen and John Leeke bought the Wading River property is unclear,

Courtesy of Horace Somes, Jr.

The Leek/McKeen House as seen from the old Wading River Bridge

but there were three surveys made for John along the east side of the Wading River in 1738. A 1747 survey mentions that the property surveyed was a mile from "John Leek's house." This means that the original house had to have been built between 1738 and 1747, presumably near their wharf property. There are no surveys listed for Steven Leek.

The Leeks, Stephen and Sarah, John and Phoebe, probably built a modest home in Wading River that must have sat only a few yards from the bank of the river itself. How long they actually lived in this little house is not known, but they had great plans. John had is eye on the river trade, and the Leeks built a wharf quite near their house.

A will exists for Stephen Leek dated March 14, 1753, and, by the terms of his will, John was to be his executor and would *inherit the homestead property* on the death of his stepmother. We do know that at the time of his death in 1753, Stephen was living with his third wife, Sarah, and his son, John and his wife, Phoebe, in Wading River.

Courtesy of Horace Somes, Jr.

The Adams/Leek Cemetery
New fence and sign spruced things up for the Bicentennial Celebration in 1976

After his father's death, John and Phoebe continued to live in the homestead on the Wading River which his father had purchased in the house father and son had built together. The couple had at least five children that were alive at the time of John, Sr.'s death in 1777: John, Jr., Mary, Phoebe, Martha, and Achsah.

In a very intriguing note, Bisbee (*Signposts*) quotes a reference from the New Jersey Archives, Volume xxI, p. 148, 1742 viz. that "John Leek had performed an operation upon himself and 'made himself a Eunick.'" The Leek Genealogy does not give birthdates for John and Phoebe's children, but John, Jr., the eldest child, was born in 1735 since he died in 1790 at the age of fifty-five.

If all of John's six children were born within the eight year period between 1735 and 1742, he may well have castrated himself, although other families in the area would easily outdo that record. In any case, John, Sr. did not lack for progeny.

John and Phoebe welcomed John Brainerd, the well-known Presbyterian missionary, into his home and apparently gathered like-minded neighbors to worship in the Presbyterian fashion. Brainerd had to content himself with preaching under a widespreading oak until a meeting house was constructed.

The famous missionary noted in his journal: "*The next Friday* [the 17th of April, 1761] *I rode to Wading River twenty miles on my Road to Manuhocking* [Manahawkin] *and preached a Lecture to a considerable congregation.*" In November, Brainerd was back in Wading River: "*The next day I rode 20 miles and preached at Wading River; and the day following returned home*" [November 1761].

John Leek, Sr. was a strong supporter of the revolt against English rule and loaned money to the patriot cause during the War for Independence. He was simply getting too old to be traipsing around the countryside. He left that to John, Jr. who was actively involved in the prosecution of the Revolutionary War. Now the family could boast another "Captain "John Leek, even though the son's title was military rather than nautical. He served from 1775 to 1783 in the Second Regiment, Company of Rangers of the Burlington County Militia.

Captain John, Sr. wrote his will on May 5, 1777 and named his cousins from Cumberland County: Samuel, Recompence, and Nathan Leek, as his executors. Amongst the provisions of his will was one which left a portion of his property on which he had built a Presbyterian Meeting House. Historians of the area have always considered this plot of ground to have been the one including the Leek family burial ground immediately behind their house, but this is not the case.

The provision in John Leek, Sr.'s will clearly shows that the ground left for the church was that on which the French Cemetery is located.

In the Name of God Amen I John Leek of little Egg harbour in the County of Burlington in the Western Division of New Jersey yeoman I do this fifth day of May in the Year of Our Lord One

Thousand Seven hundred and Seventy Seven . . . give and bequeath unto the several inhabitants of Wading River and Bass River in Little Egg Harbour, and to their heirs forever, they being Presbyterians, for the use of the Presbyterian Meeting House and burial Ground, one certain lot of land, containing sixty-five perches, butted and bounded as followeth: northwestardly from Willis creek about seven or eight chains from an old footway across said Willis Creek on an Old Beaver Dam, beginning at a young white oak marked on four sides and extends 1st south thirty-six degrees two chains and sixteen links to a stump, about a perch from the meeting house; 2nd north thirty-three degrees east one chain and ninety-five links to a white oak; then 3rd north thirty-two degrees and a half west one chain and fifty links; then 4th To the beginning. All which sixty-five perches of land and meeting house and burial ground for the use of a Meeting House for Presbyterians to carry on the worship of God in. But in case it should so happen in the process of time, that there should be a vacancy when there is no Presbyterian minister or other person set apart to carry on the worship of God, in said meeting house by said Presbyterians, in that case it is my will that any Protestant minister of any society that is well recommended by the society they belong to, to have the liberty to preach in said meeting house, until the Presbyterians can be enabled to carry on the worship of God in said meeting house themselves; and it is my desire that the Presbyterians belonging to said meeting house, when there is a vacancy as aforesaid, that they lovingly receive those of other societies that come to minister in said house with Christian love and forbearance as much as possible.

The foregoing was given to me by Pete Stemmer of New Gretna who has been doing research on Bass River Township. "Willis" or "Willitt's" Creek is the Ives Branch of the Wading River, and the description encompasses the current site of the "French" cemetery, so called because some of the remaining stones are those of the French family who succeeded the Leeks in ownership of this property. All traces of the structure are gone. It is quite possible that Route 542 covers the original site of the building or at least that its construction obliterated it.

The Leeks, however, did not use this site as their place of burial. Most of that family were buried on the hill behind their house, now known as the Adams/Leek/McKeen cemetery. There is even a stone in that cemetery on which observers fifty years ago could find carved simply "SL" which may indicate that John's father, Stephen, was buried on the property when he died in 1753.

It has been believed that a small cellarhole near the Adams/Leek/McKeen Cemetery is the site of the Leek house in Wading River. The site is close to that of the former Leek Wharf, and it is certainly possible that Stephen and Captain John had their house here. It is equally possible that the current house beside the road was built on the site of the original structure, although the old road ran behind the house rather than in front of it.

The Leek Wharf ran along the river for some distance above the current bridge, and perhaps stretched down river as well. The original channel in the river ran close to the Bass River side at the Leek property. Evidence suggests that much of this land was filled in by the river and by dumping over the years. Most of the land towards the southwest along the New Gretna road is land that was filled when the old drawbridge was constructed in the 1920's. The channel was dredged farther from the shoreline at this time also. Towards the northeast, though, the wharf ran along the Goldacker Road for a distance up river. Some years back, digging was done in this area, revealing a twenty foot depth of silt from the river that had filled in a deep basin that used to exist right next to the presumed location of the Leek Wharf. The original channel would have led directly to the wharf rather than heading out into the river as it does today. The Leeks built a sizable enterprize over the years including a store and storehouse, a large wharf, a shipyard, a sawmill, and perhaps several other outbuildings related to both their wharf activities and their farm.

Adams descendant, Steve Eichinger, points out that the Goldacker Road used to run a little farther inland than it does today and that several cellar indentations in the area indicate the location of other buildings. Just upriver, local legend says, stood a log cabin that seems to have been the center for the cordwood shipping part of the wharf's trade.

When John, Sr. died in 1777, he had assembled property totaling at least 336 acres. John, Jr. had another fifty-one in his own right. Both he and his wife, Phoebe, were buried in the little cemetery behind their home beside the little river they had grown to love so well. Captain John Leek, Jr., a surveyor by trade, had married the reputed beauty, Martha Rose and the couple had eight children: John III, Samuel, Martha, William, Achsah, Mary, and Phoebe. His youngest son he named after his beloved former commander and the sitting first President of the United States, George Washington.

Phoebe Leek, John, Jr.'s sister, married the Great John Mathis's son, Job, who died in 1770 and was buried in the Quaker cemetery in Little Egg Harbor (Tuckerton). Job and Phoebe (Leek) Mathis had a son, Daniel, who married the daughter of the famous privateer captain, Micajah Smith of Chestnut Neck. Daniel's brother-in-law, Micajah, Jr. was married to Jeana Sooy, the daughter of Noah Sooy, granddaughter of Joseph Sooy (Yoos II), and niece of Nicholas Sooy I of Green Bank.

Daniel and Phoebe (Smith) Mathis had a daughter, Sarah, who married James Austin Downs, and lived in the town of her grandmother, Wading River. Her daughter, Leah Eleanor Angeline Downs married John J. Maxwell, the son of James and Bethia (Gale) Maxwell. Their daughter, Helen Bethia Maxwell married James McAnney. All of these surnames will figure prominently in the history of Wading River.

When Captain John Leek, Jr. died in 1790 at the age of fifty-four, his house stood in the middle of a large plantation that reached up the river for some distance and inland towards the Bass River Tavern and what would become known as Leektown and also down river to the Merrygold Branch on the New Gretna road. He had a profitable business based on river trade, controlling the transshipment of goods from upriver. He had a shipbuilding enterprize on his property, the actual location of which is not known, but it has been suggested that it stood near the lower landing below the current bridge directly opposite the Taylor land and burial ground on the northwestern side of the river. It is also likely that John had cleared extensive acreage for farmland to support his family and those of his employees. All in all, it was an estate of which this honored captain in the Revolution could have been justly proud.

John Leek III married Hepsibah, the daughter of William and Esther (Cramer) Grant and started right in on producing heirs. He and Hepsibah had seven children: Achsah, William Grant, Hester A., Margaret B., Ann, Beulah, and John C. Achsah married into the Adams family (she married Ellis Adams); William Grant Leek married another Adams, Phoebe; and Margaret married John H. Shourds, of another local family.

Achsah (Leek) and Ellis Adams lived near Calico, a village in the vicinity of Martha Furnace. John Milton Adams, Jr., their grandson, says that they actually lived at nearby Perry Field most of their lives. They were buried in Hillside Cemetery at New Gretna. Their children: Samuel B., John F., William, Charles Tower, Ellen Smith, Achsah, Beulah, and Amanda generally married into other local families as well. Those who remained in the area lie in New Gretna's Miller Cemetery.

John III and Hepsibah's son, William, drowned in Bass River in 1852 at the age of 49. His granddaughter, Phoebe, born in Wading River on November 8, 1863, married Andrew Etheridge at Hammonton on January 3, 1882. The couple lived first in Batsto and had four children: Florence, Sarah, Maymie and John. Andrew became the manager of Atsion for Wharton and lived there for many years until his death. The last remains of the neglected Etheridge House at Atsion were a gaunt reminder of the past until they burned on March 1, 1998. John C. Leek, another son of John Leek III and Hepsibah (Grant), married a woman whose surname is not known but whose given name was Martha.

The Leeks, who still have a boat-building business on the Mullica, descend from Captain John Leek, Jr. and Martha's son Samuel, who married Sarah Mathis. Samuel and Sarah's son, still another John, married a Bass River girl by the name of Roseanna. John and Roseanna's son, William, born in 1813, married Hannah, the daughter of Noah Sooy, granddaughter of Yoos Sooy II, and niece of Nicholas Sooy I. Their oldest son they called Charles Platt Leek.

Charles Platt Leek's brother, yet another William, and his wife Rebecca (Cramer), named their second child Charles Platt Leek also. Mother Rebecca was the daughter of Richard and Mary Ann (Van Sant) Cramer of Lower Bank. This Charles Platt Leek organized the C.P. Leek Boat Works in Lower Bank which later was known for its Pacemaker Yachts. He married Edith Young and became the parents of Cecil Gilbert Leek, Olga Winona Leek, and John Everett Leek. John E. Leek is the father of John E. (Jack) Leek, Jr. (b. 1930), who owns (1995) Ocean Yachts and lives on the Atlantic County side of the Mullica, his sister, Marie Lee (b.1927), and his brother, Donald (b.1933).

For the better part of eighty years, the Leeks had remained on their homestead in Wading River, but early in the nineteenth century, however, something happened with John Leek III. John III is not buried in the family cemetery, or at least there is no marked grave for him and his wife. It is known that, on February 12, 1817, he sold all the land in Wading River which he had inherited from his father and grandfather and disappeared. A portion of the old homestead by the river came into the possession of Robert McKeen, Esq., whose family would own it for most of the nineteenth century. Though John III vanished from the town of his ancestors, the rest of his family remained in the area. An 1821 letter, written by his father-in-law, William Grant, mentions that his daughter, Hepsibah, was a widow. Though his birthdate is not known, John Leek III could not have been very old when he died.

Just when did the Leeks build their second house which stands hard by the New Gretna road? No one seems to know. There are indications that it wasn't built by the Leeks at all but by the property's next owner, Robert McKeen, Esq. A reference is made in the William F. Augustine Collection at Rutgers University Libraries to an 1815 date for the construction of this house, but that is two years prior to the sale of the corner to McKeen. The tiny cellar hole behind the big house seems rather small to have been the location of a house for this wealthy family over the entire eighty year period of their residency. It is possible that the Leek family did build a newer house on the site of the present structure that was incorporated into a larger building when Robert McKeen purchased the property from John Leek III.

Regardless of *when* or *who* built it, for the better part of the nineteenth century, this building housed a store, the post office of Wading River, and served as a stop on the Mail Stage Road which branched off from the Stage Road in the vicinity of Bodine's. We don't know much about Robert McKeen except that he was born in Wading River in 1779, but we do know something about his wife's background. Laura Blackman (*History of Little Egg Harbor*) relates a wonderful story about one Joseph Burns. Joseph did not have a safe, happy voyage from England when he sailed to this country in the eighteenth century. His ship went down at sea, and he was the only survivor. He clung to a wooden plank, adrift in the Atlantic for four days and four nights. The rough seas eventually tore all the clothes from his body, and the roughness of the plank that was his savior chafed the flesh off his arms. When all hope seemed lost, he was finally rescued by the crew of another vessel that just happened to be in the area and found him at the last possible moment.

Anna M. McKeen
1869-1968
Daughter of
John Franklin and Hannah (Carter) McKeen

Joseph Burns settled in New Jersey and married Hannah Cranmer, the daughter of Joseph Cranmer, Sr., and the couple's daughter, Margaret, born in Wading River in 1795, married Robert McKeen on the 8th of January 1818. The previous year, McKeen had purchased property from John Leek III that included the site of this house and stretched down river into the marshes. Thanks to the efforts of Murray and Jean Harris of New Gretna, we know that Robert and Margaret had eight children: William (b. 1818), Samuel (b. 1821), John Franklin (date of birth unknown), Catharine [sic] Ann (b. c. 1825), George Towers (b. 11 June 1826), Robert Forman (b. 1 June 1828), Mary (b. circa 1825), and Maria Jane (date of birth unknown).

Theirs was a time of prosperity for Wading River/Bridgeport, with traffic both across the new bridge and on the river to Martha Furnace and later to McCartyville. Robert McKeen is listed in the Batsto Store Books as the owner of the schooner *Huntress* in 1854 and as part owner of the *Packet* with his partner, Samuel Taggart. The wreck of the *Huntress* lay off the old Leek Wharf property near McKeen's house for many years until the county built the new bridge and removed the remains from the river. McKeen and Taggart kept their own vessels busy, scowed iron ore to Martha and returned with pig iron, carried rags to McCartyville and returned with paper, brought fence posts and rails downriver, and ran a store to the rear of the McKeen house.

Of the McKeen children, George Towers McKeen died at the age of sixteen on August 30, 1842, and William B. was drowned in the Wading River on October 10th, 1850, five years after his father's death and the year before his mother's demise.

John Franklin McKeen married Hannah Carter (b. 1830 d. 1909), the daughter of John and Lavinia (Cramer) Carter of Bridgeport on the 23rd of July 1848, and they had seven children who survived to adulthood: Charles Augustus, George T., William H. (b. 1854), Samuel L., Mary (b. 1860), John F. (b. 1862), and Anna M. (b. 1869). John McKeen is mentioned in the Batsto Store Books as master of the sloop *Cora* in 1859. He died in 1878 at Bridgeport.

Three times John Franklin and Hannah tried to have a son named George Towers, and three times they trudged up the hill to the old Leek/McKeen cemetery with their children. The first George T. lived less than a year after he was born in 1848. The Second George T. was born in 1849 and died in 1851. The third George T. was born in 1853 and died in 1854. The name was certainly ill-fated in two generations. A daughter, Margaret, was born about 1851 and died in 1865.

Robert Forman McKeen married Sarah Lavinia Loveland (b. 17 January 1829 d. 22 July 1913), daughter of John and Rachel J. (French) Loveland, on June 2, 1850.

Maria Jane McKeen married Samuel Adams (not the Samuel Adams of Massachusetts but a local Samuel whose grandfather was Hezekiah Adams of Bass River).

"Forman" McKeen is listed on the 1850 census as being twenty-one years old and a waterman. His brother William is listed as a farmer, and 1850 is the year he drowned in the river. Mother Margaret is listed as possessing $11,000, quite a sum in those days. Brother Samuel is also listed as a waterman, while Catharin [sic] has no occupation listed after her name. This would seem to indicate that the McKeen house was not yet used for a hotel at this time. By 1860, "Robert F." had become a "sea captain" and his sister, Catharine, a "hotel keeper." Brother Samuel had shifted to being a "laborer."

Robert McKeen died October 19, 1845 at the age of sixty-five. Robert's wife, Margaret, died six years later at the age of fifty-six. Robert and Margaret still lie in eternal slumber on the hillside beside their home in the Adams-Leek-McKeen cemetery along with several of their children. The story of Margaret's father isn't finished yet, though. It has one ironic twist. After his miraculous rescue, Joseph Burns was known to have said, time and time again, that "those that was born to be hung would not be drowned." Years later, he fell off a ship that was anchored at the Virginia capes and drowned. The sea had finally reclaimed its own.

When Robert McKeen had purchased the property, the area was experiencing a slump and the Leek Wharf was in decline. Up river, Martha Furnace was in operation, and McKeen saw possibilities for the area. After McCarty built his paper mill in 1832, it, too, needed a means to both ship and receive goods, and, although they used the Landing below the town (Beaver Branch), only smaller boats could make it even that far upriver. Two other landings existed upstream from Leek's Wharf, but the river became too shallow for ships of any size to continue. Thus, the larger vessels had to stop at the Leek's rather than proceed upstream. No doubt some of the business moved to the lower wharf after the construction of the first bridge in 1814 somewhat discouraged passage to sailing vessels beyond that point, but that is precisely the property purchased from the Leeks by Robert McKeen.

In 1975, as part of a conversation with the Cramers of Ship Bottom, Martina Adams Eichinger gave the following description of the McKeen storehouse behind the house on the corner. It is given here, courtesy of her son, Steve Eichinger.

> *The McKeen storehouse was a retail store as well as a storehouse. Its northwest corner was used as a reference point in certain deed descriptions. It had a stone foundation as shown by the remaining cellar walls. Later, there was a two-story residence of one room on each floor added to the storehouse. This was on the east side of the storehouse, that is, the side away from the river. Martina remembers seeing this structure and being warned to avoid the cellar hole as it was deep and had water in it. There was no tunnel from the cellar to the river.*
>
> *The road at that time ran along the south face of these two, joined structures, somewhat along the course of the present Cemetery Lane; it did not run where the present county (or township) road lies. The road now known as the Leektown Road came later. The wharf was in line with the storehouse or the old road. At that time the road running, along the west, or river, side of the storehouse was the main road to Martha. It is now called River Road or Goldaker Road. This road extends about a half mile, beyond the Rudolph cottage to a few summer homes. Topographical maps show it continuing, more or less, to join the New Gretna-Harrisville road south of Harrisville, a short way below Chips Folly Camping Ground. Bridges are out over small streams and trees have grown in the roadway.*

Steve remembers his mother and aunt pointing out the cellar hole in the above location as the site of the original Leek house which makes this transcription doubly interesting. Here, Martina is obviously saying that it was a McKeen structure, not a Leek one. Where was the original Leek house? No one seems to have a clue. Perhaps it stood on the site of the current McKeen/Adams house. There was a map of the Leek Wharf in the Batsto archives at one time, but it couldn't be located. Perhaps if we are able to find it someday, we will know for sure.

When Robert McKeen died in 1845, the will he had written in 1832 was probated. He basically left the bulk of his property to be equally divided amongst his sons, with provision made for his widow and daughters. He also left his sons the schooners *Samuel* and *Franklin*, and the sloop *Huntress*. In 1848, his widow and children apparently wished to settle the estate, and the Orphan's Court issued a decree on December 9th of that year, ordering his properties to be sold. McKeen's daughter, Catharine, bought the homestead and adjacent lands. She never married. At some time between 1850 and 1860, she began using the McKeen house as a hotel. Steve Eichinger of Wading River found a copy of her license for the year 1879. Dated April 15th of that year, the Inferior Court of Common Pleas of Burlington County issued to Catharine McKeen a license to maintain an "inn and tavern" for a period of one year. It was signed by the clerk of the court, John B. Deacon.

From her photograph on this page, Catharine must have been a serious and commanding person. Though she remained unmarried, she wasn't alone in the house become tavern. Her brother, Samuel, also did not choose to marry and continued to live in the family house with his sister.

Catharine McKeen served as postmistress from the time of the establishment of the Wading River Post Office on February 8, 1858 until her death on September 19, 1890. Though some people seem to remember the post office being on the Washington Township side of the river during the latter part of the nineteenth century, it is unlikely that it was so until after Catharine's death. Copies of the postmaster's "location" sheets dated October 29, 1863 and May 24, 1884 indicate that it was probably kept in this house from the time of its inception in 1858 until she died.

After Catharine's death, the post office may have been kept by Edwin Clark Sooy in his store on the Washington Township side of the river until William A. Maxwell took over as postmaster. Possibly Charles "Ed" Leek was postmaster in the same building when he ran the store for Sam Ireland. In any case, the "location sheets" indicate that Maxwell was postmaster in 1914 and probably remained so until the post office was eliminated in 1923.

Catharine and Samuel had lost two brothers, several nephews and a niece. Even though they both remained unmarried, they were not spared tragedy in their own lives. In the 1880's, the home, tavern, store, post office caught on fire and burned to the ground. Steve Eichinger tells a comical yet sad tale of human nature that is said to have happened during this fire. Since there were no banks in the area, families often kept whatever coins they had accumulated stashed all over their houses. When the fire broke out, Catharine McKeen dashed around the house, frantically digging out hoard after hoard of gold coins from their hiding places and throwing them out the windows. Outside, everyone for miles around had gathered to watch the blaze. There were no fire companies at the time and no way to pump the river water onto the flames, so there was nothing they could do but watch. When the gold coins started raining from the windows, however, temptation proved too much, and these poor people, who may not have even possessed a single gold coin before, dove to the ground to gather them up and squirrel them away for themselves.

The McKeens rebuilt their house on the same foundation, much as it had been before and continued their business until their deaths. Catharine McKeen died on the 19th of September, 1890 at the age of sixty-five and her

Courtesy of Steve Eichinger

Catharine McKeen
1825 - 1890

brother, Samuel, followed her on November 21st a year later at the age of seventy. Thus came to the end the second family to live in the homestead beside the river.

In their later years, the elderly brother and sister were cared for by their niece, Anna Staza Adams, and they left their property to her when they died. Anna Staza Adams was the eldest child of Samuel and Maria Jane (McKeen) Adams, and was born to the couple in 1849.

Something is missing from the records, however. As her great-grandson, Steve Eichinger, remarked: "I think I've found my skeleton in the closet!" Anna Staza Adams had one son, George Henry Adams. "Harry," as he liked to be called, took his mother's family name. In the family records, there is no mention of his father's name. Anna spent the middle years of her life taking care of her elderly aunt and uncle. In the year of her death, Catharine McKeen signed the papers necessary to give her brother, Samuel, a life interest in all of her property along the river and making Anna Staza Adams the sole heir after his death. Samuel McKeen, a year later, also signed the necessary documents making Anna Staza Adams the legal owner of all the properties accumulated by the McKeens along the river throughout the century. Apparently, though others in the McKeen family were unhappy with a settlement that left them out, there was nothing that could be done. A review of the documents indicated that the transfer to Anna Staza Adams was completely legal.

Catharine McKeen must have been very grateful for her niece's care in their later years and felt she needed the support the house and property would provide. A single woman of fifty-two when her uncle died, she certainly must have appreciated receiving the house which had become her home. Perhaps Catharine, a spinster all her life, sympathized with the situation of her neice. After the deaths of her aunt and uncle, Anna Staza Adams did marry George Coffee (1856-1926) , but she was beyond her childbearing years by that time.

Courtesy of Steve Eichinger

Anna Staza Adams Coffee
1849 - 1930
Anna is standing at the west end of the Leek/McKeen/Adams House in Wading River during the 1920's.

Anna Staza Adams Coffee's only son, Henry (1870-1926), married Martha Downs (1874-1955), the daughter of Benjamin Franklin and Ellen Chew Downs across the river. The couple were joined in holy wedlock by the Rev. Nicholas Van Sant, Jr. of Lower Bank on October 2, 1892. "Harry" Adams (He hated the name Henry!) ran a steam-powered sawmill that used to stand in the woods behind the house on the V formed by the Leektown and New Gretna roads.

One of his Adams forebears, Isaiah Adams, ran the Bass River Tavern on the old road from Camden to Tuckerton, though he was a total abstinence man. Isaiah had become a rich man, though not just from keeping a tavern. He had developed a large farm in the vicinity and carried on an extensive lumber and shipbuilding trade. Isaiah was Harry Adams's great great uncle.

Martha Stranger Downs Adams could trace her family back to the Great John Mathis of Bass River. Her grandfather, James Downs, had married Sarah Mathis. Sarah's father, Daniel Mathis II, was the grandson of the Great John Mathis, and her mother, Phoebe (Smith) Mathis, was the daughter of the famous privateer captain, Micajah Smith, Sr. of Gloucester County (now Atlantic County).

As we have found so many times before, every old family along the river is related to every other old family. Daniel Mathis II was the son of Job Mathis and Phoebe Leek, the sister of Captain John Leek, Sr. Another of his sisters, Mary, married Joseph Sooy, who later moved to Green Bank. After Job Mathis died, Phoebe Leek Mathis married Caleb Cramer (or Cranmer) and joined another local family into linkage. It's impossible to figure it all out, but right there you have interrelationship of Mathis, Sooy, Leek, Downs, Adams, and McKeen. Steve Eichinger of Wading River can claim all of them as his ancestors. So can Jessie Lewis and Betty Crowley Rubsam of Green Bank. So, too, can all the various Cavileers of Lower Bank, Jack Leek, Jr. and his family across the river, Horace Somes, Jr. of Wading River, the Weeks clan, Marjorie Downs Cavileer of Lower Bank, and a good many others I *don't* know.

Back to George Henry Adams. Remember him? Anna Staza Adams Coffee's only son? "Harry" and Martha Downs Adams had four daughters: Nora Ellen (1893-1899), Alice Rose (1897-1973), Anna Engel (1912-1912), and Martina Engel (1913-1989). They also had two sons: Burrel Morten Adams and Levi Henry Adams. After Harry's death in 1926 at the age of fifty-six, Martha married Samuel W. Merchant (1874-1955).

Alice Adams Weber did not have a happy marriage and was close to her grandmother in her declining years. According to her nephew, Steve Eichinger, Alice's husband, Tom Weber, was a rumrunner who brought proscribed goods into Clarks Landing. The marriage didn't last long,

Courtesy of Horace Somes, Jr.

Alice Adams Weber
1897-1973

under the circumstances. Perhaps that shared sympathy was why, when Anna Staza Adams Coffee died in 1930, Alice Rose Adams inherited the McKeen house and property. When sister Martina married Stephen Eichinger (1903-1974), they, too, moved into the old Leek-McKeen house. Their son, Steven, and his brother, were born there.

Steve doesn't remember exactly when the Leek-McKeen-Adams house was sold, but in 1941, when Henry Charlton Beck interviewed old Watson Lippincott at his boat building business beside the bridge, Alice Adams was still living in the Leek-McKeen Homestead and had faithfully tended the drawbridge over the Wading River for many years. Nephew Steve, by the way, was the last official bridge tender of the Wading River bridge, succeeding his aunt in the position. Alice did make the move to the house on the "V" and the old homestead was sold.

The sisters were very interested in the history of their town, and it was on the instigation of Alice Adams, long Alice Weber, in 1959, that the Old Bridgeport Society was organized. In that year, Alice was seventy-five years old and was concerned that the history of her beloved town would be forgotten. By this time, the old homestead had been sold from the Adams family. The Old Bridgeport Society is still in existence and Martina's son, Steve Eichinger, who lives with his wife, Joyce in Alice's house on the "V," continues the family support. Steve and Joyce have two children, Christina Alice and Wilson Lewis.

According to Steve's memory, the Leek-McKeen-Adams house was either sold or rented to a family by the name of Cook for several years. In the 1960's, a family by the name of Narien ran the Wading River Bakehouse there. George and Marion Mushett bought the house from the Nariens on the day President Kennedy was shot, November 22, 1963, but he and his wife never actually lived there. They rented the house to a couple named Hack and Jean. This was the age of the "flower children," and George remembers that they lived in a tent in the rear yard, made pottery from the river clay, and talked to the flowers. Joseph Aubrey bought the property from the Mushetts in 1964, and he rebuilt the entire structure, inside and out. Mike O'Neill succeeded Joe Aubrey as the owner. The house is now owned and loved by Harry ("Skip") and Janet Dixon.

In her last years, Alice Adams Weber lived in the little house on the "V" between the Leektown and New Gretna Roads where her nephew lives to this day. Back in the 1960's, when this author came canoeing with his scout troop, we had to pull out just below the Wading River bridge. The landing was on private property, and the woman who owned it collected $.50 per canoe for the privilege of landing on her property. She also had to charge us $.50 to make a telephone call back to Belhaven Lake to get them to come and pick us up. She apologized profusely, but it was a toll call to phone the other half of Wading River/Bridgeport, let alone all the way to Green Bank! Seems the telephone lines don't cross the river, and the calls are routed through Egg Harbor! In any case, twenty-five years later, when meeting her nephew, Steve Eichinger, I realized that I had, indeed, known his aunt. For that old lady who collected $3.50 from our Scout troop that day was none other than Alice Rose Adams Weber! Now, she, too, is gone. Though, like many of her ancestors, she hasn't gone very far, just to the hill overlooking her beloved home and the river, always the river, running to the sea.

The Leek/McKeen/Adams Homestead still stands proudly beside the road, river, and bridge it has guarded, through at least two reincarnations, for over two hundred years!

NOTE: The 1933 article mentioned on the following page says that the McKeen hotel burned exactly fifty years prior to the date of the article: 1883. Steve Eichinger of Wading River has a letter from the county clerk, Levi French, to Catherine McKeen, dated June 13, 1888, in which Mr. French advises Catherine McKeen that she could probably get away with selling liquor by the quart "where you now live. Yet there is a strong doubt as to your right to sell by the drink at any place except the house you lived in when your license was granted. You could rebuild on the old foundation and sell after you rebuild until the license expires." This would seem to indicate that the original home burned in either late 1887 or early 1888. In any case, Catherine did rebuild prior to her death on September 19, 1890.

Photograph by John Pearce

The Leek-McKeen-Adams House - 1995

Faded Flag With Black Calico Edging Memento of Night Lincoln Was Shot

Courtesy of Steve Eichinger

Flag of Mourning for a Martyred President

In 1933, an unknown newspaper published the above photograph and this American flag which had become the symbol of mourning for an assassinated President. On the night of April 15, 1865, three women sat in the the Bridgeport Tavern sewing an American flag to celebrate the end of the Civil War: Sarah McKeen, Hess Rake, and Hannah Prince.

The ladies had sewn the thirty-six stars in the field in the pattern of one big star in thanksgiving for the reuniting of the country as one nation. They had just finished their sewing when a traveller brought the shocking news of Abraham Lincoln's assassination at Ford's Theatre the evening before and of his death at 7:22 A.M. that very morning.

Shocked and saddened, the ladies got out their needles and thread once more and sewed vertical black stripes over the flag as symbols of mourning. They then hung the flag on a rope across the street in front of the McKeen Hotel, to tell all who passed that Bridgeport mourned the death of a beloved President.

The newspaper remarked that, in 1933, the three women who had sewn the flag were dead, the town's name had been changed to Wading River, and the hotel had burned fifty years before, but Martina (pictured above) and Steve Eichinger still had the old flag and displayed it on their porch as a tribute to the martyred President on his birthday, February 12. Even they are gone now. Their son, Steve, still lives with his family in their house across from the rebuilt McKeen Hotel, now also a private home.

The Quaker Meeting House of Wading River

The date of this photograph is unknown.

The Religious Society of Friends had been founded in England by George Fox in the seventeenth century. Fox and his followers believed that every person had direct access to God through the Holy Spirit and needed no intermediary. They refused to take oaths in English courts, participate in the Church of England, or bear arms. Their quaint form of dress and their habit of using the archaic informal singular address "thee" instead of "you" set them apart from the general Christian populace. Their open "testimony," with which they disrupted church services and civil meetings, made them convenient subjects of persecution. The king of England was glad to get rid of some of them when William Penn asked for a land grand in the American colonies. As has been mentioned earlier, Penn also came into the trusteeship of West Jersey, which had been settled by many of the Quaker persuasion. Little Egg Harbor had been settled by Quakers, though the Lovelands and Leeks were Presbyterians.

Early in the nineteenth century, the Society of Friends was faced with a schism which disrupted their peaceful existence, and, for a while, caused a split in practically every Friends' Meeting in the country into Orthodox, Hicksite, and Conservative branches. Those of the Little Egg Harbor Meeting who adhered to the teachings of the Hicksites built a meeting house at Bass River. In June of 1824, a committee was appointed to open a subscription for buying a lot and building a meeting house at Bridgeport/Wading River. In January of 1825, Bridgeport Meeting succeeded Bass River as an indulged meeting. The new building was completed on February 10, 1825 at a cost of $385. Some of the materials for the construction were donated and $280 was raised through subscriptions. In addition, Nathan Bartlett and David Mapps, an overseer of the meeting, gave their note to Jesse Evans for the remainder and reported the account settled in March of 1825. The first wife of Martha Furnace's manager, Lucy Evans, was also a leader of this splinter group.

Steve Eichinger locates the depression where this old meetinghouse stood between the Adams-Leek-McKeen Cemetery and the Leektown Road. Early in the nineteenth century, Martha was directly connected to Wading River by road, and Lucy Evans travelled down the road from Martha to Bridgeport each First Day for meeting. The Methodists were sweeping the area during these years, and many Quakers joined the churches built for that denomination, but Lucy remained faithful. Lucy Evans remained so faithful that the time came when she was the sole minister and member of the congregation at the Bridgeport Meeting, sitting in solitary and silent meditation each First Day until her death in 1834 at the age of sixty-six.

Quakers did not, as a rule, use gravestones to mark the final resting places of their beloved dead, but Lucy Ann has one. Between the Adams-Leek-McKeen Cemetery and the cellarhole of the old Wading River Meeting, her stone still keeps silent sentinel in the woods. It has been suggested that her husband, Jesse, was not of the "Friendly Persuasion" though he attended meeting occasionally with his wife. Perhaps it was he who erected this rather non-Quaker tribute to the bride of his youth. Maybe he needed something to salve his conscience when he married his ward, the second Lucy Ann, who was only twenty-five to his sixty-six. In any case, the first Lucy Ann Evans, wife of one of Washington Township's "great" men, lies in a marked grave in the woods of Wading River on the Bass River Township side.

There are others stones in the vicinity of hers as well, and it is supposed that these belonged to other members of the Wading River Friends Meeting, but this need not be the case. Steve Eichinger points out the shallow indentation nearby where legend has it that an African-American was supposedly buried at some time in the last century. Legend has it that, prejudice being what it was, some local men felt that the body of a Black man should not share the same sacred ground as that of white people, so late at night, they dug up the body and reburied it elsewhere. True or not, near Lucy Evans grave, a grave-sized impression in the ground bears mute testimony to the extent to which hearts hardened by prejudice will go.

This building was still standing early in the twentieth century but was reclaimed by time and the elements. On May 28, 1975, Marjorie K. Cramer and Frederic M. Cramer of Ship Bottom and Martina Adams Eichinger (Steve Eichinger's mother and Alice Adams Weber's sister) taped a conversation amongst themselves at the site of the old Bridgeport Friends Meeting, a transcription of this conversation is included here, courtesy of Steve Eichinger.

When I (Martina, b, 1913) was a child it was all green lawn, grass; the trees were not here, a few big ones but no small growth like now. There was nothing then to show where the people who attended meeting may have left their wagons. There was no carriage shed after I can remember.

We used to tell the location of the meeting house by the lot of plaster on the ground. There used to be so many more stones laid where the foundation was but somebody who lived in Alice Weber's house carted them all off for a rock garden, years ago. This is the location, the bare spot. One corner is here with the stones; another corner is over by Dr. Rudolph's line.

The building had a pitched roof; the ridge pole ran lengthwise toward the Leektown Road. It was about a foot and a half off the ground, just a couple of steps. It was ordinary height, not high enough for two stories. There was Jersey stone, solid all the way around, for the foundation. The entrance was two, big, solid doors, in the center, on the Leektown Road end of it. They had a big step outside, but no roof over it, just a step. On the other end was the chimney, the end toward the cemetery; it was brick. The outside was done in wide weatherboard; the roof was pretty well deteriorated, when I can remember it, but I think it was shingled. The building was never painted, left natural wood. The meeting house had, I think, two long windows on each side; they were squared-out, but long, just plain glass. I don't think there were any windows on the end with the chimney, only on the sides. There had been shutters but they had been taken off.

The inside was lath and plaster. There is still some plaster left; we used to pick it up and remark about all the years it had been there, in the weather, and it still was whole and hadn't crumbled. That may be a marking (looking at a piece of plaster) of where the lath was. (The piece showed a rough base-coat about 5/16 of an inch thick with a white finish-coat on it.) The inside walls were all there when I saw it.

The church was empty when I was a child; even the benches were taken out. There were about fifteen of them and they were stored in an old barn for a while; then they were gotten rid of. On Aubrey's front porch is one of the pews [This bench, now in poor condition, was photographed this date by Frederic. It measured about ten feet in length.]. There were two of them at Aubreys when Alice left there. That's the old McKeen (Anna Coffee) property. Anna Adams, or Coffee, took care of her aunt and inherited her property, which didn't suit the other heirs in the family. It then passed to Alice. The bench that wasn't any good the Aubreys didn't keep [it]. Another bench, supposed to be in good condition, is on the porch of a friend of ours who lives on the road to New Gretna on the other side (south) of the bridge over the Merrygold. These are the only two I know of in existence. The stove was taken out; Alice let it go for junk. Those cathedral stoves are worth so much money today. There were beautiful spires sticking up on it.

I don't remember anything about lights. They must have had some because, when my mother (Martha Stranger (Downs) Adams, 1874-1955) was a child the Methodists held their meetings here and they must have had some kind of light, probably oil lamps. They held their meetings here until they built the church that used to be over the (Wading River) bridge. It hasn't been too many years since that church was altogether gone. It was opposite the white house that is on the (southeast) corner of the road to Batsto and the Turtle Creek road. (Marjorie remembered the church as standing in the mid-1940's.)

The meeting house burned, I would say, somewhere about 1924. It burned to the ground. A forest fire went right through the cemetery. That was the first one. About 1931 or '32 another one went through.

I don't remember any other markers or tombstones in the Friends' part except just what you see there. None has disappeared since I can remember. There must have been more than that. But in any of the records, you never read that anybody has been buried here. When you read about Martha, they've all been taken to Lower Bank or somewhere else. People are so surprised that Lucy Evans is buried here.

I have no idea how large the Friends congregation was. I imagine they came from as far away as Martha. Of course, there was a lot of houses around here through these woods then. You find old stone piles. They had been there a good many years because my grandmother Adams (Anna Staza Adams, 1849-1930) remembered them only as stone piles. So, they had been long before her and she would be well over a hundred now.

Steve says that this building was known as the Chickeree Chapel during the last half of the nineteenth century, though he doesn't know if services of any kind were actually held here. While reading microfilm copies of the Mount Holly *Herald* from the late 1800's, he came across the following notes under the Wading River section. Unfortunately, he failed to note the dates of publication.

Chickeree Chapel would have but few worshipers of a Sunday were it not for the indefatigable efforts of Prof. Billy Gale, who starts out early in the morning to drive in enough people to form a congregation and in this way the Professor manages to keep them "filled full" of religion.

Daniel E. Cale lost a valuable cow the other day. It appears that Dan had been feeding the animal on corn and neglected to give her any water for about a week, and when he finally did give her some, the corn began to swell and soon choked her to death. Since that occasion he has accepted the office of sexton of Chickeree Chapel.

The only thing that remains of the old Bridgeport Quaker Meeting is a depression in the woods off the Leektown Road. Scattered through the woods, outside the confines of the Adams-Leek-McKeen Cemetery, Lucy Evans of Martha lies buried these hundred and sixty years, along with a few of her fellow Quakers, but the casual passerby would never know that these woods that now shelter them in death, once shaded them in life as they sat in silence with their God.

The French Family

According to Leah Blackman in her book *History of Little Egg Harbor Township*, the French family of Bass River was one of the wealthiest and most influential families in the area. She relates that Francis French, Sr. settled at Bass River at some time prior to the Revolutionary War. He was the owner of a grist mill and sawmill on Willits Creek in Bridgeport/Wading River that later came into the possession of Charles Cramer. This seems misleading. Research by Pete Stemmer of New Gretna indicates that John Leek, Sr. bought one hundred fifty acres of land from *William* French in 1747. This William has to be the father of Francis French, Sr. though there is no indication that he actually lived on his four hundred acres at Wading River. His son, Francis, Sr., may well have moved here at a later date.

No deed is apparent for the Willit's Creek property, but, of course, John Leek, Sr. left part of it in his 1777 will for the cemetery and Presbyterian meeting house. The stones are so worn in the little cemetery beside the Willits Creek (also called the Ives Branch) that we don't know who is buried there today except those of the French family. The earliest graves must have lost their markers long ago. John, Sr.'s will doesn't mention a mill in the vicinity of the plot for the church, but a sawmill *is* mentioned in an 1814 sale from John Leek III to Francis French. Thus it is probable that either Captain John Leek, Jr. or his son, John III, built the sawmill after John Sr.'s death. A grist mill in the location is not mentioned in the sale of John III to Francis French but is noted in a sale from his heirs, Jacob and William French to Isaac Cramer in 1823. Therefore, it is probable that the Leeks built the sawmill and Francis French built the grist mill.

Blackman did not know the name of Francis's first wife but said that she was the mother of Thomas French, Sr. When his first wife died, Francis married Phoebe, the daughter of Jacob Cranmer of Bass River. Thomas French, Sr. married Hannah Johnson, whom Blackman says was from Atlantic County (then Gloucester County), and they had twelve children: William, Francis, Joseph, Thomas, David, John, Rachel, Sarah, Ann, Mary, Abigail, and Eliza.

Referral can be made to Leah Blackman's history for the full genealogy of this family, but it seems that the eldest son, William, was a sea captain and a very wealthy man. He married Lavinia, the daughter of Isaac Cramer, whose farm bordered the Merrygold Creek, just a short way from the French mills. The couple only had one daughter, Hannah, who moved to Philadelphia. When Lavinia died, he married Phoebe Mathis, the daughter of Daniel Mathis, II, and they had eight children.

Thomas French, Sr.'s second son, was named after his grandfather. Francis II, became a wealthy man also. He married Ann Mathis, the daughter of Daniel Mathis II and sister of his brother William's first wife, Lavinia Mathis. Their children were Thomas E., Daniel, Lewis, Burrows, Levi, Francis III, Mary Ann, Phoebe, Leah, Ellen, and Anna.

Both Thomas and his father, Francis, were known and respected in Washington Township and in the Bass River section of Little Egg Harbor, and their names crop up from time to time as executors and witnesses to legal papers. Joseph French, Thomas, Sr.'s third son, always seems to have the title "Esquire" attached to his name. He married Martha Cale, daughter of Josiah Cale. Of their six daughters, two married Adamses, one married Arthur Sooy, and one Caleb Mathis. Thomas, Jr.'s first wife was Harriet Mathis, the granddaughter of John Mathis and daughter of Micajah, but he moved away from the area. Thomas, Sr.'s fifth and sixth sons, David and John, died unmarried. Then come the girls: Rachel married John Loveland. Sarah married Charles Adams. Ann married Sylvanus Seaman. Mary married John Hewlings and "went west." Abigail married Captain George Allen, and Eliza married Lewis Giberson.

The name is rarely mentioned in the Washington Township records, but the name of William and Elizabeth French appears at the birth of their daughter, Anna in December of 1848. William is listed as a clerk at Atsion. That of Mary Jane French, daughter of William and Elizabeth French, appears for her wedding to John Batterson on November 3, 1849. Residence of the couple is given as Martha Furnace, and the Battersons were from Toms River. The April 7, 1858 wedding of Lewis French to Elizabeth Cavileer, daughter of Reuben and Eliza Cavileer, is also recorded, but that of her sister, Mary, to David Cavileer is not. Blackman does *not* list a William French married to an Elizabeth, and the only Mary Jane is William's sister who married Josiah Hackett, of Salem, N.J., not John Batterson. That is a curiosity.

The only time that the name French appears on the Washington Township Committee records is in the 1848 election, held on March 14th of that year at Mrs. Giffords, Quaker Bridge. The name of William B. French is listed with that of Bodine Coffin as the two Freeholders. He is also a member of the township committee, along with Nicholas S. Thompson and Jesse Richards. His name appears again in 1850 as a member of the township committee for that year, then disappears entirely. So who was William B. French? Was he the one married to Elizabeth whose daughter, Mary Jane married John Batterson of Toms River? Lewis French was the son of Francis French II and Ann (Mathis) French and should be of the same generation, but there is no "William" in Leah Blackman's lists.

The little cemetery is all that remains in Bridgeport/Wading River of the illustrious French family. Driving by, one hardly notices it, let alone the sites of the grist mill and sawmill that once bore the names of Leek and French. The farms have all returned to trees, so that the present-day explorer can hardly imagine the early prosperity that the French family once gained from farming, trade, and industry at the beginning of the nineteenth century.

The Cranmer/Cramer Family of Wading River

Cranmer, Cramer, Crammer, however one chooses to spell the name, there are and have been a lot of them around for the past three centuries. Leah Blackman, in the last part of the nineteenth century, repeated the old tale of their descent from Henry VIII's famous archbishop and suggested that all of the family in the Little Egg Harbor region came from three brothers and a cousin who emigrated to this area from Long Island. Local members of the extended family deny any relationships among themselves and proudly vary both the spelling of their name and its pronunciation. You have already read about one branch of the family in Lower Bank. Now we have to deal with one in Wading River. Thank goodness that Murray and Jean Harris just published a Cramer genealogy through the Gloucester County Historical Society. It's as thick as a telephone book, but Jean and Murray claim that each and every local Cramer, Cranmer, or Crammer comes from one particular couple, William and Elizabeth (Carwithy) Cranmer (Murray and Jean spell it that way).

William Cranmer was one of the early settlers of Southold, Long Island, and his wife, Elizabeth, was from there, too. The couple moved to East Jersey around 1665, for in that year, William took an oath of allegiance to the King of England at Elizabethtowne and gave his occupation as carpenter. William and Elizabeth Cranmer had three sons and a daughter: Thomas (b. c. 1662), William (b. c. 1664), John (b. c. 1666), and Elizabeth (no birth date given).

The Bridgeport/Wading River Cramers (or Cranmers) go all the way back to this couple's third son, John. John married Sarah Osborne before 1694. Sarah was born about 1663 at Easthampton, Long Island. Apparently, a whole group of Quakers from Long Island moved to the Elizabethtowne area during the last part of the seventeenth century, for her father wrote his will there in 1694. John and Sarah themselves are mentioned in the minutes of the Rahway and Plainfield Monthly Meeting minutes and also in those of the Woodbridge Monthly Meeting.

Murray and Jean Harris note that John bought land at "Barnagate" on May 9th, 1702. He must have intended it as an investment, for he later settled in Essex County at Whippany, not in the Barnegat area, and his will was probated there on June 22nd, 1716. He and Sarah had had four sons and possibly a daughter before his death at the age of fifty. The Harrises note that two of his sons, Thomas and John, were left four pounds each. Sarah, his widow, was left the remainder of the estate to bring up his children. This is curious, since they list the couples' children in order as 1) John, 2) Thomas, 3) Jeremiah, 4) Stephen, and possibly 5) Grace, meaning that Stephen was the youngest son.

John seems to have remained in the Elizabethtown area. Murray and Jean don't say where Thomas lived, but he married a Willetts who was related to the Pharos, and both of those families were in the Little Egg Harbor area.

Jeremiah and Stephen certainly relocated to the Little Egg Harbor area. Jeremiah is recorded as having married Abiah Tuttle in Barnegat on September 19, 1738 and was one of the signers of the petition of 1749 to create Stafford Township. Stephen married Sarah Andrews, the daughter of Edward and Sarah (Ong) Andrews of Little Egg Harbor. After his wife's death about 1748, he married Sarah Little on October 31, 1749. The following year, his loving neighbors, John Ridgway and Jacob Henry, testified against Stephen Cranmer before the Little Egg Harbor Monthly Meeting, which condemned him for "marrying out of unity." He apologized in 1750 and all was forgiven.

Between his two wives, Stephen had a total of sixteen children, eight by each. The Wading River Cranmers are descendants of their child, Caleb.

About 1755, Caleb married Sara Andrews and they had one son: Isaac, born on September 1, 1756. He married Dorcas Adams about 1783. Dorcas (b. November 23, 1766) was the daughter of Hezekiah Adams.

Isaac Cranmer lived on a "plantation" on the Bass River side of Bridgeport/Wading River, on the south side of the Merrygold. It is now the home of the George McCartens. Since Isaac's son, Charles, seems to have owned all his property north of the Merrygold, it may have been that much of his father Isaac's land was on that side as well. We do know that Isaac bought the Leek/French mills on Willett's Creek from Francis French's heirs, his sons Jacob & William & wife Phebe, in 1823, and these were later the property of his son, Charles.

After the death of Sarah (Andrews), Caleb Cramer married Mary Baker as his second wife on the 29th of July, 1760, and they had five sons and two daughters: Caleb, Jr., Chalkley, Stephen, Eli, Martha, Mary, and John.

Chalkley (b. September 12, 1773, d. March 9, 1810 at Martha) married Achsah Leek, daughter of Captain John and Martha (Rose) Leek (b. January 29, 1773, d. July 8, 1858). Her aunt, Phoebe, the widow of Job Mathis Sr. and the sister of Captain John Leek, Jr., became the third wife of Chalkley's father, marrying the prolific Caleb on August 16th, 1792. Martha (b. June 29, 1762, d. April 12, 1842) married John Mathis, son of Micajah and Mercy (Shreve) Mathis, (b. December 23, 1753, d. October 20, 1824) on August 16, 1781. They are buried at Chestnut Neck where they made their home.

Eli (b. between 1770 and 1780, d. before 4 March 1848, when his will was probated in Burlington County) married Hannah Gifford, daughter of Jonathan and Catharine Gifford, about 1800.

Stephen married Nancy Robbins. No further data is available on this couple.

Mary married David Cavileer, Sr. in September 19, 1782. David was the son of John, who is buried next to Yoos Sooy in Lower Bank and was the son of the first Peter.

John Cranmer married a girl named Mary and lived within the limits of Philadelphia county. Sarah Cramer, married a Taylor, but his first name is not known.

Isaac Cramer is the one we are concerned with at the moment. He served in the Revolutionary War prior to marrying Dorcas Adams. Isaac died on November 17, 1839, and Dorcas followed him to the Isaac Cramer Cemetery in New Gretna nine years later on August 6, 1848.

Isaac and Dorcas had nine children: George A., Charles, Bethiah, Uriah, Mary, Isaac, Lavinia, Hope, and Lucy Ann. George A. married Lucy Cale; Charles married Mary Gaskill; Bethiah married Archibald Sooy; Uriah married Maria Franklin; Mary married Isaiah Robbins; thirty-five year old Isaac died unmarried and was buried in the Isaac Cramer family cemetery; Lavinia married William French; nothing is known about Hope; Lucy Ann married Edward Johnson.

Charles is the one we can pinpoint most closely with a particular piece of property, for, by the time of his death on September 29th, 1872, he had accumulated a sizable amount of land between the Merrygold Creek and Willitts' Creek (Mill Creek, Ives Branch), including the former Leek sawmill and French grist mill which he inherited from his father. On April 6, 1809, he married Mary Gaskill, the daughter of Ebenezer and Martha Gaskill of West Creek, and the couple had twelve children, eight boys and four girls. It seems that Charles acquired the Leek/French mills himself, though it was "all in the family" anyway. His sister, Lavinia was married to William French. Both Charles and his wife, Mary, are buried in Hillside Cemetery, New Gretna.

Some time back, I asked Murray Harris how the Cramers of Wading River were related to the Cramers of Lower Bank. He was basking in the sun in Arizona while I was freezing in New Jersey at the time, and I could just see his broad grin over the phone when he told me I was just going to have to wait until his book was published. It was just too complicated to explain. Actually, it isn't all that bad. The Cranmers (or Cramers) of Wading River, as I have shown above, were descended from William and Elizabeth (Carwithy) Cranmer of Elizabethtown through their third son, John. The Cramers of Lower Bank are also descendants of William and Elizabeth Cranmer of Elizabethtown, but through their second son, William. Isn't that simple? Just don't try to figure out how any of the present-day Cramers or Cranmers are related. It's just too far removed!

Oh yes, two more things before we leave this family. Murray and Jean standardize the spelling of the name to "Cramer." That is, all local Cramers, Cranmers, Crammers, with either long "a" or short "a" are nevertheless descendants of the same William and Elizabeth (Carwithy) Cranmer of Elizabethtown. The differences in spelling don't mean anything.

Courtesy of John Milton Adams, Jr.

Unfortunately for romantics, they also have to say that there is just no evidence that the family is descended from Henry VIII's unfortunate Archbishop of Cantebury. That doesn't mean they aren't. It just means that no evidence exists to verify the connection.

The Isaac Cramer House
Autumn 1958

This house sits to the east of the Merrygold and is currently the home of George and Nancy McCarten

This house stood on the southeastern side of the Ives Branch (Willett's Creek). It belonged to
Steven Silkotch before it was torn down and was the last recorded place visited by the Jersey Devil.
It is believed to have been the home of Charles Cramer, son of Isaac Cramer.
The photograph above, and those on the next page, were taken in the late 1950's by Budd Wilson, Sr.

View of the
Cramer/Silkotch House
from Route 542
1958

End View of the Original Section of the Cramer/Silkotch House

The Cramer/Silkotch Barn

617

The Wading River Hotel

The Works Progress Administration survey of the Wading River Tavern indicates that the first warrent for the West Jersey Council of Proprietors on the western side of the river was made to a James Wetherill for 1,664 acres of land on May 23, 1722. Parcels of this property were transferred to a John Darnell, beginning in 1741. One of the earliest surveys on record was a resurvey made for the estate of John Darnell on May 30, 1760. The Darnells were an important early family which seems to have gradually disappeared from the area during the nineteenth century, and there is little information about them. Lewis Darnell's land is shown on an 1836 map of McCartyville as two parcels of fifty-one and 69 3/4 acres lying on the north side of the the 1808 road (Rt. 542) along Ridge Road. Edmund Darnell and Benjamin H. Lippincott had a resurvey made on 501 acres adjoining the Lewis Darnell land in 1817. The date of 1761 shows on the land of Lewis Darnell. None of this acreage seems to have included the land on which the Wading River Hotel stands.

Names and places from the eighteenth century seem obscure to the residents of today. Place names have long been forgotten: Stories Road, Marks Road, Nickers Swamp. Even the

name of the original builder of the Wading River Hotel is no longer known.

The style of its architecture indicates a construction date during the second half of the eighteenth century. A note from Mildred Honeker in the collection of Dorothea Somes suggests it was originally constructed by a man named Miller and may, at some time, have been called "Townsend's Inn."

This house was built in the finest style that was practical for a rural area at the time. The interior woodwork was beautiful as the Works Progress Administration photographs on these pages indicate.

William Leek, the brother of John Leek III and son of Capt. John, Jr. and Martha (Rose) was born on March 18, 1772. On November 27, 1790, he married Catherine Loveland, the daughter of Charles (Sr.) and Mary (Gleason) Loveland. Their first son they named after William's brother, and the sitting first President of the United States, George Washington. George Washington Leek II was born on the 5th of September, 1793.

George married Hannah B. Mathis and, according to Mrs. Honeker, worked at Harrisville, which was then called McCartyville. She suggests

Anna Bush Maxwell Leek
with George W. Adams, her grandson.

that George and Hannah Leek purchased this house when they "came down" from Harrisville. McCartyville was not started until 1834, but there is no indication where G.W. lived during this period. In any case, this house did come into the possession of the Leeks in the first part of the nineteenth century.

George and Hannah's son, Maja Leek, the second of five children, was born on February 18, 1818. Maja married Sarah Louisa Cavileer who was not even a month older than he was, she having been born on the 13th of March in the same year. Sarah Louisa was the daughter of Peter and Eleanor (Sooy) Cavileer of Lower Bank.

Maja Leek bought the upper Leek Wharf property on the Washington Township side of the Wading River and Leek property at Cranberry Point on the Bass River side from his father and his aunt Elizabeth, children and heirs of his grandfather William Leek, for $100 on the 12th of May, 1852 (*Burlington County Records*, Vol. H-5, Page 300). They seemed to have gotten the property from their father's estate on the 15th of July, 1833, but this is ten years after father William's death in 1823.

Hannah Mathis Leek died on the 1st of September, 1851. The couple had raised six children: Charles Loveland, Maja, Catherine, William Hammond, George T., and Mary W. George died at the age of twenty, three years before his mother.

After a respectable wait of four years, George Washington Leek II married Charlotte (Loveland) Cramer. Charlotte passed away on February 11, 1869, and this time, G. W. remained a widower until his death on June 7, 1880 at the age of eighty-seven.

This photograph was taken by the Works Progress Administration and shows both the fine woodwork of the fireplace surround and the deteriorated condition of the interior at that time.

619

Maja and Sarah Louisa had five children: Charles W., who fought in the Civil War and died at home in 1862 at the age of twenty from a fever he had contracted during his service; Josephine (b. March 25, 1846), who died eleven days before her ninth birthday; Maja Towers (b. January 28, 1850), who married Anna Bush Maxwell; George Washington III, who married Annabelle Crowley, the sister of James Morrell Crowley of Green Bank, and Sarah Josephine, who died at the age of eleven on March 11, 1870.

Maja Towers Leek and George Washington Leek were housing contractors, as was their uncle, mother Sarah's brother, Charles Cavileer. Sarah's husband, Maja, was a sea captain but also acted as a partner with his sons and brother-in-law in the construction business.

Anna and Maja Towers Leek had only three children who survived them: Sarah Virginia, who married Walter Edgar; Anna Augusta, who married George Adams; and Ila Mae, who married James Ellsworth Leek. Their other children all died young: Maja A., died when he was seven years old; Charles W., died at the age of five months; Maja Towers, Jr., died at six months of age; and Matilda M., died at the age of eight.

On the sixth of January, 1890, Sarah Leek signed her name to a deed of sale selling, for fifty dollars, a 60' by 70' lot to the trustees of the newly-organized Methodist Episcopal congregation that had been formed in Wading River. This piece of property bordered the Batsto Road a few hundred feet towards the northeast from her home.

Old Sarah was smart. She stipulated in the deed that the church had to be started by the trustees within three years of the contract date, or the property would revert to her. In addition, she also stipulated that, should the church be destroyed by fire, the trustees would have to rebuild it within five years or would lose the property to its original owner.

Courtesy of Mildred Honaker

Ann Wooler (standing)
Anna Bush Maxwell Leek,
wife of Maja Towers Leek (seated)
with her great granddaughter,
Twila Rae Honaker

Courtesy of Mildred Honaker

Ila Mae Leek
Daughter of Maja Towers Leek
and Anna Bush Maxwell Leek
and mother of Mildred Honaker

When Sarah died on October 8, 1899, she, like her daughter-in-law, had experienced the ultimate grief. Of her five children, only George Washington Leek III survived her. Her son, Maja Towers, had died at the age of forty-four on August 1, 1894, almost six years before. It is interesting to note that Sarah Leek transferred the Wading River Tavern property to her daughter-in-law on November 20, 1893, a year before the death of her son, Maja Towers (*Burl. Co. Records*: Bk. 313, Folio 8). Anna Bush Maxwell Leek continued to live in the old tavern another thirty-four years. She finally sold it to John Quigley for $1,200 on the sixth of December, 1927 (*Burl. Co. Records*: Vol. 704, Page 263).

The Quigley family has lived on the property ever since. John Quigley, Jr. currently occupies the old house, while his mother lives in a newer house built on the property. The old tavern was almost lost to an electrical fire on the twenty-ninth of December in 1986, but fortunately the Lower Bank Fire Company prevented disaster.

Ccourtesy of Budd Wilson

Curtis, Roy, and Ralph Leek
Photo by Mrs. John (Wobbar) Maxwell - Sept. 1905

Courtesy of Mildred Honaker

Irene Mildred (Leek) Honaker
daughter of Ila Mae Leek and James Ellsworth Leek and
granddaughter of Maja Towers Leek and
Anna Bush Maxwell Leek;

Ellis Honaker
Mildred's husband

Augusta (Leek) Adams,
daughter of Maja Towers and Anna Bush Maxwell Leek,
sister of Ila Mae,
and Mildred's aunt

Note: Mildred's brother, Warren Montgomery Leek, married
Lillian Sadenvasser and later, Emma Nash

The boys are standing on the main road, which is now Route 542. The house to the right in the picture is the rear of the John (Wobbar) Maxwell house which stood at the intersection of Turtle Creek Road and Route 542. The bridge is out of sight up the road. The Wading River Tavern, home of Maja Towers and Anna Bush Maxwell Leek cannot be seen for the trees but would be in the distance on the left side of the road.

The first on the left is Curtis Maxwell, son of John (Wobbar) Maxwell, whose mother took the photograph. He lived with his family in the house shown in the picture.

The other two boys are the sons of George Washington Leek III and Annabelle (Crowley) Leek.

Ralph was born on December 20, 1896. He married Ida Harris Knight in 1921, and they had no children. On December 6, 1928, he married Annie Ethel (Bosarge) Cambre. He and Annie had two children: Ralph Herbert, Jr. and Annabelle. Roy (Leroy) was born on August 13, 1900.

Fireplace Detail

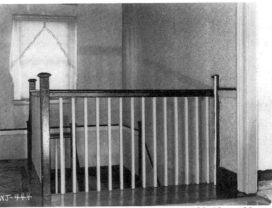

Stairwell and Railing

An Old Shed Near the Wading River Hotel

The Wading River Tavern in 1998

Uncle "Gus" Maxwell's First Store

Courtesy of Horace Somes, Jr.

William Augustus Maxwell, son of William (Billy) and Rachel (Herrington) Maxwell, was raised on his father's farm at the last bend on Turtle Creek Road before the road enters the swamps. His family was large: he had three brothers and six sisters! He was born in 1846 and died in 1936 at the age of ninety. William Augustus, called "Gus," built himself a house near his father's farm and also set up a store in this little building next to the Wading River Tavern on property owned by Anna Bush Maxwell Leek, the widow of Maja Towers Leek. How many years he used this building for a store is not known, but he purchased the large building across the street from Sam Ireland sometime after 1907.

We know from the postal records that W. A. Maxwell was postmaster of the Wading River Post Office at least from 1914 to its demise on March 31, 1923. It is not known if the actual post office was ever in this building or whether Gus Maxwell had purchased the Sooy/Ireland store across the street when he became postmaster. Apparently, he was living in his home on Turtle Creek Road when he ran a store from this building.

A notation in the collection of Dorothy Somes suggests that William Augustus Maxwell was a sea captain, and he may indeed have been so in his early years. It was quite common for a captain to retire to the land in his late thirties or early forties, having made sufficient money in his younger years to support himself in a less strenuous and hazardous occupation. By 1910, Gus would have been sixty-four years old, a respected sea captain, postmaster, and storekeeper.

Photograph by John Pearce

Gus Maxwell's First Store - 1995

623

The Sooy/Ireland/Maxwell Store
1714 Route 542

Photograph by Dudley Lewis

This photograph was taken in February 2000

According to notes in the Somes's collection from Ralph H. Leek, the son of George Washington III and Annabelle (Crowley) Leek, this building was originally constructed by William H. Sooy (b. 1798, d. 1861), the son of Nicholas Sooy I of Green Bank. This means that the house had to have been built after William H. Sooy's majority in 1819.

William's son, Edwin Clark Sooy (b. 1833, d. 1873) married Jane Ann Leek (b. 1833, d. 1911), the daughter of Captain William Loveland Leek and Mary (Cavileer) Leek. Captain William was the son of William and Catherine (Loveland) Leek. Edwin and Jane operated a store (the notes add, "and post office") there from about 1880 to 1906. Edwin's son Edwin, Jr.(b. 1833, d. 1903) and his wife, Anne (Turner) Sooy continued his parents' business. When Edwin, Jr. died in 1903, Anne (Turner) Sooy tried to continue the operation of the store but finally sold the building to a Sam Ireland about 1907.

Sam Ireland was an entrepreneur who had purchased quite a bit of timberland in the area of Wading River and did not intend to run the store himself. He hired "Ed" Leek as the store manager. Mildred Honaker remembered Ed running the store and may have mistakenly thought he owned it, too. Sam Ireland finally sold the building and the business to William Augustus "Gus" Maxwell, who had been operating a store in the little building across the street, next to the Wading River Tavern. By the way, "Gus" Maxwell's second wife, Etta (Sooy) Maxwell, was the great granddaughter of the original builder of this building, William Sooy.

It seems that Robert McKeen may have owned the building after Gus Maxwell and the Groff family lived there for a while, too. Eugene Groff, Sr. built a house on one section of the original property. The Mazza family has made the old store their home for many years.

When was the post office moved across the river? We don't know. We do know that Catherine McKeen was post mistress at its inception on February 8, 1858 and was still postmistress in 1884. Her death in 1890 may have been the time when it was moved to the Sooy store. By 1914, it was being operated by W. A. Maxwell, who signed the post office documents in that year identifying the location of the Wading River Post Office and himself as postmaster. This means that there is a window of twenty-one years during which the Wading River Post Office was probably moved across the river and operated by Edwin Sooy, Jr. Alice Adams Weber, in her article "Jack and Jill by the River," included in this chapter, says she remembers going to Ed Sooy's store for the mail around 1901. It is very unlikely that Edwin, Sr. and his wife, Jane, had the post office in their store while Ed, Sr. was still alive.

Courtesy of Horace Somes, Jr.

The actual date of this photograph is not known,
but it was probably taken in the 1960's.

Mildred Honaker, in a note written in March of 1980, remembered that there was once a "town hall" in Wading River. It stood next to this house and apparently was used for social gatherings into the twentieth century. As far as the Washington Township records are concerned, no township meetings were ever held in Wading River. However, Wading River was a part of Randolph Township from its inception in 1870 until it was reincorporated into Washington Township in 1893, and it is possible that this building was used for some of the meetings during this twenty-three year period.

Mildred remembered that band concerts were held there nearly every Saturday evening. There was good entertainment and even square dances held in the building. In the early part of the twentieth century, it was quite an attractive place. Unfortunately, the band members gradually moved away [or died], and outsiders were rowdy, so it was closed. After being left vacant for a while, the town hall was turned into a carriage house, then became part of a barn next to the road and was finally torn down.

This house, too, was almost lost to an electrical fire on October 20, 1974, but the Lower Bank Volunteer Fire Company managed to save it.

William (Billy) Maxwell
1816-1908

James Maxwell, Sr. was born in Ireland in 1777 and migrated to Wading River at some time prior to 1800. He married Berthia (or Bethia) Gale, the daughter of James and Sarah (Cramer) Gale in 1804. While Berthia (or Bethia) died in 1865, no date is known for James's death, but he died in Wading River. James and Berthia had six sons: James Jr., John J., William, Robert, Samuel, and George.

James, Jr. (1810-1887) married Sarah Leeds, the daughter of Robert Leeds. They had nine children: Roxanna, James Albert, Mary Elnora, John Robert, William F., John W., Rebecca, Frank, and Edwin.

John Maxwell, Sr. (1812-1890) married Leah E. Downs, daughter of James and Sarah (Mathis) Downs of Wading River. They had ten children: George Socrates, Samuel A., John F., James, Helen Berthia (or Bethia), Leah Ann, Sarah Jane, Mary Frances, Marthia Olive, and Phoebe Arabella. Their daughter, Helen Berthia (or Bethia), married James McAnney.

William (Billy) Maxwell married a New York girl, Rachel A. Herrington, and the couple had their homestead far out towards the marshes on the west side at the third bend of Turtle Creek Road. As is evident from the Taylor Will, James Maxwell had property adjoining the Taylor estate in this area. William may have built a new home on the property or succeeded to the home of his parents. It is not certain which is the case.

Rachel and Billy Maxwell had ten children over the years, four boys and six girls. The boys were William Augustus, George S., Joseph B. and James Foster. The girls were Sarah Berthia, Anna M., Mary Malinda, Sarah Josephine, Sophia Elizabeth, and Rachel Matilda. Sarah married Maja Leek, Jr. Billy was a farmer, and he and Rachel and the children spent most of the nineteenth century in Bridgeport working the land and serving the community.

William and Rachel Maxwell raised John H. Wobbar (son of Otto and Hannah) when he was given away at the graveside on the death of his mother. Though John took the name of Maxwell, he was never formally adopted by them. He married Martha Southard of Batsto and lived in the house which stood, until recently, on the southwest corner of Turtle Creek Road and Route 542.

Memories say that Billy Maxwell's house burned down when firewood was stored too close to a woodstove, but the date of the destruction is unknown.

A cute note which has come down through time about Billy Maxwell: One time, Rachel got sick from eating pancakes that William had made with Bobbit's Washing Powder which he thought was Bobbit's flour! Sure must have cleaned her out inside.

Isn't it funny what people remember. Almost ninety years has passed since Billy died, and the only personal thing anyone remembers about him was this bit of humor. Billy's farm lies overgrown and vacant, much of it taken over by marshland and swamp. Not a single building remains. An abandoned well, a shagbark hickory, and a nauseating experience are all that are left of Billy Maxwell and his wife, Rachel.

To the southwest of the old homestead site of the Maxwell family is Poplar Hill. The hill is a slight rise between marshes and two ponds, but there is no evidence of poplar trees there today.

In the swamps along the road below where the house stood are evidences of ditches which used to surround old fields, now overgrown. Orville McAnney remembered these as corn fields where now maple and gum trees grow.

Courtesy of Horace Somes, Jr.

The remains of the well on the homestead of
William (Billy) Maxwell
Photograph - 1977

The William Augustus Maxwell Family

Courtesy of Horace Somes, Jr.

William A. Maxwell House
Turtle Creek Road

William A. Maxwell was one of the sons of William (Billy) Maxwell and the brother of George S. Maxwell. He was born in 1846 and died in 1936. William A., like his brother, became a sea captain. After he retired, he set up a little store on a piece of property on the main road which he purchased from Anna Bush Maxwell Leek. Later, he bought the Sooy/Ireland store on the other side of the road and served as postmaster at least from 1914 until the post office closed in 1923.

The house is currently the last house on Turtle Creek Road but originally was the second house on the west side of the road, his father William's being the first. He married Angie Adelia Jones and had five sons and three daughters: William Haines (married Martha Regensberger), James H. (married Mary Bozarth), Harold (married Hannah Cavileer), Jarvis (married Estella Adams), Otis (died young), Leda S., Rachel (died young), and Rose. Angie (Jones) Maxwell died in 1899 at the age of 38 (probably worn out by child-bearing!).

After his wife died, he married Etta Sooy (1876 - 1918), by whom he had another four sons and five daughters: Earl (b. 1906), Preston (1907), Rose (1908) [She only lived eighteen days], Amy (1909), Burris (1911), Eugene (1913), Irene (1914-1915), Elinora (no date given) and Otise (1891 or 1892).

William and Angie's first son, William Haines Maxwell moved to Egg Harbor City where he became active in politics. He served as mayor of that town and was active in the Hiram Dewey Lodge 226, Free and Accepted Masons, for over fifty-three years. He lived at 146 Liverpool Avenue.

The Maxwell house has had a series of owners after the Maxwells: Smith, Hines, Grundmier, Orville McAnney, the Atlantic City Police Club, Menge and Ruth Horn. The George Menge family built a new home on the property adjoining this one.

On November 27, 1978, a fire somehow got out from a woodstove in the living room and threatened to burn this house down like so many others in Wading River, but the Lower Bank Fire Company saved it. The current occupants are Buddy and Cookie Fisher.

The William A. "Gus" Maxwell House - 1995

The Sooy Family of Wading River

William H. Sooy (b. Jan. 15, 1798, d. May 7, 1861), a lawyer and *son* of Nicholas I and Sarah (Sears) Sooy and *brother* of Nicholas II, built his homestead near his father's tavern at Washington. (Nicholas II also had a son named William H. Sooy who lived in Green Bank.) William H. married Rebecca Weeks of Weekstown. (b. May 1, 1796, d. April 16, 1860). He and Rebecca had five sons and four daughters: Benjamin, Samuel, William Henry, Jr., Edwin Clark, Arthur, Elizabeth, Maria, Frances Ann, and Sophia.

Son Benjamin was born on the 17th of September, 1819. He married Eunice Bevis Kimble (b. Jan. 6, 1824, d. March 30, 1902), the daughter of Samuel and Hannah Kimble of Pleasant Mills. Sam Kimble was a sea captain. Benjamin and Eunice raised eight sons and three daughters. William Henry Sooy, Jr. would marry Lydia Ursula Collins and be Green Bank's blacksmith for many years. Son Edwin Clark Sooy would run the store across from the Wading River Hotel.

William H. and Rebecca (Weeks) Sooy bought land in Wading River, and it is believed that this became the Sooy farm on old Swan Bay Road off Turtle Creek Road, a farm that boasted a landing on the Turtle Creek, just below the forks. It is also thought that Benjamin and his wife lived there.

Like so many families, tragedy was to visit this farm on the Turtle Creek. Benjamin and Eunice Sooy suffered the loss of two fine sons in the Civil War: Stephen Bodine Sooy (b. July 23, 1843) and Samuel Kimble Sooy (b. June 15, 1845). Stephen died in either 1864 or 1865 at about the age of twenty-one. All that is known about his brother, Sam, is that he died in the war, somewhere between the ages of sixteen and twenty-one.

Benjamin and Eunice's third son, William H., III was born on the 27th of June in 1847 in Wading River, married Sarah Mesereau (b. October 7, 1852, d. April 15, 1883), and continued to live in Wading River, probably on the family farm.

Benjamin and Eunice's first daughter was born on the 29th of March in the year of 1849. They must have been overjoyed at being blessed by a daughter after having three sons in a row. They named the baby girl Hannah Emily. She married Joseph Crowley, who died in 1875. She later married George Burroughs of Delaware. After his death in 1890, she married William Whitcraft, also of Delaware. She died at Newport News, Virginia on March 17, 1896 and was buried there.

Two years after the birth of Hannah, Benjamin and Eunice welcomed Benjamin Franklin Sooy into the world. Born on the 12th of May, 1851, Benjamin F. became a coastal sailor and married Frances Wright. He died on the Fourth of July, 1890 and lies buried somewhere between Elwood and Batsto.

Daughter Sophia was born on April 22nd, 1853 and died at the age of twenty-one.

Brainard Clark Sooy was born on the Sooy farm on October 16, 1855. On the Fourth of July, 1877, he left New Jersey for the state of Iowa where he married Caroline Kinber a year later, and the couple had six children. In 1892, he and his family moved from Iowa to Mapleton, Nebraska where he died on October 14, 1893.

Daniel W., the next son, was born on November 6th, 1857 and became the captain of a schooner. He married Catherine (Carrie) Sooy, who was his third cousin once removed, and the couple had three girls: Waverly, Sabrina, and Nellie. He was shipwrecked in 1887 or 1888 and died the following year.

Thomas Kimble Sooy was born on September 16th, 1859. He married Martha Crowley, and they had five children: Katheryn, Hattie, Watson, Lewis, and Gertrude. They lost Hattie, Gertrude, and Watson in infancy and Katheryn at twenty-nine. Thomas and Martha lived in Green Bank at 1032 River Road. Thomas was very active in politics, serving on the Board of Chosen Freeholders for Burlington County for several terms and also was a member of the Washington Township committee. He ran a general store in Green Bank and was postmaster there for many years. When Martha died, he moved to Egg Harbor City, where he died on the twenty-first of October, 1937, at the age of seventy-eight after a life full of community service and honored by the citizens of both Washington Township and Egg Harbor City. His funeral was at the Green Bank church and he is buried in the adjoining graveyard.

Howard Sooy was born to Benjamin and Eunice on August 14, 1861, but they lost the child at an early age.

Their eleventh child was a daughter, Rebecca Josephine, who was born on the sixth of June, 1865. The tantalizing records of the Sooy Genealogy note that she married William H. Whitcraft of Wilmington, Delaware, but this poses a complication. According to that same genealogy, her sister Hannah's third husband is purported to have been William Whitcraft of Wilmington, Delaware. Of course, she was sixteen years younger than her oldest sister, and would only have been thirty-one in 1896 when her sister died. Maybe she did marry her sister's third husband. Who knows. Stranger things than that have happened.

Benjamin Sooy died on the sixteenth of September, 1872 at the age of fifty-one. Eunice lived another thirty years. When was their old farm abandoned? As has been mentioned above, William H., III probably continued to live on the Wading River land after the death of his father. He was only twenty-five when his father died, and he did live in the township. If William H. III and his family continued to live with his widowed mother until her death in 1902, the farm may have been occupied at least until his own passing on the 10th of May, 1920. He and his wife, Sarah (Mesereau), had five children: Samuel Horace, Retta, William Leander, Amanda Edna, and John E. Carey.

The Lippincott Family

According to Leah Blackman, the story of the Lippincott family of Bass River begins with Joseph Lippincott, Sr. who came from England and bought a farm in Freehold, Monmouth County. His son, Joseph, Jr., eventually settled in Egg Harbor and practiced his trade as a weaver as well as working his farm. The "Egg Harbor" mentioned is presumably in Gloucester (now Atlantic) County, but not necessarily so. The area incorporated in 1798 as Little Egg Harbor Township was known simply as Egg Harbor from 1740 until 1798. Many of the early references to "Egg Harbor" may well mean "Little" Egg Harbor as we now know it.

In 1744, he married Esther Andrews of Little Egg Harbor. Esther was the daughter of Samuel Andrews and the granddaughter of Edward Andrews of Little Egg Harbor Meeting, now Tuckerton, who owned the farm and mill on the northeast side of Lake Pohatcong. Joseph, Jr. and Esther (Andrews) Lippincott had two sons and a daughter: Samuel, Peter, and Elizabeth. Samuel married a girl from Barnegat, Deborah Arnold, and they also had three children: Samuel, Joseph, and Elizabeth.

Their son, Samuel, married a girl by the name of Hannah Snow, also of the Little Egg Harbor area. The family was of the "Friendly Persuasion" and the remains of Joseph, Jr., his wife, Esther, Samuel, and his wife, Hannah, lie in the Friends cemetery at Tuckerton.

Gideon Lippincott (b. Aug. 9, 1817 d. March 10, 1890), son of Samuel and Hannah (Snow) Lippincott, grandson of Samuel and Deborah (Arnold) Lippincott, and great grandson of Joseph and Esther (Andrews) Lippincott, married Sarah Wetherby (frequently spelled "Weatherby") of Wading River (b. February 1, 1832 d. March 2, 1874). Sarah J. Wetherby was the dauther of William and Phoebe Wetherby. A note in the Mount Holly newspaper for March 10, 1881 says that a tornado destroyed G.R. Lippincott's house, barn, and outbuildings the previous Friday. Gideon's property is described as being between Lower Bank and Maxwell's Point which is just about the spot where an 1849 map shows the house of William Weatherby. Perhaps Gideon and his wife took over the property of her parents when they passed away.

Gideon and Sarah (Wetherby) Lippincott had five sons and only one daughter: Samuel S. (b. January 20, 1857), Amanda E. (b. May 24, 1860), George W. (b. September 5, 1862), Watson "Wad" Atwood (b. August 18, 1865), John W. (b. November 15, 1867), and Charles H. (b. July 23, 1870). A sixth son, William C. Wetherby (b. March 1, 1852), may have been born to Sarah prior to her marriage to Gideon.

Their first son, Samuel, became well-known for his abilities as a carver of decoys. He married Leah Maxwell and is buried in Hillside Cemetery in New Gretna. Samuel and Leah (Maxwell) Lippincott's son, Robert, was also a decoy carver of some renown. He married Jeanette Watson and continued to live in Wading River until his death in 1970.

Their third son, Watson, was the "Wad" Lippincott who built Mullica River Skiffs beside the Wading River bridge late in life and was interviews by Henry Charlton Beck for a newspaper article.

This information was supplied by Alice (Downs) DeCamp, the great granddaughter of Gideon Lippincott and agrees with one exception with that given by Leah Blackman in her *History of Little Egg Harbor*. Mrs. Blackman adds a generation, which I have shown above, to Alice (Downs) DeCamp's material, namely, that of the first Samuel, who was married to Deborah (Arnold). Mrs. DeCamp's material omits this generation.

The Benjamin Maxwell Family

Courtesy Fay Bartling 1982

Benjamin Maxwell House
(No longer in existence)

This house used to stand on the west side of Turtle Creek Road on the property now (1995) owned by Super Kwick Inc., a trash-hauling firm.

It originally belonged to a Benjamin Maxwell and was the homestead farm of his family. This Benjamin Maxwell may have been the one who was the son of John F. and Elizabeth L. (Adams) Maxwell, grandson of John J. and Leah Eleanor Angeline (Downs) Maxwell, and great-grandson of James and Berthia (Gale) Maxwell.

This Benjamin Maxwell was born in 1879 and married Louella Gibbs (b. 1885, d. 1925). They had four children: Elizabeth, Thomas, Alma, and Isaac. (There is also a possibility the couple had another son, Marvin.) The house appears to be of an older archetectural style than the late 1800s, however, and it may have been the home of Benjamin's parents and grandparents. After Benjamin Maxwell, Walker, Clark, Bartling and Otto Schmetcke owned the property. David Bartling built a new house for himself south of the old one, in which the Bartlings still reside.

"Sonny" Schmetcke ran a trash-hauling business and had various other interests as well. For a while, he ran a donkey baseball team which even included a zebra! The house was later occupied as an office by Super Kwick Inc. and burned in a fire in 1991 or 1992.

This view is of the rear wing of the house. The porch which is clearly visible in the lower photograph is to the right in this one.

Both photographs courtesy Fay Bartling 1982

The George S. Maxwell Family

Home of George S. Maxwell
(No longer in existence)

George S. Maxwell was the son of William "Billy" Maxwell. He was born in 1848 and became a sea captain. He married Rebecca A. Adams, the daughter of Benjamin and Sarah Adams and built this house on Turtle Creek Road which was the first house on the right from Billy's Landing. Rebecca was born in 1855 and died in 1931.

Rebecca and George had eleven sons and three daughters: William Augustus II, George Benjamin, Lemuel Hopkins, Morris Haines, Joseph Holock, Charles Albert, Maja Leek, Philip S., Rudolph Conn, Matthew Henry, Lewis Israel, Mary Jane, Rachel Anna, and Ruth Elizabeth. Rebecca is pictured in the photograph taken on a boat at the fish factory on Crab Island at the end of this section on Wading River.

William Augustus Maxwell II married Lida Loveland, daughter of Ruben and Mary Loveland and had one son, Norris. William A. II followed in his father's footsteps, becoming a sea captain but was lost at sea near Cape Lookout, North Carolina, in 1905 when he was thirty years and seven months old.

George served as Freeholder, Township Clerk, and Registrar of Deeds of Washington Township at various times during the last part of the nineteenth century.

The house went through a series of owners after the deaths of George and Rebecca including: Brytezak, Plicta, Fessler, Budd, and Glasser. At some unknown time, it fades from history. Notes in the Dorothea McAnney Somes collection indicate that it burned during the occupancy of the Glassers, but others say that the Glassers remodelled an existing bungalow which had been occupied before them by the Fesslers.

George S. Maxwell

Fred Fessler trapped the marshes and hunted the meadows of Turtle Creek. He kept his gunning boat moored at Billy's Landing where the road now ends.

In November, 1950 a northeaster hit the area on a full-moon, which meant that the tides were at their highest point. The men of Turtle Creek went down to the landing to secure their boats and returned up the road to their homes with the tidal water following them.

Fred Fessler became separated from the others in the dark, and it was feared that he was lost. The following morning, however, he turned up on the porch of Howard McAnney's house safe and well, although looking a bit worse for the wear.

Everyone who lived near the marshes knew that, when the tidal level came up as high as it had during the storm the previous night, the "trash" reeds and grass floated off the

George S. Maxwell and one of his sons

marsh in large mats. Fred Fessler's boat had gotten caught in it which made it impossible for him to row against the wind through the thick mat of "trash" reeds in the water.

Fred told Howard McAnney he had floated downriver all the way to the Mullica and then on down to the old Iron Bridge (the pre-Parkway bridge of Route 9 across the Mullica). He was then blown back upriver, into the mouth of the Wading River, and on up to the Wading River Bridge, where he arrived the following morning. During the long, miserable night, he could only wait out the storm, constantly bailing out his boat, and hope for the best. The night was so dark, he had no idea where he was except when he got near Iron Bridge. Throughout the long night, muskrats washed out of their homes by the high tide sought refuge in Fred's "lifeboat," their fear of drowning outweighing their fear of a human. Even a hawk joined this unwilling "ark." At first light, Fred found his boat banging up against the Wading River Bridge, and he simply stepped out onto it and made his way to Howard McAnney's house on Turtle Creek Road, drenched and cold but alive.

The storm decimated the muskrat population in the area. The storm tides had washed away their houses and drowned many of the "rats" themselves. The water level from the storm actually had come all the way up Turtle Creek Road past the Billy Maxwell homestead site. Orville McAnney, Howard's son, said that there were so many dead muskrats floating in the creeks that one could go out and collect them with a dip net. It took years for the "rat" population to recover from this devastating storm.

The Taylor Family

When Thomas Taylor made out his will on November 22, 1825, he had good reason to be proud of his accomplishments. He and his beloved wife, Elizabeth, had six sons and two daughters to brighten their lives: Benjamin, Thomas, John, Joseph, Henry, William, Mary, and Elizabeth. At the time of his death, Thomas had assembled an estate that included most of the upper part of the land from the Wading River to the Great Swamp on both sides of Turtle Creek Road. To the south lay the property of his friend and neighbor James Maxwell (the father of "Billy" Maxwell).

Thomas and Elizabeth Taylor apparently built their homestead on Turtle Creek Road [now #12, the home of the Horace Somes, Jr. family] about 1796. This homestead property he bequeathed to his son, William upon his death. His son, Thomas, received the house and property on which he lived at the time of his father's death which included the land where William F. Gale later built his home on Cedar Lane. Son John got the west end of the property. Benjamin received the land to the northward of the homestead towards what is today Route 542. Son Joseph received sixty acres of land south of Thomas's and John's land, east of James Maxwell's land, and west of William's land. His other sons and daughters received still other portions of his land.

Though little is known of this family and the houses they built have long returned to dust, the gravestones of a tiny cemetery still huddle in the woods off Cedar Lane. This cemetery, known by the family name, may contain the unmarked graves of Thomas and Elizabeth Taylor, but the stones which have survived mark the resting places of their son, Thomas, Jr. and his family.

Thomas, Jr. married Esther Loveland prior to his father's death in 1825. As has been noted, they lived in a house that stood somewhere near where William F. Gale later built his home on Cedar Lane in what is now the Turtle Run Campground. They had at least three children: Charles Henry, Theodore C., and Esther.

Tragedy seemed to haunt their little family. Their first child, Theodore C., was born on April 14, 1829 but lived only nineteen years. He died on March 6, 1848, and the engraving on his stone reads enigmatically: "His days of affliction are over; the hours and nights of illness. We see him in anguish no more. He has gone to his happy release."

Courtesy of Victor Roma

The Taylor Cemetery

When Theodore was seven years old, his sister, Esther, named for her mother, was born. Like her brother, Esther would die at the age of nineteen, on August 7, 1855.

The couple's third child, Charles Henry Taylor, was born on April 5, 1845, and actually lived to an old age, dying on September 2, 1909. Esther Taylor, his mother, was not so fortunate. She died on the first of May, 1851, not quite fifty-one years of age. Her death at least spared her the suffering that she would have experienced at the death of her daughter, four years later. Thomas, Jr., at fifty-one, was left with a six year-old son and a fifteen year-old daughter.

Charles Henry married Hannah Darby, the daughter of John and Mary (Robbins) Darby on February 27, 1867. Hannah was a descendant of the Leeks, the Allens, and the Cramers, while her new husband laid claim to the Loveland (and through them to the Mathis and Leek families) as well as to his own. They had seven children, two of which died at very early ages. Charles and Hannah were buried in the Miller cemetery in New Gretna.

The whole family, with the exception of Charles Henry, lies buried here beside the Wading River, on land that was once the homesite of their grandparents. Or at least, we presume something is still left of their remains after hogs rooted up their bones in one final, tragic humiliation.

Esther Taylor
Wife of Thomas Taylor, Jr.
b. September 2, 1800
d. May 1, 1851

Courtesy of Victor Roma

Thomas Taylor, Jr.
b. March 30, 1794
d. August 29, 1863

Esther Taylor
Daughter of Thomas and Esther Taylor
b. March 28, 1836
d. August 7, 1855

Theodore C. Taylor
Son of Thomas and Esther Taylor
b. April 14, 1829
d. March 6, 1848
in the 19th year of his age
"His days of affliction are over; the hours and nights of illness. We see him in anguish no more. He has gone to his happy release."

The James Franklin Downs Family

The Downs family lived in Wading River before the beginning of the nineteenth century and intermarried with all the old families of the area. The earliest data now available begins with the marriage of Sarah Smith Mathis to James Austin Downs.

Sarah was the daughter of Daniel Mathis and Phoebe (Smith) Mathis. Her grandparents through her father were Job and Phoebe (Leek) Mathis, and her great grandparents were John and Phoebe Leek of Wading River and Great John and Alice (Andrews-Higbee) Mathis of Bass River.

James Austin Downs was the son of Samuel and Abigail (Austin) Downs. James Austin Downs was born in Tuckerton on June 10, 1789 and married Sarah Smith Mathis on January 17, 1814. The couple lived in Wading River, though the exact location is not known. They had six children: Daniel James Austin, Frances A.E., Leah Eleanor Angeline, Phoebe Jane, Benjamin Franklin, and Sarah. Frances married William Clifton Gale (see THE WILLIAM F. GALE FAMILY) and Leah Eleanor Angeline married John J. Maxwell, the son of James and Bethia (Gale) Maxwell.

Frances (Downs) and William Clifton Gale had five children, including William F. (who married Matilda Heineman); Sally (who married Albert Sooy); Edward (who married first Julia Adams and later her sister, Sarah. James A. Downs married Deborah Hilliard, and Mary Frances married Josephus Weeks as his second wife.

It was William F. and Matilda (Heineman) Gale who lived in the house on the north side of Cedar Lane in the Thomas Taylor, Jr. homestead where the Turtle Run Campground is now located.

Benjamin Franklin Downs married Ellen Chew. Among their eleven children were James Franklin Downs (b. March 27, 1856; d. March 13, 1931), Sarah Ellen, and Martha Stranger. James Franklin married Amanda Lippincott, and they had twelve children. Sarah Ellen married Reuben Cavileer of Lower Bank and sister Martha married first, G. Harry Adams, and later Samuel Merchant. Martha (Downs) and G. Harry Adams were the grandparents of Steve Eichinger of Wading River.

James Franklin Downs lived near the end of Cedar Lane. Nothing remains of the little house in which he and his wife, Amanda, raised their children. Horace Somes, Jr. relates a story

Courtesy of Harvey LeMunyon

James Franklin Downs

he heard that James Franklin's hogs got loose one day and rooted up all the bones in the old Taylor cemetery on the property. It must have been a gruesome sight to see human bones scattered all over the ground by the hogs. The gravestones still stand sentinel in their accustomed position off Cedar Lane, but who knows whether they mark any of the beloved remains.

Edward Downs, the son of James Franklin and Amanda (Lippincott) Downs, was born on the 25th of April, 1881and married Hannah Adams. Hannah was the daughter of Theophilus and Sarah (Mick) Adams and was born in 1889. Edward and Hannah (Adams) Downs lived in the little house on Turtle Creek road which now is in ruins but once stood proudly on what was called the Fountain Cramer Estate. A sister, Leona Downs, married Daniel Lemunyon. They were the parents of Harvey Lemunyon.

Hannah (Adams) and Edward Downs had four children: Alice, Edward, Jr., Marjorie, and Bertha. Marjorie married Walter Knickerbocker Cavileer, Jr. of Lower Bank. Their daughter, Nancy, married Jesse Souders. Alice married Harry DeCamp. It isn't recorded whether Edward, Jr. ever married, and Bertha died at the tender age of fourteen months.

Hannah (Adams) Downs died on the 21st of May, 1931, and Edward died on the 23rd of July, 1956. Both were buried in the Lower Bank cemetery.

Courtesy of Ruth Updike

Hannah (Adams) Downs
(Mrs. Edward Downs)

Photograph by John Pearce

The Fountain Cramer Estate

This was the home of Edward and Hannah (Adams) Downs.

The "Fountain Cramer" for whom it is named was the son of Caleb W. Cramer and Mary Ann Mott, the grandson of Achsah (Leek) and Chockley Cramer, and the great-grandson of John and Martha (Rose) Leek and Caleb and Mary (Baker) Cramer.

No dates are given for Fountain Cramer, but his father died in 1851. Since Edward Downs was not born until 1881, it is assumed that Fountain Cramer built this house in which he and his wife could raise their children. After his death, it was probably sold to Edward Downs for the same purpose.

Today, only ruins are left of this old house that has seen a century and a half pass by.

Hammonton Peddler about 1910
Harvey Downs in baseball team togs! Dora Maxwell, Carlton Maxwell

Harvey Downs was the son of James Franklin and Amanda (Lippincott) Downs and the brother of Edward Downs. He was born on February 20, 1892 and died at the age of twenty-eight on June 30, 1920 of tuberculosis.   Here, he is in the prime of young manhood, smiling, happy, and ready to play baseball.

Marjorie (Downs) Cavileer

Marjorie is the daughter of Edward and Hannah (Adams) Downs and is the widow of Walter Knickerbocker Cavileer, Jr. Born in the house on the Fountain Cramer Estate, she still lives in nearby Lower Bank along the Mullica. No longer proud of her early hunting days, she now delights in the many ducks and geese that gather in front of her house.

The Levi Downs Family

Courtesy of Horace Somes, Jr.

The Levi Downs Residence
Turtle Creek Road and Route 542

Levi Austin Downs was the son of Benjamin Franklin (1824 - 1906) and Ellen (Chew) Downs (1837 - 1900) and the brother of James Franklin Downs. He was born on the twenty-third of September, 1857 and married Ella Williams, who was born on September 5th, 1864. They built this house on the corner of Turtle Creek Road across from the John (Wobbar) Maxwell house site in which to raise their children.

Levi Austin and Ellen only had two children: William and Levi Austin, Jr.

William married Sadie B. Valient, and the couple had two children, a boy and a girl: Thelma and Delvin. Sadie died in Atlantic City at the ripe old age of eighty-eight in 1971.

William's brother, Levi, Jr., was born on June 22, 1884. He married Ella M. Bozarth, daughter of William and Margaret (Ford) Bozarth. They had four children: William Lloyd (who died at the age of two years old), Sabrina (who died at the age of forty), Ann, and Georgia.

Courtesy of Steve Eichinger

Levi Austin Downs

640

The William F. Gale Family

The William F. Gale Residence
Cedar Lane
(No longer in existence)

Thomas Taylor had his homestead where Horace Somes, Jr. and his wife Barbara live at #12 Turtle Creed Road. He once owned most of the land in the upper Turtle Creek Road area, and, in his 1825 will, left various pieces of his property to his sons. This particular farm was left to Thomas Taylor, Jr. and was listed in his will as the "farm where Thomas now resides."

On September 10, 1846, William Clifton Gale and Frances (Downs) Gale, both of local families, were blessed with the birth of a fine son whom they named William F. William was the third child and second son of the couple. Three years later, Frances gave birth to twins: James A. and Mary Frances.

William F. became a schoolteacher. He met and married another schoolteacher, Matilda Heineman, who had been born in Harrisville on February 10, 1856 and had taught school in East Orange, New Jersey. It is presumed that William F. and Matilda built this house off Cedar Lane in Wading River at sometime during the last quarter of the nineteenth century, and William left teaching to raise a family and work his farm. No one seems to know just what happened to the original farmhouse of Thomas Taylor, Jr., but the architecture of the Gale house indicates a construction date during the second half of the nineteenth century.

The couple had three children: Anna Frances (b. June 25, 1884), William C. (b. August 31, 1888) and E. Ruthven (b. June 5, 1895). Anna never did marry, but William married Maude Wetherby, and the couple had five children. E. Ruthven married a girl by the name of Louise, but her maiden name is not known.

William F. and Matilda lived in this house for some years around the turn of the century, and both died within a year of each other, William in 1929 and Matilda in 1930.

Robert McKeen owned the property after the Gales, and Paul and Dini Maurer bought it from him. Prior to World War II, Paul Mauer had a business hauling bone and meat scrap from area resturants for rendering. The Mauer family is now mostly from New Gretna. Their sons, Bill and Norman, are deceased. Naomi still lives in New Gretna where she served as postmaster for many years.

Duncan Doyle established a campground on the property after he purchased it from the Mauers which he called the Turtle Run Campground.

On January 13, 1982, a fire started in an unlined chimney. Horace Somes, Jr. remembers that he first heard it was a chimney fire, but when he looked out from his house, he saw flames shooting thirty feet in the air off the ridge line of the house and knew it was a working fire. The Lower Bank Fire Company did its best but to no avail. It was just too fully involved before they arrived on the scene. After the fire was out, nothing remained of the old Gale house.

Duncan Doyle replaced the old house with a modular one which still stands on the property. In 1995, the Turtle Run Campground continues under the ownership of Scott Hazard of New Gretna, who also owns the Pilgrim Lake Campground in Bass River.

Courtesy of Horace Somes, Jr.

Matilda Heineman Gale
wife of William. F. Gale - circa 1912

Courtesy of Horace Somes, Jr.

William. F. Gale
Schoolteacher and farmer

The James McAnney Family

The Home of James and Helen (Maxwell) McAnney
L. to R. Dauthter Leah Ann, Laura (son Charles' wife) holding her son Willis, mother Helen Bertha (Maxwell) McAnney, and father JamesMcAnney. The two children in front of the fence are Elton and Elmira McAnney, son and daughter of Charles and Laura McAnney and grandchildren of James and Helen.

James McAnney was the son of Samuel and Sarah McAnney who are buried at Pleasant Mills. Samuel was born on June 2, 1785 and died on June 9, 1855. His wife, Sarah, was born in 1791 and died on September 8, 1863.

James was born on August 5, 1827 in Batsto where his father worked, and, at the age of thirty-four, joined the Union Army as part of the First Calvalry of New Jersey Company C1, on August 17, 1861. He seems to have had either illness or wounds which kept him from his unit from time to time, but he kept going back. He finally mustered out on July 24, 1865. After the war, he was a proud member of the Grand Army of the Republic, Post 68.

On December 26, 1862, he married Helen Bertha Maxwell, daughter of John Maxwell and Leah Eleanor Angeline (Downs) Maxwell, in Lower Bank who apparently was his third wife. Leah was the daughter of Sarah Mathis and James A. Downs, granddaughter of Daniel Mathis II and Phoebe (Smith) Mathis [daughter of the famous privateer captain, Micajah Smith of Chestnut Neck], great-granddaughter of Job Mathis and Phoebe (Leek) Mathis, and great, great-granddaughter of the Great John Mathis of Little Egg Harbor and of John Leek of Wading River.

James and Helen had nine children: Charles H. (b. 1864, m. Laura F. Garrison), James Socretes (called "Crate"; b. 1869, m. Sophia Ford), Irene A. (b. 1872 and died in 1881), Howard W. (b. 1874, m. Alice Vincent), George A. (b. 1876, m . 1) Amanda M. Wescoat and 2) Annabella Headley), John F., Leah Ann (b. 1878), Minerva (b. 1884), and Alvin B. (no birth date given, m. Della Loveland).

James worked at the paper mill in Harrisville. Both he and his wife were buried at Lower Bank.

Charles, Socrates, George, and Howard are covered separately in this section on Wading River.

John McAnney served in the Coast Guard and married Sophie Bozarth. The couple lived in New Gretna between Route 9 and Hillside Cemetery, which became their final resting place. John is pictured in Beck's *Jersey*

Genesis with a double-barreled shotgun. Their children were: Talbert, a bayman who married Dorothy Robbins and lived across from the school in New Gretna; Theora, whose married name is not known but who lived in Absecon and had children; James lived in Manahawkin with his wife but left her and went to California. She later rejoined him there.

Alvin married Della Hickman and lived in New Gretna at the end of the first road across from and above the Presbyterian Church. Their children: Marie (married a bayman and lived in Oceanville), Irene (married a man named Bishop and lived in Collingswood), and Rubin, called "Ruby" (married Margaret "Peg" Cramer and lived in New Gretna). Ruby managed docks on the Bass River which he rented from Chet Allen just below the parkway and Route 9 bridge. The boat yard is still known as "Allen's Dock" in 1995.

Minerva married Malcolm Billsborough who was originally from England and captained one of the DuPont family yachts. His brother-in-law, Charles McAnney served as his mate, and Wilbur McAnney, Charles' son, was the cook. Minerva and Malcom lived in Wilmington, Delaware, and had only one child, Helen, who married a funeral director. He died of cancer, and Minerva remarried to a man appropriately named "Money" who worked in real estate. He died of a heart attack and was buried in Middletown, Delaware. Minerva continued to live in Middletown and worked in a bank in Wilmington.

James McAnney

Leah Ann married Louis Loveland and lived in New Gretna near her brothers, John and Alvin, in the first house on the north side of the road to Wading River, fifty yards east of the sharp bend at the western end of the town. Their daughter, Anna, married Melville Parker, only son of wealthy parents. Apparently Melville had sufficient means to do what he chose, and he chose to be a bayman. He was an excellent organist but never pursued it.

Daniel had some problems with marriage. He married a woman by the name of Myrtle, but they didn't get along. Apparently, if he asked her to pass something to him at dinner, she threw it at him. He worked as a carpenter and lived in the home of his parents. The couple finally divorced, but not until after a daughter, Doris, was born.

The Home of James McAnney - 1995
waits forlornly for the fire or bulldozer which will forever banish the memory of the Civil War veteran who built it in the town he loved. The property is owned by Fay Bartling who lives in Massachusetts.

Doris married Walter McAnney, the son of Jenny McAnney (the unwed daughter of Socrates McAnney), making her husband her first cousin once removed.

Irene died as a child at the age of nine.

James McAnney was locally famous for being the proud owner of one of the "Big Guns." Back in the last half of the nineteenth century, no one had ever heard of raising ducks and geese for food. Nor would they know what to make of farming oysters and clams. Like the Lenape before them, they could not have conceived of the need for such practices. God had paved the waters of the Chesapeake and Delaware Bays, of the bays and rivers of South Jersey, with so many oysters and clams that it was beyond rationality to suggest that they would ever disappear from their accustomed places. Likewise, all manner of wildfowl filled the marshes and skies of this blessed land for the benefit of those who lived on it. By the end of the Civil War period, prosperity had passed them by, and they had to use any means available to make a living. One of those means that God himself had placed at their disposal was commercial hunting.

The hotels of New York, Philadelphia, Baltimore, and Washington paid comparatively well for fresh clams, oysters, ducks, geese, and fish from these bountiful country areas, and the local men were willing to supply their wants. Some of these men had invested in very large guns of various types that they could lay in a sturdy boat and blast hundreds of birds at a time as they settled on some secluded waters for the night.

Courtesy of Ann (Loveland) Parker

James McAnney
A Proud Veteran

James wasn't a bad man. He wasn't thinking about slaughtering God's creatures when he set out in his skiff with his six-bore big gun. He was thankful that God, in His mercy, had blessed James McAnney's homeland with such abundance. He was thinking that the few extra pennies he made from his hunting would get the family through another winter. Not hunting to the best of his ability would mean watching his children starve in the midst of plenty, and that he was not about to do. James McAnney's big gun was supposed to have taken over a quarter pound of black powder to load, and when it went off, you must have been able to hear it clear to Green Bank!

The State of New Jersey, like her sisters along the waterways, finally woke up to the fact that the unthinkable was actually happening: the wildfowl were dwindling in number. Regulations were needed, and one of the first was the abolition of big guns. Every one they could find was confiscated and destroyed. It must have broken old McAnney's heart.

James McAnney, the old soldier, answered his last muster call on the 31st of March, 1909.

The house was later occupied by Bob and Jeanette Lippincott. Bob worked at the Leek Boatworks. Now the tiny home where James and Helen McAnney raised their nine children lies vacant, forsaken these many years. Soon it will be completely forgotten, like so many of its neighbors.

The Charles McAnney Family

Courtesy of Super Bros.

The First Home of Charles and Laura McAnney
(No longer in existence)

Charles McAnney, son of James and Helen (Maxwell) McAnney, was born in 1864 and married Laura Garrison. (Another source lists her as a McKeen, but no "Laura McKeen" appears in my McKeen genealogical information.) Laura and Charles were supposed to have been first cousins. Their "honeymoon" house stood on the west side of the road to "The Islands" off what is today Cedar Lane. Charlie is pictured at the age of twelve in the photograph of the Wading River Cornet Band towards the end of this chapter. This house was supposed to have belonged to a McKeen before Charlie McAnney bought it.

To accomodate his growing family, he soon built a second house next to this one but actually on the road.

Laura and Charles had seven children: Elsie, Mary, Elton, Elmira, Wilbur, Willis, and Irvin.

Elsie married Paul Taylor, who worked for the Atlantic City Gas Company. The couple had no children and are buried at the Pleasant Mills churchyard. Elsie died in 1964.

Mary married David Wescoat who worked as a carpenter. They lived in Nesco and owned a store there. Mary and David were not blessed with children either.

Courtesy of Stephen Eichinger, Feb. 1992

Charles McAnney's House - a visit from the peddler

646

Elton worked as a carpenter and lived in Egg Harbor City. He met and married Dora Jerue, but the marriage was not successful. She left him to live with the husband of her best friend, George Bozarth, betraying both husband and friend. She died only a few years later of a brain tumor. Elton, meanwhile, married again, this time to a woman named Edith, who had been previously married. Edith had a child from her former marriage, and the couple added Victor, Warren, Joseph, Marian, and Mirtle to the list.

Elmira married Jack Super, from whom several of the photographs in this section come. Jack worked in sawmills, and both are buried in Hammonton. They had four children: Jack, George, Burtis ("Burt") and Nelson. Elmira died in the spring of 1965, and Jack followed her soon after. They lived in Pleasant Mills most of their married life, but later moved to Elm on the White Horse Pike.

Wilbur settled at Edgewater, New Jersey, and worked on boats. He married a girl named Helen from Odessa, Delaware, but the couple was later divorced. They had a boy and a girl prior to the divorce. Next he married a woman named Winifred ("Winnie") of Edgewater, who had several children from her previous marriage. They had no children together. He died in the spring of 1965 of a heart attack and is buried in Edgewater.

Willis married Mary Bird of Tuckerton and lived in that town for many years before moving to Toms River. He worked as a carpenter, and the couple had one daughter.

Irvin married Edith Ford of Green Bank. Irvin worked at odd jobs in the woods and on the bay. They had to live in a shack for a while that stood between the Bartlings (the Benjamin Maxwell House where Super Kwick is in 1995) and Howard McAnney's first farm. Later they lived in Green Bank. The couple had one boy and two or three girls but their names and whereabouts are not known. He died in 1960.

During the 1970s, Charlie Nichols of Bulltown lived in the house. Horace Somes, Jr. remembers the day the house burned quite well. On October 21, 1971 about 6:30 A.M., Charlie came over to the Somes's house and pounded on the door. It was in the middle of duck season, and Horace Sr. and Jr. were having breakfast. Charlie was quite inebriated, and neither Horace nor his father could make much sense out of what he was saying. He kept saying something about the kids running off into the woods. Horace, Sr. and Jr. soon started to get things straightened out. Charlie's wife, it seems, had left him a while back and wasn't at home. Charlie had heard a noise outside and had let go a couple of shotgun blasts through his bedroom window. That scared the kids who took off into the woods. "Yeh, " Charlie slurred, "and the house is on fire too. Let it burn!"

Courtesy of the Super Bros.

The Second Home of Laura and Charles McAnney
(No longer in existence)

Horace Sr. and Jr. were wide awake by now and immediately dove for the phone to call the Egg Harbor City Fire Company which was serving Wading River at that time. Then they ran to the house and got a garden hose on the burning mattress, keeping the fire under control until the fire company arrived. Apparently, Charlie had been smoking in bed and had let the lighted cigarette fall on the mattress when he took the shot out the window.

When Charlie Nichols moved out, the old house was vacant for a few years and finally burned to the ground on April 8, 1975. Horace and Dorthea Somes purchased the property and added it to their farm. Their son, Frank, built a new house near the old home site and lives there with his family.

Two towering red oak trees used to stand in the front yard of the old house. These were known as "witness" trees and marked the north line of the property on a division line cited in the 1825 will of Thomas Taylor. When the house burned, one of the ancient trees was killed by the fire. When it was cut down, it was found to have a huge, rotten core. In the outer area of good wood, the Somes's counted over two hundred and fifty annual rings. Estimating the size of the rotten portion, the tree's total age must have been at least three hundred and probably closer to four hundred years old. Thus the two trees may have taken root long before the original settlement of the area. The second tree still stands to the west of the house site near Turtle Creek Road.

The Howard McAnney Family

Courtesy of Howard Somes, Jr.

The First Home of Howard and Alice McAnney

Howard McAnney, the son of James A. McAnney, was born in Wading River on March 19, 1874 and attended school in the little schoolhouse on Turtle Creek Road. He lived with a Mr. and Mrs. Perry for several years when he was young. The McAnney family was large and the finances were not. The Perrys were rather well off but could have no children.

His first work away from home was cutting marl in Marlton. He met Miss Alice Marion Vincent and soon the young couple were deeply in love. Alice was the youngest of nine children of Myers and Dora Vincent of Milton, Delaware. Howard and Alice were married by L.C. Wainwright on the 19th of January, 1903, and they built the house shown in the photographs on this page in Wading River in the year of their marriage. Howard worked as a cook out at Fish Factory and also cooked on yachts from Massachusetts to North Carolina. Later, he worked for Zurn at "Half Moon," the mini-resort across the river.

They soon had two children, Orville Otis and Dorothea Helen. This house and farm were a bit small for their growing family, so they purchased another home on Turtle Creek Road from the Gale family for $800. Ed Gale lived downstairs and Francis Gale lived upstairs.

It is believed that their second house had been built around 1796 by Thomas Taylor as his homestead farm. It is possible that the original part of the house was built prior to the birth of his son, Thomas, Jr., in 1794. In his 1825 will, Taylor left parcels of his land to his five sons. The homestead farm was given to his son, William B. Taylor and his wife Letitia, with the provision that wife and mother, Elizabeth, have the use of the two easterly rooms, one bed, bedstead and bedding of her choice, the eight-day clock, a large looking glass desk, one walnut table, six new Windsor chairs and such kitchen furniture as she wanted, one cow and his gray mare.

Photograph by John Pearce

The First Home of Howard and Alice McAnney - 1995
Turtle Creek Road

649

In 1838, Captain William Loveland Leek, son of William and Catherine (Loveland) Leek and grandson of John and Mary (Rose) Leek, bought most of the parcels from the Taylor family and lived here. The date of sale was recorded on March 28, 1838. Son Benjamin had died unmarried and without issue, but all the rest of the remaining family signed off on the deal on the second parcel. A third parcel was sold to Leek on October 13th of 1838 by son Joseph

Leek completed the purchase of the Thomas Taylor homestead ten years later when he bought the fourth parcel from Thomas Taylor, Jr. John Maxwell, William C. Gale, and John A. Downs apparently had an interest in yet another parcel of land which was a part of Thomas Taylor, Jr.'s land by this time and they also signed the agreement. Thus by Febraury 12, 1848, William L. Leek had Thomas Taylor, Sr.'s entire homestead, with the exception of that belonging to Thomas, Jr.

Courtesy of Horace Somes, Jr.

The Second Home of Howard and Alice McAnney
as it looked when they purchased it in 1911

An 1849 map in the possession of Horace Somes, Jr., the current owner, shows this house belonging to W. Gale. Gale no longer had an interest in the property by 1849, having sold it the year before.

William Loveland Leek died on August 7, 1848, the same year in which he had finally reassembled the Taylor homestead, and his son, William Towers Leek inherited it. Levi H. Chew and his wife, Hope, bought the homestead from the Leeks in 1861. In 1895, Benjamin F. and Ellen (Chew) Downs acquired it from Chew.

Courtesy of Horace Somes, Jr.

The Second Home of Howard and Alice McAnney as remodeled.
The old barn in the rear of this house, seen in the photograph above, is interesting in its own right. It has ten inch, hand-hewn beams and is of pegged construction. It was built with angle bracing which were actually ship's "knees," betraying the hand of a ship's carpenter and/or the use of recycled material from an old ship. Both are likely.

Downs may have owned the homestead until his death in 1906. When Howard and Ida Bozarth bought the property on October 11, 1911, it was in the estate of Edward B. Gale. George S. Maxwell and Sallie Gale, acted as executors for Gale.

That same day, the Bozarths sold it to Howard and Alice McAnney. This farm was larger than McAnney's old one down the road and included several outbuildings. This sizable piece of land enabled him to raise all types of garden products, and he marketed corn, peas, strawberries, and blueberries. He also raised cows, chickens, and turkeys.

Courtesy of Horace Somes, Jr.

The Second Home of Howard and Alice McAnney
as remodeled.

He net-fished on the Mullica in the winter for perch, striped bass, and cat fish, which were shipped to New York's Fulton Fish Market and to Philadelphia. Each spring, he would net herring for fertilizer. Herring were also smoked and "potted" (pickled) for eating.

Howard and Alice owned over four hundred acres of salt hay meadows from Turtle Creek to Swan Bay on the Mullica, and Howard mowed it for the use of his own animals as well as for sale. During the season, he trapped for muskrat and mink.

Both Howard and Alice were active in the Wading River Methodist Church, and Howard was a member of the Knights of Pythias in New Gretna. Over the years, Howard worked on the house, changing the roofline and

Photograph by John Pearce

The McAnney/Somes Residence - 1995

Summer Beauty on the Wading River Farm of
Howard and Alice McAnney

moving a room from the northeast end to the rear for a summer kitchen. Horace Somes and his sons later cut this room off the house and moved it across Turtle Creek Road for storage.

Orville quit school when he was in the eighth grade and worked on the bay. Orville always told a good story about his last day as a clammer. He was happily treading clams in deep water as always when he spotted the profile of a triangular sail on the horizen over towards Atlantic City. He kept treading for clams but kept an eye on the sail as it seemed to draw nearer across the bay. It suddenly shocked him to realize that the "sail" didn't belong to a boat at all but was the dorsal fin of a large shark heading directly for him. Orville said he scrambled out of the water and into his garvey as quickly as he possibly could with little regard for grace and style, and that was the last time he ever went out for clams.

Orville tried his hand at a little of everything during the depression years: boat building, car repair, scooping cranberries, electrical work, plumbing. Later, he worked for L.N. Renault and Sons, Inc., the wine makers in Egg Harbor City, where he met his future wife, Olive Henderson. He married her in her home in Lower Bank. Orville and Olive had two children: Howard Orville (who served on the carrier *Midway* and on the cruiser *Los Angeles*, married a girl named Susan Ann, and had two children, Rebecca and Daniel, and adopted James McAnney; Howard Orville McAnney lives in Point Pleasant); and Diane (went to Glassboro for a year and worked as a legal secretary). Orville later worked for DuPont.

Dorothea Helen attended the New Jersey College of Commerce and also worked at the Renault Winery in Egg Harbor City. She married Horace Arthus Somes of Montclair, New Jersey, who was in the area as part of the Civilian Conservation Corps. Horace had lost his first wife, Mary Cramer of New Gretna, in an automobile accident. Dorothy and Horace rented Alice Weber's house on the "V" between Route 542 and the Leektown Road until the end of World War II.

Horace was sent to Europe in 1944 with the HQ Battery of 718th Field Artilery of the 63rd Division. He advanced to Second Lieutenant and won the Air Medal and the Bronze Star.

When he returned home, he worked at the Northeastern Forest Experimental Station of the U.S. Forest Service, Department of Agriculture at New Lisbon, New Jersey, where the couple lived. He also attended Penn State for two years. The couple built a home in Pemberton and another on Turtle Creek Road when they returned to Wading River in the 1970s. This house stands opposite the old homestead on a two-acre parcel where the Watsontown Gun Club had been until it burned in the 1920s.

Horace and Dorothea had two children: Horace, Jr. (b. September 6, 1947) and Frank Robert (b. August 29, 1951). Dorothea worked at the station in New Lisbon until it closed in 1965. She then worked for a year as a typist for the 2017th Communications Squadron on McGuire Air Force Base and in June of 1966, began working at Fort Dix.

Howard McAnney died on May 27, 1958, at the age of eighty-four and was buried in Lower Bank. His wife, Alice, passed away ten years later. Son Orville died on October 1, 1982 at the age of seventy-five.

Horace, Sr. and Dorothy, along with their sons, Horace, Jr. and Frank, turned their farm into a Christmas tree farm some years ago, and the family has continued to operate it as such through the years.

Dorothy (McAnney) Somes died in 1992. Horace, Sr. remarried and lives in Tuckerton. Horace Somes, Jr. continues to live on the old homestead with his wife, Barbara, the former Barbara (Cavileer) Ryder of Lower Bank, and their two sons, Robert and Howard. Horace currently works for the Forestry Department of the State of New Jersey.

Robert Somes
Son of Horace and Barbara Somes

Both photographs courtesy of
Horace Somes, Jr.

Orville McAnney and his sister, Dorothea,
with the farm horses - circa 1928

Courtesy of Horace Somes, Jr.

Friends!
Jean Weiner and Dorothy McAnney - circa 1928
Turtle Creek Road is on the right with the old school in the
background. This picture was taken before Jim Updike
built his house.

Proud of his Fish!
Orville McAnney

Courtesy of Horace Somes, Jr.

Proud of his corn!
Howard McAnney

Courtesy of Horace Somes, Jr.

Alice (Vincent) McAnney making soap.
She is pouring the liquid soap into molds.

Howard McAnney making cider

Howard McAnney and his turkeys

All photographs on this page are courtesy of Horace Somes, Jr.

In Dorothea (McAnney) Somes'
notes, this picture is labeled simply,
"Turkey". Indeed it is!

Orville McAnney and Robert Lippincott

Orville and Howard McAnney

Wood Chopping for the
Winter's Fuel

During the summer, the cows on the farm were sent to the
meadows to fend for themselves.

Orville and Dorothea McAnney

Orville & Dottie McAnney
Easter 1946

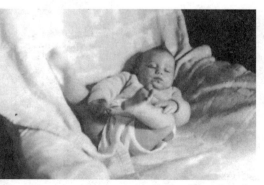

Diane McAnney

Orville McAnney's children: Howard and Diane
and their cousin Jack

Alice and Howard McAnney

At Valley Forge, on a trip to see the dogwoods in bloom:

Howard McAnney, Dorothea McAnney,
Alice McAnney,
Ruth Updike, Marguerite Updike,
James Updike

Both photographs are courtesy of Horace Somes, Jr.

Orville McAnney at 42 with Horace Somes, Jr. at 1 1/2 - 1949

A flooded field is fun for skating!
Dorothy McAnney and her father, Howard

Winter Fun
Jim Updike with the dog, Pal; Howard McAnney
and his daughter, Dorothea, and Marguerite
Updike, Jim's daughter.

Courtesy of Horace Somes, Jr.
Orville's Son, Howard Orville McAnney

Years had passed
Since we moved away;
I returned at last
One soft spring day.

I looked at the house,
The road, the trees . .
But I saw only
Memories.

- Dorothea (McAnney) Somes

Horace Somes, Jr. adds a note about possums: "Possums seem to be common on our farm. We have caught five near our chicken coop this Fall (1995). Dot put a coconut custard pie out on a bench next to this shop to cool one evening. When we looked out later, a big, three-footed possum was standing in the middle of the pan and had eaten out the entire center of the pie. He was working his way outward towards the crust. Although much of the pie was left, we went back inside and let him have the rest - we didn't want it."

The Samuel Maxwell Family

Courtesy of Steve & Millie Potter

Mrs. Samuel Maxwell poses proudly before her house on Turtle Creek Road.
L. to R.: Mary Margaret (Cramer) Maxwell, Ralph Maxwell, and Helen Maxwell
This house is no longer in existence.

Samuel Maxwell, son of John and Leah (Downs) Maxwell, was born on the nineteenth of July, 1850 and married Mary Margaret Cramer (b. 3/27/1856, d. 3/2/1932). The couple built this house on Turtle Creek Road opposite the Benjamin Maxwell House (now the Super Kwick property).

Samuel and Mary Margaret Maxwell had four children:

Grover, who married Dora Cramer and had a son, Carlton;

Mary Maud, who married Daniel T. Sooy, Jr.. and was the mother of Helen (Sooy) Williams and Ethel (Sooy) Robbins.

Mabel, who married Samuel Leonard ("Len") Sooy. Len Sooy (b. 1873, d. 1941) was the son of Daniel T. and Esther L. Sooy; Mabel and Len's daughter, Esther, married Stephen Potter of New Gretna.

Ralph L. (b. 1892, d. 1958). Ralph married first Viola Townsend (b. 1887, d. 1945) then Hilda (surname unknown).

Samuel Maxwell died slightly more than a month after his wife on the seventh of April, 1932.

It is not known when this house met its demise but the lot is now (1995) abandoned and overgrown by trees. The old site is marked by a stone foundation, old ditches outlining long-forgotten fields, and a stand of persimmon trees.

Courtesy of Steve & Millie Potter

Mabel, Ralph, and Helen Maxwell

Mabel (Maxwell) Sooy
Esther (Sooy) Potter
Ethel (Sooy) Robbins

These photographs were taken at the farm in New Gretna which Steve Potter, the grandson of Len and Mabel (Maxwell) Sooy, sold recently.

Mabel (Maxwell) Sooy
The wife of Len Sooy

Ethel & Grover Maxwell
Grover was a grandson
of Mabel and Len Sooy

All the photographs on this page are courtesy of Stephen Potter and his wife, Millie. Stephen is the grandson of Mabel (Maxwell) Sooy and "Len" Sooy.

The John (Wobbar) Maxwell Family

House Built by Charles Cavileer which became the home of John (Wobbar) Maxwell
(No longer in existence)

This house stood on the corner of Turtle Creek Road and Route 542 until 1994. It was originally built by Charles Cavileer, the brother of Sarah Leek for John (Wobbar) Maxwell. John (Wobbar) Maxwell was the son of Otto Wobbar and Hannah Gaunt (see GREEN BANK: South Bend). Hannah died at an early age, and Otto was unable to take care of their three children by himself. At Hannah's funeral, John, Lizzie, and Mary were given away to other families who took them in.

John Wobbar was raised by William (Billy) and Rachel Maxwell as part of their family, and the boy took the Maxwell name. His children also kept the surname of "Maxwell."

John had only one child, a boy named Curtis, who is pictured in a photograph in this chapter. The property was bought about 1960 by Susan Bartling and her husband, who built a new house next to this one in John (Wobbar) Maxwell's old orchard. Susan was a nurse and worked in Atlantic City. They sold this property about 1964.

In 1991, renovations were underway to restore this attractive old house. The then-owner, Miss Adams of Philadelphia, was in the process of selling it to Henry and Minnie Stroback when a water pump under the stairway started a fire which gutted the house.

Barbara Somes, who lives just down Turtle Creek Road and was a member of the Lower Bank Fire Company, got the call and rushed up the road to the corner, arriving long before the first fire truck. She found Henry Stroback on his way back into the burning house to recover valuables that were still inside. Following him through the kitchen to the front room, they found the smoke very intense. She grabbed his belt and walked him backwards, retracing their steps through the kitchen. They just managed to escape out the door when the entire downstairs flashed over. Both were very fortunate to escape with their lives. The burned-out remains were torn down in 1994, but the house is currently being reconstructed (1999).

The John (Wobbar) Maxwell House

The Summer Kitchen at the side of the John Wobbar Maxwell House

The John (Wobbar) Maxwell
House after the fire
Courtesy of Budd Wilson, Jr.

The Charles Edward Leek Family

Charles Edward ("Ed") Leek, the son of Charles T. and Anna Maria (Reynolds) Leek, was born on December 27, 1868 and married Lucretia Applegate on the fifteenth of February, 1890 in Egg Harbor City. They built their home on the west side of the main road north of the intersection with Turtle Creek Road.

Lucretia (Applegate) Leek was born in Pasadena, New Jersey, then called "Wheatlands" (see Henry Charlton Beck's *Forgotten Towns*) on July 16, 1873. She and Ed had eight boys and five girls: Merritt, Harry, Major, Frank, George, Charles, Jr., Leslie, Norris, Ida (Hilliard), Emma (Bower), Leola (Hughes), Anna (Sooy), Bessie (Oser).

Ed ran the store east of Turtle Creek Road for Sam Ireland after the death of Edwin Sooy and may have served as postmaster after the death of Catherine McKeen in 1890.

Ed also had cranberry bogs and engaged in the fur trade, buying and selling muskrats, minks, coons, and skunks both for their meat and for their furs. He shipped as high as six tons of meat to Philadelphia one year. It seems he also had a lumber and sawmill business and sold all his lumber through Atlantic City and Pleasantville.

Sometime after Sam Ireland sold the store to William "Gus" Maxwell in the first part of this century, Ed and Lucretia moved to the Smithville area where he operated a service station. Later he had a grocery business in Pleasantville, a restaurant business in Egg Harbor City and spent years as a firefighter.

Once when he lived in Leektown, he remembered in later years, "I had to fire the whole road (about a mile and a half) myself. . . . Saved my own place and three-four others." [newspaper story by Gwen Pettit - Atlantic City Press - 1955]

Lucretia (Applegate) Leek passed away on August 28, 1958, and Ed Leek died three years later on the twenty-eighth of September, 1961.

The property on which their home stood was owned by the Souders for a while and is now owned by King/Scott.

Courtesy of George Leek

Mrs. Lucretia (Applegate) Leek
circa 1920

There is an interesting story from the era of prohibition. Apparently "someone" operated a still somewhere down the road to the Bozarth sawmill which ran past Ed's house on the main road. One of his neighbors, being somewhat unneighborly, notified the federal authorities. They came swooping down on Wading River - but there the story ends. It isn't recorded whether the miscreat still operator was arrested, the still destroyed, or the unfriendly neighbor treated to the cold shoulder afterwards. The inquirer is simply left hanging with these few details.

The Benjamin Franklin Downs and John Updike Families

Courtesy of Burrel Adams

The Downs/Updike House
Turtle Creek Road
(no longer in existence)

On October 18, 1855, in the city of Philadelphia, thirty-one year old Benjamin Franklin Downs of Wading River married eighteen year old Ellen Chew. The young bride was the daughter of Hope and Levi Chew, an old, respected name in the Quaker City. The couple lived in this house, which used to stand on Turtle Creek Road, and raised a family of seven children: James Franklin, Levi Austin, Zebulon Henry, Sarah Ellen, Mary Augusta, Emma Jane, and Martha Stranger.

James Franklin (b. March 27, 1856) married Amanda Lippincott and lived out towards the end of Cedar Lane. Levi Austin (b. September 23, 1857) married Ella Williams and lived on the corner of Turtle Creek Road and Route 542. Zebulon Henry (b. Mary 12, 1860) died in infancy. Sarah Ellen (b. June 23, 1862) married Reuben Cavileer. Mary Augusta (b. March 8, 1865) married Charles Robbins, and Martha Stranger (b. November 9, 1874) married Harry Adams, the son of Anna Staza Adams Coffee.

Benjamin Franklin Downs was the fifth of six children born to James and Sarah (Mathis) Downs, who herself was the great granddaughter of the Great John Mathis. James and Sarah were residents of Wading River, though it is not known whether they, too, lived in this house. From the photograph, it is certainly older than the mid-nineteenth century.

Courtesy of Steve Eichinger

Ellen Chew Downs

Marjorie Downs Cavileer of Lower Bank and Steve Eichinger of Wading River are the great grandchildren of Benjamin Franklin and Ellen (Chew) Downs and the great great grandchildren of James and Sarah (Mathis) Downs.

Ellen (Chew) Downs just made it into the new century. She died in 1900 at the age of sixty-three. Before she passed away, though, she planted the pine tree in her front yard which appears so prominently in the above photograph. In 1997, only that old pine remains to tell the story of the generations which made that forgotten homestead their home. Benjamin Franklin Downs survived his wife by only six years, dying at the age of eighty-two in 1906. James and Sarah lie buried in unmarked graves in the old Lower Bank cemetery. The Lower Bank graves of Benjamin Franklin and Ellen (Chew) Downs are marked with stones.

The next resident of the Downs farm was John Updike. John was born in 1845 to a Pennsylvania German family from Pottstown, Pennsylvania, and served in the Civil War in Company I, 5th Regiment, Maryland Volunteers. He was captured, along with his whole regiment, and became a prisoner of war. John survived the imprisonment, and was a proud member of the Grand Army of the Republic when that organization was founded after the Civil War came to an end.

He first married "Maggie" Garrison, but, while she was buried next to him, her name is not on the gravestone. Only that of his second wife appears there. He had one son by his first wife, a boy they called Samuel, who married a girl named Louise and lived in Hillside, New Jersey.

Annie Auerbach, his second wife, was born in Germany in 1852 and was brought to this country when she was about thirteen months old, her family settling in Egg Harbor City. For a while, she worked as a housekeeper in Philadelphia, but on a visit to Laura McAnney, a friend who lived in Wading River, she met John Updike and fell in love. The exact year that they moved to the Benjamin Downs farm is not known. Annie and John had five children: John, Henry, James, Sadie, and Emil. Emil died at the tender age of four.

Sadie Updike married Joseph Ware and lived at Batsto with his parents, Frank and Ida. It was here that their first child, Annie, was born. By the time son Howard was born three years later, Sadie and Joe had moved in with her parents on the Downs farm in Wading River. That would mean that the Wares moved to Wading River between 1918 and 1920 when the senior Updike's died. They were living in Lower Bank when their second son, Nelson, was born.

Howard married Sara Allen and lives on North Maple Avenue in New Gretna. Nelson married Evelyn Simpkins and lives on Old Church Road in Lower Bank, and Anna married Dr. H. Cory Walling. The Wallings live in Randolph, New Jersey, but spent most of their married life in Morristown where he was a doctor of osteopathy. Sadie (Updike) Ware died of tuberculosis in 1928.

Jane Helena (Garrison) Updike
the first wife of John Updike
whom the family knew as "Maggie"

Annie (Auerbach) Updike
1852 - 1920

668

John and Annie's son, John (b. 1886), worked on pleasure boats that sailed from the Wading River area and was a famous decoy carver. He married Ina Jagmitty (b. 1905), and they had one child, a daughter by the name of Barbara Sue. Ina Jagmitty was a member of the Leek family. John and Ina lived in Green Bank during his last years at 1037 River Road in the Reverend Joseph C. Clark house, and his decoys became famous all over the area. John Updike, Jr. died in 1955. His wife, Ina, passed away in 1980.

Son James (b. 6/18/1894, d. 6/19/1969) served in the infantry during World War I, during which he was wounded and spent some time in Walter Reed Hospital. James was a cabinetmaker by trade and worked in a shipyard during the Second World War. He married Ruth Huntley, the daughter of William and Edith (Jones) Huntley of Philadelphia.

Edith (Jones) Huntley later married a second time to George Thomas. George was a cranberry grower and also worked for the State Forestry Service. George also had talents in surveying and mapmaking, jobs which he performed for the state. He died of a heart attack in 1930 while fighting a forest fire which threatened to engulf all of Wading River.

James and Ruth (Huntley) Updike originally lived with his parents at the Downs farm at the same time as Joe and Sadie Ware were living there. After his parents' deaths in 1920, he purchased property on Turtle Creek Road at the end of Cedar Lane from Howard McAnney and also acquired a piece of land that had been attached to the old school property. Here they built a home in 1927. The couple had a daughter, Marguerite, who was given the nickname "Chick" (short for "Chickaru") by her father when she was a small child. "Chick" married a Methodist minister, the Rev. Blaine Detrick. Margaret now lives in the home her father built on Turtle Creek Road.

Son Henry served in the military during World War I and married Minnie Vincent. Henry Updike was a fur-buyer and lived in New Gretna. He also had blueberry fields in Wading River.

The old house was abandoned after the James Updike family moved into their new home. In 1959, it was listed as one of the oldest houses in South Jersey, but it was in such bad shape that it was eventually torn down. The pinetree planted by Ellen (Chew) Downs stands silent, solitary sentinel where once the old homestead sheltered generations of at least two families.

Courtesy of Burrel Adams

The Downs/Updike House

The James Socretes "Crate" McAnney Family

The Home of "Crate" McAnney
Turtle Creek Road
(no longer in existence)

James Socretes "Crate" McAnney was the son of James McAnney. "Crate" married Elizabeth Maxwell and built this house on Turtle Creek Road directly across from his father and mother's home. "Crate" and Elizabeth had four children, three of which are pictured with their parents on the following page: Jenny, Beatrice, George, and Sarah.

This house, like so many others, was destroyed by fire while the McAnney's were living there, and the family moved to Tuckerton rather than rebuilding in Wading River. After the death of his wife, "Crate" moved to a house on the north side Merrygold Branch of the Wading River just above the bridge towards New Gretna on the Bass River side of the Wading which was also consumed by fire at a later date.

After her marriage, Jenny moved to Merchantville where she and her husband operated a greenhouse. Jenny had a son out of wedlock, probably prior to her marriage when she lived in Tuckerton with her parents. Her son, Walter, took the McAnney name. It was believed that his father was a married man who owned a garage in Tuckerton. Walter was raised by his grandfather "Crate" at Merrygold.

Beatrice married and lived with her husband and children somewhere on the White Horse Pike.

George married Annabelle Headley, and the couple lived in Wildwood. Later in life, they moved to Erma where he died of a heart attack while cutting grass. After seeing her husband properly buried in the Methodist Church at Erma, Annabelle moved back to Wildwood.

Sarah, Elizabeth and "Crate's" youngest child, was never strong. At the age of seventeen, she married a young man who was in the Coast Guard and lived in Wildwood near her brother and his wife. She died from a heart condition at the age of twenty-five. She is listed in the Somes' notes as having five children, of whom, only the name of one is known: Ruth. If she was weak in the first place, having five children over eight years certainly didn't help any.

The Turtle Neck Gun Club, owned by Tony and Sidney Caruso, stands on the property in 1995.

Beatrice McAnney, Elizabeth (Maxwell) McAnney, Jennie McAnney, Susie Maxwell,
Robert Lippincott, "Crate" McAnney;

Turtle Neck Gun Club
Site of home of Socrates McAnney

671

The Lemuel Maxwell Family

Photograph by John Pearce

The Home of Lemuel and Etta Maxwell - 1995

Lemuel Hopkins Maxwell (1882-1954) was the son of John F. Maxwell (1855-1898) and Elizabeth (Adams) Maxwell, the grandson of John J. Maxwell (1812-1890) and Leah Eleanor Angeline (Downs) Maxwell, and the great grandson of James Maxwell, Sr. (1777-1844) and Berthia [or Bethia] (Gale) Maxwell.

John F. and Elizabeth (Adams) Maxwell had three boys and a girl: Benjamin (1879-1954), Lemuel Hopkins, Robert, and Leah. Benjamin married Louella Gibbs (1885-1925); Robert married Margaret Holloway (1893-1955) and later Elsie Smith (1903-1979), and Leah married Samuel Lippincott.

Lemuel married Mary Etta Rosell (1887-1959), the daughter of Lewis G. and Susan (Grant) Rosell. Susan (Grant) was the daughter of Job and Elizabeth Grant of Tuckerton.

The couple built this house after they were married around the turn of the century and raised four children here:Lemuel, Jr. (1906-1964), Susie, Bernice, and Marie. Susan married Harold Emmons; Lillian Bernice ("Bunn") married Louis Michael Carpo, Sr. and later Charles Floyd Dickinson; Norma married Irvin Ford; and Marie married Lawrence Goad.

This property was originally part of the land attached to the Wading River Hotel, home of Maja and Sarah Leek. Apparently Anna Bush (Maxwell) Leek and Maja Towers Leek sold him the property on which to construct his home.

The house still stands on the Batsto-Bridgeport Road (Route 542) and is the home of Fred Quigley. Fred's father, John Quigley, owned the old Wading River Hotel for many years.

The Wading River Methodist Episcopal Church was the next building up the road towards the west and was also built on property originally attached to the Wading River Hotel.

The Wading River baseball field was located on land behind this house until it was moved to the far corner of Ridge Road and the Batsto-Bridgeport Road.

Brian Maxwell, who has the Maxwell Funeral Homes in Manahawkin and Mystic Islands is the grandson of Lemuel Maxwell, Jr., the young child standing next to his father in the photograph at right.

The Lemuel and Etta Maxwell Family - Circa 1913
L to R.: Susie, Lemuel, Lemuel, Jr., Etta, Bernice Maxwell

The Maxwell Girls: Susie, Marie, and Bernice

The children are standing on the front porch of this house, and the Wading River Church can be seen in the background. Lillian Bernice "Bun" Maxwell, the little girl on the right, married Louis Michael Carpo, Sr. She later married Charles Floyd Dickinson and is still living in New Gretna in 1996.

Etta Maxwell with Susie
Lemuel Maxwell with Lemuel, Jr.

Captain Jesse Williams

Captain Jesse Williams was a sea captain and respected member of the Bridgeport community. He was a member of the Wading River Cornet Band and was photographed with them in 1876.

An article in the Atlantic City newspaper dated April 30, 1902 tells a tragic tale of the Williams's family:

UNFORTUNATE FAMILY.

Father Sick, Mother Seriously Ill, Son in Hospital.

The little 13-year-old messenger boy, George Williams, who was run over on May 1 by a Reading passenger train at Baltic and New York avenues and is now lying in the city hospital with his right arm cut off, a fractured skull and broken teeth, is the son of Jesse Williams, probably one of the best known sea captains on the coast. Captain Williams, ten years ago, lost a freight steamer on Ship Shoal off the Carolina coast, and since that time has not taken any long voyages. When the Brigantine Transit Co. was organized, he was put in charge of the passenger steamers, and the past three years he has been captain of Mr. Young's steam yacht Nada, Mr. Williams is slowly recovering from a severe attack of grip, while Mrs. Williams, the wife and mother of the unfortunate boy, has been lying at the point of death.

HUMANITY

Courtesy of Horace Somes, Jr.

Cold Cellar on the Homestead of Captain Jesse Williams
circa 1981

Jesse's daughter, Sabrina, married William Towers Cramer, whose mother was Catharine Leek, the daughter of George Washington and Hannah B. (Mathis) Leek.

Jesse's granddaughter, Georgia (Cramer) Lutz, was born in New Gretna and taught school here for one year in 1907. She was well-known to the young people of her time and apparently visited her grandfather at other times than just this one year.

Almost nothing is known about the Williams home which used to stand on this property. When it disappeared or what happened to it is another pine barrens mystery.

The Capt. Williams homestead, however, did change hands many times in the course of the years. John Maxwell owned the property early in the nineteenth century. In 1845, he transferred it to James Maxwell, who sold it to William Williams in the same year. In 1882, William Williams transferred it to Jesse Williams. On the 15th of August, 1908, Jesse and Amanda Williams sold ten acres to Isaac Updike. Howard McAnney bought the same ten acres on April 18, 1919. Howard McAnney apparently sold 2.16 acres to a man named Fiscus the same year. In 1920, Howard McAnney acquired another 5.12 acres of the original estate.

Orville McAnney acquired the property from his father in 1945, had his houseboat brought up from Zeagle's Ditch and set it up on this property as a summer cottage. Orville lived in Penns Grove at the time and worked for DuPont. Horace Somes, Jr. still remembers the old houseboat, hull and all, sitting near this old cold cellar. At some time, it, too, was torn apart and a mobile home moved onto the lot.

The estate was later sold to a man named Davis, and is currently owned by Mike Brown. The old cold cellar is still in existence in 1995.

Photograph by John Pearce

The Cold Cellar on the
Jesse Williams Homestead - 1995

Georgia (Cramer) Lutz

Georgia Cramer was the granddaughter of Captain Jesse Williams, whose homestead stood on Turtle Creek Road, and the great, great granddaughtrer of Captain John Leek of Wading River.

She was born in New Gretna at the site of the Great John Mathis Homestead on land now a part of Viking Yachts on the 22nd of October 1886. She was only fourteen when she began teaching school.

Georgia taught first in New Gretna, then in Wading River in 1907 at the little one-room schoolhouse on Turtle Creek Road. She then moved to the Pleasantville district, where she spent the next forty-six years.

Apparently, she visited the home of her grandfather many times over the years and was well-liked by everyone in Wading River.

According to Eleanor Yaeger, principal of the Leeds Avenue School where Georgia taught the fourth grade, she was a born teacher.

"Teaching was my whole life," she commented on her retirement. "I loved every one of the children I taught, and I hope some of them loved me." (Quoted in *The Beacon* for October 21, 1982 on her 96th birthday.)

After retirement in 1950, she moved to Tuckerton to live with her neice and nephew, Warren and Florence Cramer. During her lengthy career in Pleasantville, she was active in the Parent-Teacher Association, the Order of the Eastern Star, in which she served as Worthy Matron for two years, and was a member of Daughters of the American Revolution, Great John Mathis Chapter.

"Every day is a gift," she said on her 96th birthday. "The first 96 years were the easiest." Georgia died at her home on the 21st of December, 1982, at the age of ninety-six.

Courtesy of Horace Somes, Jr.

Georgia Cramer

Courtesy of Warren & Florence Cramer

Georgia Cramer and George Bamford

Courtesy of Horace Somes, Jr.

Georgia Cramer

Photographs courtesy of Horace Somes, Jr.

The Wading River Bridge

The first bridge to be constructed over a navigable portion of any of the area rivers was that over the Wading River. Built in 1814, the original bridge was completely made of wood and had a swing span over the channel on the eastern side of the river.

It lasted for a hundred years, with repairs of course, being replaced in the 1920s. Its successor was a narrow lift bridge, constructed mostly of wood, pilings, supports, and decking, with a steel guardrail and a steel lift.

This bridge was, in turn, replaced in the late 1980s by a new concrete and steel structure, although much of the wooden pilings and bulkheading of the approaches were retained.

This photograph seems to have been taken during the period when the swing bridge was dismantled.

Courtesy of Steve Eichinger

The First Wading River Bridge
Built in 1814 as a Swing Bridge

Dorothea McAnney on the old bridge - 1924

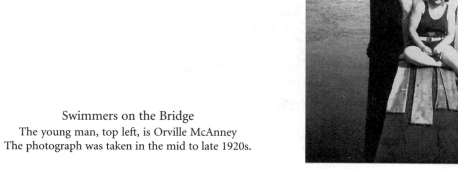

Swimmers on the Bridge
The young man, top left, is Orville McAnney
The photograph was taken in the mid to late 1920s.

Sketch of the old Swing Bridge
This sketch was commissioned by the Old Bridgeport Society for the
bicentennial of the United States in 1976.

The Second Wading River Bridge
The early swing bridge was replaced by this draw bridge about 1925.
The view is looking west towards the Washington Township side.

Captain "Gus" McKeen's Christmas Village of Wading River

The following information about Gus McKeen's village was taken from a newspaper article of unknown origin. Though some of the information given is inaccurate, it does present a verbal picture of Captain Gus's Wading River. The only peice of this marvelous work which is known to have survived the passage of years is the model of the McAnney house, now owned by Horace Somes, Jr. and his wife, Barbara.

Captain Gus McKeen, who in 1949 lived in Egg Harbor City, lovingly built a Christmas display that year in which he faithfully reproduced a model of the old town of Wading River almost completely from memory. Many years had passed since he was a youngster, but Captain Gus remembered the smallest details of the town of his birth: his old home, the little one-room schoolhouse, the grocery store, the park and picnic grounds, the bridge, the old tavern, the naked ribs of an old vessel sticking up through the water on the river bank, his father's schooner *Cora*, even a duck hunter shooting from his sneakbox surrounded by his decoys.

The old Chickeree Chapel, long ago fallen into the dust of the ages, surrounded by its cemetery, still stood in McKeen's model. Gus's great uncle, Thomas, had signed the Declaration of Independence, and Thomas's nephew, Kirk Loveland, had helped to build the Presbyterian chapel.

A stagecoach drawn by four horses waited infront of the old tavern. The stage, in Capt. Gus's memory, was driven by the father of Captain Jack Jones, a retired Coast Guard officer, who claimed it took six days to go from Tuckerton to Philadelphia.

The farm of the McKeen's neighbor, Captain William Cale, contained every detail imaginable: wheat, both freshly mowed and still standing in the field, watermelons, cabbages, tomatoes, and other crops in their fields, cordwood stacked and ready for the the winter, rail fences, laundry hanging on the clothesline, bird houses, cows and horses, even a hog hanging up after it had been killed next to the boiler and the other items necessary for its butchering.

Capt. Gus built the country store of his childhood as he remembered it. Storekeeper John F. McKeen had sold liquor by the pint, directly from a barrel for a yearly licence fee of $15.

Captain McKeen's grandfather had once owned over 22,000 acres in the vicinity of Wading River, and used the land to produce charcoal for the New York market. Gus himself had worked on the farm as a boy for $5 a month. He later went to sea with his father and also served as chief steward onboard ocean liners.

679

The Wading River Cornet Band

Wading River was proud of its cornet band, especially when it played in Philadelphia for the Centennial Celebration in 1876. Many of the men in the town were members:

1	Maja Leek	8	William Gale
2	Charles H. McAnney	9	Capt. George Valiant
3	Edward Sooy	10	James Gale
4	George Leek	11	John Maxwell
5	Levi Downs	12	Austin Downs, Sr.
6	Capt. Jesse Williams	13	Samuel Maxwell
7	Frank Downs		

These names should be old friends by now. Maja Leek lived in the Wading River Tavern. Charles McAnney would only have been a boy of twelve if the date of this picture is 1876 as it is presumed. He was born in his father James's house on Turtle Creek Road and later had homes on Cedar Lane. Ed Sooy ran the store on the Batsto-Bridgeport Road across from the Wading River Hotel. George Leek was probably Maja Leek's son, George Washington Leek III. Levi Downs lived on the corner of Turtle Creek Road and the Batsto-Bridgeport Road. Capt. Jesse Williams lived on Turtle Creek Road. Frank Downs lived on the Fountain Cramer property on Turtle Creek Road. William Gale was a schoolteacher who lived on Cedar Lane. James Gale may have been the brother of William Gale.

A note in the Wading River section of the Mount Holly *Herald* circa 1881-1883 recalls a wrenching incident in the life of this town band:

> *There is a sorrowful feeling in Bridgeport. The treasurer of the cornet band recently disappeared in the dead of night and all efforts to discover his whereabouts were futile. The first thing that was done rather shocked the feelings of a few. They commenced going over his accounts and soon discovered the cause of his flight. The amount of money he had in his possession at the time he left is not definitely known. His bondsmen feel very dubious and are confident that they will be called upon to make good the deficiency. The defaulter is well known throughout this section and his sudden departure has caused a genuine sensation.*

Though the culprit may have been well known in the 1880's, his name remains a mystery a century later.

The Wading River Methodist Church

Courtesy of Elton McAnney

A beautiful view of the old Wading River Methodist Church.
The two little girls are Mary McAnney on the left and
Dorothea McAnney (mother of Horace Somes, Jr. of Wading River)
on the right. The building is no longer in existence.

"There are only two lasting bequests we can hope to give our children
. . . one of these is roots; the other is wings." - Hodding Carter, 1907 - 1972

On the sixth of January, 1890, Sarah L. Leek, widow of Maja Leek, sold a sixty by seventy foot parcel of land on the north side of the main road (Route 542) in Wading River/Bridgeport to the trustees of a newly-organized Methodist Episcopal Church for the purpose of constructing a church building in the town. Sarah knew how things often were with church people and insisted in the Deed of Gift that the construction of the new building begin within three years or the property would revert to her or her family. She also stipulated that, if the building were destroyed by fire, the church trustees would have to rebuild it within five years or face the loss of their property. What she didn't envision in 1890 was the dereliction and collapse of the building due to neglect.

Her signature on the Deed of Gift was witnessed by two of the most eminent men of Washington Township at the time: Nathaniel D. Vansant, the son of the late minister of the Lower Bank and Green Bank churches and E. C. Sooy, Jr., the largest single property owner in the vicinity of Green Bank and a very religious man in his own right.

The trustees got to work immediately and, by November 8, 1890, they had completed a beautiful building which included an attractive bell tower. The first bell placed in the structure was made of South Jersey iron and cracked almost immediately. The second bell was more professionally manufactured and outlasted the building. It was a gift of the Rev. Christian Heineman.

This bell was supposed to have been the one which hung in the tower over the old paper mill at Harrisville, and the Rev. Heineman may have purchased it when Harrisville went bankrupt during the same year that the church was built.

James McAnney was one of the first trustees of the congregation, and Horace Somes, Jr.'s grandmother, Alice (Vincent) McAnney, wife of Howard McAnney, was the organist. Dorothy (McAnney) Somes also grew up playing the old reed organ. James McAnney, a veteran of the Civil War, delighted in "giving testimony" and preaching in this church, which he had helped to build.

Each Sunday, that bell would call the faithful of Bridgeport/Wading River to wor-

Courtesy of Elton McAnney

ship, its melodious song echoing down along the houses that lined Turtle Creek Road and reaching across the river to the other half of the community as well.

Church-sponsored picnics and socials provided a means for the social interaction so important to the community health of a small town. Whether or not a family was active in church affairs, everyone could enjoy the wonderful fellowship which the church supported.

Mrs. Estelle Peterson had organized a Sunday School in the town even before the church building was constructed. She was only fourteen years old when she started the first Sunday School in the old Quaker Meeting House on the Bass River side of the town, and she became the first teacher in the Sunday School which met in the new Methodist building. When the growth of the congregation and the youngsters attending classes warranted it, the trustees appointed Mrs. Peterson as Superintendent of the Sunday School, a post she held until she moved to Batsto in 1911.

The old building is remembered to have had a rather unique feature. It was heated by two potbellied stoves, one on each side of the nave. There was, however, only one chimney in the middle of the ridge. The chimney was split, and part ran down each side of the roof to the two stoves. These long and angled dual chimneys that merged into one were the cause of several chimney fires.

In March of 1980, Mildred Honaker thought back and tried to list the names of the ministers who served this congregation: Garrison, John Veal, Dempster, Towers, Joseph Horner, William B. Magsum, Louden, Alfred Burr, and John Cramer.

Parishioners gather outside of the Wading River Church after a service.
The date of this photograph is not known, but it is likely, given the ladies' dresses,
that they were taken in the first decade of the twentieth century

As the years passed, however, something happened to the community spirit which had always sustained both church and town. Old familiar faces were laid to rest in the Lower Bank cemetery and younger families moved elsewhere. The church reached its fiftieth anniversary, which was duly celebrated, but it would not see many more.

The Great Depression and World War II had left the Heart of the Pines desolate. There had been no industry in the area since the railroads had stolen the river traffic three-quarters of a century before. People had been able to get by on small farms and by fishing, hunting, logging, clamming, oystering, sphagnum moss and pinecone collecting, and cranberry culture.

After the Second World War, the fish no longer appeared in the Mullica, and the swamps were depleted of their giant white cedars. There was no demand for Sphangnum moss, and oysters were practically nonexistent. Most of the small farms had been abandoned and were fast growing over with scrub. The automobile and paved roads took people farther afield to find work which was no longer dependent on the land. Many of the old houses stood empty and gaunt, their broken windows allowing the elements to sweep through and destroy the interiors. One by one, fire gutted them, or they fell apart.

Wading River had been a vital and happy community at the turn of the century. By 1950, it was only a shadow of its former self. Some scions of old families still remained in the land they loved, but most moved away.

The Wading River Methodist Church, last of the Washington Township churches to be built, lay derelict. There had been an effort to have the Methodist Conference help restore it and appoint a minister, but they came to naught. Depression and World War had taken away its parishioners, and the remaining families would not afford to support it.

After years of weathering, the bell tower could no longer support the weight of its bell and collapsed. The old bell, once ringing the hours from the cupola of the main plant at Harrisville, now lay on the debris-strewn floor of the Wading River church. One of the Groffs hauled it to the home of Alice Adams Weber across the Wading River. Zeke Forman of Green Bank later had it moved to that town for use in the Green Bank Methodist Church, but the old bell was never to be installed there either. Zeke also brought the reed organ to the Green Bank Church where it remains to this day.

Henry Charlton Beck led a bit of a rescue mission of his own. He was serving as a summer priest at St. Peters at the Light in Barnegat Light and had been familiar with the old Wading River Church for decades. He saw to it that at least some of the pews were transported to the old building on Long Beach Island that housed the congregation of St. Peters. This was recently confirmed to this author by Canon Gilbert Martin, currently vicar of St. Peters, who was the rector of Holy Innocents' Church in Beach Haven at the time. It was Father Martin who had called the attention of St. Peter's to the availability of the pews at Wading River and had urged Father Beck to make the arrangements. What was left of this well-loved church, built with so much hope, was torn down and carted away in 1959.

"The old church was a grand meeting place for all the people of the village. I can remember Uncle Jimmy [McAnney], as we used to call him. He was a good preacher...we owe the McAnneys a great deal in our Christian growth." (Mildred Honaker, January 1, 1980).

"The old church had her day, and I think all of us have memories that will not let her be forgotten," wrote Mildred Honaker on December 14, 1978. "The Quakers tried it and the Presbyterians, also the Methodist. It looks like it wasn't in the plan of things. But we can always hope for a greater tomorrow."

The following is taken from an actual church bulletin from the dates given
that was saved by Dorothy (McAnney) Somes.

"THE HEART WARMING CHURCH"
WADING RIVER M.E. CHURCH
WADING RIVER, N.J.

A Weekly Church Bulletin
Take it home with you and give it to your friends

SUNDAY WORSHIP
1:30 P.M.

Prelude
Hymn
Prayer
Psalter
New Testament Lesson
Announcements and Offerings
Hymn
Sermon
Hymn
Benediction

EPWORTH LEAGUE 6:45 P.M

PRAYER SERVICE
7:30 P.M. Thursday

A good wholesome song service
Preaching at 8:00
Testimonial Meeting
Voluntary Prayers
Benediction

If you want to be helped nearer to God come to prayer meeting. It is a long step
from Sunday to Sunday

TRUSTEES

Howard McAnney   Treasurer
Levi Downs
Ella Downs
Wm. Maxwell
Geo. Maxwell

                                    Stewards

Howard McAnney
Alice McAnney   Communion
Geo. Maxwell
Wm. Gale
Mary Peterson
Ruth Updike   Secretary and Treasurer
James Updike

December 1926 - January 1927
Courtesy of Horace Somes, Jr.

The Wading River Church lies forlorn and forsaken about 1950.

Her bell had fallen in and her windows were broken. There are few things more sad than an abandoned church that once vibrated with the sound of hymns sung with spirit by loving parishioners now silent and cold. Preachers and people alike have entered into glory beyond the touch of such decay, but their beloved church stands unneeded and unloved by a new generation.

The Rev. Henry Charlton Beck
Wading River - 1950

Courtesy of John Milton Adams, Jr.

Silent and Abandoned
The Old Harrisville/Wading River Bell
c. 1950

The Wading River School

Courtesy of Horace Somes, Jr., and the Super Bros.

The School - circa 1915

In this little, one-room schoolhouse, the children of Bridgeport/Wading River received their education in the "3 R's" for a great many years. According to a note from Mildred Honaker to Dorothy Somes in March of 1980, the building is not the first to have been built for this purpose at this spot.

> *"The first school was built by Grandfather Maxwell and Uncle George . . . in that same grove of trees. It had <u>two rooms</u> and was taught by Miss Mary Griffen. She lived in the back room."*

Mrs. Honaker noted that, in those days, taxes for educating children were not levied on all property owners, but families with children paid a "head tax" on each child to pay for their instruction. Mary Griffin was a retired missionary, and her reputation for being a very wonderful woman was remembered for many years.

Courtesy of Horace Somes, Jr., and the Super Bros.

View of the School from Cedar Lane
The road that runs in front of the school is
Turtle Creek Road.

> *"She died at our place before I was born,"* writes Mrs. Honaker, *"but I used to play with one of the dolls she made for grandma's children. She lived for several years in the little one-room house Grandfather Maxwell built for her on our*

back lot. It later became our summer kitchen. She came from a very notable family. Her nephews were famous Philadelphia surgeons."

The first mention of taxes collected in the township for schools is listed in the record of the town meeting for March 9, 1830, when the sum of fifty dollars was approved to "educate the poor children in the year." During the early nineteenth century, the township tax for roads varied from a low of $100 to a high of $500 annually. In this year when $50 was collected for the education of poor children, $400 was raised for work on the roads. No mention is made of a "head tax," but one was collected until free public education became a reality in New Jersey beginning in 1847.

Mary Griffin's name is first mentioned on a balance sheet report the year Thomas H. Richards replaced his father, Jesse, as Town Superintendent of Schools. Mary was paid $36.40 on the 16th of September, 1854. Richards reports that a balance of $31.74 was on hand for School No. 7 (Bridgeport/Wading River) as of March 14, 1855.

The old two-room school building was replaced by the building pictured sometime in the last half of the nineteenth century. It was in this

Courtesy of Horace Somes, Jr.

Georgia Cramer

building that Georgia Cramer, a local girl from New Gretna, taught the children of Bridgeport/Wading River in 1907.

The last year for the little schools of Washington Township was 1919. A new "central" school was built in Green Bank for all the children of the township, and the little local schools were consolidated in one town. Children were then bussed to school, and the one-room schoolhouses became superfluous. A man by the name of Ben Parsons bought the old school building and added porches and a machine shop. Parsons had been the foreman for Sun Shipbuiding Company. He had one son, Ben, Jr. After Ben Parsons, the building was owned by William MacDonald, head ranger at the Bass River State Forest through the mid-1960s.

The building remains basically the same in 1995 as it did after Ben Parsons made his additions. The old school pushes its way through enclosed porches and additions as though trying still to maintain its dowager dignity despite the abuse of time. Nicholas and Laverne Waters are the owners in 1995.

One of the truly fun days in the year was spent in the schoolhouse grove. Sponsored each year by the local churches, young and old would come for a day of excitement

Photograph by John Pearce

The Wading River School in 1995

Courtesy of Horace Somes, Jr.

Ben Parsons

and enjoyment. They would come by the wagon-loads for the afternoon and evening festivities. There were games for everyone. Music was provided (each town had its own band), and everyone would join in the singing. The church groups provided refreshments, including candy and root beer. Oyster suppers, cakes, pies, and popcorn were sold in great quantities.

These happy annual picnics are no more. The Wading River Methodist Church no longer exists to host them, and the churches in Lower Bank and Green Bank barely have enough people on a Sunday morning to keep the doors open. It's sad that so much happiness is only a memory for the older people of a more innocent time.

Courtesy of Horace Somes, Jr.

The Children of the Wading River School - 1915

The teacher in 1915 was a "Miss Weeks" whom students remembered for years as having only one arm. Her right arm had been amputated at the elbow. That did not seem to alter her effectiveness, however. Orville McAnney recollected that she could get the attention of an unruly student using a quick jab with the hard stub of her amputated arm.

Front Row: Orville McAnney, Kenneth Bozarth, Isaac Maxwell, Elsie McAnney, Lemuel Maxwell, Susie Maxwell, Unknown
Middle Row: Miss Weeks (teacher), Elizabeth Maxwell, Allie Lippincott, Mary McAnney, Beatrice McAnney, Myrtle Lippincott, Glada Downs
Back Row: Stanley Downs, Wilbur Lippincott, Matthew Maxwell, Charles Lippencott, Lewis Maxwell

Half Moon/Chip's Folly

Courtesy of Horace Somes, Jr.

Aerial View of Half Moon/Chip's Folly - circa 1976.

Imagine you are standing beside a pinelands river, looking out over a huge cove of wild rice. The day is warm but not hot. The season verges on autumn. A gentle breeze gently caresses your face as your gaze hovers over a view that has changed little over the last three hundred years. A flock of Canada geese honks overhead as its "V" formation points south for the coming winter. Soon after, wild ducks fly low over the brown waters. They seem so close you could just reach out and touch their beauty. In the shallows not far upstream, the gentle Great Blue Heron pauses in its stately passage, its eyes staring into the waters as if transfixed. If it were not for a couple of power boats anchored out near the channel, you would think you'd been transported back to a more pristine time in some wonderful dream of paradisial perfection.

This is Chip's Folly, a strange name for Elysium, but not the less ambrosial. This special spot on the east side of the Wading River is a trailer park today, but that makes it no less beautiful. Owned and maintained by the Ludwig family for three generations, access is limited to paying guests, but for those who spend their summers and weekends here, it must be a welcome relief from the congestion of the cities.

The old name for the area is Half Moon. Steve Eichinger and Horace Somes, Jr. said that the name came from the huge bend in the river at that point which resembled a half moon. Yet in this century, the name never seems to have been used by those who owned the land. "Half Moon" was what the locals called it. Long months went by, and I never particularly thought about Half Moon. Then I picked up Charles S. Boyer's *Old Inns and Taverns in West Jersey*. Boyer had noted the references in the *Martha Diary* which mentioned the Half Moon Tavern.

According to the *Martha Diary*, the workers used to frequent local taverns much too regularly to suit good, old Jesse Evans. A couple of miles was no distance to walk at all when your throat was parched, and you longed for a relaxing drink of rum to wash away the aches and pains of a hard day's work. There in the diary stand the names: Sooy's, Bodine's, and . . . Half Moon.

690

Charles S. Boyer knew exactly where Sooy's Inn and Bodine's Inn were located, but the only "Half Moon" he could identify was over in the Flyat area, north of Indian Mills and two and a half miles west of Tabernacle. Henry Bisbee (*Sign Posts* and *Martha: The Complete Furnace Diary*) followed Boyer in making the same identification.

Oct. 30, 1808	*John Cumming gone to the Half Moon*
April 23, 1810	*Pat'k Hambelton drunk at Moon*
May 25, 1812	*James M'Entire bro't home his Daughter from the half Moon for fear her Morals would be corrupted*
Aug. 8, 1813	*McEntire at the half Moon drinking whiskey*

I had read these entries in Bisbee's full copy of the diary long before I encountered Boyer, but the name had meant nothing at the time. When I read them in Boyer, the thought struck me: *how far* did they go just to get a drink? I made a mental note to ask Budd Wilson if he had ever encountered a "Half Moon" a bit closer to Martha. Neither of these otherwise astute men ever seemed to question just how long it would take a man from Martha Furnace to walk or ride all the way to Flyat. Then again, they must have had quite a drunk, passing Sooy's, Bodine's, Quaker Bridge, and probably other taverns on their day-long trip just to get a drink!

Yet that was how lost in the pines was the knowledge of the old Half Moon Tavern, which sat just about four miles down the road from Martha, almost the same distance as it was from the old iron town to Sooy's Inn. Not long after reading this passage from Boyer, I met Budd haunting the Green Bank cemetery.

"Hey, Budd," I yelled out. "I need to ask you something."

When Budd got over to where I was waiting, I was just about to open my mouth when he said, "I just remembered something that I want to tell you. A long time ago, Alice Adams Weber took me up the Chip's Folly Road and pointed out a depression near an old buttonwood tree, saying that was the location of the Half Moon Tavern."

I was floored! Budd and I had never talked about the Half Moon Tavern before, to my knowledge.

I started to laugh and said, "You won't believe it but that's exactly the question I wanted to ask you!"

That was on a Sunday. On Monday morning, I opened my mail to find a note from Lois Ann Kirby, former editor of the Batsto Citizens Gazette, relating information on the Birdsall family which I'd requested from her. Along with it was a copy of an article written by Henry Charlton Beck back in the 1930's about, of all things, the Half Moon Tavern. Two elderly local men had taken him up the original road to Harrisville that ran along the river and showed *him* the location of the Half Moon Tavern. He gave almost no information on the old inn and quickly shifted the subject to the McKeen Tavern in Wading River, but there it was. Once again, completely out of the blue, came the Half Moon Tavern.

Later in the week, I met Steve Eichinger, Alice Adams Weber's nephew, for a visit to Chip's Folly, and, of course, I asked him about Half Moon. Yes, he said. He remembered his aunt taking him up the Chip's Folly road years ago and pointing out a huge catalpa tree as the site of the tavern. "Catalpa?" I inquired, and told him about Budd Wilson's memory of a buttonwood tree.

"Catalpa . . . buttonwood . . . yeh, it could have been. I don't know. It was a long time ago."

We didn't find the tree, but we found a house depression right near the gates of Chip's Folly on the old Harrisville Road. Was this the site of the old Half Moon Tavern? Beck's informants had said that there was a small village there, but we only found one depression. Perhaps. One thing is sure. James McEntire did not have to go all the way to Flyat to save the morals of his daughter. The Half Moon Tavern frequented by the workers at Martha Furnace was surely *not* in Flyat. It was right here on the Martha-Wading River Road.

Back before the turn of this century, a group of businessmen organized a hunting club and purchased land on the east bank of the Wading River near the site of the old Half Moon Tavern. Calling their club the Riverside Game Association, these gentlemen hunters enjoyed themselves amongst the profusion of wild birds and deer that frequented the Wading River valley.

The land was ideally designed to enable wealthy businessmen from Camden and Philadelphia to get away from the grind of the city and enjoy a bit of relaxation in the Pine Barrens of New Jersey. Their club house was an old building that had stood on the property for many years prior to their coming. Now comes the joke on both Steve Eichinger and myself. Read "Jack and Jill by the River" which is included in this section. Alice Adams Weber says that the first club house of the Riverside Game Association stood on the old road (the Mail Stage road) across from the Joseph Gail (probably "Gale") place. Clearly, we had discovered the foundations of the Gail house and surmised the tavern stood across the road. This was indeed the site which Alice Weber and Beck's informants had pointed out as that of the old Half Moon Tavern. The first club house and the tavern building were one and the same.

Courtesy of Steve Eichinger

"In the Good Old Days"

The club house in the photograph was originally the Half Moon Tavern and it burned to the ground soon after this photograph was taken in 1901. #1 is John Zurn; #9 is Harry Adams, Steve Eichinger's grandfather.

One of these turn-of-the-century members of the Riverside Game Association was John Zurn. John M. Zurn was president of the O. F. Zurn Company, an oil company based in Philadelphia. Born in the City of Brotherly Love in 1866, Zurn was one of the founders of the Quaker City Chemical Company of Philadelphia, Pennsylvania and Knoxville, Tennessee. He was also the treasurer of the Quaker City Chemical Company of Canada, Ltd. which was headquartered at Hamilton, Ontario. Zurn moved in all the right circles amongst the elite of the East Coast and joined in all the recreational pursuits so popular at the time, including his chief passion, yacht racing.

When John Zurn posed with other members of the hunting club in front of their old club house in the pines, the year was 1901. Harry Adams, Steve Eichinger's grandfather, worked for the club as a guide. It was in that very year when that original club house, the old Half Moon Tavern, burned to the ground. In the spring of 1902, Zurn proceeded to build a new one close by the river on a commanding hill with a beautiful vista of the wild rice. The building is still in existence today, but it is not used very much. Scout groups use it for weekend camping trips, and hunters still frequent it during the Fall hunting season, but it has sadly deteriorated over the years from the fine "hunting lodge" it once was.

Zurn's Club House was, and is still, a two story building completely paneled in tongue-and-groove boards. It has two rooms that enter off the porch facing the river and several rooms upstairs of varying sizes for the guests. One of those rooms appears to have had closet space for seven in numbered cabinets. Other rooms are set up for three or two people. A commercial kitchen dominates the rear of the first floor, and another room was subdivided by the building of a hall and

Courtesy of Horace Somes, Jr.

John M. Zurn
Circa 1929

bathroom. The single upstairs bathroom seems to have been added after the building was built. I suppose, Zurn soon found that outhouses were not as attractive to wealthy businessmen as they once had been. They may have wanted "rustic" but not *that* rustic! They were, after all, *gentlemen*!

In 1910, the land taxed included 640 acres and a dwelling. In 1911, only 540 acres seems to appear. In 1912, the "Bennett Tract" of 100 acres is included with the 540 acres and house. Apparently, this 100 acres was not treated as a separate parcel in 1910.

An item in the Mount Holly *Herald* for December 10, 1904 says that "the Wading River Realty Company, a Newark Corporation, has just purchased of Miss Hattie Kauffman, a tract of 2,200 acres of land in Bass River Township. It cannot be ascertained what they are going to do with the property." What this Newark company had to do with John Zurn is not known, nor does the name of the Wading River Realty Company appear on the tax records of the period. The same edition of the newspaper mentioned that "The Riverside Game Association owns 660 acres of land in Bass River Township and has a handsome club house. To avoid the state license demanded of non-reisdents, a portion of the property has been transferred to members." There seems to have been no apparent connection between the two corporations at this time.

Thanks to Steve Eichinger's painstaking research in the Bass River Township tax records, we know that, in 1917, the Wading River Realty Company is listed on the tax records *in place of* the Riverside Game Association as owners of this same 640 acres. Its address was given as 2740 North Broad Street, Philadelphia. John Zurn was president and Charles S. King of Camden was secretary.

Courtesy of Steve Eichinger

The Riverside Game Association Club House: Formerly the Half Moon Tavern

The tavern stood on the old Bridgeport-Harrisville Road across from the Joseph Gail place. It was that very tavern building that was used by the Riverside Game Association as their first club house. It burned in 1901, apparently soon after the above photograph was taken, and John Zurn built the new club house by the river the following spring. Thanks, Alice! When we look at the building in the above photograph, we really are seeing the long elusive Half Moon Tavern, where "James M'Entire bro't home his Daughter from the half Moon for fear her Morals would be corrupted."

Bass River Township tax bills from that year indicate that the Wading River Realty Company was billed for a dwelling, an icehouse, a sunhouse, a garage, a barn, a shed, and 540 acres of land. John Zurn and Joseph L. Sweigard were billed at Broad and Lehigh Avenue in Philadelphia for a boathouse, two high-power launches, as well as other boats and accessories. Thus it seems that the several parcels of land owned by the Riverside Game Association were assumed by the Wading River Realty Company, now headed by John Zurn, and it has become a Philadelphia corporation rather than a Newark-based entity. No further mention is made in the tax records of the original 2,200 acres purchased by the company in 1904.

In 1921, the "George Townsend Tract" of 96 acres appears. The *total* acreage, however, doesn't seem to change very much. According to the 1836 map of Martha, a George Townsend had a house in the area at the time, possibly the Half Moon Tavern. In 1923, John Zurn is listed as having meadows at Broad Creek, managed by W. Roy Mathis, in addition to the other properties. In 1925, Zurn is taxed for 656 acres and a bungalow appears. The total acreage taxed is now 934 3/4 acres.

The actual organization running the "camp" was the Wading River Game Association. As the envelope engraving below indicates, Charles King is secretary, and the address given is one in Camden. Perhaps the Wading River Game Association and the Wading River Realty were organized seperately for legal or tax reasons, even though the same men served as officers in each.

It must have been a real pleasure for city dwellers to find a refuge in the pines from summer's heat and the hectic pace of business in a major metropolitan center. Here beside the Wading River, they could relax amongst friends and associates or simply enjoy a few days of tranquility with their wives. When the air turned cold, a weekend of hunting in the "wilderness" was just the thing to make them feel revitalized. The nearest railroad station was miles away, either in Hammonton, Elwood, or perhaps Harris Station, Chatsworth, or Tuckerton, and the trip out to the Wading River would have made them tired and dusty. If they drove out from Camden and Philadelphia, the rutted sand roads must have made a nightmare out of the better part of a day. But when they got here! Ah, they could bask in the same beauty that persists today.

During the teens and twenties, Zurn dammed three tributaries of the river to form three small lakes. He even interconnected the lakes with canals so that more water flowed to the one nearest the Club House. Though

WADING RIVER GAME ASSOCIATION, INC.
WADING RIVER, N. J.

———

CHARLES S. KING, SECRETARY
225 MARKET STREET   CAMDEN, N. J.

An Envelope Engraving of the new Club House
built by John Zurn and what was called the Riverside Game Association at the time.

The Wading River Game Association Dock

Proud Hunters!
On the left is John Zurn, the owner of the Wading River Game Association, alias "Half Moon."
On the right is Harry Adams, Steve Eichinger's grandfather.
They are standing in front of the new Club House.

picturesque, they were highly practical. Despite the nearness of the river, the first club house had burned because there was no way to get water onto the fire. Zurn had a ram pump installed to run a generator. He also built a windmill which pumped water into a large tank in the attic of the Club House. In 1925, he had Ben Broome build a bungalow on the property, and Zurn added a swimming pool nearby the following year.

One of the unique features of Zurn's Wading River Game Association was a huge, two-story floating barge. The autumn may have been reserved for the men and their hunting, but the summers were enjoyed with the ladies present. Realizing that the heat of the pinelands could be overwhelming, he built a screened barge so that his "guests" could loll away the hot afternoon hours, anchored leisurely out in the center of the river where they could enjoy the breezes off the water. Horace Somes, Jr.'s grandfather, Howard McAnney, cooked for John Zurn both in the kitchen of the Club House and on board the barge. Steve Eichinger's grandmother, Martha Adams, also worked as cook at "Half Moon," and Harry Adams worked as a laborer/carpenter. Roy Mathis acted as a hunting guide.

When John Zurn died in 1929, his "playground for the rich and famous" ceased to be an attraction for that class. The stock market crash deprived Half Moon's wealthy clients of their resources, and few had the cash to take holidays in the woods any more. Taxes on the property continued to be paid by his estate, in care of the O.F. Zurn Company in Phildelphia or Charles King through 1937. It was sold to Alfred W. Lasher, 1110 Park Avenue, New York City, for $100.00 on May 14, 1937. The sale included all tools, equipment for water and electrical light plants, furniture, furnishings, kitchen utensils, bedding, cutlery, and glassware in the bungalow and Club House and tools in and around the tool house and garage.

Steve Eichinger, who was a boy at the time, remembers that Mr. Lasher was known for arriving from the city in a fancy car and a couple of exceedingly beautiful women in tow. He kept a car and a yacht stored at his new retreat and made the most of them on the weekends. If the times had been as idyllic as they had seemed in the 1920's, the local people would simply have chuckled at the antics of another city slicker who had more money than brains. Unfortunately, the 1930's had an entirely different - and much darker - character.

These were the exciting and frightening days when the European continent was in turmoil and America was engulfed in Depression. Germany had been hit with financial disaster and humiliation after World War One, and

Courtesy of Steve Eichinger

Club Members of the Wading River Game Association
No one in this photograph has been identified, nor is the date known, but it was certainly prior to John Zurn's death. The building behind the people is the Zurn-built Club House.

The Half Moon Barge
The wealthy "campers" at Zurn's Wading River Game Association spent many a leisurely hour
on the Wading River when the summer's heat over whelmed them on shore.
Howard McAnney, who served as cook aboard the vessel, stands proudly at the bow.

Another View of the Half Moon Barge

the chaotic situation was crying for a savior. The German people seemed to have found him in the person of an Austrian with a comical little mustache who certainly had mastered the German language and knew how to inspire people. Little did they realize that his strong-hand tactics were only the beginning of new tragedies that would eventually devour the entire world.

During the 1930's and '40's, Half Moon seems to have been surrounded by intrigue and dark secrets, at least in the minds of some of the local people. These were the heady years when all of Europe was caught up in the drama of Hitler's rise to power in Nazi Germany. Many Americans, especially those of German origin, were happy to see their native county rebuild itself and proudly take its place amongst the nations of the world once again. Hitler's rise to power seemed brutal to some, but great crowds cheered his inspiring speeches and rejoiced that Germany was being rebuilt after the devastation of World War One. When he did finally achieve the chancellorship, he set about rebuilding Germany's industry almost overnight. Hitler's rebuilding program seemed, at least from a distance, to be achieving miracles, and German-Americans, shamed and abused by their neighbors during the Great War, were delighted in his achievements.

When war broke out in Europe, some German-Americans sided with their homeland, though the vast majority supported their new country. Once again, though, people were suspicious. Small villages were adept at isolating those who were different from the majority, and many Americans of German extraction had their homes or barns burned by their neighbors out of fear and distrust.

Their fears were not completely without foundation. Some German-Americans founded support groups called "Bunds" to further the interests of their fatherland in Europe, and many prominent Americans spoke favorably of Hitler. Charles A. Lindburgh was a fan. So was Ambassador to the Court of St. James, Joseph Kennedy. The pinelands were not free from rumors of such machinations. Their relative obscurity was a boon to those who schemed and plotted. German-Americans really had no idea what was actually going on in Germany. They only knew they were supporting their families and friends.

Local people were always looking for juicy gossip, and the German background of the new owner of Half Moon was fuel for the fire. His actions were looked on with suspicion. Remember that bevy of beautiful women he brought with him from New York each summer weekend? People in Bridgeport/Wading River would catch a glimpse of Lasher and his girls as their yacht passed through the Wading River drawbridge on its way to the sea. Quite visible were crates labelled "Freihoffers Bakery" in the stern cockpit. When they returned to Half Moon through the bridge which Alice Adams Weber had opened for them, the crates were nowhere to be seen. That was sufficient to arouse suspicion and encourage rumor.

Those journeys started the people talking. There must have been more than met the eye in those crates marked "Freihoffer's." German submarines were known to patrol off shore long before actual war broke out between America and the Axis powers.

Perhaps . . .

There was the time that a ten year-old local boy was standing on the Wading River bridge near sundown. A small boat came up river containing two men that the boy didn't know. Voices carry quite a way over water, and the men didn't notice the boy on the bridge as they motored quietly upstream. The boy could hear their "German" quite distinctly, despite the fact that they tried to keep their voices low. They were startled when they finally saw someone on the bridge and stopped the engine - and their talking. They allowed the ebbing tide to carry them back downstream until the growing dusk hid them from view. Were they heading for Half Moon? Were they really German spies? Ah, what dreams must have filled a young boy's mind!

A German Bund along the Wading? Who knows! Probably the "memories" were just the products of a young and fertile imagination, yet, we, too, are caught up in the excitement of the possibility of deception and deceit on the dark waters that flowed amongst the lonely pines. It certainly makes a good story, though it doesn't much matter in this day and age. We've made friends of old enemies and found new enemies to excite the dull times.

The Bungalow at Half Moon - built in 1925

Another German-American couple came to Half Moon during those years. Paul and Elsie Ludwig arrived to act as caretakers for the Lasher estate. Paul Ludwig II says he thought they came around 1933, but Steve Eichinger thinks it was a bit later than that. A 1933 date would mean that they came before the property was sold to Mr. Lasher. Steve remembers when the senior Paul's son, Werner, started school with him about 1939 or 1940. Both boys were about five years old at the time.

Martina and Steve Eichinger, our Steve's parents, were very friendly with the Ludwigs, but some of the local people entwined them in the rumors as well. No one was free from suspicion in those days. Paul Ludwig, grandson of the first Paul, told us that a small, Mediterranean-style villa used to stand overlooking the river at Half Moon. On one dark night, it caught fire and burned to the ground. The Ludwigs heard that local people burned it down. Bridgeporters whispered that "others" had burned it so that its secrets would remain hidden from prying eyes. This is the stuff of which legends are made!

The reality seems to be that the structure in question, according to the tax records, was not a "villa" but the "round house," whatever that was, that actually burned in 1931. A huge fire was sweeping across the pinelands at that time, and the owner of the Maja Leek bogs on the western side of the river set a backfire to protect his property. It did that, but this fire got out of control, leaped the river, and burned all the way to West Creek. In the process, it destroyed part of the Wading River Realty Company's property, including the "round house." So, yes, you could say that "local people" burned it down, but the fire had nothing whatsoever to do with German sympathizers. Yet even something as common as fire in the pines became sinister and the source of rumor and innuendo as the years passed.

On December 1, 1945, Paul and Elsa Ludwig bought the property from Alfred and Isabelle Lasher for $7,000, subject to an existing mineral rights lease with Shell Oil Company. Ludwig was to share any future profits from the lease with Lasher on a fifty-fifty basis. For several years, the Ludwigs used the land to raise all kinds of pheasants, especially silver and golden pheasants, as well as specialty chickens. When the camping industry started to grow in the 1950's, they renamed their property "Chip's Folly" and set up a campground. The Paul Ludwig, who now manages Chip's Folly, is the son of Werner and grandson of Paul and Elsie Ludwig. He thought that the name came from his father's nickname, Chip, but Steve Eichinger remembers the children at school calling Werner by his given name.

Photograph by John Pearce
Paul Ludwig II and Steve Eichinger - 1997
They are standing in front of the "New" Club House,
built by John Zurn in 1902.

He didn't gain the nickname "Chip" until his teen years, and then the Egg Harbor boys called him that because he came from Chip's Folly. So we still don't know the origin of the name. The "folly" part is easy to understand. In the postwar era, no one could imagine the profitability of a campground in the pines, but Chip's Folly still goes on.

Where once the wealthy friends of John Zurn had enjoyed the "cool" pre-air conditioning breezes of the Wading, now the slightly less rich and famous set up tents and trailers for the same purpose. On the day Steve Eichinger and I journeyed to the Folly, Paul acted as our guide for six and a half hours! It was the first time that Steve had been to the area since he was fourteen years old. All three of us had a great time. Paul was a gracious host, and meeting his wife and daughter at the end of the day was a delightful treat.

The Club House of John Zurn - 1997

The Bungalow - 1997

Looking north (above) and south (below) across the Half Moon cove.

Black and white just does not do justice to these photographs by the author. Just imagine the carpet of wild rice in the foregrounds of both pictures as a beautiful and shining russet gold with a cerulean sky and cobalt blue water in the foreground. Absolutely gorgeous!

The Boat Docks at the Bridge

Courtesy of Horace Somes, Jr.

The Boat Dock at the Wading River Bridge

Courtesy of Horace Somes, Jr.

Boat Launching on the Wading River

Boat at Leek's Landing - Wading River
Bridge - YMCA Boys were brought
from Atlantic City for outing at Harrisville. About 1912.

Both photographs courtesy of
Horace Somes, Jr.

The following article was written by Alice Adams Weber in 1958 and is presented here as a voice from the past, courtesy of her nephew, Steve Eichinger. Many of the places mentioned will be familiar to the reader by now, and the people she talks about will be old friends, not strangers.

Jack and Jill By The River
By Alice Weber
Old Bridgeport, Jan. 16 , 1958

When Pat and I were quite young, to us the world was big and we thought we were much older. The first Christmas I remember, Uncle Dick and Aunt Mell came home for Christmas. They lived in Atlantic City and they trimmed Christmas trees for all the nieces and nephews in the family. Uncle Dick made a beautiful garden under the tree and made a pond with swans and little men and little lead boats. Of course my brother and I had to take the little lead men and boats out in the middle of the room, on the floor and play. Uncle Dick, a big, tall man, not watching his step, our little men and boats were flat and that was the sad end of them.

Our sister, Nora, the oldest, had died with Diptheria. I could just remember her. We had a play house around the old picket fence. I was 3 and 1/2 years old when she died. We all had Diptheria, but mother. Daddy nearly died with it. Pat ran around with it, and I was in bed. Dr. Duncan was our doctor. I still remember the pretty little pink pills in little bottles in his satchel, how I wanted them. I thought they were so pretty.

Then the next summer, mother went to a picnic at Fred Miners. Late in the afternoon, Daddy took us to get mother. This was the first time we had ever seen a wind mill. It must have been at Lower Bank. Capt. Jesse Cavileeer had one and Mom Weaver had one at Weekstown. We had Fred Horse. He was so pretty and very fast. Daddy had a rubber tired wagon, no top.

Then, another trip was Memorial Day, over to the old church by the cemetery. They had lunch under the big oak by the church. It had seats made out of planks. The Reverend N. VanSant spoke. I remember the lunch was boiled ham, potato salad and a banana on wooden plates. I remember Aunt Emma and Uncle Charlie Robbins were there. I wore a little white lacy hat, all trimmed across the crown with old rose baby ribbon. I loved that little hat. I thought I was so big. Pat and I played around the river. Jim Kelly fished Pat out of the deep water once, I don't remember that.

The summer of 1901, Daddy was on the fish steamer. Pat and I would go with him on Sunday afternoon and take him to Bass River at the dock to the steamer. There we had old Topsy. Fred horse was dead. Topsy was the mule and daddy turned her around, then she brought us home. Pat did the driving.

We had a bad storm in Fall of 1901, in September. The dam at Harrisville broke. The tide was over the bridge. They rode to Ed Sooy's store, also the postoffice to get the mail.

Then we had our cow, Naby. Daddy pastured her with the Updikes. They charged a $ a head for the Summer. Nearly everybody in the place put theirs out there. During the storm Naby drowned. She was soon to have her calf. Sam Maxwell had two yearlings that drown. Uncle Billy Maxwell was way up in his eighties. He walked down to the meadows to see what had happened to Naby. She was near a ditch and caught her nose in the barbed wire fence. The tide come up over her. The yearlings died the same way, so Jack and Jill had to do with less milk.

The two master ships used to sail in and bring loads of shells to make lime for the fields. They used some shells on the roads. Some of the ships carted pine cordwood. There used to be so many rows of cordwood along the river, that we played on it. They took a lot from the Goldecker landing. One ship had a negro crew. Nights they used sing after their work was done, it sounded so nice. When they dumped the shells, we used to get pretty shells and found so many little sea horses.

As we grew older, they had the one masted boats. The baymen sailed to the bay. There used be from 8 to 12 boats below the bridge anchored on weekends. They stocked up Mondays and sailed to the bay and returned on Friday. In their time, they used bring in mussels in the spring of the year. Farmers broadcast them on the corn fields and potato patches. Judge French used to have his boat brought in at Leeds Point. He put the mussels around his fruit trees in his orchard.

Around 1901, we saw our first automobile. It was like a Fall Top and had rubber tires on wagon wheels. They had to push it up the hill from the bridge up to the house. It belonged to George Gossler who had the Wading River Cranberry Bogs. The road there was a two rut road. In the spring of 1902, they widened and graveled the road from Bass River to Atsion Creek.

March 30th my mother had twin boys, one born dead. My nose was cut off . I no longer was the baby. There were no girls around on this side of the river, so I was a Tom Boy.

It was late in the Fall of 1901 when Fred horse got hurt. Daddy was working on the bogs with Fred and Topsy. She jumped and upset the wagon off of the dam and it threw Fred on his back and broke it so badly, that they had to put him out of his misery. Fred was buried by the ridge road near the sand hole. Eva Leek, was older than I. We picked flowers a lot of time and put them on Fred's grave. I used to play at Eva's. You had to pass her home to go to the bogs and the old ridge road.

In the Spring of 1902, they built the Clubhouse. It was sometimes called John Zurn's Clubhouse. They were members of well-to-do families of Philadelphia. The first Clubhouse was on the old main road to Harrisville, just across the road from the site of the old Joseph Gail place. At that time, some of the foundation was there and a large buttonwood tree. Waricks lived for awhile as caretakers for the first Clubhouse. Then Ed Wolf was caretaker and it burned down. Ed and his wife Bertha came and stayed with my parents until they built the Clubhouse that's still standing today 1902 - 1968. It's built out along the river of the old Wading River Game Assn. They had a wide walkway built through the Half-Moon Swamp to the river. The river is very wide and at one time was called Christians Bay. Half-Moon today [is called] Broad Place. In the 20's it was noted for the best duck shooting blind on the Wading River and still is. It has such good feed. John Zurn had wild rice planted in the teens. It's quite heavy every year and spread all along the river for some distance.

Daddy took me up in the new clubhouse when they were building it. I was so afraid I would fall. There was just the stairway and studding. Pat and I had our pictures taken in the field of the Old Wading River Assn. One of the members, Henry Homes, took them. My sister has a picture of that clubhouse of my Daddy, Fred and Topsy and some members in the open wagon, going on a hunting party to old Harrisville. Then in 1913, my Daddy was janitor for the new clubhouse for 3 years.

Our Sunday School teacher, Estella Peterson, named us Jack and Jill. When we were little we were always together. We all walked to Sunday School, young and old and to evening service. There was quite a crowd and they used to kick up the dust. There were lots of mosquitoes. There was Stella and Lizzie, Frank and his wife Lizzie and Billy G. Cramer, their father. There was Edna and Dora Cramer and Georgia Ann and Rebecca Williams and Cora Cramer and her Uncle Kirk. They all walked in those days. When I was about 6 or 7 they had a beach party. All the Sunday School children and some grownups. They went on the boat, *New Jersey*. I don't know if it was a state boat at that time. Dan Sooy owned it. I think Jack and Jill were the only children that didn't go. Mother wouldn't let us go, she said it would blow up. But they went to Bonds Beach. Bonds old hotel was standing then with all the furniture was in it. The only way you could get there, I guess, at that time was by boat. Jack and Jill wanted to go so bad. It hurt worse when all the other children went. It wasn't long after that, that Bonds hotel was gutted. I don't know what happened to the old hotel.

My mother used to have quilting parties and Lizzie, Dora, Edna, Georgie, and Rebecca used to sew. Lizzie and Dora almost lived at our house. They liked my cousin, Joe, who lived with us. My youngest brother, the girls used to tickle him, so he stammered. He was about 3 years old. They would take him home from Sunday School with them. He was quite a swimmer and diver at the age of five. Jill was seven years old when she learned to swim. We didn't have any water wings. Uncle Billy Maxwell told us to get a piece of plank to float us, then use our feet and arms. That's how Jack and Jill learned to swim.

The Maxwells brought the old *F. P. Stoy* naptha launch with an engine and a canape. They took the engine out, tore the canape [*sic*] off and built a pilot house and large room and then an engine room on it. They were going to run produce. They never put an engine in it and it layed on our shore for years. It became the swimming hole and bath house for different generations of children. All the children of Wading River remembers the old *Stoy*. When they could swim good there, they would go to the bridge and swim in deep water. They brought *F. P. Stoy* from Atlantic City. It was named for the Mayor of Atlantic City at that time.

Commercial Fishing

Courtesy of Horace Somes, Jr.

Crew of Fishing Steamer *Adroit* out of Little Egg Harbor

1	Mark Leeds	New Gretna	
2	Ira Jereu	New Gretna	
3		Tuckerton	Mate
4	Asbury Mathis	New Gretna	
5			
6	Joseph Hickman	New Gretna	Captain
7	Austin Downs	Wading River	
8	Levi Chew	Mathistown	
9	John Nickols	Lower Bank	
10			Asst. Eng.
11	Reuben Cavileer	Lower Bank	
12		West Creek	
13	Malcolm Billsborough	New Gretna	Pilot
14	Ford	Green Bank	
15	Jones	West Creek	
16	Joe Loveland	New Gretna	
17	Marvin Mathis	New Gretna	
18	Charles Cavileer	Lower Bank	
19			Chief Eng.

Courtesy of Helen (Billsborough) Ludlam, June 1977

Commercial fishing played a tremendous role in the local economy of the entire Mullica valley in the nineteenth and early twentieth centuries. Nicholas Sooy II was reputed to have owned several fishing stations on the lower Mullica, including one on Crab Island in Great Bay, which employed local men in both fishing and processing. Huge sturgeon were caught and processed for many uses. Their caviar was a delicacy and many people liked to eat the meat pickled. They were also used for oil, glue, and isinglass. Isinglass was made from fish bladders, by the way.

On boat at Crab Island "Fish Factory"
Alice and Howard McAnney with their son Orville and daughter Dorothy,
Sadie Updike, Grace Updike, Rebecca Maxwell - c. 1913

Late in the nineteenth century, a Sooy, probably Ephraim C. Sooy, Jr., owned a fish factory on Crab Island out in Great Bay. Henry Beck records, in *Jersey Genesis*, that John Wesley Ford of Lower Bank clearly remembered the Sooy fish factory. It was managed by Jim Otis and later by one of the Mathises. By this time, the fish of preference was the inedible but incredibly oily mossbunker or menhaden, sometimes also called "Sam Days" and "greentails." "'Sometimes,' said Jack, 'we just called 'em bony-fish and mud-shad, but greentails was always the fav'rite. Maybe they got a name like that because they always left a slick behind 'em in the water.'"

Joe Wharton also owned fish factories all along the east coast, including one at the mouth of the Mullica. These larger entrepreneurs owned steam fishing boats as well as the factories which processed the fish, but independent ship owners competed with them for the catch. Beck reports that it was "a messy, slippery business. Jack [John Wesley Ford] said it was. You had to be beyond 'mindin'' smells. 'But it was a job,' he explained, 'and most of us liked to keep workin'.'"

Beck recorded one of the traits of the men along the Mullica and Wading Rivers:

> *"When berrying fell off and all the wood that was needed was chopped and sold, men of the Mullica drifted down to the shore and signed aboard fish steamers. The wages were never much, nor was the food; but there was living in the business if the greentails were running and nobody worried any more about the morrow than they do down there today."* [*Jersey Genesis*]

After the steam fishing boat had cleared the inlet, the skipper and mate aboard the independent boats went aloft. From the masthead, they could sight schools of menhaden from their oil slick. The men would call down to those standing by below to put off in their dories and head for the menhaden. Each dory held two men who would throw over the nets and drift until they were full. When the mother ship's hold was full, they put in to the nearest fish factory.

In the twentieth century, the J. Howard Smith Processing Company and the Fish Products Company owned the Crab Island fish factory and ground up the menhaden for fertilizer. Workers would come by boat from the shore from both New Gretna and from a dock which used to stand on Seven Bridges Road (now Great Bay Boulevard) out of Tuckerton.

About 1960, the great schools of menhaden disappeared, and the factory on Crab Island was abandoned. The buildings were sold to Hanson Inc. in the 1970s which tore everything apart for salvage. Hanson then donated the island to the state as part of the Great Bay Wildlife Refuge. Originally, the state thought about turning the buildings into a fish study center, but by 1978, the authorities had determined to demolish everything.

On the eighteenth of April in 1982, somehow everything caught fire. Thirty mile per hour winds fanned the flames and the conflagration took on holocaust proportions. About twenty-five firefighters from the mainland tried to fight the fire for four hours, but it was impossible to make any headway without fire equipment. According to the Atlantic City Press article on the fire, a representative of the state Department of Environmental Protection reputedly told the firefighters to let the buildings burn. They were going to be torn down anyway. In the Press article, firefighter Tim Hewitt of Tuckerton Borough Fire Company told the reporter that "burning tar paper that lined the tin sides of the factory building sent black clouds of smoke shooting into the air which could be seen several miles away."

Ships were not the only way in which fishing was carried on, nor were menhaden the only fish sought after. Local men used to take their nets down to the frozen Mullica in winter and catch some pretty impressive fish. Striped bass, perch, and catfish were shipped to Philadelphia and to the Fulton Fish Market in New York. Records kept by Dorothea Somes indicate that her father, Howard McAnney, sold fish through several buyers.

Studies in the 1930s were being made by various government groups to determine the migratory habits of striped (or Rock) bass. A letter from Daniel Merriman, in charge of the Connecticut striped bass investigation, to Mr. Arthur L. Clayton of Island Heights dated December 14, 1937 (also in the Somes collection) indicates that one tagged fish caught on December 4th in Barnegat Bay had been tagged in the Thames River above New London, Connecticut on September 8th and had grown exactly one inch in the intervening three months. Another letter from Merriman to Walter Cavileer, Jr. of Lower Bank, who was then president of Jersey Coast Fishing and Clamming (Mullica Branch), thanks that fisherman for returning the tags of striped bass he had caught in the Mullica.

An idea of the wholesale price of these fish can be gained from examining the accounts of purchase receipts included in the Somes papers. Though the year is not filled in, the date is in the 1940s on several such receipts and list: John Dais Co., Fulton Fish Market, to Howard McAnney on December 22nd: 19 1/2 Bass, $7.80; 15 Perch, $1.88; 20 Perch, $2.00; 75 Perch, $6.00; 138 Cats, $6.90; totalling $24.58; expense $2.50; commission, $3.07; leaving a total to be paid McAnney of $19.01. Another such receipt from the same company to McAnney dated January 16th lists: 37 Bass, $12.95; 39 Perch, $7.02; 65 Perch, $6.50; 28 Perch, $2.80; and 77 Cats, $5.39; totalling $34.66; less expense of $3.00 and commission of $4.33; leaving a total to be paid McAnney of $27.33. A handwritten note lists a profit on fishing (assuming for the year) of $2,601. The same list records the profit from muskrats at $1,016.27.

The Fish Factory on Crab Island in Great Bay

Ice Fishing on the Mullica

Net Fishing Through the Ice on the Mullica
Orville and Howard McAnney

Ice Fishing
Orville and Howard McAnney

"Striped Bass"
Howard and Orville McAnney

708

Cranberries

Courtesy of Horace Somes, Jr.

The Laurel Cranberry Company
Mr. Smith, manager

Cranberries became a major financial resource in the Washington Township area not long after Samuel Crowley, Jr. planted the first cultivated bog in the middle of the nineteenth century. So many of the inland cedar swamps had been stripped of their great trees by that time that some use was needed for their forsaken lowlands, and cranberry cultivation fit the bill precisely.

All along the upper Mullica, Batsto, and Wading Rivers, lowlands were turned into bogs. To the north of Wading River/Bridgeport, the Ridge Road runs along an actual ridge of high ground which divides the lowlands of the Wading River to the east from the Great Swamp to the west. During the nineteench century, cranberry bogs

Cranberry Sorters
Lunch Break - 1910

Left to Right:
Elmira McAnney
Sadie Updike
Alice Adams
Ruth Maxwell
Jennie McAnney
Ada Lippincott

Courtesy Super Bros.

were created along the Washington Township side of the river above the intersection of Ridge Road with Pike Hole Road. These bogs were made with a complex of braided drainage ditches. They are opposite Cranberry Point on the Bass River side between Goldackers and Chip's Folly.

Initially, water for the bogs was taken directly from the Wading River. In recent years, however, brackish water has been found farther and farther up the river, so that today, water has to be brought down in a canal from a mile above Charcoal Landing. Maja Leek and his wife, Sarah, had a large area farther upstream that was used in cultivating both cranberries and, at a later date, blueberries.

For many years, the berries were hand-picked. Then scoops were invented and used to harvest the berries. In the middle of the twentieth century, the first gasoline-powered machines were developed (see BULLTOWN) which harvested the berries in dry bogs. In recent decades, the bogs are flooded at harvest time. The bogs are agitated and the berries float to the surface.

A Mr. Smith had the idea of developing a larger cranberry-growing business than the usual small, family holdings in the area. Around the turn of the century, he sold stock and built an extensive business on the north side of Route 542 on both sides of Ridge Road. Houses and buildings were concentrated near the main road and included the large building shown on the previous and following pages that was used for sorting, packing, and storing the cranberries for shipment to market, and a large home for himself. This large building stood near the northwest corner of Ridge Road and the Batsto/Bridgeport Road, a site that is now completely reforested. Other houses for workers were also con-

Courtesy of Ruth Updike

Mr. Powers

structed in the vicinity. A couple of the original buildings had at least six small, individual rooms for the convenience of the workers. The bogs stretched between the Ridge Road and the Wading River towards the east.

Howard McAnney and his wife, Alice, lived in a house along the Wading River near the bogs and acted as Smith's foreman. He was in charge of seeing that the land was cleared and the bogs properly prepared for setting the plants. A novel idea was tried. Quite a few hogs were purchased and fenced in the areas to be cleared in the hope that their rooting would dig out everything which the entrepreneurs wanted removed. Unfortunately, it is reported that all the hogs died of cholera. The company then employed Polish immigrants to do the work the hard way with axes and hoes. The hard-working Poles cleared the ground and planted the bogs, and, to the delight of the investors, the cranberry harvest was plentiful.

Unfortunately, the investors were not. Despite success in production, the Laurel Cranberry Company was never properly capitalized. Ed Leek succeeded Howard McAnney as manager and had to sue for his pay. He was finally awarded some of the bogs and buildings. Others were sold to George Gosler who hired a World War I veteran by the name of Powers as manager. Mr. Powers lived on Route 542 in the last house on the left, going west before reaching the Great Swamp. The Powers house had a succession of owners including the Jamisons, Hoffmans, and Doheneys. The Jamisons were from Canada, and Mr. Jamison was fond of telling his Wading River neighbors that the geese in his homeland were so plentiful that he could ride a wagon through a cornfield and return with a load of geese.

Courtesy of Mildred (Leek) Honaker

Mrs. Etta Powers
Mrs. Mildred (Leek) Honaker

In 1943, the house was struck by lightning and burned to the ground. A new house was built on the location of the Powers house by Harry Herbert which included a wood-working shop. Bob Jones ran Flyway Decoys out of the shop for some years.

The Powers and the Updikes had been close friends, and Henry Updike succeeded Powers as manager of the Gosler bogs. George Gosler's nephew, Joe Palmer, also had bogs in the area which Henry managed for him.

Luck didn't get any better for the Laurel Cranberry Company under the new owner. Ed Leek built a bungalow between the original main house and the river for his son, George, and his wife. Not long after, his wife was cooking on the stove when it caught on fire and burned the house down. George Leek's wife was injured but recovered from her burns. In 1930, a forest fire destroyed all the buildings of the former Laurel Cranberry Company. The high winds generated carried pieces of burning shingles far across the river.

The Laurel Cranberry Company tried to put Bridgeport/Wading River on the map. On the east end of the main

The Cranberry House Under Construction - circa 1905

building was emblazoned: 490 mi. Portland, Me., 3,000 mi. Portland, Oregon. At the present time, the Wading River Cranberry Company is the last remnant of this important business in the Wading River area.

Photographs courtesy of Horace Somes, Jr.

711

The New Cranberry House is almost ready for business.
The Bridgeport-Batsto Road (Route 542) is just to the right of the picture. Ridge Road runs right behind this building.

An idea of the position of these no longer existing buildings can be gained from these three pictures.

The corner of the building just showing in the picture at left is the corner of the little section of the Cranberry Building shown in the top photograph at the extreme right. The road is Route 542.

In the lower picture, the photographer has taken a couple of steps out into the roadway and pointed his camera a little farther down the road towards the east. The house visible in the distance is the rear of the John (Wobbar) Maxwell house that used to stand on the corner of Turtle Creek Road and Route 542. The bridge is about a quarter mile down the road.

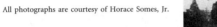

The Wading River Bogs are Ready for Harvest

The Harvest

Back when the Laurel Cranberry Company was in operation, the cranberries were handpicked from dry bogs which was very hard labor indeed.

After scoops were developed, pickers used the scoops to gather the berries from the plants rather than simply using their hands.

This may have been easier on their hands, but the scoops were heavy and the work was still back-breaking.

The first machines (pictured in the chapter on Bulltown) knocked the berries from the plants in dry bogs.

The modern machines in the photographs on the preceding page were designed to be used in wet bogs. The machines vibrate the berries off the plants which then float to the surface and are corralled together in one place.

Trucks are then brought into the bogs and large conveyor belts are rigged from the trucks into the bogs.

Workers rake the floating berries from the bogs into the mouth of the conveyor belt which then lifts them into the trucks.

Most of the cranberries grown in South Jersey today are grown for processing. The Ocean Spray Cooperative has a huge packing house in Chatsworth which serves as the reception center for all the berries of the growers in this region.

Photographs courtesy of
Horace Somes, Jr.

714

The Intersection of the Batsto-Bridgeport Road (Route 542),
Ridge Road, and Turtle Creek Road
The heavily-wooded area on the right hand side of the photograph was where the Laurel Cranberry Company had its buildings. The cleared fields in the center of the picture are those of the farms on Turtle Creek Road. At the top of the picture is the Great Swamp. The bogs are off the lower right side of the photograph.

An Autogyro - Forerunner of the Helicopter
This hybrid was basically a small airplane, complete with wings and propeller, with non-tilting horizontal blades for lift which enabled it to take off vertically and hover. It was used for spraying the cranberry bogs.

Helen Wilkinson
at the Gosler's Cranberry Bog Dam - circa 1924

Watson "Wad" Lippincott

West End of the Wading River Bridge on the South Side - Circa 1935

Watson Lippincott was seventy-five years old when Henry C. Beck wrote an article for the Atlantic City Press about him in 1941. Watson built Mullica River Gunning Skiffs for anyone who wanted one and could pay him. Not that he'd built boats all his life, you see. Watson Lippincott, scion of one of the oldest families in Wading River/ Bridgeport, had been a farmer, then a bayman. In the 1930's, he lived on a houseboat in the Wading River and built skiffs.

Mullica River Gunning Skiffs, it seems, were uniquely designed for hunting in the Mullica and Wading River estuaries. They were bateau-sided, flat-bottomed skiffs that were very maneuverable in the little creeks and shallows of the two rivers. Their counterpart developed for use on the bays behind Long Beach Island were the sneakboxes, though the gunning skiffs of this region never seemed to have been built for sailing, just rowing. The skiffs actually built for hunting had flat decks, much like their sneakbox cousins, and their flat bottoms were a great asset in the shallow, calm waters of the rivers.

Born in Green Bank on August 18, 1865 where his father had worked in the glass factory for Nicholas Sooy II, Watson had tried his hand at making a living from the bay and rivers before forsaking life on the water for a farm on the land.

Clams and oysters were plentiful throughout the nineteenth and early twentieth centuries, though they didn't sell for much by today's standards. Beck asked him how much they were selling for in 1941, "Three dollars a hundred?"

"Three dollars a thousand, more like," was his answer from Lippincott. "The highest I ever knew them to be was in the last war [World War I]. That was $1.20 a hundred for big chowder clams."

When Beck asked him why he had started building rowboats, Watson's laconic reply was, "You have to do something. ... You have to work or starve. And there's always work if you want it."

Henry Beck wrote that Lippincott got his boat-building wood from New Gretna. "Good Jersey *red* cedar," Beck wrote. Shows how much Henry Charlton Beck knew about boat building and wood. *Red* cedar indeed! If Watson was building cedar closets, Beck would have been right. *White* cedar, good Jersey *white* cedar from the surrounding swamps that hugged the shores of the Wading and Mullica Rivers, that's what boats were made from!

Wading River once had its own real shipyard. During the nineteenth century, the river had teemed with cargo vessels which hauled the products of the pines to New York and Philadelphia. There was a market for sloops and schooners of some size at that time. The demand for ships decreased rapidly towards

The Wreck of the *Huntress* lay just upriver from the bridge on the Bass River side off what was once the Leek Wharf.

the end of the century with the coming of the railroads. Martha Furnace folded at mid-century. Harrisville was closed by the end of the century. When the cordwood and lumber trade ran out early in the twentieth century, so did the demand for ships. By 1941, the glory days of shipping were long past, and the only local market was for rowboats.

Lippincott told Beck about the old hulks that still lay submerged in the river nearby. One was of the *Huntress*. She had been owned by Captain Robert McKeen, who had lived in the old Leek/McKeen Homestead on the Bass River side of the Wading River bridge. The *Huntress* had been a sixty-foot sloop, according to Watson. "Probably a freighter. ... She's been here longer than me, pretty much as you see her now," he said.

"That one close by here was built down in Atlantic City," he told Beck. "A man had the idea of gathering truck [farm produce] from the farms here and running it to Atlantic City. The idea didn't work and the ship went to the dogs. There came a big tide and she washed from over there to over here where she laid. Some boys got aboard her after that and set her afire."

Watson Lippincott was referring to the *Old Stoy*, pictured to the right on the east side of the river. She was fast aground and abandoned at the time this photograph was taken, and children used her as a bath house.

Watson remembered that storm tide which washed her across the river from Bass River to Washington Township. The fire must have been a spectacular site to watch as the old hulk disintegrated in a roar of flames and sank hissing into the brown waters of the river. One more quaint reminder of the past was gone.

Watson Lippincott lies in an unmarked grave in the Lower Bank cemetery. His old houseboat long ago decayed with the twin assaults of time and the elements. Even the land on which he worked is no longer quite so solid in 1995 as it was in 1941. Like the *Old Stoy*, white cedar planking, oak ribs, horse-glue, galvanized fasteners, and the smell of paint no longer shelter by the bridge. There is beauty there still, but a way of life is gone.

The *Old Stoy*

The Logging Industry

The Sam Ireland Sawmill
Charles and Eva Kauflin managed the mill for Sam.
This view is the north side of the sawmill about 1908.
Ed Leek is on the left.

Logging was a major industry along the Mullica and Wading Rivers and their tributaries for over two hundred fifty years. The first families to settle along the rivers found extensive swamps filled with towering white cedar trees. Surrounding the swamps were stands of large oaks, mixed with some pines. Further inland in the Pine Barrens, the trees grew smaller and smaller on the uplands, but the cedars still towered in the swamps along the rivers.

Enterprising businessmen as they were, these early farmers cut timber for their own needs and loaded handhewn lumber onto small sailing craft for shipment down river to distant markets. Along with the homesteaders came entrepreneurs who set up sawmills on the numerous streams of the area, and towns frequently grew up around them. Each of the little towns of Washington Township boasted at least one, if not more, waterpowered sawmills. An export trade in charcoal and roundwood used as firewood for Philadelphia and New York developed quite early in the history of the area.

The white cedars of New Jersey became famous for ships' timbers, masts, and planking. It resisted rot and was prime lumber for shipbuilding. It wasn't long before ships' carpenters were setting up shipyards and practicing their trade right on the spot. Bridgeport/Wading River, Lower Bank, and Green Bank all had shipyards in them for most of their first two hundred years.

White cedar also was used for building houses, and most the local homes built in the eighteenth century were made from this termite/rot resistant wood. Great cedars felled by windstorms or killed by salt water lay submerged in the swamps for centuries and provided particularly good material for shingles and clapboards. Some men were engaged in shingling almost completely.

They would first probe the muck in the swamp with iron rods called "progues" to find the buried logs. A cutting spade was then used to chip a foot-long piece from the submerged log to determine if it was felled by wind or had been killed by the rising salt water. Windfalls made the best shingles. Those which had been destroyed by

Shingles at sawmill along road running south past the store/post office.
In the background can be seen a house (one occupied by Milton Kauflin's family) and further back can be seen
chimney of Maja Towers Leek's house. The sawmill was located on the old stage road (according to Mildred
Honaker who lived in the Maja Towers Leek home.)

the salt water had raised their dead trunks to the air and had partially rotted before they had toppled into the swamp. Growing trees which were knocked down by great storms were well-preserved by the enfolding muck of the swamps. Some of these buried trunks measured three or four feet in diameter. If the shingle miner decided that the log was good, he dug out the muck, sawed off the ends, and raised it. He used a crosscut saw to cut the log into the length of shingle wanted, then used a froe and mallet to split the log into blocks. Each block or "bolt" would be split into a rough-hewn shingle which was trimmed on a shaving horse with a draw knife. Shingles were also cut in sawmills such as that pictured above. In this case, they were made from standing trees rather than cut from ones buried in the swampy muck.

The Great Swamp, stretching from the Mullica River northward across Route 542, was divided into a series of long, narrow strips of land, each with a different owner. A logger would start cutting into his section, laying a corduroy road made from logs as he cut. There was so much water in the swamp that cutters could not venture far off the road, hence the long, narrow parcels of land.

Great cedars and oaks were cut where they stood and hauled to the nearest sawmill to be cut into lumber and framing materials. Smaller trees were generally cut for firewood, charcoal production, and feeding the vast appitites of the iron furnaces and the later glassworks. Early waterpowered sawmills were usually operated with a breast wheel and had vertical saw blades attached to a frame. Powered by belts and wooden gears, the frames moved up and down with the supported saw blade cutting through the logs. The log to be cut rested on a log carriage. A small tub wheel, forerunner of the turbine, provided the power to move the log carriage away from the saw blade.

The circular saw was invented in 1796 but was only used for cutting verneer. It did not come into common use as a rip saw until the mid-19th century. When it did, it made the process much quicker and easier. By this time, the huge breast wheels had been replaced by the turbines (See "The Sawmill" under Batsto). Late in the century, steam engines made sawmills less dependent on location near a water source, and the twentieth century use of kerosene or gasoline engines made them quite mobile. Small sawmills could be moved around from place to place wherever there was timber to be cut.

During the first part of the twentieth century, Sam Ireland owned a sawmill behind his store in Wading River which stood on the Washington Township side of the bridge. Charles and Eva Kauflin managed it for him. There used to be a road which left the main road between the river and the Sooy/Ireland/Maxwell House and Store and ran down along the river to the Landing where the Downs family lived. The Kauflins and their children,

Milton and Thelma, lived in a house which stood near the road. Milton Kauflin later relocated the mill to South Maple Avenue in New Gretna where he continued to operate it until his death. Walt Downs moved one of the outbuildings to the end of Cedar Lane. Gus Chiriani owned this building for a while but it now (1995) stands abandoned.

A steam-powered blower used to exhaust sawdust from the mill out into the swamp down river. Older residents remembered that sawdust was found as far down river as half a mile from the mill. Howard McAnney and Henry Updike used some of the sawdust produced in the mill to mulch blueberry plantings (as per Orville McAnney).

Corduroy roads made from logs laid side by side through the swamps enabled wagons, and later trucks, to make their way through the muck to haul out the logs. Finished lumber was loaded onto sloops and schooners for shipment to the New York and Philadelphia markets. After the railroads came through Hammonton and Egg Harbor City, wagons, and later, trucks, hauled the final products overland to be shipped by rail.

Another mill was built by Charles Bozarth on the south side of Route 542 on property now occupied by King and Scott homes. A bunkhouse for the workers stood behind this mill and a road stretched southward through Rob Maxwell's farm into the Great Swamp.

The mill was abandoned by the 1920s, and some enterprsing local man had a bootleg still on the property after the Prohibition Amendment was passed. It is said that spilled liquor ran down the sides of the Batsto-Bridgeport Road (Route 542) when the still was raided by the authorities. Some of the whiskey barrels were saved for local use however.

Yet another mill must have been operated at the head of the cranberry bogs at Millic Field where a high bank overlooks the Broad Place below Devil's Elbow. A sawdust pile was there into the 1960s.

On the Bass River side, two mills operated on the Willits Creek/Mill Creek/Ives Branch. Route 542 passes over what had been the site of the mill dam with the pond and sawmill to the north and a grist mill to the south of the road. The saw mill was originally built by John Leek, Sr. John Leek III sold the mill to Francis French in 1823. Francis then built the grist mill. Charles Cramer mentions the saw mill in his 1870 will, which means that at least the sawmill was still standing and operating at that time. No mention is made of the grist mill, so it is likely that it was gone by 1870.

The early settlers and businessmen of the eighteenth, nineteenth, and early twentieth century looked on the natural resources of the area as unlimited and renewable. Thus they clear-cut most of the land we now call the Pine Barrens. Clearcutting lasted into the late 1970's, when cedar swamps still fell to the loggers. During the 1920's and 1930's, much of the land lay denuded. Small farms stretched from Bridgeport/Wading River through Green Bank and on towards Batsto. Denuded swamps were turned into cranberry bogs and empty fields were later cultivated with blueberries. In the interior, abandoned farms were slowly returning to second-growth forests as the land lay fallow.

George Leek logging cedar - c. 1930

Photographs courtesy of George Leek

George and Merrit Leek - c. 1930

The State of New Jersey, in those days, was actively involved in returning the land to forest and engaged in reforestation. In some areas, stands of white pine were planted as well as other species which had greater commercial value than the local pitch pine. The State also became involved in both road improvement and in firefighting.The depression-era Civilian Conservation Corps (C.C.C.) did extensive work in rebuilding the local area.

There were two C.C.C. camps in Washington Township. In Green Bank, the camp was located on the northeast corner of Routes 542 and 563. A maintenance shop and nursery was operated at what is now the State garage on Lover's Lane. This camp was known for its production of seedlings which were shipped to other camps, including the one in Bass River, for use in reforestation. Much of the area had been destroyed by numerous fires early in the twentieth century, and vast areas were replanted by the Civilian Conservation Corps.

The Green Bank camp built the park on River Road in Green Bank and also constructed an extensive road system in Great Swamp where the state acquired large tracts when it bought properties there and organized the Green Bank State Forest.

One road stretched from Route 542 all the way to the lower end of the Great Swamp near Log Bay. They also built a road from Lower Bank (a portion of which is now Charlie Bell Lane) which crossed the above road and ran on through to Wading River, exiting onto Turtle Creek Road at the last house toward the west.

The site of the old C.C.C. camp in Green Bank now lies abandoned and grown over. The last building burned on July 10, 1978. Even the roads back to the camp are impassable to motor vehicles because of the extensive regrowth.

Courtesy of George Leek

George Leek logging in the Great Swamp - c. 1930
This photograph seems to be a double exposure, but it certainly does make George Leek appear to be a ghost standing on the cordoroy road.

The second Washington Township camp was located on the Jenkins Road in Penn Forest above Lake Oswego. This camp built several miles of roads and the recreation area at Bear Swamp Hill. The boys also replaced the wooden dam at Lake Oswego with the present concrete one.

There are still stands of large cedars along the Mullica and Wading Rivers that reminds us of size of those ancient swamps of years past. Areas that once supported farmland now has returned to forest, but the growth is much smaller than it used to be, at least along the river valleys.

It takes more than a single lifetime to restore that which has been lost. Stripped of its trees, the land can recover. Develop it, and it's gone forever.

Courtesy of Horace Somes, Jr.

Cedar in the "Great Swamp"
John Simpkins of Green Bank
No one knew quite what to do with this huge tree.
None of the sawmills in the area had the means to cut it!
The original publication of this photograph identified the man as "Chink" Simpkins, but
Nelson and Evelyn (Simpkins) Ware say it is actually "Chink's" brother, John.

Hunting and Trapping

Henry Grundmeier and Orville McAnney - c. 1924

The following article is taken from an unpublished manuscript by Horace Somes, Jr. and is used with his permission.

The winter was a great time to be out and "walk" the meadows - no flies, reeds thinned out and flattened by storms, and the marsh surface easily walked when frozen. If you took the trouble, you could take along your shotgun to jump-shoot ducks before the waterfowl season ended in January. Low tide was the time to go, so that you could get to the deeper muskrat runs and reach your traps. Blowout tides caused by strong westerly winds were great, because you didn't have to hurry to finish before the water came back in. It was also a time to discover sunken and abandoned relics in the creeks and mud - old massive cedar logs, boat wrecks, and evidence of haying. To make it easier to cross small creeks and ditches, many of the mouths were "fenced" or "gated" - basically a simple but precarious footbridge consisting of a row of cedar posts, with a single long stringer that was set at the high tide level.

Changes in our area probably combine both natural and human impacts with profound results for the game of the [upland and] marshlands. . . . Deer had been exterminated from most of the State by the end of the 19th century, and my grandfather saw the first one cross our farm sometime about 1920. Although the loss of deer had eliminated a source of wild game, it also would have made farming easier back then. My grandfather grew large fields of corn and sweet potatoes, and this probably became harder as the deer population grew. The absence of deer also may have favored the regrowth of cedar swamps after logging, where the young growth otherwise would have been a favored browse for deer. In recent decades, the failure of regrowth in some cedar areas has been attributed to the large deer population. . . .

Trapping for muskrats - with incidental catches of raccoon, mink, and fox - was once a source of revenue in the broad meadows which spread below Lower Bank to Wading River. Further downstream, the short-growth saltmarshes of the Mullica did not support "rats." The winter trapping period worked well with the other seasons of the land and water - bridging a gap between the fall waterfowl hunt and spring replanting of the farms. Both my grandfather [Howard McAnney] and uncle [Orville McAnney] trapped the meadows of Turtle Creek and Swan Bay, and twenty plus rats were a good - and heavy - haul for one low-tide's tending of the traps. The rats could be sold whole to the fur-buyer, who made weekly collections; or the pelts skinned out and stretched, for later sale - with the meat sold either locally or to markets as "marsh hare." My mother recalled taking meat into Egg Harbor

City for delivery when she went to high school there. Before I was old enough to trap the meadows, I ran a mouse trapline in my grandparents' cellar - and was rewarded with a dime per catch by the "furbuyer."

Although outlawed by today's Fish and Game laws, rabbits also used to be trapped at the woodlines around the farms. A wooden box trap, baited with an apple slice on a trip stick and with a brick counterweight on the trap door, was an effective way to live-catch rabbits - which also probably were more abundant when there used to be more farms and fewer deer.

The muskrat population crashed in the late 1980s in our area - although anti-fur sentiments and foreign imports had already hurt prices and reduced trapping. "Rat houses," which had once dotted the marsh, were gone, and you could no longer see their white caps when it snowed in the winter. I can remember as many as twenty-plus houses in several acres of three-square grass on a piece of our marsh. The cause [of the decline in the "rat" population] is not known, because the State Fish and Game [Commission] never gave much attention to the "sport" of trapping - too politically incorrect for research. It was not [due] to overtrapping, because reduced prices had reduced the harvest a decade before [the decline]. Perhaps it reflects the increasing salinity and dominance of the Phragmites, but I doubt it. The only consolation is that other furbearers have returned to the area. Otters are regular inhabitants of my duck blind, although their fish diet and housekeeping habits leave much to be desired. They probably have been favored by the brackish water which improved fishing and brought in crabs as a side-dish. Beaver have also returned to the inland streams and are a great pest to the

Courtesy of Horace Somes, Jr.

Orville McAnney

cranberry growers (including the Wading River Bogs), as well as the road crews who have a struggle to keep some culverts and bridges unclogged.

The duck population also has been lower in recent years, although the federal Fish and Game Service indicates that populations are now rebounding - although this October's (1995) opening season didn't show it. Probably the weather is at fault, because the birds don't seem to move into our area without cold temperatures - we haven't had a hard frost yet. Without a little nighttime ice on the ponds, the ducks remain inland and dispersed. The loss of valuable wildlife plants from our marshes hasn't helped either. Duck blinds

Courtesy of Horace Somes, Jr.

Duck Blind on Bill's Creek off Wading River - 1970's

These heavy, flat-bottomed work boats were called "row garveys"
and were used to haul nets and salt hay and for fishing.

now are scattered and used infrequently, whereas every marsh property with a good creek or riverfront formerly hosted one or more blinds. Duck season used to be a big family time on our farm. My father would take off from work to hunt almost every day during the peak of the season. The kids would help grandmother pluck the ducks, seated around a large tub in an outbuilding; and the small feathers and down would be used to stuff pillows. We freeze the ducks today, but they used to be "canned" in Mason ball jars - just as the jellies and applesauce were put up in the cellar.

While the ducks have declined, larger waterfowl have come into the area. Goose hunting on a regular basis was unheard of in the past, and few people had their decoys - although you might get a lucky shot during the October migration flight. Resident geese, as well as the ubiquitous mallard, are now year-round occupants of our rivers and even of our lawns. Whistling or tundra swans also arrived in the state in the 1950s, and we now host a winter population of over five hundred on the remaining rice beds as well as in the cranberry bogs. In turn, these large waterfowl have served as winter prey for our national symbol, the Bald Eagle, and Wading River is one of the recognized places in the state where these large raptors have returned.

Scrape and Paint:
Billy's Landing
1940
Howard McAnney

These boats were batteau-sided hunting boats called gunning skiffs which were unique to the Mullica estuary.

Dorothy (McAnney) Somes - October 13, 1945

Howard McAnney - October 13, 1945

Horace Somes, Jr. - 1948

Horace Somes, Sr.,
Horace Somes, Jr.,
Howard McAnney,
and Lady
1948

Photographs courtesy of Horace Somes, Jr.

Frank Somes and Duke
Bill's Creek - 1970

Barbara Somes
Wife of Horace Somes, Jr. - 1980

Howard and Robert Somes
with their father, Horace Somes, Jr.
December 28, 1992

A Proud Hunter - 1993

All photographs courtesy of Horace Somes, Jr.

727

Salt Haying

Abandoned Salt Hay Mower

Salt haying was one of the seasonal occupations of this area for over a hundred years. Both the road through Sooy Place and Turtle Creek Road had extensions that reached all the way out into the meadows to the Mullica River, providing access for the wagons and horses of the salt hay farmers. Scow Ditch at the end of the Swan Bay Road and Zeagles Ditch at the end of Turtle Creek Road offered shelter for the flat-bottomed salt hay barges.

Nature provided an ideal situation for this type of "farming." The ground did not have to be tilled. No seed had to be planted. Each winter, the salt hay farmer simply burned off the stubble that remained which contributed to a healthier growth the following year. When the meadows were ready for mowing, the farmer moved his barge, his horses, his wagon, and his mowing machine to his salt hay lot and went to work. The horses pulling the mowers had to wear boots called "mudboots" to protect their hooves from constant contact with the wet muck and to help keep them from sinking into the meadows. The effect was somewhat like seeing a pair of horses on snowshoes. Even with this insurance, a second team was often kept within shouting distance in case the other team sank too deeply into the mud and had to be hauled out.

After the hay was cut, it was raked into stacks. The horses were then hitched to wagons and the stacks shovelled into them. Sometimes the hay was shovelled directly on to barges and hauled as far up the river or creek as they could be taken. It was then unloaded, carted to a man's farm in wagons and baled for shipment.

Salt hay barges were usually flat-bottomed scows about thirty feet long. Often these barges had a two-room cabin on them which provided a sleeping quarters and kitchen facilities for the salt hay mower so that he didn't have to make the long journey back and forth to his home each and every day.

All of the meadows on the lower Wading River were surveyed by a man named Braddock in 1858 and divided into lots. Each lot was numbered and were of varying sizes up to about twenty-five acres each. Residents of the area would always buy some of these lots, in addition to their upland and cedar swamp land, to add to their income. If they didn't choose to cut the hay themselves, others would often rent their salt hay marshes from them.

Salt hay farmers could recognize the three varieties of salt hay which grew in their meadows but which were not separated at harvest. "Black grass" is actually a rush and grows on the higher meadows where there is a fresh water flow onto the marsh. It gets its common name from the fact that, if it isn't cut by July, it turns oily and black. At the lowest marshes, "Yellow salt" grass grows. This is the finest of the salt hay types and is the most prized. Between the "Yellow salt" and the "Black grass" grows another type which has a hollow stem and no particular local name but is called "Spike grass" elsewhere along the coast. Unlike the other two "grasses," spike grass grows straight.

Salt hay has had a variety of uses over the years. In the eighteenth and nineteenth centuries, farmers cut it by hand with scythes and used it extensively on their upland farms for feed and mulch. As Dorothy Somes noted in one of her photographs, the cows were sent to the meadows in the summer to graze on the lush grass. As a mulch, the salt hay was great. It wouldn't sprout as a weed on the upland farms, which was an asset indeed. The actual harvesting was done from June to the end of the year.

McCarty and the Harris brothers also found an excellent use for the salt hay mown on the meadows of the Wading and Mullica Rivers. They made paper out of it. They probably started the first commercial usage of the hay in any quantity. Their quality of paper was equivalent to our butcher's paper of today, but it was a marketable product that sold well throughout the nineteenth century. Salt hay cut on the Mullica and Wading could be barged upstream as far as the McCartyville/Harrisville Landing above Charcoal Landing where it was loaded onto wagons and carted the mile or so remaining to the papermill.

The glasshouses of Washington Township in mid-century used salt hay for packing their precious and highly breakable product for shipment. Sand roads and springless wagons were hard on glass products, especially window glass, and salt hay made a perfect packing material. Pottery plants, like the one up in Pasadena (above Route 72) used it for the same purpose, and many an old sand road saw much wagon traffic during the late summer when the salt hay was being cut and hauled overland.

Salt hay had another advantage: it doesn't rot very quickly. Bales of salt hay could be stored by the glass, pottery, and brick plants throughout the winter without fear of it turning into a mushy mess. There were even a few places in New Jersey where salt hay was used in making rope.

While salt hay farmers didn't have to plow and plant and hoe to raise their crop, they did have to work closely with nature. Farmers cut a series of floodgated ditches into their meadows to regulate the flow of saltwater. If too much saltwater flowed over the meadows, they grew into sedges. Without care, meadows turned into "rotten marsh" that could no longer be safely harvested.

The last salt hay farmer on the Mullica and Wading Rivers was old Charlie Weber who lived on Route 542 at the end of Church Road outside of Lower Bank. He kept his horses, mower, and barge busy into the 1940s, though, by this time, there were no others joining him in the harvest.

What a mound of salt hay! Dorothea McAnney, Helen Wilkinson (from Canada) and Jean Weiner (from Egg Harbor - her father was a tailor)

You can tell the "real" salt hay (Yellow salt) by its distinctive curve.

Courtesy of Horace Somes, Jr.

Ownership Map of the Swan Bay Meadows

"From map made by W. R. Braddock on February 18, 1858, for sale of area by heirs of William Richards (built up Batsto Ironworks during final era of prosperity; 9/12/1738 to 8/31/1823). A copy was given to each purchaser. One of these was in the hands of the late Edward Downs (died about 1946). Orville McAnney copied the following information about 1930:" Horace Somes, Jr. sketched the map from the data gathered by his uncle, Orville.

1	L. Mathis, 8 acres	16	B.T. Downs, 25.20 acres, $2.25 - $56.70
2	L. Mathis, 13.93 acres	17	J.S. Cramer, 45.67, $3.75 - $171.07
3	I. Weeks, 11 acres	18	S. Cavileer, 13.86 acres
4	5.4 acres	19	T. Clark, 6.22 acres
4 ½	R. , 7.5 acres	20	T. Clark, 13.93 acres
5	J. French, 6.91 acrea	21	M. Adams, 6.29 acres
6	J. Marshall, 4.43 acres	22	Joe Allen, 27.75 acres, $5 - 138.75
6 ½	W. Gale, 4.53 acres	23	B. T. Downs and Wm. Gale, about 25 acres, $3.75 - $87.22
7	C.W. Cavileer, 6.52 acres	24	B. T. Downs, 25.18 acres, $2.25 - $56.65
7 ½	S. McKean, 4.36 acres	25	not sold, 55.49
8	R. Cavileer, 22.24 acres, $17 per acre: $378.08	26	T. Sooy, 39.71 acres, $8.25 - $327/60
9	J. Weeks, 24.69 acres, $10 - $246.90	27	G. Wetherby, 20.17 acres, $2.75 - $55.46
10	about 25	28	B. Wetherby
11	about 25	29	B. Wetherby, 20.48 acres, $4.50 - $91.93 ½
12	about 25	30	B. T. Downs, 102.92, $2.50 - $257.30
13	about 25	31	B. T. Downs, 50.25 acres, $4.75 - $238.68
14	about 25	?	J. Townsend, 28.95 acres
15	B. Downs, about 25, $4.50 - $104.76		

Sphagnum Moss

No one knows at what period sphagnum moss was first gathered, but early settlers seem to have discovered that it had excellent absorption characteristics and helped in healing wounds. Henry Charlton Beck (*Jersey Genesis*) says that it was used for medicinal purposes in Europe as early as the Napoleonic Wars. During the Russo-Japanese War, the Japanese soldiers were given sphagnum dressings, which they found better than cotton for wounds.

During World War I, the British adopted it for dressings in 1915 after the Germans and Japanese had been using it extensively. Beck quotes George E. Nichols of the Sheffield Scientific School as saying that "*a pad* [of cotton] *will absorb five or six times its weight in water. . . .Exceptionally good moss will absorb as much as twenty-two times its own weight of water. The moss retains liquids better than cotton so that a dressing need not be changed as often.*"

Sphagnum moss (*sphagnum papillosum*) grows best in white cedar swamps from New Jersey northward, and was gathered extensively by local residents for the first half of this century. It was raked out of the swamps into piles on higher ground, slung in hammocks to drain out the moisture, then baled and sold. Florists used it for floral arrangements, prior to the invention of styrofoam. They still use it to wrap around the roots of plants that are to be shipped. Its excellent water retention properties keep the roots moist during transit. "Mossies" worked hard and long for the sixty–ninety cents they received per bale.

Moss was out and cotton in during World War II, and styrofoam swept the floral market in the sixties. Now the moss grows undisturbed in the remaining cedar swamps of the Mullica estuary.

The Gateway to Atlantic City

Wading River, it seems, had its equivalent of Florida real estate promoters. The first part of this century was not a profitable time for the residents of the Mullica and Wading River estuaries. The railroads had caused the collapse of river-dependent shipping. The iron and glass industries were only memories. Farming was being challenged by the mid-west. Hunting, fishing, and chicken farming didn't make anyone wealthy. Then came a brainstorm.

Atlantic City was at the peak of its popularity, and property in that fashionable seaside resort was expensive. Wading River was somewhat near the shore. Why not cash in on Atlantic City's renown? A developer, whose name isn't even remembered today, bought up property on both sides of the Batsto-Bridgeport Road (Route 542) and hired surveyors to lay out streets just west of the intersection with Turtle Creek Road. Each street was marked with shingle-like markers, and a large gateway was built over the new development's entrance road to the north of the main road. "The Gateway to Atlantic City," the archway read. Orville McAnney remembered helping those surveyors lay out the dream development when he was about sixteen years old which would make the date about 1923.

Dreams were soon shattered, however. Not one house was ever built on those carefully laid out streets. The tax maps of Washington Township still clearly show the development, though now the land is overgrown with trees and not a single street remains to be seen.

This planned development stood just off Route 542 to the west of the Beebe lot which was just across the road from the former Applegate property.

Other residents tried to sell property as well. The William A. "Gus" Maxwell house on Turtle Creek Road was sold three times to folks from Missouri. They gave up their homes in that state to move to Wading River but simply couldn't make a living and had to move again. The Smiths, the Hines, the Grundmeiers - all are remembered for being nice people, but all had to move away. Orville McAnney owned it for a while, then sold it to the Atlantic City Police Club.

The William F. Gale house on Cedar Lane was sold to three different families from north Jersey who tried to make a living raising raspberries, sheep, and even by canning jams - all to no avail. A bulkheading company owned it for a while but finally left town. Only when Duncan Doyle established the Turtle Run Campground was some success found.

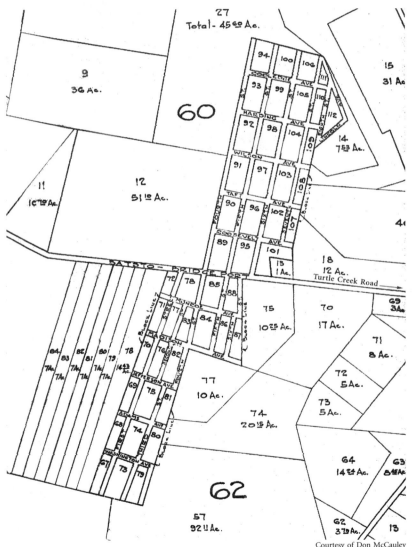

Courtesy of Don McCauley

Layout of the Gateway to Atlantic City
from the Washington Township tax maps of 1937

Route
542

The People of Wading River

Courtesy Mildred Honaker

Amy (Maxwell) Weeks
Charles and Rae

Courtesy of Horace Somes, Jr.

Mr. Grundmeier & Orville McAnney - 1922

Courtesy of Horace Somes, Jr.

Lavinia (Bryant) McCarten

Courtesy of Virginia Steber

Elsie and Mary McAnney

Courtesy of Horace Somes, Jr.

Mary McCullough
Lived in former home of Lemuel
Maxwell, now Fred Quigley's

L. to R.: Ruth Updike, Floyd Sawyer, Elsie McAnney, Robert Lippincott,
Dorothea McAnney, Orville McAnney

All photographs on this page are
courtesy of Horace Somes, Jr.

Dot McAnney - 1935

L. to R. : Sadie Updike, Unknown, Rachel Maxwell,
Mildred Leek

Anna Adams

L. to R.: Martha Downs Adams Merchant
Glada (Downs) Cramer, Elsie (McAnney) Taylor
Mary Maxwell

734

The People of Wading River

Alice (Downs)DeCamp, Marjorie (Downs) Cavileer,
Mary McAnney, Stanley McCarten

Leah Kirby, Amy Maxwell, Helen Wilkinson, Dorothea McAnney

Mary McCullough, Sadie Updike Ware,
Mrs. Smith, Ruth (Huntley) Updike,
Anna Ware, Howard Ware

735

The Way Thro' the Woods
or
"The Lost Road Thro the Woods"

They shut the Road thro' the Woods
      Seventy years ago!
Weather and rain have undone it again,
      And now you would never know
There was once a Road thro' the Woods
      Before they planted the trees.

It is underneath the Coppice and Evergreen Shrub And the thin anemones
      Only the traveller sees
That where the Wooddove broods
      And the wild-folk play at ease,
There was once a Road thro' the Woods!

Yet, if you enter the Woods
      Of a Summer-evening late,
When the night air Cools on the trout-pools
      Where the wild deer Calls his mate.
They fear not folk in the Woods,
      Because they are so few.

You may hear the beat of a horse's feet
      On the Sandy Road in the dew;
Steadily Cantering thro'
      These misty Solitudes,
As tho' they perfectly knew
      The old, last Road thro' the Woods. . . .
But the Old Road is gone thro'
      The Woods!

Used by Laura Larrabee McConeghy in her work,
"The Lure of Roads" and believed to have been written by her about 1935.
All of Mrs. McConeghy's work was written by hand,
and there seems to be no division in the first line of the second stanza.

The Truly Forgotten Towns of the Pines

On the Road to Little Egg Harbor:

Bass River Tavern

Bodine's Tavern

Washington Tavern (Sooy's Inn)

Mount

Penn Swamp

Quaker Bridge

Hampton Gate,

Hampton Furnace, Hampton Forge

The Eagle Hotel

Also:

Friendship

Sandy Ridge

Penn Place

Union Forge

Godfrey's Bridge

Tulpehocken

Brotherton

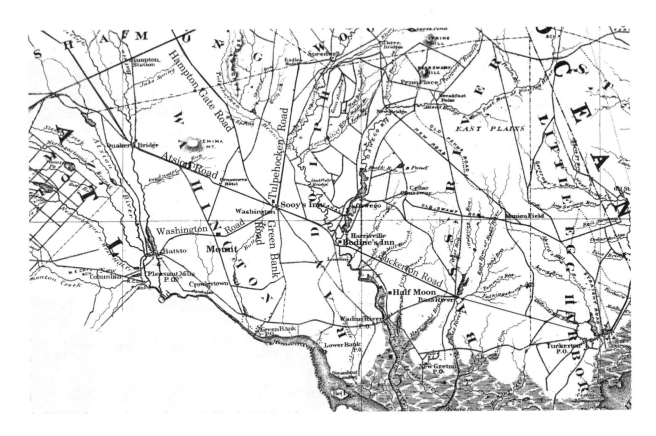

The Road to Little Egg Harbor

Using the 1870 F.W. Beers Map

Spirit of the Pines
written at Calico
by John Milton Adams

All day long I heard her cry
In early morn, and when the sun rose high.
Slanting down to bring the evening star
The plaintive notes came echoing afar.

I've searched and search through woods and mossy glades
Into the tangled swamps lone paths I've made
Beside the stilly shores my footsteps take
To hear her cry come floating o'er the lake.

Perhaps I'll never see this vision fair
This loveliness of wood, stream and air.
Yet do I know that she is mine
Even though I seek and seek, yet never find.

February 11, 1940

The Road to Little Egg Harbor

During the middle years of the eighteenth century, colonial businessmen were casting a favorable eye on the natural resources of the New Jersey Pinelands. The little rivers with their strong flow seemed just waiting to turn mill wheels of every sort. The bogs were filled with iron-ore in abundance. Along their banks stood thousands of acres of pines and oaks that would provide timber for both lumber mills and for feeding iron furnaces. Huge white cedars filled the swamps that promised excellent wood for boat-building. The tidal section of the Mullica was deep enough to provide a smooth avenue for the shipment of goods to the New York and Philadelphia markets. The first travellers to the shore either took the long way around via the Delaware Bay, the Atlantic Ocean, Great Bay, and up the Mullica, or they travelled by Indian paths through the forest.

The first road to Little Egg Harbor from Philadelphia started at Cooper's Point in what is now Camden and ran through the Marlton area. It then turned southeast, crossed the Taunton Road, then the Jackson-Medford Road. Just south of the present-day Medford Lakes, the Road to Little Egg Harbor split. The middle route passed through Pipers Corner, Flyatt, Oriental (below Tabernacle), Hampton Gate, and High Crossing. The more southerly route connected Charles Read's iron enterprises of Taunton, Aetna, and Atsion. Still a third ran from the Tabernacle area southward past the Eagle Tavern and through Tulpehocken. All three of these roads merged at or near the crossroads of the pines: Sooy's Inn, later called the Washington Tavern. Here, a single road continued to the crossing of the Wading River, the Bass River, and on into Little Egg Harbor.

The middle route may have been the earliest section, because there would have been no need for the more southerly route prior to the construction of Atsion Forge in 1765. It is said that the first settlers in the Tuckerton area had to cart their grain all the way to Medford to the nearest grist mill for grinding until the Andrews brothers built one of their own on what became known as the Tuckerton Creek. From the time of the founding of Little Egg Harbor Yearly Meeting early in the eighteenth century, Quakers had made the annual journey from the Burlington and Mount Holly area down through the pines to the little meeting by the bay. We know that by 1774, they had used the southerly route for some time, for in that year, they built a bridge at the Batsto River crossing, which, ever since, has borne the title of "Quaker Bridge."

Traces of this road survive into the twentieth century, though parts of it are almost impassable except by foot. From Washington to the Wading River, the road is called Iron Pipe Road. A portion is fenced off in cranberry bogs where it approaches the Wading River crossing. The bridge over the Wading River has been gone for over a century, and the modern-day state campground at Bodine's Field below Harrisville has obliterated most traces of this primal road. It seems that a portion of it ran very much where the present Route 679 does today. The construction of that modern road destroyed all signs of the old road in that area. From the Harrisville-New Gretna Road (Route 679), the old road is paved through Bass River State Forest into Tuckerton and is called "Stage Road."

Early travellers were on their own. At first there were no taverns along the route and no regular stages ran through the pines, though private coaches could and did travel to Atsion and Batsto. Heavily laden wagons made their laborious way through loose sand and swamp from the various early iron enterprises and from Little Egg Harbor itself. People travelled on foot or on horseback, making the best of a lengthy trip through a huge extent of wilderness. The sand road was always deeply rutted from usage, filled with huge, water-filled potholes. Occasionally a stream had to be forded which was always a harrowing experience for all concerned. Eventually, bridges were built, mostly by local people who had settled in the area of a crossing.

Most of the early taverns seem to have been built about the same time as the first regular stage ran in the area at the end of the eighteenth century. The exception was that of Nicholas Sooy I at the major crossroad where the southern and northern branches of the Road to Little Egg Harbor met. The middle route merged with the southern just a short distance to the west. At this point also, roads from Speedwell and Eagle, from Green Bank, and from Batsto, joined the main road. Nicholas Sooy I is reputed to have built his tavern at the crossroads on this Road to Little Egg Harbor about 1773. When the war was successfully concluded, he named his tavern the Washington Tavern, although it would long continue to be known as "Sooy's Inn."

By 1795, there were so many iron furnaces and forges spread throughout the pines as well as a growing population along the Mullica, Wading, and Bass Rivers, that a stage line became financially feasible. As soon as there was a stage, there was a necessity for more taverns. Enterprising men, taking note of the possibilities, built taverns, the lifelines of colonial travelling. Every few miles, horses had to be changed, passengers refreshed and fed, and perhaps even bedded down for the night. At a maximum of five miles an hour, more likely two or three was the average, the stage would make its way from the Cooper's Point ferry to Philadelphia to the bay and back. Only after the stage started running on a regular schedule could this road be properly called "Stage Road."

The actual "stage" taverns were limited by law in number and location. They had to be a half day's journey apart. In what would become Washington Township, additional inns were built at Hampton Gate and Quaker Bridge (where the road crossed the Batsto River). Another would be built on the Quaker Bridge Road at Mount. The last stop before the "town" of Little Egg Harbor Meeting was the Bass River Hotel, where the stage route crossed the river of that name. After Tuckerton received its name in 1798, this old Road to Little Egg Harbor became known as "The Tuckerton Road."

For a hundred years, this route bisected what would be, by 1802, Washington Township, and the little towns along the way were prosperous. Next to the Mullica itself, this road was the artery along which flowed the lifeblood of the pines. The taverns were the central meeting places, the voting stations, the gathering places for local militia training, and the hangouts for the workers in the iron furnaces and forges which dotted the area. The names of the taverns along the way, and those of the hosts, were as well known two centuries ago as the major towns along the Garden State or the New Jersey Turnpike today.

THE BASS RIVER TAVERN

The Road to Little Egg Harbor left the vicinity of the Andrews' mill in what would be known as Tuckerton by 1798 and ran in a straight line to the only place where a crossing of the Bass River could be made. A section of the road remains in use today, leaving Tuckerton behind the Acme on Route 9 and travelling straight as an arrow through the woods past the entrance to Bass River State Forest. Just beyond, a road from New Gretna joins it for the river crossings. There are two bridges, one for each branch. These bridges come in the middle of a winding, tortuous section of the road which was built through a small section of swamp between the two river branches. The bridge over the easternmost branch is known as Fir (or perhaps Fur) Bridge. No name seems to have been attached to that over the main branch of the Bass River. In this vicinity, Thomas French built a tavern that went by the name of French's Tavern. The second host was Isaiah Adams who seems to have called his inn the Bass River Hotel. Colloquially, it was called the "Red" Tavern, perhaps because it was painted that color rather than simply left weathered wood as were most other structures. Isaiah was unique among the tavern keepers of old in that he was a teetotaller. The Red Tavern closed in 1855, probably with the death of the proprietor.

The tavern was quite near the present location of the Pilgrim Lake Campgrounds building where Allen Road intersects with Stage Road. An 1849 map indicates a building in this location, and a cellar depression can still be found there also.

Minutes of the Township Committee of Little Egg Harbor Township, as signed by Ebenezer Deacon, the Town Clerk, include the following resolution: "Resolved that the new laid out road from Tuckerton to Bass River be opened between this and the next town meeting." Unfortunately, no date is attached to this page in the clerk's minutes book. Road Returns indicate that the road was laid out as it exists today between 1798 and 1810. The 1798 survey is for a road to be laid out from "the Province Line" (Keith's Line) and Atsion, ie. from about West Creek to Atsion through Tuckerton. Other Road Returns indicate that portions of this road were resurveyed during the next twelve years.

BODINE'S TAVERN

The present road splits after passing the site of the Bass River Tavern, the right fork being the original route towards Bodine's Tavern. Today, the old "Road to Little Egg Harbor" ends on Route 679, the modern road from New Gretna to Chatsworth, but in the eighteenth and nineteenth centuries, it followed the course of Rt. 679 to a point just below the bridge over Beaver Branch. Here it headed directly for Bodine's Tavern where it crossed the Wading River. For almost a century, this was the lowest spot on the river where a traveller could cross the Wading by bridge. After the lower Wading River Bridge was built in 1814, a mail stage to Bridgeport, Lower Bank, Green Bank, and Crowleytown used a road paralleling the river from Bodine's through what is now Chip's Folly to the new swing bridge. The Bridgeport end of this road is known as Goldacker's today and comes in right beside the bridge. By this time, though, all traffic along the Road to Little Egg Harbor had headed off into the woods towards Sooy's Inn for almost a hundred years, an area which remains much the same as it was three centuries ago.

The tavern on the Road to Little Egg Harbor where it crossed the Wading River was built by John Bodine. The Bodines were an old and illustrious French Huguenot family, and John's great, great grandfather, Jean, had left his native country prior to 1677 and settled on Staten Island. His son, Jean, Jr., was born at Medis, France on May 9, 1645 and had been naturalized in London, England, on March 21, 1682. Jean, Jr. married twice and fathered ten children, the last of whom was Francis, who was probably born in England. Francis Bodine, Sr. was a resident on

Staten Island in 1726 when he was charged with a minor offence and fined. Mary Elizabeth Sinnott (*Annals of the Sinnott, Rogers, Coffin, Corliss, Reeves, Bodine, and Allied Families*) believes he moved to Cranbury, Middlesex County, New Jersey, with his sons, Vincent and Francis, Jr., where he died. Francis, Jr. married Maria Day and they had three children in Cranbury: Joel (b. 1742), Francis III (b. 1744), and John (b. 1746). They may have also had a son, James (b. c.1747) who later moved to Tennessee, and possibly a son, Thomas.

In 1773, Francis III acquired a tract of 20 acres from Amos Pharo at Tranquility Swamp, and a part interest in another twenty-two acre piece. Also in that year, James Pharo made a quit claim to Francis Bodine III for five and a half acres on the Pappoose Branch. Ms. Sinnott notes that, on November 1, 1775, Francis, Jr. purchased thirty acres at Tranquility Swamp in what would become Washington Township and moved to the vicinity at that time with his three sons. She also says that the deed for this property is found in the Burlington County Deeds, Liber M2, 335. The deed listed only has the name "Francis Bodine," leaving open the possibility that it was Francis III, not Francis, Jr. who acquired the property. Francis, Jr. may never have left Cranbury, but certainly his sons were in the area by this date. Francis III may have been in the area that would be Washington Township at an even earlier date than his first property purchase suggests, for on March 20th, 1768, he married Mary Rose (b. 1748), who may have been from the same local family as John Leek, Jr.'s wife, Martha.

In 1784, Francis III bought another one hundred twenty acres at Tranquility Swamp from Daniel and Enoch Mathis, a sale which was not recorded until 1846. On August 10, 1790, he apparently bought the remaining interest in Pharo's twenty-two acres from the sheriff. On January 8, 1822, a few months before his death, Francis III transferred one hundred twenty acres at Tranquility Swamp to his son, Daniel Bodine.

Francis's brother, John, enlisted as a private during the Revolutionary War, served for seven years, and was mustered out as a captain. John married Mary Roundtree, and they had five children together. On her death, he married Ann Taylor, by whom he had ten more children. Ann had been born in Hillsborough District, Orange County, North Carolina, in 1765. Two of John's sons became clergymen: The Rev. John and the Rev. Stacy Bodine. His eighth child, Sarah, married Joseph Allen of Lower Bank. His seventh son, Joel, married Sarah Gale of Wading River, and eventually became the owner of the Williamstown Glass Works. Joel's grandson, John Forman Bodine, was elected to the State Assembly from Camden County in 1864 and was State Senator from Gloucester County in 1874. John Forman Bodine's brother, J. Alfred Bodine, married Phebe J. French, the daughter of Francis French of Bass River. Francis's son, James, married Sarah Sooy, daughter of Nicholas Sooy I.

In 1791, John Bodine bought land on the Road to Little Egg Harbor about a seven-mile ride from Tuckerton where it crossed the Wading River. Here, he built a tavern. Francis III and his wife, Mary (Rose) seem to have lived on the Bodine property by this time as well, and the couple had eight children. He later removed to a plantation about a half mile from Lumberton, and two and a half from Mount Holly. He died on September 27, 1822 and is buried in Lumberton. His wife had preceded him in death by two years. Her passing was on December 15, 1820.

Brother Joel was living at Swago (the site of Martha) when, in 1771, he married Mary Corlies. He finally settled in Long-a-Coming (Berlin) where he died in 1819. According to Ms. Sinnott, both Joel and Mary Bodine are buried in the cemetery of Saint John's Episcopal Church at Chew's Landing, where they had been parishioners.

Photograph by John Pearce

The Road to Little Egg Harbor crossed the Wading River on a large bridge at Bodine's Tavern, one section over a side branch and one over the main branch. All that remains of either bridge are the pilings. It was called the "Great Bridge" in Little Egg Harbor township records.

The first mention of the bridge across the Wading River in the minutes of the township committee of Little Egg Harbor Township is that of 1779, when money was appropriated to redeck the bridge that carried the Road to Little Egg Harbor. Subsequent references indicate that it had to be redecked every four years, which means that the bridge had to have been built at least as early as 1775.

Bodine's received increased business after the founding of Martha Furnace in 1793 and of the Wading River Forge and Slitting Mill two years later. Martha's workers were delighted (a little too delighted to suit Jesse Evans) to travel the two or three miles down river to drown their aches in Bodine's liquor.

When the infant Washington Township needed a place to hold its first meeting in 1803, Bodine's Tavern was chosen. Francis Bodine III was elected as President of the meeting, and John Bodine was elected to the first Township Committee, along with Jonathan Johnson of Lower Bank, Joseph Walker of the Wading River Forge and Slitting Mill, Thomas Richards of Batsto, and Jesse Evans of Martha. William Saltar, Esq. of Atsion served with Jesse Evans as Chosen Freeholders. John Bodine served with Thomas Richards as Commissioner of Highways. Francis Bodine III was elected Overseer of the Poor. Francis III was fifty-nine when the first township meeting met at the tavern and his brother, John, fifty-seven. Though president of the first Washington Township meeting, Francis III did not stay long in his new position. It was that in that same year that he bought his plantation in Lumberton and moved from the area.

There were others there at Bodine's Tavern that day in March of 1803 whose names would become familiar in the township over the years and some who would vanish from memory as well. Jacob Barnhart, the owner of the Eagle Tavern, was elected Collector, William Weatherby of Wading River - Clerk, Lewis Mingen and James Gale - Overseers of Roads, and Edward McBride and John Cramer - Constables.

Without doubt, the tavern was jammed with voters from such far-flung parts of the township as Atsion, Batsto, Green Bank, Lower Bank, Wading River (no bridge yet), and Speedwell. The Bodines probably made a bundle off the hard-drinking voters.

Town Meeting was held at Bodine's Tavern from 1803 through 1808. Only for a brief period of three years would it again venture that far east in the township, though. In 1820 through 1822, the annual meeting returned to Bodine's, but by that time, it was operated by Samuel Bodine, not John. This Samuel had to have been Samuel H. Bodine, son of Francis III, Samuel, son of John, was only ten years old in 1820. Samuel H. Bodine had married Pharnelia (Parnell) Sooy, daughter of Nicholas Sooy I and Sarah (Sears) Sooy in August of 1813. Their daughter, Mary, twin to Francis V, was buried in Lower Bank one month after she was born in 1815.

John Bodine's last recorded position for the township was that of Surveyor of Highways in 1816. On June 9, 1821, John took a mortgage on fifty acres and the tavern from his son, Joel, but Joel doesn't seem to have actually operated the tavern. That chore was left to his cousin, Samuel, who ran it from 1820 - 1822. Early in 1823, Samuel H. Bodine seems to have taken over the operation of Sooy's Inn after the death of Nicholas Sooy I, but his tenure did not last the year. His father, Francis III, had died the year before, and Samuel moved to his plantation near Mount Holly. John Bodine's second wife, Ann, and their son, Jesse (1804-1879), tried to carry on at their tavern, apparently without nephew Samuel, but they were not successful.

It is not known just when Bodine's ceased to operate, but it is presumed to have closed around 1840. After the construction of the swing bridge on the lower Wading River, traffic tended to move southward to include the Mullica River towns, and business decreased along the old route.

Township meetings continued to be held at the lost towns along the Tuckerton Road through 1852, but Bodine's was no longer the focus of attention. One of the numerous forest fires that have swept through the area probably erased it from the earth and from memory long before the twentieth century was born. Joseph Wharton bought the land along with that of Harrisville when he purchased that latter town, and the State of New Jersey acquired it from his estate.

The Bodine name is preserved in the area by a huge campground which the State calls "Bodine's Field." During the heyday of Harrisville, The Landing was located just downstream from the old hotel where Beaver Branch meets the Wading River. From this point, most of the goods produced at the Wading River Forge, Martha Furnace, local sawmills, McCartyville, and later Harrisville, were loaded on small transports for shipment down river to the Leek Wharf. Here everything was reloaded on to coastal vessels which then headed for New York, Philadelphia, and other cities.

The pilings of the old bridge(s) for the stage road can still be seen in the river as it flows through Bodine's Field today, and the site of the tavern is nearby. It is marked by a small clump of trees in a shallow hole.

One interesting discovery has come to light during a lengthy drought in 1995. A 1,500 foot sluiceway was discovered near Bodine's Field. A note in Bisbee's *Sign Posts* under "Bodine's Tavern" says that Thomas F. Gordon in his *Gazetteer and History of the State of New Jersey* (Trenton, 1834) records that Bodine operated a sawmill near his tavern.

THE WASHINGTON TAVERN: SOOY'S INN

Nicholas Sooy I, whose father, Joseph (Yoos II) lived in Sam Driver's house in Green Bank, owned the next tavern on the Road to Little Egg Harbor. From Bodine's, the road travelled on a straight course through the woods to a point where several local roads came together. Near the junction of the first Stage Road via Hampton Gate with the newer route via Quaker Bridge and Atsion, Sooy built a tavern at around the time of the Revolutionary War. A direct road connected Green Bank with the crossroads on the Road to Little Egg Harbor.

Nicholas Sooy I had married Sarah Sears, the daughter of Paul Sears, a colonel during the Revolutionary War and scion of a well-respected Massachusetts family. The young couple are thought to have purchased land and built a tavern in the Sweetwater/Pleasant Mills area. About 1773, he bought land on the Road to Little Egg Harbor at the major crossroads of all the roads from everywhere in the area and built another tavern. There is a deed of record showing land transferred to Nicholas I from his father, Joseph, in 1770 that lay across the Tulpehocken Road, but it is not known whether this was the tavern site. Nicholas's and Sarah's tavern was called colloquially Sooy's Inn, and it quickly became the focus of life in Washington Township for seventy-five years. Charles Boyer, in his 1931 book *Old Inns and Taverns of West Jersey*, says that he could find no record attaching the name of Nicholas Sooy I to the tavern prior to 1795, but admits that it was opened before the Revolutionary War.

Nicholas Sooy I was proud of his new country and its General-in-Chief and named his tavern the "Washington Tavern." It is said that the tavern sign bore a likeness of the general, surrounded by a laurel wreath. The legend on the sign read, "Our Country Must Be Free." Some even started calling the area "Washington," but the place was known as "Sooy's" through the 1830's. An 1839 map shows the location as "Washington."

A small town actually grew up around Sooy's Inn, and the place bustled on voting day and "training" day. Sooy's Inn was the meeting place for the local Committee of Safety. It was sufficiently far from the peace-loving Quakers further to the east to give the revolutionaries some sense of privacy and secrecy. Those devoted to the patriot cause were always suspicious that the Quakers would betray them to the loyalists, though it seems that the Sooy family itself had been Quaker prior to the commencement of the war.

Sooy's Washington Tavern must have been a busy place, with travellers coming to and from Philadelphia. All roads crossed at or near Sooy's, so everyone had the opportunity to stop there. On "Training Day," militiamen from all over the area would congregate at this tavern for a boisterous drinking binge, relishing the time off from work and the only socialization they probably had enjoyed in some time.

The Martha Diary has at least three entries relating to Sooy's Inn:

October 10, 1809	*Election at Sooy's. Several of the hands went.*
March 13, 1810	*Town Meeting at Sooy's*
July 15, 1813	*Capt. Townsend made a draft of militia at Sooy's*

When Atsion was left to decay in 1815, the United States Government moved the post office from that place down the road to Sooy's. Some writers in the past have confused this location with that of Green Bank, thinking that Nicholas Sooy I lived in that latter town, but there is little doubt that the post office was moved to this town on the Tuckerton Road.

Town Meeting was held here for eleven years from 1809 through 1819. At the time when the meeting moved from Bodine's to Sooy's in 1809, Nicholas Sooy I was elected to the Township Committee for the second time. He had served as Pound Keeper (the public animal impoundment supervisor) in 1804, was first elected to the Committee at Bodine's in 1805, went off the Committee in 1806 but served with Jesse Evans of Martha and John Bodine as Commissioners of Appeals in that year and again in 1807, went back on the Committee in 1808, and continued to serve the township in various capacities until his death in 1822. In 1808, a "Nicholas Sooy" is listed as constable, but this was probably his son, Nicholas II, the job of constable requiring the stamina of a young man. Also, the township records always indicate Nicholas I as "Sr." when he is listed.

The township annual meeting would return to Sooy's for one more year in 1823, but by that time it would be run by Paul Sears Sooy, the brother of Nicholas Sooy II, Nicholas I having died the year before.

Nicholas and Sarah parented thirteen children at their tavern: Hannah, Elizabeth, Noah, Nathan, Nicholas II, Jemima, Josephus, Sarah, Parnell (or Pharnelia), Sophia, Archabold, William H., and Paul Sears.

Nicholas II married Esther Weeks, daughter of Ezekiel Weeks of Weekstown and sister of Samuel Weeks, Lower Bank tavern keeper, and Job Weeks, a Lower Bank farmer.

Hannah married Samuel Pettit who was related to Charles Pettit, Quartermaster General of the Continental Army, Secretary of New Jersey from 1772-1778, and who later represented Pennsylvania in the Continental Congress. Their oldest daughter, Sarah, married Job Weeks, her Aunt Esther's younger brother.

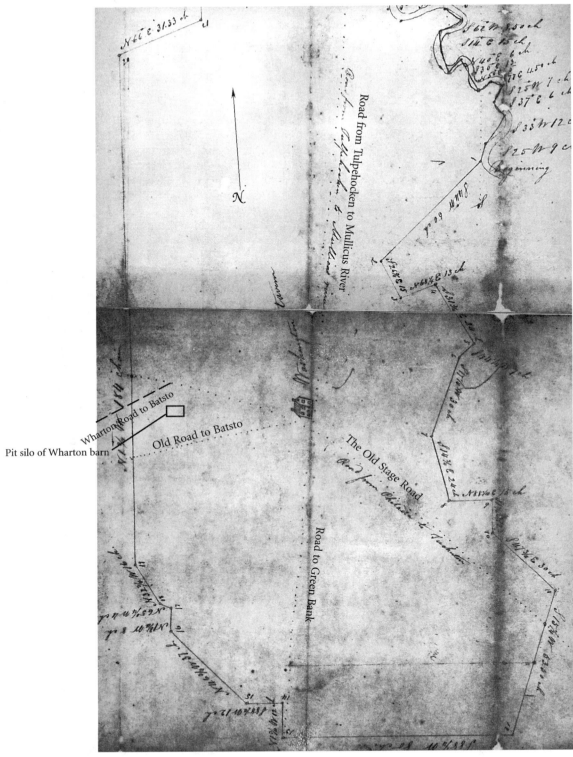

Courtesy of Budd Wilson

From an Old Map of the Washington Tavern Area
(Sooy's Inn)
The roads have been labeled and the map turned for purposes of orientation. The road to Batsto
which Joseph Wharton built (the current road) has been drawn in on this map. Also, the location
of the pit silo of the Wharton barn has been marked.

Elizabeth married Arthur Thompson. The couple bought land at Quaker Bridge from her father and built the first tavern at that site. Noah Sooy married Sarah Harriet Weeks. Jemima married Alexander Thompson. Alexander Thompson would go into partnership with Jemima's brother, Nicholas Sooy II, in building the glass factory at Green Bank.

Josephus Sooy first lived in Green Bank and married Sarah Thomas. He and Sarah later moved to the Pemberton area.

Sarah married James Bodine, son of Francis Bodine, Jr.

Parnell (or "Pharnelia" as on her gravestone) married Samuel Bodine. Archabold married Bethia Cranmer and lived near Mount Holly.

William H. Sooy married Rebecca Weeks and lived just up the Road to Little Egg Harbor from his father's tavern. *His* son, William H., was the Green Bank blacksmith for many years, and son Benjamin lived on a farm off Turtle Creek Road in Wading River. Paul Sears Sooy, their youngest, married Elizabeth Cavileer, daughter of Peter and Eva Cavileer.

Sarah (Sears) Sooy died on June 7, 1819 and was laid to rest in the old burying ground of the Pleasant Mills church. Nicholas I was placed next to her when he passed away three years later on the 22nd of December, 1822. Nicholas Sooy I had run the Washington Tavern for approximately forty-nine years when he died.

An intriguing tidbit concerning Nicholas Sooy I arises from his will, a copy of which is at Batsto and in the New Jersey Archives. In that document, he left the Washington Tavern "where I now reside" to "my dearly beloved wife," and on her death, to "my son, Sears Sooy." That much we know. In addition, though, he bequeaths his son Josephus "one of my cows in addition to the plantation and tavern which I purchased of Rever Elton and for which I have already given him a Deed." I haven't had time to research this second tavern of Nicholas Sooy I and have no idea where it was located, but then there are always mysteries to challenge the mind in the study of history. There is no mention in the Sooy Genealogy of Josephus owning a tavern. Perhaps this is the one Nicholas I is rumored to have owned prior to the building of Sooy's Inn at Washington.

Paul Sears Sooy, only twenty-two in the year of his father's death, inherited the tavern from his father and became concerned with the daily management. Charles Boyer says that Samuel Bodine took over the actual operation Sooy's Inn at Nicholas I's death but was soon succeeded by "Sears" Sooy.

Paul Sears Sooy ran it for two years, followed by Eldad Cook for the next two years. Once again, Paul Sears Sooy took over the operation of the inn. William DeBow leased it from Paul Sears Sooy in 1829, and six years later, John Hammell became the proprietor. At some time, Boyer doesn't say just when, Paul Sears Sooy took the tavern back again and "was here as late as 1854." He died in 1868.

The notes from the Washington Township records show the annual meetings were held at Paul Sears Sooy's in 1823, Eldad Cook's in 1824 and 1825, "Town House" (Quaker Bridge) in 1826, and at Paul S. Sooy's in 1827, confirming Boyer's research. The last meeting held at Sooy's Inn was that of the third of three meetings in the year 1832 which declared the previous two meetings, held at Quaker Bridge, to be invalid.

After 1823, Sooy's Tavern would no longer be the center of the township, although it seems to have existed at least until the 1850's. According to the late Theda Ashton, long member of the Batsto Citizens Committee, it had ceased being a tavern by about 1860 and probably burned within the following decade.

The last births recorded at "Sooy's Inn" were those of Merret [sic] Sooy, born April 1, 1866, and Joseph F. Sooy, born August 22, 1867. The parents of both children were Arthur and Martha Sooy who had a farm in the area, probably his father's just up the stage road from his grandfather's tavern. Arthur was the son of William H. Sooy and Rebecca (Weeks) Sooy and grandson of Nicholas I and Sarah (Sears) Sooy. He was also the brother of Benjamin (farmer in Wading River), Samuel, and Edwin Clark (storekeeper in Wading River). The name "Sooy's Inn" was probably applied to the little town rather than to the tavern, because the latter had ceased operations by this time.

In the list of marriages for the township, it is recorded that Abrham [sic] Nichols married Elizabeth Wintlin at Sooy's Inn on March 9, 1859. Abrham Nichols is listed as a "landlord," and his residence is given as Lower Bank. He and Elizabeth were married by W. "W." Sooy. The residence of Abraham Nichols in Lower Bank is interesting. We know he ran a tavern and had a landing just beyond Crowleytown, but there does not seem to be anything indicating that he had a residence or a tavern in Lower Bank other than this notation.

On April Fool's Day of that year, W. H. Sooy, J.P., married Henry Ford and Charlott [sic] Beebe at Sooy's. The next month, on May 7th, W. "W." Sooy married Benjamin Harris and Hannah Palmer at Sooy's Inn. These three weddings seem to be the last conducted at this lost town in the pines. This William H. Sooy was probably the *brother* of Nicholas Sooy II and not his *son*. He was the one who lived near Sooy's Inn, the location of which is marked on the 1836 map of McCartyville. He was a lawyer, so it is logical that he was the Justice of the Peace. An 1849 map still has this location marked as his house. It stood about 750 feet west of the tavern on the Tuckerton Road, and a cellarhole and well are in this location. This William H. died in 1861, and there are no entries in the town records with his name attached after that date, so it is presumed that he is the William H. in question.

Three other weddings relating to Sooy's Inn were performed by W.H. Sooy, Justice of the Peace, during this period. On November 4, 1848, George Myers married someone named Margaret Reed. The couple was married at Batsto, but their residence is listed as Sooy's Inn. On November 26th of 1848, John [no surname given] married Catherine McDogul, with W. H. Sooy conducting the ceremony. On October 1st, 1854, W. Sooy married Abram Brown and Isabella McCane at "Washington Tavern." This couple also lived at "Washington Tavern."

In an article printed in the Spring/Summer edition of the Batsto Citizens Gazette for 1997, Theda Ashton is quoted as having said,

> *My great-grandparents on the Coleman side, Richard and Hannah Coleman, lived in the old stagecoach stop at Washington, 5 miles out of Batsto on the Washington Turnpike. It wasn't a stagecoach stop and it wasn't a bar then. The Colemans were the last family to live in this house, as it later burned down.*
>
> *Grandpop Jesse Coleman was born there in 1861 and that's where he was raised. He was the youngest of eleven children. He remembers where the bar was and he played in the bar.*

After Joseph Wharton bought the surrounding area late in the nineteenth century, he had extensive fields in this area, just up the road from the site of the old tavern. He even built an entirely new road from Batsto to what he called "Washington Fields." It is difficult to imagine that, at one time, a great deal of this area along the Old Tuckerton Road was open lands, some cultivated in farms, with houses and barns. Today, it is deep in the pines, a lonely spot in the midst of nowhere, a condition it has not known since the Revolution. The sand roads still come together at this crossroads in the pines, but they bear little traffic. If you are sharp, you can find the remains of Wharton's barn and pit silo. You'd have to know where to look to find the cellar hole of Nicholas Sooy's Washington Tavern. The cellar hole and well are still visible where the Tulpehocken/Green Bank Road crosses the Tuckerton Road, not far from the merging of the Atsion Road and the Hampton Gate Road.

Courtesy of Budd Wilson

The Pit Silo at Washington

This is all that is left of the Wharton barns at this location. Many have confused this ruin with the site of the Washington Tavern, but Wharton's Washington Farms was further up the Tuckerton Road from the tavern towards Atsion.

MOUNT

Very little is known about the Mount Tavern on the Tuckerton Road between Washington and Quaker Bridge. Zebedee Wills deeded the site of the tavern to Jonathan Cramer on March 27, 1839 for the sum of $900. Cramer apparently built the tavern in that year and ran it for perhaps as long as twenty years. The tavern was abandoned by the 1860's.

Township records show that Town Meeting was held at Jonathan Cramer's Mount Tavern from 1843 through 1846. In the years just prior to this, the meeting had been held up the road at Quaker Bridge. Apparently there was some interest in moving the meeting to a more central location. These were the years that the old Sooy Tavern at Washington was fading away. At the first meeting held at his establishment, Jonathan was elected as a Commissioner of Appeals, but he does not seem to have served the township in any capacity after that year.

Where in the world did the tavern ever get the name of "Mount?" The one impression gained by the traveller through the New Jersey pinelands is of flatness. Some areas have slight, undulating hills, but there are certainly no "mounts" of any size. However, about a mile due north of the site of the Mount Tavern on the Mount/Sandy Ridge Road which skirts the Penn Swamp, lies Jemima Mount. Jemima Mount "towers" above the swamp and flat landscape beyond almost one hundred feet! Don't get me wrong. I haven't lived in South Jersey long enough to call this a "mountain." Elsewhere, it would barely rate being called a "hill." In the pinelands of South Jersey, though, its hundred-foot height qualifies it for at least the designation of "mount."

Who was Jemima? Jemima was a popular name at the time. Nicholas Sooy I had a sister by that name who died at twenty-one in 1782 and is buried in the Green Bank cemetery. His daughter, Jemima, born in 1784, two years after her brother, Nicholas II, married Alexander Thompson, the brother of Arthur Thompson who bought property from Sooy at nearby Quaker Bridge in 1808 and ran the Quaker Bridge Tavern for several years. Was "Jemima Mount" named after the girl who died so tragically young or after the niece born two years after her death?

When did Mount Tavern cease to be? We don't even know that. No further mention is made of it in the township records as a meeting place after 1846, nor does the name of Jonathan Cramer appear again, though other Cramers are active in township politics after that time.

It is recorded that Thomas Cramer, son of Charles Cramer of Mount, married Rebecca, daughter of Jonathan Cramer of Bridgeport in Lower Bank on September 20, 1857. W. Sooy conducted the ceremony. William and Mary Cramer, who had a farm in Lower Bank, gave birth to a little girl, Georgia Anna, on November 27, 1865 at Mount Tavern. That is the last mention of Mount in the township records.

An 1867 map of the area indicates two buildings at Mount, one of which was undoubtedly the tavern. The other was the home of Richard (1814-1884) and Hannah (Ford) Coleman . An article in the Batsto Citizens Gazette in 1980 records that committee member Theda Ashton remembered that her grandfather, Jesse Coleman, told the story of how he grew up in Mount in the last years of the nineteenth century. He and his siblings used to delight in playing in the old, abandoned tavern of Jonathan Cramer. Of course, she also said he "grew up" at the Washington Tavern, and Theda is no longer around to clarify her thoughts. The Coleman family may have moved from Washington to Mount during Jesse's youth, perhaps when the old Washington Tavern burned. In any case, the laughter of children at Mount echoes only in memory.

PENN SWAMP

Early travellers on the Road to Little Egg Harbor met a real obstruction after leaving Cramer's Mount Tavern in the form of a dense cedar swamp. Here it would have been necessary to actually build a road by cutting down trees and laying the logs side by side in the path. These early "corduroy" roads were the only practical method for crossing areas which remained wet all year.

Cedar swamps are dark and mysterious, the light from the sun almost blocked by the tall trees, sphangum moss floating around their water-soaked bases. Travellers in either direction on this old road must have been mighty happy to see the lights of the Mount Tavern or the Quaker Bridge Tavern after traversing this foreboding place.

The township records list three births in Penn Swamp: Nancy, daughter of William and Rachel Gifford, born on the fifth of February, 1853; John, son of James and Mary Dillet, born two weeks later; and Nancy, daughter of Edward and Catherine Gumner, born on the sixth of March following. Their fathers are all listed as laborers, so the families may have been living here on a temporary basis. Perhaps they were working as woodcutters or colliers.

QUAKER BRIDGE

For years, the Quakers on the western side of the state were inconvenienced by the Mullica River crossing deep in the pines on their way to Yearly Meeting at Little Egg Harbor. Finally in 1774 (some say 1772), they had had enough, planned their journey a day earlier than usual, and built a bridge, and the location has been "Quaker Bridge" ever since. At some time early in the nineteenth century, probably by 1809, Arthur Thompson built an inn near the old "Quaker" bridge. Called "Town House" or "Townhouse," this tavern was the scene of the annual township meeting from 1826 through 1833 (though the information for the year 1827 is not given in the records). In 1833, the inn is called "Elizabeth Thompson's Town House."

The Wharton ledgers show the story of Quaker Bridge. The property was comprised of several surveys, one of which had been made for John Monrow for 165 acres. Monrow conveyed that piece, along with others, to Charles Read of Batsto and Atsion in 1767 and 1768. William Richards took over the property when he bought the Batsto Works. Richards sold the property to Nicholas Sooy I on January 30, 1801 for the sum of $100.00. Nicholas, it will be remembered, owned the Washington Tavern further down the Stage Road.

On September 20, 1808, Nicholas and his wife sold the Quaker Bridge property to Arthur Thompson for $2,400, not a bad profit for an eight-year investment. Thompson had become their son-in-law when he married their daughter, Elizabeth. Thompson proceeded to build a tavern at that spot. Charles Boyer notes that his first license was issued in 1809.

June Methot in *Blackman Revisited* traces Thompson's family back to a Thomas and Elizabeth Thompson who had two sons in Yorkshire, England: John (b. 1635) and Andrew (b. 1637). In the year 1658, the family moved to the

Quaker Bridge - c.1940

vicinity of Dublin, Ireland. John Thompson married Jane Humbly in 1665, and his brother, Andrew, married Isabella Marshill, daughter of Sir Humphrey Marshill, the same year. Both families sailed on the *Mary of Dublin* and arrived in Salem County on the 22nd of February, 1677/8. June Methot could not determine whether they were Quakers when in England, but Salem had been founded only two years before their arrival by John Fenwick's Quakers, and the Thompson name appears on their lists after their arrival.

Andrew and Isabella (Marshill) Thompson had four children, three of which were born in Ireland: Elizabeth (b. 1666), William (b. 1669), and Andrew (b. 1676/7). Their fourth child, Benjamin, was born in Salem County. Ms. Methot provides no birth date but found him on the list of contributor's to the Salem Friends by 1698.

This William was the great-grandfather of our Arthur Thompson. Arthur's father, also a William, served as a private in Captain Jacob Dubois's company of the Salem militia during the Revolutionary War, so this branch of the family must have left the Quaker faith by this time. William married Mary Nieukirk on January 2, 1772 and the couple had two known sons: Arthur (b. 1773) and Alexander (b. October 2, 1781).

When the part of the Atsion Works owned by the Quaker Henry Drinker was reopened at the end of the war, the Thompson family moved there to find work. William bought a farm in Evesham, Burlington County, in 1789, and, as Ms. Methot notes, he described himself as a "Hammer Man" in the deed. In 1811, they deeded their farm to their son, Alexander.

Arthur, meanwhile, had gone to work at the Atsion Works, but seems to have had greater ambitions. As has been mentioned, he married the daughter of the wealthy host of the Washington Tavern on the Phildelphia/Tuckerton Road on March 7, 1797 (Methot has May 11th). He bought "10 undivided 16th parts of the Atsion Iron Works and lands thereto belonging or therewith used or occupied - part of 530 acres lying west of a hill called Jemima's Mount lying in the Township of Northampton," on February 13th, 1802. Six years later, his father-in-law sold him the piece of land on the "Batsto Creek north of the bridge known as Quaker Bridge." Brother Alexander, meanwhile, had married another daughter of Nicholas and Sarah Sooy, Jemima. Unfortunately, no date for the event is given by either Methot or the Sooy Genealogy. The two brothers and sisters worked together to build and open the Quaker Bridge Tavern.

A stone in the Green Bank cemetery notes that Arthur Thompson, Sr. died on the 21st of November, 1819 at the age of forty-six. His wife, Elizabeth (Sooy) Thompson, tried to continue operation of the tavern. Boyer says she kept the place going until 1836 when James G. Sears took over the operations. This is confirmed, as far as Sears is concerned, by the Washington Township records that show the town meeting held there in 1837 when the inn was under the Sears name. In 1833, the town meeting was held at "Elizabeth Thompson's Town House, Quaker Bridge." In 1834, it was held at "Town House, Quaker Bridge, William W. Sloan." From 1835 to 1836, no name is given for the host/hostess of Quaker Bridge.

General Elias Wright, when tracing the history of the property at Quaker Bridge for his boss, Joseph Wharton, noted in the Wharton ledgers that Arthur Thompson died intestate *in 1832*, leaving his sons, William *and Nicholas*, as his heirs. Now William was definitely Arthur's son, but, according to June Methot, Nicholas was his brother Alexander's son. If they had some type of partnership agreement, Alexander may have continued the operation at Quaker Bridge, but there is no indication that this was the case. On his death, then, his only son, Nicholas Sooy Thompson, and his brother Arthur's oldest son, William, were the heirs. On the other hand, the Sooy Family Genealogy lists "Sooy" Thompson as *Arthur's* oldest son. If this is correct, "Nicholas Sooy" Thompson may have been Arthur and Elizabeth's son, not Alexander and Jemima's as per Methot, and Wright would have been quite correct that "William and Nicholas" were Arthur's heirs.

In any case, the Wharton ledgers continue: Jesse Evans, Nicholas Sooy II, and William Braddock were appointed commissioners on March 16, 1832. They determined that the property could not be divided without great prejudice and appealed to the court to permit them to sell the property. The order to sell was issued on May 13, 1832. The fact that the township records call this tavern "Elizabeth Thompson's Town House" in 1833 also seems to indicate that Arthur died in 1832. The curious thing is that stone labelled "A. Thompson, Sr." in the Green Bank cemetery next to Elizabeth Thompson's with the date of November 21, 1819. The stone attests that he died at the age of 46 which would be correct for his 1773 birthdate. It is entirely possible that Arthur did die in 1819, but that it was not until 1832 that his widow and children petitioned to have his estate sold. This may have confused General Wright.

The commissioners sold the Quaker Bridge property to Samuel Richards on December 17, 1832, for $1,805. Thus the property dropped 30% in value over the intervening thirty-four years and the addition of the tavern since Nicholas Sooy I sold it to Thompson in the first place. The Quaker Bridge tract contained about 100 acres at this time. Also sold to Richards at this time as the "Mount Tract" of 100 acres. This tract seems not to have been the site which Jonathan Cramer would purchase in 1839 but was west of Jemima's Mount, part of a survey of 741 acres which Josiah Foster had conveyed to the owners of Atsion Iron Works and part of 536 acres surveyed to Henry Drinker and conveyed to Arthur Thompson on February 13, 1802. No indication is given as to when it left Samuel Richards' ownership, but he died in 1842. According to her stone in the Green Bank cemetery, Elizabeth (Sooy) Thompson died on March 4, 1840. Her brother-in-law and sister, Alexander and Jemima (Sooy) Thompson, were buried in Pleasant Mills.

Quaker Bridge proves an enigma. Township meetings were held here for years, but every year indicates a different name: 1837, James G. Sears; 1838, John Nixon's; 1839, Mahlon Pettit's; 1840-42, Jonathan Heartman's; 1847-1848, Mrs. Gifford's Quaker Bridge House; 1849-1852, Jonathan Heartman's again. The town meeting was not held in Quaker Bridge after 1852, indicating that it had probably lost its importance at about that time. There are no marriages listed during the period of the extant town records (1848 -1877) that were conducted at Quaker Bridge, nor is anyone who was married during that time listed as a resident of the area.

Were all the places different? Were some meetings held in private homes? Did one tavern have several successive owners? The answers have been swallowed up by the pines. It is unlikely that any meetings were held in private homes. There is no indication that any ever was. Most would have been entirely too small to contain the number of people in attendance. Besides that, township residents needed food and refreshments after travelling so far for the meeting. If every one of these places was a different inn, Quaker Bridge must have been a bustling place! It is more than likely that one inn did change hands through the years, but there may have been at least two inns located at this Mullica crossing. Three buildings are known to have been at the crossing, at least one of which was a dwelling. Perhaps Samuel Richards leased the inn to different tavern keepers. No one knows. Such a lively spot was Quaker Bridge a hundred and fifty years ago. Now there is nothing there at all.

HAMPTON GATE, HAMPTON FURNACE, AND HAMPTON FORGE

The middle route of the Road to Little Egg Harbor originally ran from Sooy's Inn (Washington) through Hampton Gate towards Tabernacle. It actually went a little south of Tabernacle to Aetna Furnace. This portion near Tabernacle is known as The Tuckerton Road today. After joining what we know as the Carrenza Road, it ran on to Hampton Gate. Here, about the midway point on the Washingting/Tabernacle road, Daniel Cavileer operated a tavern called The Gate. To the southwest, the Batsto River and its branches run through extensive marshland in this area, and due south of the tavern stood the Hampton Forge and Furnace.

Apparently, both were built before 1795, probably by Clayton Earl, near the point where the Robert's (or Robbin's) Branch flows into the Batsto proper. Bisbee notes that the 1849 map of the area shows a pond on both Robert's Branch and the Batsto River which are listed as "Furnace Pond" and "Forge Pond."

The Wharton ledgers list a 1795 transfer from Restore Shinn and wife to Richard Stockton and Clayton Earl for 1,000 pounds, an enormous sum for ten acres of empty land, if that is indeed what it was. There may well have been more to it than meets the eye. As noted in the quote below, this purchase seems to have been for land that became part of the Hampton Furnace and Forge property. In 1796, Clayton Earl would become a partner of Samuel Richards in purchasing Pleasant Mills from Joseph Ball.

Again, the ledgers note that Clayton Earl conveyed one half part of Hampton Furnace and one-half of the Saw Mill known by the name of "Unknown Mill" to William Lane and John Godfrey in May of 1795 for the sum of 4,000 pounds. Charles Boyer, in *Early Forges and Furnaces*, found the original deed listed in the Burlington County Book of Deeds, Book E, p.3, and that the sale included a one-quarter interest in a skit mill somewhere on the property as well. Richard Stockton still owned the other half interest in the property.

According to Boyer, Stockton's heirs sold that interest to "Garret" and William Ashbridge on January 2, 1797. This was actually George Garret Ashbridge and his brother, William, who were also briefly involved with the Wading River Forge and Slitting Mill, not his cousin, George, of Martha and Weymouth. Lane and Godfrey sold their half share to the Ashbridges on May 3, 1799 (BCD Book F, p. 206).

The Restore Shinn property as part of the Hampton Furnace property is mentioned in a legal agreement dated 29th December, 1800 between George and William Ashbridge and Job Prickett which states

Whereas disputes have sometimes past arisin, and are still subsisting between George G.
Ashbridge and William Ashbridge of the one part to claim two surveys viz: - one survey of one

hundred and ninety three acres surveyed to Philo Leeds recorded in the surveyor General's at Burlington in Lib a. folio 331. - one survey of ten acres surveyed to Restore Shinn, recorded in the office aforesaid in Lib. - P. folio 34, . . .

The Ashbridges seem to have built another forge on the Batsto River south of Hampton Furnace and Forge about two miles above Quaker Bridge which was called the Washington Forge. There is a deed dated February 19, 1810 which conveys "one half of Hampton Furnace and Forge lately erected called Washington Forge," and one half of "Unknown Mill" from George to William Ashbridge.

Boyer says that the Ashbridges added a considerable number of acres to the property and notes a tax duplicate from Old Washington Township to Joseph Doran assessing him for 4,900 acres and a forge with six fires in 1812. Doran may well have been running the forge at the time, though the Ashbridge's owned the property. Tax bills seem to have been sent to the operator rather than to the actual owner of the property at this period. Boyer seems to assume that this 4,900 acres included everything, but then why is there no mention of the furnace, sawmill, and skit mill? Perhaps the acreage was even larger and someone else was operating the furnace and mills at that time.

The Martha diary mentions that "Wm. Warner gone to Hampton and Atsion after bellowses stuff" on June 10 of 1813, and again, that Mr. Evans and his wife gone to Hampton" on July 5th of 1814.

According to Boyer, Hampton Furnace made "wagon tires, wagon axles, flat and round bar iron, 'wagon arms,' sledge hammers and hollow ware." Finished goods were transported to a Lumberton wharf and then shipped downstream to Philadelphia by boat. When the iron ore beds at Hampton Furnace ran out, ore was shipped in to the Lumberton wharf and then carted over to the furnace.

William Ashbridge died intestate, and his children were all minors. Jonas Preston and Richard Thomas, Jr. were appointed guardians, and an act of the state legislature, approved on December 5, 1823, authorized the sale of the William Ashbridge property:

> *Mansion house, Furnace, forges, mills, and other real estate in the County of Burlington, leaving a widow and 4 minor children that the furnace had been burned down, the forge dam broken, the buildings in a state of decay, the real-estate unproductive, and depreciating in value; that the widow and guardian and some of the relatives of the minor children had represented to the Legislature that the interest of the children would be promoted by sale of real estate and had prayed that the guardians might be authorized to make sale of the same. It was enacted etc. etc.*

A deed was thereby executed by James Preston and Richard Thomas, Jr., trustees under act of the legislature dated March 18, 1825, transferring the Hampton Forge and Furnace property to Samuel Richards of Atsion in consideration of the sum of $9,050 (Burl. Co. Clerk's office, Book R 2, p. 534).

According to Boyer, the last person to operate the works was Joseph Austin, who dismantled the forge and moved it to Dover (Tom's River) prior to 1828. He also says that the furnace was abandoned soon after Samuel Richards bought the property. By 1834, Boyer notes, both furnace and forge were in ruins for T.F. Gorden's *Gazetteer of New Jersey*, published in that year, said as much.

When Samuel Richards died in 1842, his will left his Weymouth Furnace property to his daughters, Elizabeth Richards and Sarah (Richards) Colwell and his Atsion property to his daughter, Maria, and his son William H. It does not mention the Hampton Furnace and Forge property. Maria and her husband, William Walton Fleming, did seem to own the property in 1860, but by then, all traces of both forge and furnace had vanished.

After the railroad was built through the area, there was a station called "Hampton" due south of the site of the forge and furnace near where the railroad crossed the Batsto River. There is still a sand road running south from the furnace/forge site to the crossing.

In the twentieth century, there were extensive cranberry bogs in the vicinity of the forge and furnace sites. They were called the Hampton Gate bogs, though they centered on the Batsto River where the old Hampton Forge and Furnace had stood rather than on Hampton Gate itself. The latter was actually on the periphery of the Hampton Gate bogs.

Access to the forge and furnace sites today is by a sand road from Atsion, most of which is in decent shape, but whose final journey through swampland to Hampton Forge and Furnace is blocked to vehicles by deep, water-filled potholes. There are still remnants of walls to entice the visitor but little more to indicate the activity that must have filled this place almost two centuries ago. All now is buried in the quiet of the pines.

THE EAGLE HOTEL

There was a third road out of Washington to Tabernacle and on towards Cooper's Ferry. This is known as the Washington/Speedwell Road but the main road bypassed Speedwell Furnace to the west and went on up past the Eagle Tavern. There was, however, a direct road to Speedwell that branched off this road above Tulpehocken.

The site of the Eagle Tavern is northwest of Speedwell, a little more than a mile down the road towards Friendship and a mile or so up the Tulpehocken Road. It provided the refreshments so well liked by the men who worked in the iron industry. This was one tavern that never seemed to come to mind when the township meetings were planned. It was just too far out of the way to be practical for the residents of the rest of the township to even consider going there. Today, the Washington Tavern of Nicholas Sooy is famous compared to the total obscurity of the Eagle Hotel.

Photograph by John Pearce

The Grave of Charles Wills
near the site of the Eagle Hotel

According to Bisbee, the Eagle Tract is mentioned in a survey made in 1786, from which the hotel probably gained its name. Charles Boyer, in *Old Taverns and Inns in West Jersey*, says that the first licensed keeper he could find was Gideon Pharo, licensed in 1798. He also notes that a 1799 road return marks the beginning of a road "leading from Eayre Town to Tulpehawkin [sic], a short distance south of the public house of Gideon Pharow." Jacob Barnhart was "mein host" in 1810 and the inn was known as Barnhart's Tavern, though he served as Collector of Taxes in the township in 1803, indicating he had at least been around prior to the 1810 date. John Shield succeeded Barnhart for a year, and Abner Cross took over after Shield.

Photograph by John Pearce

Site of the Eagle Hotel - 1996

James McCambridge operated it between 1826 and 1849. McCambridge printed an advertisement in 1826 noting that "he now dwells at that old and noted stand known by the name of Barnhart's tavern." (Boyer)

The Wharton ledgers mentions the Barnhart Tavern in 1831, indicating that it was still called by the name of its original owner four years after McCambridge bought it. Since it was the closest hotel to Speedwell Furnace, it was patronized by both the workmen at the furnace and by visitors to the area. The 1849 map of Burlington County indicates the location of the old Eagle Tavern, but Boyer says it was abandoned by that time. Actually, he is somewhat wrong. While it may have ceased being a tavern, the McCambridge family still lived there.

Stephen V. Lee, Jr. of Speedwell remembers that three McCambridge brothers were in residence when the old building caught fire and burned to the ground, but the actual date of the conflagration escapes him. The first Stephen Lee married James McCambridge's sister, and McCambridge sold him the Speedwell Tract in 1868.

On the old road from Sooy's Inn through Hawkin Bridge and Eagle towards Tabernacle, near the site of the old tavern, stands the marker for a single grave. Once there was a sizable cemetery here, and its headstones were made of ironwood. After the State of New Jersey took control of the area, a forest fire swept through, damaging the headstones, and the State decided to replace them. The State workers were not familiar with the lasting qualities of ironwood and replaced the charred headstones with neatly-lettered pine slabs. Unfortunately, pine rots rather quickly, and there is no trace of the graves today. Neither was a record kept of their location and identity. A single stone headstone remains, marking the last resting place of a child, Charles Wills, who died in 1848. Back in the woods behind the grave is a clearing that marks the site of the village of Eagle, those houses and outbuildings associated with the families and workers who operated the tavern. There is no evidence of the life that went on here for so many years. Once again, the pines have swallowed up the memories.

The Road To Little Egg Harbor - Reprise

A well-equipped four-wheel drive vehicle can still travel the Old Tuckerton Road from Atsion almost to the Wading River in 1996, just as the stages did in the first part of the nineteenth century. Today, however, there are no inns along the road to break the boredom of the long, sand road and relieve dry, parched throats. In fact, today there is nothing at all between Atsion and Route 563 (the Chatsworth/Green Bank Road). East of Route 563, extensive cranberry bogs and private land ownership bar the passage to the Wading River at Bodine's field, but the old road is still there. Only the section between Bodine's and the current Harrisville/New Gretna road is missing entirely. After intensive study of maps and aerial photographs with Steve Eichinger of Wading River, we've decided that the last route of the Stage Road ran where Route 679 does today from the point where the present Stage Road ends on Route 679 to just below Bodine's Field. Here it turned off the present course of the road and ran directly for Bodine's where it crossed the Wading River on the "Great Bridge." This was confirmed by an old map in the New Jersey Archives.

All evidence of human habitation and early importance has been erased by time from the sides of this old roadway through the pines. Quaker Bridge boasts only a small steel bridge over the upper Mullica. Mount is unidentifiable. Washington is but a crossroads of several sand roads coming from nowhere and going nowhere. Bodine's is a campground maintained by the State.

The road from Washington to Tulpehocken is almost non-existant, but the current road to Hawkin Bridge (Tulpehocken) from just west of Godfrey's Bridge is used by both campers and canoers and is in good shape (as sand roads go). From Hawkin Bridge, there is a road open through to the Carrenza Memorial. From there it is paved into Tabernacle. The original Hampton Gate Road lies to the west of the Friendship-Carrenza Road.

The Hampton Gate Road, the middle of the routes to Little Egg Harbor and eventually Philadelphia, ran northwesterly from Washington (Sooy's Inn) and crossed the (later) Central of New Jersey tracks at High Crossing. It ran on until it joined the present Carrenza Road a little over a mile north of that monument. It then followed the present road through Hampton Gate, after which it diverged more westward to Oriental and eventually to Read's Aetna Furnace. Only the Tabernacle Township section of this road is passable today.

The third road ran from the Tulpehocken crossing (Hawkin Bridge) northward to the Eagle Tavern. From there, it went in a more northwesterly direction, skirting Apple Pie Hill to the south. It seems to have joined the present road from Chatsworth to Tabernacle, running in the same course until diverting more to the north. Most of this road is impassable today, except on foot.

The southern route, from Route 563 to Route 206 at Atsion is passable, at least by four-wheel drive vehicles. Thus, most of the old road(s) are lost deep in the woods. Only the Tuckerton end of the southern branch and the northeastern ends of the southern and middle branches are paved. Otherwise, all sleeps in the pines where once there was life.

Photograph by John Pearce

Friendship
1996

FRIENDSHIP

The road through Speedwell from Route 563 ends at what used to be the town of Friendship. Late in the last century, a nice little village grew up on the Washington to Tabernacle road which runs past the Carrenza Memorial. Until recently, the explorer would have been treated to the sight of a couple of old, weather-beaten houses, but the last one succumbed to arson about thirty years ago.

In 1868, the same year when the first Stephen Lee built his house at the site of Speedwell Furnace, a marriage took place between two Quakers in Medford that would have far-reaching consequences for the nearby area that would be called "Friendship." Joseph Evans and Lydia E. Wills, daughter of Henry and Lydia (Stokes) Wills, stood before Meeting and bound themselves as husband and wife.

The bride's father, Henry Wills, in partnership with his brothers, John and Joseph, owned 1200 acres in what was called "Friendship Neck," which was partly in old Washington Township and partly in the newly-formed Woodland Township. The brothers visited the property once a year for a jaunt, bringing home an occasional deer which one of them had shot and gathering cranberries which grew wild in isolated natural bogs.

Bridegroom Evans quickly became fast friends with his wife's brother, Joshua, and the two young men became interested in the cultivation of cranberries, a fad which seemed to be sweeping the area. Henry Wills offered his share of the land at Friendship Neck to his son and son-in-law if they could buy out his brothers' interests.

Joshua Wills and Joseph Evans wasted no time in doing just that, and, in the same year as Joseph's wedding, the pair concluded the land transactions and constructed a village, including houses, a school, a huge cranberry packing house, a store, and several other associated buildings.

Over the next two decades, the two men built bog after bog on their acreage, setting out the natural wild cranberries which had grown on their property into the cultivated bogs. Fourteen years after they had become partners in Friendship, Joshua's mother and Joseph's mother-in-law died, and the two men bought some land in Medford Township that had been part of her estate at a place called Quoexen. Here they also created two bogs for cranberries.

Photograph by John Pearce

The Ruins of the Packing House

Dudley Lewis (left) of Green Bank and Vince Laganella of Manahawkin explore the huge foundation of the packing house at Friendship on a weekend early in 1996. The building was about 120 feet long by fifty feet wide.

In 1893, Evans and Wills obtained title to another 810 acres which joined their Friendship lands to the north, giving them a total of 2010 acres. On this newly-acquired property, they built bogs with names like Storey, Columbia, Nevada, and Vernal. The Friendship Bogs were the largest cranberry-producing operation in the area at the time.

Joseph Evans died in 1909, but Joshua Wills continued to produce cranberries in partnership with the Evans' estate. The concern was finally incorporated in 1930 as Evans and Wills, Inc. Unfortunately, Joshua Wills died only four years after the incorporation papers were signed. Joshua Wills had had two daughters, Katherine and Mary, who had married two brothers, Jesse and Allen Sharpless. Since Katherine Wills had died before her father, the interest in his properties passed to his daughter, Mary, and to Francis Sharpless, his grandson by Katherine.

Francis had acted as manager of all the Evans and Wills properties prior to his grandfather's death, but, in 1951, Sharpless and the Evans heirs decided to divide the properties between them. Francis received those lands nearer Medford while the Evans heirs received the Friendship bogs.

The Friendship lands were eventually purchased by Andy Andrews, who held them for several years. He finally was persuaded to sell them to a real estate speculation company for $42 an acre. Stephen Lee rented the bogs for a year, but the company wanted so much for the rental, that the bogs would not have been profitable for Lee to operate. He declined a second year's lease. The company, Friendship Forest Lakes, then sold the tract to the State of New Jersey for $525 an acre. Not much of a bargain for the people of New Jersey as it turned out.

Most of the houses had been abandoned by this time, as was the packing house. The schoolhouse that used to stand on the property was moved to Tabernacle. A Puerto Rican family was the last to reside in Friendship, and the Washington Township School had to send a bus down the long, miserable road from Speedwell to pick up one little girl. Finally the family moved away, and arsonists struck.

Now there is nothing at all at Friendship. The road from Speedwell to Friendship used to be paved. Today it is little more than a corrugated sand road. The state's interest, as always, is to allow the area to return to wilderness, although on a recent weekend, the number of dirt bikes participating in an organized rally would seem

Site of the Friendship Store
This store sat on the Washington/Hawkin Bridge/Friendship Road. The Packing House ruins are in the right rear.

to subvert their purpose. Stephen Lee, Jr., still decries the fact that the state will not allow the bogs to be rented and planted.

    The former town of Friendship has one other importance. The Alloway family spent three generations at the Friendship Bogs. Mark Alloway had worked in Friendship. His son, Garfield Alloway, worked for Francis Sharpless's wife in the feed business in Philadelphia before he returned to Friendship. *His* son, Mark, also managed the Friendship bogs. Garfield Alloway's daughter, Gladys, born in one of the little houses of Friendship, married Tony DeMarco, the picker boss at the Godfrey Estate in Woodland Township. The two became the parents of Garfield and Mark DeMarco. Today, the DeMarcos own the Chatsworth Cranberry Company, the largest cranberry farm in Woodland Township. Garfield and Mark DeMarco built the new Municipal Building for the Township of Woodland and dedicated it to the memory of their parents. Garfield is the former chairman of the Burlington-Bristol Bridge Commission, and an important figure in the Republican Party of Burlington County. The DeMarcos placed a monument deep in the pines to commemorate James Garfield Alloway and his wife, Anna (Shinske) where they set out their first blueberry field that became the basis for the DeMarco enterprise of today. It lies off the Hawkin Bridge/Friendship Road below Friendship, sheltered by the silence of the forest. The monument also commemorates Gladys (Alloway) DeMarco's brother and sister: Mark Andrew and Ruth Alloway.

    The Evans, Wills, and Alloways are gone now, their memory commemorated only by shallow depressions in the ground.

Site of Gladys (Alloway) DeMarco's Birthplace at Friendship

756

The Foundation of the Last Remaining House at Friendship - 1996

Called "The Bungalow," this house stood on the corner of the Carrenza Road and the Speedwell Road. Herb Gerber of Tabernacle remembers that his father's house was the next one up the road towards Speedwell. Then came the school, and finally, his father's barn.

As is the fate of every other forgotten town in the core area of the pines, no marker illumines the site of this cranberry town in the pines. The State of New Jersey seems to prioritize abandoning buildings and lands to their fate. That's what the citizens of the state get for all their tax money. Historical markers cost too much and probably would be vandalized anyway.

Dirt bikes roar through this area today, their riders paying little heed to the triumphs and tragedies of the past as they play on and thus destroy the last remnants of another forgotten town.

The Friendship School

This tiny schoolhouse was built in 1890 to serve the children of Friendship. One of its last teachers was Helena Davidson, who took the train in from Hammonton to Harris Station, where a youthful Walt Priest picked her up and drove her to Friendship.

Helena would later marry Haze Wobbar of Green Bank and become the principal of the consolidated school in that town for many years.

The building was moved from Friendship to Tabernacle and restored by the local historical society. It stands next to the elementary school on the Carranza Road which eventually joins one of the branches of the Stage Road at Hampton Gate, after which it leaves that ancient trail for its continued journey to Friendship, Hawkin Bridge, and Washington.

SANDY RIDGE

Just to the west of Friendship lie bogs that were developed as part of Joseph Wharton's business ventures in the pines. Little is known about this area, but there are indications that there were at least three houses located near these bogs. There is no evidence of a packing house at the site, however.

PENN PLACE

Directly towards the east from Speedwell was a village called Penn Place, a truely "forgotten town." Almost nothing is known about it. It lay on the Pappoose Branch of the upper Oswego River (the East Branch of the Wading River) in what is today Penn State Forest. It is assumed that this was a small village of the type that was frequently found in the central pinelands, and the 1867 map on the following page shows five structures. The 1868 map of George H. Cook, State Geologist, also shows five structures in Penn Place on the intersection of Penn Place Road and Old Penn Road. An 1888 map from the Geological Survey of New Jersey has only three structures indicated at this location, and Old Penn Road is not shown.

Penn Place Road began at Speedwell and ran in a southeasterly direction through extensive bogs and swamps to this little village. All along the East Branch of the Wading River there is a swamp. Both the road from Martha and that from Bass River had to cross extensive swampland before reaching Penn Place also. Old Penn Road (and New Road which replaced it) ran across the Pappoose Branch and the East or Oswego Branch of the Wading River and on to Munion Field.

Penn Place gained its name from a scion of that famous family who lived there. According to Leah Blackman (*History of Little Egg Harbor*), William Penn had a neer-do-well son from whom the Washington Township family descended. If so, James Penn, Sr., the first Penn to live in the township, had to have been, at very least, Penn's great-grandson.

Blackman says that James, Sr. was born in 1752 and died in 1840 at the age of eighty-eight. Mrs. Blackman did not know his wife's name, but gave his children as: William, James, Joel, Jonathan, Stacy, John, Elizabeth, Rhoda, and Hannah. She says that his eldest son, William, married Sarah Jenkins (ah, that illusive Jenkins family) who may have been a sister of Isaac Jenkins, the early stage entrepreneur. Isaac and his wife, Hannah (Stiles), had no children, so Sarah couldn't have been his daughter. The Jenkins name crops up yet again in that William's sister, Rhoda, married one Zachariah Jenkins. Jesse and Zephaniah Penn married sisters, the daughters of Jacob Headly: Rebecca and Hope. Though noting that the progeny of James Penn, Sr. were numerous, Leah Blackman made no attempt to trace them and says that several of them went West.

Henry Bisbee (*Sign Posts*) postulates that James Penn, Sr. was a descendant of John Penn, a grandson of the famous William Penn, who arrived in this country on November 30, 1752, but this would make a 1752 birthdate for James, Sr. a bit of a problem.

The Jersey Shore, a publication of the Lewis Historical Publishing Company in New York, traces the lineage of Captain Elvin Penn of Waretown using the "History of Burlington County" (no further reference is given) to an *adopted* son of William Penn, the founder of our neighboring state and trustee of West Jersey. It goes on to say that James Penn, "a member of this family, settled on West Plains about 1710 and married, about 1720, a Miss Alloway. It traces Captain Elvin Penn's line through their son, William, who married Sarah Jenkins. William's son, Zephaniah, it says, married Hope Headley, daughter of Jacob Headley. Their son, Jesse, was the father of Captain Elvin.

Historian Charles Kier researched the Penn line for genealogist Henry J. Grant and made his report in 1982, a copy of which is on file at the Burlington County library. Kier began with one William Penn (b. 6/2/1605, d. 1696) a sea captain who purchased 350 acres in the vicinity of St. George's Creek in Maryland in 1678. He had three sons: Mark, Moses, and Edward. It was Edward, according to Mr. Kier, who was the father of our James.

James Penn, Sr. was born in Cumberland County, N.J. about 1729 and seems to be in Washington Township at least by the beginning of the nineteenth century. He eventually settled with his grown sons and their families near where the East and West Plains meet, the only portion of the true "barrens" in the township, dying in 1814.

Kier says that he married Elizabeth Judith Alloway in 1749, and they had at least seven children: Richard (1760-1843), Thomas (1751-1831), James, Jr. (1756-1839), William (1763-1837), Joseph (1768-1827), Mary, and Sarah. James, Jr. married Rebecca Headley (a Washington Township family name).

Confusing and conflicting? Well, what else is new in the pines? Quite frankly, I'd bet on Charles Kier. He had Leah Blackman, *The Jersey Shore,* and Henry Bisbee in front of him when he did his research.

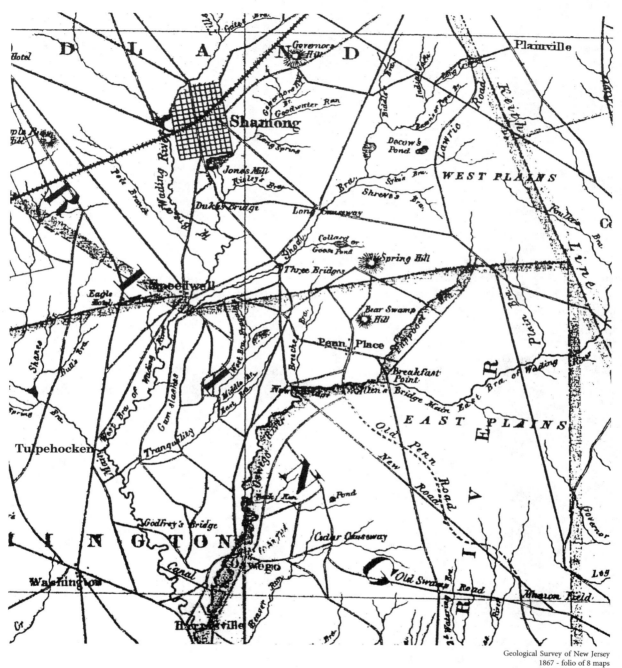

Geological Survey of New Jersey
1867 - folio of 8 maps

On this 1867 map, note the location of Penn Place, the East Plains, the West Plains, Speedwell, the Eagle Tavern, Tulpehocken, and the planned town of Shamong, now Chatsworth. Harrisville and Washington are at the bottom. Route 563, the Chatsworth-Green Bank Road, had not been constructed when this map was drawn. There certainly are roads to everywhere, but Washington and Speedwell appear as hubs. Neither was important by the time this map was made. Note the name "Oswego" appearing instead of Martha or Chitwood. The stream now known on the topographic maps as "Hospitality" is here labelled "Tranquility." The Bodine family first settled at "Tranquility Swamp," and this is the only known identification of the name "Tranquility" in Washington Township. Christopher Estlow, through his father, Godfrey, also owned property on the "Tranquility Branch."

759

Kier lost his source, but notes that James Penn (1729-1814) "operated a sawmill with his son, Thomas, at Brotherton (Indian Mills)" in 1772. This would be during the period that the land was still being used as an Indian reservation.

Bisbee's *Martha: The Complete Furnace Diary and Journal 1808-1815* mentions a William Penn paying a head tax from 1796 through 1811. It also notes him as a woodcutter in 1808, and his name appears under July 21, 1809. Joseph Penn is also on the list as a woodcutter in 1808. William Penn, Sr. is listed as a householder in 1809 and paid tax to Washington Township as part of the Martha Company. In 1809, the name Joel Penn appears as a woodchopper. James Penn, Sr.'s name is noted on February 15, 1812 as a "victualer." William Penn, Sr.'s name does not appear on the 1812 tax list. Leah Blackman mentions a "Joel" but no "Joseph." Kier lists a "Joseph" but no "Joel." Oh well.....

In any case, the family did end up out in the swamps of northeastern Washington Township. Henry Bisbee says that they were here by 1795 and remained in the vicinity at least as late as 1850. Charles Kier's investigations pushes the date of first settlement to 1810 and the latter date to 1890. The Martha Diary does seem to place this family very near the location of Penn Place by 1812. Perhaps James, Sr., the victualer, had his farm there, and his sons worked for Jesse Evans as woodcutters, living with their families out in the woods.

Kier had "off-the-record" permission to do some exploratory excavations in the area in three shallow depressions back in 1982 and found springs (floor nails) which he believed dated back to about 1810, cut nails, home-made red clay bricks, very thin window glass (from at least two different eras), fragments of a lamp chimney, and fragments of plaster.

Kier notes that, during the 1930's, a camp of the Civilian Conservation Corps was located directly south of Penn Place. He had just recently discovered (1982) that the camp was "occupied solely" by African Americans. Kier found evidence of fires other than forest fires in the cellar holes he examined and surmised that the C.C.C. had demolished and burned the "surviving structural ruins" at Penn Place.

Before leaving Mr. Kier, the historian gives a hint as to the further movement of this family when they left Penn Place. It seems that at least one branch removed to the Waretown/Barnegat area, another to Winslow Township, and yet a third to Cedar Bridge. He seems to believe that at least part of the family moved to Waretown through the Reevestown area but can't document the names and dates. Kier thinks that the family moved from Burlington County into Ocean County when "farming, woodcutting, and coaling were no longer sustaining."

The area's claim to fame is one of the oddities of South Jersey: a "mount." Bear Swamp Hill rises almost one hundred fifty feet into the air at this location. It once boasted a fire tower, but a National Guard aircraft on a practice bombing run took it out around 1966. Apparently the pilot didn't believe there was a mountain in South Jersey either. It was a fatal mistake.

UNION FORGE

The original boundary of Washington Township ran considerably north of its present-day line just south of Speedwell. It included the location of the Union Forge, now in Woodland Township and even Union in Tabernacle Township.

According to Arthur Pierce (*Iron in the Pines*), Union Forge was built by William Cook, Sr. in 1800. Somewhat later, it was owned and operated by Anthony S. Earl and William Fenimore. Boyer (*Forges and Furnaces*) notes the name of William Cook and the date of 1800 in a tax duplicate he located. In a footnote, Boyer says that Nelson's *New Jersey Coast for Three Centuries*, II, 413, mentions that it was established by S. Jones and J. Biddle. He also writes that Hageman and Woodward, in their *History of Burlington and Mercer Counties*, say that Thomas and Samuel Richards built the forge. Apparently neither Pierce, Boyer, nor Woodward & Hageman are correct. Nelson comes closest to the mark.

A deed in the Wharton ledgers notes that, on March 1, 1791, *Abraham* and Elizabeth Jones sold a one-third share of the site on the "West branch of Wading River *whereon the Forge called Union Forge is erected*," to Alexander Shreve for 625 pounds. This wasn't recorded until January 6, 1812 (in Burl. Co. Book X, page 224).

The Batsto Ledgers go on to record that in 1792, Joseph Biddle conveyed by will his one-third share in Union Forge to Stacy Biddle. In 1810, Abraham Jones and his wife sold their one-third share to William Fenimore for 550 pounds, and in 1812, Stacy Biddle did likewise for 600 pounds.

What is likely, then, is that Joseph Biddle and Abraham Jones seemed to have owned (and perhaps themselves built) the Union Forge prior to 1791, with Jones owning two-thirds and Biddle one-third.

Boyer's tax duplicate for William Cook, Sr. for the year 1800, indicates that Cook was at least operating the works in that year, even if he doesn't seem to have owned it. Another tax duplicate Boyer found, this one from 1806, shows Cook being billed for taxes on 1500 acres of land "valued at two dollars per hundred acres and for two forge fires." Yet another for 1809, lists both William Cook, Sr. and William Cook, Jr. and also shows that the property included a slitting mill by this time. What we can says is that from 1792 to 1810, the land was owned by Alexander Shreve, Stacy Biddle and Abraham Jones, with William Fenimore succeeding Jones in 1810, while William Cook, Sr. operated the forge from at least 1800 to 1809.

From 1810 to 1812, Fenimore owned two-thirds of the property, while Shreve retained one-third. The Wharton ledgers do not give a date for the sale of Alexander Shreve's one-third share, but it must have been 1812 as well, because William Fenimore was the sole owner of the works when he sold it in the same year he had gained complete control of it. It is possible that Cook had purchased Shreve's 1/3 share before 1800, but the fact that Shreve's original purchase was not recorded until its sale to Fenimore in 1812 seems to indicate that he did not. Fenimore received $4,300 for three tracts of land including 4573 $^{1/2}$ acres "all the premises now belonging to the Union Forge Tract."

This forge just seemed to have faded away as well. Boyer says it was located on Horner's *Map of New Jersey*, published in 1855, but it was listed as a furnace, which is wrong. It was definately a small forge using primarily pig iron from Speedwell and fashioning it into bar iron. Boyer records that the water power was used to run a sawmill as early as 1843, which may mean that the forge was no longer operating at this time. Speedwell Furnace had ceased its operations prior to the death of Samuel Richards in 1842, leaving Union Forge without a local source of pig iron. It is not unreasonable that it was gone by that time, too, leaving the dam and race to be used for a sawmill.

When the railroad was built through the area in about 1859, a station called *Shamong* was sited about a mile east of the old Union Forge and a hotel was built for travellers on the railroad. In 1866, this area was taken from Washington Township to form Woodland Township. Buzby's Store was built in 1865, one year before Woodland Township was formed. It is currently being restored by Marilyn Schmidt, formerly of Cranbury and Barnegat Light and author/publisher of *Exploring the Pine Barrens of New Jersey: A Guide*. The town of *Shamong* did not become *Chatsworth* until 1893. It is interesting to note that there was another town called Shamong in Washington Township. This town, also known as Hartford, was just south of the old Brotherton Indian Reservation at Indian Mills.

GODFREY'S BRIDGE

A fine, paved road heads westward from Route 563 near Jenkins and leads to a campground maintained by the State of New Jersey called "Godfrey's Bridge." On the eastern side of the West Branch of the Wading is a private campground, and a state-maintained bridge crosses the river to the state campground. This old road continues on through the woods to the junction with the Tuckerton Road and the road to Batsto. The bridge is shown on an 1868 map and mentioned in the road returns for 1908 and is named for Godfrey Estlow (or Estilow), who had married Phebe Sooy, the daughter of John Sooy of Green Bank/Herman, and niece of Nicholas Sooy I. Godfrey operated a sawmill that stood on the river in the southeastern corner of his property.

The fifty acres Godfrey Estlow bought in 1791, goes back to an early survey to Samuel Smith for 400 acres of land (SurGenOffice Lib. E, p. 156). The 400 acres was conveyed through Robert Smith to Daniel and Sarah Smith, the wife of James Pemberton, and finally, on August 17, 1790, to Robert (1/3rd), Sarah (1/6th), Daniel (1/3rd) Smith and their sister, Catherine Allinson (1/6th). Within the year, Catherine had died, leaving her one-sixth share to her children, William and Mary Allinson.

The following year, Godfrey Estlow bought fifty acres of this 400 acres from the Smiths (of Burlington County) and the Allinsons (of Waterford, Gloucester - now Camden - County). His property line ran down the Tulpehocken Road, then cut across to the West Branch of the Wading River, northward up the river, and back over to the place of beginning. The actual location of the Estlow sawmill seems to have been upriver from the present Godfrey's Bridge campground, at least according to the 1836 map of McCartyville. At the top of the following page, a section of that map shows that there were two bridges just south of Godfrey's property, one labelled simply "bridge," the other called "Old Bridge." The one labelled "bridge" seems to be in the location of the current Godfrey's Bridge. It is known that Godfrey ran a sawmill on the river for some years, though the only confirmable date is 1831 for the mill's operation. Family legend says that he also worked for Jesse Evans as an ore hauler over at Martha.

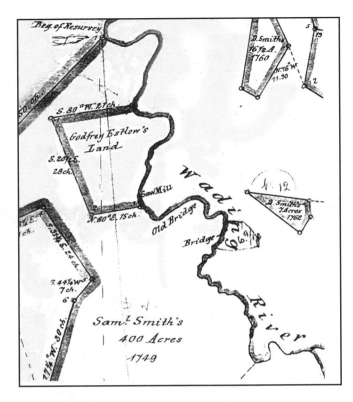

Godfrey Estlow's Mill

This is a portion of the 1836 map of McCartyville as copied by Samuel Downs in 1861. The section shown is that near the current Godfrey's Bridge. Godfrey Estlow's land and mill site and most clearly indicated. I believe that the crossing marked "Bridge" is the current Godfrey's Bridge.

On April 8, 1836, Godfrey's son, James, bought his father's fifty acres as well as all his other parcels of land in the area. According to Henry Beck, quoting the Charles Cramer diary, Godfrey Estlow died on October 14, 1836 and was buried at Barnhart's Place (the Eagle Tavern) two days later. His other son, Christopher (b.1815), took title to the same lands his brother had purchased from their father, on January 9, 1844 but the transaction wasn't recorded until March 28, 1848. Christopher was a sawyer at Martha, and according to the township records, his wife, Ann (Robineau), gave birth to a boy on Christmas Eve in 1848 whom they named "Hezekiah."

We don't know just where Christopher lived with his family, but he may well have remained on his father's land. It does seem that the Estlow land could be described as "Martha." Though they seem far apart today, they are really very close together - as the crow flies.

Christopher and Ann (Robineau) bought a house and lot from Jesse and Lucy Ann Evans of Martha on August 8, 1846 for $5.00. This property is described as lying "on the east side of Beaver Run in the Gore between Beaver Run and Bodine's 73 acre Survey and on the bank where the road crosses the Run, containing 3/4th Acre." This was quite near his mother-in-law's property which lay just below the junction of Beaver Run and the Wading River near Bodine's. Perhaps Christopher and Ann planned to move to this house to be closer to her mother.

Christopher's own mother, Phoebe (Sooy) Estlow, died in 1849 "at Martha." Estlow, his wife, Ann Robineau, and his children: Jesse A., Godfrey II, Francis, Christopher, Jr., Winifield, and Hezekiah are listed on the 1850 census and probably still lived at Martha. Son Sadock was born in 1854 "at Martha," so they hadn't moved as of this date.

Francis B. Chetwood had purchased the Martha site by this time, but his dreams of a real estate development never materialized. Apparently the sawmill where Christopher worked ceased operations during this decade, for, by the time Christopher sold his father's mill property on January 21, 1860, he and his wife and family were living in Dover Township, New Jersey. The mill land was sold to Joseph Holloway, Christopher's brother-in-law. Godfrey Holloway, Joseph's son, received the property on October 24, 1874. Godfrey, listed as being "of Mullica Township," sold it to Joseph Wharton on December 23, 1881.

When they left the township, the Estlow family moved to Red Oak Grove in Lacey Township, Ocean County and later purchased Wells Mills on February 6, 1874. Christopher died in 1881 and was buried in the Reevestown cemetery, not far from Warren Grove. His wife, Ann (Robineau), was laid beside him when she passed away six years later. A new stone graces their gravesites. Nearby, his son, Jesse A. Estlow and his wife, Deborah, have simple, sandstone headstones with just their names carved into them. Jesse and Deborah's son, also Jesse A., Jr., was born in 1890 and died in 1892 at the age of two years, two months.

Francis Mick of Jenkins says he remembers that the original Jenkins schoolhouse stood on the Godfrey's Bridge road just before it joined the Philadelphia/Tuckerton Road, and that it burned down. Walt Priest of Green Bank confirmed that there once was a schoolhouse just west of Godfrey's Bridge and that it burned. The annual school report of the Burlington County Superintendent in 1885 mentions that "The small school-house in District No. 103 was destroyed by fire, and a new one costing some $300 has been put in its place." District No. 103 was the school at Washington, then in Randolph Township. Three years later, this new building also burned to the ground. There was some discussion prior to this about moving the school out to the new main road (Route 563) due to the declining population of the Washington area. After this second building burned, its replacement was built in Jenkins and appears in the superintendent's 1890 report.

TULPEHOCKEN

If you take the road from Jenkins through Godfrey's Bridge (the Washington-Jenkins Road), there is a road on the right that leads today to Hawkin Bridge campground that is maintained by the State of New Jersey. Actually, there are two roads leading in that direction: the Maxwell-Friendship Road and the Washington-Speedwell Road. This latter is what was once known as the Road to Tulpehocken.

When you reach the bridge over the Tulpehocken Branch that flows into the Speedwell or West Branch of the Wading River, you have reached old Tulpehocken. The name in Lenni Lenape means "Place of the Turtle." There is little known about this site, though there are references to the Tulpehocken mill in old records.

The Tulpehocken Creek was dammed where the present-day road to Friendship crosses it today, and apparently a sawmill stood nearby. At a recent period of low water, evidence of a millsite was located near the Hawkin Bridge campground, but this mill was on the Wading River, not on the Tulpehocken branch.

Budd Wilson of Green Bank used to think that an entry in the Wharton Ledgers indicated Tulpehocken when it mentioned Smith's Old Mill on the "Old Road to Washington." The same reference mentions a George DuPre,

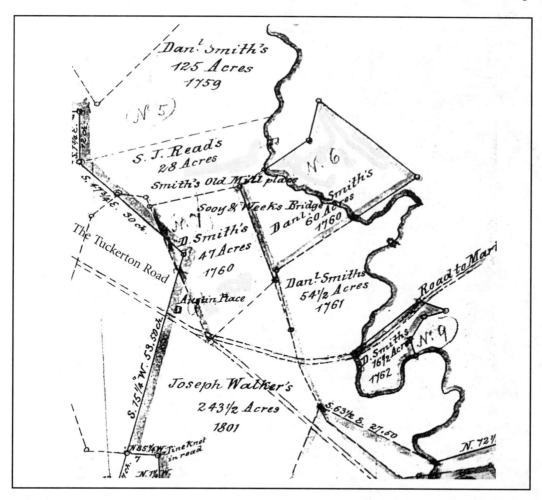

This is also a portion of the map of McCartyville, copied by Samuel Downs in 1861. The portion shown here lies just upstream from Harrisville/McCartyville and downstream from Godfrey's Bridge. It clearly indicates the location of "Smith's Old Mill" as just above a spot called "Sooy and Weeks Bridge." I think that the current Evans Bridge of Route 563 is just between the millsite and the Sooy/Weeks Bridge.

whose house stood near the mill by the graveyard. This latter is interesting because there is no known cemetery at Hawkin Bridge. The "Smith" referred to was Daniel Smith, who owned extensive property around Tylertown during the last half of the eighteenth century. A map in the Wharton Ledgers (Vol. 9, p. 299) shows the lands around Tylertown that Daniel Smith owned and labels the Washington Road as "the "Road from Batsto to Smith's Old Mill and to Wading River." The land was all surveyed in the 1760's. If this is when Smith's mill was in operation, then the mill was certainly "old," even during the nineteenth century when it was only a memory. Unfortunately for Budd's original interpretation, the 1836 map of McCartyville indicates the location of "Smith's Old Mill" on the west branch of the Wading River, just upstream from the present Evans Bridge, a millsite also confirmed recently. According to the map, Daniel Smith owned hundreds of acres in this area also.

Steve Eichinger, with his interests in old road returns (the recording of roads as they were laid out) found the return for the Tulpehocken Road. One of the marks on this road was where it crossed the Tulpehocken branch at Hawlings Mill. This must, indeed, be the long, lost name of the mill at Tulpehocken, though its years of operation are unknown. The road today makes an "S" bend just before Hawkin Bridge. Originally, it made only one turn and ran down the earthen dam, the remains of which are still clearly visible on the west side of the current road. A cut in the dam may indicate the location of the mill, though no race is visible.

THE BROTHERTON INDIAN RESERVATION

Believe it or not, Indian Mills, site of the only Indian reservation in New Jersey, was once part of Washington Township. The Indians who lived along the Delaware and throughout this area of the province of New Jersey were from the Unami tribe of the Lenni Lenape or "True Men." C.A. Weslager, in his book, *The Delaware Indians*, says that the actual translation is more like "Common People." Those who inhabited the more northern areas were from the Munsi group of the same people.

Ancient traditions and legends recounted their initial journey from the west into the Delaware River area long before their contact with the first Europeans. They were organized in autonomous bands with no common structure or chief. Each band acted independently from the others, which made them vulnerable to outside intrusion and influence. The various bands frequently called themselves by the name of the location in which they lived for the better part of the year. They were not a warlike people and tried to get along with the Swedes and Dutch settlers from the first contact, but constant pressures from the Europeans and from the Susquehannocks to the west gradually pushed them out of the lower Delaware area.

Both the Swedes and the Dutch tried to extinguish Indian claims to the lands on which they settled, but there were controversies. William Penn attempted to deal honestly with these early Americans. He made every effort to purchase their lands from them at a fair price, even though his grant from the English crown gave him complete control and rights to the lands that became Pennsylvania without obligating him to extinguish their claim to the land. After his death, his sons had no compunction about cheating the Delawares in any land transactions they negotiated, as the infamous "Walking Purchase" so amply demonstrated.

The Iroquois Confederacy in upstate New York, basically allied to the British against the French and their Indian tribes, claimed to have defeated the Lenape and brought their territories under Iroquois domination. It suited the Pennsylvania authorities to emphasize Iroquois control over their more peaceful neighbors to ensure that the Delawares would not give them any problems in ceding their lands.

By the outbreak of the French and Indian War in the mid-eighteenth century, most of the Lenape in Delaware and Pennsylvania had been resettled to the west, first along the Susquehanna River, and later along the Juniata. European settlers had not pressured the Native Americans in New Jersey too greatly at first, and, with the Quaker heritage of West Jersey, they had been treated fairly by the newcomers in most cases and learned to coexist quite well. By the late 1750's however, increasing settlement was causing them ever greater discomfort. They had to contend with land grant after land grant pushing them from their settlements and hunting grounds.

A young Presbyterian missionary, David Brainerd, ministered to the Lenape that lived near the forks of the Delaware River in Pennsylvania (near Easton) for about a year in about 1744. He also visited their relatives on the Susquehanna for a short time. The following year, he went to Crosswicks, near Bordentown, New Jersey, called by the Lenape, Crossweeksung. Here he lived in a hut which the Indians had built for him and travelled around the area, visiting the various bands that lived in the vicinity. It was apparently during this time that he came to the area of The Forks of the Little Egg Harbor River. For the most part, he received attention from the women and children, but the men were somewhat hostile. Jonathan Edwards, who edited Brainerd's journals under the title *Memoirs of the Reverend David Brainerd*, in 1822, as quoted in Weslager, cites an entry in Brainerd's journal that gives the reason for this hostility towards Christianity. A Lenape man told Brainerd that *the white people lie, defraud, steal, and drink worse than the Indians . . . that the English have by these means, made [the Lenape] quarrel and kill one another, and in a word, brought them to the practice of all those vices which now prevail among them. So that they are now vastly more vicious, as well as much more miserable, than they were before the coming of the white people into the country.*

Brainerd's fervor did meet with some success, however, and Crosswicks grew to a settlement of about one hundred thirty by March of 1746. The land could not sustain the growing population, so the people decided to move to a site that was two miles northeast of Cranbury, New Jersey, and start a new town, called Bethel. Some local Native Americans did remain near the present-day Vincentown on land that had been granted to Mahamickwon, known as "King Charles" to the English.

David Brainerd died in 1747, and his brother, John took up the mission at Cranbury. The outbreak of the French and Indian War brought fear to the hearthside of every white family. The French employed Canadian Indians to fight for them, which they did with particular ferocity. New Jersey's Governor Jonathan Belcher notified his council that murders by the French and their Indian allies had been committed "near our borders." Some Delawares in the northern Delaware River area took advantage of the hostilities to cross the river into New Jersey to avenge supposed wrongs done to them before they had left the colony.

Meanwhile, the peaceful Christian Indians at Cranbury became increasingly worried. Most settlers considered all Indians as hostile and had no compunction about shooting first and asking questions later, if ever. They, too, were afraid of marauding war parties of French Indians from the north. The New Jersey legislature passed a resolution that enabled the Cranbury Indians to go to a magistrate and get a certificate that showed that they were not hostile Indians. The magistrate would also give each Indian a red ribbon, that, when worn in the hair, identified the person as a friend, rather than an enemy.

Governor Belcher panicked in June of 1756 when a war party of hostile Delawares, apparently from Pennsylvania, carried out a raid in Sussux County. He issued a proclamation, recorded in the *New Jersey Archives*, vol. 17, pp. 30-31, that called the Delawares "Enemies, Rebels, & Traytors to his most Sacred Majesty" and went on to "require all his Majestys Subjects within this Province to be Assiduous Within the Government in taking or Destroying the said Delaware Indians." He also offered a scalp bounty of 150 Spanish dollars on every male Indian above the age of fifteen, and 130 dollars on every scalp, from male or female, under the age of fifteen.

The governor was thinking of hostile Indian scalps, of course, but terrified or angry settlers wouldn't discriminate. Money was money, and the authorities wouldn't know whether the presented scalp once graced the head of a hostile or a friendly Indian. The Indians at Cranbury feared for their lives, and they were told to stay within set bounds around their town for protection.

Sir William Johnson, the British Indian agent in New York, negotiated a treaty with a Delaware chieftain in Pennsylvania at about the same time that Governor Belcher issued his proclamation. When the governor received word of the treaty on July 11, 1756, he immediately issued another forbidding any depredations against the Delawares in New Jersey. The Quakers and Presbyterians of the colony felt that the Indian problems were the result of past abuses committed against the Indians, and the New Jersey government decided to prevent further warfare by righting some of those wrongs. The governor appointed commissioners who listened to the Indians and advised the legislature to pass several laws to correct the abuses.

In 1757, the New Jersey legislature did precisely that. Amongst other things, it made it illegal to sell liquor to the Indians and prohibited the imprisonment of an Indian for debt. The commissioners met with the Lenape at Crosswicks on February 20, 1758. Present were representatives of Delawares from Pennsylvania who had been forced off their lands in northern New Jersey some time back. These demanded payment for those lands as compensation. A solution also had to be found for protecting the peaceful Indians in the southern part of the colony.

Governor Francis Bernard, newly appointed to his position, called a meeting of the Provincial Assembly to deal with the problem. The tribal leaders, particularly Chief Teedyuskung of the Unamis and Chief Benjamin of the Minsis, were invited to attend the meeting. They met in Burlington on August 9, 1758, and the Indians presented a written request for a permanent home in the area known as Shamong in Evesham Township, Burlington County.

The legislature of the Province of New Jersey, wanting to insure that the Lenni Lenape, residing in the province, had just treatment, made provisions for land to be purchased and set aside as a reservation for their exclusive use forever. When the lands were purchased, the reservation was a part of Evesham Township, though it was later included within the bounds of Washington Township when it was formed in 1802 and became part of Shamong Township in 1852.

On the 12th of August, 1758, the legislature enacted a law which authorized the purchase of lands for the benefit of the Lenni Lenape or Delawares, as they were called, which is recorded in the State Library at Trenton in the Book of Pamphlet Laws Vol. 111.1757.Acts 1758, page 20.

Basically, this law recites that the colonial legislature, wishing to have a good understanding with the Indians and to satisfy their just demands, appointed Andrew Johnson, Richard Saltar, Charles Read, John Stevens, William Foster, and Jacob Spicer as commissioners and authorized the treasurer of the colony to pay them jointly, or any three of them, the monies required to purchase the "right and claim of all or any of the Indian Nations of the Colony." It provided that the sum thus expended should not exceed sixteen hundred pounds, and that the sum expended to satisfy the claims of the nation called "the Delawares, South of the Raritan, near Cranberry [sic]" should not exceed eight hundred pounds.

It states that the Delawares wanted part of the money spent on land for them to live on, and the legislature wanted them to have a "Lasting Monument of Justice" of the colony towards them. It was enacted that any three of the said commissioners, with the Governor's consent, shall purchase some tract and take deeds for the same in the name of the Governor in trust for the use of the Indians South of the Raritan and their successors forever. It also provides that the Indians could not lease or sell any part of the said land to be bought, and that no person, Indians excepted, should be permitted to settle on that land, nor would they be allowed to cut or remove any timber from it.

Money for the purchase would be raised by a lottery in the amount of six hundred pounds in October of 1759, five hundred pounds in October of 1760, and five hundred pounds in October of 1761. It also provided that the purchase would not "prejudice the right" of the Indians to hunt and fish on any unlocated lands.

On August 29, 1758, Benjamin Springer and Hannah, his wife, sold a tract of land in the vicinity of what became known as the Brotherton Reservation to Francis Bernard, Governor of New Jersey, and the commissioners appointed by the legislature, for the consideration of seven hundred forty pounds. The transaction was recorded in the Surrogates of the States Office in Book O of Deeds, page 394. Other contiguous purchases were subsequently made until the reservation totalled 3,284 acres (Weslager says 3,044 acres). It included an orchard, an old mill on the Edgepillock Branch, and a new mill on another branch. A second house on the Springer property was occupied by James Denight, and exception was made for this house and a hundred acres of land around it to be reserved for Denight. The Indians were to have full possession of the lands, without taxes, and without the right to sell it.

Approximately two hundred Native Americans settled on their new lands, and people of European extraction were excluded. While the legislature later extended settlement privileges to Narragansetts, Mohicans, Pequots, of New England, Mohawks from New York, and Nanicokes from Maryland, very few of these people settled permanently on the Brotherton Reservation.

A conference was held at Easton, Pennsylvania, on October 8, 1758, with people from the Iroquois Confederacy, the Nanticokes, Tutelos, Unamis, Munsies, Mahickon from New York, and the Pomptons, who were New England Indians who had established a home near Patterson . The Munsies claimed that they had been deprived of their lands in the northern part of New Jersey and asked for recompense. Governor Bernard and his advisors, having already spent almost half the money appropriated by the legislature on the new reservation, offered the intended eight hundred pounds to the Munsies and the Pomptons to completely extinguish their claims. The offer was accepted.

About two hundred of the three hundred Indians remaining in New Jersey moved to the new reservation on the Edgepollock Creek, which lent its name to the settlement. They built cabins, a gristmill, and a log meeting house on the land. Governor Bernard, in a letter written on June 15, 1759, noted that he had travelled to Edgepollock and laid out a town "to which I gave the name of Brotherton."

In 1762, John Brainerd was appointed superintendent of the Brotherton Reservation, but, as would be common on reservations for the next two centuries, there was never enough money. He did get small amounts from the Presbyterian churches and from the College of New Jersey (Princeton), but he actually "loaned" $200 to the reservation so that the Indians could build a church. John taught the Indians farming methods and various trade skills and generally helped them to live very much as their white neighbors lived.

As early as 1767, the Brotherton Indians received an invitation from Delawares living in Ohio to come and join them. John Brainerd wrote their reply which said that they were ready and willing to join the Ohio Delawares but that they needed money for their moving expenses, had a church, schoolhouse, and residences which would be lost if they moved, and needed the support of the New Jersey authorities. Perhaps this was a polite way of refusing the Ohio Delawares' offer.

The Ohio Delawares didn't forget the Brothertons, however. In 1771, when Governor William Franklin was in Philadelphia on business, he met with "Captain" Killbuck, one of the Ohio Delawares and representative of their chief. Killbuck asked Franklin for help in selling the reservation as this was the only thing holding back the Brotherton Delawares from joining the rest of their tribe in Ohio. Franklin promised to tell his council and the Assembly of the request. On June 1, 1777, some of the Brothertons met with the governor and council at Burlington to request the sale of their lands, but there had been several Delawares from Brotherton who had not signed the petition for sale. The governor and council decided that those who wanted to join their people in Ohio could do so, but the land wouldn't be sold.

John Brainerd died in 1781. Not everyone can be replaced. John couldn't be. From that time on, the Indians were on their own. There is some suggestion that a few of the Indians may have found employment in local iron furnaces, but there is scant evidence to support this. They did build a sawmill and grist mill on their land. By the end of the century, though, barely a hundred of the original two hundred had survived.

Needing money, they asked the legislature to permit the lease of some of their lands with the proceeds going to the tribe. Consequently, on the 17th of March, 1796, the legislature appointed Joseph Saltar, Josiah Foster, and Thomas Hollingshead as commissioners to take charge of the lands and gave them power to lease it in a way that would be advantageous to the Indians. It stipulated that leases should not be entered into for a period longer than ten years, with rents to be paid quarterly or yearly. The proceeds should be paid to the Indians in necessaries, clothing etc., and the commissioners were to make an accounting with the Burlington County court in the May term each year.

The Indians of Brotherton received an invitation from the Stockbridge Indians, who lived among the Oneida in western New York State, to join them. The Stockbridge Indians were Mahicans originally from Massachusetts. The language they spoke was an Algonkian dialect related to Lenape, and they were considered relatives. The elders of the Brothertons felt that they would soon all die or be absorbed into the surrounding population if they did not make the move, so they asked the legislature to sell their lands and give them the proceeds to finance their relocation.

It seems strange that they would join the Stockbridge Indians in Oneida rather than join their Delaware kinsmen in Ohio, but it was actually a smart move. During the Revolutionary War, the western part of the Delwares were split between factions that supported either the Americans or the British, and there was much hard feeling against those on the losing side. There would be continued hostility on both sides. Joining the Stockbridges meant a choice for peace by the Brothertons, even at the expense of losing their national identity.

On December 3, 1801, the legislature passed another law appointing commissioners to "sell and convey the said Indian Lands at 'Brotherton' for the benefit of the Indians." The act states that the Indians had memorialized the legislature for an outright sale of the lands rather than the lease arrangement made in 1796 and stated that they wanted to go to the settlement at "New Stockbridge" in New York State. They had formed a union with the Stockbridge Indians that was "mutually agreeable" and wanted to go and live with them.

The legislature, "regarded it as its duty to promote the happiness of the Indians," enacted that William Stockton, William Saltar, and Enoch Evans be appointed commissioners "to cut and divide said lands at 'Brotherton' into lots not exceeding 100 acres as would be beneficial to the Indians." They were authorized to sell the lots at public sale and use the money to convey "the Indians to Stockbridge, purchase clothing, utensils, furniture, etc., to buy land, stock, etc. to see to it that the understanding of the two tribes was friendly etc." It stipulated that all documents associated with the division and sale of the Indians' lands should be deposited in the office of the Secretary of State. It required the commissioners to give a $15,000 bond. Terms of any sale would be one third of the purchase money to be paid in thirty days, one third in a year, and one third in two years with interest. It required that the commissioners could not act until John Beatty and James Ewing reported that not less than three quarters of the Indians "of full age consent to the sale and conveyance of the said land."

William Saltar and Enoch Evans resigned their duties as commissioners, and Governor Bloomfield appointed Charles Ellis to fill the vacancies. In compliance with the act, the commissioners divided the lands into thirty-four lots, and they were subsequently sold at from two to five dollars per acre to twenty-two different buyers.

There remained only sixty-three adult Indians who had any rights to the property at the time of the sale. The Indians rented twelve wagons and loaded them with all the goods they possessed, and, in May of 1802, they set out for New York. Their last chief, Elisha Ashataina (also called Lashar Tamar) led them away for their home for the past forty-four years to an uncertain future. The greatest number of the tribe removed to New York State as they had wished, though some did remain in the area.

Those who had moved to New York were reduced to about forty in number by the 1830's, and these few decided to move west to the area of Green Bay, Wisconsin. In 1832, the New Jersey legislature, which had kept much of the reservation land sale proceeds in trust for the tribe rather than lift them out of poverty in New York, appropriated $3,551.23 to resettle the remaining members of the tribe in Wisconsin.

In thanks, Bartholomew Calvin (Shawuskukhkung - "Place of the Wilted Grass"), the member of the tribe who had conducted the negotiations with the State, wrote to the lawmakers in gratitude:

> *Not a drop of our blood have you spilled in battle; not an acre of our land have you taken but by our consent. These facts speak for themselves and need no comment. They place the character of New Jersey in bold relief, a bright example to those States within whose territorial limits our brothers still remain.*

The tale of the Brotherton Reservation is not over yet, though. The original act setting up the Brotherton Reservation had provided that the land would be tax free "for all times." The 1801 act which authorized the sale of those lands did not include a provision to make them subject to local taxes again. Consequently, the Washington Township tax assessor, William Saltar, who had been appointed as one of the original commissioners to sell the lands in the first place but had resigned, declared that they were now taxable. The new owners took the case to court and, in September, 1804, the assessments were set aside. The legislature of the State of New Jersey repealed the act of 1758 which had created the reservation in an act passed in December of the same year.

In 1805, the tax assessor, this time Lewis Wilson, once again assessed the properties. Two years later, the State Supreme Court upheld the assessment, but the owners continued their appeal all the way to the Supreme Court of the United States, which ruled in 1812 that the act of 1804 repealing the act of 1758 was unconstitutional. Two years later, James Maxwell, the new tax assessor of the township, ignored the Supreme Court's ruling and assessed the properties anyway. The owners gave up and paid their taxes.

The story still isn't over. In 1877, sixty-three years after Maxwell had successfully assessed the properties, the then owners of the property once again refused to pay their taxes and cited the Supreme Court's decision of 1812. The State Supreme Court finally ruled that the tax assessor had the right to make the assessments on the grounds that the owners had acknowledged that right of the township, by now Shamong Township, to tax them and surrendered their right to exemption. The case was appealed no further.

At least one Lenape family returned to the site of their former home. Chief Lasha Tamar, as he was known in later years, brought his family back to the area and settled on a farm in Rancocos. His daughter was long remembered as "Indian Ann," a local basket maker. Ann's first husband was Peter Green who was supposed to have been a former slave. When he died, she married John Roberts, an African American who had served in the Civil War in Company A, 22nd Regiment of Colored Troops.

The couple lived in a house on the Dingletown Road, not a great distance from the old Brotherton Reservation in the area now called Indian Mills. Ann had seven children: Peter, John, Samuel, Richard, Hester, Ann, and Lydia. In 1880, she applied for a pension from the government, based on her husband's service and gave her age as seventy-five. If that was accurate, she could not have been born until her father had returned to New Jersey in 1805. She died in 1894 and was buried in the Methodist cemetery at Tabernacle. Her grave is marked by a stone placed there by the Burlington County Historical Society. Indian Ann was the last full-blooded Native American of the Lenape Brothertons known to have lived in the area of old Washington Township.

The Mullica:
Pathway to the World

The Ship That Never Returned
Maude M. Maxwell
March 8, 1892

On a summer's day when the waves were rippled
By the softest, gentlest breeze
Did a ship set sail with cargo laden
For a port beyond the seas —

There were fond farewells, there were loving signals
While a form was yet discerned —
Though they knew it not, t'was a solemn parting
For the ship — she never returned.

Did she ever return?
She never returned — her fate is still unlearned.
Tho' for years and years their loved ones were watching,
Yet the ship never returned.

Said a feeble lad to his anxious mother
I must cross the wide, wide sea
For they say perchance in foreign climate
There is health and strength for me.

T'was a gleam of hope in a maze of danger
And her heart for her youngest yearned.
Yet she sent him forth with many a blessing
On the ship that never returned.

Only one more trip, said the gallant seaman
As he kissed his weeping wife.
Only one more bag of that golden treasure
And 'twill last us through life.

Then I'll spend my days in my cozy cottage
And enjoy the rest I've earned.
But, alas, poor man, for he sailed commander
On the ship that never returned.

Maude M. Maxwell: The notation on the poem is "as by Dan Sooy." Mary Maude Maxwell was the daughter of Samuel and Mary Margaret (Cramer) Maxwell. She married Daniel T. Sooy, Jr. and was the mother of Helen (Sooy) Williams and Ethel (Sooy) Robbins. The page notation says that she died young.

For over a hundred years, the rivers that flowed to the sea along the North American coastline provided the major means of communication and trade among the British colonies and the new American nation. Roads were poor and few in number, while the rivers allowed access to the interior of the country and a comparatively easy means of moving people and goods throughout the coastal plain. Even travel between nearby towns was often by water, rather than by roads that were no more than glorified Indian trails through dense woods.

The Mullica River pointed inland towards Philadelphia, and its head of navigation at The Forks brought goods within reach of that city without having to round Cape May and sail up Delaware Bay. Goods could be brought to The Forks, loaded into wagons, and taken to the navigable part of the Rancocos Creek for reshipment to the capitol of Pennsylvania or carried overland to Cooper's Ferry, now Camden, and enter the city by crossing the Delaware at that point.

Early settlers like Yoos Sooy, Peter Cavileer, John Leek, Sr., and Thomas Clark depended on the river for their very lives. The Mullica and Wading Rivers gave them the only means of contact with the outside world, and their prosperity depended on the dark waters of the pines.

Wartime Prosperity

During the Revolutionary War, merchants and the Congress found it an alternative pathway for goods blocked from sailing up the Delaware by British men-of-war in the lower bay. Local privateersmen knew its tortuous channel and inlet sandbar sheltered their activities from the patrolling British.

John Leek, Sr. of Wading River was reputed to have built a shipyard down river from his home near the Leek Wharf, but no hard evidence has been found to establish a date for this enterprise. John Van Sant bought land at The Forks from Richard Wescoat in 1760 and built a shipyard that would be active for a period of about thirty years. Though information is sketchy, there may well have been another shipyard at The Forks as well. At this focal point of activity, local ships were outfitted for trade and privateering, and many new vessels slipped down the ways into the brown waters of the Mullica. It is indeed unfortunate that no data exists on just how many ships were built on the Mullica and Wading Rivers, but occasional glimmers do shed some light on the tremendous traffic that plied the rivers for almost two hundred years.

Advertisements appearing in Pennsylvania newspapers announced the sale of many captured vessels during the war. Public notice was given for a 1778 sale on July 28th at Richard Wescoat's of : *Industry*, a brig of 150 tons; *Poly's Adventure*, a sloop; and *Speedwell*, a sloop. During 1779, April and July sales were conducted that included *Fortune*, a schooner; *Rattlesnake*, a schooner; *Chance*, a sloop; *Hornet*, a sloop; and *Retrieve*, a sloop. The year 1780 saw the following vessels sold: *Betsy*, a schooner; *Little Molly*, a schooner; and *Revenge*, a sloop. Another *Betsy*, this one a brigantine, was sold at The Forks in 1782.

Tons of captured goods made their way up the river to the docks of Richard Wescoat and Elijah Clark, then on to New Jersey's interior, Philadelphia, and to the Continental Army. Larger vessels that could not navigate the river were tied up and sold at Chestnut Neck. Their goods were often loaded into smaller vessels and brought upriver to The Forks to be sold or used as supply for the army.

Batsto was operating at full blast during the war, and at least some of her goods were shipped down river, though British patrols on the high seas made water shipment rather risky. Carting goods by wagon up the Philadelphia-Little Egg Harbor Road brought them safely to Washington's army when it was in the vicinity, though the speed at which they travelled must have left much to be desired.

A New Nation and A New Prosperity

The end of the war brought an end to the prosperity of The Forks at least as far as British largesse in captured goods was concerned, and shipbuilding in the area took a tumble. Both Elijah Clark and Richard Wescoat took their fortunes and moved away, Clark to retirement and Wescoat to Mays Landing and more profitable prospects. Even John Van Sant, now in his sixties, closed up shop and moved to the Bass River, where he spent a few years building small boats.

Shipping, on the other hand, was set for boom times. The end of the war brought renewed vigor in the iron industry, and the furnaces and forges in the area kept local sea captains and their ships busy transporting goods to and from the industries. Batsto took on new life with the arrival of William Richards. On the Wading River, the Wading River Forge and Slitting Mill and Martha Furnace shipped their products via the river system.

This second century of Mullica life would see the charcoal, lumber, and wood products trade provide lucrative profits for local ships and their owners. Men like Nicholas Sooy II in Green Bank set up shipping facilities along the river, bought wood products from the woodchoppers and sawmills, and shipped them to market in their own vessels. When glassmaking beckoned, Nicholas II needed vessels to transport the products of his glass factory also. He and others like him organized commercial fishing and built fish factories in the Great Bay area.

Jesse Richards of Batsto and Jesse Evans of Martha placed heavy demands on shipping. They not only had products to send to market, they started importing "foreign" (or as Evans would have called it, "mountain") ore from the northern part of the state, as well as limestone to feed their furnaces. The growing populations of Lower Bank, Green Bank, Martha, Batsto, and the areas more inland required goods which couldn't be manufactured locally. When Jesse Richards added glass to the production schedule at Batsto, even more cargo was provided for the local shipping industry. Many of the area residents were sea captains and crew members aboard coastal vessels. Others were watermen, the name used to include oystermen, clammers, and fishermen. Still others plied the various trades needed in maintaining wooden vessels.

THE LOCAL SHIPYARDS

The new century also brought a new generation into positions of managing old businesses. John Van Sant's son, Joel, set up a shipyard near the area of the Green Bank store, and, according to an article in the Batsto Citizens' Gazette (Summer, Fall, Winter 1987) by R. Craig Koedel, at least one known vessel, the *Mary*, a 43-ton schooner, was built at Green Bank in 1854. Later in the century, his sons, Joel, Jr., and Doughty would live in Joseph Sooy's old house near the little church and their brother, Samuel lived just down the road. The brothers built rather large vessels right across from the cemetery. The Van Sants constructed at least three three-masted schooners of over a hundred feet in this location at the end of the third quarter of the century: the *L.A. Seiver*, the *Lillie Falkinburg*, and the *Harvey W. Anderson*.

Nothing is known about the *L.A. Seiver*'s dimensions, but the *Lillie Falkinburg* was 115.8 feet long, had a beam of 30.8 feet and a gross tonnage of 216.58. The *Harvey W. Anderson* is mentioned in the List of Merchant Vessels of the United States for 1888 as being a schooner 132 feet in length, 32-foot beam, 9.5-foot draft, and a gross tonnage of 394.29. She was built in 1877, four years after the *Lillie Falkinberg*. The Mullica of today is a far cry from what it was in earlier centuries. After natural sediments and the wash of speedboats did their dirty work, the channel is now narrow and very shallow in some places. It is almost impossible to imagine how anyone could get a 132-foot ship with a 9.5-foot draft *out* of Green Bank and into the sea. Quite frankly, it seems like the modern equivalent of walking on water.

The 1888 list includes other vessels built at Green Bank, though they are all of small size: the *Tormentor* (1873), forty-five feet long, 13-foot beam, and draft of 2.1 feet; the *Susan Jane* (1876), 66.6 feet long, beam of 23.9 feet, and draft of 5.5 feet; the *E.A. Cranmer* (1881), 45 feet long with a 17-foot beam and a draft of 5 feet; and the *Laura Hope* (1883), 27 feet in length with a 12-foot beam and a draft of 2.8 feet;.

There seem to be no records concerning the nineteenth century yard at Lower Bank, but stories of the building of Levi Johnson's first ship, the *Walter Lemuel*, tell of her being built where River Road meets the Mullica and heads downstream. Also according to the Koedel article, another schooner *Mary*, 104 tons, was built at Lower Bank in 1839.

Wading River is even more of a puzzle. Legend has it that John Leek, Sr. built the first boatyard there, but there are no records about it, just faint hints. It seems that Robert McKeen and Samuel Taggart, his partner, had ship construction as one of their interests, but they were gone by the time that the vessels on the 1888 list were built. So who built them? The answer to that, I'm afraid, will take much more research.

Wading River's credits include: the *I Don't Know* (1872), 53 feet long, 19.9 feet wide, and a draft of 5.2; the *Lela* (1873), 32.3 feet long, 11-foot beam, with a 2.5-foot draft; the *John Lonsdale* (1874), 46.4 feet long, 15.3 feet in width, and a draft of 4.0 feet; and the *John D.* (1883), 41.6 feet long, 14.2 feet in beam, and a draft of 2.3 feet.

The first recorded vessel built at Pleasant Mills, according to Mr. Kroedel's article, was the *Batsto*, built in 1804 "at Batsto" and registered in 1815. Pleasant Mills is given as the place of construction of the 63-ton schooner *Elizabeth*. Five vessels between 63 and 134 tons were built there during the 1830's while eight more were built in the 1840's. A second schooner *Batsto* is listed as being built in 1837, but it doesn't appear on any registry. The *Atsion* was built at Batsto in 1836 and enrolled in 1844. The 1830's saw the construction of a 134-ton schooner *Emeline Peterson*, and a smaller schooner, the *Phoebe and Margaret*. Yet another schooner was built at Batsto in 1840: the 90-ton schooner *Stranger*. In 1840, Batsto saw the *Frelinghuysen* go down the ways, and in 1844, the *John*

Wurtz, 84-tons, followed in the wake of the *Frelinghuysen*. These vessels were used to carry Batsto's iron and glass products, as well as lumber to Philadelphia and New York, until the railroads provided cheaper transportation. On their return, they brought back supplies for the local communities.

STEAMBOAT FIASCO

Throughout the nineteenth century, steam vessels gained in popularity both for hauling cargo and for carrying passengers. The age of sail reached its zenith prior to the Civil War, but the growing demand for fast, reliable service doomed the industry. Sail hung on into the twentieth century, because the entire hold could be devoted to cargo and operated on a cheap resource. Steamboats, though considerably more reliable, had to haul tons of coal or wood to power their great engines, taking up a generous proportion of space which otherwise would have been devoted to cargo. Even so, the age of sail was on its inevitable way out. When the destructive War Between the States came to its conclusion, northern industry was in high gear, and prosperity beckoned. While the shallow waters of the western rivers were dominated by the well-known stern-wheelers, the eastern bays and rivers saw huge, side-wheel steamboats making regular runs to all the major and most of the minor ports along the eastern seaboard.

The side-wheel design of these wooden behemoths made them very stable. As the boat leaned towards one side, the huge wheel paddles dug more deeply into the water, forcing the vessel back towards the level. They were colorful, artistic, practical, and popular. Steamboat companies were organized in every major city and set up regular runs all along the coast, as well as up the Chesapeake Bay, the Delaware Bay, the Hudson River, and the Connecticut River.

It is no wonder that local entrepreneurs from Egg Harbor City decided that the Mullica needed the fast, efficient passenger service to New York and Philadelphia that steamboats could provide. They were organized under a general act of the New Jersey legislature on March 17, 1854, but their plans were disrupted by the commencement of hostilities between the Union and the Confederate states. No sooner had the Civil War ended, however, when they began to plan for the day when steam-driven vessels would make regular runs from the Mullica towns to the big cities, carrying both freight and passengers. Egg Harbor City was planned as a community that would stretch from the railroad to the Mullica, as it still does today, so it was reasonable that someone should develop the river end of things.

Courtesy of Budd Wilson, Jr.

One Share of Stock in the Egg Harbor Navigation Company

The entrepreneurs of the Mullica valley were excited by this new idea. They had set their hopes on a railroad through the pines that would enable their little communities to grow into bustling cities in the next century, but the railroads had not been built into the area - yet. A steamship company might be the answer to their prayers, at least in the short run. July 4th, 1866 was the date set for the festivities that would introduce the new service to the world - or at least to South Jersey. We are indebted to Dorus Snow of the *South Jersey Republican* for his account of the "first day" and to J.G. Wilson's article in the Batsto Citizens Gazette, Spring and Summer edition of 1985. Though their words, we find the truth of that eternal principle, if something can go wrong, it will.

Dignitaries from all over South Jersey had been invited to the great event. The Egg Harbor Navigation Company had purchased two steam vessels for their run to New York, and they were to employ one of those for the inaugural trip. The first problem encountered by the invited guests had nothing whatever to do with steamboats and everything to do with railroads. Egg Harbor City might have one end on the Camden and Atlantic rail line and the other on the Mullica, but there was no way that anyone could take the train from Hammonton and points west to the Egg Harbor City station, then travel overland the several miles necessary to reach the steamboat landing on the river beyond the old Gloucester Furnace Landing by horse-drawn coach in time to board the steam vessel for its trip. Snow and five other Hammonton residents [Hammonton seems so close in this day of automobiles, a short twenty minute ride.] boarded the train to Atlantic City, stayed there overnight, then got on the train again for the ride back to Egg Harbor City. This got them to the station in time to ride overland to the steamship landing.

The boat was scheduled to leave the dock at 9:00 A.M., but there were the inevitable delays. When the Hammonton folks arrived at the dock, they found that many other invitees had come down from New York on the steamship. The festivities were to include a trip back to New York, complete with plenteous food and a party atmosphere, so all looked forward to a great day. Hah! They should all have remained home in bed.

As everyone knows so well, nothing ever gets started when the organizers say it will, and this day's event was no exception. The guests had plenty of time to get acquainted as they paced the deck impatiently, but the delay did give time for late arrivals to board. The German Band from Egg Harbor City (they're still umpahing away - different musicians, of course!) had been hired to play before the boat left the dock, and they cheerfully continued to play, and play, and play, and play as the delay increased. At least their music helped to lessen the aggravation.

Right at the outset, the plans had been changed. The owners announced that the day's trip would only extend to Atlantic City, not all the way to New York. Snow never did find out why the plans had been altered, and one wonders how the New York City folk felt about not returning home on the schedule they had been promised. The owners of the steamboat company were positive and ebullient, as all promoters are required to be. They informed the guests that the trip down river and across the bay to Atlantic City was the one which posed the most hazards to navigation anyway. The trip to New York would be a piece of cake. Getting to Atlantic City was the hard part. A few of the invited guests had taken a long look at the huge steamboat that lay tied up at the dock on the Mullica and had wondered about the vessel's size relative to the width of the channel it had to navigate, but they figured the captain and pilot knew their business and had everything well in hand. Wrong.

Actually, the trip down river from Lower Bank to Chestnut Neck went without a hitch and was delightful. At that old scene of Revolutionary havoc, the steamer made a landing to take on the distinguished State Senator, D. S. Blackman of Atlantic County and his entourage. Still no problem. The next scheduled stop was to be on the Bass River for even more dignitaries. Reporter Snow noted that the steamer turned into the Bass River, which must have been caused by a misunderstanding between the captain and the pilot. Actually, it had to travel up the Bass River if it was going to pick up anyone unless the guests were going to traipse through a couple of miles of marshland, their shoes squishing in the sticky mud, to get to the mouth of the river on the Mullica. The problem was that the steamer was a bit big for the river. Snow noted that "an hour was lost before we were again underway in the main stream." Actually, it takes twenty minutes at ten knots to get from the mouth of the Bass River to New Gretna, though they may have met their new passengers at Amasas Landing and cut the time in half. What they must have had great difficulty in doing was turning their vessel around after they'd gotten up that far.

So, a late departure and an hour's delay in a river too small for the boat, the celebrating [?] party were once again bound down river on the Mullica, heading for the open bay. Now, two things that the planners hadn't counted on were the weather and the tide (Strange, when you're navigating a boat!). The delays had allowed the morning to wear well away, and the strong, afternoon wind picked up early. As anyone who has been on Great Bay knows very well, a stiff easterly wind can kick up quite a chop as it builds across that expanse of water, especially when accompanied by a falling tide. Captain, pilot, and owners must have had a heated discussion in the pilot house about the resulting rough waters, but they finally announced to the passengers [reluctant captives by this time?] that the trip would end at Little Egg Inlet. In other words, they weren't even going to get to Atlantic City! Well, they *had* said that getting to Atlantic City was the hard part.

After tossing about in the short chop of the bay off the inlet, the vessel turned around and headed back across the open water for the mouth of the Mullica, hardly visible in the distance. Spume from the wind-tossed waves splashed across the deck, soaking the brave-hearted [or foolhardy] who had remained outside the main cabin. It was also well past the noon hour, and the passengers had seen nothing of the great quantities of food promised for their voyage. With growling stomachs, they approached the owners, who turned red in the face but admitted that no food had been brought aboard. The trip should only have taken a couple of hours at the most, and the party was to be held in Atlantic City. The guests were just going to have to go hungry.

Now came the supreme humiliation. The captain ran the boat up on a mud bank to let off the people from Port Republic. That's not unusual practice for a paddle-wheeler, but what he didn't count on was the rapidly falling tide. When he went to pull away, the mud just sucked and sucked, and the vessel was stuck tight. There were no rescue services you could call on back in 1866, so there they were for the next twelve hours until the tide came back in.

The Port Republic folks proved the saviors of the day. They certainly wouldn't have wanted to remain on board the stuck steamer with no food and no place to sleep, so they invited all the other passengers back to their homes for the night. As Snow reported, the passengers left the stranded boat "with no regret." The following day, the Hammonton delegation boarded the train at Patcong [Pomona] and were home in no time flat. One wonders how the steamship promoters ever had the nerve to show their faces around Egg Harbor City and Hammonton for a long while.

The tragicomedy of the initial day did not wreck the company's plans, unusual as that might seem from the mishaps. Three months later, the company announced that they had bought still another vessel, a screw-driven steamer called the *Eureka*, that had been built in Wilmington, Delaware, two years before. As J.G. Wilson noted in the Batsto Citizens Gazette, the new boat had a keel of 110 feet, a beam of 23 feet, could carry 140 tons of cargo, forty-two cabin passengers and twelve deck passengers, at a speed of twelve knots. Passenger steamers continued to ply the Mullica for several years, though not without mishap. Apparently, one ran into the Lower Bank Bridge (the old, wooden swing bridge), and Atlantic County officials expressed their intention to sue the company to recover repair costs in December of 1867.

Lower Bank, Green Bank, and Herman City continued to see the steamboats make their regular runs for several years, as old maps showing their steamboat docks attest. Unfortunately, the railroads that had doomed sail transportation would be no more kind to steamship transportation. The rails could simply provide faster and cheaper service than could waterborne vessels. The steamer entrepreneurs should have taken warning from the fateful first day and just packed up and gone home. They probably would have saved money. The one share of stock that Budd Wilson, Jr. still cherishes is totally worthless, except, of course, to historians and sentimentalists. Seeing William Sooy's signature on the stock certificate as president of the company, one wonders if this is how he lost his inheritance to the Union National Bank of Mount Holly in 1879. Perhaps he sank the borrowed $5,000 into the steamship line that was doomed to failure, and, risking all, he lost all.

The following is a list of ships owned or captained by local men that was gleaned from the Batsto Store Books by Edna Wilson, the mother of Budd Wilson, Jr. The date given is that of the entry in the books. In most instances, no indication is given whether the name given was the owner or the master of the vessel. Where there was such an indication, I have included it. Most of the time, the master of a ship had a part interest in it. One can possibly gain insight into whether a particular person is the owner or the master of a vessel by noting the date. If it is early in his life, he is probably the master. If it is later in his life, he is no doubt the owner. The sea was a difficult mistress, and most men who lived through their seafaring experience retired early, usually in their forties.

Owner/Master	Ship	Type	Year
Allen, Jesse	*John Little*	Schooner	1852
Allen, Jesse	*John Fritts*	Schooner	1853
Allen, Jesse	*John Fitchell*	Schooner	1853
Allen, Jesse (Master)	*Vulcan*	Schooner	1841
Cale, Josiah	*Speedwell*	Sloop	1830
Cale, William	*Eureka*	Steamer	
Cale, William	*Ida*	Schooner	1861
Cavileer, C.	*Arcadia*	Schooner	1852
Cavileer, Peter	*Pearl*	Schooner	1836
Cavileer, Reuben	*Archelaus*	Schooner	1838
Cavileer, Reuben	*L. Reeves*	Sloop	1847
Cramer, Caleb (Master)	*Maryland & Julia*	Schooner	
Crowley, Samuel	*July R. Clark*	Schooner	
Crowley, Samuel	*Anna Maria*	Schooner	1837
Crowley, Samuel	*Stranger*	Schooner	1846
Crowley, Samuel, Jr.	*Belvidier*	Schooner	1832-1834
Crowley, Samuel, Jr.	*Rebecca*	Sloop	1857
Crowley, Sebastian	*Anna D. Coffee*	Schooner	1841
Crowley, Sebastian	*Patriot*	Schooner	1843, 1847
Crowley, Therman	*July R. Clark*	Schooner	1854
Crowley, Thomas	*First Consul*	Schooner	1832-1834
Crowley, Thomas	*Ida*	Schooner	1861
Edwards, B.	*Batsto*	Schooner	1837
Edwards, B.	*Pilgrim*	Schooner	1838
Edwards, (Benjamin?)	*Mark*	Schooner	1847
Edwards, Benjamin	*Chesepeke* [sic]	Schooner	1849
Gale, Joseph	*J.W. Conklin*	Schooner	1838
Hall, Capt.	*Laura*	Schooner	
Johnson, J., (Captain)	*John Wurts*	Schooner	1847
Johnson, Jacob	*Georgianna*	Sloop	1859
Johnson, Levi G.	*Confidence*	Schooner	1830
Johnson, Levi G.	*Henry Clay*	Schooner	1832, 1852
Johnson, Levi G.	*First Consul*	Schooner	1837
Leek, Maja (Captain)	*Adjutant*	Schooner*	1838
Leek, Maja (Captain)	*Adjutant*	Sloop*	1841
Leek, William	*Hannah & Mary*	Schooner	1838
Leek, William (Master)	*Ann*	Schooner	
Maxwell, James (Owner)	*Albert*	Sloop	1838
Maxwell, William	*Bush*	Sloop	1860
McKeen, John	*Cora*	Sloop	1859
McKeen, Robert & Taggart, Samuel	*Packet*	Schooner	

* These are probably the same vessels. The clerk making the entry may have made an error in the type of vessel though it is entirely possible that Maja Leek had a sloop built with the same name as his former schooner.

Owner/Master	Ship	Type	Year
McKeen, Robert & Taggart, Samuel	*Huntress*	Schooner	
McKeen, William (Owner)	*Conroy* (or *Convoy*)	Schooner	1827
Nichols, S.	*Jesse Richards*	Schooner	1846
Richards, Thomas H.	*Frelinghuysen*	Schooner	1846
Richards, Thomas H.	*Gypsy*	Schooner	1846
Sooy, Benjamin (Captain)	*Elkinslaw*	Schooner	1847, 1849
Sooy, Benjamin	*E. Winslow*	Schooner	1847
Sooy, Noah, Jr.	*Lady Godfrey*	Schooner	1844
Van Sant, Joel	*Bodine Coffin*	Schooner	1852
Weeks, Capt.	*E & Larry*	Schooner	1838
Weeks, Job	*Esther & Sarah*	Schooner	1847
Weeks, Samuel	*Winslow*	Schooner	1837
Weeks, Samuel (Master)	*Morning Star of Washington*	Schooner	
Wharton	*Albert*	Schooner	
Wharton	*Alert*	Schooner	
Wharton	*Acktine*	Schooner	
Wooslten [sic], William (Captain)	*Mary*	Schooner	1851*
Woolston, W.	*Mary*	Sloop	1851*

* These are probably the same vessels. The clerk making the entry may have made an error in the type of vessel.

SHIPBUILDING IN THE MULLICA - LITTLE EGG HARBOR REGION

(Figures taken from an article entitled, "Shipbuilding: An Early Shore Industry", by R. Craig Koedel, published in the Journal of the Atlantic County Historical Society, 1985-1986)

	Number of Vessels			Tonnage	
Decade	Built	Registered	Not Registered	Total Registered	Average Each Vessel
1790-1799	2	2	0	229.00	114.50
1800-1809	3	3	0	112.77	37.59
1810-1819	1	1	0	79.00	79.00
1820-1829	6	6	0	421.80	70.30
1830-1839	45	43	2	4399.69	102.32
1840-1849	28	27	1	2853.63	105.69
1850-1859	36	33	3	5354.44	162.26
1860-1869	32	17	15	2922.82	171.93
1870-1879	14	13	1	1847.69	142.13
1880-1889	7	7	0	105.68	15.10
Total	174	152	22	18326.52	120.57

One can easily see from the above figures that ship construction peaked in the area in the three decades before the Civil War, though the average size of the vessels were greatest in the 1850 through 1870 period. Registered tonnage was at its height from 1850 - 1859. The 1880 - 1889 period shows the full impact of the railroad on shipping and the decline of area industry with a dramatic drop in vessels registered.

Workboats on the Mullica

The *Mabel E. Horton* was owned by Captain James Morrell Crowley and inherited by Bert Crowley, his son. Bert sold her and used the proceeds to purchase his first little red school bus. She appears to be a small, wooden tug or work boat from around the turn of the century. She may be steam. Though no stack is visible, she does have either an air or a steam whistle. She is docked at the slip that used to be in front of Captain Crowley's home at 1027 River Road.

Only the name of this vessel is known, but the *Burlington* appears to be a small turn-of-the-century workboat. She has a straight-front main cabin. Steam can be seen coming from her stack as she approaches the dock. She appears to be heading for the same slip as that used by the *Mabel E. Horton* in the above photograph.

Captain Crowley Loveland, obviously a descendant of both the Crowleys and the Lovelands, used to winter his yawl, *Vagabond*, in front of 1027 River Road, the home of Captain James Morrell Crowley at the time. In the photograph above, the Wobbar Store would have been just to the left, if it had been there when this photograph was taken. A close examination of the background seems to indicate that the Green Bank bridge is the old swing bridge, built in 1855 and replaced in 1926, which would date this photograph as prior to 1926 anyway. The *Vagabond* was used by Captain Loveland as a charter boat.

Budd Wilson, who lives there now, was told that her masts were brought through the third story gable in the house and stored in the rear wing, which had been added in the 1880's. This would have entailed getting the heavy masts almost horizontal before pulling them into the house three stories up, an almost impossible task!

There is, however, a square section cut in the floor of the third story, directly above the second story window. More than likely, the masts were placed over the porch roof into the second story window, up through the ceiling of the second floor and into the hallway of the third floor. This would make the task of pulling them into the hall through the doorway to the back section a much more reasonable task.

In the photograph at right, the *Vagabond* is all the way up in Maine and loaded (overloaded, rather) with vacationers.

Vagabond - Captain Crowley Loveland

Augusta (Gussie) Weeks and her grandfather, Otto Wobbar, relaxing on board his sailboat.

Delwyne P. Crowley
and His *Nemo*

Courtsy of Budd Wilson, Jr.

Courtsy of Budd Wilson, Jr.

Relaxing aboard his boat is Delwyne P. Crowley, owner of Crowley's Basin, home of the Tuckerton Seaport.

Yachting on the Mullica

This little vessel was called *L-Tiger* and belonged to Ezekiel Forman, father of Jessie (Forman) Lewis. Zeke's boat was named after a silver mine owned by his father-in-law, Ephraim C. Sooy, Jr.

This photograph is probably pre-1940. The boat is tied to the "upper" dock, just downriver from the Old Store. The house in the picture appears to be the Braun House at 1045 River Road.

A large Chris Craft Motor Yacht from the 1950's

A Matthews Motor Yacht - early 1950's

Courtesy of Dudley H. Lewis

The *Unvarnished Truth*, a 1937 32-foot Elco Motor Yacht, Captain Dudley Lewis of Green Bank - 1994

A brand new Ocean Yachts is put through her trials on the Mullica below Lower Bank during the summer of 1995. Ocean Yachts is owned by Jack Leek, formerly of Pacemaker Yachts, whose home and shipyard are on the Atlantic County side of the river between Green Bank and Lower Bank.

A century ago, there were several shipyards in Washington Township. Today there are none, but Jack Leek and his family have such close ties to this heart of the pines for over two centuries that he is forgiven for living on the other side of the river.

Photograph by John Pearce

Another "Last Wooden Boat Built on the Mullica"

This magnificent vessel might be considered the last wooden boat built on the Mullica. Ian Arnot, an Australian by birth, educated in England, but a resident of the United States for many years, bought this 1926 50-foot Elco Motor Yacht a few years ago and began "restoring" it in the old Pacemaker Yachts building in the background of this photograph. He has proceeded with such painstaking care that almost every piece of wood in her hull and superstructure is new. He had to berth her in Atlantic City for two years, where a storm removed her deckhouse. She has an apt name: *Patience*! He constructed a new one and continues the rebuilding of her interior. In the autumn of 1997, he was able to return to Lower Bank where this photograph was taken.

So much of *Patience* is new that he can claim her as the last wooden boat built on the Mullica. He vies with Jack Leek for the title. Jack Leek had *Miss Heritage* built in his boatyard in 1996. She is a runabout built to plans drawn by his grandfather in 1919 (See V. 2 p. 135).

The Bridges Over the Mullica and Its Tributaries

THE WADING RIVER BRIDGE

During the eighteenth century, the Road to Little Egg Harbor crossed the Wading River far inland at Bodine's Tavern. The only bridge across the Mullica was at Batsto-Pleasant Mills. The first major drawbridge authorized to be built across the Mullica or any of its navigable streams was that which spanned the Wading River, crossing from Washington Township to Bass River (then Little Egg Harbor) Township, was authorized on the 18th of January, 1814.

> *An Act authorizing the board of chosen freeholders of the county of Burlington, to build a Draw-bridge over Wading River, at or near Leakes wharf.*
>   *1. Be it enacted by the Council and General Assembly of this state, and it is hereby enacted by the authority of the same, That it shall and may be lawful for the board of chosen freeholders in and for the county of Burlington aforesaid, to build and maintain a good and sufficient bridge over Wading river, at or near Leakes wharf, where the main road leading from Longacoming to Tuckerton crosses the same, with a suitable draw therein, of a sufficient width for the convenient passage of vessels navigating the same.*
>   *A. Passed at Trenton, January 18, 1814.*

The bridge as built was a wooden swing span and lasted, with repairs, until it was replaced about 1924-5. At that time, the old bridge was torn out and a new lift span was built. It was similar to those constructed at Green Bank and Lower Bank over the next two years. At the time the bridge was built, the river channel was dredged away from the eastern shore of the river, and the level of the eastern shore across from the McKeen house was raised with fill. This bridge was replaced in 1983-4 by a more modern structure that is wider than the bridge it replaced but was designed to look like the earlier bridge. Dreamers in the State bureaucracy wanted to put in a high-rise bridge at the time, but considerable local opposition prevented the destruction of a major portion of old Bridgeport. The State of New Jersey also wanted to replace the Green Bank bridge with a high rise, which would have annihilated most of that town as well, but once again, they were foiled in their dastardly deed. The photographs of all the Wading River bridges may be found in the chapter on Wading River/Bridgeport.

THE BASS RIVER BRIDGE

Traffic through Bass River had headed inland from Tuckerton and crossed the Bass River by the upper road at the Bass River Tavern. In 1821, a lower road was laid out, crossing the river two and a half miles below the old road, which made a larger bridge across the Bass River a necessity. The drawbridge was actually constructed in 1824. This meant that traffic avoided the inland route by the Bass River Tavern in favor of the more seaward route of New Gretna, then on to Wading River.

The first bridge over the Bass River at New Gretna - Circa 1906

THE NACOTE CREEK BRIDGE

The third bridge built over the navigable part of the Mullica or one of its tributaries had nothing at all to do with the traffic patterns on the northern side. As previously mentioned, anyone bound northward from Great Egg Harbor was obliged to head either out to Swimming-Over Point or inland northwestward around the Nacote Creek and eventually the Mullica. To make life easier, the state legislature planned a drawbridge over the Nacote Creek at Port Republic. According to Charles Werner, this bridge was authorized on February 7th, 1829 and stood next to the old tavern on the upper road in Port Republic.

THE GREEN BANK BRIDGE

This still left coastal north-south travel almost impossible. The road would have headed up from Great Egg Harbor, then inland to Port Republic, then even farther inland on the west side of the Mullica, all the way up to the Forks and Batsto. Life would be so much easier for the traveller if a crossing of the Mullica could be made somewhere a little closer to the shore.

In 1855, the legislature authorized the construction of a draw or swing bridge over the Mullica at the town of Green Bank, which was subsequently built. Actually, these authorizations simply permitted the counties to enter into a bond to build the bridge and required the local residents of Green Bank and Weekstown to build the connecting road. It wasn't supposed to cost the State of New Jersey one cent!

> *An Act to authorize the erection of a draw or swing bridge over the Mullicus River.*
> *1. Be it enacted, by the Senate and General Assembly of the State of New Jersey, That it shall and may be lawful for the boards of chosen freeholders of the counties of Burlington and Atlantic to build and maintain a good and sufficient bridge over the Mullicus river, at Green Bank, in the township of Washington, in the said county of Burlington; to a point opposite in the township of Mullicas, in the county of Atlantic, with a suitable draw or swing therein, which said draw or swing shall be at least thirty-five feet in width, for the convenient passage of all*

The Green Bank bridge as built in 1855 - circa 1909.

vessels navigating the said river; provided that before the freeholders construct said bridge, the inhabitants of Greenbank and Weeksville enter into bond to construct the causeway connecting the bridge with the main land free of expense to the said counties.

2. And be it enacted, That this act shall take effect immediately. Approved March 15th, 1855.

This bridge was a steel swing bridge and lasted until 1926 when it was replaced by a wider drawbridge.

THE LOWER BANK BRIDGE

It is rumored that a ferry ran from Lower Bank to Clark's Landing during the eighteenth century. It is even more probable that one ran from the lower end of Lower Bank across the river to Gloucester Furnace Landing. These ferrys would have provided the only connecting link between Old Gloucester (now Atlantic) County and the east bank of the Mullica below Batsto/Pleasant Mills until the Green Bank bridge was built in 1855.

Lower Bankers had to take this ferry to the Atlantic County side of the river, then make the journey to Egg Harbor City, where they could catch the Camden and Atlantic Railroad (after 1854) on their journey to Philadelphia or Atlantic City. They finally persuaded the legislature to authorize a bridge to be built at Lower Bank even though the Civil War was then raging.

Photograph by John Pearce

The Green Bank Bridge - 1995
The boat is the *Unvarnished Truth*, a 1937
32-foot Elco,
Captain Dudley Lewis

Publ. by H. Kirscht
Egg Harbor City, N.J.

MULLICA RIVER BRIDGE – Lower Bank, N.J.

Courtesy of Pete Stemmer

The Lower Bank bridge built as authorized in 1863
Photo date unknown

The new Lower Bank Bridge - 1995

AN ACT to authorize the erection of a draw or swing bridge over the Mullicus River at Lower Bank.

1. Be it enacted, by the Senate and General Assembly of the State of New Jersey, That it shall and may be lawful for the boards of chosen freeholders of the counties of Burlington and Atlantic to build and construct, or cause or permit to be built and constructed, a bridge over the Mullicus river, commencing at the terminus of the road running from Capt. J. Johnston's store to the river, at Lower Bank, in Washington Township, Burlington County, to a point opposite in the township of Mullicas, in the county of Atlantic, meeting and connecting with a road now being constructed by the Egg Harbor Association, from Egg Harbor City to said river, and to place in said bridge a draw or swing of at least thirty-five feet in width, of such construction as to impede as little as possible the navigation of said river.

2. And be it enacted, That this Act shall take effect immediately.

Approved February 25th, 1863

The road mentioned was River Road, and the bridge was to be built where the road reached the Mullica. Surveys of the Atlantic County side must have been completed when it was determined that there was simply too much swamp over which to build a causeway which would connect this bridge with the road to Egg Harbor, for in the same year, the site of the bridge was moved downstream to a point opposite the then home of Samuel Cavileer, at its present location.

A SUPPLEMENT to an act entitled "An Act to authorize the building of a bridge over the Mullicus river, at Lower Bank."

1. Be it enacted by the Senate and General Assembly of the State of New Jersey, That the bridge which by the act to which this is a supplement, the boards of chosen freeholders of the counties of Atlantic and Burlington, were authorized to build and construct, or cause or permit to be built and constructed across the Mullicus River, shall commence near the residence of Samuel Cavileer, at Lower Bank, in Washington township, Burlington County, and end at a point on the opposite side of the river in the township of Mullicus, county of Atlantic, meeting and connecting with a road now being constructed by the Egg Harbor Association for Egg Harbor city to said river; instead of being built as in said original act is directed; and they shall place in said bridge, over the deepest channel of said river, a draw or swing of at least thirty-five feet in width, of such a construction as to impede as little as possible the navigation of said river.

2. And be it enacted, That the said act to which this is a supplement, in so far as the same is inconsistent with the provisions hereof, be and the same is hereby repealed.

3. And be it enacted, That this act shall take effect immediately.
Approved March 24th, 1863.

This information was gathered by Mr. Charles Werner of New Gretna in 1930. Mr. Werner notes that the Lower Bank bridge was in very poor repair in the early 1920's and was the cause of several automobile accidents. The authorities of Burlington and Atlantic counties wanted to do away with the bridge altogether, rather than repair or rebuild it. They wanted to force the residents to travel to Green Bank to get across the river, adding several miles to their travel toward Egg Harbor City. Mr. Lewis Adams successfully led the Lower Bank residents in protest and the counties agreed to build a new bridge to replace the old span. The original bridge had been a narrow, wooden swing bridge. This was replaced with a steel drawbridge as had also been done in Green Bank.

They say that there is nothing new under the sun. The two counties involved with these bridges are at least consistent. Every time the bridges are in need of extensive repair, at least one of the two counties proposes to do away with it entirely. Someone in the state government even proposed that a high-rise bridge be built in Green Bank, which would effectively destroy the entire town. Burlington and Atlantic counties finally reached an agreement in the 1980s that Burlington would maintain the Lower Bank span and Atlantic the Green Bank span. The bridges were in desperate need of repair in the early 1990s, and Burlington County completely rebuilt the Lower Bank bridge. Though maintaining the looks of the earlier drawbridge, they widened the roadway considerably. Atlantic County, on the other hand, has simply repaired the old 1926 Green Bank bridge, after years of trying to keep heavy trucks from crossing it failed miserably. They erected 10' height barriers over the bridge a couple of years ago, which were taken out every other night, it seemed like, by small trucks and even by tractor-trailers. They finally gave up and repaired the bridge. Someday they may even replace it with a new structure like that of Lower Bank and Wading River.

THE ROUTE 9 BRIDGE

Until the late nineteenth century, all traffic along the shore had to go inland to cross the Mullica. Early Quakers had used Swimming Over Point, but that involved a lengthy trip through marshes on both sides of the river, and the Mullica itself was wide, deep, and fast-flowing at that point. In 1856, the legislature authorized the counties of Burlington and Atlantic to construct a bridge which later became the main bridge over the Mullica, carrying Route 9 southwards.

> *1. BE IT ENACTED by the Senate and General Assembly of the State of New Jersey, That it shall and may be lawful for the boards of chosen freeholders of the counties of Burlington and Atlantic, to build and maintain a good and sufficient bridge over the Mullicus river, at or near Chestnut Neck, in the township of Galloway, in the said county of Atlantic, to a point opposite, in the township of Little Egg Harbor, in the county of Burlington, with a suitable draw or swing therein, which said draw or swing shall be at least thirty-five feet in width, for the convenient passage of all vessels navigating the said river.*
> *2. And be it enacted, That this Act shall take effect immediately.*
> *Approved, March 14th, 1856.*

Unfortunately, the respective Boards of Chosen Freeholders failed to appropriate the necessary funds to build the authorized bridge. The issue was still being debated almost thirty years later when the Mount Holly *Herald* reported that it had become a political issue.

> *One of the candidates for Freeholder in this township has hit upon the novel plan to gain the support of unpledged voters by agreeing in case of his election to unite Burlington and Atlantic counties by a bridge over Mullicas River, and that the cost of such a structure would only be about $400,000. It is more than likely he will have to erect the bridge at his own expense, and if he is willing to do that we hope he will be elected.*
> *- Mount Holly Herald, June 6, 1885.*

Apparently, the Freeholder candidate in question did not wish to provide the whopping sum of $400,000 himself, for the question of a bridge over the Mullica continued to be debated. In May of 1886, Mark W. Adams wrote a letter to the editor of the *Herald* extolling the virtues of New Jersey's farms. Mr. Adams comments:

New Jersey farms are exceeded in value (size considered) by the farms of but few, if any, states in our country. Is it because the soil of New Jersey is naturally better than that of other states? Is it because the farmers are more wide awake, more industrious, more energetic than the farmers of other states? No! It is because New Jersey lies between the two largest cities of the United States which afford a never failing market for the vegetables, fruits, and other things which the New Jersey farms produce in abundance. - Mount Holly Herald, *May 15, 1886*

Mr. Adams goes on to note that Atlantic City land was very valuable, and that city's hucksters and butchers come within two miles of New Gretna, but could not get across the river to purchase farm products. "It would take 14 miles driving over a miserable road" to get to Port Republic from New Gretna, which meant that the farmers of Bass River were losing out on a major market for their produce. He concludes that, "we in New Gretna are somewhat like a vessel without a jib, a toad without legs, a bird without wings, a wagon without wheels, a house without windows, doors or chimneys. How long will it be so?"

The following week, a rebuttal from "Another Independent Voter" graced the pages of the *Herald*.

Our beautiful little village on the main road from Tuckerton to Egg Harbor City, 6 miles from Tuckerton, on water navigable to Atlantic City and the outside world is just now attracting much attention. Chestnut Neck is just two miles away and can be reached in half an hour. We have 3 general stores, 2 churches, 5 schools, supplied by third grade teachers and two butcher wagons from Tuckerton give us a good supply of fresh meats, when we get tired of fish, clams and oysters, which are unsurpassed. We have good markets for our produce, everywhere except in China, and we might get in there if we had a few more enterprising men. If we were all of the same opinion we might reach it in some way, about as soon as we get that bridge over the Mullica River. We are already making heavy drafts on the county treasury for bridges and I doubt if the tax-payers up your way [in the western portion of the county] are willing to spend $20,000 for the bridge. ... We have only $3,350,000 of taxable property and the applicants for the proposed road over the meadows to the bridge represent about $15,000 of that amount. An investigation of the strong statements made by the writer in last week's HERALD sets him down as a mad or crazy man. - The Mount Holly Herald, *May 29, 1886*

On September 11th of the same year, another startling notice appeared in the *Herald*:

The new road from New Gretna to Chestnut Neck via tunnel [!] under the Mullica river is still being agitated. When the application was made, surveyors were appointed who viewed the ground, laid out the road and made their return. . . . The object of it all is to get a **bridge over the Mullica river.**

- Mount Holly Herald, *September 11, 1886*

Four years later, there was still no bridge. There was movement, however, which was promising. Apparently Atlantic and Burlington Counties had at least built a road to the river on their respective sides, for the December 13, 1890 issue of the *Herald* reported that "Burlington County was invaded Thursday last by Atlantic county Board of Freeholders."

The expedition was organized to view the site of the proposed Mullica river bridge near Chestnut Neck. Leaving Absecon in carriages at 11 A.M., the party drove through not very picturesque nor mountainous scenery to Chestnut Neck arriving there at 12:30. They inspected the road which is being built and is nearly finished to the Mullica river bank as an extension of the Port Republic road. . . . It consists of a foundation of pine log trimming, apparently coming from the mill, varied on both sides and filled in with meadow muck, to be topped with gravel.

Crossing the historic battlefield of Chestnut Neck the company swooped down upon Capt. Daniel Rose's oyster scow, which for once was turned into a private yacht or ferry on which the invaders were soon safely landing in Burlington County. They were met by Winfield S. French,

Two Views of the Original Route 9 Bridge over the Mullica River

The above photograph is of the New Gretna end of the bridge and is courtesy of Thomas Cramer. On the right is Captain Hezekiah Adams of Bass River, who became the bridge tender in 1899. The photograph below is of the Atlantic County side of the bridge and is courtesy of Thelma Cramer Eppolite.

RT-9. BRIDGE OVER MULLICA RIVER - PORT REPUBLIC — NEW GRETNA 1920's AR/2.00

William R. Lipponcott and Horace G. Ireland, the committee appointed by Burlington county to receive them.

Winfield S. French, as chairman, explained that the site was the narrowest part of the Mullica river which they found feasible for the building of a bridge. The channel was 28 feet deep, and the tide very swift during its rise and fall. It will require a bridge about 700 feet long, and the one they had in view would be substantial as well as ornamental, an iron bridge with a driveway 16 feet wide and the draw 23 to 25 feet in length. The bridge will cross the river obliquely so as to better withstand the swift current.

One carriage and two "jump seat" wagons were at the landing to convey the party to New Gretna, four miles distant to dine.

They were driven over the new road one mile and half in length built expressly in anticipation of the bridge, and runs through a fine expanse of meadow land. It is built similarly to the one on the Atlantic county side.

A ten minute conference was held in the post office, deciding that Director Currie should call a special meeting of the Board of Freeholders between the 10th and 15th of June to decide whether the bridge is to be built or not, half at the expense of Atlantic county.

When work is started it will require about three months to complete the bridge.

Mount Holly *Herald*, December 13, 1890.

In the same issue, the *Herald* announced that

The new bridge to be built over the Mullica river to connect Burlington and Atlantic counties is to be 750 feet long, made up of four spans of 150 feet each, and a draw span of the same length having two clear openings of about 63 feet, and with a roadway, 16 feet wide. The entire superstructure will be iron and steel, except planking. The piers will be concrete, 12 x 22 feet at the river bottom, tapering to 16 4 1/2 x 7 feet at the top and covered with an iron sheathing. This construction was adopted as being one that would withstand the elements and be a permanent improvement. Work will commence about April 1st, 1891, and the bridge completed by August 1st, 1891. Then the people of New Gretna and Port Republic propose having a meeting to celebrate the event. - Mount Holly *Herald*, December 13, 1890.

Thirty-five years of talking had finally produced results. No data has come to light on the name of the first bridge tender, but the May 22, 1897 issue of the *Herald* reported that "Jesse French has assumed the duty of draw tender fo the Mullica River iron bridge." Two years later, Hezekiah Adams took over the job on the 15th of May, 1899. In 1907, the *Herald* mentioned that Hezekiah's salary was $30.00.

Unfortunately, the first iron bridge proved an expensive debacle.

After having dragged along for nearly a year it is likely that something will be done shortly by the Atlantic Board of Freeholders towards repairing the iron bridge over the Mullica river at Chestnut Neck that is said to contain mushy concrete in the abutments and to be unsafe. There is a great deal of travel over the bridge. The bridge committee of the Atlantic Board will meet a similar committee from the Board of Freeholders of Burlington county at the bridge in September. It will be inspected in order to ascertain whether or not it will stand the storms and pressure of ice during the coming winter. Plans were prepared months ago for the repair of the structure and were approved by the war department and the Atlantic county authorities but did not find favor with the Burlington county folks. They thought the plan called for too great an outlay of money and wanted something cheaper. It is likely now that the two counties will come to an understanding, advertising for bids and award the contract that the operation may be started before the cool weather sets in as a great part of it will be concrete work. It will take about $35,000 for it [Atlantic County Review].

- Mount Holly *Herald*, August 15, 1908.

The concrete pylons of the seventeen-year-old bridge were disintegrating, yet no immediate action was taken to repair the bridge. Two years later, the *Herald* did report that:

County supervisor of roads, Joseph Hilton and county engineer Earl Thompson Tuesday inspected the Mullica river bridge in conjunction with E. D. Rightmire Atlantic county's engineer and supervisor Smith. They were taken to the bridge in an auto which is furnished by the county for the use of the supervisor and the structure was found to need rebuilding but no action can be taken at this time. - Mount Holly *Herald*, February 19, 1910.

It was finally decided to replace the iron bridge, built less than twenty years before, rather than try to repair it. This time around, the construction of this second bridge gave the two Freeholder boards just as many headaches as before. The counties hired George S. Bennett and approved the contract in March, 1915, but work was stopped on February 20, 1917 by the county engineers due to shoddy construction. Legal problems with the contractor resulted. At the point at which work had been stopped, the counties had paid Bennett forty thousand dollars. It cost them another sixty-three thousand to complete the job.

This "Old Iron Bridge" was replaced by the Garden State Parkway bridge in the early 1950's. Tater Cramer, the last bridge tender, faithfully stood to his post at the draw until the new Parkway bridge was opened. The Route 9 causeway to the old bridge was abandoned, and the road was rerouted onto the parkway, across the parkway bridge, and off on the other side, to rejoin its old course to Smithville and Leed's Point.

I am indebted to Peter Stemmer, Steve Eichinger, and Harry Deverter of Bass River for providing me with a copy of their Mount Holly *Herald* research work, from which the above quotations have been taken.

The Second "Iron Bridge" Across the Mullica Carrying Route Nine - early 1950's
This photograph was actually taken from the northern end of the new Garden State Parkway bridge.

795

The Spell

Emma Van Sant Moore

I have an understanding with the pines,
Magnolia, laurel and green-briar vines.
They weave about me such a spell
Of quiet peace, that I know full well—
Although my feet have wandered far,
It is for me a sure lodestar
That draws me back and e'er inclines
My weary heart to rest for aye
'Mid Jersey pines.

from *Mullica*, 1960

The Headless Ghost
of the Pines

Tales of bodies disposed of in the pines by New York crime families have always been common. People outside the area have thrilled to mysterious and intriguing occurrences that titillate the senses and suggest deep, dark secrets carried by the cedar-stained waters of the little rivers lost in the vastness of the woods.

They picture the isolated settlements and extensive back-country as prime territory for unrecorded movements and secret burials. Stories abound of half-wit trigger-happy pineys who would let loose their 12 gage at you and leave your corpse to the turkey buzzards deep in the fastness of the unexplored wilderness. Nothing could be farther from the truth, of course.

There are isolated houses where the inhabitants are wary of strangers poking their noses where they don't belong, but the vast majority of the inhabitants of this heart of the pines are happy, cordial, well-adjusted, and sociable people. Occasionally, a body does turn up. A hiker once discovered the remains of a buried Corvette. Generally, though, organized crime would rather execute a victim and leave their body around as a lesson to others or dump them into the Hudson than travel all the way to South Jersey for disposal. Today there are simply too many people in the pinelands to ensure secrecy.

There are stories of rape and murder in the pines which are all too true, though. The Revolutionary War was a civil war in a very real sense. John Adams' estimate that the population of the colonies was divided into thirds in their opinion was probably accurate. If a third of the populace believed in the justice of the War for Independence, another third was indifferent one way or the other. Quakers were against war in any form for any reason, and South Jersey had quite a large number of people of that faith. Then there were those who were loyal to Mother England and openly supported the efforts of her troops and of Royal Governor William Franklin in his effort to stamp out the rebellion.

What John Adams didn't consider in his estimate were those who supported neither side but were hardly indifferent. These men, who would have been criminals in stable societies, had but one loyalty: to themselves. They used the turmoil and confusion of the times to line their own pockets at the expense of their neighbors and get away with it. They lived for the excitement of the raid, the gratification of a rape, the thrill of watching a house burn to the ground, the begging of husband, wife ... or *very* recent widow ... for life and/or sanctity of their persons. These men were sensualists of the cruelest sort who found their stimulation in the agony of their fellow human beings. These were the Refugees.

Claiming to be Tories, loyal to the Crown of England, they would swoop down on unguarded cabins, looting, raping the innocents, burning homes down over the heads of their victims, stimulated by the action and the blood lust. Many times, they waited until the men of the house had joined the militia to protect the area from outside assault, little suspecting that the threat would come from inside. Yet they were no respecters of political loyalties either. Staunch support for King George III was no defense. Ultimately, the Refugees didn't care which side in the conflict the inhabitants of an isolated cabin supported, they still became targets.

The nineteenth century romantics saw these men as heroic Robin Hood-like characters. They definitely were not. They were feared and hated by the inhabitants of the pines and dealt with harshly when captured.

Such was Joseph Mulliner, scourge of the pines. He could be charming and debonair, occasionally gallant, but he could also be cruel, hard-hearted, and completely selfish. A "Philadelphia Bulletin" article by Frank Toughill in 1958 described Mulliner as "tall, broad-shouldered, narrow waisted, mighty of muscle, and outrageously handsom e . . . It was thirst for adventure rather than wickedness of nature that took him into outlawry... He had a gaiety of nature that could be thought frivolous."

Joe Mulliner, a man of English extraction, settled with his brother, Moses, in the pines prior to the beginning of hostilities with Great Britain. Moses became a private and a drummer in the New Jersey Line as a substitute for Job Mathis (Blackman, *History of Little Egg Harbor*). Joe didn't see things the same way. He saw the immediate advantages of the confusion caused by the conflict and organized a gang which grew to upwards of one hundred men who roamed the forests and towns along the Mullica for excitement and pillage.

They made their headquarters in Cold Spring Swamp near The Forks on an island surrounded by impassable, water-soaked terrain. Here they planned their raids, piled up their ill-gotten booty, and avoided contact with whatever militia could be organized to search for them. Whether the night were darkened by clouds or bright as day from a full moon mattered not to these brigands. They had the largest armed force in the area and feared neither God nor man.

From their fastness, they would lead their horses through the swamp to high ground, mount up, and gallop down a sand road towards their latest chosen victim. Out of the night, a lonely forest cabin would be surrounded, its inhabitants rudely awakened by shouts and threats. Old men, women, and children would be hauled from their beds and dumped in a pile outside their rude home, forced to watch as their few possessions were thrown from windows or carried to the yard. When excitement gripped the Refugees and lust burned within them, the women would be raped, even right before the horrified eyes of their helpless husbands.

Loaded with whatever valuables they could carry on their horses, the Refugees would set fire to the cabin and the remaining possessions of their victims and dash off for their swamp refuge. Many a protesting man was left lying in front of his house, a bullet through his heart, amidst the wailing of wife and children, the whole scene lighted by tongues of fire from their burning house.

To give Joe Mulliner his due, he does not seem to have been directly involved in the worst of the crimes ascribed to the Refugees of the pines. It seems that he, himself, was rather a jovial, fun-loving sort who robbed stage coaches, way-stations, and taverns. One of the stories told about him relates that he showed up at a tavern intent on having a good time. At gunpoint, he ordered the fiddler to continue playing and chose the prettiest girl in the place as his dancing partner. The girl's young lover took about all he could and finally stepped forward and challenged the famous Refugee, punching him in the jaw. Everyone present expected Mulliner to react with anger and kill the youth, but Mulliner simply laughed. Joe announced that, since the young man was the only one in the place with enough guts to defend his "lady," he deserved the girl. He then ordered his gang out of the tavern.

Another story has it that Mulliner pulled a raid on the Washington Tavern which was hosting a wedding at the time. When he and his men dismounted in the yard, Joe found the young bride-to-be crying. He asked her why she was so sad on her wedding day, to which the girl replied that she didn't want to marry the intended groom. Gallant to the end, Mulliner proceeded to run the man off the premises at the point of a gun, leaving the girl far happier than when he found her.

These rogues knew that they could flaunt themselves with little fear of capture, for what authority there was had more than enough to do with fighting the war far distant from The Forks of the Mullica. Arthur Pierce, in *Iron in the Pines*, relates a story about an impromptu raid by Mulliner's gang one Sunday afternoon. The target was a large and fearless widow who was just returning from services at Clark's Log Meeting House, the predecessor of the Batsto-Pleasant Mills Church.

The woman's name was Bates. Of her eight sons, four were away with the militia, and the others were too young to fight though they helped her farm her land. She and her deceased husband had apparently brought several pieces of fine furniture and silver plate into their forest home when they had moved there, and the knowledge of that plate had reached Cold Spring Swamp.

On this particular Sabbath afternoon, several members of Mulliner's gang decided to part the widow from her prized possessions and paid an unexpected call on her. When the Widow Bates and her young family got back from church, they found the gang rampaging through their home. Undaunted, the widow used her powerful lungs in a tongue-lashing that was vitriolic.

Pierce records the remembered dialogue which followed:

"'Silence, woman!' cried the leader of the gang, 'or we'll lay your damned house in ashes.'

'That would be worthy of cowardly curs like you,' snapped the widow. 'But you'll never stop my mouth while there's breath in my body.'"

The Refugees promptly took logs from the woman's own fireplace and set the house ablaze. When she tried to put the fire out and her children threw rocks at the men, Mulliner's gang tied them all up and left them to watch the only shelter they had turn to ashes. After seeing the family well-secured, the men mounted their horses and galloped away.

Mrs. Bates and her family found sympathy with their neighbors, several of whom were wealthy from the privateer goods sold at The Forks, and these kindhearted people came to her aid. Her silver was gone, but at least she and her children had their lives, and they would have another roof over their heads before long. Several weeks after the incident, someone left her $300 in coin, a rather large sum in those days. Since the gift had been anonymously made, the rumor spread that Joe Mulliner had been so upset with his gang's actions in his absence that he, himself, had given the sizable gift. Knowing the character of the Refugees, it more than likely came from the manager of Batsto, Joseph Ball, or one of the masters at The Forks, Richard Wescoat or Elijah Clark.

Throughout much of the war, Mulliner continued his raids throughout the area, not confining himself to the Mullica valley but ranging over into Old Gloucester (now Atlantic) County and also into Monmouth (now Ocean) County. Regardless of the romantic tales that spread about him after the fact, he was roundly hated by everyone wherever his greed led him.

Thinking that the local men were too busy to occupy themselves in chasing him, he became more bold in showing up in public places. This imprudence finally resulted in his downfall.

The story has it that there was a party at a tavern in Nesco, then called New Columbia, in the year 1781 which drew the famed Mulliner to its festivities. The tavern, a private residence, is presently known as the Indian Cabin Mill Inn. Captain Baylin and his Rangers, the local militia, were waiting for just such impudence on the outlaw's part, and they, too, planned on being present at the tavern. Mulliner must have been shocked and furious when he was suddenly surrounded by the Rangers. Taken to Burlington City, he was tried and convicted six weeks later. Sentenced to "hang by the neck until dead," the famed Refugee was nearing his end, but Mulliner caused a stir by a jail-cell conversion.

Watson Buck tells the story of what followed in an excellent article, "The Refugee Chieftain Joseph Mulliner", in a 1970 "Batsto Citizens Gazette." A later edition of the "Gazette," that of Fall 1974, reprinted the original article from which Buck got his information. The story originates with a Rev. G.A. Raybold, Methodist minister and son-in-law of William Coffin, Sr. who built a sawmill and glassworks at Hammonton in 1812 and 1813 and later also ran the glassworks at Green Bank. Raybold apparently got the story from an eyewitness to the hanging of the infamous Refugee of the Pines. The tale was probably well-treasured by the Methodist clergy of the time.

During his imprisonment, it seems that Joe was visited by at least three ministers bent on saving his soul: the Rev. William Budd, New Mills (Pemberton), the Rev. Joseph Cromwell, and the Rev. Pedicord. Painting the appropriate picture of the flames of hell (which probably reminded him of the many houses he had burned to the ground) they "convinced" the notorious thief, murderer, and rapist to confess his crimes to save his soul. Raybold noted that the ministers attempted to

> *induce his soul, so guilty and so nigh God's judgement-bar, to hear the words of warning, and to accept the offers of grace through the crucified Jesus. He [Mulliner] became alarmed and repented most sincerely, confessing all his baseness. They uttered to him the words of invitation, and the trembling, repentant sinner believe in the name of Jesus and was pardoned . . . The cell of the condemned prisoner became the altar of his salvation.*

No doubt he also thought it might save his life. Fortunately, at that time at least, the law was the law.

Thousands came to witness the spectacle of Mulliner's hanging. At the appointed hour, Mulliner arrived with the faithful three, Budd, Cromwell, and Pedicord in tow, and was led out of the city to Gallows Hill (now the site of a Roman Catholic cemetery). The throng of thrill-seekers flowed after him and surrounded the soldiers who had formed a hollow square around the gallows tree and the cart containing the criminal. His flare for the dramatic functioning to the end, Mulliner lifted his face to the crowd, who, it is said, saw a man contemplating heaven with serenity.

He sat down and seemed as if in prayer. The Rev. Pedicord used his considerable eloquence, standing in the cart alongside the butcher of the pines turned "victim," and brought tears to the eyes of the crowd. One of the other clergymen followed the sermon with an equally eloquent prayer. Mulliner then stood and asked all in attendance to sing a familiar hymn.

As if deeply moved by the experience, the former arch fiend clapped his hands and shouted, "I've found him. I've found him! Now I'm ready!" Mulliner adjusted the noose around his neck, bade farewell to the faithful clergymen in attendance and said to the carter, "I am ready. Drive off."

The driver shook the reins and the horse started up, leaving the hapless brigand twitching at the end of the rope. He swung slowly around a couple of times, spasmed again, then hung still. The famous Refugee of the Pines was dead.

Raybold concludes, "So died Joe Mulliner, according to this old account, with repentance in his heart, the sound of a hymn sung by the thousands who had come to watch him die, one of the last still echoing across the countryside." With these dramatics, it's strange that Hollywood hasn't made a film hero out of him.

After the crowds had gone, his body was cut down and laid in the cart for his final trip back to the pines. His remains were presented to his wife (the story doesn't say what *she* thought of his numerous escapades and infidelities), and she had it buried beside the Sweetwater/Weekstown Road near where she lived.

Drunken woodsmen dug up the bones seventy-odd years later, but kindhearted Jesse Richards, Patriarch of Batsto, saw to it that they were returned to their original grave.

Though the clergy seem to have seen the heavens opened and angels escorting this miscreant into the realm of eternal light, local legend has a far different tale to tell about the spirit of Joseph Mulliner. It is said that, on moonless nights when the wind howls in the pines, a lonely wanderer near the Mullica might see a huge, headless figure, clad in an enveloping cloak, rise from the waters at The Forks, his head carried beneath its arm. Story goes, old Mulliner is still searching for gold he buried somewhere along the Mullica. People swear they have seen this fantom of the night, and it terrifies them. They are not given to flights of imagination, these denizens of the pines, and they would rarely admit to strange happenings they can't explain.

Perhaps the clergy were taken in by the seeming deathbed confession of the infamous robber. Perhaps he received his eternal justice after all. Maybe he didn't like his bones being dug from the ground by those drunken woodsmen. I don't know. I do know that it will be a cold day in hell before I'm going to spend a dark and stormy night several miles down the forest trail that was once the Batsto road to The Forks, but if I do and a shadowy cloaked figure rises up out of the Mullica, I'm getting out of there fast! Quite frankly, the woods and swamps give me the creeps at night anyway. Far away from the friendly lights of cars and houses, deep in the pines, one can believe almost anything to be true. I sincerely hope that kindly, old Jesse Richards, who himself lies peacefully in the Batsto-Pleasant Mills churchyard nearby, helped to set Joe Mulliner's soul free for all time by seeing that his bones were returned from whence they came.

NOTE:

In the above account, I have kept to the traditional location of Mulliner's burial. There is, though, a question of that location that is over a hundred years old. A news item in the Mount Holly *Herald* dated November 21, 1885 mentioned the hanging and burial of Joseph Mulliner at Crowleytown near a point where several huge sycamore trees grew.

> *Near Crowley's Landing there are three ancient buttonwood trees of gigantic size, which for more than a century have served as landmarks for voyagers up and down the river. Upon one of these trees a refugee leader named Mulliner was hanged for treason during the revolutionary war. Subsequently a summer house was built among the branches of the same tree by a member of the Richards family of Batsto.*

Mulliner was, of course, hung in Burlington, but his body was brought home to the Mullica Valley for burial. The question is, on which side of the Mullica was his final resting place? References to the buttonwoods of Crowleytown sound strangely familiar. The famed buttonwoods that served as lookouts and range markers stood on the Pleasant Mills side of the Mullica where Richard Wescoat had his home (see BATSTO: Sweetwater/Pleasant Mills). Is it possible that there has been some confusion here?

Henry Charlton Beck, in one of his newspaper articles, mentioned a "legend" of Mulliner's hanging in Crowleytown, but indicated that he knew that the grave was in Pleasant Mills. He notes that the gang was rounded up after Mulliner's hanging and that one, a deserter from the army, was hung on a tree at Crowleytown. Beck also understood that the scene of the punishment was in Woodbury, the county seat of Old Gloucester County, rather than in Burlington, county seat of Burlington County. He seems to have been wrong. A "New Jersey Gazette" report of the day noted that the trial and execution was in Burlington. Rev. Raybold's relation of an eyewitness account also places the execution in Burlington.

Beck, in the same article mentioned above, noted that a wooden sign had been erected over an old stone in the Pleasant Mills area announcing simply: "Joseph Mulliner, 1781. No one today seems to know the location of this stone. It is common knowledge that, in more recent years, Mulliner's "grave" on the Sweetwater/Weekstown Road was marked by some local men as a prank in 1965. They had to have spent some money, though, for this stone was made of granite and read "The grave of Joe Mulliner: Hung 1781." The location of the original stones seems to have been unknown when the men placed this latter memorial to the "Robin Hood of the Pines."

A further curiosity is that no one seems to have heard of "Cold Spring Swamp" where Mulliner is supposed to have had his hideout. The name doesn't seem to appear in the Wharton Ledgers. Beck mentions "Hemlock Swamp" as the location of Mulliner's hideout, but I can't find a swamp by that name either. Robbie Wills (see CROWLEYTOWN) used to assert that he had found this particular location deep within Mordecai Swamp, which lies between Crowleytown and Batsto. Mr. Wills was born at Crowleytown in the old Buttonwood Hill Tavern on the edge of Mordecai Swamp in 1891. His 1967 death precluded further investigation into his assertion. David Gauntt, in a 1989 "Batsto Citizens Gazette" article, quotes Frank Toughhill's article in the "Philadelphia Bulletin," January 26, 1958, that "Mulliner lived in the hemlock swamp about eight miles from Sweetwater while his wife lived at the Forks of the Mullica at the main road intersection."

The Jersey Devil

Sketch by Kathie Howe

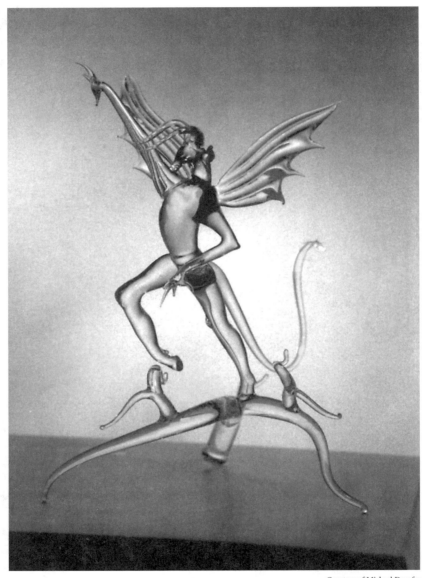

A representation of the Jersey Devil, sculptured in glass by Michael Dorofee of Bass River Township, Route 9, RFD Box 278, Tuckerton, N.J.

A Dark and Dangerous World

In a world of space travel, of planes, trains, automobiles and interstate highways, of television and satellite communications, it is almost impossible for most of us to feel the sense of isolation which gripped the European settlers who first set foot upon this dark and brooding continent. Their world was a world of limitations. Two hundred fifty years ago, there were no highways, no telephones, no means of quick and easy travel.

The voyage across the Atlantic took months and was fraught with dangers. Death in dark and swirling waters was a reality for all too many who ventured into the New World. There were no real cures for illnesses, and doctors, such as they were, probably did more harm than good.

A man who dared to dream of a new life and took his wife and children aboard some leaky vessel at a European port was saying good-bye to his mother and father forever. The settled life of the European world, where there were laws and troops to enforce them, where great cities teemed with a mixed populace of all sorts, was left behind. In its place, was a land where the cities were mere towns, huddling near the seashore and rivers, surrounded by a vast and forbidding forest that seemed to stretch westward forever.

We can appreciate the fortitude with which such men and women ventured into this dark unknown land, but we can never fully comprehend their bravery and their terror. For them, the forests were evil, filled with wild animals and even wilder Indians, whose war-painted faces, bloody tomahawks and unearthly shrieking struck terror into the strongest heart.

One thing the European settlers shared with their terrifying neighbors. They believed that the world was alive with unseen spirits, who were always ready to spring upon the tardy and stray to rip them apart, piece by piece. Every shadowy movement, each unidentified sound, each breath of wind moaning in the pines, bespoke of the very real presence of evil in the forest fastness.

A man gathered his wife and children around the hearth at the first suggestion of the coming night, shivering not only against the cold of winter, but also against the shrieks and moans that accompanied the howling wind. Families clustered in villages and towns at first, but when a man hungered for land he could call his own, he had to take his family into that threatening forest, following only Indian trails or deer paths, build a cabin far from his neighbors, and live almost completely to himself.

Small settlements grew for mutual protection, but these only mitigated the ever-present sense of impending doom which hung over the uncertain lives of these venturous men and women of the past. Without roads, the rivers alone were the highways for these early pioneers, and, in some places, were the only spaces clear enough for the sun to shine in their lives, for huge trees with their lofty canopies shut out most of the light, even at high noon.

No wonder, then, that these early settlers told tales around their hearthfires on a long winter's evening. With the snow piled deeply outside and the wind howling through the chinks of early log and frame huts, children's stories took on a somber reality. The native peoples, in wigwam and longhouse, told similar tales of dark and brooding danger which threatened to engulf even the most watchful.

In New England as the seventeenth century drew to a close, an epidemic of witchcraft fear swept over otherwise intelligent people. Before it had run its course, eighteen people had been hung and one pressed to death for a crime whose only evidence was spectral. Let the girls and young women of Salem Village but "see" a spirit or familiar over anyone, and that person was doomed. No weight of testimony to good conduct and steadfast faith was allowed to mitigate the guilt.

Not much more than a century later, Washington Irving spun his tale of old Dutch New Amsterdam, where a headless horseman clattered down lonely forest paths, waiting to destroy the unwary. Even in the post-Revolutionary age, he could relate, with only a hint of laughter, the story of a man who slept twenty years after playing ninepins with Henry Hudson's crew in their Catskill mountain retreat.

The Jersey Devil Is Born

The Pine Barrens of New Jersey were no different in this respect than areas all over the eastern seaboard. Without any form of rapid communications between towns and isolated houses, with no electric lights to make day of the night, tales of strange happenings took on a life of their own to chill the souls of God-fearing Christians.

Exactly when or where this strange story originated, no one will ever know, but it came from the hearts and spirits of a people isolated from their own kind and from minds for whom devils and evil spirits were as real as men and women of flesh and blood.

A half-eaten chicken, torn apart by a fox, a sheep or cow mauled by a marauding bear or mountain lion, an unearthly shriek, howled on a dark and stormy night had but one explanation: evil was afoot in the world.

Down a sandy road towards the bay on old Leed's Point lay the home of Mother Shourds. The Shourds family were not the only denizens of the place. Daniel Leeds, early pioneer and surveyor, had settled there early in the 1700's. So had Nicholas Sooy, Sr., son of old Yoos Sooy of Lower Bank. So had the Shourds family and several other families with still-familiar surnames. Of all the legendary "mothers," Mother Shourds' name lives on.

Back in the 1950's, a Mrs. Bowen pointed out to Henry Beck the collapsing ruins of the Shourds' house, whose darkened and rotting timbers begged the romance of a tale. Mrs. Shourds, you see, was a woman hard-pressed by the twelve children she had already borne. The thirteenth was one too many. "May it be a devil," she spat through her pain, though she was undoubtedly shocked when she got her wish.

The boy-child was born perfectly normal, but, before the horrified eyes of mother and midwife, it soon became horrendously distorted. Its head began to resemble that of a dog, its face a horse, its feet the cloven hoof of a pig (or perhaps, more like those of his satanic majesty himself), and its tail quite forked.

It grew bat-like wings, and, with an ear-piercing screech, it flapped those great wings and flew up the chimney and out of his birthplace forever. Some even suggest that it paused to dine on the whole Shourds family before it finally flew away. Devil that it was, it made itself known in countless little ways over the next two and a half centuries.

There's A Devil to Pay in New Jersey

Was it Mother Shourds who bore the ill-fated child? Or was it Mother Leeds, as other versions of the story relate? Was it born at Leed's Point, or Pleasantville, or even right in Lower Bank itself? What does it actually look like? The descriptions are as varied as the witnesses to its appearances over the years. Surely there have been nights of unearthly screams and mornings on which the torn bodies of chickens, sheep and other livestock were found caked with their own blood.

Early witnesses included Captain Stephen Decatur and Joseph Bonaparte, the former a renowned sea captain of the American Navy, the latter a brother to Napoleon and once King of Spain. Why does the Jersey Devil reappear every seven years and why do appearances always seem to coincide with war? Why is he considered a harbinger of evil? Why are there nights when sturdy pinelands folk hesitate to venture far from the comforting lights of their homes, even in these days of automobiles and streetlights?

In 1909, the Jersey Devil really got devilish. He roved far afield from the Pine Barrens of his birth to Haddonfield, Woodbury, Burlington, Mount Holly, and even managed to fly across the Delaware for a visit to Pennsylvania. He was spotted as far north as the New York border. As late as 1951, he made an unmistakable visit to Gibbsboro.

One moonless night in August of 1955, the residents of Green Bank heard an unearthly deep-throated screaming echoing from the swamps and marshes on the Atlantic County side of the Mullica that sent shivers up their spine. The men of the town, and some of the women, poured out of their houses by the river and hurried across the old bridge. Ahead of them in the darkness, they could hear the sounds of the unearthly roaring as it crossed the Weekstown road, heading into the swamps on the upriver side of the road.

Several of the men had grabbed their shotguns and rifles but none would venture into the depths of the swamp at night to chase after the horrible cries. At sunrise, the men gathered on the Atlantic County side of the bridge to seek reasonable explanations for the previous evening's frightful screams, but, though they searched for days, they found nothing. Was it the Jersey Devil? Months later, the carcass of a bear was found in the upstream swamps, but they could never be sure whether the awful cries were those of a wounded bear or whether they issued from the lungs of the bear's killer.

The men of Green Bank would never talk about that night. Asked about the incident in later years, they would laugh uproariously at the gullibility of the outsiders, but when they turned away, the smile would quickly fade, and their eyes would tell the very real fear which engulfed them that dark night. Not one would ever actually talk about it. Most of those hearty men who stood frozen to the Weekstown Road that night are gone now, but the few people who remain remember that night vividly.

806

In 1959, a Wall Township judge fined a group of boys $50, though they claimed they were out hunting some kind of monster. The following year, the people of Dorothy were terrorized. Two years later, screams pierced the night near Atsion, and eleven inch long tracks were found the next day.

The last appearance recorded was in April, 1966 at the farm of Steven Silkotch of Wading River/Bridgeport. Something had mauled thirty-one ducks, three geese, four cats, and two large dogs. One of the dogs was a ninety pound German Shepherd, whose body had been dragged a quarter of a mile from where it had been attacked!

Though the roadways today are lighted and are far more highly travelled than they were just a few years ago, the miles and miles of dark woods still shelter the ghostly tale of Mrs. Shourds' thirteenth child. Are you a nonbeliever? Stop your car along some lonely stretch of sand road far out in a cedar swamp on some dark night, and see if you, too, don't hear the cries of the Jersey Devil, even in this skeptical scientific age as we approach the third millennium.

Leed's Devil
Emma Van Sant Moore

Long ago—thus the tale goes—
A babe was born, and quickly arose
From lying in bed and his mother's side,
And flew through the window with cry so shrill—
The sound—folk could scarce abide!

Startled and frightened by the piercing cry,
Mother and midwife, and folk near by
Trembled, and drew together in fear—
Praying that never again in life
So weird a sound they'd hear!

But on many a night, through many a year,
The regretful mother was doomed to hear
The discordant cry of her devil-son—
Prenatally hated by his mother and cursed—
Cursed, ere life had begun!

This woman, who had given birth oft before,
Hated the thought of one child more;
Thus in dismay and rage when she learned
That another child was on its way—
The joys of motherhood spurned.

She cursed the unborn child and said:
"Although I be a woman wed,
I hate this innocent, unborn child!"
And she called on the Devil to take it away—
With curses weird and wild!

Ah, but curses—she was to learn—
Like well-known fowl, must need return
Home at night. And though she had won
Her desire of the Devil, she knew not the power
Of the curse laid upon her son!

Sketch by Kathie Howe

The Devil took him and shaped him well.
He looked like a monkey, yet one could tell
By his pointed ear and arrow-tipped tail,
That the Devil had fostered this cloven-hoofed
    child—
This child with the dismal wail!

At night, from the tops of nearby trees,
This mournful wail was borne on the breeze
To the mother, who listened with 'bated breath
For his cry. And on her heart fell a chill
More horrible than death!

Unwanted, unloved—forced ever to roam
Throughout the forest in lieu of a home—
This little devil is said to play
Many a prank and freakish trick—
Now here—now far away.

From county to county, South Jersey folk say,
This Leeds' Devil his pranks will play.
And upon this fact they all agree:
That his tricks are not evil; he does no harm—
A mischievous imp is he.

Some folk have told of a ghostly light
That lured them into the woods at night.
Others, of a scratching upon the roof—
A sulphurous smell and a piercing cry—
And by the door, the print of a hoof!

There's no question at all but this creature forlorn
Can change his appearance like a sheep that is shorn.
Hunters have said that when stalking deer,
They have drawn a bead on an antlered buck
Which would magically disappear!

It would vanish completely—not run away—
And they have also been heard to say,
That instead of the tracks a startled deer
Would make in the soil—they found in tile sand
One hoofprint—and it filled them with fear!

It is told that a housewife in response to a rap,
Opened her door and a man doffed his cap.
He asked for food, but the woman said
She had none in the house; and the stranger replied:
"You have cakes, I know—if no bread!"

"Go look in your cupboardl" said the stranger bold.
And the woman did as she was told;
Finding, much to her surprise,
A plate of cakes; and she took some to feed
This stranger, who seemed so wise.

But when she had brought the cakes to the door,
The stranger was gone; and from the floor
Came a smell of brimstone and a faint blue light,
While the sound of laughter, impish and wild,
Echoed into the night!

Trembling with fear, the woman once more
Returned and opened the cupboard door.
And was very frightened when she could find
Neither cakes nor plate; but only a note
On which, "The Leeds' Devil" was signed!

Thus down through the years the Leeds' Devil goes!
His mother—long since in death's repose—
No longer hears those plaintive cries,
When infrequently her son appears
Close by the grave where she lies.

Many years may pass with no tales being told
Of the unfortunate outcast from the Leeds' family
    fold.
Then, quite suddenly, the word goes 'round:
"The Leeds' Devil wails—is abroad once more—
And single hoofprints are found!"

Then the gullible worry, and wonder why
Clouds of evil o'er a peaceful sky
Must gather when Leeds' Devil is seen to roam—
Why wars and calamities of various kinds
Threaten country and home!

'Twas ever thus down through the years.
In spite of a mother's penitent tears,
The Leeds' Devil abroad must ever foretell
That in the affairs of the human race,
Troubles loom—and naught is well!

Originally published by the Poets of America
Publishing Company in 1960 as part of a collection of
poems by the author entitled, *Mullica*.

An Epilogue

Remove not the ancient landmark

which your fathers have set.

— Proverbs 22:28

A Chantey

Emma Van Sant Moore

Could I once more feel the fine salt spray,
And see the blown spume on the waves of Great Bay,
I'd stow my worries, and I'd reef my cares
And shout like a fishwife crying her wares:
     Let's away! Let's away! Let's away!

"Make way!" I'd shout to the winds that blow,
"No matter how you rage, I'll not go below."
Now I'm happy again — I'm blithe and free;
For I'm cruising on the wonder-ship Jubilee!
     Let'er blow! Let'er blow! Let'er blow!

"Make Way!" I'd shout to the common craft,
As I paced the deck, from fore to aft.
"I'm living again — I'm laughing with glee
"To be sailing on the good ship Jubilee!"
     Oh, ho! Sailor, abaft!

Though I'd stow my worries, we would not reef sail;
For the ship will ride easy in wind a near gale.
O, I'm dreaming I know — but happy I'd be
Could I go for a cruise on the Jubilee!
     Hail! Captain, hail!

O, her bowsprit points to the wind-swept sky,
Where the white clouds scud, and the gray gulls fly.
We'll cross Great Bay to the Mullica's mouth
As we went on our way up from the south.
     Fly! Seagulls, fly!

While passing through the draw with light cargo,
Will I hear Jesse Johnson sing the "Old Argo?"
Ah! 'Tis a later day; it's "Tater" now we hail,
As we glide through the bridge with short-trimmed
    sail!
     Hail! Horatio, ho!

Then up the river and through Swan Bay,
Where the meadows lie teeming with good salt hay —
On up the river where sires of yore
Built many a ship on the Mullica shore.
     O, smell the hay, the hay!

O, it's a fine day, and I seem to see,
As we sail up the river on the Jubilee,
A gath'ring of the clan on that same broad shore,
Where they built fine ships in those days of yore!
     Oh, ho! Oh, ho! The shore!

There's father, and grand'ther, and Nicholas too —
Beckoning to me — calling to you.
Yes, mingling with the present, the past is here,
And I seem to hear singing as I draw near.
     O, hail to me — to you!

Could great-grandsire Nicholas through the gall'ry
    ports see,
He would know why the ship's called the Jubilee.
On companionway-header is carved this verse:
(A passage from the Bible in words true and terse)
     "O, day of Jubilee!"

"Proclaim thou liberty throughout the world,"
(Let's look and make sure the flag's unfurled)
"To all the inhabitants: (to you and to me)
It shall be unto you a Jubilee."
     Proclaim to all the world!

If old Yoos Sooy's in the gathering on shore,
He'll think a Dutch tub is sailing as of yore —
With her saucy, tilting bowsprit and rather high stern,
The Jubilee will make him for the Netherlands yearn!
     Oh, ho! Oh, ho! The shore!

O, where am I living — in the present or past?
I'm dreaming I know — how I wish it could last!
Yes, I'm dreaming a dream; but happy I'd be
Could I sail up the river on the Jubilee!
     Oh, ho! The port at last!

From a collection of poems entitled *The Mullica* by Emma Van Sant Moore
which was published by the Poets of America Pulbishing Company in 1960.

The sun is setting in the southwest over the dark waters of the Mullica. Fall and winter have been beautiful this year, and temperatures have allowed woods-walking with only light jackets. "Cruel" December has been kind, though the lack of rain has made the little rivers of the pine barrens run at half their normal volume and the woods tinder-dry. Another old year will be forgotten in the rejoicing over the arrival of the new, and a third millennium will soon sweep this old earth into new challenges, threats, and experiences undreamed of just a few short years ago.

The challenges are there to be grasped, the threats to be met with boldness, and life embraced to the fullest. Yet there is a deep sadness as those who have met those challenges and threats in past generations recede into the dim recesses of our collective memories. As I said in the very beginning of this work, we are not alone. Surrounding us are the ghosts of all who have gone before us, who have lived, and loved, and been laid to rest in the earth within the sheltering arms of God.

Someday all too soon, we, too, shall join them, and we will be forgotten in the mists of time. "Tomorrow belongs to me," may be the cry of youth, but the older we get, the more the past becomes our tomorrow. Today is the only day we have to reach for the challenges of the future. It is also the only day we have to comprehend the past and remember those who have gone before us.

It is almost impossible for us to imagine the Atlantic coast as it was two hundred years ago, a wilderness of trees broken only by small farms and villages. Now city and suburban sprawl, highways and turnpikes, shopping malls and parking lots shove aside the last glimpse of the earth that nourished us. Our fast-paced lives envelop us as once the land comforted us. Our need for excitement and entertainment propels us over the land and through the water at speeds so fast we destroy what we value and fail to see the remaining beauty.

New Jersey has begun a quest to purchase thousands of acres of yet-undeveloped land, so that our children and grandchildren and great-grand children might know a postage-stamp park, the last small vestige of once vast forests. We have not yet learned that simply buying open space isn't nearly enough. Left unprotected by good management and care, we will destroy those lands by our carelessness and quest for momentary pleasure. Good stewardship requires more than mere acquisition. It demands trusteeship — responsible care for those lands. We are no longer the beneficiaries of a vast wilderness. Let's not kid ourselves. We are trustees for parks. We still risk losing our last natural beauties unless we are willing to deal with them responsibly.

Preserving our past is a vital part of that responsibility. We need to know. We need to care. We need to live and breathe with those who have gone before us. Only when we can appreciate their struggle for life and their acceptance of death can we find our own fulfillment in the world of today and tomorrow.

I am loathe to close this tale for the people and the land have become so familiar to me, a part of my life. Their spirits have breathed into me a love for the land they cherished and an appreciation for their courage. An end brings loneliness. Yet I know that the end is only a beginning. There is so much more to learn. Another battle in the war to remember has only just begin. Our struggle to preserve thrusts into tomorrow, into the next century, into the next millennium, so that hundreds of years from now, those who come after us may know the joys and sorrows of our lives, the challenges we have met, the dreams we have dreamed. I walk the long-abandoned Road to Little Egg Harbor and stand beside an empty cellar hole of old Sooy's Inn, trying to feel the excitement of an election day long ago, of travellers heading for Philadelphia, or tired ironworkers drowning their aches and broken dreams in a pint of ale. I stand, lost in the woods, surrounded by ghosts. Soon, I, too, must join them, but, God willing, I will make one small contribution towards the end that those who come after us may learn from the past. We are still building on the foundations laid by those who have gone before us. I remind myself, as did Benjamin Franklin, that the sun is not a setting one but a rising one, a sun shining with hope.

I can find no more fitting words with which to close than those with which I commenced:

On a star-spangled night deep in the pines, near a tannin-stained little river, the voices of the past still call to us. Those spirits breathing, sighing, reaching out to touch in the blackness of the enveloping night which I first encountered in the Green Bank churchyard were not threatening, but crying out for empathic consciousness. The faded names on crumbling stones are old, familiar friends now, and life's meaning has found increasing depth and breadth beside the brown waters of the Mullica. Blushing bride and hoary grandam, hearty youth and ancient sire, long in their graves and almost forgotten, have come to life again. They speak to us of our roots, formed in the soil of this land though coming here from far-distant realms. Their spirits fashioned their dreams into realities, a process with which we still struggle in ongoing reincarnation.

This has been their story. The people themselves are the real Heart of the Pines.

JOHN E. PEARCE
December 10, 1998

The Cemetery

They stand in quiet rows
Gleaming white by pencil day
And in ghostly gray, repose
The silhouette of night away.

Touched only by elements of time,
The shielding tomb
Impels their heart to mine
Above their mounded shrine.

Lettered memories etched in
Bold embrace on silent stone,
Heritage of joy and grieving echoes,
Find peace where sleep atones.

This keeping marble watches
Beyond endless dreaming,
Lifting music above the seasons
Into spheres of ceaseless glory,
No more the human needing.

Jessie Lewis
Green Bank
2000

Additional Photographs

Unfortunately, these photographs were given to me too late to incorporate into the text.

Charlie Weber, Sr. - Last of the Salt-Hayers

Charlie Weber, Jr.

A "Typical" Load of Hay
Edward Weber is on the left
Charles W., Jr. on the right

Emilie (Weber) Ware
Daughter of Charlie and Pauline Weber
Second Wife of Joe Ware

Photographs are courtesy of Elaine Weber Mathis,
daughter of Charles W. Weber, Jr.

Sarah Ellen and Samuel Ford and and their Children
Samuel was the brother of Julia Belle Ford and the son of Samuel
Pitman and Margaret Emeline Ford.

Photographs are courtesy of Elaine Weber Mathis,
daughter of Charles W. Weber, Jr.

Frank and Susann Ford

The Green Bank Fords
Standing L. to R.   Henry, Gertrude, Clayton
Sitting L. to R. Bertha, Margaret, Arwilda, Elsie

Bibliography

Bibliography

Barber, John W. and Howe, Henry. *Historical Collections of the State of New Jersey*. New York: S. Tuttle, 1844.

Batsto Citizens Gazette. All Issues. Batsto, N.J.: The Batsto Citizens Committee, 1966-1996.

Bear, Christopher T., Coxey, William J., and Schopp, Paul W. *The Trail of the Blue Comet: A History of the Jersey Central's New Jersey Southern Division*. Palmyra, N.J.: The West Jersey Chapter, National Railway Historical Society, 1994.

Beck, Henry Charlton. *Jersey Genesis: The Story of the Mullica River*. New Brunswick, N.J.:, Rutgers University Press, 1991 printing, 1945.

Bisbee, Henry H. and Colesar, Rebecca Bisbee. *Martha: The Complete Furnace Diary and Journal 1808-1815*. Burlington, N.J.: Henry Bisbee, Publisher, 1976.

Bisbee, Henry H. *Sign Posts: Place Names in History of Burlington County, New Jersey*. Willingboro, N.J.: Alexia Press, Inc., 1971.

Blackman, Leah, *History of Little Egg Harbor Township, Burlington County, N.J., from the First Settlement to the Present Time*. Toms River: The Great John Mathis Foundation, Inc., 1963.

Blake, Mrs. Georgiana C. "Early Atlantic County." Reprinted by the Atlantic County Historical Society from the Atlantic City Press, April 22, 1934.

Boyer, Charles S. *Early Forges and Furnaces in New Jersey*. Philadelphia, Pa.: University of Pennsylvania Press, 1931.

Boyer, Charles S. *Old Inns and Taverns in West Jersey*. Camden, New Jersey: Camden County Historical Society, 1962.

Braddock-Rogers, K. "Fragments of Early Industries in South Jersey." *Journal of Chemical Education*. Vol. 8, 10, 11, October and November, 1931.

Buchholz, Margaret Thomas, Editor; Shore Chronicles. Harvey Cedars, New Jersey: Down the Shore Publishing, 1999.

Cadberry, Henry Joel. "Negro Membership in the Society of Friends". *Journal of Negro History*. Volume 21, 1936, pp. 186-190.

Chard, John. "Historic Ironmaking." Northeast Historical Archaeology, Vol. 1, No. 1. Spring, 1971.

Craig, Peter Stebbins. *The 1693 Census of the Swedes on the Delaware*. Winter Park, Florida: SAG Publications, 1993.

Daniels, Peggy Kneffel and Schwartz, Carol A., Editors; *Encyclopedia of Associations*. Detroit, Washington, D.C., London: Gale Research Inc., 1994.

Dellomo, Jr., Angelo N. *Harrisville: A Journey Down the Sugar Sand Roads of Yesteryear*. Atlantic City, New Jersey: Angelo Publishing Company, 1977.

Dew, Charles B. *Bond of Iron: Master and Slave at Buffalo Forge*. New York: W. W. Norton and Company, 1994.

Edwards, James T. *The Edwards Family*. Randolph, N.Y.: Randolph Pulbishing Company, 1903.

Evans, Ezra. Manuscript chronicle of Evans and Wills, Inc. February, 1953.

Federal Writers' Project of the Works Projects Administration of New Jersey. *The Swedes and Finns in New Jersey*. New Jersey Commission to Commemorate the 300th Anniversary of the Settlement by the Swedes and Finns on the Delaware; 1938.

Fowler, Michael, and Herbert, William A. *Papertown of the Pine Barrens: Harrisville, New Jersey*. Eatontown, New Jersey: Environmental Education Publishing Service, 1976.

Green, Charles F. *Pleasant Mills, New Jesey, Lake Nescochague: A Place of Olden Days*. No publisher or date of publication given.

Hawthorne, William J. "Early Life on the Wading River," *South Jersey Magazine*, Winter and Spring, 1976.

Kemp, Franklin W. *A Nest of Rebel Pirates*. Egg Harbor City, New Jersey:The Batsto Citizens Committee, 1966.

Lyght, Ernest. *Path of Freedom: The Black Presence in New Jersey's Burlington County 1659-1900*. Cherry Hill, New Jersey: E & E Publishing Company, 1978, pp. 8-11.

Mack, Helen Leek. "The Cavileer Family". A manuscript in the posession of the Atlantic County Historical Society; Somers Point, N.J.

Mack, Helen Leek. *The Leek Family of Southern New Jersey*. Woodbury, New Jersey: Gloucester County Historical Society, 1988.

McCloy, James F. and Miller, Ray Jr. *The Jersey Devil*. Wilmington, Delaware: The Middle Atlantic Press, 1976.

McMahon, William. *South Jersey Towns*. New Brunswick, N.J.: Rutgers University Press, 1973.

Methot, June. *Blackman Revisited*. Toms River: Ocean County Historical Society, 1994.

Miller, Pauline S. *Joel Haywood: The Founding Father of Ocean County*. Ocean County Cultural & Heritage Commission, 1997.

Moore, Harvey. *An Old Jersey Furnace*. Baltimore, Md.: Newth-Morris Printing Co., 1943.

Morris, Richard B. (ed.) *The Era of the American Revolution.* New York, Evanston, and London: Harper and Row, 1969.

Norton, James S.; *New Jersey in 1793: An Abstract and index to the 1793 Militia Census of the State of New Jersey.* Salt Lake City, Utah, 1973.

Patriotic Order Sons of America. *Brief History Pennsylvania Accomplishments and Legislative Interests, Message, Membership Qualifications, Social and Fraternal Activities of the Patriotic Order Sons of America.* Arsenal Ctr. Bldg. 107, Suite 217, 5301 Tacony Street - Box 136, Philadelphia, Pa.

Pepper, Adeline. *The Glass Gaffers of New Jersey.* New York: Charles Scribner's Sons, 1971.

Perinchief, Elizabeth M. "Adams Cemetery". Manuscript written by Ms. Perinchief for Barry Cavileer, 1991.

Perinchief, Elizabeth M. *History of the Cemeteries in Burlington County, N.J. 1687 - 1975.* Privately published. A copy is in the possession of the Atlantic County Historical Society, Somers Point, N.J.

Pierce, Arthur D. *Family Empire in Jersey Iron: The Richards Enterprises in the Pine Barrens.* New Brunswick, New Jersey: Rutgers University Press, 1964.

Pierce, Arthur D. *Iron in the Pines: The Story of New Jersey's Ghost Towns and Bog Iron.* New Brunswick, New Jersey: Rutgers University Press, 1990.

Pierce, Arthur D. *Smugglers' Woods.* New Brunswick, New Jersey: Rutgers University Press, 1960.

Pomfret, John E. *The New Jersey Proprietors and Their Lands 1664-1776.* Princeton, New Jersey: D. Van Nostrand Company, Inc. 1964.

Salter, Edwin. *A History of Monmouth and Ocean Counties.* Bayonne, N.J.: E. Gardner & Son. 1890.

Snyder, John P. *The Story of New Jersey's Civil Boundaries 1606-1968.* Trenton, New Jersey: Bureau of Geology and Topography, 1969.

Stanger, Frank Bateman. *The Methodist Trail in New Jersey: One Hundred Twenty-five Years of Methodism in the New Jersey Annual Conference 1836-1961*; The New Jersey Annual Conference of the Methodist Church, 1961.

Steelman, Robert B. *What God Has Wrought: A History of the Southern New Jersey Conference of the United Methodist Church*; Pennington, N.J.:The United Methodist Church, Southern New Jersey Conference, 1986.

Stewart, Mrs. M. Alice. "Weymouth, New Jersey, Over One Hundred Years Ago." Reprinted by the Atlantic County Historical Society from an article in the Atlantic City Press, July 1, 1934.

Van Name, Elmer Garfield. *The Weeks Family of Southern New Jersey*; Haddonfield, N.J.: Privately published, 1967.

Vansant, The Honorable Samuel R. Manuscript Letter in the possession of the Atlantic County Historical Society; Somers Point, N.J.

Weslager, C.A. *The Delaware Indians.* New Brunswick, New Jersey: Rutgers University Press, 1972.

Werner, Charles J. *Eric Mullica and His Descendants: A Swedish Pioneer in New Jersey; together with a Description of the Mullica River Region in Burlington and Atlantic Counties, N.J. and An Account of the Early Generations of the Family in the Vicinity of Mullica Hill and Swedesboro, Gloucester County, N.J.* New Gretna, N.J.: Charles J. Werner, 1930.

Wilson, Budd. "The Batsto Window Light Factory Excavation." Archeological society of New Jersey, Number 27. Trenton, N.J.: MacCrellish & Quigley Company, December, 1971.

Wilson, Budd. "The Batsto Window Light Factory Artifacts." Archeological Society of New Jersey, Number 29. Trenton, N.J.: MacCrellish & Quigley Company, December, 1972.

Woodman, Henry. *The History of Valley Forge.* Oaks, Pa.: John U. Framncis, Sr., 1920.

Woodward, Major E.M. *History of Burlington County,* Philadelphia: Everts and Peck, 1883.

Works Progress Administration. *The Records of the Swedish Lutheran Churches at Raccoon and Penns Neck: 1713-1786;* Sponsored by the New Jersey Commission to Commemorate the 300th Anniversary of the Settlement by the Swedes and Finns on the Delaware, 1938.

Index

Index

Leeds, Daniel 598, 806
Leeds Devil 530
Leeds, Jane 474
Leeds, Levi 530
Leeds, Lydia 530
Leeds, Margaret Jane 496
Leeds, Mark 705
Leeds, Moses 530
Leeds, Mother 806
Leeds, Philo 121
Leed's Point 66, 364, 411, 431, 795
Leeds, Rachel 530
Leeds, Robert 626
Leeds, Sarah 626
Leeds, Solomon 430
Leeds, Vincent 60
Leek, Phoebe Devinney 599
Leek, Rachel 599
Leek, Achsah 600, 602, 614, 638
Leek, Aimee Jean 534
Leek, Anna 305, 602, 666
Leek, Anna Augusta 620
Leek, Anna Bush Maxwell 620—621, 623—624, 627, 672
Leek, Annabelle (Crowley) 250, 620—621, 624
Leek, Annie Ethel (Bosarge) Cambre 621
Leek, Beatrice (Yanko) 534
Leek, Bessie 666
Leek, Betty 307
Leek, Beulah 602
Leek Boatyard 432
Leek, C.P. 449
Leek, Catharine 674
Leek, Catherine 249, 619
Leek, Catherine Loveland 619
Leek, Cecil 533, 534
Leek, Cecil Gilbert 531, 602
Leek, Charles Edward ("Ed") 605, 666
Leek, Charles, Jr. 666
Leek, Charles Loveland 619
Leek, Charles Platt 602
Leek, Charles Platt I 474, 491
Leek, Charles Platt II 219, 448, 474, 491, 525, 528, 531—532, 534, 539, 542, 602
Leek, Charles T. and Anna Maria (Reynolds) 666
Leek, Charles W. 620
Leek, Charlotte (Loveland) Cramer 619
Leek, Curtis 621
Leek, David Charles 534
Leek, Donald 533—534, 537, 602
Leek, Donald, Jr. 534
Leek, "Ed" 625, 710—711, 718
Leek, Edith 525
Leek, Edith (Young) 531, 534, 602
Leek, Elizabeth 619
Leek, Emma 666
Leek, Emma Nash 621
Leek, Frank 666
Leek, George 250, 666, 680, 711, 720—721
Leek, George and Merrit 720

Leek, George T. 619
Leek, George Washington 594, 602
Leek, George Washington and Hannah B. (Mathis) 674
Leek, George Washington II 619, 680
Leek, George Washington III 620, 621, 624
Leek, Hannah 599
Leek, Hannah B. Mathis 619
Leek, Hannah Sooy 602
Leek, Harry 666
Leek, Hepsibah Grant 602—603
Leek, Hester A. 602
Leek Homestead 592
Leek, Ida 666
Leek, Ida Harris Knight 621
Leek, Ila Mae 620—621
Leek, Irene Mildred 621
Leek, James Ellsworth 620—621
Leek, Jane (Hofheimer) 534
Leek, Jean (Corbett) 534
Leek, Joanna Ackeley 599
Leek, John, Jr., Captain 602, 614, 638, 448, 463, 601
Leek, John C. 602
Leek, John Everett 531, 533, 602
Leek, John Everett, III 534, 537, 541, 589—590, 602, 607, 619, 783—784
Leek, John F. 602
Leek, John IV 537, 541
Leek, John Everett, Jr. (Jack) 448, 533—534, 537, 539, 588, 600, 602, 675, 741
Leek, John, Sr., Captain 473, 534, 544, 587, 588, 599, 601, 606, 613, 643, 720, 771, 772
Leek, Kim Michele 534
Leek, Leola 666
Leek, Leslie 305, 666
Leek, Lillian (Warner) 533
Leek, Lillian (Sadenvasser) 621
Leek, Lucretia Applegate 666
Leek, Maja A. 430, 590, 593—594, 619—620, 624, 672, 680—681, 710
Leek, Maja Towers 620—621, 623—624, 672, 719
Leek, Maja Towers and Anna Bush Maxwell 621, 624
Leek, Maja Towers, Jr. 620
Leek, Major 666
Leek, Margaret 602
Leek, Margaret B. 602
Leek, Marie Lee 602
Leek, Martha 600, 602
Leek, Martha (Rose) 448, 588, 602, 614, 638
Leek, Mary 588, 600, 602
Leek, Mary Ella (Johnson) 491, 500
Leek, Mary W. 619
Leek, Matilda M., 620
Leek, Merritt 666
Leek, Mildred 734
Leek, Miriam 307, 313
Leek, Nathan 600
Leek, Norris 666
Leek, Olga Winona 531, 602
Leek, Phoebe 588, 602, 606
Leek, Phoebe Adams 602

Leek, Phoebe Devinney 600
Leek, Rachel (Cope) (Schindler) 533
Leek, Ralph 537, 621
Leek, Ralph H. 624
Leek, Ralph Herbert, Jr. 621
Leek, Ralph Nicholas 534
Leek, Randel 307
Leek, Rebecca 451
Leek, Rebecca (Cramer) 491, 531, 602
Leek, Recompence 600
Leek, Richard 309
Leek, Roseanna 602
Leek, Roy (Leroy) 621
Leek, Samuel 600, 602
Leek, Sarah 588, 593, 599
Leek, Sarah Josephine 620
Leek, Sarah Louisa (Cavileer) 619—620, 624, 663, 672, 681, 710
Leek, Sarah Mathis 602
Leek, Sarah Virginia 620
Leek, Stephen 587
Leek, Virginia 306, 311
Leek, Walter 531
Leek, Warren Montgomery 621
Leek Wharf 589, 601, 603, 605, 742, 771
Leek, William 434, 589, 602, 603, 619
Leek, William, Captain 272
Leek, William and Catherine (Loveland) 430, 624
Leek, William Grant 602
Leek, William Hammond 619, 624
Leek, William Loveland 430
Leek, William Loveland and Mary Cavileer 624
Leek, William Spafford 448, 491, 531
         (See also: Leak, Leeke)
Leek-McKeen-Adams Cemetery 607, 611
Leek/McKeen/Adams House 598, 717
Leeke, Ebenezer 599
Leeke, Elizabeth Dayton 599
Leeke, Hannah Baker 599
Leeke, Joanna 599
Leeke, John 599
Leeke, Mary 599
Leeke, Mary Shaw 599
Leeke, Phillip 599
Leeke, Phillip, Jr. 599
Leeke, Sarah 600
Leeke, Stephen 599
Leeke, Thomas 599
         (See also: Leak, Leek)
Leek's Creek 593
Leek's Landing 702
Leektown 592, 602
Lela 772
Lemunyon, Daniel 638
Lemunyon, Harvey 638
Lemunyon, Leona Downs 638
Lenni Lenape 11—12, 14, 764, 765
Leonard, Azariah 144
"Letters of Marque" 64, 140
Lewis, Bill 476

Lewis, David 430
Lewis, Dudley H. 3, 180, 204, 209—210, 348, 783, 789
Lewis, Herb 202
Lewis, Irma 476
Lewis, J. Herman 476
Lewis, James Hansell ("Hans") 7, 202—204, 209—210, 218
Lewis, Jessie (Forman) 3, 180, 193, 196, 203—204, 210, 218—219, 265, 270, 300, 400, 492, 782
Lewis, John 476, 525
Lewis, Phyllis 202
Lewis, Robert 202
Life Saving Service, Father of 262
Lightman, Paul 151, 154, 156
Lillie Falkinburg 205—206, 772
Lilly, Wm A 299
Limonite 100
Line Ditch 593
Lingerfield, John 240
Lippencott, Charles 689
Lippencott, Joshua 119
Lippincott, Ada 709
Lippincott, Allie 689
Lippincott, Amanda 637, 667
Lippincott, Amanda E. 630
Lippincott, Benjamin H. 618
Lippincott, Bob and Jeanette 645
Lippincott, Charles H. 630
Lippincott, Deborah Arnold 630
Lippincott, Earl, Jr. 382
Lippincott, Earl, Sr. 382
Lippincott, Elizabeth 630
Lippincott, Esther Andrews 630
Lippincott Family 630
Lippincott, George W. 630
Lippincott, Gideon 630
Lippincott, Hannah Snow 630
Lippincott, Jeanette Watson 630
Lippincott, John W. 630
Lippincott, Joseph 630
Lippincott, Joseph and Esther (Andrews) 630
Lippincott, Joseph, Jr. 630
Lippincott, Joseph, Sr. 630
Lippincott, Joshua 119, 146, 148, 365
Lippincott, Leah Maxwell 630
Lippincott, Myrtle 689
Lippincott, Peter 630
Lippincott, Robert 305, 630, 656, 671, 734
Lippincott, Samuel 630, 672
Lippincott, Samuel and Deborah (Arnold) 630
Lippincott, Samuel and Hannah (Snow) 630
Lippincott, Samuel and Leah (Maxwell) 630
Lippincott, Samuel S. 630
Lippincott, Sarah Wetherby 630
Lippincott, Watson "Wad" Atwood 607, 630, 716
Lippincott, Wilbur 689
Lippincott, William 146
Lippincott, William C. Wetherby 630
Lippincott, William R. 794

M

Mabel E. Horton 778
MacDonald mill 467
MacDonald, Ruth (Cramer) 449
MacDonald, William 170,—172, 449, 457, 688
MacDonalds of Glencoe 135
MacGregors 135
MacLaren, Donald H. 299
Magee, John W. 299
Magsum, William B., Rev. 682
Mahamickwon 765
Mahicans 767
Main Street 129
Maja Leek bogs 699
Makepiece scoop 385
Malich, Pål 407
Manahawkin 292—293
Manchester, Lucius 299
Mandrona, Frank 439
Maple Swamp 124
Mapps, Anne 453
Mapps, David, Captain 195, 424, 441—444, 446—
        447, 451—454, 456, 459, 473
Mapps Estate 453
Mapps, Grace 442—444, 446—447
Mark Richards 574
Markley, Albert W. 35
Marks Road 618
Marple, George 30
Marsh Grass (salt hay) 343
Marsh hare 723
Marshall, J. 730
Marshill, Isabella 749
Marshill, Sir Humphrey 749
Martha 34, 69—70, 118, 301, 320, 402, 691, 741—
        743, 750, 758, 761, 762, 772
Martha Diary 393, 395, 555, 558—559, 690, 743, 751

Martha Furnace 553—566

Martha Furnace, other references
        21, 62, 321, 326, 349, 366, 394—
        396, 399, 555, 575, 602, 604, 610, 612—
        613, 691, 742, 771
Martha: The Complete Furnace Diary and Journal 180,
        562
Martinsburg, North Carolina 31
Marvin Gardens 501
Mary 772
Mary Clinton 487
Mary of Dublin 749
Mason jars 169, 189
Mason, Jarvis 35
Mason, John 188
Mateland, Mary 184
Mathews, Daniel Leeds 246
Mathis, Ann 613
Mathis, Asbury 705
Mathis, Caleb 613

Mathis, Clarance Lloyd 184
Mathis, Daniel 442, 452, 602, 741
Mathis, Daniel II 606, 613, 643
Mathis, Elaine (Weber) 184
Mathis, Elizabeth 434
Mathis, Enoch 741
Mathis, George 309
Mathis, Hannah B. 619
Mathis, Harriet 613
Mathis, Job 588, 602, 606, 643, 799
Mathis, Job, Sr. 614
Mathis, John 587, 598, 602, 606, 613—614, 643, 667
Mathis, John, Homestead 675
Mathis, L. 730
Mathis, Marjorie Nevada 513, 529
Mathis, Marvin 705
Mathis, Mary 606
Mathis, Micajah 613
Mathis, Micajah and Mercy (Shreve) 614
Mathis, Phebe (Leek) 614
Mathis, Phoebe (Leek) (or Phebe) 588, 606, 613—614,
        643
Mathis, Phoebe (Smith) 606, 643
Mathis, Richard C. 267
Mathis, Roy 696
Mathis, Sarah 602, 606, 643
Mathis, Sarah Smith 637
Mathis, W. Roy 694
Matthews, Rt. Rev. Paul 400
Matthews, Sarah Augusta (Cavileer) 525, 527
Mauer, Bill 641
Mauer, Naomi 641
Mauer, Norman 641
Mauer, Paul and Dini 641
Maxwell, James 626
Maxwell, Adelia 311
Maxwell, Alma 631
Maxwell, Amy 627, 735
Maxwell, Angeline Adelia (Jones) 489, 627
Maxwell, Anna Bush 620
Maxwell, Anna M. 626
Maxwell, Benjamin 631, 661, 672
Maxwell, Bernice 305, 672, 673
Maxwell, Bethia (Gale) (or Berthia) 602, 672
Maxwell, Brian 672
Maxwell, Burris 627
Maxwell, Carlton 639, 661
Maxwell, Charles Albert 633
Maxwell, Curtis (Wobbar) 663
Maxwell, Dora 639
Maxwell, Dora Cramer 661
Maxwell, Earl 627
Maxwell, Edwin 402, 563, 626
Maxwell, Elinora 627
Maxwell, Elizabeth 631, 670, 689
Maxwell, Elizabeth U. 269
Maxwell, Elsie (Smith) 672
Maxwell, Estella Adams 627
Maxwell, Estelle Vivian 489
Maxwell, Ethel 662

Miller, Alfred Hance 177
Miller, Augustus "Gus" 87, 132, 178
Miller, Caleb 177
Miller Cemetery 602
Miller, Cora 178
Miller, Edward James 177, 178
Miller, Ella 178
Miller, Elmer 178
Miller family 168
Miller, Jesse Lemuel 177
Miller, John Wesley 87, 177—178
Miller, Jonathan Sprague 177
Miller, Joseph 173, 177—178
Miller, Josephine A. (Weeks) 475
Miller, Maggie 178
Miller, Mary 177
Miller, Pauline 142, 261
Miller, Rebecca (Cobb) 173, 177—178
Miller, Ruby 474, 499
Miller, Ruth Ann 177
Miller, Sarah Ann 168, 173
Miller, Susanne (Ford) 183
Miller, The Rev. James 162
Miller, Thomas Stewart 177—178
Miller, W. B. 125
Miller, William 268
Miller, William A. 475
Millers 168
Mills, Nathaniel B. 158, 291
Miners, Fred 703
Mingen, Lewis 742
Minnies 359
Minsis 765
Minuit, Peter 415
Miss America 229
Miss Heritage 539, 541, 784
Miss New Jersey 229
Mission Marine 537
Missions in the Pines 49
Missouri Compromise of 1820 254
Moelke 407
Molding room 103
Molicka, Eric 408
Mollica, Anna 409
Mollicas 410
Mollicka, Olave 409
Mollicka, Olof 409
Möllika, Anders 409
Möllika, Widow 409
Money, Minerva McAnney Billsborough 644
Monrow, John 138
Montgomery, Burke 218, 448
Montgomery, Ella (Cramer) 218, 219
Montgomery, Frances 219
Montgomery, James Burke 193, 218—219, 246
Montgomery, Judge *(See also: Montgomery, Russell)* 193, 219
Montgomery, Margaret 219
Montgomery, Margaret (Higgins) 219
Montgomery, Robert 232

Montgomery, Russell 193, 218—220, 532
Montgomery, Russell, Jr. 219
Montgomery, Ruth (Cramer) 496
Montgomery, Shirley Janet 219
Montgomery, William 496
Moore, Byrd 460, 532
Moore, Emma Van Sant viii, xviii, 2, 199, 403, 770, 807
Moore, Gerald 460
Moore, Harvey 559
Moore, Mary 395
Moore, S.K. 299
Mora Parish 408
Mordecai Landing 67, 124, 187
Mordecai Swamp 802
Morey Field 564
Morgan, John 145, 158
Morton, Charles 582
Mossies 731
Mossybunkers 359
Mott, Mary Ann 638
Mount 739, 740, 745, 747, 749, 753
Mount Holly 29, 60
Mount Holly Iron Works 120
Mount Tavern 747
Mount/Sandy Ridge Road 747
"Mountain" ore 560, 561
Mud-shad 359, 706
Mudboots 728
Mulford, Ann 430
Mulica, Ingeri 408
Mulicka, Ingrid 410
Mulicka, Stephen 410
Mullica 21, 23, 25, 26, 64, 69
   (See also: Mollica, Molica, Molika, Moelke, Mulicka, Mollika)
Mullica, Anders 407
Mullica, Annakin 407
Mullica, Catherine 408
Mullica, Christian 407
Mullica, Eric 3, 15—16, 59, 136, 407—409, 410—412, 414, 430, 527, 533, 545
Mullica, Eric, III 410
Mullica, Eric, Jr. 407, 409—410, 527
Mullica, Helena 408, 409
Mullica, Hendrick 407
Mullica Hill 410
Mullica, Ingabor 408
Mullica, Ingeri 407
Mullica, John 407—410
Mullica, Marget 410
Mullica, Olof 407
Mullica Pirates 65
Mullica River 29, 59, 64, 66, 319, 414, 416, 421
Mullica River Boat Basin 26
Mullica River bridge 26
Mullica, Stephen 408
Mullica Township 434
Mullica, Widow 412
Mullicas River 197

Tumbling Dam 324
Turbine 719
Turner, Abby Ann 430
Turner, Catherine 279
Turner, Samuel 279
Turnes, Father 163
Turtle Creek 402, 592—593, 629, 723
Turtle Creek Cove 438, 592
Turtle Creek Road 303, 592—593, 629, 635, 640,—
    641, 648—649, 652, 654, 661, 663, 666—
    667, 669—670, 675, 682, 687, 712, 715,
    721, 728, 732, 745
Turtle Neck Gun Club 670, 671
Turtle Run Campground 635, 637, 641, 732
Tuttle, Abiah 614
Twing, Rev. Cornelius W. 400
Two Bridges 382
Two Mile Landing 125
Tyler, Alwilda 167
Tyler, Emily 167
Tyler, Samuel 167
Tyler, Sarah 167
Tylertown 167, 169, 764

U

Umstead, Mary E. 475
Unamis 765
Uncle Thannie 428
Underground Railroad 82
Underhill, Charles Reginald 474, 492, 499
Underhill, Ella Howell (Johnson) 451, 457, 474,
    477, 479, 492, 499, 529, 530
Union 760
"Union Extra" 115
"Union First" 115
Union Forge 573, 760—761
Union Forge Tract 761
United Sons of America 254
Unknown Mill 750—751
Unvarnished Truth 783, 789
Updike, Annie (Auerbach) 668
Updike, Barbara Sue 669
Updike, "Chick" 669
Updike, Emil 668
Updike, Grace 706
Updike, Henry 668, 669, 711, 720
Updike, Ina Jagmitty 669
Updike, Isaac 674
Updike, James 455, 658, 668—669, 684
Updike, James and Ruth (Huntley) 669
Updike, Jane Helena (Garrison) 668
Updike, Jim 654, 659
Updike, John 668
Updike, John, Jr. "Jack" 243, 532, 668, 669
Updike, Louise 668
Updike, Marguerite 307, 658—659, 669
Updike, Minnie Vincent 669
Updike, Ruth Huntley 658, 669, 684, 734—735
Updike, Sadie 455, 668, 706, 709, 734
Updike, Samuel 668

Upland 408
Upper Bank 195
Upper Dock 208, 237

V

Vagabond 251, 779
Valiant, Captain George 594, 680
Valient, Sadie B. 640
Valley Forge 66, 255, 320, 555
Valley Forge State Park 255
Van Buren, Martin 382
Van Name, Elmer G. 433
Van Sant 21—22
Van Sant, Isaac 428
Van Sant Bible 427
Van Sant, Capt. Joel Frank III 205
Van Sant, Captain John 123, 426, 429
Van Sant, Christopher 426
Van Sant, Doughty 199, 205, 772
Van Sant, Doughty 461
Van Sant Family 426
Van Sant family 193, 199
Van Sant, Florence (Johnson) 474
Van Sant, Frank 474
Van Sant, Higbee, Jr. 200
Van Sant, Higbee, Sr. 200
Van Sant, Honorable Samuel R. 426
Van Sant, Isaac 446, 477
Van Sant, James 428, 429, 446
Van Sant, Joel 200, 205, 427, 446
Van Sant, Joel II 199, 205
Van Sant, Joel, IV 426
Van Sant, Joel, Jr. 427, 772
Van Sant, Joel Nicholas IV 200
Van Sant, John 123—124, 200, 205, 426, 771
Van Sant, John Wesley 427, 446
Van Sant, Lillie 200
Van Sant, Mary Ann 428, 448
Van Sant, Mary Ann (Cramer) 446
Van Sant, Mercy (Davis) 429, 446, 493
Van Sant, Nathaniel 477, 483
Van Sant, Nathaniel D. 266, 428, 446—447, 493, 682
Van Sant, Nicholas, Jr. 446
Van Sant, Rachel 426
Van Sant, Rebecca 426, 428—429
Van Sant, Rev. Nicholas 178, 200, 205, 423, 426,
    446, 447, 452—453, 503
Van Sant, Rev. Nicholas, Jr. 200
Van Sant, S. Monroe 428
Van Sant, Samuel 205, 221, 428, 446, 772
Van Sant, Samuel R. 427
Van Sant shipyards 200
Van Sant, Stanley 461
Van Sant, The Rev. Nicholas
    426, 429, 446, 464, 477, 493, 495, 518, 703
Van Tienhoven, Cornelius 15, 415—416
Van Tienhoven, Dr. Lucas 15, 415
Van Tienhoven, Sarah 15, 415—416
Van Tienhoven, Tryntje (Broding) 415

Weeks, Sam 457
Weeks, Samuel 301, 366, 424, 430, 435, 451—453,
 456—457, 459, 464, 470, 475, 498, 743
Weeks, Samuel B. 453
Weeks, Samuel, Jr. 452,—453, 503
Weeks, Samuel, sawmill 456
Weeks, Sarah 187, 225, 287, 434
Weeks, Sarah Elizabeth 470
Weeks, Sarah Harriet 745
Weeks, Sarah Pettit 743
Weeks Tavern 460
Weeks, Thomas 433
Weeks, William 434, 435
Weeks, William and Margaret (Bevis) 435
Weeks, William Henry 453, 459
Weekstown 366, 433—434, 436, 458, 788
Weeksville 366, 434, 789
Weex, Ezekiel 433
Weex, James 433
Weex, Job 433
Weimer, Dudley 202
Weiner, Jean 654, 729
Weist, Donald 299
Wells Mills 394, 762
Werner, Charles 408, 410—411, 412, 791
Wescoat, Amanda M. 643
Wescoat, Daniel 138
Wescoat, Daniel, Jr. 138
Wescoat, Daniel III 138
Wescoat, David 646
Wescoat, Deborah (Smith) 138
Wescoat, Elizabeth 138
Wescoat, Margaret 144
Wescoat, Margaret (Lee) 138
Wescoat, Mary McAnney 646
Wescoat, Richard 60—61, 64—66, 124, 137,
 140, 144, 427, 434—435, 771, 800, 802
  (See also: Westcott)
Wesickaman 30
Wesley, John 158, 242, 290—291
Wessler 265
West, Caleb 559
West Creek 261, 293, 448
West Creek Forge 557
West Jersey Circuit 157
West Jersey Council of Proprietors 618
West Jersey District 158
West Jersey Society 473
West Mill Branch 119
West Mill Tract 32
West Plains 758
West Point 19
Westcott, Arthur 433
Westcott, Boarden 213
Westcott, Richard 433, 434
  (See also: Wescoat)
Westecunk Forge 557
Western dry-picking machine 171
Wetherby, (See also: Weatherby)
Wetherby, B. 730

Wetherby, G. 730
Wetherby, Maude 641
Wetherby, Sarah 630
Wetherill, James 618
Weymouth 34, 49, 69, 395, 750
Weymouth diary 395
Weymouth Furnace
 33, 34, 43, 347, 437, 557, 575, 589, 751
Weymouth Junction 303
Weymouth Station 70, 115, 125
Wharton Estate 24, 46, 327
Wharton, Joseph
 23, 39, 43, 50, 71, 73, 74, 75, 80, 85, 95—
 96, 125, 193, 199—200, 249, 327, 335, 356,
 411, 564, 706, 742, 744, 746, 749, 758, 762
Wharton School of Finance 71
Wharton State Forest 25
Wheatlands 666
Wheaton, Frank 533
Wheaton Glass 533
Whelan, The Rev. William 162
Whitcomb Manor 60, 77
Whitcraft, Hannah Emily Sooy Crowley Burroughs 629
Whitcraft, Rebecca Josephine Sooy 629
Whitcraft, William 629
White, Ada 279
White, Alanson 279
White, Alfred 279
White, Amy 279
White, Benjamin 279
White, Blanchard 382
White, Catherine 279
White cedar 718
White, Cordelia 279
White, David 279
White, Emmaline 279
White, Hannah 279
White, Howard 279
White, Lemuel B. 279
White, Lenora 279
White, Lucy Ann 279
White, Mary 279
White, Rachel 279
White, Rebecca Jane 279
White, Reuben 279
White, Sarah 279
White Town 279
Whitewater Creek 593
Whitney Mullen 116
Widden, Charles 327
Wiilson, Ruth 177
Wild Cat branch 121
Wild Oak Island 593
Wild Oat Cove 593
Wilhelmina 333
Wilkinson, Helen 715, 729, 735
Willett's Creek 616
William F. Gale house 732
William III 135
William Lippincott and Company 146—147

Wright, Elias
Wright, Frances 629
Wright, General Elias 71, 82, 94—95, 128, 188, 194, 327, 335, 411, 441, 452, 456, 749
Wright, Thomas 464

X

Xantippe 142

Y

Y.M.C.A. 327, 333, 349
Yanko, Beatrice 534
Yates, Bing 310
Yates, Mabel 362
"Yellow salt" grass 728—729
York, Edward 146
York, L. David 299
York, William 146
Youle, John 321, 556
Young, Edgar 531
Young, Edith 531, 602
Young, Phoebe Ann (Headley) 531

Z

Zeagles Ditch 592, 674, 728
Zimbalist, Efrem, Jr. 150
Zitto, Sal 532
Zurn, John M. 692—696, 699, 704
Zurn's Club House 692, 694—696, 699—700, 704

LAWS OF THE STATE OF NEW JERSEY
COMPILED AND PUBLISHED UNDER THE
AUTHORITY OF THE LEGISLATURE.
By Joseph Bloomfield

Printed by James Wilson
Trenton N.J. - 1811.

An Act to incorporate into a township a part of the townships of Northampton, Evesham, and Little Egg-Harbour in the county of Burlington, by the name of Washington.

Passed November 19, 1802

Whereas a number of the inhabitants of the township of Northampton, Evesham, and Little Egg-Harbour, in the county of Burlington, have, by their petition, set forth to the Legislature the disadvantages they labor under by reason of the great extent of the said township; for remedy whereof,

Sec. 1. Be it Enacted by the council and general Assembly of this state, And it is hereby enacted by the authority of the same,

That all that part of the townships of Northampton, Evesham, and Little Egg-Harbour, lying *within* the following bounds; Beginning at the mouth of Wading River, and running up the same the several courses thereof, to the mouth of Tub Mill branch; thence up the said branch, the several courses thereof, to the head; from thence to a point of fast-land known by the name of Breakfast-point; from thence a direct course to a bridge called Joseph M. Laurie's bridge, near the head of a stream of water called Poppuse-run; from thence, on a direct course, until it strikes a bridge at the head of the Union Forge-pond; from thence a straight line, to Muskingum bridge; from thence on a straight line, to Atsion-creek, above Goshen-Mill; from thence down Atsion-creek, the several courses thereof, to Mullicas-river, and down the same, the several courses thereof, to the place of beginning, at the mouth of Wading-river, shall be, and is hereby set off from, the said township of Northampton, Evesham, and Little Egg-Harbour, and made a separate township to be called by the name of Washington.

2. And be it enacted, That the inhabitants of the said township of Washington be, and they are hereby vested with, and entitled unto all the powers, privileges and authorities, and shall be and are hereby made subject to the like regulations and government which the *inhabitants* of the aforesaid townships of Northampton, Evesham, and Little Egg-Harbour, are subject and entitled to; and that the inhabitants of the said township of Washington be, and they are hereby incorporated, styled and known by the name of "The inhabitants of the township of Washington in the county of Burlington, "and entitled to all the privileges, authorities and advantages, that the other townships in the said county are entitled unto by virtue of an act, entitled, "An act incorporating the inhabitants of townships, designating their powers and regulating their meetings."

Passed the twenty-first day of February, in the year of our Lord one thousand seven hundred and ninety eight.

3. And be it enacted, That the first town meeting of the inhabitants, after the passing of this act, shall be on the second Tuesday of March next, at the house of John Bodine, at Wading River bridge, and that all town meetings thereafter, shall be held on the second Tuesday of March, annually, at such place as the electors of said township shall, from time to time, direct and appoint.

Reverie on a Pinelands Stream

A quiet stream flows
In still grace
Where God placed His hand,
Blue-eyed grass and mellow rose
Interpose banks edged
With cool white sand.

Minarets of cedar strands
Stay in changeless watch
Composing lyrics on the wind,
Of muted chords long lost
In purling race are found again
By waters of Seraphim.

Here poetic interlude
Of seasons linger
In timeless measured scan,
Only sun and shadow
Trace intervals of age,
Unveil an elegy of talisman.

I would remain and dream
Beside this silver stream,
Bid the tide pass me by,
Leavening the gossamer of my wing
That I might touch the hand of God,
To become an everlasting sigh.

Jessie Lewis
Green Bank
1987